Raptors at Risk

Edited by
R. D. CHANCELLOR & B.-U. MEYBURG

Proceedings
of the V World Conference
on Birds of Prey and Owls

Midrand, Johannesburg, South Africa
4–11 August 1998

WORLD WORKING GROUP ON
BIRDS OF PREY AND OWLS

ISBN 0-88839-478-0
Copyright © 2000 World Working Group on Birds of Prey and Owls

Cataloging in Publication Data
World Conference on Birds of Prey and Owls
(5th : 1998 : Johannesburg, South Africa)
   Raptors at risk

   Copublished by: Hancock House Publishers and World Working
Group on Birds of Prey and Owls.
Includes bibliographical references.
ISBN 0-88839-478-0

   1. Birds of prey--Congresses. 2. Owls--Congresses. I. Chancellor, R.
D. (Robin D.) II. Meyburg, B.-U. (Bernd-U) III. World Working Group
on Birds of Prey and Owls. IV. Title.
QL696.F3W65 1998   598.9   C00-910215-9

All rights reserved. No part of this publication may be reproduced, stored in a retrieval system or transmitted, in any form or by any means, electronic, mechanical, photocopying, recording, or otherwise, without the prior written permission of Hancock House Publishers.
Printed in Canada—Printcrafters

Front cover photograph: B.-U. Meyburg
Indian Vultures with dogs at a carcass in northern India, taken in the late 1970s. Today, only 25 years later, such a once commonplace gathering would be almost impossible to find.

Back cover photograph: B.-U. Meyburg
Portrait of an adult male Lesser Spotted Eagle (*Aquila pomarina*) when captured on 7 July 1996 near its eyrie (at "Viereckwiese") in northern Germany and marked with a solar-powered satellite transmitter (PTT16867). This bird has now been monitored by satellite for more than three years migrating every northern winter to Zambia.

Published simultaneously by

WORLD WORKING GROUP ON
BIRDS OF PREY AND OWLS

**World Working Group on
Birds of Prey and Owls**
Wangenheimstr. 32, D - 14193 Berlin, Germany
Phone: ++49-30-893 881-33
Fax: ++49-30-892 80 67
Email: WWGBP@aol.com

Published for distribution to institutes and individuals by

HANCOCK HOUSE PUBLISHERS LTD.
19313 Zero Avenue, Surrey, B.C. V4P 1M7
HANCOCK HOUSE PUBLISHERS
1431 Harrison Avenue, Blaine, WA 98230-5005

(604) 538-1114   Fax (604) 538-2262
(800) 938-1114   Fax (800) 983-2262
Web site: www.hancockhouse.com
Email: sales@hancockhouse.com

The World Working Group on Birds of Prey and Owls (WWGBP)

The WWGBP has been active for thirty years now and today plays an important role in the promotion of raptor conservation and research on an international level. Its membership list today comprises over 1,000 raptor specialists and enthusiasts in all parts of the world, and anybody with an interest in raptors is welcome to become a member.

For further information contact:
- World Working Group on Birds of Prey and Owls, P.O. Box 52, Towcester NN12 7ZW, England. Tel/Fax: +44 -1604- 86 23 31, E-mail: WWGBP@aol.com
- Weltarbeitsgruppe für Greifvögel und Eulen e.V., Wangenheimstr. 32, D-14193 BERLIN, Germany. Fax: +49 30 892 80 67, Tel: +49 30 893 881 33, E-mail: WWGBP@aol.com, or
- Groupe de Travail Mondial sur les Rapaces, 31 avenue du Maine, F-75015 PARIS, France. Tel/Fax: +33 1 42 22 22 27, E-Mail: WWGBP@aol.com.

In addition to issuing to all members and subscribers a newsletter (in English, German and French), thereby keeping them informed of current research, forthcoming conferences, status reports, recent publications, etc. one of the Group's major activities is to organise a World Conference every five years as well as other international meetings.

The following scientific publications are still available from WWGBP:

RAPTOR CONSERVATION TODAY (1994)
Proceedings of the IV World Conference on Birds of Prey and Owls.
799 pages, size 15,5 x 23 cm, with colour cover, contains 88 original papers in English from a large number of authors world-wide. Price US $ 23, £ 15, DM 45, FF 150.

RAPTORS IN THE MODERN WORLD (1989)
Proceedings of the III World Conference on Birds of Prey and Owls.
612 pages, size 15,5 x 23 cm, with colour cover, contains 72 original papers in English by 112 authors from 27 countries. Price US$ 21, £ 14, DM 40, FF 132.

EAGLE STUDIES (1996)
549 pages, size 21.3 x 15 cm, with colour cover, comprises 64 original papers by a wide range of authors from many different countries. Price US $ 16, £ 10, DM 30, FF 99.

BIRDS OF PREY BULLETIN No. 4 (1991)
302 pages, size 14,5 x 21 cm, with colour cover, many black and white photographs, contains 28 papers by 41 authors from 20 countries world-wide on birds of prey and owls covering a wide range of topics concerning the biology, ecology, status and conservation of these birds. Price US$ 10, £ 6, DM 18, FF 60.

HOLARCTIC BIRDS OF PREY (1998)
Proceedings of an International Conference
680 pages, many diagrams, maps, line drawings and photographs.
At present out of print. To be reprinted.

Preface

In conjunction with the Raptor Conservation Group (RCG) and Vulture Study Group of the South African Endangered Wildlife Trust, the World Working Group on Birds of Prey (WWGBP) held the V World Conference from 4-11 August 1998 in the splendid setting of the ESKOM Centre at Midrand, Johannesburg. Some 250 participants came from all continents to attend the conference, the emblem of which, lending prominence to South Africa, the host country, was a soaring Bateleur Eagle (*Terathopius ecaudatus*). To commemorate the occasion, a special set of postage stamps was issued depicting different birds of prey and, during the opening ceremony, an official representative of the South African government solemnly presented framed sets of these to the chairmen of the WWGBP and the RCG.

In addition to the faultless organisation of the ESKOM Centre, other noteworthy contributions to the event were a piece of music specially composed for the occasion and a liberal supply of specially pressed "Lesser Kestrel" red wine, making the conference opening a conspicuous success. During the next few days the participants fused into a well-knit community, many new contacts were established, friendships sealed and ways of co-operation agreed on.

Following the formal opening on 4.8.98, the scientific programme consisted of 14 sessions held concurrently in two separate lecture halls, during which over 130 oral presentations and 35 posters were delivered. Parallel with the World Conference, the 3rd International Raptor Biomedicine Conference was also held at the ESKOM Centre from 9-11 August, 1998. Midway through the conference, so as to make a break and allow participants to relax, an excursion was organised to view a breeding colony of Cape Vultures at Magaliesberg and to visit the De Wildt Cheetah and Wildlife Centre nearby. On this trip it was possible to observe the numerous Cape Vultures and occasional White-backed Vultures (*Gyps coprotheres* and *G. africanus*), together with Black and Fish Eagles (*Aquila verreauxii* and *Haliaeetus vocifer*), Milky Eagle Owl (*Bubo lacteus*) and Pearl-spotted Owlet (*Glaudicium perlatum*), not to mention other characteristic examples of the South African avifauna. That same evening the participants were invited as guests to a splendid banquet held to celebrate the Silver Jubilee of South Africa's Endangered Wildlife Trust.

In the immediate vicinity of the ESKOM Centre, in the undulating grassland, there was a low-lying marsh to which one could pay useful visits in between sessions. Here, in addition to numerous passerines, plovers and water birds, one could see the occasional Lanner Falcon (*Falco biarmicus*), Black-shouldered Kites flying in every evening and, regularly at dusk, the Marsh Owl (*Asio capensis*). Before and during the conference, which closed on 11 August with the adoption of 15 resolutions and a WWGBP members' meeting, guided tours and individual excursions could be made to many parts of the Republic of South Africa. A number of participants also went on to attend the 22nd International Ornithological Conference, held at Durban from 18-22 August.

This volume comprises a major part of the oral and poster presentations given during the conference, conditional on their being original contributions as yet unpublished, even in a different language. A number of authors did not finally submit their papers, whilst several others were, for various reasons, not acceptable.

We are grateful to the conveners of each session and the anonymous referees for the time and trouble they took over checking and editing the texts. Without their close involvement, before,during, and after the conference, this volume of proceedings might never have seen the light of day and, on behalf of all the participants, we warmly thank both them and all the authors.

Our unreserved gratitude is also due to Dr. John Ledger of the Endangered Wildlife Trust for so generously inviting us to hold the conference in South Africa, and to Prof. Gerhard Verdoorn, Chairman of the RCG, and his indefatigable team for their faultless organisation and running of the meeting. The management of the ESKOM Conference Centre is also to be congratulated for the high level of accomodation and facilities which they provided.

The title which we have selected may not seem appropriate to some readers since many species of raptors, especially in Europe and North America, are recovering and are not at risk any more. However, the example of the very recent, dramatic and unexpected decline of two species of *Gyps* vultures in India shows that Birds of Prey are always at risk and that one can never be sure that their populations will be stable for the foreseeable future. The situation of the White-backed Vulture *Gyps bengalensis* and the Long-billed Vulture *G. indicus* must now be regarded as critical. Extinction of either or both species, which were extremely common throughout India until as recently as only three years ago, breeding in cities and villages appears to be inevitable unless the factors responsible for their decline can be identified and corrected. Views like the one on the front cover may sadly soon be history.

R. D. Chancellor   Bernd-U. Meyburg
Hon. Secretary   Chairman

World Working Group on Birds of Prey (WWGBP)

Contents

Preface
R. D. Chancellor & B.-U. Meyburg   5

Part 1
Current Studies of African Raptors

Stability and long-term changes in a West African raptor community
Jean-Marc Thiollay   15

Raptor Studies in Kenya: Past, Present and Future
Munir Virani   27

Status and conservation of raptors on the Masoala Peninsula, Madagascar
Russell Thorstrom & Lily-Arison Rene de Roland   35

A new Subspecies of the Booted Eagle from Southern Africa, inferred from biometrics and mitochondrial DNA
Reuven Yosef, Gerhard Verdoorn, Andreas Helbig & Ingrid Seibold   43

Nesting behaviour of a pair of Bat Hawks *Macheiramphus alcinus* in South Africa, recorded by time-lapse video images
T. Harris, A. Kemp & J. Dunning   51

Flight, foraging and food of the Bateleur *Terathopius ecaudatus*: an aerodynamically specialized, opportunistic forager
R. T. Watson   65

Causes of Cape Vulture *Gyps coprotheres* mortality at the Kransberg colony: a 17 year update
P. C. Benson   77

Ecology of Taita *Falco fasciinucha*, Peregrine *F. peregrinus minor* and Lanner *F. biarmicus* Falcons in Zimbabwe
R.R. Hartley   87

Breeding biology of Henst's Goshawk *Accipiter henstii* on Masoala Peninsula, northeastern Madagascar
Lily-Arison Rene de Roland   107

Behaviour and Range Movements during the post-fledging dependence period of the Madagascar Fish-eagle *Haliaeetus vociferoides*
Simon A. Rafanomezantsoa   113

Taxonomic problems in African diurnal raptors
William S. Clark & R.A.G. Davies   121

Advances in the molecular systematics of African raptors
Michael Wink & Hedi Sauer-Gürth   135

Part 2
Biology & Conservation of the Vultures of the World

The Status of Vultures in Africa during the 1990s
P.J. Mundy   151

Vultures in Asia
S.M.Satheesan   165

The Current Status of North American Vultures
Lloyd F. Kiff — 175

The Status of Vultures in Latin America
Marsha A. Schlee — 191

Habitat Loss and Vultures: a Case Study from Israel
Reuven Yosef & Ofer Bahat — 207

The role of avian scavengers in locating and exploiting carcasses in central Saudi Arabia
Mohammed Shobrak — 213

Regular Long-distance migration of Eurasian Griffon *Gyps fulvus*
Goran Susic — 225

The Farming Community and the Conservation of the Cape Griffon Vulture *Gyps coprotheres* in the Western Cape, South Africa
H.A. Scott, R.M. Scott & A.F. Boshoff — 231

The Ecofunctional positions of Palaearctic Vultures
W. Baumgart — 239

Part 3
Falcons in Asia and the Middle East

Saker *Falco cherrug* and Peregrine *Falco peregrinus* Falcons in Asia: Determining migration routes and trapping pressure
C.P. Eastham, J.L Quinn & N.C. Fox — 247

The Saker Falcon *Falco cherrug* in Kazakstan
Anatoliy Levin, Mark Watson, Helen Macdonald & Nicholas C. Fox — 259

The Saker Falcon *Falco cherrug* in Mongolia
Damdinsuren Shijirmaa, Eugene Potapov, Samdangiin Banzragch & N. C. Fox — 263

The Saker Falcon *Falco cherrug* in the Kyrgyz Republic
Erin J. Gott, Helen J. Macdonald & N. C. Fox — 269

The Saker Falcon in European Russia
Vladimir Galushin & Valery Moseikin — 275

Are Peregrine Falcons in Northern Siberia still affected by organochlorines?
J.L. Quinn, Y. Kokorev, J. Prop, N. Fox & J.M. Black — 279

New Developments on the Western Border of the Saker Falcon *Falco cherrug* range in Middle Europe
W. Baumgart — 295

The Status of the Lugger Falcon *Falco jugger* in Pakistan
M. Ahmed, N.C. Fox & C.P. Eastham — 301

Part 4
Conservation Models for Raptors of the World

The California Condor Recovery Programme
Lloyd Kiff — 307

Appearances vs Performance; managing endangered Tasmanian Wedge-tailed Eagles in forestry operations
Nick J. Mooney — 321

Madagascar Fish-Eagle and Community-based Wetland Conservation
R. T. Watson, A. Andrianarimisa, D. Razandrizanakanirina & L. Kalavaha   333

Progress in Translocation of Diurnal Raptors
Tom J. Cade   343

Falconry as a Conservation Tool in Africa
R.R. Hartley   373

Black Sparrowhawks in the Southwestern Cape: Benefits of cooperative conservation
E. E. Oettlé, M. Walters & D. Pepler   379

People and Hyrax in the Conservation of Black Eagles in the Matobo Hills, Zimbabwe
N. Chiweshe   383

The Black Eagle Radio Telemetry Project in the Matobo Hills, Zimbabwe
W. J. Goodwin   395

Evaluating the long-term effectiveness of conservation practices in Montagu's Harrier *Circus pygargus*
Beatriz Arroyo & Vincent Bretagnolle   403

On the Demography of the Imperial Eagle *Aquila heliaca* in Kazakhstan
Evgeny A. Bragin   409

Ecological Research and its relationship to the Conservation Programme of the Golden Eagle and the Japanese Mountain Hawk-Eagle
T. Yamazaki   415

Part 5
Raptors in Urban Environments

Raptors in Urban Landscapes: A Review and Future Concerns
Oliver P. Love & David M. Bird   425

Urban Landscapes and Raptors: a review of factors affecting Population Ecology
David E. Andersen & David L. Plumpton   435

Nest Sites of Five Raptor Species along an Urban Gradient
R. W. Mannan, C. W. Boal, W. J. Burroughs, J. W. Dawson, T. S. Estabrook & W. S. Richardson   447

Overwintering by Urban-nesting Peregrine Falcons *Falco peregrinus* in Midwestern North America
Greg Septon   455

Adaptation of two Falcon species *Falco femoralis* & *Falco subbuteo* to an urban environment
Klaus Dietrich Fiuczynski & Paul Soemmer   463

Red-Shouldered Hawks *Buteo lineatus* nesting on human-made structures in Southwest Ohio
Jeffrey L. Hays   469

Part 6

Understanding Distribution - the Whys and Wherefores of Geographical Ranges of Raptors

Understanding the Distribution of Australia's Diurnal Raptors
William K. Steele & David J. Baker-Gabb   475

Radio Telemetry studies of dispersal and survival in juvenile White-tailed Sea Eagles *Haliaeetus albicilla* in Norway
Torgeir Nygård, Robert E. Kenward & Kjell Einvik — 487

The ups and downs of a Northern Goshawk *Accipiter gentilis* population over a 30 year period - Natural dynamics or an artefact?
Volkher Looft — 499

Part 7
Predation and Feeding Ecology

Effects of Predators on their Prey: some generalisations
I. Newton — 509

The Influence of Predation by Black Eagles *Aquila verreauxii* on Rock Hyrax numbers in the Arid Karoo
R. A. G. Davies & J. W. H. Ferguson — 519

Can Raptor predation limit Red Grouse populations?
S.J. Thirgood & S.M. Redpath — 527

The Impact of Rabbit Calicivirus Disease on Raptor reproductive success in the Strzelecki Desert, South Australia: A preliminary analysis.
I.D. Falkenberg, V. G. Hurley & E. Stevenson — 535

Can the Common Kestrel *Falco tinnunculus* provision Increased broods in a mid-latitude environment?
Anthony J. van Zyl — 543

Feeding ecology of Javan Hawk-eagle *Spizaetus bartelsi* during the nestling period
Dewi M. Prawiradilaga, Nils Rov, Jan Ove Gjershaug, Hapsoro & Adam Supriatna — 559

Socio-Economic Problems and Solutions in Raptor Predation
R.E. Kenward — 565

Part 8
Conservation Biology of the World's Migratory Raptors

Conservation Biology of the World's Migratory Raptors: status and strategies
Keith L. Bildstein, Jorje Zalles, Jennifer Ottinger & Kyle McCarty — 573

Conservation Strategies for the world's largest known Raptor Migration Flyway: Veracruz, the River of Raptors
Ernesto Ruelas Inzunza, Stephen W. Hoffman, Laurie J. Goodrich, & Ruth Tingay — 591

The Value of extensive Raptor Migration Monitoring in Western North America.
Jeff P. Smith & Stephen W. Hoffman — 597

Conservation of migrating raptors through banding; results of over 30 years of the Cape May Raptor Banding Project
William S. Clark, Christopher Schultz, & Olin Allen — 617

Where have 30,000 Lesser Spotted Eagles *Aquila pomarina* gone?
Dan Alon — 627

Part 9
Islands and Raptors

Biodiversity, Island Raptors and Species Concepts
Clayton M. White & Lloyd F. Kiff — 633

Biology and molecular genetics of Eleonora's Falcon *Falco eleonorae*, a colonial raptor of Mediterranean islands
Michael Wink & Dietrich Ristow — 653

Status of Réunion Marsh Harrier *Circus maillardi* on Réunion Island
V. Bretagnolle, J.M. Thiollay & C. Attié — 669

Population density, territory size and habitat use of Gurney's Eagle *Aquila gurneyi* in the North Moluccas, Indonesia
Nils Røv & Jan Ove Gjershaug — 677

Recent Observations on Peregrine Falcons *Falco peregrinus* of the Cape Verde Islands, Atlantic Ocean
Clifford M. Anderson & Clayton M. White — 685

The Status of the Christmas Island Hawk-Owl *Ninox natalis*
F.A. Richard Hill — 691

Dispersion in the Seychelles Kestrel *Falco araea*
Jeff Watson — 697

The Peregrine Falcon *Falco peregrinus* in Fiji and Vanuatu
Clayton M. White, Daniel J. Brimm & Jon H. Wetton — 707

The Osprey *Pandion haliaetus* in the Cape Verde Islands: distribution, population trends and conservation problems
João Ferreira & Luis Palma — 721

Ecomorphology of island populations of the Kestrel *Falco tinnunculus* on Cape Verde
S. Hille & H. Winkler — 729

Part 10
Impact of Electricity Utility Structures on Raptors

Raptor Mortality on Powerlines in South Africa
Chris S. van Rooyen — 739

Steel Distribution Poles – Environmental Implications
Richard E. Harness — 751

Evaluating the Risk existing Powerlines pose to large Raptors by utilising Risk Assessment Methodology: the Molopo Case Study
Rudi Kruger & Chris. S. van Rooyen — 757

Raptor Electrocutions and Outages – A Review of Rural Utility Records spanning 1986-1996
Richard E. Harness & Kenneth R. Wilson — 765

Powerlines and Raptors, using Regulatory Influence to prevent Electrocutions
Leo R. Suazo II — 773

Part 11
Biology of Owls with Emphasis on Vocalisations

Owl Vocalizations as Interspecific Differentiation-Patterns and their taxonomical value as Ethological Isolating Mechanisms between various Taxa
Claus König — 781

Distribution and population size of the Sokoke Scops Owl *Otus ireneae* in the Arabuko-Sokoke forest, Kenya
Munir Virani — 795

Relationships between Foraging Range, Prey Density and Habitat Structure in the Tawny Owl *Strix aluco*
C.F. Coles, S.J. Petty & C.J. Thomas   803

How Many Seychelles Scops Owls *Otus insularis* are there?
Jeff Watson   813

Molecular Systematics of Owls (Strigiformes) based on DNA-sequences of the mitochondrial cytochrome b gene
Michael Wink & Petra Heidrich   819

Part 12
Taxonomy, Phylogeny, Developments in Raptor DNA Studies and other Theoretical Aspects

Advances in DNA studies of diurnal and nocturnal raptors
Michael Wink   831

Preliminary Genetic Analysis of some Western Palaearctic populations of Bonelli's Eagle, *Hieraaetus fasciatus*.
Pedro Cardia, Bárbara Fráguas, Miguel Pais, Thomas Guillemaud, Luís Palma, M. Leonor Cancela, Nuno Ferrand & Michael Wink   845

Phylogenetic relationships between Black Shaheen *Falco peregrinus peregrinator*, Red-naped Shaheen *F. pelegrinoides babylonicus* and Peregrines *F. peregrinus*
M. Wink, H. Döttlinger, M.K. Nicholls, & H. Sauer-Gürth   853

The application of DNA technology to enforce Raptor Conservation Legislation within Great Britain
Nick P. Williams & Justin A. Evans   859

Part 13
General Studies

Contaminants and Wintering Areas of Peregrine Falcons, *Falco peregrinus*, from the Kola Peninsula, Russia
Charles J. Henny, William S. Seegar, Michael A. Yates, Thomas L. Maechtle, Sergei A. Ganusevich & Mark R. Fuller   871

A Multisensor Telemetry System for studying Flight Biology and Energetics of free-flying Griffon Vultures *Gyps fulvus*. A Case Study
R. Bögel, R. Prinzinger, E. Karl & C. Walzer   879

Footedness Bias in hunting Birds of Prey
Davide Csermely   885

Resolutions   893

Part 1

Current Studies of African Raptors

Bateleur *Terathopius ecaudatus*

Conveners:
Alan Kemp & Warwick Tarboton

Stability and long-term changes in a West African raptor community

Jean-Marc Thiollay

ABSTRACT

Breeding and non-breeding diurnal raptors were censused in 1972 and 1996 over the same 2,700 ha palm savanna and gallery forest mosaic at Lamto Reserve, central Côte d'Ivoire. This protected area, once part of the Guinean savanna belt of West Africa, became increasingly isolated within highly degraded, deforested, cultivated and overhunted habitats. All seven large forest raptors and resident savanna eagles disappeared before the mid 1980's. Among the 12 remaining breeding raptors, four species increased (including two seasonal migrants), four species remained stable (including two forest accipiters) and four species decreased, but not significantly (including the 2 largest species). All 14 non-breeding raptors (Palaearctic and African migrants), remained stable or increased. With an average of 63 breeding pairs/1000 ha, this area supports one of the highest densities of diurnal raptors ever recorded. Some savanna species, here at their southernmost extension, may have shifted their distribution southward or increased in the southern portion of their range (Gabar Goshawk *Micronisus gabar*, Black Kite *Milvus migrans*, Wahlberg's Eagle *Aquila wahlbergi*) after droughts and habitat losses that occurred between the two censuses. Deforestation and large scale cultivation around the reserve may have favoured European Marsh Harrier *Circus aeruginosus* and Lanner Falcon *Falco biarmicus*, while resulting fragmentation of natural habitats probably drove larger eagles to extinction. Within the reserve, decreasing oil palm fruits as food may have affected specialized consumers (Palm-nut Vulture *Gypohierax angolensis*, African Harrier-hawk *Polyboroides typus*).

INTRODUCTION

There are still few studies of the long-term dynamics of a complete raptor community, least of all in the tropics. In Africa, the pioneering population monitoring of eagles in Kenya by Brown (1952-1955) and in Zimbabwe by Gargett (1990) are noteworthy. Furthermore, the consequences of habitat fragmentation and isolation on bird commmunities, currently a deep concern, have been throughly analyzed in temperate forests (Wilcove & Robinson 1990; Saunders *et al*. 1991; Villard *et al*. 1995) and open habitats (Soulé *et al*. 1992; Herkert 1994; Knick & Rotenberry 1995), as well as in tropical forests (Laurance & Bierregaard 1997) but rarely in Africa (Newmark 1991) and never specifically on a raptor community.

Reserves that protect natural habitat patches are often bound to become isolated within a matrix of initially similar but soon degraded habitat increasingly unsuitable for at least some species that eventually survive only in the reserve. Moreover, edge effects add their negative consequences to those of isolation and further imperil the survival of small populations (Burkey 1989; Andren 1994). This process, well known in forest fragments, may also occur in grasslands (Saunders 1989). Raptors are highly sensitive to prey availability, vegetation structure, pollution and human disturbance and thus are good indicators of environmental changes (Newton 1979).

The Lamto Reserve, Côte d'Ivoire, offered an opportunity to monitor long-term changes in an undisturbed patch of natural savanna, more and more isolated in an increasingly modified and impoverished landscape. The protected area was studied continuously since 1962, against which the dynamics of the raptor population over the last thirty years could be interpreted, owing to the data accumulated on the distribution and habitat of the species involved (Thiollay 1972, 1975a, 1975b, 1975c, 1977b, 1985, 1988). It was exposed to three major threats of outside origin:

1) Climate changes that occurred in sub Saharan Africa in recent decades, especially dry spells and a general deficit of rainfall before 1990, from the Sahel to humid coastal Côte d'Ivoire (Paturel *et al.* 1995; Servat *et al.* 1996). This will be referred to as global changes.
2) Increasing human pressure on the regional landscape, particularly around the Lamto Reserve, leading to fragmentation and degradation of natural habitats and probable extinction of some raptor populations. This will be distinguished as regional changes.
3) Vegetation changes inside the reserve (increasing tree cover, invasion of exotic shrubs, exploitation of palms). These will be called local changes.

STUDY AREA

The 2,700 ha Lamto Reserve is a gallery forest-palm savanna mosaic in south central Côte d'Ivoire, West Africa (6°13'N; 5°02'W). On the north-south gradient from the Sahara desert to the rain forest along the Gulf of Guinea coast, it is at the southernmost tip of the savanna belt, and one of the very last natural remnants of the humid South Guinean Savanna that typically fringed the northern edge of the dense forest zone beween 6° and 8° N. During the last 35 years (J.L. Tirefort, comm. pers.), the mean annual rainfall, by 5-year periods, averaged 1,240-1,383 mm in 1962-1966 and 1987-1996, but between 1967 and 1986, it was consistently lower (1,120-1,186 mm) in connection with the generally drier climate over most of West Africa, culminating in drought years in the early 1970s and 1980s (Servat *et al.* 1996). The rains increase from late February to May, peak in June and September-October and quickly decrease in November. Each year, all the savanna is burnt in January (height of the dry season) to maintain the vegetation in a steady state and avoid more damaging late fires.

The network of gallery forests stems from a wide riverine forest along the Bandama River, becoming narrower away from it along small watercourses, and ultimately giving way to isolated woodlots on gentle upper slopes (Fig. 1). From 1963 to 1988, the total forest coverage of the reserve increased from 15.6% to 17.9% (Gautier 1989). There has been also a significant increase of the mean tree density of savanna woodlands (Gautier 1990). The savanna can be divided into three broad habitat categories (Table 1), all of them dominated by 20-m tall Borassus palms (*Borassus aethiopium*), 3-15-m tall deciduous trees (mostly *Crossopteryx*, *Piliostigma*, *Cussonia*, *Terminalia* and *Vitex*) and a thick continuous grass cover (1.0-1.5 m) in the rainy season. In the early 1980s, an introduced shrub, *Chromolaena odorata*, began to invade the reserve and now forms dense thickets, 2-3 m high, along most gallery forests, in woodlots and little-burnt woodlands. This is the major habitat change since the early studies. The Oil Palm *Elaeis guineensis*, once a common tree in gallery forests and an important fruit source for several large birds, decreased through overexploitation by poachers for wine. Most large mammals have been extirpated and only a few Kob *Kobus kob*, Busbuck *Tragelaphus scriptus*, Buffalo *Syncerus cafer*, Hippopotamus *Hippotamus amphibius* and monkeys *Cercopithecus* spp. survive.

Figure 1. Vegetation map of the study area, Lamto Reserve. The lower edge is the Bandama River with forested islands. Gallery forests and woodlots are in black, and increasingly lighter shades sketch the three progressively less wooded savanna types (Table 1).

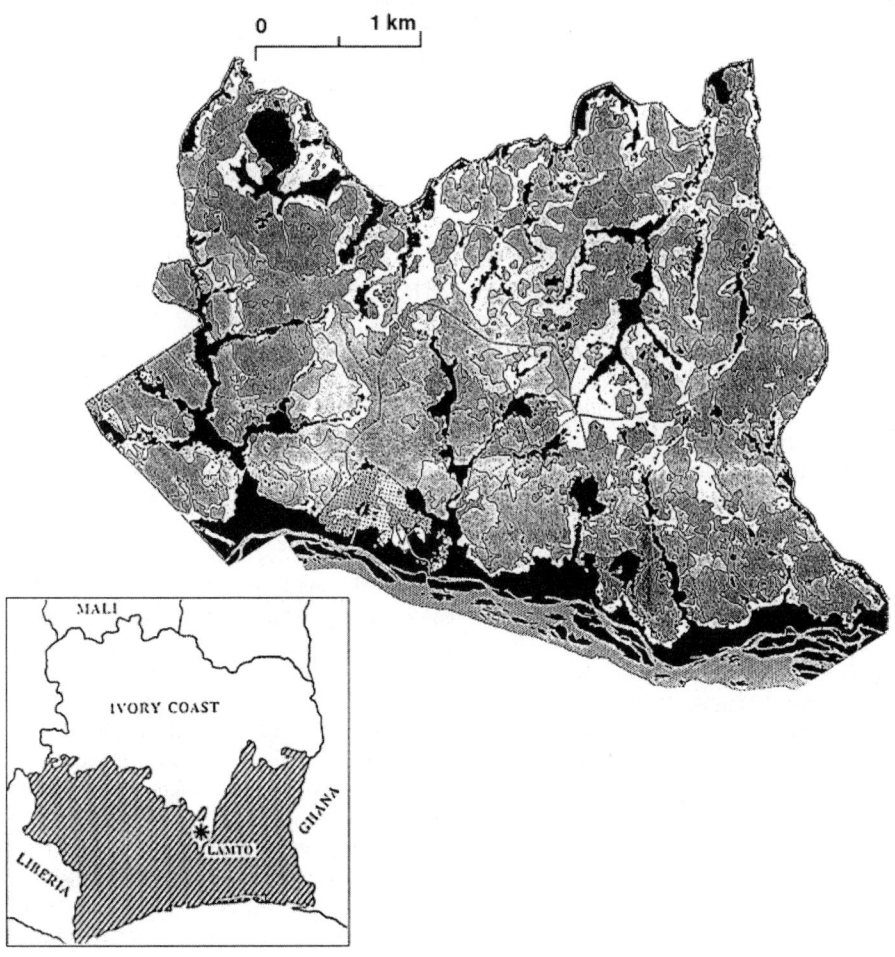

In the 1960s, the surrounding region was still covered with natural savannas and extensive forest tracts. Signs of increasing human pressure were already apparent, i.e. a general decrease of Borassus and Oil Palms, overhunting, and clearing of forest patches for logging and agriculture. This large scale process of habitat degradation continued unabated and is still going on. Additionally, agricultural development schemes have turned large areas of savanna and forest into rice fields, oil palm plantations, cattle pastures and extensive coffee or cocoa plantations. Logged forests and plantations, which burnt during the drought years, are now dense thickets of *Chromolaena* dominated by isolated trees (*Ceiba*, *Bombax*, *Sterculia*) and dead trunks. A dam on the river, just upstream from the reserve, prevented the seasonal flooding of the riverine forest and turned its formerly open understorey into an impenetrable thicket. Thus, the Lamto savanna progressively became an island of little- disturbed natural habitat, within an increasingly modified region this is covered by a variety of secondary vegetation types which are often unsuitable for some of the original raptor species.

Table 1. Structure, composition and relative area of the three main types of savanna on the Lamto Reserve. Gallery forests, woodlots, a few tracks and buildings account for the remaining 18% of the study area (see Thiollay 1970a).

Main types of savanna	Mean palm + broadleaf tree cover	Dominant graminean species	Proportion of the total reserve area
Open grassland	<=7%	*Loudetia simplex*	19.2%
Thin woodland	8-36%	*Hyparrhenia* sp.	37.7%
Dense woodland	37-80%	*Imperata cylindrica*	25.1%

METHODS

The raptor community was intensively surveyed from 1967 to 1973, both within the reserve and in a sorrounding radius of about 50 km (Thiollay 1975a, 1975b, 1976, 1977a, 1978a). After one-month visits in 1983 and 1984, the whole 2,700 ha study area was searched again in February-March 1996, but not the surrounding region. The most complete census was carried out from November 1971 to May 1972, thus covering the entire breeding season of every species. This was the year of reference, compared to the shorter survey of February-March 1996 that concentrated on the peak of the reproduction of most species (Thiollay 1976). The 1972 census was fairly representative of a stable population from 1967 to 1973, as suggested by the 75 active breeding sites found in early 1968 that were all still occupied by a pair of the same species in 1972 (some of them using alternative nests).

I censused all territorial pairs, whether sucessfully breeding or not, and whether resident or seasonal migrants. Additionally, I tried to make conservative estimates of the number of unmated individuals of each breeding species and of non-breeding migrants. Only the latter birds were counted separately in February and March, because they steadily decreased after their maximum numbers of early February (Thiollay 1975a, 1975b).

During day-long walks, I searched the entire area carefully, crossing at least twice every 100 x 100 m square (grid-cell superimposed on Fig. 1) and passing within less than 50 m of every spot at least once. Absolutely all individual Borassus palms and large trees in savanna and gallery forests were checked for nests and each nest structure was controlled repeatedly for signs of occupation. All nests were actually visited throughout the breeding season in 1972, but not in 1996 where the only goal was to assess the number of breeding pairs. All nests and observed individuals with their behaviour were located on enlarged vegetation maps.

All pairs of Black Kite *Milvus migrans*, Long-crested Eagle *Lophaetus occipitalis* and Grey Kestrel *Falco ardosliaceus* and most pairs of other species were identified when their nest was found, at any stage. Alternatively, the following criteria, recorded on at least two different days over the same area, were used to record breeding presence: African Cuckoo Hawk *Aviceda cuculoides* = display flight of an adult; Bat Hawk *Macheirhamphus alcinus* = 2 adults hunting at dusk; Palm-nut Vulture *Gypohierax angolensis* = a pair of adults calling or chasing other raptors; African Goshawk *Accipiter tachiro* = adult displaying at dawn; Western Little Sparrowhawk *A. erythropus* = adult calling or carrying prey; Shikra *A. badius* = a pair calling or mobbing other raptors; Lizard Hawk *Kaupifalco monogrammicus* = one or two adults singing simultaneously with a neighbouring pair; African Hobby *F. cuvieri* = pair repeatedly calling and mobbing raptors. Non-soaring forest species (Congo Serpent Eagle *Dryotriorchis spectabilis*, Long-tailed Hawk *Urotriorchis macrourus*) were located by searching throughout the undergrowth of the wide gallery forests, mainly along the Bandama River, and especially by listening for calls early and late in the day. Eagles were mostly observed from outside the forest when they were hunting along edges or soaring and displaying over the canopy.

The monthly number of non-breeding migrants and additional unmated individuals of resident species was probably underestimated, because no bird was marked and individuals moved often, sometimes over long distances. The study area was divided into savanna patches, bounded by the network of galleries and woodlots. Along transects allowing a thorough visual coverage of the study area, I recorded the number and position of all individuals not referable to a known pair in as many contiguous patches as possible ($>=3$) during the same half-day, and only when they stayed within the same patch all the time that they were in view. For each month, I summed over the whole reserve the minimum number of birds that were seen in each patch at every passage. For resident species whose immature plumage was easily recognized (Palm-nut Vulture, African Harrier Hawk *Polyboroides typus*), I counted as extra birds only non-adult birds. For other breeding species, only individuals seen together with a territorial pair were considered as extra birds. Black Kites were counted at roosts and other large gatherings, assuming that breeders may have also joined such groups.

Numbers of raptors were full counts over the total reserve area. The between-year differences in population size were tested by a chi-square test with Yates correction and one degree of freedom, in a 2 x 2 Goodness-of-fit test based on the null hypothesis of equal numbers from the two sample periods. However, only considerable changes were statistically significant, whereas smaller differences may also have been real, since counts were accurate and exhaustive.

RESULTS

Breeding diurnal raptors

This raptor community exhibited a remarkable long-term stability (Table 2). Among the 13 breeding species (excluding extinct forest species), only the status of the two rarest species changed. A single pair of Long-crested Eagle bred on the reserve at least until 1973. It was last seen on the study area in 1983 and none was recorded in 1996. The Lanner Falcon *F. biarmicus* was a scarce resident in open areas, including towns, in the Lamto region and it was sighted only twice on the reserve before 1973. By 1983, one pair had already settled in the study area. In 1996, a breeding pair was still found but it was defending its territory against 1-2 additional individuals and observations throughout the reserve also suggested that the actual population size may have been more than one pair. Both the eagle's demise and the falcon's increase may be related to the large scale anthropogenic changes in the region around the reserve, namely deforestation and woodland clearing that mean habitat losses for the former and benefits for the latter.

Among the eleven other species, different trends were detectable in 1996 (Table 2):
  i) The Grey Kestrel, a sedentary and solitary species of the most open grasslands, had a stable population from 1967 to 1973 and increased to 5 pairs in 1996. Its habitat requirements are quite similar to those of the Lanner Falcon and the growth of its population may also come from regional habitat changes, since the trend towards increasing woodland cover in the reserve should not have favoured this species.
  ii) The two African migrants increased. The rise of the Shikra population, from 12 to 15 pairs, though not significant ($Chi^2 = 0.148$, $P>0.7$), was probably real because the 1972 survey was more complete than the shorter 1996 survey where early or late nesting attempts may have been missed. The four-fold increase of the Black Kite breeding population (10 to 43 pairs) was striking ($Chi^2 = 19.32$, $P<0.001$), while the non-breeding individuals were still at least as numerous as in 1972. Only isolated pairs of Black Kites were formerly breeding in the reserve. In 1996, there were also two colonies, of 8 and 10 active nests respectively and 30-50 m from each other.
  iii) The two small forest raptors, the African Goshawk and the Western Little Sparrowhawk, had stable populations: the same number of pairs were found in the same portions of the large riverine forest of the Bandama River over the 25 years interval. This was in strong contrast with the disappearance of all larger forest raptors. Even the more widespread Bat Hawk showed at least a 50% decrease and no nest was found in 1996. However, it is often an unpredictable nester and it is unclear whether this was a real population decline.

Table 2. Raptor population size on the 2,700 ha savanna-forest mosaic of Lamto Reserve. Pairs included all settled pairs identified, even when breeding was not proved or was unsuccessful. Individuals = minimum number of unpaired residents and migrants in February and March separately in 1972 and in late February - early March together in 1996. Res = resident (breeding) species: Afr = African migrant (locally breeding or not); Pal = Palearctic wintering migrant. Names from Dowsett & Forbes-Watson (1993).

Species	Status	Breeding pairs		Non-breeding individuals	
		1972	1996	1972	1966
African Cuckoo Hawk	Res	10	6	4-3	2
European Honey Buzzard	Pal		1-3	1	
Bat Hawk	Res	4	2	?	?
Black-shouldered Kite	Res			1-0	0
Black Kite	Afr	10	43	152-58	125
Palm-nut Vulture	Res	13	11	20-18	15
Brown Snake Eagle	Afr			0	1
W. Banded Snake Eagle	Afr			0-1	2
African Harrier-hawk	Res	34	29	13-12	9
Montagu's Harrier	Pal			1-0	0
Eurasian Marsh Harrier	Pal			0	3
Gabar Goshawk	Afr			0	1
African Goshawk	Res	4	4	?	?
Shikra	Afr	12	15	4-7	6
W. Little Sparrowhawk	Res	3	3	?	?
Grasshopper Buzzard	Afr			88-45	69
Lizard Hawk	Res	38	36	12	11
Common Buzzard	Pal			2-1	2
Red-necked Buzzard	Afr			2-1	1
Tawny Eagle	Afr			1-0	0
Wahlberg's Eagle	Afr			3-1	6
Long-crested Eagle	Res	1	0	1	0
Common Kestrel	Pal			1-0	0
Grey Kestrel	Res	3	5	1	1
European Hobby	Pal			1-1	1
African Hobby	Res	17	15	9	7
Lanner Falcon	Res	0	1	0	1
TOTAL		**149**	**170**	**317-174**	**264**

iv) The 5-10% drop of the two most abundant small resident raptors, the Lizard Buzzard and the African Hobby (Table 2) was not significant (Chi^2 = 0.014 and 0.031, P>0.8) and unlikely to be real because both species were begining to breed during the 1996 survey and some late-settling pairs may have been overloooked.

v) The two large common raptors, so characteristic of the palm savanna-forest mosaic, Palmnut Vulture and African Harrier-hawk, both decreased by 15% (Table 2). This limited decline was not significant (Chi^2 = 0.042, P>0.8 and 0.254, P>0.6 respectively), but may have been real, because adult pairs and their nests were very conspicuous and unlikely to be missed. The number of birds in immature plumage also decreased consistently by about 20%. The two species shared the same staple diet of oil palm fruits in this area (Thiollay 1978a). Many of these palms have been felled on the reserve during the last two decades. This may have reduced a major food source and may explain a decline of these two specialized raptors.

vi) The African Cuckoo Hawk also decreased from 10 to 6 pairs, though not significantly (Chi^2 = 0.563, P>0.4). Mostly a foliage gleaner of large insects from open woodlands to dense forest (Thiollay 1977a, 1978a), it was a secretive and late breeder and the 1996 census may have been incomplete. Nevertheless it was a sensitive indicator of habitat impoverishment (Thiollay 1988) and its apparent decrease may have been real.

Overall, the breeding raptor population decreased from 1972 to 1996 by a mere 8.6%, excluding Black Kites, and it actually increased if Black Kites were included. The total density was still 47 breeding pairs of raptors per 1000 ha and even 63 pairs/1000 ha with Black Kites. This density may be overestimated because some peripheral pairs had home ranges extending outside the reserve although their nest was within the boundaries.

Non-breeding raptors

The fourteen non-breeding species recorded in February-March in the Lamto savanna (Table 2) could be divided into three categories (see Thiollay 1977b and 1985b for their regional status):

i) The resident Black-shouldered Kite *Elanus caeruleus* was common around the reserve in the most open cultivated areas but only occasional individuals came to forage in the dense natural savanna woodland of the protected area.

ii) Among the six Palearctic wintering migrants, three species were regular (1-2 individuals) in both February and March surveys in 1972 and 1996: European Honey-Buzzard *Pernis apivorus*, Common Buzzard *Buteo buteo* and Eurasian Hobby *F. subbuteo*. Montagu's Harrier *Circus pygargus* and Common Kestrel *F. tinnunculus*, widespread in West Africa but uncommon in southern savannas, were not resighted in 1996. The Eurasian Marsh Harrier *C. aeruginosus*, a rare vagrant in the Lamto savanna before 1973, was seen hunting daily in 1996. It may have actually increased in the surrounding areas, attracted by new large ricefields and dams, becoming as a result more frequent on the reserve.

iii) Of seven Ethiopian seasonal migrants, only the occasional Tawny Eagle *Aquila rapax* was not resighted in 1996. The Brown Snake Eagle *Circaetus cinereus* and Gabar Goshawk *Micronisus gabar* were previously rare in the Lamto region and exceptional on the reserve. Conversely, they were observed several times in 1996 within the reserve alone. This suggests a southward shift of their southern limit. Two regular migrants on the reserve (1-2 individuals) Western Banded Snake Eagle *C. cinerascens* and Red-necked Buzzard *B. auguralis*, were at least as frequent in 1996 as in 1972. The Wahlberg's Eagle *A. wahlbergi* had increased 2-3 fold by 1996. The number of individuals was too small to detect a statistical difference ($Chi^2 = 1.125$, $P<0.3$), but they were seen consistently more often in 1996 than in 1972. The abundant Grasshopper Buzzard *Butastur rufipennis* had a population size not significantly different in 1996 ($Chi^2 = 0.017$, $P>0.9$), compared to 25 years ago. Since foraging birds tended to be regularly spaced and aggressively maintained a minimum inter-individual distance, the Lamto area was probably saturated. In the early years, the density of Grasshopper Buzzards was much lower outside the reserve. This suggests that undisturbed savanna was preferred over degraded grasslands. Because of this concentration effect, any overall increase of the population would not show up within the reserve and evidence of any decrease would be delayed.

Vanished forest raptors

Six medium-sized to large species were associated with the wide gallery forest along the Bandama River and disappeared in the 1970's. Their demise was coincidental with the clearing of contiguous and extensive forests and savanna woodlands on the opposite side of the river, whose former breeders may have sustained their marginal populations of the Lamto area. Congo Serpent Eagle was recorded three times and Black Sparrowhawk twice in 1967-1970 on the reserve. Two pairs of Long-tailed Hawk were established in 1967-73. I located the species in 1983-84 in a single area but in 1996 none could be found. One pair of Ayres' Hawk Eagle *Hieraaetus dubius* was resident until 1972 and was not seen subsequently. One pair each of Cassin's Hawk Eagle *Spizaetus africanus* and Crowned Eagle *Stephanoaetus coronatus* were observed from 1967 until they disppeared after 1970, apparently without having bred successfully during this period (nest of Crowned Eagle found).

DISCUSSION

In spite of serious environmental degradation in the region, the overall stability of local raptor populations on the Lamto Reserve is remarkable. It may be questionable to infer a long-term trend and the influence of environmental changes from only two brief surveys, for a locally dynamic bird population in which stochastic between-year fluctuations may occur. Moreover, any detectable response of a population inside a protected area may be delayed and buffered by locally suitable conditions with resultant saturated population density, by a high longevity of many tropical species and by the concentration of birds attracted by better conditions and security inside the reserve. Therefore the following interpretations of the results remain tentative, even though they are supported by extensive surveys over most of West Africa and by a comprehensive experience of Côte d'Ivoire (Thiollay 1977b, 1978b, 1985). The long-term changes in this raptor community may have three different origins, that can be called global, regional and local.

Global changes in West Africa come mainly from decreasing rainfall and are more spectacular in the Sahel than at humid southern latitudes. Rainfall may affect vegetation, food supply and breeding success and this may influence bird population size, timing and extent of seasonal migrations and/or a shift of geographical range. The Lamto area being one of the wettest and southernmost extensions of natural savanna in West Africa, a decrease of rainfall may result in the appearance of new species from northern zones or in an increase of migrants formerly staying further north. In fact, the few cases found of increases were of migrants (Black Kite, Gabar Goshawk, Wahlberg's Eagle) and no significant decrease that could have suggested worsening conditions somewhere along their seasonal distribution.

Regional changes are driven mainly by the effects of human population growth and conversion of natural habitats. Large scale deforestation, clearing of savanna woodlands for plantations, heavy exploitation of Borassus and oil palms, large ricefields, dams and persistent hunting pressure, all occur throughout Central Côte d'Ivoire and in the immediate vicinity of Lamto Reserve. As a result of this habitat degradation or destruction, as well as direct killing, some species should decrease or disappear outside the reserve. Small remaining populations inside the protected area are thus increasingly isolated. This was probably how the eagles became extinct. The expected consequences are also an increasing occurrence, inside the reserve, of species that have successfully adapted to the new man-made habitats in the surrounding region. Such a spill-over may be illustrated by the Marsh Harrier and Lanner Falcon. Even without a population increase, a species sensitive to habitat loss outside the reserve may use the natural savanna as a refuge and cause a local increase.

Local changes are those affecting the vegetation inside the reserve and, as a result, the bird community. Three main factors emerged that could be related to observed changes in species abundance: developing tree cover, illegal felling of palms and invasion of *Chromalaena* thickets. The long-term trend towards an increasing density of savanna woodland (Gautier 1989, 1990) has had no obvious consequences on raptors up to 1996. The reduction of oil palm fruits may explain the moderate decrease of the Palm-nut Vulture and African Harrier Hawk, major consumers of this food resource (Thiolllay 1978a). The more adaptable and successful Black Kite, another important consumer of palm fruits in the Lamto area, may have turned to alternative food sources or may exercise stronger competition, including outside the reserve, with the above raptors on this critical resource during the dry (breeding) season. The dramatic invasion of *Chromolaena* thickets, in and along gallery forests and woodlands, has changed the structure of what was a specific foraging habitat of African Cuckoo Hawk and African Goshawk. Most of the savanna species did not seem to have experienced extinctions predicted as a consequence of fragmentation (Robinson & Quinn 1992). This may be because the grassland area on the reserve was sufficient to hold viable populations and/or they were still connected with healthy populations outside.

Forest species, conversely, have suffered significantly from habitat fragmentation. Forest patches around the reserves were more reduced or degraded than savanna stands. As a result, their populations could not rescue those of the reserve. The protected forest area was also six times smaller than that of savanna, and was highly fragmented into narrow galleries. Extinction is known to increase exponentially with the degree of fragmentation (Burkey 1989), whereas small patch size and isolation worsen the effects of habitat loss on declining populations (Andren 1994). Finally, forest birds are less mobile than many savanna birds, and this greatly increases their extinction probability in isolated fragments (Burkey 1989). Local extinctions involved large forest species, but not migrant savanna eagles (*Aquila, Circaetus*).

The overall density of breeding raptors in the Lamto Reserve is still one of the highest ever documented for a community of non-colonial Falconiformes (Thiollay 1975b). Among possible reasons is the dominance of small to medium-sized species, with very few large eagles or vultures which are prominent in other African savannas (e.g., MacDonald & Gargett 1984). The lush vegetation, the short dry season and the high habitat heterogeneity, combining forests, open grasslands and woodlands, are also likely to promote both species diversity and high densities through abundant and varied food sources. The high raptor species-richness, however, is outmatched in some (much larger) national parks of Côte d'Ivoire (Table 3) or elsewhere in Africa (e.g., Thiollay 1970b, 1978c; Hartley 1993) and in comparable grassland-forest mosaic in the Neotropics (38 species in an area of similar size in Venezuela, Thiollay 1996).

Table 3. Species richness of breeding raptors in the (small) Lamto Reserve compared to three (large) national parks surveyed in Côte d'Ivoire (Tai, in the southwestern rain forest area; Maraoué, in the central forest-savanna contact-zone; Comoé in the northern Guinea savanna: Thiollay 1975c).

	Vultures	Savanna eagles	Other savanna species	Forest raptors	TOTAL
Taï	1	0	3	8	12
Lamto	1	3	9	8	21
Maraoué	2	5	11	6	24
Comoé	4	7	12	3	26

Implications for conservation

Three consequences of human population growth and of unsustainable exploitation were found to be especially damaging:

1) clearings and unburned patches of savanna are quickly invaded by *Chromolaena* thickets which prevent natural regeneration,
2) the hunting pressure eliminated almost all game (including large birds) outside the reserve and may threaten raptors ranging across the boundaries, and
3) palms which provide important nesting, roosting and perching sites (*Borassus*) or food supplies (*Elaeis, Raphia*) are drastically reduced.

Therefore, it is crucial to prevent such encroachment if this last refuge is still to play its conservation role. The area of protected savanna, albeit small (about 2200 ha), maintained a stable population of most raptors over three decades in spite of important habitat changes all around. Conversely, the less than 500-ha forested area, fragmented into narrow galleries, then isolated by regional deforestation and degraded by invasion of *Chromolaena*, lost its larger species, which already had small populations. Such a protected area may act as a refuge and contribute significantly to the conservation of the regional biodiversity. The Borassus palm savanna-forest mosaic occurred within a narrow belt along the northern edge of the rain forest zone. African Harrier Hawk, Lizard Hawk and African Hobby, at least, reached a higher density here than in any degraded area and in any other vegetation zone (Thiollay 1988). There is no other protected area in Côte d'Ivoire that includes a sizeable patch of this palm savanna and it is barely possible to increase the size of the Lamto Reserve owing to the unavailability of pristine habitat around. The annual burning management maintains this palm savanna and limits the increase of both natural woodland and *Chromolaena* thickets, as proved by the comparative evolution of the surrounding region. Burning remains a critical tool for the conservation of this original habitat and its associated avifauna.

ACKNOWLEDGMENTS

The 1968-72 studies were supported by the Ecole Normale Supérieure, Paris and supervised by Prof. M. Lamotte, director of the Ecology Department. The 1996 field work was funded by the SALT Programme under the responsibility of J.C. Menaut. The manager of the Lamto station, R. Vuattoux, also provided invaluable assistance.

REFERENCES

ANDREN, H. 1994. Effects of habitat fragmentation on birds and mammals in landscapes with different proportions of suitable habitat: a review. *Oikos* 71: 355-366.
BROWN, L.H. 1952-1955. On the biology of the large birds of prey of the Embu District, Kenya Colony. *Ibis* 94: 577-620, 95: 74-114, 97: 38-64, 183-221.
BURKEY, T.U. 1989. Extinction in nature reserves: the effect of fragmentation and the importance of migration between reserve fragments. *Oikos* 55: 75-81.
DOWSETT, R.J & A.D. FORBES-WATSON 1993. *Checklist of birds of the Afrotropical and Malagasy Regions.* Tauraco Press, Liège.
GARGETT, V. 1990. *The Black Eagle. A study.* Acorn Books, Randburg.
GAUTIER, L. 1989. Contact forêt-savane en Côte d'Ivoire: évolution de la surface forestière de la réserve de Lamto (sud du V-Baoulé). *Bull. Soc. Botanique de France* 136: 85-92.
GAUTIER, L. 1990. Contact savane-forêt en Côte d'Ivoire centrale: évolution du recouvrement ligneux des savanes de la réserve de Lamto (Sud du V-Baoulé). *Candollea* 45: 627-641.
HARTLEY, R. 1993. The Batoka gorges, haven for birds of prey. *Afr. Wildl.* 47: 74-78.
HERKERT, J.R. 1994. The effects of habitat fragmentation on mid-western grassland bird communities. *Ecological Applications.* 4: 461-471.
KNICK, S.T. & J.T. ROTENBERRY 1995. Landscape characteristics of fragmented shrubsteppe habitats and breeding passerine birds. *Conserv. Biol.* 9: 1059-1071.
LAURANCE, W.F. & R.O. BIERREGAARD (eds). 1997. *Tropical forest remnants. Ecology, management and conservation of fragmented comunities.* University of Chicago Press, Chicago.
MACDONALD, I.A.W & V. GARGETT 1984. Raptor density and diversity in the Matopos, Zimbabwe. In: *Proc. V Pan-Afr. Orn. Cong.*, pp. 287-308. Southern African Ornithological Society, Johannesburg.
NEWMARK, W.D. 1991. Tropical forest fragmentation and the local extinctions of understory birds in the eastern Usambaras mountains, Tanzania. *Conserv. Biol.* 5: 67-78.
NEWTON, I. 1991. *Population ecology of raptors.* T. & A.D. Poyser, Berkhamsted.
PATUREL, J.E., E. SERVAT, B. KOUAMÉ, J.F. BOYER, H. LUBES & J.M. MASSON 1995. Manifestations de la sècheresse en Afrique de l'Ouest non sahélienne. Cas de la Côte d'Ivoire, du Togo et du Bénin. *Sécheresse* 6: 95-102.
ROBINSON, G.R. & J.F. QUINN 1992. Habitat fragmentation, species diversity, extinction and the design of nature reserves. In: Jain, S.K. & Botsford, W. (eds.), *Applied population biology*, pp. 223-248. Kluwer Academic Publishers, Dordrecht.
SAUNDERS, D.A. 1989. Changes in the avifauna of a region, district and remnant as a result of fragmentation of natural vegetation: the wheat belt of Western Australia. A case study. *Biol. Conserv.* 50: 99-135.
SAUNDERS, D.A., R.F. HOBBS & ?. MARGULES 1991. Biological consequences of ecosystem fragmentation. A review. *Conserv. Biol.* 5: 18-32.
SERVAT, E., J.E. PATUREL & H. LUBÈS 1996. La sécheresse gagne l'Afrique Tropicale. *La Recherche* 290: 24-25.
SOULÉ, M.E., A.C. ALBERTS & D.T. BOLGER 1992. The effects of habitat fragmentation on chapparal plants and vertebrates. *Oikos* 63: 39-47.
THIOLLAY, J.M. 1970a. Recherches écologiques dans la savane de Lamto (Côte d'Ivoire): le peuplement avien. Essai d'étude quantitative. *Terre et Vie* 24: 108-144.
THIOLLAY, J.M. 1970b. Les rapaces du Parc National du Niokolo Koba. Données préliminaires. *Oiseau Revue Française Ornithologie* 40: 115-130.
THIOLLAY, J.M. 1972. L'avifaune de la région de Lamto (moyenne Côte d'Ivoire). *Annales Université d'Abidjan* E (IV, 1): 5-132.
THIOLLAY, J.M. 1975a. Les rapaces d'une zone de contact savane-forêt en Côte d'Ivoire. Présentation du peuplement. *Alauda* 43: 75-102.
THIOLLAY, J.M. 1975b. Les rapaces d'une zone de contact savane-forêt en Côte d'Ivoire. Densité, dynamique et structure du peuplement. *Alauda* 43: 387-416.

THIOLLAY, J.M. 1975c. Les rapaces des parcs nationaux de Côte d'Ivoire. Analyse du peuplement. *Oiseau Revue Française Ornithologie* 45: 241-257.
THIOLLAY, J.M. 1976. Les rapaces d'une zone de contact savane-forêt en Côte d'Ivoire. Modalités et succès de la reproduction. *Alauda* 44: 275-300.
THIOLLAY, J.M. 1977a. Les rapaces d'une zone de contact savane-forêt en Côte d'Ivoire. Modes d'exploitation du milieu. *Alauda* 45: 197-218.
THIOLLAY, J.M. 1977b. Distribution saisonnière des rapaces diurnes en Afrique occidentale. *Oiseau Revue Française Ornithologie* 47: 253-294.
THIOLLAY, J.M. 1978a. Les rapaces d'une zone de contact savane-forêt en Côte d'Ivoire. Spécialisations alimentaires. *Alauda* 46: 147-170.
THIOLLAY, J.M. 1978b. Les migrations de rapaces en Afrique occidentale, adaptations écologiques aux fluctuations de production des écosystèmes. *Terre et Vie* 32: 89-133.
THIOLLAY, J.M. 1978c. Population structure and seasonal fluctuations of the Falconiforms in Uganda National Parks. *E. Afr. Wildl. J.* 16: 145-151.
THIOLLAY, J.M. 1985. The birds of Côte d'Ivoire: status and distribution. *Malimbus* 7: 1-59.
THIOLLAY, J.M. 1988. The Guinean savanna belt of West Africa: a case study of the raptor community. *ICBP Technical. Publications.* 7: 159-169. ICBP, Cambridge.
THIOLLAY, J.M. 1996. Distributional patterns of raptors along altitudinal gradients in the northern Andes and effects of forest fragmentation. *Journal Tropical Ecology* 12: 535-560.
VILLARD, M.A., G. MERRIAM & B.A. MAURER 1995. Dynamics in subdivided populations of neotropical migratory birds in a fragmented temperate forest. *Ecology* 76: 27-40.
WILCOVE, D.S. & S.K. ROBINSON 1990. The impact of forest fragmentation on bird communities in Eastern North America. In: Keast, A. (ed.), *Biogeography and ecology of forest bird communities*, pp 319-332. SPB Academic Publ., The Hague.

Jean-Marc Thiollay
Laboratoire d'Ecologie, E.N.S.
46, rue d'Ulm
75230 Paris Cedex 05
France

Raptor Studies in Kenya: Past, Present and Future

Munir Virani

INTRODUCTION

Kenya supports one of the richest avifaunas in Africa and contains a mosaic of different habitats determined by altitude and rainfall distribution. This natural spectrum includes montane forests, dry and moist forests, woodlands, savannah grasslands, scrublands, deserts, marshes and mangroves. These diverse habitats support a total of 75 species of diurnal birds of prey and 16 of nocturnal owls - a raptor richness that is among the highest of any country in the world.

In contrast to its rich natural resources, Kenya also has one of the highest human population growth rates in the world and a severely limited area of fertile land. Nearly eighty-eight percent of Kenya's human population is directly dependent on rain-fed agriculture (IUCN 1992). Furthermore, small-scale subsistence agriculture and livestock grazing is the most prevalent land-use throughout much of Kenya (Sorley & Andersen 1994). This has resulted in many of its areas exceeding their carrying capacity (KNR 1972). As a result, the country has reached a situation where land-use interests such as agriculture, tourism, ranching, wildlife management, forestry and water conservation - each of them valid and nationally productive usages of land -are in competition and often in conflict over large areas of the country. Not only are various arms of the Government in disagreement or confusion on these issues, but the problem is compounded by the demands of the landless, burgeoning population which are haphazardly realised in the absence of clear policies. This lack of land-use policy has clearly affected the country's wildlife resources. For example between the period from 1920 to 1970, this resource had, as a direct result of increasing human pressure, been depleted by as much as 50% (KNR 1972). Raptor abundance and diversity have also suffered as a result of increasing human population pressure. For example, a recent survey on raptor abundance in south-central Kenya in relation to land-use patterns showed that differences in land-use practices between undisturbed and man-altered habitats are directly responsible for significant changes in raptor community structure (species richness, density and species identity) related to human land-use (Sorley & Andersen 1994).

There is an urgent need for a clear-cut national policy on land and habitat use that should aim to protect the country's precious wildlife resources, while at the same time meeting the needs of the local people. Understanding the ecological requirements of key indicator species that are sensitive to habitat change can bring about effective land-use policies based on sound conservation principles. Raptor studies have been used as effective tools for conservation in a number of projects around the world (e.g. Peregrine Falcon – USA; Mauritius Kestrel – Mauritius; Madagascar Fish Eagle – Madagascar) (Burnham *et al.* 1992). In the East African region, information obtained from ecologically-based raptor studies can be used to achieve conservation goals. For example, a study on the ecology of raptors in the Impenetrable Forest in Uganda provided vital information on seven raptor species and, in consequence, aided in the long-term conservation policy of the forest (Muhweezi 1990). In order to achieve conservation using raptors as indicators, knowledge about their basic ecology is vital. However, there is a large gap in the knowledge about the basic ecology of most raptors in the East African region. In a recent study on the state of ecological knowledge and conservation status of raptors in Africa, almost 61% of raptors were rated as poorly understood in aspects of distribution, population dynamics, breeding biology and feeding ecology (Virani & Watson 1998). Furthermore, in a recently compiled list of East African birds in jeopardy, almost 40% of all the breeding raptors that occur in the East African region (n = 79) have been listed as either Endangered (1), Vulnerable (14) or Near Threatened (15) (Bennun & Njoroge 1996). Thus a lack of sufficient knowledge about the basic biology of East African raptors, coupled with their high local conservation importance, has fuelled the need to better understand the basic ecological requirements of key raptor species. Raptor studies are thus an ideal tool to focus on conservation strategies, especially in areas prone to changes in habitat, both natural and anthropogenic (see Reichholf 1974; Watson 1991; Thiollay 1992; Burnham *et al*. 1992; Virani & Watson 1998).

The aims of this paper are a) to outline the steps taken in the revival of raptor studies in Kenya, b) to highlight some of the raptor studies recently and currently conducted in Kenya, and c) to discuss the direction and future of raptor research and conservation in Kenya.

REVIVAL OF RAPTOR STUDIES IN KENYA

Prior to 1980, the late Leslie Brown published almost a quarter of all that is known about raptors in Africa (Virani & Watson 1998) and thus provided a solid framework to build on for future raptor studies. The majority of his fieldwork was conducted in Kenya, and his classical studies on the African Fish Eagle *Haliaeetus vocifer* at Lake Naivasha and the eagles of Embu Hill are still being referred to at this date. Sadly, after his death in 1980, raptor studies in Kenya came to a virtual halt, save for a handful of raptor enthusiasts who continued watching and enjoying Kenya's raptors. Small-scale raptor studies were also conducted intermittently by overseas researchers, including distribution studies on the African Fish Eagle (Cambridge University 1979; Reading University 1986; Smart 1991), distribution and density survey of the Sokoke Scops Owl *Otus ireneae* (Kelsey & Langton 1984), pesticide studies (Lincer *et al*. 1981), just to mention a few. These studies were short, spanning a few days, or were part of an overall expedition focussing more on other aspects such as vegetation analysis or species counts. There was still an urgent need for a focused, more co-ordinated study on individual raptor species threatened by anthropogenic impacts.

In 1992, exactly 12 years after the demise of Leslie Brown, the Peregrine Fund Inc., World Center for Birds of Prey, included Kenya in its Pan-African Raptor Conservation Project. The Kenya Project, initiated by Rick Watson (Programme Director, Africa and Madagascar), was modelled after the Peregrine Fund's successful partnerships in the Philippines and Madagascar, where a focus on birds of prey is used to achieve conservation goals. The main aim in Kenya was to develop national expertise and ability to achieve conservation of biodiversity. This would be achieved by gathering important ecological and socio-economic information on which to base conservation and management interventions that are specific to the unique problems of each target site. Under a joint memorandum of understanding with the National Museums of Kenya (NMK), and under the managership of local raptor expert Simon Thomsett, the Peregrine Fund's Kenya Project was initiated. Over the last six years, three students have undergone post-graduate training in raptor biology. In addition, self-supporting overseas students have been encouraged to help in on-going or independent raptor projects (see below).

KEY-SITES OF RAPTOR STUDIES IN KENYA

Raptor research activities in Kenya have focused on three important sites, the Arabuko-Sokoke forest along the Kenyan coast (ranked as the second most important forest in mainland Africa for bird conservation by Collar and Stuart (1985)), the Lake Naivasha area in the Great Rift Valley (now declared a Ramsar site), and the Athi-Kapiti grasslands south-east of Nairobi (Fig 1).

Figure1. Map of Kenya showing major sites of raptor reserved activities.

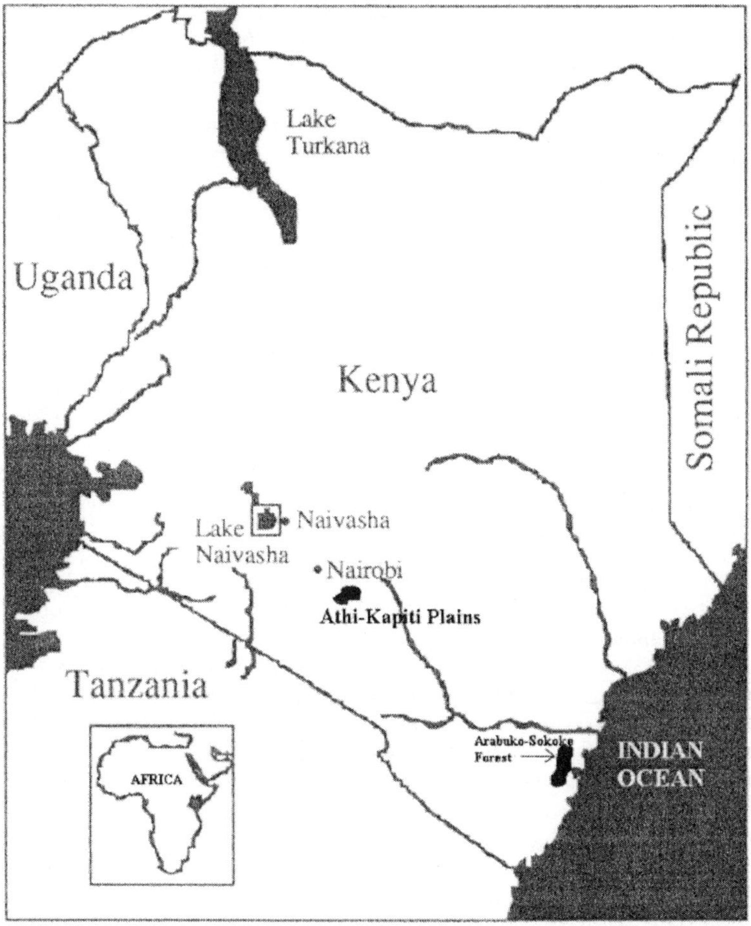

Arabuko-Sokoke forest

The Arabuko-Sokoke forest contains the greatest area of natural complete forest cover in coastal Kenya (Robertson & Luke 1993). It covers an area of 372 km² and is a vestige of the coastal forest that once stretched along the entire coastline of East Africa (KIFCON 1994). The forest is a vital habitat for a number of endangered and rare species of animals, among them the Sokoke Scops Owl which is virtually confined to the *Cynometra* woodland habitat within the forest. As the forest faced a major threat from increased clearance of its valuable timber trees, it was believed that the owl population might be further threatened (Kelsey & Langton 1984). In 1993, a year-long study on the ecology of the Sokoke Scops Owl commenced. The aims were to better understand the owls' ecological requirements so that an effective conservation and management plan could be implemented to ensure the species' survival (see Virani 1995; Virani *this proceedings*; Virani *in press*). A distribution and density survey of the Barred Owlet *Glaucidium capense*, in relation to the Sokoke Scops Owl, was also conducted (Virani & Tarpley *in litt.*).

Lake Naivasha

Lake Naivasha, Kenya's largest freshwater lake, is located in the Great Rift Valley. The lake covers an area of about 120km^2 and has a shoreline of approximately 50 km (Melack 1979). The Lake Naivasha area has always been an important ecological site to Kenya (Harper *et al.* 1990). Its diversity of flora and fauna, and the range of vegetation-zones associated with the lake and its hinterland, is greater than that of other Rift Valley lakes (Lincer *et al.* 1981). This importance has been maintained even though the lake has no statutory protection or reserve status. In 1995, the lake was recognised as a Ramsar wetland site of international importance.

The Lake Naivasha area has a high economic value; it is the fount of Kenya's upcoming horticultural industry. The lake's waters irrigate thousands of hectares of fertile volcanic loam which burgeon with vegetables and flowers. The lake area is also a focus for tourism (particularly bird watching) and recreation (boating and sport fishing) which earn the country foreign exchange. In addition, a commercial fishery has also been built up over the past 30 years on the basis of introduced species, the products being transported to Nairobi and Nakuru in addition to local consumption (Harper *et al.* 1990). The area is also industrially significant as a consequence of the development of Olkaria, just to the south of the lake, a geothermal energy generation site that produces about 43 megawatts (15%) of Kenya's total energy consumption (Harper *et al.* 1990).

The lake has experienced, over the years, tremendous fluctuations in water level, plant structure, animal populations and nutrient composition. The increasing human population around the lake has resulted in clearing of riparian forests along the lake shore for agriculture and settlement. The recent proliferation of flower and other horticultural enterprises has accelerated this trend, which in turn may have had an impact on the flora and fauna of the lake and its environs.

In order to determine whether the rapid changes in land use patterns around the Lake Naivasha area are having a significant impact on the animal communities, a study focusing on the ecological requirements of the Augur Buzzard *Buteo augur*, Egyptian Vulture *Neophron percnopterus* and African Fish Eagle was initiated.

The Athi-Kapiti plains

The Athi-Kapiti plains are ecologically linked to Nairobi National Park and are an important migratory corridor for the thousands of plains game that occur in the park. The plains consist of rolling savannah grasslands, riverine woodland, man-made dams and rocky gorges. The area is an important migratory route for Lesser Kestrels *Falco naumanni* and other migrating birds. The migratory patterns of plains game animals are becoming increasingly constrained by sprawling settlements and industrial development on the Athi-Kapiti plains. The plains were originally set aside as a game conservation area, but land hunger around Nairobi became acute in the 1970s and people were allowed to settle there. This resulted in ranches being fenced off, small-scale agricultural plots mushroomed and human-wildlife conflicts became intense.

A study on the Martial Eagle *Polemaetus bellicosus*, commenced in 1996, aims to determine the ranging patterns and habitat utilisation of the eagle in order to determine the impacts of rapidly changing land-use patterns on the birds' ecology.

HIGHLIGHTS OF CURRENT AND RECENT RAPTOR STUDIES IN KENYA

Sokoke Scops Owl (Virani 1995)

A study of the Sokoke Scops Owl was conducted between January and December 1993. Elicited-call surveys were used to determine the owls' distribution, abundance and calling behaviour, while radio-telemetry was used to study the owls' home range and movement patterns. Owl pellets were also collected to determine their contents.

The owls were found mainly in the dense *Cynometra* woodland, where they occurred at a density of 7 pairs/km^2. They occurred at lower densities in adjacent habitats of lower canopy height. The total owl population in the forest was estimated at 1,000 pairs. Three neighbouring owl pairs were radio-tracked for a month-long period each. They occupied exclusive territories of about 12-14 ha, roosting and foraging mainly within the lower canopy level of *Cynometra* woodland. Owl activity was linked with lunar cycles, as they tended to forage nearer to their roosts and travel smaller distances on moonlit nights. Calling activity was significantly higher during the first quarter and full moon phase. Most calling activity and movement took place two hours after dusk and two hours before dawn. Females were found to be 20% heavier than males. Based on pellet analysis, the owls fed almost entirely on insects. As a result of the Sokoke Scops Owl study, the status of the owl was downlisted from endangered to its present status of vulnerable (Collar *et al.* 1994).

Barred Owlet (Virani & Tarpley *in litt.*)

Barred Owlet surveys in Arabuko-Sokoke forest were conducted between October and December 1993. The owlets were found mainly in the *Brachystegia* woodland and intermediate *Cynometra* woodland. The interest in the distribution of the owlet stems from a hypothesis of mutual exclusivity with the Sokoke Scops Owl. Both owl species co-existed in the intermediate *Cynometra* woodland, although at much lower densities than in their preferred habitats. Barred Owlets occurred at a density of 4.4 pairs/km2 in *Brachystegia* woodland and their total population size in the forest was estimated to be about 300 pairs.

Augur Buzzard (Virani *in litt.*)

The Augur Buzzard study was conducted between January 1995 to January 1998. The aims were to determine the impacts of different land-uses on the ecology of the species. Populations of Augur Buzzards were studied in three different land-use areas; Hell's Gate National Park, undisturbed *Acacia* woodland and agricultural areas. Productivity of Augur Buzzards was highest in undisturbed *Acacia* woodland (1.32 chicks/pair/year) and lowest in agricultural areas and Hell's Gate National Park (0.64 and 0.53 chicks/pair/year respectively). Mortality rates were lowest in undisturbed *Acacia* woodland and highest in agricultural areas. Forty percent of mortality (n = 15) was a result of human persecution and poisoning. Rainfall did not influence timing of laying, although 76.4% of pairs (n = 74 pairs over 3 years) laid between April and September of each year. The diet of Augur Buzzards comprised mainly rodents (74.4%) while birds (6.4%), reptiles (3.9%), dassies (3.8%) and arthropods (1.3%) formed the rest. Prey delivery rates to the nest differed at different stages of the nestling period as well as when there was more than one chick in the nest.

African Fish Eagle (Virani & Harper *in litt.*; Virani *et al. in litt.*)

Prompted by previous data on population size of the African Fish Eagle at Lake Naivasha (Brown & Hopcraft 1973; Cambridge University 1979; Reading University 1986, Smart 1991; and African Waterfowl Census 1990-1993), an ongoing study on the eagles began in April 1994 (Virani *et al.* 1997; Parsons 1997; Virani & Harper *in litt.*). The aims of the study were to compare present-day fish eagle population size with that which existed in the early 1970s, and to correlate population trends with parameters such as lake-levels, transparency, prey availability and habitat parameters.

The population of the African Fish Eagle has declined by around 50% since 1970, to around 110 adults (all territory-holding pairs). Proportions of juveniles:adults have declined from 20% to 4% over the same period. At present, shoreline density ranges from 2.6 adults/km (western shore with mature trees, continuous papyrus fringe and rocky hinterland) to 0.6 adults/km (eastern shore with intensively farmed riparian edge, degraded papyrus and no trees). The overall decline in adults has been caused by loss of about one-third of the shoreline since the lake has receded after 1970, exacerbated by degradation of fringing papyrus vegetation around half the shoreline through various forms of human activity. Decline in productivity has been caused by reduction in available food. Appropriate-sized fish have declined through over-fishing and higher levels of sediment and phytoplankton growth have reduced water transparency. Appropriate-sized birds have almost disappeared, following a catastrophic decline in aquatic littoral plants. A total of 37 fish eagles have been trapped and measured. Females weighed 2.30-3.31 kg (mean 2.99, n = 20); males 2.10 - 2.65

kg (mean 2.34, n = 17). The mean weight of female birds was lower than those published in existing literature (Brown *et al.*, 1982) suggesting that they may be catching just enough food to maintain body weight but not enough to sustain breeding. In 1997, only four active nests existed. The most effective conservation measure for the eagle will be effective management of the fishery.

A new study to determine the nest-site characteristics of the eagles began in July 1998 (Virani *et al. in litt.*). A total of twenty nests and twenty random sites have been quantified. Data are presently being analysed.

Martial Eagle (Ong *in litt.*)

A study on the home range and habitat use of the Martial Eagle on the Athi-Kapiti plains was conducted between October 1996 and October 1997, and at the time of writing C. Ong was writing up her thesis. A total of six Martial Eagles from three adjacent pairs were radio-tagged and tracked during this period. Data were also obtained on their nest-site characteristics, breeding success and diet (analysed from prey remains found beneath nests).

Egyptian Vulture (Mburu *in litt.*)

The ecology of the Egyptian Vulture was studied in the southern Lake Naivasha area and, at the time of writing, B. Mburu had completed his field work. He observed a total of five adjacent pairs and focused mainly on aspects of breeding biology and ranging patterns.

Other raptor projects

Since 1992, a number of other projects have been proposed and/or conducted. These include 1) collection of blood and muscle tissues from various raptors in the Rift Valley for the analysis of organo-chlorine residues (Thomsett *in litt.*), 2) raptor road counts in the Rift Valley region and along the Nairobi-Mombasa road (Virani *in press.*), and 3) re-introduction of the Bearded Vulture *Gypaetus barbatus* in Hell's Gate National Park (Thomsett, pers comm.).

THE FUTURE OF RAPTOR CONSERVATION IN KENYA

The revival of raptor research activities in Kenya has provided a firm platform on which to base future conservation work. International organisations such as the Peregrine Fund Inc. – World Center for Birds of Prey (USA), Earthwatch Institute (USA) and the Aga Khan Foundation (Switzerland), in collaboration with local institutions such as the National Museums of Kenya and the Elsamere Conservation Centre, have been instrumental in the revival of raptor research activities in Kenya. It is imperative that these partnerships continue to grow and flourish. The concept of establishing an autonomous raptor group to coordinate raptor activities in Kenya has been discussed by various partners. In May 1998, the structure of a Kenya Raptor Working Group (KRWG) was officially approved by members of the Bird Committee of the East African Natural History Society (EANHS). The KRWG will serve as the 'raptor arm' of the EANHS, one of the oldest natural history societies in Africa (founded 1909) with a firm commitment to promoting the study of natural history and conservation of biodiversity in the East African region. The objectives of the KRWG will be

1) to coordinate and facilitate conservation-based ecological studies on predatory birds, 2) to understand factors that influence their distribution and abundance, 3) to continue and expand ecological monitoring programmes on existing raptor projects, 4) to initiate a countrywide raptor monitoring programme through a series of annual road counts and intensive banding programme, 5) to build and maintain a database for all ecological and conservation work related to predatory birds, 6) to develop and implement a community-based raptor conservation project in the Lake Naivasha region, 7) to conduct annual certificate courses on 'Raptor Biology and Conservation', targeted mainly towards undergraduate and graduate students as well as other institutions such as tour guide associations, park rangers and amateur naturalists, 8) to train individuals in aspects of identification, handling and banding of raptors, 9) to distribute through the EANHS, a newsletter on the latest developments and news regarding aspects of raptor biology and conservation, 10) to develop a detailed atlas on the distribution and status of raptors in Kenya (and East Africa), 11) to maintain and

foster close links with other environmental NGO's and research organizations on conservation and management issues, and also to identify and implement new projects with existing research organizations such as the International Centre for Insect Physiology and Ecology (ICIPE) and the International Centre for Research on Agro-forestry (ICRAF) in new sites such as the Ngurumans (projects under discussion include 'Understanding the impacts of Tse-tse control on raptor communities' (ICIPE) and 'The value of re-afforestation projects and their impacts on nesting raptors' (ICRAF)), 12) to work closely with the Wildlife Clubs of Kenya and arrange visits to school wildlife clubs in key raptor conservation areas, and give talks and education materials concerning the conservation of raptors (and birds in general), 13) to facilitate raptor research opportunities for visiting students/volunteers by identifying small projects and providing guidance and logistical support where possible, and 14) to work in collaboration with other world-wide raptor organisations such as the Raptor Conservation Group of the Endangered Wildlife Trust (South Africa), International Birdwatching Centre (Israel), Raptor Research Foundation (USA), among others. These collaborations are vital for project funding, further training of scientific and technical staff, for example on aspects of captive breeding, and the initiation of new raptor projects such as the use of satellite-transmitters on the little known Ruppell's Griffon Vulture *Gyps rueppellii*.

ACKNOWLEDGEMENTS

I would like to thank the Peregrine Fund Inc.- World Center for Birds of Prey, Earthwatch Institute and the Aga Khan Foundation for their financial and logistical support in various raptor projects. The Department of Ornithology, National Museums of Kenya and the Elsamere Conservation Centre provided logistical support. I am deeply indebted to all my field assistants and volunteers for their help. I would also like to thank the Raptor Conservation Group for enabling me to attend the V Raptor Conference in Midrand, SA and Dr Alan Kemp for allowing me to contribute in his African raptors session. I am grateful to Dr Leon Bennun for his comments. This paper is dedicated to Simon Thomsett for his contribution to raptor research in Kenya.

REFERENCES

AFRICAN WATER FOWL CENSUS. 1990-1993. *Data extracted from the annual African Water fowl censuses conducted on Kenyan Rift Valley lakes*. National Water Fowl Census Co-ordinator, National Museums of Kenya, Nairobi.
BENNUN, L.A. & P. NJOROGE 1996. *Birds to watch in east Africa: a preliminary Red Data list*. Research Rep. 23. Centre for Biodiversity, National Museums of Kenya, Nairobi.
BROWN, L.H. & J.P.D. HOPCRAFT, 1973. Population structure and dynamics in the African Fish Eagle *Haliaeetus vocifer* (Daudin) at Lake Naivasha, Kenya. *E. Afr. Wildl. J.* 11: 255-269.
BROWN, L.H., E.K. URBAN & K. NEWMAN 1982. *The Birds of Africa*. Vol. I. Academic Press, London.
BURNHAM, W.A., D.F. WHITACRE & J.P. JENNY 1992. The Maya Project: use of raptors as tools for conservation and ecological monitoring of biological diversity. In: Meyburg, B.-U. & Chancellor, R.D. [eds], *Raptor Conservation Today*, pp. 257-264. World Working Group on Birds of Prey, Berlin.
CAMBRIDGE UNIVERSITY EXPEDITION. 1979. *University of Cambridge Kenyan Eagle Study Expedition of 1979*. Unpublished report, not seen, cited in: Reading University Expedition 1986.
COLLAR, N.J. & S.N. STUART 1985. *Threatened Birds of Africa and related islands: the ICBP/IUCN Red Data Book*. International Council for Bird Preservation and International Union for Conservation of Nature and Natural Resources, Cambridge.
COLLAR, N.J., M.J. CROSBY & A.J. STATTERSFIELD 1994. *Birds to Watch 2. The world list of threatened birds*. Birdlife Conserv. Series: 4. Birdlife International, Cambridge.
HARPER, D.M., K.M. MAVUTI & S.M. MUCHIRI 1990. Ecology and management of Lake Naivasha, Kenya, in relation to climatic change, alien species introductions, and agricultural development. *Environ. Conserv.* 17: 328-336.
INTERNATIONAL UNION FOR CONSERVATION OF NATURE. 1992. *The Conservation Atlas of Tropical Forests*. IUCN, Gland.
KELSEY, M.G & T.E.S. LANGTON 1984. The conservation of Arabuko-Sokoke forest, Kenya. *International Council for Bird Preservation Study Report*: 4. ICBP, Cambridge.

KIFCON 1994. *Kenya Indigenous Forest Conservation Programme (KIFCON)*. Phase I Report. KIFCON, Nairobi.
KNR 1972. *Kenya National Report to the United Nations on the human environment*. Professional printers and stationers, Nairobi.
LINCER, J.L., D. ZALKIND, L.H. BROWN & J. HOPCRAFT 1981. Organochlorine residues in Kenya's Rift Valley lakes. *J. Applied Ecol.* 18: 157-172.
MELACK, J.M. 1979. Photosynthetic rates in four tropical African fresh waters. *Freshwater Biol.* 9: 555-571.
PARSONS, M. 1997. A study of the African Fish Eagle *Haliaeetus vocifer* and its habitat at Lake Naivasha. Unpublished B.Sc. dissertation, University of Leicester.
READING UNIVERSITY EXPEDITION. 1986. Report of the Reading University Kenyan Eagle Survey. Unpublished report, Royal Geographic Society, London.
REICHHOLF, J. 1974. Artenreichtum, Haufigkeit und Diversitat der Greifvogel in einigen Gebieten von Sudamerika. *J. Orn.* 115: 381-397.
ROBERTSON, S.A. & W.R.Q. LUKE 1993. *The report of the NMK/WWF Coast Forest Survey*. WWF Project 3256: Kenya, Coast Forest Status, Conservation and Management.
SMART, A.C. 1991. Density and distribution of the Fish Eagle *Haliaeetus vocifer* on Lakes Naivasha and Oloidien, Kenya. *Scopus* 14: 76-83.
SORLEY, C.S. & D.E. ANDERSEN 1994. Raptor abundance in southcentral Kenya in relation to land-use patterns. *Afr. J. Ecol.* 32: 30-38.
THIOLLAY, J-M. 1992. A world review of tropical forest raptors. Current trends, research objectives and conservation strategy. In: Meyburg, B.-U. & Chancellor, R.D. [eds], *Raptor Conservation Today*, pp. 231-239. World Working Group on Birds of Prey, Berlin.
VIRANI, M.Z. 1995. Ecology of the endangered Sokoke Scops Owl *Otus ireneae*. Unpublished M.Sc. thesis, University of Leicester.
VIRANI, M.Z. *in press*. Home range and movement patterns of the Sokoke Scops Owl *Otus ireneae*. ?
VIRANI, M.Z. *in press*. Changes in raptor populations around the Naivasha-Elementeita area using indices from roadside counts. *Kenya Birds*.
VIRANI, M.Z. *in litt*. The impacts of different land-uses on the ecology of the Augur Buzzard *Buteo augur* in the southern Lake Naivasha area, Kenya. Ph.D. research, University of Leicester.
VIRANI, M.Z. & D.M. HARPER *in litt*.. The African Fish Eagle *Haliaeetus vocifer* at Lake Naivasha, Kenya.
VIRANI, M.Z. & H. TARPLEY *in litt*. Distribution and density of the Barred Owlet *Glaucidium capense* in the Arabuko-Sokoke forest, Kenya.
VIRANI, M.Z., R. THORSTROM & D.M. HARPER 1997. What is happening to Naivasha's Fish Eagles? *Kenya Birds* 5: 98-100.
VIRANI, M.Z. & R.T. WATSON 1998. Raptors in the East African tropics and western Indian Ocean islands: State of ecological knowledge and conservation status. *J. Raptor Res.* 32: 28-39.
VIRANI, M.Z., M. WILSON & D.M. HARPER *in litt*.. Nest-site characteristics of the African Fish Eagle *Haliaeetus vocifer* at Lake Naivasha.
WATSON, R.T. 1991. Using birds of prey as an environmental conservation tool: The Peregrine Fund's World Programme. *Environ. Conserv.* 18: 269-270.

Munir Virani
Peregrine Fund Kenya
Dept. of Ornithology
National Museums of Kenya
P.O Box 40658
Nairobi, Kenya
and
Dept. of Biology
Leicester University, U.K.

Status and conservation of raptors on the Masoala Peninsula, Madagascar

Russell Thorstrom and Lily-Arison Rene de Roland

ABSTRACT

Madagascar is the fourth largest island in the world and has a high degree of floral and faunal endemism. One hundred and seven (53%) of the 203 resident bird species are endemic, including 11 of the 22 diurnal and nocturnal raptor species. Since 1990, The Peregrine Fund has been conducting studies on the forest raptor community of the Masoala Peninsula in north-eastern Madagascar, where the largest intact lowland rainforest on the island exists. Of the 22 raptor species recorded for Madagascar, 19 have been found on the peninsula, with nesting records documented for Madagascar's two most endangered raptors, Madagascar Serpent-eagle and Madagascar Red Owl, plus Bat Hawk, Madagascar Harrier-hawk, Frances's Sparrowhawk, Madagascar Sparrowhawk, Henst's Goshawk, Madagascar Buzzard, Madagascar Kestrel, Banded Kestrel, Madagascar Long-eared Owl, White-browed Owl and Malagasy Scops Owl. Status, threats and conservation measures are discussed for each of the raptor species found on Masoala Peninsula. Information gathered on the Madagascar Serpent-eagle was important in the justification and size of the newly inaugurated Masoala National Park, encompassing 220,000 ha of pristine lowland rainforest.

INTRODUCTION

Madagascar is the fourth largest island and largest oceanic island in the world, with an area that comprises about 0.4% of the land surface of the planet Earth (Mittermeier 1997). Madagascar lies in the Indian Ocean, about 400 km off the eastern coast of continental Africa, and has been isolated for more than 150 million years. This long isolation has contributed to a high species endemism of plants and animals. Today, many ecosystems on Madagascar are threatened, by increasing human population pressure from slash-and-burn farming and fuelwood collecting, including what little natural forest remains.

The Masoala Peninsula was recognized by the government of Madagascar as a high-priority area for conservation of biological diversity, because of endemic flora and fauna such as the Madagascar Serpent-eagle *Eutriorchis astur*, isolation from the otherwise continuous north-south rainforests, and the occurrence of extensive lowland forest. In October 1997, the new Masoala National Park was inaugurated to protect the unique and endemic biological diversity of the Masoala Peninsula. The survival of many endemic fauna and flora will depend upon maintaining the intact primary forests of Masoala National Park.

Madagascar has 22 species of diurnal and nocturnal raptors, of which 11 are endemic to Madagascar: two are considered critically endangered, the Madagascar Fish-eagle and the Madagascar Serpent-eagle and one endangered, the Madagascar Red Owl (Collar *et al.* 1994). Both the Madagascar Serpent-eagle and Madagascar Red Owl are known from the eastern rainforest region (Langrand 1990), and recently from the Masoala Peninsula (Thorstrom & Watson 1997). Although some species of Malagasy raptors have benefited from the degradation of forests (e.g. Madagascar Kestrel), most forest species have been adversely affected. Other causes of species declines have been persecution by man for food, superstition and protection of poultry.

In this paper we will provide information on the status and threats, and make recommendations for conservation measures needed to preserve, the 19 raptor species occurring on the Masoala Peninsula of northeastern Madagascar.

SPECIES ACCOUNTS

Madagascar Cuckoo-falcon *Aviceda madagascariensis*

An endemic and sparsely distributed species throughout Madagascar. Reported to inhabit all types of forest, most often encountered at edge of forests or around clearings in forests, and ranges from sea level to 1800 m (Langrand 1990). Mainly feeds on lizards and insects. Its nesting and breeding biology poorly known but appears to be a forest- or woodland-nesting species. Reported to be in the Masoala forests by visiting bird enthusiasts but not substantiated. This species is easily confused with the common and highly variably-plumaged Madagascar Buzzard *Buteo brachypterus* (Langrand 1990; del Hoyo *et al.* 1994). The Madagascar Cuckoo-Falcon is an easily overlooked species throughtout its broad range. If it does occur in Masoala forests it is extremely rare. This species is not under any great threat overall but declining forest is bound to negatively affect the species. Considered a near-threatened species and populations need to be identified and habitat protected against human disturbances and degradation.

Bat Hawk *Macheiramphus alcinus*

A rarely observed species in Masoala and throughout Madagascar. Probably breeds at an extremely low density throughout its range. One nesting pair was observed in the northeastern region of the Masoala Peninsula on 18 December 1993. Local villagers showed us this species, claiming it to be the Madagascar Serpent-eagle. The nest was in an isolated tree on a small hill surrounded on all sides by land cleared for subsistence agriculture. One individual was observed in 1992 perched in a tree at Tampolo, 7 km south of Andranobe Field Station, The Peregrine Fund's research station and 2 km from the ocean. One individual rarely seen every year near the AFS and probably an individual from Tampolo. Difficult to ascertain the status of this secretive species but forest felling may open up more habitat for it. Little is known about this species' breeding biology in Madagascar. A study on its ecological needs is warranted.

Black Kite *Milvus migrans*

Occasionaly observed at Maroantsetra, the port to Masoala Peninsula, flying along the coastal beaches or along the rivers and, on the eastern side of the peninsula, flying over agricultural fields, villages and coastal beaches. During our raptor survey in 1992, we observed several individuals flying over a field at Nandrahanana north of the village of Ambanizana on the west coast of Masoala Peninsula. This species is abundant in the western region of Madagascar. Appears to be under no great threat but suspected that human persecution to protect poultry may frequently occur.

Madagascar Serpent-eagle *Eutriorchis astur*

An elusive, endemic and endangered bird of prey found only in primary forests. Virtually unknown until rediscovery, repeated sightings and capture in 1993-1994 (Thorstrom *et al.* 1995). A shy, secretive species, easily overlooked and confused with Henst's Goshawk. The ranging area of a radio-tagged individul was important for determining the size and justification of the Masoala National Park. Recently found nesting on the west and east side of the peninsula. One nesting pair, studied during the 1997 breeding season, constructed a nest in an epiphytic fern. Both adults incubated, the female attended the nestling, and prey deliveries to the nest were mainly chameleons (*Furcifer* and *Calumna* spp.) and leaf-tailed geckos (*Uroplatus* spp.), plus some arboreal and terrestrial frogs. The nestling fledged at nine weeks of age.

We have located 15 different individuals of serpent-eagles at nine sites throughout the Masoala Peninsula. Currently, the new Masoala National Park and peninsular forest contain the greatest number of sightings and known density of serpent-eagles in Madagascar. We have estimated that about 104 territorial pairs may exist in the Masoala National Park and peninsula, with the assumption that the forested habitat is homegenous and the species' breeding density is saturated. The Madagascar Serpent-eagle is a forest-dependent species that relies on intact forest for its ecological needs. It is critical that the primary Masoala forest be maintained in this park for survival of one of the least known and most endangered raptors in the world. The loss of primary forests will definitely affect the survival of this species.

Madagascar Harrier-hawk *Polyborodies radiatus*

An endemic and common nesting species in the Masoala forests. Found from primary to degraded forest and wooded habitats. Easily observed and heard throughout the Masoala forests, soaring frequently above the forest canopy. Appears to breed at a low density throughout the Masoala Peninsula. We observed four nesting attempts during a 1992 raptor survey on the west coast of Masoala Peninsula (one at Rantabe, two at Ambanizana and one at Andranobe). The Andranobe pair has nested at the same site for 7 years, from 1991-1997, laying two eggs each year but fledging only one young in 1994 and 1996. This species has a broad diet and occasionally hunts by hanging on vegetation and thrusting its feet into holes. Diet consists of insects, amphibians, reptiles, birds and mammals (Langrand 1990; del Hoyo et al. 1994), and was observed feeding on Henst's Goshawk nestlings (Rene de Roland et al. 1996) and a dwarf lemur *Cheirogaleus* sp.)(G. La Marca pers. comm.) on the Masoala Peninsula during the 1995 and 1997 breeding seasons, respectively. Local villagers on the east coast of Masoala Peninsula trapped, killed and ate a harrier-hawk because it predated on their domestic fowl. Probably persecuted in areas where it preys on domestic livestock. In the future, this species could be impacted by human persecution as more local people raise and protect domestic fowl.

Madagascar Marsh-harrier *Circus maillardi*

A large harrier for an island species. May be a different species from the subspecies found on Réunion (R. Simmons pers. comm.). Uncommon and infrequently observed coursing over fallow rice fields and marsh or wetland habitat. Rarely observed on Masoala Peninsula, mainly on the east side where more forest alteration has taken place, and sighted once at the airstrip of Maroantsetra. As forests are converted to large rice fields on the peninsula this altered habitat will probably benefit this species to a slight degree. It may move along the coastal rice fields to more open habitat in north-western and eastern regions of the Masoala Peninsula. One of the main threats to this species is grassland fires that usually occur during the dry period, which is its nesting season (Pauven 1995).

Frances's Sparrowhawk *Accipiter franescii*

A small, common forest raptor on the Masoala Peninsula. This species inhabits any woodland and secondary or primary forests. It has a high nesting density in the Masoala forests, with six nests within 30 minutes by foot from Andranobe Field Station (Rene de Roland in press). Diet mainly insects, lizards and birds. At 14 nests under study on the Masoala Peninsula, 13 (93%) were successful in fledging at least one young (Rene de Roland in press). Normally changes nest site from one year to the next, with a mean internest distance of 105 m from 1994 to 1995 (n = 9 nests). Occasionally hunted for food by local villagers on the Masoala Peninsula (pers. obs.).

Madagascar Sparrowhawk *Accipiter madagascariensis*

An endemic, uncommon and secretive medium-sized forest accipiter. Inhabits mainly primary forest and rarely occurs in secondary vegetation. Confused easily with Frances's Sparrowhawk and occasionally with Henst's Goshawk. Three nesting attempts were observed at two different nest sites from 1993-1996, north of Andranobe Field Station. Diet composed mainly of birds, and builds a small stick nest, slightly larger than Frances's Sparrowhawk but placed near the top of the tree. Vocalization similar to Frances's Sparrowhawk and appears to hunt in the upper canopy for birds. Rarely observed in the forest, except at its nest, and due to its secretiveness it is a difficult species to detect. Does not appear to be threatened but as forested habitat declines this will surely affect this species in the future.

Henst's Goshawk *Accipiter henstii*

The largest endemic accipiter in Madagascar and considered of near-threatened status. During the breeding season this raucous hawk is easy to find, which contrasts with its activity during the nonbreeding season. Occasionally heard and seen soaring above the forest canopy. Easily confused with the rare and endangered Madagascar Serpent-eagle. Most reports of serpent-eagles by local villagers are of this species. A rapacious hawk feeding on large birds and lemurs (*Avahi laniger* and *Eulemur* spp., Goodman *et al.* in press). Neighbouring nests in the interior of Masoala Peninsula were approximately 7-12 km apart. Breeds at a low density and estimated to be about 26 breeding pairs in the Masoala National Park. Probably lives at a lower population density in the Masoala forests than the Madagascar Serpent-eagle. We know of six past and present nesting territories found throughout the peninsula from 1991 to 1997. May use the same nest from previous nesting season or build a new nest 300-500 m from old nest. Occasionally persecuted by local villagers for attacking poultry. A forest-dependent species that needs a large area to survive. Maintaining the forest of the Masoala National Park is important for its protection.

Madagascar Buzzard *Buteo brachypterus*

Endemic and common hawk found in the Masoala forests, forest clearings, and secondary vegetation. An obvious buteo, heard and observed soaring above and perched in the forest canopy. Appears to be an adaptable species found in a wide range of habitats from degraded openings, woodlands and primary forests. In a study on the Masoala Peninsula, Berkelman (1996) found a high breeding density for the Madagascar Buzzard of a pair per 0.8 km^2 in 1991 and 0.5 km^2 in 1992 at Andranobe Field Station. This species is an opportunistic hunter that feeds on a wide range of prey species from invertebrates such as terrestrial crabs to lizards, snakes, birds and rodents (Berkelman 1994, Del Hoyo *et al.* 1994). Occasionally hunted for food by local villagers (pers. obs.).

Madagascar Kestrel *Falco newtoni*

Ubiquitous species in grasslands, croplands, secondary vegetation, and degraded woodland habitats, and in and around villages. Nests in tree cavities and large hollows on the Masoala Peninsula and is vocal at its nest. Six nests were observed during the 1997 breeding season. Feeds mainly on insects and lizards. A common raptor found in fields, slash-and-burn clearings and other human-altered habitat. This species has probably increased with deforestation, cultivation and urbanization. Found throughout the Masoala Peninsula in any vegetation-covered opening or slash-and-burn clearing. No antagonistic behaviour was observed between a nesting pair of Madagascar Kestrels and Banded Kestrels separated by 100 m, but it is frequently harassed by cavity-nesting Broad-billed Rollers *Eurystomus glaucurus*.

Banded Kestrel *Falco zoniventris*

An endemic and secretive species that lives on the forest edge or in woodland clearings. About twice the size of the Madagascar Kestrel. A difficult species to detect, even during the breeding season, because of its secretive and relatively non-vocal behaviour. Three nests have been discovered on Masoala Peninsula from 1995-1997. Stamps out a nest in the centre of a epiphytic fern situated in a large tree fork (Thorstrom in press). Feeds mainly on chameleons and insects. Considered a near-threatened species but probably more abundant than was once thought due to its secretive nature. An increase in deforestation may lead to a decline in the population status. Protection of forest edge and woodland habitat is critical for the survival of this species.

Eleonora's Falcon *Falco eleonorae*

An austral migratory species usually arriving in December in Madagascar and in January to the Masoala Peninsula. Observed in groups or pairs feeding on large flying insects over the forest canopy. Common on the Masoala Peninsula from December to March but appears to have decreased from 1991 to 1997 (René de Roland pers. obs.).

Sooty Falcon *Falco concolor*

An austral migratory species usually arriving in December in Madagascar and in January to the Masoala Peninsula. Observed in groups or pairs feeding on large flying insects over the forest canopy. Uncommon on the Masoala Peninsula from December to March.

Madagascar Red Owl *Tyto soumagnei*

The endemic Madagascar Red Owl was first rediscoved in Marojejy in 1993 (Halleux & Goodman 1994). Peregrine Fund biologists then discovered this species at sea-level on the Masoala Peninsula in early 1994, which considerably extended its known range. A strictly nocturnal species that is extremely rare, one pair was studied on the Masoala Peninsula (Thorstrom *et al.* 1997). Nearly all the information known about this species comes from this one study pair. Radio-telemetry helped identify foraging habitat, which included secondary degraded forest, rice paddies, and day-roosts in exotic plantations of bananas and cloves. The study pair occurred on the forest edge and hunted in active and fallow rice fields, cattle pastures, slash-and-burn agriculture areas, and the forest edge. This species is not a forest obligate as previously believed, and may simply have been overlooked. The nest was located in a cavity of an isolated tree surrounded by subsistence agricultural lands (Thorstrom & René de Roland 1997). Feeds mainly on native insectivores and rodents (Thorstrom *et al.* 1997; Goodman & Thorstrom in press). This species has also been heard at three sites on the peninsula with all vocalizations coming from large subsistence agriculture plots along the main forest block (Thorstrom 1997). The study female was used as an important conservation practice, where birding enthusiasts were shown the day-roosting owl if they contributed funds to the building of a local school in the village nearest to the owl's territory (Thorstrom 1997). Over $450 American dollars went to the building of the school. The creation of protected areas in eastern rainforest domain, such as Masoala National Park, may be sufficient to conserve the species (Watson & Thorstrom 1997). Basic research on the ecology of the Madagascar Red Owl is needed in areas where it occurs in primary forests.

Barn Owl *Tyto alba*

A common species living in towns, large villages and openings. Feeds mainly on introduced mammals (Goodman *et al.* 1993; Goodman & Thorstrom in press). Common in the town of Maroantsetra and infrequently at Ambanizana village. As deforestation continues the species will probably increase in areas of large clearings and openings, and where populations of introduced rodents become abundant.

Malagasy Scops Owl *Otus rutilus*

A common nocturnal species found in any forested or wooded area. Population status not known but probably affected by loss of wooded and forested habitat. Feeds chiefly on insects and nests in small tree cavities. The loss of forested habitat would decrease the availability of nesting sites. Basic research on the ecology of this scops owl is needed.

White-browed Owl *Ninox superciliaris*

A poorly-known endemic and nocturnal species, sometimes active during the crepuscular periods. Occupies a variety of habitats from towns to primary forests. Two nests have been observed on the peninsula in tree cavities, one in the forest interior and the other on the forest edge. A vocal species that calls sometimes during the day. Observed feeding on insects and lizards, with several prey deliveries to nests occurring during the early morning hours. Basic research on the ecology of this owl is needed to understand its habitat requirements.

Madagascar Long-eared Owl *Asio madagascariensis*
A large, poorly-known endemic owl found in degraded, secondary and primary forests. One nest, observed in a patch of littoral forest in November 1994, was in a large epiphytic fern. Two weeks after finding the nest we visited the site and found two fledglings 20 m from the nest. Feeds on rodents, small lemurs and birds (Langrand 1990; Goodman *et al.* 1993). Basic research is needed on the ecology of the Madagascar Long-eared Owl.

ACKNOWLEDGEMENTS
We thank Bill Burnham and Rick Watson of The Peregrine Fund for providing support to the Madagascar Project. We are grateful to Lloyd Kiff, Rick Watson and Alan Kemp for comments on earlier versions of this manuscript. We also thank all the field technicians involved in the field work of this project.

REFERENCES
BERKELMAN, J. 1994. The ecology of the Madagascar Buzzard *Buteo brachypterus*. In: Meyburg, B.-U. & Chancellor, R.D. (eds). *Raptor conservation today*, pp. 255-256. WWGBP & Pica Press, East Sussex.
BERKELMAN, J. 1996. Breeding biology of the Madagascar Buzzard in the rain forest of the Masoala Peninsula. *Condor* 98: 624-627.
COLLAR, N.J., M.J. COSBY & A.J. STATTERSFIELD 1994. *Birds to Watch 2: The World List of Threatened Birds. BirdLife Conservation Series*: 4. Birdlife International, Cambridge.
DEL HOYO, J., A. ELLIOT & J. SARGATAL 1994. *Handbook of the Birds of the World*. Volume 2. New World Vultures to Guineafowl. Lynx Edicions, Barcelona.
GOODMAN, S.M., O. LANDGRAND & C.J. RAXWORTHY 1993. The food habits of the Barn Owl *Tyto alba* at three sites on Madagascar. *Ostrich* 64: 160-171.
GOODMAN, S.M., O. LANDGRAND & C.J. RAXWORTHY 1993. Food habits of the Madagscar Long-eared Owl *Asio madagascariensis* in two habitats in southern Madagascar. *Ostrich* 64: 79-85.
GOODMAN, S.M., L.-A. RENE DE ROLAND & R. THORSTROM In press. Predation on the eastern woolly lemur *Avahi laniger* and other vertebrates by Henst's Goshawk *Accipiter henstii* in Madagascar. *Lemur News*.
GOODMAN, S.M. & R. THORSTROM In press. The diet of the Madgscar Red Owl (*Tyto soumagnei*) on the Masoala Peninsula, Madagascar. *Wilson Bull.* 110.
HALLEUX, D. & S.M. GOODMAN 1994. Rediscovery of the Madagascar Red Owl *Tyto soumangei* (Grandidier 1878) in north-eastern Madagascar. *Bird Conserv. Intn.* 4: 305-311.
LANGRAND, O. 1990. *Guide to Birds of Madagascar*. Yale University Press, New Haven.
PAVERNE, L. 1997. Nidification et comportement du Busard de Maillard (*Circus maillardi*) dans la région d'Ankozobe au nord-ouest d'Antananarivo. *Newsletter of the Working Group on Birds in the Madagascar Region* 7: 21-24.
MITTERMEIER, R., P.A. GIL & C.G. MITTERMEIER 1997. *Megadiversity: Earth's biologically wealthiest nations*. Agrupacíon Sierra Madre, S.C., Mexico.
RENE DE ROLAND, L.-A. In press. Breeding biology of the Frances's Sparrowhawk *Accipiter francesii* in a lowland rainforest of northeastern, Madagascar. *Ostrich*.
RENE DE ROLAND, L.-A., R. THORSTROM & R.T. WATSON 1996. Breeding records and nestling predation of Henst's Goshawks on Masoala Peninsula, Madagascar. *Ostrich* 67: 168-170.
THORSTROM, R. In press. A description of nests, diet and behaviour of the Banded Kestrel. *Ostrich*.
THORSTROM, R., J. HART & R.T. WATSON 1997. New record, ranging behaviour, vocalization and food of the Madagascar Red Owl *Tyto soumagnei*. *Ibis* 139: 477-481.
THORSTROM, R. & L.-A. RENE DE ROLAND 1997. First nest record and nesting behaviour of the Madagascar Red Owl *Tyto soumagnei*. *Ostrich* 68: 42-43.
THORSTROM, R. & R.T. WATSON 1997. Avian inventory and key species of the Masoala Peninsula, Madagascar. *Bird Conserv. Intn.* 7: 99-115.
THORSTROM, R., R.T. WATSON, B. DAMARY, F. TOTO, M. BABA & V. BABA 1995. Repeated sightings and first capture of a live Madagascar Serpent-eagle *Eutriorchis astur*. *Bull. Brit. Orn. Club* 115: 40-45.

WATSON, R.T. & R. THORSTROM 1997. Birding and ecotourism as a conservation tool on Masoala: The Madagascar Red Owl and The Peregrine Fund's nest reward program. In: Watson, R.T. (ed.). *Masoala Project: Use of raptors and other avifauna for conservation, monitoring and evaluation of rain forest on Masoala Peninsula, Progress Report IV*, pp. 123-126. The Peregrine Fund, Boise.

Lily-Arison Rene de Roland
The Peregrine Fund's Madagascar Project
B.P. 4113 Antananarivo 101
Madagascar

Russell Thorstrom
The Peregrine Fund
566 West Flying Hawk Lane
Boise, Idaho 83709
U.S.A.

Chancellor, R. D. & B.-U. Meyburg eds. 2000
Raptors at Risk
WWGBP / Hancock House

A new Subspecies of the Booted Eagle from Southern Africa, inferred from biometrics and mitochondrial DNA

Reuven Yosef, Gerhard Verdoorn, Andreas Helbig and Ingrid Seibold

ABSTRACT

The population of Booted Eagles *Hieraaetus pennatus* breeding in Southern Africa is proposed to comprise a new subspecies, *H. p. minisculus*, based on its small size and three differences in the DNA sequence of 1041 base pairs of its mitochondrial *cytochrome b* gene. It is suggested that its common name be the Southern Booted Eagle.

ACCOUNT

Only two subspecies of the Booted Eagle *Hieraaetus pennatus* are recognized at present, *H. p. pennatus* (Gmelin), 1788 and *H. p. harterti* Stegmann, 1935 (Brown & Amadon 1968). The breeding range of the nominate subspecies is described as south Europe to North Africa and the Caucasus, and of *H. p. harterti* as in southwest and central Asia. Cramp and Simmons (1980) state that there is a cline of increasing size from west to east, but that birds in central Asia do not warrant recognition as a third subspecies, *H. p. milvoides* Jerdon 1839. For further discussion of the sub-specific taxonomy and nomenclature of this species refer to Porter (1970) and Brooke (1974).

It appears that early researchers were unaware of the breeding population of Booted Eagles in southern Africa (e.g. Brown & Amadon 1968). Upon discovery, it was assumed that these birds were of the nominate subspecies that had recently initiated breeding in the region (Tarboton 1994). Furthermore, Tarboton mentioned that a nest found in 1917 in the southern Cape region was incorrectly ascribed to a different species, and so was paid no further attention. In 1972, a pair of Booted Eagles was discovered nesting in the western Karoo, and since then many other breeding pairs have been discovered in the southern Cape.

Tarboton (1994) contends that "despite other uncertainties, it is clear that the Booted Eagle has established itself as a breeding species in southern Africa in comparatively recent times." Steyn (1996) reports that an estimated 400 pairs breed in the Western and Eastern Provinces of South Africa, and that the previously unrecorded Booted Eagle may actually be the most common breeding eagle in the region. Brown *et al.* (1982) contend that the European and North African breeding populations are not racially distinct from the Southern African population, but Steyn (1996) thought that the situation required "further elucidation", with which we concur.

On a visit to South Africa in February 1997, RY and GV observed that a Booted Eagle *Hieraaetus pennatus* at the RESCUE (Raptor Education and Special Care Unit) rehabilitation centre was smaller than those on migration at Eilat and those that breed in Europe and Asia. Blood samples were taken from this individual and from three others held at the World of Birds aviaries, Cape Town, and sent to AH and IS for DNA-sequencing. In addition, biometrics were taken from specimens of skins in the Transvaal Museum at Pretoria, South Africa, and in the Natural History Museum at Tring, United Kingdom.

Table 1. Data on specimens of *Hieraaetus pennatus* examined at the Transvaal Musem (TM), Pretoria, the Natural History Museum (NHM), Tring, at the United States National Museum of Natural History (USNMNH), Washington, D.C., and at the Museum of Comparative Zoology (MCZ), Harvard University.

Date (Specimen Number)	Location	Sex/ Age	Wing length	Tail length	Body length	Culmen	Hind claw
Holotype	RESCUE, South Africa	U	330	175	430	23.0	23.5
10.05.1935 (21178; TM)	Assab, Namibia	M Ad	343	186	461	19.5	24.0
19.08.1937 (21179; TM)	Klipfontein	M Ad	343	181	446	20.5	24.5
24.02.1909 (5491, TM)	Transkei	F Ad	364	187	485	22.0	25.0
POSSIBLE *H. p. minisculus* SKINS:							
??.??.1864 (342, NHM)	Chibisa, Zambesi	U	345	188		23.7	23.9
97.??.???? (43.2.28.62, NHM)	South Africa	U	355	191		21.1	23.1
20.02.1923 (404158, USNMNH)	Malawi	M	346				
29.12.1914	Kugersdorp	F	407	204	542	25.0	30.0
24.12.1891 (18001, TM)	Vryburg, Kalahari	F Ad	399	206	522	25.0	29.0
28.11.1915 (13331, TM)	Pretoria	F Ad	399	226	546	25.0	29.0
17.11.1912 (4830, TM)	Matatiele, NE Cape	F Juv	384	184	526	26.0	30.0
14.02.1912 (9284, TM)	Pretoria	F Ad	388	205	555	24.5	28.0
29.12. 1914 (14574, TM)	Krugersdorp	F Ad	407	204	542	25.0	30.0
??.09.1903 (1484, TM)	Rhodesia	? ?	374	188	478	23.5	28.0
12.02.1884 (343, NHM)	Rustenberg Transvaal	F Ad	385	200		24.3	28.7
??.??.1877 (56031, USNMNH)	Greece	M	362				

Date (Specimen Number)	Location	Sex/Age	Wing length	Tail length	Body length	Culmen	Hind claw
22.03.1877 (56032, USNMNH)	Hungary	F	342				
29.03.1894 (152787, USNMNH)	Egypt	F	391				
30.12.1945 (399824, USNMNH)	India	F	408				
30.12.1945 (399825, USNMNH)	India	F	365				
12.12.1948 (408023, USNMNH)	Nepal	F	394				
28.12.1912 (433525, USNMNH)	South Africa	?	360				
10.04.1910 (152792, MCZ)	Caucasus	M	368				
29.07.1917 (152793, MCZ)	Turkestan	F	399			24.0	25.0
??.05.1886 (71035, MCZ)	Palestine	?	386			26.0	27.0
??.??.???? (71036, MCZ)	Palestine	?	423			broken	30.0
??.??.???? (71037, MCZ)	Palestine	?	383			25.0	27.0
??.??.1879 (33601, MCZ)	India	?	364			23.0	24.0
??.??.???? (92686, MCZ)	India	?	427			24.0	31.0

We compared our data with the biometrics of Eurasian birds and with skins in museums. Because Palaearctic birds mingle with the local breeding population during the austral summer, we follow Brooke (1974) in separating the data for museum specimens collected during the austral summer from those collected during the breeding season in southern Africa (Tables 1 & 2). Our conclusion from the morphometric data is substantiated by the DNA-sequencing done later.

Nucleotide sequences of the mitochondrial *cytochrome b* gene (1041 base pairs) were compared between three Booted Eagles of the Palearctic breeding population (one from Germany; two migrants caught in Eilat, Israel) and two individuals of the South African breeding population (holotype plus one captive bird from the World of Birds, Hout Bay near Cape Town). Total cellular DNA of each individual was isolated from blood samples. The *cytochrome b* gene was amplified via polymerase chain reaction and sequenced directly as described in Seibold and Helbig (1995). Both South African birds differed from the Palearctic ones at three out of 1041 (0.29%) nucleotide positions (Table 3). The sequences are deposited at the EMBL databank under accession numbers Y15760 (*H. p. pennatus*) and Y15761 (*H. p. minisculus* (ssp. nov.)).

The sequence divergence of 0.29% between the Palearctic and the South African populations indicates that some genetic differentiation has taken place since both last shared a common ancestor. It is not important how large the percentage difference is, but whether the differences are consistent, and so the differences should be confirmed by sequencing samples from more specimens for both areas. All three substitutions are synonymous third codon position transitions, i.e. they do not affect the amino acid sequence of the gene product. The sequences presented correspond to positions 14995 through 16023 of the *Gallus gallus* mitochondrial genome (Desjardins & Morais 1990).

The result is consistent with a recent colonization of southern Africa by Booted Eagles from the Palearctic, probably within the Holocene. Therefore morphological differences seen today between the subspecies must have evolved rapidly, probably due to strong selection pressures in the newly colonized, southern African environment.

Table 2. Comparison of biometrics of specimens of *Hieraaetus pennatus* examined at the Transvaal Musem (Table 1) with data from literature and field studies. Data presented: mean (± SD) and range. Blank columns indicate lack of data.

Sex	N	Wing Chord (mm)	Tail length (mm)	Body Mass (g)	Culmen (mm)	Hind Claw (mm)
H. p. minisculus ?						
Male	2	343.0 (0)	184 (3.5)	540 (holotype)	20.0 (0.5)	24.3 (0.4)
Female	1	364	187	22.0	25.0	
Eilat, Israel (migratory birds)						
Male	8	357.1 (4.1) (352-362)	193.6 (8.4) (185-213)	590 (523-659)	22.4 (1.3) (21.1-25.4)	26.1 (1.3) (23.9-28.5)
Female	28	385.7 (9.1) (370-413)	204.8 (6.2) (194-220)	774 (642-1025)	25.0 (2.4) (22.4-36.4)	29.0 (0.9) (28.0-31.9)
Brown & Amadon (1968)						
Male		361 (352-378)	(188-192)			
Female		391 (375-403)	(205-211)			
Brown *et al*. (1982)						
Male	9	369 (353-390)	195 187-202	709 (510-770)		
Female	10	409 (380-428)	211 (196-218)	975 (840-1250)		
Weick (1980)						
Male		347-412	187-202	595-770	21.0-24.0	
Female		355-435	196-230	840-1145	24.0-26.0	
Cramp & Simmons (1980)						
Male	14	358 (10.7) (342-378)	195 (5.7) (186-204)	709 (n = 9) (510-770)	21.9 (1.0) (20.0-23.5)	24.4 (0.9) (22.9-25.4)
Female	24	393 (12.6) (374-425)	205 (4.2) (198-215)	975 (n = 10) (840-1250)	24.6 (1.2) (22.0-26.2)	29.1 (1.8) (25.0-31.0)

We appreciate that the taxonomy of the *Hieraaetus* eagles is still full of uncertainties, but this distinctive form cannot, on present evidence, be assigned to or treated as either of the two known subspecies of the Booted Eagle. We therefore consider that it should be treated as a new sub-species, and because it is the smallest of the three subspecies, we propose the name:

Hieraaetus pennatus minisculus subsp. nov.

English name

We suggest Southern Booted Eagle, after the region in which this sub-species is known to breed.

Holotype

Adult, unsexed, alive at the RESCUE rehabilitation centre, South Africa; private collection of GV. Found injured (fractured wing) by Jacques Fuller and Johan Esterhuizen in the Free State Province of South Africa in October 1995. Measurements were taken on 9 February 1997.

Table 3. Nucleotide sequences of the mitochondrial cytochrome b gene of three Booted Eagles of the Palearctic breeding population and two individuals of the South African breeding population. Both South African birds differ at three out of 1041 nucleotide positions (0.29%) from the Palearctic ones.

pennatus	GGCTCCCTAC	TGGGAATCTG	CCTACTAACA	CAAATCCTAA	CTGGCCTCCT	ACTAGCCATA
miniscules	....	....	....	....	....	....
pennatus	CACTACACCG	CAGACACCAC	CCTAGCCTTC	TCGTCCGTTG	CCCACACATG	CCGAAACGTA
miniscules	....	....	....	....	....	....
pennatus	CAGTACGGCT	GACTAATCCG	CAACCTACAT	GCCAATGGAG	CGTCCTTCTT	CTTCATCTGC
miniscules	....	....	....	....	A.........	....
pennatus	ATCTACCTAC	ATATCGGCCG	AGGACTCTAC	TACGGCTCGT	ATCTATATAA	GGAAACCTGA
miniscules	....	....	....	....	....	....
pennatus	AACACAGGGA	TCATTCTCCT	ACTGACCCTT	ATAGCAACCG	CCTTCGTAGG	CTATGTCCTC
miniscules	....	....	....	....	....	....
pennatus	CCATGAGGAC	AGATATCCTT	CTGAGGGGCC	ACAGTCATCA	CCAACCTATT	CTCAGCAATT
miniscules	....	....	....	....	....	....
pennatus	CCGTACATTG	GACAAACCCT	CGTAGAGTGA	GCCTGAGGCG	GATTCTCCGT	AGATAACCCC
miniscules	....	....	....A.....	....	....	....
pennatus	ACCCTCACCC	GTTTCTTTGC	CCTACATTTT	TTACTCCCAT	TCCTTATCGC	AAGTCTTACC
miniscules	....	....	....	....	....	....
pennatus	CTAATCCACC	TCACCTTCCT	GCACGAATCC	GGATCCAACA	ACCCTCTAGG	AATTATCTCA
miniscules	....	....	....	....	....	....
pennatus	AACTGTGACA	AAATCCCATT	CCACCCATAC	TTCTCCTTAA	AAGACATTCT	AGGATTCTTA
miniscules	....	....	....	....	....	....
pennatus	CTAATACTAC	TCCCACTAAC	AACCCTAGCC	CTATTCTCAC	CCAACCTATT	AGGTGACCCA
miniscules	....	....	....	....	....	....
pennatus	GAAAACTTCA	CCCAGCAAA	CCCTCTAGTT	ACACCCCCTC	ACATCAAACC	AGAATGATAC
miniscules	....	....	....	....	....	....
pennatus	TTCCTATTTG	CATATGCTAT	CCTACGCTCA	ATCCCCAACA	AGCTGGGGGG	AGTACTAGCC
miniscules	....	....	....	....	....	....
pennatus	CTAGCTGCCT	CAGTACTGAT	TCTATTCCTC	ATCCCCCTTC	TCCACAAATC	CAAACAACGC
miniscules	....	....	....	....	....	....
pennatus	ACAATAACCT	TTCGACCCCT	CTCCCAACTC	CTATTCTGAA	CCCTAATCGC	CAACCTCCTT
miniscules	....	....	....	....	....	....
pennatus	ATCCTCACAT	GAATCGGCAG	CCAACCAGTA	GAACACCCAT	TTATCATCAT	TGGCCAACTC
miniscules	....	....	....	....	....	....
pennatus	GCCTCCCTCA	CCTACTTCTC	CACCCTCCTA	ATCTTCTTCC	CTTTAATTGG	AGCCCTCGAA
miniscules	....	....	.....T....	....	....	....
pennatus	AATAAAATGC	TCCACCCCTA	A.........			
miniscules	....	....	....			

End (chicken position 16023)

Measurements of holotype

Wing chord 330 mm, tail length 75 mm, wing span 1050 mm, total body length 430 mm, tarsus 59 mm, culmen 23 mm, hallux 23.5 mm and body mass 540 g. The beak was bluish at the base and black at tip, the cere yellow, and the eye brown in colour.

We consider the holotype to be a poor indicator of the subspecies because it is an individual with a broken wing and living in captivity. As with most captive birds held in cages, we expect that the biometric measurements may not represent the wild population. In the holotype, we suspect that the measurements of the wing and the tail length (and hence the total body length) are influenced by exaggerated abrasion of the feathers. In contrast, the culmen has grown because of the lack of natural abrasion.

Measurements of other individuals.

Of the 10 skins in the Transvaal Museum (TM), one is from Roumania and seven were collected during the austral summer. The other three skins collected were distinctly small for a Booted Eagle (Fig. 1). Specimen #'s 21178 and 21179 are adult males and each had a wing chord of 343 mm, with tail length 186 mm and 181 mm, total body length 461 mm and 446 mm, culmen 19.5 mm and 20.5 mm, hind claw 24 mm and 24.5 mm respectively (Table 1). Specimen #5491 is an adult female with the wing chord 375 mm, tail length 187 mm, total body length 485 mm, culmen 22 mm, and hind claw 25 mm.

At the Natural History Museum at Tring, there are two specimens that were collected in southern Africa and one from Zambesi (Table 1). The biometrics of the two southern African birds are similar to those reported above. However, lack of collector's information (especially date) prevents us from adding them to the southern African list with certainty.

This uncertainty also holds for the individual collected in Malawi (specimen #404158) which is at the United States National Museum of Natural History, Washington, D.C. The date on which the bird was collected is within the period when Palaearctic wintering birds are still present. However, the wing chord is comparatively short in relation to the other skins (Table 1). Although total body length was also measured, the data are not included because differences in preparation style have influenced the measurement, and skins ranged from understuffed with very short necks to overstuffed and expanded skins (Christopher Milerisky, USNMNH).

None of the seven skins at the Museum of Comparative Zoology, Harvard University, are from southern Africa (Table 1). Four of the specimens were collected in the late 1800s, two in India and two in Palestine (present-day Israel). The other three were collected in the first two decades of the century, one in the Caucasus region, one at Karabura, Turkestan, and one in Palestine.

It has been shown that in Eurasia the Booted Eagle is clinally larger from west to east, i.e., birds from Spain and North Africa have the shortest wing, increasing to the largest in Turkestan and Siberia (Cramp & Simmons 1980). The birds that breed in southern Africa are smaller than both Eurasian subspecies. They are also local and either do not migrate at all or migrate shorter distances than those of the Palearctic populations. Hence, we would expect the wing to be shorter (Table 2) and more rounded, i.e., primary feathers less elongated (cf. Jenni & Winkler 1994). This is borne out by the fact that, for the migratory subspecies, the primary feather projection is usually P7 (or P6 because of abrasion) and the primary projection of the holotype is P5.

Based on the morphological, genetic, and geographical distribution findings mentioned above, we suggest that the Booted Eagle that breeds in southern Africa is a different, as yet undefined, subspecies.

ACKNOWLEDGMENTS

We thank Erez Yosef for his help and insight in the early stages of this discovery. Hadoram Shirihai examined skins at the Natural History Museum, Tring, on behalf of RY. Christopher Milensky kindly identified and measured the skins at the United States National Museum of Natural History. Dr. R. Paynter, Jr., Museum of Comparative Zoology, Harvard University, allowed RY access to skins. We thank J. Fuller, J. Esterhuizen and Neil Greenwood for the care and rehabilitation of the type specimen. Financial support was received from the Leslie Brown Award (Raptor Research Foundation). David Parkin and Peter Alden commented on an earlier draft of the manuscript.

REFERENCES

BROOKE, R. K. 1974. On the material evidence of *Hieraaetus pennatus* in southern Africa. *Bull. Brit. Orn. Club* 94: 154-158.
BROWN, L. & D. AMADON 1968. *Eagles, Hawks and Falcons of the world.* McGraw Hill Book Co., New York.
BROWN, L. H., E. K. URBAN & K. NEWMAN 1982. *The Birds of Africa.* Vol. 1. Academic Press, London.
CRAMP, S. & K. E. L. SIMMONS (eds). 1980. *The Birds of the Western Palearctic.* Vol. 2. Hawks to Bustards. Oxford University Press, Oxford.
DEL, HOYO, J., A. ELLIOT & J. SARGATAL (eds). 1994. *Handbook of the Birds of the world.* Vol. 2. New World Vultures to Guineafowl. Lynx Edicions, Barcelona.
DESJARDINS, P. & R. MORAIS 1990. Sequence and gene organization of the chicken mitochondrial genome. *J. Mol. Biol.* 212: 599-634.
HOWARD, R. & A. MOORE 1984. *A complete checklist of the birds of the world.* Oxford University Press, Oxford.
JENNI, L. & R. WINKLER 1994. *Moult and ageing of European Passerines.* Academic Press, London.
PORTER, R. F. 1970. Studies of less familiar birds - 161. Booted Eagle. *Br. Birds* 63: 333-337.
SIEBOLD, S. & A.J. HELBIG 1995. Evolutionary history of New and Old World vultures inferrred from nucleotide sequences of the mitochondrial *cytochrome b* gene. *Phil. Trans. Royal Soc. London B* 350: 163-178.
STEYN, P. 1996. *Nesting birds - the breeding habits of Southern African birds.* Fernwood Press, Vlaeburg.
TARBOTON, W. 1994. *South African birds of prey.* Struik Publishers, Cape Town.
WEICK, F. 1980. *Birds of Prey of the world.* Collins, London.

Reuven Yosef
International Birding & Research Center in Eilat
P. O Box 774
Eilat 88000
Israel

Gerhard Verdoorn
Endangered Wildlife Trust
P.O. Box 72155
Parkview 2122
South Africa

Andreas Helbig and Ingrid Seibold
Vogelwarte Hiddensee
Univ. Greifswald
D-18565 KIoster
Germany

Nesting behaviour of a pair of Bat Hawks *Macheiramphus alcinus* in South Africa, recorded by time-lapse video images

T. Harris, A. Kemp and J. Dunning

ABSTRACT

We studied activities at a Bat Hawk nest over almost the entire 126-day nesting cycle (52 day incubation, 74 day nestling periods), during September 1991 to February 1992. We recorded parental and chick behaviour using time-lapse video images, taken each second over 24 hours and under infra-red at night. The sexes shared incubation almost evenly (male 48%, female 52%), but the female brooded more (81%), almost all in the first 40 days of the nestling period. Most prey (89%) was delivered around dusk and dawn, but with some deliveries throughout the night. Nocturnal deliveries were more frequent and inter-prey delivery times longer on moonlit nights, although the mean prey delivery rate was the same as on moonless nights. Bats comprised the main prey, together with a few small birds.

The male brought twice as many prey items to the nest during incubation, but did not provision the female. During the nestling period, both sexes delivered equal numbers of prey, but the female fed the chick more often (58%). Nightly prey deliveries averaged 1.2 (range 0-5) during the incubation and 4.7 (range 0-9) during the nestling period. The long breeding cycle is equivalent to that of a petrel rather than a raptor of the same body mass.

INTRODUCTION

The Bat Hawk *Macheiramphus alcinus* is the size and shape of a large falcon (body mass about 600g), but with no obvious sexual dimorphism in size or colour. The sooty-brown plumage is relieved only by white eyelids, nuchal patches, concealable belly feathers and thin bars across the tail, by pale grey feet and cere, and by large yellow eyes. The nest of sticks is usually built on an uncluttered horizontal branch, high up in an emergent pale-barked tree (Harris *et al.* 1990). The Bat Hawk is remarkable among diurnal birds of prey, order Falconiformes, for being primarily crepuscular and nocturnal, for feeding mainly on bats that are caught and swallowed in flight (Eccles *et al.* 1969; Fenton *et al.* 1977; Black *et al.* 1979), and for its single chick reared over a prolonged nesting cycle (Steyn 1982; Harris *et al.* 1990; Hartley & Hustler 1993; Hartley 1995).

We report here on the breeding biology of a pair of Bat Hawks at the southern tip of their African and Asian range, assisted by time-lapse video images. This was part of a broader study of two neighbouring pairs, which included analysis of pellets and prey, use of telemetry to determine their large 200-250 km² home and hunting range, and taped recordings of their vocalisations and behaviour (Harris et al. 1990).

METHODS

Study sites and pairs

Two neighbouring nest sites of Bat Hawks were observed in the Tzaneen area (23°56'S, 30°07'E), Northern Province, South Africa, from 1986-1992. Both nests were built on 50 x 50 cm metal mesh platforms that we attached 25-30m above the ground on a lateral branch of a large *Eucalyptus* tree. The nest tree and surrounding trees were larger than others in the area and were situated within mixed exotic plantations of smaller *Eucalyptus* and *Pinus* trees. Both nests were in hilly country and on the crest of a ridge. The adults hunted in valleys around the nest area and over flat lowlands about 5km to the east. At least one member of each pair was marked with a coloured or metal leg band to facilitate separation of the sexes during observations.

Nest observation techniques

We monitored one nest with a video camera and time-lapse recorder during September 1991 to February 1992. We then analyzed the recordings for 24 hours of each day and covering almost the full nesting cycle. Additional observations at both nests, during the same and previous seasons back to 1988, were made from about 40-50m away on the ground. We used night-vision binocular equipment mounted on a tripod, plus a mirror angled above each nest surface.

At the study nest, a video camera was mounted on a bracket approximately 3m above the level of the nest and 5m from it. A recorder and monitor were housed 80 m away on the ground, in a small lockable trailer that was parked inside a tent and protected externally with a security fence. A 220V AC power supply for the system was drawn from a powerline about 100m away. To reduce time lost due to power failures, usually caused by the earth-leakage relay tripping because of lightning strikes, a radio transmitter was fitted to the system to alert an assistant who lived nearby and changed the tapes at 4-day intervals.

The nest was monitored continuously by a Panasonic CCD video camera (model WV-CD22) with a 50mm f/1.8 auto-iris lens (model WV-LA50). The camera was linked with 80m of co-axial cable to a Panasonic time-lapse video recorder (model AG-6010) and monitor (WV 5340). To record at night, an external light source was used that was switched on and off automatically by a light-sensitive switch. The lighting came from one of two 6V 15W halogen lights and the second acted as a standby that could be switched on by remote control. The lights were fitted with a RG830 Schott longpass filter and so provided light in the near-infrared range (wavelength >700 nm) that was invisible to humans.

The camera's internal IR filter was removed to obtain maximum sensitivity. The camera was modified to focus automatically from daytime (normal) to nighttime (near-infrared) recording by means of a small geared DC motor coupled to a ring-gear mounted on the lens and controlled by limit switches. The light-sensitive switch simultaneously activated the external light and the focus motor.

Sound recordings could be made when the recorder was switched manually from time-lapse to continuous-record mode. An AKG D900 microphone, its signal boosted with a pre-amplifier, was mounted on rubber above the nest.

Equipment protection

The camera was mounted in a sealed weather-proof housing, extended in front to reduce glare from direct sunlight. The recorder was mounted in a dust-proof, fan-ventilated (negative pressure) container with dust-filtered vents. All cables were enclosed in a PVC tube which, on the tree, was supported by saddles nailed to the trunk and, at the base of the tree, was buried underground in a pipe. Experience showed that all cables, secured to the tree on sturdy galvanised brackets, had to be attached to threaded stainless steel pegs that projected at least 30mm away from the trunk. This gap provided sufficient tolerance for growth to take place without forcing the brackets off the tree. A number of protruding flat metal bars (50cm x 30mm x 6mm) were mounted about 50cm above the camera and lights, and the microphone was housed in a 75mm PVC tube. This provided protection from the wind, weather, falling strips of bark and loose branches, which proved to be a major problem with alignment of equipment.

Initially, lightning proved a major problem that resulted in loss of equipment, particularly when cables were slung above ground. This necessitated a rigorous protection system which consisted of an earth-leakage unit on the main supply cable and an 8mm bare copper cable, connected to the camera and its housing and earthed with 3 x 1m copper-coated spikes over a length of 5m at the base of the tree. At both ends of the system, the 220V power cables were linked together and down to earth with voltage dependent resistors (varistors), rated at 275V applied voltage and capable of clamping currents up to 4000 amps. The 12V DC supply on the camera was similarly protected with 12V varistors and the video cables were also protected at both ends by in-line coaxial earthing connectors. The audio circuit was protected using commercial in-line protection connectors at the microphone output and recorder input (Strike-Tek 250mA, Vmax 17.5). Finally, the main supply cable was earthed with an 8mm copper cable via earthing spikes, and the security fence, trailer and recording equipment were also earthed to this. The whole system later sustained a direct strike with no damage to equipment.

Recording and analysis of data

Data were collected, from egglaying to fledging, as a series of video frames, recorded each second and annotated with date and time. Frames were collected in 96-hr bouts of continuous recording, achieved using a 4-hour video tape with the recorder-selector set on 72-hour mode. This necessitated a tape change only every four days.

The monochrome video recordings were then played back in sequence. The onset and cessation of each category of Bat Hawk behaviour was noted to the nearest second, using the date and time data which formed part of the original recordings. The sex of each adult at the study nest was noted whenever possible, based on the presence of a leg band on the male and the absence of bands on the female. Dates and times for phases of the moon, moonrise and moonset were supplied by the South African Weather Bureau.

RESULTS

Data were collected on 30 4-hour video tapes, representing about 2880 hrs of recording. Time lost due to power failures, tape changes and other technical problems were logged as 'no-data'. Over the 126-day nesting cycle, a total of 7.4 (5.9%) days were lost, in 47 no-data periods ranging from 24-86400 secs (86400 secs = 1 day, Table 1). Behaviours prior to brief time losses of <383 secs were scored as continuing across that interval (25 of these were tape changes of <164 secs (2.7 mins) made during the day when the Bat Hawks were inactive). However, complete days were excluded from the analysis when time loss >=383 secs (6.4 mins). Most of these longer periods occurred during the periods of crepuscular or nocturnal activity and only a few were for long periods during the day. Their omission from various data sets resulted in a maximum exclusion of 4/52 days from the incubation period and 17/74 days from the nestling period.

Table 1. Duration and timing of data losses due to various technical problems with time-lapse video recording at a Bat Hawk nest.

No-data periods due to technical problems	secs	days
Continuous time loss <383 secs	1416	0.02
Continuous time loss >=383 secs	640567	7.4
Time lost during incubation period	57681	0.7
Time lost during nestling period	583553	6.7

Identification of sex

Individuals were identified to sex as either 'definite', when a good view was available of the legs to record the presence or lack of a leg band, or 'probable' if there was any doubt (Table 2). The level of certainty increased for activities during the nestling period, probably because the birds tended to stand for longer periods and offer a better chance of seeing both legs.

Table 2. Accuracy of definite sex determination for members of a pair of Bat Hawks during different behaviours at their nest, as recorded from video images.

Nesting behaviour	% definite sex determination (n)	
	Male	Female
Incubation	74 (226)	74 (284)
Brooding	82 (68)	90 (197)
Prey delivery	77 (187)	86 (169)
Feeding	100 (56)	83 (78)

Incubation period

The incubation period (egglaying-hatching) was recorded at just over 52 days (1250.4 hrs, Table 3). At the second nest, a period of 53+-0.5 days was recorded in the same season, based on morning and evening observations via the nest mirror. Egglaying and hatching at the study nest took place in the early evening (Table 3). At the second nest, these activities took place between dusk and dawn, after the last evening check. At the study nest, egglaying occurred six days after, and at the second nest 14 days after, the full moon. Hatching then occurred two days before and 7 days after full moon respectively.

Table 3. Exact laying, hatching and fledging details at the Bat Hawk study nest, recorded from time-lapse video.

Activity	Date	Time	Duration to next activity			
			days	hrs	mins	secs
Egglaying	30.Sep.91	18:28:37	52	02	26	18
Hatching	20.Nov.91	21:54:55	74	07	20	38
Fledging	02.Feb.92	05:15:33				
		TOTAL:	126	09	46	56

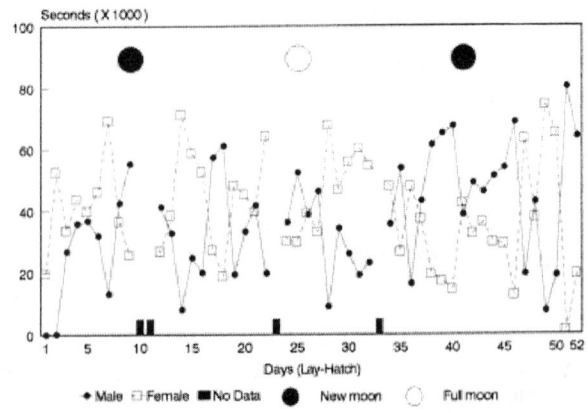

Figure 1. Incubation role for each sex of a pair of Bat Hawks, in relation to moon phase (full moon = open circle; no moon = solid circle; excluding four "no data" days from the 52-day incubation period).

Both sexes at the study nest shared incubation almost evenly overall (male 48%, female 52%, Table 4, Fig. 1), but with considerable individual variation between days. Female effort appeared to show a slight decrease over time, which was countered by a slight increase in male effort.

Table 4. Sex roles of members of a pair of Bat Hawks during the 52-day incubation period.

Activity	Comparison of sex roles	
	Male	Female
Days recorded incubating	51	52
Days analyzed (less 4 no-data days)	47	48
Total incubation effort (hrs)	491.9	537.8
Percent of incubation effort	48	52
Mean daily incubation (hrs)	10.5	11.2
Minimum daily incubation (mins)	3.5	22.6
Maximum daily incubation (hrs)	22.2	20.6
S.E. daily incubation bouts	5.3	4.8
Mean daily dark phase incubation (hrs)	8.0	5.0[a]
Mean daily light phase incubation (hrs)	5.3	5.6[b]
Mean daily daytime incubation (hrs)	5.1	5.6[c]
Mean daily nighttime incubation (hrs)	5.6	5.4[d]

[a] Dark phase of the moon. In general this spanned 7 days before to 7 days after New Moon, with a variation of +- 2 days (1800-0500 hrs).
[b] Light phase of the moon. In general this spanned 7 days before to 7 days after Full Moon, with a variation of +- 2 days (1800-0500 hrs).
[c] daytime = 0600-1700 hrs.
[d] nighttime = 1800-0500 hrs.

Nestling period

The nestling period (hatching to first flight from the nest) was recorded at just over 74 days (1735.3 hrs) and the chick fledged in the early morning (Table 3), two days before no moon. There was a noticeable change in parental behaviour at about 41 days after hatching, four days before no moon (Table 5, Figs. 2 & 3). Up to this time, the chick was regularly brooded and fed by the parents and after this, for the remaining 33 days of the nestling period, it fed and maintained itself. During the first 41 days, the chick was brooded for 81% of the time by the female and 19% by the male (Table 5, Fig. 2).

Figure 2. Brooding role for each sex of a pair of Bat Hawks, in relation to moon phase (full moon = open circle; no moon = solid circle; excluding 17 "no data" days from the 74-day nestling period).

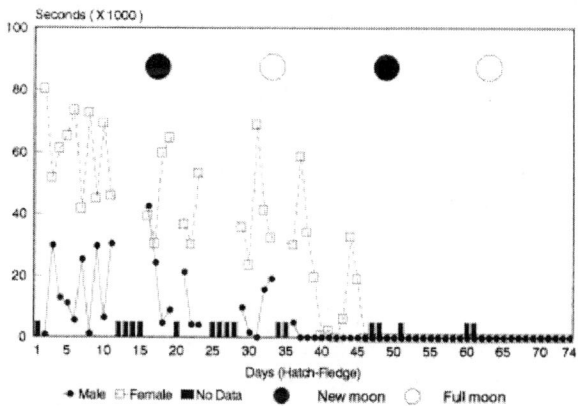

Table 5. Sex roles of members of a pair of Bat Hawks during the 74-day nestling period, divided into the periods before and after the chick requires no further brooding and feeding.

Activity	Comparison of sex roles Before/after 41 days	
	Male	Female
Number of days of brooding behaviour	36/0	41/4
Days analyzed (less 12/5 no-data days)	24/0	29/4
Total brooding effort (hrs)	87.1/0	365.2/16.2
Percent of total nestling period	4.9/0	20.5/0.9
Percent of brooding effort	19/0	81/100
Mean daily brooding (hrs)	2.7/0	12.6/0.6
Minimum daily brooding (mins)	0/0	13.4/0
Maximum daily brooding (hrs)	8.4/0	22.3/0
S.E. daily incubation bouts	2.9/0	5.7/2.0
Mean daily dark phase brooding (hrs/day)	3.8/0	12.3/1.2[a]
Mean daily light phase brooding (hrs/day)	2.3/0	13.7/0[b]
Mean daily daytime brooding (hrs/day)	2.2/0	4.6/0[c]
Mean daily nighttime brooding (hrs/day)	1.4/0	8.0/4.0[c]

[a] Dark phase of the moon. In general this spanned 7 days before to 7 days after New Moon, with a variation of +- 2 days (1800-0500 hrs).
[b] Light phase of the moon. In general this spanned 7 days before to 7 days after Full Moon, with a variation of +- 2 days (1800-0500 hrs).
[c] daytime = 0600-1700 hrs.
[d] nighttime = 1800-0500 hrs.

Figure 3. Total daily prey deliveries and feeds given to the chick by a pair of Bat Hawks, in relation to moon phase and nights with dense mist (full moon = open circle; no moon = solid circle; excluding 12 "no data" days from the 74-day nestling period).

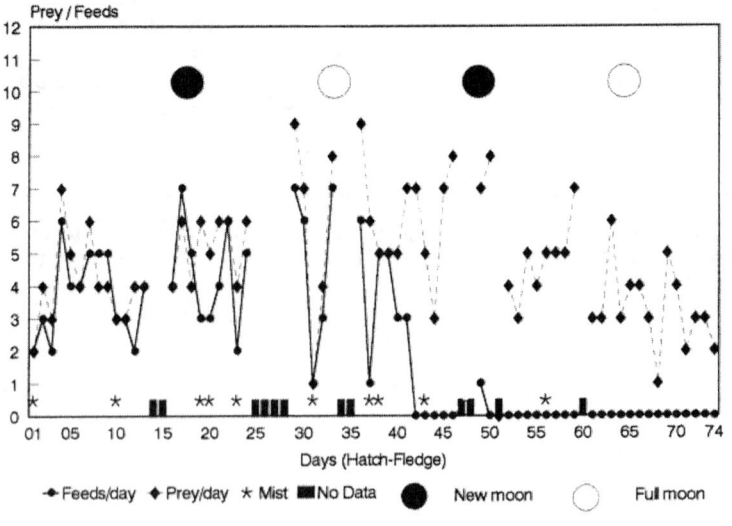

Diet and prey delivery

Identification of prey species was usually not possible in this study. The majority of identifiable prey appeared to be bats, with only two suspected birds delivered based on the plucking behaviour of the Bat Hawks. However, a previous analysis of prey at this nest site, based on pellets collected over a two year period, showed that prey during the breeding season consisted mainly of *Pipistrellus*, *Tadarida* and *Scotophilus* bats, together with some small birds (swifts, swallows, small diurnal passerines, nocturnally-migrating button-quail).

Usually, the adult that arrived with prey fed the chick. The male only passed nine prey items to the female, who then fed the chick, while the female only passed a single item to the male, which he then passed to the chick.

During the 52-day incubation period, the male delivered almost twice as many prey items as the female (Table 6, Fig. 4). The first recorded delivery of prey, by the male, only took place on day-10 of the incubation period (not shown on Fig. 4 because it was one of the excluded 'no-data' days). A maximum of five prey items/day were delivered to the nest during this period.

Table 6. Sex roles in prey delivery to the nest by members of a pair of Bat Hawks.

Nesting stage and activity	Comparison of sex roles		
	Male	Female	Combined
Incubation period:			
Days with prey deliveries	26	18	26
Days analyzed (less 3 no-data)	49	49	49
No. prey items delivered	39	21	60
Percentage contribution	65	34	100
Prey items/day (n = 49 days)	0.8	0.4	1.2
Range per day	0-3	0-3	0-5[a]
S.E. of daily deliveries	0.8	0.6	1.0
Nestling period:			
No. prey items delivered	148	148	296
Percentage contribution	50	50	100
Prey items/day (n = 63 days)	2.35	2.35	4.70
Range per day	0-5	0-6	0-9
S.E. of daily deliveries	1.3	1.4	1.9
Nestling period, before/after 41 days			
Days with prey deliveries	-	-	42/33
Days analyzed (less 8/3 no-data)	-	-	33/30
Prey items delivered	88/61	78/69	166/130
Mean prey items/day	2.7/2.0	2.4/2.3	5.1/4.3
Percentage contribution	53/46	47/54	100/100
Prey range/day	0-5/0-5	0-6/1-6	1-9/1-8[b,c]
Mean prey/day, dark phase[d]	2.8/2.3	3.0/2.2	5.8/4.5
Mean prey/day, light phase[e]	3.3/1.9	2.4/2.8	5.7/4.7
Prey deliveries before midnight	45/33	39/35	84/68
Prey deliveries after midnight	43/27	39/35	82/62
Timing over total nesting cycle:			
No. prey items delivered	187	169	356
During dark phase (n = 48 days)[d]	89	90	179
During light phase (n = 50 days)[e]	98	79	177
Prey items/day, dark phase[d]	1.85	1.87	3.72
Prey items/day, light phase[e]	1.96	1.58	3.54
Prey deliveries before midnight	90	79	169
Prey deliveries after midnight	97	90	187

[a] Although individual maxima was 3, the combined total on a given day was never more than 5.
[b] A least one sex delivered a minimum of 1 prey item when the other sex delivered nothing.
[c] Although individual maxima were 5 and 6, the combined total on a given day was never more than 9.
[d] Dark phase of the moon. In general this spanned 7 days before to 7 days after New Moon, with a variation of +- 2 days (1800-0500 hrs).
[e] Light phase of the moon. In general this spanned 7 days before to 7 days after Full Moon, with a variation of +- 2 days (1800-0500 hrs).

Figure 4. Total daily prey deliveries by each sex of a pair of Bat Hawks during the incubation period, in relation to moon phase (full moon = open circle; no moon = solid circle; male n=39, female n = 21; excluding three "no data" days from the 52-day incubation period).

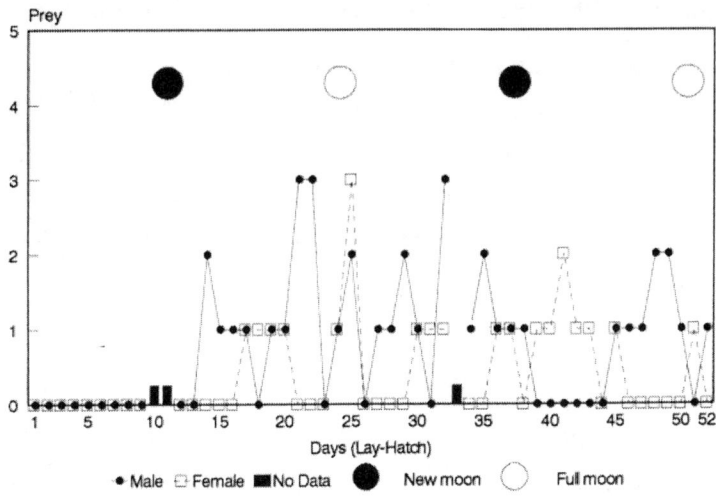

Figure 5. Total daily prey deliveries by each sex of a pair of Bat Hawks during the nestling period, in relation to moon phase (full moon = open circle; no moon = solid circle; male n=148, female n = 148; excluding 12 "no data" days from the 74-day nestling period).

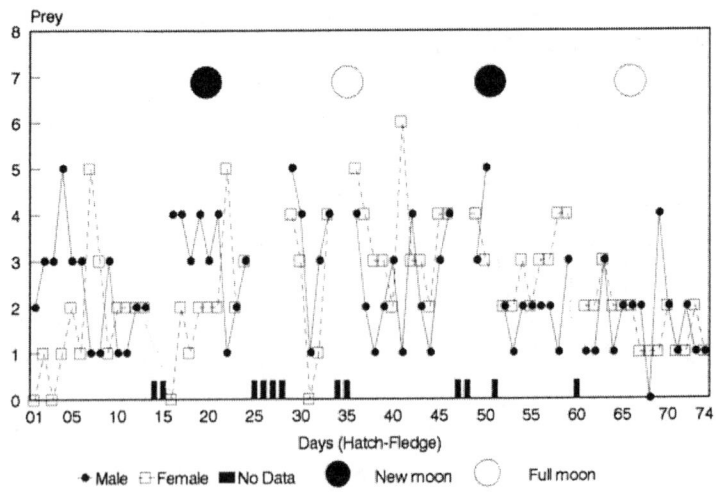

During the 74-day nestling period, deliveries continued throughout, from hatching to fledging, with a maximum of nine prey items delivered in one night (Table 6, Figs. 3 & 5). The chick swallowed prey items whole at the age of 15 days and was feeding itself at 41 days old. During the period up to 41 days of age, the male delivered more items than the female (53:47%), but this was reversed during the period from 42 days of age to fledging (46:54%). Overall, the male and female shared deliveries almost equally, but the female fed the chick on the nest slightly more often than the male (58:42%, Table 7).

Table 7. Sex roles on the nest in feeding of the chick up to 41 days old by members of a pair of Bat Hawks.

Activity	Comparison of sex roles		
	Male	Female	Combined
No. of feeding bouts	56	78	134[a]
Percentage contribution	42	58	100
Mean no. of bouts/day	1.7	2.4	4.1
Mean duration of bouts (mins)	3.7	9.8	1.2
Minimum bout duration (secs)	7	11	54
Maximum bout duration (mins)	46	35	1.5
S.E. of bout duration	-	-	12 secs
Mean no. of bouts/day, dark phase	1.7	2.1	-
Mean no. of bouts/day, light phase	2.9	2.4	-
No. bouts before midnight	27	32	59
No. bouts after midnight	30	46	76

[a] Male delivered 9 prey items which were handed to the female, who then fed the chick. The female only handed the male a single prey item which he then handed to the chick. Only a single bout of feeding was recorded when the chick was older than 42 days, when an item was delivered by the male and fed to the chick by the female.

Prey deliveries took place at dusk, dawn and in the night, between about 17:30-06:00 hrs. Prey delivery was strongly bimodal, with 89% of deliveries taking place between 17:00-20:00 hrs and 04:00-06:00 hrs (Table 8, Fig. 6). Overall, more deliveries occurred at dawn (after midnight, 53%) than at dusk (before midnight, 47%). This result is also reflected in data on feeding of the chick (Table 7, Fig. 7), with 44% of feeds before midnight and 56% after. More prey was also brought during these peaks in the dark phase of the moon than in the light phase (Fig. 8). Although the total number of prey items delivered during these two peaks was similar, during the light phase of the moon more prey (4%) was brought between these peaks, in the middle of the night, than during the dark phase (1%).

Table 8. Number of prey deliveries and chick feeding bouts recorded per hour during the dark and light phases of the moon by a pair of Bat Hawks during their total nesting cycle.

Activity and moon phase	Hour initiated recording																		%	(n)
	0	1	2	3	4	5	6	7	8	9	/	16	17	18	19	20	21	22	23		
Prey delivery:																					
Dark phase	0	1	0	3	70	18	1	0	0	0	/	0	0	10	75	0	0	1	0	50.3	(179)
Light phase	3	4	3	4	53	26	1	0	0	0	/	0	1	7	55	2	3	11	4	49.7	(177)
Total	3	5	3	7	123	44	2	0	0	0	/	0	1	17	130	2	3	12	4	100.0	(356)
Feeding bouts:																					
Total	3	1	1	8	58	3	1	0	1	0	/	0	1	8	42	0	0	6	2	100.0	(135)

DISCUSSION

The main limitation with video recording is that the effective field of vision is restricted by the camera lens and, in this study, includes only a single nest and its immediate surroundings. However, this is balanced against the feasibility of monitoring the entire nesting cycle of the inaccessible, little-known and nocturnal Bat Hawk.

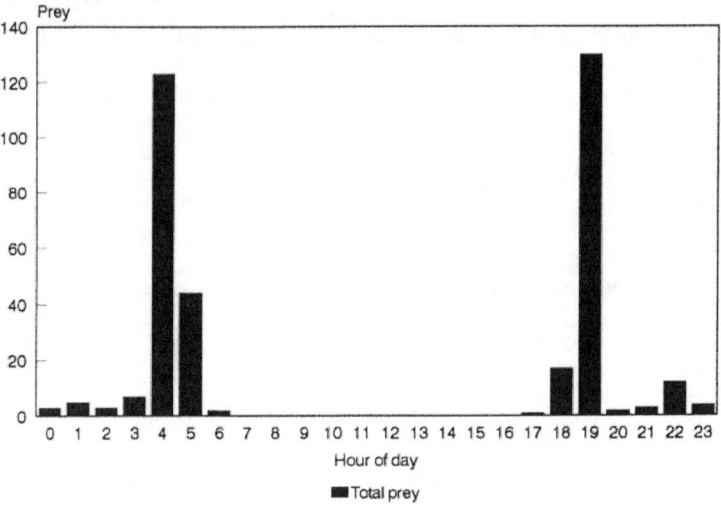

Figure 6. Prey deliveries per hour by a pair of Bat Hawks during the entire nesting cycle (n = 356; within one hour of starting time indicated; excluding 15 "no data" days from the 126-day nesting period).

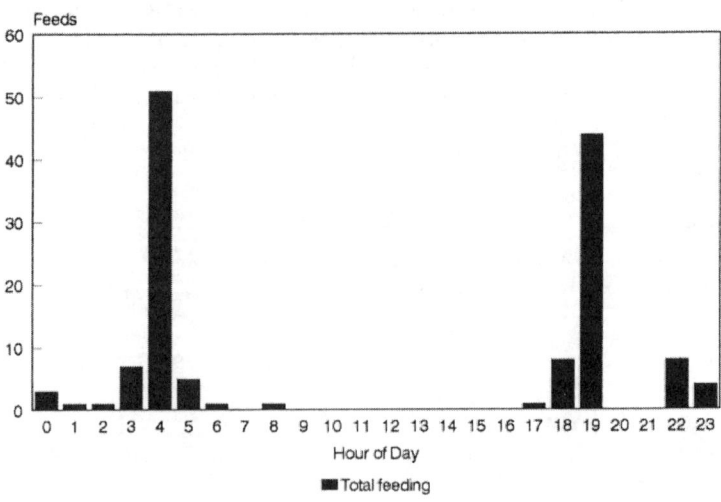

Figure 7. Feeding bouts per hour of the chick by a pair of Bat Hawks during the 74-day nestling period (n = 135; within one hour of starting time indicated; excluding 12 "no data" days from the 74-day nestling period).

Both sexes shared incubation and brooding, even though definite identification of the male, based on the presence of a leg band, was only 74% and 82% respectively (Table 2). The sexes shared incubation about equally, but the female brooded the chick more than the male (Tables 4 & 5). Previous briefer studies suggested that only the female incubated (Hartley 1988, 1995), or that the male incubated much less than the female (Hustler 1983), and there might be some individual variation between pairs. Brooding was intense up to about 20-30 days (cf. to 22 days, Hartley 1995) but then declined to almost nothing by 40 days and for the rest of the nestling period (Fig. 2).

Figure 8. Total prey deliveries to the nest by a pair of Bat Hawks during the entire nesting cycle, for different hourly periods of the day, and for the weeks preceding and following full and no moon respectively (n=356; excluding 15 "no data" days from the 126-day nesting period).

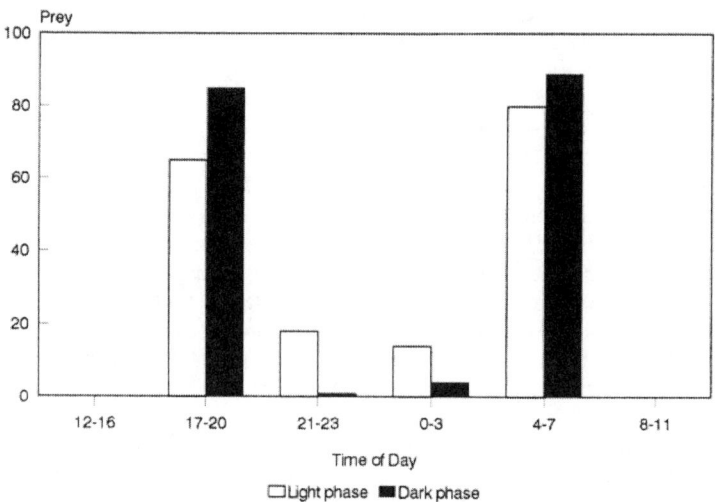

Our two accurate records of a 52-53 day incubation period agree with one of 53 days reported by Hartley (1995), but our record of a 74-day nestling period is slightly more than the 67 days that he reported. While little variation is expected in the incubation period, more variation might be expected in such a prolonged nestling period, due to the effects of weather (e.g. mist, Fig. 4), food availability and hunting success on chick development.

The total nesting cycle of 126 days greatly exceeds that of about 70 days for a 600g falconiform, as predicted by an allometric regression against female body weight (Newton 1979). One of the principal factors to influence the fledging period in birds is growth of their relatively long wing bones (Carrier & Auriemma 1992). African Bat Hawks, with a mean ulna length of 124mm (SD 7.1, n = 35, our measurements of museum specimens), do have markedly longer bones than equivalent-sized falcons, such as Lanner *Falco biarmicus* (99mm, SD 4.8, n = 27) or African Peregrine *F. peregrinus minor* (86-98mm, n = 2, Mendelsohn *et al.* 1989).

Such long wing bones, a clutch size of one, slow development, a prolonged nesting cycle and nocturnal habits are, however, typical for petrels of similar size to Bat Hawks (Anonymous 1992; Carrier & Auriemma 1992; Hartley & Hustler 1993; Hartley 1995; Warham 1996). The long nestling development of the single petrel chick has been related to low provisioning rates by the parents, where they alternate incubation and brooding and where food delivery to the chick is at long and erratic intervals. In the Bat Hawk, the sexes shared incubation, brooding and hunting for the chick, but still achieved only a low and erratic food supply (mean 4.7 prey items/day, range 0-9, Table 6, Fig. 3).

As expected, bats comprised the main prey, with only a few items of small birds (Harris *et al.* 1990; Hartley 1995). The bimodal dusk and dawn delivery of prey conforms to the mainly crepuscular foraging reported for the Bat Hawk (Eccles *et al.* 1969; Black *et al.* 1979; Brosset & Erard 1986; Hartley 1995). It also conforms with dusk and dawn peaks of insect and bat activity (Fenton *et al.* 1977; Erkert 1982; Rautenbach *et al.* 1988). However, other studies have mainly recorded Bat Hawk activity at dusk, while we found that even more prey was delivered after (53%) than before (47%) midnight. Although many factors will influence provisioning rates, it does suggest that the dawn peak in aerial arthropod and bat activity may not be smaller than the dusk peak in all seasons or for all species. Different species of bats are also active at different times of the night and at different altitudes above ground (Fenton et al. 1977), and bat activity is further influenced by the weather, especially by rain and cold (Fenton et al. 1977), all of which could affect Bat Hawk hunting behaviour (Fig. 3).

The nesting cycle of the Bat Hawk covers 4.5 lunar cycles. Although the nightly number of prey deliveries to the nest was similar during dark and light phases of the moon, the time at which prey was delivered differed. During the light phase, and particularly around full moon, some prey was brought in throughout the night. Similar observations were made at both nests, using night-vision and telemetry studies of hunting adults (Harris et al. 1990). Despite improved visibility on moonlit nights, and prey delivery at similar overall rates to moonless nights, the crepuscular delivery of prey on moonlit nights was lower and the mean interval between deliveries longer. This suggests that prey was less available than on dark nights and that the Bat Hawks had to hunt for longer periods throughout the night. A similar increase in foraging behaviour has been observed in the insectivorous Common Poorwill *Phalaenoptilus nuttallii* (Brigham & Barclay 1992).

During moonlight, bats are known to alter their roost departure time, to decrease their activity and to resort to the shadows of more densely foliaged areas (Fenton et al. 1977; Beith 1982; Law 1997). These changes in bat activity have been interpreted as predator-avoidance behaviour, but the situation may not be that simple since many insects are also known to be lunaphobic, especially moths (Mills 1986).

However, Bat Hawks are also capable of catching prey when there is no moon- or starlight (Harris et al. 1990, Fig. 8). We even have an observation at the second nest, where an adult left the nest and caught a bat within 50m on a pitch black night. The emergent pale-barked trees favoured as nest sites (Harris et al. 1990; Hartley 1995) may also be important 'beacons' when Bat Hawks return to their nest after dark.

Bat Hawks at perch and on the nest at night often twitched their heads from side to side, as if listening for something. Tests with natural bat sounds elicited no obvious response, nor were any obvious specialisations to the external ear found on museum anatomical specimens, so the exact technique by which Bat Hawks locate some of their prey in the dark remains unresolved. Hunting Bat Hawks are attracted to towns and artificial lights (Hartley & Hustler 1993; Hartley 1995; pers. obs.), but this might be due to the lights attracting insects that attract bats, rather than improved visibility for the Bat Hawks.

Since Bat Hawks lack marked sexual size dimorphism, despite hunting agile prey, the sexes are expected to share hunting and provisioning to the nest (Mendelsohn 1986, 1987; Auburn 1987). In this study, both sexes brought prey to the nest during the incubation period, with the male bringing almost twice as much as the female. However, no provisioning of the female by the male was recorded during incubation, although during the nestling period the chick was fed mainly by the female on the nest, as in previous studies (Hustler 1983; Hartley 1995). During the nestling period, the female delivered more prey to the nest than the male (58%:42%), and Hartley (1995) also reported deliveries by both sexes to the chick (12 prey deliveries, male 7, female 4, unknown 1).

ACKNOWLEDGEMENTS

Many individuals and organisations contributed to make this research possible. Menno Klapwijk, Dylis Hoets and Meg Kemp are particularly thanked for their commitment, as are M. Amm, P. Baleca, C. and K. Begg, B. Bertelsman, J. Beukus, T. Cassidy, Mr and Mrs Cousins, Mr and Mrs R. Cromarty, D. Dailtz, P. Desmet, B. de Souza, W. Ferguson, J. Harman, B. Harris, J. Harris, D. Harty, B. Hersov, B. Ilsley, C. Lambrechts, C. Leach, M. Louw, D. Luther, M. Melle, L. Minter, W. Neser, J. Thomé, M. Whiting and A. van Zyl. Sponsorship from the following organisations is gratefully acknowledged; City Lab (Pty) Ltd., Eloptro (Pty) Ltd., Hunt Leuchars & Hepburn Timber Products (Pty) Ltd. (HL&H), Lotzaba Forests (Pty) Ltd. (Rand Mines), Memortech (Pty) Ltd., National Panasonic (Pty) Ltd., Sage Life Limited, Westfalia Estate (Hans Merensky Holdings (Pty) Ltd.). Additional support was obtained from the Department of Environment Affairs (Forestry), North-

Eastern Bird Club (NEBC), Northern Transvaal Ornithological Society (Pretoria Bird Club), South African Ornithological Society (SAOS), Transvaal Museum and Tzaneen City Council Electricity Department.

REFERENCES

ANONYMOUS. 1992. The Bat Hawks have fledged. *TM Bird Department News* February 1992: 1.
AUBURN, J. 1987. RSD and the agility of the Bat Hawk. *Gabar* 2: 15-16.
BEITH, C.C. 1982. Insectivorous bats fly in shadows to avoid moonlight. *J. Mamm.* 63: 688-690.
BLACK, H.L., G. HOWARD & R. STJERNSTEDT 1979. Observations on the feeding behaviour of the Bat Hawk (*Macheiramphus alcinus*). *Biotropica* 11: 18-21.
BRIGHAM, R. M. & R. M. R. BARCLAY 1992. Lunar influence on foraging and nesting activity of Common Poorwills (*Phalaenoptilus nuttallii*). *Auk* 109: 315-320.
BROSSET, A. & C. ERARD 1986. *Les oiseaux des régions forestières du nord-est du Gabon.* Vol. 1. Ecologie et comportement des espèces. Société Nationale de Protection de la Nature, Paris.
CARRIER, D. R. & J. AURIEMMA 1992. A developmental constraint on the fledging time of birds. *Biol. J. Linn. Soc.* 47: 61-77.
ECCLES, D. H., R.A.C. JENSEN & M.K. JENSEN 1969. Feeding behaviour of the Bat Hawk *Ostrich* 40: 26-27.
ERKERT, H.G. 1982. Ecological aspects of bat activity rhythms. In: Kunz, T.H. (ed.). *Ecology of Bats*, pp. 201-242. Plenum Press, New York.
FENTON, M.B., N.G.H. BOYLE, T.M. HARRISON & D.J. OXLEY 1977. Activity patterns, habitat use, and prey selection by some African insectivorous bats. *Biotropica* 9: 73-85.
HARRIS, T., J. DUNNING & D. HOETS 1990. The darker side of Bat Hawks. *Birding in Sthn. Afr.* 42: 86-89.
HARTLEY, R.R. 1988. Bat Hawks in Mutare. *Honeyguide* 34: 28-29.
HARTLEY, R.R. 1995. Notes on the breeding biology and productivity of a pair of Bat Hawks in Mutare. *Honeyguide* 41: 6-17.
HUSTLER, K. 1983. Incubatory behaviour of the Bat Hawk. *Ostrich* 54: 156-160.
HARTLEY, R. & K. HUSTLER 1993. A less-than-annual breeding cycle in a pair of African Bat Hawks *Machaeramphus alcinus*. *Ibis* 135: 456-458.
LAW, B.S. 1997. The lunar cycle influences time of roost departure in the Common Blossom Bat, *Syconycteris australis*. *Aust. Mamm.* 20: 21-24.
MENDELSOHN, J. M. 1986. Sexual size dimorphism and roles in raptors - fat females and agile males. *Durban Mus. Novit.* 13: 321-336.
MENDELSOHN, J. M. 1987. Comments on RSD and the agility of the Bat Hawk by J Auburn. *Gabar* 2: 16-17.
MENDELSOHN, J.M., A.C. KEMP, H.C. BIGGS, R. BIGGS & C.J. BROWN 1989. Wing areas, wing loadings and wing spans of 66 species of African raptor. *Ostrich* 60: 35-42.
MILLS, A.M. 1986. The influence of moonlight on the behaviour of goatsuckers (Caprimulgidae). *Auk* 103: 370-378.
NEWTON, I. 1979. *Population ecology of raptors.* T. & A. D. Poyser, Berkhamstead.
RAUTENBACH, I.L., A.C. KEMP & C.H. SCHOLTZ 1988. Fluctuations in availability of arthropods correlated with microchiropteran and avian predator activities. *Koedoe* 31: 77-90.
STEYN, P. 1982. *Birds of prey of southern Africa.* D. Philip, Cape Town.
WARHAM, J. 1996. *The behaviour, population biology and physiology of the petrels.* Academic Press, San Diego.

Tony Harris, Alan Kemp & John Dunning†
c/o Department of Birds
Transvaal Museum
P O Box 413
Pretoria
0001
South Africa
†died 17 June 1992

Chancellor, R. D. & B.-U. Meyburg eds. 2000
Raptors at Risk
WWGBP / Hancock House

Flight, foraging and food of the Bateleur *Terathopius ecaudatus*: an aerodynamically specialized, opportunistic forager

R. T. Watson

ABSTRACT

The low altitude, soaring flight of the Bateleur *Terathopius ecaudatus* is unusual and characteristic of the species. Wing and tail measurements showed that their aspect ratio (8:1) is only slightly higher than other soaring raptors (7:1), but their relative tail length is considerably less (Bateleur tail:wing-length = 0.2, other eagles >0.4). Observations of Bateleur behaviour showed that foraging was performed from low altitude soaring, in which a limited range (45-55 km^2) was repeatedly searched for up to 70% of daylight hours. Strikes at prey (n = 229) were conspicuous and at slow speed. Analysis of prey remains showed that prey was either carrion or, possibly captured live, was nocturnal mammals, reptiles, or insectivorous birds. Feeding trials (n = 40) showed that Bateleurs were adept at locating small-sized carrion (67% of 131 baits) and were first on 94% of occasions. I hypothesize that the specialized aerodynamics of Bateleurs allows them to soar and forage at low altitude, to opportunistically take carrion and live prey, and thus to occupy a food niche that apparently is used rarely by other diurnal avian scavengers.

INTRODUCTION

The flight of the Bateleur *Terathopius ecaudatus* is often mentioned as an extraordinary and identifying characteristic of the species (Watson 1987, Brown & Amadon 1989, Tarboton 1990). Their low altitude, canting flight (Pennycuick 1972) is shared with few other raptors and their relatively long, narrow wings and short tail are unique among terrestrial birds (Watson 1986). The relationship between these characteristics and their natural history has not been thoroughly explored. In this paper I describe and quantify pertinent aspects of the Bateleurs' flight, foraging and food, and propose a relation between their morphology, aerodynamics, foraging behaviour and diet.

METHODS

This study was conducted between 1981 and 1984 in the Kruger National Park (KNP, 22°32'-25°32'S; 30°50'-32°02' E), South Africa. The KNP is just over 350 km long, 90 km wide at its widest, and covers an area of about 20,000 km^2. Habitat within the KNP is generally described as eastern lowveld and can be divided into several landscape types (Gertenbach 1983). Most behavioural observations occurred in the central part of the KNP, within a 15-km radius of Satara rest camp, and in two landscapes known respectively as *Acacia welwitschii* Thicket and *Sclerocarya caffra/Acacia nigrescens* Savanna.

Flight

Bateleur flight behaviour was studied by 'focal bird observations' of known individuals from two high vantage points (a rock outcrop called Matikiti Kopje and an unnamed rock outcrop on the Sweni River) that allowed up to 3 h of uninterrupted observation per individual. Two adjacent territorial pairs were observed from each point for 192 h between 1982 and 1983. Individuals were readily identified by their sexually dimorphic plumage and their visits to known nests.

Birds were observed through a 25-50x zoom spotting scope. At 1-minute intervals the focal bird's horizontal distance from the observer was visually estimated to the nearest 0.5 km using landmarks of known distance, its magnetic compass bearing measured from a sighting compass mounted on the telescope, and its behaviour described. Data were recorded on a tape recorder for later transcription so that the observer never lost sight of the focal bird.

Focal bird flight direction was calculated from successive locations, assuming that travel was in a straight line between locations at one-minute intervals. Home ranges were measured by plotting successive, sub-sampled, statistically independent (Schoener 1981) locations of observed birds. Convex polygons were drawn around outermost locations and the map-maker's formula used to calculate the polygon area.

Foraging

Foraging behaviour was recorded during the same focal bird observations described above. In addition, observations of every Bateleur seen and recorded during the study period ('ad-libitum' observations, n = 4255 from 1981 to 1984) were used to increase sample sizes of rarely seen behaviours, such as attempted and successful strikes at prey.

Food

Diet was determined by identification of prey remains collected at nests and from birds observed feeding during focal bird and ad-libitum observations. Prey remains were either 'bulk' items such as skin, bones, scales and feathers, or they were pellets. Feathers were only considered to have come from prey if more than one was found below the nest, otherwise they were disregarded as being moulted. The numbers of each prey type were conservative minima because as many pieces as possible from each sample were combined to represent one prey item and only parts clearly belonging to different individuals were counted separately.

Mammal remains were identified to species, if possible, otherwise they were placed into an ungulate size class suggested as appropriate for the classification of antelope bone remains (Brain 1974). Bird remains, feathers, bones, mandibles and claws were identified to family, as were reptile and fish parts (mainly skulls, skin and scales).

Pellets were dissected dry and separated into component parts for identification. Mammal hair was identified to species, using gelatin impressions of scale patterns that were compared with reference collections (Keogh 1974, 1979, 1983). Feathers and other bird parts were identified macroscopically from reference collections. Reptile scales were identified based on shape, colour, presence of apical pits, ridges or spines and calcification using museum reference collections. Fish scales were classed simply as unidentified fish. Insect parts were identified to order where possible from reference collections.

The importance to diurnal scavengers of small items of carrion (fist-sized lumps of meat or other carrion of similar size) was measured experimentally by setting meat baits in plain view, then watching them from a concealed vantage point until the first animal arrived and ate the bait. Two or three baits, each >150 m apart, were usually put out around 08:00 hrs, after Bateleurs began flying, and observed simultaneously until discovered by scavengers or until dusk.

RESULTS

Flight

Bateleur flight was distinguished by continuous low-altitude soaring flight (low directional flight, LDF, Fig. 1, Watson 1986), at elevations of roughly 2-3x tree-top level (about 40-80 m above ground level, a.g.l.). Flight from the ground or elevated perch usually began with a brief period (e.g. 10 - 30 seconds) of flapping flight (FF, Fig. 1), but proceeded thereafter for long periods (e.g. 10 - >360 minutes) without flapping. Soaring Bateleurs exhibited a characteristic irregular canting motion of the wings, that resembled movements expected of an unstable aircraft or bird which must frequently correct its flight attitude (roll) as it flies through turbulent air. Low wide- or low tight-circling (LWC, LTC, Fig. 1) occurred occasionally during flight, often associated with loss of height as the bird appeared to inspect potential prey on the ground. Circling in thermals (thermalling) to gain height was most often seen in the afternoon, associated with high flying (HF, Fig. 1) at much higher elevations than low flight and often exceeding 300 m a.g.l..

Figure 1. Bateleurs' diurnal activity pattern in (a) summer and (b) winter from focal bird and ad-libitum observations combined. NF = non-flying. All other abbreviations described in the text.

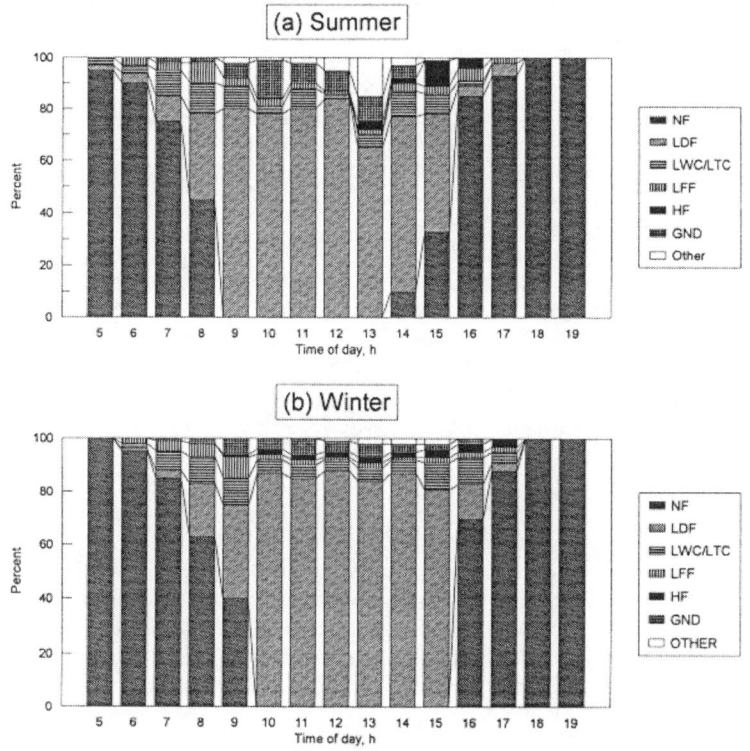

Diurnal activity patterns for summer and winter (Figs. 1a & 1b respectively), derived from focal bird and ad-libitum sampling, revealed that the majority of Bateleurs began flying about 2-3 h after sunrise, and continued for 6-8 h until 2-3 h before sunset. During this active period of 50-70% of daylight hours, most time (40% of daylight hours in summer and 57% in winter) was spent in low directional soaring flight (LDF, Fig. 1). Much smaller proportions of time were spent in low wide circling (LWC), low flapping flight (LFF), high flight (HF), on the ground (GND) or other activities (Other, Fig. 1). Activities on the ground (GND, Fig. 1) included feeding and bathing. Flight began and peaked earlier in the day in summer than in winter, suggesting a dependence on heating by the sun to generate thermal energy for soaring flight. Flight terminated earlier in the day in summer than winter, suggesting that termination of flight was not solely determined by thermal factors, but also possibly social behaviour or satiation.

Low directional flight speed was crudely measured by driving a vehicle at the same speed as a Bateleur as it flew over or parallel to a road. Opportunities to do this occurred fortuitously 3 times during the study period and all measured a ground speed of 50-60 km/h. By inference, Bateleurs could travel 250-480 km in low directional flight in a normal activity period of 6-8 h.

Focal bird observation revealed that Bateleur pairs used low directional flight to repeatedly traverse a limited home range of 45-55 km^2 (n = 4, mean = 51.6 km^2, SD = 4.8) measured by the convex polygon method. Flight direction was measured from successive 1-minute interval locations during focal bird observations of the same individual under strong wind (>25 knots) and calm conditions (Fig. 2). Flight direction was not significantly different from random or uniform under either strong wind (Rayleigh's z = 1.57, n = 110, P = <0.05) or calm conditions (Rayleigh's z = 0.10, n = 109, P = <0.05, Zar 1984).

Figure 2. Flight directions and distances of one individual Bateleur in (A) calm and (B) windy conditions.

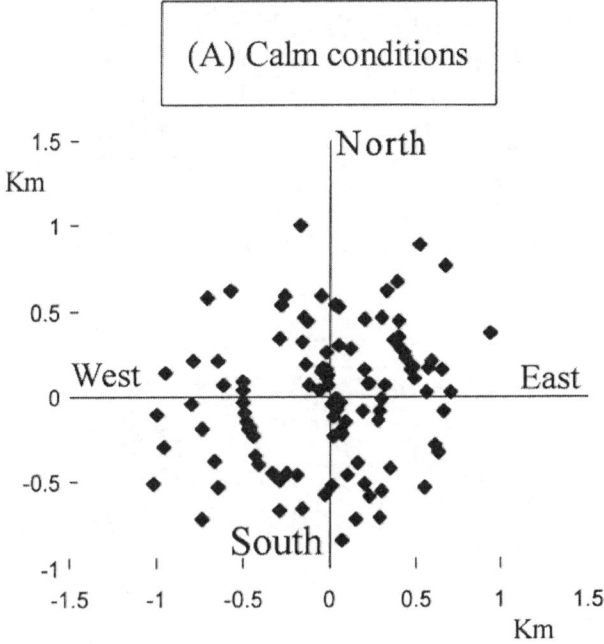

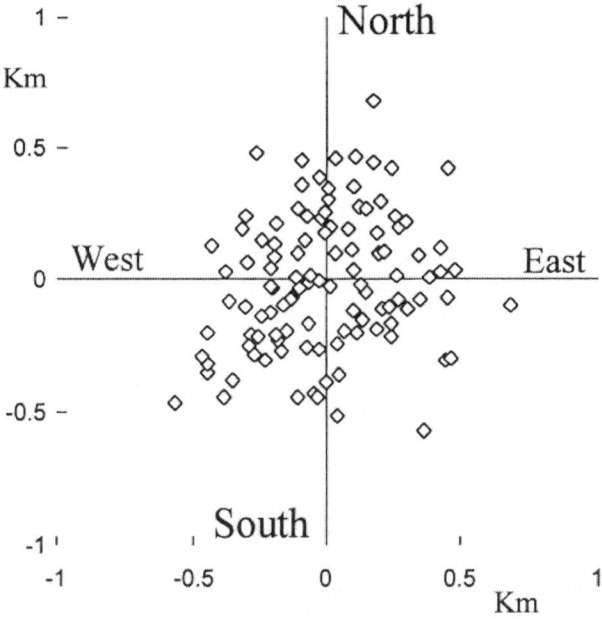

Foraging

Strikes at prey and descents to carrion by Bateleurs were observed 229 times during focal bird and ad-libitum observations combined. Three types of prey strikes and one type of descent to carrion were readily distinguished. 'Kill Strike-A' began with low tight circling followed by a wings up, slow descent onto prey on the ground. 'Kill Strike-B' was a slow descent, with wings held out to break the descent, to land in a tree, apparently capturing arboreal prey. 'Kill Strike-C' began with a fast, shallow dive below tree-top level, followed by recovery in flight with prey in the talons. This was seen once, and was the only attempt at prey capture in flight. 'Approach to carrion' began with low tight, or low wide circling, followed by landing on the ground or on an elevated perch at a distance from the carrion, followed by landing on or walking up to the carrion. Apart from Kill Strike-C, all strikes and approaches to carrion were slow and conspicuous, requiring a wings-up ('parachute-like') descent and wing flapping to break the descent just before touch down. Kill strikes or descents to carrion were always associated with low flying. The temporal pattern of foraging was illustrated in the daily activity pattern (Fig. 1) by all low flying and ground activity combined. Change in foraging success and foraging effort through the day was illustrated by indices derived from observations at feeding trials. A foraging success index was calculated as the difference between the number of baits found and the number expected to be found based on the proportion of bait-hours available (Table 1). An index of foraging effort was calculated from the number of baits located by Bateleurs per bait-hour (Table 1). Indices of foraging success and foraging effort before 08:00 hrs and after 16:00 hrs were too influenced by small sample size to be meaningful. Otherwise, foraging success was positive during 10:00-13:00 hrs and greatest from 10h00 to 11h00, while foraging effort was greatest during 10:00-12:00 hrs but remained high and fairly constant until 16:00 hrs (Table 1).

Table 1. Temporal distribution of foraging success and effort by Bateleurs determined from feeding trials with baits.

Time of day	No. of bait hours, h	No. of baits found (bf)	No. of baits expected to be found (bef)	Foraging success index, (bf-bef)	Foraging effort index, (bf/h x 100)
07h01-08h00	7	1	0.9	0.1	15.4
08h01-09h00	75	6	10.4	-4.4	8.0
09h01-10h00	182	12	25.2	-13.2	6.6
10h01-11h00	203	40	28.1	11.9	19.7
11h01-12h00	187	33	25.9	7.1	17.7
12h01-13h00	154	24	21.4	2.6	15.6
13h01-14h00	129	16	17.9	-1.9	12.4
14h01-15h00	83	10	11.5	-1.5	12.1
15h01-16h00	33	4	4.6	-0.6	12.1
16h01-17h00	3	1	0.4	0.6	33.0
Total	**1046**	**145**	**145**		

Food

Analysis of Bateleur prey remains revealed 1,879 individual items, including 49 mammal species, 37 bird species, 20 reptile species, 5 fish genera, one unidentified frog, and two arthropod genera (Table 2). Any identified mammal normally weighing over 5 kg was assumed to have been picked up as carrion (Table 2). Mammals weighing less than 5kg were assumed possibly to have been captured, as were all birds, reptiles and fish, although the latter probably only became available with the seasonal drying up of dams and rivers.

Table 2. Summary of prey identified in prey remains from all known Bateleur nests in the KNP in 1982 and 1983. Identifications to species were given by Watson (1986).

	Frequency	Percentage
Mammal		
Carrion	681	36.2
Captured	346	18.4
Sub-total	1027	54.6
Bird	446	23.7
Reptile	334	17.8
Fish	37	2.0
Unidentified & other	35	1.9
Total	**1879**	**100%**

Mammalian carrion comprised the single most frequent food source (Table 2). The most frequent (>10 individuals) species included Blackbacked Jackal *Canis mesomelas*, Porcupine *Hystrix africaeaustralis*, Greater Canerat *Thryonomys swinderianus*, Cape Buffalo *Syncerus caffer*, Bushbuck *Tragelaphus scriptus*, Impala *Aepyceros melampus*, Common Duiker *Sylvicapra grimmia*, and Steenbok *Raphicerus campestris*.

Of the animals small enough to have been killed, birds were the most frequent prey item, most often (>10 individuals) including Cape Turtle Dove *Streptopelia capicola*, other dove species, Green Pigeon *Treron calva*, Lilacbreasted Roller *Coracias caudata*, Redbilled Woodhoopoe *Phoeniculus purpureus*, Yellowbilled Hornbill *Tockus flavirostris*, Burchell's Starling *Lamprotornis australis* and other glossy starlings.

Small mammals were the next most frequent prey item (Table 2), often (>10 individuals) including Cape Hare *Lepus capensis*, Scrub Hare *L. saxatilis*, Multimammate and Coucha Mouse *Praomys* spp., Veld and Rock Mice *Aethomys* spp., Bushveld Gerbil *Tatera leucogaster*, Pouched Mouse *Saccostomus campestris*, Small- and Large-spotted Genet *Genetta* spp., Slender Mongoose *Herpestes sanguineus*, and Dwarf Mongoose *Helogale parvula*.

Reptiles were almost as frequent in the diet as small mammals (Table 2), and often (>10 individuals) included various skink species, lacertid species, Plated Lizard species *Gerrhosaurus* spp., Cordylidae species, Nile Monitor *Varanus niloticus*, Olive Grass Snake *Psammophis phillipsii*, Puff Adder *Bitis arietans*, Black Mamba *Dendroaspis polylepis*, and other unidentified snake species. Amphibians and invertebrates were identified but represented <0.1% of the total. The extremely high diversity of small and possibly killed prey items in the Bateleurs' diet, plus the abundance of obviously carrion items, suggests that Bateleurs are primarily scavengers and that some or many of the small prey items may not have been killed but were scavenged as carrion.

Of 131 baits put out during 40 separate feeding trials, 94 (72%) baits were found by scavengers (Table 3). Bateleurs found 67% of all baits put out (40% adults, 60% non-adults included in four age-classes recognizable before adult, Watson 1987), and they were the first diurnal scavenger to find the bait on 94% of occasions (Table 3). Bateleurs were relatively more efficient at finding these small baits than they were at finding large carcasses, as observed by Mundy (1982) at which Bateleurs were first to arrive at only 47% of 91 carcasses.

Table 3. Species and numbers of scavengers that were first to arrive at baits that were located (n = 94) compared with all the baits observed (n = 131).

Species	*Number of baits located by scavengers*	*Percent of baits located by scavengers*	*Percent of all baits observed*
Bateleur	88	94	67
Whiteheaded vulture	2	2	2
Blackbacked jackal	2	2	2
Slender mongoose	2	2	2
Total	**94**	**100%**	**73%**

Bateleurs were seen eating, catching or carrying prey on 71 occasions during focal bird and ad-libitum observations. Of these, 70% and 85% of all items taken by adult and non-adult Bateleurs respectively were deduced to be carrion (Table 4). About 20% of the diet was large carrion items (>5 kg live weight), and 54% small carrion, such as dead birds, reptiles, and other small animals killed on the roads or in the grass fires that annually burn in savanna landscapes (Table 4). The remainder were live prey.

Table 4. Diets of adult and non-adult Bateleurs determined from focal bird and ad-libitum observations. Live-captured vs. carrion prey were deduced from the Bateleur's behaviour (Watson 1986) or direct observation.

Prey type	*Adult frequency*	*Non-adult, frequency percentage of total*	*All age classes*
Carrion			
Large carrion	10	4	20
Small carrion			
Bird	1	1	3
Reptile	2	0	3
Unidentified	20	10	42
Road kill	2	2	5
Burn kill	0	1	1
Sub-total	25	14	54
Total carrion	**35**	**18**	**74**
Live prey			
Small mammal	5	1	9
Bird	1	1	3
Reptile	8	0	11
Termites	1	1	3
Total live prey	**15**	**3**	**26**
Grand total	**50**	**21**	**100**

DISCUSSION

Soaring is a low energy method of flight (Pennycuick 1980) that is used widely among terrestrial and marine birds. Most terrestrial soaring birds use thermals as the source of lift for directional soaring flight. They circle to gain altitude in a thermal then glide, losing height between thermals (Pennycuick 1972). Alternatively, they can fly continuously in one direction by slowing their forward speed in a thermal while rising, and speeding-up in areas of sinking air to minimize altitude loss (Pennycuick 1972). In this way they maintain or even gain altitude while moving forward. Slope and undulating air currents are also used for lift when a strong and constant breeze is available (Rüppell 1977). The low altitude soaring flight of the Bateleur, without circling in thermals and under conditions of calm to light breeze, is therefore unusual among soaring birds.

Pennycuick (1972) explained the characteristic flight of Bateleurs as a form of dynamic soaring, in which they extract energy from horizontal gusts of air in the manner of sea birds, such as albatrosses (Rüppell 1977). One way this could be done is to bank alternately right and left, showing the raised wing to the swell (Pennycuick 1972). This explanation implies that wing canting by the Bateleur should be a fairly regular rocking motion and it is probable that this form of dynamic soaring alone would impose restrictions on the Bateleurs' direction of flight relative to the prevailing wind direction. To fly in another direction, they would be forced to use thermals in a manner similar to vultures (Pennycuick 1972). Careful observation of Bateleurs in flight revealed an erratic canting motion, resembling a bird's reaction to instability. Focal bird observations showed that Bateleurs' direction of flight was random or uniform and independent of wind direction (Fig. 2). It also showed that thermal soaring occurred most often only in the late afternoon, after hunting and other maintenance activities were accomplished for the day (Fig. 1). Therefore, Pennycuick's (1972) explanation of Bateleur flight would seem to be only a partial explanation.

I propose the following hypothesis as a possible explanation for Bateleur flight. At low altitude, under normal conditions of calm air to light breezes, sources of lift are probably not well defined. Air moves horizontally between areas of rising thermals and sinking air (Fig. 3a), and weak slope updrafts and undulating air (Fig. 3b), superimposed on thermals, add complexity, unpredictability and turbulence to conventional sources of lift (Fig. 3c). Irregular wing canting by Bateleurs in soaring flight resembles the motions expected of a bird in turbulent air.

For a bird to soar in any direction at this altitude, it must detect and use the slightest sources of lift and speed up through areas of sinking air. If this were so, Bateleurs would gain and lose altitude repeatedly as they flew, perhaps shifting from one state to the other so rapidly as to be unnoticeable. I suggest that the Bateleur is capable of using weak sources of lift found at low altitude that, because of its uniquely specialized aerodynamics, described below, are useless to other terrestrial soaring birds.

Efficient gliding aircraft are designed to fly in such a way as to maximize their glide ratio (forward distance to sinking distance), by obtaining maximum lift with least drag. Drag is most readily reduced by increasing the aspect ratio (wing-length:wing-width) because more elongated and pointed wings generate less induced drag (Rüppell 1977). Such a design would also be efficient for soaring birds, but it is severely limiting for other aspects of their survival. Long thin wings would be difficult to manoeuvre in confined spaces, such as negotiated by most terrestrial birds, and takeoff and landing would be increasingly difficult. Wing design of soaring birds represents a compromise between efficient gliding and other essential capabilities.

Albatrosses inhabit the marine environment, where wing length is less limited by confined space, and so come closest to the long thin wing design of efficient gliding aircraft. The aspect ratio of the Wandering Albatross *Diomedea exulans* is 20:1 (Brown 1976, Rüppell 1977), and is much greater than the aspect ratio of the Bateleur (8:1) or White Backed Vulture *Gyps africanus* 7:1 which has a glide ratio of 15:1 (Pennycuick 1972). Being limited by terrestrial confinement, the Bateleur's wing dimensions are only slightly modified to increase aspect ratio for efficient soaring.

Figure 3. Diagrams of (a) thermals that may be used by Bateleurs to gain lift at low altitude in the absence of a breeze, (b) other sources of lift at low altitude, that may be created by a light breeze, and (c) complex sources of lift at low altitude.

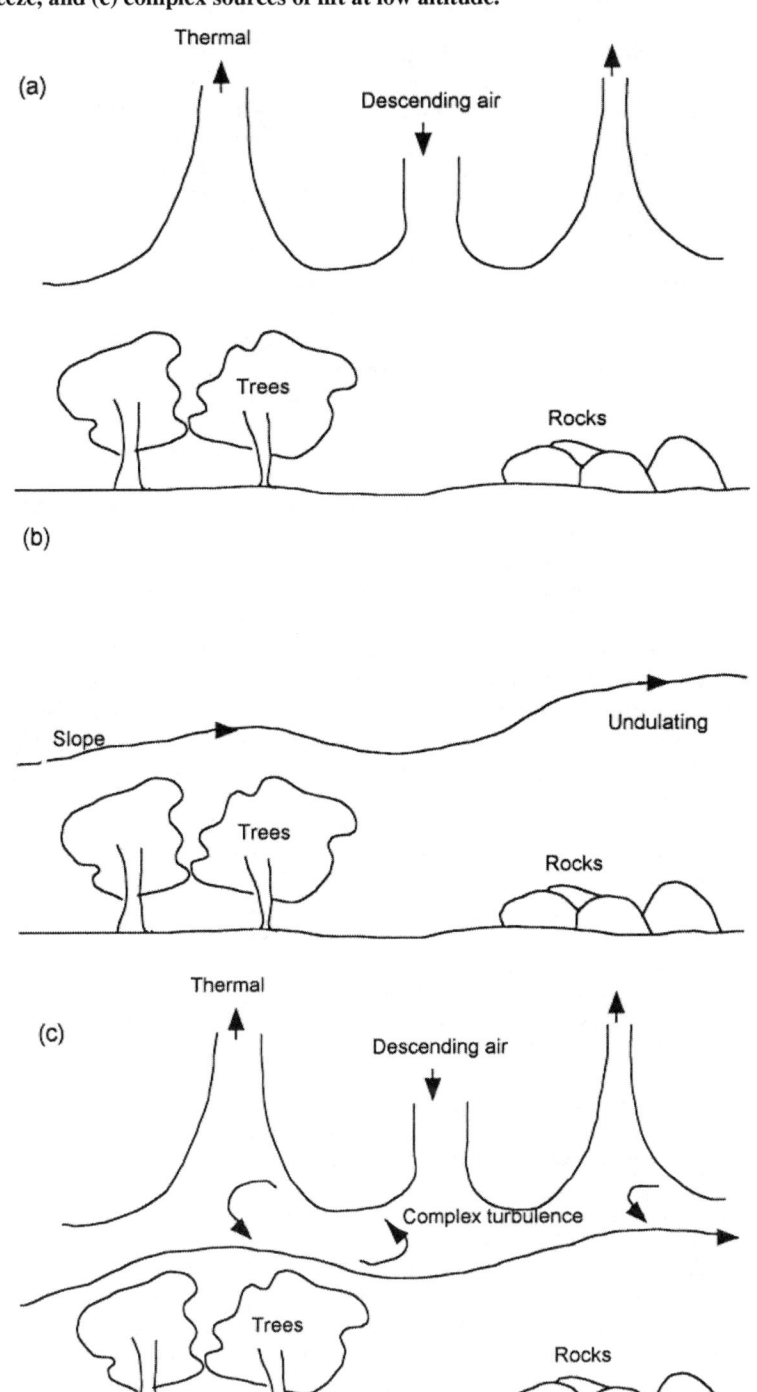

I suggest, therefore, that the Bateleur's unique ability to soar at low altitude, without using thermals, may also be attributed to its unusually short tail, an aerodynamic modification not found in other raptors. The Bateleur's tail-length:wing-length ratio is 0.2, whereas that of all other raptors are greater than 0.4 (Brown 1976).

The aerodynamic effects of tail length and shape have not been accurately measured for any bird, but it seems to be generally assumed that the tail mainly serves a stabilizing and directional function. The tail also provides lift and is a source of drag (Tucker 1992). The Bateleur's tail has a small surface area and presumably generates relatively little drag. Low drag would improve the glide ratio and, thus, may allow Bateleurs to use weak sources of lift. However, the tail also produces lift, so the short tail of the Bateleur must represent a trade off between better lift and loss of drag. For the Bateleur less drag seems to be the more important factor.

Compared with other raptors, the Bateleur's very reduced tail length and area has an obvious impact on its method of foraging. For example, a Black Kite *Milvus migrans*, which is readily seen manoeuvring in close proximity to humans, can be seen to twist, fan or angle the tail, to turn in confined spaces without rapid forward flight, and to land precisely on small targets. The tail is also used as an air-brake; when fanned and angled forward it rapidly halts a bird after a stoop at prey. If spread while hovering, the tail provides an extra lift-producing surface, like the wing-flaps on an airplane.

The Bateleur's reduced tail length must affect essential hunting abilities by reducing its ability to manoeuvre in close quarters and at slow airspeed, to brake after a stoop or to hover. It may also reduce stability in normal gliding flight (Rüppell 1977) and this may contribute to the Bateleur's irregular canting motion while flying. Presumably these abilities are important to most other raptors' survival and propagation, as no other raptors have a tail as short as the Bateleur.

The effect of a short tail can be readily seen in the Bateleur's typical approach to prey (Kill-Strikes A and B, and Descent to Carrion). The effect of a short tail was most obvious in the birds' dependence on wing-flapping to stop, but it also necessitated a slower approach with wings held up rather than tucked in for a fast stoop. This, combined with the circling before the stoop, must eliminate for Bateleurs any element of surprise that is used by other avian hunters to their advantage.

Low altitude soaring was used principally for foraging by the Bateleur and must compensate for its apparently clumsy hunting and killing method. I suggest that flying for long periods of time, repeatedly searching a limited home range of 45-55 km^2 at low altitude, brings Bateleurs into contact with an unusual food supply, namely small-sized carrion. The detailed searching allowed by low altitude soaring probably means that Bateleurs can see small dead animals that other avian scavengers, flying at higher altitude, cannot detect. Because Bateleurs are smaller than and subordinate to most other avian scavengers, preferring to leave a large carcass when they arrive (Houston 1980, Mundy 1982, Watson & Watson 1987), small carrion that can be consumed quickly by the Bateleur may be an important food source.

Feeding trials demonstrated that Bateleurs are very efficient at finding small items of carrion. Prey remains showed that at least 36% of the diet was large carrion, and ad-libitum and focal bird observations indicated that this proportion may be as high as 74%, including at least 54% small carrion.

However, Bateleurs also killed live prey (Steyn 1980, Watson 1986) and their low altitude searching can bring them into contact with many small animals. The most frequent small prey species could be described collectively as nocturnal mammals, insectivorous birds and various reptiles. I propose that the common denominator among these prey groups is that they may have to be temporarily occupied or distracted, such as insectivorous birds killing their own prey, nocturnal mammals disturbed from their diurnal lairs, or sun-basking reptiles, for the Bateleurs' approach to be effective.

In conclusion, I propose that the unique flight of the Bateleur, its foraging method and food source are linked. Bateleurs appear to be opportunistic foragers that are aerodynamically specialized, by virtue of their short tail and slightly higher aspect ratio, for low altitude soaring for long periods of time. This flight mode brings Bateleurs into contact with small carrion and temporarily distracted mammals, birds and reptiles, often enough to be an important and consistent source of food that is little exploited by other diurnal scavengers.

ACKNOWLEDGMENTS

I would like to thank Chris Watson for assistance, and comments on an earlier draft of this paper. Lloyd Kiff and Alan Kemp also made valuable comments on drafts of this paper. I thank the National Parks Board for permission to work in the KNP, and the South African Ornithological Society, South African Nature Foundation, University of the Witwatersrand, Foundation for Research and Development of the CSIR, and Sigma Motor Corporation for financial and logistical assistance.

REFERENCES

BRAIN, C.K. 1974. Some suggested procedures in the analysis of bone accumulations from southern African quaternary sites. *Ann. Transvaal Mus.* 29(1): 1-8.
BROWN, L. 1976. *Birds of prey and their biology*. Hamlyn, New York.
BROWN, L. & D. AMADON 1989. *Eagles, hawks and falcons of the world*. Wellfleet Press, New Jersey.
GERTENBACH, W.P.D. 1983. Landscapes of the Kruger National Park. *Koedoe* 26: 9-121.
HOUSTON, D.C. 1980. Interrelations of African scavenging animals. *Proc. IV Pan-Afr. Orn. Congr.*: 307-312.
KEOGH, H. 1974. Hair characteristics of thirty-nine species of southern African Muridae and their use as taxonomic criteria. M.Sc. thesis, University of Cape Town.
KEOGH, H. 1979. An atlas of hair from southern African species with reference to its taxonomic and ecological significance. D.Sc. thesis. University of Pretoria.
KEOGH, H. 1983. A photographic reference system of the microstructure of the hair of southern African bovids. *S. Afr. J. Wildl. Res.* 13: 89-132.
MUNDY, P.J. 1982. *The comparative biology of southern African vultures*. Vulture Study Group, Johannesburg.
PENNYCUICK, C.J. 1972. Soaring behaviour and performance of some East African birds observed from a motor-glider. *Ibis* 114: 178-218.
PENNYCUICK, C.J. 1980. The soaring flight of vultures. In: B. Wilson (ed.) *Birds*. Scientific American, New York.
RÜPPELL, B. 1977. *Bird flight*. Translation of Vogelflug (1975). Van Norstrand Reinhold, New York.
SCHOENER, T.W. 1981. An empirically based estimate of home range. *Theor. Popul. Biol.* 20: 281-325.
STEYN, P. 1980. Bateleur: breeding and food. *Ostrich* 51: 168-178.
TARBOTON, W. 1990. *African birds of prey*. Cornell University Press, New York, U.S.A.
TUCKER, V. 1992. Pitching equilibrium, wing span and tail span in a gliding Harris' Hawk *Parabuteo unicinctus*. *J. exp. Biol.* 165: 21-41.
WATSON, R.T. 1984. Home range and habitat utilization of the Bateleur: a preliminary study. In: Mendelsohn J.M. & C.W. Sapsford (eds), *Proc. 2nd. Symp. African Predatory Birds*. Natal Bird Club, Durban.
WATSON, R.T. 1986. The ecology, biology and population dynamics of the Bateleur eagle (*Terathopius ecaudatus*). Unpubl. Ph.D. Thesis, University of the Witwatersrand, Johannesburg.
WATSON, R.T. 1987. Flight identification of Bateleur age classes: a conservation incentive. *Bokmakierie* 39(2): 37-39.
WATSON, R.T. & C.R.B. WATSON, 1987. Interspecific piracy between Tawny Eagles and Bateleurs: how common is it? *Gabar* 2: 9-1 1.
ZAR, J.H. 1984. *Biostatistical analysis*. Prentice Hall, New Jersey.

Richard T. Watson
The Peregrine Fund
World Center for Birds of Prey
566 West Flying Hawk Lane
Boise, Idaho 83709
U.S.A.

Chancellor, R. D. & B.-U. Meyburg eds. 2000
Raptors at Risk
WWGBP / Hancock House

Causes of Cape Vulture *Gyps coprotheres* mortality at the Kransberg colony: a 17 year update

P. C. Benson

ABSTRACT

An assessment of natural and man-induced mortality factors was made at the Kransberg Cape Vulture colony from 1981 to 1998. Unhatched eggs accounted for the largest number of mortalities at this colony. Death at the nestling stage was the second highest age group affected. Nestling death was due to poisoning, predation, weather, traumatic injury and insufficient food. At the fledging stage, the juvenile's inability to return to the nest to be fed, collision with natural and man-made structures and drowning accounted for the mortalities observed. At the sub-adult and adult stage, poisoning was the only mortality factor observed. The two main factors affecting Cape Vultures at the Kransberg are food availability and poisoning. Increasing human densities, improved farming practices and changes in land-use will cause a decrease in food availability, resulting in an overall decline in Cape Vulture numbers. Total numbers of birds and reproductive output should stabilise at a level which can be supported by the available food. Total numbers could however be further affected by poisoning incidents, which can have a devastating impact on reduced numbers of birds. Eliminating poisoning incidents should be the highest conservation priority for Cape Vultures at the Kransberg.

INTRODUCTION

Documentation of bird mortality is difficult, as most carcasses go undiscovered. Of those found, there are biases toward man-induced factors (Newton 1976). The proximate and ultimate causes of death may differ and are often difficult to assess, leading to questionable conclusions. Though many causes of mortality have been suggested for Cape Vultures *Gyps coprotheres* (Benson & Dobbs 1984; Tarboton & Allan 1984; Mundy *et al.* 1997), little is known of the yearly variation in these factors or their relative importance to the total population or particular sub-populations.

This paper addresses some mortality factors documented at the Kransberg, the largest Cape Vulture breeding colony, where reproductive activities were monitored and carcasses collected as part of a long-term study of this bird's biology (Benson & Dobbs 1984; Dobbs & Benson 1984a, 1984b; Tarboton & Benson 1988; Benson *et al.* 1990). Breeding activities were followed and the pattern of nesting failures monitored over 17 seasons. A total of 464 carcasses of various age groups were collected from below the nesting cliff and surrounds. An evaluation of the cause of death for each was made and the importance of the different mortality factors are considered.

STUDY SITE

The Kransberg, 20 km northeast of Thabazimbi in the west of South Africa's Northern Province (24°28'S, 27°36'E), is on a 5.1 km section of the south-western corner of the Waterberg mountain range. A portion of the 200 m high south-facing nesting cliff is included in the recently proclaimed Marakele National Park and the remainder is on private land. Cattle and game farming are the main land-uses in the surrounding *Acacia* thornveld savanna.

METHODS

Reproductive activities

Over 2,800 sites have been identified and mapped on photos from aerial surveys of this cliff and each is assigned a unique alpha-numeric code (Tarboton & Benson 1988; Benson *et al.* 1990). From March 1981 to March 1984 the colony was monitored on a full-time basis. Subsequently, monthly ground surveys from 1-3 weeks in duration have been conducted throughout the breeding season and behavioural and/or reproductive activities documented at each site. Using the terminology of Postupalsky (1974), when an occupied site is where at least nest building behaviour is observed, and an active site is where at least an egg is laid (i.e. all active sites are occupied, but not all occupied sites are active) breeding success was determined.

The use of each site for breeding, timing of reproductive activities and nesting success has been monitored from 1981. Most sites were used for nesting in at least one season during this study. When possible, the cause of unsuccessful nesting attempts was determined. Over 14,000 nesting attempts have been documented.

Mortality factors

Carcasses of vultures have been collected from the base of the nesting cliff, the scree slope below the colony, under towers at the top of the nesting area and elsewhere around the colony. An assessment of these carcasses has been made, including chemical analyses when poisoning was suspected and conditions allowed it. Toxicological analyses were conducted at the Veterinary Research Institute - Onderstepoort. Remains of many of these carcasses are housed at the Department of Birds, Transvaal Museum, Pretoria.

RESULTS

Nesting success

During this study, the greatest number of breeding attempts occurred in 1984, when 977 occupied sites, of which 961 were active nests, were documented. The lowest number of breeding attempts occurred in 1995 when 725 occupied sites were observed, of which 697 were active. Fledging success from 1982 to 1997 ranged from 33.6% to 61.1% at occupied sites. In this period a total of 13,533 nesting attempts were monitored. The overall mean fledging success for this period was 50.3% (Fig. 1).

Figure 1. The fate of Cape Vulture nesting attempts at the Kransberg Colony (1982-1997).

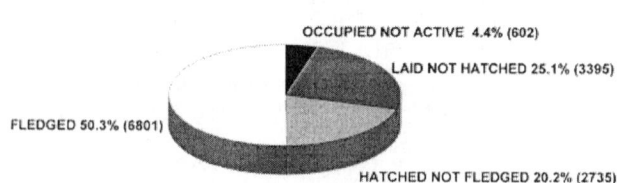

Nesting mortalities

Generally, the highest period of nesting failure was during the egg stage (11 of 16 years), when 55.4% of failures occurred. The average duration of incubation of eggs which failed to hatch was 66.7 days (N = 2366). However, some birds continued to incubate for almost 5 months (Fig. 2). Normal hatching occurs at about 56-57 days after egglaying.

Figure 2. Days from laying to abandonment of unhatched eggs by Cape Vultures at the Kransberg Colony (1983-1998).

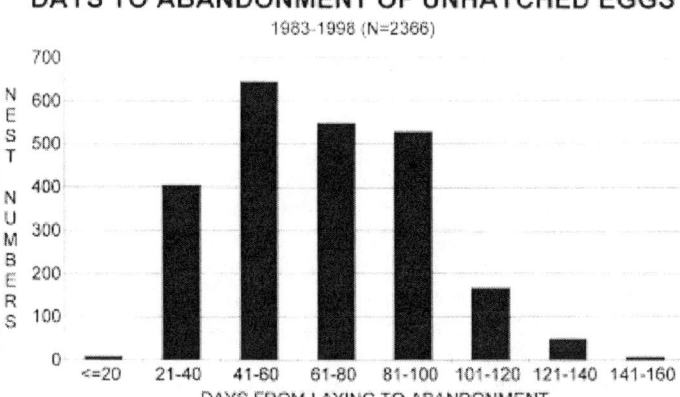

The average age at death of nestlings which failed was 69.6 days. There was an increase in mortality during the period of 20-40 days of age, with the biggest loss of nestlings occurring between 60-100 days (Fig. 3). The average hatching date is 8 July (N = 6998). Days 20-40 are during the coldest period of the winter months, which may account for this increase in loss when chicks are still quite small, but are not receiving the close brooding from parents that occurs in the first weeks after hatching. The second and larger loss occurred during the period of greatest food demand by the nestlings, when they are growing at their fastest rate.

Figure 3. Days from hatching to failure of nestlings of Cape Vulture which died at the Kransberg Colony (1983-1997).

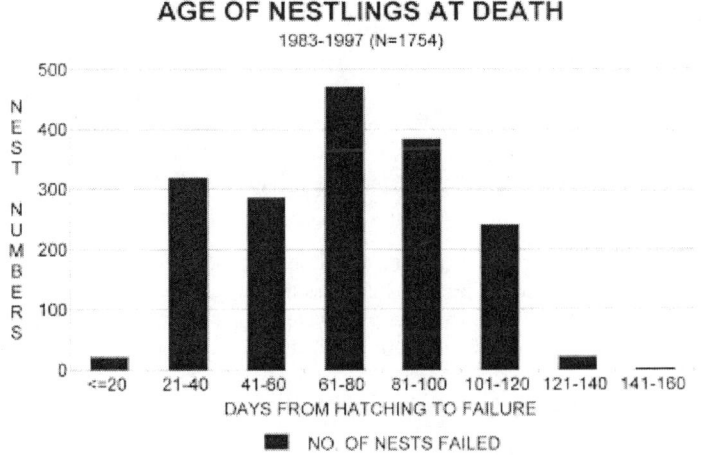

Predation

The main predator on Cape Vultures at the Kransberg is the Black Eagle *Aquila verreauxii*, which flies daily along the nesting cliff and soars in updrafts with vultures. Although only nine nestlings have actually been observed to be killed by Black Eagles at Kransberg (and two others at the Blouberg colony), many more unsuccessful predation attempts have been seen. Both adult and subadult eagles take young vultures. Adult eagles may act individually or in pairs. Subjectively, adult eagles seem more proficient than young birds at taking nestlings.

Eagles also scavenge vulture carcasses which have fallen to the base of the nesting cliff (pers. obs.). Of the carcasses found under nesting areas, 122 showed some evidence of scavenging or predation. Carcasses of poisoned adult vultures have been found scavenged, as well as nestlings which have died of poisoning or other causes. Generally it is impossible to be certain whether a carcass was scavenged or predated unless a predation event was observed. My feeling is that a predated carcass is usually fully consumed, while those scavenged are only partially eaten. Twenty-seven nestling carcasses were thus categorised as predation victims.

Depending on the vultures' reproductive state, their response to the eagles varies. During and prior to incubation there is no vocal response to the eagle's presence. When eggs begin to hatch, vultures respond to the eagles with a hoarse roar. This also varies, depending on the location of the eagle relative to the nesting areas. When the eagle is flying below the nesting areas vultures do not respond vocally, but when level with or above nest sites roaring occurs. Once fledging begins, roaring all but ceases.

Vultures attempt to defend their young by rushing at the eagle with wings spread and several birds may converge on the smaller predator. This can result in a rough and tumble event leading to the eagle being battered or the pulling from the nesting ledge of adult vultures. These latter observations occurred when young eagles attempted to take nestlings. Again, subjectively, young eagles appear less motivated than adults in their attacks on vultures. The young eagles may be more cautious or perhaps their intention is more harassment than predation.

A single event of a subadult eagle still-hunting a vulture chick was observed. The eagle landed on an unused vulture nest site, observed the potential prey and parent, then attacked successfully.

Benson & Dobbs (1984) reported on events of a lone male baboon consuming and/or destroying vulture eggs in 1982. Subsequent observations suggest that this is an uncommon occurrence. Baboon troops travelling through nesting areas generally avoid the vultures.

Traumatic injury

Bone abnormalities in nestling vultures are one source of mortality at the Kransberg and other colonies. Over 80% of the skeletal anomalies observed in live wild nestlings on the Kransberg cliff, between 1982 and 1997, were unilateral and in the wing (N = 143) (Benson in press a). The radius and ulna are often the bones affected. Though externally observable bone abnormalities may approach 3% of young at fledging stage, these birds represent about 1% or less of the annual reproductive attempts at the Kransberg.

Of the 143 nestlings with bone abnormalities, 27 (18.8%) were observed at 13 nest sites. At 12 of these sites, nestlings were observed with abnormalities in two years, at the 13th, nestlings were affected in three seasons. Though no formal assessment of nest sites has yet been conducted, some of the above are in relatively tight situations, with little space available for adults to land or stand without encountering the nestling. Others are in areas of high nesting density.

Weather

Benson & Dobbs (1983) reported weather at the Kransberg, in the form of a heavy mist covering the nesting cliff for an extended period of 2-3 days, as the ultimate cause of some nestling loss in 1981. Subsequent observations suggest this weather pattern is not a typical occurrence. Though mist regularly engulfs the Kransberg, this generally dissipates by mid-day, and poses little danger to nestlings. This same weather pattern occurs at colonies in the Magaliesberg, Soutpansberg, Drakensberg and at the Blouberg (pers. obs.).

Starvation

Of these 142 nestling carcasses, none was thought to have actually starved, even though the ultimate cause of death of most is probably food shortage. These include birds for which there was a negative result when testing for poisoning, or where no testing was done. Of 67 carcasses, collected between 2 September 1981 and 7 December 1983, and for which an approximate date of death could be determined, 50 (74.6%) died in the period 60-100 days after the average hatching date, at the same time that the highest period of nestling mortality occurs on the nests. Five additional birds died during an inclement weather period, when adults could not forage (see above and Benson & Dobbs, 1984).

Some of these 142 birds may have died of other causes, such as poisoning (see below), but could not be definitely linked to other specific mortality factors. Forty-four carcasses were scavenged and 21 had some sort of skeletal abnormality. An additional 32 nestling carcasses were observed on nests, but were not retrieved as it would have created undue disturbance to other nesting birds.

Mis-fledging

Forty-nine fledgling carcasses were found along the cliff base or the scree slope. Skeletal abnormalities occurred in 19 of these. Fifteen birds showed signs of being scavenged. Seven birds were discovered alive and some were so weak they made no effort to fly when approached. One bird was observed at the base of the cliff on 7 December 1983, and nine days later the bird was in the same place, too weak to flee. Three birds had severe recent unhealed breaks. One of those birds was flushed, and flew out from the cliff with a broken leg dangling. Upon circling several times, gaining altitude, one of its wings collapsed and the bird fell to the scree slope below.

Drowning

One fledgling was discovered drowned in a farm dam. This bird had slight unilateral bone abnormalities in the wing, on the keel and in the leg.

Collisions

There are four communication towers on the top of the Kransberg nesting cliff. The largest and most significant to the vultures is the South African Broadcasting Corporation's (SABC) radio and television transmitter (Benson & Dobbs 1984). This tower, 235 m high, is supported by 16 guy wires, attached diagonally to ground anchors from four levels. Since 1981, I have recovered 98 carcasses under this tower. Of 43 birds for which age at death could be determined, all but one were recent fledglings. The remaining bird was a subadult. Collisions occurred mainly between October and February, when all fledging occurs at the Kransberg. These values may be low as there is evidence that scavenging of carcasses does occur and that some may have been carried off by mammalian carnivores (e.g. brown hyaena *Brunea brunea*) which have increased in the area since the proclamation of Marakele National Park (pers. obs.). Despite placement of objects on the guy wires, first orange metal balls and then coiled bird diverters (Koop 1979; Koop & de Jong 1982), birds continue to be killed.

Poisoning

Chemical testing for strychnine was conducted on 90 birds from Kransberg. Poisoning was confirmed in 30 of 36 adults, one subadult, one juvenile and 24 of 52 nestlings. Testing was done between 1981-1984 while I lived full-time at the Kransberg. Though 34 of the birds tested were negative for strychnine it is likely the adult birds were also poisoned. Some breeding adults fed their young poisoned meat on returning to the nest, resulting in the nestling's death. Four additional adult carcasses were found after they had decomposed too much for sample collection.

Poisoning was suspected in an additional 88 free-flying birds, discovered from 1985-1997. After 1984, the cliff base was searched less regularly and the state of decomposition of the carcasses found precluded sample collection for testing. However, the pattern of the 1981-1984 poisoning incidents suggests probable poisoning of these 88 birds.

Poisoned adults were generally discovered along the cliff under nesting areas. For birds discovered soon after death, it was sometimes possible to correlate their location with nest failures in the areas above where the carcasses were found. Some carcasses were concentrated under areas where little or no nesting occurred. In one case 14 birds (12 adults, one fledgling and one nestling) were discovered in one area. Nine of these birds were in a "pile". Little nesting occurs above that site, though birds often roost there. Some areas on the nesting cliff are used almost exclusively by adults as roosts once fledging begins (pers. obs.). This discovery was made on 13 November 1983, well into the fledging period, when adults often roost away from their nest site.

I believe that sub-lethal doses of strychnine can ultimately cause the death of adult vultures returning to the colony, as seizures occurring from the poison induce the birds to fall from the cliff, resulting in death from traumatic injury. I have observed birds falling from the nesting cliff and sustaining such injuries at the Kransberg and at the Blouberg colony. These birds tested positive for strychnine. One such bird fell from the cliff while I was walking at the base, landing a few metres from me. When approached, it got up and ran off another ledge to fall approximately 30 m. Although still alive, it was weak, had many broken bones and subsequently died.

Several adult vultures tested negative for strychnine when poisoning was likely. Generally, groups of birds were discovered in poisoning incidents. Some of these birds tested negative while others were positive. Crop and stomach contents, and liver were collected for strychnine tests. Crop and stomach samples were not always available from carcasses, and when present, test results were not always consistent with those from the liver. Positive results from stomach and crop samples sometimes occurred when liver tests were negative, while other birds tested positive for all three.

At least 23 incidents of poisoning occurred at the Kransberg between 1982 and 1997, affecting a minimum of 124 free-flying birds. The number of carcasses discovered per chemically-confirmed incident varied greatly from 1-19 birds. It is unlikely that carcasses of all of the poisoned birds returning to the colony were found and others probably died at the poison site or elsewhere. Nestlings discovered during the period 1985-1997 were not tested and none have been considered as dying of poisoning, though some probably did. Those birds are classified above as having died of starvation.

DISCUSSION

Nesting mortalities

Eggs and nestlings were the age groups with the highest mortality at the Kransberg colony. Eggs not hatching was the greatest cause of nesting failures. The group with the second highest mortality was nestlings 60-100 days of age (Fig. 3). Nestling growth rate is fastest and food consumption greatest during this period (Komen 1991). This high mortality rate, when the nestlings' energy demand is greatest, suggests that food availability limits reproductive success.

Predation

The impact of predation on Cape Vultures is difficult to quantify as observations of interactions with predators are irregular. Although Black Eagles do interact with adult vultures, it is usually when attempting to capture the latter's nestling. Little interaction occurs at the egg stage. The large number of carcasses discovered which had been fed upon and the attempts to take live nestlings indicates that eagles recognise vulture nestlings as a food source. The adult vultures' roaring indicates recognition of the eagles' threat and serves as an alarm to other nesting birds. This interaction has certainly occurred for as long as both birds have been present on the cliffs and eagles must represent little threat to the vultures' long-term viability as a species.

Traumatic injury

The nature of the bone abnormalities observed in Cape Vulture nestlings suggests that traumatic injury is the origin. The high incidence of unilateral abnormalities of the wing is consistent with other studies where traumatic injury of birds has been studied (Howard & Redig 1993; Goodman & Glynn 1988). Though some authors suggest that Cape Vulture bone anomalies are due to a calcium deficiency (Mundy & Ledger 1976; Richardson *et al.* 1986), no evidence has been presented indicating this is the case. Abnormalities in those studies are also primarily in the wings (Ledger & Mundy 1976; Mundy & Ledger 1977; see also Fig. 3.2 of Mundy 1983, p. 61). In most nutritional or metabolic disorders, the entire skeleton will be impacted and weight-bearing bones (i.e. legs, pelvis) are usually those most affected (Fowler 1981). This is not the type of abnormality observed in the great majority of nestlings with bone anomalies. Observations of adult and subadult skeletal material collected from poisoning and other events also indicate that additional abnormalities occur which are not externally observable but which do not interfere with the bird's normal functioning and breeding (Benson in press a).

There is evidence that some of the abnormalities observed may be of a genetic or developmental disposition, and a few may have a metabolic or nutritional origin (Benson in press a). It is however impossible to determine the aetiology of these last two categories, without knowing the history of the individual involved. Developmental, genetic, metabolic and nutritional disorders appear to represent less than 5% of the total abnormalities observed (pers. obs.). Though these anomalies are interesting, they are a normal part of the Cape Vultures' biology, as they are of many other birds and vertebrates (e.g. Brandwood *et al.* 1986; Goodman & Glynn 1988), and have little significance on the long-term viability of the species.

Weather

Although prolonged periods of inundation by heavy mist may cause increased Cape Vulture nestling mortality within a single season, the extended period of cloud observed in 1981 (Benson & Dobbs 1984) cannot be considered the norm and does not represent a major long-term mortality factor for the species.

Starvation

Although data suggesting a food shortage are largely circumstantial, with the highest nestling mortality occurring at the period of greatest energy demand, it is likely that food is the main factor limiting reproduction. For Kransberg and other large colonies (e.g. Blouberg, Manutsa), the food demands of thousands of birds must increase intra- and interspecific competition, and it is likely these colonies can only exist in areas of high livestock mortality such as occurs near the communal grazing areas of the former homelands of South Africa (Huntley *et al.* 1989; Benson in press b). The existence of the largest Cape Vulture colonies in, adjacent to or very near the former homelands supports this view. It is likely that with development of these areas and improved farming practices, the food available to vultures will decline. Though it has been suggested that feeding stations can alleviate this food shortage (Butchart 1988), the high demands of large colonies makes this food source appear meagre. These feeding stations do however, have other benefits (e.g. public relations, education) which justify their continuance. It is likely that Cape Vulture populations will decline to levels which can be supported by local food availability. Breeding numbers of Cape Vultures in the Northern Province have declined from the drought years of the early 1980's (Benson *et al.* 1990; Benson in press b), suggesting that this may already have started. If lower breeding numbers persist, then greater vigilance will be required to prevent catastrophic poisoning incidents from decimating already reduced populations.

Mis-fledging

Fledging must be one of the periods of highest mortality for all birds. It is difficult to document for vultures, as individuals may travel long distances from the colony before dying. If a Cape Vulture fledgling does not return to its nest it will not be fed and more than likely will die. From October to February, fledgling vultures can be seen on many of the roads surrounding the Kransberg. Birds often land in the wooded area on the scree slope below the nesting cliff, unable to become airborne and so cannot return to their nest site.

Collection of these fledglings and attempts to return them to the wild have become the focus of several conservation efforts directed toward vultures (H. A. Scott pers. comm). Although this may have some public relations value, its biological significance to the species should be considered carefully. There are indications that some of these birds continually end up grounded, even after repeated expensive efforts to rehabilitate them. Several questions arise. Is there a genetic component to these birds' inability to survive on their own? Are we working against natural selection when attempting to put their genes back into the population? Could the time and financial effort expended on these individuals be better spent in other areas necessary for the species' conservation?

Fledglings reflect the experiential history and genetic and behavioural adequacy of their parents. The fledging process is a major hurdle, and the bird's ability to return to the nest a measure of its physical and behavioural competence. Though "accidents" may occur, it could be argued that even these gauge an individual's survival capacity. Though the inability of birds to successfully raise young might have a component based in human-caused environmental degradation (e.g. lack of food due to changes in land use) the answer to the birds' problem is not to "rescue" the weakest individuals (i.e. unsuccessful fledglings) but rather to enhance the survival potential of successful fledglings by addressing and modifying the ultimate problem.

Collisions

The impact of collisions on the Kransberg Cape Vulture population is relatively small compared to some mortality causes. Few birds are killed each year and they are a cohort which probably has a relatively high mortality rate from other factors. However, they have passed through the nestling period and have apparently fledged successfully, thus they are relatively robust individuals and perhaps fit to breed, making these deaths cause for concern.

The SABC has placed metal balls and bird diverters on the guy wires of the tower, yet collisions continue to occur. Though these diverters have proven successful in deterring collisions on horizontal power and telephone lines (Koop 1979; Koop & de Jong 1982), the diagonally placed guys blend against the background of the earth below (pers. obs.), probably making them difficult to see for birds flying above them. These devices, meant to make the guys more visible, are relatively useless, particularly for young inexperienced birds. Adults, by contrast, do fly in the area of the towers and even roost on some of them, yet seem to have no problem avoiding the offending guy wires, suggesting that birds learn to avoid the wires with experience.

Drowning

The relative lack of farm dams in the immediate surroundings of the Kransberg colony may partially account for the low numbers of birds drowned. This mortality factor is important in other areas (M. D. Anderson pers. comm., this proceedings) and should be mitigated for as it affects free-flying birds which are breeding or potential breeding individuals.

Poisoning

Poisoning is the most significant cause of adult and subadult Cape Vulture mortality at the Kransberg colony. Poisoning incidents vary in size, yet the numbers of birds discovered undoubtedly under-represents the total killed. Poisoning has been implicated in the decline of Cape and other griffon vultures elsewhere (Brown 1977; Schenk 1977; Brown & Piper 1988; Allan 1989).

Some breeding adults return to the nesting cliff and feed their young poisoned meat, resulting in the adult's and nestling's deaths. This suggests strychnine can be stored in the crop without harm to the adult, only affecting a bird once digestion occurs. I believe sub-lethal doses of strychnine can also ultimately lead to death in adult birds returning to the nesting cliff, when seizures, occurring with strychnine poisoning, cause them to fall from the cliff and ultimately die from traumatic injury.

Although extensive information is distributed to farmers, by organisations including the provincial nature conservation authorities and Vulture Study Group, poisoning continues. Poisoning is generally the unintentional result of commercial farmers placing poison over whole carcasses for Black-backed Jackal *Canis mesomelos* control. Although this method is illegal, it is impossible to control. This contrasts with poisoning incidents in the South African Lowveld, adjacent to the large Kruger National Park and private game reserves, where vultures are intentionally poisoned for parts to be sold in the traditional medicine market (van Jaarsveld 1988; pers. obs.). Other poisons have been employed in these incidents, including almost any agricultural pesticide or dip.

One must be cautious not to attribute other causes of mortality to poisoning. In spring and early summer, many newly fledged birds are found on the ground in the Thabazimbi area. These birds are often dehydrated or emaciated and unable to fly, and may have seizures similar to those caused by strychnine poisoning which leads to mis-diagnosis of their condition. The discovery of adults or sub-adults in such a condition, particularly in large numbers, may be a relatively good indicator of poisoning. However, it is impossible to attribute a recent fledgling's similar condition to poisoning without chemical analysis.

When collecting specimens for chemical analysis it is important to take as much material as possible. Crop and stomach samples are probably the best specimen source, as negative results have occurred from liver samples when crop samples were positive. This suggests the poison may act before reaching the liver, or at least in levels sufficient for positive test results.

It is likely that there is a time lag for the poison to reach the liver even though it is having an effect on the bird's nervous system. Because vultures often regurgitate crop and/or stomach contents when stressed, it is possible some of the birds discovered eliminated these contents before death, resulting in negative test results. When only liver samples are available, negative results may be misleading. These birds could also have died from other poisons untested for, although this seems unlikely considering the presence of the other carcasses with which they were discovered. From the pattern observed from 1981-1984 it is likely that some of those birds were also poisoned, suggesting that mortality due to poisoning is much higher than positive test results suggest.

ACKNOWLEDGEMENTS

The author would like to thank the following organisations and individuals for providing financial and/or logistical support during various phases of this project: Anglo American and De Beers Chairman's Fund, Billiton Development Trust, Birdlife South Africa, Colour Presentations, Department of Zoology University of the Witwatersrand, Mining Stress Systems, National Geographic Society, New York Zoological Society, Northern Transvaal Ornithological Society, Rennies Travel, Raptor Research Foundation, South African National Parks Board, South African Broadcasting Corporation, South African Department of Co-operation and Development, South African Department of Environment Affairs, The Kwêvoël, The Peregrine Fund, Transvaal Directorate of Environmental & Nature Conservation, Transvaal Museum Bird Department, Veterinary Research Institute - Onderstepoort, Western Foundation of Vertebrate Zoology, Witwatersrand Bird Club, E. Aucamp, T. Cassidy, J. C. Dobbs, L. N. Gilson, J. Harris, T. Harris, E. Joseph, A. C. Kemp, D. Solomon, W. R. Tarboton and P. van Staden.

REFERENCES

ALLAN, D. G. 1989. Strychnine poison and the conservation of avian scavengers in the Karoo, South Africa. *S. Afr. J. Wildl. Res.* 19: 102-106.

BENSON, P. C. In press a. Bone abnormalities in vultures - abstract. In: Boshoff, A. F., Anderson, M. D. & Borello, W. D. (eds.). *Vultures in the 21st century - vulture research and conservation in southern Africa*. Northern Cape Nature Conservation Services, Kimberley.

BENSON, P. C. In press b. Status of vultures in the Northern Province, South Africa - 1998. In: Boshoff, A. F., Anderson, M. D. & Borello, W. D. (eds.). *Vultures in the 21st century - vulture research and conservation in southern Africa*. Northern Cape Nature Conservation Services, Kimberley.

BENSON, P. C. & J. C. DOBBS 1984. Causes of Cape Vulture mortality at the Kransberg colony. In: Mendelsohn, J. M. & Sapsford, C. W. (eds.) *Proc. Second symp. Afr. Predatory Birds*, pp. 87-93. Natal Bird Club, Durban.

BENSON, P. C., W. R. TARBOTON, D. G. ALLAN & J. C. DOBBS 1990. The breeding status of the Cape Vulture in the Transvaal during 1980-1985. *Ostrich* 61: 134-142.

BRANDWOOD, A., A. S. JAYES & R. McN. ALEXANDER 1986. Incidence of healed fractures in the skeletons of birds, molluscs & primates. *J. Zool., Lond. (A)* 208: 55-62.

BROWN, C. J. & S. E. PIPER 1988. Status of Cape Vultures in the Natal Drakensberg and their cliff site selection. *Ostrich* 59: 126-136.

BROWN, L. H. 1977. The status of, and threats to, diurnal and nocturnal birds of prey in east Africa and Ethiopia. In: Chancellor, R. D. (ed.). *Report of Proc. World conference on birds of prey*, pp. 15-28. International Council for Bird Preservation, Vienna.

BUTCHART, D. 1988. Give a bird a bone. *Afr. Wildl.* 42: 316-322.

DOBBS, J. C. & P. C. BENSON 1984a. Behavioural and metabolic responses to food deprivation in the Cape Vulture. In: Mendelsohn, J. M. & Sapsford, C. W. (eds.) *Proc. Second symp. Afr. Predatory Birds*, pp. 211-214. Natal Bird Club, Durban. Proc. Second symp. Afr. Predatory Birds: 211-214.

DOBBS, J. C. & P. C. BENSON 1984b. Calcium requirements and bone abnormalities in the Cape Vulture. In: Mendelsohn, J. M. & Sapsford, C. W. (eds.) *Proc. Second symp. Afr. Predatory Birds*, pp. 219-228. Natal Bird Club, Durban.

GOODMAN, S. M. & C. GLYNN 1988. Comparative rates of natural osteological disorders in a collection of Paraguayan birds. *J. Zool., Lond.* 214: 167-177.

HOWARD, D. J. & P. T. REDIG 1993. Analysis of avian fracture repairs: implications for captive and wild birds. In: *Proc. Assoc. Avian Vets.* AAV Publication office, Lakeworth, Florida.

HUNTLEY, B., R. SIEGFRIED & C. SUNTER 1989. *South African environments into the 21st century.* Human & Rousseau Tafelberg, Cape Town.

KOMEN, J. 1991. Energy requirements of nestling Cape Vultures. *Condor* 93: 53-158.

KOOP, F. B. J. 1979. Vermindering van draadslachtoffers door markering van hoogspanningslijnen. *Elektrotechniek* 57: 60-63.

KOOP, F. B. J. & J. DE JONG 1982. Vermindering van draadslachtoffers door markering van hoogspanningsleidingen in de omgeving van Heerenveen. *Elektrotechniek* 60: 641-646.

LEDGER, J. & P. MUNDY 1976. Cape Vulture research in 1975. *Bokmakierie* 28: 4-8.

MUNDY, P. J. 1983. The conservation of the Cape Griffon Vulture of southern Africa. In: Wilbur, S. R. & Jackson, J. A. (eds). *Vulture Biology and Management*, pp. 57-74. University of California Press, Berkeley.

MUNDY, P. J. & J. A. LEDGER 1976. Griffon Vultures, carnivores and bones. *S. Afr. J. Sci.* 72: 106-110.

MUNDY, P. & J. LEDGER 1977. The plight of the Cape Vulture. *Endangered Wildlife* 1(4): 2-3.

MUNDY, P. J., P. C. BENSON & D. G. ALLAN 1997. Cape Vulture *Gyps coprotheres*. In: Harrison, J. A., Allan, D. G., Underhill, L. G., Herremans, M., Tree, A. J., Parker, V. & Brown, C. J. (eds.). *The atlas of southern African birds*, Vol. 1: Non-passerines, pp. 158-159. Birdlife South Africa, Johannesburg.

NEWTON, I. 1979. *Population ecology of raptors*. Buteo Books, South Dakota.

POSTUPALSKY, S. 1974. Raptor reproductive success: some problems with methods, criteria and terminology. In: Hamerstrom, Jr., F. N., Harrell, B. E. & Olendorff, R. R. (eds.). *Proc. Conf. Rapt. Cons. Techniques*, pp. 21-31. Raptor Research Report no.2, Fort Collins, Colorado.

RICHARDSON, P. R. K., P. J. MUNDY & I. PLUG 1986. Bone crushing carnivores and their significance to osteodystrophy in griffon vulture chicks. *J. Zool., Lond. (A)* 210: 23-43.

SCHENK, H. 1977. Status and conservation of birds of prey in Sardinia: with a special note on the impact of man on a griffon vulture population. In: Chancellor, R. D. (ed.). *Report Proc. World conference on birds of prey*, pp. 132-136. International Council for Bird Preservation, Vienna.

TARBOTON, W. R. & P. C. BENSON 1988. Aerial counting of Cape Vultures. *S. Afr. J. Wildl. Res.* 18: 93-96.

Patrick C. Benson, Ph.D.
Department of Zoology
University of the Witwatersrand
Private Bag 3
P.O. Wits
2050
Johannesburg
South Africa

Chancellor, R. D. & B.-U. Meyburg eds. 2000
Raptors at Risk
WWGBP / Hancock House

Ecology of Taita *Falco fasciinucha*, Peregrine *F. peregrinus minor* and Lanner *F. biarmicus* Falcons in Zimbabwe

R.R. Hartley

ABSTRACT

All Taita *Falco fasciinucha* and most African Peregrine *F. peregrinus minor* Falcons were found breeding along escarpments, gorges and inselbergs in well-wooded country, mainly along river systems in the Zambezi Valley (80% Taitas, N = 16; 37% of Peregrines, N = 50), where Peregrines outnumbered Taitas 3:1 and Lanner Falcons *F. biarmicus* 10:1. Most Lanner nests (67%,N = 155) were found in open or woodland habitats in domed inselberg and kopje terrain, where they outnumbered Peregrines 3:1 and where Taitas were rarely seen. Peregrines and Lanners competed with Taitas for breeding sites and for prey, and consequently Taitas were relatively absent from areas which also hosted the other two species. While cliffs >100 m were favoured by Taitas (38%, N = 7) and Peregrines (23%, N = 28), cliffs <25 m (25%, N = 5) and 30-35 m (31%, N = 34) were used by them respectively. All Taita and Peregrine nests were on cliffs, where cavities (Taitas 73%, N = 19; Peregrines 46%, N = 51) and sheltered ledges were used mainly. Most Lanner nests (88%, N = 203) were on cliffs (ledges 63%, N = 110; cavities 21%, N = 38) and 50% (N = 56) were on features <25 m high. Lanners also used stick nests (32%, N = 72) on cliffs (22%, N = 45), in trees (96%, N = 27) and on pylons (100%, N = 2), while Lanners (16%, N = 36) and Peregrines (8%, N = 11) also bred in quarries and on buildings.

The main prey of Taitas was small to medium sized birds (mean = 40,9 g) from woodland (64%) and cliff (32%) habitats, of Peregrines was medium sized birds (mean = 139,7 g), especially doves (39%) from woodland (84%), and of Lanners was medium sized birds (mean = 188 g) from woodland (49%) and human (45%) habitats, where key prey was feral pigeons *Columba livia* and poultry. The rarity of the Taita is probably determined by its more specialised habitat requirements and possibly also by its interspecific relationship with the Peregrine, while the population of the generalist Lanner may be expanding with land clearance in Zimbabwe.

INTRODUCTION

Taita *Falco fasciinucha*, African Peregrine *F. peregrinus minor* and Lanner *F. biarmicus* Falcons are resident in Zimbabwe (hereafter Taita, Peregrine and Lanner respectively). The much rarer Siberian Peregrine *F. peregrinus calidus* is a non-breeding Palaearctic migrant which has rarely been encountered in Zimbabwe (Irwin 1981; Hartley 1998). Throughout its range in Africa, the Taita is sympatric with the much larger Peregrine (Hunter et al.1979; Thomsett 1988; Moller 1989; Jenkins 1991; Hartley et al. 1993) and the two species may compete for nest sites and prey (Thomson 1984; Hustler 1989; Hartley et al. 1993). Throughout their shared range, the Peregrine is apparently dominant and it possibly affects the distribution and abundance of the much rarer Taita (Thomson 1984; Hustler 1989; Hartley et al. 1993). In Zimbabwe, it is possible that there are more than 60 pairs of Taitas (Hartley 1995) and 350-400 pairs of Peregrines (Hartley 1993a).

The Peregrine is a little studied, uncommon breeding resident in Africa south of the Sahara (Brown et al. 1982; Cade 1982; Steyn 1982), although it appears to be more common in Zimbabwe (Irwin 1981; Thomson 1984; Hartley 1992; Harrison et al. 1997), Kenya (Thomsett 1988) and in the Western Cape Province of South Africa (Pepler & Martin 1988; Jenkins 1994). Despite being a specialist hunter of birds (Ratcliffe 1980; Cade 1982), the Peregrine has proved highly adaptable over its cosmopolitan range (Cade et al. 1988), and in Africa it is resident over a wide range of habitats, including deserts (Braby et al. 1987). However, in Africa it appears to be best represented in tropical woodlands (Hustler 1983; Tarboton & Allan 1984; Thomson 1984; Hartley 1992) and fynbos (Jenkins 1994). Many of the investigations on the Peregrine in Africa have focussed on its apparent rarity, with suggested reasons being: a) its dependence on cliffs in woodland habitats; b) the role of water and related patchiness of food resources; c)the influence of cliff height, latitude and pesticides; and d) competition with the sympatric Lanner (Thomson 1984; Mendelsohn 1988; Jenkins 1991, 1992a & b, 1994; Hartley 1992). Both Lanners and Peregrines occur throughout Zimbabwe (Irwin 1981; Harrison et al. 1997). Lanners breed on a wide range of cliffs and also in old stick nests in trees and on pylons (Thomson 1984). Lanners are more common in more open habitats and it has been estimated that there are over 1000 pairs in Zimbabwe (Thomson 1984).

Based on subjective observations, Thomson (1984) suggested that: 1) the rarity of the Taita is determined by its interspecific relationship with the Peregrine; 2) the site requirements and breeding season of Peregrines and Lanners are the principal factors determining their respective population status in Zimbabwe; and 3) the Lanner is an open country species whose range has probably increased with recent deforestation in Africa. This study investigates these hypotheses and presents sightings and specimen data on distribution, abundance, nest site characteristics, morphology, hunting, prey, habitat requirements and habitat changes, based on 20, 136, and 231 pairs of Taitas, Peregrines and Lanners respectively.

STUDY AREA

Zimbabwe covers an area of 390,460 km^2 (Zinyama & Whitlow 1986) within the Afro-tropical region. The physical background has been described by Irwin (1981). There are four main geographical regions: the lowveld (<600 m elevation), middleveld (600-1000 m), highveld (>1000 m) and montane. Generally, temperature, rainfall and vegetation type are coincident with these altitudinal zones. Annual rainfall is mainly from November to March, with a national mean of 647 mm (range of 335-1193 mm), but varying from 147-2640 mm in different parts of the country in different years (Department of Meteorological Services *in litt*.). Although the principal vegetation type is *Brachystegia* (Miombo) woodland, 24 sub-types have been described by Wild (1965).

Key woodland habitats are mopane *Colophospermum mopane* in the drier (400-712 mm annual rainfall) lowveld and middleveld areas (zone 1 - Zambezi Valley; Fig. 1); varying combinations of *Julbernardia* and *Brachystegia* in the wetter (700-1500 mm) middleveld (zone 1) and highveld areas (zone 2 - Mvurwi-Mrewa), and *Terminalia* in granitic terrain of the middleveld (700-800 mm; zone 3 - Matobo Hills).

Topographical features used for nesting by these falcons include tors, kopjes, domed inselbergs, mesas, mountain cliffs, escarpments, river cliffs and gorges (Lister 1993; Table 1). Tors are relatively small piles of granite boulders extending 5-40 m above the general topography. Kopjes are small granite hills up to 70 m high, comprising large rectangular boulders interspersed with small patches

Figure 1. Principal falcon breeding zones in Zimbabwe

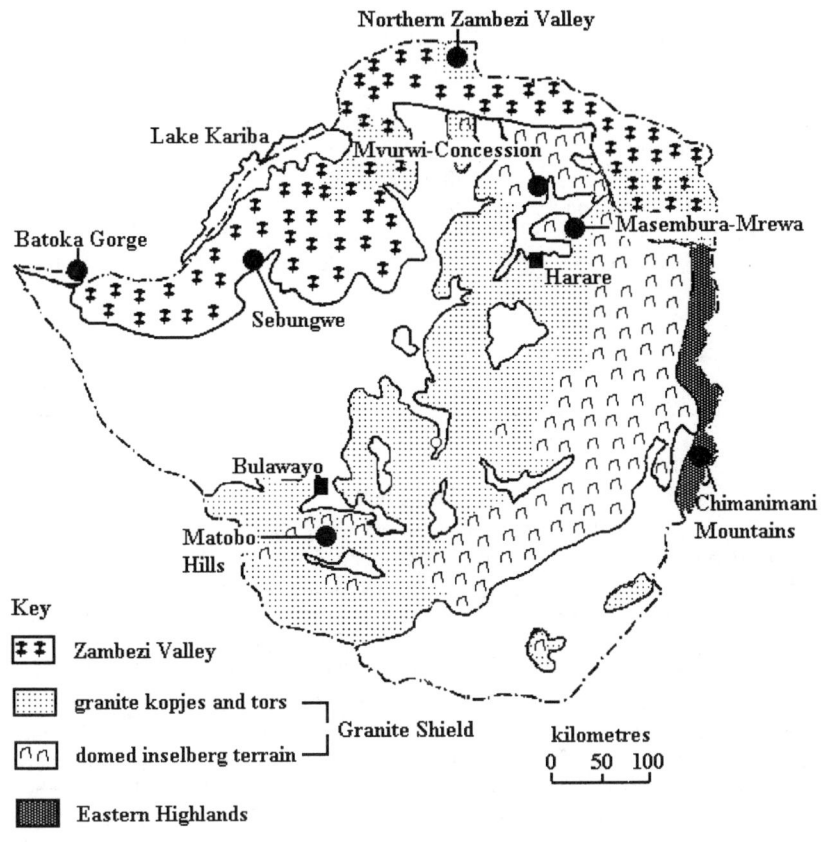

of soil and vegetation. Domed inselbergs, also called bornhardts, are large granite features which usually range from 100-500 m above the general topography and vary from almost symmetrical whalebacks to irregular sugar-loaf features. Kopjes, and sometimes tors, are found among domed inselbergs, but are also frequent over the remainder of the granite shield. All such cliff habitats are abundant over wide areas of the country, of which about 30% is covered by granitic domed inselbergs (Fig. 1; Whitlow 1980a), while mountain ranges, and escarpments and gorges, characterise the eastern border and the main river systems (especially the Zambezi and Save) respectively.

The quality and abundance of natural habitats is related to three land-use categories. State Land (National Parks Estate = 12,7%; Forestry Areas = 2,3% of Zimbabwe) comprises protected areas with natural densities of breeding raptors. General Land (32% of the country) is privately owned, has a mean density of 7,6 persons/km^2, comprises mainly ranchlands with natural habitats still intact and relatively undamaged (Whitlow 1988; Hartley et al. 1996), and in many areas has densities of breeding raptors that compare favourably with protected areas. On Communal Lands (42% of the country, but 60% of the human population at a mean density of 25,5 persons/km^2, Zinyama & Whitlow 1986), habitat quality has declined rapidly and 60% of the area is either overpopulated or grossly overpopulated (Whitlow 1988), mainly with peasant farmers. Deforestation in several of these areas has reached 10% per year (Whitlow 1980b), especially in areas with domed inselberg terrain which comprise 64% of Communal Lands (Whitlow 1980a, 1988).

Table 1. Topographical and other features used for nesting by Taita, Peregrine and Lanner Falcons in Zimbabwe.

% Feature used	Taita (n = 20)	Species Peregrine (n = 136)	Lanner (n = 231)
Tor			7.4
Kopje		1.5	26.0
Domed Inselberg (Bornhardt)		36.8	33.7
Mesa	20.0	9.5	0.9
Mountain cliff/Escarpment	5.0	12.5	2.2
River cliff		12.5	
Gorge	75.0	19.1	1.3
Quarry		4.4	13.8
Building		3.7	1.7
Pylon			0.9
Tree			12.1

METHODS

Surveys were conducted during the breeding season by members of the Zimbabwe Falconers' Club (ZFC; Hartley 1993b). Work on Taitas and Peregrines sometimes involved The Peregrine Fund Inc. (TPF) and was part of a formal programme between the ZFC and the Department of National Parks and Wild Life Management (DNPWLM; Hartley 1993b). Data were collected on habitat, nest type, cliff height, position and aspect. Nest record cards from the Natural History Museum of Zimbabwe were also used, and mainly involved Lanners (n = 58).

Three contrasting zones surveyed between 1990 and 1994 were assessed for ecological contrasts favoured by Taitas, Peregrines and Lanners. Zone 1 included three study areas in the Zambezi Valley (Fig. 1). Zone 2 included an arc of granite dwala and kopje terrain stretching from privately-owned, relatively undisturbed habitats on General Land around Mvurwi-Concession, to tribal-owned, significantly deforested Communal Lands around Masembura-Domboshava-Mrewa. Zone 3 was the mainly kopje terrain of the Matobo Hills (Gargett 1990), including National Parks Estate (protected), General and Communal Lands. For each nest site in each of these areas, a quality index (QI) was calculated that included three key components (each with a score of 0-2, maximum possible score 6, after Manzi & Perna 1994): 1) maximum height of cliff, <35m = 0; 36-100 m = 1; >100 m = 2; 2) complexity of site, single cliff = 0; group of cliffs with one aspect = 1; group of cliffs with more than one aspect = 2; 3) dominance, the angle of view with no intervening obstacles for at least 1 km, <30° = 0, 30°-90° = 1 and >90° = 2.

Table 2. Taita, Peregrine and Lanner Falcon nest sites in Zimbabwe, according to land use category.

Species (n)	% Land use category		
	N.Park/state land	General land	Communal land
Taita (n = 20)[1]	84.2		15.8
Peregrine (n = 136)	35.6	28.1	36.3
Lanner (n = 231)	10.6	56.4	32.9

[1] includes two sites on Zambian side of Batoka Gorge, Zambezi

Prey data for Taitas were sourced from Hartley et al. (1993) and my unpublished notes, for Peregrines from Hustler (1983), Hallamore (1972) and my unpublished notes, and for Lanners from the unpublished notes of myself, G.Hall and W.R. Thomson. Prey were identified from pluckings, remains, pellets and from observations at all sites, during and outside of the breeding season. Identification was based on comparisons with reference material held by the Natural History Museum of Zimbabwe and with my own catalogue of avian prey (126 species). It is likely that reptiles and mammals were under-represented for the generalist Lanner (Simmons *et al.* 1991). Captive Taitas (N = 16) and Peregrines (N = 22), and wild-caught Lanners (N = 29), were weighed to the nearest gram on an Ohaus triple-beam balance, and some were also measured (following Biggs *et al.* 1978 and Mendelsohn *et al.* 1989). Nomenclature follows Maclean (1993).

The laying date of the first egg was estimated by backdating from the estimated age of the chick(s) in each nest. It was assumed that eggs were laid at 3-day intervals and that incubation and fledging took 32 days (but 34 days for Taita, W. Heck & RRH pers. obs.) and 42 days respectively.

RESULTS

1. Status and distribution

1.1. National

The Peregrine and Lanner occurred throughout the country, while the Taita was more restricted. Of 27 Peregrines recovered or trapped since 1965, only three were *F. p. calidus* (Hartley 1998). Only two Taitas were recovered over this period. All Taitas and most Peregrines were found breeding in well wooded country along escarpments, gorges and inselbergs (Table 1), mainly along river systems in the Zambezi Valley (16/20 Taita nests; 50/136 Peregrine nests) where Lanners were less common. Taitas and Peregrines were found breeding at altitudes of 350-2200 m a.s.l. Taitas and Peregrines were also found along the montane eastern highlands, including in dry deciduous woodland and in the mountain heathlands overlooking moist miombo woodlands. Lanners were found mainly (N = 155) in open and woodland habitats on the the granite shield, where they were more frequent than Peregrines and where Taitas were rarely seen.

Peregrines predominated in undisturbed woodland habitat with isolated vertical rock formations overlooking river systems or springs. The most extreme examples of this phenomenon were: 1) along a line of 30 m high sandstone cliffs in the Save valley where three pairs of Peregrines bred at a mean internest distance of 1,4 km, and 2) on a massive sandstone mesa in the Zambezi valley where two pairs occupied back-to-back cliffs only 0,35km apart. Where there are multiple vertical rock formations offering a wide choice of cliffs, such as in long convoluted gorge systems, Taitas may co-exist as a breeding population with Peregrines. This is also true of the mountainous Chimanimani area which has at least three pairs of Taitas and six pairs of Peregrines. By contrast, Taitas were rarely encountered in areas that had been significantly altered by humans.

Of 20 different Taita sites checked from 1990-97, 15 were occupied and five were abandoned. Of 99 different Peregrines sites checked from 1990-97, 73 were occupied, seven were abandoned and 19 were replaced by Lanners, eight of these on domed inselbergs in deforested Communal Lands (Table 1). Most Taita sites and 63.7% of Peregrine sites occurred either in protected areas or on relatively undisturbed habitats on General Land (Table 2). On Communal Lands, Lanners appear to have benefited from land clearing, while Taitas and Peregrines have not.

1.2. Domed inselberg and kopje terrain

Peregrines and Lanners competed mainly for large domed inselbergs in woodlands (Fig. 1, Table 1), and nine of these features were shared by both species: in each case the falcons occupied cliffs within 0,5 km (but out of sight) of each other. Of 23 Peregrine sites occupied by Lanners, 14 were on large domed inselbergs. Of five Lanner sites occupied by Peregrines, four were on large domed inselbergs, two in well wooded General Land, and two in deforested Communal Lands. In relatively undisturbed habitats in domed inselberg terrain (Mvurwi-Concession - zone 2; Fig. 1) six pairs of Peregrines were matched by Lanners 1:1.2. Mean internest distances for Peregrines and Lanners were 24.6 km (SD = 7.64 km) and 16.2 km (SD = 16.09 km) respectively. In the deforested areas of the Communal Lands nearby (Masembura-Dombashawa-Mrewa) five pairs Peregrines were outnumbered by Lanners 1:3.3 and mean internest distances were 23.9 km (SD = 13.56 km) and 6.1 km (SD 2.62 km) respectively. Most of the deforestation was on the flat, undulating pediments, while the scree slopes remained wooded. By contrast, in the kopje terrain of the Mangwende Communal Land south of Mrewa there were no Peregrines, while the mean inter-nest distance for six pairs of Lanners was 4.8 km (SD = 0.4 km).

Throughout the granite shield tors and kopjes (33%) were used by Lanners (Table 1) and only two large kopjes were used by Peregrines: one an alternate site, and the other, a nest on a vertical granite finger, was occupied only once. As a general rule, Peregrines did not breed on tors and kopjes. This trend is further supported by the pattern in the Matobo Hills (zone 3), which consists primarily of kopjes. Here 2-3 pairs of Peregrines (mean inter-nest distance = 10.2 km, SD = 3.3 km) also bred mainly on large domed inselbergs, leaving Lanners (n = 21; mean inter-nest distance = 6.9 km, SD 3.62 km) to dominate the tors, kopjes and remaining domed inselbergs, many of which are occupied by Black Eagles. Lanners (13%) frequently use old, and sometimes even new nests of Black Eagles *Aquila verreauxii*. Peregrines and also Taitas rarely use old stick nests for breeding (Table 3). Although Taitas were seldom encountered in granite terrain and have not yet been recorded breeding in such habitats in Zimbabwe, it is likely that they do so as a Taita was seen at very close range near Centenary in 1995 (J. Hough *in litt.*).

1.3. Zambezi Valley

In the Zambezi Valley, Peregrines (N = 50) outnumbered Lanners (N = 5), and also outnumbered Taitas 3:1. In the Sebungwe area of the Zambezi Valley, two Lanner sites occurred on mesas, shared with pairs of Peregrines 1.1 km and 2.2 km away respectively. The latter zone once hosted a pair of Taitas which nested on a low cliff which faced an occupied Peregrine site 3.9 km away. However, since a pair of Lanners took over the Peregrine site, the Taitas have left and have not been relocated, while the Peregrines have bred elsewhere on the same feature. In a more rugged area nearby, a deep gorge once hosted two pairs of Taitas and two pairs of Peregrines, but they were then joined by a pair of Lanners. The Taitas originally nested 1.9 km apart, but only 0.7 km and 1.1 km from where the Lanners nested. Since the arrival of the Lanners, only one pair of Taitas has been seen, but the nearest Peregrines, 1.7 km and 3 km away respectively, were still there. Twelve pairs of Peregrines and four pairs of Taitas have been found in this rugged gorge (Peregrines = 6; Taitas = 4) and escarpment (Peregrines = 6) terrain. Mean internest distance for Peregrines was 4.96 km (SD = 2.59 km). Over the past 30 years, elephants *Loxodonta africana* have caused extensive damage to some of the woodlands in this zone, which may have favoured the Lanner. In another area of the northern Zambezi Valley, three pairs of Taitas and three pairs of Peregrines were found on isolated mesas in dry deciduous woodland. The two closest Taita sites were 5.4 km apart, while the internest distance for Peregrines was 6.3 km (SD = 2.7 km).

The highest recorded density of falcons was in the Batoka Gorge system below Victoria Falls, where 13 pairs of Peregrines and six pairs of Taitas were found. The mean inter-nest distances for Taitas and Peregrines were 4.62 km (SD = 2.38 km) and 3.49 km (SD = 2.0 km) respectively, or one pair of falcons of either species every 3.84 km. This is probably an underestimate, as it is likely that there were 8-10 pairs of Taitas and 15-18 pairs of Peregrines along this section (Hartley 1993a). As for the Sebungwe area, the extensive system of convoluted cliffs has provided many opportunities for nesting and has probably led to the significant concentration of Taitas.

1.4. Human altered environments

Both Lanners and Peregrines have adjusted to human altered environments. Both species bred in quarries (Table 1) and on dam walls. In the quarries of the Shurugwi area, up to six pairs of Lanners and two pairs of Peregrines have bred at mean internest distances of 2.6 km (SD = 1.71 km) and 12.8 km respectively. Similar clusters of Lanners occurred in the quarries of Mashava (six pairs) and Zvishavane (seven pairs).

Up to two pairs of Peregrines and a pair of Lanners have bred in Harare city. A pair of Peregrines has attempted breeding in Bulawayo city, while both species can be frequently encountered in either centre. Five and 14 Peregrines have been recovered/trapped in and around Bulawayo and Harare cities respectively. Over seven days, in agricultural lands on the edge of Harare, one Peregrine and five Lanners were trapped and ringed. These falcons were all attracted to maize and soya bean lands which hosted large numbers of doves (*Streptopelia semitorquata*, *S. capicola* and *S. senegalensis*) and Redbilled Queleas *Quelea quelea*. These grain fields have acted as 'funnels' (Hartley 1998) for falcons - tens of thousands of Redbilled Queleas usually occurred in early to mid-winter - that draw in mainly juvenile and immature Lanners. As many as seven Lanners have been seen in the air at once, while others were perched nearby either on the ground or in eucalyptus trees (Hartley 1998).

2. Nest site characteristics and breeding

2.1. Cliff height and quality index

Taitas and Peregrines mainly occupied dominant vertical cliffs, while Lanners occupied these and smaller features, as well as trees (Table 1; Fig. 2). Taitas also bred on very small vertical cliffs (25% <25 m), while Peregrines bred frequently on vertical cliffs with a modest height (30-35 m), but only in the mid- to low altitude woodlands of the Zambezi and Save catchments where they were able to outcompete Lanners. Although Peregrine nests are usually inaccessible, one could walk on to three of these sites despite their being in areas frequented by baboons *Papio ursinus*. In domed inselberg terrain, where there was probably competition with the Lanner, and in the eastern highlands, only large features and mountain cliffs (nearly all >71 m) were used. The most consistently occupied Peregrine nests in domed inselberg terrain were those on cliffs >100 m. Furthermore most cliffs used by Taitas and Peregrines had a commanding height above the valley or plains below (Taitas: range = 30-984 m, mean = 170 m; Peregrines range = 40-1020 m; mean = 251 m) and there is no significant difference between on small (<70 m) and large cliffs (>71 m, χ^2 = 2.563, P = >0,1). Half (50.3%) the cliffs used by Lanners were <25 m, and the difference between cliff heights used by Lanners and Peregrines was significant (χ^2 = 18.55, P = <0,001).

Mean QIs for all sites tested in the three sample zones were Taitas 2.56 (n = 16); Peregrines 3.92 (n = 56) and Lanners 2.97 (n = 58). Mean cliff heights were 103.5 m (range 20-350 m), 84.4 m (range 24-300 m) and 45.1 m (6-180 m) respectively. In Batoka Gorge, the QI was 4 for Peregrines and 3.8 for Taitas, the limited difference probably relating most to the relative homogeneity of the system. In the Sebungwe area, the QI was 4.19 for Peregrines and 2.8 for Taitas. In the northern Zambezi Valley, the QI was 3 for Peregrines and 0.8 for Taitas, the latter clearly occupying marginal sites. Wherever Taitas occurred, they had to fit in where possible (Hartley *et al.* 1993) and four Taita sites were located near occupied Black Eagle nests, with none of the Peregrine sites so positioned. Both Taitas and Peregrines vigorously defended their nests when eagles passed by (Hartley *et al.* 1993).

2.2. Cavities, ledges and stick nests

Taitas nested in cavities and sheltered ledges, in common with Peregrines (Table 3) and the difference in frequency of use was not significant (χ^2 = 4.83, P = >0.02). Cavities provide shade and more easily allow brooding falcons and their young to escape detection from predators. Taitas are especially secretive around the nest (Hartley *et al.* 1993). Furthermore they are able to use much smaller cavities (mean = 0.76 m wide x 0.5 m high x 0.7 m deep m; N = 4) than Peregrines (mean = 2.14 m wide x 1.2 m high x 1.5 m deep; N = 21).

Most Lanner nests were on cliffs (87%; Table 1) where ledges were used mainly, many of these open, and some cavities (Table 3). The difference in frequency of use of these nest types was significant between Lanners and Peregrines (χ^2 = 16.57, P = <0.001). Lanners also used old stick nests in trees, pylons, and on cliffs (Table 3). Lanners (15.6%) and Peregrines (8.1%) also bred in quarries and on buildings. Quarry sites used by Peregrines were deep vertical sink holes, not the large open faces used by Lanners.

Figure 2. Cliff height selection for Taita, Peregrine and Lanner Falcons in Zimbabwe.

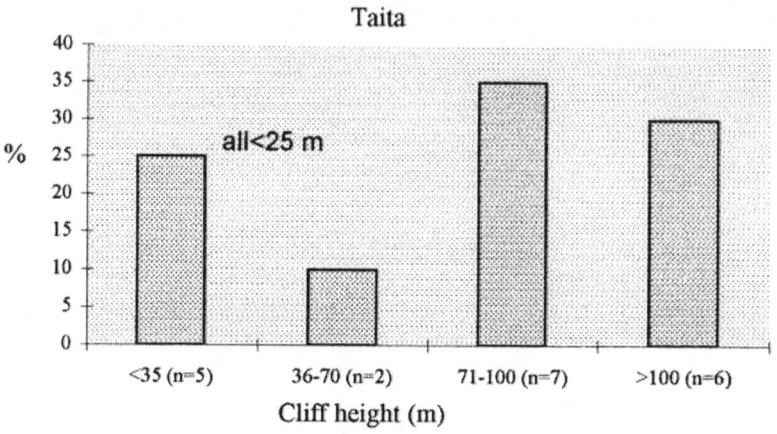
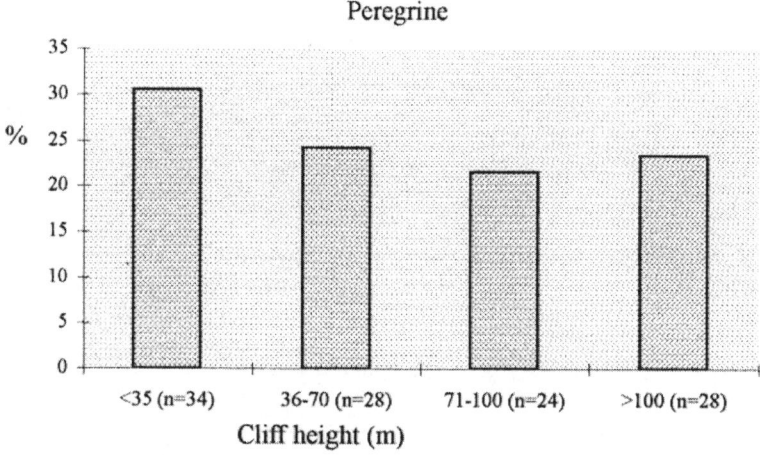
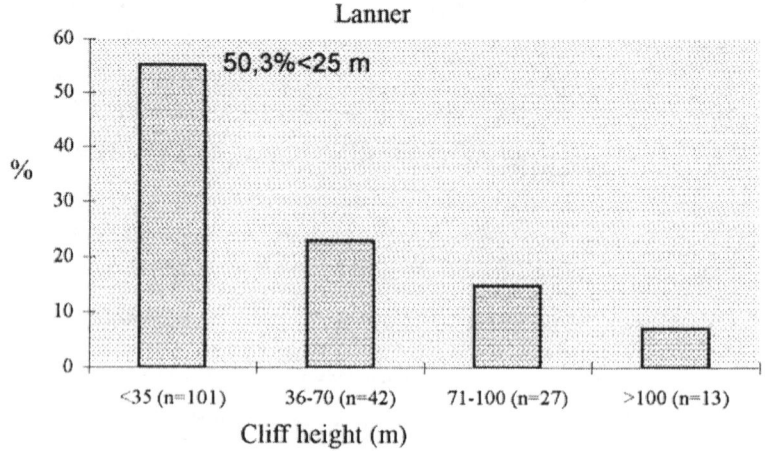

Table 3. Preferred nest sites for Taita, Peregrine and Lanner Falcons in Zimbabwe. Parentheses indicate % old stick nests in ledges, cavities and trees.

Species	%Nest sites		
	Ledge	Cavity	Tree
Taita (n = 26)[1]	26.9 (3.8)	73.1 (3.8)	
Peregrine (n = 104)	51 (2.9)	49 (2)	
Lanner (n = 183)	63.9 (16.4)	20.8 (5.5)	15.3 (96.4)[2]

[1] ledges and cavities were used alternately at three sites
[2] one nest in crotch of tree

By contrast Lanners often took over eagle nests (N = 51), especially Black Eagle (N = 23). Furthermore, there were ten records of Lanners harassing eagles and/or their chicks before they used the eagle nests. There were also suggestions that the Lanners either evicted or killed eagle chicks (N = 3) to achieve their objective. Bateleur *Terathopius ecaudatus* nests were used on eight occasions. Other eagle nests used included Martial *Polemaetus bellicosus*, African Hawk *Hieraaetus spilogaster* and Tawny Eagles *A. rapax*. Other stick nests used included Whitenecked Raven *Corvus albicollis* (N = 15) and Black Stork *Ciconia nigra* (N = 8). Aggressive encounters occurred with Whitenecked Raven (a clutch of Lanner eggs was found broken amongst raven and Lanner feathers) and Lanners also harassed Black Storks.

All three falcon species have been seen dust bathing, but only Taita and Peregrines have been seen water bathing (in small pools). In captivity, Taitas and Peregrines water bath regularly, but Lanners rarely do so. All Taita and Peregrine sites were close to permanent water (Hartley *et al.* 1993). Although a wide range of aspects was chosen by all species, southerly aspects appear to be favoured by Taitas and Peregrines while Lanners favoured east and west aspects (Table 4).

Table 4. % of aspects for nests of Taita, Peregrine and Lanner Falcons in Zimbabwe.

Facing	Species		
	Taita (n = 17)	Peregrine (n = 113)	Lanner (n = 177)
N	5.9	7.1	10.7
NNE	5.9	2.7	1.1
NE	5.9	7.1	11.9
ENE		1.7	
E	11.7	6.2	19.2
ESE		1.7	0.6
SE	5.9	8.0	7.3
SSE	11.7	7.1	0.6
S		13.3	13.0
SSW	11.7	11.5	0.6
SW	17.6	5.3	9.0
WSW		7.1	0.6
W	5.9	4.4	18.1
WNW	5.9	2.6	
NW	5.9	7.1	7.3
NNW	5.9	7.1	

2.3. Laying dates and clutch sizes

Although few observations were conducted outside of the breeding season, some Peregrines have been found at their breeding cliffs in April, at the same early stage as Lanners. However, peak laying periods for Lanners, Peregrines and Taitas were in this order and about a month apart (Table 5). Both Lanner and Peregrine young fledged by the end of September and early November respectively, near the onset of the rains. At this time there is a sharp influx of prey from three sources a) migratory birds, b) fledglings of resident passerines especially from mid-November onwards and mainly insectivores (Vernon 1978; Irwin 1981) and c) insects, including termite alates. Insect abundance is often coincident with the onset of the rains in late-October/early November, when juvenile Lanners are becoming independent.

Table 5. Laying dates for Taita, Peregrine and Lanner Falcons in Zimbabwe.

	Number per month (%)					
Species	May	June	July	Aug	Sept	Oct
Taita (n = 21)				9.5	85.7	4.8
Peregrine (n = 81)			3.7	88.9	7.4	
Lanner (n = 112)	0.9	5.4	58.0	33.9	0.9	

Clutch sizes recorded were: Taitas: 3 eggs x 2; 4 eggs x 2 (in captivity 2 eggs x 4; 3 eggs x 27; 4 eggs x 2; mean = 2,9; W. Heck *in litt.*, pers. obs.); Peregrines: 2 eggs x 11; 3 eggs x 24; 4 eggs x 11 (in captivity 1 egg x 4; 2 eggs x 14; 3 eggs x 70; 4 eggs x 34; mean = 3,1 eggs; pers. obs.), and Lanners: 2 eggs x 2; 3 eggs x 30; 4 eggs x 38; 5 eggs x 2. Although mean clutch size for Taitas is 3.5 eggs, the sample size is small and the much larger sample for captive birds may be more realistic at 2.9 eggs, similar to the Peregrine (mean = 3), while the versatile Lanner had predictably the largest (mean = 3.55).

Table 6. Selected morphometrics of Taita, Peregrine and Lanner Falcons in Zimbabwe.

	Species and sex, morphometric, S.D.(n)					
	Taita		Peregrine		Lanner	
Morphometric	male	female	male	female	male	female
Weight (g)	219.9	312.9	495.0	700.5	474.9	607.1
	8.8(7)	24.0(9)	35.7(8)	105.8(14)	51.7(20)	56.0(9)
Bill length (mm)	13.5	13.5	19.3	27.3	19.1	20.8
	0.6(5)	1.4(9)	1.7(8)	0.8(14)	1.0(20)	0.4(9)
Bill width (mm)	13.1	14.0	15.7	18.1	15.8	16.2
	0.3(5)	0.6(9)	0.5(8)	0.9(14)	0.0(1)	0.0(1)
Gape (mm)	21.2	23.3	20.5	30.4	29.0	30.6
	0.3(5)	1.2(7)	5.1(8)	1.32(14)	0.0(1)	0.0(1)
Wing (mm)	207.4	235.6	277.3	324.4	314.0	347.0
	4.4(7)	5.0(9)	5.5(8)	9.4(14)	12.3(20)	13.7(9)
Tail (mm)	94.0	106.5	129.8	153.3	164.8	183.6
	4.9(5)	6.1(9)	5.2(8)	10.1(14)	10.1(20)	9.4(9)
Tarsus (mm)	30.2	31.3	43.2	45.1	46.5	47.2
	1.0(5)	0.8(9)	1.9(8)	2.7(14)	3.0(20)	0.8(9)
Mid-toe (mm)	34.1	35.0	47.0	50.9	41.8	45.5
	1.7(5)	0.9(9)	3.4(8)	1.6(14)	2.5(20)	2.7(9)
Wing area (cm^2)	427.8	558.8	756.3	1044.8	1154.1	1286.3
	29.2(3)	59.1(6)	53.2(8)	63.8(9)	50.2(5)	108.2(3)
Wing loading (g/cm^2)	0.51	0.56	0.61	0.71	0.42	0.48
	0.03(3)	0.09(6)	0.04(8)	0.05(9)	0.04(5)	0.04(3)

3. Morphology, hunting and prey

Taitas and Peregrines are very similar in structure (Table 6), feather texture and hunting behaviour, being especially adapted to fast, attacking flights at flying birds. Both have high wing loadings, short tails and big feet. Tail/wing ratios for Taitas, Peregrines and Lanners were 45%, 47% and 52%

respectively. Taitas and Peregrines also have shorter and harder feathers, probably contributing to their superior speed.

For its size, the Taita has a particularly high wing loading, and its wing beat is fast. This suits its style of short vigorous hunts close to the nest site (Hartley *et al.* 1993). Its bill is strong with a width:length ratio of 1.0 (Peregrines = 0.81; Lanners = 0.8) so that prey can be immobilised quickly, while there is little size difference in the bill size of males and females. Furthermore the gape is large relative to its size (*contra* Peregrine and Lanner; Table 6), and this probably facilitates quick consumption of food.

The Taita and Peregrine are markedly different in mass, females of the former weighing just 44.7% of the latter to give a character ratio (larger/smaller, Hutchinson 1959) of 2.24. Ratios for selected linear measurements between these species are 2.02 (bill length) and 1.38 (wing length). Such ratios between Lanner and Taita are 1.94 (mass), 1.54 (bill length) and 1.47 (wing length). Those for Peregrine and Lanner are 1.15 (mass), 1.31 (bill length) and 0.93 (wing length). Taitas and Peregrines also have big feet (mid-toe:tarsus ratios of 1.13 and 1.11 respectively) which facilitate capturing prey on the wing, contrasting with the smaller feet of Lanners (mid-toe:tarsus ratio of 0.93) which also take prey on the ground, including mammals and reptiles.

Table 7. Taxonomic groups of avian prey recorded for Taita (T), Peregrine (P) and Lanner (L) Falcons in Zimbabwe.

Family/group	No.(%) T	No.(%) P	No.(%) L	% By weight T	% By weight P	% By weight L
Columbidae	2 (3.1)	175(39.0)	52(54.7)	8.4	48.7	73.7
Phasianidae		12(2.7)	4 (4.2)		12.9	9.3
Apopidae	4 (6.2)	21 (4.7)	6 (6.3)	6.7	1.2	0.4
Hirundinidae	10(15.6)	7 (1.6)		8.5	0.4	
Sturnidae	6 (9.4)	42 (9.4)	1 (1.1)	30.9	5.5	0.8
Coraciidae & Phoeniculidae		22(4.8)			3.0	
Bucerotidae		21 (4.7)	1 (1.1)		6.9	1.0
Ploceidae	14(21.9)	38 (8.5)	2 (2.1)	13.2	1.6	0.4
Estrildidae	8(12.5)	11 (2.4)	4 (4.2)	3.9	1.0	0.4
Other passerines	17(26.6)	28 (6.2)	6 (6.3)	15.6	2.8	1.5
Other near-passerines	1 (1.6)	41 (9.1)	4 (4.2)	10.8	7.8	3.1
Other non-passerines	1 (1.6)	31 (6.9)	2 (2.1)	2.0	8.2	0.8
Domestic poultry & budgerigars			13(13.7)			8.6
Total	**64 (100)**	**449 (100)**	**95 (100)**	**100**	**100**	**100**

Of 30 prey species taken by Taitas (mean prey mass = 40.9 g), 15 were also recorded for Peregrines (mean prey mass = 139.7 g; 79 species) and it is likely that the latter can capture all prey taken by the former. Key prey overlap by taxonomic grouping included Apopidae, Hirundinidae, Ploceidae, Estrildidae and Sturnidae (Table 7). Four species taken by Taitas were also taken by Lanners (mean prey mass = 185.7 g; 30 species), although this is likely to be an underestimate. Sixteen prey species taken by Peregrines were also taken by Lanners. Being roughly 45% the mass of the Peregrine and Lanner, the Taita specialises on smaller birds which tend to be taken close to the nest using either still-hunting from a high vantage, speculative-hunting or hunting from a soar (Hartley *et al.* 1993). Coupled with the relatively high wing loading and the presumed extra energy costs, the Taita is constrained to a smaller home range, as little as 1 km radius around the nest during the breeding season (Hartley *et al.* 1993) and 45.6% of prey (by weight) was taken from cliff habitats (Table 8). However, at four sites that were abandoned, Taitas were not seen hunting near the nest cliffs where there was a paucity of prey, but rather these pairs relied mainly on woodland habitats. Three of these woodlands had declined through elephant damage, making them a less than optimum circumstance for this species.

Table 8. Habitat preferences of avian prey for Taita (T), Peregrine (P) and Lanner (L) Falcons in Zimbabwe.

Habitat	No. of birds (%)			% by weight		
	T	P	L	T	P	L
Cliff	20(31.2)	51(11.4)	2(2.1)	45.6	9.9	2.9
Woodland	40(62.5)	379(84.4)	47(49.5)	49.5	83.0	35.6
Grassland	3(4.7)		3(3.1)	4.9		0.9
Aquatic		18(4.0)			6.5	
Human[a]		1(0.2)	43(45.3)		0.6	60.6
Other	1(1.6)					
Total	**64**	**449**	**95**	**100.0**	**100.0**	**100.0**

[a] feral and domestic pigeons *Columba livia*, poultry and budgerigars.

Taitas, Peregrines and Lanners all hunt significantly in woodland habitats for birds (Table 8), while the latter two also preyed significantly on columbids (Table 7). Ecological similarity between Taitas and Peregrines is supported by their similar hunting habits and vocalisations (Hartley *et al.* 1993). It is also supported by habitat preferences for prey, with woodland species dominating both by number and weight (Table 8), even more so than for the Lanner which has adapted well to human habitats (towns and cleared farmlands) and which took little prey from cliff habitats. However, the degree of use of these habitats was significantly different between Taitas and Peregrines ($\chi^2 = 19.8$, $P = <0.001$; cliff, woodland and other) and between Peregrines and Lanners ($\chi^2 = 216.01$, $P = <0.001$; cliff, woodland, human and other). Furthermore, Peregrines are much less dependent on cliff habitats than Taitas and have been seen hunting over woodland up to 30 km from their breeding sites. There was also a significant difference between prey selection (based on taxonomic grouping) between Taitas and Peregrines ($\chi^2 = 8.27$, $P = <0.001$) and between Peregrines and Lanners ($\chi^2 = 76.22$, $P = <0.001$).

4. Interspecific behaviour

There are three records of aggressive encounters between Peregrines and Lanners, all at cliffs shared for breeding. An encounter between two females in front of a Peregrine site degenerated into a tussle on a ledge, after which the Peregrine drove off the Lanner in a powerful aerial display. Peregrines were clearly dominant in the other interactions. Peregrines also pursued Taitas near the nest (Hartley *et al.* 1993). Away from the nest, Taitas and Peregrines have been seen soaring together without any interaction.

Peregrines killed small raptors such as Littlebanded Goshawk *Accipiter badius*, Blackshouldered Kite *Elanus caeruleus* and Barn Owl *Tyto alba* (pers. obs.). Under falconry conditions, it is not unusual for trained Peregrines to attack small raptors, and other species so killed included Gabar Goshawk *Micronisus gabar*, Ovambo Sparrowhawk *A. ovampensis*, Hobby *F. subbuteo*, Eastern Redfooted Falcon *F. amurensis*, Pearl-spotted Owl *Glaucidium perlatum* and Marsh Owl *Asio capensis*. Trained Lanners also attacked and killed Barn and Marsh Owls.

All three species attack eagles that venture within 200-300 m of their nests. Taitas also attack hornbills, presumably because the latter could rob eggs and chicks (Hartley *et al.* 1993). Lanners appear to be particularly aggressive to nesting eagles, in order to commandeer their nests which they appear to do on occasions. Taitas and Peregrines were much less drawn to old stick nests and there are no records of them commandeering such nests. Along extensive cliff systems, Peregrines appear to avoid breeding near active Black Eagle nests.

Barn Owls probably compete with these falcons for nest holes and several Barn Owls have been recorded as Peregrine prey (pers. obs.). However, the remains of an adult male and female Peregrine were found about 500 m away from their nest hole in the nest hole of a Mackinder's Eagle Owl *Bubo capensis mackinderi* (F. Couto pers. comm.). Barn Owls have been flushed from cavities frequented by Taitas and it is possible that these owls could kill these much smaller falcons at night.

DISCUSSION

Status and distribution

There is no information on internest distances for Taitas, apart from Moller (1989), Dowsett (1983) and this study, and it appears that there is some clustering of sites in areas with extensive cliff systems. A 70 km-long cliff system on Mt. Elgon, Uganda, hosted 19 pairs of Peregrines, 5 pairs of Lanners and 4 pairs of Taitas (Moller 1989), the ratio of Peregrines to Taitas being similar to the Zambezi Valley. Otherwise, distribution of Taitas is very patchy (see also Hunter et al. 1979). By contrast, Peregrines can occur at relatively high densities and those in Batoka Gorge, parts of the Sebungwe valley and in the Save system exceeded that recorded in the Waterberg Plateau of Namibia (mean = 5.1 km/nest ; Brown & Cooper 1987) and parts of the eastern escarpment of South Africa (mean = 7.5 km/nest; A.R. Jenkins & T. Wagner in litt.). Particularly dense clusters of Peregrines in Zimbabwe (two sites 0.35 km apart and three sites 1 km and 1.7 km apart) match that recorded by Thomsett (1988) in Kenya.

Where there was competition in domed inselberg terrain with Lanners, internest distance increased significantly for Peregrines in Zimbabwe, again in accord with estimates from Kenya by Brown & Amadon (1968) and Thomsett (1988), but double that recorded in the south-western Cape (Pepler et al. 1991).

On the granite shield and in three zones with high densities of quarries, Lanner Falcons occurred at comparable densities to those recorded in South Africa (8.6-9.5 km/nest; Tarboton & Allan 1984), Namibia (4 km/nest; Brown & Cooper 1987) and Zambia (3.5 km/nest; Osborne & Colebrook-Robjent 1984).

Comparative ecology

That Taitas and Peregrines shared similar ecological conditions, and that Taitas were sympatric with Peregrines, is also supported by observations in Uganda (Moller 1989), Kenya (Thomsett 1988), South Africa (Jenkins 1991), Zambia and Malawi (Hunter et al. 1979). In South Africa, a pair of Taitas bred in an old Peregrine site on an escarpment (Jenkins 1991), near a gorge which has had up to 4 pairs of Peregrines (Tarboton & Allan 1984). Taitas and Peregrines were also found in granitic domed inselberg terrain in the miombo woodlands along the Muchinga Escarpment of Zambia (J. Weaver pers. com.; J. Auburn in litt.) and Mwanza district of Malawi (Hunter et al. 1979; J. Auburn in litt.). Specimens of Taitas have been recovered near granite terrain at Mt. Darwin (Smithers 1956), Nyanga Downs (Snell 1963) and near Mutare (Black 1983).

Although Peregrines were tied to cliff habitats in woodlands in Zimbabwe (Hustler 1983; Thomson 1984; Hartley 1992), Zambia (Osborne & Colebrook-Robject 1980), the Transvaal (Tarboton & Allan 1984) and Namibia (Brown & Cooper 1987), a significant population (48-95 pairs; Pepler et al. 1991) occurred in the fynbos of the south-western Cape. Pairs have also occurred in desert landscapes, on cliffs overlooking a water hole (Braby et al. 1987) and along Fish River (Maclean 1960) in Namibia, and along the lower Orange River in South Africa (Jenkins & Van Zyl 1994). In each of these areas, Peregrines have probably retained a competitive edge over Lanners because most available prey can only be hunted consistently by aerial hunting (Thomson 1984; Brown et al. 1987; Jenkins 1995).

The ultimate factors for Peregrines were cliffs and suitable numbers of avian prey, while proximate factors were raised canopies (woodlands and fynbos, Jenkins 1994) and water (to attract avian prey), which could be exploited by their aerial hunting techniques. River valleys can also function as corridors for prey (Hartley 1992), suiting these specialised aerial attackers. Although Taitas, Peregrines and Lanners all used small cliffs in Zimbabwe, contrasting ecological requirements, especially between Peregrines and Lanners, limited competition for these sites. Taita and Peregrine sites were primarily in woodland habitats, positioned over significant river systems with permanent water nearby, either in the river and/or in a spring. This was always the case for small cliffs (Fig. 2), several overlooking permanent springs and/or close to river junctions. By contrast, Lanners occurred at lower densities in these areas and their numbers may also have been restricted by the limited variety and abundance of prey, and by competition for nest sites with the Peregrine. Furthermore most Lanner sites on small cliffs were in more open habitats and were not linked either to woodland or water. Peregrines and Lanners also bred on buildings and in quarries.

Cliff heights used by Peregrines and Lanners in Zimbabwe compared with patterns elsewhere (Tarboton & Allan 1984; Mendelsohn 1988), where Peregrines occupied significantly more dominant features that Lanners. However, in Zimbabwe (as on the Waterberg Plateau, Namibia) smaller cliffs were used more frequently by Peregrines than elsewhere in Africa, especially South Africa (Tarboton & Allan 1984; Mendelsohn 1988; Pepler et al. 1991). This is probably because where there is a good food supply less desirable nesting cliffs may be accepted (Hustler 1983; Brown & Cooper 1987), and walk-on sites have also been recorded in Kenya (Thomsett 1988). The hypothesis that Peregrines benefit on an energy/time-cost basis by selecting high cliffs has been discussed by Tarboton (1984), Thomsett (1988), Newton (1988) and Jenkins (1995). Taitas would benefit in the same way from using high cliffs, which were also the most consistently occupied features in Zimbabwe. Energy constraints, from high wing loading and relatively small size, may influence more efficient hunting near cliffs by increasing costs for efforts made further afield, especially during the breeding season when increased provisioning is necessary. It is also possible that competition with the Peregrine means that the smaller falcon is constrained to accept the least optimum cliffs. This is supported by studies in Namibia, where Rock Kestrels *F. tinnunculus* occupied the smallest cliffs, after Lanners and Peregrines (Brown & Cooper 1987).

In the Transvaal, Peregrines and Lanners avoided west, north-west and south-west aspects for their nests (Tarboton & Allan 1984). By contrast, in Zimbabwe 47% Taita, 30% Peregrine and 35% Lanner nests were on these aspects (Table 4). Tree nesting has also extended the range of Lanners into more open woodland areas without cliffs, where there is no overlap with nesting Peregrines. Lanners used stick nests more frequently than the other two species and patterns accord generally with the Transvaal (Tarboton & Allan 1984). While Gargett (1990) described both Lanners and Peregrines using old Black Eagle nests, there were no records of Lanners attempting to oust Black Eagles from their nests. Few pylon sites were used (contra 22.3% in the Transvaal; Tarboton & Allan 1984), probably owing to weaker observer effort in this context in Zimbabwe, and possibly also to the greater frequency of larger trees with old eagle nests. Owing to their morphology, Lanners are generalists with an encompassing range that breed in a great variety of sites. Consequently, they are usually the most numerous of the three species, especially today with increasing human-modified landscapes.

The rarity of the Taita is probably determined by its more specialised habitat requirements, and possibly also by its interspecific relationship with the Peregrine (Thomson 1984; Hustler 1989; Hartley et al. 1993), while the Lanner is generally an open country species whose range has probably increased with recent deforestation in Africa (Thomson 1984). Nothwithstanding their similarities, key differences in ecomorphology have probably allowed Taitas and Peregrines to co-exist. Character ratios of mass, bill and wing lengths all exceed 1.3, and so minimise overlap. Similar contrasts were seen in three North American accipiters (Storer 1966, in Wiens 1992). These body-size relationships also correspond with differences in both the range and mean of prey sizes taken by Taitas and Peregrines, suggesting that some minimal morphological separation is necessary to permit the co-existence of congeners (Wiens 1992). The large linear bill:length ratio for Taitas and Peregrines is consistent with the findings of Schoener (1965, in Wiens 1992) for food specialists using foods of relatively low abundance, which also translates into species whose body sizes are large relative to overall food abundance. Such differences in size in Taitas and Peregrines may have arisen to make foraging more effective (optimal foraging; Dodson et al. 1998), rather than competitive. Peregrines can take a much wider range of prey, from small to medium-sized birds, and can take them at much further distances from the nest, than is cost effective for Taitas. It is likely that Taitas are more agile and better adapted to taking cliff-dwelling species and small birds in close proximity to their nests.

Indeed the Taita is more specialised than the Peregrine, with its apparently greater dependance on cliff habitats for prey and its smaller home range during the breeding season. It is apparent that the Taita has a narrower niche than the Peregrine and Lanner and so is less successful numerically.

Less consistent nesting was recorded for the Taita on small cliffs, where it depended primarily on woodland habitats and was probably forced to hunt further afield. Outside the breeding season, in common with Peregrines and Lanners, Taitas may also move away from cliff habitats in search of food (Britton 1980; Muller 1989), although this has not yet been recorded in Zimbabwe.

Similarly large character ratios typify Taitas and Lanners, while for Peregrines and Lanners only the bill:length ratio exceeds 1.3. Instead, wing shape, wing beat, wing loading and foot size contrast more significantly for Peregrines and Lanners (Jenkins 1995), producing contrasts in hunting methods and so reducing compeion. Lanners are better adapted for soaring in thermals and so they possibly hunt for longer periods during the day, at different times to Taitas (Hartley *et al.* 1993), and to Peregrines which tend to be more crepuscular (Ratcliffe 1980; Hustler 1983; pers. obs.). By contrast, the more specialised Taita and Peregrine are better adapted than the Lanner at making fast attacking flights at flying birds, especially from cliffs overlooking wooded valleys. In these zones, the Peregrine may restrict the Taita, and can outcompete the Lanner whose ground-hunting opportunities are limited. High wing loadings of Taitas and Peregrines probably hinder their ability to hunt prey on the ground, and they probably expend proportionately more energy in flight than the more buoyant Lanners with their significantly lower wing loading.

Lanners can search more effectively (Jenkins 1995) and use a greater variety of hunting methods (Thomson 1984; Yosef 1991; Jenkins 1995), including successful attacks on ground prey such as rodents, locusts, reptiles and poultry, while smaller feet and longer tails assist this generalist. As they can soar more easily, Lanners are less dependent on high cliffs and consequently are better adapted than the other two species in relatively featureless terrain. Hence, Lanners can outcompete the other two species in more open habitats, especially when the number and range of avian prey is depressed (see also Jenkins 1994, 1995). Furthermore, Lanners have adapted to hunting poultry around kraals and settlements (Steyn 1982; Barbour 1971; Hartley *et al.* 1995), supporting the contention that they have been replacing Peregrines over areas in the high- and middleveld where there has been extensive clearance of land for agriculture (Thomson 1984).

Birds comprised 79% of Lanner prey in the Transvaal (Kemp 1993) and 78.5% in Israel (Yosef 1991), a similar proportion to this study. Domestic pigeons were taken commonly in towns (Mendelsohn 1988) and wild columbids comprised 43% of prey for pylon-nesting Lanners in the Transvaal (Kemp 1993). In Botswana, outside of the breeding season, Redbilled Quelea were also key prey for the migrant Lanners which occurred there, mainly from October-February (Herremans & Herremans-Tonnoeyr 1996) as opposed to March-June in Zimbabwe (Hartley 1998). It is possible that they move north during the winter and that this population breeds elsewhere in Africa (Herremans & Herremans-Tonnoeyr 1996). The significant difference in prey taken by Taitas, Peregrines and Lanners, both by habitat and by taxonomic grouping, is not surprising. It reduces competition and allows the presence of at least two species in many areas, while competition for breeding sites probably ultimately restricts the Taita.

In tropical woodlands, especially in the wet season, there can be significant avian abundance (Vernon 1985) that is enhanced by the inclusion of islands of non-miombo habitat, including: 1) the cliff habitat; 2) the contrasts above and below breeding cliffs, especially along escarpments (Zambezi valley = miombo above cliffs and mopane woodlands below); and, 3) habitats along rivers and their terraces with more nutrient-rich soils and water. In such areas, Lanners only bred where there were openings caused by elephant damage or, latterly, by human encroachment and clearance for cultivation.

Immigration of Lanners probably increases competition for nest sites (Moller 1989) and, being the smallest and most specialised, the Taita probably loses. This trend is supported in this study (Sebungwe), the Muchinga Escarpment of Zambia where Lanners now breed at 3/4 sites where Taitas used to nest, and in Malawi where Taitas seem to be absent from both areas where the species was known to occur in the late 1970's (J. Auburn *in litt.*). In 1983, J. Weaver (pers. comm.) commented on the start of land degradation along the Muchinga Escarpment, where a pair of Peregrines and Taitas nested successfully on the east faces of separate inselbergs 2 km apart. The same has probably occurred in the the degraded inselberg terrain around Mt. Darwin (Zimbabwe) where a Taita was collected (Smithers 1956).

By contrast, patchiness of certain habitats, as caused by cultivated lands for cereals in a mosaic of intact woodlands, may have assisted both Peregrines and Lanners which can hunt the local abundance of columbids and queleas. This may also have allowed Peregrines to occupy breeding sites for longer periods and be in position before, or at the same time, as Lanners. This appears to be the case on General Land in zone 2 where Peregrines have maintained fidelity to nest sites, while in neighbouring Communal Lands there were frequent nest changes with Lanners, probably owing to the circumstances, improved for the latter and declining for the former.

Deforestation has probably reduced avian prey diversity and abundance for Peregrines, which have to spend longer periods hunting and at further distances from the dominant cliff sites which still attract them. Consequently, Lanners can more easily occupy some of the Peregrine breeding sites. By contrast, in woodland habitats of the Zambezi and Save valley systems, Peregrines appear to be resident all year round. These circumstances indicate contrasting ecological conditions which favour one species and are detrimental to the other respectively, and are not examples of competition.

Since 62% of Peregrines (Table 2) were found breeding in intact and relatively intact habitats, on State and private land respectively, coupled with their competitive edge over Lanners in these habitats, the breeding season did not appear to be a critical factor determining their respective population status in Zimbabwe (*contra* Thomson 1984). Site requirements (Thomson 1984; Mendelsohn 1988) have probably been more decisive, influenced by morphology, hunting behaviour and prey of the falcons (Jenkins 1995).

Laying dates for Peregrines and Lanners accord with Irwin (1981) and Tarboton & Allan (1984). However, the June and July laying dates for Taitas in Irwin (1981) appear to be incorrectly assigned (Hartley *et al.* 1993). Peak laying dates for Taitas and Peregrines appear to coincide with peak abundance of prey when the young are flying (Olsen & Georges 1993), while the earlier peak laying date for Lanners appears to coincide with the period of lowest cover and highest availability of insects during the start of the rains in October-November. Lanners are better adapted than Taitas and Peregrines at hunting these on or just above the ground, and juveniles especially can take advantage of these circumstances soon after fledging.

Young passerines fledge from mid-November onwards, by which time most migrants have also arrived, and this should suit juvenile Taitas and Peregrines. Taitas laid, on average, 21 days later than Peregrines nesting in the same vicinity. This may be to avoid any contact when the Peregrines are displaying (Hartley *et al.* 1993), since they are aggressive around the nest at this time. Taitas then intensify their breeding activity when the Peregrines are incubating and at their most discreet and unobtrusive (Hartley *et al.* 1993).

Significant interspecific competition for nests was recorded in Kenya (Thomsett 1988) and the Transvaal (Tarboton & Allan 1984). The only other record of predation by an owl also involved a Mackinder's Eagle Owl (which took a juvenile Lanner; Steyn & Tredgold 1977). However, this was a significant problem in the USA where Great Horned Owls *Bubo virginianus* attack Peregrines (Cade 1982).

Pesticides do not appear to be a significant problem in Zimbabwe (Hartley 1993c; Hartley *et al.* 1995; Hartley *et al.* 1996), but habitat destruction has been rapid (Whitlow 1980a & b, 1988) and the policy of land acquisition threatens to accelerate this trend (Sill 1992). Habitat destruction could result in the displacement of Taitas by Lanners, and Lanners could also extend their range at the expense of Peregrines. Monitoring of Taitas, Peregrines and Lanners, with respect to habitat quality in the three land-use categories, should be continued.

ACKNOWLEDGEMENTS

Thanks are due to ZFC fieldworkers, especially A. Barnes, M. Bing, G. Bodington, N. Deacon, D. Dudman, A.S. Dunkley, C. Edy, W. Gau, R. Giesswein, N. Greaves, A. Groenewald, J. Grobler, D.M. Hartley, A. Huelin, P. Heymans, C. King, A. Langley, G. McAllister, R. Neilson, R. Querl, J.N. Smith, R.V. Teague, J. Tiffin, I. Thomson, W.R. Thomson, Falcon College and Peterhouse Falconry Clubs; and to W. Heinrich, M. Robertson, and J. Weaver (TPF). Assistance was also provided by P.J.

Mundy (DNPWLM), W.H. Burnham and R.T. Watson (TPF). My attendance at the 5th World Conference on Birds of Prey was made possible by the Raptor Conservation Fund of the ZFC, TPF and the Raptor Conservation Group of the Endangered Wildlife Trust. P.J. Mundy and A.R. Jenkins made helpful comments on the manuscript.

REFERENCES

BARBOUR, D.Y. 1971. Notes on the breeding of the Lanner. *Bokmakierie* 23: 2-5.
BLACK, R.A.R. 1983. Some observations on the Taita Falcon (*Falco fasciinucha*). *Naturalist* 27: 12-14.
BIGGS, H.C. BIGGS, R. & KEMP, A.C. 1978. Measurement of raptors. *Proc. Symp. Afr. Predatory Birds*, pp.: 77-82. Transvaal Museum, Pretoria.
BRABY, R., PATTERSON, J. & BROWN, C.J. 1987. Peregrine Falcon breeding in the Namib Desert, SWA/Namibia. *Gabar* 2: 43-44.
BRITTON, P.L. (ed.). 1980. *Birds of East Africa, their habitat, status and distribution*. East Africa Natural History Society, Nairobi.
BROWN, L.H., E.K. URBAN & K. NEWMAN. 1982. *The Birds of Africa*. Vol. 1. Academic Press, New York.
BROWN, L.H., & AMADON, D. 1968. *Eagles, hawks and falcons of the world*. Country Life Books, Feltham.
BROWN, C.J. & T.G. COOPER. 1987. The status of cliff-nesting raptors on the Waterberg, SWA/Namibia. *Madoqua* 15:243-249.
CADE, T.J. 1982. *The falcons of the world*. William Collins Sons and Co., London.
DODSON, S.I., ALLEN, T.FH., CARPENTER, S.R., IVES, A.R., JEANNE, R.L. KITCHELL, J.F., LANGSTON, N.E. & TURNER, M.G. 1998. *Ecology*. Oxford University Press, Oxford.
DOWSETT, R.J. 1983. Breeding and other observations on the Taita Falcon *Falco fasciinucha*. *Ibis* 125: 362-366.
GARGETT, V. 1990. *The Black Eagle, a study*. Acorn Books & Russel Friedman Books, Randburg.
HALLAMORE, C. 1972. Observations on the African Peregrine by a falconer. *Honeyguide* 69: 13-16.
HARRISON, J.A., ALLAN, D.G., UNDERHILL, L.G., HERREMANS, M., TREE, A.J., PARKER, V. & BROWN, C.J. (eds.). 1997. *The atlas of southern African birds*. Vol. 1: Non-passerines. Birdlife South Africa, Johannesburg.
HARTLEY, R. 1992. Status and productivity of Peregrines in low latitudes. *Gabar* 7:38-40.
HARTLEY, R. 1993a. The Batoka Gorges, haven for birds of prey. *Afr. Wildlife* 47:74-78.
HARTLEY, R.R. 1993b. Falconry as an instrument for conservation in Zimbabwe. *Proc. VIII Pan-Afr.Orn.Congr*, pp.:105-110.
HARTLEY, R.R. 1993c. DDT impact on raptors in the Zambezi Valley. Proc. Our endangered environment 1993. In: *Birds of a Feather*, pp.: 43-47. Endangered Wildlife Trust & Sunlink International, Harare.
HARTLEY, R.R., BODINGTON, G., DUNKLEY, A.S. & GROENEWALD, A. 1993. Notes on the breeding biology, hunting behavior, and ecology of the Taita Falcon in Zimbabwe. *J. Raptor Res*. 27: 133-142.
HARTLEY, R.R., NEWTON, I. & ROBERTSON, M. 1995. Organochlorine residues and eggshell thinning in the Peregrine Falcon *Falco peregrinus minor* in Zimbabwe. *Ostrich* 66: 69-73.
HARTLEY, R. 1995. What is known about the Taita Falcon? *Zimbabwe Wildl*. 80: 14-17.
HARTLEY, R. 1996. Falcons fly free in Zimbabwe. In: *Vision of wildlife, ecotourism, the environment in southern Africa*, pp.: 60-67. Endangered Wildlife Trust fourth annual, Johannesburg, South Africa.
HARTLEY, R.R., HUSTLER, K. & MUNDY, P.J. 1996. The impact of man on raptors in Zimbabwe. In Bird, D.M., Varland, D.E. & Negro, J.J. (eds.). *Raptors in human landscapes*, pp.: 337-353. Academic Press, London.
HARTLEY, R. 1998. Raptor migration and conservation in Zimbabwe. In: Leshem, Y., Lachman, E. & Berthold, P. Proc. international seminar: Migrating birds know no boundaries. *Torgos* 28: 135-150.
HERREMANS, M. & HERREMANS-TONNOEYR, D. 1996. Seasonal patterns of Lanner Falcon abundance in Botswana. *Ostrich* 67: 83-84.
HUNTER, N.D., DOUGLAS, M.G., STEAD, D.E., TAYLOR, V.A., ALDER, J.R. & CARTER, A.T. 1979. A breeding record and some observations of the Taita Falcon *Falco fasciinucha* in Malawi. *Ibis* 121: 93-95.
HUSTLER, K. 1983. Breeding biology of the Peregrine Falcon in Zimbabwe. *Ostrich* 54: 161-171.
HUSTLER, K. 1989. The ecological relationship of Taita and Peregrine Falcons. *Honeyguide* 35: 158-160.
HUTCHINSON, G.E. 1959. Homage to Santa Rosalia, or Why are there so many kinds of animals? *American Naturalist* 93: 145-159.
IRWIN, M.P.S. 1981. *The birds of Zimbabwe*. Quest Publishing, Salisbury.
JENKINS, A. 1991. Latitudinal prey productivity and potential density in the Peregrine Falcon. *Gabar* 6: 20-24.
JENKINS, A., HOFFMAN, I. & WAGNER, T. 1991. First breeding record of the Taita Falcon in South Africa. *Ostrich* 62: 78.

JENKINS, A. 1992a. A comparison of provisioning rates at Peregrine and Lanner Falcon nests in the Transvaal, South Africa. *Gabar* 7: 11-14.
JENKINS, A. 1992b. Interpretation and implications of falcon provisioning rates in South Africa - replies to Hustler, Oettle and Hartley. *Gabar* 7: 41-45.
JENKINS, A.R. 1994. The influence of habitat on the distribution and abundance of Peregrine and Lanner Falcons in South Africa. *Ostrich* 65: 281-290.
JENKINS, A.R. 1995. Morphometrics and flight performance of southern African Peregrine and Lanner Falcons. *Journal of Avian Biology* 26: 49-58.
JENKINS, A.R. & VAN ZYL, A.J. 1994. Flush-hunting and nest robbing by Peregrine Falcons. *J. Raptor Res.* : 118-119.
KEMP, A.C. 1993. Breeding biology of Lanner Falcons near Pretoria, South Africa. *Ostrich* 64: 26-31.
LISTER, L.A. 1993. Some examples of geological controls of Zimbabwean scenery. *Geographical Education Magazine* 16: 25-33.
MACLEAN, G.L. 1960. Records from southern South-West Africa. *Ostrich* 31: 49-63.
MACLEAN, G.L. 1993. *Roberts' Birds of southern Africa*. John Voelcker Bird Book Fund, Cape Town.
MANZI, A. & PERNA, P. 1994. Relationships between Peregrine and Lanner in the Marches (Central Italy). In: Meyburg, B-U. & Chancellor, R.D. (eds.). *Raptor Conservation Today*, pp.: 157-162. WWGBP/The Pica Press, Berlin.
MENDELSOHN, J.M. 1988. Double-brooded, city-breeding Lanner Falcons. *Gabar* 3: 50-53.
MENDELSOHN, J.M., KEMP, A.C., BIGGS, H.C., BIGGS, R. & BROWN, C.J. 1989. Wing areas, wing loadings and wing spans of 66 species of African raptors. *Ostrich* 60: 35-42.
MENDELSOHN, J.M. 1988. The status and biology of the Peregrine in the Afrotropical region. In: T.J. Cade, J.J. Enderson, C.G Thelander & White, C.M. (eds.). *Peregrine Falcon populations: their management and recovery*, pp.: 297-306. The Peregrine Fund, Boise.
MOLLER, P. 1989. The Taita Falcon *Falco fasciinucha*: results of a study at Mt. Elgon. In: Meyburg, B-U. & Chancellor, R.D. (eds.). *Raptors in the modern world*, pp. 315-319. Proc. III World Conference on Birds of Prey, Eilat.
NEWTON, I. 1988. Population regulation in Peregrines: an overview. In: T.J. Cade, J.J. Enderson, C.G Thelander & White, C.M. (eds.). *Peregrine Falcon populations: their management and recovery*, pp. 761-770. The Peregrine Fund, Boise.
OLSEN, J. & GEORGES, A. 1993. Do Peregrine Falcon fledglings reach independence during peak abundance of their main prey? *J. Raptor Res.* 23: 149-153.
OSBORNE, T.O. & COLEBROOK-ROBJENT, J.F.R. 1980. The status of the genus *Falco* in Zambia. *Proc. IV Pan-Afr. Orn. Congr.*: 301-306.
OSBORNE, T.O. & COLEBROOK-ROBJENT, J.F.R. 1984. Observations on the Lanner Falcon in Eastern Zambia. In: J.M. Mendelsohn & Sapsford, C.W. (eds), *Proc. 2nd Symp. Afr. Predatory Birds*, pp. 19-22. Natal Bird Club, Durban.
PEPLER, D. HENSBERGEN, H.J. & MARTIN, R. 1991. Breeding density and nest site characteristics of the Peregrine Falcon *Falco peregrinus minor* in the Southwestern Cape, South Africa. *Ostrich* 62: 23-28.
RATCLIFFE, D. 1980. *The Peregrine Falcon*. T. & A.D. Poyser, Calton
SILL, M. 1992. Cultivating a new system. *Geographical Magazine* 14: 45-50.
SIMMONS, R.E., AVERY, D.M, & AVERY G. 1991. Biases in diets determined from pellets and remains: correction factors for a mammal and bird eating raptor. *J. Raptor Res.* 25: 63-67.
SMITHERS, R.H.N. 1956. Interesting Rhodesian records. *Ibis* 98: 139.
SNELL, M.L. 1963. Birds at 2000 ft in an area of montane grassland on the eastern border of southern Rhodesia. *Ostrich* 34: 36-39.
STEYN, P. 1982. *Birds of prey of southern Africa*. David Philip, Cape Town.
STEYN, P. & TREDGOLD, D. 1977. Observations on the Cape Eagle Owl. *Bokmakierie* 29: 31-42.
TARBOTON, W.R. 1984. Behaviour of the African Peregrine during incubation. *Raptor Res.* 18: 131:-136.
TARBOTON, W.R. & ALLAN, D. 1984. The status and conservation of birds of prey in the Transvaal. *Transvaal Museum Monogr.* 3: 1-115.
THOMSETT, S. 1988. Distribution and status of the Peregrine in Kenya. In: T.J. Cade, J.J. Enderson, C.G Thelander & White, C.M. (eds.). *Peregrine Falcon populations: their management and recovery*, pp. 289-295. The Peregrine Fund, Boise.
THOMSON, W.R. 1984b. Comparative notes on the ecology of Peregrine, Lanner and Taita Falcons in Zimbabwe. In: J.M. Mendelsohn & Sapsford, C.W. (eds), *Proc. 2nd Symp. Afr. Predatory Birds*, 15-18. Natal Bird Club, Durban.

VERNON, C.J. 1978. Breeding seasons of birds in deciduous woodland at Zimbabwe, Rhodesia, from 1970 to 1974. *Ostrich* 49: 102-115.
VERNON, C.J. 1985. Bird populations in two woodlands near Lake Kyle, Zimbabwe. *Honeyguide* 31: 148-161.
WHITLOW, R. 1980a. Land use, population pressure and rock outcrops in the tribal areas of Zimbabwe Rhodesia. *Zimbabwe Rhodesia agric. J.* 77: 3-11.
WHITLOW, R. 1980b. *Deforestation in Zimbabwe, some problems and projects.* Natural Resources Board, Government Printer, Harare.
WHITLOW, R. 1988. *Land degradation in Zimbabwe.* Dept. of Natural Resources, Harare.
WIENS, J.A. 1992. *The ecology of bird communities. Vol. 1. Foundations and Patterns.* Cambridge University Press, Cambridge.
WILD, H. 1965. Vegetation map of Rhodesia. In: Collins, M.O. (ed.). *Rhodesia: its natural resources and economic development*, p.23. Collins, Salisbury.
YOSEF, R. 1991. Foraging habits, hunting and breeding success of Lanner Falcons (*Falco biarmicus*) in Israel. *J. Raptor Res.* 25: 77-81.
ZINYAMA, L. & WHITLOW, R. 1986. Changing patterns of population distribution in Zimbabwe. *GeoJournal* 13:365-384.

R.R. Hartley
Zimbabwe Falconers' Club
Falcon College
Esigodini
Zimbabwe

Breeding biology of Henst's Goshawk *Accipiter henstii* on Masoala Peninsula, northeastern Madagascar

Lily-Arison Rene de Roland

ABSTRACT

I studied the breeding biology of the endemic Henst's Goshawk *Accipiter henstii* during three breeding seasons, 1995-1997, on Masoala Peninsula, northeastern Madagascar. Breeding coincided with the end of the dry season. Five nesting attempts were documented. Nest building was from end of July to September, egg laying in September and October, incubation September to November, nestling period October through December, and post-nestling period December to February. The duration of nest construction was 53 days for a new nest and 24 days for renewal of an existing nest. The incubation period was 39 to 40 days (n = 3 nests). The nestling period was 44 days for 4 males (n = 2 nests), and the post-nestling age of dispersal was 86 to 89 days for a male and female. Overall reproductive success was 57% (number of young fledged per breeding attempt). A total of 1.14 young fledged per breeding attempt. Most reproductive losses resulted from nestling predation (n = 5 young) or bad weather (n = 1 young). I observed 145 prey items delivered and identified prey was composed of 86 birds and 26 mammals (25 being lemurs). There was a difference in prey composition between males and females, with 76 birds and 21 lemurs, respectively.

INTRODUCTION

Henst's Goshawk *Accipiter henstii* is the largest endemic accipiter on Madagascar. Little is known about this large raptor, especially its breeding biology and nesting requirements, and it is frequently confused with the recently rediscovered Madagascar Serpent-Eagle *Eutriorchis astur* (Sheldom & Duckworth 1990; Thorstrom *et al.* 1995). It is found in a wide range of forested habitat from the western dry forest to the eastern rain forest (Langrand 1990). This species is classified as near-threatened (Collar *et al.* 1994). The Peregrine Fund's Madagascar Project began working on raptors in 1991 on the Masoala Peninsula of northeastern Madagascar. One occupied Henst's Goshawk nest was found in 1991 (Borge 1993) near the Andranobe Field Station (AFS), a research site jointly run by The Peregrine Fund and Xerces Society/Wildlife Conservation Society. This pair nested in the same site in 1992. In 1993, through The Peregrine Fund nest reward programme (Watson *et al.* 1992), another occupied nest was discovered 11 km south of AFS. This pair abandoned their nest in 1994, possibly due to human disturbance within 100 m of the nest tree when forest slashing for creating lemur traps and swidden agriculture occurred during the nest building and courtship period.

In 1995, two more nests were discovered about 25 km inland from the east coast of Masoala Peninsula in undisturbed rainforest within Masoala National Park. The two nests were approximately 12 km apart on an east to west axis. The nests were discovered when, during the incubation period, the female would leave the nest for breaks and vocalize loudly. Unfortunately the nestlings at both nests were depredated by the Madagascar Harrier Hawk *Polyboroides radiatus* during the early nestling period (Rene de Roland *et al.* 1996). In 1996, the same two nest sites were occupied again, possibly by the same birds. On the west side of Masoala Peninsula, a fifth newly discovered pair began nest construction about 6.3 km south of AFS.

In 1997, the pair observed at the west side changed its nest tree and moved to another tree about 300 metres northwest of the 1996 nest. A new pair used the tree abandoned by the 1994 pair, in which I observed that the female was different from the 1994 female.

In this paper I present information from observations at these nests on the breeding biology of the Henst's Goshawk. Important findings were the predation of nestling goshawks by the Madagascar Harrier-hawk during the periods of absence of adults from the nest, possibly due to food stress, the distribution of goshawks in Masoala forests, and documentation of goshawks feeding on lemurs.

METHODS

This bird is very noisy during the reproductive period. At the end of the rainy season on Masoala Peninsula (July), I walked within the forest edge from the early morning until late afternoon to listen for the bird's call. When I localised the call, I approached and searched the surrounding trees. After nest localisation, I looked for a good place 40-50 m from the nest tree to make observations. Observations began in the early morning at 04:30, from the nest construction until the post-nestling period. During nest construction, I recorded all adult activities (role of the male and female in nest construction, distance from the nest tree at which the adult took nest material, duration and timing of mating, distance of adult roosts from nest tree, type and quantity of prey caught by adults). During the incubation period, I observed the role of the adults, the type and quantity of prey, and the duration of the incubation period. After hatching, I observed the growth of the chick, contributions of the adults to the chick, and duration of nestling period. Each chick was followed during the post-nestling period and the activity of the young noted (distance from the nest tree, date at which they catch their own prey, behaviour relative to the adults, and duration of the post-fledging period).

RESULTS

Nest building

During 1996, I observed three pairs during the nest building period for a total of 150 h 12 min. Two pairs found in 1995 reused the same nests in 1996. Nest building in 1966 at the third, newly-discovered site spanned 53 days, from the start to finish. At the other two reoccupied sites, it took 24 days to reconstruct the previous year's nests. The male was the most active in nest building, spending 4 h 9 min (68.4%), while the female spent only 1 h 55 min (31.6%). Most of the time, nest construction activity by the male was followed by mating (nest construction by male was observed 100 times and they copulated 93 times). The average duration of copulations for all three pairs was 12.87 sec ± 2.82 (range = 7-18, n = 93). The females sometimes visited the nest to arrange the nesting material (n = 30), and was very vocal during the nest construction period. Both sexes often stayed at the nest tree from around 17:00 (observed during 14 observations from 05:00 until 18:00), and I observed mating just before sunset on 3/14 afternoon observations. Nesting material was collected at 34 ± 16 m (n = 19) from the nest tree by the female and at 31 ± 15 m (n = 74) by the male.

Egg laying

In 1995 I was not able to determine when eggs were laid because the two nests were found during the incubation period. In 1996, first eggs were laid during the dry season on 12 September, 17

September and 8 October at the three nests. In 1995, one nest (Antafononana) had two eggs, but in 1996 and 1997 I did not disturb nesting to record the number of eggs in each nest.

Incubation

The female was the main incubator. The female allowed the male to incubate only while she fed away from the nest after prey had been delivered by the male. I observed that the female responded to the male's call as he flew towards the nest with prey. She would leave the nest upon his calling and arrival. During our observation periods, on average the female incubated for 79.5%, the male incubated for 6.1% and the nest was not attended for 14.4% of the time. The incubation period was 39 to 40 days (n = 3 nests). The female delivered fresh greenery to the nest from trees within the vicinity of the nest tree (50 times during 60 observations).

Nestling period

Only the female brooded the young and the male never brooded or fed the young. When the young were 14 days of age, the female began moving around but always remained in view of the nest. At the same time, the male captured and delivered prey items to the female. At 32 days after hatching, the females began searching for food, and when the female was not present the males delivered prey directly to the young in the nest. Nestlings were able to feed themselves after 29 days of age. At 38 days of age, the young began to move around among the nest branches, hopping and practising flying. Young males fledged at an average of 44 days of age (range 43 to 45, n = 4).

Fledgling period and dispersal

Young stayed within 100 m of the nest tree until 60 and 70 days of age, for males and females respectively. The adults fed the young at the nest until 65 days of age (n = 5 young, n = 3 nests). After 65 days of age, the young began intercepting the adults before they arrived at the nest and took prey directly from the adults. Two fledgling males from one nest competed vocally and aggressively for food upon the arrival of the adults. At 84 days of age, the young female unsuccessfully attacked an adult White-fronted Brown Lemur *Eulemur fulvus albifrons* (weight 2.3 Kg, Mittermeier et al. 1994) with a young on its back. At 93 days of age, I observed the radio-tagged young male catch a Madagascar Coucal *Centropus toulou* (length 45-50 cm, Langrand 1990). Natal dispersal of the radio-tagged young male was at 86 days of age and of the young female at 89 days of age.

Table 1. Prey items taken by Henst's Goshawks during the breeding seasons of 1995, 1996 and 1997.

Prey type	Male (%)	Female (%)	Total (%)
Birds	76 (52)	10 (7)	86 (59)
Mammals	4 (3)	22 (14)	26 (17)
Unidentified	23 (16)	10 (7)	33 (23)
Total	**103 (70)**	**42 (30)**	**145 (100)**

Food habits

I observed 145 prey delivered to females, nestlings and fledglings (Table 1). The identified prey was composed of 86 birds, 25 lemurs and one tenrec. Lemurs were mainly taken during the nestling (n = 10) and post-nestling period (n = 14). Three species of lemur were identified in the prey remains collected near and at the nests, mainly Eastern Woolly lemur *Avahi laniger*, a White-fronted Brown Lemur and an adult Small-Toothed Sportive Lemur *Lepilemur microdon*. Twice I observed an adult female delivering an adult White-fronted Brown Lemur missing its head and once an Eastern Woolly Lemur with complete body. The male delivered 76 birds and the female 21 lemurs during the incubation, nestling and post-nestling periods combined (Table 2).

Table 2. Prey deliveries by male and female Henst's Goshawks during the breeding seasons 1995, 1996 and 1997.

Breeding period	MALE			FEMALE		
	Birds	Mammals	Unidentified	Birds	Mammals	Unidentified
Incubation	23	1	9	0	0	0
Nestling	21	2	5	6	9	2
Post-nestling	32	1	9	4	13	8
Total	**76**	**4**	**23**	**10**	**22**	**10**

Reproductive success

In 1995, at one nest, two eggs in a 2-egg clutch hatched and in the second nest I observed one chick in the nest at hatch but was unsure of the clutch size (Table 3). In 1996, six young hatched in three nests and three young fledged. However, at the site that fledged two males, one fledgling disappeared during the first two weeks after fledging, at an age of 60 days, but it was not discovered whether it had an accident, suffered predation or dispersed. I observed the mortality of one young at 34 days of age, due to exposure to a long period of rain, and at another nest two young disappeared at 13 days, suggesting predation. In 1997, five young hatched in two nests and all fledged. A total of 14 young hatched and 8 fledged in the combined 1995, 1996 and 1997 breeding seasons, giving an average reproductive output of 1.14 young fledged per breeding attempt (Table 3).

Table 3: Reproductive success of Henst's Goshawks during the breeding seasons of 1995, 1996 and 1997.

Year	No breeding attempt	No of eggs	Average clutch size	No eggs hatched	No of young fledged	Fledglings/ breeding attempt	Nest success
1995	2	2a	2	3b	0 (0%)	0 (0\2)	0 (2)
1996	3	?	?	6	3 (50%)	1 (3\3)	66 (3)
1997	2	?	?	5	5 (100%)	2.5 (5\2)	100 (2)
Total	**7**	**?**	**?**	**14**	**8 (57%)**	**1.14 (8\7)**	**57 (7)**

a: Number of eggs documented in one nest.
b: Number of eggs hatched in two nests.

DISCUSSION

Nest building began at the end of the rainy season (last week of July) and natal dispersal occurred during the start of the rainy season (last week of January). Nest building took from 24 days (rebuilding last year's nest) to 53 days (building a completely new nest), depending on the status of the last year's nest. The breeding period from nest building to fledgling dispersal was approximately 5 months. Large raptor species have long breeding seasons, especially tropical birds, where incubation, nestling development and dependency periods are more prolonged than in temperate regions (Newton 1979). In Henst's Goshawk, the 5 months breeding period appears normal for this size of bird and the tropical environment does not appear to have prolonged the breeding cycle of this species. The breeding cycle of the congeneric, similar-sized Northern Goshawk *A. gentilis* (incubation period 35-38 days, nestling period 34-41 days, independence at 70-90 days, del Hoyo *et al*. 1994), is similar to Henst's Goshawk (incubation 39-40 days, nestling period 43-46 days, independence 86-89 days).

The nest was 70% built by the male and 30% by the female. This is comparable to the Northern Goshawk and other species of accipiter for the construction of the nest (Brown & Amadon 1989; Newton 1986). Henst's Goshawks built their nests in the early morning, similar to the Frances's

Sparrowhawk *A. francesii* (Rene de Roland, in press) and Northern Goshawk (Brown & Amadon 1989). The male and female usually departed from the nest site in the early afternoon and returned by late afternoon, when, on several occasions, I observed copulations prior to sunset. Females did nearly all the incubation except during times when they fed away from the nest and the males were allowed to incubate. During the middle of day, I observed that the female appeared to be restless, hot and stood many times at the edge of the nest with open bill. When the female left the nest during incubation breaks, she nearly always returned with sprigs of greenery collected from neighbouring trees. The greenery was always placed around the edge of the nest. I also observed this behaviour less frequently in the smaller Frances's Sparrowhawk. There are many suggestions for placing greenery around the nest edge: 1) a form of nest-sanitation for covering rotten meat and excreta, 2) boredom by a waiting female, 3) nest exchanges between incubating mates, 4) filling in the nest and consolidating its structure, and 5) advertisement announcing an occupied territory (Newton 1979). I suspect that the latter suggestion seems most plausible in the case of the Henst's Goshawk.

During the incubation period, the male was the sole provider of food and he continued this during the first few weeks of the nestling period. As the nestlings grew and were able to thermoregulate, the female began to hunt away from the nest site (32 days after hatching) and left the chicks for many hours. At two nests in 1995 (Rene de Roland *et al.* 1996), the female appeared to be food stressed and during the first few days and weeks of the nestling period was gone for 2-4 hours every day. Apparently, she was searching for food for her two nestlings and herself. On November 1995, the female at this site was observed pursuing on foot a Lesser Asian Civet *Viverricula indica* 50 m northeast of the nest tree (R. Thorstrom, pers. com.). These extended absences by the females put the nestlings in jeopardy from predation by other animals. At both nests in 1995, Madagascar Harrier-hawks were observed depredating the 1-2 week-old nestlings (Rene de Roland *et al.* 1996).

For many raptors, it has been reported that the parents decrease prey deliveries to the young to encourage them to disperse from their parents' territory (Davies 1976; Moreno 1984; Simmons 1984; Edwards 1985). I did not find this behaviour as the reason for natal dispersal in the Henst's Goshawk, because the adults always delivered prey to the young until their departure. At one nest site in 1996 (Vakoanina), the male continued to deliver prey to the young female which did not stay near her nest site. The adult male brought a subadult *Avahi laniger* and put it above an epiphyte near the nest, even after he had called for a long time and received no response from the young. The following day I climbed to the epiphyte and collected the cached lemur. Young males and females called frequently around the nest site before departure, which is similar to *A. nisus* (Frumkin 1993). Young Henst's Goshawks became independent once they were able to capture prey.

Birds were the most important prey caught by the adult male. Of six bird species identified, Blue Coua *Coua caerulea* was most frequently taken. This species is found throughout the canopy and even down to the forest floor. The Blue Coua moves from tree to tree searching for insects and lizards. The Henst's Goshawk is a sit-and-wait predator (perch hunter) in the branches of trees and I suspect that goshawks attack Blue Couas by surprise with a burst of speed. The Blue Coua is probably the most abundant large forest bird in the forests of Masoala Peninsula and hence the most common prey of Henst's Goshawks. On 3 January 1997, one adult male goshawk was observed chasing a Madagascar Wood Rail *Canirallus kioloides* on the forest floor and through dense brush, but was unsuccessful in capturing its intended prey.

White-fronted Brown Lemur and Eastern Woolly Lemur appeared to be important prey of Henst's Goshawks. Brown Lemurs are very common throughout Masoala Peninsula (Mittermeier *et al.* 1994; pers. obs.). The Eastern Woolly Lemur is a nocturnal species and it is intriguing to speculate how Henst's Goshawks might capture this species. I observed one resting on the main trunk of a tree at 09:00 in the morning. I suspect that goshawks might capture this species as it moves from its day resting place to another place if weather or another animal flushes it. Alternatively, they may be captured during the crepuscular period when they are still moving to their resting places or goshawks may actively search for resting Eastern Woolly Lemurs and capture them on their resting sites.

In spite of the abundance of prey caught by the adults, the reproductive success was very low during the three breeding seasons of 1995, 1996 and 1997. I observed 14 young hatched and 8 fledged successfully during the three-year period, with a productivity rate of 57% young fledged per breeding attempt and 1.14 young fledged per successful attempt. This 1.14 young per successful attempt is similar to reports for the Northern Goshawk, ranging from 1.4-3.1 chicks fledged per successful pair (del Hoyo et al. 1994). The main causes for reproductive failures were predation by another raptor (n = 3) and severe weather (n = 2).

ACKNOWLEDGEMENTS

I would like to thank the Peregrine Fund's technicians on Masoala for their help in the field. Special thanks to Rick Watson and Russell Thorstrom for their help and comments on this paper. Special thanks also to Robin Chancellor for his support for to me to attend this conference. I would like to thank The Peregrine Fund's Madagascar Project, the Direction des Eaux et Forets, ANGAP. The Peregrine Fund cooperates with CARE and the Masoala project. This work was supported by grants from the Liz Claiborne and Art Ortenberg Foundation, Environment Now, John D. and Catherine T. MacArthur Foundation, and USAID.

REFERENCES

BORGE, L. 1993. First studies on Madagascar Harrier-hawk and Henst's Goshawk. In: Watson, R.T. (ed.). *Madagascar Project, Progress Report I, 1991-1992*, pp. 73-74. The Peregrine Fund, Boise.
BROWN, L. & D. AMADON 1989. *Eagles, Hawks and Falcons of the World*. Wellfleet Press, Syracuse.
C0LLAR, N.J., M.J. CROSBY & A.J. STATTERSFIELD 1994. Birds To Watch 2: The World List of Threatened Birds. *Birdlife Conservation Series*: 4.
DAVIES, H.B. 1976. Parental care and the transition to independent feeding in the young spotted flycatcher (*Muscicapa striata*). *Behaviour* 59: 280-295.
DEL HOYO, J., A. ELLIOT & J. SARGATAL 1994. *Handbook of the birds of the World*. Volume 2. New World Vultures to Guineafowl. Lynx Edicions, Barcelona.
EDWARDS, P.J. 1985. Brood division and transition to independence in blackbirds *Turdus merula*. *Ibis* 127: 42-59.
FRUMKIN, R. 1993. Intraspecific brood-parasitism and dispersal in fledgling Sparrowhawks *Accipiter nisus*. *Ibis* 136: 426-433.
LANGRAND, O. 1990. *Guide to the Birds of Madagascar*. Yale Univ. Press, New Haven & London.
MITTERMEIER, R.A., I. TATTERSAL, W.R. KONSTANT, D.M. MEYERS & R.B. MAST 1994. *Lemurs of Madagascar*. Conservation International, Washington D.C.
MORENO, J. 1984. Parental care of fledged young, division of labor and the development of foraging techniques in the northern wheatear *Oenanthe oenanthe* L. *Auk* 101: 741-752.
NEWTON, I. 1979. *Population Ecology of Raptors*. Buteo Books, Vermillion.
NEWTON, I. 1986. *The Sparrowhawk*. T. & A.D. Poyser, Calton.
RENE DE ROLAND, L.A. in press. Breeding biology of Frances's Sparrowhawk *Accipiter francesii* in a lowland rainforest of northeastern, Madagascar. *Proc. 9th Pan-Afr. Ornith. Congr.* pp. 90-99.
RENE DE ROLAND, L.A., R. THORSTROM & R.T. WATSON 1996. Nesting records and predation of Henst's Goshawk on Masoala Peninsula, Madagascar. *Ostrich* 3: 168-170.
SHELDON, B.C. & J.W. DUCKWORTH 1990. Rediscovery of the Madagascar Serpent-Eagle *Eutriorchis astur*. *Bull. Br. Orn. Cl.* 110: 126-130.
SIMMONS, R. 1984. Pre-independence behaviour, morphometrics and trapping of fledgling Red-breasted Sparrowhawks. *Ostrich* 55: 158-162.
THORSTROM, R., R.T. WATSON, B. DAMARY, F. TOTO, M. BABA & V. BABA 1995. Repeated sightings and first capture of a live Madagascar Serpent-eagle *Eutriorchis astur*. *Bull. Br.Orn.Club.* 115: 40-45.
WATSON, R.T. 1992. Rapport d'avancement 1991-1992: Projet Madagascar. The Peregrine Fund, Boise.

Lily-Arison Rene de Roland
The Peregrine Fund's Madagascar Project
B.P. 4113 Antananarivo 101
Madagascar

Chancellor, R. D. & B.-U. Meyburg eds. 2000
Raptors at Risk
WWGBP / Hancock House

Behaviour and Range Movements during the post-fledging dependence period of the Madagascar Fish-eagle *Haliaeetus vociferoides*

Simon A. Rafanomezantsoa

ABSTRACT

The Madagascar Fish-Eagle *Haliaeetus vociferoides* exhibits fratricide and probably polyandry. I monitored the dispersal of six fledglings from 1995 to May 1997 in central- western Madagascar, four of which resulted from 'sibling rescue'. Observations focused on behaviour and movements. The chicks fledged at 85.8±10.7 days of age (n = 6), during September to October. They spent 88% of their time perched on trees near water, but also did short flights and spent <25% of their daily time on the ground on the lake shore. The first dispersals from the natal territory occurred on January and April, both by females when they began to hunt for themselves. Three males and one female still remained in parental territories in May 1997, but occasionally made a distant soaring flights to places without territorial pairs (n = 4). The post-fledging dependence period varied from 5 to 8 months, until the beginning of the next breeding season in May. At 20 months of age, one young, still in juvenile plumage, remained in the parental territory. I suspect that if juveniles remain in their parents' territory until reaching maturity, they become 'extra adults', or occupying the territory of their parents when they die.

INTRODUCTION

The Madagascar Fish-eagle *Haliaeetus vociferoides* is endemic to Madagascar and is one of the rarest birds of prey in the world (Meyburg 1986). Unfortunately, many wetlands on the island have been transformed into rice fields and the highest human population densities are concentrated around them since rice is the dietary staple (Langrand & Goodman 1995). The eagle exhibits fratricide and 42% of pairs have one or two helpers, which may reduce the annual potential productivity. Consequently, the rate of population size increase is low while the home range and territories are large. Many studies have been done concerning the biology and ecology of the species, but little information is available during the post-fledging period. Previous observations over several years in western Madagascar had shown that the majority of fledglings had left their parents after several months of age. Only a male, hatched in 1993, remained on the parental territory when I started this study in September 1995. This study aims to describe the main behaviours of fish-eagles during the post-fledging dependence period and the factors that may influence range movements and natal dispersal.

STUDY AREA AND METHODS

This study was conducted in west-central Madagascar, a flat lowland area liable to flooding which contains many wetlands such as lakes, mangroves, swamps and rivers. About 10% of the total population of Madagascar Fish-eagles are concentrated around a complex of three lakes in the Antsalova region (Befotaka 3.86 km^2, Soamalipo 4.86 km^2 and Ankerika 3.09km^2). These lakes determine the southern limit to the primary deciduous forest of Tsimembo (between 18° 59'- 19°03'S and 44° 24'- 44° 29'E), which covers 32,800 ha at a mean altitude of 10 m a.s.l. The lakes lie about 10 km inland from Mozambique Channel.

Observations around the three lakes were made from September 1995 - May 1997, particularly in territories of pairs with young. The technique of 'sibling rescue', first suggested by Meyburg (1974) as a method to double annual production in rare species, was successfully applied to Madagascar Fish-eagles (Watson *et al.* 1996). Three fledgling males and three fledgling females were observed during the field study, three of which hatched in 1995 and three in 1996. All young were from pairs on three lakes. [In 1995, three pairs out of 10 monitored produced chicks, namely Ankerika 3 (female and 'sibling rescue' male), Ankerika 5 and Soamalipo 2 (female). In 1996, four pairs out of 10 monitored produced chicks, namely Befotaka 3, Soamalipo 2 and Soamalipo 3 with two chicks, and Ankerika 3 with one chick. Four individuals were killed at nests and so only three chicks fledged for 1996, including two from 'sibling rescues' (42% overall mortality before fledging).

Five young were radio-tagged and I tracked their movements using a TRX-1000 S receiver (Wildlife Materials Inc.). Each eagle was banded for quick identification, by an aluminium numeric band on one leg and by one or two coloured plastic bands on the other. Sexes were distinguished by the relatively smaller size and higher-pitched vocalizations of the males. Adults were distinguished from juveniles by their vocalizations and by the completely white plumage on the tails and faces (Langrand & Meyburg 1989).

I focused my attention on the behaviours and movements of juveniles, but also observed any adults that I could see. I recorded the activities of each individual at a 10-minute sampling interval. Other important events during this period were also noted and described briefly. To quickly locate accurate coordinates during observations, I used a grid-scale drawn over a 1:40,000 scale map of the three lakes. When the eagles moved away from the vicinity of lakes, I used a global positioning system receiver (Trimble Ensign) to establish my location. To measure home range area and utilization, and the distance covered by fledglings, I used the computer programme Ranges IV (Kenward 1990).

RESULTS AND DISCUSSION

Behavioural development

A total of 1,225.27 hrs of observations were made. At about 65-75 days of age, young spent much of the time exercising their wings and flapping full strength by standing on branches about 2-3 metres from the nest (but rarely in the nest). This behaviour profited especially from the windy periods during the middle of the morning and the afternoon. The first flight occurred at 85.8_10.7 days (n = 6), during September to October which is in the dry season. Males appeared to leave the nest earlier (mean 78.66 days) than females (mean 91.33 days). I did not always directly observe the first flight from the nest, as sometimes it was difficult to determine exactly the age of fledging. This was because initially the young spent much time on branches near the nest, but even during the first two weeks of flight they returned frequently to the nest for food brought there by the adult. Aerial food transfer was not seen at this stage.

Direct sibling aggression appeared to be common the Madagascar Fish-eagles. Competition was ferocious once chicks learnt to grapple for larger items and any food not swallowed quickly is liable to be stolen by a sibling. However, juveniles were no longer aggressive when they approached the age of fledging, so that attacks from elder towards younger siblings became rare and even disappeared.

The Madagascar Fish-eagles did little flying, mainly only perch-to-perch flights. Their size and weight may have an influence on the performance, such that they spent much of the day (88%) immobile, waiting for their parents to bring food. They perched in full view on large or dead trees, usually near the nest but also over water, moving closer to the water as nest trees varied in distance of 24.5 - 640 m from the lakes. The eagles moved only during the heat of the day to leafy perches from which continued surveillance.

Soaring flight appeared at about 9-10 weeks after fledging, and in general at hot temperatures with clear skies (> 23_C, cloud < 60%). Sometimes the young eagles soared to such a high altitude that I could not detect them without the aid of binoculars. Some fledglings remained in the parental territories at this age but visited other sites using soaring flight, influenced by, among other factors, thermals. In these the raptors spiral upwards on the rising warmer air then glide down to enter another bubble of rising air, on which they may be carried effortlessly along for tens of kilometres.

Stooping was used for catching prey from an observation point. Prey capture was first observed at about 6-10 weeks after fledging, when I saw the young eagles catch fish or sometimes small crabs. At first, they tried to catch dead fish left by fishermen and then, as they became experienced, they were successful at live fish. In general, success varied between 20-35%, according to the age and experience. Training on hunting technique may not depend directly on the parents, as during this stage the young went their separate ways, not necessarily in the presence of an adult.

Calling by juveniles was an important behaviour that helped to maintain contact between parents and young. Most calling occurred when they begged for food, and calling differentiated juveniles from adults and males from females (Figs. 1-3). In general, a call was formed by 4 notes "*ko ko koy koy*", which was accentuated to 5 notes when demanding food and lasted for about 2 secs. The frequency can reach 8-10 kHz for juveniles but only 5 kHz for adults (Figs 1,2). As described by Langrand & Meyburg (1989), in the case of a duet, the calls of an adult pair are generally alternated, with the male's calls higher-pitched than the female's. The posture adopted during calling is not typical for juveniles, with and head and beak held slightly more horizontal than for adults. Calling in flight was rare, most frequently only during soaring.

Figure 1. Sonogram of a juvenile female's call.

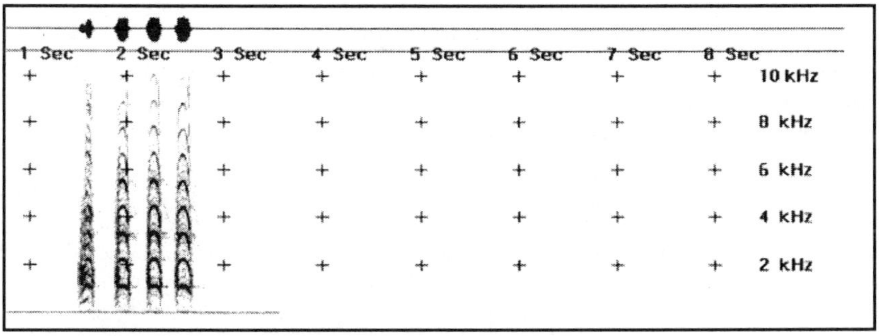

Figure 2. Sonogram of an adult's call (sex unknown).

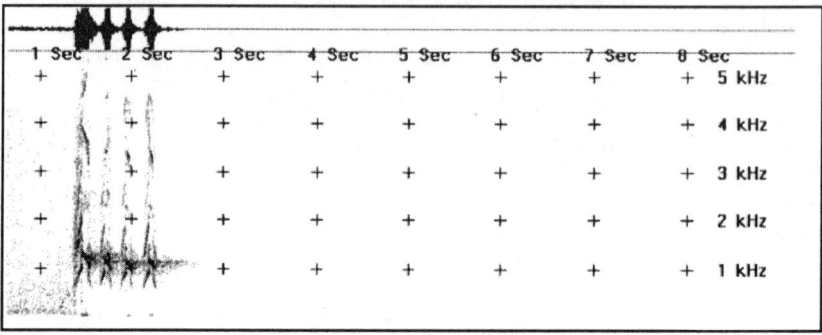

Figure 3. Sonogram of 2 adult's calls in duet.

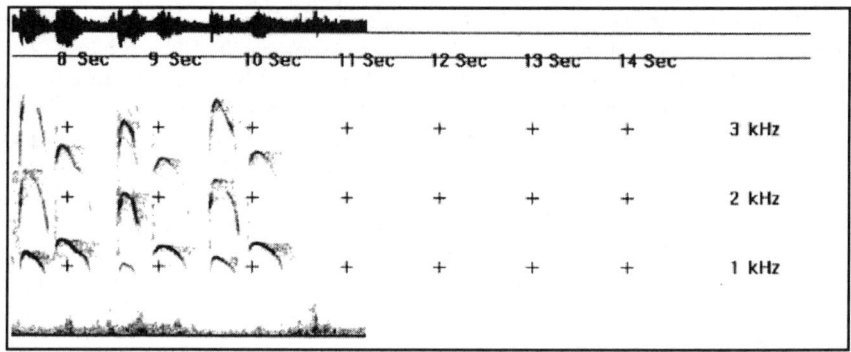

Range movements and area utilization

Young spent much time perched on a large tree near water and only rarely moved up to 80 metres from lake into the forest. Their range surrounded the nest until they were experienced in flight, after which they tended to move close to water. They did not pass beyond their parents' territories at this age, nor did they defend them. They landed on the ground only on shore, never in the middle of the forest, and spent <25% of their daily time on the ground.

The area covered varied from one young to another (Fig. 4) but, in general, it seemed to depend on the total area available in the parental territory. The young started to go beyond the three lakes after several months of age, making use of thermals. For example, I located a young male of the Befotaka 3 pair at about 19 weeks after fledging. He moved for about 3 km alongside the river that flooded the lakes during the wet season and then, after several days of getting no food, he returned to his natal site. I also located a young male of the Ankerika 3 pair at 45 weeks of age, along a river and about 18 km from his natal territory at Lake Ankerika. Effectively, some young made round trips between their natal sites and other wetlands surrounding the complex of the three lakes. Several juveniles (n = 4) were noted in other places where there was a dominance of water (rivers, lakes, mangrove swamps or marshes), so I assume that sites visited by all young were wetland areas.

The post-fledging dependence period

Parents continued to feed each individual juvenile for a variable period after leaving the nest. Young moved soon moved away from the area surrounding the nest, since they were not able to catch fish. Later, I rarely saw parents feeding young over 5-6 months of age. Some juveniles remained in the parental territory after the behaviours of the next breeding season appeared in early May. On average, there were 8-9 months between the hatching date (July) and the next breeding season (early May). This time corresponded to that in which I observed parents feeding young. The first recorded dispersal occurred in January 1996, by the young female of the Soamalipo 2 pair, 13 weeks after its first flight. A second female of the Ankerika 3 pair only left her territory after 8 April 1996, 25 weeks after fledging. I observed that these juveniles were still being fed by their parents several days before they dispersed, but that they had started to catch fish. In May 1997, the 20-month old male of Ankerika 3 (hatched in 1995), and a male and a female of Soamalipo 3 (hatched in 1996) still remained in their respective territories and were still in their juvenile plumage.

Figure 4. Area covered by young.

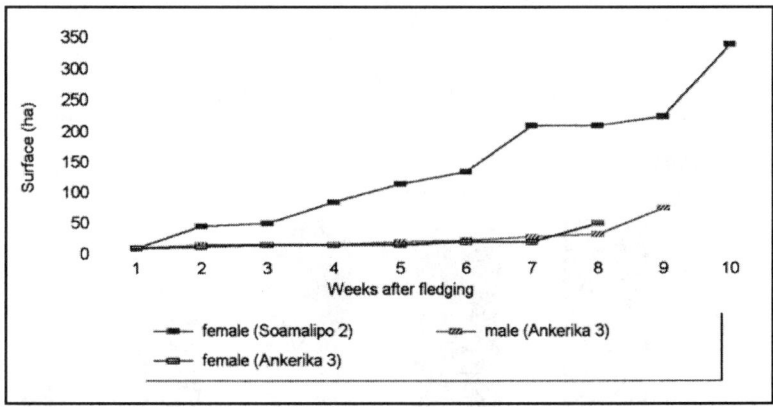

When the breeding season begins in late April, members of every pair are aggressive towards juveniles, especially of the opposite sex. The post-fledging period may vary individually and sometimes it was confusing to delimit this period exactly because of the mobility of the juveniles. Two main factors may influence young to leave their parents: non-feeding by parents and aggressive dominance by certain adults. However, prolonged care by parents characterizes most large raptors, and delayed maturity may also occur in this species. I suspect that if juveniles remain in their parents' territory until reaching maturity, they then become 'extra adults' (helpers), or occupy the territory of their parents when these die. Polyandry does not seem to be common because in this reproductive strategy, females should at least lay eggs in different nests. That may explain why there are only 42% of pairs that have 1-2 extra adult male helpers.

The success or failure of natal dispersal of young fish- eagles affects the species' population size. It also affects their ability to repopulate suitable habitat within its former range once the factors affecting the species' decline have been resolved, such as hunting, persecution and habitat degradation (Watson et al. 1993). With the conservation programme initiated by The Peregrine Fund, involving habitat preservation management and surveys, fewer than 100 pairs have been found to remain between Belo sur Mer and Antsiranana in western and north-western Madagascar (Rabarisoa et al. 1997).

In 1993, biologists from the project first tested with success the 'sibling rescue' technique. When I studied four birds from this method, I observed that this technique may really increase the population size and I did not hear of any fledglings' death since I ended my observations. In their movements, fledglings may find different habitats that ecologically and biologically satisfy the species. This may explain why some eagles did not return to their natal territories, although it was quite difficult to locate the movements of all birds, given the short range of transmitters (4-5 km). However, some young did move over long distances of up to 10 km.

Figure 5. Time passed in parental territories.

a) Young from 1995

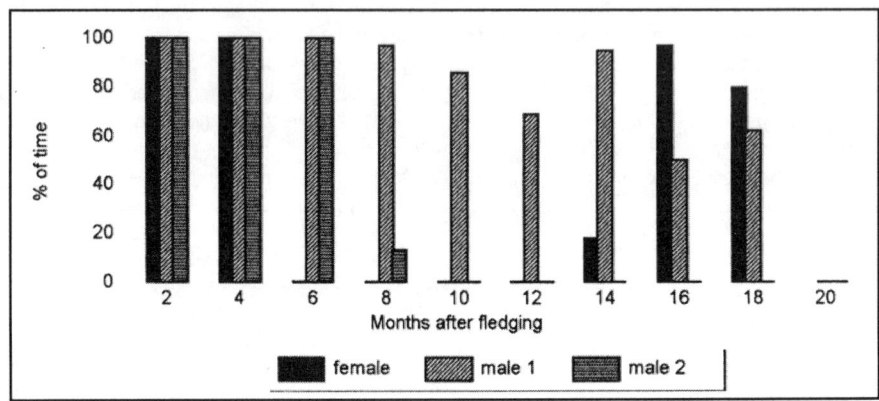

b) Young from 1996.

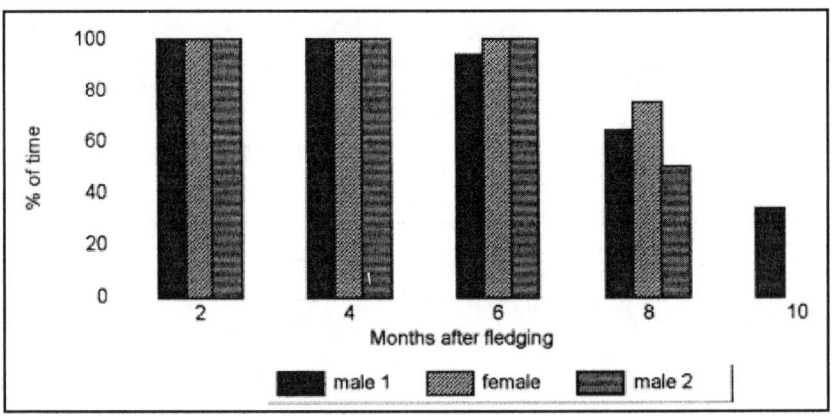

ACKNOWLEDGEMENTS

I am grateful to The Peregrine Fund for granting this study. I would like to thank especially Rick Watson, Program Director for Africa and Madagascar, and Russell Thorstrom, biologist, for their valuable comments and help during my field study and the redaction. Additional thanks are due to the staff and field technicians of the Madagascar project. My trip to South Africa was possible by the help of Robin Chancellor, Honorary Secretary of the WWGBP.

REFERENCES

KENWARD, R. 1990. *RANGES IV.* Institute of Terrestrial Ecology, Wareharm.
LANGRAND, O. & S. GOODMAN 1995. Monitoring Madagascar's ecosystems: a look at the past, present and the future of its wetlands. In: Herman, T.B., Bondrup-Nielson, S., Wilson, J.H. & Mundo (eds). *Ecosystem monitoring and protected areas*, pp.203-214. Science and Management of Protected Areas Association, Nova Scotia.
LANGRAND, O. & B.-U. MEYBURG 1989. Range, status and biology of the Madagascar Sea Eagle *Haliaeetus vociferoides*. In: Meyburg, B.-U. & Chancellor, R.D. (eds). *Raptors in the modern world*, pp. ?. Proc. III World Conf. Birds of Prey & Owls, WWGBP, Berlin.

MEYBURG, B.-U. 1974. Sibling aggression and mortality among nestling eagles. *Ibis* 116: 224-228.
MEYBURG, B.-U. 1986. Threatened and near-threatened diurnal birds of prey of the world. *WWGBP Birds of Prey Bull.* 3: 1-12.
RABARISOA R., R.T. WATSON, R. THORSTROM & J. BERKELMAN 1996. Status of the Madagascar fish-eagle *Haliaeetus vociferoides*. In: Watson, R.T. (ed.). *Madagascar Wetlands Conservation Project. Progress report III, 1995-1996.* The Peregrine Fund, Boise.
WATSON, R.T. 1993. *Madagascar project: The Madagascar Fish Eagle and Conservation Project and The Masoala Project: Use of Raptors and Other Fauna for Conservation Management and Evaluation. Progress report I, 1991 and 1992.* The Peregrine Fund, Boise. USA.
WATSON, R., S. THOMSETT, D. O'DANIEL & R. LEWIS 1996. Breeding, growth, development and management of the Madagascar fish eagle (*Haliaeetus vociferoides*). *J. Raptor Res.*.

Simon A. Rafanomezantsoa
The Perergine Fund's Madagascar Project
B.P. 4113 Antananarivo 101
Madagascar

Chancellor, R. D. & B.-U. Meyburg eds. 2000
Raptors at Risk
WWGBP / Hancock House

Taxonomic problems in African diurnal raptors

William S. Clark and R.A.G. Davies

ABSTRACT

Several sets of taxa of diurnal raptors, previously thought to be races, have now been shown to be species, e.g., Imperial Eagles *Aquila heliaca* and *A. adalberti*, Tawny Eagles *Aquila rapax* and *A. nipalensis*, Black-shouldered Kites *Elanus caeruleus* and *E. leucurus*, and Short-toed Eagles *Circaetus gallicus*, *C. beauduoini*, and *C. pectoralis*, because of differences in plumages, morphology, behaviour, food preferences, DNA sequences, and so on. On the other hand, Archer's Buzzard is most likely a colour morph of Augur Buzzard *Buteo augur*, and not a species. Three sets of allopatric African taxa now considered to be subspecies appear different enough in plumage and other characters to warrant separation as species: Forest and Mountain Buzzards (*Buteo trizonatus* and *B. oreophilus*), the Common Kestrel complex (*Falco tinnunculus*, *F. rufescens*, and *F. rupicolus*), and the African Goshawk (*Accipiter toussenelii* and *A. tachiro*, and perhaps *A. canescens*). Their differences are highlighted. Published differences in the north Africa races *Falco biarmicus erlangeri* and *F. b. tanypterus* of the Lanner Falcon and *F. pelegrinoides pelegrinoides* and *F. p. babylonicus* of the Barbary Falcon are questioned. The taxonomic status of the Yellow-billed Kite *Milvus migrans parasitus* as a subspecies is agreed to, and the genus of Wahlberg's Eagle *Aquila wahlbergi* is discussed. Further research into the differences of the problematic species listed above is needed; however, we must all first agree on what constitutes a species.

INTRODUCTION

Many species of birds, including the Osprey *Pandion haliaetus* and the Peregrine *Falco peregrinus*, were described initially, often from different areas of the world, as two or more species. Later, taxonomists working with large sets of museum specimens, combined similar taxa that were considered as separate species into races of a single widespread species. Hartert (1912-1921) was particularly active in this consolidation. Later, however, some combined sets of similar taxa were thought to be sufficiently different in plumage, behaviour, biology, and DNA, to again be regarded as separate species. Examples of this are the Spanish and Eastern Imperial Eagles, *Aquila adalberti* and *A. heliaca* (Hiraldo *et al.* 1976; Seibold *et al.* 1996), Steppe and Tawny Eagles, *A. nipalensis* and *A. rapax* (Clark 1992), and Augur and Jackal Buzzards *Buteo augur* and *B. rufofuscus* (Brooke 1975).

Some mergers that were later re-split occurred more recently, for example the combining of the American White-tailed Kite *Elanus leucurus* with the African and Asian Black-shouldered Kite *E.*

121

caeruleus, based on Parkes (1958), while Clark and Banks (1992) give many reasons why this combination was not valid. Fortunately, this merger was not recognized outside of North America.

Brown (1974) gave alleged inter-breeding of three taxa of *Circaetus* snake eagles as reasons to consider them as one species. However, as pointed out by Clark (1999), all of these can be explained by the breeding of subadult Black-breasted Snake Eagles *C. pectoralis* (shown on plate 14 in Maclean 1993 and p. 161 in Newman 1983) with adults or with another subadult. Plumages of the three, particularly juvenile plumage, are quite different (Clark 1999).

Kemp, in del Hoyo *et al.* (1994), treated the Archer's Buzzard *B. archeri* as a separate species, presumably based on Sibley and Monroe (1990). Clark (1996) presents reasons why it should be considered only as a colour morph of the Augur Buzzard, *B. augur archeri*.

During our field and museum work, and literature searches, as background for the field guide to African raptors that we are preparing, we noted many differences between and among present-day subspecies of three species: *Buteo oreophilus, Accipiter tachiro*, and *Falco tinnunculus*. We highlight these differences and couple this information with inferences on likely habitat separation to make predictions on which taxa may qualify for species status. We also identify taxa worthy of further investigation, including DNA analyses. For races of several other African species we find no distinguishing features. Our objective in this paper is to tidy up some 'loose ends' in the classification of African raptors.

SPECIES-LEVEL TAXONOMIC QUESTIONS

The three sets of allopatric Africa taxa that we believe are candidates for possible splitting into 2-3 species, based on further research, are the Forest and Mountain Buzzards *Buteo trizonatus* and *B. oreophilus*, the African Goshawks *A. tachiro* and *A. toussenelii*, and the Common Kestrel complex (*F. tinnunculus, F. rufescens*, and *F. rupicolus*).

Mountain and Forest Buzzards

The Mountain Buzzard occurs in high mountains of East Africa, from Ethiopia to northern Malawi and west to the eastern mountains of the former Zaire, usually above 2000m. The Forest Buzzard occurs in forests of the Southern Cape of South Africa. There are few, if any, records in the large gap between their ranges. Kemp, in del Hoyo *et al.* (1994), considered them races but added 'Race *trizonatus* may merit treatment as a full species.' James (1986) advocates making them full species.

From our experiences, they are easily separated by plumages. Both Rudebeck (1957) and James (1986) note striking differences in plumages between the two taxa. Forest Buzzards usually show some rufous tones on their underparts and upper tails. Forest Buzzards (Newman 1983: 171; Sinclair *et al.* 1993: 103) show a pale unmarked area between breast and belly that forms a noticeable 'U' on their underparts, a feature lacking on any Mountain Buzzard. Mountain Buzzards are overall darker, lacking any warm brown or rufous tones (Zimmerman *et al.* 1996: 131). The illustration of adult *B. trizonatus* in del Hoyo *et al.* (1994: 186) looks little like the real bird and appears more like an adult *B. oreophilus* with a white 'U' on its underparts. Juveniles of Mountain Buzzards differ little from adults in plumage, only in tail pattern and intensity of dark markings on leg feathers. However, juvenile Forest Buzzards lack the adults' rufous tones on back and tail, and have a different tail pattern.

A Meinertzhagen specimen in the British Museum of Natural History (BMNH 1965.M.1273) that was clearly an adult *B. trizonatus* was labelled as having been collected within the range of *B. oreophilus* on Mt. Kilimanjaro. See Knox (1993) for an example of Meinertzhagen's habit of stealing specimens and making up false data for their new tags. This specimen was most likely taken from a South African collection. Rudebeck had indicated on the label 'Locality probably South Africa.'

The Mountain Buzzard hunts regularly on the wing, whereas the Forest Buzzard is a perch hunter, yet soars regularly, but not for hunting. Maclean (1993) and Steyn (1992) describe the Forest Buzzard as hunting primarily from perches, whereas we observed Mountain Buzzards in Kenya hunting from the air in the manner of the Booted Eagle *Hieraaetus pennatus*.

Allan (1992) presents ring (band) recovery records to indicate that Forest Buzzards are somewhat migratory, moving north in the austral winter. No migration has been reported for the Mountain Buzzard (Brown et al. 1982).

Forest Buzzard (currently *Buteo oreophilus trizonatus*) appears to be a different species from Mountain Buzzard (*B. o. oreophilus*). Records from Malawi and Zimbabwe need further investigation to evaluate whether these populations are truly separate. Although there are mountain ranges of the Rift Valley in between the two populations, mountains in Zimbabwe, Zambia and Malawi are generally half the height of the larger mountains in East Africa, so the absence of cool forest conditions in between coastal South Africa and the highlands of East Africa may comprise an effective barrier to these populations.

We suggest that Forest and Mountain Buzzards may have both been derived from ancestral Steppe Buzzard (*Buteo b. vulpinus*) stock. The conditions that would appear to encourage such birds to become resident are cool temperate forest. These conditions are met both on the south coast in South Africa and at high altitude in East Africa. Adoption of sedentary habits by these two taxa (perhaps in the same manner as has recently been reported for the Booted Eagle in Africa) may have occurred at different times.

African Goshawk complex.

The African Goshawk has been considered by some authorities as one species, *Accipiter tachiro* (Wattel 1973; Brown et al. 1982; Amadon & Bull 1988) and by others as two species, *A. tachiro* and *A. toussenelii* (White 1965; Louette 1992; Kemp, in del Hoyo 1994). The taxa involved (Wattel 1973; del Hoyo et al. 1994) (Fig. 1) are:

1. The *tachiro* group:

A. ta. tachiro - Southern Africa.
A. ta. sparsimfasciatus - Somalia, East Africa.
A. ta. croizati - SW Ethiopia.
A. ta. unduliventor - Ethiopian highlands.
A. ta. pembaensis - Pemba Island.

The races *A. ta. tachiro* and *A. ta. sparsimfasciatus* are barely distinguishable. They differ from all other taxa (except perhaps *A. ta. croizati*, which we have not seen) in larger size and greater sexual size differences and in plumages of adult female (Figs. 2 & 3) and juvenile. Adult females lack the white tail spots shown on the other taxa. The race *A. ta. unduliventor* is much closer in characters to taxa in the *toussenelii* group than to those in the *tachiro* group and should be placed with the former group.

2. The *toussenelii* group:

A. to. macroscelides - West Africa.
A. to. toussenelii - Rain forests of Central Africa.
A. to. canescens - Rain forests of upper Zaire R. basin.
A. to. lopezi - Ferdinand Po Island.

The males of *macroscelides* are similar to those of *tachiro* but show a stronger rufous wash on their underparts, especially on flanks and leg feathers; however, the adult females are quite different from those of *tachiro* (Fig. 2), and are almost identical to the males (Fig. 1), including having white tail spots (Fig. 3). Adults of *toussenelii* and *canescens* differ little and both sexes have rufous and grey unbarred underparts (Fig. 4).

Kemp and Crowe (1994) offer compelling differences in morphometric data between both adult males and females of *A. tachiro* and *A. toussenelii* to support the two-species advocacy. Progogine (1980) shows a zone of contact between *A. tachiro* and *A. toussenelii* in Central Africa, especially in the eastern part of the Democratic Republic of Congo (formerly Zaire); however, no plumage intergrades have been reported. In this region, the two appear to be separated by habitat preference, with *A. toussenelii* in the rain forest and *A. tachiro* in the cutover edges and second growth.

We suggest that African Goshawks *Accipiter tachiro* and Red-chested Goshawks *Accipiter toussenelii* qualify as separate species, and we expect DNA studies to confirm this. Although *A.*

tachiro is generally considered to inhabit sparser forests than *A. toussenelii*, we do not consider that this habitat difference explains all the differences observed between these two taxa. *A. toussenelii* must inhabit similar sparse riverine woodland in West Africa. We propose that the two must have been separated for an extended period(s) in the past somewhere along the Rift Valley, where today so many similar taxa suddenly diverge (e.g. *A. minullus / A. erythropus*). The most likely geographic feature to have split these woodland birds is the arid corridor connecting the Kalahari to the Horn of Africa (Kingdon 1990) which was so prevalent in the cool dry glacial periods. This barrier would have effectively split the forest biomes into a Central and West African component (*A. toussenelii* group) and a South-eastern component (*A. tachiro* group). It would also explain the occurrence of an *A. toussenelli*-type goshawk (*A. to. unduliventor*) inhabiting the forests of Ethiopia (which falls to the north of the arid corridor).

Common Kestrel complex.

The Common Kestrel *Falco tinnunculus* has 5 subspecies that occur on the African continent (del Hoyo *et al.* 1994). They are:

F. t. tinnunculus – north-western Africa and palearctic migrant to sub-Saharan Africa.

F. t. rupicolaeformes – north-eastern Africa, primarily Nile drainage.

F. t. archeri - Somalia, perhaps coastal Kenya.

F. t. rufescens (= *F. t. carlo*) - Highlands of central and eastern Africa.

F. t. rupicolus - Southern Africa north to Angola and southern Tanzania.

The first three races are similar and are not separable in the field, or even in hand, as they overlap in most characters; *F. t. rupicolaeformes* averages brighter than nominate race (Meinertzhagen 1954), and *F. t. archeri* is smaller (Archer & Godman 1937). On the other hand, the last two races, *F. t. rufescens* and *F. t. rupicolus*, are quite different from the nominate race and from each other in plumages, and all are easily differentiated in the field. In particular, the adult females of the three taxa are quite different (Figs. 6 & 7). We believe that certainly *F. t. rupicolus* and possibly *F. t. rufescens* should be considered as candidates for full species status based on the differences listed herein. Further field and DNA work are required for confirmation of *F. t. rufescens* as a distinct species. More details for these potential species are presented:

A. Mountain Kestrel - The African Mountain Kestrel, as *F. t. rufescens* is called by Archer & Godman (1937) and Bannerman (1953), is resident at higher elevations in Central and East Africa, usually breeding on rocky outcrops or cliffs, but recently has descended to lower elevations to breed on buildings in cities near the rain forest, e.g., in Nigeria (Elgood *et al.* 1994).

The Mountain Kestrel is always separable from the nominate race by its overall darker colouration (Archer & Godman 1937; Bannerman 1953); it is not correctly illustrated in Zimmerman *et al.* (1996: 145) nor labelled correctly in Brown *et al.* (1982: 435, the figure labelled 'adult male' is an adult female and that labelled 'adult female' is a juvenile). Adult females are somewhat similar to adult males in that they have grey heads and tails, but with dark barring on their upperparts and more black banding in their tails (Fig. 8). Chapin (1932) noted this, but Bannerman (1953) and Archer and Godman (1937) both stated incorrectly that females had no grey on the head. We have looked at many specimens of *F. t. rufescens* and verified that all adult females had grey heads, as shown in Fig. 8. Juveniles are like adult females but have brown heads (Fig. 8). Brown and Amadon (1968) show only the adult male.

Chapin (1932) mentions that the Mountain Kestrel would seem to be specifically distinct from *F. t. tinnunculus* but for their intergradation in northeast Africa and southwest Arabia. We found no intergrades between *F. t. rufescens* and *F. t. tinnunculus* in the hundreds of specimens from those areas, nor from anywhere else; all specimens from Africa north of the range of *F. t. rupicolus* were either *F. t. tinnunculus*, (including *F. t. rupicolaeformes* and *F. t. archeri*), or *F. t. rufescens*.

B. Rock Kestrel - The Rock Kestrel, as *F. t. rupicolus* has always been called, is resident throughout Southern Africa. There are only a few records of *F. t. tinnunculus* within its range: two from Malawi (Benson & Benson 1977), two from Angola (Traylor 1963), and two from Zambia (Benson *et al.* 1971). Bouet (1955) considered it a full species.

The plumages of the Rock Kestrel are much different from those of Common Kestrels in the *F. t. tinnunculus* group and from *F. t. rufescens*. Note that Rock Kestrels are not illustrated in Brown and Amadon (1968), Brown *et al.* (1982) or del Hoyo (1994). Plumages of adult males and females differ little and resemble those of adult male *F. t. tinnunculus* in having grey heads and tails and chestnut upperparts, but the brighter chestnut upperparts of *F. t. rupicolus* are less heavily marked, and their underparts are also a bright chestnut that contrasts with nearly unmarked white underwings. Females tend to have more black bands in the central tail feathers (Newman 1983: 193; Sinclair *et al.* 1993: 123). Juvenile Rock Kestrels resemble adults but have brown heads.

Common Kestrels have fewer close competitors, however Rock and Mountain Kestrels in Africa do have (e.g.: *E. caeruleus*, Fox Kestrel *F. alopex*, Greater or White-eyed Kestrel *F. rupicoloides* and the migratory kestrels). Competition with these may explain the narrower habitat preference exhibited by Rock and Mountain Kestrels.

The full species status of Spotted Kestrel *F. moluccensis* and Australian Kestrel *F. cenchroides* is unquestioned, yet if we compare their plumages to the Common Kestrel (Figs. 9 & 10), we find several parallels to the comparison of *F. t. rufescens* and *F. t. rupicolus* with Common Kestrel. In both comparisons, sexual dimorphism of the adult plumages is far less pronounced than in Common Kestrel. In both comparisons the taxa adjacent to the range of the Common Kestrel (*F. t. rufescens* and *F. moluccensis*) have noticeably darker plumage than the Common Kestrel, while the taxa furthest away (*F. t. rupicolus* and *F. cenchroides*) are more chestnut-coloured and less heavily marked.

The plumage differences among Mountain, Rock, and Common Kestrels are no less than the differences among Spotted, Australian, and Common Kestrels. Helbig & Seibold (pers. comm.) found that *F. t. tinnunculus* is closer to *F. cenchroides* than to *F. t. rupicolus* according to mtDNA sequences. *F. cenchroides* is accepted as a distinct species, implying that *F. t. rupicolus* should be as well.

Clearly the Rock Kestrel *F. t. rupicolus* is a species separate from the Common Kestrel *F. t. tinnunculus*. Gene flow between these taxa will be restricted by two ecological barriers for kestrels: the Sahara Desert north of the equator and the Miombo woodlands to the south. In between these two barriers lies the third taxon, Mountain Kestrel *F. t. rufescens*, which appears to be distinct from both and warrants further study, including DNA comparisons, to establish its status.

SUB-SPECIES LEVEL TAXONOMIC QUESTIONS

While taxonomic questions at the subspecies level are not of as great a concern as those at the species level, it is nevertheless important to keep printed descriptions of the different taxa as accurate as possible. We have found that several subspecific differences mentioned in the literature do not hold up to close scrutiny of specimens. These are the differences between the races *Falco biarmicus erlangeri* and *F. b. tanypterus* of the Lanner Falcon; the races *F. pel. pelegrinoides* and *F. p. babylonicus* of the Barbary Falcon; and the races *Aquila n. nipalensis* and *A. n. orientalis* of the Steppe Eagle.

Lanner Falcon

Two races of this species have been described for Africa north of the Sahara, *F. b. erlangeri* for the northwest and *F. b. tanypterus* for the northeast into the Middle East. Published differences between them are size and colouration, with *F. b. erlangeri* being smaller and paler (Cramp & Simmons 1980). However, after having inspected over a hundred specimens of both, we feel that there is a complete overlap in colouration, with some specimens of *F. b. tanypterus* being paler than most of *F. b. erlangeri*. Likewise, while there is most likely a slight clinal variation in greater size from west to east, this is masked by individual size variation. We recommend merging these two subspecies into one.

Barbary Falcon

The Barbary Falcon *Falco pelegrinoides* is thought by most authorities to be a separate species (Cade 1982; Amadon & Bull 1988), but Brown *et al.* (1982) and del Hoyo *et al.* (1994) elected to treat it as two races of the Peregrine *F. peregrinus*. The two races were thought to differ by size and colouration, with *F. pel. babylonicus* being larger and paler (Cade 1982). However, we have found a complete overlap in plumages from pale to dark, with no consistent feature to differentiate specimens. Cade (1982) postulates that there may be a separation in the ranges in the Middle East, but the range map for this species in Porter *et al.* (1996) shows extensive range in this area. Any size differences between Asian and African falcons may just be according to Bergman's Rule and are not, to our thinking, sufficient for racial distinction. Helbig & Seibold (pers. comm.) found no differences in mtDNA sequences between them. Again we think that *F. pel. pelegrinoides* and *F. pel. babylonicus* should be merged.

Steppe Eagle

Cramp and Simmons (1980) state that, compared to *A. n. orientalis*, *A. n. nipalensis* is larger, with darker adults that more often have rufous nape patches. We have found the same amount of variation of plumages among eastern and western eagles, with no single character that would distinguish either race. All adults had rufous nape patches. Illustrated differences between the races in Sinclair *et al.* (1993: 93-94) appear to be only size differences between sexes; however, Steppe Eagles never have grey upperparts as illustrated. The nominate race (eastern eagles) winters only in Asia, not in Africa as stated. We believe that the racial differences are too small and suggest merging the races.

Yellow-billed Kite

We agree with Brooke (1974) that *Milvus migrans parasitus* is a valid race and not a separate species.

GENERIC LEVEL TAXONOMIC QUESTIONS

Wahlberg's Eagle

This eagle was long thought to be in the genus *Aquila*, mainly because of the dark plumage of most individuals. However Amadon and Bull (1988) placed it in *Hieraaetus*, based on field observations by Smeenk (1974) and other considerations (Amadon 1987), but go on to comment that it is intermediate in characters between these closely related genera. Read Debus (1985) and Amadon (1987) for arguments *pro* and Auburn (1988) for arguments *con* placement in *Hieraaetus*. We concur with Amadon and Bull (1988) that Wahlberg's Eagle is closer to *Hieraaetus* than to *Aquila* in many of its characters; however, we reserve final judgement until DNA evidence is presented.

DISCUSSION

We briefly present arguments why further research into the differences among taxa in three sets of African raptors would most likely verify that each taxon is a full species. These are: Mountain and Forest Buzzards, the Common Kestrel complex, and the African Goshawk complex. Further, we questioned published differences in the north African races of Lanner Falcon and those of Barbary Falcon and Steppe Eagle. More research and insight are needed to determine if Wahlberg's Eagle is an *Aquila*, a *Hieraaetus*, or in its own genus. However, to get complete agreement among taxonomic authorities, we must all first agree on what defines a species.

ACKNOWLEDGMENTS

We thank the curators and collection managers of many museums, but particularly, the American Museum of Natural History, especially Allison Andors and Mary Lecroy; the Natural History Museum, especially Robert Prys-Jones; the Transvaal Museum, especially Alan Kemp; the Kenya Museum, especially Leon Bennon and Colin Jackson; and the National Museum of Natural History for assistance and permission to look at specimens. We also thank our editor at Academic Press, Dr. Andrew Richford, for making our research on African raptors possible. R. Dowsett provided critical comments on earlier drafts.

Figure 1. African Goshawk taxa. (l to r) Adult female *A. t. macroscelides* (male alike), adult male and female *A. t. toussenelii*, adult male and female *A. t. tachiro*.

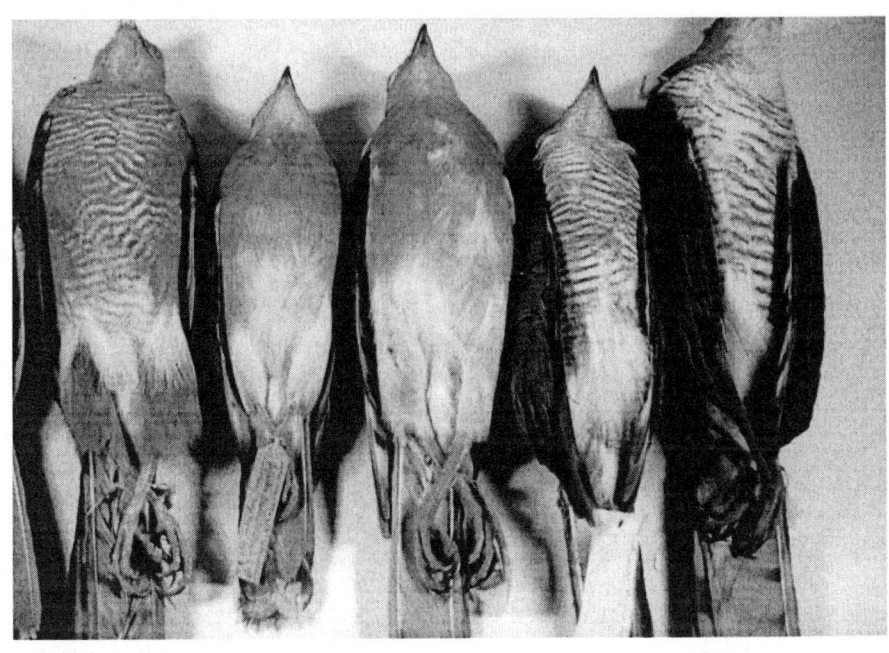

Figure 2. Adult female African Goshawk undersides comparison. Top, *A. t. tachiro*; bottom, *A. toussenelii macroscelides*. Latter has more rufous wash.

Figure 3. Adult female African Goshawk uppersides comparison. Top, *A. t. tachiro*; bottom, *A. toussenelii macroscelides*. Latter has white tail spots.

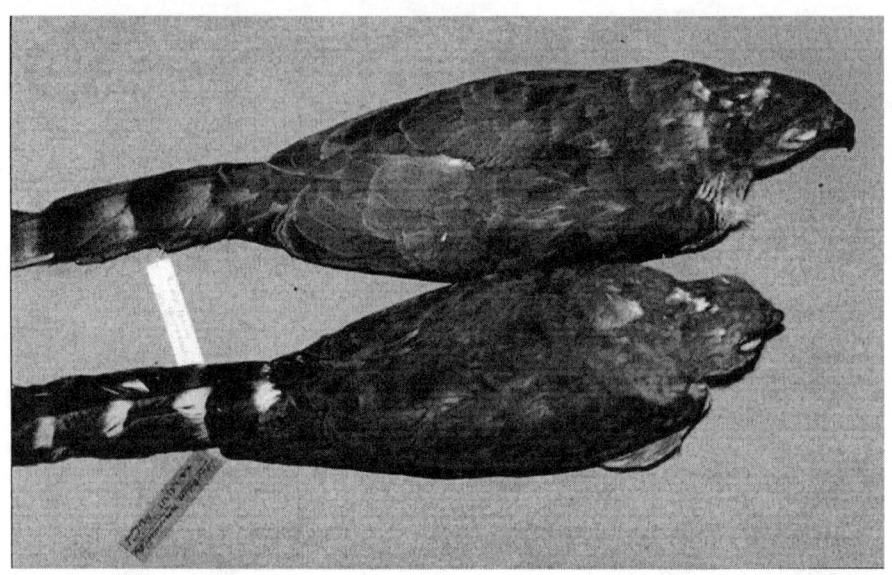

Figure 4. Adult *A. t. toussenelii*. Lacks strong rufous barring on underparts. Plumage of females is like that of males.

Figure 5. Adult *A. t. toussenelii*. Plumage of females is like that of males.

Figure 6. Comparison of undersides of adult female kestrels: (Top to bottom), *F. t. tinnunculus*, *F. t. rufescens*, *F. t. rupicolus*.

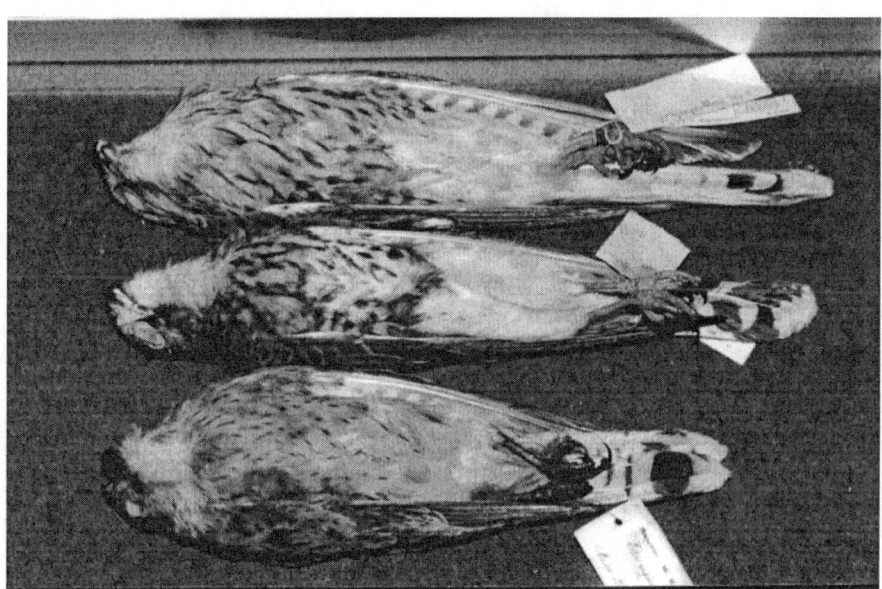

Figure 7. Comparison of uppersides of adult female kestrels: (Top to bottom), *F. t. tinnunculus*, *F. t. rufescens*, *F. t. rupicolus*.

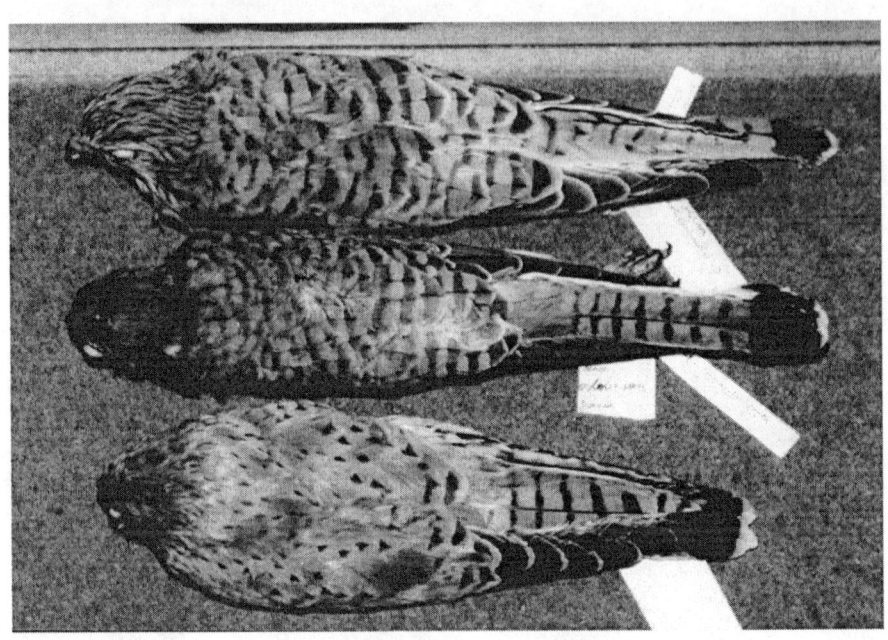

Figure 8. Mountain Kestrels *F. t. rufescens* uppersides. (l to r) Adult male and female and juvenile. Female has grey head.

Figure 9. Comparison of undersides of adult female kestrels: (Top to bottom), *F. cenchroides*, *F. moluccensis*, *F. t. tinnunculus*.

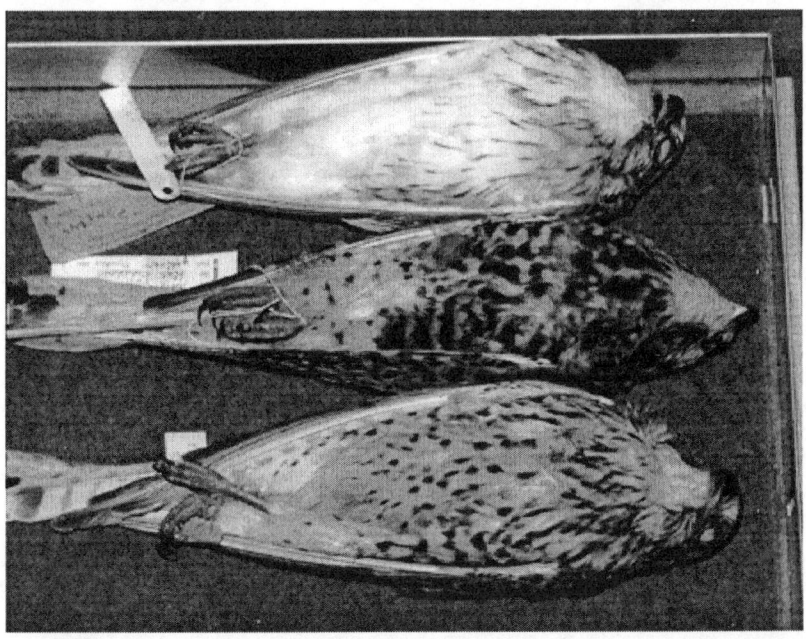

Figure 10. Comparison of uppersides of adult female kestrels: (Top to bottom), *F. cenchroides*, *F. moluccensis*, *F. t. tinnunculus*.

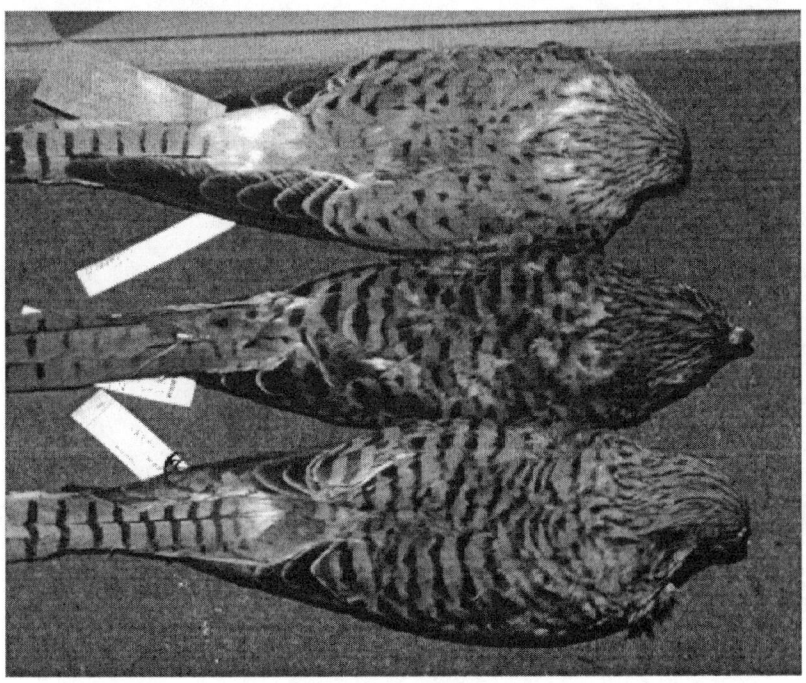

REFERENCES

ALLAN, D. 1992. Long distance movements of Forest Buzzards in South Africa. *Gabar* 7: 26-27.
AMADON, D. 1987. Comments on eagles of the genus *Hieraaetus*. *Gabar* 2: 18-19.
AMADON, D. & J. BULL 1988. Hawks and owls of the World: A distributional and taxonomic list. *Proc. West. Found. Vert. Zool.* 3(4).
ARCHER, G. & E.M. GODMAN 1937. *The Birds of British Somaliland and the Gulf of Aden*. Gurney and Jackson, London.
AUBURN, J. 1988. Why Wahlberg's Eagle is not a *Hieraaetus* eagle. *Gabar* 3: 15-18.
BANNERMAN, D.A. 1953. *The Birds of West and Equatorial Africa*. Oliver and Boyd, Edinburgh.
BENSON, C.W. & F.M. BENSON 1977. *The Birds of Malawi*. Montford Press, Limbe, Malawi.
BENSON, C.W., R.K. BROOKE, R.B. DOWSETT & M.P.S. IRWIN 1971. *The Birds of Zambia*. Collins, London.
BOUET, G. 1955. *Oiseaux de L'Afrique tropical*. Première partie. Office de la Recherche Scientific et Technique Outre-Mer, Paris.
BROOKE, R.K. 1974. The migratory Black Kite *Milvus migrans migrans* (Aves: Accipitridae) of the Palearctic in southern Africa. *Durban Mus. Novitates* 10: 53-66.
BROOKE, R.K. 1975. The taxonomic relationship of *Buteo rufofuscus* and *B. augur*. *Bull. Br. Orn. Club* 95: 152-154.
BROWN, L. 1974. The races of the European Snake Eagle *Circaetus gallicus*. *Bull. Br. Orn. Club* 94: 126-128.
BROWN L.H. & D. AMADON 1968. *Eagles, Hawks, and Falcons of the World*. Vol. 2. McGraw-Hill, New York.
BROWN, L.H., URBAN, E.K. & NEWMAN, K. 1982. *The Birds of Africa*. Vol. 1. Academic Press, London.
CADE, T.J. 1982. *The Falcons of the World*. Cornell University Press, Ithaca.
CHAPIN, J.P. 1932. The Birds of the Belgian Congo. *Bull. Am. Mus. Nat. Hist.* 65.
CLARK, W.S. 1992. The taxonomy of Steppe and Tawny Eagles, with criteria for separation of museum specimens and live eagles. *Bull. Br. Orn. Club* 112: 150-157.
CLARK, W.S. 1996. The validity of Archer's Buzzard as a species. *J. Afr. Raptor Biol.* 11: 11-13.
CLARK, W.S. 1999. Plumage differences and taxonomic status of three similar *Circaetus* snake-eagles. *Bull. Br. Orn. Club.* 119: 56-59.
CLARK, W.S. & R. BANKS 1992. The taxonomic status of the White-tailed Kite. *Wilson Bull.* 104: 571-579.
CRAMP, S. & K.E.L. SIMMONS 1980. *The Birds of the Western Palearctic*. Vol 2. Oxford University Press, Oxford.
DEBUS, S.J.S. 1985. The small *Hieraaetus* eagles on four continents: a superspecies? *Gabar* 1: 36-39.
DEL HOYO J., A. ELLIOT & J. SARGATAL (eds.) 1994. *Handbook of the Birds of the World*. Vol 2. Lynx Edicions, Barcelona.
ELGOOD, J.H., J.B. HEIGHAM, A.M. MOORE, A.M. NASON, R.E. SHARLAND & N.J. SKINNER 1994. *The Birds of Nigeria*. B.O.U. Check-list no. 4. BOU, Tring.
HARTERT, E. 1912-1921. *Die Vögel der Paläarktischen Fauna*. Vol. 2. Friedlander und sohn, Berlin.
HIRALDO, F., M. DELIBES & J. CALDERON 1976. Sobre el status taxonómico del Aguila Imperial Ibérica. *Acta Vert. Donana* 3: 171-182.
JAMES, A.H. 1986. Review of taxonomic characters in African buzzards (Genus *Buteo*). *Beaufortia* 36: 1-12.
KEMP, A. & T. CROWE 1994. A morphometric analysis of *Accipiter* species. In: Meyburg, B.U. & Chancellor, R.D. (eds). *Raptor Conservation Today*. WWGBP & Pica Press, Berlin.
KINGDON, J. 1990. *Island Africa*. Collins, London.
KNOX. A.G. 1993. Richard Meinertzhagen - a case of fraud examined. *Ibis* 135: 320-325.
LOUETTE, M. 1992. The identification of forest accipiters in central Africa. *Bull. Br. Orn. Club* 112: 50-53.
MACLEAN, G.L. 1993. *Robert's Birds of South Africa*. 6th ed. Trustees of the John Voelker Bird Book Trust Fund, Cape Town.
MEINERTZHAGEN, R. 1954. *Birds of Arabia*. Oliver and Boyd, Edinburgh.
NEWMAN, K. 1983. *Newman's Birds of southern Africa*. Southern Books, Halfway House.
PARKES, K.C. 1958. Specific relationships in the genus *Elanus*. *Condor* 60: 139-140.
PORTER, R.F., S. CHRISTENSEN & P. SCHIERMACKER-HANSEN 1996. *Field Guide to the Birds of the Middle East*. T. & A. D. Poyser, London.
PROGOGINE, A. 1980. Etude de quelques contacts secondaires au Zaire oriental. *Le Gerfaut* 70: 305-384.
RUDEBECK, G. 1957. *Buteo buteo trizonatus*, a new buzzard from the Union of South Africa. *South African Animal Life* 4: 415-437.

SEIBOLD, I., A.J. HELBIG, B.-U. MEYBURG, J.J. NEGRO & M. WINK 1996. Genetic differentiation and molecular phylogeny of European *Aquila* eagles according to cytochrome b nucleotide sequences. In: Meyburg, B.U. & Chancellor, R.D. (eds). *Eagle Studies*, pp. 1-12. WWGBP, Berlin, Paris & London.
SIBLEY, C.G. & B.L. MONROE 1990. *Distribution and Taxonomy of the Birds of the World*. Yale University Press, New Haven.
SINCLAIR, I., P. HOCKEY & W. TARBOTON 1993. *Illustrated guide to Birds of southern Africa*. New Holland, London.
SMEENK, C. 1974. Comparative ecological studies of some East African birds of prey. *Ardea* 62: 1-96.
STEYN, P. 1982. *Birds of Prey of Southern Africa*. David Philip, Cape Town & Johannesburg.
TRAYLOR, M.A. 1963. *Checklist of Angolan birds*. Comp. Diam. Angola. Museo du Dundo, Lisbon.
WATTEL, J. 1973. Geographic differentiation in the genus Accipiter. *Publns. Nuttall Ornith. Club* 13.
WHITE, C.M.N. 1965. *A revised check list of African non-passerine birds*. Government Printer, Lusaka.
ZIMMERMAN, D.A., D.A. TURNER & D.J. PEARSON 1996. *Birds of Kenya and northern Tanzania*. Princeton University Press, Princeton.

William S. Clark
7800 Dassett Court #101
Annandale, VA 22003
U.S.A.

R. A. G. Davies
P O Box 1390
Halfway House
1685 South Africa

Chancellor, R. D. & B.-U. Meyburg eds. 2000
Raptors at Risk
WWGBP / Hancock House

Advances in the molecular systematics of African raptors

Michael Wink and Hedi Sauer-Gürth

ABSTRACT

The mitochondrial cytochrome b gene was amplified and sequenced from approximately 35% of all species and 50% of genera of diurnal raptors. Nucleotide sequence data were used to reconstruct their molecular phylogeny using the Maximum parsimony, Neighbour Joining, and Maximum Likelihood methods. A number of new phylogenetic relationships were discovered in African members of the Falconidae, Pandionidae and Accipitridae. In a number of instances, DNA supports the view that certain subspecies, which differ by morphology, size and distribution, can be regarded as distinct species: such pairs are: *Falco chicquera* and *F. (c.) horsbrughi*, *F. columbarius* and *F. (c.) aesalon*, *Circus maillardi* and *Circus (m.) macrosceles*, *Circus cyaneus* and *Circus (c.) hudsonius*, *Milvus migrans* and *Milvus (m.) parasitus*, *Aquila (Hieraaetus) fasciatus* and *A. (f.) spilogaster*, *Pandion haliaetus* and *P. (h.) ridgwayi*. The genera *Aquila* and *Hieraeetus* are also found to be paraphyletic and therefore *Hieraeetus* should be merged in *Aquila*.

INTRODUCTION

Diurnal raptors have been grouped into five families, Accipitridae, Pandionidae, Sagittariidae, Falconidae and Catharthidae, and are placed in a common order Falconiformes (del Hoyo *et al.* 1994) or the infraorders Falconides and Ciconiides (Cathartidae), respectively (Sibley & Monroe 1990). Morphological and molecular data provide evidence that at least Cathartidae, Falconidae and Sagittariidae do not share direct ancestry with Accipitridae and Pandionidae (Wink 1995; Wink *et al.* 1998), indicating that the order Falconiformes or infraorder Falconides are apparently artificial units which combine birds that share a common life style, especially in behaviour and ecology. Because convergent traits are abundant in raptors, molecular data, such as DNA sequences of marker genes, which provide many characters for comparison that are less biased by parallel evolution than morphological, ecological or behavioural traits (Avise 1994; Mindell 1997), offer an opportunity to elucidate evolutionary relationships.

Nucleotide sequences of the mitochondrial cytochrome b gene have already been employed to study the systematics and evolution of diurnal raptors (Avise *et al.* 1994; Griffiths 1997; Mindell 1997; and from our laboratory: Seibold *et al.* 1993, 1996; Helbig *et al.*, 1994; Wink 1995, 1998; Wink & Seibold 1996; Wink *et al.*, 1996, 1998; Seibold & Helbig 1995, 1996). Among diurnal raptors, more than 230 species and 79 genera have been described. The molecular data published so far are based on one or two mitochondrial genes, cover approximately 50% of the genera and 35% of the species and provide a first idea of their evolutionary past. Because these conclusions rely on incomplete data sets (and may thus suffer from 'long branch attractions' and insufficient resolution) much more work is needed before we shall be able to understand the evolution of diurnal raptors with more precision.

In our continuing effort to elucidate the molecular systematics of raptors we have sequenced the cytochrome b gene of a number of African raptors for the first time. In this communication, emphasis was laid on phylogenetic relationships among African taxa that constitute a substantial subset on all raptors.

MATERIAL AND METHODS

Origin of DNA, PCR and DNA-Sequencing

Blood and tissues were stored either in an EDTA buffer or in ethanol (Wink 1998) and stored at –20°C until processing. DNA was extracted using the proteinase K protocol. The mitochondrial cytochrome b gene was amplified by PCR using primers (Table 1). PCR products of at least two or more specimens were sequenced directly using the dideoxy chain termination method with the Sequenase PCR Product Sequencing Kit (Amersham Life Science, US70170) and [α-^{35}S] labelled dATP or using the cycle sequencing Kit (Amersham Life Science, RPN 2438/RPN 2538) in combination with CY5 labelled primers (Table 1). For cycle sequencing a two stage programme containing an initial denaturing step at 94°C for 4 min and 25 cycles at 60°C (40 sec), and 94° (30 sec) was used. Radioactive fragments were separated on a PAGE gel apparatus (Stratagene, Base Ace Sequencer) while CY5 labelled fragments were analysed on an automated Sequencer (Pharmacia, ALF-Express). Sequences of >1000 nt were read from autoradiograms or obtained directly from ALF-Express and aligned. Deletions, insertions or inversions were not encountered in cytochrome b. Part of the sequences used were based on earlier studies from our laboratory (Seibold 1994) or were taken from the literature [e.g., sequences of some Cathartidae from Avise *et al.*, (1994); of Polyborinae from Griffiths (1997)]. Usually two to over 10 sequences per species are available in our laboratory so that sequences used for this analysis can be regarded as representative for each species.

Table 1. Oligonucleotide primers used for PCR and sequencing. (x = CY5 fluorescent label. Sequence in 5'- 3' orientation)

PCR	
MT-A1	caacatctcagcatgatgaaacttcg
MT-A2	gccccatccaacatctcagcatgatgaaacttcg
MT-A3	ctcccagccccatccaacatctcagcatgatgaaacttcg
L14857	gggtctttcgccctatcaat
MT-F1	agggtggagtcttcagttttggtttacaagaccaatg
MT-F2	ctaagaagggtggagtcttcagttttggtttacaagaccaatg
SMT-B	tcaaatgatatttgtcctc
Cycle sequencing	
MT-C2-CY	xgaggacaaatatcattctgagg
MT-U2-CY	xggggtgaagttttctgggtc
MT-C4-CY	xagtgttgggttgtctactga
MT-U1-CY	xtccmggctcaaacaaccccctagg
MT-CCY	xtaccatgaggmcaaacatc
SMTACY	xcaacatctcagcatgatgaaacttcg
MT-LeCY	xtcaaacccgaatgatayttcctatt
MT-V-CY	xtggagggcraaraatcgggt
SMT-FCY	xgtggagtcttcagttttggtttacaagac
SMT-BCY	xtcaaatgatatttgtcctc

Figure 1. Molecular phylogeny of raptors.

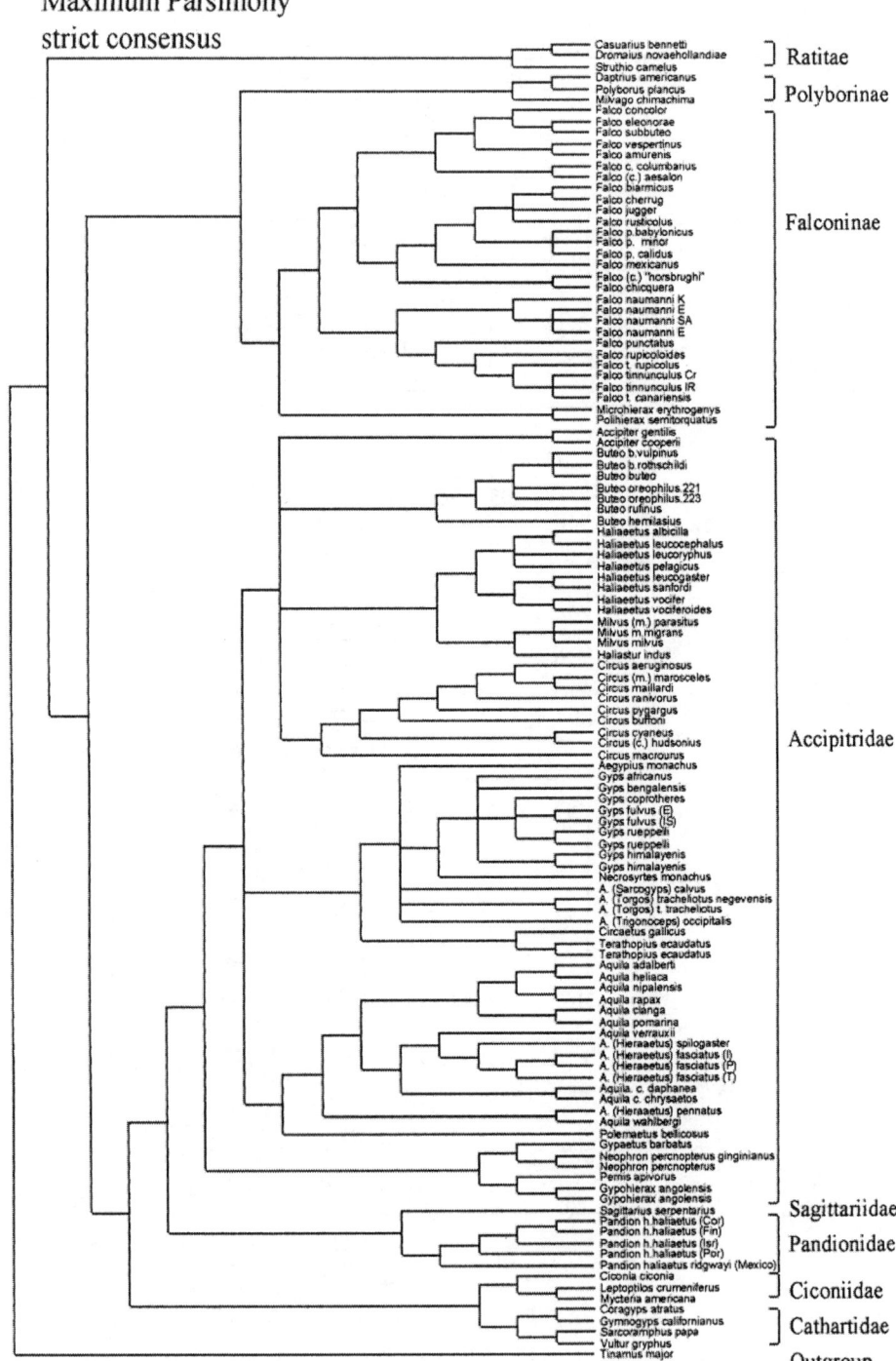

Neighbour Joining

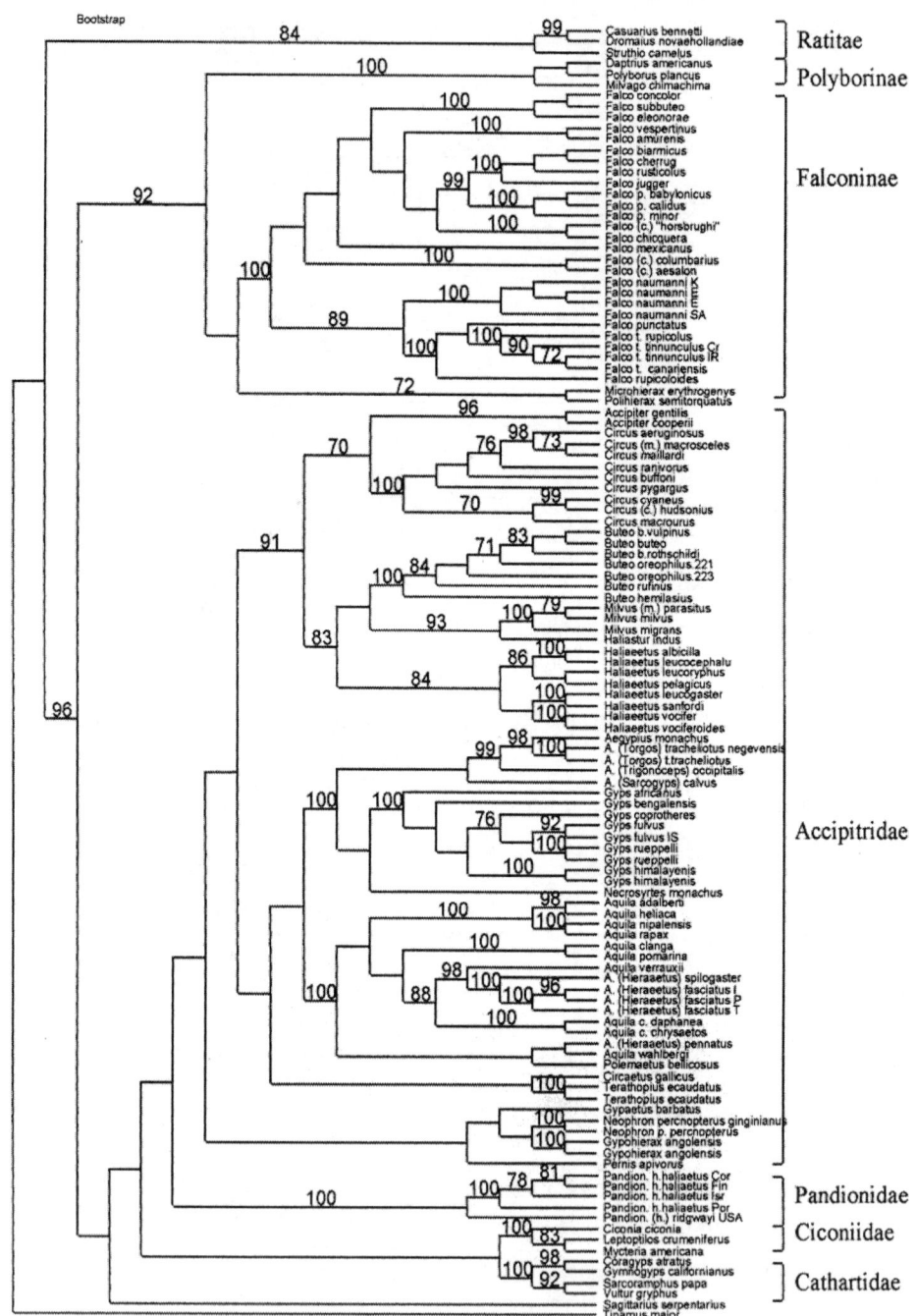

Strict consensus tree reconstructed using MP; 377 characters are constant, 267 variable characters are parsimony-uniformative and 616 parsimony-informative; tree lengths: 4691 steps; CI= 0.276; RI=0.683; HI= 0.724. Neighbour Joining bootstrap cladogram (1000 replications; p distance as distance algorithm)

Phylogenetic and statistical analysis

Phylogenetic relationships were analysed by different methods. The programme package MEGA (Kumar et al. 1993) and PAUP* were used to estimate genetic distances and to reconstruct trees with the Neighbour Joining (NJ), Maximum Parsimony (MP) and Maximum Likelihood methods (Swofford 1993). In MP, heuristic searches using the default settings were conducted without character weighting.

RESULTS AND DISCUSSION

For the present analysis, a data set was selected in which most species are represented by a single sequence. In a few instances, two or more sequences have been included from birds of different geographic origin in order to document phylogeographic variation (e.g., for *Hieraeetus fasciatus*, *Pandion haliaetus* or *Falco tinnunculus*).

Phylogenetic trees were reconstructed using the character state method MP (Fig. 1a) (represented as a strict consensus of 230 equally parsimonious trees) and the distance method NJ (Fig. 1b) (shown as a bootstrap cladogram; numbers are bootstrap frequencies (in %) at the respective furcation). ML analyses for the complete data set were not possible because of limited computation power. ML analyses which produce most reliable trees (Nei 1996), were constructed for partial phylogenies of smaller subsets. As can be seen from Figures 1a and 1b, the general topology of both MP and NJ trees is almost identical; differences can be seen in the placement of the genera *Sagittarius*, and *Circaetus/Terathopius*.

We have chosen *Tinamus* as a distant outgroup and the Ratitae as a distant ingroup; both groups of birds have evolved earlier than raptors (Feduccia 1996). The choice of other outgroups did not influence the tree topology.

Phylogenetic relationships between and within raptor families

The Falconidae, Cathartidae and probably the Accipitridae form monophyletic assemblages (Fig. 1), i.e. each of these families was derived from a common ancestor. The monotypic genera *Sagittarius* and *Pandion*, which are the sole representatives of their families, cluster at the base of the furcations which lead to the Accipitridae. Whether they share direct ancestry with the Accipitridae (as suggested by DNA-DNA hybridisation; Sibley & Ahlquist 1990) cannot be settled with the present data set, since bootstrap values indicate only small support for these furcations. However, the Falconiformes as a group apparently represent a polyphyletic assemblage, indicating that at least the families Falconidae and Cathartidae evolved independently from the Accipitridae.

Pandionidae

Ospreys form a monospecific family with a world-wide distribution. Four subspecies have been recognized, of which two are included in the present analysis. Within *P. h. haliaetus* populations (from Israel, Corsica, Portugal, and Finland) little phylogeographic differentiation can be seen, but a substantial difference (4% nucleotide divergence) can be detected between *P. h. haliaetus* and *P. h. ridgwayi* of the New World. Because similar distances have been found between distinct species and because of differences in distribution and morphology, it would be plausible to treat the New World Ospreys as a distinct species.

Sagittariidae

Sagittarius serpentarius represents a monospecific family, which has been placed near Accipitridae and storks (del Hoyo et al. 1994). Cytochrome b sequences always place this taxon outside the Accipitridae (which would agree with karyotype data) but could not find a clear sister so far; storks never appear as a direct sister group to the *Sagittarius*, as suggested by Sibley and Ahlquist (1990).

Falconidae

Members of the Falconidae are divided into the subfamilies Polyborinae and Falconinae. Also according to cytochrome b data, both groups represent monophyletic clades (Griffiths 1997) which share common ancestry (Figs. 1 & 2). The African Pygmy Falcon *Polihierax semitorquatus* and the

Philippine Falconet *Microhierax erythrogenys* represent sibling genera which form a sister group to the large monophyletic *Falco* assemblage.

Within the genus *Falco*, the following monophyletic clades can be distinguished: a) kestrels, b) merlins, c) hobbies (*Hypotriorchis*), d) desert falcons *Hierofalco* (Saker *F. cherrug*, Gyr *F. rusticolus*, Laggar *F. jugger*, Lanner *F. biarmicus*), and e) peregrines *F. peregrinus*.

Kestrels

Kestrels diverge at the base of the monophyletic *Falco* clade (Figs. 1 & 2). The Eurasian Kestrel (*F. tinnunculus*) has been subdivided into several subspecies, and some island forms have already been considered as distinct species, such as *F. newtoni*, *F. punctatus*, and *F. araea* (Sibley & Monroe 1990; del Hoyo et al. 1994). Our data set contains the subspecies *F. t. rupicolus* from South Africa, *F. t. canariensis* from Madeira, *F.t. tinnunculus* from Europe and *F. punctatus* from Mauritius. Differences in size, plumage patterns and distribution are also reflected at the cytochrome b level. DNA data support the view that these taxa derive from a common ancestor, with the Greater Kestrel *F. rupicoloides* from South Africa as a sister group. The Lesser Kestrel *F. naumanni*, which forms a sister group to the Eurasian Kestrel (Figs. 1 & 2), breeds in the Mediterranean and in parts of Eastern Europe and Asia. Cytochrome b data suggest that haplotypes of the populations of Spain and Kazakhstan differ and that sequence data can be used to determine the origin of wintering birds in Africa: A Lesser kestrel studied in South Africa came from the western Mediterranean (Figs. 1a & 2).

Merlins

Several subspecies are recognized in *F. columbarius*. Our analysis included *F. c. columbarius* from North America and *F.c. aesalon* from northern Eurasia. The cytochrome b gene shows substantial sequence divergence (2% distance) which is in the range of distinct species. Because of geographic, size and plumage differences, it would be plausible to treat both subspecies as distinct species (Wink & Seibold 1996; Wink et al. 1998).

Hobbies and red-footed falcons

Sooty *F. concolor* and Eleonora's *F. eleanorae* Falcons and Hobby *F. subbuteo* share many similaries in ecology and behaviour (food of birds and insects; breeding distribution in the Mediterranean and Europe but wintering quarters in Africa), which is reflected at the cytochrome b level (Seibold et al. 1993). These species form an unambiguous monophyletic clade (Figs. 1 & 2). In several reconstructions (Figs. 1a & 2) Red-footed Falcon *F. vespertinus* and its sibling species, the Amur Falcon *F. amurensis*, cluster as a sister group. Both species share many similarities with the Hobby group, including a mixed diet, Eurasian breeding and South African wintering quarters. Plumage patterns in this group show a light and/or a dark type, suggesting that the ancestor of this assemblage could have been a hybrid between a dark and a light falcon species.

Desert hierofalcons and peregrines

The Prairie Falcon *F. mexicanus*, which has been viewed as a member of the *Hierofalco* complex, always clusters at the base of the Hierofalco-Peregrine clade (Figs. 1 & 2) and cannot be regarded as a superspecies with *F. jugger* and *F. biarmicus* (del Hoyo et al. 1994). Distances between *F. mexicanus* and *Hierofalco* range between 6 and 9% nucleotide substitutions, indicating that the New World *F. mexicanus* has diverged about 3 to 5 million years ago from an Old World ancestor (assuming a molecular clock calibration of 2% sequence divergence = 1 million years; Wilson et al 1987; Tarr & Fleischer 1993).

F. peregrinus, of which more than 19 subspecies have been recognized (including the Barbary Falcon, *F. p. pelegrinoides*) (del Hoyo et al. 1994) does not show much haplotype variation (Figs. 1 & 2; see also Wink et al. this volume). Therefore, either *F. peregrinus* represents a young taxon or a taxon with frequent gene flow between subspecies.

Figure 2. Molecular phylogeny of the Falconidae reconstructed with the Maximum Likelihood method.

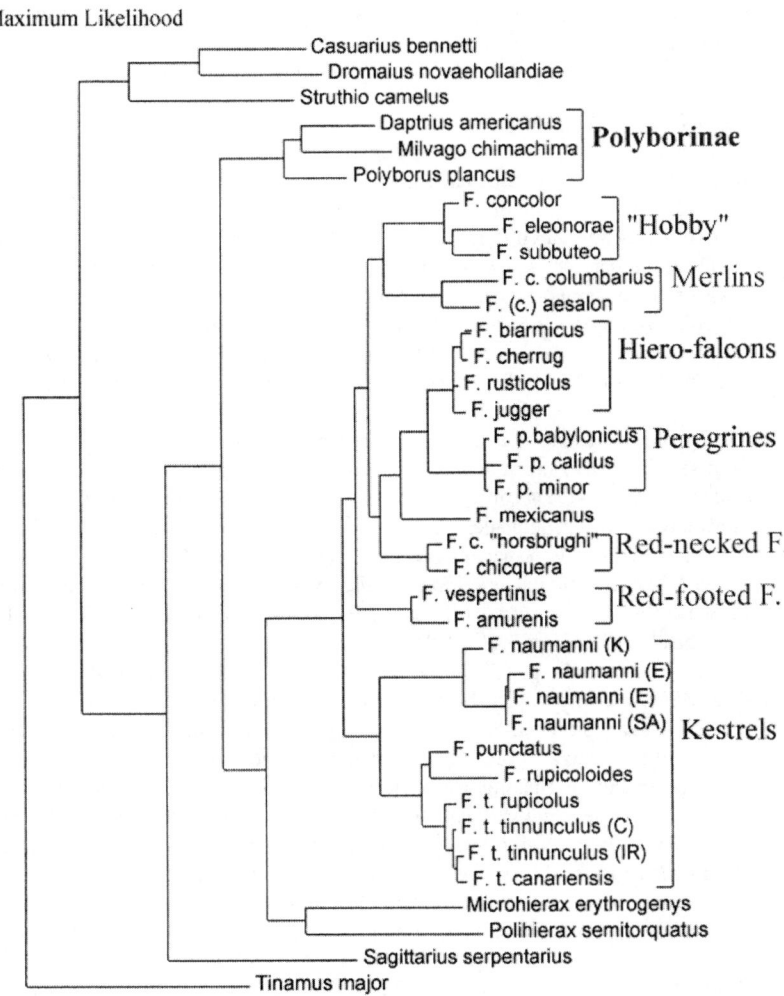

Branch lengths are proportional to evolutionary distances.

The *Hierofalco* desert falcon group, which includes *F. rusticolus*, *F. cherrug*, *F. jugger*, and *F. biarmicus*, appears as a closely related monophyletic complex of species with recent speciation. In previous studies (Seibold *et al.* 1993; Helbig *et al.* 1994; Wink & Seibold 1996; Wink *et al.* 1998) we had reported that the *Hierofalco* group formed a monophyletic complex which clustered at the base of the falcon tree. Meanwhile we discovered that a paralogous cytochrome b gene exists in this group and that our earlier data were based on the nuclear copy of the cytochrome b gene. The present position of the *Hierofalco* group, as a sister group to the Peregrine, appears more likely (Figs. 1 & 2).

Red-necked Falcon

The Red-necked Falcon *Falco chicquera* occurs in two parapatric populations in Pakistan/India (*F. c. chicquera*) and in Africa south of the Sahara (*F. c. ruficollis* and *F. c. horsbrughi*) (del Hoyo *et al.* 1994). Differences in distribution and morphology are also reflected at the cytochrome b level, in that *F. c. chicquera* and *F. c. 'horsbrughi'* (our samples derived from South Africa) differ by 1.8% nucleotide substitutions (equivalent to approximately 0.9 million years of divergence). It is unclear at the moment whether two subspecies occur in Africa (the description of *F. c. horsbrughi* was based on a single bird and has been questioned). In any case, differences in morphology, distribution and cytochrome b suggest that both taxa have reached species level already and might be treated as distinct species, as *F. chicquera* and *F. ruficollis* or *F. horsbrughi*, respectively.

ACCIPITRIDAE: *Haliaeetus*, *Milvus* and *Buteo*

Buzzards apparently form a monophyletic group with kites and sea-eagles (Fig. 1b). Phylogenetic relationships within the sea-eagle clade have already been published (Wink et al. 1996; Seibold & Helbig 1996), except for the position of the Madagascar Fish-eagle *H. vociferoides*. Because the plumage pattern of *H. vociferoides* differs substantially from that of the African Fish-eagle *H. vocifer*, but shows similarities to Sanford's Sea-eagle *H. sanfordi*, a relationship between both taxa appeared possible. However, *H. vociferoides* is clearly a sibling species of *H. vocifer* (Fig. 3). Thus Madagascar was probably colonized by an ancestor of *H. vocifer* about 2.5 million years ago, which became isolated and developed into *H. vociferoides*. Morphological similarities between *H. sanfordi* and *H. vociferoides* are probably due to the fact that these taxa shared a distant common ancestor (Figs. 1 & 3).

Kites of the genus *Milvus* are a closely related monophyletic group. The African Black Kite *M. m. parasitus* differs from the European and Australasian subspecies *M. m. migrans* by showing a yellow instead of a black beak. This difference is also reflected at the cytochrome b level (distances account for 1.6%). Because of geographic, morphological and genetic differences it would be plausible to treat African kites south of the Sahara as a distinct species (e.g., as *M. parasitus*, as suggested by some field guides). The Brahminy Kite *Haliastur indus*, which had been placed in the genus *Milvus*, is indeed the nearest relative of *Milvus* (distance 7%), so whether the genus *Haliastur* should be maintained is debatable (del Hoyo et al. 1994).

Old world members of the genus *Buteo* form a closely related monophyletic group in all reconstructions (Figs. 1 & 3). Branch lengths leading to the recognized species are very short, indicating that these taxa represent either a young group of raptors or that hybridisation between all of them has occured frequently. In other groups of raptors, such small differences were found in haplotypes of single species originating from different localities (see *Pandion, Hieraetus fasciatus, Falco peregrinus, Falco tinnunculus*). *Buteo oreophilus* from South Africa is almost identical to the Eurasian Buzzard *Buteo buteo*. Also *B. b. rothschildi* from the Azores cannot be distinguished from *B. buteo* of the mainland. In conclusion, species borders in *Buteo* cannot be confirmed by cytochrome b. Other molecular markers and a detailed morphological study is necessary to review the systematics of this genus which was always difficult because of strong plumage polymorphisms in the group.

Circus and *Accipiter*

Goshawks *Accipiter* usually cluster as a sister group to the monophyletic genus *Circus* (Figs. 1 & 3). Within species of the Marsh-harrier group, *C. aeruginosus* of Eurasia, *C. maillardi* of the Malagasy region, and *C. ranivorus* from South Africa, form a monophyletic group indicating the evolution from a common ancestor. *C. maillardi macrosceles* breeds on Madagascar and *C. m. maillardi* on Réunion. Because of geographic, morphological and genetic distances (3% divergence) both taxa have been considered to be distinct species (V. Bretagnolle, J.-C. Thibault pers. comm.). The Hen Harrier *C. cyaneus* and Pallid Harrier *C. macrourus* share close ancestry and both taxa share many similarities in plumage patterns. *C. c. cyaneus* of the Old World differs significantly (divergence 1.7%) from *C. c. hudsonius* of North America, suggesting that both taxa might be considered as distinct species (Wink et al. 1998). *C. pygargus* and *C. buffoni* are not in the *cyaneus* clade, as could have been expected on account of different plumage patterns.

Figure 3. Molecular phylogeny of the buzzards, sea-eagles, kites and harriers, reconstructed with the Maximum Likelihood method.

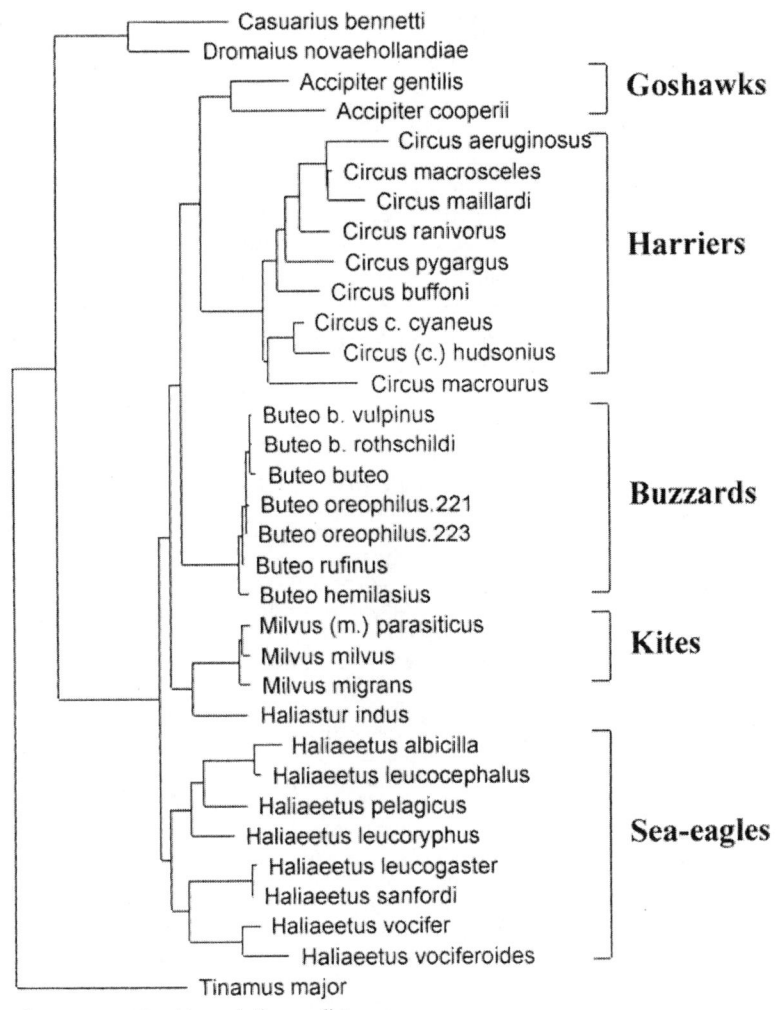

Branch lengths are proportional to evolutionary distances.

Old World Vultures

Within the group of Old world vultures two main evolutionary lineages are evident (Wink 1995; Wink & Seibold 1996; Wink *et al.* 1998; Seibold & Helbig 1995). One assemblage includes the Bearded Vulture *Gypaetus barbatus* and the Egyptian Vulture *Neophron percnopterus*. This clade shares many biological characters and is always positioned at the base of the Accipitridae cluster, indicating an evolutionarily old lineage of vultures. The Palm-nut Vulture *Gypohierax angolensis* of Africa had not yet been included in the molecular studies, but was always placed in the neighbourhood of *Gypaetus* and *Neophron*. Molecular data unambiguously confirm that *Gypohierax angolensis* is indeed a member of the *Gypaetus/Neophron* lineage (Figs. 1 & 4). The Honey Buzzard *Pernis apivorus* never clusters with buzzards but always at the base of the Accipitridae tree, close to or in the *Gypaetus/Neophron* clade.

A second lineage includes the genera *Necrosyrtes* and *Gyps* which form a monophyletic clade, with *Aegypius, Torgos, Trigonoceps* and *Sarcogyps* as a sister group (Figs. 1 & 4). The latter group is comprised of monotypic genera which, because it constitutes a monophyletic clade of species which share many morphological and behavioural characters, could be placed in a single genus. The name *Aegypius* has already been proposed for this assemblage (Mundy *et al.* 1992; del Hoyo *et al.* 1994).

Gyps rueppellii and *G. himalayensis* were not included in previous molecular analyses, but form a closely related monophyletic group with *G. coprotheres* and *G. fulvus* (Figs. 1 & 4). Its members have been considered as a superspecies (Sibley & Monroe 1990; del Hoyo *et al.* 1994). Distances in this group are small, as observed in the *Buteo* complex, suggesting that they either represent young species or a species complex which shows some past and present hybridisation. For *G. africanus* and *G. bengalensis*, which had been placed in the genus *Pseudogyps* (having 12 and not 14 rectrices), genetic data imply a close relatedness to *Gyps* and their consideration as part of a common genus *Gyps* (as proposed by Sibley & Monroe 1990; del Hoyo *et al.* 1994)

Figure 4. Molecular phylogeny of the vultures and booted eagles reconstructed with the Maximum Likelihood method.

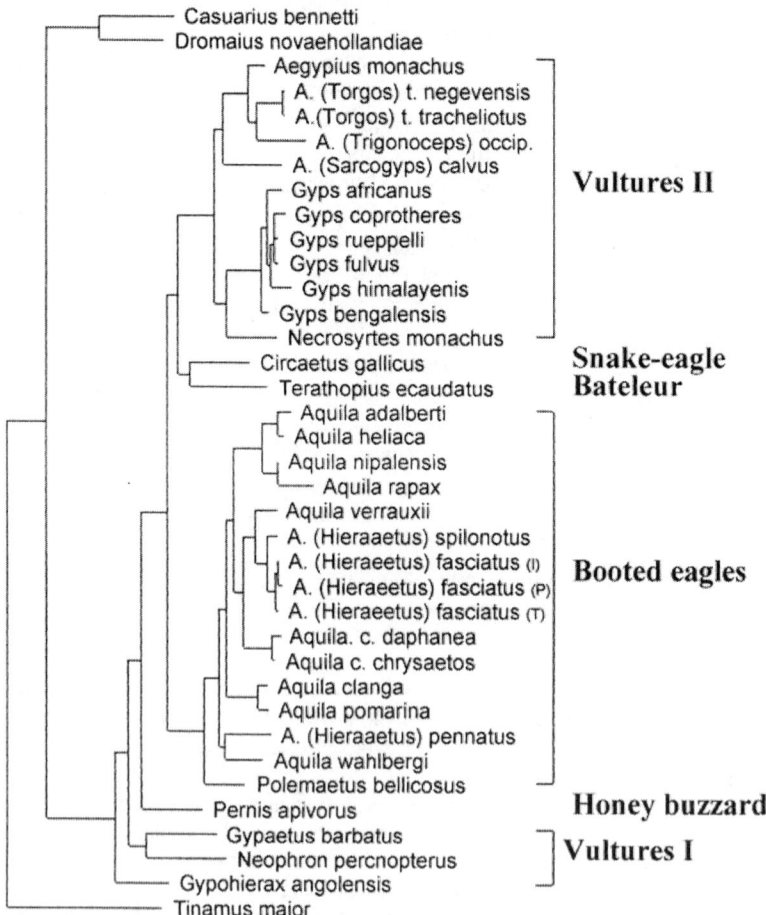

Branch lengths are proportional to evolutionary distances.

The example of Old World vultures clearly shows how convergent traits evolved in raptors; ecologically they are scavengers and evolved this 'profession' from different evolutionary origins. Therefore, vulture is an ecologically but not a systematically meaningful term.

Booted eagles and allies

Members of the genera *Aquila*, *Hieraaetus*, and *Polemaetus* share common ancestry (Figs. 1 & 4). This clade is apparently paraphyletic, indicating that the allocation of taxa to the genera *Aquila* and *Hieraaetus* does not reflect a phylogenetic sorting. Because *Hieraaetus* has been classified as a member of the genus *Aquila* before, the molecular data would support a merger of *Hieraaetus* into *Aquila*.

H. pennatus appears as a sibling species to *A. wahlbergi* (Figs. 1 & 4) and a relationship between both taxa has already been discussed, since the dark morph of *H. pennatus* is quite similar to *A. wahlbergi* (del Hoyo *et al*. 1994). *H. pennatus* breeds in Europe and Asia, but winters in Africa south of the Sahara (and in India) in the breeding grounds of *A. wahlbergi*. It could be argued that *A. wahlbergi* evolved from a dark morph of an ancestral *H. pennatus* that became resident in its winter quarters in Africa.

H. fasciatus (breeding in the Mediterranean and Asia) and *H. spilogaster* (breeding south of the Sahara) form sibling species (divergence 1.7%, Figs. 1 & 4). Morphological, geographical and genetical distances support the view to treat both taxa as distinct species (Sibley & Monroe 1990; del Hoyo *et al*. 1994). Within *H. fasciatus*, a low degree of haplotype differentiation can be seen (Cardia *et al*. this volume).

The relationships between *A. clanga*, *A. pomarina*, *A. rapax*, and *A. nipalensis*, and the recognition of *A. adalberti* as a distinct species from *A. heliaca* have been reported before (Seibold *et al*. 1996). In *A. chrysaetos* we had described two haplotypes; a new analysis clearly shows that both types can be allocated to the subspecies *A. c. chrysaetos* and *A. c. daphanea* (which breeds in East Asia) (Figs. 1 & 4).

The Short-Toed Snake-eagle *Circaetus gallicus* and the Bateleur *Terathopius ecaudatus* form a monophyletic clade in all reconstructions (Figs. 1 & 4); this clade is not obvious as far as plumage patterns are concerned, but food and feeding, and especially breeding, show some similarities in both taxa and a relationship has been proposed (Sibley & Monroe 1990). We need to include all members of the genus *Circaetus* to test whether the sister group relationship remains stable.

CONCLUSIONS

Molecular systematics of birds is still in its infancy (Mindell 1997) but will eventually provide a framework for the interpretation of anatomical, phylogeographic, and behavioural characters. Phylogenies which were reconstructed with the present data set support many relationships which had already been elaborated using detailed anatomical, morphological and behavioural data (summarized in del Hoyo *et al*. 1994). This fact shows that even a single mitochondrial gene can reconstruct phylogenetic relationships within a family with a high degree of reliability. Relationships between families are more difficult to resolve since the cytochrome b gene is at its limits under these conditions (Meyer 1994). In many instances the DNA helps to decide longstanding systematic questions, as to which genus a species might belong or if a given subspecies differing in distribution, size and morphology can be regarded as a distinct species. The latter distinction is not only important for systematics but also for conservation. The Spanish Imperial Eagle, for example, is a good species (Seibold *et al*. 1996) and as its numbers are down to 150 pairs, it becomes one of the rarest birds of prey, whereas the Eastern Imperial Eagle still comprises approximately 2000 pairs (del Hoyo *et al*. 1994). This means that conservation of *A. adalberti* gains highest priorities as a distinct species.

ACKNOWLEDGEMENTS

This work would not have been possible without the help of many ornithologists who provided blood and feather samples of raptors: Our thanks go to V. Bretagnolle, R. Simmons, W. Bednarek, C.

Fentzloff, B. Clark, H. Brünning, C. Fulquhar, M. Heidenreich, G. Ehlers, W. Scharlau, C. Kaatz, M. Pomarol, H. Prehn, P. Gaucher, R. Pfeffer, D. Schmidl, J. Thibault, O. Hatzofe, D. Bird, A. Kemp, C. Jones, M. Stubbe, B.-U. Meyburg, W. Grummt, C. König, J.J. Negro, D. Ristow, D. Peppler, B. Arroyo, B. Etheridge, H.H. Witt, B. Bed'hom, S. Ostrowski, D. Ellis, U. Höfle, R. Kenward, and N. Fox. The following co-workers have collaborated in the laboratory during earlier stages of this ongoing project: Dr. I. Seibold, Dr. A. Helbig, A. Krauthoff, Dr. P. Heidrich, H. Staudter, and F. Lotfikhah.

REFERENCES

AVISE, J.C. 1994. *Molecular markers, natural history and evolution.* Chapman and Hall, London.
AVISE, J.C., W.S. NELSON & C.G. SIBLEY 1994. DNA sequences support for a close phylogenetic relationship between some storks and New World vultures. *Proc. Natl. Acad. Sci.* 91: 5173-5177.
DEL HOYO, J., A. ELLIOTT & J. SARGATAL 1994. *Handbook of the birds of the world.* Vol. 2, Lynx Edicions, Barcelona.
FEDUCCIA, A. 1996. *The origin and evolution of birds.* Yale University Press, New Haven and London.
GRIFFITHS, C.S. 1997. Correlation of functional domains and rates of nucleotide substitution in cytochrome b. *Mol. Phylog. Evol.* 7: 352-365.
HELBIG, A.J., I. SEIBOLD, W. BEDNAREK, H. BRÜNING, P. GAUCHER, D. RISTOW, W. SCHARLAU, D. SCHMIDL & M. WINK 1994. Phylogenetic relationships among falcon species (genus *Falco*) according to DNA sequence variation of the cytochrome b gene. In: Meyburg, B.-U. & Chancellor, R.D. (eds.). *Raptor conservation today*, pp. 593-599. WWGBP & Pica Press, Berlin.
KUMAR, S., K. TAMURA & M. NEI 1997. *MEGA-Molecular Evolutionary Genetics Analysis.* Version 1.0. Pennsylvania State University.
MINDELL, D.P. 1997. *Avian molecular evolution and systematics.* Academic Press, San Diego.
MUNDY, P.J., D. BUTCHARD, J. LEDGER & S. PIPER 1992. *The vultures of Africa.* Academic Press, London.
NEI, M. 1996. Phylogenetic analysis in molecular evolutionary genetics. *Ann. Rev. Genet.* 30: 371-403.
SEIBOLD, I., A.J. HELBIG, B.-U. MEYBURG, J. NEGRO & M. WINK 1996. Genetic differentiation and molecular phylogeny of European *Aquila* eagles according to cytochrome b nucleotide sequences. In: Meyburg, B.-U. & Chancellor, R.D. (eds.) *Eagle studies*, pp. 1-15. WWGBP, Berlin, London & Paris.
SEIBOLD, I. 1994. Untersuchungen zur molekularen Phylogenie der Greifvögel anhand von DNA-Sequenzen des mitochondriellen Cytochrom b-Gens. Dissertation University Heidelberg, Hartung-Gorre Verlag, Konstanz.
SEIBOLD, I., A. HELBIG & M. WINK 1993. Molecular systematics of falcons (family Falconidae). *Naturwissenschaften* 80: 87-90.
SEIBOLD, I. & A.J. HELBIG 1996. Phylogenetic relationships of the sea eagles (genus *Haliaeetus*): Reconstructions based on morphology, allozymes and mitochondrial DNA sequences. *J. Zool. Syst. Evol. Res.* 34: 103-112.
SEIBOLD, I. & A.J. HELBIG 1995. Evolutionary history of New and Old World vultures inferred from nucleotide sequences of the mitochondrial cytochrome b gene. *Phil. Transact. Roy. Soc. Lond. Ser. B* 350: 163-178.
SIBLEY, G.C. & J.E. AHLQUIST 1990. *Phylogeny and classification of birds. A study in molecular evolution.* Yale University Press, New Haven.
SIBLEY, C.G. & B.L. MONROE 1990. *Distribution and taxonomy of birds of the world.* Yale University Press, New Haven.
SWOFFORD, D.L. 1998. *PAUP-Phylogenetic analysis using parsimony.* Version PAUP*.
TARR, C.L. & R.C. FLEISCHER 1993. Mitochondrial DNA variation and evolutionary relationships in the amakihi complex. *Auk* 110: 825-831.
WILSON, A.C., H. OCHMAN & E.M. PRAGER 1987. Molecular time scale for evolution. *Trends Genetics* 3: 241-247.
WINK, M. 1995. Phylogeny of Old and New World vultures (Aves: Accipitridae and Cathartidae) inferred from nucleotide sequences of the mitochondrial cytochrome b gene. *Z. Naturforsch.* 50c: 868-882.
WINK, M. 1998. Application of DNA-markers to study the ecology and evolution of raptors. In: Chancellor, R.D., Meyburg, B.-U. & Ferrero, J.J. (eds.) *Holarctic Birds of Prey.* pp. 49-71. Adenex & WWGBP, Berlin.
WINK, M., P. HEIDRICH & C. FENTZLOFF 1996. A mtDNA phylogeny of sea eagles (genus *Haliaeetus*) based on nucleotide sequences of the cytochrome b gene. *Biochem. Syst. Ecol.* 24: 783-791.

WINK, M. & I. SEIBOLD 1996. Molecular phylogeny of Mediterranean raptors (Families Accipitridae and Falconidae). In: Muntaner, J. & J. Mayol, (eds.). *Biology and Conservation of Mediterranean raptors, 1994.* SEO/BirdLife, Madrid; *Monografia* 4: 335-344.

WINK, M., I. SEIBOLD, F. LOTFIKHAH & W. BEDNAREK 1998. Molecular systematics of holarctic raptors (Order Falconiformes). In: Chancellor, R.D., Meyburg, B.-U. & Ferrero, J.J. (eds.). *Holarctic Birds of Prey*, pp. 29-48. Adenex & WWGBP, Berlin.

Prof. Dr. Michael Wink
Institut für Pharmazeutische Biologie
Im Neuenheimer Feld 364
D-69120 Heidelberg
Germany

Part 2

Biology & Conservation of the Vultures of the World

Vulturine Fish Eagle *Gypohierax angolensis*

Conveners:
Peter J. Mundy & Gerhard H. Verdoorn

Chancellor, R. D. & B.-U. Meyburg eds. 2000
Raptors at Risk
WWGBP / Hancock House

The Status of Vultures in Africa during the 1990s

P.J. Mundy

ABSTRACT

Since the last review on the vultures of Africa (1992), many new observations have been made. For example, more than 2000 Eurasian Griffons crossed the Straits of Gibraltar in autumn 1993; Rüppell's Griffons have been seen in Spain, Portugal, Zimbabwe and South Africa; a Cinereous Vulture (disputed) was seen north of Aswan (Egypt); some first-year Egyptian Vultures do migrate north in spring. Two major atlas projects, in Saudi Arabia (1995) and in southern Africa (1997), have considerably helped to define vultures' distributions. Several initiatives are underway to conserve the birds, particularly in South Africa (for example the reintroduction of the Egyptian Vulture, and liaison with Eskom, the electricity supply company), but also in Kenya with the Bearded Vulture. Poisons remain a major threat for vultures, and incidents of poisoning are still reported in southern Africa. Poisons and loss of habitat are implicated in the very parlous state of all vultures in Morocco. Indeed the whole of Arab Africa is something of a 'black hole' for the birds, and this situation needs urgent attention. Finally, there have been/are at least 21 human conflicts in Africa this decade, ranging from civil unrest to genocide. These must have affected the conservation status of vultures in the continent.

INTRODUCTION

Continental Africa supports, or has supported in the recent past, eleven species of vulture, and it is therefore the most vulture-rich of all the continents. The status and distribution of these birds, including comparative data on their foraging and feeding, and breeding, were recently reviewed in considerable detail (Mundy *et al.* 1992). Several questions and hypotheses were aired in that book, some of which are hopefully in the process of being answered or tested. While vulture-watching in the field remains a fairly popular pursuit, nevertheless it should be said that Africa in many areas remains a dangerous continent for ornithologists. Also its size and complexity mean that no one single person can visit more than a fraction of it, and therefore an understanding of vultures must be gained by proxy from the literature, as well as by using one's own observations and information. Fortunately, however, Africa is quite well covered by bird journals and newsletters.

In fact many interesting observations have been made since 1992. This paper aims to review these observations and the situation for vultures in general in Africa in the decade of the 1990s.

NEW OBSERVATIONS

Cape Griffon *Gyps coprotheres*

Monitoring and studies of this species continue apace. It was again sighted in southern Zambia (at Mazabuka) in May 1997, but no supporting details were listed (Demey 1998), and a juvenile was seen and photographed south of Chirundu in Zimbabwe in August 1993 (Stiles 1994). Parker (1997) confirmed the continued existence of a colony in southern Mozambique, though at the same time stating that the birds foraged mostly in Swaziland. Incredibly, a bird (not aged) was seen in a Cape Town suburb in August 1998 (T. Hardaker, SABirdNet). None of these sightings is shown on the Cape Griffon's map in the recent atlas (Mundy *et al*. 1997). However that map does emphasise the division of the vulture's range into four sub-populations, being (i) northern South Africa, eastern Botswana and southern Zimbabwe, (ii) south-eastern South Africa and Lesotho, (iii) south-western Cape, and (iv) northern Namibia. This fragmentation was already realised (Mundy *et al*. 1992:77; see also Piper 1993:88), but due to the bird's well known long flights (Scott 1991b, Oatley *et al*. 1998) it is not yet perceived as serious in terms of genetic isolation.

After detailed documentation and analysis, Piper (1993) determined that the Cape Griffon has 83 breeding colonies with a total of about 4400 breeding pairs. He estimated that the entire population of the species numbered about 12,000 birds, which made it the second vulture (after the California Condor *Gymnogyps californianus*) to be so censused. From an analysis of 'recoveries', i.e. dead ringed birds (about 600), and resightings (nearly 700), it seems that immatures find 'nursery' areas where they live temporarily, and these areas may shift in locality from year to year.

One 'recovery' was of a nestling ringed in 1975 and found electrocuted in June 1994 only 35 km away (Oatley 1994), for a longevity of nearly 19 years. To date, this is the record for the species. While it has been stated that "few birds have survived for 10 years or longer" (Oatley *et al*. 1998), some of this parlous state of affairs must be due to rings falling off the birds. Piper (1993:406) concluded that "there are no adequate estimates of survival for adult Cape Vultures" as yet, although a better model is at hand (Piper 1995).

Much monitoring of breeding pairs at colonies continues to be effected. These are particularly in the Magaliesberg, at Potberg in the south-western Cape, at the Botswana colonies, and at Wabai Hill in Zimbabwe (see province and country accounts in Boshoff *et al*. 1997). Stability or small increases are often being seen, but also decreases such as in the Eastern Cape.

Several major conservation initiatives are pursued in southern Africa, usually with the Cape Griffon foremost in mind. Supplementary feeding stations, or vulture 'restaurants', are still actively promoted, indeed such a scheme was written into the conservation plan of the Potberg colony. Over a nine-year period, 507 carcasses totalling nearly 18 tonnes in weight were supplied at the Potberg 'restaurant', though it was estimated that this mass comprised only 7%-16% of the colony's food requirements (Scott & Boshoff 1994). This 'restaurant' was shown to improve the survival rates of young griffons (Piper *et al*. in press). General advice on running vulture 'restaurants' has recently been published as a pamphlet (Scott & Anderson [1998]), and also in the farming press (Anderson & Scott 1996).

A second major initiative is the partnership between the South African supplier of electricity (Eskom) and the Endangered Wildlife Trust, in an effort to solve the problems of electrocution and collision (van Rooyen & Piper 1997). The system of mitigations will benefit all species that interact with powerlines, though the Cape Griffon is still a very frequent victim.

Incidents of poisoned and sick vultures, including Cape Griffons (Boshoff 1991, Scott 1994), still occur in the subcontinent, though "at a lower frequency" than earlier (Verdoorn 1997b). Organophosphates and carbamates are often implicated in these occurrences. For example in nine wild birds that showed some degree of paralysis, all had significantly lower cholinesterase levels in whole blood than did a control group (Wysoke *et al*. 1994). In addition blood samples taken from Cape Griffons (both wild nestlings and captive birds) had organochlorine residues, in some of which the levels could have caused eggshell thinning (Van Wyk *et al*. 1993). Since its inception in late 1991, the Poison Working Group of the Endangered Wildlife Trust has vigorously campaigned to reduce the non-target impact of poisons (Verdoorn 1997b).

And lastly, in terms of initiatives that benefit the Cape Griffon, a campaign is underway in South Africa to prevent drownings in circular farm reservoirs (Anderson [1996]).

In outdoor feeding trials of captive adult Cape Griffons, Komen (1992) determined that the average daily food intake was 497 g, and the assimilation efficiency was 86%. A single full crop of food should provide enough energy for three days. A large fat reserve in an adult in good body condition could maintain the bird for at least 20 days. Komen & Brown (1993) put many figures together to calculate that a family of Cape Griffons needed 524 kg meat per annum to survive. Its maximum food requirement of 1,98 kg per day (in the middle third of the nestling period) fell in September and early October, which coincided with peak mortalities of both wild ungulates and domestic livestock.

An alarming phenomenon being reported in recent years is that of the birds feeding or preying upon live domestic animals. Thus in the mid-1980s, Cape Griffons ate a stillborn calf and also some of the rear end of the cow (Pringle 1990). In 1996, birds were seen feeding on several live lambs (Scott 1997).

Rüppell's Griffon *Gyps rueppellii*

The most astounding aspect of this species in recent years is its incredible wanderings - and the fact that vulture watchers were there to see it. First, from 1989 to 1991, an adult atypical Cape Griffon was seen at the Potberg colony near Cape Town (34° 22'S), but its 'scaled' appearance suggested a Rüppell's Griffon (Scott 1991); it copulated with a Cape Griffon. Then in 1990 and 1992, single immature birds were seen at Wabai Hill in Zimbabwe at 20° 04'S (Mundy 1995), and in 1994 a Rüppell's Griffon was first seen at Blouberg at 29° 03'S (Snyman *et al*. 1994). In 1995 three Rüppell's Griffons were seen at Blouberg (Snyman & Snyman 1994), and one was later seen to copulate with a Cape Griffon. In 1997 an adult was seen at 18° 45'S in Zimbabwe (Mundy 1998), and also at the Kransberg colony at 24° 30'S in South Africa (Benson 1997). Meanwhile birds have been sighted in 1990-1992 in Spain at latitudes of about 37° and 39° 30'N (de Juana 1994), and again in 1993 at 36° N (de Juana 1995), and an immature was seen in Portugal in 1994 (Verdoorn 1994) at 38° 41'N. Most of these birds were photographed. A bird that was ringed in the Serengeti National Park was later found "in the middle of the Sudan" (D.C. Houston *in litt.*), a distance of about 1800 km from the place of ringing.

Small range extensions of the species are recorded in Sierra Leone (G.D. Field *in litt.*), northern (Clarke 1985) and southern (Douthwaite & Miskell 1991) Somalia, and in the Selous Game Reserve of southern Tanzania (Stronach 1993). Finally, "scores" of Rüppell's were seen with hundreds of other vultures at the Addis Ababa slaughter house in May 1995 (Allan 1995), behaviour that seems to be unusual in Africa by this species.

Eurasian Griffon *Gyps fulvus*

This species is a migrant into Africa from its breeding grounds in Europe, as well as a breeding bird in low numbers in north-west Africa. The furthest south it has been recorded is at Lake Langano (7° 35'N) in Ethiopia: two adults in late October (Vittery 1983).

It is termed "rare" in northern Niger (Newby *et al*. 1987), in fact only seen in May. An "exhausted" bird was found at the Red Sea coast in Egypt in 1997 (Demey 1998). However, on the other side of Africa, at Cap Blanc in Western Sahara/Mauritania, 50 Eurasian Griffons were seen in August 1995, and 16 in August 1996, mostly "juveniles and subadults" (Layna 1997). These dates suggest that the birds came from North Africa rather than the Iberian peninsula. Meanwhile, at the Straits of Gibraltar (actually east of Tarifa), an astounding 2,160 "mostly juvenile" Eurasian Griffons were observed crossing over to Morocco in only eight days of a 34-day period in mid-October to mid-November 1993 (Griesinger 1996). The birds used flapping flight, and needed up to 25 minutes to cross 15 km of open water. By the time they arrived in Morocco, the flocks were "at an altitude of less than 50 m above sea level"! Nevertheless, this huge number is only about one-third of the annual crop of juveniles in Spain (Griesinger 1996), and we are still left curious as to the whereabouts of 3,000 others.

African Whitebacked Vulture *Pseudogyps africanus*

Some range extensions have been noted for this species. A few are recorded in north-west Sierra Leone (G.D. Field *in litt.*), it is on the checklist for the Selous Game Reserve in southern Tanzania (Stronach 1993), and most surprisingly two young birds were seen in the Karoo region of South Africa at about 32° 30'S (Verdoorn 1995a). This last sighting is hundreds of kilometres south of its usual distribution. Other observations of interest include: "several hundred" at the Addis Ababa slaughter house in May 1995 (Allan 1995); a four-metre long Rock Python *Python sebae* was seen trying to swallow a juvenile vulture but failed (Verster 1992); another python was seen coming out of the water, catching a bird, and successfully swallowing it (W. Mullié pers. comm.); predation by Black-backed Jackals *Canis mesomelas* on vultures at a waterhole in the Kalahari Gemsbok National Park is a "regular occurrence" (Donaldson & Donaldson 1996); about 20 nests in a 'loose' colony on the western side of the Okavango Delta are all in Ebony trees *Diospyros mespiliformis*, which is a broad-leaved non-thorny species (J. Davey pers. comm.).

Poisonings and drownings still occur in southern Africa, and this species is a frequent victim. For example 64 birds were poisoned in one incident (Anderson 1995), and 38 drowned in another (Anderson *et al.* 1997). These vultures are also victims of electrocution (Anderson & Kruger 1995).

Hooded Vulture *Necrosyrtes monachus*

Range extensions for this species include eastern Guinea, where it is considered to be "common", and further south in that country (Halleux 1994). A juvenile was seen in north-west South Africa at about 500 km west of its usual range (Verdoorn *et al.* 1997).

This species, being commensal with humans, is easily attracted to slaughter houses. About 400 were seen at the one at Addis Ababa (Allan 1995), and about 500 at Kumasi in Ghana (pers. obs.). Also, "hundreds" roost in the grounds of the Nile Hotel in Kampala, where it is said "former dictators had countless people murdered and buried" (Butchart 1997a)! In Zimbabwe, Hooded Vultures are increasingly being seen on the highveld due to the increase in small abattoirs and accompanying offal dumps (Mundy 1997).

A longevity record for a vulture comes from this species - a juvenile ringed in May 1974 was recovered dead at a poisoned carcass in September 1995, in its 22nd year of life (Oatley 1996).

Lappetfaced Vulture *Torgos tracheliotos*

Some interesting information has been produced on this large and distinctive species. A few slight range extensions have been noted, particularly in Egypt: one bird at the southern tip of the Sinai peninsula (Kirwan 1993), for example, and a group of five seen in Gebel Elba in 1985 (Meininger 1996). The birds in this group were generally brown in colour, had dark bills, and their heads were pale and without conspicuous lappets, again emphasising the likelihood that these so-called *nubicus* birds are in a 'hybrid zone' (Mundy *et al.* 1992:153). More birds are being seen recently in the Kalahari region of northern South Africa, and indeed 57 were sighted at a 'restaurant' (Maritz 1998b), which is a modern-day record. In the same area, 27 nest sites have been discovered (Verdoorn 1997) when a few years ago few were known. Current estimates of the breeding population in the Kruger National Park are now up to 100 pairs (K. Herholdt pers. comm.), and in the Namib-Naukluft Park are at 72 pairs (P. Bridgeford pers. comm.). In this latter park, an amazing occurrence of two nestlings being reared together in one nest was found in 1991 (Bridgeford *et al.* 1995).

Recently an adult was seen one morning at 05h30 on a dead but still-warm White-tailed Mongoose *Ichneumia albicauda* in Zimbabwe (C. Stockil pers. comm.). In the northern Cape of South Africa in the long drought of the early 1980s, these vultures were several times seen to kill new-born lambs (A. Maritz pers. comm.).

The furthest known journey for a first-year bird was by one seen in southern Zambia at 1107 km from its place of ringing in South Africa (Oatley *et al.* 1998).

The worst poisoning incident of this species occurred in June 1995, adjacent to the Namib-Naukluft Park in west-central Namibia. By using a poison (carbofuran) on a dead donkey, a rancher managed to kill 86 Lappetfaced Vultures and eight Whitebacked Vultures (Simmons 1995). He had accused them of preying on his new-born Dorper lambs.

Cinereous Vulture *Aegypius monachus*

This species is still barely a member of the African avifauna. One bird was sighted north of Aswan in Egypt in December 1993 (Kirwan 1994), but this is considered to be a misidentification of a Lappetfaced Vulture (P.L. Meininger *in litt.*). In any case the Cinereous Vulture is an "extreme rarity" in Egypt (M. and S. Baha El Din *in litt.*). Birds were seen in the winters of 1987-1989 in Algeria (Bellatrèche 1994), but possibly not since (P. Isenmann and A. Moali *in litt.*).

Whiteheaded Vulture *Trigonoceps occipitalis*

This species attracts hardly any attention from observers. Very minor range extensions have been recorded such as in Burkina Faso (Balanca & de Visscher 1997) and in northern South Africa (Verdoorn 1995a). A sighting of "about twenty individuals seen soaring together over the carcass of an elephant on 6 Mar 1995" (Salewski 1997) in northern Ivory Coast is unique, and by far the largest flock seen in recent times; the Okavango Delta in Botswana is credited with a population of "200 pairs" (500 birds), or about one pair per 90 sq. km (Tyler & Bishop 1998). Both these statements seem barely credible to me.

Egyptian Vulture *Neophron percnopterus*

In recent years several sightings of both adult and immature birds have been made in South Africa and Botswana, to such an extent that there is a possibility of a breeding pair in this part of the subcontinent. Breeding is also thought possible in northern Namibia (Simmons & Bridgeford 1997). Elsewhere in Africa, breeding occurred in cliffs near to Lake Chad and in Cameroon (Scholte 1998). In Gambia, an immature was seen in June 1997 (Demey 1998). In December 1994, an estimated 1473 Egyptian Vultures were found roosting along a 75 km length of powerline in Ethiopia (Sigismondi & Politano 1996).

New information has been produced at migration points in the autumn (1) and spring (4), where birds were categorised as adults or immatures/juveniles (Table 1). In eight autumn counts, 1182 adults (75.6%) and 382 immatures (24.4%) were seen, and in five spring counts the numbers were >2124 (94.5%) and 124 (5.5%). These extra data produce the same conclusion as noted by Mundy *et al.* (1992:191), that very few immatures return to Europe in the spring. In a more comprehensive analysis, however, Yosef & Alon (1997) consider that immatures may return to Europe by a different route (Suez) than the one they took to get to Africa (Eilat). For young Egyptian Vultures, then, the questions remain as to what proportion stays or dies in Africa during the European winter and what proportion migrates back north; certainly more return north than originally supposed.

Table 1. Some autumn and spring migrations of Egyptian Vultures into and out of Africa.

Place	Date	Adults	Imms	Ref.
Gibraltar (Morocco)	26 Aug. - 5 Sep. 1995	209	49	(1)
Suez (Egypt)	25 Mar. -31 Mar. 1982	243	3	(3)
Suez	4 Mar. -29 May 1990	321	63	(2)
Eilat (Israel)	15 Feb. -19 May 1994	316	26	(5)
Bab-al-Mandab (Djibouti)	4 Mar. - 7 Mar. 1990	>731	4	(4)

(1) Franchimont & Moumni 1996; (2) Meininger & de Roder 1992; (3) Ullman 1985; (4) G. & H. Welch *in litt.*; (5) Yosef 1996.

A controversial aspect of the species is whether males and females show any sexual dimorphism in colour. Some years ago a photo of an Egyptian Vulture, taken by the Terrasse brothers, was labelled as an adult female by virtue of its yellow face (Jaubert 1989). It had a large black 'smudge' on its face. The male had been described as having a bright red face. This distinction between the sexes was later repeated by Davey (1994), and in good detail by Guyot & Ligor (1993-94). These latter authors saw this difference consistently in a dozen pairs - the male's face is orange-yellow and the female's is straw-yellow (and she is slightly larger than him). Unfortunately these authors made no mention of black smudges.

Meanwhile, in Israel, Levy (1990) found that among 13 pairs and one trio the male had a black 'smudge' on his face but the female did not. Some photos support this contention (Cloudsley-Thompson 1981:48), but others do not (Rodriguez 1992:116). More recently, Levy's discovery has been re-affirmed (Levy & Segev 1996) in spite of disagreement from Spanish workers (W.S. Clark *in litt.*). Very tellingly, however, a photo of a copulating pair in Tanzania (Butchart 1997b:43) shows the male with no smudge while the female has a smudge! In addition, the male's face is orange, hers is yellow. Although years ago I had examined skins of Egyptian Vultures in museums, regretfully I did not notice the presence/absence of these facial smudges, but Bill Clark (*in litt.*) determined on 20 specimens that presence or absence occurred in both sexes. Recently, through the courtesy of the Museo Nacional de Ciencias Naturales (Madrid), I examined skins of six adults and one subadult - all had black smudges; four were labelled as "females", three as sex unknown.

In summary, then, while slight sexual dimorphism does occur between the sexes - in intensity of facial colour, and in size - this is not linked to the presence or absence of black smudges on the face.

Bearded Vulture *Gypaetus barbatus*

Rather little has been noted in the last few years for this denizen of high mountains. In terms of altitude, however, an ossuary is known on Mount Kilimanjaro at 3800 m (Grimshaw 1995b), and a bird was seen there in 1998 at about 5000 m (J. Dale pers. comm.). In South Africa a search was done in July 1994, in the Drakensberg, which estimated 220 nesting pairs and 240-odd juveniles (Verdoorn 1995b), in fact a slight increase over an earlier estimate (Brown 1992). In the same area, at a vulture 'restaurant' at Nottingham Road in KwaZulu-Natal, 12 Bearded Vultures were seen together with 96 Cape Griffons (M. Glenny pers. comm.); unfortunately the date could not be remembered. These results may indicate an improved farmer awareness of scavengers. However, five birds are known to have been killed by poison collars and coyote getters in South Africa (Boshoff 1991, Colahan 1991). New food items for the species are giant rats (*Cricetomys gambianus* ?) and once a puppy dog (A.B. York *in litt.*), both on Mount Elgon in Kenya; and again in Kenya a large monitor lizard *Varanus* sp. (Brown 1963).

In the Balé mountains of Ethiopia, a nest was found at an altitude of 3950 m, which in March had two fully grown and feathered youngsters in it (Barrau *et al.*1997). This is the first observation of a brood of two. By back-dating, the clutch (normally of two eggs in this species) was laid in October.

The two characteristics for which Bearded Vultures are famous are, first, using red soils as a cosmetic to stain their otherwise white body and head plumage, and second, in their bone-breaking and bone-swallowing habits. Recent work has proved that the rufous colour of the bird's plumage comes from the external deposit of iron oxide which sticks to the ends of the feathers (Brown & Bruton 1991) . Also, it seems that the iron oxide is combined with a fine clay component (Houston *et al.* 1993). Recent work again has shown that Bearded Vultures have a digestive efficiency of 50% of a bone meal, with most being digested within 24 hours (Houston & Copsey 1994). The species is an atypical vulture in not having a crop. Its stomach cannot grind the bones, but does have a very high density of acid secreting cells.

Useful demographic data were obtained in the South African/Lesotho study (Brown 1997). Thus the annual survival rate of adults was 94%, and a bird once attaining adulthood had a further life expectancy of 21.4 years. Meanwhile the survival of young birds to sub-adulthood (at four years of age) was only 13%. These figures could probably well apply to healthy populations of other vulture species. Interestingly, the proportion of young birds sighted in an area increased as the density of adult birds decreased.

Palmnut Vulture *Gypohierax angolensis*

Some range extensions have been noted in north-east Central African Republic (Bretagnolle 1993), in the forests of the Sangha region in CAR and Congo (M. Fay and A. Turkalo pers. comm.), in southern Tanzania (Stronach 1993), in eastern Zimbabwe (Hustler & Irwin 1995, Jana 1995) where a new breeding record may have occurred (Tree 1998), and particularly in South Africa. Here vagrants have been seen in the eastern Transvaal (K. Herholdt pers. comm.), in the western Transvaal (Oberprieler 1998), and in the south-western Cape (McCall 1994, Robertson 1995). By contrast, the vulture was not seen along a 400 km length of coast in southern Mozambique (Parker 1995), due probably to severe habitat change.

Whereas the species is not generally gregarious (e.g. Butchart 1995), 18 birds (including five immatures) were once seen at a colony of River Martins *Pseudochelidon eurystomina* in Gabon (Alexander-Marrack 1994). It was suspected that the vultures were preying on nestlings of the martin. There have also been sightings of the bird scavenging on dead ungulates (Butchart 1997b, Medland 1993, Levy 1995, A. Turkalo *in litt*.), carrying food items in its talons (Harris *et al*. 1994), and even flying about on moonlit nights (Chittenden & Myburgh 1996).

Recently, detailed observations have been made at nests at Mtunzini in South Africa (Harris *et al*. 1994, Chittenden & Myburgh 1996), where there are now perhaps four breeding pairs. When in breeding condition, the upperwing coverts of the adults become rusty-brown; white coverts replace them in the non-breeding season. Slight differences were noted between partners: a female in one pair had a bright yellow eye, a reddish face, and a broad white edge to the tail, whereas the male had an amber eye, a pinkish face, and a narrow white edge to the tail (W. Goodwin pers. comm.). The incubation period for the egg was about 47 days, and both partners incubated. The period for nestlings was 90 days, and both parents fed the nestling. These nests were in palm trees, but one in Sierra Leone was "in a cleft of a cliff" (G.D. Field *in litt*.).

It is now said to be scarce in Liberia due to being shot for fun by hunters (Gore 1994).

General

Seeing six species of vulture at one carcass is very unusual. Such gatherings have been seen recently in Kenya in August (Levy 1995) and in Tanzania in July (Butchart 1997b). On both occasions the Palmnut Vulture was an attendant, which is itself most unusual. This African vulture assemblage has been subjected to functional analysis on skull and beak dimensions (Hertel 1994, 1995). Three feeding types were recognised - rippers, gulpers and scrappers - and three size classes.

Many phylogenetic analyses on the diurnal birds of prey (including vultures) have been done in recent years. They tell different stories! Various characters or elements have been used: morphometrics (Kemp & Crowe 1993), syrinx (Griffiths 1994), osteology (Holdaway 1994), chromosomes (Bed'Hom 1996), diverse including behaviour (Kemp & Crowe 1990), DNA hybridization (Sibley & Ahlquist 1990), genome DNA (Keyser *et al*. 1996), and mitochondrial cytochrome b (Avise *et al*. 1994, Siebold & Helbig 1995, Wink 1998). The most detailed of these studies as regards African vultures is that by Siebold & Helbig (1995). They stated, among other comments, that the Bearded and Egyptian Vultures are "much more primitive", there is a core group of vultures (subfamily Aegypiinae), and it was unclear to which genus the Hooded Vulture belongs.

INITIATIVES

Two major atlas projects, both of regional coverage, have appeared recently, with both defining bird distributions in hitherto new ways. That for the Arabian peninsula (Jennings 1995), strictly speaking outside Africa, nevertheless raises interesting points on the vultures in north-east Africa across the Red Sea. Four species live in Arabia. The Bearded Vulture and (probably) the Lappetfaced Vulture occur on both sides of the Red Sea (part of the Rift Valley) but as different subspecies. There is considerable doubt as to whether the Rüppell's Griffon ever actually occurred in Arabia. Both the Eurasian Griffon and Egyptian Vulture are "widespread resident[s]"; the former is an uncommon bird in north-east Africa, the latter is a common migrant, but it is not known if Arabian vultures themselves migrate to Africa. At the opposite end of the continent, nine species of vulture were sighted in southern Africa during the atlas period (Harrison *et al*. 1997). Breeding localities were not mapped, but months of breeding are shown in graphs. These are not entirely satisfactory due to the vultures' long breeding cycle. Both atlases are sterling efforts by the local bird-watching communities, but they suffer from having no data on numbers and ages. The southern African atlas dealt with the issue of numbers to some extent by employing a "reporting rate", so that the maps show areas of frequent reporting (=high density ?). Atlas projects are in operation elsewhere in Africa.

Vultures migrate into and out of Africa at four main 'gates' - Straits of Gibraltar, Sicily/Cap Bon, Suez and Eilat, and Bab-al-Mandab - and it is regrettable that comprehensive counts in both seasons, the northern autumn and spring, for all points have not yet been attempted. Admittedly it is much easier said than done! But interest in migrating raptors is still at hand, for example in Spain (Griesinger 1996, 1998) and Morocco (Franchimont & Moumni 1996), at the straits of Messina (Giordano *et al.* 1998), and at Eilat (Yosef & Alon 1997). I look forward to the year when raptor biologists are able to link up and "conduct coordinated surveys at all major migratory flyways around the Mediterranean basin and in the Middle East" (Yosef & Alon 1997).

To my knowledge, in subSaharan Africa, the only countries where vulture-focused initiatives or conservation actions are in progress, are Kenya and South Africa (and neighbouring Botswana and Zimbabwe). In Kenya the Bearded Vulture has long disappeared from Hell's Gate (Thomsett 1993a), last seen in 1984 with an isolated sighting in 1987 (Henderson 1997), and also from Mount Kenya since 1990 (S. Thomsett *in litt.*). It is planned (and permitted) to take six second-hatchlings, i.e. 'Abel' chicks, from the Balé mountains in Ethiopia, where the species is common. Unfortunately, poisoning of carnivores and vultures is considered to be common in Kenya, and has led to marked reductions in the vulture populations. This was recently emphasised again by the poisoning of Egyptian Vultures around Hell's Gate National Park "by Masai cattle herders" (Anon. 1998). Also within this park, the breeding Rüppell's Griffons have declined "very significantly" (Thomsett 1993b). Road surveys in early 1990 both in the Nairobi National Park and settled areas outside showed that vultures were much more common inside the park than outside it (Sorley & Andersen 1994).

Meanwhile in South Africa and Zimbabwe the environment for vultures is very much more friendly now than it was one or two decades ago. This happy state of affairs can be attributed to the activities of the Vulture Study Group, Raptor Conservation Group, and Poison Working Group (all under the auspices of the Endangered Wildlife Trust) and their colleagues in the nature conservation departments, and to the positive response shown by the land owners, Eskom, pesticide companies, and others. Several initiatives have already been mentioned under the Cape Griffon above. In addition efforts have been underway for some years on bringing back the Egyptian Vulture to South Africa (Verdoorn 1998), although somewhat overtaken by appearances of wild birds. Interest and actions regarding vultures in southern Africa as a whole were described at length at the 1997 Kimberley workshop (Boshoff *et al.* 1997).

While vultures can in theory find a safe haven inside national parks and game reserves, they will of course also fly to 'unprotected' areas outside. Here is the true field of vulture conservationists, in trying to change people's attitudes from negative to positive, so that the birds (and much else under their wing beats) can survive and flourish in the greater environment. Notable examples in South Africa are the farming communities around the Potberg colony (H.A. Scott pers. comm.) and in the Kalahari (Maritz 1998a). In Zimbabwe, the removal of some monopolies in the new liberalised economy has allowed many local abattoirs to appear - with advantages to vultures.

The South African experience points to three 'simple' messages:

(i) Land owners have consciences but these have to be awakened or enlightened as to the specific plight of vultures (and 'problem' animals generally) by active conservationists. Without the latter, the former is unlikely to happen.

(ii) The conservationists must have the data at their finger-tips, i.e. research results and monitoring are the essential starting points.

(iii) Debate, cooperation and compromise are likely to be more productive than confrontation. The EWT, for example, enters into "conservation partnerships" with key sectors.

THREATENED POPULATIONS

Where there are no bird watchers, there is no information. On this basis the current status of vultures in many countries of Africa is not known. Partly this is due to the fact that in the 1990s Africa is suffering yet another turbulent period. In these few years there have been at least 21 conflicts, from civil unrest (South Africa) to genocide (Burundi and Rwanda); some are still ongoing. Eritrea has been formed as a new country from Ethiopia; Somaliland is similarly trying to break away from Somalia; southern Sudan may achieve the same one day from the Khartoum regime; and Western Sahara is still dominated by Morocco. Bird watching and vulture study in such areas in Africa can be difficult to the point of dangerous, to say the least.

North (Arab) Africa is a region of great concern to vulture/raptor conservationists. In Morocco the Cinereous and Lappetfaced Vultures are extinct, and the Eurasian Griffon and Bearded Vulture could soon follow them (Franchimont & Sayad 1993). The vultures have been described as "really endangered" (Haddane 1996), they have suffered a "dramatic decline" (P. Bergier *in litt.*), and the situation "est plus qu'alarmante" (J. Franchimont and A. El Ghazi *in litt.*)! Indeed, it is thought that the Eurasian Griffon ceased to breed altogether after 1987 (P. Bergier *in litt.*). The annual reports of the Groupe d'Ornithologie du Maroc Central, published in *Porphyrio*, list few sightings of the three main species. Poisons against carnivores is likely to be the major cause, but also disturbance from increased human populations. Given the large numbers of Eurasian Griffons and Egyptian Vultures that cross to Morocco from Spain (and France and Portugal), then possibly these birds too are at serious risk of being poisoned, presuming that they do feed along their migration route. This must surely be of interest to the Bonn Convention?

Off the west coast of Morocco and Western Sahara, the Canary Islands offer no better home to the Egyptian Vulture, it seems. In this archipelago the species is sedentary, but is in decline (Blanco & Gonzalez 1992).

The situation is better in Algeria, but there are no known details as to threats (P. Isenmann *in litt.*). Indeed, in the Kabylie region in the north, three species are surviving well, even increasing; these are the Eurasian Griffon and Egyptian and Bearded Vultures (Moali & Gaci 1992). Of the other two species on record for Algeria, there are no recent sightings of the Lappetfaced Vulture but a few of the Cinereous a decade ago (P. Isenmann *in litt.*).

I have no recent information for Tunisia, but Levy (1996) quotes D. Boukhalfa to the effect that "Egyptian Vultures are very common in Tunisia during the migration seasons." But what about the local breeding birds?

What little news there is from Libya is alarming. A report from J. Svehlik in the mid-1980s stated that "everything that moves is shot at" (Meyburg 1986), and in a 30-month period he saw no vultures.

In Egypt, declines are thought to have occurred in Egyptian, Lappetfaced and Bearded Vultures during the last 10-15 years (M. and S. Baha El Din *in litt.*). There are no recent sightings of the Rüppell's Griffon and Cinereous Vulture, and perhaps they should not be expected. A sighting of the latter north of Aswan is considered to have been more likely a Lappetfaced Vulture (P.L. Meininger *in litt.*). Interestingly, M. Baha El Din remarks that Lappetfaced Vultures follow the camel trains that come through the desert from Sudan, and feed on any carcasses.

In summary then, the story varies among the countries of the Maghreb but overall the populations of vultures are in rather a bad way, being vulnerable in places to poisons, shooting, disturbance, effects of deforestation and over-grazing. They are most at risk in Morocco. This is doubly unfortunate because it is likely to affect the migrant populations from western Europe. Some positive conservation effort for vultures is desperately needed in Morocco and probably throughout the Maghreb, including the Canary Islands.

CONCLUSIONS

The document produced in southern Africa (Boshoff *et al.* 1997) is a 'position statement' on the vultures of that region. So far it is a unique document in Africa, and possibly in the world. It could be produced because of the historical and on-going connections among the countries of the subcontinent. This is the factor lacking elsewhere in Africa. Perhaps the South should reverse the North-South aid flow and initiate projects in the rest of Africa! Vulture numbers, breeding sites, food supply, utilisation and disturbance by humans, are aspects of interest everywhere and all could be easily studied with a minimum of equipment - and a dash of bravery. I therefore look forward to the activities of the new generation of vulture-conservationists in the 21st century, in monitoring, documenting, and improving the status of vultures in Africa.

ACKNOWLEDGEMENTS

I thank several persons who kindly supplied information when answering my queries. They are Mindy and Sherif Baha El Din, Patrick Bergier, Ahmed El Ghazi, J. Franchimont, Paul Isenmann, Peter Meininger, and Simon Thomsett. The Vulture Study Group kindly made arrangements for my attendance at the world conference. I thank Mark Anderson, André Boshoff and Gerhard Verdoorn for criticising a draft of this paper.

REFERENCES

ALEXANDER-MARRACK, P. 1994. Notes on a breeding colony of the African River Martin *Pseudochelidon eurystomina* in Gabon. *Malimbus* 16: 1-9.
ALLAN, D. 1995. Raptor rapture in Ethiopia. *Bird Numbers* 4: 28-31.
ANDERSON, M.D. 1995. Mortality of African Whitebacked Vultures in the North- West Province, South Africa. *Vulture News* 33: 10-13.
ANDERSON, M.D. [1996]. *Birds of prey and farm reservoirs.* [pamphlet]. Janssen Animal Health, Johannesburg.
ANDERSON, M.D. & KRUGER, R. 1995. Powerline electrocution of eighteen African Whitebacked Vultures. *Vulture News* 32: 16-18.
ANDERSON, M.D., MARITZ, A.W.A. & OOSTHUYSEN, E. 1997. Vultures drowning in farm reservoirs. Pages 98-101. *In*: A.F. Boshoff *et al.*, *op. cit.*
ANDERSON, M. & SCOTT, A. 1996. Skep 'n aasvoël-'restaurant'. *Landbouweekblad* 23rd August: 34-37.
ANON, 1998. Pan Africa conservation program. *Peregrine Fund 1997 Annual Report*: 16.
AVISE, J.C., NELSON, W.S. & SIBLEY, C.G. 1994. DNA sequence support for a close phylogenetic relationship between some storks and New World vultures. *Proc. Natl Acad. Sci.* 91: 5173-5177.
BALANCA, G. & DE VISSCHER, M.-N. 1997. Composition et évolution saisonnière d'un peuplement d'oiseaux au nord du Burkina Faso (nord-Yatenga). *Malimbus* 19: 68-94.
BARRAU, C., CLOUET, M. & GOAR, J.L. 1997. Deux jeunes Gypaètes barbus *Gypaetus barbatus meridionalis* à l'envol dans une aire des Monts du Balé (Ethiopie). *Alauda* 65: 200-201.
BED'HOM, B. 1996. Phylogenetic and evolutionary consequences of the atypical karyotype of Accipitridae. Page 136. *In*: M. Pandolfi (Ed.) *Abstracts 2nd Int. Conf. Raptors*. RRF and University of Urbino (Italy).
BELLATRECHE, M. 1994. Données nouvelles sur l'avifaune algérienne. *Alauda* 62: 136-138.
BENSON, P.C. 1997. Status of vultures in the Northern Province, South Africa. Pages 21-29. *In*: A.F. Boshoff *et al.*, *op. cit.*
BLANCO, J.C. & GONZALEZ, J.L. (eds) 1992. *Libro rojo de los vertebrados de España*. ICONA Col. Tec., Madrid.
BOSHOFF, A.F. 1991. Poison collar kills vultures in the north-eastern Cape Province. *Vulture News* 25: 15-16.
BOSHOFF, A.F., ANDERSON, M.D. & BORELLO, W.D. (eds) 1997. *Vultures in the 21st century*. Vulture Study Group, Johannesburg.
BRETAGNOLLE, F. 1993. An annotated checklist of birds of north-eastern Central African Republic. *Malimbus* 15: 6-16.
BRIDGEFORD, P.A., BRIDGEFORD, M. & ERASMUS, J. 1995. First record of two Lappetfaced Vulture chicks reared in one nest. *Ostrich* 66: 35-37.
BROWN, C.J. 1992. Distribution and status of the Bearded Vulture *Gypaetus barbatus* in southern Africa. *Ostrich* 62: 1-9.
BROWN, C.J. 1997. Population dynamics of the bearded vulture *Gypaetus barbatus* in southern Africa. *Afr. J. Ecology* 35: 53-63.
BROWN, C.J. & BRUTON, A.G. 1991. Plumage colour and feather structure of the bearded vulture (*Gypaetus barbatus*). *J. Zool., Lond.* 223: 627-640.

BROWN, G.H.H. 1963. Habits of the Lammergeyer. *J. E. Afr. Nat. Hist. Soc. Coryndon Mus.* 24 (no. 106): 72-73.
BUTCHART, D. 1995. Some observations on the Palmnut Vulture in Gabon, Central Africa. *Vulture News* 32: 19-22.
BUTCHART, D. 1997a. Silverbills and Shoebills. *Africa-Birds & Birding* 2(2): 24-30.
BUTCHART, D. 1997b. Northern Tanzania. A bounty of birding. *Africa-Birds & Birding* 2(5): 37-43.
CHITTENDEN, H. & MYBURGH, N. 1996. Vultures in the village. Mtunzini's Palmnut Vultures. *Africa-Birds & Birding* 1(1): 20-27.
CLARKE, G. 1985. Bird observations from northwest Somalia. *Scopus* 9: 24-42.
CLOUDSLEY-THOMPSON, J. 1981. *Vultures.* Wayland, Hove (England).
COLAHAN, B.D. 1991. Bearded Vultures killed with coyote getters (R) in the eastern Orange Free State, South Africa. *Vulture News* 25: 13-14.
DAVEY, P. 1994. Egyptian Vulture *Neophron percnopterus* behaviour. *Scopus* 18: 62.
DE JUANA A., E. 1994. Observaciones homologadas de aves raras en España y Portugal. Informe de 1992. *Ardeola* 41: 103-117.
DE JUANA A., E. 1995. Observaciones homologadas de aves raras en España y Portugal. Informe de 1993. *Ardeola* 42: 97-113.
DEMEY, R. 1998. Recent reports. *Bull. Afr. Bird Club* 5: 69-75.
DONALDSON, P. & DONALDSON, E. 1996. To: I-Spy. *Gyps Snips* November: 4.
DOUTHWAITE, R.J. & MISKELL, J.E. 1991. Additions to *Birds of Somalia, their habitat, status and distribution* (Ash & Miskell 1983). *Scopus* 14: 37-60.
FRANCHIMONT, J. & MOUMNI, T. 1996. Suivi partie de la migration post- nuptiale des rapaces diurnes sur la rive sud du Détroit de Gibraltar en 1995. *Porphyrio* 8: 55-76.
FRANCHIMONT, J. & SAYAD, A. 1993. Création d'une association marocaine d'ornithologie. *Proc. Pan-Afr. Ornithol. Congr.* 8: 265-270.
GIORDANO, A., RICCIARDI, D., CANDIANO, G., CELESTI, S. & IRRERA, A. 1998. Anti-poaching on the Straits of Messina: results after 15 years of activities. Pages 623-630. *In*: R.D. Chancellor, B.-U. Meyburg & J.J. Ferrero (Eds.) *Holarctic birds of prey.* WWGBP and Adenex, Berlin and Mérida.
GORE, M.E.J. 1994. Bird records from Liberia. *Malimbus* 16: 74-87.
GRIESINGER, J. 1996. Autumn migration of Griffon Vultures (*Gyps f. fulvus*) in Spain. Pages 401-410. *In*: J. Muntaner & J. Mayol (Eds.) *Biología y conservación de las rapaces Mediterráneas, 1994.* SEO/BirdLife Monogr. nr 4, Madrid.
GRIESINGER, J. 1998. Juvenile dispersion and migration among Griffon Vultures *Gyps fulvus* in Spain. Pages 613-621. *In*: R.D. Chancellor, B.-U. Meyburg & J.J. Ferrero (Eds.) *Holarctic birds of prey.* WWGBP and Adenex, Berlin and Mérida.
GRIFFITHS, C.S. 1994. Monophyly of the Falconiformes based on syringeal morphology. *Auk* 111: 787-805.
GRIMSHAW, J.M. 1995. Birds of prey and owls of the western and northern slopes of Mt Kilimanjaro, Tanzania. *Scopus* 19: 27-37.
GUYOT, A. & LIGOR, J.-L. 1993-94. Un élément de dimorphisme chez le Vautour percnoptère (*Neophron percnopterus*). *Nos Oiseaux* 42: 40.
HADDANE, B. 1996. The impact of human activities and rehabilitation of raptors: case study: current situation of raptors in Morocco. Page 111. *In*: M. Pandolfi (Ed.) *Abstracts 2nd Int. Conf. Raptors.* RRF and University of Urbino (Italy).
HALLEUX, D. 1994. Annotated bird list of Macenta Prefecture, Guinea. *Malimbus* 16: 10-29.
HARRIS, D., HARRIS, J., HARRIS, C. & GOODWIN, W. 1994. Observations on the Palmnut Vulture in South Africa. *Birding in SA* 46: 73-78.
HARRISON, J.A., ALLAN, D.G., UNDERHILL, L.G., HERREMANS, M., TREE, A.J., PARKER, V. & BROWN, C.J. 1997. *The atlas of southern African birds*, vol. 1. BirdLife South Africa, Johannesburg.
HENDERSON, I. 1997. The last record of Lammergeier in Hell's Gate ? *Kenya Birds* 5: 84-85.
HERTEL, F. 1994. Diversity in body size and feeding morphology within past and present vulture assemblages. *Ecology* 75: 1074-1084.
HERTEL, F. 1995. Ecomorphological indicators of feeding behavior in recent and fossil raptors. *Auk* 112: 890-903.
HOLDAWAY, R.N. 1994. An exploratory phylogenetic analysis of the genera of the Accipitridae, with notes on the biogeography of the family. Pages 601-649. *In*: B.-U. Meyburg & R.D. Chancellor (Eds.) *Raptor conservation today.* WWGBP, Berlin/Pica Press.
HOUSTON, D.C. & COPSEY, J.A. 1994. Bone digestion and intestinal morphology of the Bearded Vulture. *J. Raptor Research* 28: 73-78.

HOUSTON, D.C., HALL, A. & FREY, H. 1993. The characteristics of the cosmetic soils used by Bearded Vultures *Gypaetus barbatus. Bull. B.O.C.* 113: 260-263.
HUSTLER, K. & IRWIN, M.P.S. 1995. Fifth report of the OAZ rarities committee. *Honeyguide* 41: 103-106.
JANA, A. 1995. Palmnut Vultures in the Honde valley. *Honeyguide* 41: 109.
JAUBERT, J.-P. 1989. Le vautour fauve. *Bibliothèque de Travail* 1009: 24.
JENNINGS, M.C. 1995. *An interim atlas of the breeding birds of Arabia.* Natl Comm. Wildl. Conserv. Developm., Riyadh.
KEMP, A.C. & CROWE, T.M. 1990. A preliminary phylogenetic and biogeographic analysis of the genera of diurnal raptors. Pages 161-175. *In*: G. Peters & R. Hutterer (Eds.) *Vertebrates in the tropics.* Museum Alexander Koenig, Bonn.
KEMP, A.C. & CROWE, T.M. 1993. Morphometrics of African diurnal raptors. *Proc. Pan-Afr. Ornithol. Congr.* 8: 83-94.
KEYSER, C., MONTAGNON, D., SCHLEE, M., LUDES, B., PFITZINGER, H. & MANGIN, P. 1996. First isolation of tandemly repeated DNA sequences in New World vultures and phylogenetic implications. *Genome* 39: 31-39.
KIRWAN, G. 1993. Around the region. *OSME Bull.* 31: 39-46.
KIRWAN, G. 1994. Around the region. *OSME Bull.* 32: 43-48.
KOMEN, J. 1992. Energy requirements of adult Cape Vultures (*Gyps coprotheres*). *J. Raptor Research* 26: 213-218.
KOMEN, J. & BROWN, C.J. 1993. Food requirements and the timing of breeding of a Cape Vulture colony. *Ostrich* 64: 86-92.
LAYNA, J.F. 1997. Eurasian Griffons *Gyps fulvus* migrating into Cap Blanc, Mauritania, Western Sahara. *Vulture News* 36: 35-36.
LEVY, N. 1990. Biology, population dynamics and ecology of the Egyptian Vultures, *Neophron percnopterus*, in Israel. English summary, 27pp. M.Sc. thesis, Tel-Aviv University.
LEVY, N. 1995. Six species of vulture seen together in Kenya. *Vulture News* 32: 26.
LEVY, N. 1996. Present status, distribution and conservation trends of the Egyptian Vulture (*Neophron percnopterus*) in the Mediterranean countries and adjacent arid regions. Pages13-33. *In*: J. Muntaner & J. Mayol (Eds.) *Biología y conservación de las rapaces Mediterráneas, 1994.* SEO/Bird Life Monogr. nr. 4, Madrid.
LEVY, N. & SEGEV, H. 1996. Reproductive biology, courtship behaviour and status of the Egyptian Vulture *Neophron percnopterus* in Israel. Pages 415-424. *In*: J. Muntaner & J. Mayol (Eds.) *Biología y conservación de las rapaces Mediterráneas, 1994.* SEO/BirdLife Monogr. nr 4, Madrid.
MARITZ, A. 1998a. *Kalahari Raptor Project status report* [pamphlet]. Raptor Conservation Group and S.A. Eagle Insurance, Johannesburg.
MARITZ, A. 1998b. Interesting observations. Lappetfaced Vultures. *Vulture News* 39:53.
McCALL, M. 1994. Palmnut Vulture sighting. *Promerops* 214: 8.
MEDLAND, R.D. (ed.). 1993. Flora and fauna records. *Nyala*16: 77-90.
MEININGER, P.L. 1996. From the verge of the western Palearctic: birds of Gebel Elba area, Egypt. *Dutch Birding* 18: 285-292.
MEININGER, P.L. & DE RODER, F.E. 1992. The migration of birds of prey at Suez, spring 1990. *Courser* 3: 23-34.
MEYBURG, B.-U. 1986. Some observations on raptors in Libya. *Newsletter WWGBP* 4: 14.
MOALI, A. & GACI, B. 1992. Les rapaces diurnes nicheurs en Kabylie (Algérie). *Alauda* 60: 164-169.
MUNDY, P.J. 1995. Rüppell's Griffons in Zimbabwe. *Honeyguide* 41: 218-221.
MUNDY, P.J. 1997. Vultures in Zimbabwe. Pages 76-81. *In*: A.F. Boshoff *et al., op. cit.*
MUNDY, P.J. 1998. Rüppell's Griffon in Zimbabwe - a third time. *Honeyguide* 44: 23-24.
MUNDY, P.J., BENSON, P.C. & ALLAN, D.G. 1997. Cape Vulture. Pages 158-159. *In*: J.A. Harrison *et al., op. cit.*
MUNDY, P., BUTCHART, D., LEDGER, J. & PIPER, S. 1992. *The vultures of Africa.* Acorn Books and Russel Friedman Books, Randburg and Halfway House (South Africa).
NEWBY, J., GRETTENBERGER, J. & WATKINS, J. 1987. The birds of the northern Air, Niger. *Malimbus* 9: 4-16.
OATLEY, T.B. 1994. Selected recoveries from SAFRING: January 1994-June 1994. *Safring News* 23: 95-102.
OATLEY, T. 1996. Revelations from bird ringing. *Bird Numbers* 6: 16-17.
OATLEY, T.B., OSCHADLEUS, H.D., NAVARRO, R.A. & UNDERHILL, L.G. 1998. *Review of ring recoveries of birds of prey in southern Africa: 1948-1998.* Endangered Wildlife Trust, Johannesburg.
OBERPRIELER, O. 1998. Palmnut Vulture in the dry west. *Gyps Snips* July:4.
PARKER, V. 1995. The current status of some birds of prey in southern Mozambique. *J. Afr. Raptor Biology* 10: 2-3.

PARKER, V. 1997. The status of vultures in Swaziland and Mozambique. Pages 90-92. *In*: A.F. Boshoff *et al.*, *op. cit.*
PIPER, S.E. 1993. *Mathematical demography of the Cape Vulture*. Unpubl. Ph.D. thesis, University of Cape Town.
PIPER, S.E. 1995. A model of the ring-recovery reporting process for the Cape Griffon *Gyps coprotheres*. *J. Appl. Statistics* 22: 641-659.
PIPER, S.E., BOSHOFF, A.F. & SCOTT, H.A. in press. Modelling survival rates in the Cape Griffon *Gyps coprotheres*, with emphasis on the effects of supplementary feeding. *Bird Study*.
PRINGLE, A. 1990. Cape Vultures feeding on a live cow. *Witwatersrand Bird Club News* 150: 10.
ROBERTSON, I. 1995. Recent reports. *Bull. Afr. Bird Club* 2: 61-64.
RODRIGUEZ, J.L. 1992. *Monfragüe, sierra brava*. Fondo Natural, Madrid.
SALEWSKI, V. 1997. Notes on some bird species from Comoé National Park, Ivory Coast. *Malimbus* 19: 61-67.
SCHOLTE, P. 1998. Status of vultures in the Lake Chad Basin, with special reference to northern Cameroon and western Chad. *Vulture News* 39: 3-19.
SCOTT, H.A. 1991a. Atypical griffon at Potberg Cape Griffon colony in the De Hoop Nature Reserve, south-western Cape. *Vulture News* 25: 10-11.
SCOTT, H.A. 1991b. A 'miracle' Cape Griffon. *Vulture News* 25: 17-20.
SCOTT, H.A. 1994. Sick or incapacitated Cape Griffons *Gyps coprotheres* treated at the De Hoop Nature Reserve, Western Cape from May 1985 to May 1993. *Vulture News* 30: 10-18.
SCOTT, A. 1997. Reported depredation of lambs by Cape Griffons *Gyps coprotheres* in the Overberg region, western Cape. *Vulture News* 37: 28-30.
SCOTT, A. & ANDERSON, M. [1998]. *Vulture restaurants* [pamphlet]. Overberg Conservation Services, Gansbaai.
SCOTT, H.A. & BOSHOFF, A.F. 1994. *A supplementary feeding scheme for the Cape Griffon Vulture in the southwestern Cape Province, 1984- 1992*. Internal Report no. 13, Cape Nature Conservation, [Cape Town]. 33 pp.
SIBLEY, C.G. & AHLQUIST, J.E. 1990. *Phylogeny and classification of birds*. Yale University Press, New Haven.
SIEBOLD, I. & HELBIG, A.J. 1995. Evolutionary history of New and Old World vultures inferred from nucleotide sequences of the mitochondrial cytochrome b gene. *Phil. Trans. R. Soc. Lond.* B 350: 163-178.
SIGISMONDI, A. & POLITANO, E. 1996. Unusually high concentrations of the Egyptian Vulture *Neophron percnopterus* in a border area of the Dancalia region of Ethiopia, pp. 88-89. *In*: M. Pandolfi ed. *Abstracts 2nd Int. Conf. Raptors*, RRF and University of Urbino (Italy).
SIMMONS, R.E. 1995. Mass poisoning of Lappetfaced Vultures in Namibia. *J. Afr. Raptor Biology* 10: 3.
SIMMONS, R.E. & BRIDGEFORD, P. 1997. The status and conservation of vultures in Namibia, pp. 67-75. *In*: A.F. Boshoff *et al.*, *op. cit.*
SNYMAN, J. & SNYMAN, P.H. 1994. Aerial display performed by Rüppell's Griffons (*Gyps rueppellii*) in the Blouberg mountain region, Northern Province, South Africa. *Vulture News* 31: 13-15.
SNYMAN, P.H., SNYMAN, J., LAWSON, M.E. & LAWSON, N.F. 1994. Rüppell's Griffon sightings at Blouberg in the Northern Province, South Africa. *Vulture News* 31: 10-12.
SORLEY, C.S. & ANDERSEN, D.E. 1994. Raptor abundance in south-central Kenya in relation to land-use patterns. *Afr. J. Ecology* 32: 30-38.
STILES, E.K. 1994. Cape Griffon in the Zambezi valley. *Honeyguide* 40: 248.
STRONACH, N. 1993. Checklist of the birds of Selous Game Reserve. *SCP Disc. Paper* no. 15, 23 pp.
THOMSETT, S. 1993a. Bringing back the Lammergeyer of Hell's Gate. *Kenya Birds* 2(1): 24-25.
THOMSETT, S. 1993b. The raptors of Naivasha and Hell's Gate. *Kenya Birds* 2(1): 27-29.
TREE, A.J. 1998. Recent reports. *Honeyguide* 44: 35-48.
TYLER, S.J. & BISHOP, D.R. 1998. Important bird areas of Botswana. Pages 333-354. *In*: K.N. Barnes (Ed.) *The important bird areas of southern Africa*. BirdLife South Africa, Johannesburg.
ULLMAN, M. 1985. Raptor migration at Suez in March 1982. *Dutch Birding* 7: 11-17.
VAN ROOYEN, C.S. & PIPER, S.E. 1997. The effects of powerlines on vultures. Pages 102-104. *In*: A.F. Boshoff *et al.*, *op. cit.*
VAN WYK, E., VAN DER BANK, F.H., VERDOORN, G.H. & BOUWMAN, H. 1993. Chlorinated hydrocarbon insecticide residues in the Cape Griffon Vulture (*Gyps coprotheres*). *Comp. Biochem. Physiol.* 104C: 209-220.
VERDOORN, G.H. 1994. What are Rüppell's Griffon doing in the Blouberg ? *Vulture News* 31: 2-3.
VERDOORN, G.H. 1995a. Turning the tide for birds of prey in South Africa. *Birding in SA* 47: 110-113.

VERDOORN, G. 1995b. A year of vulture history for South Africa. Pages 50-59. *In*: D. Holt-Biddle (Ed.) *Vision of wildlife, ecotourism and the environment in southern Africa. 1996 Annual.* Endangered Wildlife Trust, Johannesburg.
VERDOORN, G. 1997a. Red-hot birding ... discover the Kalahari. *Africa - Birds & Birding* 2(2): 60-68.
VERDOORN, G.H. 1997b. The impacts of poison on vultures. Pages 105-108. *In*: A.F. Boshoff *et al.*, *op. cit.*
VERDOORN, G.H. 1998. The epic of Pharaoh's Chicken in South Africa. *Endangered Wildlife* 29: 4-9.
VERDOORN, G.H., TERBLANCHE, D. J.J. & DELL, S. 1997. Vultures in the North West Province, South Africa. Pages 33-36. *In*: A.F. Boshoff *et al.*, *op. cit.*
VERSTER. R. 1992. Python almost swallows a vulture. *Birding in SA* 44: 30.
VITTERY, A. 1983. Movements of palaearctic raptors in the Ethiopian Rift Valley. *Scopus* 7: 1-9.
WINK, M. 1998. Advances in the molecular phylogeny of vultures, eagles, hawks and falcons. Pages 61-62. *In*: *Abstracts Vth world conference on birds of prey and owls*. WWGBP/RCG/VSG/EWT, Johannesburg.
WYSOKE, J.M., ERASMUS, A., TRENDLER, K.O., TRENDLER, R., VAN DER TOORN, J.J.T.K. & VERDOORN, G.H. 1994. A paralysis syndrome in Cape Griffons (*Gyps coprotheres*) associated with depressed plasma cholinesterase levels. *Vulture News* 31: 4-8.
YOSEF, R. 1996. Sex and age classes of migrating raptors during the spring of 1994 at Eilat, Israel. *J. Raptor Research* 30: 160-164.
YOSEF, R. & ALON, D. 1997. Do immature Palearctic Egyptian Vultures *Neophron percnopterus* remain in Africa during the northern summer ? *Vogelwelt* 118: 285-289.

P.J. Mundy
Dept. National Parks
P.O. Box 2283
Bulawayo
Zimbabwe

Chancellor, R. D. & B.-U. Meyburg eds. 2000
Raptors at Risk
WWGBP / Hancock House

Vultures in Asia

S.M.Satheesan

ABSTRACT

Of the 15 Old World vultures eight species occur in Asia. The more common among them are the White-rumped and Egyptian Vultures, as well as the Long-billed Griffon. The less common are the Eurasian or Fulvous Griffon and the Red-headed Vulture. The uncommon and rarer ones include the Himalayan Griffon, the Cinereous and the Bearded Vultures. Human population explosion, diminishing food supply, roost and nest sites, and irresponsible hunting and trapping are the main causes of their population decline. Banning the killing and capturing of these birds by law, setting up vulture feeding stations, and providing artificial perches, roost and nest sites, will go a long way in conserving these vultures.

INTRODUCTION

Of the world total of 22 species of vultures eight Old World vultures occur in Asia. They are the Red-headed, Cinereous, White-rumped, Egyptian and Bearded Vultures and the Long-billed, Eurasian and Himalayan Griffons. This paper discusses their distribution and status, analyses the major causes of their population declines, and suggests some methods to conserve them.

DESCRIPTION, DISTRIBUTION AND HABITS

Red-headed or King or Pondicherry Vulture *Sarcogyps calvus*
This is a huge black vulture (wing span *c.*2m, wt. 3.7-5.4 kg), unmistakable because of its deep scarlet or yellowish-red naked head, neck with fleshy wattles, and legs, white patches at the base of neck and on upper thighs and a thin whitish band along underside of the outstretched wings, seen in flight (Ali & Ripley 1983; Brown & Amadon 1968).

A resident vulture of Asia, it occurs in Pakistan, India, Bangladesh, Nepal, Myanmar (Burma), Thailand, Laos, South Vietnam and Malaysia, up to *c.* 2500m in the Himalayas. It is absent from Sri Lanka. It is rare and nowhere numerically abundant (Ali & Ripley 1983), and considered a near-threatened species (Collar, Crosby & Stattersfield 1994). In SE Asia it is found in clearings in forested areas, but in S. Asia it is usually seen in deciduous and semi-desert biotopes near habitations. Robson (1997) reported recent sightings by villagers of these birds in Cambodia.

Surveys show that the population of this bird has declined in Gujarat, Rajasthan and Uttar Pradesh states of the Indian union where it used to be fairly common (Samant, Prakash & Naoroji 1995). But Keoladeo National Park in Rajasthan and Corbett National Park and Agra in Uttar Pradesh have favourable habitats and reasonable populations of these vultures (Prakash 1989; Satheesan 1989a; Samant *et al.* 1995). They are uncommon in S and NE India. Saikia & Bhattacharjee (1990b) mentioned that this bird had become very rare in Assam in the last ten years especially in Kachamari of Sibsagar district in the Brahmaputra valley, even though two nests of this bird were located in the interior of Hahkati Reserve forest near Sawkhwaghata in Assam. Unlike what the name suggests these birds shy away from competition at carcasses, preferring to feed alone away from the crowd of other vultures.

It nests on trees and rarely on bushes. Davidson (1874) found a nest of this vulture on a low prickly bush three feet above the ground in Gotekindee, Sattara district, Maharashtra. O'brien (1921) sighted their nests on thorny trees and once in a large clump of cactus. It was thought to nest on inaccessible sites by Murray (Vertebrate Zoology of Sind), but Barnes could not find any nest in Sind (Oliver 1915). Oliver sighted their nests on Babul (*Acacia* Sp.)- live and dead trees- in Murid Rais forest, Hyderabad Division, in Pakistan.

Cinereous or Eurasian Black Vulture *Aegypius monachus*

This is a huge uniformly black or dark brown vulture (wing span 2.5 – 2.7m, wt. 7-12.5kg). A naked leaden pink neck surrounded by a distinct blackish (not white) ruff, broader head (partially naked), black fur-like feathers and down on crown, occiput, lores and cheek, absence of fleshy wattles on sides of neck, and a wedge-shaped tail help distinguish it from other vultures (Ali & Ripley 1983; Brown & Amadon 1968).

The first sighting of the bird in Rajputana (now Rajasthan state) in India was made in 1899 by Newnham. The bird was sighted in different localities in Gujarat state, such as Mitli in Kaira district, Ahmedabad and Kutch. The bird was described earlier by Butler in 1870, Newnham (1900), Acharya (1950) and Aldrich (1952). Acharya (1950) mentioned that it has round nostrils, an extremely wide gape and only twelve rectrices for the tail. Hughes (1917) wrote that the legs and feet of these birds were creamy white in colour. Mitli in Gujarat, 65 km south of Ahmedabad, was the southernmost record for the bird (Ali 1960).

It is a resident bird breeding in the high mountains of northern India, semi-desert Baluchistan to Gilgit in Assam, including the Himalayan dry temperate zone between $c.1800$ and 3600m altitudes and often straggling along the Himalayas to Bhutan and east in Tibet (Baker 1910). This bird was recorded from Tibet by other ornithologists (Koelz 1940; Ali 1946; Ludlow 1950; Vaurie 1972). Baker (1910) sighted a bird in Calcutta Slaughter House which was captured later and its specimen is in the Calcutta museum collections. It breeds in the Barall range of North Cachar hills in Assam (Choudhury 1986, 1997). It was first recorded by Baker in 1888-89 in the Cachar hills on a nest from where he had taken an egg for examination. It was also recorded in November 1981 in Baligaon in the flood plains of Brahmaputra River, Darrang District, Assam. The bird fell down from a tree and was collected and moved to Assam State Zoo at Guwahati (Choudhury 1986). A pair of these birds was seen in Dimagiri in Bhutan in November 1885 (Baker 1910). It is a rare sparse winter visitor to India recorded south to c 21°N (Ali & Ripley 1983). Straggler birds were collected further south, from Karimnagar (18° 30' N, 79° 10' E) in Andhra Pradesh in 1986 (Choudhury 1987) and Pathanamthitta (9° 03'- 9° 30' N, 76° 15' - 77° 38' E) in Kerala in 1989 (Sreekumar 1991). In 1990 a Cinereous Vulture was recorded near Nalapattu Bird Sanctuary, Nelore District in Andhra Pradesh (Perennou & Shantaram 1990). An injured Cinereous Vulture was caught in Harpalwadi Village in Satara District of Maharashtra State in December 1992 and later moved to the Katraj Snake Park in Pune in Maharashtra in January 1993 (The Indian Express, 4 January 1993; Satheesan 1993). All straggler birds caught were immature, totally exhausted and some also injured (Satheesan 1993). Vagrant birds were collected in Thailand in December 1996 and January 1997 by the Bird Conservation Society of Thailand (Robson 1997).

Marshal (1911) had sighted nests of this bird on juniper trees c 12 m high (2500-2600 m a.s.l.) in May near Quetta (Pakistan). Eggs were white in colour with rusty-red markings all over, thicker at the large end. These markings were very lightly laid on, and could easily be rubbed off with a wet finger.

Asian White-rumped or White-backed Vulture *Pseudogyps bengalensis*

This is a brownish black vulture smaller in size (wing span *c.* 2m) and lighter (4.5kg) than the true *Gyps* vultures (griffons). As its name indicates this vulture has a prominent white rump (lower back) noticeable when perched or from above in flying birds. Young birds are dark or light brown with the lower back plain light brown, resembling Long-billed and Eurasian (Fulvous) Griffons.

The White-rumped Vulture is the commonest and the most abundant species of the Indian peninsula, except Sri Lanka through Myanmar to Indo-China. It breeds in SE Iran, SE Afghanistan, E Pakistan, India, Nepal, Bangladesh and Myanmar. Formerly widely distributed in SE Asia, it is now almost extinct in most areas. It is recorded in small numbers from Laos (Robson 1997). It is a sedentary bird of open country and lowlands up to *c.* 3100m in the Himalayas.

These birds generally feed on large mammal carcasses. It was also found to be feeding on a dead Bandicoot Rat (*Bandicoota indica*) and a domestic cat on two separate occasions in 1980 in Agra (Satheesan 1989b). They feed in daylight hours, retreating to the roosts before sundown. But this species was also seen feeding at night by Smith (1915), Morris (1935) and Lewis (1940). McCann (1940) noted that the primitive slaughterhouse which existed (not present now) at Bandra in Bombay attracted large numbers of these birds which in roosting on Brab (Palmyra) Palms *Borassus flabellifer* killed the plants with their acrid excreta leaving the bare "poles" standing. When the crown of one palm disappeared there was no place to perch and hence the vultures moved to the next palm, thus destroying several palms in each locality.

Large numbers of nests were observed in Keoladeo National Park in Rajasthan (Prakash 1989) and in Agra, Uttar Pradesh (Satheesan 1995). It nests on trees, and rarely on buildings in the absence of suitable trees, especially in deserts and semi-desert areas (Satheesan 1995).

Indian Long-billed Griffon *Gyps indicus*

Larger (wing span 2-2.5m) and heavier (wt. *c.* 5 kg) than the Asian White-rumped Vulture, the Indian Long-billed Griffon is recognised by its bright isabelline (yellowish-grey) plumage without a pure white back. It has yellowish eyes.

It is distributed in peninsular India through Myanmar to Indo-China except Sri Lanka. It breeds in SE Pakistan, India (not in extreme SW), Nepal and Bangladesh. It is also recorded in Laos (Robson 1997). Formerly it was widespread in SE Asia. A resident bird, it is usually seen in lowlands sometimes up to an altitude of 1500m. Two subspecies are recognised: *indicus*, occurring in Pakistan and India south of the Gangetic plain, and *tenuirostris* occurring in India north of and including the Gangetic plain east to Assam, Nepal, Bangladesh, Myanmar and SE Asia. *G.i. tenuirostris* has a longer, more slender and darker (black) bill than *G.i. indicus* (bill is yellowish grey in adult birds). The latter is a cliff-nester and seen in more numbers in hilly terrain and cliffs and in drier open country. The former nests on trees.

The nests of the tree-nesting subspecies were located in 1989 in Lower Assam area in the Kamarup district (Saikia & Bhattacharjee 1990a). Their nests were also sighted in Jaldapara Wildlife Sanctuary, West Bengal (25° 58' - 26° 52' N, 89° 08' - 89° 55' E) as well as Corbett National Park in Uttar Pradesh (29° 31' - 29° 35' N, 79° 46' - 79° 50' E). Long-billed Griffons were recorded in the south of the Indian subcontinent near Bangalore (12° N) in Karnataka and Mudumalai Wildlife Sanctuary (11° 32' - 11° 43' N, 76° 22' - 76° 45' E) in Tamil Nadu (Samant *et al.* 1995).

In earlier work on vultures several Long-billed Griffons were wrongly identified as Eurasian Griffons (Ali & Abdulali 1945). Nests of Long-billed Griffons were recorded near Chakia in Benares District, Uttar Pradesh by Gill (1921) and near Ambala in Haryana by Jones (1916). These griffons are more aggressive at carcasses than are White-rumped Vultures.

Eurasian or Fulvous or Indian Griffon *Gyps fulvus*

Larger (wing span 2.5+ m) and heavier (wt. *c* 7-8.2 kg) than the White-rumped Vulture and Long-billed Griffons, the Eurasian Griffon has a fulvous or bright cinnamon body without a white back, neck white in colour and fully covered with down. Immature Long-billed can be distinguished from Fulvous Griffon by the absence of a complete covering of white down (leaving black feathers in the mid ventral line) for the neck, and the presence of a less clearly defined pale back (paler than adjacent areas), as well as a smaller wing span (Grubh 1974).

In Asia the Eurasian Griffon breeds north to at least Pamir in Afghanistan, Pakistan, Kashmir, NW India, Nepal and West China. According to Brown & Amadon (1968) it breeds in China east to Nan Chan but this is not supported by Cheng (1989). It occurs in Tajikistan, Kyrgyzstan and SE Kazakhstan in the former USSR (Alstrom 1997). According to Ali & Abdulali (1945) a Eurasian Griffon shot in Kurla, Bombay (19° N) in February 1893 (now a specimen in the collections of the Bombay Natural History Society) is the southernmost record for the species. Thakker (1988) narrated how two naturalists saved a Fulvous Griffon from being stoned and harassed by residents near Ranip, Ahmedabad in November 1987. It used to feed on 750-1000g of meat daily in captivity. Discovering the cost incurred, the rescuers stopped feeding the bird and it flew away, not to return to the same place. In winter it occurs widely in Pakistan and N India south to *c.* 20° N, and further sometimes to Bangalore at 13° N (Satheesan 1990) and east to Assam and Nepal. It breeds in mountainous areas up to 3000m. In winter it comes down to the plains.

Two subspecies are recognised: *fulvus* - the Eurasian Griffon - breeds west of Afghanistan whereas *fulvescens*, the Fulvous or Indian Griffon, breeds in Afghanistan and eastwards in S Asia. It is a cliff-nester.

These griffons inhabit bare mountains, open savannah and semidesert country. In winter outside the breeding season they are sighted in large numbers in tropical forest and in semi-arid and arid zones except coastal and island zones in India. At carcasses seen on the Indian plains White-rumped Vultures outnumber the Long-billed and the Fulvous Griffons (the least in numbers) but the Fulvous is the most aggressive among them and it easily succeeds in competition for food and roosting sites on trees.

Himalayan Griffon *Gyps himalayensis*

Larger (2.5 - 3.1m or more) and heavier (wt. *c.* 8-12 kg), the Himalayan Griffon is distinguished from the Eurasian Griffon by its much paler body, less reddish in colour, stouter more robust bill, and the greenish grey to white legs and feet. It is purely a mountain bird and a resident at high altitudes, usually 600-4000m, occasionally up to 6100m, although immature birds winter in the plains of N India and Nepal. It breeds in C Asia north to Altaj, and in Afghanistan, N Pakistan, the Himalayas, S Tibet and C China (Koelz 1940; Ali 1946; Ludlow 1950; Vaurie 1972). It was sighted in winter at the Keoladeo National Park in the plains of Bharatpur, Rajasthan (about 27° 10' N- 77° 32' E) (Satheesan 1989b). Large numbers were sighted in the Great Himalayan National Park, Kullu District of Himachal Pradesh (77° 15'-77° 50 N, 31° 35'-32° 00' N), at elevations of 1500-6140 m. This bird was widely distributed throughout the wild uplands of Kashmir mainly above the tree line - seen in Jhelum valley over open spaces and in Baramulla. It was common in Wular Lake area in winter, afforested hillsides, valleys in Lidar about Pahlgam and in much open wooded country such as Sind (Bates & Lowther 1991). It also occurs in Tajikistan, Kyrgyzstan and SE Kazakhstan in the former USSR (Alstrom 1997). It flies in the company of Eurasian Griffons and Bearded Vultures. This bird is more common in the Western Himalayas, uncommon in the Trans-Himalayas, and rare in the Central and Eastern Himalayas.

It lays a single egg, coloured pale creamy to reddish buff, between December and February or March and the young birds leave the nest by late May or early June. In Kashmir they are reportedly breeding around 3000 m.

Egyptian or Scavenger Vulture *Neophron percnopterus*

This can be separated from other vultures by its smaller size (wing span *c* 1.5 – 1.6 m; wt 1.5 – 2 kg), creamy white body colour with black quill feathers, red eyes, bare skin of face yellow to orange, yellow feet and bill, wedge-shaped tail as well as eagle-like flight. Of the two subspecies recognized, *percnopterus*, the Egyptian Vulture, is larger and heavier than *ginginianus,* the Indian Scavenger Vulture, and has a dark brown bill (not yellow as in the Indian subspecies), and stronger feet and claws (Ali & Ripley 1983). The powerful bill opens up turtle carapaces. Scavenger Vultures are known to follow, kill and feed on turtles moving from one pond to another when ponds dry up in summer in Rajasthan (Auffenberg 1981; Breedon & Breedon 1982). Active predation by this vulture on a Checkered Keelback water snake *Natrix piscator* while negotiating a road, was recorded in Keoladeo National Park, Bharatpur (Prakash & Nanjappa 1988). Scavenger Vultures feeding on carcasses of their own species and those of White-backed Vultures were observed on a few occasions between 1980 and 1981 in Agra (Satheesan 1989c). The numbers of Scavenger Vultures were more in the afternoon and those of White-backed Vultures more in the morning hours at the primitive slaughterhouse in Agra. The White-back Vulture feeds on large chunks of meat whereas the Scavenger Vulture feeds more on tidbits, dried blood and larvae of insects at the slaughterhouse. Thus the food and feeding behaviour of the Scavenger Vulture place it in a different ecological niche and it avoids competition with the more common and abundant White-backed Vulture (Satheesan 1989c). This is a resident bird found from *c*. 3000m in the Himalayas south to Kanyakumari (not in Sri Lanka), east to Bihar and western parts of West Bengal, but not seen in Bangladesh and Assam. It is found in plains and desert around habitations in drier areas and avoids wetter areas.

The Egyptian Vulture nests on the ledges of rocks, old buildings, tombs and rarely on trees. Paynter (1924) found a nest of the Egyptian Vulture on the ground near Lahore in Pakistan. Biddulph (1937) sighted a nest of this bird on a termite mound only 1.5 m high on the water-spread of an irrigation tank in Tanjore in Tamil Nadu state. Sheromoney (1977) confirmed that the Scavenger Vultures which famously used to go to the Thirukalukundram Hill Temple to feed on the rice pudding offered by the temple priest as a religious ceremony every day around noon, still make visits to the temple. They breed around the hill. In Tamil literature this place is referred to as *Kalukundram* meaning "Vulture Hill", and dates from the seventh or eighth century A.D.

Bearded Vulture *Gypaetus barbatus*

This is a large vulture (wing span 2.5 – 3m, wt. 4.5 – 6 kg), more related to the Egyptian Vulture than other Old World vultures. The characteristic "beard" projecting downwards on each side of the beak, an upright posture, extremely long wings, long diamond-shaped pointed tail, reddish buff underside, short feathered tarsi, long blunt claws, black grey colour on wings, dirty white crown ringed with black, and a black circle around the eyes, are all pointers to the identification of this bird (Ali & Ripley 1983; Brown & Amadon 1968).

It is a resident and purely mountain species in India even though in other countries it is known to descend to the plains and steppes to forage and associate with human habitations. It is restricted to the Himalayas in Pakistan, Kashmir, and east of Nepal, Bhutan, Assam and Arunachal Pradesh, soaring to over 7000m (Ali & Ripley 1983). It was also recorded from Tibet (Koelz 1940; Ali 1946; Ludlow 1950; Vaurie 1972). It is common in the Western Himalayas, uncommon in Trans-Himalayas, and rare in the Eastern Himalayas. Whistler (1912) mentioned that this bird was abundant in the neighbourhood of Kalabagh on the river Indus in Pakistan. It was common in Mussoorie in Uttar Pradesh, India (Fleming 1956). The Bearded Vulture is a vagrant in winter in the Bhabar tract (Shivalik in the lower Himalayan foothills and the Terai) where the Corbett National Park (29° 31'- 29° 35'N, 70° 41'E) is also situated in Uttar Pradesh, but relatively common to the snowline and more so in the high altitude areas (Samant *et al.* 1995).

The Bearded Vulture does not fight with other vultures for the tidbits of a carcass. Instead, it will wait till all the vultures have left and remains there until the carcass is cleaned. This bird does not swoop down on its food (carcass) like a kite but alights nearby and feeds slowly. It will not attack a live animal. It does not carry off lambs and human babies and the name of this bird as "Lammergeier" is a misnomer. Donald (1908) pointed out that this bird rarely uses the claws as a means of offence or defence and much prefers biting. Osborn (1908) stated that one should not conclude that this bird can hurl animals such as Chamois, Ibex and Ghoral over the tremendous precipices of the Himalayas just because Jerdon had found the shoulder blade of a Ghoral and hoof of an Ibex in the stomach of a dead Bearded Vulture.

The Bearded Vulture picks up bones and tortoises and drops them from a height on the rocks to break them and feed on their contents (Osborn 1908; Donald 1921). Ali (1960) points out that the bird drops bones from a height of 50-70 m. This process is repeated if necessary until the bone splinters whereupon the bird lands to pick up and swallow the pieces (Fleming 1956). Donald (1908) had observed a vulture dropping a bone fifty times and still the bone was not broken when he left the locality.

This bird breeds between November and March. Lowther (1946) mentioned that Jones had recorded it flying in Rawalpindi (in Pakistan) over the railway station to at least 7,400 m, at which height also it was observed soaring by one of the Mount Everest expeditions. It breeds between 364 m at Campbellpur district, where Jones found a nest, and 4,300 m.. Jones found a nest of this bird with eggs in Simla at a height of 770 m. The nest was made in a recess or a small cave of a sheer cliff. One to three eggs are laid but only one chick is generally reared from a nest. Each pair of birds can have two or three nest sites (Lowther 1946).

PRESENT STATUS

The White-rumped and Egyptian or Scavenger Vultures, as well as the Long-billed Griffon are more common and abundant than others. A decade ago the populations of these vultures had risen to such an extent in some areas as to become an aviation hazard. In order to prevent bird strikes, persecution of these birds, removal of carcass dumps, and modernization of primitive slaughterhouses, were taken up in different cities and towns. As a result the vulture populations started to decline in urban areas. In Asia Eurasian Griffons and Red-headed Vultures are less common compared to the earlier-mentioned species. The Himalayan Griffon, the Cinereous and Bearded Vultures are uncommon and rare because they do not benefit much from human activities and exploit the animal waste at carcass dumps, widely available in the Asian plains, like the other vultures. However, denudation of the mountains is forcing them to forage at lower altitudes.

CAUSES OF POPULATION DECLINE

(1) Unchecked human population explosion and resultant unplanned urbanisation coupled with inefficient animal garbage disposal formerly produced a regular and super-abundant artificial food supply (carcasses) for vultures (Grubh *et al.* 1990). When man's short-sighted activities "boomeranged" in the form of bird strikes to aircraft (15 military aircraft and some human lives have been lost in India due to vulture strikes, from 1980 to 1994) (Satheesan 1994) authorities started withdrawing the food supply to vultures by modernization. Then the vultures started moving out of urban areas to natural forests and countrysides and so declined in numbers.

(2) Irresponsible shooting and killing was done in some areas, because they are a threat to aircraft safety, and belief that they probably kill cattle and sheep also reduced their populations.

(3) Felling of trees usually used by vultures for roosting and nesting and destruction of other suitable roost and nest sites due to human population pressure, also caused reduction in their populations. In Agra several of the roost and nest trees of vultures were cut to construct residential buildings and shopping complexes since 1981.

(4) Vultures were utilized by man widely in olden days (even now in some villages and towns in Asia) to pick mammal carcasses clean so that the people can use the animal hides and skeletons in industry. Rotting carcasses at regular dumps and primitive slaughterhouses or bone mills are no more a sight in many cities in Asia due to the recent wave of modernization. Hence all the large populations of vultures have disappeared from several Indian cities such as New Delhi, Bombay, Bangalore and Madras.

(5) Handsome species of vultures such as Cinereous and Red-headed Vultures make attractive exhibits in zoos. Roberts (1991) pointed out that the constant demand from animal exporters in Pakistan may have been instrumental in the decline of the Cinereous Vulture.

(6) Disappearance of natural habitats, especially on mountains and cliffs, may account for the decline of mountain-dwelling vulture species. Natural habitats of these vultures are destroyed

due to developmental and commercial activities, local community pressure and management problems. Developmental projects and activities destructive to vulture habitats include construction of roads, railway lines, cable car lanes, power stations, aerodromes (air strips and helipads) and military establishments (firing ranges and bombdoms). The commercial activities harmful to these birds and their habitats include mining, stone-quarrying, tourism, timber-felling and extraction, illegal hunting and wildlife trade. Local community pressures from grazing, fuel wood extraction, collection of non-wood forest products, fishing and poaching also disturb these birds. Management problems include pollution, fires (natural or started by settlers to clear forests), promotion of monoculture, activities of trekkers, mountaineers and tourists, local conflicts, terrorist/bandit infestation, conversion of hill slopes into agricultural fields (as in contour farming), building of roads in an environmentally destructive manner, and pollution of water bodies and soil by insecticides and herbicides, as well as dumping of coal tar (used for metalling of roads) in rivers. Above all the Himalayas is a highly seismic zone. Much of the area is unstable and frequent earth tremors occurring there cause the progressively degrading hill-sides to slide down, destroying vegetation and habitat of wild animals and birds.

(7) Accidental or purposeful poisoning can be another reason for the extinction of vultures from certain areas of their abundance. Kannan (1993) mentioned that between 1960 and 1980 chemically contaminated carcasses laid out to kill cattle-marauding leopards venturing out of the adjoining forests have finished off every vulture in and around Anaimalai Hills according to the villagers residing around the Indira Gandhi Wildlife Sanctuary in Tamil Nadu. This used to be the case 20 to 30 years ago with villagers residing near forests with lions (Gir Forest, Gujarat), tigers and leopards (several forested areas) where several vultures were killed feeding on the poisoned carcasses laid out to kill the carnivores.

(8) Until 1980 certain tribal people in Andhra Pradesh state were known to eat eggs, chicks and adults of vultures. The 'Banda' community (locally called Bandollu) residing in Guntur and Prakasam, coastal districts of Andhra Pradesh, used to catch vultures with special nets. Since 1980 vultures stopped breeding and are rarely seen in these areas (Rao 1992). In 1983 villagers of Sasan Gir in Gujarat, Bapne near Bombay, and Viswaneedam near Bangalore, mentioned that certain tribal people caught vultures using nooses and even bare hands, in order to eat them on festive days (Satheesan 1989d).

WHY AND HOW TO CONSERVE VULTURES ?

Vultures are a boon to mankind because they keep our environment clean. Vultures are nature's incinerators and they prevent the outbreak and spread of epidemics by consuming diseased carcasses. We should allow vultures to live in their own right, but at the same time check their population explosion, which may pose a serious threat to aviation safety, by denying their food in areas where airfields and airports occur (Satheesan 1996). In order to conserve vultures the following measures will be necessary.

(1) Capturing and killing of vultures should be strictly banned by law.
(2) Identifying and protecting the remaining natural habitats of these birds from use for agriculture, industry, mining, hydroelectric projects and construction of buildings, roads and airports should be given top priority.
(3) Setting up vulture "restaurants" or feeding stations will definitely put an end to the drastic decline of the endangered species.
(4) Providing artificial perching, roosting and nesting sites in natural or natural-looking sites (away from aerodromes and utility structures to avoid conflicts with man and collisions with aircraft and installations carrying power) will go a long way to conserving vultures.
(5) Protect all species of vultures by including all of them in Schedule 1 of the Wildlife Protection Act, 1972.

(6) of the Government of India. So far only the Bearded Vulture is included in Schedule 1 of the act.
(7) Ban all pesticides (biocides) and hazardous chemicals used by agriculturalists, health departments and individuals through efficient legislations.
(8) Promote organic farming and ban synthetic fertilizers.

The Buddhist Tibetans carry their corpses to high rocky areas, outside their villages, cut them into pieces and offer them to vultures (Stein 1972). The Zoroastrian community or the Parsees in India keep their corpses in "Towers of Silence" for vultures to feed on (in cities such as Bombay, Ahmedabad and Bangalore) as their last religious offering (Satheesan 1989d). Everybody will agree that theirs (Tibetans and Parsees) is the noblest of thoughts and deeds, and it works for the conservation of vultures too.

Vultures are the most wonderful of nature's creations. They are the best friends of farmers and indispensable in keeping our planet healthy and clean.

REFERENCES

ACHARYA, H.N.G. 1950. Occurrence of the Cinereous Vulture (*Aegypius monachus* Linnaeus) at Ahmedabad, north Gujarat. *J. Bombay nat. Hist. Soc.* 49: 307-309.
ALDRICH, H.C. 1952. Occurrence of the Cinereous Vulture (*Aegypius monachus* Linnaeus) in Kaira District, Gujarat. *J. Bombay nat. Hist. Soc.* 50: 945-946.
ALI, S. 1946. An Ornithological pilgrimage to Lake Mansarowar and Mount Kailas.*J. Bombay nat. Hist. Soc.* 46:284-308.
ALI, S. 1960. The Cinereous Vulture (*Aegypius monachus* Linnaeus)- an addition to the birds of Kutch. *J. Bombay nat. Hist. Soc.* 57: 408-409.
ALI, S. & ABDULALI, H. 1945. Some recent records of the Griffon Vulture *Gyps fulvus fulvescens* Hume) in peninsular India - a correction. *J. Bombay nat. Hist. Soc.* 45: 236-237
ALI, S. & RIPLEY, S.D. 1983. *Handbook of the Birds of India and Pakistan.* Oxford University Press. Bombay.
ALSTROM, P. 1997. Field identification of Asian *Gyps* vultures. *Oriental Bird Club Bulletin* 25: 32-49.
AUFFENBERG, W. 1981. Behaviour of *Lissemys punctata* (Reptilia, Testudinata) in a drying lake in Rajasthan, India. *J. Bombay nat. Hist. Soc.* 78: 487-493.
BAKER, E.C.S. 1910. Notes on the occurrence of *Vultur monachus* in Calcutta. *Records Indian Museum* 5: 81.
BATES, R.S.P. & LOWTHER, E.H.N. 1991. *Breeding birds of Kashmir.* Oxford University Press. Delhi.
BIDDULPH, C.H. 1937. Unusual site for the nest of the White Scavenger Vulture [*Neophron percnopterus ginginianus* (Lath.)]. *J. Bombay nat. Hist. Soc.* 39: 635-637.
BREEDON, S. & BREEDON, B. 1982. The drought of 1979-1980 at the Keoladeo Ghana Sanctuary, Bharatpur, Rajasthan. *J. Bombay nat. Hist. Soc.* 79: 1-37.
BROWN L. & AMADON, D. 1968. *Eagles, Hawks and Falcons of the world. Vol. I.* Country Life Books. Feltham.
CHENG. T-HS 1987. *A synopsis of the Avifauna of China.* Paul Parey. Beijing, Hamburg & Berlin.
CHOUDHARY, A. 1986. Occurrence of Cinereous Vulture (*Aegypius monachus*) in the lower altitudes in Assam (India). *Tiger Paper* 13(2): 32-33.
CHOUDHARY, A. 1997. The status of the birds of Dibru-Saikhowa Sanctuary, Assam, India. *Oriental Bird Club Bulletin* 25: 27 – 29.
CHOUDHURY, B.C. 1987. Capture of Cinereous Vulture *Aegypius monachus* in Karimnagar District, Andhra Pradesh. *Mayura* 7 & 8: 49-50.
COLLAR, N.J., CROSBY, M.J. & STATTERSFIELD, A.J. 1994. *Birds to watch 2.* BirdLife International, Cambridge.
DAVIDSON, J. 1874. Letter to the Editor. *Stray Feathers* 2(1-3): 336.
DONALD, C.H. 1908. The Bearded Vulture or Lammergeyer (*Gypaetus barbatus*). *J. Bombay nat. Hist. Soc.* 18: 913-914.
DONALD, C.H. 1921. The Lammergeier (*Gypaetus barbatus*) and the Golden Eagle (*Aquila chrysaetos*) *J. Bombay nat. Hist. Soc.* 27: 952-953.
FLEMING, R.L. 1956. The bone-dropping habit of the Lammergeier. *J. Bombay nat. Hist. Soc.* 52: 933-934.
GILL, E.H. 1921. Nidification of the Himalayan Long-billed Vulture (*Gyps tenuirostris*). *J. Bombay nat. Hist. Soc.* 27: 951-952.

GRUBH, R.B. 1974. *The ecology and behaviour of vultures in Gir forest.* Ph.D. Thesis. University of Bombay. Bombay.

GRUBH, R.B., NARAYAN, G. & SATHEESAN, S.M. 1990. Conservation of vultures in India, pp. 360-363. In: *Conservation in developing countries: Problems and prospects. proc. Centenary seminar*, Bombay Natural History Society.

HUGHES, F.L. 1917. Note on the Great Brown Vulture (*Vultur monachus*) in captivity. *J. Bombay Nat. Hist. Soc.* 25: 298-300.

JONES, A.E. 1916. *Gyps tenuirostris* (Hodgson), the Himalayan Long-billed Vulture, breeding near Ambala, Punjab. *J. Bombay nat Hist. Soc.* 24: 358.

KANNAN, R. 1993. Local extinction of vultures in and around the Anaimalai Hills. *Newsletter for Bird Watchers* 33: 58.

KOELZ, W. 1940. Notes on the birds of Zankskar and Purig, with appendixes giving new records for Ladak, Pupsha and Kulu. *Michigan Acad. Sciences, Arts, Letters* 25: 297-322.

LEWIS, E.S. 1940. Vultures feeding at night. *J. Bombay nat. Hist. Soc.* 42: 189-199.

Lowther, E.H.N. 1946. The Lammergeier (*Gypaetus barbatus Linnaeus*). *J. Bombay nat. Hist. Soc.* 46: 501-508.

LUDLOW, F. 1950. The birds of Lhasa. *Ibis* 92(1): 34-35.

MARSHAL, T.E. 1911. Nesting of the Cinereous Vulture (*Vultur monachus*) near Quetta. *J. Bombay nat. Hist. Soc.* 21: 264-265.

MCCANN, C. 1941. Vultures and palms. *J. Bombay nat. Hist. Soc.* 42: 439-440.

MORRIS, R.C. 1935. Vultures feeding at night. *J. Bombay nat. Hist. Soc.* 38: 190.

NEWNHAM, A. 1900. Occurrence of uncommon birds in Rajputana. *J. Bombay nat. Hist. Soc.* 13: 193-194.

O'BRIEN, E. 1921. Nidification of the Black Vulture or Indian King Vulture (*Otogyps calvus*). *J. Bombay nat. Hist. Soc.* 28: 284-285.

OLIVER, E.G. 1915. The King Vulture (*Otogyps calvus*) in Sind. *J. Bombay nat. Hist. Soc.* 23: 777.

OSBORN, W. 1908. Note on the Bearded Vulture (*Gypaetus barbatus*) or Lammergeyer. *J. Bombay nat. Hist. Soc.* 18: 500-501.

PAYNTER, W.P. 1924. Lesser White Scavenger [Sic] Vulture(*N. ginginianus*) nesting on the ground. *J. Bombay nat. Hist. Soc.* 30: 224-225.

PERENNOU, C. & SHANTARAM, V. 1990. Status of some birds in South Eastern India. *J. Bombay nat. Hist. Soc..* 87: 306-307.

PRAKASH, V. 1989. Population and distribution of raptors in Keoladeo National Park, Bharatpur, India. Pp. 129-137. In: *Raptors in the Modern World*. B.-U. Meyburg & R.D. Chancellor (eds.). WWGBP. Berlin.

PRAKASH, V. & NANJAPPA, C. 1988. An instance of active predation by Scavenger Vulture (*Neophron percnopterus ginginianus*) on Checkered Keelback water snake *(Xenochrophis piscator)* in Keoladeo national Park, Bharatpur (Sic), Rajasthan. *J. Bombay nat. Hist. Soc.* 85: 419.

RAO, K.M. 1992. Vultures endangered in Guntur and Prakasam districts (A.P.) and vulture eating community. *Newsletter for Bird Watchers* 32: 6-7.

ROBSON, C. 1997. From the field. *Oriental Bird Club Bulletin* 26: 60-66.

ROBERTS. T.J. 1991. *The Birds of Pakistan. Vol 1.* Oxford University Press: Karachi.

SAIKIA, P. & BHATTACHARJEE, P.C. 1990A. Indian Long-billed Vulture nesting in Assam. *Newsletter for Bird Watchers* 30: 9.

SAIKIA, P. & BHATTACHARJEE, P.C. 1990. Records of the King Vulture in Assam. *Ibid:* 9.

SAMANT, J.S., PRAKASH, V. & NAOROJI, R. 1995. *Ecology and behaviour of resident raptors with special reference to endangered species* Final Report 1990-1993. Bombay Natural History Society, Bombay.

SATHEESAN, S.M. 1989a. King Vultures in Agra. *Pavo* 27: 81.

SATHEESAN, S.M. 1989b. Birds at vulture-feeding sites in Agra, India. *Vulture News* 21:25.

SATHEESAN, S.M. 1989c. On the differences in feeding behaviour between Scavenger and Indian White-backed Vultures. *Vulture News* 22: 49-50.

SATHEESAN, S.M. 1989d. Behaviour of the Indian Whitebacked Vulture in the presence of man. *Vulture News* 22: 52-53.

SATHEESAN, S.M. 1990. A record of the Indian Griffon vulture in South India. *Vulture News* 23:22.

SATHEESAN, S.M. 1993. Note on Cinereous or European Black Vulture *Aegypius monachus*. *Zoo's Print* VIII (4): 1

SATHEESAN, S.M. 1994. The more serious vulture hits to military aircraft in India between 1980 and 1994. In: *Proc. 22 Meeting of the BSCE (Vienna)* : 163 - 168.

SATHEESAN, S.M. 1995. Roost and nest trees preferred by Indian Whitebacked Vultures *Pseudogyps bengalensis* in Agra city and environs. *Vulture News* 32: 3-9.

SATHEESAN, S.M. 1996. Raptors Associated with Airports and Aircraft, pp 315-323. In: *Raptors in Human Landscape,* D.M. Bird, D.E. Varland and J.J. Negro (eds). Academic Press. London.

SEROMONEY, G. 1977. The *Neophron* Vultures of Thirukalukundram. *Newsletter for Bird Watchers* 17: 1-4.

SMITH, O.A. 1915. Vultures feeding after sundown. *J. Bombay nat. Hist. Soc.* 23: 579.

SREEKUMAR, R.S. 1991. Cinereous Vulture *Aegypius monachus* (Linne.) in Pathanamthitta, Kerala. *J. Bombay nat. Hist. Soc.* 88: 111.

STEIN, R. A. 1972. *Tibetan civilization.* Faber & Faber. London.

THAKKER, P.S. 1988. An encounter with Indian Griffon Vulture *Gyps fulvus fulvescens* Hume- a rare variety. *Newsletter for Bird Watchers* 28: 8-10.

VAURIE, C. 1972. *Tibet and its birds.* H.F. & G. Witherby. London.

WHISTLER, H. 1912. Immature plumage of Lammergeyer (*Gypaetus barbatus*). *J. Bombay nat. Hist. Soc.* 21: 663-665.

S.M.Satheesan
B-VI/3, Airport Colony
Airports Authority of India
Mahipalpur, Gurgaon Road
New Delhi – 110 037
India.

Chancellor, R. D. & B.-U. Meyburg eds. 2000
Raptors at Risk
WWGBP / Hancock House

The Current Status of North American Vultures

Lloyd F. Kiff

ABSTRACT

Population trends of three species of North American cathartid vultures, the Turkey Vulture *Cathartes aura*, Black Vulture *Coragyps atratus*, and California Condor *Gymnogyps californianus*, are reviewed here. Both of the smaller species have undergone dramatic northward range extensions since the 1920s. A temporary decline in numbers occurred in many areas from the 1950s to the early 1970s, coinciding with the period of DDT use in North America, and widespread eggshell thinning was documented in California, Texas, and Florida during that period. Soon after the domestic use of DDT was banned in the United States and Canada in the early 1970s, vulture populations began to increase. Based on distributional data from diverse sources, numbers of both species are presently stable or increasing throughout their North American ranges. The ongoing northward range expansion has been enhanced by several factors, including increases in the deer population, increased availability of other road-killed animals, reduced pesticide use, reduced human persecution, the increased number of landfills, and a general warming trend. Given the long-term nature of the northward expansion, its continental dimensions, and parallel expansions of other, ecologically unrelated species, it seems likely that climatic changes may be the most important. The California Condor, a rare species throughout its recorded history, has shown an encouraging increase in numbers during the past decade as a result of a vigorous captive breeding and release programme. Although it is still one of the most endangered species in the world, there is increasing hope that its once all-but-inevitable extinction can be prevented.

INTRODUCTION

Three species of cathartid vultures, the Black Vulture *Coragyps atratus*, Turkey Vulture *Cathartes aura*, and the California Condor *Gymnogyps californianus*, occur in the portion of North America north of the United States-Mexico border. A status review indicates that the fortunes of all three species have improved markedly in recent years, although on different scales.

Because their recent status, distributional trends, and ecological requirements are similar in general details, the two small North American cathartids are discussed together here. In preparing this update, I have relied heavily on the valuable reviews by Pattee and Wilbur (1989), Coleman and Fraser (1989, 1990), Kirk and Hyslop (1998), Kirk and Mossman (1998), and Mossman (1991).

To prevent the impending extinction of the California Condor, an aggressive management programme, involving captive breeding and reintroduction, was initiated in 1980 and has continued to the present time. Fuller details of that programme are described elsewhere in this volume; hence, the discussion here is limited mostly to details on condor numbers and range.

TURKEY AND BLACK VULTURES

General Notes

The Turkey Vulture is the most widespread and differentiated cathartid species, occurring from southern Canada to Tierra del Fuego and the Falkland Islands, ranging from sea level to 4,300 m (Brown & Amadon 1968, Houston 1995). Four subspecies were recognized by Brown and Amadon (*op. cit.*) and Houston (*op. cit.*), but additional valid undescribed races may exist while molecular techniques may reveal that some groups are actually full species.

The northernmost temperate breeding populations are migratory. The eastern populations of North American winter mostly in the southern United States, whereas the western United States populations migrate south through Central America south to Paraguay (Brown & Amadon *op. cit.*). More than one million individuals pass each fall over Veracruz, Mexico migration hawk watch stations (E. Ruelas pers. comm.), and hundreds of thousands have been recorded in a single fall migration season over Panama (Smith 1980).

On a hemispheric basis, the monotypic Black Vulture is the most common cathartid; indeed, Brown and Amadon regarded it as the most common bird of prey in the Western Hemisphere. The species occurs from the southeastern United States and extreme southern Arizona and Texas south to Argentina and Chile (AOU 1998). Despite the abundance of the species, its migratory status is still unclear. It appears to be resident throughout most of its range, but possible migratory movements have been detected in Central America (Eisenmann 1963, Skutch 1969). Black Vultures do not occur as far south in South America as Turkey Vultures, nor as far north or west in the United States. Interestingly, in California, where the Black Vulture is presently absent, the Pleistocene equivalent, *Coragyps occidentalis*, was the most common small cathartid as recently as 10,000 years ago, judging from fossil remains from Rancho La Brea (Howard 1930).

Turkey Vultures have the most catholic habitat preferences of any member of the Cathartidae, perhaps owing in part to their ability to use olfactory clues in locating carcasses. This adaptation, shared by all *Cathartes* species, including the Neotropical Lesser Yellow-headed Vulture *C. burrovianus* and Greater Yellow-headed Vulture *C. melambrotus*, allows them to penetrate denser forests than other avian scavengers, all of which rely solely on visual cues (Houston 1986, 1988). In eastern North America, Turkey Vultures prefer a mosaic of open and forested habitats to accommodate their nesting, feeding, and roosting requirements. Although they often roost in large congregations, Turkey Vultures are usually solitary or occur as loosely associated pairs when foraging. They are usually the first species to find carcasses, but, depending on the region, they are displaced by the later-arriving Black Vultures, King Vultures *Sarcorhamphus papa*, California Condors, and Andean Condors *Vultur gryphus* (Koford 1953, Wallace & Temple 1987, Houston 1988).

Black Vultures tend to occur in larger groups at carcasses than the Turkey Vulture, and they are associated with human settlements and activities throughout their range. They seldom penetrate actual unbroken primary forest, although birds may occasionally feed just within forest edges on carcasses found first by Turkey Vultures. Probably as a consequence of its foraging strategy and its capacity to feed on smaller food items, the Turkey Vulture is more widely distributed ecologically and geographically, even though the Black Vulture is more abundant in most areas of sympatry.

Population Trends

In compiling this summary I have drawn upon data provided by the Breeding Bird Survey, Christmas Bird Counts, migration counts from hawkwatches, state breeding bird atlases, National Wildlife Federation regional raptor symposia, and the field notes sections of *American Birds*. Enumerating the various biases and sampling weaknesses of certain of these approaches has become a discrete scientific discipline in itself by now, but, in aggregate, the surveys are adequate for detecting broad population trends and changes in continental range patterns of easily detected species like vultures.

Breeding Bird Survey

The Breeding Bird Survey (BBS) is an ongoing cooperative programme initiated in 1965 and sponsored jointly by the U.S. Fish and Wildlife Service and the Canadian Wildlife Service. It was designed to estimate population trends of migratory bird species nesting in North America north of Mexico. Pairs of observers conduct surveys along highways, making 50 3-min stops 0.8 km apart during a single morning each year at the height of the breeding season. All bird species seen or heard in the vicinity of each stop are recorded. The strength of the BBS lies both in the scope of its coverage (>3,700 routes) and in the repetition of the same survey routes in successive years (> 2,900 annually) (Sauer *et al.* 1997).

In the first summary of long-term BBS results, Robbins *et al.* (1986) analysed population trends that emerged from the first 15 years (1965-79) of the survey. These data indicated that populations of both Black and Turkey Vultures were stable, and no significant changes were detected in any major region of the country. A modest population increase was detected in the Great Lakes Region for the Turkey Vulture, and a significant decrease was found in Florida.

These findings agree with later analyses, using more sophisticated statistical techniques (Sauer *et al.* 1997). An increase, albeit not statistically significant, in Turkey Vulture populations was apparent only in Canada during the early period (1966-1979), and populations elsewhere showed little or no change (Table 1). In contrast, BBS survey data from 1980-1996 revealed highly significant population increases for Turkey Vultures in all areas, particularly Canada, except for a slight, non-significant decline in the Central Region (Table 2). Black Vultures also increased in all areas in both periods, although the changes were not highly significant (Tables 3, 4).

As noted by Kirk and Mossman (1998), cathartid vultures are probably underrepresented by BBS techniques, since the surveys are conducted in the early morning before thermals develop and the birds have become active. The effects of such a bias should not have varied over the history of the BBS project, however, so overall population trends indicated by these data are probably valid.

Christmas Bird Count (CBC)

The National Audubon Society Christmas Bird Count is an early-winter survey of birds conducted annually within two weeks of 25 December by an army of observers throughout North America. Total numbers of species and individual birds are recorded within 15-mi (24 km) diam circles, and many of the same localities have been censused for decades; 1,692 counts were made by over 45,000 participants during the 1995-96 season (Sauer *et al.* (1996).

Brown (1976) analysed North American vulture population trends from CBC data between 1950 and 1973 and found that populations of both species declined steadily during that 24-year study period. Turkey Vulture populations held fairly steady through the 1950s, then dropped off more steeply after 1959. Black Vulture sighting frequencies dropped by almost 50% from the beginning to the end of the study period. Brown's study period coincided closely with the period (1946-1972) of legal DDT use in the United States and Canada.

Based on CBC data, Sauer *et al.* (1996) estimated North American bird population trends for the period 1959-88 (data for subsequent years have not yet been analysed). Based on this technique, the Black Vulture showed minor trend declines in several southern states, including Alabama (-2.5), Georgia (-3.4), Kentucky (-0.1), and South Carolina (-4.2). Only the latter was highly statistically significant ($P<0.01$). Highly significant positive trends were found in Tennessee (7.3) and Maryland (4.3), and a significant ($P<0.05$) positive trend was found in Pennsylvania (5.2). Despite the apparent declines in the southern states, the relative abundance of the species was still much higher in that region, being highest in Georgia, where 21.35 birds were counted per 100 party hours. Because this span of years overlaps between the period of greatest DDT use and 16 years following the ban on the pesticide, any population trends that might be related to that contaminant would be masked. However, a rough analysis of survey-wide data for this period show a decline in numbers between 1959 to about 1971, then a steady increase through 1988 (Sauer *et al. op. cit.*).

The equivalent data for the Turkey Vulture indicate a more or less stable North American population from 1959 to 1971, followed by a steady upward trend in numbers through 1988. Highly significant percentage increases in Turkey Vulture survey counts were found in Alabama (5.3), California (2.0), Florida (4.0), Pennsylvania (7.2), and throughout the entire survey area (2.6); none of the few reported declines in trends were significant.

In the following tables Trend = % change/yr, P = statistical significance, N = number of count circles on which trends were estimated. (Data from Sauer *et al.* 1996).

Table 1. Turkey Vulture population trends based on BBS data, 1966-79.

	Trend	P	N
United States	+1.2	0.30	816
Eastern Region	+1.2	0.38	447
Central Region	+2.1	0.19	208
Western Region	-2.3	0.24	169
Canada	+8.1	0.43	8

Table 2. Turkey Vulture population trends based on BBS data, 1980-96.

	Trend	P	N
United States	+1.6	0.00	1522
Eastern Region	+3.2	0.00	890
Central Region	-0.2	0.83	353
Western Region	+3.8	0.00	328
Canada	+17.3	0.00	49

Table 3. Black Vulture population trends based on BBS data, 1966-79.

	Trend	P	N
United States	+1.8	0.31	220
Eastern region	+1.4	0.53	149
Central region	+2.6	0.39	70

Table 4. Black Vulture populations trends based on BBS data, 1980-96.

	Trend	P	N
United States	+2.3	0.09	415
Eastern region	+2.1	0.24	284
Central region	+3.0	0.15	130

Migration hawk watches

These stations record actual observations of birds passing by established lookout points. All North American hawk watches have recorded increasing numbers of both vulture species in recent years, apparently reflecting the growth of summering populations ever farther to the north. Representative findings from some of the best known observation stations are as follows:

Cape May, New Jersey: The count of fall migrating Turkey Vultures continues to increase steadily. In 1993, the first season that the count exceeded 1,000, 1,540 individuals were recorded. Subsequent counts were 2,260 in 1994, 3,242 in 1995, and 5,425 in 1996 (Greenstone 1997). Black Vulture numbers also have continued to increase at this site, where the species was virtually unknown only a few decades ago (Greenstone *op cit.*).

Hawk Mountain, Pennsylvania: The first Black Vulture was sighted in fall migration at Hawk Mountain in 1979 (in the 35th year of observations), and the species has been detected annually since 1985. The average number sighted in fall during the last five years is 50 (L. Goodrich *in litt.*).

Over the years at Hawk Mountain, Turkey Vulture observations have been recorded only intermittently, and interpretation of sightings is complicated by the presence of a resident population. However, the number of birds recorded during the past 10 years is believed to be stable or possibly increasing (L. Goodrich *in litt.*).

Niagara Peninsula Hawkwatch, Grimsby, Ontario: Hussell and Brown (1992) reported an increase in annual indices of abundance of 8.0% in Turkey Vulture numbers in fall migration between 1975-1990 at this site, based on logistical multiple regression procedures, which permitted corrections for date and weather effects.

Hawk Ridge, Duluth, Minnesota: Based on logistical multiple regressions, Hussell and Brown (1992) found an increase of 3.6% in annual indices abundance of Turkey Vulture numbers between 1974-1989, the highest rate of change for any of the species detected at this site during the same period.

HawkWatch International: Based on their analysis of hawk watch data from four western sites (Wellsville Mountains, Utah; Goshute Mountains, Nevada; Manzano Mountains, New Mexico; Sandia Mountains, New Mexico), Hoffman *et al.* (1992, unpubl. data) concluded that the number of Turkey Vulture detections in fall migration has increased steadily (as much as 15% annually) during the past two decades along at least two distinct migration flyways in the Interior West.

Golden Gate Raptor Observatory, Marin Headlands, California: As in the case of Hawk Mountain, interpretation of Turkey Vulture observations at this site is complicated by the presence of a resident population and the apparent tendency of some migrants to remain in the area for several days. Nevertheless, the fall population has been stable, or possibly increasing, over the past five years (A. Fish pers. comm.). This coincides with the conclusions of the California Department of Fish and Game for the state in general (K. Hunting pers. comm.).

Veracruz, Mexico: The population of migrant Turkey Vultures in fall appears to be stable, and fall counts at two major observation sites averaged 1,205,707 individuals during the five-year period of 1992-1996 (E. Ruelas pers. comm.).

Breeding bird atlases and state bird books

I reviewed the status summaries for Black and Turkey Vultures in recent bird atlases and/or state bird books for most North American states and provinces and found that all reported stable or increasing resident and migrant vulture populations since the late 1970s and 1980s.

National Wildlife Federation reviews

The National Wildlife Federation organized five regional symposia between 1985-1988 on the status of United States raptors. Except for the one held in the Southwest, each proceedings volume contained a chapter on vultures, and these are still relatively up-to-date assessments of vulture status in North America. The conclusions of the respective authors were as follows:

Southeast: Turkey Vulture populations stable over the region as a whole; range expansion and increase in numbers of the Black Vulture northward (Coleman & Fraser 1990).

Northeast: Increased numbers and northward range expansion of both species (Coleman & Fraser 1989).

Midwest: Turkey Vulture populations stable or increasing overall; Black Vultures possibly declining (Mossman 1991).

Western: Turkey Vulture populations appeared stable with no evidence of recent significant changes in distribution... "the long-term outlook for the species in the West is good."(Pattee & Wilbur 1989).

American Birds

Another rich source of information on the current status of North American birds is the field notes columns of the journal *American Birds* (formerly *Audubon Field Notes*; now titled "*Field Notes*"), which were initiated in 1947, the year when DDT was first widely used in North America. Whereas there has been a strong preoccupation with vagrants in these columns over the years, they also contain frequent comments on apparent range extensions or unusual increases in abundance of more common species. The *American Birds* field notes sections represent the most comprehensive source of up-to-date, albeit subjective, information on the recent and present status of bird populations in North America.

In general, the regional reports documented declining populations of cathartid vultures in most parts of North America in the 1960s. Increasing populations were reported in most regions in the mid- to late-1970s and throughout the 1980s. During the 1990s, there has been unanimous agreement that the ranges of both species of small cathartids are continuing to expand northward, more individuals are attempting to overwinter ever farther north, and birds are arriving earlier in spring and staying later in fall than was previously the norm. For example, both species, especially the Turkey Vulture, now occur with regularity in southern Quebec, northern Ontario, and the Maritime Provinces, where they were virtually unrecorded formerly, and some birds are now overwintering successfully. There is even a recent record for the Turkey Vulture in Yukon Territory, Canada (Bowling 1996) and multiple records for southeastern Alaska (Tobish 1997)! In view of the continuing lack of documented nestings in most of this region, it is probable that many of these pioneering individuals may be non-breeders, or post-breeding wanderers, as suggested by Cadman *et al.* (1988) and others.

Limiting factors

The historical causes of mortality and/or population limitation of North American vultures include shooting, trapping, primary and secondary poisoning, eggshell thinning, human-related accidents, the lack of suitable food, and the loss of foraging habitat and nesting sites. Only the latter two factors are likely to still be of any significance.

Human persecution

Direct human persecution of these vulture species has taken the usual forms, including shooting, trapping, and deliberate poisoning. Throughout the first half of the present century, many ranchers and farmers associated Turkey and Black Vultures with the spread of livestock diseases, especially anthrax, and therefore often sought to eliminate them, usually by trapping (Parmalee 1954). In addition, there were also more valid concerns about Black Vulture depredations on calves and other newborn livestock. In some regions there were large-scale government-sponsored and private programmes to eliminate problem vultures (Howell 1928). According to Snyder and Rea (1998), literally hundreds of thousands of Black and Turkey Vultures were eliminated by trapping in Florida and Texas during the 1940s and 1950s. There are still some locally based government-sanctioned removal episodes, usually in response to Black Vulture livestock depredations. Otherwise, there appears to be little direct persecution of either species, and both are now protected by the Migratory Bird Treaty Act, a treaty between the United States, Canada, and Mexico.

Where they are sympatric, both species may roost together in large aggregations with little, if any, interspecific conflict. In some populated areas, these roosts are regarded as a public nuisance, and occasional government permits are issued to disperse the birds, generally by non-lethal means. By and large, however, shooting and directed poisoning episodes are increasingly rare throughout most of the ranges of these species and will probably continue to decline as a result of changing American attitudes toward wildlife and an increasing trend toward corporate agriculture in the United States and Canada. There is a low cost:benefit ratio for large corporations in shooting or poisoning vultures in this era of heightened environmental awareness in North America. Most find it more acceptable to endure occasional minor losses or inconveniences from the vultures than to generate disproportionate negative publicity and public outcry by shooting them.

Secondary poisoning

According to Snyder and Snyder (1991), Turkey Vultures are relatively insensitive to natural pathogens and some rodenticides, including the compound 1080, but quite sensitive to other poisons, including cyanide and strychnine, which were formerly used widely to poison coyotes and other perceived threats to cattle and sheep. These two vulture species like California Condors, may also be unusually sensitive to lead poisoning, which they can obtain in the form of bullet fragments in shot mammals carcasses and gutpiles. Little is known of the effects of range poisons on North American vulture populations, but it could have been considerable during former eras, when setting out poisoned carcasses for vermin was a widespread practice, and hunting was more pervasive.

One of the most widespread and dramatic forms of indirect poisoning of these species has been DDE-induced eggshell thinning. Wilbur (1978) first reported declines of 11%, 12%, and 18% in eggshell thickness indices of post-1947 (post-DDT) Turkey Vulture eggshells from California, Florida, and Texas, respectively. Drawing on larger samples, Kiff et al. (1983) confirmed these trends in eggshell thickness indices from post-1947 samples from the same three states, finding declines of 9.7%, 15.9%, and 10.1%, respectively, and they were associated with high levels of DDE residues extracted from the eggshell membranes. Elsewhere, Coleman and Fraser (1989) reported eggshell thinning of 8% and 14% in small Turkey Vulture eggshell samples collected between 1947-1964 in southeastern and mid-Atlantic states, respectively.

Kiff et al. (1983) also found even greater declines in thickness indices of post-1947 Black Vulture eggshells from Florida (16%) and Texas (17%), and there was a significant negative correlation with DDE residue levels of 6 ppm wet wt in the latter sample. These levels of eggshell thinning are very close to those associated with population declines in other species (Peakall & Kiff 1988) and probably led to breakage in some eggs.

Food limitation

In most other regions, the availability of eligible carcasses has probably increased greatly as a result of human activities. As soon as automobiles became part of the American scene in the early part of the this century, vultures began to profit from the new availability of road-killed creatures, despite occasionally becoming road kills themselves (Sutton 1928). Sutton (1928 *op. cit.*) may have been the first to advance the notion that a tremendous resurgence of the White-tailed Deer *Odocoileus virginianus* population and their subsequent starvation led to a marked increase in the Turkey Vulture population in Pennsylvania in the 1920s. This factor has subsequently been mentioned by various authors. e.g., Wilbur (1983) and Kirk and Hyslop (1998), as an important reason for the notable increase in the range of both vulture species in northeastern North America in recent decades.

Throughout the western portion of the United States range of Turkey and Black Vultures, cattle have become a modern staple of their diet, but changes in ranching practices, including the increased use of feedlots and the tendency of some ranchers to promptly remove cow carcasses from the open range, have led to a decline in the availability of this food source. This may have contributed to a lower density of these species in some western states, as suggested for Texas by Porter and White (1977), for Utah by Taylor (1986), and for Arizona by Rea (1998b), but it has no doubt been partially compensated by the increase in landfills and roadkills.

Habitat changes

Widespread habitat changes have probably favoured both vulture species in the eastern United States and Canada. After well over two centuries of settlement by Europeans and subsequent retreats and advances of the forests, the prevailing habitat is a mosaic of forest patches and open areas well suited to the cathartid species. However, increasing urbanization of coastal southern California, once a stronghold of Turkey Vulture populations, has probably contributed to a decline in numbers there (Garrett & Dunn 1981, Unitt 1984). Another negative anthropogenic effect on vulture habitat has been a decline in the Southeast in the availability of suitable nesting sites, principally large hollow trees, for Black Vultures as a result of modern timbering practices (Jackson 1983, Robbins & Easterla 1992).

DISCUSSION

Bagg and Parker (1951, 1953) provided detailed summaries of the spread of the Turkey Vulture into New England and eastern Canada, beginning in the second quarter of this century. Since their analysis, the limits of the range of both vulture species in North America have continued to undergo a steady expansion northward. This trend, which also occurred in northern and western New York (Allen *in* Bagg & Parker 1951) and the Midwest (Van Tyne *in* Bagg & Parker 1951), has continued into Quebec, Ontario, the Maritime Provinces, and even along the Pacific Coast , as shown in the preceding section. Based on all available evidence, it appears to be a long-term, unidirectional phenomenon that is unprecedented in the recorded history of these two species.

Wilbur (1983) and Pattee and Wilbur (1989) suggested that the United States range of the Turkey Vulture has both expanded and contracted over time regionally, citing as an example the temporary abundance of this species in Montana in the 1880s during the massive slaughter of the great bison *Bison bison* herds and their subsequent retraction to the south when this temporary food supply subsided (Cameron 1907). Other authors also noted declines of Turkey Vultures in South Dakota (Grinnell 1875) and Minnesota (Roberts 1932) which may have been related to the disappearance of the bison. This, and Webster's (1978) report of a striking increase in Texas Turkey Vulture populations in response to an increase in rat populations, shows that the species is capable of major changes in distribution and abundance. However, aside from the earlier (temporary) retreat from the northern Great Plains and upper midwestern states, the entire recent history of the Turkey Vulture appears to be characterized by a continual northward expansion.

Nevertheless, Coleman and Fraser (1989, 1990) stated that Turkey Vultures occurred in New England in the early 1800s, but were rare there by the last part of the century, implying that they began returning in the 1920s in response to a recovery of the deer population. They apparently based this on Merriam's (1877) mention that Linsley (1843) found the species "not uncommon" in southern Connecticut in the early 1800s, although Merriam himself characterized the species as "a rare visitor from the South" by mid-century, an assessment echoed by Sage and Bishop (1913). Linsley, a clergyman, also described in detail a purported incident of a Turkey Vulture attempting to carry off a chicken in its feet, which calls his reliability as an observer into question. The assertion of the Turkey Vulture's former abundance was dismissed by Bagg and Parker (1951), and there is little else in the older literature to support the notion that the species was ever numerous in New England until recent times. Indisputably, probably on the basis of hearsay, Wilson (1808-14) stated that "this species inhabits a vast range of territory, being common, it is said, from Nova Scotia to Tierra del Fuego.". However, in his later revision of Wilson's great work, Bonaparte (1825-33) injected the qualifying comment with this account that "In the northern States of our Union, the turkey buzzard is only occasionally seen. It is considered a rare bird by the inhabitants.".

Giraud (1844) reported that the Turkey Vulture was "of rare occurrence in the vicinity of New York (City)", although he noted that it was more common in New Jersey and nested there. He stated that he was unaware that this species ever reached New England, and he suggested that Long Island was the northern terminus of its range. Giraud's work was based on several decades of study, so he should have been aware of any profound declines in the numbers of Turkey Vultures. Similarly, De Kay's contemporaneous work (1844) on the birds of the whole State of New York, also showed this bird to be rare. Finally, in the most comprehensive 19th century work on North American land birds, Ridgway (*in* Baird *et al.* 1874) also stated that the species was not common north of central New Jersey, and mentioned only that "occasionally individuals have been seen as far north as New Brunswick and Nova Scotia". If the species had formerly been common in the New England area, this surely would have been noted.

The Black Vulture has also undergone a conspicuous range expansion since the 1920s. It was unknown in the Northeast, or even as far north as Virginia, until well into the 20th century. Bonaparte (1825-33) and Ridgway (*in* Baird *et al.* 1874) gave North Carolina as its northern limit, and the latter authority stated specifically that the species did not occur then as far north as (Norfolk) Virginia. Subsequently, Black Vultures have moved farther north, and the species now breeds regularly as far north as Pennsylvania and Ohio, and individual birds are routinely found much farther north, even in winter.

Farther west, Parmalee (1954) showed that the Black Vulture increased greatly in numbers in Texas in the 1920s, attributing this to changing livestock practices. The intrusion of this species into Arizona also evidently occurred at about the same time, judging from the assessment of Phillips (1934), who noted that "The Black Vulture was apparently merely casual in Arizona up to a few years ago. Now it is rather regular but still very rare in the region south of Tucson and Ajo, near the border. It probably occurs in summer, but observation here is chiefly limited to the winter months.". Subsequently, the species has increased greatly in numbers, if not in range, and it breeds regularly in the southern portions of the state (Rea 1998a).

Bagg and Parker (1951) listed several factors that, acting in combination, might have been responsible for the northward expansion of cathartid vultures, including (1) the great increase in deer populations in the Northeast, particularly since 1920, as suggested earlier by Sutton (1928) and Peterson (1948), (2) an increase in the number of road-killed animals, as automobile traffic burgeoned, (3) the deterioration of vulture habitat farther to the south, owing to the spread of civilization, and (4) the warming of the climate in the Northeast.

It is tempting to speculate that the range of the Turkey Vulture, at least, has ebbed and flowed northward and southward in eastern North America over the past two centuries as a result of the changing fortunes of the deer population, yet the historical data do not support the notion that vulture distributional changes in the Northeast, where the most conspicuous expansion has occurred, have involved anything more than a steady expansion northward. There is no evidence that vulture movements represent a cyclic response correlated with the rise and fall of deer populations, although the presence of large numbers of deer no doubt makes it easier for these scavengers to survive. By now, the expanding vulture populations have moved well beyond the portions of the continent where the deer populations have increased the most, and it is of interest that none of the birds reported from the northern extremes of the range have been feeding on deer carcasses. A more general explanation seems to be in order.

The somewhat incidental suggestion of Bagg and Parker (1951) that Turkey Vultures may have moved northward as a result of a decline in habitat quality in the South seems quite unlikely, since there has not been a long-term population decline there concomitant with the northerly range expansion, despite intense persecution in some areas. However, Mossman (1991) agreed that this might have been an important factor in the northward expansion of Turkey Vultures in the Midwest. Unquestionably, there have been deleterious widespread habitat changes for vultures in portions of both the South and the Midwest, primarily as the result of widespread conversion of formerly forested areas to agricultural uses and housing tracts.

Evidence from the CBC, *American Birds* regional reports, and various other sources, including Porter and White (1977), indicate that most North American populations of Black and Turkey Vultures were in decline from the 1950s to the early 1970s and that a recovery subsequently occurred. The timing of the decline coincided closely with the period (1946-1970) of the greatest use of DDT and other persistent organochlorine pesticides in North America. The documentation of widespread eggshell changes, presumably DDE-induced, in both species (Wilbur 1978, Kiff *et al.* 1983), and the subsequent increase in vulture numbers, which began shortly after the domestic use of DDT was banned in 1972, strongly suggest that these population effects were the result of DDE contamination. It is doubtful that eggshell thinning is still a problem for North American Turkey and Black Vultures, based on measurements of several recent samples obtained opportunistically. For example, by 1983 and 1984, Pennsylvania Turkey Vulture eggshells exhibited near historical shell thicknesses (L. Kiff & J. Coleman, unpubl. data).

Although vulture populations in some parts of the country were probably suppressed during the period of greatest DDT use, there is no evidence that the broader northward expansion was appreciably slowed. Whereas it is likely that the pattern of organochlorine pesticide use accounts for most of the trends observed in Black and Turkey Vulture numbers throughout the North American range of both species, the ongoing northward expansion was a separate matter related to other factors. It would be useful to compare BBS data for the periods 1966-1972, when DDT was still in use, and 1973-1979, the period when a rebound from the pesticide era may have occurred, but such figures are presently unavailable.

Rea (1998b) suggested that Turkey Vultures (and presumably also Black Vultures) in Latin America might still be suffering from eggshell thinning, since heavy DDT use continued in Mexico and more southern countries well after the compound was banned in Canada and the United States. In fact, Albert *et al.* (1989) reported high DDE levels and declines in eggshell thickness indices in

Black Vulture eggs from the State of Veracruz, Mexico. Presumably, Turkey Vultures migrating through the Neotropics from more northern breeding grounds would also be affected. However, DDT use in Mexico and most other Latin American countries has greatly declined during the last decade (Pesticide Action Network *in litt.*), so affected populations may now be recovering from years of DDE contamination.

The range expansion of the vultures is occurring over such a broad front that it requires a generalized explanation. Of the hypotheses suggested by Bagg and Parker (1951), the idea that northward changes in the ranges of both of these cathartids is related to a long-term warming trend is a tantalizing one that deserves further examination. Certainly, a similar northward range expansion in eastern North America over the past few decades by several weather-sensitive passerine species, e.g., Northern Cardinal *Cardinalis cardinalis*, Northern Mockingbird *Mimus polyglottos*, and Carolina Wren *Thryothorus ludovicianus*, seems to be related to an overall warming trend (Root 1988). Various *American Birds* regional editors have commented upon the apparent tendency of Black and Turkey Vultures to overwinter or to appear earlier in spring in northern areas in milder winters, and short-term movements of these species are probably greatly influenced by extreme weather conditions.

It is possible that the limits of the winter ranges of both vulture species may be imposed by minimum temperatures. From her analysis of Christmas Count data, Root (1988) concluded that, with the exception of portions of the Mississippi Valley, most of the areas in the United States where Black Vultures occur have an average minimum January temperature of above 30°F (-1°C). Cannings *et al.* (1987) and Rea (1998 a,b) suggested that the availability of unfrozen carcasses may be a important factor in limiting the winter range of both species. Obviously, an overall warming trend would push the limits of inhabitable territory farther northward. Many of the extralimital birds reported from New England and eastern Canada have been found at landfills. Naturally, such individuals are probably easier to detect than birds in more remote areas, but the increasing number and size of these facilities may provide a source of relatively unfrozen food that was previously unavailable to the vultures.

Of the two species, the Turkey Vulture is probably less vulnerable to future changes that may occur as human populations continue to increase. As a consequence of its adaptability to a wide range of habitats, perhaps related to its specialized foraging strategy, a capacity to feed on a wide range of food items, and its less restricted choice of nest sites, including even abandoned buildings (Valentine 1973), the Turkey Vulture is more widely distributed over the landscape, even though the Black Vulture is more abundant in most areas of sympatry. Within historical times, Turkey Vultures have traditionally occurred farther north and in more diverse habitats that the Black Vulture.

In the short term, there is probably little cause for concern about either of the small cathartid vulture species in the North American portion of their range, except possibly on a local basis where isolated poisoning or shooting episodes might occur. In the not-too-distant future, however, the increasingly antiseptic ranching practices of corporate agriculture and the relentless conversion of formerly open lands to housing developments will probably result in gradual declines of some local vulture populations unless these species again become fixtures in urban and suburban areas, as was the case in the early days of American history.

CALIFORNIA CONDOR

The California Condor has traditionally been the posterchild for rare and endangered bird species in North America and even globally. Warnings about its alarming decline were sounded as early as 1890 (Cooper 1890), and the inevitability of its extinction was the common refrain of most writings on the species throughout the present century. In an effort to prevent the condor's extinction, an aggressive management programme, involving captive breeding and reintroduction, was initiated in 1980. Fuller details of that programme are described elsewhere in this volume; hence, this discussion is limited to details on changes in condor numbers and range.

Range

The California Condor occurred widely in North America as recently as the late Pleistocene, and fossil remains have been found in New York, Florida, northern Mexico, Texas, New Mexico, Arizona, and California (Emslie 1990). The species became extinct throughout most of its range around the end of the Pleistocene (about 10,000 yr B.P.). Most ornithologists, including Grinnell and Miller (1944), Koford (1953), Wilbur (1978), and AOU (1998), have concluded that the range of the California Condor was limited to the Pacific Coast region, from British Columbia, Canada to Baja California Norte, Mexico, during the last two centuries.

Snyder and Rea (1998) argued otherwise, however, listing several reported condor sightings from Arizona and Utah between the 1860s and 1924. Taken singly, none of these records, which include several secondhand accounts (e.g., Brown 1899, Harris 1941), is particularly satisfactory by modern standards, and they do not differ greatly in character from other long discarded or dubious reports of condors in Alberta (Fannin 1897), Idaho (Wilcox 1917) Nevada (Dillon 1966, Ryser 1985), and Colorado and Wyoming (Harris 1941). In lieu of specimens or more detailed accounts, the matter of whether or not the species has occurred east of the California Sierra Nevada in historical times is a subjective judgement. At most, condors could only have been exceedingly rare outside of the Pacific Coast region within the past century.

Numbers

Despite its low numbers throughout its history, efforts to determine the actual size of the condor population met with little success until recently. "Best-guess" estimates between 1923 and 1943 ranged widely, but most estimators put the number of living condors at 100 or less (Table 5). Following his landmark study of the species between 1939 and the late 1940s, Koford (1953) was challenged to produce an estimate of the condor population, based for the first time on actual research throughout the range of the species. He settled on the figure of 60 birds, while admitting that this was a somewhat arbitrary figure and that the number could actually be as high as 100 (Ed Harrison pers. comm., Snyder & Johnson 1985). A National Audubon Society-sponsored survey of the status of the condor population was conducted in the early 1960s by two rancher conservationists, Ian and Eben McMillan, and together with their collaborator, Alden Miller, they concluded that there had been a decline to only 40 birds (Miller *et al.* 1965).

Table 5. Historical estimates of the total California Condor population.

Estimate	Year	Authority
<100	1923	Dawson (1923)
"a few dozen"	1925	Finley & Finley (1926)
150	1926	J. Grinnell (*fide* Phillips) (1926)
12	1933	Wetmore (1933)
< 50	1933	Willett (1933)
60+	1934	Robinson (1934)
< 50	1939	American Ornithologists' Union (1940)
100	1943	Grinnell & Miller (1944)
60-100	1951	Koford (*in litt.*)
60	1953	Koford (1953)
40	1964	Miller *et al.* (1964)
50-60	1966-71	Wilbur *et al.* (1972)
<50	1975	Wilbur (1976)
40-<50	1976	Wilbur (1978)
25-35	1978	Wilbur (1980)
21-22	1982-83	Snyder & Johnson (1985)
27	1987	Snyder & Snyder (1989)
147	1998	R. Mesta (pers. comm.)

Following formal involvement of the U.S. Fish and Wildlife Service in condor conservation, an annual survey was conducted each October between 1966 and 1980 in an attempt to monitor numbers of the species. The survey results were somewhat ambiguous, owing to the strong influence of weather conditions on the reported totals and the impossibility of detecting all extant condors in the still-vast range of the species in a two-day effort (Wilbur 1980). However, it was apparent that the condor population probably included as many as 50-60 individuals between 1966-71 (Wilbur et al. 1972) and that ever fewer birds were detected in succeeding years (Wilbur 1978, 1980).

Snyder and Johnson (1985) devised an ingenious method of censusing condors by photographing them in flight and separating them by their individual peculiarities in feather patterns. By compiling a comprehensive photographic record of condors in all parts of the known range, they concluded that the number of wild condors was reduced to 20-21 birds by late 1982. At that time there was only a single individual in captivity, and the estimate of 21-22 total condors represented the probable lowest point in the history of the species. Snyder and Johnson (1985) also re-analysed earlier estimates of condor numbers, and they concluded that both Koford and the McMillans had greatly underestimated the size of the populations during their respective eras. According to their extrapolations, there could have been as many as 180 condors during the early 1950s and 120 during the 1960s.

Management programme

Despite the imprecision of the survey results, it was generally agreed that the condor population was continuing to decline at a precipitous rate. In response, the U.S. Fish and Wildlife Service and the National Audubon Society initiated a vigorous condor management programme in 1980. One thrust of this was to radio-tag several condors to determine causes of mortality, to track movements of individuals, and to identify critical habitat. Another major component of the programme was a detailed study of the nesting habits of wild condors. This eventually came to include removal of eggs from wild condor nests for hatching in captivity and capturing several adult and juvenile birds for captive breeding purposes. Between 1984 and 1987 these manipulations resulted in a slight increase in the total population of the species, the first documented reversal in the decline of condor numbers in the recorded history of the species.

Although overall numbers were increasing, the wild flock continued to decline for unknown reasons, most likely from shooting and/or poisoning incidents. When the last wild bird was taken into captivity in 1987 for its own security and for use in the captive breeding programme, there were only 27 condors in existence (Snyder & Snyder 1989). The efficacy of the photographic censusing method was confirmed by the fact that no condors undetected by Snyder and Johnson (*op. cit.*) turned up after the presumed last free-flying individual was captured. Sadly, the photographic census had accounted for them all.

Successful captive breeding of California Condors began with the production of a single chick (Molloko) at the San Diego Wild Animal Park in 1988 (Kiff 1990). Two more were produced in 1989, four in 1990, and ever increasing numbers annually through the 1998 breeding season, when 20 birds were produced at three captive breeding facilities (Los Angeles Zoo, San Diego Wild Animal Park, and the World Center for Birds of Prey, Boise, Idaho). Since a majority of the birds presently in captivity have not attained the usual breeding age (five-six years), captive production of young may soon show a more logarithmic rate of increase.

The first release of captive-produced condors to the wild was conducted in January 1992, when two chicks hatched in 1991 were released with two similar-aged Andean Condor chicks in the Sespe Condor Sanctuary, Ventura County, California. Subsequently, 14 groups of 2-6 young condors have been released at four sites in California and one in Arizona. Survival of the released birds has been 56% (Kiff, this volume), among the highest rates enjoyed by any similar vertebrate reintroduction programme. The oldest individuals in the wild have been observed engaging in courtship display and are probably forming breeding pairs. By the end of 1998, there were 42 condors alive in the wild, and 105 were housed in the three captive breeding facilities (R. Mesta pers. comm.).

The short-term objectives of the condor programme, which would lead to the consideration of downlisting the species to threatened status, are to establish 150 pairs in at least three self-sustaining populations, being the captive flocks (in aggregate) and two disjunct wild populations, with at least

15 breeding pairs in each of the three groups (USFWS 1996). This goal has nearly been reached with the captive flock, and it is hoped these numbers can also be achieved in the wild over the next decade.

REFERENCES

ALBERT, L.A., C. BARCENAS, M. RAMOS & E. IÑIGO 1989. Organochlorine pesticides and reduction of eggshell thickness in a Black Vulture *Coragyps atratus* population of the Tuxtla Valley, Chiapas, Mexico. Pp. 473-475 *in* B.-U. Meyburg and R. D. Chancellor (eds.), *Raptors in the modern world*. WWGBP, Berlin.

AMERICAN ORNITHOLOGISTS' UNION 1940. Report of the Committee on Bird Protection, 1939. *Auk* 57:279-291.

AMERICAN ORNITHOLOGISTS' UNION 1998. *Check-list of North American birds*. 7th edition. American Ornithologists' Union, Washington, D.C. 829 pp.

BAGG, A.M. & H.M. PARKER 1951. The Turkey Vulture in New England and eastern Canada up to 1950. *Auk* 68:315-333.

BAGG, A.M. & H.M. PARKER 1953. Further information on the Turkey Vulture (*Cathartes aura*) in New England and Canada. *Auk* 70:490-491.

BAIRD, S.F., T.M. BREWER & R. RIDGWAY 1905 (1874). *A history of North America birds. Land birds.* Vol. III. Little, Brown, and Co., Boston. 560 + xxviii pp.

BONAPARTE, C.L. 1825-33. *American ornithology, or the natural history of birds inhabiting the United States, not given by Wilson*. 4 vols. Carey, Lea and Carey, Philadelphia.

BOWLING, J. 1996. British Columbia/Yukon region. *Natl. Audubon Soc. Field Notes* 50:322.

BROWN, H. 1899. The California vulture in Arizona, *Auk* 16:272.

BROWN, W.H. 1985. Winter population trends in the Black and Turkey Vultures. *Amer. Birds* 30(5):909-912.

BROWN, L. & D. AMADON 1968. *Eagles, hawks and falcons of the world.* 2 vols. McGraw-Hill. 945 pp.

CADMAN, M.D., P.F.J. EAGLES & F.M. HELLEINER (Compilers) 1988. *Atlas of the breeding birds of Ontario.* Univ. of Waterloo Press, Waterloo, Ontario. 617 pp.

CAMERON, E.S. 1907. The birds of Custer and Dawson Counties, Montana. *Auk* 24:241-270.

CANNINGS, R.A., R.J. CANNINGS & S.G. CANNINGS 1987. *Birds of the Okanagan Valley, British Columbia.* Royal British Columbia Museum, Victoria, British Columbia. 440 pp.

COLEMAN, J.S. & J.D. FRASER 1989. Black and Turkey Vultures. Proceedings of the Northeast Raptor Management Symposium and Workshop. *Natl. Wildl. Fed. Scient. Tech. Ser.* 13:15-21.

COLEMAN, J.S. & J.D. FRASER 1990. Black and Turkey Vultures. Proceedings of the Southeast Raptor Management Symposium and Workshop. *Natl. Wildl. Fed. Scient. Tech. Ser.* 14:78-88.

COOPER, J.G. 1890. A doomed bird. *Zoe* 1:248-249.

DAWSON, W.L. 1923. *The birds of California*. Vol. IV. South Moulton Co., San Diego, CA. 121 pp.

DE KAY, J. 1842-44. *Zoology of New-York, or the New-York fauna: comprising descriptions of all the animals hitherto observed within the state of New York, with brief notices of those occasionally found near its borders, and accompanied by appropriate illustrations. Part II. Birds.* Carroll and Cook, Albany, New York. 380 pp.

DILLON, R. 1966. *The legend of Grizzly Adams, California's greatest mountain man.* Coward-McCann, New York.

EISENMANN, E. 1963. Is the Black Vulture migratory? *Wilson Bull.* 75:244-249.

EMSLIE, S.D. 1990. Additional ^{14}C dates on fossil California Condor. *Natl. Geogr. Res.* 6:134-135

FANNIN, J. 1897. The California vulture in Alberta. *Auk* 14:89.

FINLEY, W.L. & L. FINLEY 1926. Passing of the Californian Condor. *Nat. Mag.* 8(2):95-99

GARRETT, K. & J. DUNN. *Birds of southern California: status and distribution.* Los Angeles Audubon Society, Los Angeles. 408 pp.

GIRAUD, J.P. Jr 1844. *Birds of Long Island.* Wiley & Putnam, New York. 397 pp.

GREENSTONE, E. 1997. New Jersey region. *J. Hawk Migration Assoc. Amer.* 23:23-30.

GRINNELL, G.B. 1875. Zoological report: Chapter 2. Birds. *In* W. Ludlow (ed.), *Report of a reconnaissance of the Black Hills of Dakota made in the Summer of 1874*. U.S. Army Engineer Dept., Washington, D.C. 121 pp.

GRINNELL, J. & A.H. MILLER 1944. The distribution of the birds of California. *Pacific Coast Avifauna no. 27.* 608 pp.

HARRIS, H. 1941. The annals of *Gymnogyps* to 1900. *Condor* 43:3-55.

HOFFMAN, S.W., W.R. DERAGON & J.C. BEDNARZ 1992. Patterns and recent trends in counts of migrant hawks in western North America, 1977-1991. Unpubl. report.

HOUSTON, D.C. 1986. Scavenging efficiency of Turkey Vultures in a tropical forest. *Condor* 88:318-323.

HOUSTON, D.C. 1988. Competition for food between Neotropical vultures in forest. *Ibis* 130:402-417.

HOUSTON, D.C. 1994. Family Cathartidae (New World vultures). Pp. 24-41 *in* del Hoyo, J., A. Elliott, and J. Sargatal (eds.), *Handbook of birds of the world, vol. 2. New World vultures to guineafowl*. Lynx Edicions, Barcelona. 638 pp.

HOWARD, H. 1930. A census of the Pleistocene birds of Rancho La Brea from the collections of the Los Angeles County Museum. *Condor* 32:81-88.

HOWELL, A.H. 1928. *Birds of Alabama*. Dept. Game Fisheries of Alabama, Montgomery, AL.

HUSSELL, D.J.T. & L. BROWN 1992. Population changes in diurnally-migrating raptors at Duluth, Minnesota (1974-1989) and Grimsby, Ontario (1975-1990). Ontario Ministry of Natural Resources, Maple, Ontario. 67 pp.

JACKSON, J.A. 1983. Nesting phenology, nest site selection, and reproductive success of Black and Turkey Vultures. Pp. 245-270 *in* S.R. Wilbur & J.A. Jackson (eds.), *Vulture biology and management*. University of California Press, Los Angeles. 550 pp.

KIFF, L.F. 1990. Back from the brink: the battle to save the California Condor. *Terra* 28:6-18.

KIFF, L.F. this volume. The California Condor Recovery Programme.

KIFF, L.F., D.B. PEAKALL, M.L. MORRISON & S.R. WILBUR 1983. Eggshell thickness and DDE-residue levels in vulture eggs. Pp. 440-458 *in* S.R. Wilbur & J.A. Jackson (eds.), *Vulture biology and management*. University of California Press, Los Angeles. 550 pp.

KIRK, D.A. & C. HYSLOP.1998. Population status and recent trends in Canadian raptors: a review. *Biol. Conserv.* 83:91-118.

KIRK, D.A. & M.J. MOSSMAN 1998. Turkey Vulture (*Cathartes aura*). *In* A. Poole & F. Gill (eds.), *The Birds of North America*, no. 339. The Birds of North America, Inc., Philadelphia, PA.

KOFORD, C.B. 1953. *The California Condor*. National Audubon Society Research Report no. 4. 154 pp.

LINSLEY, J.H. 1843. A catalogue of the birds of Connecticut, arranged according to their natural families. *Amer. J. Sci. Arts* 44:249-274.

MERRIAM, C.H. 1877. *A review of the birds of Connecticut*. Tuttle, Morehouse, and Taylor. New Haven, Connecticut.

MILLER, A.H., I. MCMILLAN & E. MCMILLAN 1965. The current status and welfare of the California Condor. *Natl. Audubon Soc. Res. Rep.* 6. 61 pp.

MOSSMAN, M.J. 1991. Black and Turkey Vultures. Proceedings of the Midwest Raptor Management Symposium and Workshop. *Natl. Wildl. Fed. Scient. Tech. Ser.* 15:3-22.

PARMALEE, P.W. 1954. The vultures: their movements, economic status, and control in Texas. *Auk* 71:443-453.

PATTEE, O.H. & S.R. WILBUR 1989. Turkey Vulture and California Condor. Proceedings of the Western Raptor Management Symposium and Workshop. *Natl. Wildl. Fed. Scient. Tech. Ser.* 12:61-65.

PEAKALL, D.B. & L.F. KIFF 1988. DDE contamination in Peregrines and American Kestrels and its effects on reproduction. Pp. 337-350 *in* T.J. Cade, J.H. Enderson, C.G. Thelander and C.M. White (eds.), *Peregrine Falcon populations, their management nd recovery*. The Peregrine Fund, Inc., Boise, Idaho.

PETERSON, R.T. 1948. *Birds over America*. Dodd, Mead and Co., New York. 342 pp.

PHILLIPS, A.R. 1934. The present status of hawks and owls in Arizona. *Annual Rept. of the Hawk and Owl Soc.* 1934:15-17.

PHILLIPS, J.C. 1926. An attempt to list the extinct and vanishing birds of the Western Hemisphere, with some notes on recent status, location of specimens, etc. *Proc. Int. Ornithol. Congr.* 6:503-534.

PORTER, R.D. & C.M. WHITE 1977. Status of some rare and lesser known hawks in western United States. Pp. 39-57 *in* R.D. Chancellor (ed.), Proceedings of the World Conference on Birds of Prey, 1975. ICBP, London. 442 pp.

REA, A. 1998a. Black Vulture *Coragyps atratus*. Pp. 24-26 *in* R.L. Glinski (ed.), *The raptors of Arizona*. University of Arizona Press, Tucson. 220 pp.

REA, A. 1998b. Turkey Vulture *Cathartes aura*. Pp. 27-31 *in* R.L. Glinski (ed.), *The raptors of Arizona*. University of Arizona Press, Tucson. 220 pp.

ROBERTS, T.S. 1932. *The birds of Minnesota*. University of Minnesota Press, Minneapolis. 693 pp.

ROBBINS, C.S., D. BYSTRAK & P.H. GEISSLER 1986. The breeding bird survey: its first fifteen years, 1965-1979. *U.S. Fish Wildl. Serv., Resour. Publ.* 157. 196 pp.

ROBBINS, M.B. & D.A. EASTERLA 1991. *Birds of Missouri: their distribution and abundance*. University of Missouri, Columbia, Missouri. 456 pp.

ROBINSON, C.S. 1940. Notes on the California Condor, collected on Los Padres National Forest, California. Unpubl. rep. U.S. Forest Service, Santa Barbara, CA. 21 pp.

ROOT, T. 1988. *Atlas of wintering North American birds; an analysis of Christmas Count data*. University of Chicago Press, Chicago. 312 pp.

RYSER, F.A., Jr. 1985. *Birds of the Great Basin: a natural history*. Univ. of Nevada Press, Reno. 604 pp.

SAGE, J.H. & L.B. BISHOP 1913. *The birds of Connecticut*. State Geological and Natural History Survey, Hartford, Connecticut. 370 pp.

SAUER, J.R., S. SCHWARTZ & B. HOOVER 1996. The Christmas Bird Count home page. Version 95.1. Patuxent Wildlife Research Center, Laurel, MD.

SAUER, J.R., J.E. HINES, G. GOUGH, I. THOMAS & B.G. PETERJOHN 1997. The North American Breeding Bird Survey results and analysis. Version 96.4. Patuxent Wildlife Research Center, Laurel, MD.

SKUTCH, A.F. 1969. Notes on the possible migration and the nesting of the Black Vulture in Central America. *Auk* 86:726-731.

SMITH, N.G. 1980. Hawk and vulture migrations in the Neotropics. Pp. 51-65 *in* A. Keast & E.S. Morton (eds.), *Migrant birds in the Neotropics: ecology, behavior, distribution, and conservation*. Smithsonian Institution Press, Washington, D.C. 576 pp.

SNYDER, N.F.R. & E.V. JOHNSON 1985. Photographic censusing of the 1982-1983 California Condor population. *Condor* 87:1-13.

SNYDER, N.F.R. & A.M. REA 1998. California Condor *Gymnopgyps californianus*. Pp. 32-36 *in* R.L. Glinski (ed.), *The raptors of Arizona*. University of Arizona Press, Tucson. 220 pp.

SNYDER, N.F.R. & H.A. SNYDER 1989. Biology and conservation of the California Condor. *Current Ornithology* 6:175-267.

SNYDER, N.F.R. & H. SNYDER 1991. *Birds of prey: natural history and conservation of North American raptors*. Voyageur Press, Stillwater, MN. 224 pp.

SUTTON, G.M. 1928. Extension of the breeding range of the Turkey Vulture in Pennsylvania. *Auk* 45:501-503.

TAYLOR, D.M. 1986. Turkey Vultures decline at a traditional roosting site. *Great Basin Nat.* 46:305-306.

TOBISH, T.G., Jr. 1997. Alaska region. *Natl. Audubon Soc. Field Notes* 51:911.

UNITT, P. 1984. *The birds of San Diego County*. San Diego Society of Natural History Memoir 13. 276 pp.

U.S. FISH AND WILDLIFE SERVICE 1996. *California Condor Recovery Plan*, Third Revision. Portland, OR. 62 pp.

VALENTINE, A.F. 1973. Nesting of a Turkey Vulture in Alpena County, Michigan. *Jack-Pine Warbler* 51:92.

WALLACE, M.P. & S.A. TEMPLE 1987. Competitive interactions within and between species in a guild of avian scavengers. *Auk* 104:290-295.

WEBSTER, F.S., Jr. 1978. South Texas region. *Amer. Birds* 29:941-944.

WETMORE, A. 1933. The eagle, king of birds, and his kin. *Natl. Geogr. Mag.* 64:43-95.

WILBUR, S.R., W.D. CARRIER, J.C. BORNEMAN & R.W. MALLETTE 1972. Distribution and numbers of the California Condor, 1966-1971. *Amer. Birds* 26:819-823.

WILBUR, S.R. 1976. Status of the California Condor, 1972-75. *Amer. Birds* 30:789-790.

WILBUR, S.R. 1978. The California Condor, 1966-76: a look at its past and future. *North American Fauna* no. 72. 136 pp.

WILBUR, S.R. 1980. Estimating the size and trend of the California Condor population, 1965-1978. *Calif. Fish Game* 66:40-48.

WILBUR, S.R. 1983. The status of vultures in the Western Hemisphere. Pp. 113-123 *in* S.R. Wilbur & J.A. Jackson (eds.), *Vulture biology and management*. University of California Press, Berkeley. 550 pp.

WILCOX, T.E. 1917. Minutes of the 572nd regular meeting. *Proc. Biol. Soc. Wash.* 30:xii.

WILLETT, G. 1933. A revised list of the birds of southwestern California. *Pacific Coast Avifauna* no 21:204 pp.

WILSON, A 1808-14. *American ornithology, or, the natural history of the birds of the United States*. 9 vols. Bradsford and Inskeep, Philadelphia.

Lloyd F. Kiff
The Peregrine Fund
566 West Flying Hawk Lane
Boise
Idaho 83709
USA

Chancellor, R. D. & B.-U. Meyburg eds. 2000
Raptors at Risk
WWGBP / Hancock House

The Status of Vultures in Latin America

Marsha A. Schlee

ABSTRACT

Conservation status, habitat requirements, and problems affecting the American Black Vulture, Turkey Vulture, Lesser and Greater Yellow-headed Vultures, King Vulture, and Andean Condor are presented as well as the management plans and recovery programmes underway for the Andean Condor. Cathartid populations are mainly affected by habitat alteration, persecution, hunting pressure, and pesticides. Improved livestock management also contributes to a decline in the food supply in many areas. The numerical status of most of the species needs to be evaluated and studies are also needed on their biology and ecology. At the present time, the Andean Condor is on CITES I, and the King Vulture has been placed on CITES III only for Honduras. The author strongly recommends placing *Sarcoramphus papa*, *Cathartes burrovianus* and *Cathartes melambrotus* on CITES II.

INTRODUCTION

Six vulture species are found in Latin America: American Black Vulture *Coragyps atratus*, Turkey Vulture *Cathartes aura*, Lesser Yellow-headed Vulture *Cathartes burrovianus*, Greater Yellow-headed Vulture *Cathartes melambrotus*, King Vulture *Sarcoramphus papa*, and Andean Condor *Vultur gryphus*. All are members of the family Cathartidae, shown by DNA sequencing and hybridization (Sibley & Ahlquist 1990; Keyser *et al.* 1996), as well as by myological, osteological and behavioural features (for reviews, see Rea 1983 and del Hoyo *et al.* 1994), to be more closely allied to storks (Ciconiidae) than to the Old World accipitrid vultures; however, more recent findings indicate that even a close relationship with storks appears unlikely (Wink *et al.* 1998). The two groups of vultures are phylogenetically distinct but have highly convergent life styles, although evolution of the tongue and bill specializations in the cathartids may not have been related to carrion-eating (Ladyguin 1996).

Previous reports on the conservation status of the New World vultures were given in 1979 at the 1st International Symposium on Vultures, Santa Barbara, U.S.A. (Wilbur 1983), and in 1982 at the 2nd World Conference on Birds of Prey, Thessaloniki, Greece (for a summary of the workshop proceedings, see Mundy 1985). This paper will update the situation for the cathartids found in Latin America and will be based on data from published and unpublished reports, general avifauna surveys and other scientific studies as well as country or species reports prepared specifically for the 5th World Conference by field workers and ornithological organizations. A latitude of approximately 20°N was used as a cut-off for separating the area covered in this paper (Neotropical region) from that to the north (Nearctic).

SPECIES ACCOUNTS

American Black Vulture *Coragyps atratus*

Found throughout most of Latin America (Ellis *et al.* 1983), this conspicuous and very common species has become known as the "town scavenger," feeding in markets, at rubbish dumps, in the streets (del Hoyo *et al.* 1994), and also from road kills (Houston 1987). Black Vultures are considered to be an "increaser species" (Ellis & Smith 1986), adapting well to habitat modification and whose populations rise in areas where primary forests have undergone agricultural development (Ellis *et al.* 1983; Stiles 1985). Originally, the species was confined to edges of rivers, swamps and wetlands (del Hoyo *et al.* 1994) and its abundance, contrary to that of the *Cathartes* species, is not related to natural mammal density (Houston 1987). In heavily forested areas, Black Vultures are found only along the edges or associated with villages and small isolated settlements, as seen in the Maya/Calakmul Biosphere Reserve Complex, Guatemala/Mexico (Berlanga & Wood 1992; Whitacre *et al.* 1991), and the species is rare in the Brazilian Amazon, its density having been recorded north of Manaus in an area having relatively closed-canopy virgin forest but in the process of being fragmented for cattle ranching (Stotz & Bierregaard 1989). In French Guiana, where the major part of the country consists of primary undisturbed forest, Black Vultures are found along the coast and near some towns, their density being particularly high in the mangroves where they eat the remains of fish (Jullien & Thiollay 1996).

Black Vultures have figured in a number of other avifauna surveys, many of which provide an abundance index. The species is common in the Serra da Capivara National Park in the Brazilian caatinga of southeastern Piauí (Olmos 1993) and in the reserves surveyed in the southeast—Serra do Tingua, Serra dos Orgaos National Park, Sooretama Biological Reserve, Poço das Antas Reserve and the Serra da Siberia (Scott & Brooke 1985); also fairly common in Parque Estadual Intervales in southeastern São Paulo in the Serra do Mar Mountains (Mañosa & Pedrocchi 1997); common along the Paraguay River but more so in the south near human dwellings, sporadic rather than seasonal variations in population numbers being shown (Hayes 1991). The species is very common throughout Argentina, the Ríos Chubut and Negro (M. Nores pers. comm.) and in Patagonia where its highest abundance is reached in the valleys and Andean grassy hills (Donázar *et al.* 1993); common throughout the Chaco (Short 1975) and in northern Bolivia at the Beni Biological Station (Brace *et al.* 1997), but uncommon in the Río Machariapo dry forests of the northern La Paz department (Pearman 1993); common along coastal southern Peru where it feeds on the remains of marine mammals and fish (R. Piana pers. comm.) and also found in the Pacific dry forests of the Bosque Nacional de Tumbes (Parker *et al.* 1995) and in the Northwestern Peru Biosphere Reserve (Cook 1996). In western Ecuador, Black Vultures are abundant at refuse dumps, in the inter-Andean valleys up to 2200-3200 m a.s.l. and in most of the areas impacted by man (Ortiz-Crespo 1986), but less common in the east where there is less deforestation (P. Greenfield pers. comm.); also common in southwestern Colombia in the mosaic of pastures, cultivated fields and disturbed forests surrounding La Planada Reserve on the Pacific slopes of the Andes, the species occurring up to 3300 m a.s.l. and being common in densely populated areas along all gradients down to the coast (Thiollay 1991); common in Venezuela in the western Llanos and in the Andes of Mérida, foraging up to about 3500 m a.s.l. and being sustained almost exclusively by human activities in highly deforested areas (Thiollay 1996). In the western Llanos of Venezuela, Black Vultures are at full carrying capacity (G. Ríos pers. comm.) but in the northern and central Llanos their abundance varies according to the type of habitat and its use (Gómez *et al.* 1989): density is very low (0.13/km^2) in the monocultures of rice near Calabozo, rises (1.40/km^2) in the areas used for sorghum and cattle near Altagracia de Orituco where remnants of dry deciduous forest remain, and is highest (6.96/km^2) in the state of Apure at Hato El Cedral where cattle are raised and capybara *Hydrochaeris hydrochaeris* are culled annually, the remains of which are left for the scavengers (del Hoyo *et al.* 1994).

Other cathartid species may be adversely affected as Black Vultures become more abundant. In Argentina, for example, the proliferation of garbage dumps and road kills in mountain habitat has brought about an increase in Black Vulture populations which in turn could limit the amount of food available for Andean Condors since the former detects carcasses sooner and consumes most of the carrion before the condors arrive (Donázar et al. 1992). Also, expansion of the species into the Chiquibul Forest Reserve in Belize could limit the amount of food available for juvenile King Vultures since the latter are very slow feeders, requiring a lot of time to fill their crops and being easily supplanted by groups of Black Vultures (J. Clinton-Eitniear pers. comm.). In general, however, high abundance of *C. atratus* does not seem to create problems for the other vulture species (M. Nores pers. comm.).

Black Vulture populations are reported as decreasing in Mexico, due to habitat availability and pollution (Ramos 1986), high levels of organochlorine residues having been found in Black Vulture body tissues in Chiapas (Albert et al. 1989a) and also in egg-shell fragments and in whole eggs in the Tuxtla Valley (Albert et al. 1989b). The species is also declining in the deserts and puna of northern Chile where food availability has decreased (Jaksíc & Jiménez 1986). The intense aerial spraying of agrochemicals in the plantations of cotton, tobacco, and rice in the Tolima Llanos of Colombia has also been incriminated for having caused declines in Black Vulture numbers in the past (Olivares 1970). Finally, the species has sometimes been persecuted, being accused of spreading disease, killing newborn lambs or calves as well as attacking livestock during parturition when trying to get the placenta (Rio Grande do Sul, Brazil: Belton 1984; western Llanos, Venezuela: G. Ríos pers. comm.).

Turkey Vulture *Cathartes aura*

Four distinct races differing in head colour and in size are recognized. The most widely distributed in South America, and easily distinguished by a large white band on the back of the head, is *ruficollis*. The status of these taxa is questioned; the races may actually be separate species.

The Turkey Vulture is the most versatile of the cathartids, living in desert habitat, grasslands, temperate and tropical forests as well as in extremely cold conditions in the Falkland Islands and Tierra del Fuego (del Hoyo et al. 1994). On the Pacific slopes of the Andes, the species is present up to 2200 m in altitude, occasionally 2600 m, where it is less numerous than Black Vultures (Thiollay 1991). Since Turkey Vultures readily colonize newly deforested areas, their hunting and breeding ranges increase during the early stages of deforestation (Thiollay 1991), and thus the species has suffered less from accelerating habitat changes than its forest dwelling counterparts (Ecuador: Ortiz-Crespo 1986). However, in the Maya/Calakmul Reserves (Guatemala, Mexico), the species is most abundant in the areas least impacted by man, the pattern being the reverse of that of the Black Vultures, possibly suggesting interspecific competition, but habitat preferences may also play a role considering that the forest is lower, drier, and more open in the Guatemalan units (Whitacre et al. 1991).

The North American races are migratory. Several hundreds of thousands of Turkey Vultures pass through Panama in October and November to northern South America where they winter with the resident race (Ellis et al. 1983; Gale 1986). In Colombia, only a small percentage of the residents are displaced since food competition is limited, the migrants using garbage and refuse around human habitations whereas the residents feed on road kills or small carcasses along the highways (Koester 1982). In the central Llanos of Venezuela, however, the subspecies have the same dietary preferences and when the races are sympatric, the residents shift from foraging over open or semi-open habitats to foraging almost exclusively in gallery forests whereas the migrants forage primarily over the savannas (Kirk & Currall 1994; Kirk & Houston 1995). The physical condition of resident Turkey Vultures also falls below the normal range when migrants are present but returns to above average when they leave (Kirk & Gosler 1994). Since some migrants visit the gallery forests, and win most agonistic encounters, food competition is minimized by the residents finding carcasses first and feeding quickly before the migrants arrive (Kirk & Houston 1995). In other areas the numbers of resident Turkey Vultures have been seen to decrease somewhat in October-November when migrants are present (Guatemala: Vannini 1989).

Turkey Vultures have been included in many avifauna surveys and are considered to be fairly common to abundant when in appropriate habitat (del Hoyo et al. 1994; Ellis et al. 1990). In French

Guiana, the Turkey Vulture is the least numerous of the smaller vulture species and mixes with the Lesser Yellow-headed Vulture in the coastal savannas and marshes (Jullien & Thiollay 1996; Thiollay 1985a), but density seems to correspond to what would be expected for the species in these habitats (J.-M. Thiollay pers. comm.). Turkey Vultures are fairly common in the Serra da Capivara National Park in the Brazilian caatinga (Olmos 1993) and are seen daily in both the Sooretama and Poço das Antas Biological Reserves in southeastern Brazil, but the species is uncommon in the Serra da Siberia and the Serra do Tingua and absent in the Serra dos Orgaos National Park, all of the latter having large tracts of primary forest (Scott & Brooke 1985). Likewise, Turkey Vultures are at low density in a well-preserved area of Atlantic rainforest in the Parque Estadual Intervales, being seen above the canopy or in small openings next to roads or hamlets (Mañosa & Pedrocchi 1997); also rare in the relatively closed-canopy forests and forest fragments north of Manaus (Stotz & Bierregaard 1989) as well as along the Paraguay River (Hayes 1991).

On the other hand, the species is common over the Argentinean wet forests to the northeast and northwest where food is abundant because of the cattle and horses kept in the clearings (Olrog 1985) and common in the valleys and Andean grassy hills of Patagonia (Donázar *et al.* 1993); common throughout Chile but most abundant in the desert areas of the north and the shrublands of the central zone (Jaksíc & Jiménez 1986). In Bolivia, the species is frequently seen at the Beni Biological Station in all zones except the cyperacean swamps and along the banks of the Río Manique (Brace *et al.* 1997); present in the northern La Paz department (Remsen & Parker 1995), but abundance was not quantified; uncommon in the dry forests along the Río Machariapo (Pearman 1993). The species is also present in Peru in the dry forests of the northwestern departments of Tumbes and Piura (Cook 1996; Parker *et al.* 1995) and it figured in a study on the guild of avian scavengers located east of the Sechura Peninsula (Wallace & Temple 1987a). In the western Llanos of Venezuela, the species is widespread and common and populations are stable (G. Ríos pers. comm.); also common in the temperate zone of the Andes of Mérida where it forages in open habitat up to about 2500 m a.s.l. (Thiollay 1996); common in the northern Llanos but replaced by the Lesser Yellow-headed Vulture in the rice fields near Calabozo and at low density at Hato El Cedral in Apure (Gómez *et al.* 1989).

Two threats are listed for the species (del Hoyo *et al.* 1994): getting killed by cars while feeding at road-side carrion and being poisoned by contaminants at rubbish dumps. In the past in southern Rio Grande do Sul, Brazil, the species was affected by poison during the campaign to eradicate the Black Vultures (Belton 1984); in Mexico, the populations of resident Turkey Vultures are declining due to pollution (Ramos 1986) and data on the status of the species are currently being prepared by Pronatura (J. Clinton-Eitniear pers. comm.). Large-scale spraying of agrochemicals has also been incriminated for bringing about local declines in Turkey Vulture populations (Colombia, Tolima Llanos: Olivares 1970).

Lesser Yellow-headed Vulture *Cathartes burrovianus*

This cathartid occurs from Mexico through Central America to northern Argentina and Uruguay; its status, distribution, breeding biology and ecological requirements are poorly known (del Hoyo *et al.* 1994). Two subspecies are sometimes recognized and some of the northern populations appear to be migratory. An influx of Lesser Yellow-heads has been reported in northern Colombia, September-March, where they mix with flocks of migrating Turkey Vultures, and the southern subspecies *urubitinga* has also been seen in Colombia from April to October (Koester 1982).

The Lesser Yellow-headed Vulture is absent in areas where heavy forest habitat predominates, as shown in surveys taken in the Maya/Calakmul Biosphere Reserves, Guatemala/Mexico, (Whitacre *et al.* 1991), French Guiana (Jullien & Thiollay 1996; Thiollay 1985a), and southeastern Brazil in the Serra da Siberia, Sooretama, and Serra do Tingua Reserves and Serra dos Orgaos National Park (Scott & Brooke 1985). The species prefers open habitat/grasslands and savannas (Ellis *et al* 1983; del Hoyo *et al*. 1994; Kirk & Currall 1994)—and especially moist terrain. In French Guiana it is the most common vulture in the coastal open areas, including mangroves and forest edges, highest abundance being reached in marshes and wet swamps and some overlap occurring with the distribution of Turkey Vultures (Jullien & Thiollay 1996; Thiollay 1985a); often seen in flocks of 10-15 (Thiollay

1985a), density corresponding to what is expected for the species in these habitats (J.-M. Thiollay pers. comm.). The Lesser Yellow-head is common in the Serra da Capivara National Park in the arid caatinga of northeastern Brazil (Olmos 1993); common in southeastern Brazil in the Poço das Antas Biological Reserve which has rolling hills and plains and extensive areas of marshes and swamps within and adjacent to the reserve, but a significant part of the marshes will be destroyed in the future by a dam that is currently under construction (Scott & Brooke 1985); frequently seen soaring low over wet meadows and rice fields in Rio Grande do Sul (Belton 1984). Seasonal abundance is reported along the Paraguay River, highest density of Lesser Yellow-heads occurring in January when water levels are lowest, and the species is most abundant in the northern sector where extensive marshes are found along the margins of the river (Hayes 1991). The species is common in Argentina in the open country and grasslands of the northcentral and northeastern provinces of Formosa, Chaco, Corrientes, and Misiones (M. Nores pers. comm.; Olrog 1985); confined to the moist eastern fringe of the South American Chaco, mainly along the Paraguay River (Short 1975); common in northern Bolivia at the Beni Biological Station in swamp forests, forest islands, seasonally wet former riverbeds, artificially created roadside pools as well as in chaco vegetation and over savannas (Brace *et al.* 1997); listed as a species expected to occur in the projected La Paz Reserve in the northern part of the country, which includes one of the most pristine major areas of grassland on the continent (Remsen & Parker 1995). Lesser Yellow-heads, however, are not common in western Venezuela where they are restricted to the humid and seasonally flooded lowland grasslands of the Llanos (Thiollay 1996); likewise in the north and central Llanos the species is most common in areas where the savanna is seasonally inundated and used for the cultivation of rice (Gómez *et al.* 1989).

In Mexico, the status of the species has been difficult to appraise and some of the Lesser Yellow-heads may only be summer visitors (Ramos 1986). As a coastal swamp resident, the species is particularly vulnerable to pollution from industrial activity, off-shore oil, and some volcanic activity as well as pesticides (Clinton-Eitniear in Mundy 1985, p. 464), but the effect of the latter is not clear since the same author reports Lesser Yellow-heads as abundant in areas of high potential contamination. At the present time, Lesser Yellow-heads are most numerous in the Yucatán, and even more so in similar habitat in Belize and Honduras, but as Turkey Vultures become more abundant and expand their ranges and as marshes are polluted or drained, *burrovianus* will be placed at risk (J. Clinton-Eitniear pers. comm.). In addition, the species was locally affected by poison in Brazil at the time Black Vultures were being eradicated from southern Rio Grande do Sul (Belton 1984) and Lesser Yellow-heads have also been affected by large-scale aerial spraying of agrochemicals in plantations in Colombia (Tolima Llanos: Olivares 1970).

Greater Yellow-headed Vulture *Cathartes melambrotus*

This vulture was described as a species only in 1964 (Wetmore 1964). Little is known of its breeding biology and no nests have yet been reported (del Hoyo *et al.* 1994). The distribution of the Greater Yellow-head is also poorly known and some records from the west-central Amazon (Ellis *et al.* 1990) show it to occur in both very dense forests and agricultural croplands along a road swath farther west than the zone indicated on the distribution map in del Hoyo *et al.* (1994). This vulture was also not indicated as occurring in Argentina, but *melambrotus* would appear to be the yellow-headed species seen in 1981 by Olrog (1985) in the Iguazú National Park in the northeast province of Misiones where the bird was common, and *melambrotus* may also have been the species seen the same year in the rainforests of the Caliegua National Park in the northwestern province of Jujuy (cited in Olrog 1985).

The Greater Yellow-headed Vulture is a true forest vulture, regularly occurring in large tracts of unbroken primary forest (Thiollay 1985a,b), but also being seen over clearings and secondary forest, usually alone or in pairs (Thiollay 1985a). Sometimes Turkey Vultures and Lesser Yellow-headed Vultures co-exist with the Greater Yellow-headed Vulture (Thiollay 1985b). In French Guiana, all three *Cathartes* species overlap in old mangroves and in areas with high forest fragmentation (Jullien & Thiollay 1996). The Greater also slightly overlaps with the Turkey in the coastal forests and in secondary and fragmented forest (Jullien & Thiollay 1996). The most detailed data on the status of the Greater Yellow-head come from French Guiana, the species being widespread and abundant there (Thiollay 1985a). In the north-central part of the country in an area of unbroken lowland rainforest near the Nouragues field station, the highest recorded concentration of Greater Yellow-heads was 12 individuals, with an estimated average population of 19 individuals/100 km^2 (Thiollay 1989). Along the Courcibo River at Saint Eugène, Greater Yellow-heads are also very common, seen several times a day, usually solitary, occasionally 2 or 3 together, and once 10 fed upon the carcass of a Brocket deer *Mazama* sp. (O. Claessens pers. comm. and in prep.). In the Brazilian Amazon some 80 km north of Manaus in an area of continuous forest as well as forest fragments and clearings for cattle pastures, the species was recorded as uncommon (Stotz & Bierregaard 1989), but in the pristine forests along the Rio Xingú, 52 km SSW of Altamira, Pará, this species was the most prevalent of the vultures, six together at the most and seen in 31/45 days of field work, data being collected on the Greater Yellow-head's use of olfaction to locate carrion (Graves 1992). At the Beni Biological Station in northern Bolivia, the species was recorded as infrequent, seen over all types of forest (terra firma, seasonally inundated, riverine, swamp, secondary and deciduous) but not over the savannas, chaco, or cyperacean swamps (Brace *et al.* 1997); also seen in northern La Paz department where the lowland forests of western Amazonia meet the humid montane forests of the eastern slopes of the Andes, but no density index was established (Remsen & Parker 1995). It can still be found in the eastern lowlands of Ecuador, where deforestation has proceeded on a smaller scale than in the western zones (Ortiz-Crespo 1986), and the species seems to be fairly common (P. Greenfield pers. comm.); also recorded in Peruvian rainforests (Tambopata Reserve) but not common (R. Piana pers. comm); abundant in Colombia in the Amacayacu National Park in the várzea forests of Matamatá and the terra firma forests of Río Cotuhé where the species' olfactory capabilities and its role in the guild of forest scavengers were studied (Gómez *et al.* 1994). The same type of study was also carried out in an area of lowland forest in northern Venezuela near El Callao (Houston 1994), but the density of the species was considerably lower than that recorded in Colombia.

The main threats to the Greater Yellow-headed Vulture are habitat destruction and human exploitation of forest areas, resulting in disturbance and high hunting pressure which cause a radical decline in mammal numbers—and mammal carcasses form the basis of the food supply for all the *Cathartes* species (Houston 1987). In turn, when the density of the *Cathartes* species is low, the vultures are no longer able to exploit carrion efficiently and other cathartids, such as the King Vulture, that greatly depend on the *Cathartes* for locating food in dense forest habitat, are adversely affected (Houston 1987).

King Vulture *Sarcoramphus papa*

Found from southern Mexico to northern Argentina, the King Vulture inhabits tropical lowland and montane forests—primary and secondary as well as forest remnants, evergreen and deciduous—but the species can also be seen over adjoining savannas, grasslands and agricultural areas searching for food (del Hoyo *et al.* 1994; Ellis *et al.* 1983; Jullien & Thiollay 1996; Kirk & Currall 1994; Reid 1989; Thiollay 1985c). The species is classified as forest-dependent, requiring sizable patches of primary forest for feeding and nesting (Stiles 1985). Reported as not adapting well to human presence (Clinton-Eitniear 1989), King Vultures are rarely seen feeding on road kills (Clinton-Eitniear 1985; Kirk & Currall 1994) or in cattle slaughter areas (Clinton-Eitniear 1985) and even when in heavily forested habitat, the species is most abundant at sites without permanent human settlement (Whitacre *et al.* 1991), but some surprising exceptions have been reported in the north-central Llanos of Venezuela (Schlee 1995).

In Mesoamerica, the strongholds of the species are in Belize, carcasses at feeding stations in the Mountain Pine Ridge and Chiquibul Forest Reserves having attracted up to 18 Kings at one time (Clinton-Eitniear 1993), and in Guatemala where the species is particularly abundant in the Maya Biosphere Reserve in the northern Petén department (Whitacre *et al.* 1991). Traditionally, however, King Vultures were shot on sight in Belize, having been accused of killing domestic fowl (Matola 1985). In 1984, an educational programme was started at the Belize Zoo to teach school children the natural history of the species and for this purpose a hand-reared juvenile was donated by the Jackson

Zoological Park, Mississippi (U.S.A.) (Matola 1985). The Belize and Jackson Zoos also collaborated in setting up a programme to reintroduce King Vultures into the wild and one juvenile, equipped with a radio transmitter, was released in 1987 and followed for three weeks (J. Clinton-Eitniear pers. comm.); later, the programme was discontinued. In Guatemala, the species is extremely rare on the Pacific versant because of extensive deforestation and scarcity of food arising from improved livestock management (Vannini 1989).

Historically in Mexico, the species was abundant and widespread in the coastal mountains (see map in Clinton-Eitniear 1989) and even in the 1950s, a dead tapir *Tapirus terrestris* could attract more than fifty Kings in the state of Veracruz (Clinton-Eitniear 1985). Now, habitat modification and pollution (Ramos 1986) have caused Mexican King Vulture populations to decrease and the species is extinct in the regions of Catemaco (Aguilar 1989) and Los Tuxtlas (Martínez-Gómez 1992). However, some unexpected sightings have been made recently in the states of Yucatan and Quintana Roo (Clinton-Eitniear & Wood 1995) and the species is frequently seen in the Chimalas region of Oaxaca and the Lacandon in Chiapas (Clinton-Eitniear 1989) as well as in the Calakmul in Campeche (Berlanga & Wood 1992; Whitacre *et al.* 1991). Nonetheless, the Lacandona forest is currently undergoing shifting agriculture, harvesting of timber and cattle raising and the survival of the King Vulture will depend on the amount of shooting in the reserves as well as the attitudes of the locals toward vultures (Clinton-Eitniear 1989). In El Salvador, the species has been extirpated from the eastern and central part of the country where it was previously fairly common (Thurber *et al.* 1987), and a recent study at El Imposible National Park rated the King Vulture as rare and placed it on the list of birds of conservation priority that are probably threatened with extinction at the national level considering the paucity of forest sites in the country (Komar & Herrera 1995). Populations have also declined in Honduras and Nicaragua, mainly because of extensive habitat loss (Clinton-Eitniear 1993), and the King Vulture is listed on CITES III for Honduras. In Costa Rica, King Vultures are known to occur in at least 7/12 of the national parks, where most of the remaining forested areas are located, the species' density being low but stable and at carrying capacity due to a lack of food (Clinton-Eitniear 1987). In the past, nearly all of Costa Rica was covered with forest of one type or another but since 1940 over half the forests have been lost and the remaining unprotected areas are rapidly being cleared for agriculture or pasture (Stiles 1985). In Panama, King Vulture populations also appear to be stable (Clinton-Eitniear 1993), but numerical status has not been evaluated.

In South America, the status of the species varies geographically from fairly common and widespread to rare and threatened with extinction. In French Guiana, which has about 70,000 km^2 of humid tropical lowland forest that has never been logged or touched by shifting cultivation, King Vultures can be seen daily throughout the forest, alone or in pairs flying high over the canopy (Thiollay 1985a), but density is much lower than that of the smaller cathartids (Jullien & Thiollay 1996). In the north-central part of the country in an area of unbroken rainforest near the Nouragues field station, seven Kings was the highest concentration recorded, the population for 100 km^2 being estimated at nine individuals and including two resident pairs (Thiollay 1989). Near Saint Eugène, however, in an area along the Courcibo River that was inundated when the Petit Saut Dam was put into operation, King Vultures are much less numerous—only 54 sightings in 21 months—but six adults comprised the highest concentration recorded (O. Claessen, pers. comm. and in prep.). In Brazil, *Sarcoramphus* is rare or absent throughout the northeast, only one or two pairs living in the Serra da Capivara National Park, where hunting and fires are commonplace, and the species has been placed on the list of birds of conservation concern (Olmos 1993). The species is also rare in the central Amazon basin as shown in an intense 7-year study of the avifauna of the forests and clearings north of Manaus (Stotz & Bierregaard 1989), in roadside counts (Ellis *et al.* 1990) as well as in a study along the Rio Xingú, 52 km SSW of Altamira (Graves 1992). In the southeast, King Vultures are listed as rare in the Serra do Tingua and the Sooretama Biological Reserve, and absent in the Serra dos Orgaos National Park, Poço das Antas Biological Reserve, and the Serra da Siberia (Scott & Brooke 1985). In fact, the species is now considered as threatened with extinction in the state of Rio de Janeiro where it has been conferred the IUCN conservation status of "Vulnerable" (Alves *et al.*, in press). The species is also absent in Parque Estadual Intervales, a well-preserved area of Atlantic rainforest in the Serra do Mar Mountains (Mañosa & Pedrocchi 1997), and rarely seen on the slopes in Catarina or in the Aparados da Serra National Park in Rio Grande do Sul (Belton 1984); also rare in the Iguazú National Park in the Misiones forest along the Paraná River on both the Brazilian and Argentinian sides (Albuquerque 1986). The latter populations are separated from each other by extensive soyabean agriculture that forms an open corridor, several hundred kilometres wide (Albuquerque 1986). In Argentina, the species appears regularly in the wet forests of Misiones in the northeast and of Jujuy in the northwest and up to 2300 m in the mountains, the population possibly being as low as 10-15 pairs (Olrog 1985) but stable, and individuals having been seen as far south as Santiago del Estero, La Rioja, San Juan and Córdoba (M. Nores pers. comm.); rare in Paraguay (M. Nores pers. comm.); uncommon to rare in the Chaco (Short 1975); reported in Bolivia in the lowland and montane forests of northern La Paz department (Remsen & Parker 1995) but status not determined, and uncommon in the "Man and Biosphere" Beni Biological Station (Brace *et al.* 1997). In Peru, King Vultures are known to breed in the southeastern rainforests along the Tambopata River near Puerto Maldonado (T. de Roy and R. Piana pers. comm.) and the species is present in the Sechura Peninsula and nearby Andean foothills where carcasses have attracted up to eight Kings (Wallace & Temple 1987a). The species is also present in the Pacific dry forests of the North-western Peru Biosphere Reserve located in the departments of Tumbes and Piura and encompassing the Bosque Nacional de Tumbes, but abundance was not determined (Cook 1996; Parker *et al.* 1995). Unfortunately, over the past 30 years, the unbroken expanses of dry forest, which formerly extended from the Cordillera de Chongón in Ecuador south to the west slope of the Andes east of Chiclayo in Peru, have been reduced to scattered small fragments of heavily exploited forest surrounded by croplands and pastures (Parker *et al.* 1995). In western Ecuador the King Vulture is very rare due to extensive deforestation (Ortiz-Crespo 1986) and only a small number remain in the dry deciduous forests west of Guayaquil (P. Greenfield pers. comm.); also uncommon in the Amazonian lowlands of eastern Ecuador (C. Canaday pers. comm.) but scattered throughout except in the oil-producing zones (Ortiz-Crespo 1986). In Colombia, deforestation has also taken its toll, the King Vulture having been eliminated from the Valle del Cauca plateau over 30 years ago when the area was cleared of its forests to make way for pastures and finally for cereal, cotton, or sugar-cane fields (Lehmann 1970). In the Amacayacu National Park in the extreme south of the country, King Vultures accounted for only 6-7% of the four vulture species present at carcasses in the várzea forests of Matamatá where human exploitation has caused the density of wild mammals to decline, but the proportion of Kings rose four-fold at Río Cotuhé, an area of terra firma forest having undisturbed mammal populations (Gómez *et al.* 1994).

King Vulture density in the Llanos of Venezuela is low (Ellis *et al.* 1983, 1990; Gómez Carredano 1994; Gómez *et al.* 1989; Gómez *et al.* 1994; Kirk & Currall 1994; Thiollay 1996), and near Guanare in the western Llanos, the species is thought to be declining because of decreasing food availability due to more efficient livestock management (G. Ríos pers. comm.). In the western Orinoco basin, King Vultures are mainly seen as scattered pairs or individuals flying over montane forests with agricultural clearings, gallery or flooded forests as well as savanna/forest mosaic dominated by forest (Reid 1989) and the species can be found up to elevations of 1000 m in the Andes of Mérida (Thiollay 1996). In Venezuela, large sections of savanna are set on fire every year (J.L. Gómez Carredano pers. comm.; pers. obs.), adjacent areas and even the fringes of very humid forest being consumed (Phelps 1970), and this takes place during the King Vulture nesting period in the Llanos (Gómez Carredano 1994; Ramo & Busto 1988; Schlee 1995). In one instance, a nest in a samán tree *Pithcellobium saman* in the dry deciduous forests of the Andean piedmont in the state of Portuguesa was affected; after the discovery of the nestling, a fire left the nest tree burning at the base and one of the branches close to the nest cavity 10 m from the ground had also burned, the tree finally falling about the time the chick fledged (Ramo & Busto 1988). Also in the Llanos, nestlings are sometimes taken home and kept as pets until they become unmanageable (J.L. Gómez Carredano pers. comm.; Schlee 1995). On the other hand, in the Valley of Las Nieves (Estado Bolívar) located in the northwest uplands of the Venezuelan Guayana, 20-43 King Vultures (adults and young) regularly gather to eat domestic carrion, the highest concentration being 68 Kings (adults and young of all plumage classes except downy or partly downy) seen at a dead horse in August 1997 (Schlee 1998); however, the foraging range of these birds is not known and many may have travelled considerable distances in search of food. Although relatively untouched at the present time, the area is slowly being developed (Huber 1995a, b): an asphalt road from Caicara to Puerto Ayacucho was completed in 1989 as well as the opening of one of the world's largest bauxite mines at Los Pijiguaos, west-southwest of Las Nieves; diamonds and gold have long been mined to the east along Río Guaniamo, and the Parguaza Forest Lot to the southwest was opened for commercial logging concessions in the early 1990s, although the latter has not yet been exploited (Huber 1995b). The burning of large tracts of land in the Venezuelan Guayana is also a problem, the savannas, shrublands, and dry forests of the northern and northwestern lowlands in Bolívar state being among the areas most heavily affected (Huber 1995b).

Andean Condor *Vultur gryphus*
This species is found among the highest peaks of the Andes from Venezuela to Tierra del Fuego and Isla Grande (Ellis *et al.* 1983), but it also descends to shrubsteppe and valleys (Donázar *et al.* 1993), to coastal areas to feed on stranded marine animals and to surrounding desert grasslands to feed on carcasses of livestock (Wallace & Temple 1987a). The Andean Condor was placed on CITES I to protect it from pressure from live animal trade, but its status varies geographically from abundant in southern Latin America to locally threatened or having become extinct or nearly so in its northern range (del Hoyo *et al.* 1994).

In Argentina, condor populations are considered to be healthy (M. Nores and L. Sympson pers. comm.) and in some areas of the Sierras Pampeanas the species may even be more numerous than before due to an increasing food supply from livestock (M. Nores pers. comm.). Some threats, however, do exist. Condors have been shot by hunters or poisoned from baits set out for foxes *Dusicyon* sp. (Jácome 1996/97), and the population in the easternmost breeding grounds of the species—the Quebrada de los Condoritos in the Achala Pampa of the Cordovan Mountains—had seriously declined by the late 1980s due to decreasing food supplies as well as constant disturbance from visitors, mineral-exploitation activities, and airforce manoeuvres (Ramallo 1990). A programme for reinforcing the population was successfully undertaken and the Quebrada was finally declared a national park (M. Terrasse, pers. comm. from F. Ramallo). Also, the Buenos Aires, Chaco and La Plata Zoological Parks drew up an agreement in 1996, later extended to two other facilities, to send Andean Condor eggs to the Buenos Aires Zoo where the young would be hand-reared and released into an established population (Jácome 1996/97). The following year, five juveniles were released in Valle Encontado, located between Río Negro and Neuquén in the Andes, the goal being to study their adaptation to conditions in the wild (L. Sympson pers. comm.). An inventory of condor roosting sites is also underway but it will take several years to determine the numerical status of the species in Argentina (L. Sympson pers. comm.).

In Chile, condors can be found throughout and in large concentrations in areas with cattle ranching (Pávez & Tala 1991), but populations are stable only in the south (Jaksíc & Jiménez 1986). The species is mainly threatened by the lack of food resulting from declines in marine mammal populations and from improved husbandry conditions for livestock, but sometimes condors are shot by farmers or used for target practice by city-dwellers on the weekends (Jaksíc & Jiménez 1986). In the basin of Río Blanco, condors gather in large numbers at a garbage dumping area some 17 km long, and in 1991 a project was drawn up to evaluate the condor's use of the refuse, to collect data on roosting and nesting sites, flight paths, etc., and to set up an artificial feeding station (Pávez & Tala 1991). A preliminary study (Anonymous 1992) proposed La Vega Piuquenes as the best site for the operations but the outcome of the project is not known.

In Bolivia (L. Jammes pers. comm.), no censuses have been taken but condors are regularly seen by plane along the east side of the Andes from the latitude of Santa Cruz to Río Pilcomaya. The species, however, seems to be slowly declining, especially in the altiplano, and is not seen as often in the dry valleys southeast of Cochabamba, droughts and desert expansion probably being contributing factors. Several studies have taken place in Peru in the Cerro Illescas on the Sechura peninsula, the Olmos and Ñaupe regions in the western Andean foothills and in the Pampa Galeras in the high Andes. The species' reproductive cycle is closely tied to El Ñino events affecting the availability of carrion, and thus coastal- and foothill-dwelling populations breed irregularly (Wallace & Temple 1988) and would have difficulties maintaining population size if human-induced activities should increase mortality (Temple & Wallace 1989). High-elevation populations, on the contrary, are probably more than able to maintain their numbers (Wallace & Temple 1988). Studies have also been made on feeding and foraging behaviour (Wallace & Temple 1987a) and hand-reared condors, released on the Sechura Peninsula, were used as surrogates to develop release procedures for the California Condor *Gymnogyps californianus* (Wallace & Temple 1987b). Andean Condors are still used in some folk festivals, serve as targets for hunters or are shot by farmers for having "stolen" domestic animals, and in the past they were shot on the guano islands by the guards (L. Paz Soldan pers. comm.).

In Ecuador (Mauricio Guerrero, national coordinator of the Save the Condor Campaign, pers. comm.; C. Canaday pers. comm.), the Andean Condor is considered as endangered, the population comprising an estimated 70-100 individuals and declining because of human persecution as well as a lack of food, native animals being replaced by domestic ones for which management practices have improved. The "Save the Condor Campaign" was started after seven condors were poisoned in the Antisa Volcano area; ranchers claimed that condors attack newborn calves but this has never been demonstrated scientifically. Also, fires are regularly started in the páramos "to ensure the rains will come" or "to have better grass" and they play a role in displacing the condors, one roost being affected in 1996. Several programmes have been implemented by CECIA, the Ecuadorian ornithological foundation, with partial financial support from either the Wildlife Conservation Society, USAid, Peace Corps or U.S. Fish and Wildlife Service. A national education campaign was started with the general public in 1991-92 to foster greater awareness of the biology of the condors and July 7 was declared National Andean Condor Day. Other programmes focus on environmental education and ecotourism, especially in buffer zones around reserves that harbour the species. A major monitoring project using aerial photography was initiated to determine the status of the populations in several areas, and the availability of food and the threats to survival are also being investigated.

In Colombia, the Condor Recovery Program went into effect in 1989, at which time the Colombian Andean Condor population numbered about 10 pairs found mainly in the Sierra Nevada de Santa Marta Mountains (Lieberman *et al.* 1993). One of the major factors contributing to the species' radical decline was the destruction of the higher altitude forests for the cultivation of potatoes, wheat, and barley, which resulted in an insufficient supply of food for the condors (Olivares 1970). A special report on the project was provided for the 5th World Conference by the programme director Alan Lieberman (pers. comm.), with additional details coming from Lieberman *et al.* (1993). In 1991, a formal Memorandum of Understanding was drawn up between the Instituto Nacional de Desarrollo de los Recursos Naturales Renovables (INDERENA) and the Zoological Society of San Diego, the latter having now provided over $100,000 in financial support. From 1989 to 1991, captive-reared condors were released in the Chingaza and Puracé National Parks and in the Chiles Indian Reserve, the number of sites later being increased to include Parque Los Nevados as well as a future site in the Sierra Nevada de Cocuy in the northeast; the recovery programme also includes a site in Venezuela (see below). All of the release sites are in the páramo zone (>3000 m a.s.l.), characterized by alpine vegetation, heavy fogs, rolling mists, gusty winds and an average temperature of 10°C. Eighteen facilities in the U.S. as well as the Cali Zoological Park in Colombia have contributed young condors for the reintroduction programme. Each bird has to be hand-carried over the high-altitude páramo to a specially prepared housing structure, releases having taken place as early as 17 days or as late as 103 days after arrival of the birds. From 1989 through 1997, 49 birds were released and 35 survived. Pairs have been formed and eggs laid and hatched. At Chiles, the six surviving birds formed a common flock with a group of wild condors from Ecuador. A recent field census in the Santa Marta shows a wild population of 32 condors consisting of various age classes from fledgling to adult.

Although the status of the condor as a former breeding species in Venezuela remains speculative, specimens have occasionally been seen in the Mérida Cordillera (Zonfrillo 1977), but they were usually thought to be transients from the neighbouring Colombian Andes or the Sierra de Santa Marta (for a review of documented sightings, see Calchi & Viloria 1991). The condor was officially declared extinct in Venezuela in 1960 and 31 years later a programme aimed at the recovery of endangered species-Andean Condor and Spectacled Bear *Oso frontino*-was started by the Banco Andino Venezolano (Fundandinos) in conjunction with the Instituto Nacional de Parques (INPARQUES), the release site for the condors being set up in the Valley of Mifafí in the Páramo de la Culata National Park (Celis Parra 1992). The project was carried out in collaboration with INDERENA, in charge of the Condor Recovery Program in Colombia, and the Venezuelan staff were trained at the Chingaza release site. Most of the information available can be found in the annual reports compiled by the general programme coordinator, Maria Rosa Cuesta (see Cuesta 1993-96). Her texts provide an excellent analysis of the housing facilities, maintenance and release procedures; feeding, foraging, and social behaviours; the association of wild condors with the released juveniles; and interactions with humans. Prior to releasing the birds, a massive educational programme was launched in the schools of Mérida, Trujillo and Táchira and a live condor mascot, donated by the Havanna Zoological Park, Cuba, was used to educate the public. In 1994, the Murcunturia Visitors Center was set up in Mifafí, an area already known for its tourist attractions.

Young hand-reared or parent-reared Andean Condors were received from the Los Angeles and San Diego Zoos. Five juveniles were released in 1993, one of which was shot at in July 1994 but not seriously wounded, the act being carried out by an inebriated local. Five more young were released in 1995, but in May of the following year, two out of the first group and two from the second were shot down by the locals. An international appeal launched by the Venezuelan Audubon Society indicated the shootings were instigated by the Mayor of Mucuchíes whose political affiliates were attacking the national parks and the condor project, seeing them as a threat to the farmers' rights to use the land as well as to the development of "mass tourism" as opposed to small-scale nature tourism. The condor project having thus been turned into a political issue, a campaign was launched by its opponents to have the two Andean national parks—the Sierra Nevada created in 1952 and the Páramo de la Culatta created in 1990—closed down, even though most of the lands are situated above the tree line where agriculture would have a devastating effect on the fragile soils and vegetation. These parks are part of the new Birdlife "Biodiversity Priority Areas for Conservation" programme. According to Alan Lieberman (pers. comm.), the situation has since been resolved and the condor recovery team, in collaboration with the Cleveland Zoo (U.S.A.), is planning new releases.

CONCLUDING REMARKS

Habitat modification, particularly deforestation, is the main factor affecting cathartid populations in Latin America, as has been pointed out in the past vulture symposia (Mundy 1985; Wilbur 1983). An estimated 200,000 ha of forest cover are lost every year, mainly for the expansion of agriculture—pastures for cattle ranching or fields for the production of soya-bean forage for the livestock industry (Tole 1998). The Atlantic rainforest of Brazil, for example, has been shattered into tens of thousands of forest fragments covering only 8% of the pre-Columbian area (Ranta *et al.* 1998). All of the primary forest of the coastal plains has been cleared in the state of Rio de Janeiro and many of the larger mammals, birds, and reptiles have become exceedingly rare if not extinct, partially due to illegal hunting in the reserves (Scott & Brooke 1985). Thus, it is not surprising to find the King Vulture, for example, listed as threatened with extinction in the area (Alves *et al.*, in press). As was pointed out in the 1982 Vulture Symposium, the survival of the King Vulture is contingent upon the rate of deforestation (Clinton-Eitniear in Mundy 1985, p. 463). The same could be said for *Cathartes melambrotus*, a species confined to undisturbed tropical lowland forest, although the latter would appear to be fairly abundant at the present time but becoming less frequent in areas where the food supply has been impoverished by heavy hunting pressure (del Hoyo *et al.* 1994). The drainage of swamps and marshes is also of concern and would put the Lesser Yellow-headed Vulture at risk. On the other hand, Black Vultures and Turkey Vultures seem to thrive with deforestation and agricultural development, although in some areas they are sustained almost entirely by human-related activities (Thiollay 1996), Black Vultures not becoming a problem when refuse is limited (Vaninni 1989).

Food availability is a problem in many areas, local mammal populations having been reduced or extirpated by habitat alteration, high hunting pressure, and disturbance (Olmos 1993; Ortiz-Crespo 1986; Jaksíc & Jiménez 1986); and in areas where habitat has been converted to pastures, the food supply is often further reduced by improved livestock management (Clinton-Eitniear 1987; Jaksíc & Jiménez 1986; Vannini 1986). In some instances, however, the scarcity of natural food is partially alleviated by the proliferation of refuse dumps (Jaksíc & Jiménez 1986), although the nutritional value of such a food source can be questioned, and the vultures are also exposed to contaminants (Pávez & Tala 1991). Human persecution exists: Andean Condors and King Vultures have been shot for target practice, for trophies, or to eliminate them as a potential "threat" to livestock; condors and some of the smaller cathartids have been poisoned.

Another important threat to raptors in Latin America is pesticide contamination (Ellis & Smith 1986; Martínez-Sánchez 1986). Organochlorines are still being used by many low-income farmers (Albuquerque 1986; Jaksíc & Jiménez 1986) and have directly affected some Black Vulture populations (Albert *et al.* 1989a, b). Although the use of the principal organochlorine biocides was ended by decree in 1984 in Venezuela, for example, DDT is still widely used in anti-malarial campaigns in the Amazonian region and organochlorines have been detected in the eggs of several raptor species in the Llanos (Basili *et al.* 1994). Large-scale aerial spraying of agrochemicals in plantations of cotton, sugar-cane, and rice caused local declines in *Coragyps atratus*, *Cathartes aura* and *C. burrovianus* in Colombia (Olivares 1970) and this claim has recently been made by some locals in the western Llanos of Venezuela in relation to King Vultures (unpubl. information). Aerial spraying of pesticides has also been incriminated for leading to the recent extinction or decline of several raptor species in parts of Ecuador (Ortiz-Crespo 1986) and for provoking symptoms of poisoning in others in Nicaragua (Martínez-Sánchez 1986), although the impact on vultures was not determined. At the last vulture symposium, one Andean Condor was reported to have been heavily contaminated from pesticides in coastal Peru but the extent of the contamination in the population as a whole was not known (S.A. Temple in Mundy 1985, p.462) and Lesser Yellow-headed Vultures are vulnerable to pollution and pesticides in coastal areas (J. Clinton-Eitniear in Mundy 1985, p. 464). Some of the above examples involve either direct or secondary contamination whereas in others, a species may have declined because of a loss or reduction in its food base. Data concerning the effects of pesticides and other environmental contaminants on vultures are extremely scarce and further study of this problem is needed throughout Latin America.

Finally, detailed studies are needed on the biology and ecology of all the cathartid species in Latin America; even the distribution of both yellow-headed species is poorly known. The populations of Andean Condors and King Vultures in high risk areas need to be numerically evaluated. At the present time, the California Condor and the Andean Condor are on CITES I and the King Vulture is on CITES III, but only for Honduras. Although the author feels that all cathartid species should as a matter of principle be placed on CITES II along with the other Falconiformes, based on the information compiled in this report, at least *Sarcoramphus papa*, *Cathartes burrovianus* and *Cathartes melambrotus* should certainly be placed on CITES II. Should the Cathartidae in the future be removed from the diurnal birds of prey and placed with the Ciconiiformes or be treated as a separate order—the Cathartiformes—all national and international legislation concerning these taxa will need to undergo the appropriate changes.

ACKNOWLEDGEMENTS

Sincere gratitude is extended to the following people who kindly made available unpublished data or provided reports for their countries: Mauricio Guerrero and Chris Canaday (Fundación Ornitológica del Ecuador—CECIA), Olivier Claessens (Muséum National d'Histoire Naturelle,

France), Maria Rosa Cuesta (Condor Recovery Program, Venezuela), Tui de Roy (The Roving Tortoise, New Zealand), Jack Clinton-Eitniear (Center for the Study of Tropical Birds, U.S.A.), Paul Greenfield (ornithologist, Ecuador), Lois Jammes (ARMONIA/Birdlife, Bolivia), Alan Lieberman (The Peregrine Fund, U.S.A.), Manuel Nores (Centro de Zoología Aplicada, Córdoba, Argentina), Luis Paz Soldan (Asociación Peruana para la Conservación de la Naturaleza), Renzo Piana (researcher, Harpy Eagle Project, Tambopata Reserve, Peru), Guilberto Ríos (Universidad Nacional Experimental de los Llanos Occidentales Ezequiel Zamora, Venezuela), Lorenzo Sympson (Sociedad Naturalista Andino Patagónica, Argentina), and Jean-Marc Thiollay (Ecole Normale Supérieure, France).

For their efforts in helping establish contact with contributors, special thanks are due to Lloyd Kiff (The Peregrine Fund, U.S.A.), Clemencia Rodner (Sociedad Conservacionista Audubon, Venezuela), and Michel Terrasse (Fonds d'Intervention pour les Rapaces, France).

REFERENCES

AGUILAR, S. 1989. Las rapaces diurnas de Catemaco, Veracruz. *2nd Western Hemisphere Meeting, WWGPB and Raptor Research Foundation*, 10-14 October, Veracruz, Mexico: Abstract No. 4.

ALBERT, L., C. BARCENAS & A. MARTINEZ 1989a. Distribución de plaguicidas organoclorados en organismos de Zopilote común (*Coragyps atratus*). *2nd Western Hemisphere Meeting, WWGBP and Raptor Research Foundation*, 10-14 October, Veracruz, Mexico: Abstract No. 5.

ALBERT, L.A., C. BARCENAS, M. RAMOS & E. IÑIGO 1989b. Organochlorine pesticides and reduction of eggshell thickness in a Black Vulture *Coragyps atratus* population of the Tuxtla Valley, Chiapas, Mexico. Pp. 473-475 *in* B.–U. Meyburg & R.D. Chancellor (Eds.), *Raptors in the Modern World*. WWGBP: Berlin, London, Paris.

ALBUQUERQUE, J.L.B. 1986. Conservation and status of raptors in Southern Brazil. *Birds of Prey Bull.* 3: 88-94. WWGBP: Berlin.

ALVES, M.A.S., J.F. PACHECO, L.P. GONZAGA, R.B. CAVALCANTI, M. RAPOSO, C. YAMASHITA, N.C. MACIEL & M. CASTANHEIRA in press. Aves. *In* H.G. Bergallo, C.F.D. Rocha, M.A.S. Alves & M. Van Sluys (Eds.), *A Fauna ameaçada de extincão do Estado do Rio de Janeiro*. Editora URJ: Rio de Janeiro.

ANONYMOUS 1992. *Informe comederos artificiales para Cóndores*. Consultores Proyecto Cóndor, División Andina: Chile.

BASILI, G., P. CARDINALE-PIZANI & R.W. RISEBROUGH 1994. Organochlorines in Venezuelan raptor eggs. Pp. 693-696, *in* B.-U. Meyburg & R.D. Chancellor (Eds.), *Raptor Conservation Today*. WWGBP, Pica Press: Berlin.

BELTON, W. 1984. Birds of Rio Grande do Sul, Brazil. Part 1. Rheidae through Funariidae. *Bull. Am. Mus. Nat. Hist.* 178: 369-636.

BERLANGA, M. & P. WOOD 1992. Observations on the King Vulture *Sarcoramphus papa* in the Calakmul Biosphere Reserve, Campeche, Mexico. *Vulture News* 26: 15-21.

BRACE, R.C., J. HORNBUCKLE & J.W. PEARCE-HIGGINS 1997. The avifauna of the Beni Biological Station, Bolivia. *Bird Conserv. Internat.* 7: 117-159.

CALCHI, R. & A.L. VILORIA 1991. Occurrence of the Andean Condor in the Perijá Mountains of Venezuela. *Wilson Bull.* 103: 720-722.

CELIS PARRA, B. 1992. *El regreso del Cóndor.* Publiandina C.A.: Mérida, Venezuela.

CLAESSENS, O. in prep. Effets de la fragmentation forestière en milieu tropical sur les peuplements et les populations d'Oiseaux: le cas de la mise en eau du Barrage de Petit Saut (Guyane française). Doctoral dissertation, Muséum National d'Histoire Naturelle, Paris, France.

CLINTON-EITNIEAR, J. 1985. King Vulture conservation and research program. *Wild Things* Sept.-Oct.: 1-3.

CLINTON-EITNIEAR, J. 1987. The King Vulture in Costa Rica. *Vulture News* 17: 21-24.

CLINTON-EITNIEAR, J. 1989. Habitat loss among hazards facing the King Vulture in Mexico. *Eyas* 12(2): 9-11.

CLINTON-EITNIEAR, J. 1993. The King Vulture in Mesoamerica: an uncertain future. *V Simposium Internacional de Fauna Silvestre, Memoria*: 44-47. Universidad Autonoma de Tamaulipas, CD.: Victoria, Mexico.

CLINTON-EITNIEAR, J. & P. WOOD 1995. Recent noteworthy sightings of King Vultures in Mexico. *Vulture News* 32: 23-25.

COOK, H.G. 1996. Avifauna of North-western Peru Biosphere Reserve and its environs. *Bird Conserv. Internat.* 6: 139-165.

CUESTA, M.R. 1993-96. *Reportes Cóndores*. Reports, Fundandino: Mérida, Venezuela.

DEL HOYO, J., A. ELLIOTT & J. SARGATAL 1994. *Handbook of the Birds of the World*. Vol. 2: New World Vultures to Guineafowl. Lynx Edicions: Barcelona.

DONÁZAR, J.A., F. HIRALDO, O. CEBALLOS, A. TRAVAINI, A. RODRIGUEZ & M. FUNES 1992. Black Vulture *Coragyps atratus* population increase can reduce food availability for Andean Condors *Vultur gryphus* in Patagonia. *IVth World Conference on Birds of Prey,* Berlin, 10-17 May. *Abstracts*: 17.

DONÁZAR, J.A., O. CEBALLOS, A. TRAVAINI & F. HIRALDO 1993. Roadside raptor surveys in the Argintinean Patagonia. *J. Raptor Res.* 27: 106-110.

ELLIS, D.H., R.L. GLINSKI, J.G. GOODWIN, Jr. & W.H. WHALEY 1983. New World vulture counts in Mexico, Central America, and South America. Pp. 124-132 *in* S.R. Wilbur & J.A. Jackson (Eds.), *Vulture Biology and Management.* University of California Press: Berkeley.

ELLIS, D.H., R.L. GLINSKI & D.W. SMITH 1990. Raptor road surveys in South America. *J. Raptor Res.* 24: 98-106.

ELLIS, D.H. & D.G. SMITH 1986. An overview of raptor conservation in Latin America. *Birds of Prey Bull.* 3: 21-25. WWGBP, Berlin.

GALE, N.B. 1986. Status of raptors in Panama. *Birds of Prey Bull.* 3: 48-50. WWGBP, Berlin.

GÓMEZ CARREDANO, J.L. 1994. *Las aves de presa de Los Llanos venezolanos.* Lagoven S.A., Petróleos de Venezuela, S.A: Caracas.

GÓMEZ, J.L., Y. CARBONELL & G. MEDINA 1989. Comparación de la densidad, diversidad y hábitos de nidificación de los Falconiformes en tres localidades de los Llanos de Venezuela. Unpubl. Report, Fundación para la Defensa de la Naturaleza: Caracas.

GÓMEZ, L.G., D.C. HOUSTON, P. COTTON & A. TYE 1994. The role of Greater Yellow-headed Vultures *Cathartes melambrotus* as scavengers in neotropical forest. *Ibis* 136: 193-196

GRAVES, G.R. 1992. Greater Yellow-headed Vulture (*Cathartes melambrotus*) locates food by olfaction. *J. Raptor Res.* 26: 38-39.

HAYES, F.E. 1991. Raptor densities along the Paraguay River: seasonal, geographical and time of day variation. *J. Raptor Res.* 25: 101-108.

HOUSTON, D.C. 1987. The effect of reduced mammal numbers on *Cathartes* vultures in neotropical forests. *Biol. Conserv.* 41: 91-98.

HOUSTON, D.C. 1994. Observations on Greater Yellow-headed Vultures *Cathartes melambrotus* and other *Cathartes* species as scavengers in forest in Venezuela. Pp. 265-268 *in* B.-U. Meyburg & R.D. Chancellor (Eds.), *Raptor Conservation Today.* WWGBP, Pica Press: Berlin.

HUBER, O. 1995a. Vegetation. Pp. 97-160 *in* P.E. Berry, B.K. Holst & K. Yatskievych (Eds.), *Flora of the Venezuelan Guayana,* Vol. 1. Timber Press, Inc.: Portland, Oregon.

HUBER O. 1995b. Conservation of the Venezuelan Guayana. Pp. 193-218 *in* P.E. Berry, B.K. Holst & K. Yatskievych (Eds.), *Flora of the Venezuelan Guayana,* Vol. 1. Timber Press, Inc.: Portland, Oregon.

JÁCOME, N.L. 1996/97. *Registro nacional de Cóndor Andino en cautiverio,* No. 5. Jardin Zoológico de la Ciudad de Buenos Aires S.A.: Buenos Aires.

JAKSÍC, F.M. & J.E. JIMÉNEZ 1986. The conservation status of raptors in Chile. *Birds of Prey Bull.* 3: 95-104. WWGBP, Berlin.

JULLIEN, M. & J.-M. THIOLLAY 1996. Effects of rainforest disturbance and fragmentation: comparative changes of the raptor community along natural and human-made gradients in French Guiana. *J. Biogeogr.* 23: 7-25.

KEYSER, C., D. MONTAGNON, M. SCHLEE, B. LUDES, H. PFITZINGER & P. MANGIN 1996. First isolation of tandemly repeated DNA sequences in New World Vultures and phylogenetic implications. *Genome* 39: 31-39.

KIRK, D.A. & J.E.P. CURRALL 1994. Habitat associations of migrant and resident vultures in central Venezuela. *J. Avian Biol.* 25: 327-337.

KIRK, D.A. & A.G. GOSLER 1994. Body condition varies with migration and competition in migrant and resident South American vultures. *Auk* 111: 933-944.

KIRK, D.A. & D.C. HOUSTON 1995. Social dominance in migrant and resident Turkey Vultures at carcasses: evidence for a despotic distribution? *Behav. Ecol. Sociobiol.* 36: 323-332.

KOESTER, F. 1982. Observations on migratory Turkey Vultures and Lesser Yellow-headed Vultures in northern Colombia. *Auk* 99: 372-375.

KOMAR, O. & N. HERRERA 1995. Avian inventory of El Imposible National Park, San Benito and Río Guayapo sectors. Pp. 6-32 *in* O. Komar & N. Herrera (Eds.), *Avian Diversity at El Imposible National Park and San Marcelino Wildlife Refuge, El Salvador.* WSC Working Paper No. 4: Bronx, New York.

LADYGUIN, A.V. 1996. Vulture assemblages in Old and New World: Are they ecological analogs? *First Joint Annual Meeting, American Ornithologists' Union and Raptor Research Foundation,* 13-17 August, Boise, Idaho: Abstract No. 271.

LEHMANN, F.C. 1970. Avifauna in Colombia. *Smithsonian Contrib. Zool.* 26: 88-92.

LIEBERMAN, A., J.V. RODRIGUEZ, J.M. PÁEZ & J. WILEY 1993. The reintroduction of the Andean Condor into Colombia, South America: 1989-1991. *Oryx* 27: 83-90.

MAÑOSA, S. & V. PEDROCCHI 1997. A raptor survey in the Brazilian Atlantic rainforest. *J. Raptor Res.* 31: 203-207.

MARTÍNEZ-GÓMEZ, J.E. 1992. Raptor conservation in Veracruz, Mexico. *J. Raptor Res.* 26: 184-188.

MARTÍNEZ-SÁNCHEZ, J. 1986. Causes affecting the survival of birds of prey in Nicaragua. *Birds of Prey Bull.* 3: 43-47. WWGBP: Berlin.

MATOLA, S. 1985. JZP vulture to Belize Zoo. *Wild Things*, Sept.-Oct.: 3-4.

MUNDY, P.J. 1985. The biology of vultures: a summary of the workshop proceedings. Pp. 457-482 *in* I. Newton & R.D. Chancellor (Eds.), *Conservation Studies on Raptors*. ICBP Tech. Publ. No. 5: Cambridge.

OLIVARES, A. 1970. Effects of the environmental changes on the avifauna of the Republic of Colombia. *Smithsonian Contrib. Zool.* 26: 77-87.

OLMOS, F. 1993. Birds of Serra da Capivara National Park in the "caatinga" of north-eastern Brazil. *Bird Conserv. Internat.* 3: 21-36.

OLROG, C.C. 1985. Status of wet forest raptors in northern Argentina. Pp. 191-197 *in* I. Newton & R.D. Chancellor (Eds.), *Conservation Studies on Raptors*. ICBP Tech. Publ. No. 5: Cambridge.

ORTIZ-CRESPO, F.I. 1986. Notes on the status of diurnal raptor populations in Ecuador. *Birds of Prey Bull.* 3: 71-79.WWGBP: Berlin.

PARKER, T.A., T.S. SCHULENBERG, M. KESSLER & W.H. WUST 1995. Natural history and conservation of the endemic avifauna in north-west Peru. *Bird Conserv. Internat.* 5: 201-231.

PÁVEZ, E. & C. TALA 1991. *Proyecto Cóndor.* Unpubl. Report, 17 pp.: Chile.

PEARMAN, M. 1993. The avifauna of the Río Machariapo dry forest, northern La Paz department, Bolivia: a preliminary investigation. *Bird Conserv. Internat.* 3: 105-117.

PHELPS, Jr., W.H. 1970. Avifauna in Venezuela. *Smithsonian Contrib. Zool.* 26: 75-76.

RAMALLO, C.F. 1990. *El Cóndor en Córdoba.* Editorial La Canada: Córdoba.

RAMO, C. & B. BUSTO 1988. Observations at a King Vulture (*Sarcoramphus papa*) nest in Venezuela. *Auk* 105: 195-196.

RAMOS, M.A. 1986. Birds in peril in Mexico: the diurnal raptors. *Birds of Prey Bull.* 3: 26-42. WWGBP: Berlin.

RANTA, P., T. BLOM, J. NIEMELÄ, E. JOENSUU & M. SIITONEN 1998. The fragmented Atlantic rainforest of Brazil: size, shape and distribution of forest fragments. *Biodiv. Conserv.* 7: 385-403.

REA, A.M. 1983. Cathartid affinities: a brief overview. Pp. 26-54 *in* S.R. Wilbur & J.A. Jackson (Eds.), *Vulture Biology and Management*. University of California Press: Berkeley.

REID, S.B. 1989. Flying behaviour and habitat preferences of the King Vulture *Sarcoramphus papa* in the western Orinoco Basin of Venezuela. *Ibis* 131: 301-303.

REMSEN, J.V. & T.A. PARKER 1995. Bolivia has the opportunity to create the planet's richest park for terrestrial biota. *Conserv. Internat.* 5: 181-199.

SCHLEE, M.A. 1995. Nest records for the King Vulture (*Sarcoramphus papa*) in Venezuela. *J. Raptor Res.* 29: 269-272.

SCHLEE, M.A. 1998. Observations on the King Vulture *Sarcoramphus papa* in the Valley of Las Nieves (Sabana Nueva), Estado Bolívar, Venezuela. *5th World Conference on Birds of Prey and Owls*, 4-11 August, Midrand, South Africa. *Abstracts*: 13.

SCOTT, D.A. & M. de L. BROOKE 1985. The endangered avifauna of southeastern Brazil: a report on the BOU/WWF expeditions of 1980/81 and 1981/82. Pp. 115-139 *in* A.W. Diamond & T.E. Lovejoy (Eds.), *Conservation of Tropical Forest Birds*. ICBP Tech. Publ. No. 4: Cambridge.

SHORT, L.L. 1975. A zoogeographic analysis of the South American Chaco avifauna. *Bull. Am. Mus. Nat. Hist.* 154: 1-352.

SIBLEY, C.G. & J.E. AHLQUIST 1990. *Phylogeny and Classification of Birds*. Yale University Press: New Haven.

STILES, F.G. 1985. Conservation of forest birds in Costa Rica: problems and perspectives. Pp. 141-168 *in* A.W. Diamond & T.E. Lovejoy (Eds.), *Conservation of Tropical Forest Birds*. ICBP Tech. Publ. No. 4: Cambridge.

STOTZ, D.F. & R.O. BIERREGAARD, Jr. 1989. The birds of the Fazendas Porto Alegre, Esteio and Dimoma north of Manaus, Amazonas, Brazil. *Rev. Brasil. Biol.* 49: 861-872.

TEMPLE, S.A. & M.P. WALLACE 1989. Survivorship patterns in a population of Andean Condors *Vultur gryphus*. Pp. 247-251 *in* B.-U. Meyburg & R.D. Chancellor (Eds.), *Raptors in the Modern World*. WWGBP: Berlin, London, Paris.

THIOLLAY, J.-M. 1985a. Birds of prey in French Guiana, a preliminary survey. *Birds of Prey Bull.* 2: 11-15. WWGBP: Berlin.

THIOLLAY, J.-M. 1985b. Falconiforms of tropical rainforests: a review. Pp. 155-165 *in* I. Newton & R.D. Chancellor (Eds.), *Conservation Studies on Raptors*. ICBP Tech. Publ. No. 5: Cambridge.

THIOLLAY, J.-M. 1985c. Composition of Falconiform communities along successional gradients from primary rainforest to secondary habitats. Pp. 181-190 *in* I. Newton & R.D. Chancellor (Eds.), *Conservation Studies on Raptors*. ICBP Tech. Publ. No. 5: Cambridge.

THIOLLAY, J.-M. 1989. Censusing of diurnal raptors in a primary rainforest: comparative methods and species detectability. *J. Raptor Res*. 23: 72-84.

THIOLLAY, J.-M. 1991. Altitudinal distribution and conservation of raptors in southwestern Colombia. *J. Raptor Res*. 25: 1-8.

THIOLLAY, J.-M. 1996. Distributional patterns of raptors along altitudinal gradients in the northern Andes and effects of forest fragmentation. *J. Tropical Ecol*. 12: 535-560.

THURBER, W.A., J.F. SERRANO, A. SERMENO & M. BENITEZ 1987. Status of uncommon and previously unreported birds of El Salvador. *Proc. West. Found. Vert. Zool*. 3: 109-293.

TOLE, L. 1998. Sources of deforestation in tropical developing countries. *Environ. Manage*. 22: 19-33.

VANNINI, J.P. 1989. Neotropical raptors and deforestation: notes on diurnal raptors at Finca El Faro, Quetzaltenango, Guatemala. *J. Raptor Res*. 23: 27-38.

WALLACE, M.P. & S.A. TEMPLE 1987a. Competitive interactions within and between species in a guild of avian scavengers. *Auk* 104: 290-295.

WALLACE, M.P. & S.A. TEMPLE 1987b. Releasing captive-reared Andean Condors to the wild. *J. Wildl. Manage*. 51: 541-550.

WALLACE, M.P. & S.A. TEMPLE 1988. Impacts of the 1982-1983 El Ñino on population dynamics of Andean Condors in Peru. *Biotropica* 20: 144-150.

WETMORE, A. 1964. A revision of the American vultures of the genus *Cathartes*. *Smithsonian Misc. Coll*. 146: 1-48.

WHITACRE, D.F., A.J. BAKER, L.E. JONES, R.V. PATRACA, J. SUTTER & C.M. SWARTZ 1991. Results of census efforts in three units of the Maya Biosphere Reserve/Calakmul Biosphere Reserve Complex. Pp. 43-58 *in* D.F. Whitacre, W.A. Burnham & J.P. Jenny (Eds.), *Maya Progress Report 4*. The Peregrine Fund, Inc.: Boise, Idaho.

WILBUR, S.R. 1983. The status of vultures in the western hemisphere. Pp. 113-123 *in* S.R. Wilbur & J.A. Jackson (Eds.), *Vulture Biology and Management*. University of California Press: Berkeley.

WINK, M., I. SIEBOLD, F. LOTFIKHAN & W. BEDNAREK 1998. Molecular systematics of holarctic raptors (Order Falconiformes). Pp. 29-48 *in* R.D. Chancellor, B.-U. Meyburg & J.J. Ferrero (Eds.), *Holarctic Birds of Prey*. ADENEX-WWGBP: Calamonte, Spain.

ZONFRILLO, B. 1977. Re-discovery of the Andean Condor *Vultur gryphus* in Venezuela. *Bull. B.O.C*. 97: 17-18.

Marsha A. Schlee
Muséum National d'Histoire Naturelle
Ménagerie du Jardin des Plantes
57 rue Cuvier
75005 Paris
France

Chancellor, R. D. & B.-U. Meyburg eds. 2000
Raptors at Risk
WWGBP / Hancock House

Habitat Loss and Vultures: a Case Study from Israel

Reuven Yosef and Ofer Bahat

Surprisingly, there is much difficulty in finding studies that relate directly to the effects of habitat loss on vulture populations. In most published papers this is hinted at, or mentioned in circumspect language. This makes it difficult to interpret past studies as to whether they do or do not relate to population fluctuations or to habitat loss. We would like to stress that we were unable to find in our literature search the exclusion of vultures from any given area by a competing or hostile species - whether mammalian, reptilian or avian. Most studies therefore hint at the fact that habitat loss is almost exclusively due to human activities.

Human-related encroachment on vulture habitats can be categorised in many different ways, but we have tried to be generalistic because, as we have all come to realize, each and every case is different and must be handled individually. Thus, we have narrowed things down to three major human-related elements. Further, we examine these points to see how they have affected the once healthy vulture populations of Israel. We feel that the situation in Israel is a good example of the complexities and conflicts (e.g., human population explosion, housing, jobs, food, recreation) that need to be taken into account in the conservation of vultures. Hence, we divided the human-related modifications of habitats as follows:

Settlement - building hydro-electric power stations (eloctrocution and drowning; e.g., Marinkovic & Orlandic 1994), bio-invasions that cause a decrease of indigenous biodiversity, building of roads in breeding gorges (Marinkovic & Orlandic 1994), subsequently causing mortality when vultures feed on road-kills, building towns and cities in non human-frequented areas.

Agriculture - transmission of diseases from carcasses, deforestation in tropical areas, poisoning (e.g., Soto 1986, Kiff 1989, Terasse et al. 1994), persecution.

Recreation - Hunting (non-sustainable) (e.g., Tewes 1994), disturbance, trade in wildlife or body-parts (Xiao-Ti 1991),

However, not all vultures are adversely affected by human encroachment. There are species that appear to have expanded their distribution and some can even be categorized as human commensals. This is especially true in areas where local religions believe in feeding vultures as a natural way of recycling their dead back into nature. Buddhists in Northern India and Tibet are known to put out cadavers for Himalyan Griffons *Gyps himalayensis*, Cinereous/Eurasian Black Vulture *Aegypius monachus* and Bearded vultures *Gypaetus barbatus* (Xiao-Ti 1991), and Parsee dead are disposed off by Red-headed *Sarcogyps calvus* and Indian White-backed *Gyps bengalensis* vultures (Satheesan 1998). Examples of species that appear to have benefited from human-related activities and habitat-modifications are Turkey *Cathartes aura* and Black *Coragyps atratus* Vultures in the New World,

Hooded *Necrosyrtes monachus* and African White-backed *Gyps africanus* in Africa, and the Long-billed *G. indicus* and Indian White-backed in the Indian subcontinent.

Evaluating the information presented for all vulture species from Mundy *et al.* 1992 and del Hoyo *et al.* 1994 we have found that in reality, of the 22 species, only half are known to be adversely affected by human encroachment (Table 1). The rest are either those that benefit or are indifferent and will adapt to scavenging human refuse. However, we emphasize that many populations that are classified as "Not globally threatened" could possibly be endangered, or suffer from local threats, and the situation for these species could deteriorate rapidly owing to unpredicted, stochastic events. Examples of such stochastic incidents are the recent (1998) mass poisoning in the Spanish Doñana reserve which resulted in high mortality amongst an established and flourishing population of vultures and other raptors; the same also holds true for a recent (July 1998) incident on the Golan Heights in Israel wherein the vulture population was badly affected. An example of vulture populations that have not successfully adapted to human-related activities is reflected in the present very severe situation in Israel.

Table 1. Status, level of knowledge based on existing literature and the ability of the species to adapt to human-induced changes to the environment. NGT denotes - Not globally threatened.

Species	Status	Level of knowledge	Effect of human disturbance
New World Vultures:			
Turkey Vulture *Cathartes aura*	NGT	Good	+
Lesser Yellow-headed Vulture *C. burrovianus*	NGT	Poor	?
Greater Yellow-headed Vulture *C. melambrotus*	NGT	Poor	-
American Black Vulture *Coragyps atratus*	NGT	Good	+
King Vulture *Sarcoramphus papa*	NGT	Poor	-?
California Condor *Gymnogyps californianus*	Endangered - I	Medium	+-
Andean Condor *Vultur gryphus*	NGT - II	Poor	?
Old World Vultures:			
Palm-nut Vulture *Gypohierax angolensis*	NGT - II	Good	+-
Bearded Vulture *Gypaetus barbatus*	NGT - II	Medium	-
Egyptian Vulture *Neophron percnopterus*	NGT - II	Good	-
Hooded Vulture *Necrosyrtes monachus*	NGT - II	Good	+
African White-backed Vulture *Gyps africanus*	NGT - II	Good	+
Indian White-backed Vulture *G. bengalensis*	NGT - II	Good	+
Long-billed Vulture *G. indicus*	NGT - II	Medium	+
Rüppell's Griffon *G. rueppellii*	NGT - II	Good	-
Himalyan Griffon *G. himalayensis*	NGT - II	Poor	?
Eurasian Griffon *G. fulvus*	NGT - II	Good	-
Cape Griffon *G. coprotheres*	Rare - II	Good	-
Eurasian Black Vulture *Aegypius monachus*	Vulnerable -II	Medium	-
Lappet-faced Vulture *Torgos tracheliotus*	NGT - II	Medium	-
White-headed Vulture *Trigonoceps accipitalis*	NGT - II	Medium	?
Red-headed Vulture *Sarcogyps calvus*	NGT - II	Medium	-?

Key:
Status: I - CITES I II - CITES II
Human disturbance effect: + Positive - negative +- indifferent ? unknown

In Israel, since the turn of the century (then called Palestine), and especially since Israel gained independence in 1948, Goverment policies have been best illustrated by the slogans they inspired - make the deserts bloom, development of the wilderness, etc. - and have led to wide scale changes being wrought on the environment. Wetlands were drained, human settlements were advocated and built in the middle of no-where in the so-called "wilderness", and large scale agriculture backed by technology and use of biocides was encouraged. Consequently, all xeric regions within Israel's boundaries have undergone extensive environmental changes that have adversely affected the region's indigenous avifauna. Some were subtle and were not discovered till recently - like the exaggerated exploitation of ground water for human purposes which has resulted in a die out of a wide range of indigenous flora and fauna and in parallel has allowed non-desert species (such as the Great Spotted Cuckoo, *Clamator glandarius*, Indian House Crow, *Corvus splendens*, or the Graceful Warbler, *Prinia gracilis*, Yosef 1996, 1997) to penetrate the desert regions. Similarly, habitat changes related to agricultural development have had, and continue to have to date, the most severe and widespread impact on vulture populations. On a global scale, these changes have reached a point where most vulture populations are dependent on domestic mammals as a major food source (e.g., 50-80% of the diet of Bearded Vulture in Macedonia, Grubac 1991).

In Israel, three out of our five vulture species have gone the way of the Dodo. The first to disappear was the Cinereous Vulture, which may have bred at the extreme periphery of its breeding range in northern Israel (see Nathan *et al.* 1996, Shirihai 1996), but certainly wintered in larger numbers, and is almost never seen today. This disappearence may not necessarily be solely linked to the changes in Israel's landscape but also probably to the widespread decline across its range in Europe and the Levant. However, the possibility of side-effects following the use of biocides in winter cannot be ruled out.

The first of the confirmed breeding vultures to go extinct was the Bearded Vulture, mainly owing to changes in habitat use due to human settlements and activity, chiefly in desert habitats, as well as foraging habits and sanitation levels of Bedouin goat and sheep herds, and the extensive use of biocides. This was a wide-spread, low population density species, that occurred in most of our mountainous regions - whether Alpine, temperate, Mediterranean, or desert (Fig. 1). However, owing to the burgeoning human population and their exploitation of the human-friendly habitats prior to venturing into the desert, and the education for environmental recreation (Leshem 1988), the last vestiges of the population were confined to the geocentric heart of the Judean Desert (Leshem 1980). The last confirmed breeding attempt was in 1981 (Bahat 1986) and since then we only have sporadic observations of loitering or migrant individuals.

In the past decade, the last surviving Negev Lappet-faced Vultures *Torgos tracheliotus negevensis* were taken into captivity for a breeding programme, and possible future reintroduction. The causes of the decline of this species in Israel are many - lack of food, increased disturbance by nature-loving hikers and recreationists, hunting, egg collecting, biocides, electrocution (Meretzky & Lavee 1991), as well as the illegal trade in Israeli birds to European zoos, of which we have knowledge of at least 12 cases. The range in mid-20th century was in most of the desert regions - Judean, Negev and the Syrian-African Rift Valley or the Arava, and several tens of pairs were estimated to have occurred (Fig. 2). In the 1980s this dropped to less than 5 breeding pairs restricted to the Arava valley and the last pair attempted to breed in 1990 (Yosef & Hatzofe 1997). From the conservation perspective - although comparatively large resources are today utilized for the captive breeding programme in Israel - the problem is that the responsibility to preserve the relevant habitats is not shouldered by any of Israel's conservation agencies and these areas are today slated for almost immediate development. Our concern is that if the propagation of the young in the breeding programme does succeed, and the young are to be released in Israels' wild in the future, the only place is the southern Arava region: this area that must be targeted immediately, a hands-off policy implemented, and held in trust for the future of the project.

The situation of the Egyptian Vulture *Neophron percnopterus* is one of ups and downs - until the mid-20th century it was a widespread breeder with an estimated 500-1000 pairs. However, owing to extensive use of biocides this population plummeted almost to extinction in the late '50s and '60s. A

Figure 1. Changes in the distribution of Bearded Vultures in Israel. The last confirmed breeding attempt was in 1981.

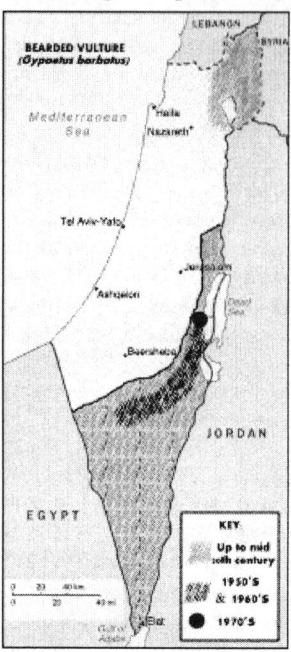

Figure 2. Changes in the distribution of Lappet-faced Vultures in Israel. The last confirmed breeding attempt was in 1990.

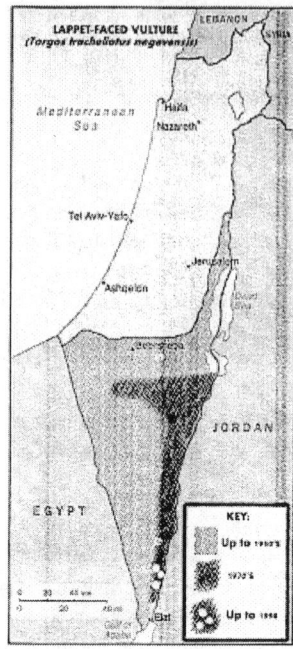

Figure 3. Changes in the distribution of Egyptian Vultures in Israel. Today an estimated 50-70 pairs breed in Israel.

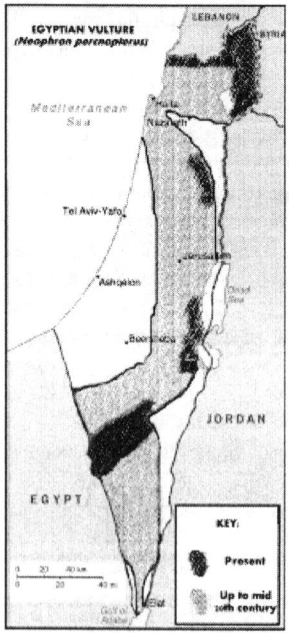

Figure 4. Changes in the distribution of Griffon Vultures in Israel. During the 1998 breeding season 45 pairs successfully reared young.

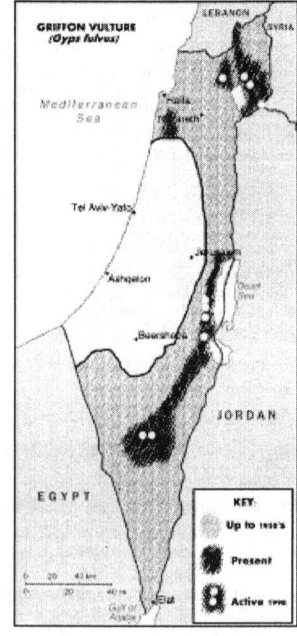

recovery occurred in the 1970s when up to 80 breeding pairs were counted. This rose further in the 1980s with 133 pairs noted, of which 129 (97%) were in the deserts or along the Rift Valley and the Golan Heights (Fig. 3). We regret to say that the 1990s have marked another decline and today only 50-70 pairs breed in Israel. From the conservation perspective this species appears to have a viable population in the wild that should be appropriately encouraged (e.g., habitat conservation, feeding stations, prevention of nest disturbance, etc.) and not necessarily by investing in the very expensive process of a captive breeding programme.

The Griffon Vulture, in our eyes, represents the critical state of Israel's environment at present. When Henry Baker Tristram, an English missionary, published accounts of his trips in the Holy Land in 1865 and 1884 he wrote: "The numbers of the Griffon Vulture in every part of Palestine are amazing." The species bred in most mountainous regions (Fig. 4) and it is estimated that in the mid-19th century about 1000 pairs bred in Israel (Shirihai 1996). However, in the 1950s it almost became extinct owing to a human-induced onslaught on its populations which included lack of food, electrocution, pesticides, hunting, etc. In the late 1970s and early 1980s only about 80 pairs, i.e., 5% of the former population, were observed to breed. There was an improvement in the late 1980s and we had about 130 pairs, but this has plummeted today to 45 pairs which successfully reared young in 1998. Many of the former known breeding sites of Griffon Vultures have been deserted due to human activity and disturbances (Court et al. 1997). The population is at present still at a viable level wherein with appropriate measures it can be rehabilitated. However, this is contingent on law enforcement (especially by education and/or harsh penalties) when poisonings occur. Recent incidents in Israel have shown that the culprits go unpunished and the problem continues. This also raises questions about the existing breeding programmes and release of Griffon Vultures into the wild when the existing problem has not been eliminated.

Although we have up to this point presented a negative side of Israel's environmental implementation policies and the subsequent results, we would like to stress, and to give examples of, the efforts underway to try and return the vultures to Israel's skies. These activities include a reintroduction project on the Carmel mountains, directed by Ohad Hatzofe. In the framework of this project, nearly 50 Griffon Vultures have been reintroduced into the wild since 1993. Another project, directed by OB, involves the Israel Electric Corporation, together with the Israeli Nature Reserves Authority and National Parks (INRANP) and the Society for the Protection of Nature in Israel (SPNI). As part of this project, electricity poles and lines have been protected against electrocution of birds, while satellite telemetry has been implemented to follow the movements of Griffon Vultures inside and outside of Israel's international boundaries. The above mentioned organizations, together with the International Birding & Research Center in Eilat (IBRCE), have undertaken a joint effort to preserve Gamla - the biggest breeding colony of Griffon Vultures in Israel. This project includes a thorough nest surveillance (e.g., Court et al. 1997), monitoring and radio-tracking of chicks in the fledging and post-fledging stages, as well as analysis of food contamination (Bahat 1997). Another important project, due to start soon in the desert regions, is a network of feeding stations in 9 different areas from the northern Judean hills down to the Elat mountains. We consider this project vital to the survival of the remaining Griffon and Egyptian vultures in the arid regions of Israel.

Vultures as a group are highly vulnerable to human persecution of any kind. Although many of the characteristics of vultures have led human communities to believe them to be, for example, God's messengers, or have aroused the scientist community's curiosity, they have suffered a major downfall over the past century. The fact that vultures are group feeders allows for an increased die-off in case of a pin point-calamity. Vultures have an important role in our nature - they are a major scavenging force which our environment needs. However, this group of birds, which has survived for the last 20 million years will most probably not survive humankind unless we take action to save the vultures and their appropriate habitats today.

REFERENCES

BAHAT, O. 1986. Raptor nesting in the Judean Desert - past, present and future trends. *Torgos* 12:8-24. (In Hebrew, English summary).

BAHAT, O. 1997. The way of a vulture in the sky - the Griffon Vultures in Israel. *Torgos* 26, 67 pp. (In Hebrew, English summary and captions).
COURT, L., R. YOSEF, O. BAHAT & D. KAPLAN 1997. Griffon Vulture *Gyps fulvus* nest surveillance project at the Gamla Nature Reserve, Golan Heights, Israel: 1996 conservation report. *Vulture News* 37:10-20.
DEL HOYO, J., A. ELLIOTT, AND J. SARGATAL. (Eds.) 1994. *Handbook of the birds of the world*. Vol. 2. Lynx Edicions, Barcelona.
GRUBAC, R. B. 1991. Status and biology of the Bearded Vulture *Gypaetus barbatus* in Macedonia. *WWGBP Birds of Prey Bull.* 4:101-117.
KIFF, L. F. 1989. DDE and the California Condor *Gymnogyps californianus*: the end of a story? Pp. 477-480 *In: Raptors in the modern world* (B.-U. Meyburg & R. D. Chancellor, eds). WWGBP, Berlin.
LESHEM, Y. 1980. The Bearded Vulture - prince of the cliffs. *Israel - Land and Nature* 23:22-28. (In Hebrew).
LESHEM, Y. 1988. Der Negev und die Judaische Wuste: Lestzte chance fur Israels Greife. *Luscinia* 46:89-95. (In German).
MARINKOVIC, S. & L. ORLANDIC 1994. Status of the Griffon Vulture *Gyps fulvus* in Serbia. Pp. 163-172 *In: Raptor conservation today* (B.-U. Meyburg & R. D. Chancellor, eds). WWGBP, Berlin/Pica Press.
MERETZKY, V. J. & D. LAVEE 1991. Conservation and management of the Negev Lappet-faced Vulture in Israel. Israel Nature Reserves Authority. vii+116 pp.
MUNDY, P., D. BUTCHART, J. LEDGER & S. PIPER 1992. *The vultures of Africa*. Acorn Books, Johannesburg.
NATHAN, R., U.N. SAFRIEL & H. SHIRIHAI 1996. Extinction and vulnerability to extinction at distribution peripheries: an analysis of the Israeli breeding fauna. *Israel J. Zool.* 42:361-383.
SATHEESAN, S. M. 1998. Vultures in Asia. pp. 13, Abstract in 5th WWGBP Conf., Midrand, South Africa.
SHIRIHAI, H. 1996. *The birds of Israel*. Academic Press.
SOTO, P. Le statut du Vatour fauve *Gyps fulvus* au Maroc. *WWGBP Birds of Prey Bull.* 3:173- 181.
TERRASSE, M., C. BAGNOLINI, J. BONNET, J.-L PINNA & F. SARRAZIN 1994. Reintroduction of the Griffon Vulture *Gyps fulvus* in the Massif Central, France. Pp. 479-491. In: *Raptors in the modern world* (B.-U. Meyburg & R. D. Chancellor, eds). WWGBP, Berlin.
TEWES, E. 1994. The European Black Vulture *Aegypius monachus* project in Mallorca. Pp. 493-498 *In: Raptor conservation today* (B.-U. Meyburg & R. D. Chancellor, eds). WWGBP, Berlin/Pica Press.
XIAO-TI, Y. 1991. Distribution and status of the Cinereous Vulture *Aegypius monachus* in China. *WWGBP Birds of Prey Bull.* 4:51-56.
YOSEF, R. 1996. On habitat-specific nutritional condition in Graceful Warblers: evidence from ptilochronology. *J. Ornithol.* 139:309-313.
YOSEF, R. 1997. First record of Great Spotted Cuckoo parasitizing Indian House Crow. *Israel J. Zool.* 43:397-399.
YOSEF, R. & O. HATZOFE 1997. Conservation aspects and former nest-site selection of the Lappet-faced Vulture (*Torgos tracheliotos negevensis*) in Israel. *Vulture News* 37:2-9.

Reuven Yosef
International Birding & Research Center in Eilat
P. O. Box 774
Eilat 88000, Israel

Ofer Bahat
Faculty of Aerospace Engineering
Technion - Israel Institute of Technology,
Haifa 32000, Israel

The Role of Avian Scavengers in locating and exploiting Carcasses in central Saudi Arabia

Mohammed Shobrak

ABSTRACT

The order in which different avian scavengers arrive at a carcass, the length of time each species spends feeding, and the methods used to reduce inter-specific competition, were investigated in central Saudi Arabia. Twenty-five observations were made at carcasses placed at sites inside and outside the Mahazat as-Sayd protected area. Observations were also made at a town rubbish dump, where permanent food is available for scavengers. The Brown-necked Raven was the first species to arrive at a carcass, whereas the Lappet-faced Vulture was the last species to find and feed from a carcass. However, the number of vultures increased rapidly once the carcass had been discovered. Competition was reduced by different species attending the carcasses at different times of the day. For example, the small species, such as the eagles and ravens, fed early in the morning and in the late evening, whereas the large species, such as the Lappet-faced Vulture, concentrated their feeding around midday.

INTRODUCTION

The potential for competitive interactions between animals increases greatly where mixed species flocks feed on patchily distributed food resources, and there are many avian examples of this amongst waders and gulls (Goss-Custard 1980; Monaghan 1980). Many field studies of closely related species living in the same area have shown differentiation in feeding habits between species, at least during periods of food shortage (Lack 1954, 1971; Krebs & Davies 1981; Perrins & Birkhead 1983). Carrion represents a resource which is exploited by many bird and mammal species. However, the avian scavengers have a considerable advantage over mammalian competitors in locating these transient, isolated sources of food, through their greater ability to locate carcasses and low energy costs of travel (Houston 1974, 1979).

Among these avian scavengers are vulture species which feed mainly on carrion, and which can locate carcasses quickly even over long distances (Mundy *et al.* 1992). The Old World vultures are known to locate carrion only by sight, whereas among the New World vultures the three species of *Cathartes* also use olfaction (Stager 1964; Houston 1984; Mundy *et al.* 1992). Studies on ecological separation of African vultures have shown that there is considerable specialisation among the avian scavengers to avoid competition over food (Kruuk 1967; Pennycuick 1972; Houston 1976, 1980; Mundy et al. 1992).

However, little is known of the scavenging guild in Arabia. In this study I aim to determine firstly the times at which the avian scavenger species arrive at carcasses; secondly, the length of time each species spends feeding at a carcass; and thirdly, to examine how the numbers and species composition of scavenging birds and mammals feeding at a carcass act to reduce competition among them. I made observations within a reserve, where only wild species were available as a source of food for scavengers, and also outside the reserve where wild animals are scarce but carcasses of domestic animals are abundant (Shobrak 1996).

STUDY AREA

The study was carried out in and around the Mahazat as-Sayd reserve, located on the arid plains of central-western Saudi Arabia, at 22° 00' - 22° 30' N and 41° 28' - 42° 13' E. The reserve (2,244 km^2) was fenced in 1989 to exclude stock and nomadic herdsmen, and was the first site for the reintroduction of the Arabian oryx *Oryx leucoryx*, sand gazelles *Gazella subgutturosa*, mountain gazelle *Gazella gazella*, Houbara Bustard *Chlamydotis undulata* and Red-necked Ostrich *Struthio camelus camelus* in Saudi Arabia (Greth & Schwede 1993; Haque & Smith 1994, 1996).

METHODS

Two types of observations were made in this study. The first involved putting out carcasses and monitoring these continuously for 2-3 days. Twenty-five observations were made at sites inside and outside the reserve during most months between April 1993 and January 1995. Inside the reserve three sand gazelles and three Arabian oryx which had died from natural causes were used. Outside the reserve a total of 12 goats and 13 sheep were placed and observed. A total of 20 days were spent monitoring carcasses inside the reserve, and 45 days outside the reserve. The second set of observations was made at a rubbish dump outside the reserve, where butchers' waste was regularly discarded.

In both areas carcasses were provided at dawn (between 04:00 and 05:30 h) or on the previous day after sunset (between 18:00 and 19:30 h). Observations were made from a vehicle, which served as a hide. Carcass sites were selected in open areas where vegetation did not impede visibility. Observations on the dominance hierarchy between the scavenging species were made by recording the maximum number of each species attending the carcass, and the number of aggressive interactions between and within the different species. In addition, a correlation coefficient was calculated between the changes in the number of species with time, to see if the arrival of one species had an effect on the numbers of the other species.

The second set of observations were made at one month intervals at a rubbish dump 40km to the north of the reserve. The observations were started in February 1994 and extended for 11 months. It was possible to watch the behaviour of scavengers at this permanent food source for up to 8 hours per day, and to note the sequence in which different species arrived and the number of birds feeding at any one time. Similar observations were made when natural carcasses were found incidentally. In this study all birds except eagles were identified to species: the field identification of the *Aquila* eagles (Steppe *nipalensis*, Greater Spotted *clanga* and Imperial *heliaca*) is often difficult, and these species are considered collectively.

RESULTS

Locating the carcasses

The avian scavengers inside and outside the reserve can be divided according to their status into three groups: resident species; those species that use the area for feeding; and winter visitors (Newton & Newton 1993; Shobrak 1996). The resident species include the Lappet-faced Vulture *Torgos tracheliotos* and the Brown-necked Raven *Corvus ruficollis*. Species that used the area for feeding

Figure 1. The mean number of scavenging birds present at carcasses placed outside the reserve (bars indicate the standard error)

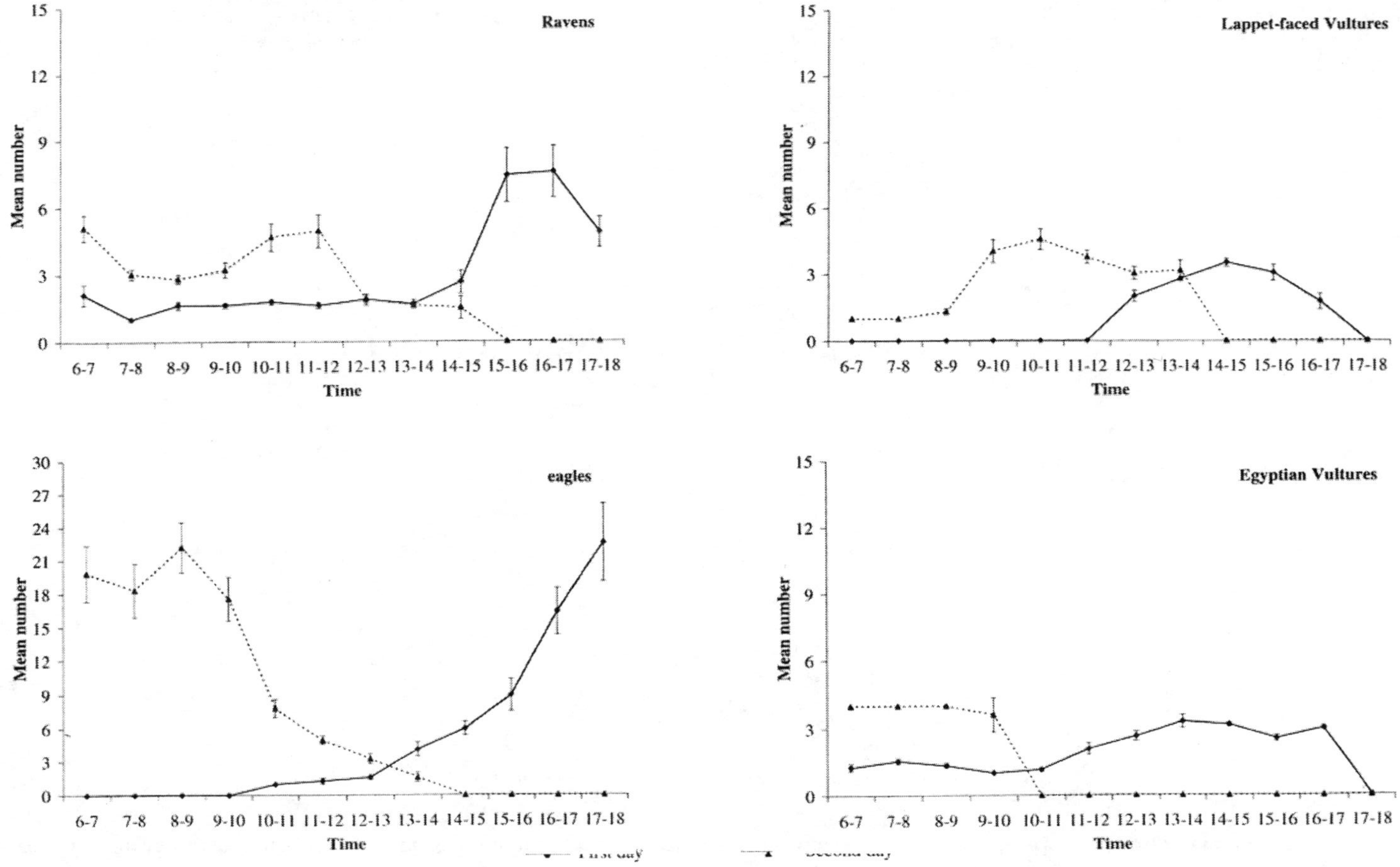

Figure 2. The mean number of scavenging birds present at carcasses placed inside the reserve (bars indicate the standard error)

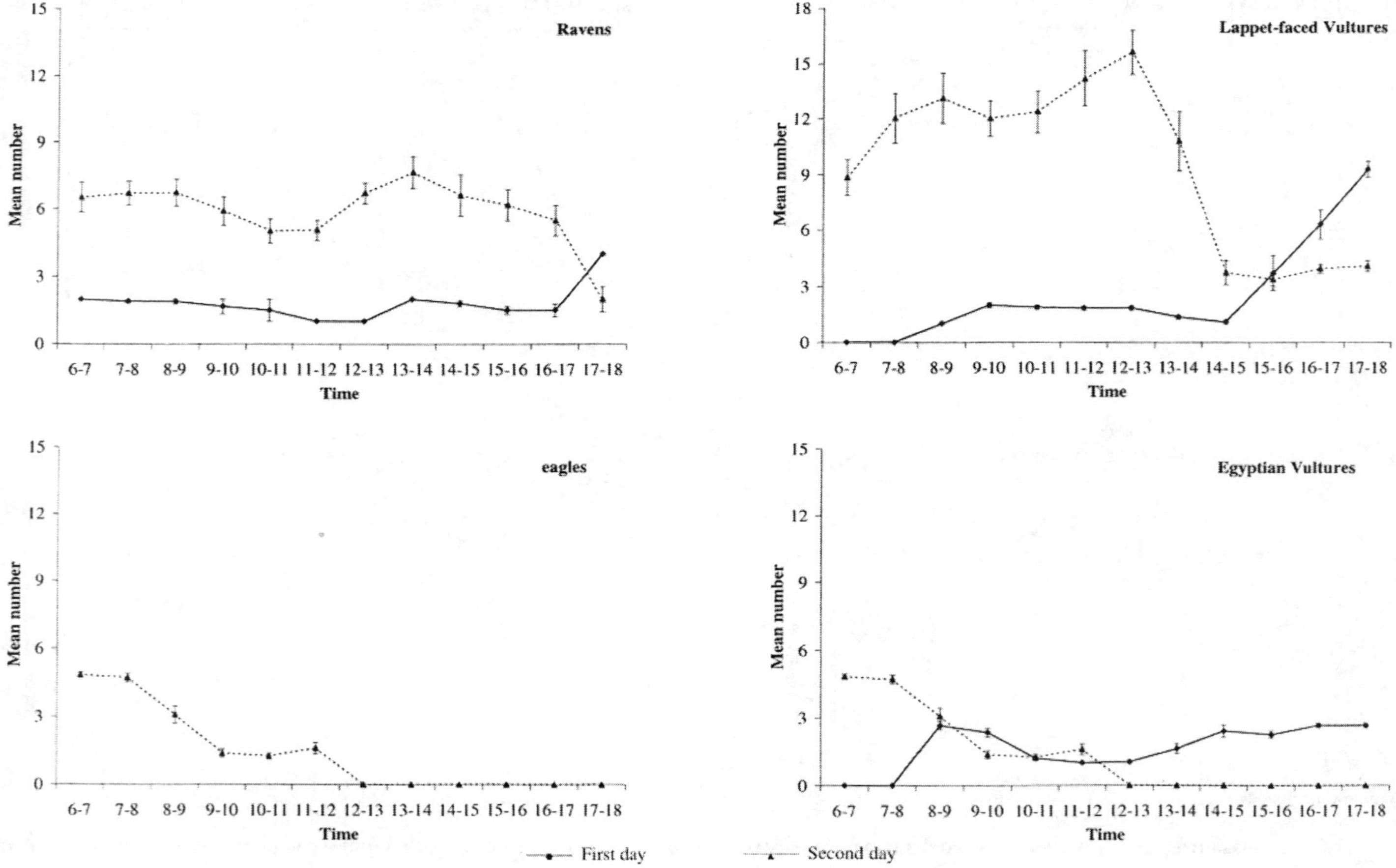

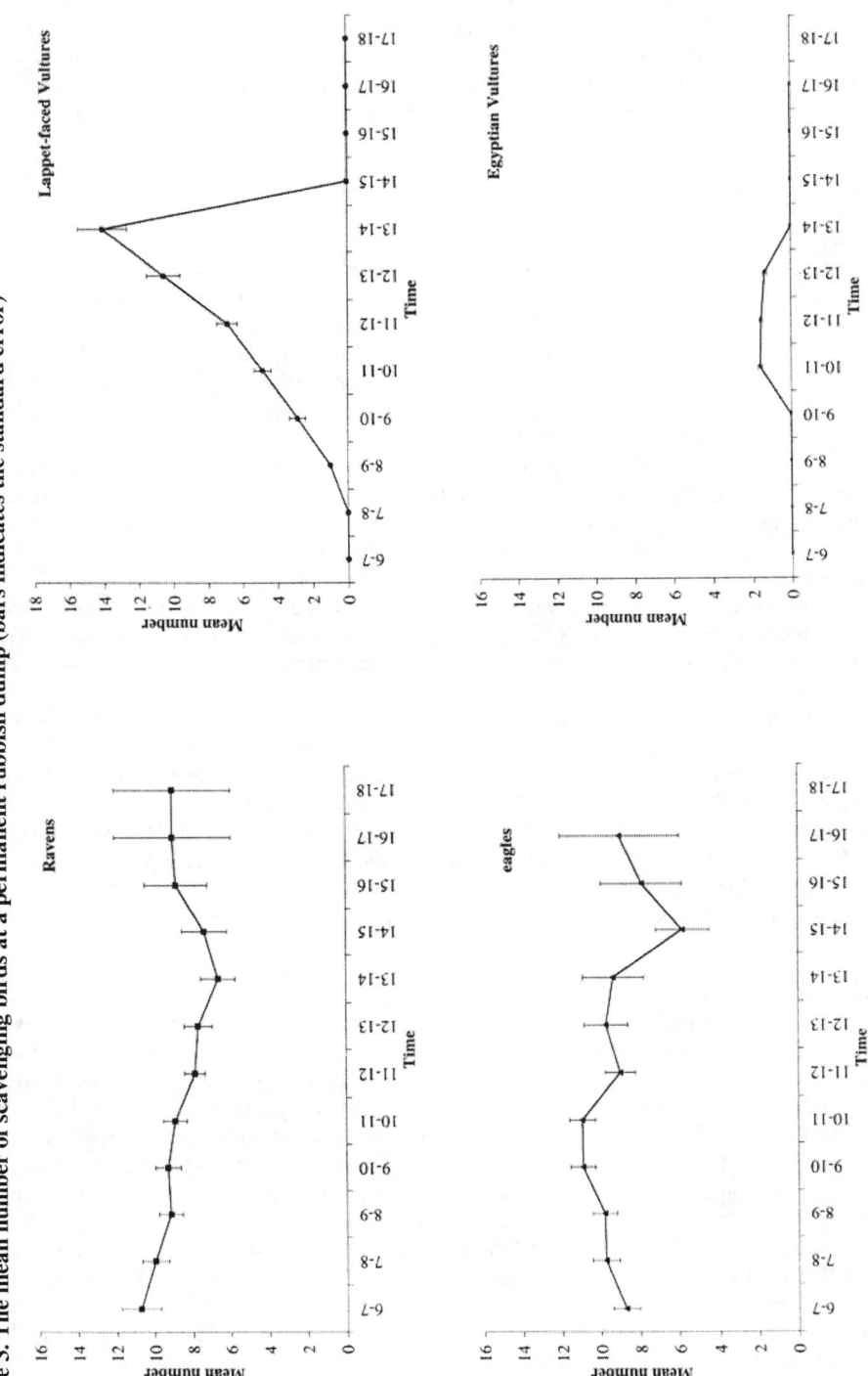

Figure 3. The mean number of scavenging birds at a permanent rubbish dump (bars indicates the standard error)

and roosting include the Griffon Vulture *Gyps fulvus* and the Egyptian Vulture *Neophron percnopterus*. Winter visitors include the Black Kite *Milvus migrans,* Cinereous Vulture *Aegypius monachus*, and Eagles, six species of which have been recorded in the reserve (Newton & Newton 1993): Bonelli's Eagle *Hieraaetus fasciatus*, Booted Eagle *H. pennatus*, Golden Eagle *Aquila chrysaetos*, Imperial Eagle *A. heliaca*, Greater Spotted Eagle *A. clanga*, Steppe Eagle *A. nipalensis*. Of the five times in which the Cinereous Vulture was observed during the study, on one occasion one juvenile was seen attending the feeding at the rubbish dump.

Resident species

Lappet-faced Vulture
On the first day Lappet-faced Vultures outside the reserve arrived after 12:00 (Fig. 1), and there were significant differences among the numbers attending the carcasses by time of day (One-way ANOVA, $F_{4,74}$ = 5.90, P<0.001). Similarly inside the reserve, the numbers changed with time, and there were significantly more birds attending the carcass later in the day (One-way ANOVA, $F_{9,176}$ = 34.96, P< 0.001) (Fig. 2). However, on the first day, birds inside the reserve arrived much later than those outside the reserve; 78% of birds coming to carcasses outside the reserve arrived before 15:00, compared with only 5% at carcasses inside the reserve.

On the second day, the birds returned at first light, although they did not start feeding from the carcasses immediately. The number of birds present at carcasses inside the reserve was significantly greater on the second day than on the first day (Mann-Whitney, *U*-test, W= 33.5, P<0.01). Outside the reserve there was no significant difference in the number of birds present at the carcass on the first and second days (Mann-Whitney, *U*-test, W= 140, P>0.05).

At the butchers' rubbish dump, where food was permanently available, the Lappet-faced Vultures arrived between 08:00 and 13:00. The number of feeding birds varied significantly with time of day (One-way ANOVA, $F_{7,263}$ = 19.90, P<0.005). The maximum numbers were observed between 13:00 and 14:00 (Fig. 3).

The Lappet-faced Vulture was seen feeding on most types of carcass. In the reserve, these vultures were most abundant at carcasses of medium size (30-60kg) such as those of Arabian oryx (Fig. 4), but overall there was no evidence that the size of carcass affected the number of birds feeding at it (One-way ANOVA, $F_{3,9}$ = 3.12, P>0.05). At the carcasses the Lappet-faced Vultures were seen feeding first from the head and from the exposed meat if the carcass was already open. Dominant birds stood on the carcasses before starting to tear the skin. At camel carcasses Lappet-faced Vultures were seen feeding only from the head, part of the neck and the rump, and rarely from the belly. After these parts had been consumed, vultures were not seen at carcasses, even though other edible parts remained.

Brown-necked Raven
There were no significant differences between the maximum numbers of Brown-necked Ravens attending carcasses on the first and the second days inside and outside the reserve (Wilcoxon Matched-pairs test, Z= -1.7529, P>0.05, n= 8 "inside"; Z= -1.2741, P>0.05 n= 13 "outside") (Figs.1 and 2).

At the rubbish dump, Ravens were seen most of the time. They arrived before 06:00, suggesting that they might roost in the area. There was no evidence that the number of ravens at the dump varied with the time of day (One-way ANOVA, $F_{10,1081}$ = 1.27, P> 0.05), (Fig. 3). The maximum number observed at the rubbish dump was 54 birds; they were mostly young and non-breeding birds.

The Brown-necked Raven was usually the first species to arrive at the carcass. Out of 17 occasions on which ravens arrived first, on 12 occasions the birds were in pairs, and on three occasions they arrived as trios; on only two occasions did a single bird arrive at the carcass. The first arrival time of ravens at carcasses was normally between 05:30 and 09:30 on the first day. But on one occasion they arrived late in the evening at 17:00. Ravens were observed three times hammering vigorously at bloated carcasses, but succeeded only once in penetrating the skin. The bill structure in this bird is not adapted to tearing tough skin, but they could succeed in opening small carcasses, such as those of young sheep, goats and gazelles. However, they were seen at all types of carcasses (Fig. 4). There was a highly significant difference in the maximum number of ravens recorded at carcasses of different weight (One-way ANOVA, $F_{3, 34} = 20.99$, $P<0.001$), showing that large carcasses attracted larger numbers of birds

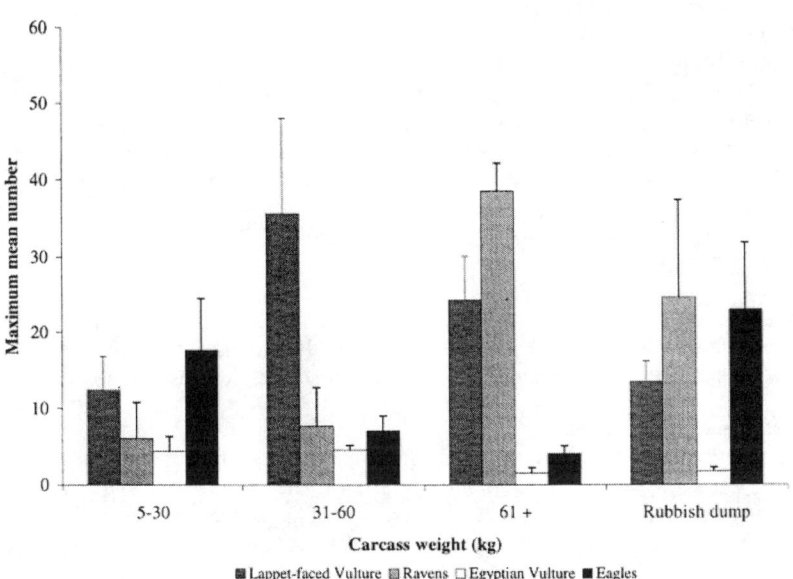

Figure 4. The mean maximum numbers of avian scavengers attending carcasses of different weights (bars represent the standard error)

The species using the area for feeding

Egyptian Vulture

The number of Egyptian Vultures feeding in the study area was low compared to other species, and no more than eight birds were recorded at any one time. Outside the reserve, the number of Egyptian Vultures increased during the day (One-way ANOVA, $F_{10, 223} = 11.16$, $P<0.001$) (Fig 1). Inside the reserve, numbers similarly changed through the day (One-way ANOVA, $F_{9, 185} = 20$, $P<0.05$) (Fig. 2). On the second day the birds were present only in the morning, and had usually left the carcass by midday. Egyptian Vultures were seen only twice at the rubbish dump, and the maximum number was two (Fig. 3).

Similarly to the ravens, the Egyptian Vultures are not adapted for tearing tough skin; they were seen tearing the skin around the skull, but not on other parts of the carcasses. More birds were recorded at small carcasses than at large ones (One-way ANOVA, $F_{3, 14} = 5.04$, $P<0.02$) (Fig. 4).

Griffon Vulture

Only two Griffon Vultures were observed: at two carcasses inside the reserve.

The migratory species

Eagles

The number of eagles at a carcass increased throughout the first day outside the reserve (One-way ANOVA, $F_{7,190}$ = 13.24, P<0.001). They were seen roosting near the carcasses, and on the second day they started feeding at first light (Fig. 1); numbers then decreased throughout the day (One-way ANOVA, $F_{7,216}$ = 14.47, P<0.001). Comparing the number of eagles which attended the carcasses in the first and second days outside the reserve, there were no significant differences (Mann-Whitney test W= 95.5, P>0.05). In the reserve there was one observation of a single bird which arrived on the first day. However, on the second day the number of birds attending the carcass had increased and there was a significant difference in the number of eagles present at different times of the day (One-way ANOVA, $F_{11,226}$ =16.55, P<0.001) (Fig. 2).

At the rubbish dump, eagles arrived before 06:00 indicating that they may roost there. The number of eagles did not vary with the time of day (One-way ANOVA, F= 1.23, P>0.001) (Fig. 3).

Similarly to the Egyptian Vultures and ravens, the eagles are not adapted for tearing tough skin, but they could succeed in opening small carcasses. A Steppe Eagle was once seen opening the carcass of an adult gazelle. It started with the soft tissue on the head and back before ripping open the belly area between the back legs. However, there was no significant difference in the maximum numbers of eagles observed at any one time attending carcasses of different weight (One-way ANOVA, $F_{3,12}$ = 0.482, P>0.05) (Fig. 4).

Other species

Black Kite and Cinereous Vulture were observed at the carcasses, but their numbers were too small for statistical analysis, and the time they spent at the carcasses was short.

Mammalian scavengers

The mammalian carnivores which could scavenge in the study area are the Arabian red fox *Vulpes vulpes* and Rüppells fox *Vulpes ruppelli*, feral dog *Canis familiaris* and wild cat *Felis silvestris*, sand cat *F. margarita*, and feral cats *F. domesticus*. Most of these species are nocturnal, and were not seen to visit the carcasses during the day. Tracks of foxes and cats were found close to carcasses in 5 of 25 cases, indicating nocturnal feeding. These tracks were found in the late summer and autumn, when the numbers of rodents and insects are known to be low and foxes may then have to seek alternative food (Olfermann 1993, 1996). Additionally, feral dogs were observed feeding on four occasions at the rubbish dump. On all occasions all the avian scavengers were observed to move away as soon as dogs arrived, and there is no doubt that dogs are dominant over the birds. However, these animals are becoming a target for persecution from the shepherds and farmers as they claim that these animals attack their livestock. Two dogs were shot in front of my car in December 1993, and the hunter was then congratulated by local people as they considered he had done them a favour.

The dominance hierarchy among scavenging species

Avian scavengers

Table 1 shows the percentage of interactions among the bird species. The Lappet-faced Vulture was the most aggressive against members of its own species. Other birds often moved aside from carcasses when dominant Lappet-faced Vultures approached. Although the Brown-necked Ravens were often the first species to arrive at carcasses, they also gathered in large numbers at the rubbish dump during summer and autumn. They showed high levels of intraspecific aggression. In groups they would also try to dominate the feeding area, by chasing other larger birds, such as the Lappet-faced Vulture, by pulling their tails and jumping on their backs. There is an excess of food at the site, and ravens rarely took advantage of a food item after it had been abandoned by the bird that they attacked. This area holds large numbers of immature ravens, rather than territorial adults.

Ravens also sometimes attack small birds which come to feed on the insects around the carcasses. Fifteen Brown-necked Ravens were observed at the rubbish dump site chasing a Hoopoe Lark *Alaemon alaudipes*. At carcasses placed at other sites I have seen the local territorial ravens behave similarly. However, on most occasions the ravens lost fights with larger species.

Table 1 also shows that most of the aggression by scavenging species was directed towards members of the same species. The eagles were the only birds to show strong aggression against the Lappet-faced Vulture. Figures 1 and 2 show that competition among the scavenging birds was reduced through species attending the carcasses at different times. The smaller species fed mainly in the morning and the evening, whereas the Lappet-faced Vultures started at mid-day.

Avian scavengers might avoid competition by leaving a carcass when more dominant species arrive. However, there was no correlation between the changes in the numbers of Lappet-faced Vultures and eagles (r_{52} =-0.056, P>0.5), nor ravens and eagles (r_{52} =-0.038, P>0.5), nor ravens and Lappet-faced Vultures (r_{52}=-0.038, P>0.5). Each species has preferred feeding times, which as a consequence avoids competition with other species, but the arrival of dominant species has no influence on the presence of birds at carcasses.

DISCUSSION

Locating the carcasses

Lappet-faced Vulture

The results showed that the Lappet-faced Vulture was usually the last species to arrive or to approach a carcass. These birds also appeared hesitant near carcasses. Their large size makes it difficult for them to take off and they are therefore more vulnerable to predation than the smaller scavenger species. This shyness at food has been observed in other small and large scavenging birds (Heinrich 1988; Mundy *et al* 1992).

Because the birds roost inside the reserve, they might be expected to locate carcasses within the reserve very quickly. But in fact very few vultures locate carcasses inside the reserve before late afternoon, possibly because there is so little food usually found within the reserve that it is not worth their time to search there and they go immediately outside the reserve as soon as they leave the roost. When birds returned to the reserve to roost later in the day they might then find a carcass located there. At all observations the birds did not start feeding from the carcasses on this first day, but they were seen resting near the carcass and then roosting in nearby trees overnight. Presumably these birds started feeding from the same carcass the next day.

Communal roosts could function as centres for the exchange of information on the location of food (Ward & Zahavi 1973; Weatherhead 1983). Studies on the New World Turkey Vulture *Cathartes aura* in southern Ontario, Canada, show that roosts do not function in this way (Prior & Weatherhead 1991), but there is good evidence that they do for the New World Black Vulture (Rabenold 1987). From my own study, I consider that Lappet-faced Vultures were not roosting communally in order to acquire information about food, but rather this might enable the birds to form a "network" in the sky and thus search effectively for food over a large area. Most birds started foraging singly or in pairs and they moved in different directions (Shobrak 1996) enabling them to cover the area effectively. Prior & Weatherhead (1991) suggested that food patches must persist for at least two days for roosts to function as information centres since most roosting birds only travel to and from the roost once each day. In the study area the majority of Lappet-faced Vultures roost near the carcass in the first day to start feeding at first light of the second day. This is especially true for carcasses placed inside the reserve, as most of these carcasses were placed between 500m and 10km from the roost site, and birds descending to food would be seen easily by the other roosting vultures.

Brown-necked Raven

There may be several reasons why the Brown-necked Raven was most often the first to arrive at a carcass. Firstly, the species is more common in the area than any other scavenging species (Jennings 1995; Newton & Newton 1993), Secondly, this species breeds solitarily and related species are known to occupy large territories (Goodwin 1976; Knight & Call 1980; Marzluff & Heinrich 1991;

Heinrich et al. 1994). According to Bossema & Benus (1985), ravens probably form lasting pair bonds and once established in a territory they occupy it for life. In all the sites where carcasses were placed there was a territorial pair of ravens occupying the area, and they usually arrived at the carcasses first. Finally, the ability of ravens to use flapping rather than gliding flight may allow them to start foraging early in the morning before the thermals form, upon which gliding birds such as vultures rely. In agricultural areas in Africa carcasses were also located most often by crows and ravens (Mundy et al. 1992).

There may be various reasons why the number of ravens at carcasses inside the reserve varied with the time of day while numbers at carcasses outside the reserve did not. Firstly, this could be due to the different numbers of ravens inside and outside the reserve. Secondly, it could be due to the difference in the size of territories and home ranges, or thirdly it could be related to the availability of food in the two areas. Newton (1979) suggested that the home range size varies depending on the food supply available to a raptor.

Eagles

As a result of hunting and overgrazing in Saudi Arabia the majority of wild prey species, which eagles could feed on during migration, have been depleted or driven to extinction in some areas (Child & Grainger 1990). As a result, the eagles instead take advantage of carrion available in the area. The number of eagles feeding at the rubbish dump was constant through the day. This does not necessarily mean that the same birds remained through the day because new birds may take the opportunity to feed when a satiated bird leaves the patch (Krebs & Davies 1981; Perrins & Birkhead 1983).

Mammalian carnivores

Large carnivores, which used to prey on wild ungulates, have started to feed on the increasing domestic herds, leading to a negative attitude of the local people towards these animals. Predators such as wolf and hyena are now absent from many areas in Saudi Arabia (Child & Grainger 1990). Although there were other mammalian scavengers in the area, such as the foxes, they have alternative food supplies and they mainly feed on insects and small mammals (Olfermann 1993, 1996). The other feral mammals occur only near the small towns and villages where they feed from the garbage dumps, but they were not responsible for removing substantial amounts from the provided carcasses. Shobrak (1996) estimated that the percentage of food utilized by the mammalian scavengers from the carcasses available around the reserve was only 4.4%.

The dominance hierarchy among scavenging species

Avian scavengers are more successful than the mammalian scavengers in utilizing these carcasses. Birds have many advantages in searching for food from the air, because they can cover large areas, and by watching other birds they can collaborate to find food. Pennycuick (1975) estimated the horizontal speed of a vulture in steep dive can reach 70km/h while the running speed of a hyena is about 40 km/h, so vultures can cover large areas with little energy while mammals use considerably more energy to reach food (Schmidt-Nielson 1972; Pennycuick 1975).

Houston's (1976) studies in the Serengeti implied that vultures do not gain an advantage over mammalian scavengers just because they get to the carcasses first. Their advantage is also that they find carcasses that the mammalian scavengers often never reach at all. In this study the mammalian carnivores are nocturnal, therefore competition at the food source was reduced between this group and the scavenging birds, but it was also found that mammalian scavengers failed to locate most of the sources of food provided. Shobrak (1996) found that the amount of food available to the scavenging species in all areas was more than they could utilize, and there were large proportions of the carcasses (65%) which were uneaten by any of the birds and mammals.

Among the avian scavengers the Lappet-faced Vultures have an advantage over all other scavenging birds, probably due to large body size which allows them to drive away competitors and to survive for longer periods between meals (Kruuk 1967; Lack 1971; Wallace & Temple 1987).

Table 1. Percentage frequency of interactions among avian scavengers at 14 carcasses, (number of aggressive attacks = 1850).

	L-f.V[1].	Raven	Eagles	Others[2]
Intraspecific	71.5	39.7	63.3	
Interspecific	28.5	60.3	36.7	
Interspecific Wins	70.9	25.8	64.8	
Interspecific Losses	29.1	74.2	35.2	
Overall proportion of interactions	41.8	25.3	30.7	2.2

1 Lappet-faced Vulture
2 Griffon Vulture, Black Kite, Egyptian Vulture and Marsh Harrier *Circus aeruginosus*.

They also require less energy per day per unit weight than do smaller birds (König 1983). The small scavenging birds have alternative food sources, and need unspecialised beaks even though carrion may be important as part of their diet for certain periods of the year. By contrast, the Lappet-faced Vulture concentrates on carrion and has a deep powerful beak with a strong hook at the tip adapted for tearing skin and feeding on the meat of mammals (Houston 1979; Mundy *et al.* 1992). This species is clearly the major scavenger on carcasses in the study area. Its ability to open the skin of large carcasses also provides feeding sites for the smaller scavenger species.

ACKNOWLEDGEMENTS

I am grateful to Professor Abdulaziz Abuzinadah, Secretary General of the National Commission for Wildlife Conservation and Development for his support and encouragement at every stage of the study. My sincere thanks to Dr David Houston and Dr. Stephen Newton for their advice and useful discussion and suggestions. In the National Wildlife Research Center I wish to thank Dr Philip Seddon for commenting on earlier versions of this paper. Lastly special thanks to Mohammed Basheer for explaining some of the computer packages.

REFERENCES

BOSSEMA, I. & BENUS, R. 1985. Territorial defence and intra-pair cooperation in the carrion crow (*Corvus corone*). *Behav. Ecol. Sociobiol.*, 16: 99-104.
CHILD, G. & GRAINGER, J. 1990. A plan to protect areas in Saudi Arabia. NCWCD and IUCN: Riyadh and Gland.
GOODWIN, D. 1976. *Crows of the world*. British Museum of Natural History. London,
GOSS-CUSTARD, J. D. 1980. Competition for food and interference among waders. *Ardea*, 68: 31-52.
GRETH, A. & SCHWEDE, G. 1993. A brief history of the reintroduction of the Arabian oryx *Oryx leucoryx* in Saudi Arabia. *Int. Zoo Yb.*, 32: 73-81.
HAQUE, M. N. & SMITH, T. R. 1994. Re-introduction of Red-necked ostriches in Saudi Arabia. *Re-introduction News*, No. 9: 5.
HAQUE, M. N. & SMITH, T. R. 1996. Reintroduction of Arabian Sand gazelle *Gazella subgutturosa marica* in Saudi Arabia. *Biol. Cons.*, 76:203-207.
HEINRICH, B. 1988. Why do ravens fear their food? *Condor*, 90: 50-52.
HEINRICH, B., KAYE, D., KNIGHT, T. & SCHAUMBURG, K. 1994. Dispersal and association among common ravens. *Condor*, 96: 545-551.
HOUSTON, D. C. 1974. The role of griffon vultures as scavengers. *J. Zool., London.*, 172: 35-46.
HOUSTON, D. C. 1976. Ecological isolation of African scavenging birds. *Ardea*, 63: 55-64.
HOUSTON, D. C. 1979. The adaptations of scavengers. *Serengeti: dynamics of an ecosystem*. Ed. Sinclair A.R.E. & North-Griffiths. Chicago University Press. Chicago, 263-285
HOUSTON, D. C. 1980. Interrelations of African scavenging animals. *Proc. IV Pan-Afr. Orn. Congr.*, 307-312.
HOUSTON, D. C. 1984. A comparison of the food supply of African and South American vultures. *Proc. V Pan-Afr. Orn. Cong.*, 249-262.

JENNINGS, M. C. 1995. *An interim atlas of breeding birds in Arabia*. NCWCD. Riyadh.
KNIGHT, R. L. & CALL, M. W. 1980. The common raven. Techn. note # 344, U. S. Dept. Interior.
KÖNIG, C. 1983. Interspecific and intraspecific competition for food among old world vultures. In: Willbur, S. R. and Jackson, J. A. (Eds.). *Vulture biology and management*. University of California Press. Berkeley.
KREBS, J. R. & DAVIES, N. B. 1981. *An Introduction to Behavioural Ecology*. Blackwell Scientific Publications. Oxford.
KRUUK, H. 1967. Competition for food between vultures in East Africa. *Ardea*, 55: 171-193.
LACK, D. 1954. *The natural regulation of animal numbers*. Oxford University Press, Oxford.
LACK, D. 1971. *Ecological Isolation in Birds*. Cambridge University Press. Cambridge.
MARZLUFF, J. M. & HEINRICH, B. 1991. Foraging by common ravens in presence and absence of territory holders: an experimental analysis of social foraging. *Anim. Behav.*, 42: 755-776.
MONAGHAN, P. 1980. Dominance and dispersal between feeding sites in the Herring Gull (*Larus argentatus*). *Anim. Behav.*, 28: 521-527.
MUNDY, P., BUTCHART, D., LEDGER, J. & PIPER, S. 1992. *The vultures of Africa*. Acorn Books. Randburg (South Africa).
NEWTON, I. 1979. *Population ecology of raptors*. T. & A. D. Poyser. Berkhamsted.
NEWTON, S. & NEWTON, A. 1993. The birds of Mahazat As Sayd reserve. Internal report. NCWCD. Riyadh.
OLFERMANN, B. 1993. Progress of the small mammal study at Mahazat As Sayd. Annual Report. NWRC, 194-203.
OLFERMANN, E. 1996. Population ecology of the Rüppell's fox (*Vulpes rueppelli*, Schinz 1825) and the red fox (*Vulpes vulpes*, Linnaeus 1758) in the semi-desert environment of Saudi Arabia. Unpublished thesis. Universität Bielefeld. Germany.
PENNYCUICK, C. J. 1972. Soaring behaviour and performance of some East African birds, observed from a motor-glider. *Ibis*, 114: 178-218.
PENNYCUICK, L 1975. Movements of migratory wildebeest population in the Serengeti area between 1960 and 1973. *E. Afr. Wildl. J.*, 13: 65-87.
PERRINS, C. M. & BIRKHEAD, T. R. 1983. *Avian Ecology*. Blackie & Son. Glasgow.
PRIOR, K. A. & WEATHERHEAD, P. J. 1991. Competition at the carcass: opportunities for social foraging by turkey vultures in southern Ontario. *Can. J. Zool.*, 28: 385-390.
RABENOLD, P. P. 1987. Recruitment to food in black vultures: evidence for following from communal roosts. *Anim. Behav.*, 35: 1775-1785.
SCHMIDT-NIELSON, K. 1972. Energy cost of swimming, running and flying. *Science*, 177: 222-228.
SHOBRAK, M. 1996. Ecology of the lappet-faced vulture *Torgos tracheliotus* in Saudi Arabia. Unpublished thesis. Glasgow University. Glasgow.
STAGER, K. E. 1964. The role of olfacation in food location by the Turkey Vulture *Cathartes aura*. *Los Angeles County Museum Contributions in Science*, No. 81.
WALLACE, M. P. & TEMPLE, S. A. 1987. Competitive interactions within and between species in a guild of avian scavengers. *Auk*, 104: 290-295.
WARD, P. & ZAHAVI, A. 1973. The importance of certain assemblages of birds as "information centres" for food-finding. *Ibis*, 115: 517-534.
WEATHERHEAD, P. J. 1983. Two principal strategies in avian communal roosts. *Am. Nat.*, 121: 237-243.

Mohammed Shobrak
National Commission for Wildlife
Conservation and Development
National Wildlife Research Center
P. O. Box 1086, Taif
Saudi Arabia

Chancellor, R. D. & B.-U. Meyburg eds. 2000
Raptors at Risk
WWGBP / Hancock House

Regular Long-distance Migration of Eurasian Griffon *Gyps fulvus*

Goran Susic

ABSTRACT

The Eurasian Griffon in Croatia breeds on island cliffs at the northernmost border of the species' distribution.

In 1990 a programme of ringing and wing marking started, and during eight years (1990-1997) 195 birds have been marked, 108 individuals were recovered or found dead (recovery rate of 55.4%) with the total of 315 re-sightings/recoveries.

All juvenile birds left their breeding colonies by the end of September of their first year, and there are no juvenile, immature or subadult Griffons on the Island. They came back when mature. Their migrational routes, when using two main directions - NW (to the Austrian and Italian Alps, then Spain?) and SE (to southern Italy, Balkans, Greece, Israel and as far south as Chad in central Africa and then, maybe, also to Spain) - are repeated every year, with the same timing.

The flight of 3.750 km made by a wing-tagged Eurasian Griffon *Ledni Zlajo*, who travelled from Croatia to Chad, is the furthest-known distance travelled by any griffon on migration.

So, although their circular movements are very complex, the conclusion could be that this is definitely not dispersal or irregular nomadism but some kind of regular migration taken by juvenile, immature and subadult birds until maturity. As a species the Eurasian Griffon should no longer be considered a sedentary or partially migrant bird, but a long distance migrant, where only non-breeding birds migrate, and their migration is complex, still not clear enough and lasts five or six years.

INTRODUCTION

The Eurasian Griffon *Gyps fulvus* is considered a sedentary and migrant ("young individuals") species (Gensbøl 1989), or as mentioned by Mundy *et al.* (1992) it is "partially migratory, that is, only a part of its population migrates annually ... into Africa." If this is true, is it known which part of its population migrates annually?

According to Bernis (1983) Spanish griffons regularly migrate, but only juvenile birds, while their aestivation in the Alps (Croatian griffon population) he called "nomadism". Various other hypotheses have been formulated to explain the phenomenon of the Eurasian Griffon's aestivation in the Alps (the critical analysis was made by Genero 1988).

The Eurasian Griffon in Croatia breeds on island cliffs above the sea, at Quarner Archipelago, northern Adriatic, at the northernmost border of the species' distribution, at 45°10'N. There was an increase of population during a period of 15 years: the number of breeding pairs has more than doubled. Extensive monitoring of the population on the Island of Cres has been conducted for nine years, and all nests are observed once or twice per month. A protected area with two Ornithological

Reserves ("Kruna" and "Podokladi"), the Island of Cres holds one of the last nesting colonies in Croatia as well as in this part of Europe. At the beginning of the 1980's there were 25-30 pairs in the colony (Perco et al. 1983), ten years ago 40-50 (Susic 1994), and today there are 72-75 breeding pairs. Such an increase is the best proof that wing-tagging is not negatively influencing the survival rate of marked birds.

METHODS

In 1990 the programme of ringing and wing-tagging started (Susic 1994). During eight years (1990-1997) altogether 195 juvenile Eurasian Griffons were marked, mainly as nestlings. All of these wing-tagged juveniles were additionally ringed with metal rings. From 1993 on we used a wing-tag slightly modified from the one described before (Susic 1994). During the first three years (1990-1992) vinyl wing-tags had dimensions of 155x95 mm (letters 95x60 mm), but then smaller and more rounded tags were used, with dimension (during the last five years) of 140x87 mm (number/letter 70x60 mm). The tags are of similar size as used for the Californian Condor, which are 150x80 mm ventral side, 130x80 mm dorsal side (Wallace 1994), and not "much larger" as mentioned by Frey & Niebuhr (1994).

At the beginning of the programme nestlings were tagged when 70-80 days old, but the best period is when they are 75-85 days old, to allow sufficient feather development for adequate marker retention. The eight years of experience have shown that there are no harmful effects on the nestlings apart from a single short period of disturbance, and if the marker is properly attached there is no injury to the bird. Selective mobbing of marked griffons, as mentioned by Frey & Niebuhr (1994), has never been observed on the Island of Cres.

The main objective of the programme is to solve why all juvenile, immature and subadult birds migrate, i.e. why all of them disappear from the colony immediately after the fledgling (dependence) period during August and September. A second aim is to discover the annual mortality rate of these griffons.

RESULTS

Out of 195 wing-tagged Croatian Griffons, 108 individual specimens were re-sighted or found dead (recovery rate of 55.4%) with a total of 315 re-sightings/recoveries (Table 1.). This number is in reality much bigger, because some birds stay in Italy or Greece near the vulture "restaurant" for months, or even for a whole year. In such a case we counted them as if they were on that location once only in a month. Wing-tagging is much more efficient compared with ringing, which has a useful recovery rate of 5% (Piper 1990) or 10% overall (Oatley et al. 1998) for the Cape Griffon *G. coprotheres*.

Table 1. Number of Eurasian Griffons *Gyps fulvus* ringed/wing-tagged on the Island of Cres (Croatia) and re-sighted or recovered dead during eight years (1990-1997).

Year	Number ringed/ wing-tagged	Number of different specimens re-sighted or found dead *	Number of re-sightings *
1990	16	11	56
1991	31	19	57
1992	29	17	39
1993	25	17	57
1994	29	18	45
1995	9	4	5
1996	26	11	28
1997	30	11	28
	195	108 (55.4%)	315

* Local re-sightings are not included.

Figure 1. Locations of Eurasian Griffons migrating from Croatia. Black spots are re-sighting locations of migrating juvenile, immature and subadult griffons wing-tagged/ringed in Croatia during eight years (1990-1997). The griffons' distribution in Africa is taken from Mundy *et al.* (1992)

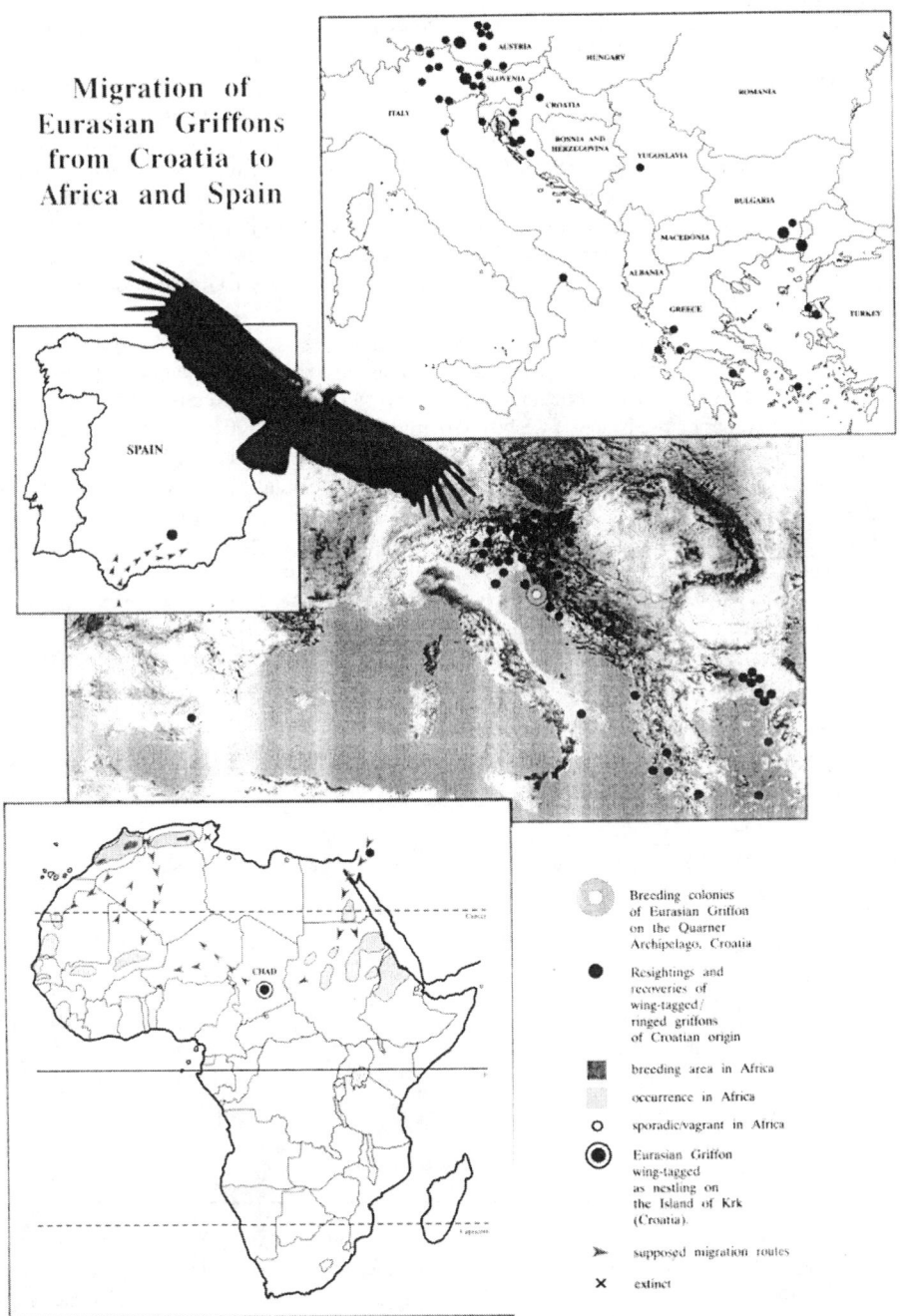

There were 22 recoveries of dead wing-tagged birds (11.3% of all marked). More than 95% of them died during the first two years of their life (13 in the first, eight in the second year).

More than 10 different specimens have been re-sighted in Italy, in Austria and in Greece (see larger black spots on Fig.1), and some birds visit the same vulture restaurant in Italy (Forgaria nel Friuli) or in Greece (Dadia Forest Reserve) every year at the same time.

One good example is griffon *Jelena* which has been visiting the vulture restaurant in Italy for eight years. The first year "she" arrived on 23 July, next year on 25 May, third year on 28 May, fourth year on 11 May, and fifth year on 11 May. After "she" became adult "she" visited the vulture restaurant only a few times in May, and for one day or two in June and/or in July.

A typical example for a type of migration pattern is that of the griffon *Maks Ubojica*. "He" was during his first year on 30 August at the breeding colony, fifteen days later "he" was in Italy (north), and one month later (middle October) in Greece (south). Next spring, on 12 May, "he" was in northern Italy again, and on 21 October again in Greece. Almost the same pattern is that of the griffon *Kizil Akbaba,* which during "his" first year was in August at the breeding colony on Cres, during September in northern Italy, and the next spring, during March, in Greece (probably on "his" way back to aestivation in the Alps).

The griffon *Laci* was during August 1998 on Cres, but on 14 October of the same year (and "his" first autumn) in the western Negev in Israel, 2.350 km to the south (O. Hatzofe *in litt.*).

The griffon *Stavros* was at the beginning of August on Cres, on 29 August near Venice (Italy) and on 12 September on the Island of Lesbos (Greece). It travelled 1.500 km in 14 days, or 110 km per day! A Spanish bird travelled no more than 80 km per day (Berthold *et al.* 1991).

The griffon *Ledni Zlajo,* wing-tagged as a nestling at the beginning of June 1992 on the Island of Krk (near the Island of Cres) had left the breeding colony at the end of August, and was found dead in Chad (central Africa) during November of the same year. During two months it flew more than 3.750 km to the south (daily migration rate not less than 65 km). At the latitude of 11°27'N, on the south side of the Sahara, it was at the southern limit of the Eurasian Griffon's distribution in Africa. Mundy *et al.* (1992) mentioned that the longest flights were made by two first-year Eurasian Griffons ringed in Spain which travelled 2.800 km to Senegal, but the recovery near Abgue, Salamat, in Chad is now the furthest-known distance travelled by a griffon on migration.

Table 2. Number of Eurasian Griffons wing-tagged in Croatia and re-sighted or recovered dead in other countries during the year.

Country	J	F	M	A	M	J	J	A	S	O	N	D
Austria					1	4	8	13	8	3		
Italy	1	1	1	1	5	10	7	7	6	3	2	2
Slovenia									1			
Greece	1	3	2	1			7	3	4	7	2	2
Bulgaria			3	1				1			1	2
Yugoslavia								1				
Israel										1		
Chad											1	
Spain											1	

But it is possible that an even much longer flight was made by the griffon *Marta*. Wing-tagged as a nestling in May 1996 (Island of Cres) it was recovered dead on 8 November 1997 near Jaén, in Spain. The bird was found about 300 km NE from the Straits of Gibraltar. This griffon died in its ("her") second year at the beginning of November, when almost all juvenile Spanish griffons have left their breeding areas in northern Spain, crossing the Straits of Gibraltar to Africa (Griesinger 1996). What was the direction this griffon used? Did it travel along the Mediterranean coast, through France and northern Spain, or just the opposite – did it come to Spain from Chad?

There are no other sightings or recoveries of Croatian griffons west of Austria. There are many birdwatchers (see for example Oreel 1988!) as well as vulture "restaurants" monitored in France and northern Spain, so one would expect that griffons migrating west of Austria would have been sighted during the last eight years if they had used that route.

The largest numbers of Croatian griffons are seen to the north (Austria, Italy and Slovenia) during the summer months of May to October (Table 2). During early autumn, griffons are migrating to the south (Yugoslavia, Bulgaria, Greece and Israel), until they reach Africa, for example Chad.

DISCUSSION

At the Island of Cres all juvenile birds (100%) leave their breeding areas at the end of August or first half of September. There are no juvenile, immature or subadult griffons on the island in winter (except for a small number of birds for a day or two when passing from the south to the north or vice versa during the spring or autumn migration). They come back to their natal colony when mature, i.e. five or six years old.

For a long time the common opinion was that after their sojourn in the Alps, Croatian griffons went back to the Adriatic islands to spend the winter in their breeding areas, because of the arrival of the cold season and snow in the Alps (Frey & Walter 1981, Perco et al. 1983, Dentesani et al. 1989). Wing-tagging proved that Croatian griffons do not spend the winter in their breeding areas, but in Africa!

So, although their circular movements are very complex, we could assume that it is not just dispersal, or irregular nomadism but some kind of regular migration taken by juvenile, immature and subadult birds until maturity. Griesinger (1996) gives similar conclusions for Spanish griffons. His results demonstrate that from northern Spain juvenile griffons are migratory birds, assembling in southern Spain and crossing over to Africa in major numbers. But Griesinger found that approximately only 30% of the juvenile griffon population in Spain crossed the Straits of Gibraltar on autumn migration to Africa, while all 100% of the juvenile griffon population leaves Croatian islands every year. Some of them spend the few summer months in Austria and northern Italy, but mainly not later than the end of October. During the late autumn they are in Greece, Bulgaria and Israel as well as in Chad and Spain! We could expect that some of them may spend the whole winter in Greece or in the Middle East, but many of them most probably continue and spend the winter months in Africa.

During the first few months (February - April) of the next spring they are again in Greece; they then pass their native island in the Adriatic in a few days only. During April and May they come to Austria and Italy again, some of them at the same feeding or roosting place, almost on the same day as the year before.

Eurasian Griffons from Croatia migrate using two main directions: NW to the Austrian and Italian Alps (and then to Spain?), and SE to southern Italy, Balkans, Greece and over the Middle East as far to the south as Chad in central Africa (and then, maybe, to western Africa and to Spain?). If griffons from Croatia regularly visit central Africa, it is possible that they travel to western Africa, where they could find Spanish griffons. Croatian griffons could then continue with Spanish griffons and travel to the north to Spain!

The migration routes are repeated every year, with the same timing. Considering their daily migration rates and the regularity of their autumn migration Griesinger (1996) calls Eurasian Griffons "medium distant migrants". Results presented in this paper show that one should call them "long distance migrants". To be more precise: Eurasian Griffons should not be considered a sedentary or partially migrant species any more, but a long distance migrant, and where only non-breeding birds are migrating, their migration is complex, still not understood, and lasts for five or six years.

ACKNOWLEDGEMENTS

I want to thank especially my Griffon-marking team, as well as all my good friends and volunteers who helped in the monitoring and protection of Eurasian Griffons on the Island of Cres during the last ten years. It is not enough to mark the birds – we need somebody to send the information about the wing-tag sightings. I would like to thank the many observers from many countries who sent in their sightings, particularly Fulvio Genero and Fabio Perco (Italy), Nina Roth Callies, Hans Frey and Dirk Ullrich (Austria), Werner Ott (Germany), Theodora Skartsi, George I. Handrinos, Joris A. Peters, Ineke J.M. Peeters-Lenglet and Kate Thompson (Greece), Stefan Avramov and Petar Iankov (Bulgaria), Ohad Hatzofe (Israel), Arturo Azorit Cañizares (Spain) and Djimadoumbaye N'Dou-Orngar (Chad). I am also very grateful to Peter Mundy who was kind enough to read and comment on an earlier draft of this paper.

Logistical support during wing-tagging was provided by Eco-centre *Caput Insulae*-Beli (non-profit organization for nature protection on the Island of Cres), and financial support by: FIMA – Varazdin (General sponsor of conservation of Griffons), Regional Environmental Centre – Croatia, Open Society Institute – Croatia, City Council of the Town of Cres and Ministry of Science and Technology of the Republic of Croatia (Eurasian Griffon-tagging project on the Quarner Archipelago colonies was partly financed as a part of the project no. 101114: Ecology and Protection of Endangered Croatian Ornithofauna).

REFERENCES

BERNIS, F. 1983. Migration of the Common Griffon Vulture in the Western Palearctic. In: Wilbur, S. R. & Jackson, J. A. (eds.) *Vulture Biology and Management*. Univ. of California Press, Berkeley. Pp. 185-196.

BERTHOLD, P., J. GRIESINGER, E. NOWAK & U. QUERNER 1991. Satelliten-Telemetrie eines Gansegeiers *(Gyps fulvus)* in Spanien. *J. Orn.* 132: 327-329.

DENTESANI, B., F. GENERO & F. PERCO 1989. *Il Grifone sulle Alpi*. Ribis Editore, Udine.

FREY, H. & K. NIEBUHR 1994. Monitoring within the International Bearded Vulture Project – an evaluation of methods. Bearded Vulture Reintroduction into the Alps. Annual report 1994: 23-31.

FREY, H. & W. WALTER 1981. Project 1075 - Griffon Vultures - Conservation Programme in Austria and Yugoslavia. *Vulture News* 6: 14-15.

GENERO, F. 1988. Considerations on the Presence of the Griffon Vulture *(Gyps fulvus fulvus* Hablizl 1783) in the Julian Alps. *Larus* 38-39:37-145.

GÉNSBØL, B. 1989. *Collins Guide to the Birds of Prey of Britain and Europe, North Africa and the Middle East*. Collins, London.

GRIESINGER, J. 1996. Autumn Migration of Griffon Vultures *(Gyps f. fulvus)* in Spain. In: Muntaner, J. y Mayol, J. (eds): *Biologia y Conservación de las Rapaces Mediterráneas*, 1994. Pp.. 401-410.

MUNDY, P., D. BUTCHART, J. LEDGER & S. PIPER 1992. *The Vultures of Africa*. Academic Press. London

OATLEY, T. B., H. D. OSCHADLEUS, R. A. NAVARRO & L. G. UNDERHILL 1998. Review of Ring Recoveries of Birds of Prey in Southern Africa: 1948-1998. Endangered Wildlife Trust, Johannesburg.

OREEL, G.J. 1988. Griffon Vulture in northwestern Europe in June - November 1986. *Dutch Birding* 10: 86.

PERCO, F., S. TOSO, G. SUSIC & M. APOLLONIO 1983. Initial data for a study on the status, distribution and ecology of the Griffon Vulture *(Gyps fulvus* Hablizl 1783) in the Quarner Archipelago. *Larus* 33-35: 99-134.

PIPER, S.E. 1990. Dispersal, nomadism and conservation in the Cape Vulture. *Ring* 13, 1-2: 217-218

SUSIC, G. 1994. Wing-marking of Eurasian Griffons *Gyps fulvus* in Croatia - Evaluation and Initial Results. In: Meyburg, B.-U. & R.D. Chancellor (eds.): *Raptor Conservation Today*. WWGBP/The Pica Press. Pp. 373-380.

WALLACE, M 1994. The use of patagial tags on Condors and other large vultures. *Gypaetus barbatus Bull*. N. 15, 11-13.

Dr. Goran Susic
Institute of ornithology, CASA
Beli 4, 51559 Beli
Croatia

The Farming Community and the Conservation of the Cape Griffon Vulture *Gyps coprotheres* in the Western Cape, South Africa

H.A. Scott, R.M. Scott and A.F. Boshoff

ABSTRACT

The Cape Griffon Vulture endemic to southern Africa, is listed as Vulnerable. The world population is estimated at 12,000 birds, including 4,400 breeding pairs. Some 90 individuals (including 30 pairs) are found in the Western Cape Province in an isolated colony near Bredasdorp. In the past, this sub-population declined from over 100 to about 45 individuals. In 1984 a three-pronged conservation strategy was implemented and comprised a colony protection plan, the introduction of a supplementary feeding scheme and a public awareness programme. A working group was established and a conservation programme drawn up. The success of the strategy is evaluated against long-term monitoring data for the sub-population. Up to the end of 1990 the population still showed a slow decline of 1.6% per year. From 1991, however, total counts rose from 59 to 94 individuals in 1998, indicating that the population had stabilised. There was a noticeable increase in both the breeding success and the fledging rate between 1981 and 1990, after which both remained constant. The survival of first-year birds increased from 42% to 69%, and this is statistically significant. These positive trends are attributed mainly to the fact that the farming community has become increasingly involved in promoting the survival of the Potberg colony.

INTRODUCTION

The Cape Griffon Vulture *Gyps coprotheres* is endemic to southern Africa. The world population is estimated at 12,000 individuals, including 4,400 breeding pairs (Mundy, Butchart, Ledger & Piper 1992; Piper 1994; Mundy, Benson & Allan 1997). The species is listed as "Vulnerable" in the South African Red Data Book: Birds (Brooke 1984).

A small isolated sub-population of some 90 birds (including 25 breeding pairs) occurs in a colony on Potberg Mountain in the Overberg region in the Western Cape Province of South Africa, near the southern tip of Africa (Fig. 1). The colony lies within the De Hoop Nature Reserve and has active links with several smaller satellite colonies about 120 km to the north-east, in the Little Karoo area. Due to both its own decline and that of the Cape Vulture population as a whole, the sub-population has attracted the attention of researchers in the past including Jarvis, Siegfried & Currie (1974), Boshoff & Vernon (1980), and Boshoff & Currie (1981).

This paper describes an integrated conservation plan that was initiated in 1984. The aims of the plan are to protect the Potberg colony and its satellites, both as a contribution to the conservation of the species, and also because of its value for educational and, more recently, ecotourism purposes (Boshoff & Robertson 1985). The strategy has a strong communication component as a means of promoting the participation of the farming community in the conservation programme. This public awareness programme is the focus of this paper. The success of the plan is measured against long-term monitoring data for the sub-population.

Figure 1. Map showing the location of the Potberg and Little Karoo colonies in the Western Cape Province, South Africa (after Boshoff & Robertson 1985; Scott 1997).

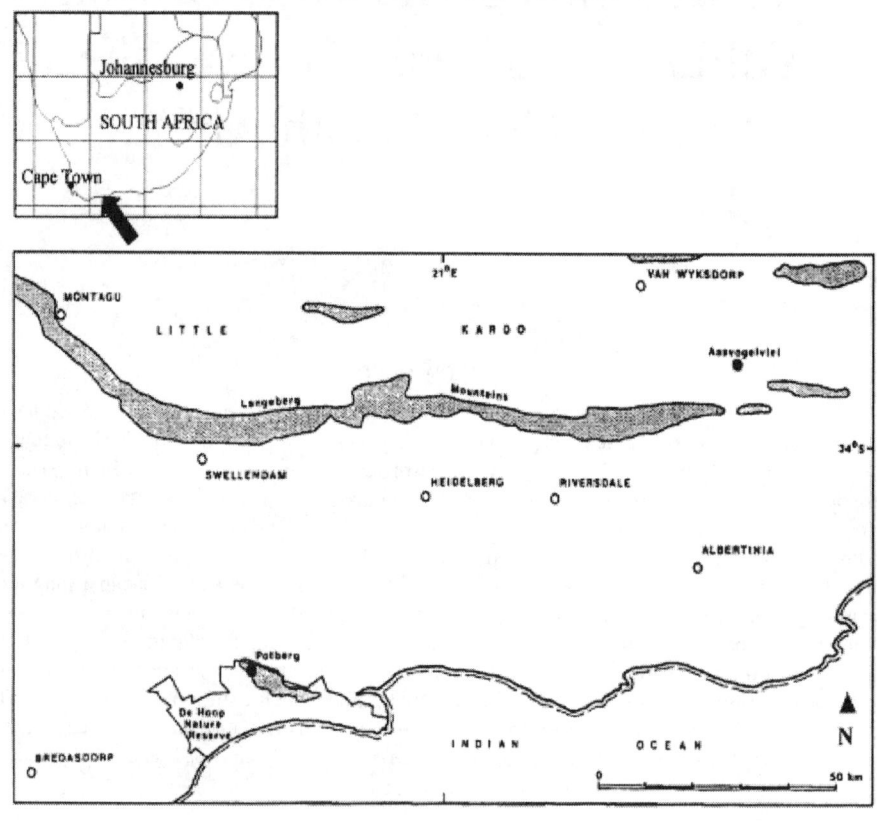

THE DECLINE OF THE POTBERG COLONY

A large-scale decline in numbers has been experienced throughout the entire distribution range of many vulture species, including the Cape Vulture (Boshoff & Vernon 1980; Mundy 1982; Brooke 1984; Collar & Stuart 1985; Mundy *et al.* 1992; Piper 1994). At Potberg, Cape Vulture numbers declined from around the turn of the century to the 1980s. Documented counts date from about 100 birds in the early 1970s to about 45 in 1983. Breeding pairs decreased from 37 in 1975 to 14 in 1980, then stabilized at around 25 pairs from 1981. The generally accepted reasons for this decline are outlined below.

232

For hundreds of years in the past, the Potberg vultures fed on the remains of large to medium-sized indigenous ungulates such as Eland *Taurotragus oryx* and Bontebok *Damaliscus dorcas dorcas* (Boshoff & Vernon 1980). These animals were most likely killed by large carnivores such as Leopards *Panthera pardus* and Lions *P. leo* and the carcasses opened up by scavengers such as Brown Hyenas *Hyaena brunnea*. These wild animals were later hunted on a small scale by indigenous Khoisan people, who also kept livestock (Robertson & February 1986). Hunting escalated with the arrival of European settlers from the 17th century onwards and the once extensive game herds were virtually exterminated.

The disappearance of indigenous ungulates and carnivores was accompanied by a large-scale human modification of the environment. Wheat farming was introduced in the Overberg region in the 1800s, and sheep farming towards the end of the 18th century; grazing pastures for cattle were planted from the 1930s. As a result of these environmental changes, the vultures were obliged to switch over to an almost exclusive diet of domestic stock around the end of the 19th century (Robertson 1983; Robertson & Boshoff 1986). Although large antelope species and Cape Mountain Zebra *Equus zebra zebra* have now been re-introduced to the De Hoop Nature Reserve, the ecosystem is still far from fully functional in terms of the original predator-prey systems.

The Overberg region is some 10,000 km² in size (Robertson 1983) and the present-day agricultural activities are still centred on grain and sheep farming, with some cattle. The Potberg vultures forage predominantly over farmland near the towns of Bredasdorp and Swellendam; this area supports a total of some 300 farmers who farm a combination of stock and grain (K. Robertson & J. Pieterse pers. comm., agricultural extension officers). Stock figures for the area in 1983 comprised some 600,000 sheep and 35,000 cattle. More recently, the trend has been towards increased numbers of cattle and fewer sheep. The vultures feed almost exclusively on dead sheep and lambs, the latter especially during lambing seasons (Robertson 1983). Initially, lambing took place from February to April and during September; more recently, a third season has been introduced, namely from June to July (N. Neethling pers. comm., local farmer).

Domestic stock carcasses ostensibly provide a readily available source of food for the birds (Jarvis *et al.* 1974; Robertson & Boshoff 1986). Seasonal and unpredictable food shortages may be experienced, however, especially at critical times for the vultures, such as the post-fledging period (December to February). Juvenile vultures, especially, are at a disadvantage at small lamb carcasses, due to the dominance of older birds (Robertson 1983; Robertson & Boshoff 1986).

Blowflies *Chrysomyia* spp. present a severe and very real problem to sheep farmers in the region, especially during wet, warm periods. The flies lay their eggs in folds of skin on the neck or rear end of the sheep and once the larvae hatch, they feed directly on the flesh of the sheep. The flies are treated by means of agrochemical preparations that are usually applied externally in the form of dips or ointments and are potentially toxic to vultures. Sheep and lamb carcasses are often buried or burnt immediately, to avoid the spread of these parasites, and are thus not made available to the vultures. Carcasses may also be treated externally with agrochemicals and left lying in the fields. Carcasses of stock animals that have been euthanased, for instance by means of barbiturates, present a further threat if not immediately removed. The dangers of pesticide residues to griffon vultures have already been noted (Mundy, Grant, Tannock & Wessels 1982; Boshoff & De Kock 1988). The indiscriminate use of these chemicals therefore presents a severe potential threat to vultures and other scavenging animals.

In the past, farmers in the region were mostly indifferent or openly antagonistic towards wildlife, including vultures. Direct persecution, through the placing of poisons, trapping and shooting was probably not uncommon in the past within the range of the Potberg vultures. These negative attitudes were often transferred to the farmers' families and to their staff. Human disturbance at the Potberg breeding colonies was a further negative factor, aggravated by disturbance by aircraft including helicopters. This threat was reduced with the incorporation of the colony into the De Hoop Nature Reserve in 1978.

A number of factors thus combined to cause a progressive decline in the size of the Potberg and Little Karoo vulture sub-population through the greater part of the 20th century.

CONSERVATION PLAN

A research programme on the decline of the Potberg Cape Vulture colony was initiated by the provincial conservation agency (Cape Nature Conservation) in the 1970s (Jarvis *et al.* 1974; Robertson 1983). The aims were to investigate the possible causes of the decline and to compile a conservation action plan to stabilize the colony and promote positive growth.

A detailed investigation into the feeding ecology of the sub-population (Robertson 1983) indicated, *inter alia*, that the vultures forage almost exclusively over farmland north and north-west of Potberg, mainly within a radius of 10-20 km from the colony, and that they feed predominantly on sheep and lamb carcasses (Robertson 1983; Boshoff, Robertson & Norton 1984). This made it possible to establish a target area for the implementation of conservation action, namely some ten farms in the immediate foraging area, and also the wider distribution area of birds from the colony.

A conservation plan was initiated in 1984, with the specific objectives of improving the survival rate of first-year birds; increasing breeding success; removing or lessening the threat of poisoned carcasses in the foraging area, and reducing pesticide levels in the eggs (Boshoff & Robertson 1985). The plan had three major components, namely colony protection, a supplementary feeding programme, and a public awareness campaign. These elements interact synergistically and are described below.

Access to the colony was restricted to one visit per month by nature reserve personnel, for monitoring purposes. Aerial protection also became possible in co-operation with the South African Air Force Test Flight and Development Centre, which was established 30 km to the south-west of the colony in the early 1980s.

The supplementary feeding scheme for the vultures was introduced in 1984. This involves the placing of a variety of carcasses, which are first slit open to facilitate entry by the birds, at predetermined sites in the vicinity of the colony (Scott & Boshoff 1990, 1994). The vulture "restaurants" aroused much interest among the local community and, in 1993, a small workshop was organized with the farmers (Scott & Boshoff 1994). As a result of the ensuing discussions the farmers largely took over the function of providing more carcasses for the vultures on their farms. Angora goat carcasses are now supplied at the "restaurant" only during bottle-neck times, for instance from December to February, when food for newly fledged birds is scarce.

An intensive public awareness campaign was launched. Pamphlets, booklets and posters were used to make appropriate information available. Communication in the home language of the target group (Afrikaans) was a vital factor. The Vulture Study Group, a working group of the Endangered Wildlife Trust, produced useful publications such as the booklet "Vultures and Farmers" (Butchart 1985), which were also widely distributed as extension tools. A positive working relationship was built with both local and national media. Extensive coverage in newspapers and magazines, on the radio and on television provided information and highlighted positive contributions by farmers and workers, who were both represented in media interviews. Displays were manned at agricultural shows and farmers' days. The vulture extension programme was facilitated by a considerable overlap with a concurrent conservation programme to conserve the Blue Crane *Anthropoides paradiseus* in the Overberg region (Scott 1993). The vulture awareness effort was also extended to the area of the satellite colonies in the Little Karoo, with the help of the Vulture Study Group. The Potberg Centre in the De Hoop Nature Reserve presents regular environmental education programmes involving mainly scholars and students, as well as farm workers. The conservation of the Cape Vulture is an integral part of these programmes. Some 3,000-4,000 people have attended these programmes per year, since 1984.

A vulture liaison group has existed in the Overberg region for some time. In 1995 it was formalized as the Overberg Vulture Group, and became affiliated to the Vulture Study Group. The group holds informal but informative gatherings twice a year, usually accompanied by an excursion to view the Potberg vultures. Members compiled a booklet containing practical guidelines for involvement in the conservation of the Potberg vultures, based on the conservation plan (Scott 1997a). Highlights of the group effort are a strong component for rehabilitating injured or poisoned vultures. This involves a dedicated local veterinary surgeon and his staff, and local farmers (including poultry farmers, who donate food for recuperating vultures). Recently there has also been an active interest in the ecotourism potential of the vultures, promoted by some of the farmers' wives who have established accommodation facilities on their farms. The vultures are now seen as a unique tourism draw-card for the region.

The increased involvement of the farming community is ascribed directly to personal liaison between conservationists and the farmers and their workers. This constructive contact is supported by increasingly outgoing policies of conservation bodies, with an emphasis on involving communities beyond the boundaries of nature reserves in conservation activities, and working towards joint solutions to problems (Boshoff 1987; Scott & Boshoff 1994; Scott 1997). Greater involvement by private landowners has increased the contribution of both farmers and their workers to aspects such as the feeding programme, monitoring and the rehabilitation of malnourished or poisoned vultures. One of the highlights has been the success story of a juvenile bird from Potberg which was rehabilitated in 1991 after indirect poisoning and subsequently flew 900 km to the Northern Cape (Scott 1991). After a second rehabilitation there, it flew back to the Potberg area, where it was yet again rehabilitated; it has subsequently been seen to occupy a breeding site at the colony. This event obtained much positive publicity for the area and especially for the involvement of the farming community in conserving its vultures.

The younger generation of farmers is showing a more enlightened attitude towards conservation. Many of them now realize that the vultures are in fact an asset to the farmer, both in terms of cleaning carcasses before diseases can spread, and for indicating stock losses. The vultures are also regarded as an invaluable ecotourism resource for the region. This change in attitude has additional positive spin-offs for the wider issues of wildlife conservation, for instance with regard to more responsible control methods for stock predators such as Caracal *Felis caracal*. The stage has now been reached where a farmer and his wife - and their workers - will readily appear on television to speak with pride about their involvement in the conservation of *their* vultures, and to expand on the usefulness of the vultures to the farming community. This is surely a conservation milestone.

EVALUATION OF THE CONSERVATION PLAN

The success of the conservation plan may be evaluated through an analysis of the long-term monitoring data for the colony (Boshoff 1981, 1987; Boshoff & Currie 1981; Boshoff & Vernon 1981; Boshoff & Robertson 1983; Boshoff & Scott 1990; Robertson 1983, 1984; Scott 1997b). These data are supplemented by a recent study on the mathematical demography of the Cape Vulture (Piper 1994; Scott 1997b), which includes the construction of a population model (updated in 1997), based on 171 ringed vultures in the Western Cape population. A total of 409 usable records comprised resightings or recoveries of 79 of these birds.

Maximum annual counts (April - December) of free-flying Cape Vultures at Potberg and the Little Karoo (Fig. 2) show that numbers at Potberg have more than doubled since the inception of the conservation plan in 1984, i.e. from 45 birds to 94 in 1998. Also apparent is the waxing and waning of the satellite colonies in the Little Karoo, up to 1990. As mentioned above, the birds from Potberg and the Little Karoo constitute a single sub-population, which is currently relatively stable. Up to 1990, the Potberg colony had an intrinsic natural rate of increase of -1.6% per year (Piper 1994); by 1995 this rate had changed to +0.1% per year (S.E. Piper pers. comm.).

Breeding success is rather low, estimated at 64.4% in 1990 (Piper 1994). The number of active pairs at breeding sites is seemingly stable from 1981 (Fig. 3), although it does not match the increase in numbers of birds. The number of eggs produced is also relatively stable. The percentages of both nestlings and fledglings produced increased somewhat from 1984 to 1986 (Fig. 3), after the inception of the conservation plan, then also stabilized. The steady increase in population size corresponds with a statistically significant increase in the survival of first-year birds, from 42.3% prior to the start of the supplementary feeding programme, to 68.9% subsequent to its implementation (chi-squared = 8.1, d.f. = 1, $p<0.01$) (Piper 1994).

Since the inception of the conservation plan there has been a general decline in the frequency of recorded cases of weak, undernourished birds (mostly immature birds, at the beginning of the year) which were brought in from the farms for rehabilitation, and of birds apparently suffering from

Figure 2. Maximum annual counts of free-flying Cape Vultures in the Potberg and Little Karoo colonies, Western Cape (April - December): 1972-1998.

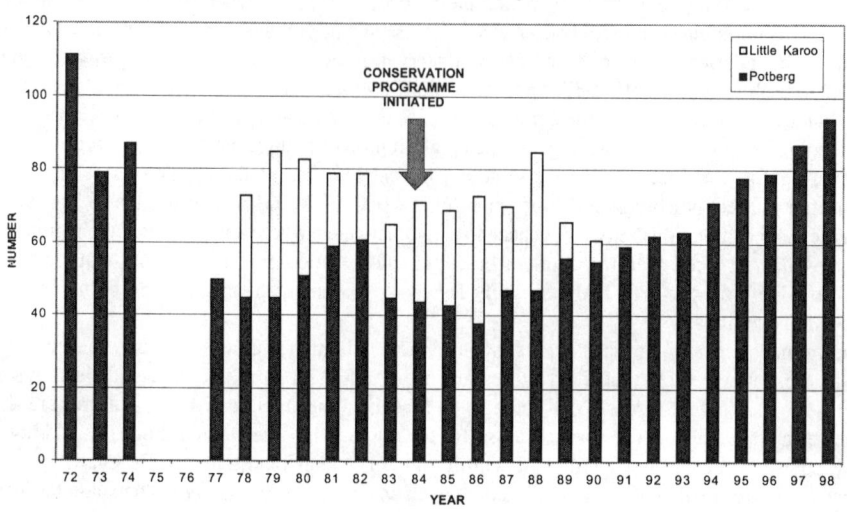

Figure 3. Breeding success of Cape Vultures in the Western Cape: Potberg and Little Karoo colonies combined, 1974-1997.

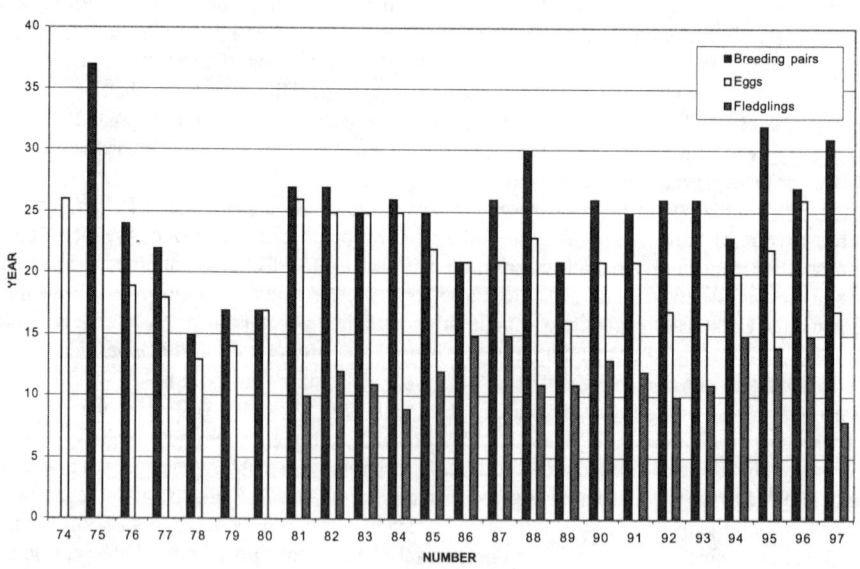

(indirect) poisoning (Scott 1994). The number of such cases decreased from a total of seven for the 1985-1987 period, for instance, to only three for the 1988-1990 period. The frequency of these cases is an important and immediate indicator of potential problems in the field.

Clearly the fortunes of the sub-population have improved since the mid-1980s and this coincides with the implementation of the conservation plan. While it cannot be categorically stated that this plan was entirely responsible for the halt of the decline in the sub-population, and the ensuing increase in numbers of birds and fledglings, it is apparent that these developments corresponded with the implementation of these far-reaching, practical management actions.

CONCLUSIONS AND THE WAY FORWARD

The increased conservation awareness among the farming community is considered to have played a pivotal role in the conservation of the Potberg/Little Karoo or Western Cape sub-population of the Cape Vulture. It is therefore vital that Cape Nature Conservation continues to implement the conservation plan fully.

The maintenance and co-ordination of the valuable long-term monitoring database is essential, to determine the effectiveness of the conservation plan and to enable adjustments to be made, as necessary. The present level of minimal disturbance at the colony should be maintained, particularly during the breeding season (May to January). Any further ecotourism developments should be handled conservatively and sensitively. Apart from its direct value to the vultures, the feeding programme is an important awareness tool for involving the farming community. Supplementary feeding is essential during bottle-neck periods.

The increasing involvement of the farming community is considered to be the single most important factor contributing to the positive trends in vulture numbers. This is directly attributed to the extension programme and in particular to liaison on a personal level and to the positive attitudes and building up of a relationship of trust between the nature reserve staff and the farming community. There is still a need for increased education programmes for farm workers, however, as these are the people who handle the agrochemicals on the ground.

The Potberg/Little Karoo sub-population is still considered to be highly vulnerable, and it is imperative that the goodwill of the farming community be maintained for its continued survival. With Cape Vulture populations continuing to be at risk, the conservation of the Western Cape sub-population presents a major challenge to today's wildlife managers and could serve as a model for conservation programmes elsewhere. An important spin-off is a more enlightened approach by landowners towards other threatened species, and to environmental conservation in general.

ACKNOWLEDGEMENTS

This work took place while the authors were employed by Cape Nature Conservation. We thank Steven Piper for updating his model with the most recent (1991-1995) field data, Kevin Shaw and Guy Palmer for commenting on an earlier draft and Peter Mundy for refereeing the paper. Tribute is also paid to the many people who have, in one way or another, been involved in the Western Cape vulture conservation plan over the years, including Cape Nature Conservation staff, university researchers, mountain climbers, agricultural extension officers, veterinarians, the media, members of the Vulture Study Group and, most importantly, the local farming communities in the Overberg and Little Karoo.

REFERENCES

BOSHOFF, A.F. 1981. Notes on two Cape Vulture colonies in the southwestern Cape Province, South Africa. *Vulture News* 5: 3-10.

BOSHOFF, A.F. 1987. Update on two Cape Vulture colonies in the SW Cape: 1981-1986. *Vulture News* 18: 37-42.

BOSHOFF, A.F. & CURRIE, M.H. 1981. Notes on the Cape Vulture colony at Potberg, Bredasdorp. *Ostrich* 52: 1-8.

BOSHOFF, A.F. & ROBERTSON, A.S. 1983. Two Cape Vulture colonies in the SW Cape Province: 1981 data. *Vulture News* 9/10: 37-39.

BOSHOFF, A.F. & ROBERTSON, A.S. 1985. A conservation plan for the Cape vulture colony at Potberg, De Hoop Nature Reserve, southwestern Cape Province. *Bontebok* 4: 25-31.
BOSHOFF, A.F., ROBERTSON, A.S. & NORTON, P.M. 1984. A radio-tracking study of an adult Cape Vulture *Gyps coprotheres* in the southwestern Cape Province. *S. Afr. J. Wildl. Res.* 14: 73-78.
BOSHOFF, A.F. & DE KOCK, A.C. 1988. Further evidence of organo-chlorine contamination in Cape Vultures. *Ostrich* 59: 40-41.
BOSHOFF, A.F. & SCOTT, H.A. 1990. The status and breeding performance of Cape Vultures at the Potberg and Little Karoo colonies, southwestern Cape: 1987-1990. *Vulture News* 24:33-40.
BOSHOFF, A.F. & VERNON, C.J. 1980. The past and present distribution and status of the Cape Vulture in the Cape Province. *Ostrich* 51: 230-250.
BOSHOFF, A.F. & VERNON, C.J. 1981. Active Cape Vulture breeding and roost sites in the Cape Province in 1979. *Vulture News* 6: 19.
BROOKE, R.K. 1984. South African Red Data Book - Birds. *South African National Scientific Programmes Report no. 97, 211 pp.*
BUTCHART, D. 1985 (third edition 1995). *Vultures and Farmers*. Vulture Study Group, Johannesburg.
COLLAR, N.J. & STUART, S.N. 1985. *Threatened birds of Africa and related islands*. ICBP, Cambridge, UK.
JARVIS, M.J.F., SIEGFRIED, W.R. & CURRIE, M.H. 1974. Conservation of the Cape Vulture in the Cape Province. *J. Sth Afr. Wildl. Mgmt Ass.* 4: 29-34.
MUNDY, P.J. 1982. *The comparative biology of southern African vultures*. Vulture Study Group, Johannesburg.
MUNDY, P.J., BENSON, P.C. & ALLAN, D.G. 1997. Cape Vulture *Gyps coprotheres*. In: *The atlas of southern African birds. Vol. 1: Non-passerines*. In Harrison, J.A., Allan, D.G., Underhill, L.G., Herremans, M., Tree, A.J., Parker, V. & Brown, C.J. (eds), pp. 158-159. BirdLife South Africa, Johannesburg.
MUNDY, P., BUTCHART, D., LEDGER, J. & PIPER, S. 1992. *The vultures of Africa*. Acorn Books, Randburg, South Africa.
MUNDY, P.J., GRANT, K.I., TANNOCK, J. & WESSELS, C.L. 1982. Pesticide residues and eggshell thickness of griffon vulture eggs in southern Africa. *J. Wildl. Manage.* 46: 769-773.
PIPER, S.E. 1994. Mathematical Demography of the Cape Vulture. Unpublished Ph.D. thesis, University of Cape Town, Cape Town.
ROBERTSON, A.S. 1983. The feeding ecology and breeding biology of a Cape Vulture colony in the southwestern Cape Province. M.Sc. dissertation. University of the Witwatersrand, Johannesburg.
ROBERTSON, A.S. 1984. Aspects of the population dynamics of Cape Vultures in the Cape Province. *Ostrich* 55: 196-206.
ROBERTSON, A.S. & BOSHOFF, A.F. 1986. The feeding ecology of Cape Vultures (*Gyps coprotheres*) in a stock-farming area. *Biol. Conserv.* 35: 63-86.
ROBERTSON, A.S. & FEBRUARY, E. 1986. Towards an historical perspective of Cape Vultures and domestic stock: a view from the southwestern Cape. *Vulture News* 15: 4-5.
SCOTT, H.A. 1991. A "miracle" Cape Vulture? *Vulture News* 25 : 17-20.
SCOTT, H.A. 1993 (compiler). *A conservation programme for the blue crane in the Overberg*. Cape Nature Conservation, Cape Town. 19 pp.
SCOTT, H.A. 1994. Sick or incapacitated Cape Vultures *Gyps coprotheres* treated at the De Hoop Nature Reserve, Western Cape, from May 1985 to May 1993. *Vulture News* 30: 10-18.
SCOTT, H.A. (compiler). 1997a. *A conservation programme for Cape vultures in the Western Cape*. Cape Nature Conservation, Cape Town. 6 pp.
SCOTT, H.A. 1997b. The status and breeding performance of Cape Vultures *Gyps coprotheres* at the Potberg and Little Karoo colonies, Western Cape, South Africa: 1991-1995. *Vulture News* 36: 2-16.
SCOTT, H.A. & BOSHOFF, A.F. 1990. Carcass preferences of Cape Vultures at the Potberg restaurant in the southwestern Cape. *Vulture News* 24: 25-32.
SCOTT, H.A. & BOSHOFF, A.F. 1994. A supplementary feeding scheme for the Cape Vulture in the south-western Cape Province: 1984-1992. *Cape Nature Conservation. Internal Report*, no. 13, 31 pp.

Ann & Michael Scott
Overberg Conservation Services
PO Box 439
7220 Gansbaai
South Africa

Dr André Boshoff
Terrestrial Ecology Research Unit
University of Port Elizabeth
PO Box 1600
6000 Port Elizabeth
South Africa

Chancellor, R. D. & B.-U. Meyburg eds. 2000
Raptors at Risk
WWGBP / Hancock House

The Ecofunctional Positions of Palaearctic Vultures

W. Baumgart

ABSTRACT

The basis of the ecofunctional differentiation of vultures in general is their social hierarchy at carcasses. Investigations of their food and foraging-range in southern Europe and central Asia showed not only clear division into "waste salvangers" and "carcass utilizers", but also a division within these groups based on actual flight performance. The Ecofunctional Positions (EFP/ÖFP - Ökofunktionelle Position) of Palaearctic vultures are in contrast to their taxonomic positions, but makes them more directly comparable to other Old World as well as New World Vultures. The following conclusions are therefore made:
- The New World condors are the intermediate functional equivalent of the large Old World solitary and carcass-using vultures, e.g. Cinereous Vulture and Eurasian Griffon respectively.
- The small New World Turkey and Black Vultures are replaced by kites in the Old World and Australia, respectively *Milvus* and *Haliastur* spp.
- The Bearded and Egyptian Vultures hold an EFP, apparently not occupied by vultures or birds of prey in the New World.

INTRODUCTION

The social dominance hierarchy of vultures at carcasses and their feeding on different parts is accepted as the basis of the ecological differentiation of this interesting group of "inactive raptors". Large species such as *Aegypius* or *Torgos* are powerful enough to tear through the skin; *Gyps* vultures eat the inner parts; and smaller species like *Neophron* pick up small leavings. *Gypaetus barbatus* takes bones at the end (Valverde 1959, Kruuk 1967, König 1974).

But this system of "cooperation" cannot be observed everywhere. Outside of Africa and India the vulture community is not complete in this way. Especially on the Mediterranean islands there are only one or two species feeding upon available resources and the ecological differentiation becomes unclear. The vultures are seeking food not only in various habitats but are also consuming rather different food items (Glutz et al. 1971, Cramp & Simmons 1980, Mundy et al. 1992). This necessitates thinking about other principles and factors of fundamental importance for vulture existence.

PERFORMANCE AND FOOD-SEARCH STRATEGIES

The Palaearctic vultures are like other vultures – incapable of active hunting in the manner of

birds of prey, their ancestors. Therefore they are without any active influence on the availability of their food supply as to dispersal, distribution or continuity. Vultures contribute to the maintenance of their existence essentially only in two ways:
- by increase of their ability to fast for weeks (by low metabolic rates and often large fat stores), and
- to travel as excellent gliders over great distances with little energy expenditure, and so to explore wide foraging ranges.

But these two abilities are negatively correlated in a fundamental antagonism!

The ability to survive a long time without food increases with weight and size (The former Pleistocene North American gigantic vulture *Teratornis merriami* can be understood not only as an adaptation to the megafauna of this time but also in high degree to a discontinuity of food supply in this period). But on the other hand, increasing weight reduces the gliding ability.

A "solution" is only possible in that all parts of the body without direct positive influence as stores for energy like muscles, bones, feathers etc., must be minimized in weight. But the minimizing of muscles decreases the active manoeuvrability! Meanwhile the passive gliding ability can be increased mainly by raising the number of secondaries to 27 (Tewes 1996), fixed to a relatively long forearm (ulna). A limitation to this development is provided by the diminishing ability of vultures in landing and taking-off rapidly. Simultaneously this prevents active hunting by vultures. The construction of the vulture's body has to correspond from the very beginning to a strongly fixed type of flight performance according to food size and sispersion. There are two alternatives:
1. Widely distributed smaller pieces sufficient for single individuals.
2. Larger animal carcasses offer plenty of food sufficient for a high number of individuals.

The representatives of these two types differ considerably in their flying abilities and shapes or silhouettes. The first group has relatively narrow and pointed wings with a longer tail, while the second group has wide rounded wings with a shorter tail.

The alternative food supplies require fundamental different search strategies (Baumgart 1998a). In the first case, birds fly low, are virtually independent of thermals (but using microthermals near the ground), and do not show inter-individual cooperation. In the second case, high thermals support the soaring of cooperating individuals.

In the negative correlation of gliding ability and weight is based the occurrence of size categories within one type. Thus the Bearded Vulture *Gypaetus barbatus* and the Egyptian Vulture *Neophron percnopterus* are interpretable in principle as size-differentiated functional "doubles" with a flight performance essentially comparable with that of gulls. They can be categorized as "mainland gulls".

The relation between these basic requisites and the derived morphological, behavioural and other patterns, is shown in Figure 1.

ECOFUNCTIONAL POSITIONS (EFP) OF EUROPEAN VULTURES

The differentiation of European vultures does not follow strict ecological principles, because one species can act in very different habitats. It seems better to speak in this case not of "niche" but of "resource base". More important is the differentiation in flight performance as basic to the Ecofunctional Positions (EFP), including the efficiency and performance criteria in using resources (Baumgart 1991). The different behaviour of vultures at carcasses, especially between "Waste Salvangers" and "Carcass Utilizers" is only the result of these principles. Vultures behave at carcasses not primarily as a functional community but only as a feeding community. Their inclusion in the family Aegypiidae was in spite of their polyphyletic descent; their inferred monophyly was one of the great mistakes of the systematiks of the past.

The functional differentiation of Bearded and Egyptian Vultures as a "Double" is easily explained. That of the Cinereous Vulture *Aegypius monachus* and Eurasian Griffon *Gyps fulvus*, ecologically, is not so clear (tree and cliff breeders in more wooded and open landscapes respectively). But they search for food in different ways.

Figure 1. The ecofunctional positions of European Vultures (principles).

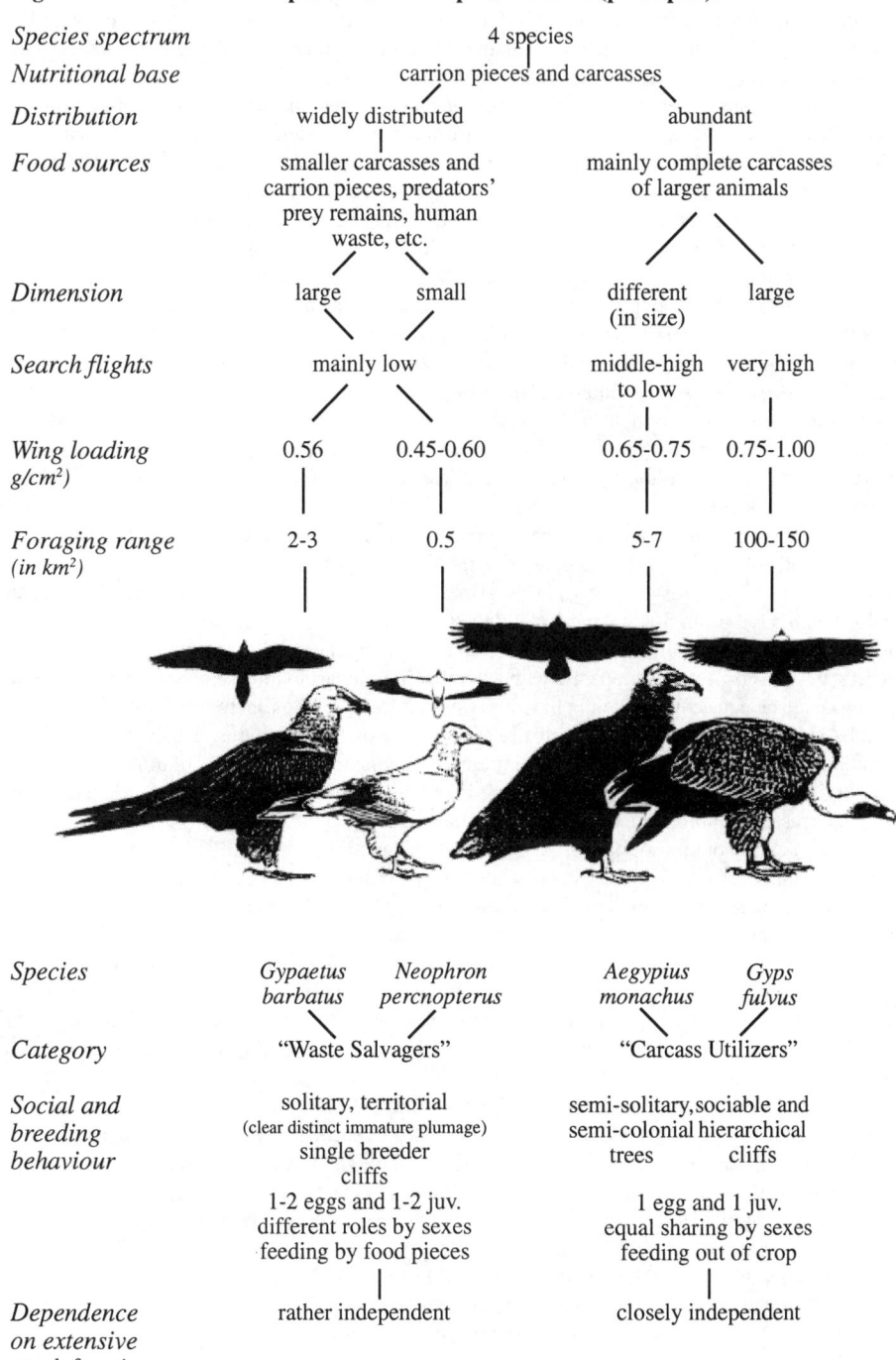

Species spectrum		4 species		
Nutritional base		carrion pieces and carcasses		
Distribution	widely distributed		abundant	
Food sources	smaller carcasses and carrion pieces, predators' prey remains, human waste, etc.		mainly complete carcasses of larger animals	
Dimension	large	small	different (in size)	large
Search flights	mainly low		middle-high to low	very high
Wing loading (g/cm^2)	0.56	0.45-0.60	0.65-0.75	0.75-1.00
Foraging range (in km^2)	2-3	0.5	5-7	100-150
Species	*Gypaetus barbatus*	*Neophron percnopterus*	*Aegypius monachus*	*Gyps fulvus*
Category	"Waste Salvagers"		"Carcass Utilizers"	
Social and breeding behaviour	solitary, territorial (clear distinct immature plumage) single breeder cliffs 1-2 eggs and 1-2 juv. different roles by sexes feeding by food pieces		semi-solitary, sociable and semi-colonial hierarchical trees cliffs 1 egg and 1 juv. equal sharing by sexes feeding out of crop	
Dependence on extensive stock farming	rather independent		closely independent	

The Cinereous Vulture has a smaller foraging range (radius about 15 km, or 700 km^2) intensively explored by a limited number of individuals. It has a lower wing loading and higher manoeuvrability in fligh than does the Eurasian Griffon. The latter's flight performance is adapted to the exploration of an extensive foraging range (radius of 60-200 km, or up to-125 000 km^2).

According to the dispersion and abundance of food sources, these two vultures may occur in different landscapes in various numbers. If there are not enough resources for a sympatric occurrence of the two species with their two types of search strategies, only one species, regularly the Cinereous Vulture, acts in an intermediate way as in Central Asia or in a certain degree on Mallorca.

The principles of sympatric occurrence of two large types of vultures, according to their different EFP (reflecting different strategies in the search for food), is also seen elsewhere in the Old World. Mostly a large solitary and a *Gyps* vulture occur sympatrically. If there are two representatives of one type because the food supply is rich then the are differentiated in size. This is the case with the Rüppell's Griffon *G. rueppellii* and African White-backed Vulture *Pseudogyps africanus* in Africa, Long-billed Griffon *G. indicus* and Indian White-backed Vulture *P. bengalensis* in India, and Lappedfaced *Torgos tracheliotus* and White-headed *Trigonoceps occipitalis* Vultures in Africa.

Other differences, for example in the breeding behaviour of Rüppell's Griffon and White-backed Vulture (cliff and tree breeder) are of less importance. Cliff breeding is more secure, but tree breeding guarantees a better distribution over an area and less travel distances. Therefore all large solitary vultures are tree breeders.

On this functional basis an objective comparison of Old World accipitrid vultures and New World cathartid vultures is possible. In contrast to the Old World situation, where mostly two sympatric types of very large vultures are found, in the Americas only one large vulture occurs: the Andean Condor *Vultur gryphus* in South America and the Californian Condor *Gymnogyps californianus* in North. Pairs of these two vultures mostly use separate foraging ranges to each other, they are solitary breeders, but can also act and cooperate with any other individuals in food searching and communal roosting (Wallace pers. com.). Their behaviour is similar to that of the Cinereous Vulture in northern Central Asia, which is without the sympatric occurrence of other vultures. This could justify an evaluation of the two condors as vultures of intermediate types under conditions of limited resources. They survived in the post-Pleistocene period perhaps because of this adaptive ability when the food supply decreased; in North America the other vultures and the teratorns disappeared.

If there is not enough food for large vultures their functions are fulfilled in a limited way by large eagles (such as *Aquila audax* in Australia or in Europe by *Haliaeetus albicilla* and *Aquila heliaca*). In these species, the adult birds regularly live like real active preying eagles but the immature birds show vulture-like features in their foraging behaviour.

Among the smaller species we now have in America two vulture groups with similar habits, the more solitary Turkey *Cathartes aura* and Yellow-headed Vultures *C. burrovianus/melambrotus* and in the clearly sociable American Black Vulture *Coragyps atratus*, compared sometimes with the small Old World Vultures like Egyptian and Hooded *Necrosyrtes monachus* Vultures. But it seems that they occupy other EFP.

In the details of food searching, the small New World vultures are in a higher degree similar to the Old World kites such as in Europe the more solitary Black Kite *Milvus migrans* and the more sociable Red Kite *M. milvus*. As smaller "doubles" they show a certain degree of functional correspondence with the Cinereous Vulture and Eurasian Griffon. In Australia the same relation between Whistling kite *Haliastur sphenurus* and *M. migrans affinus* is evident.

Under this aspect it can be explained why there are no *Milvus* kites in America. Their EFP are here occupied by the smaller New World vultures (Baumgart 1998b). But what about the small kite-like American raptors: Swallow-tailed Kite *Elanoides forficatus* and Mississippi Kite *Ictinia mississippiensis*? They can perhaps be best evaluated as seasonal equivalents of the small Old World insect-eating falcons (like *Falco naumanni* and *F. verspertinus*).

CONCLUSIONS

The above examples demonstrate clearly that the system of EFP is not closely related to the phylegentic system. The EFP appears to be a secondary independent factor in species formation. This factor is reliant on the efficiency and performance criteria of the various species in different environments, and contributes to our understanding of evolution in terms of the searching for resources.

We can now define the ecofunctional positions of western Palaearctic vultures, as follows.
- The Bearded and Egyptian Vultures are the "Large and middle-sized salvangers of dispersed wastes".
- The Cinereous Vulture and Eurasian Griffon occupy the EFP of (respectively):
- Large, solitary, intensively ranging carcass utilizer, and
- Large, sociable, hierarchical, extensively ranging carcass utilizer.

These definitions are not strictly ecological directed. They outline more a "performance-profile" realised in a variety of environmental situations. Therefore the Cinereous Vulture for instance can be found in very different habitats, from open woodlands in mountains to deserts in lowlands. Only when it occurs sympatrically with the Eurasian Griffon, its habits are then in closer correspondence with the above definition.

Nevertheless it is remarkable that the Cinereous Vulture searches especially in wooded areas, not only for carcasses of large Animals but also for rather small food items. In this way it partially resembles the Bearded Vulture (as well as even the Egyptian Vulture). In the parts of central Asia lacking *Gyps* vultures, it demonstrates some traits of the griffon´s lifestyle, becoming more gregarious, and more extensive in its searching. Under the conditions of the post-Pleistocene period in North America, but without the competition from the cathartid vultures, a Cinereous Vulture type had maybe the best chances to survive longer and alone among all the large vultures. This expresses the high ecofunctional plasticity of this type, which its substituted in other regions by representatives of other genera (*Torgos*, *Trigonoceps* and *Sarcogyps*). These may not be close generically, but they are always co-functionally related among each other.

REFERENCES

BAUMGART, W. 1991. Über die Geier Bulgariens. A. Der Schmutzgeier (*Neophron percnopterus*).- Beitr. Vogelkd. 37: 1-48.
BAUMGART, W. 1998a. Leistungsdifferenzierungen bei Greifvögeln und ‚ihre Bedeutung für artliche Existenz und Artbildung (Aves: Falconiformes) [Performance differentiations in birds of prey and their importance for existence and origin of species].- Zool. Abh. Mus. Tierkd. Dresden 50, Suppl. 125-137.
BAUMGART, W. 1998b. Probleme und derzeitiger Stand des Kalifornien-Kondor-Projektes (Frühjahr 1997).- Rundbrief WAG 25/26 (1997): 13-18. Reprint: Problems and present situation of the Californian-Condor-Project (Spring 1997).- Bearded Vulture Annual Report 1997: 66-70.
CRAMP, S. & K. E. L. SIMMONS 1980. Handbook of the Birds of Europe the Middle East and North Africa. The Birds of the Western Palearctic. Vol. II, Hawks to Bustards.- Oxford.
GLUTZ VON Blotzheim, N. U., K. BAUER & E. BEZZEL 1971. Handbuch der Vögel Mitteleuropas, Bd. 4, *Falconiformes*.- Frankfurt a. M.
KÖNIG, C. 1974. Zum Verhalten spanischer Geier an Kadavern.- *J. Orn.* 115: 289-320.
KRUUK, H. 1967. Competition for food between vultures in East Afrika.- *Ardea.* 55: 171-193.
MUNDY, P., D. BUTCHART, J. LEDGER & S. PIPER 1992. The Vultures of Africa.- London.
TEWES, E. 1996. The European Black Vulture (*Aegypius monachus* L.), management techniques and habitat requirements.- Ph. Diss. Univ. Vienna.
VALVERDE, J. A. 1959. Moyens déxpression et hiérarchie sociale chez le vautour fauve *Gyps fulvus* (Hablizl).- *Alauda* 27: 1-15.

Dr. Wolfgang Baumgart
Grumbkowstr. 2a
D-13156 Berlin
Germany

Part 3

Falcons in Asia and the Middle East

Shikra *Accipiter badius*

Conveners:
Nick Fox & Vladimir Galushin

Chancellor, R. D. & B.-U. Meyburg eds. 2000
Raptors at Risk
WWGBP / Hancock House

Saker *Falco cherrug* and Peregrine *Falco peregrinus* Falcons in Asia: Determining Migration Routes and Trapping Pressure

C.P. Eastham, J.L Quinn and N.C. Fox

ABSTRACT

New information on the migration routes of Saker Falcons *Falco cherrug* and Peregrine Falcons *Falco peregrinus* in Asia is presented using satellite tracking, recoveries of Passive Integrated Transponders (PITs or microchips) and recoveries of ringed birds. Traditionally both species are trapped whilst on migration for use in Arab falconry. Migration data reveal populations that are potentially under threat from over-trapping although more intensive studies are required to quantify this accurately. This information is essential for the conservation action plan - *Global Strategy for the Conservation of Falcon and Houbara Resources.*

Over the last five years fieldworkers have been microchipping and ringing populations of Sakers in Kazakhstan, Mongolia, Kyrgyzstan, Russia, and Peregrines in the Taymyr Peninsula, Russia. Recoveries of microchips and rings have been made in the falcon markets of Pakistan and the falcon veterinary hospitals of the United Arab Emirates.

Using 30g satellite transmitters the migration routes of six Peregrines on the Taymyr Peninsula, Russia, and one Saker in the Russian Altai Mountains were recorded. The Peregrines started their migration from Taymyr in mid September, travelling south through Russia, Kazakhstan and into south-central Asia and Arabia. The Saker migrated a total distance of 4750km from her breeding grounds in the Altai Mountains, into central China, and back to the breeding grounds in the Altai Mountains by 12 March.

INTRODUCTION

The Peregrine Falcon *Falco peregrinus* has a world-wide distribution with nineteen recognised subspecies (White & Boyce, 1988) while Saker Falcons *Falco cherrug* breed in central Asia and eastern Europe and have six subspecies (Dementiev, 1951). In the northerly parts of their range both species are migratory but are resident in the south. Sakers in the Kustany region of Northern

Kazakhstan, for example, tend to be migratory whilst those in southern Kazakhstan tend to be sedentary (Kenward & Pfeffer, 1995).

The migration routes of both species and the locations of their wintering areas are poorly known. Some Peregrines migrate into Africa, India, south-east Asia, and the Middle East. Peregrines from northern Siberia and north-east Europe (*F. peregrinus calidus*) winter as far south as South Africa (Cramp & Simmons, 1982; Stephenson *pers. comm.*). Some northern Sakers migrate into southern Asia, the Middle East, north-east Africa and southern Europe. However, very little is known about migration routes of different populations, migration speeds and the length of time spent at resting sites and on the wintering grounds.

Sakers and Peregrines have traditionally been trapped in autumn and winter and used in Arab falconry (Remple & Gross 1993) but the origins of these birds are not well known. Recently, trappers have started to move into the breeding grounds, trapping falcons earlier in the season. This has meant that even the most remote breeding grounds are now under possible threat.

It is not known whether current trapping pressure is sustainable. The National Avian Research Center (NARC) aims to answer these questions by satellite tagging and marking adults and chicks throughout their ranges, both in the wild and in captivity. NARC currently co-ordinates projects in Kazakhstan (since 1992), Mongolia (since 1994), Russia (since 1997) and the Kyrgyz Republic (1998) for Sakers, and the Taymyr Peninsula, Northern Siberia (since 1996) for Peregrines. Here we present preliminary information from some of these on-going studies.

METHODS AND MATERIALS.

Fieldworkers and biologists from the falcon-range countries were trained in ringing and microchipping techniques through workshops, videos and using the *ERWDA* (Environmental Research and Wildlife Development Agency) *Handbook of Falcon Protocols* (Fox *et al.* 1996). Rings were normally obtained through the ringing organisation of each country and ringing returns are reported through the Moscow Bird Ringing Centre and the British Trust for Ornithology.

Passive Integrated Transponders (PIT's), commonly termed microchips, were purchased from AVID PLC and inserted subcutaneously above the pectoral muscle. Each microchip has a unique number that is read using a hand-held scanner. Details are stored on the Middle East Falcon Research Group (MEFRG) microchip database. Falcon veterinary hospitals in the Middle East use the same microchips and most falcons visiting a hospital for medical treatment are routinely scanned and fitted with a new microchip if none is already present. Using data gathered from ring and microchip recoveries, with a large enough sample size, it should be theoretically possible to estimate the harvest rate from a given population. The validity of this approach is discussed below and is dependent on the assumption that the proportion of the total number of birds originally marked and subsequently detected at hospitals or elsewhere is directly related to the number actually trapped.

A small number of falcons were fitted with satellite transmitters, also called platform transmitter terminals (PTT's). Transmitters were mounted on the back between the wings at the front end using an individually fitted harness made from Teflon ribbon and bungee cord. The harness consisted of loops directly attached to the PTT, one made of Teflon positioned around the neck, and a second made from Teflon and elastic bungee cord placed around the body in front of the legs. After fitting the harness to the bird, the two loops were joined together by sewing them to a strip of Teflon lying along the sternum. The neck loop was attached to the PTT in such a way that it lay on top of the furculum and did not interfere with the bird's crop. Details of the harness design are found in the *ERWDA Handbook of Falcon Protocols* (Fox *et al.* 1996). Information from satellite tracking was gathered using the Argos Data Collection and Location System. Details of how the accuracy of a transmitter location was ensured are found in the Argos User Manual (1996). The battery life for each transmitter was approximately six months.

The NARC field-team in Russia trapped two adult female Sakers in the Altai Mountain range. One falcon was trapped near the town of Maralikha, close to the Kazakhstan border and the other one in the Kosh-Agach region near the Mongolian border. Both were ringed, microchipped and fitted with 30g transmitters before being released. Each transmitter represented 2.2-2.9% of the falcon's body-mass.

In late July/early August 1996, two adult female Peregrines were trapped using dho-gazza nets along the Pura River on the Taymyr Peninsula, Russia, and fitted with 30g satellite transmitters. The adults were trapped at their nests containing half-fledged chicks. In 1997 satellite transmitters were fitted to two adult females and two almost-fledged young females on Taymyr.

RESULTS

Saker Falcons

Ring and PIT recoveries

Saker Falcons were first microchipped or ringed in Kazakhstan in 1993, through a collaborative project between NARC and ITE (Institute of Terrestrial Ecology). Since then biologists from other parts of the Sakers' breeding range have become involved in the programme (Table 1).

Table 1. Ring and PIT recoveries of Saker Falcons since 1993.

Country/region	Year	Sakers marked	Recoveries
Northern Kazakhstan	1993	26	1. Four juvenile females - location unknown.
	1994	31	1. Juvenile male trapped in Saudi Arabia.
	1995	36	1. Juvenile female recovered at the Dubai Falcon Hospital.
	1996	24	
	1997	?	1. Juvenile female trapped south of Jeddah, Saudi Arabia.
Eastern Kazakhstan	1993	4	
	1994	20	1. Juvenile female trapped in China and recovered at the Dubai Falcon Hospital.
	1997	32	1. Juvenile female trapped in China and recovered at the Dubai Falcon Hospital.
			2. Two juvenile females trapped in Mongolia and then released.
Central Kazakhstan	1993	10	1. Juvenile female - location unknown
	1994	10	
South-east Kazakhstan	1993	19	1. Two juvenile females - location unknown
	1994	13	
	1995	16	
Kyrgyzstan	1998	15	
Russia	1997	3	
Mongolia	1994	43	
	1995	84	1. Juvenile female recovered at the Dubai Falcon Hospital.
	1998		

Of the 30 juvenile female Sakers marked in Kazakhstan in 1993, the British Trust for Ornithology reported five returns from captive female Sakers in Iraq, Pakistan, Syria, Turkey, and Yemen (Kenward & Pfeffer, 1995). Three additional microchip returns came from Sakers checked in falcon hospitals in the U.A.E., two checked in Dubai and the third in Abu Dhabi. The microchip return in Abu Dhabi corresponded to a ring return in Syria. The capture locations of these falcons are uncertain. A total of seven females captured represent 23% of the 30 marked females. Kenward & Pfeffer (1995) also give a record of one male trapped in central Kazakhstan and released again.

Only two microchip recoveries were made in 1994. One female marked in eastern Kazakhstan close to the Chinese border had reportedly been trapped in China and was subsequently recovered at the Dubai Falcon Hospital. Another male originally marked in northern Kazakhstan was trapped in Saudi Arabia. This male had also been fitted as a nestling with a radio transmitter by Robert Kenward.

Two microchip returns from female Sakers marked in 1995 were made at the Dubai Falcon Hospital. One female was microchipped in northern Kazakhstan and the other in eastern Mongolia.

In 1996 twenty-four Saker chicks in northern Kazakhstan were microchipped through Robert Kenward's study. To our knowledge no returns were made.

In 1997 four Saker returns were made, three from juvenile females marked in eastern Kazakhstan (Watson, 1997) and one from a juvenile female marked in northern Kazakhstan. The latter was trapped 100 km south of Jeddah, Saudi Arabia. Of the three Sakers marked in eastern Kazakhstan, one was recovered at the Dubai Falcon Hospital and had supposedly been trapped in China. The second was trapped by an Arab falconer in Mongolia and then released again (Upton pers. comm.). The third Saker was also trapped in Mongolia, north-east of the Hangayn Nuruu Mountains, and then released again. The two Sakers trapped in Mongolia were siblings ringed as nestlings in eastern Kazakhstan. Of the 21 females marked in eastern Kazakhstan, 3 were trapped, suggesting a harvest rate of 14.3%. However, two of these females were released.

Satellite telemetry

The transmitter fitted to the Saker Falcon trapped near Maralikha never moved and its fate is unknown. The second falcon was tracked from 12 October 1997 to 20 June 1998 (Fig. 1) and migrated a total distance of 4750km, excluding local movements.

After her release, the falcon remained in the Kosh-Agach region until 17 November 1997, occasionally moving south-east into Mongolia and returning to Kosh-Agach.

The Kosh-Agach region is a high altitude plain, approximately 2,000m above sea level and 50km^2 in area, surrounded with mountains. Over five days, fifteen adult Sakers were seen in this region where they were believed to be feeding on the Daurian Pika (*Ochotoma daurica*) which does not hibernate and so provides food throughout the winter.

After 17 November the Saker began moving south through the Altai Mountain chain in western Mongolia and then into north-west China near the river Ulungur He. She remained in this region until 3 January 1998, moving slowly south into the Dzungaria region. The Saker then travelled approximately 1200km in six days, south-east across the Gansu plains in central China to the Datong Shan mountain range, north-east of lake Quihai Hu.

She remained in this area for two weeks before moving 350 km further south into the Bayan Har Shan and A'nyemaqen Shan range, on 25 January. She stayed here until 27 February and then moved north-west 1400 km to the Baytik Shan mountain range situated on the Chinese Mongolian border, on 8 March.

By 12 March she had travelled another 600km north-west through the Mongolian Altai back to the breeding area of Kosh-Agach, Russia. She remained in this region until the last signal was received on 20 June, 1998.

Figure 1. Movements of two adult female Sakers plotted using PTT data (1997)

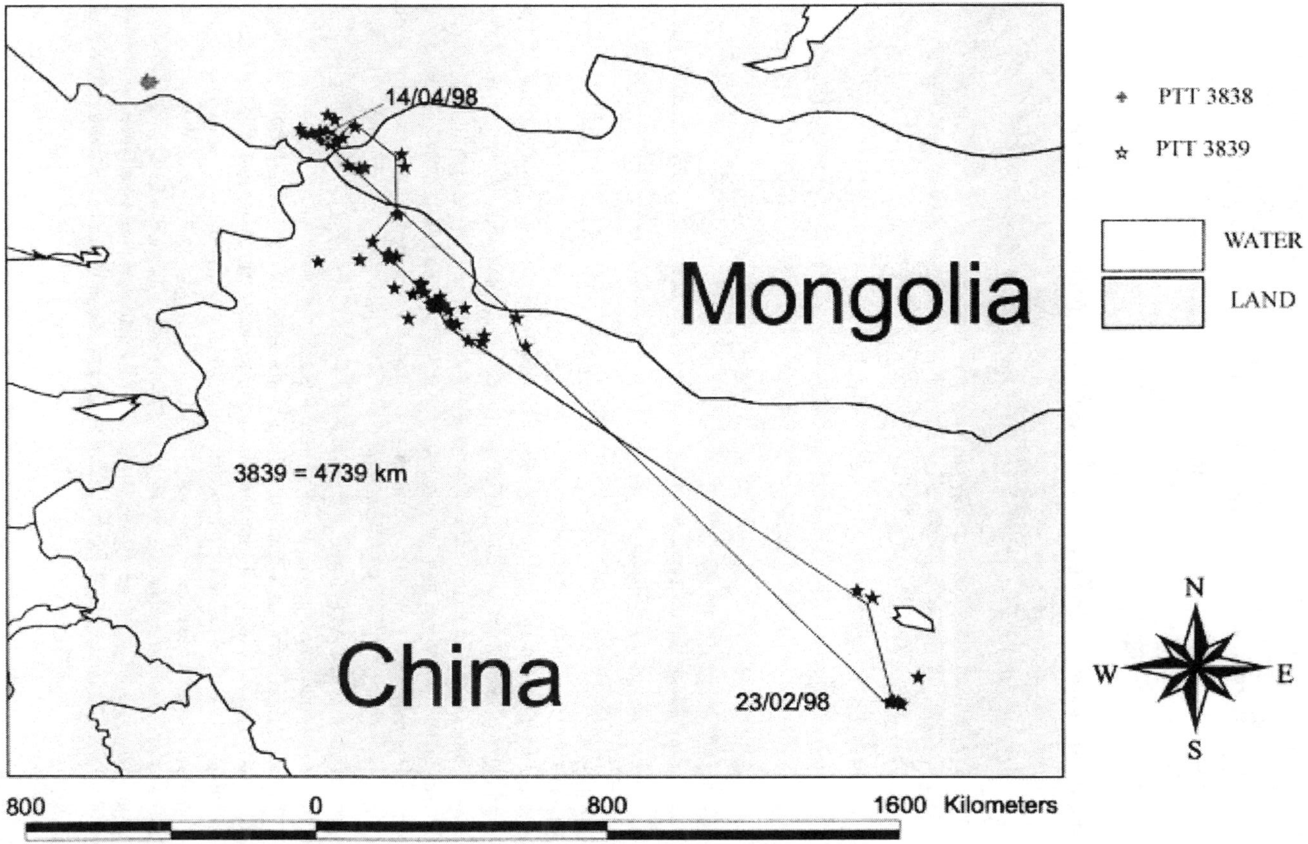

Peregrine Falcons

Ring and PIT recoveries

A total of 75 Peregrine Falcons have been ringed and/or microchipped in Taymyr since 1996 of which seven were adults. There have been no recoveries from those birds ringed in 1996 and, at the time of writing, it is too early to expect returns from the 1998 season. Two of the 17 juvenile females marked in 1997 were recovered in the UAE (see Table 2) suggesting a harvest rate of 11%. One falcon was brought to the Dubai Falcon Hospital (trapping location unknown), and Arab falconers on Qarnein Island, Abu Dhabi, trapped the other.

Table 2. Ring and PIT recoveries of Peregrine Falcons from the Taymyr Peninsula, Russia.

Year	No. ringed/chipped					Recoveries
	Adult		Juvenile		Total	
	Male	Female	Male	Female		
1996	1	2	8	5	19 (3 juveniles unsexed)	0
1997	2	2	5	17	26	1. Dubai Falcon Hospital, UAE. January, '98. 2. Qarnein Is., Abu Dhabi, UAE. November, '97.
1998					30	0

Satellite telemetry.

Falcon A migrated a total distance of 5,500 km (see Fig.2 and Table 3) from 30 July 1996 until 15 January 1997, excluding local movements. In three days she travelled 800km south-west to the Pur River. By 2 October she had travelled a further 1400km in the same direction close to a settlement named Odesskoje on the Russian Kazakhstan border, making several prolonged stops on the way. On 8 October she was in the centre of the Betpak-Dala, a large desert in central Kazakhstan. By the 18th the bird had moved a further 1800km south to the Afghanistan/Pakistan border, possibly travelling over the Hindu Kush mountain range. Shortly after she was trapped in Pakistan near Quetta.

After her release, Falcon B remained in the breeding area until 16 September. She then moved 700km south-east to the Ob Delta and reached the River Ljamin by 25 September, 800km further south. The last transmission was received from this area on 25 October (Fig.2).

The second breeding adult female, Falcon C, was tagged on 13 August 1997. She then moved 800km SSW to the settlement Tarko Sale on the Pur River. After remaining here for 11 days until 15 September, she moved south-east approximately 700km across the Tyumenskaya Oblast' on 24 September. She then travelled south-east approximately 250km on 25 September, went back north-west to almost the same previous location and then back south-east again on 27 September. The falcon changed direction moving south-west approximately 650km past Omsk and into northern Kazakhstan on 29 September. Next she moved west into the southern Ural Mountain chain, spending approximately six days on the Russian Kazakhstan border. By 13 October she had moved south approximately 1000km to the southern shores of the Aral Sea, Uzbekistan. From there she moved south-east, approximately 180km, close to the city of Tashauz on the Uzbekistan/Turkmenistan border on 15 October, after which the signal remained in the same general location.

Falcon D was trapped on 29 July 1997 at her nest site. The previous season this same territory had been occupied by a female wearing sabooks (Arab jesses) on her legs, indicating that she had previously been a falconer's bird. The bird trapped in 1997 had no jesses but did show some sign of minor scale damage on one of the legs and is thought to have been the same bird. The eyrie was checked one week after fitting the transmitter and both adults and all of the young were still doing well. Despite this the signal from this transmitter remained roughly in the same position, and we must conclude that either the falcon died or the transmitter fell off the bird.

The signal from the first juvenile, Falcon E, started transmitting on 15 August 1997 from her nest site on the banks of the Pyasina River. This falcon was approximately 40 days old when fitted with the transmitter and only a few days from fledging. She remained in the nesting territory until 19 September. The next accurate signal was received on 29 September, 750km south-west on the Ob Delta. The falcon remained in this place for two weeks until 12 October, and then travelled 400km south by 14 October. On 19 October she had travelled a further 600km, changing direction and heading south-west. The signal remained at this location, close to a settlement named Serginskiy.

Figure 2. Migration routes of two female Peregrines plotted from PTT data (1996/7)

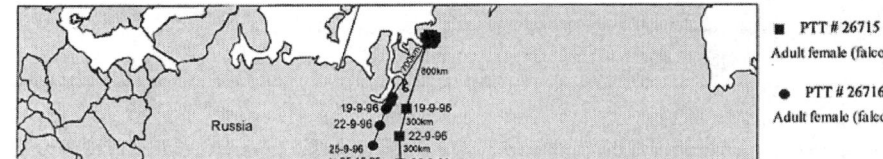

The second juvenile female (Falcon F) was tagged on 13 August. This bird had already fledged from a different nest to Falcon E when the transmitter was fitted. She remained in the nesting territory until 16 September and then travelled approximately 700km south-west to the Ob Delta where she remained from 26 September to 13 October. She then travelled approximately 2500km in a southerly direction before reaching the northern shores of the Aral Sea in Kazakhstan eighteen days later on 1 November. The signal did not change position after this date.

Figure 3. Migration routes of four female Peregrines plotted from PTT data (1997/8)

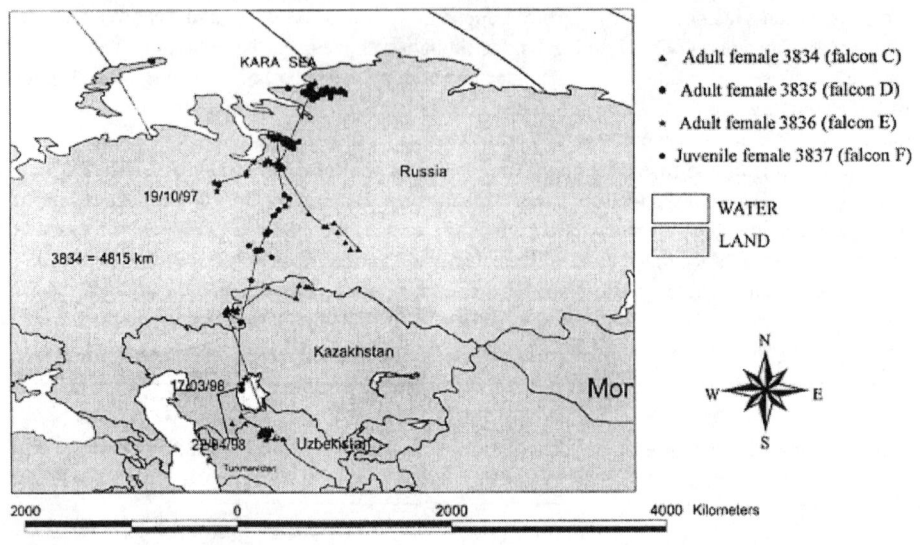

Table 3. Satellite telemetry data of Peregrine Falcons from the Taymyr Peninsula, Russia. * indicates a juvenile bird.

Falcon	Trans-mitter no.	Date fitted	Place fitted	First day movement	Last detected day of movement	Last date transmitted	Distance travelled (km)
A	26715	30-Jul-96	Lower Pura	16-Sep-96	12-Nov-96	15-Jan-97	5,500
B	26716	29-Jul-96	Upper Pura	16-Sep-96	25-Sep-96	25-Oct-97	1,500
C	3834	13-Aug-97	Middle Pyasina	4-Aug-97	15-Oct-97	27-Apr-98	4,815

DISCUSSION

Falcon harvest rates

Saker Falcons

The number of marked Sakers detected was low in most years. As estimates of harvest rates, the accuracy of these values is very likely to be poor and most potential sources of error would lead to an underestimate of the harvest rate. For example, we have no knowledge of juvenile falcon mortality before they reach those areas in which they are likely to be trapped. Such mortality would effectively increase the estimated harvest rate. The method also assumes that all of the marked falcons that are trapped are brought to hospitals, identified and finally reported to the MEFRG. This is likely to be the most serious source of error leading to an underestimation of harvest rate because 1) many trapped birds are never brought to hospitals or detected; 2) some trapped birds pass through the falcon hospitals undetected; 3) some young falcons are likely to die before being sold at falcon markets; and 4) ringed birds are less likely to be brought to a hospital by a suspicious owner. Although it may well be possible to determine the actual number trapped, it would be extremely expensive and logistically difficult to do so since this would require monitoring numbers of falcons offered for sale at markets throughout the Far and Middle East. The second point could be tackled in the long-term by gaining the participation of all falconry hospitals. It would be difficult to estimate what proportion die before reaching the markets, but in the meantime NARC is working towards improving handling practices in the Far and Middle East. The fourth point could be partly alleviated by only using microchips and discontinuing the use of metal rings.

Some falcons undoubtedly escape or are released into the wild and this is probably the only source of error that could lead to an overestimate of the harvest rate. In the case of Peregrines, for example, one of the 12 wild adult females observed on the Pura River in Taymyr in 1996 had jesses. A goose biologist reported a similar sighting in eastern Taymyr the following year (T Aarvak, *pers. comm.*). Similar records undoubtedly exist for Sakers. It is sometimes thought that the constant annual demand for new falcons is primarily a result of birds being lost or returned to the wild. The general feeling amongst concerned delegates at the current conference is that high demand is caused by high mortality amongst captive birds, especially during the summer months when falcons first arrive in the Middle East and their training begins. Clearly more information is needed to determine annual survival and release rates of captive falcons.

So far this project has concentrated on migratory Saker populations in a few areas. Obviously any harvest rate estimate that is eventually calculated will still be valid only for those populations actually marked. From a global point of view, nothing is known about trapping pressure or population size in other more remote areas where many Sakers are resident, for example in China, south-eastern Russia and Mongolia. To combat these, and other problems a conservation action plan called the *Global Strategy for the Conservation of Falcon and Houbara Resources* is being developed by NARC. This conservation plan aims to ensure the future of falcons, other species affected by falconry and the habitat in which the falcons and prey species live.

Peregrine Falcons

Data from microchipped and ringed Peregrines suggested an apparently low trapping rate amongst juveniles. For the same reasons given for Sakers, the net impact trapping has on the population is likely to be many times higher than the tagging data suggest. Even with a very low tagging effort, it was still possible to show that a minimum of 11% of tagged young females were trapped and it is suggested that over-trapping could be having a potentially wide-ranging impact on the falcon population. It is not known whether the size of the breeding population is affected by trapping or whether the effective mortality is compensatory. Quinn *et al*. (this volume) suggest that the recovering population in Taymyr is probably well below carrying capacity. In addition they found no evidence of a surplus breeding population in 1996 or 1997 which would otherwise have indicated competition for nesting sites and, hence, a population at carrying capacity.

Exposure to pesticides can probably be ruled out as being a major limiting factor because breeding success was high in 1996 and 1997. Mean organic residue levels in blood samples also suggested the population was not adversely exposed to pesticides although the sample size was small and some individuals had apparently high levels (Quinn *et al*. this volume). Trapping on migration, therefore, may well be one of the main factors preventing a complete recovery of the Peregrine breeding population in the Taymyr.

Satellite tagged birds were not included in the harvest rate estimate. We know that at least one of the six Peregrines tagged was trapped for falconry in Pakistan, but it is also quite possible that the other two birds that had apparently stopped moving when they reached Turkmenistan and Uzbekistan had actually been trapped. Birds with satellite tags are undoubtedly stressed to some degree and thereby more likely to be tempted by a trapper's bait. Nevertheless the fact that at least one of four tagged adult falcons was trapped supports the suggestion that the population suffers high trapping pressure.

Satellite telemetry

Saker Falcons

Sakers in the eastern part of their breeding range are either transitory or resident, depending on whether prey species, such as pikas and Brandt's voles (*Microtus brandtii*), are active throughout the year. Populations of Sakers marked in eastern Kazakhstan migrated east into China and Mongolia where they were trapped by Arab falconers. In Kyrgystan, Uzbekistan, Turkmenistan, and southern Kazakhstan, populations of the Saker subspecies *F. c. coatsi* are believed to be resident and remain in their nesting territories throughout the winter (Baumgart, 1991). In the Tibetan highlands Sakers are also resident due to minimal snowfall and constant availability of food (Baumgart, 1991).

Very little is known concerning the migratory behaviour of Sakers from the Altai Mountains. The female Saker tagged near Kosh-Agach showed transient migratory behaviour. She remained in the Altai Mountain chain until late November, but then moved further south, probably due to a lack of food and to cold weather.

We can conclude that the migratory behaviour of eastern Sakers is dependent on local conditions and varies from year to year. It is not known whether these Sakers follow any common migratory routes, or share wintering grounds. Satellite tagging of larger numbers of eastern Sakers would reveal more information concerning their migratory behaviour, which could be possibly explained by linking with weather patterns for central Asia.

Peregrine Falcons

All birds began their migration in mid-September, about three to four weeks after the young birds had fledged. All of the five falcons that began migrating moved approximately 700km south-west to the shores of the Ob Delta, an extremely important staging area for the migrating waterfowl on which they feed. Scott & Rose (1996) give maximum counts of 810,000 Pintail (*Anas acuta*) and 165,000 Wigeon (*Anas penelope*) alone in this area. Undoubtedly the Ob is a crucially important staging area for young falcons in particular because in September most of their main prey has left the tundra breeding grounds. In late September and October the falcons passed through Russia and into Kazakhstan. Three of the six falcons moved as far as 40° S between the Caspian Sea and Kyrgystan and one of these reached 30°S in Pakistan, where it was trapped.

It is difficult to say for certain whether the latter three falcons had reached their intended wintering grounds. Certainly *calidus* winters in these areas (Dementiev & Gladkov 1951; Roberts 1991) but it is also possible that they had been either trapped in these areas or died prematurely before they had finished their migration. This is possible because the transmitters continued working for several months with no further movement.

None of the birds tagged, microchipped or ringed were detected in Africa or India. One ringed juvenile was trapped, however, on the Arabian Gulf in November, presumably on its way to Africa. In another study a female *F. p. calidus*, satellite tagged in Saudi Arabia in autumn, moved as far as Cape Town, South Africa (P. Paillat, *pers. comm.*). Jenkins (1994) considers *F. p. calidus* to be a rare migrant to South Africa but Alan Stephenson has trapped *calidus* Peregrines on the south-east coast regularly and considers them to be reasonably common there. Jerdon (1877) says of *F. p. calidus* in India, "The Bhyri does not breed in this country, nor even, I believe, in the Himalayas but migrates to the North in April and returns about the 1st week of October". Clearly larger numbers need to be marked in different areas to determine the relative importance of India, Africa and the Middle East to *calidus* Peregrines.

Survival of satellite-tagged birds

Our data suggest that satellite tags on Peregrines and Saker Falcons may have a significant impact on their mortality. The fact that two of the eight transmitters never left the place the tags were fitted and another two travelled less than 1,600 km suggests that these birds died prematurely although it is possible the latter two could also have been trapped. It is highly unlikely that the harnesses fell off on their own. Of the three birds that travelled more than 3,000 km, one was definitely trapped for falconry but the fate of the other two is unknown.

P. Paillat (*pers. comm.*) thinks that a bird tagged with a satellite transmitter might be more vulnerable to predation by other raptors. His reasoning is that the tagged bird may provoke an aggressive or predatory response either because the falcon looks unwell or because it looks as if it is carrying prey. The idea seems plausible, bearing in mind that raptors are abundant during autumn migration in western Asia.

The tag itself, however, is also likely to have directly affected the mortality of the birds. Although dummy transmitters were tested on captive falcons and gave the birds no problems in a confined space, we have no idea how birds cope under continuous flight or when hunting. Larger birds of prey including Ospreys, Lesser Spotted Eagles and Steller's Eagles do not seem to be affected by satellite transmitters (Meyburg, *pers. comm.*). Apart from the obviously greater bird-weight to transmitter-weight ratio these larger birds have, they also fly more slowly and have much slower wing-beats. Swainson's Hawks in the Americas tagged with satellite transmitters were also not adversely affected (Fuller, *pers. comm.*). The same team also tagged Peregrines in North America using a similar harness design to ours and also thought that the mortality of this species might have been affected by the transmitters, although this has not been quantified (Fuller, *pers. comm.*).

The weight of these transmitters is unlikely to have been a problem since it accounted for just 3% of total body-mass, well within the normally accepted range. We feel that the constrictive nature of the harness itself is likely to be the main problem through its influence on muscle performance and the ease with which prey are captured. Further tests on captive falcons using different harness designs will be conducted before further tagging takes place. Ongoing efforts to reduce transmitter size will undoubtedly help reduce these problems.

CONCLUSION

So far the numbers of young falcons ringed or microchipped have been too small to estimate accurately the trapping pressure faced by Saker Falcon and Peregrine Falcon populations in the Far and Middle East. To improve the estimate, it will be essential to increase the number of birds marked and to improve our knowledge of detection rates and mortality of marked birds before being sold for falconry. Nevertheless even with a relatively small marking and 'recapture' effort, trapping pressure is detectable and could be very high in some years. For example, 23% of young Saker Falcons marked in 1993 were detected in falcon hospitals throughout the Middle and Far East. An absolute minimum of 5% of young Peregrines ringed in 1997 (11% of females) were similarly detected and at least one of six satellite tagged Peregrines was trapped on migration.

While we can conclude little from tagging a single bird, it appears that Sakers in the Altai mountains winter in central China, presumably in response to low prey availability on the breeding grounds in the non-breeding season. The data from satellite tagged Peregrine Falcons showed that the Ob Delta is an important staging area for Peregrines nesting in western Taymyr and that birds generally migrate directly south. The data also suggest that the area between the Caspian Sea and Pakistan is important for Taymyr Peregrines although it was not clear whether the tagged birds had reached their intended winter grounds.

ACKNOWLEDGEMENTS.

We would like to thank Abu Dhabi Crown Prince and Deputy Supreme Commander of the Armed Forces His Highness Sheikh Khalifa bin Zayed Al Nahyan, and Minister of State for Foreign Affairs, His Highness Sheikh Hamdan bin Zayed Al Nahyan, for their support throughout this work. We also greatly appreciate the advice and assistance given by Mohamed Al Bowardi and Dr Fred Launay. Many thanks also to Helen Macdonald for help during the research and editing the paper. To those people involved in the National Avian Research Center Falcon Programme, we would like to thank Dr Anatoli Levin, Prof. Anatoli Kovshar, Dr Robert Kenward and Mark Watson for their work in Kazakhstan, to Prof. Vladimir Galushin and Dr Valery Moseikin in Russia, to Seth Layman and Dr Yakov Kokorev for their work on the Peregrines on the Taymyr Peninsula, and to Jaime Samour and Nigel Barton for collecting ring and microchip returns in Arabia. Thanks also to Sergei Kharitonov and the Moscow Bird Ringing Centre for kindly providing rings and sending details of ring returns. Dr. J.M. Black and The Wildfowl & Wetlands Trust were originally responsible for initiating this project.

REFERENCES

ARGOS USER MANUAL. JANUARY 1996. CLS. France.
BAUMGART, W. 1991. *Der Sakerfalke*. Neue Brehm Bucherei, A. Ziemsen Verlag, wittenburg, Germany.
CRAMP, S. & K.E.L. SIMMONS 1980. *The Birds of the Western Palearctic*. Vol. 2. Oxford.
DEMENTIEV, G.P. 1951. The order of hunting birds. In *Birds of the Soviet Union*, Vol. 1. Moscow: Soviet Science.
FOX, N.C., C.P. EASTHAM & H.J. MACDONALD 1997. *The ERWDA handbook of falcon protocols*. Produced by ERWDA.
JENKINS, A.R. 1994. The influence of habitat on the distribution and abundance of Peregrine and Lanner Falcons in South Africa. *Ostrich* 65: 281-290.
JERDON, T.C. 1877. *The birds of India*. Vol 1. P.S. D'Rozario & Co., Calcutta.
REMPLE, D. & C. GROSS 1993. *Falconry and Birds of Prey in the Gulf*. Motivate Publishing, U.A.E.
ROBERTS, T.J. 1991. *The birds of Pakistan*. Vol. 1. Karachi, Oxford University Press.
SCOTT, D.A. & P.M. ROSE 1996. Atlas of Anatidae Populations in Africa and Western Eurasia. *Wetlands International Publication 41*.
WATSON, M. 1997. Saker Falcon Ecology and Conservation in North East Kazakhstan. MSc Thesis. Durrell Institute of Conservation and Ecology.
WHITE, C.M. & A. BOYCE JR. 1988. An overview of Peregrine Falcon Subspecies. In *Peregrine Falcon Populations - Their Management and Recovery*. by Cade T.J, Enderson J.H., Thelander C.G., and White C.M. (Eds.). The Peregrine Fund, Inc.

C.P. Eastham & N.C. Fox
The National Avian Research Centre,
The Falcon Facility, Penllynin Farm,
College Road, Carmarthen,
Carmarthenshire SA33 5EH
Wales, U.K.

J.L Quinn
The Edward Grey Institute of Field Ornithology
University of Oxford
South Parks Road
Oxford OX1 3P5
UK

also
The Wildfowl and Wetlands Trust
Slimbridge
Gloucestershire
UK

Chancellor, R. D. & B.-U. Meyburg eds. 2000
Raptors at Risk
WWGBP / Hancock House

The Saker Falcon *Falco cherrug* in Kazakstan

Anatoliy Levin, Mark Watson, Helen Macdonald and Nicholas C. Fox

ABSTRACT

In 1993 the National Academy of Science of the Republic of Kazakstan (NAS RK) and the National Avian Research Center (NARC), Abu Dhabi, initiated a monitoring project to assess the distribution, density and productivity of Saker Falcons *Falco cherrug* in Kazakstan. The harvest of Sakers in Kazakstan has increased over the past five years. Historically, only a small proportion of falcons were trapped during migration. Now, adults and juveniles are being taken from their breeding grounds, resulting in local extinctions. The Saker, especially in southeast Kazakstan, may become extinct at the present level of trapping. It is expected that trapping will continue in these areas and possibly in other remote areas of east Kazakstan on the borders with China and Russia. Field biologists will continue to monitor existing study areas, and survey new ones in order to assess the impact across the whole country. Continued co-operation between the NAS RK and NARC, and the development of the Global Strategy for the Conservation of Falcon and Houbara Resources, is hoped will conserve and restore the Saker in Kazakstan.

INTRODUCTION

The current project is a collaboration between the National Avian Research Center, Abu Dhabi (NARC) and the National Academy of Science of the Republic of Kazakstan (NAS RK). It commenced in 1993, following a two year pilot study contracted to the Institute of Terrestrial Ecology UK, assisted by NAS RK scientists.

The project is carried out by biologists from the Institute of Zoology of NAS RK, joined in the field in 1997 by NARC fieldworker Mark Watson. Its aims are to assess the distribution, density and productivity of Sakers, to study their migration, and to obtain biomedical and morphometric data on the population in Kazakstan. Valuable data has been obtained on habitat use, morphometrics, biomedical aspects, natal dispersal and genetics of the population over this study period. This paper concentrates on the breeding success of Sakers in Kazakstan in the years 1993-1998.

Kazakstan

Kazakstan's 2,700,000 km² represent more than half the species' longitudinal distribution and at least two-thirds of its latitudinal distribution (Kenward, *et al* 1995). The Saker is irregularly distributed in Kazakstan and only occupies habitat where suitable prey and nesting places coincide. This includes rocky mountains in the south, east and north of the country up to 2,500 m in alpine ranges (Zailiysky and Dzhungarsky Alatau, Altai). Estimates of density range from 10-20 pairs per 1000 km^2 to 0.1-2 pairs per 1000 km^2, according to habitat (Kenward & Pfeffer, 1995).

Study Areas

The study areas were three mountain sites in southeast Kazakstan within a radius of 200 km east (Great and Small Boguty, Turaigyr), west (Anarhay and Serektas) and north of Almaty (Malaisary). The area of these varies from 260 to 540 km^2 with one site in the central part of the Republic (Betpakdala desert) about 15000 km^2, 500 km distant from Almaty. In 1997 Watson initiated survey and monitoring of sub-populations in the Alakul depression and Altai mountains.

METHODS

Study areas were visited between April and July. Traditional sites were visited to ascertain occupancy and breeding success and study areas were searched for signs of new Saker nesting attempts. A Yaz off-road vehicle was used to travel within each study area; where this was impossible, areas were searched on foot. The location of each new nest was recorded using a Global Positioning System GPS. Wherever possible, adult and young birds were ringed, fitted with subcutaneous passive integrated transponders (microchips), photographed, measured and weighed. Blood and feather samples were taken for pesticide, biomedical and genetic analyses. Prey remains and pellets were collected. In 1997, additional data were obtained on local prey-bases. Sampling and measuring techniques followed NARC protocols (Fox *et al* 1997). Chicks were assumed to have fledged successfully if they were over 80% of the average age of first flight (Steenhof & Kochert 1982) when last observed.

RESULTS

Saker breeding numbers have declined over the years of the study. This began in 1992, and has been especially marked in the more accessible southeast of the Republic. By 1998 the number of occupied nests was reduced to a critical level, with the complete removal of sub-populations from some monitored regions (Anarhay, Malaysary). The number of breeding pairs in different regions are shown in Figures 1 and 2.

Figure 1. The decline of Saker nesting pairs in Southeast and Central Kazakstan

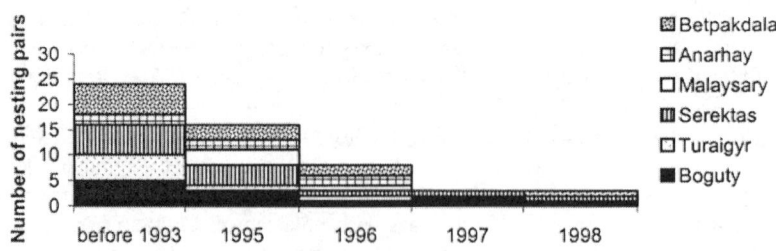

Figure 2. Decline of Saker nesting pairs in East Kazakhstan (No data for areas other than Dzhungarskiy Mts until 1997)

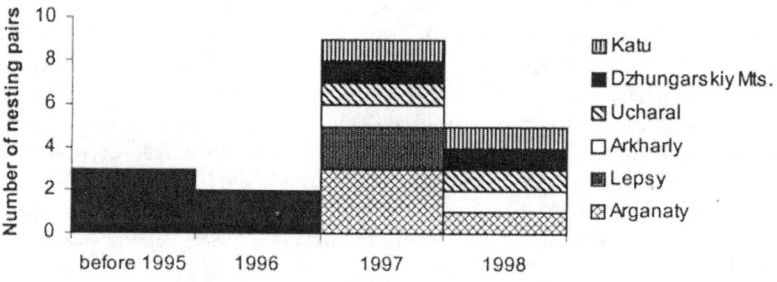

The nest success and productivity of the Saker in Kazakstan reached an all-time low in 1998 (Table 3). Birds were absent from most traditional territories in southeast Kazakstan. Single adult males were observed near some nests. Chicks were not recorded as having been stolen this season, but all three nests with eggs were abandoned in Betpakdala and in southeastern Kazakstan. A dead female was recorded on one nest in the Arharly Mountains. The fate of the nests in eastern Kazakstan remained unrecorded in 1998 as the team were filming Sakers in Arharly.

Table 3. Saker falcon nest success & productivity 1995-98 in Southern, Central & Eastern Kazakstan

Area	Number of nests checked	Number of nests occupied	Number of nests robbed	Number of nests successful	Number of chicks fledged
Southern, Central					
1995	22	13	6	2	5
1996	21	8	5	1	5
1997	21	?	1	2	?
1998	23	3	0	0	0
Eastern					
1995	3	3	0	3	?
1996	3	2	0	1	1
1997	?	16	0	9	30
1998	11	5	?	3	?

DISCUSSION

Although a full understanding of the issue of sustainability in taking wild birds for falconry cannot be addressed until the extent of variable productivity in relation to fluctuating food resources is measured (Watson 1997), it is clear that the main reason for the decreasing Saker population in Kazakstan is trapping for falconry. Initially carried out only by trappers from Arabian countries, local people quickly became involved, many of whom have little knowledge of falcons and falcon husbandry. Initially they concentrated on taking birds between 25-40 days old, but as demand increased, chicks were taken at increasingly young ages, often when still downy. It was soon realised that these birds were unsuitable for Arab buyers because they had been hand-reared, so attention was switched to trapping adult falcons at their nests. On 10 February 1997 in the Serektas mountains, the team observed 4x4 tracks running through the snow from one nest to another, and on the furthest nest a dead male Saker was found trapped in a noose. Loops of synthetic cord had been placed on both the nest and adjacent cliffs. Seven adult birds trapped on their nest sites were seen for sale that same spring in local dwellings in the Malaisary region. In 1993, official permission was given to members of the Royal Family of Saudi Arabia to catch Sakers in Kazakstan.

Many falcons die in captivity before they can be sold, further exacerbating demand. The 1997 monitoring results appeared to show an improvement in the situation in southeast Kazakstan, with successful breeding attempts in the Boguty mountains, where there had been extensive trapping in previous years One nest site was re-occupied and single males defended territories, suggesting some re-colonisation. However, this improving trend did not continue in 1998. Trappers from Saudi Arabia with official permission to harvest 30 birds visited this area in the autumn of 1997. In two months they caught 60 birds, half of which were released. Saudi trappers have also made trips to the east of the Republic, surveying the Kazakh regions of the Altai. This raises fears for Sakers breeding in previously inaccessible areas of Kazakstan.

In summary, the current situation appears to be threatening the status of the Saker as a breeding bird in Kazakstan. In conjunction with its long-term monitoring programme in Kazakstan, Russia, Mongolia and Kyrgyzstan, the National Avian Research Center is working on a Global Strategy Plan for the Conservation of Falcon and Houbara Resources. This publication aims to influence the end-users of falcons and educate Arab falconers and policy makers on the importance of sustainable use of natural resources.

ACKNOWLEDGEMENTS

Significant assistance in the field was rendered by Jacek Strek and O.Belialov. The necessary technical condition of a vehicle was supported by S.Levin. To all these listed people Anatoliy Levin expresses deep gratitude.

REFERENCES

BAUMGART, W. 1991. *The Saker Falcon*. Der neue Brehm-Bucherei, Berlin.
FOX, N. C., C.P. EASTHAM & H.J. MACDONALD 1997. *Handbook of Falcon Protocols*, ERWDA, The Falcon Facility, Wales.
KENWARD, R. E. & R. H. PFEFFER 1995. Saker Falcons in Central Asia, Final Report of the Pilot Study, Institute of Terrestrial Ecology, the Natural Environment Research Council.
STEENHOF, K., & M.N. KOCHERT 1982. An evaluation of methods used to estimate raptor nesting success. *J.Wildl. Manage.* 46:885-893
WATSON, M. 1997. Saker Falcon Ecology and Conservation in North East Kazakstan. MSc thesis, Durrell Institute of Conservation and Ecology.

A. Levin
The Institute of Zoology
National Academy of Science
of the Republic of Kazakstan

M. Watson
The Game Conservancy
Fordingbridge
Hampshire SP6 1EH
U.K.

H. Macdonald & N. C. Fox
National Avian Research Centre (Abu Dhabi)
Penllynin Farm, College Road
Carmarthen SA33 5EH
Wales, U.K.

Chancellor, R. D. & B.-U. Meyburg eds. 2000
Raptors at Risk
WWGBP / Hancock House

The Saker Falcon *Falco cherrug* in Mongolia

Damdinsuren Shijirmaa, Eugene Potapov, Samdangiin Banzragch and Nicholas C. Fox

ABSTRACT

Mongolia is a stronghold for the Saker Falcon in Asia, but, as in many other countries, the species is increasingly pressured in Mongolia by the illegal taking of birds for falconry. In this study it is estimated that there is a total of 2,823 territorial pairs of Sakers of which 1993 pairs participate in breeding producing an estimated 6,382 young Sakers per year. The average density of Sakers in Mongolia was measured as 2.7 pairs per 1000 km^2. 1998 saw the commencement of a joint research and monitoring programme for this species between the Environmental Protection Agency (EPA) of the Mongolian Ministry of Nature and the Environment and the National Avian Research Center (NARC). The programme is investigating the numbers and distribution of the Saker Falcon in Mongolia in order to conserve the species. The project also seeks to obtain data for other NARC projects in its Falcon Programme on falcon species used or affected by Arab Falconry. These include data on migration, behavioural and breeding data, dietary studies on the species, and the gathering of morphometric data and biomedical samples such as blood and feathers. This paper presents the results from the 1998 field season.

INTRODUCTION.

Studies of Saker Falcons in Mongolia have traditionally been carried out by ornithologists during surveys of Mongolian fauna (Kurochkin & Mikhailov 1994, Ostapenko *et al.* 1977, Potapov 1986, Rogacheva *et al.* 1988, Smirenskiy *et al.* 1991, Tugarinov 1932, Zabelin 1993). A number of accounts of Saker distribution occur in classical books on Mongolian ornithology as well as in special papers on systematics (Dementiev 1970, Dementiev & Shagdarsuren 1964, Kozlova 1930, 1932, 1940, 1969, Shagdarsuren 1964, Sushkin 1915, Stepanyan *et al.* 1988). At this time, Mongolia was not actively involved in the international trade of live birds and visiting Mongolia was difficult. A pilot study of Saker population was carried out by Tsengeg and Ellis in 1997 (Tsengeg *pers. comm*).

When the Republic of Mongolia started to open up, as it underwent a transition towards a market economy, the Saker became a focus for bird traders as well as conservationists. The Ministry of Nature and the Environment faced considerable difficulties working out conservation policies to protect and sustain Saker Falcon populations in Mongolia and to enforce Saker protection. The major difficulties faced were caused by a lack of funding for research and modern scientific methods. Estimates of the Saker population in Mongolia varied from 1500 to 20,000 individuals.

Such inconsistency in figures convinced the Ministry of Nature and the Environment to launch its own nation-wide research project aiming to reach an unbiased estimate of Saker population numbers and productivity. The project began in 1998 and was backed by all leading bird specialists in Mongolia.

METHODS.

Two field teams established 5 control areas across Mongolia in May-June 1998. The teams surveyed the steppes from 4WD vehicles using various optical equipment, including gyroscopic binoculars which allowed observations from moving cars. Essentially surveys on foot were carried out in the terrain where access by car was difficult. All nest locations of territorial pairs as well as position of the control territories were mapped in the control territories using Garmin 45XL GPS receiver with subsequent processing with MacGPS Pro (James Associates, PO Box 60, Nederland, Co 80 466, USA). The nest sites were described according to the standard NARC guidelines (Fox *et al.* 1997) mentioning the position of the nest, nest substrate, building material, orientation of the nest. Brood size was determined in most cases.

The control areas are large enough to represent a significant proportion of the breeding population, and are located in places accessible in the future, to ensure repeatability of surveys. The area of the control plots totals 16,948 km^2. This represents 1.1% of all Mongolian territory as estimated from the official figures (Sondom & Yanshin 1990), and 1.6% of all possible breeding habitat of Sakers in Mongolia (total area, less land higher than 3,000m, less flat sand deserts and densely forested areas estimated from Batjargal & Enkhabat 1998). In the future we plan to extend this control area to cover 2% of possible Saker breeding habitat in Mongolia.

RESULTS AND DISCUSSION

In Mongolia the Sakers were found breeding in mountain, open steppe, semi-desert and forest-steppe habitats. A remarkable distinction of breeding habitat of Mongolian Sakers is that the number of nests found on artificial nest substrates (electric poles, bridges, buildings) outnumber those nests located on natural substrates such as cliffs and rock ledges (Figure 1). Amongst artificial nests the falcons prefer poles of electric lines of various kinds (Figure 2).

Figure 1. Proportion of nests located on artificial substrates vs. natural nest sites.

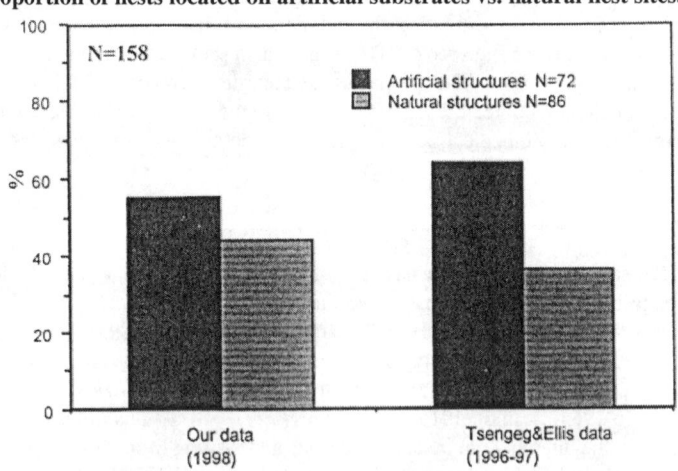

Electric poles are not the only nest sites available for falcons in flat steppe areas. It is not unusual to see falcons nesting on abandoned wells, metal and wooden electric poles, even close to busy roads and railways on deserted concrete and log cabins. Peaceful attitudes of local people towards these falcons are based on Buddhist traditions which prohibit the killing or disturbance of birds. Moreover there is also an ancient belief that to kill a falcon means to kill a soul (Simakov 1998).

Figure 2. Types of artificial nest-sites.

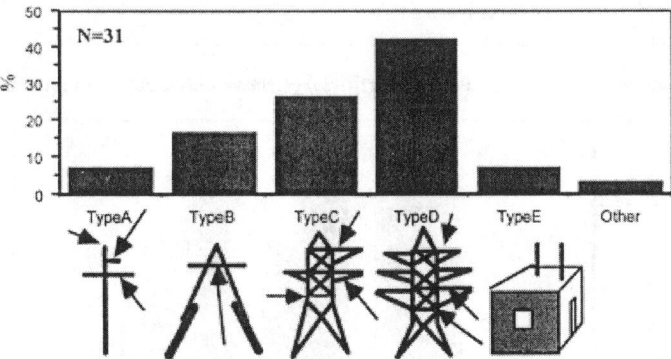

Direct human persecution of falcons has not been recorded during field trips. Nevertheless, we have found human causes of mortality acting indirectly on both parents and chicks. This is the littering of the steppe with rope and string. Faced with a shortage of nesting material, birds pick up pieces of string and parts of horse harnesses and bring them to the nests. The string sometimes acts as a set of nooses, and birds become entangled and die. This year our field team saved one chick caught in this way. It had a badly wounded tarsus, and would not have survived without our visit. One adult bird was found dead at the nest caught by string used as building material for the nest.

Other causes of mortality include death by chilling, and significant differences in hatching dates which causes some chicks to lose out in competition for food amongst the broods (Figure 3). Overall mortality does not appear to be high - out of 172 hatched young 153 fledged or reached fledgling age. The average brood size in 1998 was 3.2±0.99, N=53. Brood size distribution is given in Figure 4.

Figure 3. Clutch/brood mortality causes

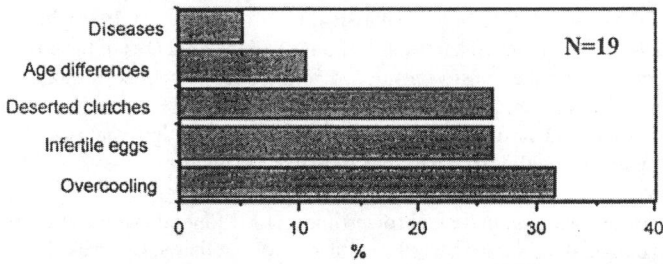

Figure 4. Brood size distribution

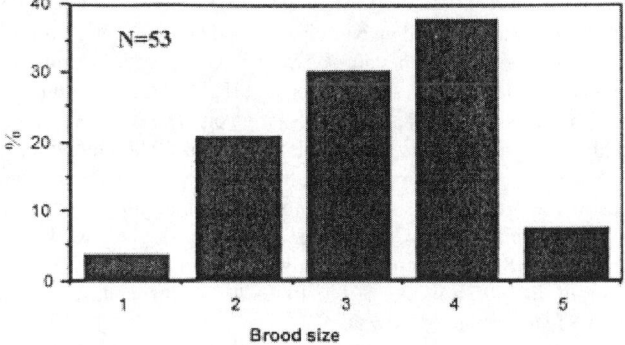

There was no significant difference between brood sizes of pairs breeding on artificial and natural sites (F=0.968254, P = 0.5311) (Figure 5).

Figure 5. Brood sizes of pairs breeding at artificial (electric poles, etc.) and natural (cliffs) sites.

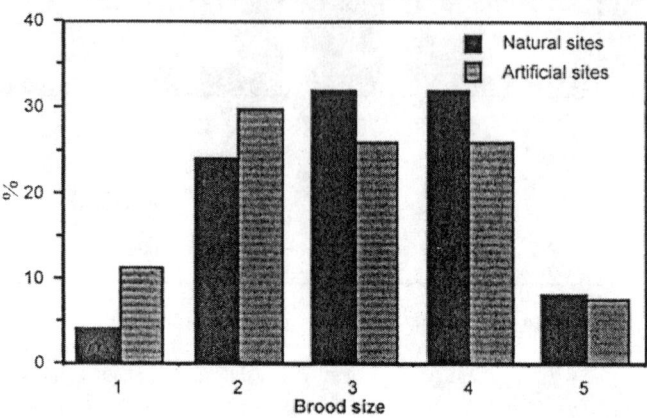

The average density of breeding Sakers in Mongolia, measured in the control areas, is 2.7 pairs per 1000 km^2. Projecting this density on the 1,540,681.8 km^2 Mongolian territory, remembering that 96,500 km^2 of the country is covered by thick forests, and a further 4% lies above 3,000m where Sakers do not breed, we reach a projected total Mongolian population of 2,823 territorial pairs of Sakers. Galushin (1971) reported a density a much lower for Sakers in the forest zone in the Rysan District, Oka Nature Reserve - 1 pair per 1000 km^2. Some other papers give unrealistically high breeding density: as high as 5-44 pairs per 1000 km^2 for Uzbekistan (Abdulnazarov 1990); 26-105 pairs per 1000 km^2 for Tula region (Likhachev 1957); 13-23 pairs per 1000 km for Tuva (Baranov 1989); and 20-30 pairs per 1000 km^2 in Khakassia (Prokofiev & Kustov 1988). In all these cases the sampled population was limited to a few pairs of birds and the total area of the control territory was not given. It appears that the density mentioned in the cited papers corresponds to some places which represent breeding clusters of the falcons, and does not give representative data for estimation of real density for large territories. The estimated breeding density in Uzbekistan recalculated from the data of Abunazarov (1990) is 0.26 pairs per 1000 km^2, i.e. about 10 times lower than in Mongolia.

With the average brood size of 3.2, and providing that the percentage of pairs participating in breeding is 70.6% as measured in the control territories, the Mongolian population of Saker Falcons produce 6382 young Sakers per year. The brood size in Mongolian Sakers was close to that reported for Kopet-Dag, Turkmenia (Polozov 1983) and for Baikal Region (Ryabtsev 1997).

CONSERVATION AND PROTECTION STATUS.

This figures of both numbers, breeding participation and breeding rate, has given a solid ground to restart discussions on the protection status of Sakers in Mongolia. Currently absent from the Mongolian Red Data Book, the Saker is still on Appendix II of CITES. Mongolia became a signatory to CITES in 1996. The decision to delist Sakers was based on the basis of one unverified estimation which estimated the numbers of Sakers in Mongolia as high as 20,000 individuals. Although there are no immediate threats to the Saker population, the Ministry of Nature and the Environment of Mongolia is concerned with the increasing number of illegal smuggling attempts. In 1997 a total of 43 Saker Falcons were confiscated by Customs and released back to the wild.

A restricted number of Saker Falcons are legally exported each year under license. In 1994, 80 falcons were exported; in 1995 a further 80, in 1996, 20 falcons, and in 1997 150 falcons were exported, mainly to Saudi Arabia and Kuwait.

Mongolian Sakers are protected in a wide network of strict Nature Reserves covering approximately 20% of Mongolian territory. In addition, the hunting, trapping and taking from the wild of all Mongolian birds of prey is prohibited. Currently the Ministry is planning to expand the current research and work out new policies more adjusted to the wildlife needs of Sakers.

REFERENCES.

ABDUNAZAROV, B.B. 1990. The expert estimation of rare raptor numbers in Uzbekistan. In: *Rare and little-studied birds of Middle Asia.* Proceedings of III Rep. Ornithological. Conf. Bukhara, Oct. 1990. :57-60.(In Russian).
BATJARGAL, Z. & A. ENKHABAT 1998. *Biological Diversity of Mongolia.* Ulanbaatar.
BARANOV, A.A. 1989. The Saker Falcon in the Tannu-Ola and Tsagan-Shibetu mountains In: *Fauna, ecology and zoogeography of vertebrates and Arthropoda.* Novosibirsk: 75-82.
GALUSHIN, V.M. 1971. Numbers and territorial distribution of birds of prey of the European Center of the USSR. Proceedings of Oka State Nature Reserve. Issue VIII. Works of Central Orn. Station, 3. Moscow, Lesnaya Promyshlennost: 3-132. Saker Falcon on : 85-86.
DEMENTIEV, G.P. 1970. On Zoological expedition of 1959 y. in the Gobi desert, Mongolian People's Rep. In: *Wildlife of Turkmenia. Ashkhabad*, "Ylym" Publ. P.44-57. (In Russian).
DEMENTIEV, G.P. & O. SHAGDARSUREN 1964. On the Mongolian Saker and the taxonomic position of the Altay Gyrfalcon. Archives of Zoological Museum Moscow University. Moscow 9: 3-37. (In Russian).
FOX, N., C. EASTHAM & H. MACDONALD 1997. *ERWDA Handbook of falcon protocols.* ERWDA.
KOZLOVA, YE. V. 1930. Birds of the South-Western Trans-Baikalia, Northern Mongolia and Central Gobi. Ac. of Sc. of the USSR. Materials of Commission on Study of Mongolia and Tuva People's Republics and Buryat-Mongolian ASSR. (In Russian).
KOZLOVA, YE. V. 1932. Birds of the high-elevation Khangai by observations of zoological detachment of Mongolian expedition 1929. L., Publ. House of the USSR Ac Sc. *Proc. of Mongolian Commission N3.* 93 p. (In Russian).
KOZLOVA, YE. V. 1940. General review of ornithofauna of the Central Asia. Izvestiya VGO *Proc. of All-Union Geogr. Soc.72* (4-5): 679-689. (In Russian).
KOZLOVA E. V. 1969. Systematic relationship between Saker and Gyrfalcons and possible history of their distribution. *Zool. Zhurlal* 58(12): 1838-1850. (In Russian).
KUROCHKIN, YE. N. & K.YE. MIKHAILOV 1994. Breeding avifauna of the Gobi territory of Mongolia. Sovremennaya ornitologiya 1992 M., "Nauka" Publ.: 50-75. (In Russian).
LIKHACHEV, G. N. 1957. An essay on breeding of large birds of prey in the broad-leaved forest. In : Proceedings of II Baltic conference, Moscow.
OSTAPENKO, V.A., V.M.GAVRILOV, A. BOLD, & N. TSEVENMYADAG 1977. Ecology-faunistical studies of birds in Mongolia Abstracts of VII All-Union Ornithological. Conf.. Part 1. Kiev: 92-94. (In Russian).
POLOZOV, S.A. 1983. Falconiformes of Western Kopetdag. In: Galushin, V. - ed. [Ecology of Birds of Prey]. M., "Nauka" Publ.: 134-136.
POTAPOV, R.L. 1986. On ornithofauna of Mongolian Altai and adjoining areas. In: Potapov R.L. (ed.). Distribution and biology of birds of the Altai and Far East. *Proc. of Zool. Inst 150*: 57-73. (In Russian).
PROKOFIEV, S.M. & YU.I. KUSTOV 1988. Rare and endangered bird species of Khakasia and their conservation. In: Rare terrestrial vertebrates of Siberia. Proceedings. of Symposium, Shushenskoe 17-21 March, 1986. Novosibirsk: 180-185.
ROGACHEVA, E.V., E.E. SYROECHKOVSKIY, D.YU. ALEKSANDROV, KH. SUKHBAT, M.A. ZHUKOV & N. GANBATAR 1988. Materials on bird fauna of Darkhat (Northern Mongolia). Materials on fauna of Middle Siberia and adjoining regions of Mongolia: 166-174. (In Russian).
RYABTSEV, V. V. 1997. Saker Falcon in the Baikal Region. Russian Journal of Ornithology, Express issue 10: 3-14. (In Russian).
SMIRENSKIY, S.M., D. SUMYAA & TS. BOLDBAATOR 1991. Ornithological investigations in Dornod, Almak Mongolian People's Republic. *Ornitologiya.* M., Moscow Univ. Press. 25: 116-126. (In Russian).
STEPANYAN, L.S., A. BOLD & V.E. FOMIN 1988. Taxonomical list of birds of the Mongolian People's Republic. *Ornitologiya 23*: 26-35. (In Russian).
SHAGDARSUREN, O. 1964. Birds of Prey of the Central and Southern parts of Mongolia and their practical significance Unpublished PhD thesis. Abstract. Moscow 19 p. (In Russian).
SIMAKOV, G.N. 1998. Falconry and cult of birds of prey in the Middle Asia. Pererburgskoe Vostokovedenie, St. Petersurg. (In Russian).
SONDOM, N. & A. YANSHIN 1990. National Atlas of the Mongolian People's Republic. Ulan-Baatar, Moscow.

SUSHKIN, P.P. 1915. Trip in south-eastern and southern part of the Russian Altai and North-Western Mongolia and notes about birds of this area. *Ornitologicheskiy 4*: 273-289. (In Russian, Engl. summ.).
TUGARINOV, A.YA. 1932. Birds of Eastern Mongolia by observations of expedition of the year 1928. Proceedings of the Mongolian Commission of the Academy of Sciences of the USSR. Academia of Sciences Publishers 1: 46. (In Russian).
ZABELIN, V.I. 1993. Taxonomic list of birds of the Ubsu-Nur depression. Kyzyl. 94 p. (In Russian).

Damdinsuren Shijirmaa and Samdangiin Banzragch
Ministry of Nature and the Environment
Baga toiruu 44
Ulaanbaatar - 11, Mongolia.

Nicholas C. Fox and Eugene Potapov
National Avian Research Center (Abu Dhabi)
Penllynin Farm, College Road,
Carmarthen SA33 5EH
Wales, UK

The Saker Falcon *Falco cherrug* in the Kyrgyz Republic

Erin J. Gott, Helen J. Macdonald and Nick C. Fox

ABSTRACT

In 1997 the Central Administrative Board of Hunting of the Republic of Kyrgyzstan and the National Avian Research Center, Abu Dhabi, NARC initiated a monitoring project to undertake research on the biology of the Saker Falcon in the Kyrghyz Republic. The Republic is mountainous: over half is above 3000m, and the resident Saker population is thought to be of the subspecies *F.c. coatsi*. Sakers also migrate across the country to and from breeding grounds further north. As part of NARC's Falcon Programme on species of falcons used or affected by Arab falconry, the project is investigating the numbers and distribution of the Saker in the Kyrgyz Republic, with the aim of permanently conserving this species in the future. The project also seeks to obtain data for other NARC projects in the falcon programme, including behavioural and breeding data on the Saker Falcon, morphometric data and biomedical samples such as blood and feathers. These samples will be analysed for both pesticide and heavy metal contamination, and will also be used for genetic analysis. This paper presents the results from the first field season, 1998.

INTRODUCTION

The breeding range of the Saker Falcon *Falco cherrug* extends throughout most of Central Asia, but information on the status of the Saker in Kyrgyzstan is minimal. At the beginning of this century it was described as abundant (Sushkin 1908), but more recent investigations have described the population as suffering a decline during the 1970s and 1980s due to increased disturbance and, to a lesser extent, the taking of young birds for falconry (Shalna & Sorokin 1981, Vorobyov & Shukarov 1985). Estimates for a total breeding population in the Lake Issyk-kul area have been given as 12-15 pairs (Shalna & Sorokin 1981, Galushin and Pereva 1983).

In June 1997 The National Avian Research Center, Abu Dhabi, signed a Research Agreement with the Central Administrative Board of Hunting of the Republic of Kyrgyzstan to undertake a collaborative research programme on the status, productivity and biology of the Saker Falcon in Kyrgyzstan. A team of local biologists were trained in fieldwork techniques in November 1997. The first field expedition took place from 1 May - 15 June 1998, with a local team joined by fieldworker Erin Gott.

KYRGYZSTAN

Kyrgyzstan occupies an area of approximately 198,500 km^2. Bordered on the north by Kazakhstan, on the west by Uzbekhistan, on the east by China and on the south by Tajikistan, 94% of the country is mountainous. Around 40% of the country is 3000m or above, with three-quarters permanently under snow and glaciers. The dominant geographical feature is the Tian Shan range, running southeast to south-west, defining a natural border between Kyrgyzstan and China. The mountains of the Pamir-Altai system occupy its southern part.

Habitat types vary considerably, from the hot deserts of the southwestern Osh and Kazarman areas to moist coniferous woodland in the northeastern Karakol. The Lake Issyk-Kul area varies between these two climatic types and vegetation type may change from desert to mountain steppe within a twenty minute drive. The lake itself, 170km long and 70km across, is 700m deep.

Kyrgyzstan has a population of approximately 5 million. In the summer, rural families and their livestock move to the mountain steppe, known locally as the jilo, until winter weather forces them back to the villages. The average monthly wage is approximately US $25. Peregrines *Falco peregrinus* are not recorded as breeding in Kyrgyzstan, although there is a small population of Red-naped Shaheen *F. babylonicus*.

STUDY AREA

The 1998 study area was composed mainly of the area around Lake Issyk-Kul and adjacent jilos. This area was described as a traditional Saker breeding area by local people. The western end of Lake Issyk-kul (Balykchy) has an elevation of 1600m and is 195km from Bishkek. This area shows the most open landscape around the perimeter of the lake, mainly desert with craggy mountains and hills. The rest of the lake is surrounded by mountains exceeding 4000m. A single trip was also made into high altitude jilo around At-Bashy.

METHODS

Nest sites were discovered by the presence of faecal stains, perched or flying adults, screaming chicks or by local knowledge of sites previously used by Sakers. If a site looked active, but adult falcons or chicks appeared absent, then a closer look was taken by gaining a direct vantage point on an adjacent cliff or hill and/or searching for prey remains at the base of the nesting cliff. If no results were found at a nest site traditionally used by Sakers, then the site was recorded as empty. Once a nest was discovered to be used by breeding Sakers, the age and number of young within were assessed through direct observation by spotting scope or binoculars. The location and altitude of all active and inactive nests were recorded using a Magellan 2000 Global Positioning System (GPS). Nest coordinates were marked on 1:50,000 regional air charts. Each nest was given an id code based on the name of the study area and the number of the nest: eg. the first nest found in study area Clara has the id code *Clara nest 1* (CN1).

For each nest we recorded the amount and type of vegetation, distance to water, height and aspect of cliff and nest, distance to nearest source of prey, possible disturbances and nest type. Prey remains and pellets were collected and analysed visually.

Clutch size was recorded and, where possible, the number of fledged chicks per nest. A series of morphometric measurements were taken from chicks as described in the ERWDA Handbook of Falcon Protocols. (Fox *et al*, 1997) The age of chicks was estimated using reference photographs from the Handbook, and chicks were sexed by comparing their measurements with tabulated values in the Handbook. Blood smears were taken for later biochemical study. Young birds were fitted with leg rings and passive integrated transponders (microchips). Blood samples were taken from the brachial vein for later genetic, pesticide and biomedical analysis.

RESULTS

Of 35 traditional Saker nests, 5 were occupied by breeding Sakers. Three of these 5 nests were found in separate traditional study areas around Lake Issyk-kul. The 3 Issyk-Kul nests were similar, with variations in surrounding vegetation percentage and type. Nest AN1 near Balykchy was located in semi-desert and BN1 and CN1 were found in mountain steppe 'jilo' type habitat. All three were found at approximately the same altitude, between 1778 and 2125m. Each active nest was found within a cluster of abandoned traditional nests. The nearest inter-nest distance for the nests we found was 47.1km (AN1-BN1); the greatest 178.6km (BN1-CN1). The two remaining active nests were found in the Ak-Say Study area (DN1 and DN2) with an internest distance of 15.9km. Nests DN1 and DN2 were found in high altitude mountain steppe (3528m and 3405m) where the dominant vegetation was short grass. At night temperatures at these nests dropped below zero, with frequent snow, before climbing to 23-25 degrees during the day.

Abandoned nest sites appeared similar to the active sites. Habitat type does not seem therefore to be a limiting factor for the breeding Saker population in Kyrgyzstan.

Feeding Ecology

Low altitude nests AN1, BN1 and CN1 showed a variety of avian prey remains, most of which were of Rock Dove (*Columba livia*) and Chukar (*Alectoris chukar*), Jackdaw (*Corvus monedula*) and small, unidentified birds. 25 - 50% of castings recovered from these similar sites were of mammalian origin. Rock Doves, Chukars, Jackdaws and small birds were abundant around these sites. Nests DN1 & DN2 were found in high altitude mountain steppe at approximately 4000m above sea level. 13 castings were collected from DN1, 5 of which were mammalian in origin, with remaining castings composed primarily of Red-billed Chough (*Pyrrhocorax pyrrhocorax*). Prey remains were also mainly of Red-billed Chough, the only exceptions being Rock Dove and 1 young marmot skin. Of 17 castings collected from DN2 only 4 were mammalian in origin, the remainder composed mainly of Red-billed Chough and Rock Dove. Red-billed Chough remains were also well-represented at this nest site, with few Rock Dove and other small bird remains. There appeared to be fewer prey available at Ak-cy compared to Issyk-kul. Pigeons, Ravens (*Corvus corax*), and marmots were the commonest species seen. Wing remains of Red-billed Choughs found at sites DN1 and DN2 were of full-grown birds rather then newly-fledged and inexperienced corvids (Bagyura, Haraszthy & Szitta 1994).

Table 1 Prey from 5 Saker nests

Common name	Scientific name	Prey remains	Nest
BIRDS			
Rock Dove	*Columba livia*	18	AN1, BN1, CN1, DN1, DN2
Chukar	*Alectoris chukar*	5	AN1, BN1, CN1
Collared Dove	*Streptopelia decaocto*	1	AN1
Jackdaw	*Corvus monedula*	1	BN1
Red-billed Chough	*Pyrrhocorax pyrrhocorax*	22	DN1, DN2
Carrion Crow	*Corvus corone*	1	BN1
Unidentified small birds	-	17	AN1, BN1, CN1, DN1, DN2
Total		65	
MAMMALS			
Red-tailed Jird	*Meriones erythrourus*	1	AN1
Bobby Marmot	*Marmota bobac*	2	DN1, DN2
Unidentified		16	AN1, BN1, CN1, DN1, DN2
Total		19	

Quantifying diets using prey remains and pellets can result in a bias in favour of avian prey (Bagyura, Haraszthy & Szitta 1994). However, it appears from this initial survey that the diet of Sakers in Kyrgyzstan does differ from that of Sakers in Kazakstan and Mongolia. There was little evidence of a single major prey base supporting the breeding population, and Kyrgyzstan's prey base seems to be largely avian. 76.5% of collected prey remains were avian species, while 40% of castings were mammalian. Differences between sites also showed a strong difference between diets in two habitat types used by Sakers in Kyrgyzstan. Prey remains appeared to be periodically cleared from nests by the adult Sakers, a phenomenon previously reported in Hungary (Bagyura, Haraszthy & Szitta 1994).

Breeding Ecology

The 5 nests held a total of 19 chicks, 10 male, 6 female and 3 unsexed, of which 15 fledged successfully (see Table 2). Hatch date was around 1 May. One nest contained 3-5 day old chicks on 4 May and another contained 42-45 day old chicks on 14 June, with some variation either side of this date. It was difficult to assess chick mortality as 3 of the 5 nests were found after the chicks were 30 days old. Of the 5 nests, chicks from AN1 and BN1 fledged successfully and recently-fledged chicks were found at DN2. All the 6 chicks at nests CN1 and DN1 were close to fledging when last seen. No unhatched eggs were found within any of the nests. Four unrelated Saker chicks, one from each of the 4 nests, were sampled for DNA and pesticide analysis. At the time of writing, initial results show that no blood parasites were present in the samples taken.

Table 2. Numbers of chicks in each successful nest surveyed

Nest	Male	Female	Unsexed	Total fledged
AN1	2	3		5
BN1	1		3	1 male (rest stolen)
CN1	3	1		3
DN1	2	1		3
DN2	2	1		3 (in very poor condition)
Total:	**10**	**6**	**3**	**15**

Evidence of illegal trapping was plentiful. Chicks from BN1 were presumed stolen. On May 5, BN1 held four 10-12 day old chicks. On May 26, only a single male chick remained. We found signs of human interference. Nest DN2 contained three recently-fledged chicks, one of which was seen perched in an inaccessible site near the nest. The remaining chicks were found on the ground short distances from the nest. These chicks were near to starvation, could be picked up without protest, and were approximately 200g lower in body mass than an average chick of their ages. Although the chicks were in very poor physical condition, their overall plumage was in fair condition; they showed relatively few 'stress marks' on their feathers. The adult male falcon was present at the nesting cliff but we did not see the female.

PROBLEMS AND DISCUSSION

The falcon trade

The falcon trade has become a severe problem for Kyrgyzstan's nesting raptor populations. After the fall of the Soviet Union, Kyrgyzstan and Kazakhstan were the first of the newly independent CIS countries to openly welcome foreign trade and travel. As the demand for falconry birds rose in the oil-rich Middle East and the rumour of high prices being paid for 'wild' birds reached the CIS, it took little time for the Kyrgyz people to begin 'harvesting' falcons with the prospect of getting rich. There were also rumours of people shooting raptors and trying to sell them. We were informed that a small population of breeding Sakers near Nyrin had been wiped out by such persecution. The biggest problem is thought to come from people robbing nests of both eggs and chicks, and trapping adults, primarily the female. Females are much preferred as falconry birds in the Middle East because they are larger than males. There are local reports of single male Sakers returning to traditional nest sites. The taking of adult birds, and especially female birds, exerts a far greater pressure on the population than the taking of juvenile birds on migration, the traditional source of falcons for Arab falconry.

The field team was approached on three occasions by local people selling falcons. On the first occasion the 'falcon' was in fact a Long-legged Buzzard (*Buteo rufinus*) kept in a chicken pen in a back yard. The second was an immature Saker just beginning its first moult. Kept in a wood shed, this falcon's asking price was $3000 USD. We were told by the owner that an Arab had looked at the falcon that day and was likely to buy it. The third occasion, we were approached by a man who told us he had 5 chicks from 2 different nests for sale. By the time we got around to looking at them, we were told that they had all died, but that he could probably get more.

Because the average Kyrgyz has little or no knowledge of raptors, Sakers are not the only birds suffering from this trade. Many different species of raptors are trapped and offered for sale. The problem is exacerbated by poor husbandry, leading to high mortality in trapped birds.

In conclusion, neither habitat nor prey base appear to be a limiting factor for the breeding Saker population in Kyrgyzstan. Pressure on the population by illegal trapping appears to be the main factor affecting the Saker, and, by association, other raptors in this country.

REFERENCES

BAGYURA, J., L. HARASZTHY & T. SZITTA 1994. Feeding Biology of the Saker Falcon *Falco cherrug* in Hungary. *In* Meyburg, B-U. & R.D. Chancellor (eds). *Raptor Conservation Today*, WWGBP/ The Pica Press: 397-401.
BAUMGART, W.1991. *The Saker Falcon*, (English translation by Nigel Barton), der neue Brehm-Bucherei, Berlin.
FOX, N.C., C.P. EASTHAM & H.J. MACDONALD 1997. *ERWDA Handbook of Falcon Protocols*. ERWDA, Carmarthen.
GALUSHIN, V.M. & V.J. PERERVA 1983. Status of Rare Raptors in the USSR. W.W.G.B.P., Bull. Nr. 1: 212-214.
SHALNA, A.A. & A.G. SOROKIN 1981. On rare species of birds of prey of the Issyk-Kul depression. *Ecology and conservation of birds: abstracts of VIII All-Union Ornithological Conference*, Kishinev: 237.
SUSHKIN, 1908. *Birds of the Mid-Kirghiz Steppes*. Moscow.
VOROBYOV G.G. & E.D. SHUKAROV (eds.)1985. Birds: *Red Data book of Kirghiz SSR*, Frunze: 33-56.

Erin J. Gott, Helen J. Macdonald & Nick C. Fox
National Avian Research Center (Abu Dhabi)
The Falcon Facility
Penllynin Farm
College Road
Carmarthen SA33 5EH
Wales, UK

Chancellor, R. D. & B.-U. Meyburg eds. 2000
Raptors at Risk
WWGBP / Hancock House

The Saker Falcon in European Russia

Vladimir Galushin and Valery Moseikin

INTRODUCTION

The world Saker population in the early 1980's was assessed as 35,000-45,000 pairs (Baumgart, 1991). The number of Sakers in Europe was roughly estimated as 400-600 pairs (Tucker & Heath, 1994). The precise number of Sakers in Russia is unknown. At the beginning of the 1980's it was supposed to be "probably not less than 1000 pairs" (Red Data Book, 1983). Within European Russia (west of the Urals) the Saker population was likely to be between 80 and 150 pairs (Tucker & Heath, 1994) or about 100 pairs (Galushin, 1994, 1995).

The Saker Project started in European Russia in 1997 and continued in 1998 with the support by NARC (Abu Dhabi, UAE) and the Falcon Facility (Wales, UK) as a part of the overall Saker Eurasian Project (Fox,1995; Fox & Eastham, 1996; Fox *et al.*, 1996). Its major objectives for European Russia were:

(1) to survey the Saker breeding range and populations within European Russia;
(2) to assess the current state of nesting and feeding habitats for the Saker in the region.
(3) to study Saker migrations in the south of European Russia.
(4) to reveal present and potential threats to the Saker in the region.
(5) to disseminate up-to-date knowledge on the species' status in the country in order to arouse people's awareness.

METHODOLOGY

Saker populations were assessed by two major methods: (1) surveys by mobile teams and (2) precise studies of the promising former and potential nesting sites of the species within the breeding range.

Two large regions were selected, namely the Don river basin (over 450,000 km^2) and between the Lower Volga and Ural rivers (340,000 km^2). Data on former records of Saker breeding found in literature and archives were studied, compiled and mapped. Reliable records by experienced local game-keepers, hunters and bird watchers were also taken into account. According to Sakers' behaviour and other particular indications, three categories of records have been accepted:

(1) proved nesting area - active nest with eggs or young found;
(2 presumed nesting area - Sakers repeatedly recorded during one breeding season at one site, hunting or defence behaviour, sighting of fledglings, proved nesting one-two years back.
(3) questionable area - isolated records of Sakers, reliable information from local game-keepers, hunters and bird watchers.

RESULTS

Don River Basin

This occupies over 450,000 km^2, which is almost 1/5 of European Russia and encompasses 14 administrative regions (some of them partly). At the beginning of the 20th century the entire Don river basin was a part of the Saker breeding range and covered 2/3 of the latter within European Russia. Six spring and summer surveys in 1997 embraced 11 regions west of the Lower Volga river. In 1998 two areas within the Don river basin were surveyed.

Totally 35,000 - 50,000 km^2 or about 10% of the Don basin were presumed to be potentially suitable for Sakers, due to their favourite combination of both nesting (forest edges, wood groves, river cliffs or high pylons of electric power lines) and hunting habitats (suslik colonies as most preferable food and also rook aggregations).

In 1997 10 Saker breeding areas, including the only proved one with a living nest, were recorded while in 1998 only 4 nesting areas were noted. So the average density of Saker populations was 0.55 (1997) - 0.25 (1998) pairs per 1000 km^2 of potential nesting habitats. Extrapolation allows one to suppose that 20-30 Saker pairs in 1997 and 10-15 pairs in 1998 inhabited almost 0.5 mln km^2 of the entire Don basin. The Saker breeding range lost at least three nesting "islands" in one year. Populations of susliks also continue to decrease, however some local specialists still expect some kind of population recovery for susliks in a south-eastern part of European Russia.

Volga-Ural Inter-rivers

This covers 5 administrative regions and occupies 340,000 km^2 between the Volga and Ural rivers. Two surveys were performed in 1997 and one in 1998 by mobile teams. Potential Saker habitats roughly composed 120,000 km^2 or about 30% of the entire Volga-Ural inter-river area.

In 1997 22 Saker breeding areas (5 proven ones with active nests) and in 1998 24 areas (10 proven) were recorded there. The average population density was 0.92 (1997) and 0.96 (1998) pairs per 1000 km^2 of potential nesting habitats and a total number was assumed at 100-120 pairs of Sakers between the Volga and Ural rivers.

Total European Russia

The Saker population status and trends differ in the western (Don river basin) and eastern (Volga-Ural inter-rivers) parts of the region. In short, in the west populations the breeding range is decreasing, while in the east Sakers are relatively stable at a low level. The recent position of Saker populations throughout the whole of European Russia is as follows:-

	Don River Basin	Volga-Ural inter-rivers	European Russia
Former breeding range (km^2)	450,000	340,000	790,000
Potential nesting habitats within the whole areas (km^2)	40,000	120,000	160,000
The same (%)	9	35	20
Actual breeding range (km^2)	9,000	40,000	ca.50,000
Number of breeding pairs recorded in 1997	10	22	32
The same in 1998	4	24	28
Density within surveyed potential nesting habitats (pairs/1000 km^2)	0.25	0.96	0.68
Density within former breeding range (pairs/1000 km^2)	0.02	0.32	0.15
Total population over whole areas (pairs)	12	110	ca.120
The same in limits (pairs)	10-15	100-120	110-140

The total number of Sakers was assessed as *ca.*120 pairs which is more or less the same as in 1997. Predictions are bad for the Don river basin where Saker populations will continue to decline but rather favourable for the Volga-Ural inter-rivers where stability is expected.

Autumn Migrations

The North-Caucasus autumn migration route for raptors is well known. However Sakers are very scarce there. Special observations were carried out 12-19 September 1998 in vicinities of Kislovodsk city at the northern foothills of a central part of the Caucasus mountains. In one week three Sakers were recorded flying south-west along the foothills, whereas hundreds of other raptors migrated daily. That scarcity of migrating Sakers supports the conclusion that the nesting Saker population in European Russia is very small. The raptor migration study to the south of the Caucasus ridge was similar. From 26 August till 29 October 1997 only 11 Sakers were recorded, comprising 0.009% out of over 120,000 raptors (Abuladze, 1998). As for wintering places to the south of the Caucasus ridge, Alexander Abuladze recorded only 4 Sakers through December 1998.

In general the autumn migration of Sakers in 1998 was tiny in the south of European Russia.

Breeding Range

The first result of the Project was a clear picture of overall shrinkage and fragmentation of the Saker breeding range in Eastern Europe during the last 20-30 years.

All handbooks on raptors (Dementiev & Gladkov, 1951; Brown & Amadon, 1968; Baumgart, 1978; Cramp & Simmons, 1980; Cade, 1982) including recent editions (Baumgart, 1991; del Hoyo *et al.*,1994; Snow & Perrins, 1998) show a continuous breeding range of the Saker Falcon stretching over 1 mln km^2 of the southern half of European Russia and Ukraine. It embraces, for example, the entire basin of the Don river. However only single Sakers were met there along thousands of km of survey roads. Recent surveys made it apparent that the present breeding range is quite fragmented and formed of separated areas, localities and even individual nesting sites. Today it looks spotty and is unlikely to exceed 50,000 km^2 (about 10,000 km^2 in the Don river basin and 40,000 km^2 within the Volga-Ural inter-rivers), that is 20 times less than the former range 30-50 years ago.

Threats and Conservation

The Saker population crash in Russia was caused by habitat destruction, human disturbance, lack of ready-made nests and most of all by the heavy pressure of illegal taking and smuggling of the best birds. According to some official data in the autumn of 1997 alone, over 300 Sakers were confiscated by customs at Russian airports (mostly in Siberia). Therefore a total number of smuggled Sakers in 1997 was probably close to 1000 birds. However in 1998 smuggling of Sakers decreased: less than 50 people (mostly Syrians) were stopped at the customs with falcons. For the first time in Russia four men were sentenced as Saker smugglers. There is some hope that the customs in Russia have become more watchful for illegal trade in falcons including Sakers.

As for the lack of nests constructed by ravens or raptors on trees or other suitable places during the last decade, Sakers demonstrate remarkable adaptability to nesting on electricity pylons (Piluga, 1991) and other artificial sites. These recent adaptations promoted a significant increase in the Saker population over huge areas in Mongolia, very rich in food but poor in nesting sites (Potapov *et al.*, 1999).

For European Russia a major cause of the Saker population decline was the almost overall decrease and local disappearance of its principle food namely two species of susliks (*Citellus citellus* and *C.pygmaeus*). This could have resulted from natural phenomena like changes in climate, growing more humid and warm. In turn, that led to grass growing tall and dense and less acceptable for susliks. At the same time the recent collapse in agriculture led to a sharp decrease in live-stock and grazing pressure on pastures, which finally also overgrew with tall and dense grass and shrubs, accelerating further shrinkage of suitable suslik habitats. The very existence and, moreover, probable recovery of the Saker populations and range could be possible only if susliks restore their previous numbers through forest-steppe areas of European Russia.

ACKNOWLEDGEMENTS

The authors are sincerely thankful to NARC and the Falcon Facility, to the Project supervisors and managers, namely Mr. Mohamed Al Bowardi, Dr. Nick Fox, Dr. Chris Eastham, Dr. Eugeny Potapov, Ms. Helen Macdonald and all those who helped, encouraged and favoured the Project's implementation.

REFERENCES

ABULADZE, A.A. 1998. Daten zum Greifvogelzug Herbst 1997. In *Georgien. Ornithologische Mitteilungen*, N 12, pp.369-371.
BAUMGART, W. 1978. *Der Sakerfalke*. Die Neue Brehm-Bucherei. A. Ziemsen Verlag, Wittenberg.
BAUMGART, W. 1991. *Der Sakerfalke*. Die Neue Brehm-Bucherei. A. Ziemsen Verlag, Wittenberg.
BROWN, L. & D. AMADON 1968. *Eagles, Hawks and Falcons of the World*. Vol. 1 and 2. Country Life Books, Great Britain.
CADE, T. 1982. *The Falcons of the World*. Cornell Univ. Press.
CRAMP, S. & K.E.L. SIMMONS (Eds) 1980. *The Birds of the Western Palearctic*. Vol.2. Oxford University Press.
DEL HOYO, J., A. ELLIOTT & J. SARGATAL (eds.) 1994. *Handbook of the birds of the world*. Vol.2. New world vultures to guineafowl. Lynx Editions, Barcelona.
DEMENTIEV, G.P. & N.A. GLADKOV 1951. [*Birds of the Soviet Union*]. Vol.1. "Sovetskaya Nauka", Moscow. [In Russian]
FOX, N. 1995. The National Avian Research Centre Falcon Programme. Middle East Falcon Research Group. Proceedings of the Specialist Workshop, Abu Dhabi, United Arab Emirates, pp.57-60
FOX, N.C. & C.P. EASTHAM 1996. The conservation programme on the Saker Falcon (*Falco cherrug*) in Kazakhstan, Mongolia, Pakistan and the Middle East. 2nd International Conference on Raptors. Abstracts, p.129. Urbino, Italy
FOX, N.C., C.P. EASTHAM & H.J. MCDONALD 1996. The Middle East Falcon research group. 2nd International Conference on Raptors. Abstracts, p.132. Urbino, Italy
GALUSHIN, V.M. 1994. Long-term changes in birds of prey populations within European Russia and neighbouring countries. *Bird Numbers 1992*. E.J.M.Hagemeijer, T.J.Verstrael (Eds). Statistics Netherlands, Voorburg/Heerlen. Pp.139-141
GALUSHIN, V.M. 1995. [Recent population status of rare raptors in European Russia. 2nd International Proceedings tributed to Professor V.V.Stanchinsky, Vol.2.] Smolensk. Pp.12-17 [In Russian]
PILUGA, V.I. 1991. [New data on nesting of rare and threatened birds of the Odessa region and neighbouring areas. Rare birds along the Black Sea]. Kiev-Odessa, pp.139-164 [In Russian]
POTAPOV, E., S. BANZRAGH & D. SHIJIRMAA 1999. The paradox of industrialisation in Mongolia: expansion of Sakers into flat areas is dependent on industrial activity. *Falco* 13, pp.10-12
[RED DATA BOOK OF RSFSR. ANIMALS.] 1983. N.V.Eliseev (Chief Editor), Rosselkhozisdat, Moscow [In Russian]
SNOW, D.W. & C.M. PERRINS (Eds.) 1998. *The Birds of the Western Palearctic*. Concise edition. Vol.1 and 2. Oxford Univ. Press.
TUCKER, G.M. & M.F. HEATH 1994. *Birds in Europe: their conservation status*. Cambridge, U.K. BirdLife International.

Vladimir Galushin and Valery Moseikin
Russian Bird Conservation Union
Moscow and Saratov
Russia Shosse Enthuziastov, 60
111123 Moscow
Russia

Chancellor, R. D. & B.-U. Meyburg eds. 2000
Raptors at Risk
WWGBP / Hancock House

Are Peregrine Falcons in Northern Siberia still affected by organochlorines?

J.L. Quinn, Y. Kokorev, J. Prop, N. Fox and J.M. Black

ABSTRACT

Tundra-nesting Peregrine Falcons *Falco peregrinus calidus* in Northern Siberia are highly migratory. In the face of uncertainty about their exposure to pesticides on their wintering grounds, the breeding density and success of Peregrines on the Taymyr peninsula was monitored in1996-98. The number of occupied territories per 100 km of river surveyed in 1996-98 was 3-4 times higher on the Pyasina and Pura Rivers compared with similar data from the early 1970s. Egg hatching success and nest productivity from 12 occupied territories in 1996, 21 in 1997 and 15 in 1998 all suggested that the population is not currently obviously affected by pesticides. Blood plasma samples taken from 5 adult and 17 young birds were analysed for p,p-DDE, HEOD, p,pTDE, p,pDDT and the most toxic PCB congeners. Pesticides were virtually absent in three of the five adults. One of the remaining two had moderate levels of both PCBs and DDE while the fifth had moderate levels of DDE. There is no evidence to suggest that the Peregrine population in western Taymyr is currently adversely affected by pesticides, although nesting attempts may occasionally fail due to high pesticide loading amongst some individuals.

INTRODUCTION

Approximately 19 races of the Peregrine Falcon *Falco peregrinus* are distinguished world-wide. Five of these breed at high latitudes and are highly migratory. The breeding grounds of the migratory *F. p. calidus* race are in the Eurasian Arctic above 62°N and eastwards from the White Sea just east of the Fenno-Russian border (35°E) to the Lena Delta (130°E) (White & Boyce 1988). The remoteness of their breeding grounds has meant that there is little recent information concerning the population's biology and to what extent they are currently affected by pesticides.

Many of those Peregrine populations that were severely affected by pesticides in the 1960s and 1970s have now largely recovered (various studies in Cade *et al.*1988; Crick & Ratcliffe 1995) but there is still much concern for populations either breeding or wintering in many, predominantly third-world countries. Concern is justified on the basis of a lack of even a basic knowledge of some of these populations, coupled with the fact that organic pesticides are still widely used illegally. In Russia's 'Red Data Book', the Peregrine was listed as a rare species of special concern (Flint 1978).

Galushin (1977) stated that there was a general consensus in Russia that there had been a rapid decline in Peregrine populations throughout the USSR, although there are few data to demonstrate this. Kucheruk et al.(1975) found that six sites known to be occupied on the Yamal in the late 1930s were all empty in 1973. Significant egg-shell thinning was reported from Siberian eggs collected in the early 1960s and the presence of DDE in the shell membranes suggested the likely cause (Peakall & Kiff 1979).

There is little published information concerning the present status of Peregrines in Russia. Potapov (1996) sent a questionnaire to Peregrine workers throughout former member states of the USSR and found some evidence of a widespread decline, although he pointed out that monitoring was sporadic. Henny et al. (1994) found that presumed *calidus* Peregrines on the western edge of their range were breeding well and had variable, but low, levels of pesticides in 1991. Potapov (1994), however, recorded poor breeding success and high pesticide levels in a population of a different migratory race in eastern Siberia in the 1980s. In other parts of the world there is still evidence that organochlorine pesticides are affecting Peregrines. Egg shells from *F. p. tundrius* in Arctic Canada still have high levels of DDE which they get from prey on the wintering grounds in Central and South America where organic pesticides are poorly controlled (Johnstone et al. 1996).

In an attempt to assess the health of the *F. p. calidus* population in western Taymyr, their breeding density and success was studied from 1996-1998. The importance of this basic information is well illustrated by the statistics from Britain during the pesticide crash. Here territory occupancy in 1962 was down to 56% of the 1930-39 average, just 21% of territories produced young and fledging success was much reduced. To examine evidence for a long term change in the breeding density of Peregrines in Taymyr, we merge our data with those collected by others over the last 20 years and collated by Kokorev (1995). In addition, blood samples were taken from adult and young birds to determine levels of key pesticides, a less than ideal but nevertheless useful indication of likely pesticide levels in the eggshells themselves (Court et al. 1990; Johnstone et al. 1996).

STUDY AREA

The Taymyr Peninsula is the most northerly part of the Eurasian continent and stretches from 71° to 78° North, and 80° to 114° East. The study area was along 270 km of waterway in the Pura basin (including the Bystraya, Mala Bystraya, Buotangkaga tributaries) and 800 km of the Pyasina River (Fig. 1). The length covered in any one year varied. Taymyr shows the full range of geobotanical zones from polar desert to sub-arctic areas (Andreev & Aleksandrova 1981). Most of the study area is located in the southern Arctic zone of the tundra which is typically dissected by rivers and lakes flowing through loamy substrates. The upper reaches of the Pyasina River run through shrub tundra and, near Norilsk itself, the edge of the northern forests.

METHODS

Nest separation and density

Peregrines in most parts of the world usually nest near water (Ratcliffe 1993). This is supported by extensive surveys in Taymyr by one of us (YK). In parts of Alaska, however, it has recently been found that, as Peregrine density increased to levels higher than ever previously recorded, they began to occupy sub-optimal sites several kilometres from the river where they were once thought to be absent (T. Cade, *pers. comm.*). It is thought that densities in Taymyr are a lot lower than in Alaska and that such sub-optimal sites are not used in Taymyr. Searches for eyries in Taymyr were therefore limited to the banks of the main rivers and some of their tributaries.

Nest spacing and density estimates were calculated for 1997 when 1,050 km of river were surveyed. Locations where Peregrines were seen but where no nests were found were assumed to be territories where a nesting attempt had been made, if the habitat was suitable. Early-failed territories on the Pyasina may have been overlooked although on the Pura river, failed breeders normally stayed on their territories for most of the summer. To facilitate comparison of abundance found in other areas, territory spacing was estimated in three ways by calculating: 1) the distance travelled along the river (DAR) between nests (starting from the mouth of each river, heading upstream); 2) the straight line distance (SLD) between nests on any given river (distances were not calculated between nests on different rivers; map used had scale 1:100,000); and 3) the linear density, i.e. the number of pairs per 100 km surveyed.

Detailed information on Peregrine abundance before the pesticide era was not available. Using data collated by Kokorev (1995), it was possible to compare linear territory densities estimated in this study for the Pura and Pyasina Rivers separately with estimates from the 1970s and 1980s. An estimate was included only when more than 100 km of river was surveyed on any one river in a given year. Data from 1998 on the Pura and 1996 from the Pyasina were much less comprehensive than in other years and were excluded from the comparison. Mean annual lengths of river covered for each river basin were as follows: Pyasina (mean 322 km, range 170-542 km) and the Pura (mean 219 km, range 140-288 km). Additional data are presented from the Agapa, a tributary of the Pyasina, (mean 194 km, range 100-450 km).

Detailed information on individual territory occupancy in any given year for the study area was not available so territory occupancy in the usual sense of the phrase could not be calculated. It was known, however, where eyries have been located in the Pura basin at some stage during the last 25 years. Our estimate of territory occupancy, therefore, reflects the proportion of possible territories currently occupied rather than the proportion that have ever been occupied in any one year. It is perhaps best viewed as an indicator of whether the current population is close to carrying capacity. Possible territories had to be more than 3 km apart to be classified as separate territories; those less than 3 km apart were classified as alternative eyries within the same territory.

The key physical features of nest-sites selected by Peregrines were also described to help assess, albeit subjectively, whether density within the area was likely to be restricted by the availability of nest sites.

Breeding success

A sample of nests was checked during incubation to record clutch size when the rivers became ice-free in early July making travel by boat possible. Brood size was recorded close to fledging time in 1997 (from 7-19 August); in 1996 and 1998 it was recorded when the young were at least two weeks old (late July). Although the available evidence suggests that most nest mortality in Peregrines occurs during incubation and early brood-rearing (Ratcliffe 1993), Peregrines bred 2 weeks later in 1998 than in 1996. This may have had a significant impact on survival of young owing to reduced availability of prey in late seasons. Nesting success was expressed in terms of 1) the numbers of young per successful nest and 2) the number of young per occupied territory. The latter was a conservative estimate because it included territories in which no eggs were laid and territories in which only a single bird was recorded.

Pesticide analysis in blood lipids

Blood samples were taken from the brachial vein of five adult falcons and 17 nestling falcons (2-6 weeks old). Mammals are thought not to accumulate organochlorines which means that blood samples taken from the young of lemming specialists, like the Snowy Owl and the Rough-legged Buzzard, should make a good control for contamination from other sources (e.g. Johnstone *et al.* 1996). Blood samples were taken, therefore, from three Snowy Owl and two Rough-legged Buzzard chicks. These 1-1.5 ml blood samples were stored initially for 1-2 months in sealed heparinized containers and preserved with several drops of formalin solution. They were later sent for analysis to the Institute of Terrestrial Ecology, Monks Wood, using Gas Chromatography (GC) with Electron Capture Detector in four different batches. Full details of how the samples were prepared and cleaned can be obtained from ITE, Monks Wood or from the authors on request.

Within each batch, a duplicate sample of blood was spiked with each organochlorine tested (i.e. the analyte), with concentrations varying from 0.1 to 1 ug and percentage recoveries measured. The number of different organochlorines used in the first two batches collected in 1996 was 15 and 30 in

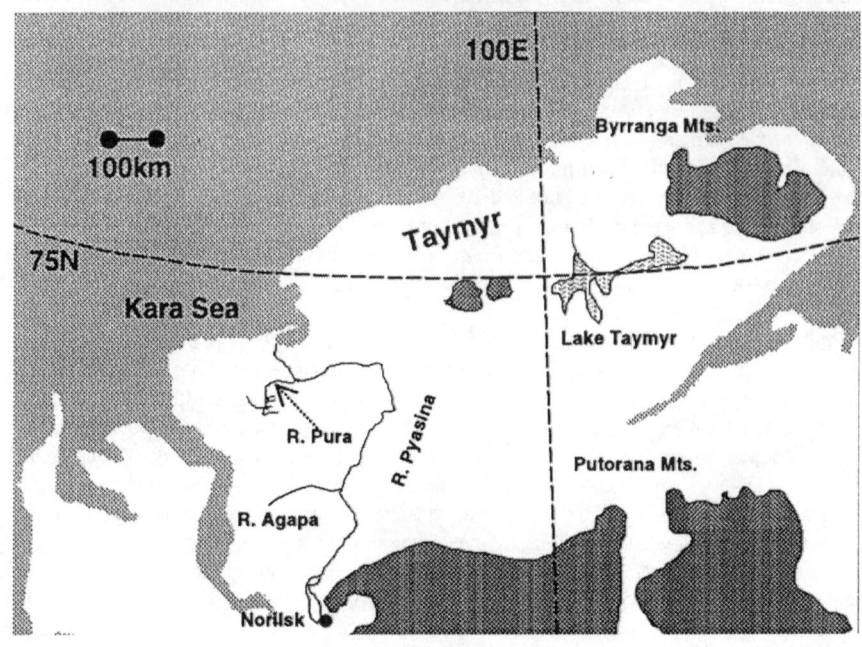

Figure 1. Map of the Taymyr Peninsula showing the location of the Pyasina, Pura and Agapa Rivers. The 100°E line of longitude and 75°N line of latitude are shown.

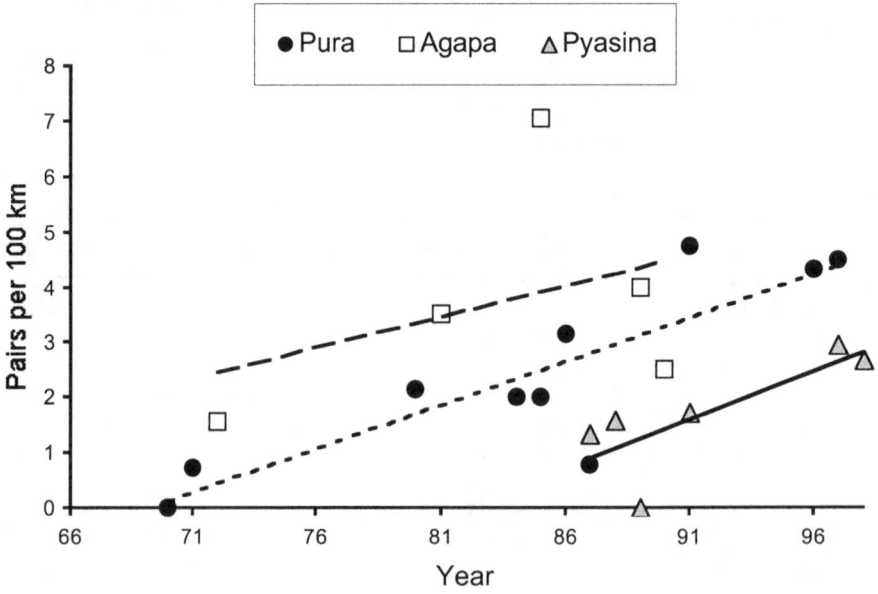

Figure 2. Numbers of occupied Peregrine territories per 100 km on the Pyasina, Pura and Agapa rivers in selected years over the period 1969 to 1997. The lines indicate the best-fit through the points.

the second two from 1997. A blank sample was spiked with each analyte which was then extracted and cleaned using the same procedure as for the real samples. Details of how the GC was calibrated and how the compounds were identified can be obtained from ITE, Monks Wood or from the authors. Individual Chlorobiphenyl congeners are numbered according to Ballschmitter and Zeil (1980) and include the primary list agreed for monitoring purposes by the International Council for the Exploration of the Sea (ICES). Limits of detection (LOD) were determined by analysing seven sample blanks and calculating the mean + 3 x standard deviations of the blank signals. LODs are expressed as total micrograms in the whole extract. For any given sample where an organochlorine was not detected, the LOD was calculated by dividing the given LOD for that compound by sample weight, the result representing the maximum level of that specific organochlorine that could have been in the sample but was not detected.

RESULTS

Territory spacing and occupancy

The average distance between occupied territories was 29.2 km along rivers or 3.37 territories per 100 km and 23.1 km in a straight line (Table 1). Territories were unevenly distributed within rivers. Large stretches held no eyries at all while others held clusters. Eyries on the Pura river were closer together (20.7 km) than on the Lower and Middle reaches of the Pyasina (36.1 km). There were no eyries on the Pyasina River south of 71°40'N to Norilsk, largely because the riverbanks were gently sloping and did not provide suitable habitat for Peregrine eyries. There was also considerable variation within each river, especially on the Pura where the DAR in section 1 was 7.2 km compared to 49 km on the rest of the river. One small stretch of the Pyasina held five pairs separated by an average DAR of 8 km compared to an average of 38 km for that whole section.

Table 1. Distance along rivers (DARs) and straight line distances between occupied Peregrine territories on the Pura River, selected tributaries and on the Pyasina River in 1997.

	Total	Pura Basin	Section 1	Section 2	Tributaries	Lower and Middle Pyasina River	Lower Pyasina	Middle Pyasina
Distance along river								
Mean (km)	29.2	20.7	7.2	49.0	19.3	36.1	35.4	38.0
Standard Error	4.7	6.3	2.5	13.9	7.2	6.5	8.3	9.8
Minimum	1	1.0	1	26.0	5.0	2.5	2.5	21
Maximum	90	74	16	74	28	90	90	66
Count	27	12	6	3	3	15	11	4
Straight line distance								
Mean (km)	23.1	15.6	6.3	34.5	15.3	27.6	27.9	26.8
Standard Error	4.2	4.9	2	14.8	5.5	6.0	7.2	12.2
Minimum	2	1	1	17.5	4.5	2	2	10
Maximum	80	64	13	64	22	80	80	63
Count	27	12	6	3	3	15	11	4

Of all eyries ever occupied in the Pura basin and lower Pyasina in the past, 60% were occupied in 1996 (n=20 territories checked), 63% in 1997 (n=24) and 67% in 1998 (n=15) (Table 2). The trends in number of pairs per 100 km were plotted against time for three rivers (Fig. 2). Data from at least two of the three rivers suggested an increasing trend in the breeding Peregrine population. In the Pura basin, there was less than 1 pair per 100 km in 1970 and 1971. By the early 1980s this

Figure 3. Features of Peregrine Falcon eyries in Taymyr, 1996-97.

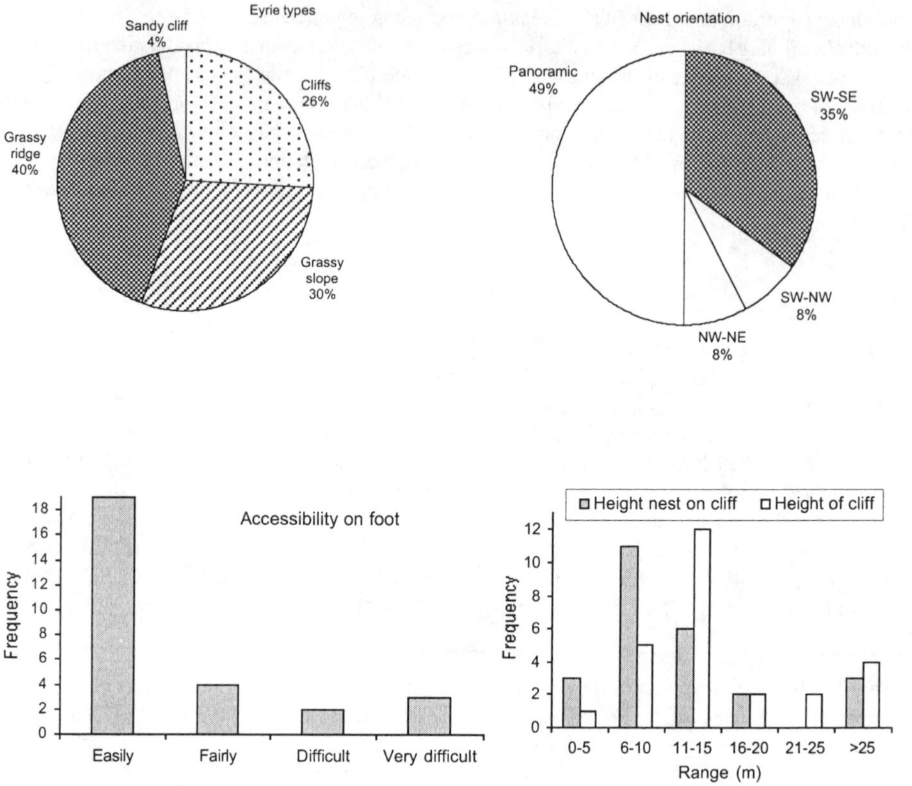

Figure 4. Breeding success of Peregrines in the Pura and Pyasina basins in 1996-98 (open circles, mean value, n = 3 years) compared with that found for other populations categorised into those thought to be depressed, recovering or close to normal (population status = 1, 2 or 3) as listed in Appendix 2.

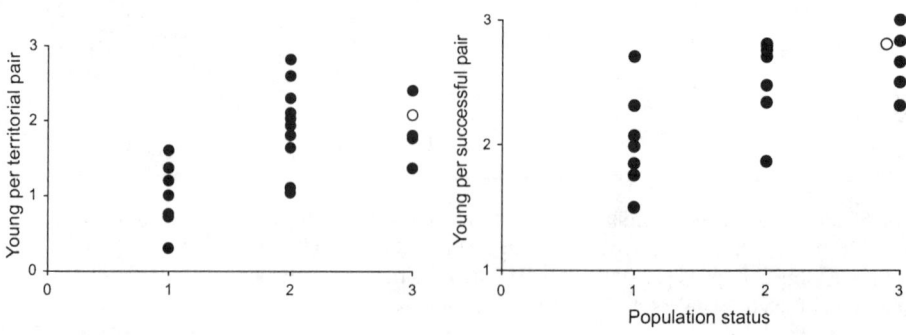

increased to just over 2 pairs per 100 km and to 4-5 pairs per 100 km by the 1990s. Data from the Pyasina were available only from the late 1980s when densities were very low - fewer than 2 pairs per 100 km - compared to the almost 3 pairs per 100 km recorded in 1997. Data from the Agapa are less numerous and clear-cut. The general trend is increasing but an exceptionally high density was recorded in 1985 when 13 territories were found along 184 km. In other years, 3-4 territories per 100-114 km were recorded so a likely explanation is that the extra 70 km of river or so surveyed in 1985 held an unusually high density. The very low density recorded in 1970 was likely to be an accurate estimate because 450 km of river yielding just seven territories were surveyed. Except for 1985, it seems that densities on the Agapa increased from 1-2 territories per 100 km in the 1970s to 3-4 in the 1980s. In general, linear densities increased by about 3-400% from the 1970s to the 1990s but appear to be currently stable.

Table 2. Breeding productivity in Taymyr Peregrines in 1996 and 1997. "n/a" = not available.

Year	River basin	Terri-tories checked	Territories occupied (pair/single)	Clutch size	% Eggs Hatched (no. eggs)	Territories success-ful (%)	Young per occupied territory[2]	Young per successful territory
1996	Pura & Pyasina	20	12 (60%)	3.50±0.29 (4)	85 (14)	67	1.92±0.43 (12)	2.88±0.23 (8)
1997	Pura & Pyasina	n/a	n/a	3.50±0.22 (6)	95 (21)	81	2.24±0.30 (21)	2.77±0.22 (17)
	Pura	24	13 (63%)	n/a	n/a	84[1]	2.33±0.53 (9)	3.00±0.38 (7)
	Pyasina	n/a	15	n/a	n/a	77	2.17±0.37 (12)	2.60±0.27 (10)
1998	Pura & Pyasina	21	17 (81%)	3.50±0.27(8)	86% (28)	73	2.0±0.38 (15)	2.73±0.27 (11)

[1] Includes two territories occupied by lone male falcons. Both females from these territories were satellite tagged in 1996; one probably died or was trapped on migration, the other was trapped. It is assumed that both would have bred successfully in 1997, had they not been tagged in 1996.
[2] Including territories occupied by lone birds.

Eyrie description

Of the seven eyries on the Pura River where eggs were laid in both 1996 and 1997, only one laid in exactly the same nest. The others moved distances of between 2 m and 1,500 m (mean 450 m ±200, SE). Twenty-six percent of all eyries (n=28) were on rocky cliffs but 41% were on sandy or grassy, river-bank ridges that normally ran perpendicular to the river and 30% were on grassy slopes (Fig. 3). Eyries were on average 20 m from water at time of survey and 6m from the highest spring water level mark (medians; n=29). Cliff or river-bank height on which eyries were located varied considerably from 3 m to 45 m (median 14 m) and the median location of nests on the cliff was 10m high. Sixty-four percent of eyrie-cliffs (n= 31) faced in a southerly and just 4% in a northerly direction. No nests faced in a northerly direction; the majority were on the tops of ridges (50%) or on south-facing slopes (35%). Eighty-two percent of nests were either easy or relatively easy to approach on foot from some angle while 11% were inaccessible on foot. Although many of the nests were accessible, this was normally only from a limited area around the nest. On average, nests were easy to approach over an angle of 20° (median; n=25). In summary, although there was a general tendency to avoid north facing slopes, eyries were found in a very wide variety of nest site types.

Breeding success

Mean clutch size (excluding pairs that laid no eggs) was 3.5 in all years (Table 1). Eighty-five percent of eggs that laid in 1996 (n=14) hatched successfully, 95% in 1997 (n=21) and 86% in 1998 (n=28). Of the 3 eggs that did not hatch in 1996 and 1997, one had broken from an unknown cause while the other two were unhatched. Most nests had very young nestlings by the second week of

July in 1996, by the first week of July in 1997, and by the second-third week of July in 1998. This suggests that clutches were completed in early June in early years and mid June in late years.

The percentage of occupied territories in a year that produced young to at least two weeks of age varied from 67% to 81% (Table 1). The number of young produced per successful territory was 2.88 (n=8) in 1996, 2.77 in 1997 (n=17) and 2.73 in 1998 (n=11) (Table 1), of which 43% (n=23), 36% (n=42) and 43% (n=30) were males respectively. The number of young per occupied territory was 1.92 (n=12), 2.24 (n=21) and 2.0 (n=15). Comparing the number of young per occupied territory on the Pura River, which is almost totally undisturbed, with the number on the Pyasina River, where hunter-fishermen operate on the rivers every 50-100 km, showed there was no difference between the two in 1997 (two-tailed t=0.80, P=0.26, df=15). The same was true for the number of young per successful territory (t=2.18, P=0.87, df=12).

Blood samples

One of the five adults (a male) had high levels of both DDE (3.31 ppm) and PCBs (4.1 ppm), another female had high levels of DDE (1.45) and the remaining three were almost totally clear of all organochlorines (Appendix 1). Male 92-1 bore the heaviest pesticide loading and tested positively for 22 of the 30 individual organochlorines tested. Spiked recoveries of samples taken from adults that contained high levels of pesticides were poor and the correction factor was therefore high. Whether or not this affected the accuracy of the test is unknown but caution should be excercised in interpreting these results.

DDE was detectable in very small amounts (0.01-0.09 ppm) in eight of the 17 juvenile falcon plasma samples and in one of the five control samples (0.03 ppm). Similar levels of HEOD were present in 7 young falcons but PCBs were almost totally absent from young falcons and control samples. Most of the young falcons that tested positive for HEOD and DDE were sampled when 4-6 weeks old (in 1997) while the falcons that tested negative were sampled when 2-3 weeks old (in 1996). Given that organochlorines are stored cumulatively, this may explain why the 2-3 week old young from 1996 tested negative.

DISCUSSION

Territory spacing and density compared to other countries

Peregrines in Taymyr occur in moderate density when compared to other parts of the world. Coastal populations in North America are particularly high, presumably because both food and suitable nest sites are more abundant. In the Keewatin district, Northwest Territories, for example, it was estimated a Peregrine territory was found in every 17 km^2 pair^{-1} (Court et al. 1988) compared to 406 km^2 pair^{-1} in this study (Quinn & Kokorev, in prep.). Various other higher estimates in Appendix 2 (from 186-285 km^2 pair^{-1}) are associated with coastal areas. It remains to be seen whether similar high densities are found on the Siberian coast. Density estimates for temperate Britain (21-119 km^2 pair^{-1}) are also much higher (Ratcliffe 1993) for similar reasons.

Pre-pesticide crash DAR estimates for the Colville and Yukon Rivers in the Alaskan interior (9.5 km and 20 km) suggest a higher density than most of the Pura and Pyasina where such high densities were found only on two small stretches of river. However, Cade's equivalent area per pair estimates were only 520 km^2 pair^{-1} and 775 km^2 pair^{-1} respectively, compared to 406km^2 pair^{-1} in Taymyr. The difference was presumably due to a lower density of rivers than in Taymyr. Based on data from several different areas in Taymyr from the 1970s and 1980s when the population was depressed, Yakushkin et al. (1993) estimated a density of 1,200-1,250 km^2 pair^{-1}. In Southern Yamal in the late 1980s, Mechnikova & Gizzatova (1991) estimated a density of 270-416 km^2 pair^{-1} and Morozov (1991) estimated 592 km^2 pair^{-1} in the Bolshezemel'skaya tundra (NE Europe). It is not clear whether comparisons between different studies are entirely valid because not all describe exactly how the estimates were made. Our estimate, nevertheless, agrees with those found in other parts of Siberia when the population was thought not to be depressed by pesticides.

Population trend: evidence for a recovery

The trends in nest density suggested that Peregrines were almost absent from western Taymyr in the early 1970s but that the population has increased substantially since then. No detailed information on densities has been published from Taymyr pre-1970s. Kretschmar and Leonovich (1967) found that eyries 'in some parts' of the Pyasina basin in 1960-62 were on average 7-10 km apart. Such high densities were also found on two stretches in 1997 so it is quite likely that population density today is not greatly different to the early 1960s. Similarly, territory spacing estimates from other parts of the *F. p. calidus* range before the pesticide crash are like those found in the Pura and Pyasina basins today. In the Lower Lena basin during the early 1960s, DARs were 10-20 km, similar to the best areas on the Pura and Pyasina in 1996-97, and on the Upper Lena, densities were similar (20-40 km) to the whole study area (Uspenskiy *et al.* 1962). Dementiev (1951) gives straight line distances between nests in Kolyma (north-eastern Siberia) and southern Yamal Peninsula (west of Taymyr) of 15-20 km, suggesting a slightly higher density than that found in Taymyr today.

It is difficult to say to what extent the increasing trend in western Taymyr reflects the situation in other parts of Siberia. Morozov (1991) estimated that 65-75 pairs nested in 41,500 km^2 in the Bolshezemel'skaya tundra (NE Europe) or 592 km^2 pair^{-1} compared to 406 km^2 pair^{-1} for the Pyasina basin in 1997 (Quinn & Kokorev, in prep). On the Yamal Peninsula, Kucheruk *et al.* (1975) reported that Peregrines were absent from former historical haunts but, by the late 1980s, Mechnikova and Gizzatova (1991) found densities that suggested a recovery. Recent reports from expeditions to several other parts of Northern Siberia suggest good numbers of Peregrines (Lower Kolyma, NE Yakutia, Sokolov 1994; Lena Delta in 1997, Zockler *pers. comm.*; Logata River in 1997, eastern Taymyr, Aarvark *pers. comm.*). Peregrines were thought to be absent from Vaygach Island in the 1980s but 10 pairs were recorded there in the early 1990s (Morozov, *pers. comm.*). It seems, therefore, that the recovery has been widespread.

Kretschmar and Leonovich (1967) showed that Peregrines were still common on the Pyasina in the early 1960s. This suggests that the population crashed in the mid-late 1960s since active eyries were almost absent in 1971 from the same area. The timing of the decline in other parts of the world varied considerably. In North America, Peregrines were extinct over much of its range by 1965. Declines occurred later in areas where DDT was introduced later. For example Alaskan Peregrines that winter in Central and South America did not show a decline until after 1967 (White & Cade 1977) and it is probable that the decline in Siberian Peregrines also lagged behind that observed in the USA and western Europe.

Although the population on the Pura River seems to have stabilised, just 60-70% of territories that have ever been occupied are occupied today, perhaps suggesting a population below carrying capacity. The latter does not rule out the possibility that the population has returned to pre-pesticide crash levels but other limiting factors may be in operation. In Britain, for example, the number of territories occupied today is even higher than before the pesticide crash (Crick & Ratcliffe 1995) when, it is suggested, the population was held below carrying capacity through the effects of persecution. The population in Taymyr may well be still limited by another similar density independent factor. A lack of suitable nesting sites is unlikely to be one of these because we found that Peregrines nested in a wide variety of habitat types, many of them a seemingly unusual choice given the surrounding habitat. In one case Peregrines chose to nest on an accessible, unstable scree slope instead of an inaccessible cliff ledge overhead. It is more likely that winter mortality, trapping pressure on migration or food availability is important in limiting Peregrines in Taymyr.

Reproductive success

Clutch size estimates for Taymyr are similar to those found in other parts of the world (Appendix 2). In itself this says little about the exposure of birds to pesticides because other studies have shown that clutch size changed very little during the pesticide crisis. The proportion of eggs that hatch successfully is a better indicator. In Northern England and Southern Scotland, 36% and 48% of eggs laid failed to hatch at the height of the pesticide crisis in the 1970s respectively compared to 23% and 26% in the 1970s and 27% and 32% in the 1980s (Ratcliffe 1993). In this study 91% of eggs hatched successfully suggesting that pesticide-related egg-shell thinning is not a current problem.

Ratcliffe (1993) suggests that mean fledged brood size was a good indicator of the health of the British population over the last 40 years. The estimate of 2.6-3.0 young per successful brood in this study is similar to the highest estimates from other parts of the world not affected by pesticides. Typical brood sizes from North America were from 2.6-2.8 young per successful pair when the population was not affected by pesticides, and 2.0 or less during the height of the pesticide crisis (Fig. 4a, Appendix 2). In Ungava Bay, Quebec, brood sizes were 1.71-1.78 during the pesticide crisis in 1970 and 1975 but from 2.36-3.21 during their recovery from 1980-85 (Bird & Weaver 1988). On the Colville river in Alaska, mean brood size from 1969-79 was 1.98 but 2.75 from 1980-85. Similar figures for the Yukon River in Alaska were 1.85 and 2.47 (Ambrose *et al.* 1988). The only data we could find from Russia that suggest a decline in breeding success was from Yamal. Osmoloskaya (1948) reported a breeding success of 2.7 young per nest in the early 1940s but Kalyakin (1983) recorded a breeding success of just 1.5 young per nest. From 1988-90 breeding success of Peregrines on Yamal increased again to 2.54 young (Mechnikova & Gizzatova 1991).

The number of young per occupied territory, as opposed to per successful pair, is thought to be a better indicator of a population's health. Once again the estimate for Taymyr in 1996-97 of 2.1 is similar to (if not higher than) healthy populations in other parts of North America (Fig. 4b, Appendix 2). For example, estimates for the depressed and recovery periods were 0.75 and 1.64 for the Colville, and 1.2 and 1.8 for the Yukon Rivers in Alaska (from Ambrose *et al.* 1988). Values below 1.5 were associated with populations suffering from exposure to pesticides. The breeding success of Peregrines in the Pyasina basin in 1996-98, therefore, suggests that the population is not currently seriously affected by pesticides.

Pesticide levels

Most published information on pesticide loading in birds of prey relates to residues in the lipid membranes on the insides of eggshells. Little has been published on residues in blood plasma and we have had to limit our discussion to DDE and PCBs. Organochlorines in blood plasma are thought to be a good predictor of organochlorines in the internal organs (Henny & Meeker 1981) but there is uncertainty as to how well they predict levels in egg membranes. Court *et al.* (1990) found the two were not very strongly correlated in individual Peregrines ($r = 0.66$) although Henny and Meeker (1981) did find a stronger correlation in other small raptors. Court *et al.* (1990) suggest that, despite these doubts, mean values derived from large samples taken from a large number of individuals should give an indication of pollution burden at the population level.

The mean DDE level in adult Peregrines from this study was 0.95 ppm (n=5) compared to 0.8 ppm in Peregrines in Rankin Inlet (North West Territories) during 1981-86 and 0.5 ppm during the early 1990s (Court *et al.* 1990; Johnstone *et al.* 1996). Maximum values obtained in 1981-86 were much higher (up to 8.2 ppm for males and 6.6 for females) than the 3.3 ppm in this study. They concluded that the average DDE levels in plasma samples from their study were representative of a population that did not face a critical pollution problem but that some of the nesting failures they witnessed could have been due to organochlorine poisoning. They also suggested that the high levels found in some of their birds could lead to direct mortality of adults in times of stress. We conclude the same is likely to be true of Peregrines on the Pura and Pyasina Rivers while acknowledging that our sample sizes are much smaller than those of the other studies and that more samples are needed. Some breeding attempts may fail due to pesticide poisoning, although the high hatching success we observed suggest these are infrequent. We cannot assume that the same conclusions can be made about *F. p. calidus* populations elsewhere because they have such a wide wintering range (see Eastham *et al.* this volume). Furthermore in North America it was found that individual populations of *F. p. tundrius* had markedly different pesticide burdens (Johnstone *et al.* 1996).

PCBs were virtually absent in young Peregrines and the control species, as they were in the Rankin Inlet birds during the 1980s but not in the 1990s. They were detected in significant quantities in one adult (4.1 ppm) and the mean value for five adults was 0.83 ppm. Although our sample size is very small, it suggests that PCB levels in Taymyr Peregrines may be twice as high as in those in Rankin Inlet (Court *et al.* 1990) and several times higher than in Greenland Peregrines (Jarman *et al.*

1994). PCB residues in eggshells have been implicated in nesting failure but it is not known how they relate to levels in blood plasma. As for DDE, we suggest that these levels are also not obviously damaging the productivity of the population in western Taymyr but future monitoring would be wise.

The very low levels of organochlorines detected in young Peregrines and their absence in the control species suggests that most of the pesticides found in adults originate primarily from prey taken on the wintering grounds and not from migratory prey species in the Arctic.

Reasons for population changes

In Russia, some believe that disturbance has been a significant factor in the decline of Peregrines (Borodin 1984). Kokorev (1995) felt that local declines in Taymyr Peregrines were primarily related to disturbance. Certainly river traffic is now lower in the Pyasina basin than it has been for many years (Kokorev, pers. obs.) and official protection measures, for example the creation of several reserves throughout Taymyr, have undoubtedly helped in the recovery of Peregrines. Given the inaccessibility and remoteness of the entire peninsula, however, and the fact that Peregrines are tolerant of some disturbance (Ratcliffe 1993), it is unlikely that disturbance had a major influence on the decline. The sheer width of the rivers means that obvious disturbance would only occur if boats landed on or near the river banks beside the eyrie, although for the last three weeks of the nestling period, Peregrines react to boats from a greater distance. On the Pyasina and Pura rivers, we found that most hunter-fishermen were aware of local 'Sapsan' eyries and on one occasion knew how many young were in the nest. Some were also aware of their potential monetary value but there was no evidence that any eyrie had been interfered with in any year.

The trapping of falcons for falconry has occurred in Asia for many hundreds of years. Traditional levels of falconry are intuitively sustainable provided the population is not under any pressure from other factors, yet little is known about the actual impact of falconry on Peregrine populations. Remple (1988) postulated that 3,000 falcons are "kept" annually on the Arabian Peninsula, approximately 30% of which are Peregrines (some of which belong to the *calidus* race). He suggests that traditionally about 60% of all falcons are released each spring, although the general consensus amongst concerned delegates at this conference was that this practice is rare and it seems that falcons may well suffer high mortality in captivity. EWRDA is currently conducting tagging studies of *calidus* Peregrines in Taymyr and elsewhere in an attempt to assess the impact of trapping on the population (Eastham *et al.*, this volume).

There is no reason to believe that trapping pressure has increased this century and, therefore, pesticides undoubtedly played a major role in the decline. Galushin (1977) believed pesticides were at least partly responsible for the then suspected decline. The timing of the decline in Peregrine populations in Taymyr seems to have coincided with the pesticide-induced decline observed elsewhere but this has not been fully established because it is based on scant data. It is likely that the timing of the decline varied geographically. There is some evidence of egg-shell thinning amongst museum egg specimens collected from Siberia in the early 1960s (Peakall & Kiff, 1979) although it is suggested in this paper that the densities of Peregrines on the Pyasina were similar in the 1960s to today. Critically high levels of DDE were found in Peregrine egg-shells collected from Kolyma in eastern Siberia in the 1980s (Potapov 1994) when the population was beginning to recover in Taymyr, although the birds in Kolyma were from a different race. More recently Henny *et al.* (1994) reported variable, but generally low, levels of organic pesticides in migratory Peregrines on the Kola Peninsula in north-western Russia and that the population was recovering.

Pesticides have been widely used throughout Asia but in the last ten years their use has been controlled in many countries like India and Pakistan. Some pesticides intended for malaria control are believed to be sold on the black market but it is unlikely the level of usage is anywhere near as high as in previous decades. Nevertheless it was noticeable that there is a distinct lack of precise information on the level of POP usage in Asia and it is suggested that there is a clear need to review the current situation throughout Asia.

One other factor could theoretically have at least contributed to a large scale decline in the *F. p. calidus* population. Ratcliffe (1993) mentions that some high altitude nesting Peregrines in Britain fail to breed if their haunts remain snow bound late in the season. In the Canadian Arctic it was found that high variability in breeding success over a 13 year period was associated with severe weather (Bradley et al. 1997) although apparently even severe weather could be survived as long as it was not prolonged. Although poor weather may directly affect breeding success through its effects on the progeny, indirect affects through reducing prey availability may be more important. Peregrines on the Aleutian Islands bred less successfully when rough seas in spring forced seabirds to spend more time far offshore (White 1975). There is some evidence that weather could have been important in Taymyr. Unpublished information on weather patterns in Taymyr show that, while mean June temperature from 1929 to 1990 was in the order of 5°C on average, it was only 2°C between 1961 and 1965 (data not available for 1966 to 1976, J. Mooiji, unpublished data). Although it seems unlikely that an unusual run of bad springs could alone have led to population decline on the scale that is thought to have occurred in Taymyr, it may well have been a contributory factor.

CONCLUSIONS

A comparison of present with historical data suggest that the Peregrine population in Taymyr seems be recovering well from low populations in the 1970s and 1980s. The presumed decline was likely to have been pesticide linked. Breeding productivity data suggest that the population in western Taymyr is not currently adversely affected by organochlorines. Two of the five adults tested did hold high levels of organochlorines in their blood plasma, however, while the others were almost completely clean. This suggests that organochlorine usage on the wintering grounds is patchy but it also shows that we need to continue to monitor the breeding success and pesticide burden of *F. p. calidus* throughout their range.

ACKNOWLEDGMENTS

This work was carried out whilst John Quinn was reading for a D.Phil. at the University of Oxford and was funded by the Environmental Research and Wildlife Development Agency, UAE. Additional funding was provided by the European Union INTAS fund, the Wildfowl & Wetlands Trust and the Peter Scott Trust for Education and Research in Conservation. Thanks to Ian Newton (ITE) and to Claire Wyatt (ITE) who did the pesticide analyses. Additional thanks go to the following people for logistical support away from the field: Olga Kokorev in Norilsk and Helen MacDonald (EWRDA). A special thanks to the fisher-hunters of Taymyr whose logistical support was essential to the success of this project and to the following who helped with data collection: Janet Hunter, Chris Eastham, Seth Layman and Sonya Rosenfield. Thanks also to Chris Perrins and Andy Gosler for commenting on the manuscript and to Lady Scott for her encouragement.

REFERENCES

AMBROSE, R.E., R.J. RITCHIE, C.M. WHITE, P.F. SCHEMPF, T. SWEN, & R. DITTRICK 1988. Changes in the status of peregrine falcon populations in Alaska. In: *Peregrine Falcon Populations. Their management and recovery*, ed. T.J. Cade, J.H. Enderson, C.G. Thelander & C.M. White. The Peregrine Fund, Inc., Boise, Idaho.
ANDREEV, V.N. & V.D. ALEKSANDROVA 1981. Geobotanical divisions of the Soviet Arctic. In: Bliss, L.C., Heal, O.W., & Moore, J.J. (Eds.). *Tundra ecosystems: a comparative analysis*. Cambridge University Press, Cambridge. pp 25-34.
BIRD, D.M. & J.D. WEAVER 1988. Peregrine Falcon populations in Ungava Bay, Quebec, 1980-1985. In: *Peregrine Falcon Populations. Their management and recovery*, eds. T.J. Cade, J.H. Enderson, C.G. Thelander & C.M. White. The Peregrine Fund, Inc., Boise, Idaho.
BORODIN, A.M. (Ed.) 1984. *The Red Data Book of the USSR: rare and endangered species of animals and plants*. Vol 1. Animals. Second edition, Moscow, Promyshlennost.
BRADLEY, M. R. JOHNSTONE, G. COURT & T. DUNCAN 1997. Influence of weather on breeding success of Peregrine Falcons in the Arctic. *Auk* 114:786-791.

BROMLEY, R.G. 1988. Status of the Peregrine Falcon in the Kitikmeot, Baffin, and Keewatin regions, Northwest Territories, 1982-1985. In: *Peregrine Falcon Populations. Their management and recovery*, eds. T.J. Cade, J.H. Enderson, C.G. Thelander & C.M. White. The Peregrine Fund, Inc., Boise, Idaho.

BROMLEY, R.G. & S.B. MATTHEWS 1988. Status of the Peregrine Falcon in the MacKenzie River Valley, Northwest Territories, 1969-1985. In *Peregrine Falcon Populations. Their management and recovery*, eds. T.J. Cade, J.H. Enderson, C.G. Thelander & C.M. White. The Peregrine Fund, Inc., Boise, Idaho.

BURNHAM, W.A. & W.G. MATTOX 1984. Biology of the Peregrine and Gyrfalcon in Greenland. Meddelelser om Grønland, *Bioscience* 14. 28 p.

CADE, T.J. 1960. Ecology of the Peregrine and Gyrfalcon populations in Alaska. *University of California publications in Zoology*, 63(3): 151-290.

CADE, T.J., J.H. ENDERSON, C.G. THELANDER & C.M. WHITE (EDS.) 1988. *Peregrine Falcon Populations. Their management and recovery*. The Peregrine Fund, Inc., Boise, Idaho.

COURT, G.S., D.M. BRADLEY, C.C GATES, & D.A. BOAG 1988. The population biology of Peregrine Falcons in the Keewatin District of the Northwest Territories, Canada. pp729-740. in *Peregrine Falcon Populations. Their management and recovery*, eds. T.J. Cade, J.H. Enderson, C.G. Thelander & C.M. White. The Peregrine Fund, Inc., Boise, Idaho.

CRICK, H.Q.P. & D.A. RATCLIFFE 1995. The Peregrine Falcon's *Falco peregrinus* breeding population of the United Kingdom in 1991. *Bird Study* 421:1-19.

DEMENTIEV, G.P. 1951. The Peregrine Falcon in the U.S.S.R. Pp 80-100 in *The Birds of the Soviet Union*, Vol. 1, eds. G.P. Dementiev and N.A. Gladkov. Soviet Science, Moscow (translated version from Russian).

FALK, K. & S. MOLLER 1988. Status of the Peregrine Falcon in South Greenland: population density and reproduction. Chapter 5 in *Peregrine Falcon Populations. Their management and recovery*, eds. T.J. Cade, J.H. Enderson, C.G. Thelander & C.M. White. The Peregrine Fund, Inc., Boise, Idaho.

FLINT, V.E. (ED.) 1978. Krasnayo Kniga CCCP (Red Data book of USSR). Part ii. Birds. Moscow, Lesnaya Promyshlennost (In Russian).

GALUSHIN, V.M. 1977. Recent changes in the actual and legislative status of birds of prey in the USSR. In: (ed.) Chancellor, R.D. *World Conference on Birds of Prey, Vienna, 1-3 October, 1975: Report of proceedings*. International Council for Bird Preservation. London. Pp152-159.

GLUTZ VON BLOTZHEIM, U.N., K.M. BAUER & E. BEZZELL 1971. *Handbuch der Vogel Mitteleuropus*, Vol.4. Frankfurt am Main, Aka demische Verlagsgesellschaft.

HENNY, C.J. & D.L. MEEKER 1981. An evaluation of blood plasma for monitoring DDE in birds of prey. *Environmental Pollution* (Series A) 25:291-304.

HENNY, C.J., S.A. GANUSEVICH, F. PRESCOTT WARD & T.R. SCHWARTZ 1994. Organochlorine Pesticides, Chlorinated Dioxins and Furans, and PCBs in Peregrine Falcon *Falco peregrinus* eggs from the Kola Peninsula, Russia. In: Meyburg, B.-U. & Chancellor, R.D. (eds). *Raptor Conservation Today*. WWGBP, The Pica Press.

JARMAN, W.M., S.A. BURNS, W.G. MATTOX, & W.S. SEEGAR 1994. Organochlorine compounds in the blood plasma of Peregrine Falcons and Gyrfalcons nesting in Greenland. *Arctic* 47:334-340.

JOHNSTONE, R.M., G.S. COURT, A.C. FESSER, D.M. BRADLEY, L.W. OLIPHANT & J.D. MACNEIL 1996. Long-term trends and sources of organochlorine contamination in Canadian tundra peregrine falcons, *F.p. tundrius*. *Environmental Pollution* 93(2):109-120.

KALYAKIN, V. N. 1983. Fauna of birds of prey and status of rare species populations in the Southern Yamal. In: *Ecology of birds of prey*: materials of the 1st meeting on ecology and conservation of birds of prey. Nauka, pp 120-124. [in Russian].

KOKOREV, J.I. 1995. Zur Bestandssituation des Wanderfalken (*Falco peregrinus*), der Rothalgans (*Branta ruficollis*) und des Zwergschwanes (*Cygnus bewickii*) auf Taimyr. In: Prokosch, P. & Hotker, Hrsg. (Eds), *Faunistik und Naturschutz auf Taimyr - Expeditionen 1989-1991*. *Corax* 16, Sonderheft.

KRETSCHMAR, A.V. & V.V. LEONOVICH 1967. Distribution and biology of the Red-breasted Goose during the nesting period. *Problems of the North*, No. 11, 229-234. (In Russian).

KUCHERUK, V. V., YU. V. KOVALEVSKIY, A. G. SURBANOS 1975. Changes of population and bird fauna of Southern Yamal for the last 100 years. *Bulletin of Moscow Naturalistís Society* 80(1):52-54.

LINDBERG, P., P.J. SCHEI & M. WIKMAN 1988. The Peregrine Falcon in Fennoscandia. Chapter 18 in *Peregrine Falcon Populations. Their management and recovery*, eds. T.J. Cade, J.H. Enderson, C.G. Thelander & C.M. White. The Peregrine Fund, Inc., Boise, Idaho.

MATTOX, W.G. & W.S. SEEGAR 1988. The Greenland Peregrine Falcon survey, 1972-1985, with emphasis on recent population status. In: *Peregrine Falcon Populations. Their management and recovery*, eds. T.J. Cade, J.H. Enderson, C.G. Thelander & C.M. White. The Peregrine Fund, Inc., Boise, Idaho.

MEARNS, R. & I. NEWTON 1988. Factors affecting breeding success of Peregrines in south Scotland. *J. Anim. Ecol.* 57, 903-916.

MECHNIKOVA, S. A. & M. M. GIZZATOVA 1991. Some data on numbers and distribution of birds of prey in the southern Yamal. Materials of the 10th All-Union Ornithological Conference. Minsk, *Navuka i tekhnika*, Part 2, Book 2, pages 72-74.

MOROZOV, V.V. 1991. The Peregrine Falcon and Gyrfalcon in the far North East of Europe. *Bulletin of Moscow Naturalist's Soc.* Vol.96,1:57-65. (In Russian).

OSMOLOVSKAYA, V.I. 1948. Ecology of birds of prey of the Yamal peninsula. Proc. of Inst. of Geography of the Russian Academy of Sciences. M.-L. Issue 41. P.5-77.

PEAKALL, D.B. & J.F. KIFF 1979. Eggshell thinning and DDE residue levels among Peregrine Falcons *Falco peregrinus*: a global perspective. *Ibis*: 121:200-204.

POTAPOV, E.R. 1994. Time budget, Organochlorines and Productivity in the Peregrine Falcon *Falco peregrinus* in the Kolyma Lowlands Region (North-Eastern Siberia). In: Meyburg, B.U. & Chancellor, R.D. (Eds). *Raptor Conservation Today*. pp195-201. WWGBP, The Pica Press.

POTAPOV, E.R. 1996. Peregrines in the former USSR: what do we know? *Raptor-link* 4(1)1-4.

RATCLIFFE, D.A. 1993. *The Peregrine Falcon*. Second edition, T & AD Poyser, London.

REMPLE, J.D. 1988. An overview of Arab Falconry, its medical lore, and the introduction of avian medicine in the Arabian Gulf. In: *Peregrine Falcon Populations. Their management and recovery*, eds. T.J. Cade, J.H. Enderson, C.G. Thelander & C.M. White. The Peregrine Fund, Inc., Boise, Idaho.

SOKOLOV, A. 1994. Peregrine in the Lower Kolyma Region, NE Yakutia, 1994. *Raptorlink* 2(3)2.

USPENSKIY, S.M., R.L. BOEHME, S.G. PRIKLONSKIY & V.N VEKHOV 1962. *Birds of North-East Yakutia*. Moscow University Press No.5 pp49-67.

WHITE, C.M. 1975. Studies on Peregrine Falcons in the Aleutian Islands. *Raptor Res. Rep.* no. 3, 33-50.

WHITE, C.M. & D.A. JNR. BOYCE 1988. An overview of peregrine falcon subspecies. In: *Peregrine Falcon Populations. Their management and recovery*, eds. T.J. Cade, J.H. Enderson, C.G. Thelander & C.M. White. The Peregrine Fund, Inc., Boise, Idaho.

WIKMAN, M. 1990. The Peregrine Falcon in Finland 1980-89. *Lintumnies* 25 (2): 54-58.

YAKUSHKIN, G. D., V. F. DOROGOV, B. B. BORZHONOV, V. A. KUKSOV & L. A. KOLPASHCHIKOV 1983. Status of the Peregrine Falcon population in Taymyr. Birds of Taymyr, Vashnil, no. 7, 42-45. (In Russian).

J.L. Quinn
EGI, Department of Zoology
University of Oxford
South Parks Road
Oxford, OX1 3PS
UK

Y. Kokorev
Extreme North Agricultural Research
Institute
Komsomolskaya 1
663302 Norilsk
Russia

also

The Wildfowl & Wetlands Trust
Slimbridge
Gloucestershire
UK

N. Fox
Environmental Research and Wildlife
Development Agency
Penllynin Farm, College Road
Carmarthen, SA33 5EH
UK

J. Prop
Zoological Laboratory
University of Groningen
PO Box 14
9750 AA Haren
The Netherlands

J.M. Black
Department of Wildlife
Humboldt State University
Arcata, California
95521-8299
USA

Appendix 1. Concentrations of organochlorine pesticides (numbers in column heading refer to names of specific PCBs) found in blood plasma taken from Peregrines and control species (young Snowy Owls and Rough-legged Buzzards) on the Pura & Pyasina Rivers in Taymyr. Batches 50 and 51 were collected in 1996; batches 90 and 91 in 1997. All concentrations are given in micrograms per gram (i.e. ppm). Total A is sum of all pesticides detected excluding PCBs. Total B is sum of PCBs detected which is not the total amount of PCB in the sample since not all PCBs were measured. These values are therefore minima. Underlined values indicate samples where the organochlorine tested was detected; these were corrected for recovery of chemicals from spiked samples. All other values are for samples where the chemical was not detected; values given refer to the detection limit of the test; i.e. due to sensitivity of chemical tests, concentrations below the given values would not have been detected if they were present. "nt" = sample not tested for the given organochlorine; "nd" = not detected.

Batch-sample	Species	Age	Sample wgt (g)	HCB	α-HCH	g-HCH	p,p-DDE	HE-OD	p,p-TDE	p,p-DDT	8	18	28	31	52	77	101	105	114	118	124	126	128	138	149	153	156	157	167	169	170	180	209	Tot A	Tot B
Adult Peregrines																																			
50-5	PF-M	A	0.34	nt	nt	nt	0.00	0.00	0.00	0.00	nt	nt	nt	nt	nt	0.00	0.00	nt	nt	0.00	nt	0.00	0.00	0.00	0.00	0.00	0.00	nt	nt	0.00	0.00	0.00	nt	nd	nd
92-1	PF-M	A	0.39	0.03	0.02	0.00	3.31	0.12	0.01	0.11	nt	nt	nt	nt	nt	0.01	0.01	0.04	nt	0.13	nt	0.01	0.06	0.45	0.00	1.70	0.17	0.01	0.02	0.08	0.29	0.82	0.02	3.6	4.1
50-9	PF-M	A	0.24	nt	nt	nt	0.00	0.00	0.00	0.00	nt	nt	nt	nt	0.02	0.00	0.00	nt	0.19	0.00	nt	0.00	0.00	0.00	0.00	0.00	0.00	nt	nt	0.00	0.00	0.00	nt	nd	nd
51-5	PF-F	A		nt	nt	nt	0.01	0.00	0.00	0.00	nt	nt	nt	nt	nt	0.00	0.01	nt	nt	0.00	nt	0.00	0.00	0.00	0.00	0.00	0.00	nt	nt	0.00	0.00	0.00	0.01	0.01	0.04
92-4	PF-F	A	0.42	0.00	0.00	0.00	1.45	0.01	0.00	0.05	0.00	0.00	0.00	0.00	0.02	0.01	0.01	0.00	nt	0.01	nt	0.00	0.00	0.01	0.00	0.03	0.00	0.00	0.02	0.00	0.00	0.01	0.00	1.51	0.04
Young Peregrines																																			
50-1	PF	Y	0.52	0.00	0.00	0.00	0.00	0.00	0.00	0.00	nt	nt	nt	nt	0.01	0.00	0.01	0.00	0.00	0.00	nt	0.00	0.00	0.00	0.00	0.00	0.00	nt	nt	0.00	0.00	0.00	nt	nd	nd
50-3	PF	Y	0.52	0.00	0.00	0.00	0.00	0.00	0.00	0.00	nt	nt	nt	nt	0.02	0.00	0.01	0.00	0.00	0.00	nt	0.00	0.00	0.00	0.00	0.00	0.00	nt	nt	0.00	0.00	0.00	nt	nd	nd
50-4	PF	Y	0.37	0.00	0.00	0.00	0.00	0.00	0.00	0.00	nt	nt	nt	nt	0.02	0.00	0.01	0.00	0.00	0.00	nt	0.00	0.00	0.00	0.00	0.00	0.00	nt	nt	0.00	0.00	0.00	nt	nd	nd
50-6	PF	Y	0.51	0.00	0.00	0.00	0.00	0.64	0.01	0.00	nt	nt	nt	nt	0.04	0.00	0.01	0.00	0.00	0.00	nt	0.00	0.00	0.01	0.00	0.00	0.00	nt	nt	0.00	0.00	0.00	nt	0.65	0.01
50-7	PF	Y	0.37	0.00	0.00	0.00	0.00	0.00	0.00	0.00	nt	nt	nt	nt	0.02	0.00	0.01	0.00	0.00	0.00	nt	0.00	0.00	0.00	0.00	0.01	0.00	nt	nt	0.00	0.00	0.00	nt	nd	nd
51-3	PF	Y	0.51	0.00	0.00	0.00	0.00	0.01	0.00	0.04	0.00	0.00	0.00	0.00	0.02	0.00	0.01	0.00	nt	0.00	nt	0.00	0.00	0.00	0.00	0.00	0.00	0.00	0.00	0.00	0.00	0.01	0.00	0.03	0.02
91-4	PF	Y	0.63	0.00	0.00	0.00	0.03	0.00	0.00	0.04	0.00	0.00	0.00	0.00	0.02	0.00	0.01	0.00	0.00	0.00	nt	0.00	0.00	0.00	0.00	0.00	0.00	0.00	0.00	0.00	0.00	0.01	0.00	0.03	0.02
91-5	PF	Y	0.58	0.00	0.00	0.00	0.03	0.00	0.00	0.04	0.00	0.00	0.00	0.00	0.02	0.00	0.01	0.00	0.00	0.00	nt	0.00	0.00	0.00	0.00	0.01	0.00	0.00	0.00	0.00	0.00	0.01	0.00	nd	nd
91-6	PF	Y	0.53	0.00	0.00	0.00	0.03	0.00	0.00	0.04	0.00	0.00	0.00	0.00	0.02	0.00	0.01	0.00	0.00	0.00	nt	0.00	0.00	0.00	0.00	0.00	0.00	0.00	0.00	0.00	0.00	0.01	0.00	0.03	nd
91-7	PF	Y	0.25	0.00	0.00	0.00	0.01	0.00	0.00	0.09	0.00	0.00	0.00	0.00	0.04	0.01	0.02	0.00	0.00	0.00	nt	0.00	0.00	0.00	0.00	0.01	0.00	0.00	0.00	0.00	0.00	0.01	0.00	nd	nd
91-8	PF	Y	0.51	0.00	0.00	0.00	0.02	0.01	0.00	0.04	0.00	0.00	0.00	0.00	0.02	0.00	0.01	0.00	0.00	0.00	nt	0.00	0.00	0.00	0.00	0.01	0.00	0.00	0.00	0.00	0.00	0.01	0.00	0.03	nd
92-2	PF	Y	0.55	0.00	0.00	0.00	0.09	0.01	0.00	0.04	0.00	0.00	0.00	0.00	0.02	0.00	0.01	0.00	0.00	0.00	nt	0.00	0.00	0.00	0.00	0.01	0.00	0.00	0.00	0.00	0.00	0.01	0.00	0.10	nd
92-3	PF	Y	0.59	0.00	0.00	0.00	0.05	0.01	0.00	0.04	0.00	0.00	0.00	0.00	0.02	0.00	0.01	0.00	0.00	0.00	nt	0.00	0.00	0.00	0.00	0.01	0.00	0.00	0.00	0.00	0.00	0.01	0.00	0.06	nd
92-5	PF	Y	0.55	0.00	0.00	0.00	0.03	0.01	0.00	0.04	0.00	0.00	0.00	0.00	0.02	0.00	0.01	0.00	0.00	0.01	nt	0.00	0.00	0.00	0.00	0.01	0.00	0.00	0.00	0.00	0.00	0.01	0.00	0.04	nd
92-6	PF	Y	0.49	0.00	0.00	0.00	0.02	0.01	0.00	0.05	0.00	0.00	0.00	0.00	0.02	0.00	0.01	0.00	0.00	0.01	nt	0.00	0.00	0.00	0.00	0.01	0.00	0.00	0.00	0.00	0.00	0.01	0.00	0.03	nd
92-7	PF	Y	0.37	0.00	0.00	0.00	0.00	0.01	0.00	0.06	0.00	0.00	0.01	0.00	0.03	0.01	0.01	0.00	0.00	0.01	nt	0.00	0.00	0.00	0.00	0.01	0.00	0.00	0.00	0.00	0.00	0.01	0.00	nd	nd
92-8	PF	Y	0.39	0.00	0.00	0.00	0.01	0.01	0.00	0.06	0.00	0.00	0.00	0.00	0.02	0.01	0.01	0.00	0.00	0.01	nt	0.00	0.00	0.00	0.00	0.01	0.00	0.00	0.00	0.00	0.00	0.01	0.00	0.02	nd
Controls																																			
50-2	SO	Y	0.51	nt	nt	nt	0.00	0.00	0.00	0.00	nt	nt	nt	nt	nt	0.00	0.00	nt	nt	0.00	nt	0.00	0.00	0.00	0.00	0.00	0.00	nt	nt	0.00	0.00	0.00	nt	nd	nd
51-2	SO	Y	0.47	nt	nt	nt	0.00	0.00	0.00	0.00	nt	nt	nt	nt	nt	0.00	0.00	nt	nt	0.00	nt	0.00	0.00	0.00	0.00	0.00	0.00	nt	nt	0.00	0.00	0.00	nt	nd	nd
51-4	SO	Y	0.57	nt	nt	nt	0.03	0.00	0.00	0.00	nt	nt	nt	nt	nt	0.00	0.00	nt	nt	0.00	nt	0.00	0.00	0.00	0.00	0.00	0.00	nt	nt	0.00	0.00	0.00	nt	0.03	nd
50-8	RLB	Y	0.31	nt	nt	nt	0.00	0.00	0.00	0.00	nt	nt	nt	nt	nt	0.00	0.00	nt	nt	0.00	nt	0.00	0.00	0.00	0.00	0.00	0.00	nt	nt	0.00	0.00	0.00	nt	nd	nd
51-1	RLB	Y	0.56	nt	nt	nt	0.00	0.00	0.00	0.00	nt	nt	nt	nt	nt	0.00	0.00	nt	nt	0.00	nt	0.00	0.00	0.00	0.00	0.00	0.00	nt	nt	0.00	0.00	0.00	nt	nd	nd
Batch 50&51	Proportion recoveries			nt	nt	nt	0.94	0.87	1.00	0.75	nt	nt	nt	nt	nt	0.92	0.83	nt	nt	0.93	nt	0.97	0.97	0.96	0.92	0.96	nt	nt	nt	0.94	1.00	0.98	nt		
Batch 50&51	LODs (ng)			nt	nt	nt	0.10	0.10	0.20	0.20	nt	nt	nt	nt	nt	0.30	0.30	nt	nt	0.10	nt	0.20	0.10	0.10	0.30	0.20	nt	nt	nt	0.20	0.10	0.10	nt		
Batch 91&92	Proportion recoveries			0.23	0.22	0.00	0.94	0.87	1.00	0.75	0.24	0.24	0.25	0.26	0.24	0.31	0.26	0.33	0.32	0.32	0.32	0.33	0.33	0.33	0.33	0.31	0.34	0.34	0.34	0.35	0.10	0.34	0.42	0.35		
Batch 91&92	LODs (ng)			0.13	0.14	0.09	0.40	0.27	0.09	6.67	0.23	0.46	0.12	0.18	2.21	0.73	0.99	0.36	0.10	0.82	0.08	0.09	0.39	0.96	0.13	0.77	0.22	0.15	0.06	0.06	0.35	0.17	1.48	0.17		

Appendix 2. Breeding density and success of British and Arctic Peregrine Falcons around the world. The symbols [1], [2] and [3] represent areas where the populations were thought by the original authors to be depressed, recovering or close to (or actually) normal. Entries without a symbol are for areas where status was unknown or where the time spanned periods of variable status.

Location	Distance along river (km)	Straight line distance (km)	Density km² per territory	% territories occupied	%pairs fledged young	Clutch size	Y/pair	Y/succ pair	Reference
NORTH AMERICA									
[3]Mackenzie River Valley, NWT, USA 1969-85				23-53			1.4-2.3	2.2-2.9	Bromley & Matthews (1988)
[1]Aleutian Islands 1970-72		7-11			66		1.77	2.66	White (1975)
[3]West Greenland 1981-85				70	80		2.4	3.0	Mattox & Seegar (1988)
[3]S. Greenland 1981-85			240	70	73		1.8	2.7	Falk & Møller (1988)
[2]Colville River, Northern Alaska 1980-85				74	56		1.64	2.75	Cade (1960); Ambrose et al. (1988)
[2]Yukon River, Interior Alaska 1970-80				55.7	71		1.8	2.47	Cade (1960); Ambrose et al. (1988)
[2]Ungava Bay, Quebec 1980-85				64	77		2.3-2.9	2.4-3.2	Bromley (1988)
[2]Kitikmeot, Northwest Territories 1982-85				44			2.8[a]	2.79	Court et al. (1988)
[2]Keewatin District, Northwest Territories 1981-86			186				2.03		Bromley (1988)
[3]Baffin, Northwest Territories 1982-85			17 (50% water)		73	3.62	2.8[a]		Burnham & Mattox (1984); Mattox & Seegar (1988)
[3]West Greenland 1972-81		7.7	285	73	85		2.3	2.7	
[1]Ungava Bay, Quebec 1970 & 1975				59	89		1.3-1.8	1.7-1.8	
[1]Yukon River, Interior Alaska 1951-68	20		775	45	65		1.2	1.85	Cade (1960); Ambrose et al. (1988)
[1]Colville River, Northern Alaska 1969-79	9.5		520	58	35		0.75	1.98	Cade (1960); Ambrose et al. (1988)
SIBERIA									
[3]Pura-Pyasina 1996-97	29	24	406	63	70	3.5	2.08	2.83	This study; Quinn & Kokorev, in prep.
[3]Yamal Peninsula (1940s)								2.7	Osmoloskaya (1948)
[3]Lower Lena, Northern Siberia	10-20								Glutz et al. (1971)
[3]Upper Lena, Northern Siberia	30-40								Glutz et al. (1971)
[3]NE Yakutia	15-20								Uspenskiy et al. (1962)
[3]R. Pyasina, Taymyr 1960-62		7-10 (n=20?)							Kretschmar & Leonovich (1967)
[3]Kola Peninsula 1987-91						3.5	1.94		Henny et al. (1994)
[3]Bolshezemel'skaya Tundra, NE Europe 1980s			592						Morozov (1991)
[3]Yamal Peninsula, early 1980s			800					1.5	Kalyakin (1983)
[3]Southern Yamal, late 1980s			270-416					2.54	Mechnikova & Gizzatova (1991)
[3]Tributaries of Pyasina, Taymyr, 1970s & 1980s	74 & 42								Kokorev (1995)
[3]Central Taymyr, 1970s & 1980s	69 & 79								Kokorev (1995)
[3]Eastern Taymyr, 1970s & 1980s	81 & 53								Kokorev (1995)
[1]Lower Kolyma, NE Siberia 1988-92						3.4	1.04		Potapov (1994)
[1]Lower Kolyma, NE Siberia 1983-87						3.75	0.30		Potapov (1994)
FINLAND									
[2]Northern Finland 1981-85		15.9	300			3.1	2.1	1.86	Lindberg et al. 1988; Wikman (1990)
[2]Southern Finland 1981-85							1.0		Lindberg et al. 1988
BRITAIN									
Britain, up to 1979			21-119			3.63	1.36	2.23	Ratcliffe (1993)
[3]Great Britain 1980-91				120	63			2.31	Ratcliffe (1993)
[3]S. Scotland 1974-82					47	3.53	1.1	2.33	Mearns & Newton (1988)
[1]Great Britain 1960-70				62	20		0.71	2.07	Ratcliffe (1993)

Chancellor, R. D. & B.-U. Meyburg eds. 2000
Raptors at Risk
WWGBP / Hancock House

New Developments on the Western Border of the Saker Falcon *Falco cherrug* range in Middle Europe

W. Baumgart

ABSTRACT

The population of the Saker in the western part of the European range (Hungary, Slovakia, Czech Republic and Austria) has increased in the 1990s. The species has been breeding for the first time in the Czech-Poland border area (since 1990) as well as in Germany (1997) and since 1998 in Poland.

This marks a real extension. In the course of this process the Saker became progressively independent of the suslik (*Citellus citellus*), its former predominant prey, starting to breed outside the present and former suslik range. Here it preys mainly on birds, especially pigeons (*Columbidae*), becomes resident and is very flexible in its choice of breeding sites (cliffs, stick nests on trees and pylons etc.).

The new orientation in the feeding behaviour of the Saker is a result of ecological changes in Middle Europe, namely the conversion of agricultural landscape suitable for pigeons. The Saker exploits this food supply, which is not effectively available to Peregrines *F. peregrinus* and Goshawks *Accipiter gentilis*. Permanent colonisation by the Saker in Central Middle Europe seems possible.

INTRODUCTION

The Saker Falcon *Falco cherrug* , which was the banner-bird of Attila with the name *Turul*, ranges across Europe to nearly the same extent as did the Huns in their time. The westernmost breeding population was on the Hungarian plains together with adjoining parts of Romania, Yugoslavia (Serbia), Croatia, Austria (Wienerwald), Czech Republic (Bohemia) and Slovakia (Glutz *et al.* 1971, Cade 1982, Baumgart 1994).

Here the Saker is found in open, steppe-like habitats with low vegetation. During the breeding season the diet comprises mainly susliks. The range of the Saker in South-eastern Middle Europe was not long ago clearly correlated with that of the suslik. In the past no breeding of the Saker outside the suslik range was recorded. Past breeding records from Germany, for instance, are uncertain (Baumgart 1991).

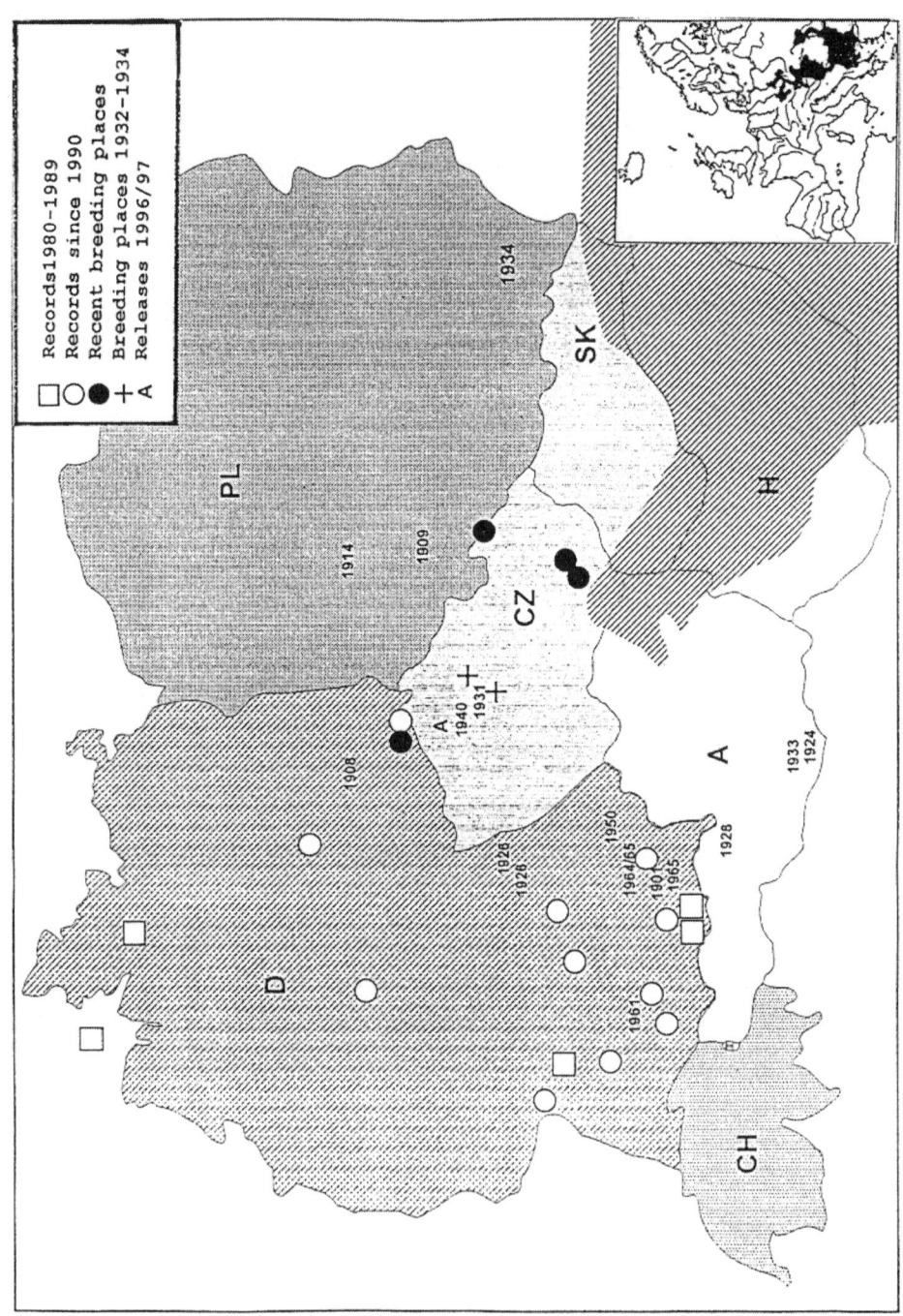

Figure 1. Saker records in Central Middle Europe during the 20th century (according to Augst 1998). The small map shows the range of the suslik in Europe (according to Van der Brink 1972).

The range of the Saker decreased in the late 19th and early 20th centuries. The main reason was the destruction of steppes and dry grasslands or their cultivation leading to increase in vegetation cover. These habitat changes led to a reduction in susliks. The diet of Sakers in remaining mountain populations became more avian orientated. In the beginning partridges *Perdix perdix* were preyed upon, but with their disappearance the importance of pigeons grew. In some local Saker populations Lapwings *Vanellus vanellus*, Rooks *Corvus frugilegus*, Starlings *Sturnus vulgaris*, Thrushes *Turdus* etc. were an important food source (Frey & Senn 1980, Janossy 1983, Baumgart et al. 1993, Bagyura et al. 1994b). This situation is comparable with the one in Kazakstan. In this period the susliks decreased remarkably but in the newly cultivated areas the pigeons increased in such a way that they could substitute the appropriate positions in the Saker´s prey composition (Korelow 1962).

Due to strong and effective conservation measures, as well as changes in diet, the Saker population in the western part of its European range has remarkably stabilised, especially in Hungary during the late 1980s and early 1990s (Bagyura et al. 1994a). The population estimate in this western region was 200-250 breeding pairs. But up until this time all breeding places were located in the range of actual or former suslik distribution.

EXTENSION OF SAKER BREEDING RANGE

A new situation occurred in 1990, when the species bred for the first time in the Czech-Poland-border area, outside the former range of suslik distribution. The diet of the 3 to 4 breeding pairs comprised almost exclusively feral Pigeons *Columba livia* and Wood Pigeons *C. palumbus*. The habitat comprises partly cultivated open fields with areas of higher vegetation cover. The falcons use nests in trees. Nothing is known about a former or recent suslik occurrence in this area (Kodelka & Petro 1994).

A real sensation was the first breeding of Sakers in Sächische Schweiz (Germany) in 1997 (Augst 1997). The breeding place is only a little more than 50 km north of the former northernmost breeding place in Duba (Bohemia), but also clearly located outside the former suslik range. The Sakers breed here on majestic cliffs sympatrically with some Peregrine pairs. They prey nearly exclusively on birds of different species with clear dominance of feral pigeons (up to now no Wood Pigeons). In 1997 and 1998 the Sakers bred unsuccessfully. In the first year the three chicks were robbed by Eagle Owls *Bubo bubo*. In 1998 there were disturbances around the time of hatching, possibly caused by problems in food supply.

According to Trommer (in Augst 1998) the Saker already breeds in Poland. In May (1998) three nestlings were found in a former Buzzard *Buteo buteo* nest approximately 8km north of the breeding sites in the Czech Republic.

The number of Saker records in Middle Europe during the last two decades, however, increased steadily (Augst 1998). The source of the falcons in Germany probably came from lost captive birds (for falconry or breeding). A young bird, however, found in Schleswig-Holstein in 1983 was banded in Hungary. Also the localisation of records in the region of the upper Danube and North German plains in the course of the river Elbe gave evidence for a natural origin of these birds. Here the last recorded Sakers of natural origin surely came from the breeding population in Bohemia in the years around the turn of the century.

DISCUSSION

What are the causes for this development? A warming up of climate is not very plausible as a promoting factor. The Saker has very high resistance to cold, and starts to breed in Inner Asia at temperatures of minus 20°C (Baumgart 1978). Clear changes in behaviour, feeding or breeding biology are not detectable. But what made Middle Europe so attractive for the Saker in last few decades?

In my opinion the main cause of this process is the transformation of the Middle Europe agricultural landscape. In farming more and more industrial methods of cultivation and harvest are introduced, wide areas under crops have become common. Grassland species such as partridges, larks (*Alaudidae*) or bustards (*Otididae*) as well as hares (*Lepus*) and susliks disastrously decreased. The resources on these wide plains became exploitable only for species living and flying in from outside. The main representatives are pigeons (instead of partridges), starlings (instead of larks) and maybe even geese and cranes (for bustards). Because pigeons are the most characteristic and noticeable representatives of this process, it can be described in its essence as the conversion of the Middle European agricultural landscape in a way suitable for pigeons.

Pigeons benefit not only from their excellent flying abilities. Up to now they do not have any real predators in this sector. In open landscapes they mostly fly too low for the Peregrine and the plains are often too wide for effective attacks by Goshawks. They can be caught only by an enduring pursuit hunter able to fly very fast near to the ground with good acceleration and manoeuvrability (Baumgart 1996).

Hierofalcons, especially the Saker and Lanner, are suitable for this type of predation in Middle Europe. The Saker, however, has the advantage because its breeding range already reaches this area.. Because the falcon now preys primarily on birds in level flight, the height of vegetation cover is no longer a critical factor, as it was when searching for susliks.

Although the Saker, Peregrine and even Goshawk all rely on pigeons, they hunt them differently and do not directly compete with each other even if they breed sympatrically. The change from mammalian to avian prey might also lead to pesticide problems for the Saker.

Long-term breeding of Sakers in Central Middle Europe seems possible with this new prey base. The Saker's high variability in selection of breeding sites is an additional advantage. Maybe the bird-hunting Sakers will show (or have already shown) some slight biometrical differentiations compared with the mammal-hunting Sakers (Pererva & Grazhdankin 1994), directed towards a slightly changed performance profile.

The Sakers of South-east Europe, depending on seasonal food supply in susliks, were previously highly migratory. The remaining population is now more resident with a continuous food supply. Especially immature birds now appear to move in a north-west direction. This could promote the formation of a Middle European breeding population. This change in migratorial behaviour may also be the result of intensified trapping of Sakers in the Middle East (Bär 1997) leading to a near extinction of the migratory part of the population. It needs to be clarified whether this new orientation in migration behaviour is natural or due to human interference.

The extension of the Saker breeding area to Central Middle Europe raises questions concerning the complex understanding of changes to their environment. Transformations in the agricultural landscape may bring not only losses but also new prospects.

REFERENCES

AUGST, U. 1997. Der Würgfalke (*Falco cherrug*) – ein neuer Brutvogel Sachsens. *Mitt. Ver. Sächs. Orn.* 8: 111-113.

AUGST, U. 1998. Die Ansiedlung des Wurgfalken *Falco cherrug* als Brutvogel in Deutschland. *Limicola* 12: 297-313.

BAGYURA, J., L. HARASZTHY & T. SZITTA 1994a. Methods and Results of Saker Falcon *Falco cherrug* Management and Conservation in Hungary. In: Meyburg, B.-U. & R. D. Chancellor (eds): *Raptor Conservation Today*. WWGBP/Pica Press, Berlin.

BAGYURA, J., L. HARASZTHY & T. SZITTA 1994b. Feeding Biology of the Saker Falcon *Falco cherrug* in Hungary. In: Meyburg, B.-U. & R. D. Chancellor (eds): *Raptor Conservation Today*. WWGBP/Pica Press, Berlin.

BÄR, N. 1997. Falkenfang und Falkenhandel in der Arabischen Republik Syrien. *Mitt. Frank. Geogr. Ges.* 44: 191-223.

BAUMGART, W. 1978. Über Gefiedermerkmale, Existenzbedingungen und Züge der Brutbiologie östlicher Sakerfalken (*Falco cherrug milvipes*).- *Mitt. Zool. Mus. Berlin* 54, *Suppl. Ann. Orn.* 2: 145-166.

BAUMGART, W. 1991. Der Sakerfalke *Falco cherrug*.- NBB 514, Wittenberg Lutherstadt, 3. Aufl.

BAUMGART, W. 1994. Saker *Falco cherrug*. In Tucker, G. M. & Heath, M. F.: *Birds of Europe: Their Conservation Status*. BirdLife International Cambridge: 198-199.

BAUMGART, W. 1996. Functional aspects in the taxonomy of large falcons.- Proc. Specialists Workshop, Abu Dhabi (UAE), 14th-16th Nov. 1965, S. 93-110.
BAUMGART, W. 1997a. Funktionelle Positionen und Taxonomie der Eigentlichen Falken (Gattung *Falco*) [Functional Positions and Taxonomy of True Falcons (Genus *Falco*)].- *Mitt. Zool. Mus. Berl.* 73 1997) *Suppl.:.Ann. Orn.* 21. 103-129.
BAUMGART, W. 1997b. Der adaptive Charakter morphologischer Merkmale bei Greifvögeln und ihre taxonomische Relevanz. *Greifvögel und Falknerei* 1995: 54-69.
BAUMGART, W., A. GAMAUF, J. BAGYURA, L. HARASZTHY, J. CHAVKO & A. PEKLO 1993. Biologie und Status des Sakerfalken in Osteuropa. *Greifvögel und Falknerei* 1992: 102-106.
CADE, T. 1982. *The Falcons of the World*. London, Auckland, Sydney, Toronto, Johannesburg.
GLUTZ VON BLOTZHEIM; U. N., K. BAUER & E. BEZZEL 1971. *Handbuch der Vögel Mitteleuropas*, Bd. 4, Falconiformes, Frankfurt a. M.
JANOSSY, D. 1983. Beiträge zur Nahrung des Sakerfalken (*Falco cherrug*). *Puszta* (1/10): 5-10.
KODELKA, D. & R. PETRO 1994. Der Würgfalke (*Falco cherrug*) brütet in Schlesien. *Cas. Slez. Muz. Opava* (A) 43: 287-288.
KORELOW, M. N. 1962. In: Gawrin, W. F., I. A. Dolguschin, M. N. Korelow & M. A. Krzimina. Ptizy Kazachstana. Bd. 2 Odrjad chischny ptizy – Falconiformes. *Aschabad*: 498-508.
PERERVA, V. I. & A. V. GRAZHDANKIN 1994. Possible Effect of Anthropogenic Environmental changes on Morphological variation of some European Birds of Prey.- In: Meyburg, B.-U. & R. D. Chancellor (eds): *Raptor Conservation Today*. WWGBP/Pica Press, Berlin.
VAN DEN BRINK, F. H. 1972. *Die Säugetiere Europas*. Hamburg und Berlin.

Dr. Wolfgang Baumgart
Grumbkowstr. 2a
D – 13156 Berlin
Germany

Chancellor, R. D. & B.-U. Meyburg eds. 2000
Raptors at Risk
WWGBP / Hancock House

The Status of the Lugger Falcon *Falco jugger* in Pakistan

M. Ahmed, N.C. Fox and C.P. Eastham

ABSTRACT

Lugger falcons *Falco jugger* are traditionally used as a decoy or *barak* to trap migratory Sakers *Falco cherrug* and Peregrines *Falco peregrinus*. Falcon trapping is an important source of income for people in the rural areas of Pakistan. However, trapping is seriously affecting Lugger populations, with an indicated 50% decrease over the last 10 years. An estimated 2,000 - 2,500 Luggers are trapped each season, with most of these birds dying after capture due to the poor conditions in which they are kept. Other factors affecting populations in Pakistan and northern India are reduced prey availability due to urbanisation and agricultural development including the use of pesticides.

In a joint conservation project the Falcon Foundation International (FFI) and the National Avian Research Centre (NARC), are tackling the factors threatening Luggers. A series of workshops to improve the care and management of captive falcons were organised for trappers in the rural areas of Punjab. Trappers were interviewed to reveal which are the most common health-related problems in trapped falcons. Field biologists are continuing to monitor and estimate the distribution and density of the Lugger population in Pakistan. Blood and feather samples are collected for pesticide, heavy metal analysis, and phylogenetic studies.

INTRODUCTION

The Lugger Falcon *Falco jugger* is distributed in Pakistan and east through India, Assam and Burma, and locally in southern Afghanistan and south-eastern Iran (Del Hoyo *et al*, 1994). It inhabits arid to semi-arid open country. In Pakistan, it is resident throughout the drier, less intensively cultivated tracts of the Indus plains, and is widely but thinly distributed in southern Baluchistan, Sindh, Punjab and the lower plains of the North West Frontier Province (Roberts, 1991). Its status in Pakistan is considered to be scarce (Roberts, 1991) with some reports indicating the Lugger population to have decreased by around 50% over the last 10 years (Fox *et al*, 1996). Surveys are currently being undertaken by the FFIP (Falcon Foundation International Pakistan) and NARC (National Avian Research Center) to determine the size of the population (Fox *et al*, 1996; Ahmed, 1996).

Population declines in Pakistan and northern India are thought to be due to a reduction in prey availability caused by urbanisation and agricultural development including the increased use of agricultural pesticides and widespread trapping (Del Hoyo *et al*, 1994; Fox *et al*, 1996; Ahmed, 1996). Falcon trapping and trading is a traditional and important source of income for people in the rural areas of Pakistan. Concern that mortality of trapped birds in captivity may contribute to the decline of this species, has prompted FFIP and NARC to collect information on health of trapped birds and to initiate a series of workshops for trappers to improve the captive management of falcons. This paper describes the work carried out in 1997.

THE USE OF LUGGERS BY FALCON TRAPPERS IN PAKISTAN

In Pakistan, Lugger Falcons are trapped and are used as decoy birds to catch large falcons, such as Saker Falcons *Falco cherrug* and Peregrine Falcons *Falco peregrinus* which are sold to falconers in the Middle East. Fieldworkers from the FFIP estimate that between 2,000-2,500 Lugger Falcons are trapped in Pakistan each year (Fox *et al*, 1996; Ahmed, 1996). Most trapping takes place between June and August in the Fort Abbas and Bahawalpur districts of the Punjab, although some birds are trapped in Sindh.

After trapping, birds are maintained in captivity by local dealers for up to two months before being sold either to prominent falcon dealers in Karachi and Peshawar, or direct to the Saker trappers in other regions of Pakistan who use them until November when the trapping season is over.

A Lugger Falcon is prepared for its role as a decoy by having its eyelids "sealed" and attaching a small feather-noose bundle or "nigil" to its leg which acts as a prey item (Remple & Gross, 1993). When a large falcon is spotted, the "seeled" Lugger Falcon is thrown up into the air. Because it cannot see, it flies upwards in circles. To the larger falcon this presents an opportunity to rob the Lugger and, after it is ensnared, both birds will flutter to the ground. It is estimated that 90% of the Lugger Falcons die during the trapping season (Shahid Iqbal, *pers. comm.*). The remainder are either released or kept until the next season.

SOCIO-ECONOMIC IMPORTANCE OF FALCON TRAPPING TO RURAL COMMUNITIES

Trapping of falcons is an important source of income for rural communities in Pakistan. Data on the species, numbers and economic values of trapped falcons were obtained following interviews with trappers in the Yazman Mandi district of Punjab and are presented in Table 1. In 1996-97 season this trade was worth approximately 3.3 million rupees and with an estimated 350 people involved, this works out at Rs. 10,000 ($250 US) per person. This trade is secretive, so it is difficult to obtain accurate data and Rashid (1997) considered that trappers may earn three times this amount ($750 US). To put these figures into context, the Gross National Product per capita in Pakistan is estimated to be around $420 US per year (Nevo, 1995) and therefore either estimate represents a significant source of income for both trappers and the local economy.

Table 1. Species and numbers of falcons trapped in the Yazman Mandi district of Punjab in 1996/97 and revenue earned by the sale of these birds.

Species	Numbers	Total cost (Pakistan Rupees)
Saker Falcon *Falco cherrug*	3 females, 4 males	2,200,000
Lugger Falcon *Falco jugger*	500-600	1,000,000
Peregrine Falcon *Falco peregrinus*	1 female, 3 males	40,000
White-eyed Buzzard *Butastur teesa*	50-300	30,000
Red-headed Merlin *Falco chiquera*	100	10,000
Kestrel *Falco tinnunculus*	100	10,000
Hobby *Falco subbuteo*	50	5,000
Total revenue		32,95,000

MORTALITY OF TRAPPED LUGGER FALCONS

Trappers and dealers in Multan, Peshawar, Fort Abbas and Yazman Mandi were interviewed to determine the common health problems in captured Lugger Falcons. Some trapping facilities were visited to observe the management of the birds and to examine falcons.

In general, birds were kept on unsuitable perching material, ranging from bricks to perches covered in cloth material, often heavily contaminated with faeces and food remains. It is not surprising that bumblefoot is frequently seen in birds kept for periods longer than a month. Birds were fitted with poor quality jesses, often string, which cause abrasive injuries. Luggers were often housed in large groups in brick outhouses and consequently traumatic injuries were a common problem. The presence of domestic poultry and pigeons exposes falcons to common avian viruses including pox and Newcastle disease. Although no serological surveys have yet been carried out to determine the exposure to viral diseases in Luggers in Pakistan, pathological and serological investigations have been undertaken in trapped Houbara Bustards *Chlamydotis undulata* maintained under similar captive conditions in Pakistan (Bailey *et al*, 1996; Bailey *et al*, 1997).

Trappers were unwilling to elaborate on the numbers of Luggers dying after trapping, and although most said only one or two died, one admitted to losing 150 of a group of 200 birds in 1996.

Concern for the health and welfare of trapped Lugger Falcons prompted FFIP to organise a series of workshops in February and December 1997, in the Yazman Mandi and Fort Abbas districts of Punjab, which were attended by approximately 200 trappers.

DISCUSSION

Neither NARC nor FFIP condone the trapping of wild falcons. But it is likely that in Pakistan this trade will continue for as long as there is a demand for wild-caught Saker and Peregrine Falcons for the Middle East market. The primary objective of these workshops was to promote better care and management of trapped Luggers by targeting the people directly involved in the trade and making them aware of the negative effect they may be having on the wild population. These workshops also represented an opportunity to gather information from the trappers and to promote a conservation message through literature, posters and videos. Improvements in the health and welfare of trapped birds may reduce some of the excessive mortality associated with this trade. This presents a step forward in bringing together conservationists and trappers to find solutions to this complex problem. Population surveys must continue in order to estimate distribution, density and productivity.

ACKNOWLEDGEMENTS

We thank Brigadier Humayun Malik, Lt Col Syed Mushtaq Hussain, Mr Shahid Iqbal, Dr Tom Bailey, the FFIP team and Mr Mohamed Al Bowardi from NARC for his continued interest and support in this work.

REFERENCES

AHMED, M. 1996. Survey report on the Lugger Falcon in Pakistan by the FFIP and NARC, Abu Dhabi, 1996. FFIP 14pp unpublished report.

BAILEY, T.A., U. WERNERY, R.E. GOUGH, R. MANVELL & J.H. SAMOUR 1996. Serological survey of Houbara bustards *Chlamydotis undulata macqueenii* in the UAE for antibodies against some avian viruses. *Veterinary Record 1996*; 139: 238-239.

BAILEY, T.A., O. COMBREAU & A. MUKHTAR 1997. A report on the Houbara Research and Rehabilitation Centre of the FFIP, March 1997. NARC, Abu Dhabi unpublished report for FFIP & NARC.

DEL HOYO J., A. ELLIOTT & J. SARGATAL 1994. *Handbook of the Birds of the World*, Vol 2. New World Vultures to Guineafowl. Barcelona. Lynx Editions 1994: 273.

FOX, N.C., A. MUKHTAR, C.P. EASTHAM & H.J. MACDONALD 1996. Research and Conservation of the Lugger Falcon *Falco jugger* in Pakistan. Second International Conference of the Raptor Research Foundation, Urbino, Italy, 1996. Unpublished.

NEVO, M. 1995. *New Internationalist*. Pakistan. No 36.
RASHID S. 1997. When the last falcon has been hunted! *Natura*, Newsletter of the WWF - Pakistan, 1997: 19-21.
REMPLE D. & C. GROSS 1993. *Falconry and birds of prey in the Gulf*. Motivate Publishing, Dubai, 1993: 20.
ROBERTS, T.J. 1991. *The Birds of Pakistan*. Oxford University Press, Karachi, 216-218.

M. Ahmed
Falcon Foundation International
4-E/2, Gulberg III
Lahore
Pakistan.

N.C. Fox & C.P. Eastham
The National Avian Research Centre
The Falcon Facility
Penllynin Farm, College Road
Carmarthen, Carmarthenshire, SA33 5EH
UK

Part 4

Conservation Models for Raptors of the World

Madagascar Fish Eagle *Haliaeetus vociferoides*

Conveners:
Richard T. Watson & Ron R. Hartley

Chancellor, R. D. & B.-U. Meyburg eds. 2000
Raptors at Risk
WWGBP / Hancock House

The California Condor Recovery Programme

Lloyd Kiff

ABSTRACT

Relatively widespread over North America through the late Pleistocene, the California Condor has been a rare bird throughout its recorded history. Despite much habitat preservation, research, education, and enforcement measures, it steadily declined in numbers for nearly 200 years, reaching a low point of 21-22 birds in 1983. Losses were due almost entirely to direct human persecution, primarily shooting and indirect anthropogenic causes, including lead and possibly other forms of poisoning. In 1980 a "hands-on" management programme was initiated by the United States Fish and Wildlife Service and the National Audubon Society. Wild birds were equipped with radios to determine causes of mortality and to identify critical habitat, breeding behaviour was studied intensively, and several eggs, young, and adults were taken to zoos to establish a captive breeding programme. Despite efforts to sustain the wild population, the species suffered a disastrous decline in the winter of 1984-85 to only one known breeding pair, and authorities decided to trap the last free-flying individuals for their own security and to add them to the captive breeding programme. The last free-flying individual was brought into captivity on 19 April 1987. The first successful captive breeding was accomplished in 1988, and productivity of the captive flock has increased annually since then at breeding facilities at the San Diego Wild Animal Park, Los Angeles Zoo, and World Center for Birds of Prey. The first releases of captive progeny occurred in 1992. Subsequently, 16 releases have been conducted at four sites in California and two in Arizona. By the end of 1998 there were 147 condors in existence, including 42 in the wild (22 in Arizona and 20 in California) and 105 in captivity. As a result of the aggressive management programme, the total condor population has increased by seven times since the early 1980s, and there is increasing hope that this unusual species can be saved from extinction.

INTRODUCTION

The California Condor *Gymnogyps californianus* has always been rare in modern times. Judging from fossil evidence, it was more common and widespread in the Pleistocene, ranging eastward all the way to Florida (Brodkorb 1964) and New York (Steadman & Miller 1987), but by historical times it occurred only along the Pacific Coast from British Columbia south to northern Baja California Norte, Mexico (Koford 1953). Following the arrival of European man on the Pacific Coast about 200 years ago, condor numbers and range declined even more precipitously, almost entirely because of anthropogenic factors. As recently as the 1970s, many writers began predicting the California Condor's certain and imminent demise. However, an aggressive management programme begun in 1980 may yet save it. Knowledge gained from both the positive and negative aspects of the programme might be useful to persons attempting to save other problem species.

BACKGROUND

Early history of condor research and management

The first detailed study of the California Condor of any kind was conducted by the wildlife photographers William Finley and Herman Bohlman at Eaton Canyon, Los Angeles County, California in the spring of 1906. The four-part account of their exploits at a condor nest and the behaviour of the nestling, which they took into captivity, still makes fascinating reading (Finley 1906, 1908a, 1908b, 1910).

There was little formal attention paid to the species until three decades later when Cyril S. Robinson, a British-born employee of the U.S. Forest Service, made a pioneering field study of the roosting and feeding habits of condors in the Los Padres National Forest, mostly in Santa Barbara County, California, between 1936-40 (Robinson 1940). The first actual governmental land management action on behalf of the condor was the establishment of the 1,198-acre Sisquoc Condor Sanctuary by the U.S. Forest Service in 1937 at the urging of local rancher-conservationist Robert E. Easton and the National Audubon Society (Koford 1953). The sanctuary area included an important condor roost, nest sites, and bathing pool. In a sense, the condor management era began with this event, since the sanctuary was henceforth closed to public entry without permit.

At about the same time, a prominent amateur ornithologist and wildlife film maker from Pasadena, California, J.R. "Bill" Pemberton, began efforts to film condors in the Sespe area of Ventura County, California. He interested John Baker, president of the National Audubon Society, and Joseph Grinnell, a professor at the University of California at Berkeley and the leading ornithologist in the state, in the idea of supporting a graduate student to conduct a comprehensive study of the California Condor under Grinnell's direction. With financial support from Pemberton and the National Audubon Society, thanks to Baker's efforts, Carl Koford was assigned by Grinnell to the project, and he conducted a landmark study of the species and its breeding behaviour between 1939-46 (Koford 1953). Koford worked mainly in the back country of Ventura County, and his findings led to the establishment of the 35,000-acre Sespe Condor Sanctuary, which was enlarged to 53,000 acres in 1951 (Wilbur 1978). In his 1953 monograph, Koford (*op cit.*) estimated that the total condor population consisted of only 60 individuals, although he privately admitted that this was a conservative figure and that the population might contain as many as 100 birds (Koford *in litt.*).

Condor numbers continued to decline, however, and the National Audubon Society commissioned a short-term assessment of the status of the population in 1963-64 by two California conservationist ranchers, Ian and Eben McMillan. Their findings, which were published with the collaboration of Alden H. Miller of the University of California, Berkeley (Miller *et al.* 1964), suggested that the condor population had declined to 40 birds.

In 1965, Fred C. Sibley became the first U.S. Fish and Wildlife Service biologist charged with studying the condor population with the specific assignment of predicting the effects of a proposed dam on Sespe Creek, which flows through the Sespe Condor Sanctuary, on the species.

Also in 1965, the National Audubon Society hired John Borneman as a "condor warden," armed only with a strong sense of public relations and a finely developed sense of humour. The U.S. Forest Service soon had its own condor biologist, Dean Carrier, and his assignment was to prepare a condor management plan for the vast Los Padres National Forest, which, by then, comprised a large portion of the condor's range (Carrier 1971). Carrier's position was maintained between 1968 to 1973.

Sibley's assignment lasted for four years, and his conclusion that the dam would likely have a disastrous impact on the condor population (Sibley 1969) coincided with the defeat of the project by the local electorate. During his tenure, Sibley, Robert D. Mallette (California Department of Fish and Game), and Borneman, initiated an annual survey of the condor population, which was held for two days each October from 1966 to 1980 and involved the participation of 50-100 trained observers (Mallette & Borneman 1966). The combined results of several surveys indicated that the total condor population was between 50-60 individuals between 1966-70 (Wilbur 1978) and confirmed what many had suspected, i.e., that the population estimate of the McMillans (Miller et al. 1964) was probably too conservative.

Sanford R. Wilbur followed Sibley as the U.S. Fish and Wildlife Service condor biologist in late 1969, and he held that position until 1980. During this entire period, he was the only U.S. Fish and Wildlife Service employee assigned to the condor "programme." Wilbur produced a monographic account on the species, including an exhaustive bibliography (Wilbur 1978), and made detailed studies on condor food resources (Wilbur 1972), plumages (Wilbur 1975), and population status (Wilbur et al. 1972, 1976). He also collaborated in a study of DDE-induced eggshell thinning in condors (Kiff et al. 1979), conducted supplemental feeding experiments near the Sespe Condor Sanctuary (Wilbur et al. 1974), and made several expeditions to the Sierra San Pedro Martir, Baja California Norte, Mexico in a fruitless attempt to confirm the existence of condors in that range (Wilbur & Kiff 1980). Finally, he organized the First International Symposium on the Vultures, co-sponsored by the Western Foundation of Vertebrate Zoology and held at the Santa Barbara Museum of Natural History in 1979. The proceedings appeared as a major book on Old and New World vulture biology and conservation (Wilbur & Jackson 1983), and the symposium greatly facilitated collaboration between vulture researchers on several continents.

As a part of the Federal mandate to recover condor populations, a "California Condor Recovery Team" was established in 1972. Consisting of five members, representing the four government agencies cooperating in the programme, plus the National Audubon Society, the Team prepared a recovery plan for the species (U.S. Fish and Wildlife Service 1974). It was formalized in 1975, the first of its kind ever approved by the U.S. Fish and Wildlife Service. The plan was heavily oriented toward protecting condor habitat as a means of saving the species.

Habitat protection, nest protection, and enforcement had been the themes of condor recovery for many years, yet the trends in the annual survey results and the complete disappearance of condors from areas where they had occurred regularly up until very recent years indicated that the species was continuing to decline. By the late 1970s, Wilbur (1978) estimated that the total condor population consisted of no more than 50, and possibly as few as 40, individuals. By now, even some biologists were predicting the inevitable extinction of the California Condor.

CALIFORNIA CONDOR RECOVERY PROGRAMME

Modern management era

Reacting to the increasingly hopeless situation, Richard Plunkett, then vice-president of the National Audubon Society, proposed enlisting the help of the American Ornithologists' Union to convene a panel of experts from various subdisciplines of biology to consider the situation and suggest steps that might be taken to save the condor. Following several meetings, the panel, headed by Robert Ricklefs, soon recommended that a vigorous condor management programme be set into motion immediately. The principal ingredients of the such a programme were to include radio tracking to obtain information on causes of mortality and critical habitat, detailed behavioural observations of birds in the wild, especially at the nest, and, if necessary, captive breeding (Ricklefs 1978). This amounted to an endorsement of a draft "California Condor Contingency Plan," prepared by the Condor Recovery Team in 1976 under Sanford Wilbur's direction and approved by the U.S. Fish and Wildlife Service in 1977, that had also recommended captive breeding and other "hands-on" actions (U.S. Fish and Wildlife Service 1996).

The appearance of these reports gave momentum to the establishment of the Condor Research Center, situated in Ventura, California, by the U.S. Fish and Wildlife Service (USFWS) and the National Audubon Society in 1980. Noel F.R. Snyder was chosen to serve as the USFWS condor biologist, replacing Wilbur, and John Ogden was placed in charge of the National Audubon Society portion of the programme. The California Department of Fish and Game also maintained a condor biologist position between 1982 to 1989.

A division of labour was determined early in the programme, and Ogden's crew focused on the identification of critical habitat, while Snyder's group located nests and made observations of birds throughout their breeding cycle. In May 1980 Federal and State permits authorizing the capture of a condor for captive breeding and equipping 10 wild condors with radiotelemetry devices were approved, but they were rescinded in the following month when a condor chick died while being examined by a field team from the Condor Research Center. After nearly two years of hearings and difficult negotiations, the California State Fish and Game Commission granted permission for researchers to place radios on condors, and nine individuals were eventually tagged by the NAS field crew. Partly as a device to capture birds, the NAS group engaged in supplemental feeding of condors on large ranches where they were known to forage. Captured birds were weighed, blood samples taken, and equipped with patagially-mounted radio transmitters with bold numbers specific to each individual.

Up until this time, the perennial problems in condor management included (1) obtaining an accurate estimate of the number of birds still in existence, (2) understanding the actual range of the species and identifying critical habitat, and (3) identifying causes of mortality.

Noel Snyder and Eric Johnston developed a novel technique to answer the first question (Snyder & Johnston 1985). They censused the population by comparing the distinctive wing patterns, produced by differential patterns of feather loss and replacement, of individual condors from photographs. Based on analyses of hundreds of photographs from all parts of the condor's range, they concluded that the wild population consisted of only 22 birds in 1982 (Fig. 1). This was the lowest number of California Condors in the recorded history of the species. It was also the first time that the entire condor population had ever been accurately counted down to the last individual, a feat that would not have been possible with conventional observational techniques.

Figure 1. Condor Populations since 1982

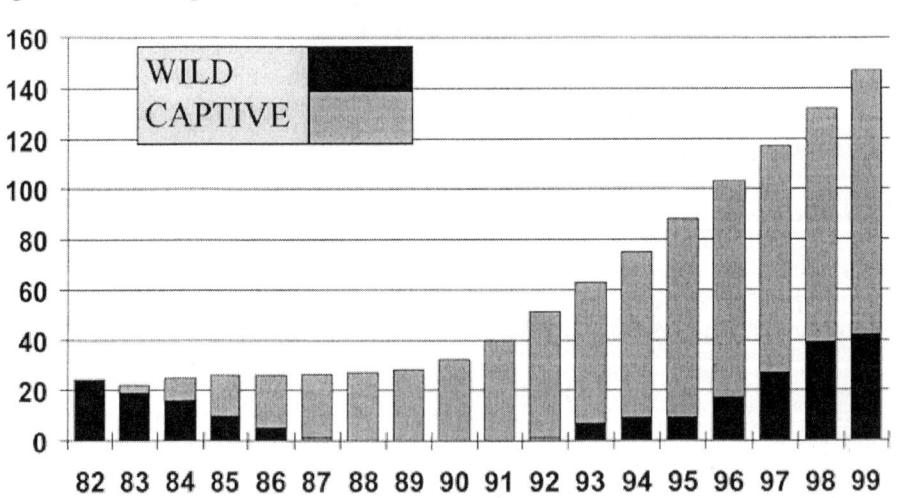

Building on the years of information about condor movements compiled by Koford, the McMillans, Sibley, Wilbur, and the annual October surveys, the NAS crew obtained a much better understanding of the current range of the condor by following radioed birds with fixed-wing aircraft and on the ground. In addition, simply having more condor observers in the field led to increased understanding of the whereabouts of the birds. It was obvious that the effective range of the species had declined greatly since the early 1970s with a particularly conspicuous decline in the number of birds recorded in the coastal mountains north of Santa Barbara County. Meretsky and Snyder (1992) integrated data from the radiotelemetry studies and the photographic survey, reporting that individual condors occasionally travelled more than 200 km, visiting all portions of the still vast condor range in a single day.

Despite the size of the birds and the prominence of the recovery programme, surprisingly little is known about the causes of condor mortality, even in recent times. Shooting was probably by far the most frequent cause of condor losses historically, but such incidents were also more likely to come to the attention of condor chroniclers, especially since many shot birds were saved as museum specimens (Wilbur 1974, 1978). Other known causes of condor losses historically included killing condors for Indian ceremonial use, capturing birds for sport or for pets, egg collecting, and accidental deaths, including striking man-made objects (Koford 1953, Wilbur 1978). Poisoning from various agents may have been a major problem at certain times and places in the condor's history, but convincing documentation of such episodes is surprisingly lacking. Severe DDE-induced eggshell thinning occurred in the condor population during the 1960s, and probably earlier (Kiff *et al.* 1979), but after the banning of DDT use in the United States in 1972, the incidence of thin-shelled eggs declined almost immediately. Inexplicably, two badly thinned eggs were laid by a single female in 1986 (Kiff 1989), but by then this phenomenon was no longer a problem for the condor population as a whole.

Partly as a result of the radiotelemetry programme, the cause of death of three wild condors in the 1980s was shown to be from a previously undocumented cause - lead poisoning (Snyder & Snyder 1989). The birds had apparently ingested lead bullet fragments or lead shot from shot deer or other carcasses within their range in sufficient amounts to cause their deaths. This finding had implications for the past, present, and future of the species. As for the past, this could have been the cause of death of several condors reportedly found sick and unable to fly (Koford 1953). Based on an admittedly small sample size, it was the major cause of condor losses during the 1980s, when the most intensive field studies were made of the species. In the western United States, where hunting and carrying guns are jealously guarded privileges, the incidence of shooting on the open range does not seem likely to decline soon, so lead poisoning could still figure prominently in the future of the condor. Unfortunately, only one of the six birds lost from the wild flock in the winter of 1984-85 was radioed, and the other birds were never found, so the actual causes of their deaths remains unknown.

Snyder and his associates made detailed observations at condor nests, adding greatly to the information provided earlier by Koford (Snyder 1983, Snyder *et al.* 1986, Snyder & Snyder 1989). Following other difficult negotiations with state officials, the team was finally allowed in 1983 to begin taking wild-laid eggs for hatching in captivity in an effort to gradually build up a captive breeding flock. It had already been confirmed that California Condors, like the related Andean Condors, would lay replacement clutches (Harrison & Kiff 1980, Snyder & Hamber 1985), and biologists took advantage of this behaviour to double- and sometimes triple-clutch wild pairs. From 1983 to 1985 15 eggs were taken from the wild and incubated at the San Diego Wild Animal Park with hatchability of 86.7% and a survival rate of 92.3% (Kuehler & Witman 1988, Kuehler *et al.* 1991). The overall condor population began to increase for the first time in recorded history, following the low point in 1981-82 (Fig. 1).

Even though the number of birds in the wild continued to decline (Fig. 1), the situation was looking more hopeful by the fall of 1984, when it seemed possible that there could be as many as five breeding condor pairs in the coming breeding season (Toone & Wallace 1994). Unexpectedly, however, six out of the remaining 15 wild birds (40% of the entire wild population) were lost in the winter of 1984-85, and the number of known breeding pairs was reduced to one. This prompted USFWS officials to recommend in the fall of 1985 that the last remaining individuals be captured for their own security and to bolster the captive flock. Since the principal problem for the condor has always been excessive adult mortality, this was one way of reducing it, i.e., bringing the birds into captivity where they were safer. The plan was strongly opposed by the NAS, who obtained an injunction to block capture of the birds, but the USFWS position, which was supported by the majority of condor biologists, prevailed in court in June 1986. The last free-flying condor, a male bearing the tag "AC-9" (= adult condor no. 9), was captured on Easter Sunday, 19 April 1987.

Captive breeding:

When AC-9 was brought into captivity, the captive flock totalled 27 birds, including 10 captured as free-flying individuals between 1967-87, 13 from eggs laid in the wild and hatched in captivity between 1983-86, and 4 removed from the wild as nestlings between 1982-86. Fortuitously, the sex ratio was about even among the 27 birds. The flock was about evenly split between two facilities, one at the San Diego Wild Animal Park at San Pasqual, California and the other at the Los Angeles Zoo. A third major breeding facility was established in 1993 at the World Center for Birds of Prey in Boise, Idaho.

Captive breeding was first accomplished in 1988, when a pair of wild-caught condors at the San Diego Wild Animal Park produced a chick christened "Molloko" (Toone & Risser 1988). Four young were produced in the following year, and chick production of the captive flock has increased annually (Fig. 2), albeit more slowly than anticipated.

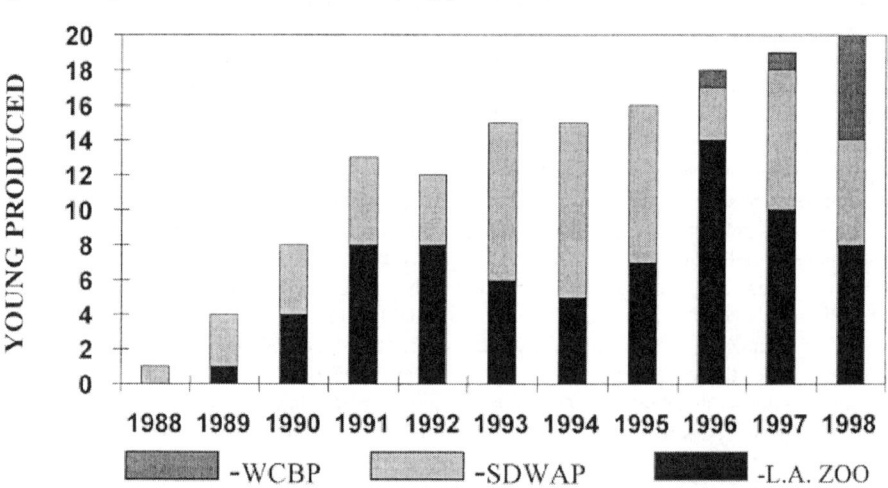

Figure 2. Captive California Condor breeding production

DNA fingerprinting analyses revealed that the captive condor flock included 14 founders from three "clans" in which the between-group relatedness seemed to be significantly less than the within-group relatedness (Geyer *et al.* 1993). The implication for condor managers is that the founder gene contributions of the subgroups are more important than the contributions of individual founders. These considerations weigh heavily in determining pairs of the captive birds, which are computer-model generated to maximize heterozygosity in the progeny. There is already known to be a lethal gene within the population that causes embryonic skeletal dysplasia (M. Wallace *in litt.*). Since the homozygous gene responsible is possessed by both members of one of the most productive pairs, it led to greatly reduced egg success in this pair before the cause was determined.

From 1988 to 1998 226 eggs were laid by the captive flock. Of these eggs, 167 (73.9%) were fertile, and 141 (84.4%) hatched. A high rate of infertility among first-time breeders and the effects of the aforementioned deleterious gene account for most of the non-hatching. Of some interest has been the high frequency of egg laying in January, far earlier than any recorded historically in the wild (Snyder & Hamber 1985, Harvey *et al.* 1996), and breeding attempts by five-year old birds (one successful) and even one four-year old bird. Previously, the age of first breeding in the species was thought to be six years, when the full adult plumage is attained, or later (Koford 1953).

Reintroduction to the wild

Following the capture of the last free-flying California Condor in 1987, the Condor Recovery Team recommended the initiation of an experimental release of the similar Andean Condor in southern California to refine condor release techniques, test the criteria being used to select release sites, field test condor rearing methods, identify potential problems peculiar to the California environment, evaluate radiotelemetry packages and other equipment, and train a field crew for anticipated California Condor releases (U.S. Fish and Wildlife Service 1996). Between 1988 to 1991, 13 yearling female Andean Condors were obtained from several U.S. zoos and released from three different sites in the vicinity of the Sespe Condor Sanctuary area (Wallace 1991). Only one of the 13 birds, an individual that struck a power line, was lost during the experiment. Following their recapture, the female Andean Condors were sent to Colombia and Venezuela to be re-released in areas where males of the same age had been released earlier (Lieberman *et al.* 1991). The surrogate release experiment was judged to be highly successful, and it helped the condor recovery programme and habitat protection efforts to maintain momentum during the period when California Condors were not in the wild.

In October 1986 the Condor Recovery Team established several criteria to be satisfied before a release of captive-bred California Condors could take place. These included having three actively breeding pairs of condors, three chicks behaviourally suitable for release, and retaining at least five offspring from each breeding pair contributing to the release (U.S. Fish and Wildlife Service 1996). In June 1989, a provision was added to retain a minimum of seven progeny in captivity for founders that were not reproductively active.

By 1991, several years earlier than originally predicted, two of the captive-produced chicks met these criteria. Although the aforementioned criteria had called for a minimum of three eligible birds, it was decided to go ahead and seize the earliest opportunity to conduct a release, using two Andean Condor young of the same age to create a larger social group. The first release of captive-reared California Condors occurred on 14 January 1992 in the Sespe Condor Sanctuary, when "Xewe" (a female) and "Chocuyens" (a male) were set free. The Andean Condors were returned to captivity in September 1992, officially marking the end of the experiment with the species in California. Chocuyens was found dead on 8 October 1992, having died from ingesting ethylene glycol, a principal component of anti-freeze, which the bird probably found in a campground parking lot.

Other releases soon followed, however, with six more condors being released on 1 December 1992 at the same Sespe Condor Sanctuary site. By the end of 1998, 16 separate releases of captive-produced California Condors had been conducted at six localities in two states (Fig. 3, Tables 1, 2). The Arizona releases were finally initiated in 1996 by The Peregrine Fund, eight years after the recovery team had recommended such an action and following years of contentious public hearings, lawsuits, and negotiations between a myriad of governmental agencies and Native American tribes.

The Condor Recovery Team established a protocol for the selection of release sites, and it includes such criteria as remoteness (but with sufficient access for the field team), protection from mammalian predators, availability of suitable roost sites and water, historical condor use, and proper wind conditions for soaring. Not least, areas have been selected where local community support for releases exceeds local opposition, although all of the release sites are on land owned by the Federal government. Part of the overall strategy in adding new release sites has been to find localities that are sufficiently disjunct from earlier sites to allow the new birds to develop their foraging and flight skills without interference from older birds, yet close enough to expect that birds from separate release sites will eventually meet and, over time, incorporate the interstitial areas into their effective ranges.

Although there has been quite a bit of variability in release procedures, depending as much (or more) on political factors as biological ones, the main ingredients have remained the same: Birds selected for release are usually raised together in a specially designated pen at one of the breeding facilities for four-five months (equivalent to their normal nestling period) or less, then helicoptered to the release site, where they are held in an open pen covered with netting for a period ranging from only two weeks to three months, during which the birds become acclimatised to their surroundings and further socialize with each other. During this period of confinement, they are provided with unlimited food, using techniques to minimize the association of food with humans. The actual release is initiated by the removal of the netting from the enclosure during nighttime, so that the birds are free to leave the pen when they choose. Most birds have been released at about the age when they would have left a nest site normally, but members of one cohort were not released until well into their second year.

Figure 3. Condor Release Sites

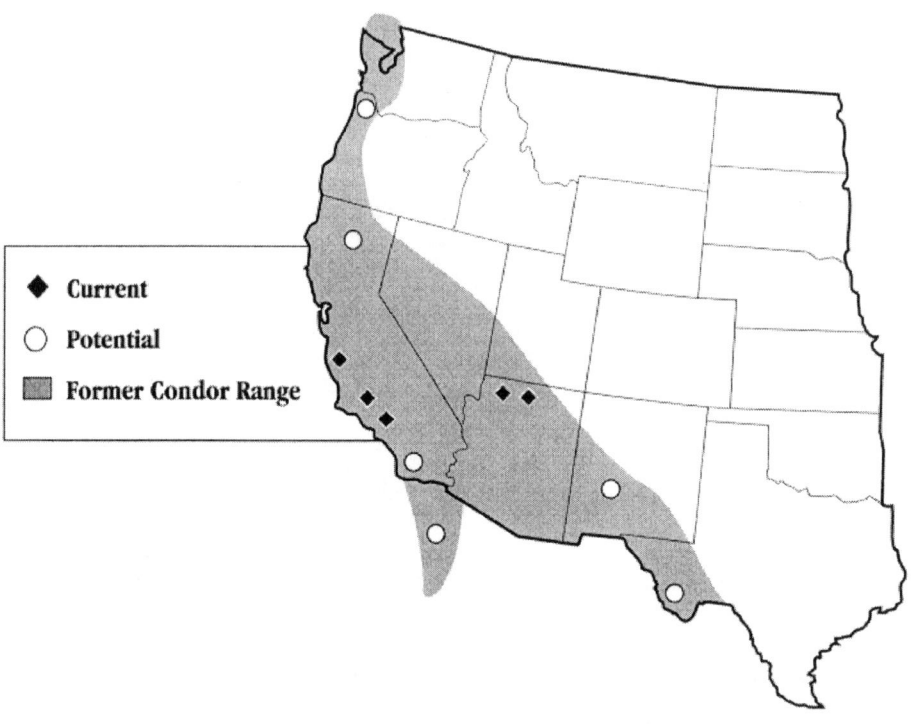

Released birds are provided with food (stillborn dairy calves) at designated feeding sites, which are moved from time to time, as long as they continue to utilize such sources. Although released birds have tended to begin feeding to some extent on items they have found on their own after about two years in the wild, all still depend mostly on the food provided to them by biologists. This assures them of a contaminant-free food source, and at least in the early months following release, it encourages them to remain in the more secure area near the release site. It is probable that this species will always utilize such "vulture restaurants" to some extent in the future, depending on the seasonal availability of "natural" food sources (including livestock).

The released birds in California have not proved to be particularly more mobile than the historical condor population, but, as might be expected, they tend to wander more widely as they grow older. As a part of the recovery process, the original Condor Recovery Team designated critical habitat in various portions of the vast (>2 million hectares) recent historical range of the species, and it has been gratifying to see the released birds gradually begin to reoccupy many of these areas. Certain of the individuals released at the Vermilion Cliffs in Arizona have routinely moved widely throughout the region from southern Utah to the central portion of the Grand Canyon. One bird even wandered as far north as Flaming Gorge, Wyoming, located on the Colorado River, before returning to its release site, a distance of 560 km (S. Farry pers. comm.). Three others also moved north along the channel of the Colorado River to Grand Junction, Colorado, where they spent several days in the vicinity of a park visitor's centre. They returned to the release site, nearly 400 km SW, in less than a day (S. Farry *op cit.*).

Table 1. History of California Condor releases, 1992-1998.

	Male	Female	Unknown
Sespe Condor Sanctuary, Ventura Co., California:			
14 January 1992	1	1	
2 December 1992	2	4	
Lion Canyon, Santa Barbara Co., California:			
8 December 1993	3	2	
8 February 1995	5	1	
29 August 1995	1	7	
19 November 1996	2	2	
14 November 1997	1	3	
Castle Crags, San Luis Obispo Co., California			
13 February 1996	2	2	
Ventana Wilderness Area, Monterey County, California:			
19 January 1997	3	1	
12 December 1997	3	2	
Vermilion Cliffs, Coconino Co., Arizona:			
12 December 1996	2	4	
14 May 1997	2	2	
27 May 1997	3	2	
20 November 1997	4	4	
23 November 1998	1		
Hurricane Ridge, Coconino Co., Arizona:			
18 November 1998	3	2	2

Table 2. Summary of California Condor release results, January 1992-December 1998 (compiled by Robert Mesta, U.S. Fish and Wildlife Service)

Total releases	16
Total condors released	75
Total died 19	
Losses in wild:	
Collisions with power lines	5
Drowned	2
Cause unknown*	2
Poisoned	1
Electrocuted on power line	1
Killed by Golden Eagle	1
* One possibly killed by coyote	
Disappeared and presumed dead:	4
Recaptured & died in captivity:	
Malnutrition	1
Cancer	1
Gunshot wound	1
Total recaptured for behavioural reasons	14
Total surviving in wild	42
Percent of released birds still in wild	56

Early in the release programme, the birds were attracted to power poles as perch sites, and this led to several fatal collisions with power lines. To address this problem, Michael Wallace, Los Angeles Zoo Curator and also the Condor Recovery Team Leader, placed fake power poles in the pens where the birds were held prior to release, wiring them so that birds landing on these structures received mild electrical shocks. Judging from the fact that only one bird has been lost subsequently from striking a powerline and that none have been recorded attempting to perch on power poles since this technique was initiated, the method seems to have worked.

The principal problem for the release programme, and one not yet solved, is the tendency for many of the birds to be drawn to human structures and activities. This has resulted in many bizarre episodes involving released condors and humans, much to the concern and frustration of the field crews following the birds. In California, some birds have tended to land on the roofs of houses and other structures, where they have torn out insulation and caused other property damage, even to vehicles. In Arizona, the birds have been attracted to the camps of fishermen along the Colorado River, where they have torn up tents, sleeping bags, and other gear. All of these behaviours seem to derive more from the curiosity of the condors and their natural tendency to play, rather than from hunger. While some episodes are initially entertaining, they eventually annoy the general public, especially the victims of condor vandalism, and they erode support for the recovery programme.

In an effort to discourage such behaviour and to make condors warier, some of the earlier release cohorts were subjected to various forms of "aversive conditioning," or systematic harassment, by the Los Angeles Zoo staff. Some biologists have also strongly favoured parent rearing of the birds to be released over puppet rearing, arguing that such individuals remain warier of humans in the wild (see discussion in Wallace 1994). Empirically, however, there seems to have been little correlation between these earlier experiences in the zoo setting, and the eventual behaviour of birds once they are released. The pressure to release as many birds as possible, regardless of their provenance, in an effort to establish the species in the wild as soon as possible has precluded rigorous field testing of rearing methods. Regrettably, the tendency of some individuals to be constantly attracted to anthropogenic situations has forced condor biologists to recapture 14 of them and remove them from the wild permanently (Table 2).

The results of the releases to the end of 1998 are summarized in Table 2. It is encouraging that there is no primary cause of mortality, especially now that the incidence of collision with power lines has been minimized, and it is also encouraging that only one of the birds has been shot. Only about 25% (19 of 75) of the released birds have actually died, and including the birds recaptured and returned to captivity for behavioural reasons as losses, survival of the released condors has been 56%. This is remarkably good for the early, still experimental years of such a programme, and, if this rate of success can be maintained or improved, it is likely that the condor can be successfully re-established in several regions.

One ominous undercurrent of the release programme is that several birds have been recaptured and brought back into captivity because of elevated lead levels in their blood. They were subjected to chelation treatment to reduce the lead levels, apparently recovered, and were re-released to the wild. In the opinion of the attending veterinarian (C. Stringfield pers. comm.) the birds would not have survived without such treatment. One bird has suffered two such episodes, yet is now back in the wild. In one instance, several condors were actually observed feeding on a deer gutpile that was suspected to contain lead bullet fragments, and they were soon trapped by the field team. Blood analyses confirmed that the birds had alarmingly high lead levels. There is some hope that there will be a general conversion to safer non-lead alloys for bullets in the near future, aided by a push from the U.S. military establishment. Short of the abandonment of lead as the bullet of choice by hunters and other shooters in open country, this factor remains a serious threat to wild condors.

Additional release sites being credibly considered or suggested (in descending order of probability) are in Baja California Norte, Mexico (Sierra San Pedro Martir), New Mexico (Ladder Ranch), various portions of northern California, and San Diego County, California (Fig. 3). The Condor Recovery Team has formally recommended that releases be conducted at the first two sites. Other areas, including the Channel Islands off southern California, the Columbia River Gorge of Oregon, and the Big Bend area of West Texas have also been suggested.

Present situation and future directions

The condor recovery programme is unusual among rescue efforts of this type in that both the captive and wild populations are being built up in parallel, and, so far, this strategy seems to be working. By the end of 1998 there were 147 condors, including 105 in captivity and 42 in the wild (Fig. 1), a seven-fold increase in the population since the low point of 1982. From this standpoint the recovery programme has been remarkably successful. Some of the older birds (now five years old) released in California are beginning to form pair bonds and engage in adolescent versions of courtship displays (R. Mesta pers. comm.). Successful breeding by condors in the wild is the last remaining proximate milestone, short of establishing a completely self-sustaining population, always the ultimate goal of the recovery programme.

According to the most recent revision of the California Condor Recovery Plan (U.S. Fish and Wildlife Service 1996) "the minimum criterion for reclassification to threatened is the maintenance of at least two non-captive populations and one captive population. These populations (1) must each number at least 150 individuals, (2) must each contain at least 15 breeding pairs and (3) be reproductively self-sustaining and have a positive rate of population growth. In addition, the non-captive populations (4) must be spatially disjunct and non-interacting, and (5) must contain individuals descended from each of the 14 founders."

The most serious remaining obstacles to achieving these objectives, as I see it, are: (1) Increasing the rate of captive breeding, which has never approached the level theoretically possible, (2) solving the problem of condor attraction to humans and areas of human activities in the wild, and (3) solving the problem of lead use in the range of the condor. Of probable future concern are (1) the possibility of additional deleterious genes appearing in the population, (2) habitat loss in some regions, and (3) political opposition to the condor recovery programme and endangered species programmes in general, resulting in the withdrawal of essential government support.

Funding the programme has always been a problem. It costs The Peregrine Fund about $2,000/year to maintain each individual condor (W. Burnham pers. comm.), so merely maintaining a captive population of at least 150 individuals would cost $300,000 annually at that rate. Indeed, some (e.g., Tom Cade) are questioning the wisdom of keeping 150 or more condors in captivity indefinitely. Perhaps eventually the captive flock could be dispersed to many zoo facilities so that the financial burden could be shared by more organizations and more educational opportunities could be created. The field efforts are also quite expensive, since the programme is still at the level where biologists attempt to monitor the whereabouts of each individual. With time and more birds in the wild, this intensive level of management can probably be reduced without harm to the overall wild population.

In the meantime, the condor recovery programme can only survive through the partnership of private sector organizations like The Peregrine Fund and the Zoological Society of San Diego and governmental entities, especially the Los Angeles Zoo and the U.S. Fish and Wildlife Service. Above all, it is the continued success of the programme that maintains broad public interest and support, without which this species would have little hope of survival.

ACKNOWLEDGEMENTS

The California Condor Recovery Programme is succeeding because of the efforts of hundreds of dedicated government officials, non-government organizations, biologists, and volunteers, and I owe most of them a personal debt. In specific regard to this update, the assistance of Robert Mesta, who faithfully maintains the scorecard of condor gains and losses, is especially appreciated.

REFERENCES

BRODKORB, P. 1964. Catalogue of fossil birds. Part 2 (Anseriformes through Galliformes). *Bull. Fla. State Mus., Biol Sci.* 8:195-335.
CALIFORNIA CONDOR RECOVERY TEAM. 1974. California Condor Recovery Plan. U.S. Fish and Wildlife Service, Ojai, California.

CARRIER, W.D. 1971. Habitat management plan for the California Condor. U.S. Forest Service. 51 pp.
FINLEY, W.L. 1906. Life history of the California Condor. Part I. *Condor* 8:135-142.
FINLEY, W.L. 1908a. Life history of the California Condor. Part II. *Condor* 10:5-10.
FINLEY, W.L. 1908b. Life history of the California Condor. Part III. *Condor* 10:59-65.
FINLEY, W.L. 1910. Life history of the California Condor. Part IV. *Condor* 12:5-11.
GEYER, C.J., O.A. RYDER, L.G. CHEMNICK & E.A. THOMPSON. 1993. Analysis of relatedness in the California Condors from DNA fingerprints. *Molecular Biol. Evol.* 10:571-589.
HARRISON, E.N. & L.F. KIFF 1980. Apparent replacement clutch laid by wild California Condor. *Condor* 82:351-352.
HARVEY, N.C., K.L. PRESTON & A.J. LEETE 1996. Reproductive behaviour of captive California Condors *(Gymnogyps californianus). Zoo Biol.* 15:115-125.
KIFF, L.F. 1989. DDE and the California Condor *(Gymnogyps californianus)*: the end of a story? Pp. 477-480 *in* B.-U. Meyburg and R.D. Chancellor (eds.), *Raptors in the modern world*. WWGBP, Berlin.
KIFF, L.F., D.B. PEAKALL & S.R. WILBUR 1979. Recent changes in California Condor eggshells. *Condor* 81:166-172.
KOFORD, C. 1953. The California Condor. *National Audubon Society Research Report no. 3*, New York. 154 pp.
KUEHLER, C.M., D.J. STERNER, D.S. JONES, R.L. USNIK & S. KASIELKE 1991. Report on captive hatches of California Condors *Gymnogyps californianus*: 1983-1990. *Zoo Biol.* 10:65-68
KUEHLER, C.M. & P.N. WHITMAN 1988. Artificial incubation of California Condor *Gymnogyps californianus* eggs removed from the wild. *Zoo Biol.* 7:123-132.
LIEBERMAN, A., J. WILEY, J.V. RODRIQUEZ & J.M. PAEZ 1991. First experimental reintroduction of captive reared Andean Condors *Vultur gryphus* into Colombia, S.A. Pp. 129-131 *in* American Assoc. Zoological Parks and Aquariums Conf. Proc. 1991, AAZPA, Wheeling, West Virginia.
MALLETTE, R.D. & J.C. BORNEMAN 1966. First cooperative survey of the California Condor. *Calif. Fish Game* 52:185-203.
MERETSKY, V.J. & N.F.R. SNYDER 1992. Range use and movements of California Condors. *Condor* 94:313-335.
RICKLEFS, R.E. (Ed.) 1978. Report of the advisory panel on the California Condor. *Natl. Audubon Soc. Conserv. Rept.* no. 6. 27 pp.
ROBINSON, C.S. 1940. Notes on the California Condor, collected on Los Padres National Forest, California. U.S. Forest Service, Santa Barbara, California. 21 pp.
SIBLEY, F.C. 1969. Effects of the Sespe Creek Project on the California Condor. U.S. Fish and Wildlife Service, Laurel, Maryland. 19 pp.
SNYDER, N.F.R. 1983. California Condor reproduction, past and present. *Bird Conserv.* 1:67-86.
SNYDER, N.F.R. & J.A. HAMBER 1985. Replacement-clutching and annual nesting of California Condors. *Condor* 87:374-378.
SNYDER, N.F.R. & E.V. JOHNSON 1985. Photographic censusing of the 1982-1983 California Condor population. *Condor* 87:1-13.
SNYDER, N.F.R., R.R. RAMEY & F.C. SIBLEY 1986. Nest-site biology of the California Condor. *Condor* 88:228-241.
SNYDER, N.F.R. & H. SNYDER 1989. Biology and conservation of the California Condor. Pp. 175-267 *in* D.M. Power (ed.), *Current ornithology*. Vol. 6, Plenum Press, New York.
STEADMAN, D.W. & N.G. MILLER 1987. California Condor associated with spruce-pine woodland in the Late Pleistocene of New York. *Quaternary Research* 28:415-426.
TOONE, W.D. & A.C. RISSER 1988. Captive management of the California Condor *Gymnogyps californianus. Int. Zoo Yearbook* 27:50-58.
TOONE, W.D. & M.P. WALLACE 1994. The extinction in the wild and reintroduction of the California Condor *(Gymnogyps californianus)*. Pp. 411-419 *in* P.J.S. Olney, G.M. Mace, and A.T.C. Feistner (eds.), *Creative conservation: interactive management of wild and captive animals*. Chapman & Hall, London.
U.S. FISH AND WILDLIFE SERVICE 1996. California Condor recovery plan, third revision. USFWS, Portland, Oregon.
WALLACE, M.P. 1991. Methods and strategies for releasing California Condors to the wild. Pp. 121-128 *in* American Assoc. Zoological Parks and Aquariums Annual Conf. Proc. 1991, AAZPA, Wheeling, West Virginia.
WALLACE, M.P. 1994. Control of behavioural development in the context of reintroduction programs for birds. *Zoo Biol.* 13:491-499.
WILBUR, S.R. 1972. The food resources of the California Condor. U.S. Fish and Wildlife Service, Patuxent Wildlife Research Center, Laurel, Maryland. 18 pp.
WILBUR, S.R. 1974. California Condor specimens in collections. *Wilson Bull.* 86:71-72.

WILBUR, S.R. 1975. California Condor plumage and molt as field study aids. *Calif. Fish Game* 61:144-148.
WILBUR, S.R. 1976. Status of the California Condor, 1972-1975. *Am. Birds* 30:789-790.
WILBUR, S.R. 1978. The California Condor, 1966-76: a look at its past and future. *North American Fauna* no. 72. 136 pp.
WILBUR, S.R., W.D. CARRIER, J.C. BORNEMAN & R.D. MALLETTE 1972. Distribution and numbers of the California Condor, 1966-1971. *Am. Birds* 26:819-823.
WILBUR, S.R., W.D. CARRIER & J.C. BORNEMAN 1974. Supplemental feeding program for California Condors. *J. Wildl. Manage.* 38:343-346.
WILBUR, S.R. & J.A. JACKSON, JR. 1983. Vulture biology and management. Univ. Calif. Press, Berkeley. 550 pp.
WILBUR, S.R. & L.F. KIFF 1980. The California Condor in Baja California. *Am. Birds* 34:856-859.

Lloyd Kiff
The Peregrine Fund
566 West Flying Hawk Lane
Boise, ID 83709, U.S.A.

Chancellor, R. D. & B.-U. Meyburg eds. 2000
Raptors at Risk
WWGBP / Hancock House

Appearances Vs Performance; managing endangered Tasmanian Wedge-tailed Eagles in Forestry Operations

Nick J. Mooney

INTRODUCTION

Forestry is an important industry in Tasmania and logging of old-growth eucalypt forests for export woodchips has been the backbone of the industry since the early 1970s. Where trees are to be regrowing, plantations (usually of hybrid eucalypts and exotic pines) vie with clear-fell, burn and wide-cast sow regimes in wet areas and thinning (removal of old-growth) in dry areas. Some old growth forest is cleared for agriculture and industrial/urban areas, while some agricultural land is replanted to a plantation.

The endemic Tasmanian Wedge-tailed Eagle *Aquila audax fleayi* is the only threatened population of this species, being *endangered* at the federal level and *vulnerable* at the State level (Garnett 1992).

Like many of its genus, the Tasmanian Wedge-tailed Eagle uses traditional nests, sometimes for many decades. Unfortunately, it also has the trait of being a shy nester and few pairs will tolerate frequent or heavy disturbance when breeding. In Tasmania, nests share many physical characteristics. With rare exceptions only large, high-limbed, old-growth eucalypts on sheltered aspects are used and nests in less than 10ha of attached forest are rarely used for breeding. Thus, forestry with its loss and disturbance of critical nesting habitat is the species' key threatening process (Mooney & Holdsworth 1991). If nests are secure and the species is not persecuted, like many other raptors that appear to require forest (eg. *Accipiter gentilis*, Reynolds *et al.* 1992), the Wedge-tailed Eagle does well in mixed-age native forest, grassland and wetlands (Marchant & Higgins 1993), a mosaic sometimes promoted by limited forestry. Wedge-tailed Eagles do not reach their highest densities in large areas of continuous, closed forest. Therefore, reserves of such are not needed for the Tasmanian Wedge-tailed Eagle, as distinct from some totally forest dependent species (Thiollay 1989; Lamberson *et al.* 1992; Blakerseley *et al.* 1992) and hence, nest by nest management has been chosen as the key for its conservation.

As a wholly protected species, the eagle, its eggs and nests have straight-forward legal protection under the National Parks and Wildlife Act 1970 but as a threatened species the eagle is also accommodated in commercial forestry under the Forestry Act 1985.

A radical increase in forestry in the early 1970's (due to the advent of wood chipping for export) coincided with gradually increasing interest in nature conservation. One result was that increasing numbers of eagles' nests were reported, giving opportunities to experiment in their conservation (Mooney & Holdsworth 1991).

Raptors do not necessarily have special conservation problems in regard to forestry although they often get special attention, probably because of their charismatic nature. However, large raptors with their conservative k type breeding strategies and low mortality rates (Newton 1979) are more at risk than most other wildlife because forestry rarely stands alone. Usually it is one of a plethora of problems (eg. Meyburg 1989).

Although superficially not as sophisticated as some management regimes for threatened raptors (eg. Reynolds *et al.* 1992), ostensibly, Tasmania has a useful system for managing Wedge-tailed Eagles in forestry operations (or managing the effects of forestry operations on Wedge-tailed Eagles). There is adequate legislation, a Forest Practices Code with mechanisms for regular updating (Forestry Tasmania 1993; Jackson & Taylor 1994) and protection prescriptions that can work (Mooney & Taylor 1996), a semi-independent body to administer such and an active wildlife conservation authority with experienced specialists. Moreover, the State has a high standard of living (arguably with sufficient resources to manage the issue), few disputes over land ownership, the island is small (6,500,000 ha) with a low human population (480,000) and reasonably good communications and access. All in all, the conservation of eagles in forestry should be comparatively successful in Tasmania, but is it?

The aim of this paper is to compare the potential and actual performance of the system by evaluating a sample of nests in forestry operations. Prescriptions themselves, rather than breeding success, were fundamental in these comparisons, because their full application results in successful conservation of eagles, i.e. more breeding (Mooney & Taylor 1996).

METHODS

The conservation process

In Tasmania, nature conservation in commercial forestry is controlled through the Forest Practices Code by the Forest Practices Unit (FPU), a semi-independent government body funded by the industry and the State. Before commercial harvesting can begin in a coupe a Timber Harvesting Plan (THP) undersigned by a Forest Practices Officer (FPO) must be approved by the FPU for that proposed operation. Amongst other things, the THP has to take account of threatened species such as the Wedge-tailed Eagle. Each district of Forestry Tasmania (FT) has a Fauna Liaison Officer who promotes and facilitates the application and improvement of the Code.

Tasmania's Code is rather unique in that it applies equally to private and government land. However, conservation actions are only endorsable for the duration of the THP, unless a legal covenant has been put in place. A THP is also needed where land is being cleared for agriculture and logs are being sold. The Code and its attendant manuals are updated every five years with interim prescriptions issued in between as the need arises.

The number of THPs approved each year has slowly increased from 830 in the 1995/96 financial year through 895 in 1996/97 to an anticipated 1000 in 1997/98 with about 40% having notification of threatened species. Most notable is the dramatic increase in notifications for Wedge-tailed Eagles, from 13 in 1995/96, through 110 in 1996/97 to an estimated 250 in 1997/98 (Forest Practices Board 1997).

Conservation of Wedge-tailed Eagle nests in commercial forestry involves:
- Establishing a reserve of at least 10ha around a nest, concentrated uphill (usually the windward side of a nest tree). Even if this area has been encroached on by logging, areas of a regrowth are dedicated to the reserve to make up the 10ha.
- Restricting heavy disturbance during breeding (July - January inclusive) to at least 500m from active nests (1000m if in line of sight).

If a nest is found during forestry operations in the breeding season, disturbance must immediately cease within the 500/1000m limit and the FPU zoologist must be notified immediately. This person and/or the Tasmanian Parks and Wildlife Service (TASPAWS) specialist will make a priority visit to check the nest's breeding status, perhaps using an aircraft. Depending on the nest status the specialist will make recommendations to the FPO responsible for the coupe, as to placement and sequencing of further forestry operations to maximize any breeding opportunity for the eagles and minimize disruption to the operator. Amendments to the THP are made and approved by the FPU zoologist.

If a nest is discovered during a forestry operation during the non breeding season forestry activities must stay outside a 10ha area (i.e., a circle of about a 360m diameter) around the nest and the FPU zoologist is notified immediately. After he and/or the Tasmanian Parks and Wildlife Service (TASPAWS) specialist visits the site the responsible FPO and preferably the contractor(s) finalize details of the nest reserve. Removal of logs felled before the nest was found and inside the 10 ha boundary may be allowed. Other activities to rehabilitate the site in terms of erosion control, facilitation of regrowth and control of access by people may also be undertaken. Negotiations of detail (road and log landings' placement and use, fire protection boundaries etc.) usually occur and such amendments to the THP are made. Instructions for conserving nests follow pre-agreed, published protocols and are modified in detail by negotiation to suit the local situation. Instructions are tiered to account for the finding of a nest in or adjacent to the coupe, before or during forestry operations (including road work and site preparations). In an attempt to streamline the process, recommendations and instructions are now also being offered to FPOs through a software 'Expert Systems Program' (basically an electronic flow chart).

To facilitate the planning process, FPOs have access to a shared TASPAWS and Forestry Tasmania database of eagle nests and must notify the FPU of nests or potential nesting habitat existing in a proposed coupe. This database is provided on a 'need to know' basis where certain map sheets are flagged as having a nest(s). If the coupe falls on such a map sheet the FPO contacts the FPU zoologist for details, the TASPAWS specialist then being consulted for an update on the nest's status. Recommendations about searching for nests in potential habitat and instructions on conserving known nests are sought from the TASPAWS specialist through the FPU zoologist (mainly for reasons of accountability). Searches are recommended for about 60% of the THPs on which there is notification of eagle nesting habitat.

In Tasmania, it is not obligatory to search for eagle nests in areas due for harvesting, although once known they must be accommodated. However, searches are increasingly encouraged through text, training and peer pressure. TASPAWS and FPU specialists conduct training and they, FPOs, FT officers, experienced consultants and volunteers from the Australasian Raptor Association, help searches. Other concerned people local to the logging area are also guided in searches for nests, due attention (usually) being given to safety and legalities of access. Thus, nests can be discovered by a variety of methods and/or people. During logging operations nests are invariably found by the road work or logging contractors, or an FPO alerted by them.

Practical, map-based methods for prioritising areas for nest searching are established (Mooney 1996) based on a simple model of the physical characteristics of the nearest known eagle nest sites (the area within 50 m of a nest tree) and nearest neighbour distance. Any area can be ranked for its likelihood of containing a nest/nests, allowing easy prioritization of searches, necessary because resources are limited and in any case nests are found in specific habitats. More sophisticated GIS-based models of eagle nest sites can also be used to predict where nests should be (eg. Brown & Mooney 1997). As a policy, coupes are not searched more than three years before operations, to minimise the likelihood of a new nest being built after searches. Monetary rewards (A$200/nest) for those first reporting nests have been tried on a limited basis.

Several FPU officers have the task of auditing THPs, the aim being to check 10% per year in terms of how they were researched (eg. was the data base checked?), presented and applied in the field. FPUs and/or the TASPAWS specialist occasionally conduct spot checks on operations and react to complaints from the public. Where there are serious breaches of the Code, FPOs can lose their licenses which affects their income.

Efforts are made to monitor the productivity of nests that have undergone active conservation in forestry for comparison with a sample of undisturbed nests (Mooney & Taylor 1996).

Under the National Parks and Wildlife Act 1970, compensation can be claimed by private landowners for losses of forest production due to instructions on a THP. Compensation applies where losses to the area to be logged exceed 5% where the conservation of a significant value would require the total exclusion of forest practices, or 10% where the conservation of a significant value could be achieved with some constraints, eg. selective logging instead of clear felling (this 5%/10% is considered a 'duty of care' under the relevant legislation). If compensation is paid, a specific conservation covenant is placed on the area. Claims for compensation follow strict protocols (Appendix 1).

Measuring performance

Issues of the conservation process that were examined were:
- Access to database: the updating process, availability and application of FPOs.
- Notification of nests or potential nesting habitats: did FPOs research the database and/or report potential nesting habitat?
- Finding nests. The method for finding nests, before or during forestry operations, was examined over time to see if the establishment of search mechanisms has reduced 'accidental' discovery of nests during operations. Usefulness of predictive models and times between discovery and reporting were also of interest.
- Reporting nests. The interval between finding and reporting nests can be critical.
- Responses to reports of nests. How credible were authorities' responses?
- Application of prescriptions. How well nests are protected from disturbance by reserves. Encroachment on the 10 ha to be reserved around a nest was scored in preference to amount of habitat left in the 10 ha, because nests might be left on the very edge of large forest blocks.
- Auditing and checks of conservation measures. How seriously were they taken?
- Permanence of conservation techniques. Techniques are only enforceable for the period of the THP so it is important to see if reserves were later cleared or disturbance protection curtailed.
- Disruption to contractors. The inconvenience/cost to the industry of stopping or moving operations is of great interest.
- Monitoring of nests. Few managed nests have the exact same prescriptions applied, giving *de facto* evolution of conservation measures. To take advantage of this, managed nests and controls have to be monitored.
- Compensation: the system makes much of compensation so the success of applicants must be examined.

RESULTS

Performance of conservation measures

Access to database. Access to the database was very good. However, hard copy lists of maps with nests can quickly become dated, putting 'new' nests at risk if searches are not carried out. If a nest is on the edge of a map, it may be affected by an operation on the adjacent edge of the neighbouring map on which it would not be flagged.

Notification of nests or potential nesting habitat

FPOs usually consulted the database. However, if a search was not conducted, a nest might be compromised. This happened only once in the past five years and there were negative repercussions for the FPO. By its very nature, logging of old-growth usually involves potential nest habitat - hence the high rate of notifications. Plantation harvesting and some thinning operations do not involve some nests or potential habitat, unless they are adjacent.

Finding nests

Searches are recommended on about 60% of the forms notifying eagles and some others are done 'just in case' (usually by FPOs who have compromised nests previously and wish to avoid a repetition). Prioritized searching, really a process of risk assessment, seems efficient at finding nests before forestry operations. This style usually shows that less that 20% of a coupe need be searched and some need not be searched at all. Although 20-40 nests are found per year, not all are in areas covered by THPs. They might be in a stream side reserve and their conservation administered by a slight alteration to that reserve as a recommendation (as distinct from an instruction) to the THP. Usually one nest is found every 30-40 coupes. Over the past decade the rate of nest 'findings' has dramatically increased (Figure 1).

Figure 1. Methods of finding nests and the stage of forestry operations during which nests became known (total n = 6 for 1970-1975, 12 for 1975-1980, 8 for 1980-1985, 18 for 1985-1990, 46 for 1990-1995 and 33 for 1995-July 1998).

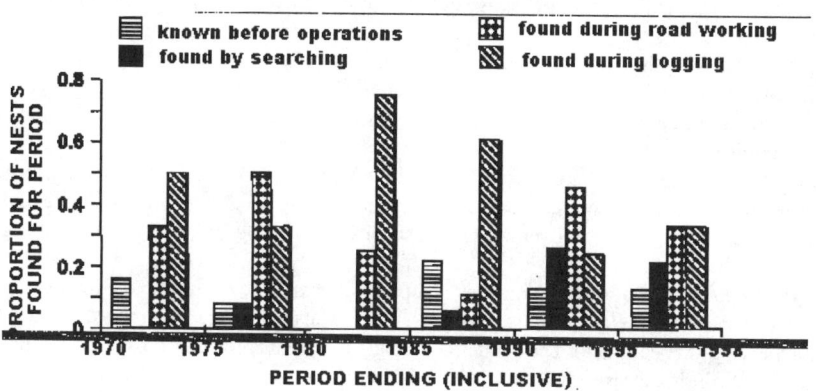

If high search standards are maintained, few nests are missed (to be later found during road making or logging). In four of the five cases where a nest was missed in a search the actual searchers were in haste and/or inexperienced and/or also asked to do other tasks or using a search method not suitable to the habitat, eg. ground searching a forest with dense understorey where a helicopter would have been both more effective and efficient, or searching with fixed wing aircraft (an efficient method for checking, not finding nests; Mooney 1988).

Once the FPC was applied and searching was encouraged and facilitated the proportion of nests found before forestry operations increased slightly with a corresponding fall in the proportion found during operations (Figure 1), still the most common way nests were found in forestry areas (67% cf. 21% of 33 found from 1995 to mid-1998, compared to 72% and 26% of 46 from 1990-1995). This trend of the minority being found by searching applies by degrees both in State forest and on private land (33% of 43 and 21% of 29 respectively since 1990).

Although GIS-based modelling has great potential for suggesting where nests should be, there are a number of practical restrictions. Adequate ground proving is essential but can be very expensive. Where the physical environments of areas differ, models might have to be formed for each area. Consider the aspects of slopes nest trees are on, a key feature of many models (eg. Brown & Mooney 1996). In the eastern district of Tasmania a model using an aspect range of 90° (from 90° -180°) will pick up 77.2% of nests. However, looking at the spread of aspects in different regions, aspect spread would only pick up 45.7% in the central north, 31.8% in the north-west, 71.4% in the west, 54.3% in the central, 55.9% in the south-east and 58.2% of all the nests known. Some regions have a great variety of aspects, reflecting complex wind and precipitation regimes and aspects may be of little use in a model since they may result in a greatly increased area predicted for nests. In such areas where physical characteristics of nest sites vary greatly, almost as many nests are needed to create a model as actually exist in the region, amounting to an academic exercise rather than a practical tool.

Nearest-neighbour distances have great potential for narrowing possibilities of nest placement for such territorial species as Wedge-tailed Eagles. However, where there has been much development, deserted nests may exist and the proximity of nests alone may not be a useful predictor; what is needed are active nests, necessitating regular monitoring. Again, the productive efficiency may be reduced to the point where the chances of an 'unpredicted' nest being found justify most areas of potential habitat being searched. Predictions incorporating nearest-neighbour distances seem to work much better where there has been less development, i.e. where territories are more stable and fewer nests exist.

Forestry's pace and time/cost of searches

Reporting nests. One concern is that some nests are reported well after after being found. In several cases investigations strongly suggested that nest trees were found by the contractor several days before being reported. Meanwhile, logging continued in the trees' vicinity with the report being made only when thay had finished logging, or a forestry officer was due to visit the operation. In several cases nests next to roadworks were only reported once the roadworks were so far advanced that they could not be moved. Always the claim was that the nest was not seen until immediately before reporting.

The offer of financial rewards by a large, private logging company for the first reporting of a nest were an attempt to defeat this time lag. This seemed a successful strategy with one claim and several enthusiastic false alarms over a period of several months. Unfortunately, senior management discontinued the practice.

*Response to reports of nests .*With rare exception the response of the FPU, FTs' Fauna Liason Officers and the TASPAWS specialist has been reliable and on time, lessening uncertainty and inconvenience to the contractor and reducing damage to eagles' breeding prospects. Responses to reports of nests during the breeding season have all been managed within two days, most in one, and outside breeding in three to five days.

Application of prescriptions. Once a nest was known, protection from disturbance was adequate in 90% of cases, about the same proportion in State forest and on private land (Table 1). The 10ha area around a nest tree was physically compromised 61% of times with the worst performance on private land. In most cases compromise of the area was from logging coming too close but in others it was due to roadworks being established before the nest was reported (not always the same as found).

Table 1. Adequacy of protective measures placed on nests in coupes since 1991, as prescriptions in the Forest Practices Code.

	LEVEL OF PROTECTION FROM DISTURBANCE OF 10 ha AROUND NEST TREE					
	During operations once known		Actions After THP Expired			
TENURE	adequate	inadequate	in place	none	compromised	intact
Private Land	27	2	15	14	22	7
State Forest	38	5	31	12	22	21

Permanence of prescriptions. Non-compulsory actions, those designed to reduce disturbance after the THP expires (eg. restricting access in the long term), were in place 63.8% of times in total

(46 of 72) but only in a clear majority in State forest (72%, 31 of 43). The best endurance of prescriptions was on areas of private land and State forest where access was strictly controlled, eg. little or no firewood cutting, trail bike riding etc. About 20% of nests in State forest have some restrictions such as locked gates. Most areas of private land have tightly restricted access but rarely is this meant to protect the eagles. Consequently, disturbance by careless users is common, even occasioning the felling of trees close to nests.

Despite conservation prescriptions not being compulsory beyond the lifespan of the THP no eagle nest reserves are known to have been cleared although a few have been burned. In their embracing of conservation, there seemed a slight tendency for owners of larger properties (and FPOs contracted to them) to be more positive about conserving eagles (Table 2) but there was no significant difference in the average size of properties where post-THP measures were in place or not.

Table 2. Degree of enthusiasm of private landowners and Forest Protection Officers for eagle conservation measures since 1991 as prescribed by the Forest Practices Code.

	BASIS OF CONSERVATION		
AREA	*Enforced Prescriptions* (resentment)	*Passive Cooperation* (ambivalence)	*Active Cooperation* (enthusiasm)
0 - 100 ha	1	2	1
100 - 500 ha	3	6	11
500 + ha	0	2	5

The system has benefited considerably from the FT policy of conservation measures applied to THPs in State forest being permanently applied under FT's own reserve system. Beyond operational protection this also provides all important priority protection from fires, wood cutting etc.

Auditing and checks of conservation measures. The diligence of auditing FPU officers has meant auditing has generally been of a high standard with FPOs generally concerned with the results and potential consequences. Spot checks have given more mixed results. Typically a visit was made immediately after instructions were given on moving the operation due to the reporting of a nest. The advantage of aircraft is that a check can be made without reference to the contractor, FPO or landowner. On about half the checks operators did not meet the letter of the instruction, contractors invariably claiming a misunderstanding. Later spot checks often showed that the logging area had been revisited to retrieve logs etc. This type of mismanagement has lessened as auditing has become further entrenched and some FPOs have been officially cautioned; it is in their direct interest to follow the FPC.

Disruption of contractors. It was clear that operations were far more likely to suffer disruption, especially having to move to a another site, if nests were found during road work or logging as distinct from before (Table 3 categories pooled to before vs during works finding X planned changes vs disruption, chi-squared=4.5, df=1, .05>p>.01). Obviously the finding of a nest during works meant they were too close.

Costs of disruptions were very hard to estimate, different contractors making wildly varying claims about identical circumstances, possibly reflecting their frustration/chagrin or perhaps other financial pressures. Forestry operations are disrupted for many reasons (usually for soil and water conservation) and contractors/FPOs habitually keep areas in reserve in case of unforeseen moves. Moving or stopping to wait for a nest status assessment usually costs 0.5 to 1.5 days of productive work but is probably less of a consequence nowadays since the operations are so mobile and work is on a contract basis rather than an hourly rate. Most contractors agree the problem is one of inconvenience and nuisance rather than monetary cost, and many accept such disruptions as part of modern forestry.

Table 3. Effect on forestry operations of the prior knowledge of nests compared to finding nests during works.

NESTS KNOWN	DISRUPTION TO FORESTRY OPERATIONS		
	Work Schedules Changed Before Works	On GroundWorks Affected	
		Temporary Halt	Moved
Before Works			
database	4	0	1
search	23	1	1
During Works			
roading	3	8	10
logging	0	7	20

Monitoring of nests. Until recently productivity of most managed nests and a control sample (in 30 territories) could be monitored by aircraft using TASPAWS funds. However, with recent 'fiscal challenges' and an ever growing list of nests, rarely has the full task been possible. Recently a sample has been used, usually restricted to those nests at which there is some history of eagle activity.

Compensation. Although straightforward on paper, the compensation process is extremely cumbersome. This inevitably leads to confusion and great frustration on the part of claimants and embarrassment to conservation authorities since there was never money actually dedicated to the compensation legislation. Of the four claims so far lodged, three claimants gave up within months and only one is still pursuing the issue, nearly a year from lodging the claim.

DISCUSSION AND CONCLUSION

The increasing rate of nest reporting seems somewhat in excess to areas logged. Some areas are being re-logged as part of changing harvesting regimes and those areas are far less likely to have nests. New areas of undisturbed old-growth forest logged per year are reasonably consistent but likely to fall as that resource lessens. Increasing numbers of nests recorded maybe due to a cocktail of:

- Methods of finding nests. Logging is a very thorough, if *de facto*, 'search' compared to anecdotal knowledge (more the case in early years). However, logging is now encroaching on a remnant habitat (typically slopes) that eagles prefer but previously were of little interest to forestry.
- Improving attitudes of people in forest industries. In the past, many nest trees were felled, some when it was not allowed by law, and few nests were reported. Nowadays this is very rare and nearly all nests are reported promptly. Conservation of eagles has demonstrated that, although often nuisances to contractors, rarely do the measures seriously affect the economics of the operation. The vast majority of the industry has accepted that non-timber forest values are here to stay.
- Improved policing of forestry activities. This has accentuated the above point.
- Numbers of nests per territory are closely related to disturbance (Mooney & Holdsworth 1991). Increasing numbers of territories undergoing disturbance might indicate more nests to find. There is a limit of course. Some territories have few remaining nest trees and although occupied, these territories often have low productivity. Often these remnant nest sites are sub-standard in extent and shelter from wind and disturbance. In some areas, competition with White-bellied Sea Eagles *Haliaeetus leucogaster* for remaining nest sites is intense (Terry & Wiersma 1997).

The reluctance of industry to accept compulsory searches may in part be a resistance to ever increasing bureaucracy and partly due to cost. However, searching is not very expensive - most coupes are 30-70ha, a day's work for an experienced searcher, but obviously a cost many contractors/landowners/FPOs gamble that they can avoid. Without doubt, those in the industry that have been disrupted by eagle conservation are more inclined to do searches but since individual contractors may only ever deal with a few nests in their careers, the change in habit is slow.

Despite the cost of searches and their not being compulsory, attempts to find nests before logging are increasing. Doubtless this is partly due to peer pressure, changing professional standards and changing public expectations but the wish to avoid disruptions is a powerful influence. Making searches of certain habitat compulsory and/or making disruptions more 'expensive' could accelerate this trend. However, rapid change (for such a conservative industry) is occurring without aggressive conservation measures and public opinion should continue the process. As finding nests before any road work or logging operation becomes part of industry 'culture' the whole process will be more successful. Searching very early in planning, at the catchment level is the ideal and can be greatly aided by predictive modelling, but these models have to be funded and ground proved.

A key characteristic is even nest spacing by eagles (eg. Ridpath & Brooker 1987; Watson & Rothery 1986) and this gives models great potential. In areas with a history of human disturbance or unusual/complex winds they must be used with caution and all habitats assessed, models perhaps being best used to prioritise and plan, not just in forestry but also with recreation and rural residence (eg. Cline 1990). In such areas predictive parameters may be hard to identify and a large number of nests can be needed, sometimes almost all the nests in the area, defeating the exercise.

Of concern is delay between finding and reporting nests. This problem seems restricted to a few contractors, interestingly in regions where they have little competition. They may therefore feel that disciplinary measures may not be applied as stringently. Such people have local political power through their providing work. As frustrating to conservation authorities as these attitudes might be, they are a minority and it is important to balance the time spent trying to change them. To defeat the problem, it may be possible to introduce regional compulsion for searches.

The success of conserving Wedge-tailed Eagles in forestry has been minimally described (Mooney & Taylor 1996). However, since protocols are continually being refined, ongoing monitoring is essential, especially if the hoped for adaptation to land 'development' (i.e. a improvement in population productivity) is to be detected, possibly allowing down listing of the species. Monitoring must involve both affected and undisturbed nests. One problem is that the control sample of nests used itself is being compromised. Some nests are now disturbed and eagles no longer use others, probably having moved elsewhere in their territory to an unknown site. Obviously efforts must be made (i.e. resources committed) to maintain a credible control sample. This means finding alternate nests and identifying undisturbed nests.

A key to the success in Tasmania might be that conservation of Wedge-tailed Eagles in forestry was introduced well before it was compulsory, avoiding serious conflict (eg. Gup 1990) and at a time in history (the late 1970s) when Tasmania's economy was buoyant and conservation/forestry conflict was limited. This allowed the introduction of new concepts and ideas via the most interested parties. Considerable debate and negotiation were undertaken on a personal level and protocols developed with the voluntary cooperation of particularly interested forestry officers, landowners and contractors (all of whom were by no means unwilling to try new ideas). Thus, early efforts were heavily reliant on favour, goodwill and personalities. Interestingly, despite considerable recent conflict in forestry management and a worsening economic climate, the momentum has remained.

As much as industries and conservation are 'rationalised', truly successful conservation relies heavily on the human touch. People, it seems, still like to deal with people (eg. Alvarez *et al.* 1996).

About 80% (175 of 220) of Tasmania's eagle territories are in State forest or on private land, areas prone to development (Mooney & Holdsworth 1991). Consequent disturbance and habitat loss reduces eagle productivity and with continuation of the process more nests are becoming disturbed (Mooney 1998). Without deliberate efforts to conserve eagles in forestry it is possible that in several decades 150 of the 175 territories at risk will undergo serious disturbance. However, the increased application of the Code has slowed the attrition (nests being lightly instead of moderately, or moderately instead of heavily disturbed), especially if searching is further consolidated.

Generally, conservation measures are more fully and consistently applied in State forest, perhaps because of the luxury of community ownership - any particular THP amendment is not key to the economy of the project. This can be very different on private land where the compensation issue must be settled. Perhaps an eagle chick production bounty could be more effective; it would be then in a landowner's interest to follow the best conservation advice. However, compensatory measures must be of clear benefit to affected people, otherwise they will not work (Salvador 1994).

One surprising result of this assessment was the loose connection between landowner enthusiasm and property size (one might expect owners of small properties to resist conservation measures). However, Tasmanian landowners are a diverse group and many have financial interests elsewhere, so total assets might be a better comparison than the size of one property.

ACKNOWLEDGEMENTS

I would like to thank Mark Wapstra and Sarah Munks of the Forest Practices Unit and the plethora of contractors, landowners, Forest Protection Officers, Fauna Liason Officers and forestry planners and assessors for their enthusiasm and patience in what can be trying circumstances.

REFERENCES

ALVAREZ, E., ELLIS, D.H., SMITH, D.J. & LARUE, C.T. 1996. Diurnal Raptors in the fragmented rainforest of the Sierra Imataca, Venezuela. pp. 263-273 *in* D. Bird, D. Varland & J. Negro (eds) *Raptors in Human Landscapes.: adaptions to built and cultivated environments.* Academic Press, Toronto

BLAKESLEY, J.A., FRANKLIN, A.B. & GUTIERREZ, R.J. 1992. Spotted owl roost and nest site selection in Northwest California. *Journal of Wildlife Management.* 56(2): 388-392.

BROWN, W.E. & MOONEY, N.J. 1997. Modelling of the Nesting Habitat of the Wedge-tailed Eagle *Aquila audax fleayi* in Tasmania. Report to Tasmanian Regional Forest Agreement Environment & Heritage Technical Committee, Hobart.

CLINE, K. 1990. Bald eagles in the Chesapeake: a management guide for landowners. Instit. Wildlife Res., Natl. Wildl. Fed., Washington, D.C. USA.

FOREST PRACTICES BOARD. 1997. *Annual Report 1996-97.* Forest Practices Board, 30 Patrick St, Hobart Tasmania 7000.

FORESTRY TASMANIA. 1993. *Forest Practices Code.* Forestry Tasmania, 199 Macquarie St, Hobart Tasmania 7001, Australia.

GARNETT, S. 1992. *The action plan for Australian Birds.* Aust. Nat. Parks & Wildlife Service, Canberra, Australia.

GUP, T. 1990. Owl vs man. *Time* Magazine. June.

JACKSON, J. & TAYLOR, R. 1994. Threatened Fauna Manual for Production Forests in Tasmania. Forest Practices Unit, Forestry Tasmania.

LAMBERSON, R.H., MCKELVEY, R., NOON, B.R. & VOSS, C. 1992. A dynamic analysis of Northern Spotted Owl viability in a fragmented forest landscape. *Conservation Biology.* 6(4): 505-512.

MARCHANT, S. & P. HIGGINS 1993. *Handbook of Australian, New Zealand and Antarctic birds.* Vol. 2. Oxford Univ. Press, Melbourne, Australia.

MEYBURG, B.U. 1989. The Spanish Imperial Eagle *Aquila (heliaca) adalberti*: its biology, status and conservation. *In* B.U. Meyburg & R.D. Chancellor (eds) *Raptors In The Modern World.* Proc. 111 World Conf. on Birds of Prey, WWGBP.

MOONEY, N.J. 1988. Efficiency of fixed-wing aircraft for surveying eagle nests. *Australian Raptor Association News* 9: 28-30.

MOONEY, N.J. 1996. Predictive searching for Wedge-tailed Eagle nests in Tasmania. *Australasian Raptor Association News* 17(1): 45-46.

MOONEY, N.J. 1998. Conservation of Wedge-tailed Eagles in Tasmania: the Blunderbuss approach.*in* (eds) G. Czechura and S. Debus. *Australian Raptor Studies II.* Birds Australia Monograph 3.

MOONEY, N.J. & HOLDSWORTH, M.C. 1991. The effects of disturbance on nesting Wedge-tailed Eagles *Aquila audax fleayi* in Tasmania. *Tasforests* 3: 15-31.

MOONEY, N.J. & TAYLOR, R. 1996. Value of nest site protection in ameliorating the effects of forestry operations on Wedge-tailed Eagles in Tasmania. pp. 275-282 *in* D. Bird, D. Varland & J. Negro (eds) *Raptors in Human Landscapes: adaptations to built and cultivated environments.* Academic Press, Toronto.

NEWTON, I. 1979. *Population ecology of raptors.* Buteo Books, Vermillion, South Dakota USA.

REYNOLDS, R.T., GRAHAM, R.T., REISER, M.H., BASSETT, R.L., KENNEDY, P.L., BOYCE D.A. JR., GOODWIN, G., SMITH, R. & FISHER, E.L. 1992. *Management Recommendations for the Northern Goshawk in the Southwestern United States.* United States Department of Agriculture, Forest Service, Fort Collins, Colarado, USA. General Technical Report RM-217.

RIDPATH, M.G. & BROOKER, M.G. 1987. Sites and spacing of nests as determinants of Wedge-tailed Eagle breeding in arid Western Australia. *Emu* 87: 143-149

SALVADOR, D.J.I. 1994. Socio-economic incentives for the conservation of the rainforest habitat of the Phillippine Eagle *Pithecophaga jefferyi.* pp. 277-282 *in* B.U. Meyburg & R.D. Chancellor (eds) *Raptor Conservation Today.* WWGBP/Pica Press, London.

TERRY, T. & WIERSMA. 1997. Competition betweenWedge-tailed Eagles and White-bellied Sea Eagles for nests. *Australasian Raptor Association News.* 17(1): 22-23

WATSON, A. & ROTHERY, P. 1986. Regularity in spacing of Golden Eagle *Aquila chrysaetos* nests used within years in northern Scotland. *Ibis* 128:406-408.

THIOLLAY, J.M. 1989. Area requirements for the protection of rainforest raptors and game birds in French Guiana. *Conserv. Biol.* 3: 128-137.

Nick Mooney
TASPAWS
GPO Box 44A
Hobart 7001, AUSTRALIA.

Appendix 1. Process to be followed in claiming compensation for loss of income to conservation requirements for threatened species under timber harvesting plans

1. Before any commercial logging operation can legally begin, a Timber Harvesting Plan (THP) must first be lodged with the Forest Practices Board (FPB) for approval under the *Forest Practices Act 1985*. The THP may include special recommendations about conserving a threatened species before it is approved; it may even be refused.

2. You are entitled to claim compensation for loss of income due to these special recommendations or refusal of the THP.

3. Firstly, you must appeal against the recommendations or refusal by writing to the Forest Practices Board at 30 Patrick Street, Hobart 7000.

4. If your appeal to the FPB is successful, then your Timber Harvesting Plan without some, or all, of the special recommendations will be approved.

5. If your appeal is unsuccessful and you still want to claim compensation, you then become an 'affected owner' and you have 180 days to appeal to the Minister of the Parks and Wildlife Service for compensation under the *National Parks and Wildlife Act 1970*.

6. If the Minister rejects your claim then you can reapply to the FPB for approval of your original THP without special recommendations. The FPB cannot then refuse the THP or add conditions regarding the threatened species already considered.

7. If your claim is accepted, the Minister will call the Conservation Compensation Committee (CCC) together to arbitrate and negotiate a settlement.

8. A payment for compensation will be accompanied by a conservation covenant - that is a legal agreement between the Parks and Wildlife Service and the landowner.

9. If the payment is not made within 180 days of agreement to pay, then you can reapply to the FPB for approval of your original THP without special recommendations. The FPB cannot then refuse the THP or add conditions regarding the threatened species already considered.

Chancellor, R. D. & B.-U. Meyburg eds. 2000
Raptors at Risk
WWGBP / Hancock House

Madagascar Fish-Eagle *Haliaeetus vociferoides* and Community-based Wetland Conservation

R. T. Watson, A. Andrianarimisa, D. Razandrizanakanirina and L. Kalavaha

The Madagascar Fish-Eagle is one of the world's most endangered birds of prey, with a known population of about 75 breeding pairs, and an estimated total of 100-120 pairs. Ten pairs breed on three adjacent lakes in western Madagascar. The lakes were fished by an autochthonous population of about 30 fishermen until 1993 when seasonal migrant fishermen arrived for the first time and began fishing in disobedience of local traditional rules, taboos, and sanctions. By 1996 fish stocks were so depleted that fishermen gave up trying to fish. In 1997 fish-eagle breeding success was significantly reduced. A central problem is a lack of resolve among community authorities to organize and implement sanctions against those who abuse natural resources. The Peregrine Fund's Community-based Wetland Conservation Project aims to reinstate traditional authority by empowering the local community to manage their natural resources, including fishing and tree cutting in surrounding forest. This approach to conservation has potential for long-term sustainability, but short-term results are slow to be realized. Public education to reduce direct persecution of eagles and management of the fish-eagle population are additional interventions necessary to secure the future of the species.

INTRODUCTION

The known breeding population of the Madagascar Fish-Eagle *Haliaeetus vociferoides* in 1998 was 75 pairs and the total breeding population was estimated in 1995 to be around 100-120 pairs (Rabarisoa *et al.* 1997). The fish-eagle was considered abundant when first discovered (Owen 1833) but today it is rare and among the most endangered eagles in the world (Langrand & Meyburg 1989). Habitat degradation and human persecution are the most likely causes for the species' decline (Watson 1997, Watson & Rabarisoa in press).

Most wetlands have been turned into rice fields to provide the Malagasy staple food. Remaining lakes and rivers are often over-fished or turbid from high rates of soil erosion from deforested land. Deforestation has destroyed much nesting habitat and selective use of the largest trees adjacent to rivers or lakes for dug-out canoe construction has degraded what forest remains (Watson *et al.* 1997, Berkelman *et al.* in press). In some parts of Madagascar the nestlings of the Madagascar Fish-Eagle are eaten by local people who sometimes fell the nest tree to obtain the birds. Others capture adult eagles to remove a foot for use by "*ombiasy*" or "*moasy*" (traditional healers). The foot of a living eagle is said to increase the strength of the healer's "treatment" (Razandrizanakanirina & Kalavaha 1997).

Conservation of the Madagascar Fish-Eagle requires three simultaneous actions: conservation of remaining suitable habitat and possibly habitat restoration, control of human persecution, and management of the species in the wild to slow population loss and eventually speed its recovery (Watson 1997). This paper describes our efforts to conserve important fish-eagle habitat by empowering the local community around lakes Befotaka, Soamalipo and Ankerika, western Madagascar, to sustainably manage and harvest the lakes and forest on which they depend and which they share with about 10% of the Madagascar Fish-Eagle breeding population.

METHODS

The Peregrine Fund first proposed the idea of a community-based conservation project to protect important wetland habitat shared by local *Sakalava* people and endangered Madagascar Fish-Eagles in 1993 by enhancing existing traditional laws and sanctions (Watson 1995). In 1996, the government of Madagascar passed a law to empower local communities to manage their own natural resources by creating a Gestion Locale Securisée (GELOSE). A GELOSE is a "management contract" or "promise" between the local community and the stake-holders that have an interest in natural resource use, such as migrant fishermen, non-governmental organizations, businesses, local authorities, and representatives of the Direction des Eaux et Forêts. Since 1996 we have worked as a "catalyst for action" to help the local community implement a GELOSE project. First, we had to learn more about the social, cultural, political and economic life of local people, as well as the ecology of natural resources and biodiversity of the area, so that our role as catalysts in the process of developing the community-based conservation project could be founded on a thorough understanding of local needs.

The Peregrine Fund team has worked with the local community since 1991 (Strzalkowska *et al.* 1995, Watson & Rabarisoa in press). In 1996 we placed the sociological side of this conservation project entirely in the hands of a Malagasy sociologist (D.R.) to bridge the cultural gap between local residents and The Peregrine Fund team. We have come to be accepted as part of the community and have developed the trust and respect essential for success of a community-based conservation project. Field work has been led by our Malagasy sociologist (D.R.) and our field manager (L.K.), a knowledgeable local resident who has been trained by The Peregrine Fund for several years. Together, this team planned each day's objectives and activities. Methods involved discussions and interviews, although sometimes observation was used when feasible and more reliable.

The ultimate goal of our work in 1996 and 1997 was to create the GELOSE, but the process required sensitivity and understanding on our part. Therefore, initial objectives in 1996 were (1) to understand the geography of the site and to meet local people and seek their acceptance, (2) to write down existing traditional laws and taboos and seek to have them recognized by local official authorities, and (3) to learn about the way of life of local residents, migrant fishermen, and others to better understand the sociological, cultural and economic forces at work in the region. These were followed in 1997 by (1) improving public awareness and involvement, and (2) forming the local association that would be responsible for creating a GELOSE and the management of the natural resources once a GELOSE is in place.

RESULTS & DISCUSSION

The team visited and involved most community leaders several times during 1996. They interviewed many villagers and fishermen, and met with government officials and leaders of other non-governmental organizations (NGOs) operating in the region (Razandrizanakanirina & Kalavaha 1997). Significant results included (1) integration and acceptance of our sociologist and The Peregrine Fund team by most local people, (2) understanding the local socio-economic forces (Razandrizanakanirina & Kalavaha 1997), (3) documenting local traditional laws and their official recognition (Appendix 1), and (4) understanding the causes of economic problems, social strife, and cultural breakdown that leading to over-fishing and degradation of forest around the lakes.

Integration and acceptance of our sociologist and The Peregrine Fund team by local people was an important step needed to ensure that we would be taken seriously by the community, and that our intervention would be accepted. This process, which involved multiple meetings with community leaders and members and participation in a variety of cultural rites, took many months, results were difficult to measure, and it seemed to even slow progress in the early stages of the project. Although frustrating at the time, it was an important step for long-term success (Razandrizanakanirina & Kalavaha 1997).

Our sociologist and her team collected information about the economic and social factors at work in the region, travelling on foot as far as Antsalova 60 km to the northeast, Trangahy village 20 km east, Masoarivo village 15 km west and Ambereny village 15 km northwest from Ankivahivahy camp (The Peregrine Fund's base camp) to meet with villagers, business owners and authorities (Razandrizanakanirina & Kalavaha 1997). The understanding gained from this study covered the history of the region, including its settlement in time and space; the population's demography including distribution, socio-professional groups, and migration; the local social structure including organization, relational system, lineages, territorial organization, traditional beliefs and religion, habitation, social relations, social conventions, village community strategy and administration; agricultural production, including land use, food production, stock breeding, fishing, and harvest of wild produce; and lastly, human impacts on the environment (Razandrizanakanirina & Kalavaha 1997)

An important step in the process of developing the community conservation project was to hold meetings with key members of the community at which existing traditional laws and taboos were discussed, agreed upon and formalized by writing them down as edicts. In addition to existing laws and taboos, the participants were encouraged to consider new rules that were relevant to the current situation and new knowledge about the state of the environment and endangered species. The final meeting took place during June 1996, and included traditional authorities such as the *Tompondrano* (traditional "keeper of the lakes"), official authorities such as the Mayor of Masoarivo township, the Sub-Prefect, and the representative for the Direction des Eaux et Forêts, as well as The Peregrine Fund's staff who took responsibility for writing the laws and taboos and, later, presenting them to the meeting participants. Having been translated from the original Malagasy Sakalava dialect to French and thence to English, the subtleties of the rules may have been lost but the meaning is generally clear (Appendix 1). Traditional rules were officially recognized at the traditional opening of the fishing season ceremony in 1996, but were largely ignored by resident and migrant fishermen alike.

Another important result was understanding the causes of economic problems, social strife, and cultural breakdown that was leading to over-fishing and degradation of forest around the lakes. Migrant fishermen had begun arriving at the lakes in 1993 and were rapidly over-fishing the lakes and degrading the surrounding forest by cutting trees for firewood and dug-out canoe construction (Watson *et al.* 1998). They began arriving at the lakes due partly to the death of an important traditional leader in the local community, but also due to strong economic incentives at the time related to devaluation of the currency and a lack of fish elsewhere (Razandrizanakanirina & Kalavaha 1997). The migrants violated many traditional rules, such as camping on the lakes' shores, using nets of a small mesh size, fishing out of season and using trawl net methods instead of passive gill nets (Watson *et al.* 1998).

Local residents feared the exploitation of fish by migrant fishermen would leave them economically disadvantaged. Rather than try to control their competitors by enforcing traditional laws, the residents joined them and began violating their own rules in order to be competitive, a classic case of the "tragedy of the commons," in which people compete harder for a limited resource in order to gain the most for themselves before it is gone. Possible future consequences are ignored. A lack of action by local authorities contributed substantially to this situation. With inaction by authorities, came lack of respect for the authorities by migrants and residents alike (Razandrizanakanirina & Kalavaha 1997).

By the end of 1996 it was obvious to us that public education, helping develop social cohesion and creating a natural resource management association from among local leaders were urgent priorities for 1997.

Conservation awareness fêtes

In a subsistence community, little happens of such great importance that it draws people from their fields and subsistence labour. Our objective was to create an event that was of historic proportions among the community, to attract people to the event and to instill its significance in their minds. At the beginning of the 1997 dry season (May and June) we involved local traditional and official leaders in two public awareness events conducted at the nearest major villages of Soatana and Ambalakazaha. These were conducted in partnership with two other non-governmental organizations (NGOs) working in the area.

Events began with an official opening by a senior official with speeches by important delegates, a youth parade through the village and a flag raising ceremony. Educational slide shows were given in the evening to cover themes on the environment in general, the different elements that form the environment, and the causes and consequences of forest degradation. We also covered the goals and activities of the three NGOs, worldwide, in Madagascar and in the local region. The following day we quizzed pupils of the Primary Public School about the themes of the slide show from the previous evening, focusing on their region, its vegetation, animals, protected species, and the local activities of the three NGO projects. Other activities, such as a soccer game between neighbouring villages, traditional dances and music, and a feast, helped to attract attention, draw people to the event, and increase its importance.

Surveys conducted in the weeks following the fêtes indicated that almost 100% of the village residents participated, and they drew people from neighbouring villages. Because of the importance of these events the fêtes became known by word of mouth, and the main messages were conveyed to people up to 20 km away. The fêtes served to inform communities immediately involved, inform people further from the affected area, and elevated the importance of the need to conserve the lakes' resources among the local officials, who vowed to support the effort to protect endangered species and control resource use.

Creating the natural resources management association, FIZAMI

After the fêtes, we helped the local traditional and official authorities create the natural resources management association, FIZAMI, a Malagasy acronym for "Association of Indigenous People of Andranobe". We believed our biggest obstacle in this task was the lack of social cohesion among traditional and official authorities and local fishermen. We were unsure if they could organize themselves into any kind of association, so we enlisted the help of the Deputy of Antsalova, an elected member of the Government's National Assembly.

Although this measure risked alienation of fishermen (especially migrants) its effect was immediate and positive. The Deputy encouraged the township's Mayor to seek police support from the main town, about 90 km away along a foot trail, to evict illegal fishermen on Lakes Befotaka and Soamalipo. The previously reluctant Mayor accompanied the police on their tour of the lakes four days later (having covered 180 km round-trip on foot) and personally helped evict illegal fishermen.

This impressive show of speed and commitment was all that was needed to galvanize the local traditional and official authorities to work together towards a common cause. We used the opportunity to further the work towards the "community management association" by visiting all the authorities over a large area and inviting them to meet. Of 36 people invited, 31 attended the meeting on November 9, 1997. The FIZAMI association was discussed, its goals, objectives and statutes defined, and a founding Board was elected that same day.

Work in 1998

The next step is to help FIZAMI mediate ways in which stake holders can manage natural resources sustainably. Once these "cahiers de charges" have been lodged with the mediator we will begin a series of debates on how they can be melded into one management contract, the GELOSE

(Figure 1). Ultimately, a single consensus will be reached and agreed upon by the FIZAMI who will then take responsibility for seeking authority from the government to become the local natural resource management authority for applying the GELOSE. We also need to repeat this whole process for the neighbouring Lake Ankerika, which, even though it is within 1 km of Lakes Befotaka and Soamalipo, lies in a different community jurisdiction.

Figure 1. Process followed by the environmental mediator for development of a "Community Contract for Management of Natural Resources" or "GELOSE".

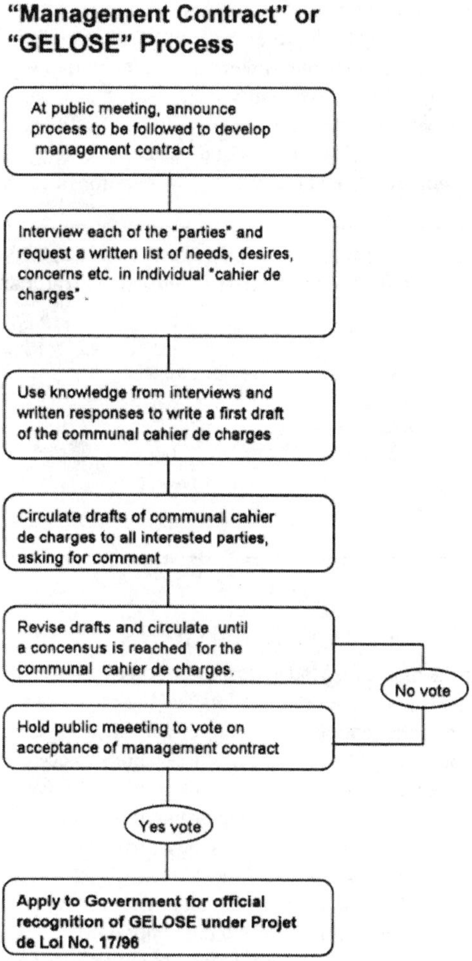

"Management Contract" or "GELOSE" Process

- At public meeting, announce process to be followed to develop management contract
- Interview each of the "parties" and request a written list of needs, desires, concerns etc. in individual "cahier de charges".
- Use knowledge from interviews and written responses to write a first draft of the communal cahier de charges
- Circulate drafts of communal cahier de charges to all interested parties, asking for comment
- Revise drafts and circulate until a concensus is reached for the communal cahier de charges.
- Hold public meeeting to vote on acceptance of management contract
  - No vote → (back to revise)
  - Yes vote ↓
- Apply to Government for official recognition of GELOSE under Projet de Loi No. 17/96

Ramsar Convention

The Peregrine Fund has also been instrumental in helping Madagascar sign the Ramsar Convention on Wetlands of International Importance. Lakes Befotaka, Soamalipo and Ankerika are listed as the first Ramsar site. International recognition of this site has helped elevate the importance of the area at government level, and is perceived by local communities as a positive step towards improving their livelihood.

Madagascar Fish-Eagle management

Despite the progress with the community-based wetland conservation project, the Madagascar Fish-Eagle remains threatened with extinction. The species is still subject to persecution and the effects of habitat degradation. Breeding success in 1997 on the all but fished-out Lakes Befotaka, Soamalipo and Ankerika was less than replacement level at two fledglings from ten pairs. Management of this population in the wild is necessary to ensure that it remains stable while habitat conservation and public awareness improve. In 1993, 1995 and 1996 we trained our Malagasy technicians to apply the "sibling rescue" (thwarting the inevitable death of one sibling in two-egg clutches) technique to increase annual production (Table 1, Watson et al. 1996). In 1997 we successfully applied sibling rescue with "hacking" (release to the wild) to increase the species' density in unoccupied areas of its present range (Table 1). Two young birds were successfully released at Lake Mangily, about 60 km northeast of their natal Lakes Befotaka and Ankerika. The technique will be used again in 1998 at the same site, with the objective of eventually establishing a new breeding pair. A full scale management program will begin only once we can be sure that sufficient suitable habitat remains to be colonized by sibling rescued birds. We have begun a satellite imagery and GIS project that should answer this question, but anticipate about two years of work before a conclusive answer is obtained.

Table 1. Results of sibling rescue trials for Madagascar Fish-Eagles breeding on Lakes Befotaka, Soamalipo, and Ankerika, western Madagascar. *First hacking attempt.

Year	No. of siblings rescued	No. of rescued siblings that fledged	No. of remaining siblings that fledged
1993	3	2	2
1995	3	1	2
1996	2	1	2
1997	3	2*	0
Total	11	6	6

CONCLUSIONS

Essential elements in the model for Madagascar Fish-Eagle conservation included (1) appropriate studies of their ecology and natural history to understand the causes of the species' decline, and (2) implementing conservation interventions that dealt directly with the causes and aimed to slow the rate of species loss. The community-based wetland conservation project addressed habitat degradation and human persecution of eagles, aiming to protect an important breeding site for the fish-eagles. We attempted to create a long-term solution to the problem of habitat degradation by empowering local communities to conserve the natural resources they share with fish-eagles. Important elements in the community-based conservation approach included:

1). taking time to develop trust with the local community and involving and training local people as representatives of The Peregrine Fund to the local community;
2). taking time to learn about the socio-economic factors at work in the community, to understand why migrant fishermen suddenly converged on these important lakes, and how that caused a breakdown in social-cohesion;
3). using and enhancing local traditional laws and taboos rather than creating and imposing an entirely new set of laws;
4). not being afraid to use powerful people to help propel the local population into taking action;
5). being there to help, organize, cajole or otherwise persuade people, including providing transport and communication in an area that lacks both, without expecting anything in return;
6). recognizing that our part was to act as a catalyst in the process of developing the community-based conservation project, and always letting others take credit for achievements;

7). and last, more time, recognizing that community-based conservation is not a quick fix, but rather a long-term commitment.

Conceptually, community-based conservation is a very different approach to conservation than the top-down, restrictive approach developed over the last century, in which communities were excluded from areas of biological importance by the creation of protected areas (e.g. National Parks). It is increasingly believed that creation of protected areas, while important for protecting areas rich in biodiversity, will never protect sufficient area for many species, especially far ranging species, such as birds of prey, and that conservation must be addressed on a wider scale if we are to conserve even some of the world's biodiversity. Community-based conservation puts the responsibility and the benefit of conservation outside of protected areas into the hands of the local community. Community-based conservation has been tried with varying degrees of success in many countries worldwide, but is only now being promoted in Madagascar. The government of Madagascar recently recognized the value of empowering local communities to look after their own resources by signing into law the means by which authority for natural resource management can be transferred to communities (Law No. 17/96). The time is ripe for community-based conservation efforts to be developed throughout Madagascar and we believe that the lessons learned from our experience in this Wetland Conservation Project will be important for directing and encouraging new efforts elsewhere.

ACKNOWLEDGMENTS

This project is funded in part by the Liz Claiborne and Art Ortenberg Foundation, the John D. and Catherine T. MacArthur Foundation, the Little Family Foundation, Disney Conservation Fund, and the U.S. Embassy in Madagascar. The Peregrine Fund works in cooperation with the Tripartite Commission represented by the Direction des Eaux et Forêts, National Office of the Environment, and others. We collaborate with Jersey Wildlife Preservation Trust and the UNESCO Bemaraha Project. We thank Ron Hartley and Lloyd Kiff for their constructive review of this paper.

REFERENCES

BERKELMAN, J., J. FRASER & R.T. WATSON in press. Nesting and perching habitat use of the Madagascar Fish-Eagle. *J. Wildl. Mgmt.*

LANGRAND, O. & B.-U. Meyburg 1989. Range, status and biology of the Madagascar Sea Eagle *Haliaeetus vociferoides*. Pages 269-278. *In* Meyburg, B.-U. & R. Chancellor (Eds.), *Raptors in the modern world*. World Working Group on Birds of Prey, Berlin.

OWEN, W.F.W. 1833. *Narrative of voyages to explore the shores of Africa, Arabia and Madagascar*. Vol. II. Richard Bentley, Publisher to His Majesty, London.

RABARISOA, R., R.T. WATSON, R. THORSTROM, & J. BERKELMAN 1997. Status of the Madagascar Fish-Eagle *Haliaeetus vociferoides* in 1995. *Ostrich* 68(1):8-12.

RAZANDRIZANAKANIRINA, D. 1997. Community-based wetland conservation project: 1996 mission notes. Pages 105-120. *In* R.T. Watson (Ed.): *Progress Report III, Madagascar wetlands conservation project*. The Peregrine Fund, Boise.

RAZANDRIZANAKANIRINA, D. & L. KALAVAHA 1997. Socio-economic status of the region around the three lakes, Befotaka, Soamalipo, and Ankerika, in western Madagascar. The Peregrine Fund, Boise.

STRZALKOWSKA, S., L. KALAVAHA, & J. MAMPIANDRA 1995. Village dialogue: gaining information through participatory discussions. Pages 81-109. *In* R.T. Watson (Ed.): *Report II, Madagascar Project*. The Peregrine Fund, Boise.

WATSON, R.T. 1995. Summary of achievements. Pages 21-33. *In* R.T. Watson (Ed.): *Progress Report II*. The Peregrine Fund, Boise.

WATSON, R.T. 1997. Madagascar Fish-Eagle conservation. Pages 45-49. *In* R.T. Watson (Ed.): *Progress Report III, Madagascar wetlands conservation project*. The Peregrine Fund, Boise.

WATSON, R.T., S. THOMSETT, D. O'DANIEL & R. LEWIS, R. 1996. Breeding, growth, development, and management of the Madagascar Fish-Eagle *(Haliaeetus vociferoides)*. *J. Raptor Res.* 30(1): 21-27.

WATSON, R.T., J. BERKELMAN, R. RABARISOA, R. THORSTROM, & C.R.B. WATSON 1997. Description of nesting and foraging habitat of the Madagascar Fish-Eagle *Haliaeetus vociferoides:* a conservation initiative. Pages 315-327. *In* R.T. Watson (Ed.): *Progress Report III, Madagascar wetlands conservation project.* The Peregrine Fund, Boise.

WATSON, R.T. & R. RABARISOA in press. Sakalava fishermen and Madagascar Fish-Eagles: enhancing traditional conservation rules to control resource abuse that threatens a key breeding area for an endangered eagle. *Proc. Pan-Afr. Ornith. Congr.* 9.

Richard T. Watson
The Peregrine Fund
566 West Flying Hawk Lane
Boise, ID 83709
U.S.A.

Aristide Andrianarimisa, Daurette Razandrizanakanirina, & Loukman Kalavaha
Ankoay TRUST for Conservation
B.P. 4113, Antananarivo (101)
Madagascar

Appendix 1. Traditional edicts, laws and *Dina*, translated from Malagasy.

TRADITIONAL EDICTS, LAWS AND *DINA* AGREED BY THE *FOKONTANY* OF AMBALAMANGA WITH RESPECT TO LAKES SOAMALIPO AND BEFOTAKA, AND THEIR SURROUNDING FORESTS. THE FOLLOWING LAWS CONCERN FISHING, THE USE OF NETS, COLLECTION OF FISH AND THE FOREST.

The following laws concern fishing, the use of nets, collection of fish and the forest.
* Before the currently existing situation concerning the exploitation of fish and the innumerable people who practice it,
* In consequence of the non-respect of traditional taboos, some existing laws aimed at Lakes Soamalipo and Befotaka and the degradation of their surrounding forest,
* For the economic expansion of the region, for the conservation and the preservation of the rural world, are:
* Hereby, *Raiamandreny* and the *Fokonolona* of Ambalamanga in order to apply the corresponding *dina*, under the direction of the Mayor of Masoarivo and the Director of the Forestry Division of Antsalova,
* Realize and advance the following decisions:

1. TRADITIONAL EDICTS

Article 1:
The decision about the LOA-DRANO, "the opening of the fishing season", depends on the *Tompondrano* ("keeper of the lakes") and the *Raiamandreny*.

Article 2:
Until the fishing season is officially opened, it is forbidden to:
- slap the water or
- hit the dug-out canoes (to drive the fish into the nets).

Article 3:
In the daily life, it is taboo since forever to:
- salt the fish catch
- transport live charcoal embers on the water
- relieve ones "needs" in the water
- bring women to the islands, such as *Nosy Sarotsy, Rehampy, Nosindambo*.

Those who violate these daily taboos will be considered malefactors (of the *Tompondrano* and his family) and will be brought to justice before the people responsible for the administrative hierarchy.

Article 4:
Those that commit an infraction of the traditional edicts must pay (a fine of) a very fat (healthy) cow and 20 litres of rum. Without waiting for the "fatality does not make credit"

2. LAWS

It is stressed that the official laws are set down by the following responsible people:
- The President of the Committee for Local Security (PCLS).
- The Mayor (of Masoarivo)
- The Sub-prefect
- The person responsible for the Direction des Eaux et Forêts, representing the Fishing authority
- The Provincial Director

Article 5:
The opening and closing of the fishing season:
The opening and the closing of the fishing season will be decided by the meeting of:
- the Mayor
- the agent for the Direction des Eaux et Forêts, representing the fishing authority
- the President of the Committee for Local Security (PCLS)
- the *Tompondrano*
- the *Raiamandreny*.

Article 6:
If the opening of the fishing season is not official, only static gill nets (*jonoky*) and fishing lines (*firango*) are allowed.

Article 7:
During the fishing season:
- Every fisherman must have a authorization (permit) to allow him to fish in calm water
- Fees must be paid to the hierarchical authorities (Fokontany, Village, Sub-prefect) for all export of fish from the region.
- Only nets of four-finger (about 8 cm) mesh can be used
- It is forbidden to use trawl nets
- It is forbidden to camp on the lakeshore outside the existing villages or hamlets, according to the decision made during this meeting.

Article 8:
The transgression of the two aforementioned articles:
The transgression or non respect of the fishing season limits or the prohibitions during the open fishing season will result in:
- the immediate application by the *Fokonolona* of sanctions and *corresponding Dina* and will be brought to justice before the hierarchical authorities starting with the *Fokonolona*, then the Mayor and the Forestry Division Director.

3. DINA
Seeing the innumerable people practicing fishing and the complexity of life, we think that it is beneficial to add some *Dina* (rules) to facilitate organization and to anticipate the future.

Article 9:
It is agreed that every fisherman should pay 5000 Fmg (about $1.25) to participate in the opening of the fishing season. The (sacrificial) zebu cattle comes from Tompondrano.

Article 10:
It is forbidden to destroy the natural environment and the forest around the Lakes Soamalipo and Befotaka.
For that:
- It is forbidden to damage the forest, to make clearings that lead to the destruction of the lakes.
- It is forbidden to kill and to hunt any of the protected animals like the *Ankoay* (Madagascar Fish-Eagle), the lemurs, the *Sifaka* (lemur), the *rere* (turtles), the water birds (except the *Vivy* "White-faced whistling duck", and the *Angongo* "Knob-billed Duck" which can be hunted during the hunting season).
- It is necessary to move away from the locality where one finds the *Ankoay* so as not to disturb its habitat.

Article 11:
In order to avoid any problems, anyone wishing to fish must join the villages indicated by the decision made during the meeting.

Article 12:
It is forbidden to cut living trees for firewood, especially *Manary, Hazomalany* and *Katrafay* in order to provide for the future. Only dry (dead) wood is reserved for this purpose.

Article 13:
For the respect of the lakes and the environment
For the respect of the lakes and the environment, it is necessary to move away from the beaches to clean the fish and bury the scales and garbage in a hole.

Article 14:
Anyone taken in flagrant offense of violating these conventions will be taken in hand by the *Fokonolona* and submitted to the authorities concerned.

These written conventions and corresponding *Dina* concern especially the region of Lakes Soamalipo, Befotaka and surrounding forests, namely *Antsingilo, Bemolaky, Analabombo.*

Progress in Translocation of Diurnal Raptors

Tom J. Cade

ABSTRACT

Since my review in 1986, no fewer than 52 projects involving translocation (reintroduction *sensu lato*) have been conducted on at least 25 species of diurnal raptors. Using a questionnaire and a survey of literature, I evaluated these translocations and identified principal factors involved in their outcomes. Of 28 projects carried out on sufficient scale to judge degree of success, 21 resulted in establishment of breeding populations that appear viable. Most of the others show initial success— establishment of individual animals and some breeding pairs in nature. Hacking has been the main method of release, but other methods are useful. Most releases have used captive-bred young, but wild-taken young and mature birds also work. Successful translocation seems related to intensity of effort, number of birds released, and habitat quality. The higher success rate (c.75 %) in translocating raptors compared to other birds (<67%) may be explained by (1) raptors being less affected by predation, (2) physically stronger, (3) more resistant to diseases, and (4) easier to raise and keep in confinement; (5) hacking was well-developed long before its use for translocation; and (6) people who work with raptors have "green thumbs" and are fanatically devoted to their projects. Ethical and societal concerns about translocation as a method of conservation have been unduly emphasized in the literature of the past 20 years and have little relevance to raptor projects. Translocation has proved to be important for the preservation of rare and threatened raptors in nature.

INTRODUCTION

Since my earlier review (Cade 1986), reintroduction or, in a broader sense, translocation as a method for restoring raptor populations has increased greatly. In 1984 I was able to summarize only some 15 examples of diurnal raptor reintroduction (see, also, Garcelon and Roemer 1988), but by now there have been well over 50 translocation projects involving more than 25 species. The Richard R. Olendorff Memorial Library at the Raptor Research Center, Boise State University, Idaho contains more than 1,000 catalogued references on raptor translocation. In recognition of the general, worldwide interest in reintroduction and related techniques as methods of conservation, the IUCN Species Survival Commission established a "Re-introduction Specialist Group" in 1989, under the chairmanship of Dr. Mark R. Stanley Price, to coordinate and guide efforts in reintroductions among the many scientists and managers involved and to establish and administer a set of guidelines for acceptable protocols. In addition, many European projects have long operated under the criteria for assessing the suitability of translocation set forth by the UK Committee for International Nature Conservation under the Nature Conservancy Council of Great Britain (Anon. 1976; see also Cade 1986).

Although the term has been used to refer to several kinds of activities involving the release of animals into natural habitats, "reintroduction" has a specific meaning, namely : "the re-establishment of a species by the release of individuals in an area where it naturally occurred but has been extirpated, usually through human influences"(Cade 1986). Since that is only one of several kinds of human intervention involving the release and establishment of animals in outdoor environments, a more inclusive term has been needed to cover all activities involving the manipulation of individuals to establish or bolster wild populations—including such actions as "restocking" or augmenting existing populations, island marooning (Williams 1977), and introduction into previously unoccupied range. The term "translocation" as used by the IUCN (1987; see also Griffith *et al.* 1989) serves that need: "Translocation is the intentional release of animals to the wild in an attempt to establish, reestablish, or augment a population." Thus, it covers such micro-manipulative techniques as "sibling rescue" (Meyburg 1978) and "fostering" (Cade 1978) to major introductions of species outside their natural ranges.

In the past 20 years there has been an increasing number of reviews and discussions about the technical effectiveness of translocation for species restoration and also about the ethical desirability of such methods, particularly as compared to more inclusive ("holistic") approaches such as habitat preservation and ecosystem management (see, for example, Myers 1979, Pitelka 1981, Csuti *et al.* 1987, Hutto *et al.* 1987, Newton 1988, Griffith *et al.* 1989, 1990, Povilitis 1990, Varner & Monroe, 1990, Cade & Temple 1995, Snyder *et al.* 1996, and Wolf *et al.* 1996). My purpose here is to review the work on translocating raptors against this background of discussion about technological effectiveness and ethical validity and to show how translocation complements other methods of conservation. As a technique how successful have raptor translocations been in establishing or significantly augmenting viable, self-sustaining populations in nature? Do artificially established raptor populations fit naturally into their ecological communities and function as their wild counterparts do or did?

METHODS

To answer these questions I have reviewed much of the literature and unpublished reports on translocations. In addition, I sent out a questionnaire to 32 workers known to be involved in one or more raptor translocations and received usable replies from 31 of them. From these sources I obtained information on 52 translocation projects involving 25 species of diurnal birds of prey. There are a number of other translocations involving diurnal raptors, but these 52 projects are the ones for which I could obtain sufficient information for an evaluation, and they represent the spectrum of programmes and techniques being used.

I have not analyzed these data statistically, because each translocation represents a complicated synergism of details about species, location, time, methods, and people. When such complex variables and interactions are reduced to a few numbers for statistical analysis, I believe important and probably essential perspectives for evaluating success or failure get lost. Although it may be tedious and old-fashioned to analyze projects on a case by case basis, as Cade and Temple (1995) did, I believe that one often ends up with a better understanding of why some projects succeed while other fail than when projects are reduced to unidentifiable numbers that are then fed into high-powered computer programmes, the workings and significance of which many researchers have to accept on faith.

RESULTS

The data are summarized in Tables 1, 2, and 3. I judged 28 of the 52 projects to have been carried out with sufficient scope (based on number of birds released, area of releases, time, monitoring effort) to warrant evaluation of their success in establishing a self-sustaining population (Table 1). By "self-sustaining" I mean that given the current characteristics of the population (its size and

Table 1 Projects carried out with sufficient scope to warrant evaluation of success or failure.

Project	Area (Km²)	No. Years	No. Birds	No. Rel. per Year	Age	Captive or Wild	Years Breeding	No. Pairs (Yr.)	% Suc.	Release Method	Habitat	No. Workers	Remarks
Peregrine—Eastern USA	>10⁶	20	>1300	16-100	J/n	C/w	19	132 ('97)	>60	H/f	A	10²	Young produced in 1997 = 185.
Peregrine—Midwest USA	>10⁶	15	>850	5-116	J	C	12	95 ('98)	c. 60	H	P/a	10²	Estimated 1/2 wild population derived from released birds.
Peregrine—Rocky Mts. USA	>10⁶	20	2112	2->100	J/N	C/w	17	438 ('97)	c. 80	H/f	P	10²	Some cross-fostering; estimated >1/2 wild pop. derived from released birds.
Peregrine—California	>10⁵	15	754	2-81	N/J	C/W	17	140 ('97)	c. 50	F/H	A/p	10²	Note: first captive-bred & fostered bird nested at Chipp River, n. Alberta, 1977.
Peregrine—So. Canada	>10⁶	20	1550	5-120	J/n	C	17	105 ('98)	>50?	H/f	A/p	10²	First tree-nesting pairs in 1996-98.
Peregrine—Germany	>10⁵	20	803	7-62	J/N	C	15	>70 ('98)	>50?	H/f	P/A	Many?	Still increasing and considered self-sustaining.
Peregrine—Sweden (Norway)	>10⁴	16	>419	2-40	J/n	C/w	15	48 ('97)	74	H/f	P	10²	Breeding success = 72% in East, 58% in West; 3 pops.
Mauritius Kestrel	>10²	10	350	1-63	J/N	C/W	12	>100 ('97)	c. 65	H/f	P/A/M	1	Max. no. pairs in 1980s; currently estimated <5 pairs.
Seychelles Kestrel	40	1	13	13	A/I	W	19	>10 ('80s)	?	M	A	?	
Lesser Kestrel—NE Catalonia	10²	9	378	40-66	J/n	C/w	8	12 ('98)	38	H/f	A	c. 10	Breeding success ranged from 0 to 80%.
Lesser Kestrel—W Catalonia	>50	8	329	8-73	J/n	C/w	5	16 ('97)	72	H/f	A	c. 10	Breeding success ranged from 27 to 100%.
Bald Eagle—New York State	>10⁴	13	213	2-33	J/n	W/c	19	40 ('98)	66	H/f	P	10²	First bred at 4 years in 1980.
Bald Eagle—So. Cent. USA	>10⁶	8	275	12-61	J	W	8	>50 ('98)	?	H	P	10²	Wild eggs hatched in lab, and chicks raised to 8 weeks.
Bald Eagle—Calif. Coast Ra.	>10⁴	9	66	>8	J	W/c	6	7 ('98)	71	H	A	c. 4-5	Reproduction above state average.
Bald Eagle—Catalina Island	>10³	19	57	1-8	J/n	C/W	12*	3 ('97)	0	H/f	M	4	*Attempted breeding—none successful.
Bald Eagle—Massachusetts	>10³	7	41	?	J	?	10*	9 ('98)	?*	H	A	?	*Total production = 89 young fledged.
Bald Eagle—Tennessee	10⁴	19	>269	av. 14	J	C/W	16	37 ('98)	>50	H	P	?	18 of 30 occupied territories produced 34 fledglings in 1997.
Bald Eagle—Indiana	10⁴	5	73	av. >14	J	W	7	19 ('98)	59	H	A	?	11 of 19 occupied territories produced 20 fledglings in 1998.
White-tailed Eagle—Scotland	10⁴	11	82	av. >7	J/I	W	14	c. 14 ('97)	c. 42	H	A	?	46 more released in 1993-1997.
Osprey—Pennsylvania	10⁴	12	236	av. >20	J	W	12	c. 35 ('97)	80	H	P	10²	Some wild birds attracted to settle.
Osprey—Tennessee	10⁴	10	165	av. >16	J	W	c. 15	>97 ('98)	>90	H	P	?	In 1998, 91 pairs produced 171 young, but not all are released birds.
Osprey—Twin Cit.es, Minn.	>10²	12	144	av. 12	J	W	10	>15 ('97)	?	H	A	40	High survival of releasees and conspecific attraction = success.
Griffon Vulture—France	>10²	6	61	1-17	A/I/j	C/W	16	71 ('97)	c. 60	A/H	P	5	
Goshawk—Great Britain	10⁵	15-20	c. 250	c.>20	J/A	W	>30	c. 400	?	Hd/h	P/A	10²	Falconry escapees, 1965-1980s and 25 deliberate releases.
Red Kite—South England	>10³	6	93	av. >16	J	W	7	>51 ('97)	90	H	P	12	High survival and productivity = quick success.
Red Kite—North Scotland	>10³	5	93	av. 18	J	W	6	23 ('97)	>75	H	A	c. 10	Ditto above.
Harris' Hawk—So. California	>10²	12	220	18-40	J/I/a	C/w	16	3-5 ('90s)	80	H/hd/f	M	c. 10	Limited and marginal habitat = dispersal.
Montagu's Harrier—Catalonia	>25	10	198	av <20	J/n	C/w	?	2-5 ('90s)	?	H/f	A-M	c. 10	Weak philopatry results in few returns to release area.

Table 2 On-going translocation projects.

Project	Area (Km²)	No. Years	No. Birds Released	No. Rel. per Year	Age	Captive or Wild	Years Breeding	No. Pairs (Yr.)	% Suc.	Release Method	Range	Habitat	No. Workers	Remarks
Aplomado Falcon So. Texas	10⁴	5	214	10-101	J	C	4	4 ('98)	75	H	P	A	c. 20	24 birds released experimentally 1985-89 prior to current project.
Lanner Falcon Israel	10³	6	46	av. >7	J	C	0	0	0	H	P	A	?	Releases spread: 1990, 1992, 1995, 1997.
White-tailed Eagle Israel	10³	5	13	c. 3	J	C	?	?	0	H	P	M	?	Poor habitat and small number of releasees make project problematic.
Andean Condor Colombia	10⁴	9	42	c. 5	J	C	3	3	?	H	C	P	>10	Sexual maturity at 6-7 years.
Andean Condor Argentina	?	1	7	7	J	C	0	0	0	H	P	P	c. 5	Project just starting in 1997.
California Condor So. Calif.	10⁴	>6	39	2-8	J	C	0	0	0	H	C	P	19	11 removed; 19 remain in wild June 98; some pairing started.
California Condor Arizona	>10⁴	<2	19	6-13	J	C	0	0	0	H	P	P	5-6	15 birds survive to Aug. 1998; 2 dead, 1 lost, 1 returned to captivity.
California Condor Cent. Calif.	>10²	1	10	5+5	J	C	0	0	0	H	C	P	?	First 5 removed because of behavioural problems; 6-8 yrs to sex maturity.
Griffon Vulture Israel	10³	5	41	7-8	A/I	C/W	4?	>2? ('97)	?	A?	P	A?	?	Some released birds have joined a wild colony 100 km away.
Bearded Vulture Euro. Alps	10⁴	12	72	av. 6	J	C	2?	2 ('97)	50	H	C	P	10²	Good survival of released birds, 38-43 of 65 fledged up to 1996.
Euro. Black Vulture Mallorca	10³	9	33	9-10	A/I/J/n	C/w	6	10 ('97)	50	H/A	P	A	>10	Last release in '92; bred 9 years after 1st release; total pop.= 60 birds.
Euro. Black Vulture France	>10²	7	26	av. >3	A/I/J/n	C/w	2	4 ('98)	25	H/A	P	A	>10	Breeding after 4th yr; young adults will promote pop. growth.
Osprey England	c. 25	2	14	6-8	J	W	0	0	0	H	C	P	.10	First 2 yrs of 5 year project; 1 dead in Senegal, 12 migrated
Red Kite Midlands, England	>10²	3	49	16	J	W	2	4 ('97)	c. 90	H	C	P	>10	On the way to successful establishment.
Red Kite Central Scotland	>10²	2	37	18-19	J	W	1?	2?	0	H	P	A	?	High survival of releasees; attempted breeding in 1997 after first year.

Table 3 Experimental or casual translocation projects.

Project	Area (Km^2)	No. Years	No. Birds	No. Rel. per Year	Age	Captive or Wild	Years Breeding	No. Pairs (Yr.)	% Suc.	Release	Range Method	Habitat	No. Workers	Remarks
Bat Falcon Guatemala	<10^2	2	16	av. 8	J	C	0	0	0	H	P	M	1-2	11 of 16 young fledged and dispersed; none settled to breed.
European Hobby England	<10^2	8	10	>1	J	C	0	0	0	F/H/t	C	A	1-2	10 young from one captive pair successfully released.
Madagascar Fish Eagle	10^2	3	9	av. 3	N	W	0	0	0	SR	C	P	2-3	7 survived and increased productivity from 0.15 to 0.28 per pair.
Osprey No. Scotland	<10^2	1	4	4	J	W	0	0	0	H	P	A	1?	Late hack of fledged juveniles in September,1929.
Spanish Imperial Eagle	>10^2	7	12	1-2	N	W	0	0	0	SR	C	A?	?	8 of 12 fledged successfully (see text for significance).
Golden Eagle Sweden	>10^2	13	25	c. 2	J	C	?	1?	?	H/f	P	M?	1	All offspring of one captive pair.
Andean Condor Peru	>10^3	1	12	12	a/I/N	C	0	0	0	H/hd	C	A	c. 5-6	7 of 11 captive bred survived >2 yrs at termination; good integration with wild birds.
Common Buzzard England	c. 570	5	44	5-17	J	W/C	2	3 ('97)	100	H	C	P/A	11	Exptl. study: high dispersal reduces settlement in release area, but dispersal and survival normal for the species.

Footnotes to Tables 1-3.

Key to symbols used. Upper case letters mean primary use; lower case mean secondary use. <u>Age</u>: A = adult, I = immature (more than 1 year old, J = juvenile (including fledglings), N = nestlings. <u>Release method</u>: A = use of acclimation cage, F = fostering, H = hacking, Hd = hard release, M = island marooning. <u>Range</u>: C = central, P = peripheral. <u>Habitat</u>: P = prime, A = average, M = marginal.

numerical trend, survivorship, breeding success, contact with other populations) and the prevailing environmental conditions, the population should persist indefinitely, barring some unpredictable catastrophic event (see Mace & Lande 1991 for non-parametrical but objective ways to assess population viability). I have not used population viability analysis or any other probability model (see Beissinger & Westphal 1998 and Reed *et al.* 1998 for the limitations and pitfalls in using such models), although such models have been applied to specific raptor translocations, as indicated beyond. For 15 on-going projects only an interim evaluation is appropriate (Table 2), while nine others were either experimental in nature or lacked the scope required for success (Table 3). The projects are further described in the following sections by grouping them according to the main functional (or phylogenetic) categories of diurnal raptors—falcons, eagles, fish-hawk, Old World vultures, condors, and hawks *sensu lato*.

Falcons

1. Peregrine Falcon *Falco peregrinus*, Table 1—Although there were a few half-hearted attempts to translocate raptors in the early decades of this century and even before, the first coordinated and systematic efforts involved the Eagle Owl *Bubo bubo* in Germany and Sweden beginning in the 1960s and 1970s (Cade 1986). Also, about the same time, a partly organized and partly clandestine effort to release Fennoscandian Goshawks *Accipiter gentilis* resulted in the reestablishment of that species in Great Britain (Marquiss & Newton 1982, Cade 1986). It was, however, the plight of the Peregrine on two continents that called forth the largest, most sustained, and coordinated programmes to restore an endangered species by captive breeding and translocation (Hickey 1969, Cade 1988a, Cade *et al.* 1988, Cade 1990, Enderson *et al.* 1995, Cade *et al.* 1997, Cade 1998).

The idea to breed Peregrines in captivity and to release the progeny back into the wild developed at the International Peregrine Conference held at the University of Wisconsin in 1965 (Hickey 1969, Cade 1988a), consequent to the realization that the species was severely threatened on two continents. There have been seven major, regional programmes, five in North America and two in Europe (see Table 1), as well as several other smaller or recently started projects, particularly in Europe.

In 1970 a programme of research and management to reintroduce captive-bred Peregrines into the vacant range of the eastern United States began at the Laboratory of Ornithology, Cornell University—soon to become known as The Peregrine Fund (Cade & Temple 1977). In 1974 The Peregrine Fund established a second breeding facility and release programme for the Rocky Mountain region at Fort Collins, Colorado, in association with the Colorado Division of Wildlife (Burnham *et al.* 1988). Later, in 1984, a permanent headquarters for the entire organization became established in Boise, Idaho at a facility known as The World Center for Birds of Prey, under the leadership of William A. Burnham.

In 1972 the Canadian Wildlife Service established a falcon breeding centre at Fort Wainwright, Alberta under the supervision of Richard Fyfe, to produce the endangered *anatum* Peregrine for reintroduction into southern Canada where, as in the eastern United States, the species had been totally extirpated (Fyfe 1976, 1988). In California, a Pacific Coast programme—the Santa Cruz Predatory Bird Research Group—got underway at the University of California, Santa Cruz around 1975. Originally founded by James C. Roush III, it has been directed by Brian J. Walton since 1977 (Thelander & Walton 1988). The fifth programme, in the upper Mississippi River valley and western Great Lakes region (Midwest USA), began in 1982 under the leadership of Patrick Redig at the Raptor Center and Harrison B. Tordoff at the Bell Museum of Natural History, University of Minnesota (Redig & Tordoff 1988).

Guided by endangered species recovery plans approved by the U.S. Department of the Interior. Fish and Wildlife Service and Canadian authorities, and involving the collaboration of dozens of federal, state, and provincial agencies, numerous non-governmental organizations, and more than 1,000 individual workers, these programmes have resulted in the release of more than 6,000 Peregrines across the North American continent since 1974 (Enderson *et al.* 1995, 1998). They unquestionably constitute the largest, coordinated effort ever mounted to recover an endangered species. Most of the principals involved were or are falconers, and the influence of falconry on the success of these programmes needs to be acknowledged (Cade 1988a).

The release of Peregrines by hacking (Sherrod *et al.* 1981) began in the eastern USA in 1974. By 1980, when some 204 falcons had been released in nine states, the first three established pairs nested successfully, and that year fostering of captive-bred chicks into wild nests was added as a second method of release (Barclay & Cade 1983). Large scale releases by hacking and fostering continued through the 1980s up to 1992; at the same time the number of established breeders grew at rates of 25 per cent per annum or more (Barclay 1988, Enderson *et al.* 1995). By 1991 when the major release effort ended, more than 1200 captive-bred Peregrines had been released in 13 states and the District of Columbia, at least 91 territorial pairs had been established, and annual production of fledged young exceeded 100 birds. Since then the breeding population has continued to grow on its own (annual releases have averaged only a dozen or so birds) at an average rate of >7 per cent per year, yielding 132 territorial pairs counted in 1997 (Mesta 1998), slightly more than one third of the number estimated to have existed before the DDT-induced extirpation (Hickey 1942). More than 900 young fledged from 1992 through 1997 (data compiled by L. Kiff, The Peregrine Fund archives). About one third of the breeding pairs nest on natural cliff eyries, mainly in the mountains of northern New York State and New England; but most of the others are found in urban habitats (Frank 1994, Cade *et al.* 1996a) and on nesting towers in coastal salt marshes (Steidl *et al.* 1991,Therres *et al.* 1993).

The continuing rate of increase in population size, the current number of breeding pairs, and their rate of reproduction all indicate that this eastern population is now self-sustaining and will continue to grow to whatever the current carrying capacity of the eastern environment may be (Cade *et al.* 1997). In addition, this population is known to have exchanged dispersing individuals with the expanding Canadian population to the north and with the midwestern population in the USA, so that it is no longer a demographically or genetically isolated population (Barclay 1995, M. Martell *et al. in litt.* 1998).

Following two earlier attempts to hack Peregrines in habitats infested with Great Horned Owls *Bubo virginianus* along the upper Mississippi River, the midwestern programme got under way in 1982, using young, captive-bred falcons produced by private breeders, mostly falconers (Redig & Tordoff 1988). The first successful breeding of released falcons occurred in 1987, following the hacking of 102 young birds. The population grew rapidly at first with the continued annual release of 18 to >100 birds, most of the pairs settling in metropolitan and urban areas, where they nest on buildings, bridges, and power plant smokestacks (Cade *et al.* 1996a). The released birds failed to establish themselves as breeders at historical eyries along the Mississippi owing to depredation of the Great Horned Owl (Cade *et al.* 1989), but they have done so along the northern shore of Lake Superior and elsewhere where owls are not a problem. By 1998, after 857 Peregrines had been released in 12 states and two Canadian provinces, the known adult population consisted of 99 territorial pairs, 84 of which nested and produced 205 young (H. B. Tordoff *et al.*, unpubl. rept.1998). A demographic analysis of this population, considering data on dispersal, survival of territorial adults, age of first breeding, longevity, lifetime reproduction, and fidelity to mate and territory from 1982-1995 indicates that this population is self-sustaining and capable of growing to the current carrying capacity based on the number of serviceable breeding locations in the region (Tordoff & Redig 1997). Even an earlier population viability analysis, carried out when this population consisted of only 52 territorial pairs in 1991, showed that under a variety of supposed conditions calculated extinction rates over 100 years varied from 0 to 5.2%, mostly <1.0 % (Moen & Tordoff 1993). Also, because of its high reproductive capacity and long range dispersal of individuals, this population likely serves as a source for repopulating adjacent regions, particularly to the west where few Peregrines as yet have resettled in the northern Great Plains.

Restocking of Peregrines in the Rocky Mountain states and Pacific Northwest began in 1977 and ended in 1997. The total number of birds released by hacking and fostering (a few also cross-fostered to pairs of Prairie Falcons, *Falco mexicanus*) was 2,122 falcons. Released falcons were known to begin breeding in Colorado by 1980, and by 1997 the total number of known pairs in the eight states of Washington, Oregon, Idaho, Montana, Wyoming, Colorado, Utah, and New Mexico was 438, whereas the known number before restocking started was only 21 pairs (Burnham 1998).

The number of reported pairs must be taken as a minimum figure, because it is now difficult for field workers to survey all potential nesting locations in these states in a given year.

It is also difficult to know how much of the increase in breeding numbers can be attributed to restocking and how much to natural increase, as both processes occurred simultaneously; but with so few wild pairs present at the start, restocking must have accounted for most of the population growth, particularly in the early years. For example, in the three states of Idaho, Montana, and Wyoming there was but one known wild pair in 1980 when restocking started. In 1997 these states held a minimum of 77 pairs; in the early years of reestablishment all closely observed adults at eyries wore bands identifying them as captive-bred and released birds. Similarly, in Colorado, perhaps the most intensively monitored state in the West, there were only six known pairs remaining when restocking started in 1977; after the release of 405 young falcons through 1990, the number of breeding pairs had grown to more than 80 in 1996 and 1997, three times the number known in Colorado before the DDT-induced decline (Enderson *et al.* 1988, Enderson *et al.* 1995, Mesta 1998). Again, during the early years most of the breeders wore bands identifying them as released birds (Cade *et al.* 1997).

Fewer than 10 surviving pairs of Peregrines were known in California before restocking began in 1977 (systematically in 1980), whereas more than 200 historical eyries had been catalogued for the state (Walton & Thelander 1988, Walton *et al.* 1988b). Using hacking, fostering, and crossfostering with Prairie Falcons, and young hatched from salvaged, thin-shelled wild eggs as well as captive-produced young, Walton and his associates released 754 falcons in California through 1997 (Walton 1997). By 1992 there were 116 occupied breeding territories in the state. Although no statewide count has been made since then, continued increases in several regions and an extrapolation of the known population growth from 1975 to 1992 indicate that there were around 140 pairs in the state in 1997, and the prediction is that the California Peregrines will exceed 200 pairs before reaching a limit imposed by environmental carrying capacity (Walton 1997), contrary to the population model developed by Wootton and Bell (1992).

From 1976 through 1996, Canadian workers released 1,550 Peregrines, mostly by hacking, in southern Alberta, s. Saskatchewan, s. Manitoba, s. Ontario and Quebec, and in the Maritime provinces, a region in which only one wild pair is known to have persisted until 1980. By 1988, after 563 young falcons had been released in 24 areas of southern Canada, only 12 nesting pairs could be located in the entire region, and the programme underwent re-evaluation (Holroyd & Banasch 1990). One reason for the apparent low success rate might have been high mortality related to long distance migration, but a more likely reason has to do with the great expanses of wild country in Canada and the limited number of observers available to find Peregrines. Following recommendations that more young (20-30) be released per area per year and that a more intensive monitoring scheme to locate nesting pairs be instituted, by 1995 there were 41 known nesting pairs in southern Canada out of 100 sites surveyed; 32 unsurveyed sites could have been occupied by an additional 12-13 pairs (U. Banasch *in litt.* 1997). In 1998 the number of known occupied sites had climbed to 105 for southern Canada excluding British Columbia (G. Holroyd *in litt.* 1998, Mesta 1998). Although this population is thinly spread over a vast landscape, it is now growing rapidly, and it probably receives some wild recruits from Labrador, the northern tier of states, and from northern Alberta.

Owing in part to the success of these regional translocations and in part to natural recovery, the U. S. Fish and Wildlife Service published a formal notice to remove the American Peregrine Falcon *F. p. anatum* from its list of threatened and endangered wildlife (Mesta 1998). The final notice delisting this subspecies is expected in 1999.

The German programme has been largely a private initiative of the Deutscher Falkenorden carried out under the general supervision of Prof. Dr. Christian Saar, with help from other groups and government agencies (Saar 1988, *in litt*.1998). The effort has been concentrated in regions north of the River Main in both former West Germany and East Germany where the Peregrine had been totally extirpated by pesticides in the 1960s, with only a small population of some 70 pairs remaining to the south in Bavaria and Baden-Württemberg (Mebs 1988). Young falcons produced in captivity by falconers, mainly at Saar's Wanderfalken-Zucht-und-Forschungsstation in Berlin (and later,

Hamburg) were released by hacking, fostering, and cross-fostering. Releases began in 1977 and have continued to the present. By 1997, 803 Peregrines had been released and a minimum of 70 territorial pairs established in Northern Hessen, Lower Saxony, Schleswig-Holstein, Hanover, Berlin, Brandenburg, Mecklenburg-Vorpommern, Saxony, and Thüringen. In addition, an unknown number of released Peregrines dispersed southward and joined the expanding wild populations in Bavaria and Baden-Württemberg, but so far no southern, cliff-nesting falcons have dispersed northward. The reintroduced falcons are nesting mostly on cliff sites or on man-made structures in urban habitats and on offshore lighthouses in the North Sea (Saar 1988). Work to establish cliff-nesting Peregrines ended in 1996 with a project in Sächsische Schweig National Park, where 12 pairs are now nesting (C. Saar *in litt.* 1998).

The remaining goal in northern Germany is to reestablish the tree-nesting population of Peregrines that formerly lived in the low country adjacent to the Baltic Sea, a population that extended through northern Poland and into the Baltic states. This task is being accomplished by hacking from artificial nests in trees and by cross-fostering young Peregrines with Goshawk parents. The first tree-nesting pair bred in a natural tree nest in 1996 and has raised three young each year through 1998; two other unsuccessful pairs have been reported (Langgemach *et al.* 1997, C. Saar *in litt.* 1998). A similar project started in northwestern Poland in 1990 in the expectation that birds from the two sources will link up to establish a viable population across the border of the two countries (Wisniewski 1995, Trommer 1997).

The Swedish project has been supervised by Peter Lindberg at the University of Göteborg and involves the Swedish Society of Nature Conservation, Swedish Environment Protection Board, and a number of other organizations, and many individuals, including some in Norway. The original goal was to restock a region of some 15,000 km^2 in SW Sweden where only a few pairs remained, until a breeding population of 30 pairs (half the pre-1955 number) had been achieved (Lindberg 1988). Release of captive-bred falcons began in 1982 and continues to the present, with a total of 419 young hacked or fostered into nests of wild Peregrines. By 1997 there were 23 pairs in SW Sweden and another 25 pairs in SE Norway just across the border (Lindberg 1997, *in litt.* 1998). The project has taken longer than originally anticipated in part because of depredations on the young falcons by reintroduced Eagle Owls.

Other small, lesser known or just starting projects to restore Peregrines are underway in various European countries. The idea, apparently promoted by the Wisconsin Peregrine Society, to establish nesting Peregrines in cities is especially popular (e.g., Warsaw, Luniak 1995).

2. Mauritius Kestrel *Falco punctatus,* Table 1—Several other species of falcon have been the subjects of translocation projects. Certainly the most outstanding has been the programme to restore the Mauritius Kestrel (Jones 1980, Cade & Jones 1993, Jones *et al.* 1995), perhaps the most significant rescue of any endangered species so far effected by captive breeding and translocation. Carried out under the direction of Carl Jones since 1979 and supported by the Government of Mauritius, the Mauritius Wildlife Fund, Jersey and International Wildlife Trusts, and The Peregrine Fund, the programme released 350 birds by hacking and fostering in the years from 1984 to 1994, using both captive-bred kestrels and birds hatched from wild eggs. The population on the island has grown from only two known pairs in 1974 (Temple 1977) to more than 100 pairs in 1997 distributed in three geographic locations covering much of the 30,000 hectares now estimated to be suitable habitat, and it seems likely that the population will eventually grow to 200-250 territorial pairs and several hundred total individuals (Jones *et al.* 1995, C. Jones, *in litt.*1998).

3. Seychelles Kestrel *Falco araea,* Table 1—Jeff Watson's (1989) project with this species on Praslin Island is unique among the raptor translocations considered here in that it consisted of a single, hard release by island-marooning of three immature and 10 adult kestrels trapped on Mahé and released within two days on the smaller island (4,000 hectares), where the species had been extirpated following extensive deforestation and fires in the first half of the 20th Century. This project probably belongs in the experimental category, but I have included it in Table 1 because it was a deliberate attempt to reintroduce a population by the hard release of a minimum number of individuals.

It was thought that by the 1970s sufficient regrowth of forest had occurred to provide suitable habitat once again. Kestrels began nesting soon after release, and by 1980 at least 10 pairs were present. Unfortunately there has been no systematic, island-wide survey since 1980. Casual observations by staff of the Conservation Division on Praslin indicate that the early momentum of population growth has not been sustained, as there appear to be no more than two or three pairs remaining, perhaps owing to the use of predator-accessible nest sites in coconut palms and on buildings (J. Watson *in litt.* 1998). A thorough re-survey needs to be done.

4. Aplomado Falcon *Falco femoralis*, Table 2—Following a few experimental releases in 1985-1989, The Peregrine Fund began a large scale, continuing project to release captive-bred Aplomado Falcons by hacking in south Texas (Laguna Atascosa National Wildlife Refuge and adjacent private properties), in cooperation with the U. S. Fish and Wildlife Service and the Texas State Parks and Wildlife Department (Cade *et al.* 1991). The northern subspecies *F. f. septentrionalis* is listed as endangered in Mexico, and the southwestern USA where it had been extirpated as a breeding species by the 1940s and 1950s, probably owing to habitat changes. Suitable savanna-like habitat appears to have returned to southern Texas following brush-removal programmes and lowered chemical contaminant levels in the environment (Mora *et al.* 1997). Since 1993, more than 300 young Aplomado Falcons have been hacked in south Texas, more than 200 of them in the last two years. The first established pair bred in 1995, and there have been four or five pairs located on and around the Laguna Atascosa refuge in 1996-98 (P. Jenny *in litt.* 1998), but much suitable habitat remains to be surveyed. Many single birds are also present. Predation by Great Horned Owls and other predators has been a problem (Perez *et al.* 1997), and there could be a scarcity of suitable nest sites (old stick nests of other hawks and ravens); but it appears that successful establishment of a viable breeding population is just a matter of continuing to release birds for a few more years. An intensive search in 1999 located >15 territorial pairs, (W. Heindrich *in litt.*).

5. Lesser Kestrel *Falco naumanni*, Table 1—In Catalonia, Spain, where the species last bred naturally in 1986, there are two projects to reestablish nesting colonies of the Lesser Kestrel, mostly by hacking but also by fostering and cross-fostering to Common Kestrel *Falco tinnunculus* parents; about 95 per cent of the kestrels were produced in captivity (Pomarol 1993). These projects are carried out under the direction of the wildlife service of Catalonia (Sevei de Protecció i Gestió de la Fauna, Direcció General del Medi Natural) and the supervision of Manel Pomarol.

At the site in Alt Emporda county, 378 kestrels have been released since 1989, and between 70 and 76 per cent have survived their first year. Two pairs first bred in 1990, and by 1998 there were 12 pairs in the colony; but annual breeding success has varied from 0 to 80 per cent, averaging only 38 per cent. Problems that retarded population growth but that have now been corrected include (1) a rat poison used in the building where the kestrels are nesting, killing half the chicks and breeders in 1993, (2) high predation of adults and chicks by the marten (*Martes foiva*) in 1994-95, and (3) a vineyard pesticide that caused reproductive failure in 1997.

At the site in Noguera county, 329 birds have been released since 1993, and there were 16 established pairs in 1997. Their annual breeding success rate has varied between 27 and 100 per cent, averaging 72 percent over five years. Only one serious problem of mammalian predation occurred in 1994 and 1995.

Despite the high mortality, these colonies have grown slowly over six to seven year periods. Continued release of birds for a few more years, combined with providing the colonies with superior, manufactured nest-sites (Pomarol 1996), should result in self-sustaining, even expanding populations (M. Pomarol, *in litt.* 1998).

6. Lanner Falcon *Falco biarmicus*, Table 2—There is an on-going project at Mount Carmel, carried out by the Society for the Protection of Nature in Israel, to establish breeding Lanners in the area by hacking captive-produced fledglings (Getreide & Hatzofe 1991). A total of 45 falcons has been released in 1990, 1992-95, and 1997. Returning birds have been seen around Mount Carmel, but so far no breeding has been observed. Releases are continuing (O. Hatzofe *in litt.* 1998).

7. Other *Falco* spp.—There have no doubt been several other exploratory attempts to translocate falcons. After all, falconers have been hacking birds for a thousand years or more, and enough falcons have escaped during hack to have suggested to more than a few minds that the process might be used to establish wild breeding pairs in new or unusual locations.

J. P. Vannini (1989, 1990), Fundacion Interamericana de Investigacion Tropical, in cooperation with the Comission Nacional de Areas Ambiente, hacked 16 captive-produced Bat Falcons *Falco albigularis* in mixed degraded forest and agricultural lands on the Pacific Versant of Guatemala, where the species is now virtually extirpated. Post-hacking survival was good (11 of 16 birds), but no pairs became established, possibly because the environment is no longer suitable (Table 3). In Devon, England, Heather Woodland (1993) bred a pair of Hobbies *Falco subbuteo* in captivity and released 10 of their young by hacking, fostering, and one trained by a falconer before release (Table 3). She concluded, correctly I think, that hacking was the preferred method, the one least likely to have unintended, adverse side effects.

Eagles

1. The Bald Eagle *Haliaeetus leucocephalus,* Table 1—This species has been the subject of numerous translocation projects in the United States since the first efforts by The Peregrine Fund in New York State in 1976 (Cade 1983, Nye 1988). By 1985, Nye (1988) was able to summarize information on the hacking and occasional fostering of 390 Bald Eagles in 13 states and the province of Ontario, Canada. Unfortunately, there has been no continent-wide assessment of all these projects since then, but well over 1,000 eagles have been translocated in various parts of the country. The seven projects summarized here show the range of accomplishments.

The Peregrine Fund hacked the first Bald Eagles (wild eaglets from Wisconsin) in New York State in 1976 and 1977 under contractual arrangements with the State Department of Environmental Conservation and the U. S. Fish and Wildlife Service (Milburn 1979). At that time there was only one poorly reproducing pair in the state. Afterward, the state's Endangered Species Programme took over the project under the leadership of Peter Nye, and through 1988 the state hacked a total of 198 eaglets (mostly from Alaska) at four different locations (Nye 1990). The first two eagles hacked at the Montezuma National Wildlife Refuge in 1976 were found paired and breeding at a nest in Jefferson County about 135 km north of their release site, where they produced young nearly every year well into the 1990s. Although the original birds are gone, the territory remains occupied by a breeding pair (P Nye *in litt.* 1998).

The nesting population in New York grew steadily, and by 1998 there were 40 territorial pairs, and the total production of young for all years through 1997 had exceeded 230 fledglings (P. Nye *in litt.* 1998). In addition, a number of the released eagles dispersed into other states and Canada (Nye 1988). This has been the best documented and most successful of the various Bald Eagle translocation projects, and it demonstrates the important point that it is easier to translocate and establish a viable population of long-lived birds with a high survival rate, even with delayed sexual maturity and a low reproductive rate, than it is to work with so-called r-selected species. The latter require a larger number of releases over a shorter period of time to be successful.

The George M. Sutton Avian Research Center in Oklahoma adopted a variation of the hacking procedure by obtaining eaglets for release from wild eggs collected in Florida from nests containing 3 eggs (Sherrod *et al.* 1987, 1989). Eaglets hatched from artificially incubated eggs were reared in captivity to 8 weeks of age before placement at hack. Between 1985 and 1992, 275 eaglets were successfully hacked at 15 locations in Oklahoma, Mississippi, Alabama, Georgia, and North Carolina. By 1991 some released eagles were nesting (Jenkins & Sherrod 1993), and by 1997 there were 26 pairs known in Oklahoma; in Georgia the population increased from 17 pairs in 1993 to 31 pairs in 1997; in Alabama 9 or 10 pairs consisted of one or more released birds; and in Mississippi the population had grown from 8 pairs in 1993 to 13 in 1996 (Jenkins 1996, *in litt.* 1998).

Unfortunately, thorough monitoring of post-release results has not been possible throughout the region of releases, and the wild eagles have been increasing at the same time; but it seems likely that released birds have accounted for a good part of the population growth. Meyers and Miller (1992) found no difference in initial hacking success between eaglets reared at the Sutton Center and wild-taken eaglets, but the captive-reared eaglets showed a tendency to remain near the hack-site for a longer time after fledging than the wild birds and to feed more on artificially provided food. These authors concluded that the captive-reared birds might have developed a stronger site tenacity for the release location by remaining longer and also may have had a higher first year survival by feeding longer on provided food before dispersal.

The Ventana Wilderness Sanctuary Research and Education Center in Monterey, under the direction of Glenn Stewart, initiated a project in 1986 to establish Bald Eagles in the Central California Coast Recovery Zone by hacking wild-taken eaglets at a site on the coast near Big Sur (Lucido & Sorenson 1997). In all 66 eaglets have been released through 1997, and seven territorial pairs are known to be established in 1998, ranging from Alameda County in the north to Santa Barbara County in the south (K. Sorenson *in litt.* 1998). It is likely that more intensive searching in this extensive range would yield additional pairs. Although the project was intended to establish nesting pairs along the coast, so far all breeding pairs have gone inland to rivers and reservoirs in the mountains of the Coast Range, probably an adaptive choice considering the results of the next project.

On Santa Catalina Island, off the coast of California from Los Angeles, David Garcelon and associates of the Institute for Wildlife Studies, Arcata have been trying to reestablish Bald Eagles for 19 years, in association with the Santa Catalina Island Conservancy (Garcelon 1988, Garcelon *et al.* 1989). Using both captive-bred and wild-taken eaglets, they have hacked and fostered 57 birds on the island. Survival of translocated eagles has been good, and one or more pairs (three from 1991 to 1997) have been attempting to nest on the island for 12 years (Garcelon *et al.* 1995); but their eggs fail to hatch owing to high residue levels of DDE in the eagles' food, mainly gulls that forage in waters where organochlorine residues remain high (Garcelon *et al.* 1989, Jenkins *et al.* 1994). On the other hand, the established pairs are perfectly able to rear fostered young (D. K. Garcelon *in litt.* 1998). In this case, a technique for translocation that worked well has failed to reestablish a viable nesting population because the environment is still not suitable for breeding eagles.

In Massachusetts, a state where only two or three pairs of Bald Eagles are known to have bred prior to c. 1905 (Forbush 1929), a translocation project began in 1982 at the Quabbin Reservoir in the central part of the state (Nelson 1986), a joint effort of the State Wildlife Division and the U. S. Fish and Wildlife Service. Through 1988, 41 eaglets were hacked in Massachusetts: the first pair nested in 1989, and in 1998 there were nine territorial pairs, five of them on the Quabbin Reservoir, three along the Connecticut River, and one in the southern part of the state; a tenth pair settled in New Hampshire (T. French, pers. comm. 1998).

In 1980, a major translocation project began in Tennessee in the Land Between the Lakes and spread elsewhere, a joint effort of the State Wildlife Resources Agency, U. S. Fish and Wildlife Service, Tennessee Valley Authority, and the National Foundation to Protect America's Eagles (Hammer *et al.* 1983a and b, Hatcher 1983, 1991). No eagles were known to be nesting in the state between 1961 and 1983. Through 1997, 269 eaglets had been released at seven hack-sites. Only captive-bred birds have been used recently. The first pair formed in 1983 and produced one young; two other pairs are known to have bred at three years of age (R. M. Hatcher pers. comm. 1998). In 1997 there were 30 occupied territories, 18 of which produced 34 fledged young; in 1998 there were 37 occupied territories, not all of them by eagles hacked in Tennessee (R. M.. Hatcher pers. comm. 1998).

From 1985 through 1989 the Indiana Department of Natural Resources conducted a Bald Eagle translocation project at Lake Monroe in the central part of the state, supported entirely by the Nongame Wildlife Fund through a citizens' income tax checkoff (Castrale 1991, Iverson 1991, Castrale & Parker 1998). Eagles were last reported to nest in Indiana in 1897. Seventy-three eaglets from Alaska and Wisconsin were hacked at the lake. The first territory became occupied in 1988, the first nesting attempt occurred in 1989, and the first two successful nestings in 1991. By 1998 there were 19 occupied territories, with 15 breeding attempts and 11 successful pairs raising 20 young. Not all of these breeders were eagles released in Indiana, as some wild birds and birds hacked in other states have dispersed into Indiana, just as Indiana's released eagles have dispersed as far west as the Mississippi River, north into Michigan and New York, and south into Texas. The Alaskan birds have ranged significantly farther from Monroe Lake than those from Wisconsin, but there was a decided tendency for all the birds to range closer to home, under 160 km, as they reached an age of more than three years (Castrale 1991).

It should be noted that many of these Bald Eagle translocation projects have taken advantage of new habitat created by dams and artificial reservoirs, so that eagles are now nesting in some localities where they had not occurred historically. Also, as with the Peregrine Falcon, the contribution of translocation to the recovery of regional eagle populations has sometimes been obscured by a simultaneous increase in the number of wild birds; but an interesting phenomenon, noted particularly in Indiana and Tennessee, has been the clustering of new nests and territories in localities where hack-towers were situated. In part this clumping no doubt reflects the well known philopatry of this species, but since not all of the eagles nesting in these areas are released birds, it must also reflect conspecific attraction (Stamps 1988) of wild eagles into locations frequented by released birds (Iverson 1991, B. Hatcher pers. comm. 1998).

2. White-tailed Sea Eagle *Haliaeetus albicilla*, Tables 1 and 2.—In Europe there has been interest in using translocation to reestablish breeding sea eagles in parts of the range where the species has been extirpated or greatly diminished in number (Love & Ball 1977, Fentzloff 1984, Cade 1986). The best documented and most successful has been the project in Scotland carried out initially by the Nature Conservancy Council and subsequently by the Scottish Natural Heritage and the Royal Society for the Protection of Birds (Evans *et al.* 1994), with the field work in the early years under the supervision of John A. Love (1983). From 1975 through 1985, 85 eaglets from Norway were hacked from cages (a few were released in other ways) on the Isle of Rum (also Rhum) in the Hebrides. Survival was good, and the eagles dispersed widely over western Scotland, northern Ireland, and Shetland; however, all reestablished nesting locations have been within 100 km of Rum (Green *et al.* 1996). The first territorial pair was found in 1981, the first recorded young produced in 1985 (6 pairs on territories); 10 pairs were located in 1991, and by 1997 there were 13 to 15 territorial pairs and a total of 64 young fledged to the wild (Evans *et al.* 1994, Roy Dennis *in litt*, 1998).

An evaluation of the results of the programme through 1992 led to a long-term viability analysis of this reintroduced population (Green *et al.* 1996). Because the estimated population growth rate based on available demographic data had a 95% confidence interval that encompassed both a decline of 11% per year as well as an increase of 11% and because simulation models indicated that there was a probability of 0.6 that the present population would become extinct in 100 years even if all demographic parameters operated at their maximum-likelihood values, the managers concluded that a further release of 60 juveniles would substantially reduce the risk of extinction. An additional 46 young from Norway were released in the northwest Highlands in 1993-1997, and more are scheduled for 1998 (Roy Dennis *in litt.* 1998). This study shows the usefulness of demographic analysis in estimating the success of a translocation project.

At the Hula Nature Reserve and at Kfar Rupin in the northern part of the Rift Valley in Israel there is a small project to reestablish sea eagles (Ohad Hatzofe *in litt.* 1998). In 1992-95 and 1997, 13 eaglets were hacked. One or more pairs had formed by 1997, but no successful breeding has occurred as yet (Table 2).

3. The Madagascar Fish Eagle *Haliaeetus vociferoides*, Table 3—The young of this globally endangered species apparently engage in obligate siblicide or "Cainism", as two eggs are frequently laid but never more than one chick fledges (Watson *et al.* 1996, in press). Some time ago Meyburg (1978, 1983) carried out experiments and described a procedure now referred to as "sibling rescue" by which the reproductive output of such species can be increased by various human interventions to save the weaker chick, "Abel," and allow both birds to fledge. Watson *et al.* (1996, in press) used sibling rescue by constructing a "double nest" with a barrier between the two parts and returning Abel to one side of the nest at 4 weeks of age. They were able to increase the productivity of a local population of Madagascar Fish Eagles ($n = 10$ pairs) to 0.28 young per territory over a three year period, compared to a productivity of 0.15 young in an unmanipulated population. While this procedure had a significant effect on productivity, there are important unanswered questions about (a) the quality of fledglings when two chicks must be fed and reared simultaneously and (b) the influence of this increased effort on survivability of the parents. A better tactic might be to take the extra offspring from nests of two, hand-rear them, and then hack them out in unoccupied habitat in an attempt to increase the number of nesting pairs by increasing the distribution or by creating additional populations (Watson *et al.* 1996).

4. The Spanish Imperial Eagle *Aquila adalberti,* Table 3—Ferrer and Hiraldo (1991) also used sibling rescue to increase the productivity of this species in Doñana National Park, Spain. Broods of up to three chicks occur, and the young engage in facultative siblicide. The technique was to transfer chicks in nests with three young to nests with one (Meyburg & Garzón 1973), but no significant difference in productivity was detected between manipulated and unmanipulated nests, and in any case the main limitation on productivity was low hatching success, not survival of nestlings. Again, a better use of chicks from large broods would be to hack them out in unoccupied habitat.

5. The Golden Eagle *Aquila chrysaetos,* Table 3—In southern Sweden, Dag Peterson has released 25 captive-produced eaglets (22 by hacking after fledging in a cage and 3 by fostering), all from a single breeding pair. Survival to independence has been high, and possibly one breeding pair in southern Sweden originated from these releases (Peter Lindberg *in litt.* 1998).

6. The Harpy Eagle *Harpia harpyja,* Table 3—Considered a flagship and umbrella species for conservation of the neotropical forests, the Harpy Eagle has virtually disappeared from the northern portion of its original distribution from Panama into Mexico. Despite the effort to establish tropical forest reserves, many are too small to maintain more than a few, isolated pairs of Harpy Eagles. Captive propagation and translocation will be necessary to maintain the genetic diversity of these isolates and to mitigate stochastic and catastrophic losses of individuals in these small and increasingly isolated populations. For several years The Peregrine Fund, Inc. has worked cooperatively with the Zoological Society of San Diego, and other zoos, to breed this eagle in captivity, with the goal to restore breeding pairs in suitable habitats throughout Central America (Burnham 1998).

The first exploratory hacking began in the Soberania National Park, not far from Panama City, in 1998, in cooperation with INRENARE, the Panamanian federal authority in charge of wildlife, and the Panama Audubon Society. Five eaglets were hacked at different times during the year from a 14-foot tower erected in a small glade within the forest. Since a young Harpy may remain with its parents for one to two years before becoming independent, we expected that continual monitoring and food-provisioning would be necessary for a long time . The eagles are tracked daily by radio telemetry. Surprisingly, the birds have already been observed to make kills on their own, including adult three-toed sloths and howler monkeys. Unfortunately, a poacher shot one of the birds, an all too common cause of death throughout the range of this majestic species, and another disappeared under suspicious circumstances (J. P. Jenny, W. Heinrich, pers.comm. 1998).

Ospreys

Roy Dennis has pointed out to me that interest in translocation of the Osprey *Pandion haliaetus* apparently antedates the contemporary spate of raptor projects by several decades. The British falconer and exhibitionist, Capt. C.W.R. Knight, obtained four nestlings from Gardener's Island, New York in August of 1929, transported them home, and released them in September as fully fledged juveniles on an islet in Loch Arkiag, Invernes-shire, Scotland, where the species reportedly had last nested in 1908 (Knight 1932, R. Dennis *in litt.* 1998.). The young Ospreys were artificially provisioned with food until they learned to fish for themselves, but nothing more is known about the fate of these birds (Table 3).

More recently Larry Rymon, East Stroudsburg University of Pennsylvania, undertook a reintroduction of the Osprey in five western counties of Pennsylvania (Schadtt & Rymon 1981, Rymon 1989). He hacked 111 wild-taken Ospreys from 1980 through 1985, and a further 125 birds from 1990 through 1995, in a region where no nesting Ospreys were known in 1981 (Houghton & Rymon 1997). Released birds began nesting five years after the first hack, and by 1998 there were approximately 35 pairs breeding widely across Pennsylvania, many of them released birds but also wild birds that were attracted into the population by the released ones; other hacked birds had dispersed into adjacent states (Houghton & Rymon 1997, L. Rymon *in litt.* 1998). (Table 1.)

Additional, extensive hacking of Ospreys in West Virginia, Kentucky, and Tennessee has allowed these birds to move into previously unoccupied range and to take advantage of new habitat created by artificial reservoirs and waterways (Westall 1990). "Overall, the Osprey population in these states surged from five nesting pairs in 1981 to 105 in 1994" (Houghton & Rymon 1997). The project in

Tennessee, for example, hacked 165 Ospreys from 1980 through 1989 (Hammer & Hatcher 1983, B. Hatcher *in litt* 1998); by 1998 there were 97 to 98 territorial pairs in the state, and 91 breeding pairs produced 171 young, most of them nesting on man-made structures (B. Hatcher *in litt.* 1998). Again, this breeding population consists of birds hacked both in and outside Tennessee, as well as some naturally occurring wild birds that have been attracted to settle in the region. (Table 1.)

In 1983, Larry Gillette and Judy Voigt-Englund of Hennepin Parks began a project to translocate Ospreys by hacking in suburban areas of the Twin Cities; they were joined later by the Raptor Center at the University of Minnesota (Martell *et al.* 1994, Martell 1995). The project has released 155 young Ospreys in five different locations (M. Martell, pers.comm 1998). In recent years there have been 12 to 15 nesting pairs in the greater metropolitan area of St. Paul and Minneapolis, and others scattered more widely through Minnesota. As elsewhere, some of the breeders in this population are wild birds that appear to have been attracted to the area by the released ones. (Table 1.)

At the Rutland Water Nature Reserve in central England, a project is underway to translocate Scottish Ospreys into vacant range, under the auspices of the Highland Foundation for Wildlife, Leicestershire and Rutland Trust for Nature Conservation, and Anglian Water, plc. The project officer is Helen Dixon. In the first two years (1996-97) of a five year effort, 14 Ospreys have been hacked at a c.>1,000 hectare lake; 12 migrated, and one was reported dead in Senegal in February, 1997. Pairing is not expected until the third summer (Roy Dennis *in litt.* 1998). (Table 2.)

Old World Vultures

In Europe and Israel there are many projects underway to reestablish populations of four species of Aegypine vultures, all threatened in one degree or another. The first, best reported, and most notable of these projects has been the successful effort in France to reestablish a breeding colony of the Griffon *Gyps fulvus* in the Grands Causses area south of the Massif Central from 1981 through 1986, spearheaded by the Fonds d'Intervention pour les Rapaces (Terrasse 1980, 1990, Terrasse *et al.* 1994, Sarrazin *et al.* 1994, Sarrazin *et al.* 1996). The release of 61 vultures over a period of six years eventually led to a population of 71 pairs in 1997 (F. Sarrazin *in litt.* 1998). The main reasons for this outcome are (1) release of adult or near adult vultures from acclimatisation cages, resulting in early establishment of breeding pairs within one year after release, (2) high survival rates of both young (0.858) and adult (0.987) vultures, (3) subsequent breeding success of released and wild-produced offspring equal to that of wild birds in other areas (0.82 yng/pair), (4) high degree of philopatry (85% of wild-produced offspring settled in their natal gorges, and (5) conspecific attraction of dispersive individuals from other populations into the colony. The one drawback has been the necessity to support the colony with artificially provisioned food (mostly sheep carcasses), although the vultures have started foraging more on natural sources of carrion in recent years (Terrasse *et al.* 1994). (Table 1.) The success of this project in the Grands Causses area has led to several other Griffon translocations in France and in the Alps.

The international programme to restore the Bearded Vulture *Gypaetus barbatus* in the Alps (Austria, Germany, Italy, France), started in 1978, is also well publicized and has involved the cooperative effort of several zoos where the birds are bred for release, as well as various conservation groups, eg. Zoological Society of Frankfurt and World Wildldife Fund-Austria, all coordinated by the Foundation for the Conservation of the Bearded Vulture (Bijleveld 1979, Frey & Bijleveld 1984, Annual Reports, Foundation for the Conservation of the Bearded Vulture, 1994-96, Frey & Llopis 1998, H. Frey *in litt.*1998). (Table 2.) Bustamente (1996) has developed PVA models for both the captive and the translocated populations, emphasizing the need for more demographic data on the released birds.

In a similar way, the Black Vulture Conservation Foundation, started in 1986 and now headquartered in Majorca, Spain under the direction of Evelyn Tewes, coordinates several translocation projects for the European Black or Cinereous Vulture *Aegypius monachus* (Terrasse 1989, Tewes 1994, Tewes *et al.* 1998, E. Tewes *in litt.* 1998). (Table 2.)

Translocation projects for the Egyptian Vulture *Neophron percnopterus* are also underway or planned in France and Italy.

Condors

1. Andean Condor *Vultur gryphus*, Tables 2 and 3—In the New World, captive breeding and reintroduction programmes have been established for both the Andean Condor and the California Condor. At first the Andean Condor was used experimentally as a "surrogate species" to develop techniques of translocation to be used for the critically endangered California species (Wallace & Temple 1987, Wallace 1991). In one project, 11 juvenile and immature, captive-bred condors were hacked, and one wild adult hard-released with back-pack transmitters on the Sechura Peninsula, northern Peru. The adult died after two months, but seven of the 11 captive-bred condors survived for more than two years when monitoring stopped. These birds had integrated socially with the local wild condors, but it is not known whether any of them became breeders. In 1980-1983 a release of 12 female Andean Condors was undertaken in southern California to test the current environment for future release of California Condors and to gain experience in the release of condors; the birds were later trapped and returned to captivity (Wallace & Temple 1987).

Because Andean Condors breed readily in captivity, a number of zoos keep breeding pairs, and several zoos in the American Zoological Association, under the leadership of the Zoological Society of San Diego, banded together to provide captive-bred condors for translocation projects in South America. The first of these projects started in the trans-Andean region of Colombia (four hack sites) in 1990, a cooperative venture of the Colombian Ministry of the Environment, the San Diego Zoological Society, the Cali Zoo, and The Peregrine Fund, Inc. (Lieberman *et al.* 1990, 1993, Lieberman 1994). A total of 42 condors has been released through 1998, and after nine years three breeding pairs are known to be established, one involving a wild mate (A. Lieberman *in litt.* 1998). Other projects are starting up, such as the one in Venezuela and one north of San Carlos de Bariloche, Argentina, on the eastern slope of the Andes where condors are rare, carried out in cooperation with the Buenos Aires Zoo (M. Wallace *in litt.* 1998).

2. The California Condor *Gymnogyps californianus*, Table 2—One of the few critically endangered species for which it was decided to remove all individuals from the wild for breeding in captivity, the last wild California Condor was trapped in 1987. At that time the entire population consisted of 27 condors, 10 captured as wild birds, four taken as nestlings, and 13 hatched from eggs taken in the wild (Toone & Wallace 1994, Kiff in press). The wisdom of this highly controversial decision can be seen 10 years later with the production of more than 110 young condors in captivity (1988-1998).

The California Condor Recovery Plan calls for the establishment of three separate populations of 150 birds each, two in the wild and one in captivity, but the plan has not been followed strictly. The release of captive-bred condors began in southern California in 1992, a cooperative effort of the U. S. Fish and Wildlife Service, San Diego Zoological Society, and Los Angeles Zoological Society. A total of 39 birds has been released over six years (through 1997) at three different release sites; eleven had to be returned to captivity owing to behavioural problems (perching on electric transmission structures, interacting with human beings at campgrounds, etc.). Of the remaining 28, nine have died as of 1998, but some of the older birds are beginning to show signs of pairing.

A second translocation project started in northern Arizona near the Grand Canyon in 1996, a cooperative effort of the Arizona Department of Fish and Game, U. S. Fish and Wildlife Service, U.S Bureau of Land Management, and The Peregrine Fund, Inc. Nineteen birds have been hacked through 1997: Two have been killed, one disappeared (presumed dead), and one had to be trapped and removed to captivity because it was accepting food from human beings. Fifteen remained alive as of August 1998 and range widely over northeastern Arizona and southern Utah but still return to the hack-site on the Vermilion Cliffs for food.

A third project began in the Ventana Wilderness of the Los Padres National Forest, Monterey County, California in January of 1997, under the management of the Ventana Wilderness Sanctuary Research and Education Center). The first four condors had to be trapped and taken back because of too many behavioural interactions with human beings. A second group of five condors released in December of 1997 has fared better so far.

It is too soon to be certain, but it appears likely that California Condors will be breeding again in the wild before long. See Lloyd Kiff's paper in this volume for more details of this work.

Hawks and other Accipitrids

1. The Goshawk *Accipiter gentilis*, Table 1.—Always a rather rare bird in Great Britain, at least in recent centuries (Bannerman 1958), the Goshawk had more or less disappeared there by the end of the 19th Century. Breeding became regular again in the mid-1960s, and the species increased significantly in the 1970s and 1980s (Marquiss & Newton 1982), so that by the 1990s the population could be estimated as c. 400 territorial pairs (Petty 1994), with major centres around the Welsh-English border, the Peak District of Derbyshire/Yorkshire, and especially the English/Scottish border. In other areas, gamekeepers have kept the number of Goshawks at a low level (I. Newton, *in litt.* 1998). This population expansion resulted from the establishment of captive-held birds. Although 25 Goshawks of Fennoscandian origin were released experimentally by hacking or by hard-release of older birds, most of the introduced Goshawks were trained birds that escaped from falconers or were deliberately let loose after a period in captivity (Kenward *et al.* 1981, Marquiss & Newton 1982). It was estimated than an average of 20 imported Goshawks per year successfully entered the wild in the decade of the 1970s, when falconers were able to bring many birds into the country. Others have no doubt become established since then.

2. The Red Kite *Milvus milvus*, Tables 1 and 2—A highly organized effort to increase the distribution and numbers of the Red Kite in Britain has been underway since 1989, sponsored by the Joint Nature Conservation Committee, English Nature, Royal Society for the Protection of Birds, Scottish Natural Heritage, and the Forestry Commission of England (Ian Carter *in litt.* 1998, Roy Dennis *in litt.* 1998, Ian Evans *in litt* 1998). Four locations were chosen in Scotland and England where the species had long been extirpated by human persecution but where the habitat appears to be highly suitable. Wild young for hacking have been obtained from Spain, Germany, Sweden, and a few from Wales. In southern England, workers hacked 93 kites between 1989 and 1994: Breeding occurred in the second year, and by 1997 there were >51 territorial pairs. Similarly, in northern Scotland, 93 kites were hacked between 1989 and 1993: Breeding first occurred in the third year, and in 1997 23 pairs were on territory. A project started in central England in 1995 has hacked 49 kites in three seasons, and four breeding pairs were found in 1997. The fourth project started in east central Scotland in 1996 has released 37 kites in two years, and two territories were occupied in 1997. The stunning success of this programme can be attributed to (a) optimum, vacant habitat, (b) high survival of the released kites from the first year on, (c) early breeding at 1 to 2 years of age, (d) a high reproductive rate, and (e) intelligent and dedicated management (Evans & Pienkowski 1991, McGrady *et al.* 1994, Carter *et al.* 1995, Evans *et al.* 1997, Evans *et al.* in press).

3. Harris' Hawk *Parabuteo unicinctus*. Table 1—The Santa Cruz Predatory Bird Research Group, in collaboration with the U. S. Bureau of Land Management, U. S. Fish and Wildlife Service, California Department of Fish and Game, and other agencies, undertook a reintroduction of the Harris' Hawk along a 320 km riparian corridor of the lower Colorado River from 1979 through 1990 (Stewart 1981, Walton *et al.* 1988a, B. Walton *in litt.* 1998). The project was part of a planned ecological restoration programme to re-vegetate a badly disturbed riparian zone with native shrubs and trees (Rosenberg *et al.* 1991), but unfortunately the plant restoration was never completed, leaving limited suitable habitat for the hawks, especially nesting sites. The Predatory Bird Group released 220 hawks by hacking, fostering, and immediate hard-release of adults including already paired birds. Some of the adults bred in the area within the first year of release; young birds began breeding in their second year. According to Brian Walton (*in litt.* 1998), the Harris' Hawk proved to be especially easy to translocate; however, because of the limited habitat, most of the released birds dispersed out of the riparian zone as soon as the few suitable nesting locations became occupied. Even so, three to five pairs of hawks have now bred in the area for 16 years, and a much larger population would no doubt have become established if the planned re-vegetation had taken place (B. Walton *in litt.* 1998). [It should be noted that Beck *et al.* (1994) incorrectly included the Harris Hawk among the 16 successful reintroductions out of the 145 projects they analyzed.]

4. Common Buzzard *Buteo buteo*, Table 3—An experimental study of buzzards translocated into Norfolk and Sussex, England, where wild buzzards are very sparse, has been undertaken by the Institute of Terrestrial Ecology, in collaboration with the Natural Environment Research Council,

National Trust, Nature England, and the British Falconers' Club, Robert E. Kenward, principal investigator (Kenward *et al.* 1996). A total of 44 radio-tagged birds were released by hacking from 1994 through 1998. A high dispersal from the release area has reduced the opportunity for local pairing, but even so five pairs were found on territory in 1998 (R. E. Kenward *in litt.* 1998), and continued releases would no doubt build up a viable population in this part of England.

5. Montagu's Harrier *Circus pygargus*, Table 1—At the Parc Natural dels Aigüanollis del' Empordà in northeastern Catalonia, the Wildlife Service of Catalonia State has undertaken to restock Montagu's Harrier in a region where the species has been greatly diminished, using both captive-produced and wild-taken young for hacking (Pomarol & Parellada 1989, Pomarol 1994). Since 1988, 198 birds have been hacked, but few have returned to the area despite the high rate of survival to independence. Although hacking has been effective in releasing independent, capable juveniles into the wild, Montagu's Harriers have poorly developed philopatry, and most juveniles disperse widely across the landscape and do not settle near their natal localities to breed. Moreover, the habitat for harriers in Catalonia has been highly degraded by agriculture. Interestingly, since 1990 between two and six pairs of harriers have nested near the release site each year, but most of them are not released birds. Do they represent another instance of conspecific attraction? In such cases, a better technique might be to establish paired harriers in flight cages located in the desired habitat and then release them after their chicks have hatched. Site tenacity might then hold them to the area in future years, but harriers are noted for moving around from one area of high prey density to another in different years. Hacking is now being used to rescue wild nestlings in agricultural lands where nests are likely to be destroyed by ploughing or haying operations (M. Pomarol *in litt.* 1998).

Summary of Results

In summary, of the 28 well executed and documented projects (Table 1), I consider 21 (75%) to have succeeded in establishing or substantially aiding in establishing self-sustaining populations. Only three (10.7%) appear to have been failures, all owing to adverse environmental influences and not to inherent technological problems. The ultimate success or failure of four other projects cannot be clearly predicted at this time. Of the 15 on-going projects (Table 2), 10 (66.6%) appear highly likely to succeed, only two (13.3%) show a low likelihood, and four are too recent to judge. One of the experimental projects (Table 3), Common Buzzard in Britain, although designed for basic biological studies, appears likely to lead to significant augmentation of breeding numbers in a depopulated region. Work with the Harpy Eagle looks promising so far and could lead to successful reintroductions in Central America, where the species is virtually extirpated.

DISCUSSION

Successfulness of Raptor Translocations

In a detailed, stepwise regression analysis of variables associated with 134 translocations of birds and 64 of mammals, Griffith *et al.* (1989) identified eight factors associated with "success" (creation of a self-sustaining population). Their most significant findings were: (a) projects involving threatened species were less successful than those involving native game species (44% versus 86%), (b) releases in excellent habitat were more successful than those in poor habitat (84% versus 38%), (c) releases in the core of the historical range were more successful than those at the periphery or outside (76% versus 46%), (d) release of wild-caught animals was more successful than release of captive-reared ones (75% versus 38%), and (e) herbivores were more frequently established than carnivores (77% versus 48%). A re-analysis of their data further emphasized the difference in success between using captive-reared and wild-caught animals and also suggested that captive-reared birds are less often successfully translocated than captive-reared mammals (32% versus 62%) (Griffith *et al.* 1990). They offered the opinion that a greater than 50 per cent chance of success should usually be the minimum criterion for starting a translocation project.

A follow-up study (Wolf *et al.* 1996), also using multivariate analysis, mostly confirmed the original findings after six additional years, except that the earlier difference between captive-reared and wild animals was reduced to marginal significance ($P = 0.034$), although for birds as a subset the difference remained 71% versus 40%. Beck *et al.* (1994) also reviewed 145 reintroductions of captive-produced animals, and reported only 16 cases (11.0%) of successfully established populations in nature, based on a minimum establishment of 500 self-sustaining individuals or a PVA demonstrating self-sustainability.

Contrary to some of the figures and analyses summarized above, my evaluation of raptor translocations indicates a high rate of successful establishments—at least 75 per cent of those projects that have been carried out with sufficient scope (Table 1), a figure that could grow to 80 per cent or more in time. This degree of success compares to a reported 63-67 per cent for birds in general, 72-73 per cent for mammals in general, 48 per cent for "carnivorous" birds, 94 per cent for carnivorous mammals, 48 per cent for herbivorous birds, 67 per cent for herbivorous mammals, 81 per cent for omnivorous birds, and 67 per cent for omnivorous mammals (Wolf *et al.* 1996). Griffith *et al.* (1989) also found that success rates approaching 70 per cent were associated with the release of large numbers of threatened and endangered birds in habitats of high quality; 68 per cent of the translocations in Table 1 involved the multiple release of >100 individual birds in good to high quality habitat.

Considerable caution needs to be exercised, however, in comparing estimates of success among different studies and even among compared projects in the same study, because different assumptions and perceptions of population characteristics often underlie an individual researcher's determination of success or failure (Sarrazin & Barbault 1996). In the absence of a PVA or other probability analysis based on real data (Bustamente 1996), such determinations are best made on the basis of objective criteria like those adopted by the IUCN Species Survival Commission for its "Red List categories" (Mace & Lande 1991, Cade *et al.* 1997). For example, the evaluations by Griffith *et al.* (1989, 1990) and Wolf *et al.* (1996) give the appearance of rigour and scientific objectivity because they employ complicated statistical analyses yielding all kinds of coefficients, chi-square values, and P-values; but in the final analysis, all these statistical results are based on the independent and subjective evaluations of *ca.* 200 respondents who decided whether or not their projects had resulted in "self-sustaining populations," the criteria for which were not specified.

Furthermore, there is the problem of scope in defining individual translocation projects and its influence on project outcome. How meaningful is it to compare a single translocation of x number of individuals at one location with multiple translocations at several sites? In their analysis, Griffith *et al.* (1990) included 18 Peregrine Falcon projects and 15 Bald Eagle projects among a total of 39 "carnivorous bird" translocations. I was surprised to learn that there were 18 Peregrine projects in North America! What they must have done was to obtain state agency reports on hack-site projects within their respective borders and considered each state as a separate project, whereas I have always considered the activity within states to be part of a regional programme. One can reach quite different results from these two perspectives. If I were to judge each of the 15 eastern USA states where Peregrines have been released as separate projects uninfluenced by the others, I would probably find two complete failures, at least five that had not achieved a self-sustaining population, and no more than eight that were successful, but when they are viewed as integral parts of one overall regional programme they represent a highly successful reintroduction (Cade *et al.* 1997).

The scope of a project also has a temporal dimension that must be taken into account. A project may fail to achieve a self-sustaining population in its first 10 years but will do so in the following five to 10 years. The period of translocation for the 21 successful projects in Table 1 averaged 13 years, ranging from 5 to 20 years, and Beck *et al.* (1994) reported an average of 11.8 years for the projects they identified as successful. Griffith *et al.* (1989) also found that length of effort, as well as number of released animals, was highly correlated with successful translocation. Thus, there is little heuristic value in comparing recent, on-going, or short term projects with these longer running efforts.

Wilson and Stanley Price (1994) noted that raptor translocations are among the more successful avian projects. There are both intrinsic, species-specific factors and extrinsic, environmental factors that probably account for the relative ease with which raptors can be successfully translocated. I can only list them here as hypotheses for further study. Intrinsic factors: (1) Raptors, especially the larger ones, are less subject to predation than many other kinds of birds; (2) they appear to be physically stronger than other birds of comparable size; (3) they are often easier to keep in captivity with less physical deterioration; (4) they appear to be more resistant to diseases than many other birds; (5) many species show strong philopatry, making re-population of a specific area by translocation easier; (6) raptors tend to be K-selected species with high rates of juvenile and adult survival, so that a high percentage of translocated individuals remain in the population and survive to breed; even though delayed sexual maturity and low rates of productivity are associated with the high survival, once established a breeding pair can be expected to produce young over periods of 5 to >10 years, depending on the species; (7) raptors show conspecific attraction (Stamps 1988, Smith & Peacock 1990, Reed & Dobson 1993), and individuals can find each other over vast distances, so that a small translocated population has the capability of recruiting wild individuals into its ranks (both conspecific and heterospecific attraction occur, especially among colonial nesting birds, McIlhenny 1934, Cade 1986, Cade & Temple 1995); and (8) raptors have a high degree of behavioural acceptance of, and adjustment to, hands-on manipulations in the field, and they can often be acclimatized to new or modified environmental conditions, thereby expanding their distributions and increasing their abundance.

Extrinsic factors: In addition to those relating to the natural environment (see Griffith *et al.* 1989, 1990; Wolf *et al.* 1996), I would like to call attention to two that are especially relevant to the birds of prey. First, the methods employed in the sport of falconry, particularly hacking, have contributed a ready-made, centuries-old and tested technology that, with little modification, has been adapted to raptor translocation with a high degree of success. When I contemplate the large number of hacking projects and the thousands of hack-site attendants of the past 25 years, I sometimes wonder what the Emperor Frederick II of Hohenstaufen, were he to be re-enthroned amongst us, would think of all this activity occurring 700 years after he established a scientific basis for the practice of falconry in his famous treatise, *De Arte venandi cum Avibus.*

Finally, most of the people who become involved in raptor translocation tend to have "green thumbs" as Dillon Ripley (1975) aptly noted: People "who have an innate skill which probably could never be learned and certainly has nothing to do with the possession of a higher educational degree." They become fanatically devoted to their birds, so that they willingly exert the extra effort and insight needed for success. "A sense of kinship with nature and a single-mindedness of purpose appear to be the touchstones of success in this work" (Ripley 1975). Statisticians have not yet learned how to factor this human dimension into multiple regression analysis.

Ethical and Societal Concerns

These topics range from concerns about animal welfare and humane treatment of captive held and translocated animals, and the degree of naturalness that can be expected from such manipulations, to worry about the need for greater participation by professional scientists and use of scientific method in translocation projects. All of these concerns have been repeatedly addressed by one official body or another beginning with the 1976 "Manifesto on Animal Reintroductions" produced by the British Section of the World Wildlife Fund, continuing to the 1987 "IUCN Position Statement on Translocation of Living Organisms," to the most recent "Re-introduction Guidelines" (1998) of the IUCN Species Survival Commission's Re-introduction Specialist Group (see Kleinman *et al.* 1994); but discussion of these issues continues unabated. For instance, a round table discussion on bird reintroductions at the International Ornithological Congress at Durban, South Africa in August of 1998 focused all its attention on "Improving the rigour of re-introduction project assessment, planning, and execution," starting from the premise that in the past many projects have been characterized by poor planning, absence of theoretical scientific underpinnings, and lack of involvement by professional biologists (from summary provided by the Chairman of the Bird Section, IUCN SSC Re-introduction Specialist Group, Philip Seddon, *in litt.* 1998). In the following paragraphs I consider some of these concerns as they relate to raptor translocations.

Ethics and moralistic sentiments about humane treatment aside (Polivitis 1990), it should go without saying that animals reared or held in captivity for the purpose of translocation must be maintained in good health and in fit condition both physically and psycho-behaviourally for survival and eventual reproduction in the wild after release (Cade 1980). It is hard to imagine that managers of a legitimate translocation project would consider releasing physically or behaviourally handicapped animals. Raptor translocations enjoy a great advantage in this regard, because the techniques for handling and maintaining raptors in fit condition in captivity have been perfected over a period of 3,000 years in the practice of falconry, and many new innovations in husbandry and health care have also been added in recent years (Redig 1993, Fox 1995, Heidenrich 1997). There is no excuse based in lack of technology for maintaining captive or manipulated raptors in poor condition.

As to the naturalness of raptors re-established by translocation, generally speaking they appear to be virtually indistinguishable from their wild counterparts in behaviour, demography, and ecology, particularly after one or two generations beyond the released founders (e.g., Green *et al.* 1996, Sarrazin *et al.* 1996, Tordoff & Redig 1997). On the other hand, some captive-produced or hand-reared individuals of certain species do show behavioural modifications that can be either disadvantageous or advantageous for survival and reproduction after release. Perhaps the commonest of these manifestations is increased tameness or tolerance of close human activities. This has been a problem for released California Condors, because these big, conspicuous birds are extremely inquisitive and exploratory, especially in their early years of life, and they often investigate human activities ranging from remote fishermen's camps to tourist centres in national parks. Released Peregrines and Mauritius Kestrels have shown remarkable plasticity in their settlement behaviour for breeding, and in addition to choosing natural sites for nesting, many of them historically known eyries, they also accept a wide variety of new, often man-made sites in drastically altered habitats (Cade & Jones 1993, Jones *et al.* 1995, Cade *et al.* 1996a). The same is true to a lesser extent for Bald Eagles and Ospreys. Such behaviour has allowed these species to extend their breeding distributions into areas formerly considered to be unsuitable. Also, in a few instances it has been necessary to provide supplemental food to reintroduced raptors—particularly the carrion-feeders [e.g., Griffon Vulture in France (Terrasse *et al.* 1994), and California Condor in California and Arizona (Kiff in press)], although artificial provisioning should not be required indefinitely.

Population geneticists, and people persuaded by them, worry incessantly about what happens to genotypes and gene pools during the process of captive breeding and translocation (see Templeton 1990 for a balanced view). Snyder *et al.* (1996) stressed seven negative aspects of using captive-bred animals for translocation, especially the influence of "domestication" (loss of genetic fitness for existence in the wild). Loss of fitness for the wild from unnatural selection in captivity usually occurs in higher vertebrates only after many generations, and the way to avoid this problem is to design the breeding programme so that all birds needed for release are produced in the first few generations in captivity. To my knowledge no diurnal raptor translocation involving captive-bred birds has gone beyond the F_3 to F_4 generations. The more serious concern, actually, is the potential for phenotypic modification or loss of essential behaviour patterns in captivity, especially for species that rely heavily on social transmission of "traditions" from one generation to the next, as Snyder *et al.* (1996) correctly point out. In other matters of concern to geneticists, inbreeding depression, if it has occurred, has not been a problem for the Mauritius Kestrel, which was reduced to only two surviving pairs at one time in its history but now numbers several hundred wild-ranging individuals; nor has the cross-breeding of half a dozen subspecies of Peregrine Falcons for release in the eastern third of the United States (Temple & Cade 1988) been associated with any noticeable outbreeding depression. Some of these "hybridized" Peregrines are among the most superb specimens to be seen anywhere in the world, and so are their numerous offspring.

Adverse impacts on biotic communities have also been concerns, especially the potential spread of diseases from translocated animals to existing wild populations (Woodford & Rossiter 1994, Snyder *et al.* 1996, Cunningham 1996). Although diseases have infrequently ravaged captive populations of raptors, there is no evidence so far that any translocation of raptors has been associated with the spread of disease to wild animals. It remains a *potential* problem, which the precautions set forth by Cunningham (1996) and the Re-introduction Specialist Group's guidelines adequately address, while the stricter regimen advocated by Snyder *et al.* (1996) is unnecessarily restrictive and costly. Common sense precautions such as quarantine prior to release and observation of physical and behavioural signs of poor condition are sufficient in most cases. Problems associated with predation by translocated raptors on domestic livestock and poultry, and on endangered species of prey, sometimes occur locally and have to be dealt with by negotiations among the concerned parties on a case by case basis (Cade et al. 1996b). Competition with other predatory species is also a possible problem, but I am unaware that a case has arisen so far.

Translocation and associated "single species" programmes are often criticized for competing with "better techniques" such as habitat preservation and ecosystem management for the scarce money allocated to conservation (Myers 1979, Pitelka 1981, Csuti et al. 1987, Hutto et al. 1987, Varner & Monroe 1990, Snyder et al. 1996). This criticism presumes that there is an objective basis for judging which methods are better than others. It also presumes that if particular allocations of money were not spent on translocation they would automatically go to support the better methods. Neither assumption has credibility. Much of the money that supports captive breeding and translocations comes from sources that otherwise would not be funding conservation at all (Conway 1995). Government agencies do have to prioritize the use of their appropriations for conservation, and tough decisions often have to be made; consequently some constituencies will not be satisfied by how the money is spent.

Conservationists should spend less time coveting one another's sources of income and more time convincing the rest of humankind to use a greater portion of its wealth on conservation. The world economy is measured in the many trillions of dollars, much of it wasted on frivolous and unnecessary, if not dysgenic, activities. The 100's of billions of dollars spent annually on drug addictions alone would more than support all needed conservation efforts (see Cade 1988b).

A related fear has to do with the danger that some people will view hands-on methods such as captive breeding and translocation as convenient, substitute strategies for habitat preservation and maintenance of natural ecosystems (Snyder et al. 1996). The fact that politicians and some bureaucrats, and some corporate executives, find this argument expedient is not a fault of the methodology or of its practitioners; it is the fault of those who attempt to beguile the public with such notions. For example, the mere suggestion that captive breeding and translocation could be valuable aids in supporting the distribution and abundance of the Spotted Owl *Strix occidentalis* was met with irrational resistance by the entrenched conservation establishment associated with the owl from fear that the forest industry would latch onto the idea as an excuse to forgo needed forest habitat protection (Jack Ward Thomas, *in litt.* 1990). Again, it is up to the conservation community to keep the record clear, without denigrating a proven and valuable methodology.

Lastly, there is the repeated plea that scientists and the scientific method should be more involved in translocation projects (Scott & Carpenter 1987, Nisbet 1988, Griffith et al. 1989, 1990, Kleinman et al. 1994). Sarrazin and Barbault (1996) decry the lack of cooperation between scientific ecologists and conservation managers in the field and make the point that reintroduction (translocation) projects are an important way to do field experiments relevant to theoretical ecology (e.g., Sarrazin et al. 1996, R. Kenward, unpublished data on the Common Buzzard). They expressed disappointment that Beck et al. (1994) found "professional biologists" involved in only a little more than half of the 145 reintroduction projects they analyzed; what Beck et al. (1994) actually reported was professional training of graduate students in biology associated with 56 per cent of all projects. That percentage is higher than one might have expected. Among the 52 raptor projects listed in Tables 1-3, no fewer than 32 (61.5%) enjoyed the close involvement of professional biologists at the Ph.D. level, and all but four (92%) were managed by professionals trained in some aspect of applied biology such as wildlife management.

While I agree that translocation projects offer unique opportunities to investigate certain scientific questions relating to demography, behavioural ecology, and other matters and that the application of biological theory and principles to management is essential for optimum success (Cade 1974, 1980, 1988b, Cade et al. 1996b), I am less certain that academic scientists necessarily make the best managers or should be the ones in charge of translocation projects, unless they are done solely for research purposes. I rather suspect that most should not be, because pure scientists tend to be mainly interested in their theories and in testing hypotheses, not in practical results. A good translocation manager is someone who combines common sense and hands-on abilities with a practical concept of how to make a project work.

Scientists, on the other hand, are undoubtedly the best people to interpret the results of a translocation and to predict outcome from an analysis of relevant data. Scientific input can help in adjusting the tactics of translocation to fit the demographic and behavioural characteristics of particular species. For example, what is the optimum pattern of release for K-selected species versus r-selected species: is it better to release a large number of individuals simultaneously for the latter, while spreading the releases out over a longer period for the former, or does it matter one way or the other? How does one go about re-establishing a highly dispersive species that has poorly developed philopatry, e.g. Montagu's Harrier? Whenever possible scientists and managers should work together on translocation projects, but only a few academic or pure scientists have shown serious interest, despite the unique opportunities available to them (Sarrazin & Barbault 1996).

CONCLUSION

In 1984, the role of translocation in raptor conservation was just beginning to be defined when I offered some speculations on its future (Cade 1986). Work in the intervening years has largely confirmed the view I outlined then: Techniques such as captive breeding and translocation should be used as methods of last resort when it becomes clear that a species or population cannot survive in the wild without such intervention. Given that caveat, translocation can be used in several ways to promote conservation. (1) It can be used to restore populations to vacated range, or, in some cases, to extend the range of a species into new areas. (2) It can be used to increase the size of small populations, especially by augmenting reproductive output by the addition of nestlings or juvenile birds. (3) It can be used to maintain the presence of a species in patches of habitat (e.g. parks and reserves) that are too small to support a self-sustaining population through time. (4) It can be used to replenish the genetic composition of small populations that suffer from inbreeding depression or other genetic problems, by the addition of individuals with different genotypes, and (5) it can be used to modify behaviours and ecological adjustments that allow individuals to survive and breed in degraded or changed habitats, thereby increasing overall species distribution and abundance (Cade 1986).

In short, translocation has proved to be effective in restoring rare and threatened raptor populations in nature, and its importance will no doubt increase as more and more birds of prey become threatened by habitat degradation, fragmentation, and loss. Like other forms of hands-on management, it lies at one end of a spectrum of actions needed to conserve biological diversity, with ecosystem management at the other end (Cade & Temple 1995). It is no better than other methods of conservation, but it also is no worse. Although the more holistic actions focused on ecosystems and habitats are essential to maintain maximum diversity, to prevent additional species from becoming vulnerable to extinction, and to provide ecological scope for the recovery of endangered species, once a species becomes threatened, it usually requires special attention focused on its particular needs for restoration to a safe population size and demographic composition. Translocation can often meet those needs more effectively than natural processes.

On the other hand, the general impression that one is likely to gain from reading all the discussions and commentaries in the literature of the past 20 years is that translocation and related hands-on methods are largely failures, and a waste of time and money, if not actually harmful in their consequences. This is a false impression as far as birds of prey are concerned, and I believe it is likely false in a more general sense as well. Because of this derogatory attitude prevalent in some quarters of the scientific and conservation communities, the practitioners of translocation have indulged themselves in an inordinate amount of introspection, self-criticism, and rule-making (see, e.g., letters on pp. 3-5 in *Conservation Biology*, 11(1), 1997). I suggest it is now time to accept that there will be some failures, to continue learning as much as we can from our efforts, take justifiable satisfaction in our considerable successes, and move on to the work ahead of us.

ACKNOWLEDGMENTS

I thank the following for taking their time to answer my questionnaire or for providing other helpful information: U. Banasch, I. Carter, J. Castrale, R. Dennis, J. H. Enderson, I. M. Evans, T. French, H. Frey, D. K. Garcelon, R. M. Hatcher, O. Hatzofe, W. Heinrich, G. L. Holroyd, M. A. Jenkins, J. P. Jenny, C. G. Jones, R. E. Kenward, L. F. Kiff, A. Lieberman, P. Lindberg, M. Martell, I. Newton, P. Nye, M. Pomarol, L. M. Rymon, C. Saar, F. Sarrazin, K. Sorenson, K. Swinnerton, J.-F. Terrasse, E. Tewes, H. B. Tordoff, M. A. Wallace, B. J. Walton, J. Watson, and R. T. Watson. L. F. Kiff also kindly read the entire manuscript and offered useful comments, as well as checking the accuracy of many citations. I also especially thank B. Griffith, F. Sarrazin, and J. M. Scott for providing critical, peer review of an earlier draft of this paper.

REFERENCES

ANONYMOUS. 1976. Re-introduction: techniques and ethics. Manifesto World Wildlife Fund (British Section). *In* Wildlife introductions to Great Britain. Report by the working group on introductions. UK Committee for International Nature Conservation. Nature Conservancy Council, London.

BANNERMAN, D. A. 1956. *The birds of the British Isles*. Vol. 5. Oliver & Boyd, Edinburgh.

BARCLAY, J. H. 1988. Peregrine restoration in the eastern United States. Pp. 549-558 *in* T. J. Cade *et al.*, eds., *Peregrine Falcon populations, their management and recovery*. The Peregrine Fund, Inc., Boise, Idaho.

BARCLAY, J. 1995. Patterns of dispersal and survival of eastern Peregrine Falcons derived from banding data. BioSystems Analysis, Inc., Santa Cruz, CA. 24pp + 7 tables & 44 figs.

BARCLAY, J. H. & T. J. CADE. 1983. Restoration of the Peregrine Falcon in the eastern United States. *Bird Conservation* 1:8-40. ICBP-US.

BECK, B. B., I. G. RAPAPORT, M. R. STANLEY PRICE & A. C. WILSON. 1994. Reintroduction of captive-born animals. Pp. 265-286 *in* P. J. S. Olney, G. M. Mace & A.T. C. Feistner, eds., *Creative conservation: interactive management of wild and captive animals*. Chapman and Hall, London.

BEISSINGER, S. R. & M. I. WESTPHAL. 1998. On the use of demographic models of population viability in endangered species management. *J. Wildl. Manage.* 62:821-841.

BIJLEVELD, M. 1979. Preface: Meeting on reintroduction of the Bearded Vulture, *Gypaetus barbatus aureus* (Hablizl 1788), into the Alps. Report of proceedings, Morges, 17-18 Nov. 1978. IUCN, Morges.

BURNHAM, W. A., ED. 1998. *The Peregrine Fund 1997 Annual Report*, p. 1. The Peregrine Fund, Inc., Boise, ID

BURNHAM, W. A., W. HEINRICH, C. SANDFORT, E. LEVINE, D. O'BRIEN & D. KONKEL 1988. Recovery effort for the Peregrine Falcon in the Rocky Mountains. Pp. 565-574 *in* T. J. Cade, *et al.*, eds., *Peregrine Falcon populations, their management and recovery*. The Peregrine Fund, Inc., Boise, Idaho.

BUSTAMENTE, J. 1996. Population viability analysis of captive and released Bearded Vulture populations. *Cons. Biol.* 10:822-831.

CADE, T. J. 1974. Plans for managing the survival of the Peregrine Falcon. Pp. 89-104 *in* F. N. Hamerstrom, Jr., B. E. Harrell & R. R. Olendorff, eds., Management of raptors. *Raptor Research Report 2*.

CADE, T. J. 1978. Manipulating the nesting biology of endangered birds. Pp. 167-170 *in* S. A. Temple, ed., *Endangered birds: management techniques for preserving threatened species*. Univ. Wisconsin Press, Madison.

CADE, T. J. 1980. The husbandry of falcons for return to the wild. *Int. Zoo Yb.* 20:23-35.

CADE, T. J. 1983. Restoration of Bald Eagles in New York and elsewhere. *Bird Conservation* 1:109-112. ICBP-US.

CADE, T. J. 1986. Reintroduction as a method of conservation. *Raptor Research Report* 5:72-84.

CADE, T. J. 1988a. The breeding of Peregrines and other falcons in captivity: an historical summary. Pp. 539-547 *in* T. J. Cade *et al.*, eds., *Peregrine falcon populations, their management and recovery*. The Peregrine Fund, Inc., Boise, Idaho.

CADE, T. J. 1988b. Using science and technology to reestablish species lost in nature. Pp. 279-288 *in* E. O. Wilson & F. M. Peter, eds., *Biodiversity*. National Academy Press, Washington, D. C.

CADE, T. J. 1990. Peregrine Falcon recovery. *Endangered Species Update* 8(1):40-43.

CADE, T. J. 1998. Delisting the Peregrine Falcon: Management and mismanagement under the endangered species act. Pp. 475-485 *in* K. G. Wadsworth, ed., *Trans 63rd No. Am. Wildl. Resour. Conf.* Wildlife Management Institute, Washington, D. C.

CADE, T. J., J. H. ENDERSON, L. F. KIFF & C. M. WHITE 1997. Are there enough good data to justify de-listing the American Peregrine Falcon? *Wildl. Soc. Bull.* 25:730-738.

CADE, T. J., J. H. ENDERSON & J. LINTHICUM, Eds. 1996B. *Guide to management of Peregrine Falcons at the eyrie.* The Peregrine Fund, Inc., Boise, Idaho. 97pp.
CADE, T. J., J. H. ENDERSON, C. G. THELANDER & C. M. WHITE, Eds. 1988. *Peregrine falcon populations, their management and recovery.* The Peregrine Fund Inc., Boise, Idaho. 949pp.
CADE, T. J., J. P. JENNY & B. J. WALTON 1991. Efforts to restore the northern Aplomado Falcon *Falco femoralis septentrionalis* by captive breeding and reintroduction. *Dodo, J. Wildl. Preserv. Trust* 27:71-81.
CADE, T. J. & C. G. JONES. 1993. Progress in restoration of the Mauritius Kestrel. *Conserv. Biol.* 7:169-175.
CADE, T. J., M. MARTELL, P. REDIG, G. SEPTON & H. B. TORDOFF 1996a. Peregrine Falcons in urban North America. Pp. 3-13 *in* D. M. Bird, D. E. Varland & J. J. Negro, eds., *Raptors in human landscapes.* Academic Press, London.
CADE, T. J., P. REDIG & H. B. TORDOFF 1989. Peregrine Falcon restoration: expectation vs. reality. *Loon* 61(4):160-162.
CADE, T. J. & S. A. TEMPLE 1977. The Cornell University falcon programme. Pp. 353-368 *in* R. D. Chancellor, ed., *World Conference on birds of prey: Report of proceedings.* ICBP, London.
CADE, T. J. & S. A. TEMPLE 1995. Management of threatened bird species: evaluation of the hands-on approach. *Ibis* 137 (Suppl. 1):S161-S172.
CARTER, I, I. EVANS & N. CROCKFORD 1995. The Red Kite re-introduction project in Britain—progress so far and future plans. *Brit. Wildl.* 7:18-25.
CASTRALE, J. 1991. Bald Eagle restoration efforts in Indiana, 1989-1990. *Indiana Audubon Quarterly* 63(3):167-176.
CASTRALE, J., & A. PARKER 1998. Bald Eagle reproduction in Indiana. *Wildlife Management and Research Notes* No. 714:1-3. Indiana Dept. Nat. Resources.
CONWAY, W. G. 1995. Wild and zoo animal interactive management and habitat conservation. *Biodiversity and Cons.* 4:573-594.
CSUTI, B. A., J. M. SCOTT, & J. ESTES. 1987. Looking beyond species-oriented conservation. *Endangered Species Update* 5:4.
CUNNINGHAM, A. A. 1996. Disease risks of wildlife translocations. *Conserv. Biol.* 10:349-353.
ENDERSON, J. H., W. HEINRICH, L. KIFF & C. M. WHITE 1995. Population changes in North American Peregrines. Pp. 142-161 *in* K. G. Wadsworth & R. E. McCabe, eds., *Trans.60th No. Am. Wildl. & Natur. Resourc. Conf.* Wildlife Management Institute, Washington, D. C.
ENDERSON, J. H., C. M. WHITE & U. BANASCH 1998. Captive breeding and releases of Peregrines *Falco peregrinus* in North America. Pp. 437-444 *in* R. D. Chancellor, B.-U. Meyburg, & J. J. Ferrero, eds., *Holarctic birds of prey, proc. of an internatl. Conf.* ADENEX & WWGBP, Merida & Berlin.
EVANS, I. M., R. H. DENNIS, D. C. ORR-EWING, N. KJELLÉN, P.-O. ANDERSSON, M. SYLVÉN, A. SENOSIAIN & F. COMPAIRED CARBO 1997. The re-establishment of Red Kite breeding populations in Scotland and England. *Brit. Birds* 90:123-138.
EVANS, I. M., J. A. LOVE, C. A. GALBRAITH & M. W. PIENKOWSKI 1994. Population and range restoration of threatened raptors in the United Kingdom. Pp. 447-457 *in* B.-U. Meyburg & R. D. Chancellor, eds., *Raptor conservation today.* WWGBP/The Pica Press, Berlin.
EVANS, I. & M. W. PIENKOWSKI. 1991. World status of the Red Kite: a background to the experimental re-establishment to England and Scotland. *Brit. Birds* 84:171-187.
EVANS, I. M., R. W. SUMMERS, L. O'TOOLE, D. C. ORR-EWING, R. EVANS, N. SNELL & J. SMITH In press. Evaluating the success of translocating Red Kites *Milvus milvus* to the United Kingdom. *Bird Study__*.
FERRER, M. & F. HIRALDO 1991. Evaluation of management techniques for the Spanish Imperial Eagle. *Wildl. Soc. Bull.* 19:436-442.
FORBUSH, E. H. 1927. Birds of Massachusetts and other New England states. Part II. Commonwealth of Massachusetts. Norwood Press.
FOX, N. 1995. *Understanding the bird of prey.* Hancock House Publishers Ltd., Surrey, British Columbia. 375pp.
FRANK, S. 1994. *City Peregrines: a ten year saga of New York City falcons.* Hancock House Publishers, Blaine, Washington.
FREY, H. & M. BIJLEVELD 1994. The reintroduction of the Bearded Vulture, *Gypaetus barbatus aureus* into the Alps. Pp. 459-464 *in* R. D. Chancellor, B.-U. Meyburg & J. J. Ferrero, eds., *Raptor conservation today.* WWGBP. The Pica Press, Berlin.
FREY, H. & A. LLOPIS 1998. Situación del proyecto de reintroduccion del Quebrantahuesos *Gypaetus barbatus* en los Alpes. Pp. 395-402 *in* B.-U. Meyburg, R. D. Chancellor & J. J. Ferrero, eds., *Holarctic birds of prey, proc. of an internatl. Conf.* ADENEX & WWGBP, Merida & Berlin.

FENTZLOFF, C. 1984. Breeding, artificial incubation and release of White-tailed Sea Eagles *Haliaeetus albicilla*. *Int. Zoo Yb.* 23:18-35.
FYFE, R. W. 1976. Rationale and success of the Canadian Wildlife Service Peregrine breeding project. *Can. Field-Nat.* 90:308-319.
FYFE, R. W. 1988. The Canadian Peregrine Falcon recovery programme 1967-1985. Pp. 590-610 *in* T. J. Cade *et al.*, eds., *Peregrine Falcon populations, their management and recovery.* The Peregrine Fund, Inc.., Boise, Idaho.
GARCELON, D. K. 1988. Reintroduction of Bald Eagles to Santa Catalina Island, California. M.S. thesis, Humbolt State Univ., Arcata, Calif.
GARCELON, D. K. & G. W. ROEMER, Eds. 1988. *Proceedings of the international symposium on raptor reintroduction, 1985.* Institute for Wildlife Studies, Arcata, California. 148pp, including bibliography of raptor reintroduction.
GARCELON, D. K., R. W. RISEBROUGH, W. M. JARMAN, A. B. CHARTRAND & E. E. LITTRELL 1989. Accumulation of DDE by Bald Eagles reintroduced to Santa Catalina Island in southern California. Pp. 491-494 *in* B.-U. Meyburg & R. D. Chancellor, eds., *Raptors in the modern world.* WWGBP, Berlin.
GARCELON, D. K., G. L. SLATER & C. D. DANILSON 1995. Cooperative breeding by a trio of Bald Eagles. *J. Raptor Res.* 29:210-213.
GETREIDE, S. & O. HATZOFE 1991. Return of the Lanner Falcon. *Israel Land Nat.* 16(4):167-172.
GREEN, R. E., M. W. PIENKOWSKI & J. A. LOVE 1996. Long-term viability of the re-introduced population of the White-tailed Sea Eagle *Haliaeetus albicilla* in Scotland. *J. Applied Ecol.* 33:357-368.
GRIFFITH, B., J. M. SCOTT, J. W. CARPENTER & C. REED 1989. Translocation as a species conservation tool: status and strategy. *Science* 245:477-480
GRIFFITH, B., J. M. SCOTT, J. W. CARPENTER & C. REED 1990. Translocations of captive-reared terrestrial vertebrates, 1973-1986. *Endangered Species Update* 8(1):10-13.
HAMMER, D. A. & R. M. HATCHER 1983. Restoring Osprey populations by hacking preflighted young. Pp. 293-297 *in* D. M. Bird, N. R. Seymour, & J. M. Gerrard, eds., *Biology and management of Bald Eagles and Ospreys.* Harpell Press, Ste. Anne de Bellevue, Quebec.
HAMMER, D. A., J. L. MECHLER, R. ALTMAN, N. J. DOUGLAS & R. M. HATCHER 1983a. Bald Eagle restoration at Land Between the Lakes. Pp. 20-33 *in* T. N. Ingram, ed., *Bald Eagle restoration: proceedings of Bald Eagle days 1982.* Eagle Valley Environmentalists, Apple River, Illinois.
HAMMER, D. A., J. L. MECHLER & R. M. HATCHER 1983b. Restoration of Bald Eagle populations in the Midsouth. Pp. 107-125 *in* D. M. Bird, N. R. Seymour, & J. M. Gerrard, eds., *Biology and management of Bald Eagles and Ospreys.* Harpell Press, Ste. Anne de Bellevue, Quebec.
HATCHER, R. M. 1983. Bald Eagle hacking project at Reelfoot Lake, Tennessee, 1981. Pp. 43-57 *in* T. N. Ingram, ed., *Bald Eagle restoration: proceedings of Bald Eagle days 1982.* Eagle Valley Environmentalists, Apple River, Illinois.
HATCHER, R. M. 1991. Computer model projections of Bald Eagle nesting in Tennessee. *J. Tennessee Acad. Sci.* 66:225-228.
HEIDENRICH, M. 1997. *Birds of prey, medicine and management.* Blackwell Science Ltd., Oxford.
HICKEY, J. J. 1942. Eastern population of the Duck Hawk. *Auk* 59:176-204.
HICKEY, J. J., ED. 1969. *Peregrine Falcon populations, their biology and decline.* Univ. Wisconsin Press, Madison. 596pp.
HOLROYD, G. L., & U. BANASCH 1996. The 1990 Canadian Peregrine Falcon (*Falco peregrinus*) survey. *J. Raptor Res.* 30:145-156.
HOUGHTON, L. M. & L. M. RYMON 1997. Nesting distribution and population status of U. S. Ospreys 1994. *J. Raptor Res.* 31:44-53.
HUTTO, R., S. REED & P. LANDRES 1987. A critical evaluation of the species approach to biological conservation. *Endangered Species Update* 4:1-4.
IUCN. 1998. *Guidelines for re-introductions.* Prepared by the IUCN/SSC Re-introduction Specialist Group. IUCN, Gland, Switzerland and Cambridge, UK. 10pp.
IVERSON, G. C. 1991. Bald Eagle restoration in the Midwest: 1980-1988. *In* B. G. Pendleton *et al.*, eds., Proc. -midwestern raptor workshop and symposium, 1989. *Natl. Wildl. Fed. Scientific and Tech. Ser.*15:235-242.
JENKINS, M. A. 1997. Bald Eagle population grows. *The Sutton Newsletter* 9:4. George Miksch Sutton Avian Research Center, Bartlesville, Oklahoma.
JENKINS, M. A. & S. K. SHERROD 1993. Recent Bald Eagle nest records in Oklahoma. *Bull. Oklahoma Ornith. Soc.* 26(3):25-32.

JENKINS, M. J., R. M. JUREK, D. K. GARCELON, R. MESTA, W. G. HUNT, R. E. JACKMAN, D. E. DRISCOLL & R. W. RISEBROUGH 1994. DDE contamination and population parameters of Bald Eagles in California and Arizona, USA. Pp. 751-756 *in* B.-U. Meyburg & R. D. Chancellor, eds., *Raptor conservation today*. WWGBP/The Pica Press, Berlin.
JONES, C. G. 1980. The Mauritius Kestrel, its biology and conservation. *Hawk Trust Annual Rept.* 10:18-27.
JONES, C. G., W. HECK, R. E. LEWIS, Y. MUNGROO, G. SLADE & T. CADE 1995. The restoration of the Mauritius Kestrel *Falco punctatus* population. *Ibis* 137(Suppl. 1):S173-S180.
KENWARD, R. E., M. MARQUISS & I NEWTON 1981. What happens to Goshawks trained for falconry. *J. Wildl. Manage.* 45:802-806.
KENWARD, R. E., S. S. WALLS & K. H. HODDER 1996. Studies of released raptors and buzzard populations by radio-tagging in 1994-6. *The Falconer* 1995:43-47.
KIFF, L. (this volume). The California Condor *Gymnogyps californianus* recovery programme.
KLEINMAN, D. G., M. R. STANLEY PRICE & B. B. BECK 1994. Criteria for reintroductions. Pp. 288-303 *in* P. J. S. Olney, G. M. Mace & A. T. C. Feistner, eds., *Creative conservation: interactive management of wild and captive animals*. Chapman & Hall, London.
KNIGHT, C. W. R. 1932. Photographing the nest life of the Osprey. *Natl. Geogr. Mag.* 62(2):247-260.
LANGGEMACH, C., T. P. SÖMMER, W. KIRMSE, C. SAAR & G. KLEINSTAUBER 1997. Erste Baumbrut des Wanderfalken *Falco p. peregrinus* in Brandenburg zwanzig Jahre nach Aussterben der Baumbrüterpopulation. *Vogelwelt* 118:79-94.
LIEBERMAN, A. 1994. Release of 5 Andean Condors. *World Birdwatch* 16(3):5.
LIEBERMAN, A., V. RODRIGUEZ, J. WILEY & J. M. PAEZ 1993. The reintroduction of Andean Condors into Colombia, South America: 1989-1991. *Oryx* 27(2):83-90.
LINDBERG, P. 1988. Reintroducing the Peregrine Falcon in Sweden. Pp. 619-628 *in* T. J. Cade *et al.*, eds, *Peregrine Falcon populations, their management and recovery*. The Peregrine Fund, Inc., Boise, Idaho.
LINDBERG, P. 1997. Projekt Pilgrimsfalk 1996. SOF 1997, *Fågeläret* 1996:56-61. Stockholm.
LOVE, J. A. 1983. *The return of the Sea Eagle*. Cambridge Univ. Press, Cambridge.
LOVE, J. A. & M. E. BALL 1979. White-tailed Sea Eagle *Haliaeetus albicilla*. Reintroduction to the Isle of Rhum, Scotland 1975-1977. *Biol. Conserv.* 16:23-30.
LUCIDO, S. & K. SORENSON 1997. Summary of results of a Bald Eagle reintroduction to the central California coast. Rept. to California Bald Eagle Working Team, April 17, 1997. Ventana Wilderness Sanctuary, Monterey, California. 5pp.
LUNIAK, M. 1995. Peregrine Falcon (*Falco peregrinus*) in cities—the background for its planned reintroduction in Warsaw. *Acta Ornithol.* 30:53-62.
MACE, G. M. & R. LANDE 1991. Assessing extinction threats: toward a reevaluation of IUCN threatened species categories. *Conserv. Biol.* 5:148-157.
MARQUISS, M. & I. NEWTON 1982. The Goshawk in Britain. *Br. Birds* 75:243-260.
MARTELL, M. 1995. Osprey *Pandion haliaetus* reintroduction in Minnesota, USA. *Vogelwelt* 116:205-207.
MARTELL, M. S. , H. B. TORDOFF & P. T. REDIG 1994. The introduction of three native raptors into the midwestern United States. Pp. 465-469 *in* B.-U. Meyburg & R. D. Chancellor, eds., *Raptor conservation today*. WWGBP/The Pica Press, Berlin.
MEBS, T. 1988. The return of the Peregrine Falcon in West Germany. Pp. 173-177 *in* T. J. Cade *et al.*, eds., *Peregrine Falcon populations, their management and recovery*. The Peregrine Fund, Inc., Boise, Idaho.
MESTA, R. 1998. Endangered and threatened wildlife and plants; proposed rule to remove the Peregrine Falcon in North America from the list of endangered and threatened wildlife. *Fed. Register* 63(165): 45446-45463.
MEYBURG, B.-U. 1978. Sibling aggression and cross-fostering of eagles. Pp. 295-300 *in* S. A. Temple, ed., *Endangered birds, management techniques for preserving threatened species*. Univ. Wisconsin Press, Madison.
MEYBURG, B.-U. 1983. The significance for captive breeding programmes of fratricide and cainism in birds of prey. *Int. Zoo Yb.* 23:110-113.
MEYBURG, B.-U. & J. GARZÓN 1973. Sobre la protección del Aguila Imperial Ibérica (*Aquila heliaca adalberti*) aminorando artificialmente la mortalidad juvenil. *Ardeola* 19:107-128.
MEYERS, J. M. & D. L. MILLER 1992. Post-release activity of captive- and wild-reared Bald Eagles. *J. Wildl. Manage.* 56:744-749.
MCGRADY, M. J., D. C. ORR-EWING & T. J. STOWE 1994. The re-introduction of the Red Kite *Milvus milvus* into Scotland. Pp. 471-477 *in* B.-U. Meyburg & R. D. Chancellor, eds., *Raptor conservation today* WWGBP /The Pica Press, Berlin.
MCILHENNY, E. A. 1934. *Bird City*. Christopher Publishing House, Boston.
MILBURN, E. H. 1979. An evaluation of the hacking technique for reestablishing Bald Eagles (*Haliaeetus leucocephalus*). M.S. thesis, Cornell Univ., Ithaca. 184pp.

MOEN, S. M. & H. B. TORDOFF 1993. The genetic and demographic status of Peregrine Falcons in the upper Midwest. Rep. for U.S. Fish and Wildl. Serv. And Minnesota Dep. Nat. Resour., Non-game Wildl. Program. Bell Mus. Nat. Hist., Univ. Minnesota, St. Paul.

MORA, M. A., M. C. LEE, J. P. JENNY, T. W. SCHULTZ, J. L. SERICANO & N. C. CLUM 1997. Potential effects of environmental contaminants on recovery of the Aplomado Falcon in south Texas. *J. Wildl. Manage.* 61:1288-1296.

MYERS, N. 1979. *The sinking ark.* Collins, London.

NELSON, D. H. 1986. Reintroduction and wintering ecology of Bald Eagles in Massachusetts. M.S. thesis, Univ. Massachusetts, Amherst. 98pp.

NEWTON, I. 1988. Reintroduction and its relation to the management of raptor populations. Pp. 1-15 *in* D. K. Garcelon & G. W. Roemer, eds., *Proceedings of the international symposium on raptor reintroduction, 1985.* Institute For Wildlife Studies, Arcata, California.

NISBET, I. C. T. 1988. Summary. Pp. 851-855 *in* T. J. Cade et al., eds., *Peregrine Falcon populations, their management and recovery.* The Peregrine Fund, Inc., Boise, Idaho.

NYE, P. E. 1988. A review of Bald Eagle hacking projects and early results in North America. Pp. 95-112 *in* D. K. Garcelon & G. W. Roemer, eds., *Proceedings of the International Symposium on Raptor Reintroduction, 1985.* Institute for Wildlife Studies, Arcata, California.

NYE, P. 1990. A second chance for our national symbol. *The Conservationist,* July/August. N. Y. State Dept. Environ. Cons., Albany.

PEREZ, C. J., P. J SWANK & D. W. SMITH 1996. Survival, movements and habitat use of Aplomado Falcons released in southern Texas. *J. Raptor Res.* 30:175-182.

PETTY, S. J. 1996. History of the Northern Goshawk *Accipiter gentilis* in Britain. Pp. 95-102 *in* J. S. Holmes & R. J. Simons, eds., *The introduction and naturalisation of birds.* Her Majesty's Stationery Office, London.

PITELKA, F. A. 1981. The condor case: An uphill struggle in a downhill crush. *Auk* 98:634-635.

POMAROL, M. 1993. Lesser Kestrel recovery project in Catalonia. Pp. 24-28 *in* M. K. Nichols & R. Clarke, eds., *Biology and conservation of small falcons.* The Hawk and Owl Trust, London.

POMAROL, M. 1994. Releasing Montagu's Harrier (*Circus pygargus*) by the method of hacking. *J. Raptor Res.* 28:19-22.

POMAROL, M. & X. PARELLADA 1989. Plan de protección de les rapaces amenazadas de Cataluña. *Quercus* 37:29-31.

POVILITIS, T. 1990. Is captive breeding an appropriate strategy for conservation? *Endangered Species Update* 8(1):20-23.

REDIG, P. T. 1993. *Medical management of birds of prey.* Third edition, revised. The Raptor Center. Univ. Minnesota, St. Paul. 182pp.

REDIG, P. T. & H. B. TORDOFF 1988. Peregrine Falcon reintroduction in the upper Mississippi valley and western Great Lakes region. Pp. 559-563 *in* T. J. Cade et al., eds., *Peregrine Falcon populations, their management and recovery.* The Peregrine Fund, Inc., Boise, Idaho.

REED, J. M. & A. P. DOBSON 1993. Behavioural constraints and conservation biology: conspecific attraction and recruitment. *Trends Ecol. Evol.* 8:253-255.

REED, J. M., D. D. MURPHY & P. F. BRUSSARD. 1998. The efficacy of population viability analysis. *Wildl. Soc. Bull.* 26:244-251.

RIPLEY, S. D. 1975. Foreword. Pp. 7-9 *in* D. R. Zimmerman, *To save a bird in peril.* Coward, McCann & Geoghegan, Inc., New York.

ROSENBERG, K. V., R. D. OHMART, W. C. HUNTER & B. W. ANDERSON 1991. *Birds of the lower Colorado River Valley.* Univ. Arizona Press, Tucson. 416pp.

RYMON, L. M. 1989. The restoration of Ospreys *Pandion haliaetus* to breeding in Pennsylvania by hacking (1980-1986). Pp. 359-362 *in* B.-U. Meyburg & R. D. Chancellor, eds., *Raptors in the modern world.* WWGBP, Berlin.

SAAR, C. 1988. Reintroduction of the Peregrine Falcon in Germany. Pp. 629-635 *in* T. J. Cade et al., eds., *Peregrine Falcon populations, their management and recovery.* The Peregrine Fund, Inc. , Boise, Idaho.

SARRAZIN, F. C., C. BAGNOLINI, E. DANCHIN & J. CLOBERT 1994. High survival estimates of Griffon Vultures *Gyps fulvus fulvus* in a reintroduced population. *Auk* 111:853-862.

SARRAZIN, F., C. BAGNOLINI, J. L. PINNA & E. DANCHIN 1996. Breeding biology during establishment of a reintroduced Griffon Vulture *Gyps fulvus* population. *Ibis* 138:315-325.

SARRAZIN, F & R. BARBAULT 1996. Reintroduction: challenges and lessons for basic biology. *Trends Ecol. Evol.* 11:474-478.

SCHADDT, C. P. & L. M. RYMON 1981. The restoration of Osprey by hacking. Pp. 299-305 *in* D. M. Bird, N. R. Seymour, & J. M. Gerrard, eds., *Biology and management of Bald Eagles and Ospreys*. Harpell Press, Ste. Anne de Bellevue, Quebec.
SCOTT, J. M. & J. W. CARPENTER 1987. Release of captive-reared or translocated birds: what do we need to know? *Auk* 104:544-545.
SHERROD, S. K., W. R. HEINRICH, W. A. BURNHAM, J. H. BARCLAY & T. J. CADE 1981. *Hacking: a method for releasing Peregrine Falcons and other birds of prey*. The Peregrine Fund, Inc., Ithaca, N.Y. 61pp.
SHERROD, S. K., M. A. JENKINS, G. MCKEE, S. TATUM & D. WOLFE 1987. Using wild eggs for production of Bald Eagles for reintroduction into the southeastern United States. Pp. 14-20 *in* R. R. Odom, K. A. Riddleburger, & J. C. Ozier, eds., *Proc.of the third southeastern nongame and endangered species symposium*. Georgia Dept. Nat. Resour., South Circle, Georgia.
SHERROD, S. K., M. A. JENKINS, G. MCKEE, D. A. WOLFE & S. TATUM 1989. Restoring nesting Bald Eagle *Haliaeetus leucocephalus* populations to the southeastern United States. Pp. 353-357 *in* B.-U. Meyburg & R. D. Chancellor, eds., *Raptors in the modern world*. WWGBP, Berlin.
SMITH, A. & M. M. PEACOCK. 1990. Conspecific attraction and the determination of metapopulation colonization rates. *Conserv. Biol.* 4:320-323.
SNYDER, N. F. R., S. R. DERRICKSON, S. R. BEISSINGER, J. W. WILEY, S. B. SMITH, W. D. TOONE & B. MILLER 1996. Limitations of captive breeding in endangered species recovery. *Conserv. Biol.*10:338-348.
STAMPS, J. A. 1988. Conspecific attraction and aggregation in terrestrial species. *Am. Nat.* 131:329-347.
STEIDL, R. J., C. R. GRIFFIN, L. J. NILES & K. E. CLARK 1991. Reproductive success and eggshell thinning of a reestablished Peregrine Falcon population. *J. Wildl. Manage. 55:294-299.*
STEWART, G. R. 1981. Re-establishing the Harris' Hawk on the lower Colorado River. *Cal-Neva Wildl. Trans.* 1981:169-175.
TEMPLE, S. A. 1977. The status and conservation of endemic kestrels on Indian Ocean islands. Pp. 74-82 *in* R. D. Chancellor, ed., *World conference on birds of prey: Report of proceedings*. ICBP, London.
TEMPLE, S. A. & T. J. CADE 1988. Genetic issues associated with recovery efforts for three endangered raptors. Pp. 17-30 *in* D. K. Garcelon and G. W. Roemer, eds., *Proceedings of the international symposium on raptor reintroduction, 1995*. Institute for Wildlife Studies, Arcata, California.
TEMPLETON, A. R. 1990. The role of genetics in captive breeding and reintroduction for species conservation. *Endangered Species Update* 8(1):14-17.
TERRASSE, J.-F. 1989. Le Vautour moine (*Aegypius monachus*) appartient encore a la faune Française. *Alauda* 57:231-232.
TERRASSE, M. 1980. Réintroduction du Vautour fauve dans les Cévennes. *Le Courrier de la Nature* 70:32-35.
TERRASSE, M. 1990. Réintroduction du Vautour fauve dans les grands Causses et renforcement de population du Vautour percnoptère. Compte rendu du colloque Saint Jean du Gard, Revue d'Ecologie. *Terre Vie 5 (Suppl):*213-226.
TERRASSE, M., C. BAGNOLINI, J. BONNET, J.-L. PINNA & F. SARRAZIN 1994. Reintroduction of the Griffon Vulture *Gyps fulvus* in the Massif Central, France. Pp. 479-491 *in* B.-U. Meyburg & R. D. Chancellor, eds., *Raptor conservation today*. WWGBP/The Pica Press, Berlin.
TEWES, E. 1994. The European Black Vulture *Aegypius monachus* project in Mallorca. Pp. 493-498 *in* B.-U. Meyburg & R. D. Chancellor, eds., *Raptor conservation today* WWGBP/The Pica Press, Berlin.
TEWES, E., M. TERRASSE, C. BAGNOLINI & J. J. SÁNCHEZ ARTÉZ 1998. Captive breeding of the European Black Vulture *Aegypius monachus* and the reintroduction project in France. Pp.417-435 *in* R. D. Chancellor, B.-U. Meyburg & J. J. Ferrero, eds., *Holarctic birds of prey, Proc. of an internatl. conf.* ADENEX & WWGBP, Merida & Berlin.
THERRES, G. D., S. DAWSON & J. C. BARBER 1993. Peregrine Falcon restoration in Maryland. *Wildl. Tech. Publ.* 93-1:1-24. Maryland Dept. of Natural Res. Fish, Heritage & Wildlife Adm., Annapolis, Maryland.
TOONE, W. D & M. P. WALLACE 1994. The extinction in the wild and reintroduction of the California Condor (*Gymnogyps californianus*). Pp. 411-419 *in* P. J. S. Olney, G. M. Mace & A. T. C. Feistner, eds., *Creative conservation: interactive management of wild and captive animals*. Chapman and Hall, London.
TORDOFF, H. B. & P. T. REDIG 1997. Midwest Peregrine Falcon demography, 1982-1995. *J. Raptor Res.* 31:339-346.
TROMMER, G. 1997. Wanderfalken-Auswilderungs-bericht aus Polen 1996. *Greifvögel und Falknerei, Jahrbuch des Deutschen Falknerordens* 1996:90-91.
VANNINI, J. P. 1989. Reintroduction of Bat Falcons (*Falco albigularis*) on Guatemala's Pacific versant. Pp. 203-208 *in* W. Burnham, ed., The Peregrine Fund, Inc. Operation Report, 1989. World Center for Birds of Prey, Boise, Idaho.

VANNINI, J. P. 1990. Reintroduction of Bat Falcons (*Falco albigularis*). Pp. 61-62 *in* W. Burnham, ed., The Peregrine Fund, Inc. Operation Report, 1990. World Center for Birds of Prey, Boise, Idaho.

VARNER, G. E. & M. C. MONROE 1990. Ethical perspective on captive breeding: is it for the birds? *Endangered Species Update* 8(1):27-29.

WALLACE, M. P. 1991. Methods and strategies for releasing California Condors to the wild. Pp. 121-128 *in* American Association of Zoological Parks and Aquariums Annual Conf. Proc., San Diego, Calif.

WALLACE, M. P. & S. A. TEMPLE 1987. Releasing captive-reared Andean Condors to the wild. *J. Wildl. Manage.* 51:541-550.

WALTON, B. J. 1997. Natural history and restoration of Peregrine Falcons in California. Unpubl. rept. 56pp. Box 7445, Santa Cruz, CA 95061.

WALTON, B. J. & C. G. THELANDER 1988. Peregrine Falcon management efforts in California, Oregon, Washington, and Nevada. Pp. 587-597 *in* T. J. Cade *et al.*, eds., *Peregrine falcon populations, their management and recovery.* The Peregrine Fund, Inc., Boise, Idaho.

WALTON, B. J., J. LINTHICUM & G. STEWART 1988a. Release and re-establishment techniques developed for Harris' Hawks—Colorado River 1979-1986. Pp. 318-320 *in* R. L. Glinski, B. G. Pendleton, M. B. Moss, M. N. Lefranc, Jr., B. A. Millsap & S. W. Hoffman, eds., *Proc. southwest raptor manage. symp. and workshop.* Natl. Wildl. Fed., Washington, D. C.

WALTON, B. J., C. G. THELANDER & D. G. HARLOW 1988b. The status of Peregrines nesting in California, Oregon, Washington, and Nevada. Pp. 95-104 *in* T. J. Cade *et al.*, eds., *Peregrine Falcon populations, their management and recovery.* The Peregrine Fund, Inc., Boise, Idaho.

WATSON, J. 1989. Successful translocation of the endemic Seychelles Kestrel *Falco araea* to Praslin. Pp. 363-367 *in* B.-U. Meyburg & R. D. Chancellor, eds., *Raptors in the modern world.* WWGBP, Berlin.

WATSON, R. T., S. RAZAFINDRAMANANA, R. THORSTROM, & S. RAFANOMEZANTSOA. In press. Breeding biology, extra-pair birds, productivity, siblicide, and conservation of the Madagascar Fish-Eagle. *Ostrich.*

WATSON, R. T., S. THOMSETT, D. O'DANIEL, & R. LEWIS 1996. Breeding, growth, development, and management of the Madagascar Fish-Eagle (*Haliaeetus vociferoides*). *J. Raptor Res.* 30:21-27.

WESTALL, M. J. 1990. Osprey. *In* B. G. Pendleton, ed., Proc. Southeast raptor management symposium and workshop. *Natl. Wildl. Fed. Sci. Tech. Ser.* No. 14:22-28. Washington, D. C.

WILLIAMS, G. R. 1977. Marooning: a technique for saving threatened species from extinction. *Intern. 200 Yearbook* 17:102-106.

WILSON, A. C. & M. R. STANLEY PRICE 1994. Reintroduction as a reason for captive breeding. Pp. 243-264 *in* P. J. S. Olney, G. M. Mace & A. T. C. Feistner, eds., *Creative conservation: interactive management of wild and captive animals.* Chapman and Hall, London.

WISNIEWSKI, G. 1995. Programme for the reintroduction of the Peregrine Falcon (*Falco peregrinus*) in Poland. *Acta Ornithol.* 30:74-78.

WOLF, C. M., B. GRIFFITH, C. REED & S. A. TEMPLE 1996. Avian and mammalian translocations: Update and reanalysis of 1987 survey data. *Conserv. Biol.* 10:1142-1154.

WOODFORD, M. H. & P. B. ROSSITER 1994. Disease risks associated with wildlife translocation projects. Pp. 178-200 *in* P. J. S. Olney, G. M. Mace & A. T. C. Feistner, eds., *Creative conservation: interactive management of wild and captive animals.* Chapman and Hall, London.

WOODLAND, H. 1993. Captive breeding and release of Hobbies (*Falco subbuteo*) in the UK. Pp. 201-206 *in* M. K. Nichols & R. Clarke, eds., *Biology and conservation of small falcons.* The Hawk and Owl Trust, London.

WOOTTON, J. T. & D. A. BELL. 1992. A metapopulation model of the Peregrine Falcon in California: viability and management strategies. *Ecol. Appl.* 2:307-321.

Tom J. Cade
The Peregrine Fund
566 West Flying Hawk Lane
Boise, ID 83709
U.S.A.

Chancellor, R. D. & B.-U. Meyburg eds. 2000
Raptors at Risk
WWGBP / Hancock House

Falconry as a Conservation Tool in Africa

R.R. Hartley

ABSTRACT

Falconry can assist raptor conservation, especially in Africa with its meagre financial resources and expertise. Falconers can assist by monitoring nest sites, ringing raptors, establishing captive breeding programmes for endangered species, assisting with raptor rehabilitation, running educational programmes and providing specimens. This model has been applied successfully for the past 21 years in Zimbabwe, as a result of the government falconry policy, consisting of a formal arrangement between the Zimbabwe Falconers' Club (ZFC) and the Department of National Parks and Wild Life Management (DNPWLM). A vital component in this relationship has been the linkages between a ZFC research coordinator and a senior ecologist (DNPWLM). The ZFC established a Raptor Conservation Unit (RCU) in 1989 which has also worked in joint programmes with The Peregrine Fund Inc., including studies on: DDT impact on the Peregrine Falcon *Falco peregrinus minor*; status, ecology and captive breeding of the Taita Falcon *F. fasciinucha*; and the raptor community in the Batoka Gorge (site of a proposed dam). The ZFC has produced over 200 Peregrines in captivity and 70 have been released. The ZFC also supports falconry clubs at two private secondary schools.

INTRODUCTION

Falconry has been a legal pursuit in Zimbabwe (Hartley 1993a) for 30 years and the special falconry policy established in 1976 by the Department of National Parks and Wild Life Management (DNPWLM) has led to a systematic and concerted effort to conserve both raptors and their prey by falconers (Hartley 1993a, 1994a). The methods and structure of the programme were described in Hartley (1991, 1993a). The Zimbabwe Falconers' Club (ZFC) conservation strategy has four components: education and public awareness through talks and demonstrations by experienced falconers and also from two falconry clubs at private schools; veterinary care and rehabilitation of raptors; a research data base on raptor nest sites used for studies of populations, comparative ecology, DDT impact and the prey base of hawks; and, a captive breeding and release programme mainly on the African Peregrine Falcon *Falco peregrinus minor*, but recently including the Taita Falcon *F. fasciinucha* as well (Hartley 1993a, 1996, in press a).

Guidance and professional input on the conservation programme was achieved by regular linkage between the Chief Ornithologist of DNPWLM and the Club's Research Coordinator (Hartley 1993a), as a consequence of official policy and also the commitment of the respective personnel concerned.

A cornerstone for the success of the programme has always been the falconers' access to birds from the wild (Hartley 1993a).

Joint conservation and research programmes have been set up between the ZFC and The Peregrine Fund (TPF), Overseas Development Agency (ODA) and the DNPWLM (Hartley 1993a). The Raptor Conservation Fund was established by the ZFC in 1989 to provide financial support to the research programme (Hartley 1993a). A separate breeding fund was established by the ZFC thereafter as well. Material and financial support has been supplied by TPF and the Endangered Wildlife Trust of southern Africa (EWT; Hartley 1993a). Material support has also been supplied by the National Birds of Prey Centre (UK; Hartley 1993a), while The Institute of Terrestrial Ecology (UK) has sampled eggshell contents for pesticide residues (Hartley *et al.* 1995).

The aim of this paper is to review the conservation activities and projects of the ZFC since 1992 (Hartley 1993a), to verify the usefulness of this approach, and also to review developments in other countries of southern and east Africa with a view to promoting the Zimbabwe model.

RESULTS AND DISCUSSION

Routine activities

Annual monitoring has continued, with the maintenance of the nest record card system which has continued to grow and a further 13 Peregrine and three Taita sites have been added since 1992 (Hartley 1993a). The system also has nesting data on: Black *Aquila verreauxii*, Tawny *A rapax*, Wahlberg's *A. wahlbergi*, African Hawk *Hieraaetus spilogaster*, Ayres' *H. ayresii*, Martial *Polemaetus bellicosus*, Crowned *Stephanoaetus coronatus*, Blackbreasted Snake *Circaetus gallicus* and African Fish Eagles *Haliaeetus vocifer*; Lizard Buzzard *Kaupifalco monogrammicus*; Redbreasted *Accipiter rufiventris*, Ovambo *A. ovampensis*,Little *A. minullus* and Black Sparrowhawks *A. melanoleucus*; Littlebanded *A. badius*, African *A. tachiro* and Gabar Goshawks *Micronisus gabar*; and Lanner Falcon *F. biarmicus*.

Numerous specimens (eggs and shell fragments; dead birds) have been measured and submitted to the Natural History Museum of Zimbabwe (NHMZ) in Bulawayo. Species included: Black, Wahlberg's, Crowned and Blackbreasted Snake Eagles; Black, Ovambo and Little Sparrowhawks; Littlebanded, Gabar and African Goshawks; and Taita, Peregrine and Lanner Falcons. The first specimen (live bird) of Sooty Falcon *F. concolor* collected from Zimbabwe (Hartley & Hustler 1995) is still in the care of the ZFC.

Data on prey taken by trained hawks included weights and measurements (including gonads), moult and location and were collected almost exclusively by Falcon College Falconry Club. This has amounted to over 2500 individuals of over 140 species. Some prey data were published in Hartley & Mundy (1992), Hartley (1995), Francis *et al.* 1996 and Hartley (1997). Furthermore this unit has also compiled a prey reference collection which now represents 126 species of birds, useful in the identification of prey remains. The monitoring of the raptor community around the college in the Esigodini area has continued for 16 years, providing useful understanding of long-term population trends.

Over 120 raptors have been ringed by the ZFC and numerous raptors have been successfully rehabilitated, including considerable veterinary work done by Dr. A. Huelin. *Post mortems* have revealed incidences of avian tuberculosis in a few free-living and captive Peregrine and Lanner Falcons, and a possible vulnerability to aspergillosis in some captive Black Sparrowhawks.

Education was described by Hartley (1993a). Since its inception in 1983 Falcon College Falconry Club (Hartley 1987) has produced 59 fully fledged falconer-conservationists (Hartley 1998a), all of whom have spent a minimum of two years of intensive activity in the unit . They have also hosted many groups of visitors, instructing them on the raptors at the facility and on aspects of raptor conservation. As many as 20 groups from visiting schools make organised trips to the facility each year. A similar service has been provided at the Peterhouse Falconry Club. Several falconers have put on posters illustrating the ZFC conservation and research programme at conservation workshops and at game fairs held in Harare. They have also given flying displays with trained raptors.

Special projects

On-going projects involving Peregrine and Taita Falcons (Hartley 1993a) were described in detail by Hartley et al. (1996):

1. *Status and distribution of the Peregrine and Taita Falcons in Zimbabwe* (1976-present). 16 of 20 Taita nest sites and 50 of 136 Peregrine nest sites have been found in well wooded areas in the Zambezi Valley where Peregrines outnumber Taitas 3:1, but increasing habitat destruction in this zone may favour the Lanner (currently outnumbered 10:1 by the Peregrine) in the future, possibly at the expense of the Taita (Hartley in press a). The Taita is sympatric with the Peregrine and it is likely that its numbers are constrained by the larger species, the Taita fitting in where it can (Hartley et al 1993, in press a). Nest site characteristics, productivity, prey, nesting densities and ecology are being studied. Formal, systematic investigations on the effect of organochlorines on Peregrine in Zimbabwe were completed in 1990, and it was concluded that these no longer posed a serious threat to populations (Hartley et al 1995). This was also supported by data collected on Lanners and Taitas (Hartley 1993b). The analyses were conducted by the Institute of Terrestrial Ecology in the UK, under the auspices of Dr. I. Newton, also scientific advisor to The Peregrine Fund, USA.

2. *Monitoring and managing falcons in two Zimbabwe cities.* Lanner Falcons have bred in Harare city since 1972 (Kellow-Webb & Dingley 1972) and a chick ringed in a nest at Grindlays Bank was recovered 17 years later - the greatest longevity recorded for a wild falcon in Africa. These and Peregrines have been monitored intermittently since then and the ZFC has been instrumental in assisting these falcons and the interested public. Dr. J.B. Condy (ZFC) provided supplementary feeding for the chicks (Kellow-Webb & Dingley 1972). In 1997, when the adult male Lanner disappeared, supplementary food was supplied to the nest by N. Deacon (ZFC) and T. Tanser, and all three young fledged successfully. After the laying of the first egg a nest tray was also provided, as the window ledge had no substrate. Stories were also canvassed to the two principal Sunday papers. Television coverage probably assisted the recovery of two young Peregrines which landed in the street below their nest in 1990. Both chicks had been supplied from the captive breeding project of the ZFC, as the Peregrines had lost two eggs (de la Harpe 1990). In separate incidents in 1997 two Peregrine fledglings stranded on busy streets below their nest were quickly rescued and handed in to ZFC personnel, who in turn returned them to their nest. Both fledged successfully. In 1997 a pair of Peregrines attempted breeding in Bulawayo for the first time. Unfortunately the adult female disappeared, and when replaced by an immature, the latter was recovered injured on the street and handed to the ZFC. A few days later it laid an egg.

3. *Captive breeding and release programmes involving Peregrine and Taita Falcons.*
a) *Peregrine.* The programme started in 1978 and the first successes were in 1981 (Hartley 1983, 1996a; Thomson 1984). To date 19 pairs have produced 214 young. Surplus young were produced from 1989 onwards, and 70 juveniles released to the wild. In 117 pair-years 20 pairs produced 96 male and 96 female young, 83% fledging successfully. 75 pair-years were claimed by 30 unsuccessful pairs, but five females from this set bred successfully when placed with suitable males. Of 57 Peregrines used, 56% produced young, compared with levels of 30-50% achieved elsewhere (Lindberg 1982). Three females produced young at 14 years of age, and one at 15 years. No females bred successfully after this time, following senescence patterns recorded in captive birds at The Peregrine Fund (Clum 1995). Each released falcon was ringed and 13 were recovered. There was a tendency to drift to towns and to cereal croplands near Harare, usually within 100 km of the release sites. The longest distance recovery was at Pretoria west, South Africa, for a falcon released at Peterhouse, Marondera (Oatley 1995). A five and a four year old falcon were recovered respectively, while another falcon bred successfully at a dominant, traditional Peregrine site in the Matobo Hills in 1997. All costs were borne by the falconers, and by a fund established by the ZFC (Hartley 1996a).

b) *Taita.* In 1993 four pairs of Taita Falcons were constituted from three females (Hartley 1994b) and one male taken from the wild, and three males bred in captivity by TPF (see Hartley & Mundy 1990; Hartley 1994b & c). One pair has died. Two pairs produced eggs in 1996 and 1997, and one of these produced young for the first time in 1997 (Hartley in press b).

4. *Breeding and ecology of Crowned Eagle* in Turwi River system (1994- present). 14 nesting territories were found in 180 km², although just 4-6 were occupied in any year. 123 prey items have been collected. Crowned Eagles were recorded feeding on carrion (Smith & Hartley 1996). A raptor community study in the wider Save Conservancy has been undertaken as ancillary programme, and so far 42 species of diurnal raptors and 9 species of owls have been recorded. This study is essentially an inventory, with data also being gathered on prey, breeding and nesting densities.

5. *Black Eagle study* in Marula district. A survey was started on the Black Eagles on private land in Marula district of the Matobo Hills in 1997, to complement the major study in the National Park (Gargett 1990). Private land has been much less studied in this area. Our study has focused on 14 nest sites, and two species of hyrax are being sampled to support surveys being done on the prey base in neighbouring Communal Lands and National Parks Estate (Chiweshe this volume). Useful data was also collected on all other species of raptor, so that there will also be a raptor community component to the programme. Several Black Eagle nests have been known since the early part of the century.

6. *Raptor community study* in the Batoka Gorge system, which holds the highest density of falcons recorded in Africa, with 8-10 pairs of Taita and 15-18 pairs of Peregrines occurring along the first 60 km of the 122 km gorge system (Hartley 1993c). Twelve of 29 species of diurnal raptors are eagles, including seven pairs of Black Eagles (Hartley & Smith 1995), and nine species of owls were also recorded. Information was supplied to a current environmental impact assessment, as a hydro-electric dam is planned (Hartley 1993 a & c).

7. *DDT impact on African Goshawk* at Siabuwa (Zambezi valley). The collection of eggs from selected sites is planned for December 1998 for DDT impact studies, to follow-up on the project completed in 1988-1990 (joint exercise with ODA, U.K.; Hartley & Douthwaite 1994). The impending exercise will test whether DDT levels have changed since the cessation of ground spraying in 1990, and whether productivity of goshawks has been influenced.

8. *Molecular phylogeny of Peregrine, Taita and related falcons* (1994-present). This is a joint project between RRH (ZFC) and Dr. D. Bell (California Academy of Sciences). This will be presented as a poster to the 22nd International Ornithological Conference in Durban in August 1998.

Most of these projects are joint programmes between ZFC, the DNPWLM and TPF (Hartley 1993a). The ZFC is also a member of the newly established Raptor Conservation Group of Zimbabwe, whose mandate includes the planning and prioritisation of research projects in the national interest. Other research oriented services rendered by ZFC activities included collaboration with: J. Dale (PhD student, Cornell University) during the harvesting of Redbilled Quelea *Quelea quelea* for hawk food during quelea breeding seasons in 1995-1997; P. Weeks (PhD student, Cambridge University) where a trained Peregrine was used to test behaviour exhibited by Redbilled Oxpeckers *Buphagus erythrorhychus*; and B. Davidson (M.Sc. student, Rhodes University) who studied a raptor community in the south-eastern Lowveld.

CONFERENCES

The ZFC has long been recognised as a valuable contributor in the field of raptor and gamebird conservation in Zimbabwe, and it has contributed to several conferences: Perdix VI gamebird symposium (Hartley & Mundy 1992; Mundy 1996); VIII Pan Afr. Orn. Congr. 1992 (Hartley 1993a, Hartley *et al.* 1993); Raptors and Man symposium (Hartley *et al.* 1996); Our Endangered Environment (Hartley 1996b); Migrating Birds Know No Boundaries (Hartley 1998b); and V World Conference on Birds of Prey.

FALCONRY AND CONSERVATION ELSEWHERE IN AFRICA

Falconry south of the Sahara has been largely confined to Zimbabwe and South Africa, while in north Africa activities have been largely related to hunting by Arab falconers. South Africa has the most falconers and it is likely the membership of the Cape, Natal, Free State and Transvaal Clubs is about 250 members. Of the 122 members (1998) of the ZFC, 91 have been practising falconers in Zimbabwe. There are three falconers in Botswana and one in Zambia. Although there are a few falconers in Kenya, including TPF's Simon Thomsett, there is no official policy or support towards the activity. There are a few keen falconers in Namibia, but it is currently not allowed there (Oettle *et al.* this volume).

Although there are many conservation minded falconers in South Africa, there has been a turbulent relationship between many falconers and ornithologists in particular (Raptor Conservation Group 1996; Ryan 1996). However, South African falconers have assisted ornithologists and conservationists (Tarboton & Allan 1984; Jenkins *et al.* 1991; Jenkins 1995; Lombard 1998; Oettle *et al.* this volume). There is also significant resistance to the harvesting of raptors from the wild (Raptor Conservation Group 1996), even if biologically justifiable. Ironically the same detractors praise the efforts of the ZFC, whose government falconry policy is based on the legitimate harvesting of birds from the wild.

In Zimbabwe the government falconry policy is based on the principle that those who use the resource will contribute to it (Thomson 1992). Experience shows this to be true, with users being more pro-active in conservation than most others. This has characterised Zimbabwe's falconers who have given their time, expertise and money to the conservation programme. In a continent that is chronically short of these resources, with pristine habitats diminishing steadily under the growing human population, wildlife needs all of the input that it can get. Wildlife biologists, falconers and landowners/holders need to pool their expertise and resources and commit to work together for the common cause of wildlife conservation.

ACKNOWLEDGEMENTS

My attendance at the V World Conference on Birds of Prey was made possible by the Raptor Conservation Fund of the ZFC, The Peregrine Fund and the Raptor Conservation Group of the EWT.

REFERENCES

CHIWESHE, N. (this volume). People and hyrax in the conservation of Black Eagles *Aquila verreauxii* in the Matobo Hills, Zimbabwe.
CLUM, N.J. 1995. Effects of aging and mate retention on reproductive success of captive female Peregrine Falcons. *Amer. Zool.*, 35: 329-339.
DE LA HARPE, D. 1990. The Harare Peregrines - a cause for celebration? *Honeyguide* 36: 163-166.
FRANCIS, J.D., D.S. MIDDLETON & R.R. HARTLEY 1996. Prey and hunting behaviour of Little Sparrowhawks in captivity, and evasive tactics of prey. *Honeyguide* 42: 146-155.
GARGETT, V. 1990. *The Black Eagle, a study.* Acorn Books & Russel Friedman Books, Randburg.
HARTLEY, R.R. 1983. Successful breeding of the African Peregrine in captivity. *Bokmakierie* 35:75-77.
HARTLEY, R.R. 1987. The operation of Falcon College Falconry Club. *North American Falconers' Club Association Journal* 26:6-12.
HARTLEY, R.R. & P.J. MUNDY 1990. Taita Falcons in captivity. *Honeyguide* 36: 66-69.
HARTLEY, R. 1991. The Zimbabwe Falconers' Club - current research and conservation projects. *Endangered Wildlife* 8: 9-15.
HARTLEY, R.R. & P.J. MUNDY 1992. Management of terrestrial gamebird hunting in Zimbabwe. *Gibier Faune Sauvage* 9: 837-846.
HARTLEY, R.R. 1993a. Falconry as an instrument for conservation in Zimbabwe. *Proc.VIII Pan Afr. Orn. Congr.*: 105-110.
HARTLEY, R.R. 1993b. DDT impact on raptors in the Zambezi Valley. Pages 43-47. *In* Proc. Our endangered environment 1993. Birds of a Feather, Endangered Wildlife Trust & Sunlink International, Harare.
HARTLEY, R. 1993c. The Batoka Gorges, haven for birds of prey. *Afr. Wildlife* 47: 74-78.
HARTLEY, R.R., G. BODINGTON, A.S. DUNKLEY & A GROENEWALD 1993. Notes on the breeding biology, hunting behaviour, and ecology of the Taita Falcon in Zimbabwe. *J. Raptor Res.* 27: 133-142.
HARTLEY, R.R. 1994a. Zimbabwe Falconers' Club information booklet, constitution, regulations. Zimbabwe Falconers' Club, Harare.

HARTLEY, R. 1994b. Growth and development of captive Taita Falcons in Zimbabwe from nestling to adult. *Gabar* 9: 14-19.
HARTLEY, R. 1994c. Trip to the United States of America. Report to EWT supporters. *Endangered Wildlife* 16:17-18.
HARTLEY, R.R. & R.J. DOUTHWAITE 1994. Effects of DDT treatments applied for tsetse fly control on the African goshawk in north-west Zimbabwe. *Afr. J. Ecol.* 32: 265-272.
HARTLEY, R.R. 1995. Recapture of a Shelley's Francolin. *Honeyguide* 41:110.
HARTLEY, R.R. & K. HUSTLER 1995. First Sooty Falcon specimen from Zimbabwe. *Honeyguide* 41: 229-231.
HARTLEY, R.R., I. NEWTON & M. ROBERTSON 1995. Organochlorine residues and eggshell thinning in the Peregrine Falcon *Falco peregrinus minor* in Zimbabwe. *Ostrich* 66: 69-73.
HARTLEY, R.R. & J.N. SMITH 1995. Eagles hunting in the Batoka Gorges, Zimbabwe. *Gabar* 10: 30-32.
HARTLEY, R.R., K. HUSTLER, & P.J. MUNDY 1996. The impact of man on raptors in Zimbabwe. Pages 337-353. *In* D.M. Bird, D.E. Varland & J. Negro. *Raptors in human landscapes.* Academic Press, London, U.K.
HARTLEY, R. R.1996a. Falcons fly free in Zimbabwe. Pages 60-67. *In* Vision of wildlife, ecotourism, the environment in southern Africa. Endangered Wildlife Trust, Johannesburg, South Africa.
HARTLEY, R.R. 1996b. DDT impact on raptors in the Zambezi Valley. Pages 43-47 *in* Proc. our endangered environment 1993. Birds of a Feather, Endangered Wildlife Trust & Sunlink International, Harare.
HARTLEY, R.R. 1997. Breeding condition, moult and hunting of Doublebanded Sandgrouse from Mpoengs. *Honeyguide* 43: 80-82.
HARTLEY, R.R. 1998a. Falcon College Falconry Club - a summary 1983-97. *Talon* 17 (2): 29-37.
HARTLEY, R.R. 1998b. Raptor migration and conservation in Zimbabwe. *In* Y. Leshem & P. Berthold. *Proc. Migrating Birds Know No Boundaries.*
HARTLEY, R.R. (this volume) a. Ecology of the Taita, Peregrine and Lanner Falcons in Zimbabwe.
HARTLEY, R. In press b. Taita Falcons breed in captivity. *Afr. Birds & Birding.*
JENKINS, A.R., I. HOFFMAN & T. WAGNER 1991. First breeding record of the Taita Falcon in South Africa. *Ostrich* 62: 78.
JENKINS, A.R. 1995. Morphometrics and flight performance of southern African Peregrine and Lanner Falcons. *Journal of Avian Biology* 26: 49-58.
KELLOW-WEBB, E.G.E. & G. DINGLEY 1972. Lanner Falcons nest in central Salisbury. *The Rhod. Sc. News* 6: 358-359.
LINDBERG, P. 1982. Captive breeding and programme for reintroduction of the Peregrine Falcon, *Falco peregrinus,* in Fennoscandia. *Proc. Nordic. Congr. Ornithol.* 3: 65-78.
LOMBARD, A. 1998. Peregrine rescue in the western Cape. *Talon Talk* 12: 1-2.
MUNDY, P.J. 1996. Perdix VI symposium on gamebirds. *Honeyguide* 42: 12-17.
OATLEY, T. 1995. Recent sightings, recoveries and recaptures of marked raptors. *J. Afr. Raptor Biol.*: 73-74.
OETTLE, E.E., D. PEPLER & G. PALMER (this volume). Black Sparrowhawks in the South Western Cape: benefits of cooperative conservation.
RAPTOR CONSERVATION GROUP 1996. Falconers and raptor conservation. *Talon Talk* 7: 14-15.
RYAN, B. 1996. Falconers and conservation. *Talon Talk* 8: 11-13.
SMITH, J.N. & R.R. HARTLEY 1996. Notes on Crowned Eagles in the Lowveld. *Honeyguide* 42: 103-104.
TARBOTON, W.R. & D. ALLAN. 1984. The status and conservation of birds of prey in the Transvaal. *Transvaal Museum Monogr.* 3: 1-115.
THOMSON, W.R. 1984. Comparative notes on the ecology of Peregrine, Lanner and Taita Falcons in Zimbabwe. *In* J.M. Mendelsohn and C.W. Sapsford (Eds.), *Proc. 2nd Symp. Afr. predatory birds.* Natal Bird Club, Durban, South Africa: 15-18.
THOMSON, W.R. 1992. The wildlife game. The Nyala Wildlife Publications Trust, Westville, South Africa.

R.R. Hartley
Zimbabwe Falconers' Club
Falcon College
Esigodini
Zimbabwe.

Black Sparrowhawks in the Southwestern Cape: Benefits of Cooperative Conservation

E. E. Oettlé, M. Walters and D. Pepler

ABSTRACT

A joint project undertaken between the Cape Falconry Club and the University of Stellenbosch to study the ecology of the Black Sparrowhawk *Accipiter melanoleucus* in the Boland and Peninsula regions of the south-western Cape led to the discovery that the species is widespread in alien woodlands, although not as common as either the African Goshawk *A. tachiro* or the Redbreasted Sparrowhawk *A. rufiventris*. The Black Sparrowhawk does not appear to be threatened by human impacts, and it adapts well to human activity. The food preference comprised of a wide range of bird species (N=11).

This study is a good example of mutual benefit that can be derived from cooperation between all interested parties. Cape Nature Conservation obtained quantitative data to assist in the formulation of management strategies for this species' conservation. The Cape Falconry Club is consequently able to harvest a limited number of birds annually for their purposes. The Cape Bird Club has been shown some of the nests and birds, and this input by the falconry club has resulted in a greater awareness and interest by the members, and a consequent great increase in the reported sightings of the species.

INTRODUCTION

Black Sparrowhawks have long been thought to be absent from the Boland region of the south-western Cape, in spite of historical records for the region (Boshoff *et al.* 1983). Hockey *et al.* (1989) report that it is an uncommon resident occurring in forestry plantations further eastwards. In other parts of South Africa, however, the species is widespread, except in the drier western regions (Tarboton & Allan 1984; Maclean 1995; Steyn 1982). The Black Sparrowhawk is a desirable falconry bird, but because of its local rarity, Cape Nature Conservation was unwilling to allow a harvest of birds for these purposes. The falconry club members along with the University of Stellenbosch thus decided to study the species in the Boland and Peninsula regions of the south-western Cape.

Interest in the species was initiated by a report from a Cape Town resident who had shot a female which had been catching his chickens near its nest in a gum tree in the suburb of Brackenfell in 1979. The pair had been breeding there for some years. This incident occurred 10 years prior to the publication of Hockey *et al.* (1989) indicating that they were not known from this region. Local residents and farmers were questioned, and there were numerous reports of large raptors regularly taking chickens, which is typical Black Sparrowhawk behaviour. The terrain, along with the numerous exotic plantations, led to the suspicion that the species should be present, and so a search was conducted during September 1989. Many nests were found, but none could be confirmed as being Black Sparrowhawk nests. The search was then brought forward to July in subsequent years, and these nests proved to be active Black Sparrowhawk nests. Most chicks had left the nests by the end of August, which explained why the September searches were unsuccessful. (Oettlé, 1990, 1993, 1994, 1995).

MATERIALS AND METHODS

The study area extended south-west from 33° 30" South and 19° 30" East. The climate is Mediterranean, characterized by cool, wet winters and hot, dry summers. Black Sparrowhawk nests were searched for in exotic woodlots and plantations consisting of a variety of *Pinus* and *Eucalyptus* spp. that appeared to be suitable breeding habitats. When nests were found, they were visited as often as possible throughout the breeding season. Nests were described according to plantation type and size, position of nest tree within the plantation, height of nest within the tree, type and height of tree, breeding details, and any other observations.

RESULTS

The species was discovered to be widespread in alien woodlands in the study area, although it was not as common as either the African Goshawk or the Redbreasted Sparrowhawk. While the latter two species were not quantified, extrapolation from intensively studied small areas within the study area led to the estimation that these species occurred at least at double the frequency of the Black Sparrowhawks. A total of twenty-two Black Sparrowhawk nests were found, and many more suitable sites were identified where nests are likely, but have not yet been investigated. The nests were found to be typical for the species. The trees used were either mature gum *Eucalyptus* spp. or pine *Pinus* spp. trees, usually close to the edge of the forest, or commanding a view from a high point within the forest. Nests were between 5 and 26 m high, usually at about two thirds the height of the tree. Earliest breeding was recorded in mid-May although most breeding started in June. Most nests were unoccupied by the end of August. As the last chick to have left the nest was at the end of October, this was from a suspected relaying after failure of the first. Food remains were likewise typical for the species elsewhere. Prey species identified were Feral Pigeon *Columba livia*, Redeyed Dove *Streptopelia semitorquata*, Cape Turtle Dove *S. capicola*, Domestic Poulty, Laughing Dove *S. senegalensis*, Helmeted Guineafowl *Numida meleagris*, Cape Francolin *Francolinus capensis*, Cattle Egret *Bubulcus ibis*, Red Knobbed Coot *Fulica cristata*, Moorhen *Gallinula chloropus*, and Yellow Billed Duck *Anas undulata*. One pair was unusual in that the birds fed predominantly on Cattle Egrets from a nearby colony.

DISCUSSION

Brown (1976), who studied Black Sparrowhawks at a nest near his home, stated that he had only seen these birds about 5 times away from the nest forest in 16 years of observation; furthermore, almost all he knew about the species had been learned there in about one hectare. He stated that the species is not shy, just elusive. It is thus no surprise that the species had been overlooked in the south-western Cape; having a Mediterranean climate, few bird watchers are about during the wettest months when the birds are breeding and most vocal. Also, exotic plantations are not desirable birding habitats at the best of times.

This study is a good example of mutual benefit that can be derived from cooperation between all interested parties. Cape Nature Conservation obtained quantitative data to assist in the formulation of management strategies for this species' conservation. The Cape Falconry Club is consequently able to harvest a limited number of birds annually for their purposes. Members of the Cape Bird

Club, which is predominantly comprised of amateur bird watchers, have been shown some of the nests and birds by falconry club members. This has resulted in a greater awareness and interest by the bird club members, and consequently has led to a great increase in the sightings of the species.

However, examples of lack of cooperation in Southern Africa are all too common. In Namibia, there is open antagonism by the Nature Conservation officials towards falconry. This has advanced to such a degree that it would appear that the scientists in that department have allowed emotions to blur their analysis of sound scientific data, bringing in personal bias to affect their decisions. One of the main reasons given by these scientists for rejecting a permit application to import African Peregrines *F. peregrinus minor* from captive bred Zimbabwean stock was that these birds posed a threat to the genetic integrity of the Namibian peregrines should they escape. This is in spite of the well recognized fact that Namibian and Zimbabwean peregrines both belong to the same subspecies. On another occasion, a pair of legally owned peregrines *F. p. peregrinus* were confiscated on the grounds that the housing, built as specified by The Peregrine Fund, (Weaver & Cade 1985) was inadequate and that the birds had been moved within Namibia without the required transport permit. These birds were then housed by Nature Conservation in a larger cage surrounded only by old shade cloth, which tore when the female flew into it, thus escaping. No attempt was made by Nature Conservation to recover the bird, and no compensation was forthcoming. This type of ignorance, obduracy and bias is an anathema to sound science, and has resulted in the crippling of much of the past cooperative efforts of these individuals. One aspiring Namibian falconer who used to spend a large amount of time ringing birds, took to flying racing pigeons instead (an exotic species!), and another resorted to wingshooting since falconry is illegal. The irony of the situation is obvious.

South Africa too has had its share of mistakes, some quite recently. Falconry was illegal in the Cape till seven years ago, and prior to this the wealth of knowledge built up by the falconers was unavailable to the conservators, for fear of falconers attracting unwanted attention. Since the easing of the regulations, and the legalization of falconry, over 20 articles have been published by Cape falconers, and a large amount of nest record and prey data has been given to Cape Nature Conservation. These data would all have been lost to the scientific community if falconry were still illegal. Other examples of antagonism may be found within the RCG itself; as recently as 1996 the RCG formally stated that it does not approve the removal of raptor chicks or the capture of free flying raptors for falconry (Verdoorn 1996). This is in direct conflict with the principles of sustainable use of resources, which is considered the cornerstone of modern conservation. In another article, the chairman of the RCG actively slates human interference with eagle nests, specifically, increasing production by removing the second egg or chick, or double clutching (Verdoorn 1994). By doing so, he influences the gullible public who are funding the RCG into believing that falconers are bad because they take birds or chicks from the wild. Had the chairman evaluated the data in an unbiased way, then it would have been evident that human interference in that particular case in point might have resulted in four chicks being reared from that pair that year, instead of only one. This type of protectionist attitude makes a mockery of the widely acclaimed efforts by The Peregrine Fund to recover the Peregrine, the Californian Condor *Gymnogyps californianus*, and more recently the Harpy *Harpia harpyja* and other eagles, to mention but a few. Furthermore, in 1997, the chairman stated that the RCG "enters into unpleasant battles with the conservation authorities", and "for the RCG, it is a continuous battle to keep unscrupulous characters away from birds of prey" (Verdoorn 1997). This is a good example of poor diplomacy and emotive and inaccurate journalism, resulting in alienation and not cooperation. Falconers are listed in the same article along with collectors, zoos and illegal operators, and yet in the past decade we do not know of any prosecuted illegal activity by falconers in South Africa, nor indeed of any of the other illegal activities mentioned. Such articles in glossy magazines do far more harm to conservation efforts than good.

History repeats itself because people don't listen the first time. Conservation resources are limited, now more than ever. There is no place for ivory towers and sensitive egos; all those involved, even peripherally, with conservation should work together and pool their resources, since the rewards are great. The alternative has failed dismally in the past; it is our duty as conservators to evaluate these facts, and apply the conclusions, even when they disagree with our preconceived opinions.

ACKNOWLEDGEMENTS

Thanks are extended to Guy Palmer, of Cape Nature Conservation, without whose support this study would not have been possible. Thanks are also extended to the other members of the Cape Falconry Club who assisted with the field work.

REFERENCES

BOSHOFF, A. F., C. J. VERNON & R. K. BROOKE 1983. *Historical atlas of the diurnal raptors of the Cape Province (Aves: Falconiformes).* Annals of the Cape Provincial Museums Natural History. Cape Provincial Museums, Grahamstown, South Africa.
BROWN, L., 1976. *Birds of prey: their biology and ecology.* Hamlyn, London.
HOCKEY, P. A. R., L. G. UNDERHILL, M. NEATHERWAY & P. G RYAN 1989. *Atlas of birds of the southwestern Cape.* Cape Bird Club, Cape Town.
MACLEAN, G. L., 1985. *Roberts' birds of Southern Africa.* John Voelcker Bird Book Fund, Cape Town.
OETTLÉ, E. E. 1990. Black Sparrowhawks in Muldersvlei. *Promerops* 192: 7-8.
OETTLÉ, E. 1993. Black Sparrowhawk (158) repeat breeding attempt. *Promerops* 211: 9-10.
OETTLÉ, E.E. 1994. Black Sparrowhawk breeds on the Peninsula. *Promerops* 212: 7.
OETTLÉ, E. E. 1995. Observations on Black Sparrowhawks breeding in Wellington. *Promerops* 217: 8.
STEYN, P. 1982. *Birds of prey of Southern Africa.* David Philip, Cape Town.
TARBOTON, W. R. & D. G. ALLAN 1984. *The status and conservation of birds of prey in the Transvaal.* Transvaal Museum Monograph No. 3, Transvaal Museum, Pretoria.
VERDOORN, G. 1994. Update on the Black Eagles at Roodekrans. *Talon Talk* (3): 3.
VERDOORN, G. 1996. Formal policy of the RCG on falconry. *Talon Talk* (7): 15.
VERDOORN, G. 1997. Limiting the trade in feathers. *Keeping track*, October/November, 62.
WEAVER, J. D. & CADE, T. J. 1985. *Falcon propagation. A manual on captive breeding.* The Peregrine Fund, Inc., Boise, Idaho.

E.E. Oettlé & M. Walters
Cape Falconry Club
P O Box 152
Wellington
7654 South Africa

D. Pepler
University of Stellenbosch
P/Bag X1
Matieland
Stellenbosch
7602 South Africa

Chancellor, R. D. & B.-U. Meyburg eds. 2000
Raptors at Risk
WWGBP / Hancock House

People and Hyrax in the Conservation of Black Eagles *Aquila verreauxii* in the Matobo Hills, Zimbabwe

N. Chiweshe

ABSTRACT

The raptor community in the Matobo Hills is very diverse. A project was initiated in 1995 to secure the future of this unique raptor community outside the Matobo National Park, mainly by focusing on the Black Eagle *Aquila verreauxii* which in the park is heavily dependent on two hyrax species (98%). These prey items have declined sharply in nearby communal lands from human pressure (hunting and habitat change). There were 78 Black Eagle pairs in an area of 1220 km^2 in the Matobo Hills in the 1970s, of which 26 were in the communal area. By 1993 the number of pairs had dropped to 45, with only four in the communal lands.

Since the start of the project, over 8,000 school children from 23 schools, 542 elders and 26 n'angas (traditional healers) have been given lectures on the relationship between Black Eagles, hyrax and people. Wildlife Clubs have been formed at all the schools surrounding the National Park, and students were taken on educational trips into the park.

The hyrax population is being monitored through censuses every April at 20 sampling sites in the National Park and eight outside the park, and has shown marked increases since 1995. Also Black Eagles have increased outside the park to 23 pairs. The Black Eagle diet outside the National Park was found to be more varied (86% hyraxes) than that inside.

INTRODUCTION

We believe that the density of Black Eagles *Aquila verreauxii* in the Matobo National Park and the immediate surrounds is the highest for the species in Africa. It may be among the highest density for a large eagle anywhere in the world. This community of Black Eagles is also special because of a long term study of nearly 40 years.

The study of the Black Eagle population in the Matobo Hills was started in 1959, and by 1964, 41 pairs had been located in an area of 620 km^2, and were being annually monitored (Gargett 1990). The number peaked in 1976 to 59 pairs. In 1978 a large area (1220 km^2) in the Matobo Hills had a total of 78 Black Eagle pairs. Sadly enough, a survey of the species in 1992 (Gargett & Gargett 1993a & b) revealed that this population had declined down to 44 pairs. This decline applied particularly in the communal lands surrounding the National Park and was confirmed by T. & O.

Aumann's (unpubl.) six-month study in 1993. The main reason for the decline was attributed to excessive competition for the eagles' main food, of hyraxes, with communal people, being worsened by natural droughts.

Because of the international significance of the raptors of the Matobo Hills, an on-going Black Eagle monitoring programme outside the Matobo National Park was proposed by T. Aumann in order to secure its population and the hyrax. The programme started in 1995 and has been going on since then. It involves the investigation and annual monitoring of the breeding performance of Black Eagles and other raptors outside the Matobo National Park; collecting and identifying raptor prey items from nests and feeding sites surrounding the nests; checking the population of hyraxes (through annual census) and their utilization by the local Ndebele-speaking people; interpretative work with school children, adults, chiefs, n'angas and District Councillors about raptors and hyraxes, with emphasis on the relationship between the Black Eagles and hyraxes. The interpretative work, which coincides with school terms, also includes talking to teachers and children about how they can contribute towards the conservation of hyraxes and ultimately the raptors outside the protected area. This paper details results from the first few years of the project.

STUDY AREA

The Matobo Hills is a unique area characterized by outstanding large bare granite hills and broken kopjes, interspersed with marshes and sponges that give rise to an intricate network of tributaries leading to the larger rivers of Whovi, Maleme, Mtsheleli and Tuli. Although the Matobo Hills are located in the drier western part of Zimbabwe, because of the nature of the habitats they represent a western extension for many species that are characteristic of higher rainfall areas in the eastern side of the country. The Matobo National Park is centred on (28° 30'E, 20° 30'S), and is surrounded by communal land and commercial farmland (Figure1).

Figure 1. Land-use in the study area

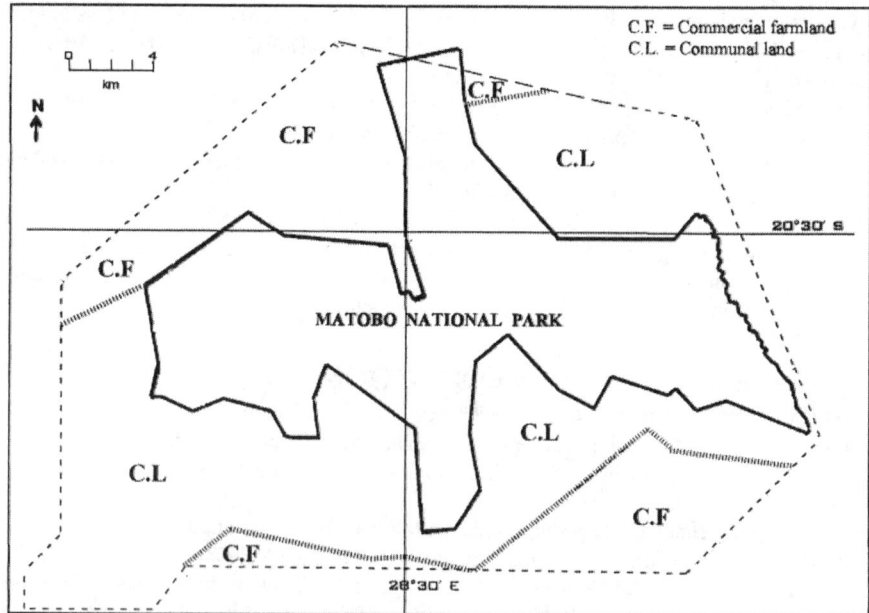

The project area is almost 800 km² in extent (Figure 1) within the Matobo Hills which themselves have an area of approximately 3,000 km²! There is an exceptional density of kopjes here, averaging three individual peaks (of 20 metres or more by elevation) per km². Coupled with the derived sandy soils, which are low in nutrients, generally the habitat is unsuitable for crop cultivation. Furthermore, the steep slopes of the kopjes cause rain water to run quickly through the drainage systems, in turn, contributing to poor soil and short-term fertility during the dry seasons.

Generally, the Matobo Hills lie in a semi-arid agricultural region which is characterized by seasonal drought spells. The average annual rainfall (November to March) from four weather stations (1984/85-1994/95 seasons; Department of Meteorological Services *in litt.*) in the Matobo Hills was 533.5 mm (range 273-819 mm). Extensive livestock production is the preferred form of agriculture.

Much of the project area is communal land, which is populated by tribal people living at a subsistence level. The commercial farmlands in the area are given over to cattle ranching.

METHODS

All the Black Eagle nest sites (occupied and unoccupied) outside the Matobo National Park were checked for occupancy once at the beginning of each breeding season (March/April). Thereafter, each of the occupied territories was visited three times to check for breeding performance: egg-laying/incubation in April-June; hatching in June/July; and fledging in August/ September. In the years of the project (1995-1998), 181 days of visits to the area were made.

Prey remains were collected from below the occupied nests and feeding sites close to the nest at the end of each breeding season (November-January). These were identified at the Natural History Museum, Bulawayo. Nomenclature follows Maclean (1993) for birds and Skinner & Smithers (1990) for mammals.

The census of hyraxes in the Matobo National Park was a continuation of the project initiated by Barry (1993), who identified 20 sampling sites inside the national park. The census was carried out by two observers each using binoculars during the early mornings only. Observations began at, or just before, sunrise and usually lasted up to four hours. The census was extended into the communal lands and commercial farmlands in 1997, where four sampling sites were identified in each and areas estimated (by eye). Hyrax were identified to species (different appearance) and age (different size) by eye; four age-classes were used.

Each of the schools (five secondary and 18 primary) near the national park boundary was visited and lectures given on wildlife conservation, particularly birds, during 1995 and 1996. As a result of the initial visits, all the 23 schools formed Wildlife Clubs. Wildlife books, pamphlets, magazines and posters were given to each to start these clubs. Each club was visited at least three times per year, to coincide with the raptor survey field trips in the hills. Local leaders (the chief, headmen and district councillors) were visited to promote the project and its objectives. By socializing with elderly people and n'angas (traditional healers) at their homes, many traditional stories and beliefs on wildlife, particularly birds, were heard.

RESULTS

Black Eagle breeding performance

The known number of territories occupied by Black Eagle pairs in the study area (outside the protected Matobo National Park) has increased from 16 in 1995 to 21 in 1996 and 23 by the end of 1997 (Table 1). The production of young per pair (y/p) was good (1995 - 0.50 y/p; 1996 - 0.81 y /p; 1997 - 0.70 y/p). This followed a major decrease in occupancy since 1978 (Figure 2).

There were only four occupied Black Eagle territories in the communal land in 1995 (Table 1), contrasting with 26 in the early 1970's (Gargett 1990). The occupied territories had, however, risen to 11 by the end of the 1997 breeding season. Three new nests were found in the communal lands (through the assistance of the local community) since the start of this project, one in 1995 and two in 1996.

Table 1. Breeding performance and territory occupancy of Black Eagles in the Matobo Hills (1995-1997)
CFL - commercial farmland; CL - communal land; P - present Br - bred successfully.

Nest No.	Land-use CL/CFL	Dates 1995	1996	1997
5	CL	Br	Br	Br
6	CL	-	-	-
7	CL	-	-	-
8/A	CL	-	-	-
16	CL	-	-	-
17	CL	-	-	-
19	CL	-	-	-
20	CL	-	-	-
21	CL	Br	Br	Br
22	CL	-	Br	Br
23/93	CL	-	-	-
24	CL	-	-	-
25	CL	-	-	-
33	CL	-	Br	Br
35	CL	-	-	-
36/A	CFL	Br	Br	Br
37	CFL	P	Br	Br
39	CL	-	-	-
42	CL	-	-	-
43	CL	-	-	-
44	CFL	Br	Br	Br
47/48	CFL	Br	Br	P
50	CL	-	-	-
52/A	CFL	P	Br	Br
53	CFL	Br	Br	p
56	CFL	-	-	-
57/A/B	CFL	P	P	Br
58	CL	-	-	-
59	CL	-	-	-
60/A	CFL	P	Br	Br
74	CFL	-	-	-
75/83	CL	-	-	-
80/A	CFL	P	P	P
84/113	CL	-	-	-
85	CL	-	-	-
87	CFL	P	P	Br
88	CFL	-	Br	Br
90/A	CFL	-	-	P
91/A	CL	Br	Br	Br
92	CL	-	Br	Br
96	CL	-	-	-
110	CL	-	-	-
116	CL	-	P	P
117	CL	Br	Br	Br
118	Cl	(?)	Br	Br
119	CL	(?)	Br	Br

	1995	1996	1997
Total occupied	16	21	23
Total breeding success	8	17	16
Total vacant	28	25	23

Figure2. Black Eagle territory occupancy outside the Matobo National Park, over a 20 year period

a. 1978

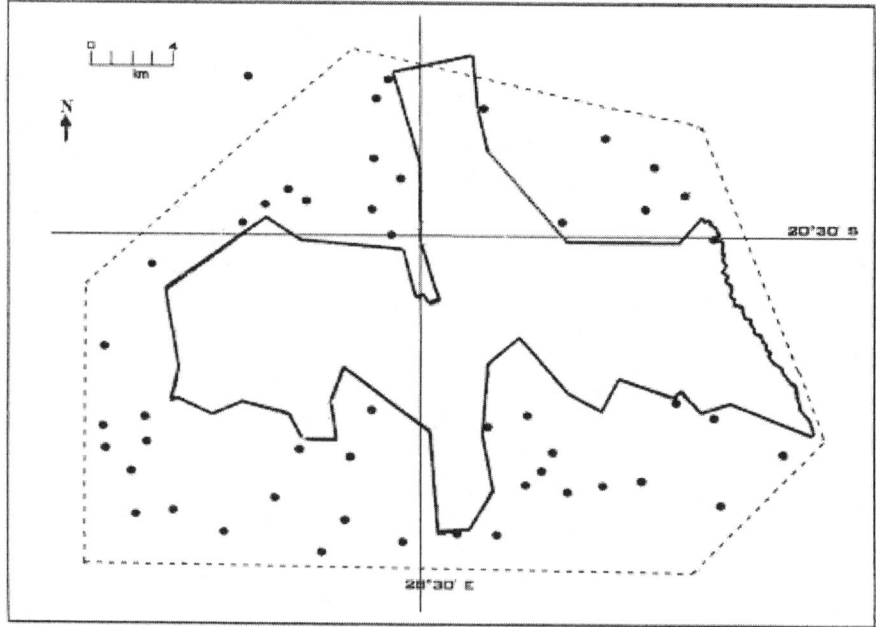

b. 1992

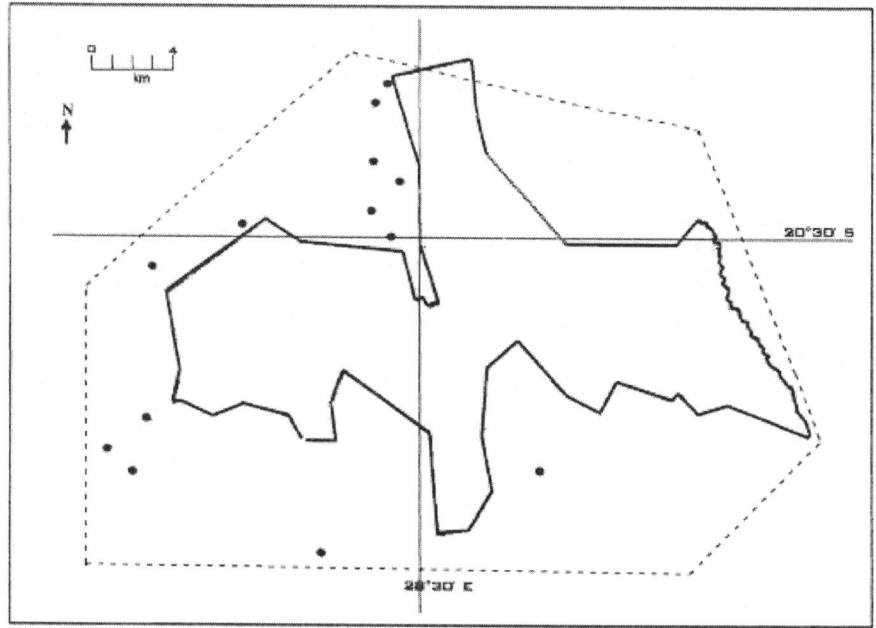

c. 1997

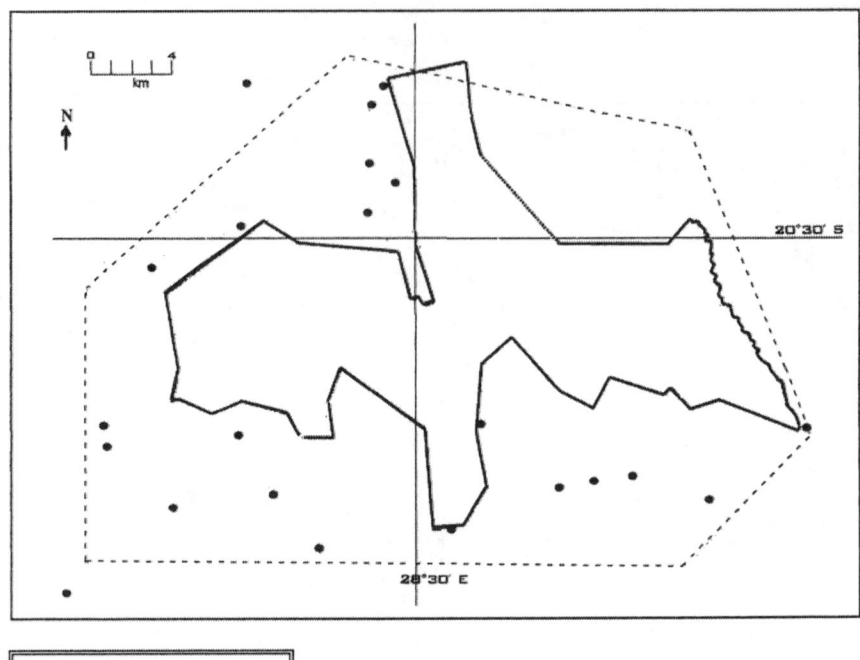

In the commercial farmland, the occupied Black Eagle territories rose from 10 in 1995 to 11 in 1997. A pair of Black Eagles was seen each time on five visits to number 90/A during the 1997 breeding season. It was assumed that a pair had resumed occupancy in this territory after being absent since 1992. The alternate nest site has not been found as yet. Nest sites 90 and 90A were still derelict by the end of the 1997 breeding season.

Six pairs of Black Eagles outside the Matobo National Park bred successfully in each of the three breeding seasons (Table 1). Four of these were in the communal land.

There was a consistently high productivity by the Black Eagles in the fewer nests of the communal lands (3-year average = 0.88 young /pair/year; Table 2). By contrast, in the national park the eagles had a lower output (3-year average = 0.49).

Table 2. Breeding performance of Black Eagles in relation to annual rainfall in the Matobo Hills, 1995–1997
BE – Black Eagle; CFL - commercial farmland; CL - communal land ; NP - national park.

Year	Rainfall (mm)	Occupied BE territories			Bred successfully		
		NP^1	CFL	CL	NP^1	CFL	CL
1995	512	29	10	4	10	4	4
1996	807	28	11	10	13	8	9
1997	569	28	11	11	19	6	9

[1] after Banfield' 1996, 1997 & 1998.

Black Eagle Prey

A total of 680 prey items of 16 species were identified from 56 collections during the project period (Table 3). The variety of species that were preyed upon by Black Eagles in the Matobo Hills during the study period was greatest in communal land, and least in the national park. Mammals accounted for 95.6% of the prey items collected, birds 2,8%, and reptiles 1.6%. The two species of hyrax - the Yellow-spotted Hyrax *Heterohyrax brucei* and the Rock Hyrax *Procavia capensis* - accounted for 92.5% (overall).

Table 3. Comparison of prey items collected from Black Eagle nest sites in the three land-use areas in the Matobo Hills

NP - national park; CFL - commercial farmland; CL - communal land.

Prey item [1]	1995			1996			1997			Total
	NP	CFL	CL	NP	CFL	CL	NP	CFL	CL	
Vervet Monkey *Cercopithecus pygerythrus*	1	-	1	-	-	-	-	-	1	3
Scrub Hare *Lepus saxatilis*	-	1	-	-	-	-	-	-	-	1
Red Rock Rabit *Pronolagus randensis*	1	-	-	1	1	1	1	3	5	13
White-tailed Mongoose *Ichneumia albicauda*	-	-	-	-	-	-	-	-	-	1
Rock Hyrax *Procavia capensis*	76	8	6	23	13	21	36	30	64	277
Yellow-spotted Dassie *Heterohyrax brucei*	80	11	11	40	41	50	35	50	34	352
Goat/Lamb (domesticated)	-	-	1	-	-	-	-	-	2	3
Helmeted Guineafowl *Numida meleagris*	1	1	-	-	-	-	-	-	-	2
Swainson's Francolin *Francolinus swainsonii*	-	-	-	-	-	1	-	1	-	2
Natal Francolin *Francolinus natalensis*	-	-	-	-	-	-	-	-	1	1
Rock Pigeon *Columba guinea*	-	-	1	1	1	1	-	2	1	7
White-necked Raven *Corvus albicollis*	-	-	2	-	1	-	-	-	-	3
Red-billed Hornbill *Tockus erythrorhynchus*	-	-	-	-	1	-	-	-	-	1
Chicken(domesticated)	-	-	-	-	-	1	-	-	2	3
Leopard Tortoise *Geochelone pardalis*	-	-	-	-	1	-	-	1	1	3
Giant-plated Lizard *Gerrhosaurus validus validus*	1	-	-	-	-	2	-	-	5	8
Collection sites	12	2	3	9	7	6	5	5	7	56

[1]Overall prey items - hyrax = 629; other = 51.

Overall, Yellow-spotted Hyraxes were taken more by Black Eagles than Rock Hyraxes (ratio - 14:11 respectively). In the national park and also in commercial farmland the Yellow-spotted Hyrax was taken more than the Rock Hyrax, whilst in the communal land the opposite occurred.

In the national park hyraxes accounted for 97.3% of prey items collected (N = 298). In commercial farmland they accounted for 92.2% (N = 166), while in the communal land hyraxes comprised 86.1% (N = 216). These figures suggest that Black Eagles in the Matobo Hills vary their diet slightly according to the location of their territories.

Hyrax census

There has been an increase of Hyraxes in the national park, as revealed by the post-birth counts of hyraxes since the start of the project (Table 4). Four (1995-1998) censuses at the 20 sampling sites (sample area = 402 hectares) in the national park gave an average of 978 hyraxes/census (range 502 - 1333), giving an average density of 2.4 hyraxes/ha (Table 4). The average density in the commercial farmland was 0.9 hyraxes/ha (sample area = 254 hectares), compared with 0.4 hyraxes/ha on communal land (sample area = 325 hectares). By contrast, decreases were recorded in the commercial farmland (by 35%) and in the communal land (by 6%)!

More Yellow-spotted Hyraxes than Rock Hyraxes were counted in the national park, whilst the ratio was the opposite outside the protected area.

Table 4. Counts of hyrax (both species combined) carried out at sampling sites in the three land-use areas in the Matobo Hills during April/May of each year.

Year	Land-use	(No. sites)	Adult	Sub ad.	Juv.	Pups		Rainfall (mm)
1995	NP	(20)	329	17	20	140	506	512
1996	NP	(20)	509	84	75	99	767	807
1997	NP	(20)	802	140	135	227	1304	569
	CFL	(4)		148	32	32	64	276
	CL	(4)		83	16	14	33	146
1998	NP	(20)	781	168	147	237	1333	482
	CFL	(4)		111	15	20	33	179
	CL	(4)		76	14	14	34	138

Poaching

There were 53 reported cases of poaching activities both inside and outside the Matobo National Park (Table 5). Most of the poachers apprehended inside the national park came from distant locations, including outside the Matobo District. These poachers killed animals through snaring around established bases. Those who were caught poaching outside the national park came from the local area. This group of people used a number of hunting methods which included group hunting with the use of dogs, spears and snares.

The most commonly poached animals in the hills were the hyraxes, which are more abundant than any other mammal. Almost every poacher had either hyrax-size snares, hyrax carcasses or hyrax skins. Table 5 also shows that more poaching activities took place during 1996 and 1997. This was likely due to the fact that armed patrols by police and army were withdrawn from anti-poaching activities in the park in 1995, and also perhaps due to the increase of hyrax in the hills (Table 4). A total of 40 hyrax skins, three hyrax carcasses, and two Bush Buck *Tragelaphus scriptus* skins were confiscated from poachers at their hideout inside the national park in June 1997. Other animals poached in the hills were antelopes.

Table 5. Poaching activities in the Matobo Hills (January 1995 - April 1998)
(Sources: Matobo National Park monthly reports & pers. obs).

Year	Poaching Reports	Poached Animals Hyrax	Other	Snares	People Convicted	Maximum Penalty
1995	8	7	7	93	8	Not spelt out.
(ZRP Support Unit pull out of the national park)[1]						
1996	13	6	5	133	10	12 months jail or $1500 fine
(Squatters illegally resettle themselves inside the national park. Later evicted through High Court's orders)						
1997	30	117	12	305	23	80 days jail with labour
1998	2	10	-	65	1	$200
(Squatters resettle themselves briefly before they were evicted once again through the High Court's orders)						
Totals	**53**	**140**	**24**	**596**	**42**	

[1] The Zimbabwe Republic Police ZRP Support Unit and the Zimbabwe National Army had been carrying out anti-poaching patrols (protecting Black *Diceros bicornis* and White *Ceratotherium simus* Rhinos) together with national parks scouts inside the Matobo National Park.

All of the poachers apprehended inside the national park were handed over to the Matobo Police Station where they were sentenced by the magistrate after appearing in the court. The maximum penalty for all the offenders was 12 months in jail (with labour), while the maximum fine was Z$1500,00 (US$50.00). Of all the poachers arrested in the hills, five were released by the magistrate, because of being juveniles (<17 years of age; four) or too old (>70 years old; one).

Squatters from Bulawayo were evicted from the Matobo National Park in September 1996, by way of a High Court order. When they re-invaded the park in March 1998 they were evicted once again, but the High Court fined the leader only Z$200,00.

Conservation Education

This programme started with 15 schools in 1995 (Table 6) and increased to 23 schools (18 primary and five secondary) in 1997, still the current membership. Each of these schools has now got a Wildlife Club, formed under this project. An important activity was an overnight camping trip for students into the Matobo National Park in 1996. However, financial constraints limited it to one educational trip per school, involving 16 schools (12 primary and 4 secondary), and four schools were combined for each trip. Each school was represented by six students and a teacher, with the exception of two schools that brought extra persons. Transport, food and camping facilities were organised and paid for from funds provided by non-governmental organizations (NGOs) and individuals.

Over 500 elderly people and 26 n'angas (traditional healers) were talked to on the relationship between Black Eagles, hyraxes and people . Stories were collected from some of the elders and n'angas on the traditional medicinal use (healing powers), superstitions and beliefs concerning some birds. A Fact Sheet (in English and Ndebele - the local language) on the relationship between Black Eagles, hyraxes and people was distributed to schools and the local community. Positive feedback included assistance from some locals in the location of raptor nests.

Table 6. Schools in the study area that are under the project's wildlife conservation education programme. C = children; T = teachers.

School name	1995 C	1996 T	per (C+T) Clubs	1997 field trip	(C+T)	Club members
Primary						
Bazha	605	15	18	7	-	21
Dopi	-	-	-	-	(342)	18
Dula	-	-	-	-	(296)	24
Fort Usher	356	11	13	7	-	23
Fumugwe	-	-	(384)	7	-	18
Gwandavale	260	6	9	7	-	19
Halale	-	-	(377)	-	-	22
Lukadzi	-	-	-	-	(281)	27
Lushumbe	156	5	14	7	-	18
Matobo Mission	-	-	(667)	-	-	38
Mazhayimbe	351	10	18	7	-	17
Nduna	178	5	13	7	-	26
Njelele	291	8	20	7	-	22
Nyumbane	396	12	18	7	-	21
Silobi	-	-	-	-	(318)	19
Silozwe	635	17	21	7	-	27
Tohwe	333	9	21	7	-	26
Whitewaters	456	12	17	8	-	14
Secondary						
Bazha	350	14	20	7	-	23
Matobo Mission	-	-	(877)	-	-	43
Silozwe	203	8	18	7	-	20
Tohwe	268	11	17	9	-	16
Whitewaters	302	12	16	7	-	19
Totals	**5140**	**155**	**2558**	**115**	**1237**	**521)**

DISCUSSION

Several factors have probably contributed towards the decline of both the Black Eagle and hyrax populations in the Matobo Hills since the late 1970s. These include a series of droughts from the early 1980s and rapid human population growth that resulted in excessive pressure on natural resources. People are destroying their habitat through extensive crop cultivation, indiscriminate cutting down of trees (for building houses and fencing, and for fuel), and overgrazing by domestic animals. By contrast commercial farmlands are characterized by controlled cattle grazing, few working people, little poaching of wild animals, and consequently relatively intact habitats.

A possible reason for the difference in hyrax populations between the communal land and the commercial farmland was perhaps due to the greater adaptability by the bigger Rock Hyrax compared to the Yellow-spotted Hyrax, which is predominantly a browser. The Rock Hyrax is a grazer but it browses heavily during the dry season when the nutritional value of grass is low (Barry 1993).

The main aim of this project is to protect the Black Eagle by protecting its food (hyraxes) and its habitats. The key problem is human population pressure. People are competing with the Black Eagle for hyraxes. While these people do not make any direct use of Black Eagles, they certainly eat hyraxes as a source of protein and also make karosses (blankets and mats) out of their skins. A double-bed kaross contains a minimum of 40 skins, while a hyrax colony consists of only 15 to 20 hyraxes. The local people told me that karosses last for more than 15 years. The way the hyraxes are hunted is well described by Walker (1989).

Five taxidermy companies visited around Bulawayo City said the current local market value of a kaross (average 40 skins) is Z$2000,00. Foreigners' prices are three times the local value. A fully mounted hyrax costs Z$1360,00 to a local buyer while it costs Z$6000,00 to a foreigner. Black market values for the karosses are most likely a lot higher. These are all incentives for poachers, who also appear to be able to get into the Matobo National Park without the fear of arrest or getting killed by armed patrolling game scouts. Furthermore, when offenders are captured and charged, penalties are mild while some are even released without conviction in court.

The education of rural communities, especially in communal lands, is particularly important as all the unique ecosystems in the national parks are at the mercy of the land use practices around them. Education from an early age helps to achieve effective wildlife conservation, and the best method should be through the school child.

However, the lack of effective strategy is the biggest problem in this context, while policy makers rarely establish supportive policies on whatever they initiate. For example, staff from the Department of National Parks did a reconnaissance patrol in 1978 to assess the deteriorating relationship between the Matobo National Park and surrounding communal people. They recommended the urgent need for an experienced researcher to undertake a sociological project in the national park and the surrounding communal land and commercial farmland, and for an African interpretative officer to start public awareness on wildlife conservation. The report that was submitted to the Parks and Wild Life Board (Ashton 1981) had sound recommendations which were partly fulfilled, while the public relations officer worked for a very short period before he was given a new job.

Socializing with people of all age groups, including the traditional leaders (chief and headmen), n'angas, and school children in the Matobo Hills helped them in getting confidence in me. They later became free to talk to me about their traditional way of living and their social problems that are related to wildlife. The local community even helped me in locating a number of raptor nests within the study area.

None of the schools under this project's educational programme had ever been visited by an education (interpretative) officer from the Department of National Parks, while the children themselves had never visited the Matobo National Park! This reflects the lack of appropriate inputs by policy makers.

Wildlife is a key resource in Zimbabwe and this project is also trying to promote conservation awareness among rural communities. Although there are many wildlife education officers in Zimbabwe (working for example through the Wildlife Society) who are willing to carry out this kind of work, funding is limited. It is hoped that through the participation of government and NGOs, more emphasis will be placed on programmes for wildlife conservation education. Changing people's attitudes towards wildlife conservation is an uphill task that cannot easily be measured over a short time, particularly in the Matobo Hills. Here the view of the Matobo National Park is deeply interwoven with strong cultural influences and traditional beliefs, and even verges towards antagonism.

ACKNOWLEDGEMENTS

I wish to thank P.J. Mundy, Tom and Olive Aumann, Valerie Gargett and George Banfield for helping me to initiate and pursue this project; staff of Matobo National Park; the Black Eagle Survey team; the Raptor Research Group; and W. and V. Goodwin for their assistance with data collection and friendship. The following people are thanked for providing some wildlife literature that was later given to schools - the late Dr H. Ashton, Mr R. Chenaux-Repond, J. Dale, Mr B. Elliot, Mrs P. Feather, Mrs P. Habgood, Martha Heath, Sandy McAdams, Mrs P.F. O'Neill, and D. Solomon. Jack Amonie and Douglas Kabale assisted with the hyrax census. P.J. Mundy provided professional advice and guidance throughout.

I thank the following major sponsors : Eagle Insurance, SAVE Foundation (South Australia), Matobo Conservation Society, Ornithological Association of Zimbabwe (Mashonaland and

Matabeleland Branches), Wildlife Society of Zimbabwe (Matabeleland Branch), and the Matabeleland Schools' Exploration Society. Wilderness Safaris and the Raptor Conservation Group are thanked for sponsoring my attendance at the 5th World Conference.

R. Hartley, P.J. Mundy and R. Watson are sincerely thanked for their comments and advice on previous versions of the paper.

REFERENCES

ASHTON, E.H. 1981. The Matopos socio-historical survey. Report to the Rhodes Matopos Committee and Parks and Wild Life Board.
BANFIELD, G.E.A. 1996. Black Eagle breeding report: Matobo National Park – 1995. *Honeyguide* 42: 57-58.
BANFIELD, G.E.A. 1997. Black Eagle breeding report: Matobo National Park – 1996. *Honeyguide* 43: 63-64.
BANFIELD, G.E.A. 1998. Black Eagle breeding report: Matobo National Park – 1997. *Honeyguide* 44: 50-51.
BARRY, R.E. 1993. Hyraxes of the Matobo National Park. *Zimbabwe Science News* 27 55-57.
GARGETT, V. 1990. *The Black Eagle: a study.* Johannesburg : Acorn Books and Russel Friedman Books.
GARGETT, V. & E. GARGETT 1993a. Hard times for the Black Eagles. *Honeyguide* 39: 7-15.
GARGETT, V. & E. GARGETT 1993b. Another look at the Black Eagles of the Matobo National Park. *Zimbabwe Science News* 27: 51-54.
MACLEAN, G.L. 1993. *Roberts' birds of Southern Africa.* John Voelcker Bird Book Fund, Cape Town, South Africa.
SKINNER, J. & R.H.N. SMITHERS 1990. The mammals of the Southern African sub-region. Pretoria: University of Pretoria.
WALKER, N. 1989. Dassie-hunters of the Matobo Hills. *Zimbabwe Wildlife* 6:23-29.

Ngoni Chiweshe
Department of National Parks
P.O. Box 2283
Bulawayo
Zimbabwe

The Black Eagle Radio Telemetry Project in the Matobo Hills, Zimbabwe

W. J. Goodwin

ABSTRACT

In 1995 a radio telemetry project was started to establish movements of juvenile Black Eagles, once they leave their natal territories. Nine transmitters were fitted to the backs of nestlings aged between 59 and 85 days. Tracking from a motor vehicle and Cessna 150 Reims aircraft had limited success. Problems included radio failure, sourcing of a suitable aircraft, and limited range of transmitters ($10km^{2)}$) in the hilly terrain, notwithstanding some successes in 1997 and 1998 with juveniles being followed through 'empty' areas and along the river valleys. It is concluded that satellite telemetry would prove a much more efficient method to achieve the aims of this study.

INTRODUCTION

Over the past 34 years Black Eagles of the Matobo Hills have been studied by members of the Black Eagle Survey team, made up mainly of amateur raptor enthusiasts. This is probably the longest ongoing study of any raptor species to date. Although much has been learned about this population, many questions remain unanswered. Over the past two decades dramatic declines in the number of breeding pairs of Black Eagle *Aquila verreauxii* (by 41%; (Gargett & Gargett 1993a; Goodwin 1997)) and the populations of hyrax (possibly 80%; Barry & Barry 1996)were noticed in the Matobo Hills. Between 1975 and 1977 there were 61 pairs of Black Eagles in the survey area which mainly includes protected areas and commercial farmland. There were only 35 occupied territories in 1997 (Banfield 1998) and 36 in 1998 (W. Goodwin unpubl.). In 1998 in the unprotected and increasingly depleted communal lands nearby only 12 of a total of 33 territories are still occupied (N. Chiweshe unpubl.). During the peak in the 1970's nowhere else were large eagles known to breed in such a density, with an average territory size of 10.3 km^2 (Gargett 1990).

An indication of a recruitment problem was highlighted in 1992 (Gargett & Gargett 1993b) when a single bird held a territory for almost nine months before attracting a replacement. In the 1970's this would have taken a few weeks or even days (Gargett & Gargett 1993). It seems therefore, that the recruitment problem is indicative of an apparent shortage of available unpaired adult birds (known as "floaters"). These birds are either moving further afield and not returning, or mortalities are occurring in excess of the normal mortality rate for immature birds produced per year, thereby leaving fewer birds for recruitment into the adult breeding population. This question, however, requires further investigation as almost nothing is known about mortality of Black Eagles and movements. (Gargett 1990).

As a result of the obvious decline in both Black Eagle and hyrax (dassie) populations, two new studies were initiated: 1) in 1992 a hyrax census in and around the study area (Barry & Barry 1996) and, 2) in 1995 the Black Eagle radio telemetry project which is described in this paper.

Figure 1. A comparison of Black Eagle nest sites in the survey area showing the decline in the number of occupied territories (Gargett 1990, Banfield 1997, W. Goodwin pers. obs.).

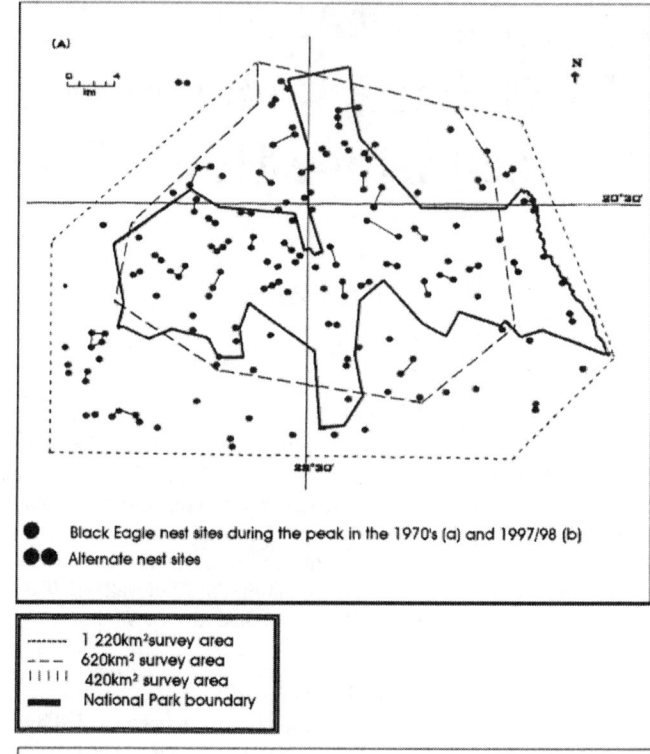

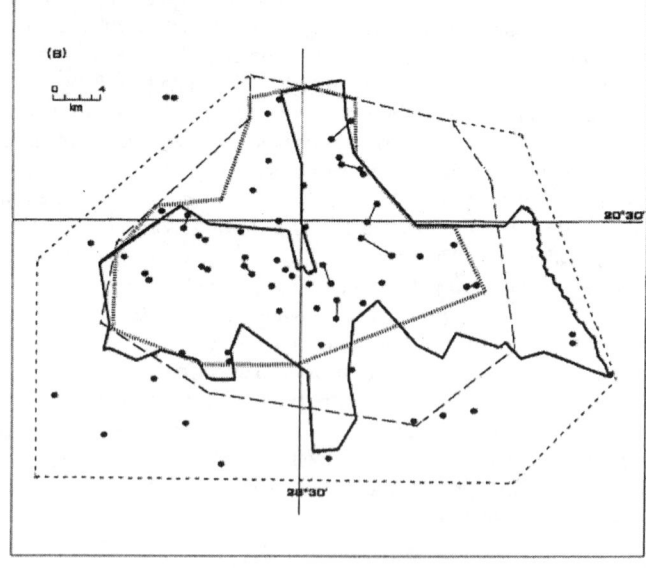

STUDY AREA

The Matobo hills are situated in Matabeleland in south- western Zimbabwe (Figure 1). The Hills are derived from an exposed granite batholith that covers 3 100 km_. This study encompasses an area from Mangwe Pass in the west, to Umzingwane Dam in the east, an area approximately 100km long by 30km wide (Figure 2). It includes the Black Eagle Survey areas of Gargett and Banfield, 1965 - 1997 (see Gargett 1990). Three land-use categories influence the quantity of the habitat: National Park is protected area with intact habitats; Commercial Farmland is used mainly for cattle grazing and is sparsely populated with some intact habitats, while Communal Land is heavily populated by peasant farmers which has resulted in widespread habitat modification inducing degradation. The average annual rainfall is about 600mm, but it is unreliable (1963-1984 = 595mm and 1985- 1997 = 547mm; Department of Meteorological Services *in litt.*).

Figure 2. Position of study area and distribution of Black Eagles in Zimbabwe in relation to the granite shield.

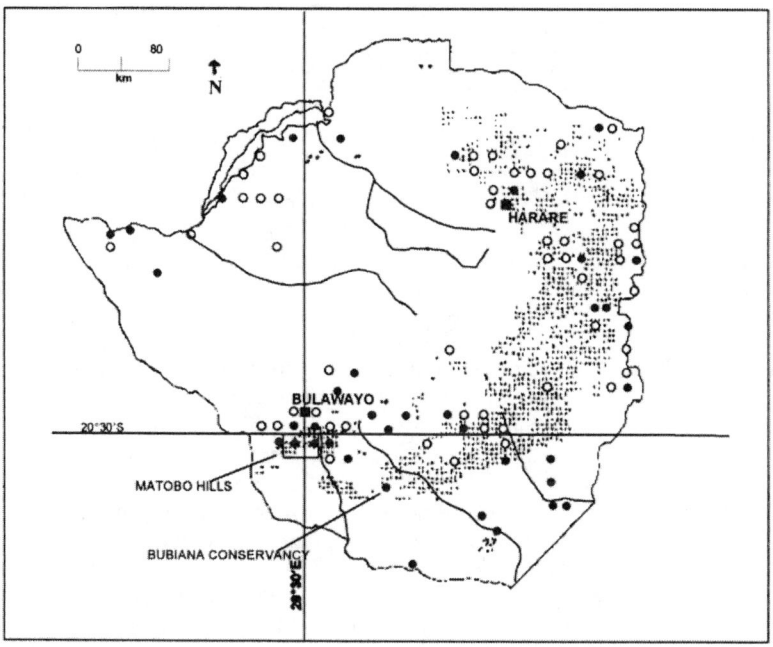

Key
- ● Black Eagle nest sites [1] (after Gargett 1990; Hartley & Smith 1995; Goodwin unpubl.)
- ○ Black Eagle sightings [1]
- ▒▒▒ On Granite Shield Domed Inselberg terrain (after Whitlow 1980)
- ☐ Study Area

[1] one or more according to quarter-degree squares

Figure 3. The Survey Area, indicating nest sites in 1995-1998, location of juvenile Black Eagles, rivers and land use categories.

METHODS

In September of the three years 1995 -1997 nine radio transmitters were attached by means of harnesses to the backs of Black Eagle nestlings between the ages of 59 and 85 days. Despite the risk of the eaglets leaving the nest prematurely, it was necessary to fit transmitters at this stage in order that the harnesses could be properly adjusted. Subject nests were selected from a cross-section of the area in order to obtain representative results. Nests also had to be easily accessible as they are on cliffs. In each instance ropes were used and eaglets were lowered to the ground in a bag.

During the second half of September 1995 radio transmitters were fitted to eaglets from four nests within the survey area. All four transmitters were fitted using a harness design adapted from that used on Cape Griffons *Gyps coprotheres* in the Cape Province (Boshoff *et al.* 1983). This harness design was first tested on a captive adult (female) Black Eagle at Larvon Bird Gardens (T. Couto pers. comm.) and adjusted accordingly. A weak link of cotton tape was used. Transmitters were AVM (California) module P2 type with a lithium battery having a current drain of 0.220 - 0.230 MA. The weight of the transmitter was 30g and had a theoretical life of around 15 months, with a range of ±50km (line of sight). Transmitters operated between 148 and 150 MHz. All transmitters were checked for operation a week before fitting and the magnets replaced. Each transmitter was again checked when fitted and all appeared to be working normally. In addition, all eaglets were ringed, weighed and examined.

Transmitters were also sourced from Merlin (Idaho). These were of a more robust design and operated between 146.47 and 146.800 MHz, having a mass of 40g, and an aerial length of 252mm. They measured 27mm x 67mm and were supplied with a teflon harness. These harnesses were fitted and then sewn with a light crochet cotton in order to facilitate a weak link as required. As these transmitters were received late in the 1996 season, only two were fitted, the remainder being fitted in 1997. Again, all transmitters were checked before fitting. However, the three that were stored for a year were periodically run for a few hours in order to allow current to flow between the battery and the transmitter, which inhibits the build-up of battery corrosion. These eaglets were checked once weekly whilst still in the nest area, and a visual record, as well as the signal, was obtained where possible.

Tracking was effected by the use of a Yagi FT-290 RII All Mode Transceiver. The various frequencies were selected manually but changed every few minutes which proved difficult. Initial tracking was done using a bulky hand-held Yagi-type antenna making use of high vantage points. A suitable aircraft was not available during 1995 and 1996. A hoop aerial was devised (Kiel Electronics, Bulawayo) for use from within the cockpit of a light aircraft, as well as from a motor vehicle. This aerial was used mainly from a motor vehicle. Towards the end of 1997, three flights were made over the Matobo Hills in a Cessna 150 Reims (130 hp) aircraft and the hoop aerial was used inside the cockpit and held out of the window. On testing over a control transmitter it was effective only when directly above the signal. Consequently "bunny ear" type aerials (Kiel Electronics, Bulawayo) were mounted over each wing strut, and were connected to the transceiver (in the cockpit) through a directional switch, to alternate receiving and give some degree of direction-finding capability. Two test flights (1997) over a fitted nestling yielded a receiving capacity of approximately 10km^2 at a height of 630m above ground. Furthermore a fairly accurate position could be obtained by monitoring signal strength whilst circling the area. All flights made in 1997 lasted about 2_ hours (1_ hours over the Matobo Hills), covering a separate section on each occasion. It was also decided to evaluate all data provided by Gargett (1990), concentrating initially on "empty areas" (where no resident pairs of Black Eagles occur) and areas to the south and west of the source of two out of five ringing recoveries.

RESULTS

Due to the early failure of the AVM transmitters, no tracking took place in 1995. One eaglet was subsequently found dead below its nest in 1996. However, this bird had a strong odour and appeared to be suffering from diarrhoea when radio-tagged in 1995. It was of interest to note that the cotton tape "weak link" had degraded and broken, possibly accelerated by the decomposition of the bird.

Merlin transmitters fitted in 1996 and 1997 operated well and the harnesses did not appear to inhibit flight or movement in any way. Both tagged juveniles in 1996 were radio-fixed only once (from a motor vehicle) after leaving their respective natal areas. The juvenile from nest 111 was flying 2km south-west of its nest on 23 February 1997, having last been located in the vicinity of the nest 35 days previously, when it was mobbed by the parent birds. The other juvenile from nest 53 was located (the same day) flying in an empty area 8.5km south-south-east of its nest. It was previously located 2km south-east of the nest 73 days earlier. It had started to move away from the nest a week or so earlier.

Table 1. Successful field trips undertaken in order to track juvenile Black Eagles after leaving the nest area.

Date Fixed	Mode Of Transport	Nest No. Of Juvenile	Distance And Direction From Nest	Time Lapsed Between Locations
23.02.1997	Motor Vehicle	111	±2km south-west	35 days
23.02.1997	Motor Vehicle	53	±8.5km south-south-east	73 days
31.03.1998	Aircraft	111	±5km north-east	87 days
03.01.1998	Motor Vehicle	29	±1.5km south-east	10 days
17.01.1998	Aircraft	29	±2km south-east	14 days
21.02.1998	Aircraft	29	±2km south-east	35 days
17.01.1998	Aircraft	86	±2.5km north-west	14 days
20.06.1998	Aircraft	86	±17km south-east	154 days

All three birds monitored during 1998 were located on a number of occasions. The juvenile from nest 29 was located from the air 2km south-east on 17 January 1998 after being last monitored 1.5km to the south-east on 3 January 1998, 14 days earlier. It appeared to be following the river valley between the hills using it as a "corridor". The juvenile from nest 86 was located in the nest area and in an "empty" area at the head of the Mtshelele valley ±2.5km north-west of its nest on 17 January, 89 days after its estimated first flight. It was located again 154 days later (20 June 1998) in the Khumalo Communal Land 17.5km south-south-east of the nest at the end of an open grassy corridor. The juvenile from nest 111 moved away from the nest area suddenly by 3 January 1998, it was seen in the nest area the previous week also ±80 days after first flight. It did not linger in the natal territory as the other two. It was found from the air in an empty area 5km north-east of its nest and north-east of the same grassy corridor as the juvenile from nest 86 on 31 March/1998, 87 days later ±130 days after first flight.

DISCUSSION

Radio telemetry, although more advanced than the previous methods (ringing, window marking, colour marking, colour flagging and patagial tagging (Gargett 1990) used in the Matobo hills, proved to be more difficult than expected and achieved little more than these earlier methods apart from more accurately ascertaining the dispersal dates. As this is the first time that this method has been attempted on wild birds in Zimbabwe, some useful lessons were learned. Transmitters that were received in 1995 all failed, due to having been stored for too long a period without being run (transmitters must be run periodically for a number of hours in order that corrosion does not build up between the battery and transmitter). This failure has occurred with AVM transmitters supplied to other users (G. Rasmussen pers. comm.). The limited range of transmitters in hilly terrain proved a major handicap for ground tracking. Availability and sourcing of a suitable aircraft, development of a suitable antenna, and a pilot willing to carry out regular flights also proved problematic. Together with the huge area to be covered, 2_ hours flying time over the Matobo hills achieved only 30% coverage. As this project was carried out by amateurs, tracking was confined to weekends only. Consequently the area was neither adequately nor systematically covered, so that results were random. In addition after 1996, extra funds had to be sourced in order to cover entrance fees to the National Park when tracking from a vehicle. Previously fees were waived for survey members.

The "corridor" theory was explored by Ferrer and Harte (1997) whilst tracking the movements of juvenile Spanish Imperial Eagles *Aquila adalberti*. In the Matobo hills immature Black Eagles were channelled via empty areas and river valleys mainly to the south, west, south-west and south-east (Figure 2) as there is little suitable habitat to the north of the area.

It also appears that, for the most part, juvenile Black Eagles do not initially wander far (Figure 2), but move in and out of the area for some time (and are harried by resident pairs) before moving further afield. The decline in resident pairs may have benefited juveniles as there is more space within the protected area, increasing their chances of survival. Recent re-occupancy (pers. obs.) of two territories within the Black Eagle breeding survey may be as a result of this.

The subject of juvenile Black Eagle mortality and movements requires further investigation in order to adequately track these birds. Satellite telemetry, although expensive, should prove to be the most successful method, as it can provide a continuous record of the movements of juvenile Black Eagles for a longer period, with much less time and manpower required than the methods used in this study. The Matobo hills cannot be viewed as an "island" but as part of a "network" of the population of this species, which occurs throughout Zimbabwe. The state of the Black Eagle is an important barometer of the well-being of the area in which it lives, and there is need to understand the movements of immature birds and possible hazards that they are subject to before they reach adulthood.

ACKNOWLEDGEMENTS

My attendance at the symposium was made possible by the Raptor Research Group, Wilderness Safaris, Russel Friedman, and the Raptor Conservation Group (RCG), RCG has assisted both with funding and the loan of equipment used for radio tracking. Eagle Insurance (Zimbabwe), Barclay's Bank (Zimbabwe), Columbus Zoo (Ohio) and the Ornithological Association of Zimbabwe provided funding for the project. The following assisted the project: P. Mundy, R. Hartley, V. Gargett, V. Goodwin, G. Banfield, N. Chiweshe, D. Beere, V. Tarr, P. Ditchburn, B. Davison and members of the Raptor Research Group and Black Eagle Survey team. I thank all of these organisations and individuals.

REFERENCES

BANFIELD, G.E.A. 1998. Black Eagle Breeding report, Matobo National Park 1997. *Honeyguide* 44: 50-51.
BARRY, R.E. & L.M. BARRY 1996. Species composition and age structure of remains of hyraxes (Hyracoidae: procaviidae) at nests of Black Eagle. *J. of Mammology* 77 (3): 702-707.
BOSHOFF, A.F., A.S. ROBERTSON & D. M. NORTON 1984. A radio tracking study on an adult Cape Griffon vulture-*Gyps coprotheres* -in the south-western Cape province. *SA Journal of Wildlife Research* 14 (3): 73-78.
FERRER, M. & M. HARTE 1997. Habitat selection by immature Spanish Imperial Eagles during the dispersal period. *Journal of Applied Ecology* 34: 1359-1364.
GARGETT, V., 1990. *The Black Eagle :A Study* Acorn Books and Russel Friedman Books, Randburg and Halfway House.
GARGETT, V. & E. GARGETT 1993a. Another look at the Black Eagles of the Matobo National Park. *Zimbabwe Sc. News* 27: 51- 54.
GARGETT, V. & E. GARGETT 1993b. Better times for the Matobo Black Eagles. *Honeyguide* 39:172-181.
GOODWIN, W. J., 1997, New Raptor Projects underway in the Matobo Hills. *Skyhost* 4 (5) : 44-45.
HARTLEY, R.R. & J.N. SMITH 1995. Eagles hunting in the Batoka Gorges, Zimbabwe. *J. African Rapt. Biology* 10: 30-32.
WHITLOW, J. R., 1980. Land Use, Population Pressure and Rock Outcrops in the Tribal Areas of Zimbabwe. *Zimbabwe/Rhodesia Agricultural Journal* 77: 3-11.

W. J. Goodwin
Black Eagle Survey
PO Box AC 592
Ascot
Bulawayo
Zimbabwe

Chancellor, R. D. & B.-U. Meyburg eds. 2000
Raptors at Risk
WWGBP / Hancock House

Evaluating the Long-term Effectiveness of Conservation Practices in Montagu's Harrier *Circus pygargus*

Beatriz Arroyo and Vincent Bretagnolle

INTRODUCTION

Evaluation of the efficacy of conservation measures is necessary at least in order to optimise the use of limited resources, such as money and/or people. However, success of conservation practices is often measured in terms of effort (number of nests saved, number of contracts attained, etc.), rather than in terms of the effect of these practices on the species' population dynamics.

The Montagu's Harrier (*Circus pygargus*) is a Palearctic raptor which breeds all across Europe (Cramp & Simmons 1980, Del Hoyo *et al.* 1994), but numbers are only significant in the Iberian Peninsula, France, and Russia. Spain and France hold around 8000 breeding pairs (Yeatman & Jarry 1994, SEO/BirdLife 1997), 80% of the European population excluding Russia. At a European level, the Montagu's Harrier is included in conservation category SPEC 4 (species with a favourable conservation status but concentrated in Europe, Tucker & Heath 1994). However, in Spain and France the Montagu's Harrier is considered as vulnerable (Blanco & González 1992, Salamolard *et al.* in press).

Montagu's Harriers nest on the ground in natural or semi-natural habitats (including marshes, meadows, grasslands, reedbeds, young conifer plantations, heaths or wastelands) and agricultural habitats (cereal fields, cornfields or hayfields). The use of crops for nesting is relatively recent in many parts of the breeding range (Elliot 1988, Clemens 1993, Krogulec 1993), but is increasing due to the decreasing availability of natural habitats. The proportion of birds nesting in agricultural habitats is relatively low (<20%) in eastern Europe (Flint *et al.* 1984, Ivanovski 1993, Krogulec 1993), but increases westwards, and in France and the Iberian Peninsula, the proportion of birds nesting in natural habitats is 20% or perhaps less (Ferrero 1995, Salamolard *et al.* in press). The use of crops for breeding makes Montagu's Harrier nests susceptible to failure due to harvesting activities, if these occur before the nestlings have fledged. Nestling deaths due to harvesting are often believed to contribute significantly to harrier decline in agricultural habitats (Berthemy *et al.* 1983, Palma 1985, Martelli 1987, Leroux 1987, Pomarol 1994). Nestling mortality due to this factor has been quoted to be very high (70-100%) in some areas (Pérez Chiscano & Fernández Cruz 1971, Berthemy *et al.* 1983, Martelli 1987, Pandolfi & Pino d'Astore 1990, Corbacho *et al.* 1997), although quantitative estimates of the impact of harvesting in a given area over several years are much scarcer (Arroyo *et*

403

al. 1995, Castaño 1995, see below). Harvesting problems have nevertheless mobilised conservationists for a long time and throughout the breeding range of the species (Salamolard et al. in press). An evaluation of the efficacy of this measure to assure the persistence of the populations is lacking, as well as any indication of how such an effort could be optimised. Therefore, the aim of this study is, with the combination of both empirical data and simulation methods, to provide some preliminary results on the evaluation of conservation measures on Montagu's Harrier population persistence, and develop ideas for future work in this direction.

METHODS

We have monitored Montagu's Harriers for 4-11 years in four different study areas. Three of them are located in western France: (i) Marais de Rochefort (45°E 57'N, 0°E 55' W, Charente-Maritime district), monitored since 1988; (ii) south of Deux Sèvres (46°E 11' N, 0°E 28' W, Poitou-Charente Region), with data available from 1994, and (iii) Baie de l'Aiguillon (46°E 24' N, 1°E 24' W, Département de la Vendée), with data collected from 1995. The fourth study area is placed northeast of Madrid, Spain (40°E 38' N, 3°E 30' W), and has been monitored since 1991. These four study sites each cover between 20,000 and 34,000 ha. All nests are located each year in each area, and are visited regularly to collect data on breeding parameters (success, timing, etc.). A wing-tagging programme of nestlings and adults has been carried out in these areas for several years, which provided data on juvenile and adult dispersal, and adult survival estimates (Leroux & Bretagnolle, in prep.).

Demographic parameters (breeding rates, age of first breeding, adult and juvenile survival) were used to model population dynamics using Vortex 7.0, a stochastic simulation programme (Lacy et al. 1995). Simulations were run for 100 years, and we performed 100 iterations per simulation. For the simulations, we used the following premises: no inbreeding depression, environmental variation in reproduction not correlated with environmental variation in survival, monogamy, sex ratio at hatching 0.500, age of first breeding for females at 2 years old on average, 3 years old for males (Leroux & Bretagnolle, in prep), and only juveniles migrate between populations.

RESULTS AND DISCUSSION

Impact of harvesting activities (i.e., the % of nestlings that would have died due to harvesting activities in the absence of conservation measures) varied among the four study areas (ranging from 7% to 50%, Table 1). This variation was partly due to habitat differences among areas: over 70% of

Table 1. Impact of harvesting activities on Montagu's Harrier productivity (i.e., proportion of nestlings that would die in the absence of conservation measures) in four different study areas.

Year	Madrid	Deux Sèvres	Baie de l'Aiguillon	Rochefort
1991	54	-	-	-
1992	23	-	-	10
1993	6	-	-	4
1994	26	67	-	0
1995	38	69	34	6
1996	33	37	36	6
1997	17	78	65	4
1998	2	47	46	5
AVERAGE	24%	49%	41%	7%

nests in Rochefort and 30% in Baie de l'Aiguillon were located in natural vegetation. Other factors were latitude (which influenced harrier breeding phenology) and weather differences among areas. Similarly, impact of harvesting varied among years within each area (reaching in particular years and areas up to 80%, Table 1), due to variations in both breeding and harvesting phenology, linked respectively to annual variations in food supply and weather. Considering each population as an isolated unit, population persistence in the absence of conservation measures was high only for populations where the impact of harvesting was lower than 30% (Fig. 1). This result indicates that, in the absence of any immigration from other populations, nest protection measures should be necessary in most Montagu's Harrier populations breeding in agricultural habitats, or many populations will become extinct. Not surprisingly, the percentage of affected nests that had to be protected to maintain stable populations increased according to the impact of harvesting (Fig. 1 & 2). In other words, the number of nests protected in a given area would determine maintenance of the population depending on the average percentage of nestlings that would die in the absence of conservation measures. This result highlights the importance of accurate estimates of the impact of harvesting in each area to determine the level of protection needed to assure population maintenance. Additionally, the annual variation of this parameter (Table 1) suggests that it would be necessary to get these estimates over several years.

Figure 1. Extinction probability of isolated populations of Montagu's Harrier with different levels of impact of harvesting, according to conservation effort (% of affected nests protected).

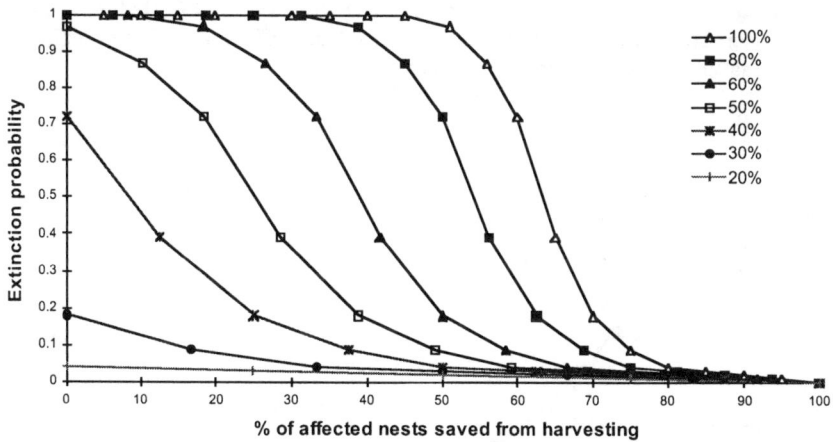

The above results apply to populations considered as isolated units. However, Montagu's Harrier populations are not isolated. Our data on nestling dispersal showed that at least 15% of juveniles disperse over 50 km from their natal site. Even without taking into account potential movements of adults among areas, our simulation analyses showed that connectivity among two populations through juvenile dispersal influenced persistence of those populations. Figure 3 shows the probability of extinction of two of our study populations in western France, one of them (Deux Sèvres) suffering a high impact of harvesting activity (Table 1), and the other one (Rochefort) breeding mainly in natural habitats, and therefore with a low impact of harvesting. Even in the absence of conservation measures in Deux Sèvres, this population could persist if 4% of the juveniles produced at Rochefort dispersed to Deux Sèvres in their first year of life (Fig. 3). Even if this is an hypothetical scenario, our results from wing-tagged birds suggest that 4% is not an unreasonable figure to describe connectivity between close (<100 km) populations.

Figure 2. Threshold levels of conservation (minimum % of nests protected) needed for population maintenance in populations with varying impact of harvesting.

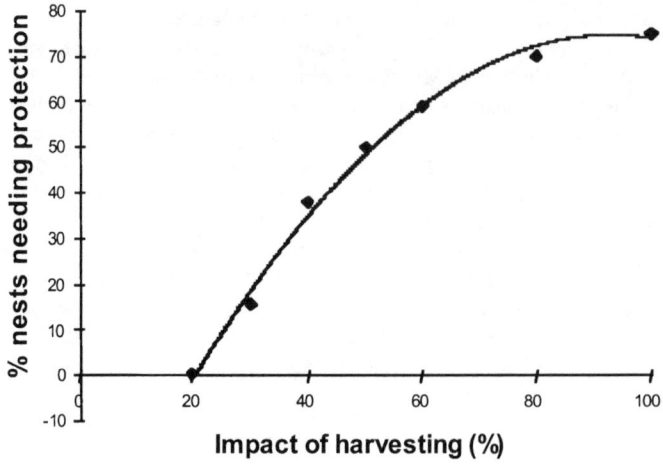

Figure 3. Probability of extinction of two study areas, Deux Sèvres and Rochefort, in the absence of conservation measures, assuming a varying degree of connectivity through juvenile dispersal from Rochefort to Deux Sèvres.

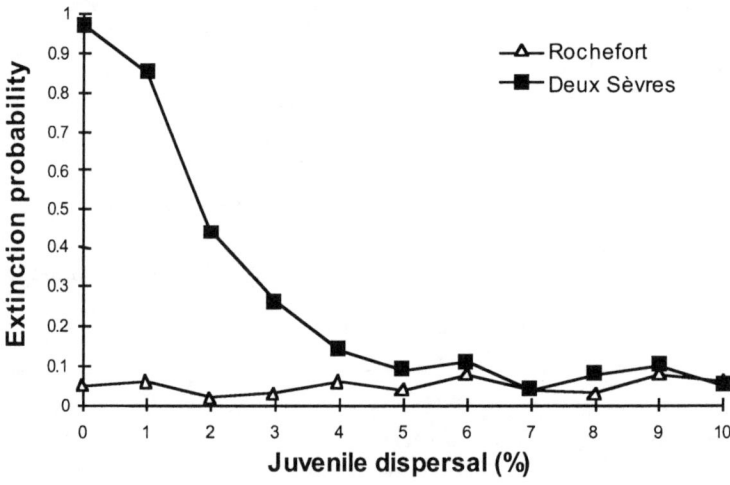

These results may have important consequences in terms of conservation of the species. First, they highlight the importance of protecting populations which are naturally productive, given that they may also have an impact on persistence of surrounding populations. Therefore, it is critical to collect accurate data with regard to the size and distribution of natural vegetation populations throughout the breeding range of the species, but especially in the core areas. Similarly, it seems urgent to evaluate the impact of the decline in habitat availability as compared to that of harvesting activities. This is particularly critical when considering that most conservation measures for the species have been based on protection of nests during harvesting activities, and that most natural vegetation populations are unprotected. Second, our preliminary results also suggest that, when working in agricultural habitats, it is more efficient to concentrate conservation effort in a given area, making sure that most nests are saved there, rather than working less intensively in larger areas, although more detailed analyses are needed to confirm this. Third, these results point out that the problem of Montagu's Harrier conservation should be addressed at the appropriate spatial scale, working regionally rather than locally. Finally, these results show the need to gather more information and understanding on patterns and ultimate causes of dispersal in the Montagu's Harrier, to assess population structure at different levels.

ACKNOWLEDGEMENTS

Many people helped with data collection, especially finding nests: A. Amar, R. Bernard, C. Bouchet, L. Courmont, T. DeCornullier, T. Dieuleveut, M.-H. Froger, T. García, A. Leroux, L. Palomares, C. Pacteau, D. Pineau and M. Salamolard. Special thanks are due to Alain Leroux, who started the wing-tagging programme at Rochefort, to Txuso García, who assured its maintainance at Madrid, and to Th. Dieuleveut, for help with the simulations.

REFERENCES

ARROYO, B., L. PALOMARES & J. PINILLA 1995. Situación y problemática de los Aguiluchos cenizo (*Circus pygargus*) y pálido (*C. cyaneus*) en la Comunidad de Madrid. *Alytes* 7: 365-372
BERTHEMY, B., P. DABIN & M. TERRASSE 1983. Recensement et protection d'une espèce protégée: le busard cendré. *Le Courier de la Nature* Jan/Fev: 10-16.
BLANCO, J.C. & J.L. GONZÁLEZ (Eds) 1992. Libro Rojo de los Vertebrados de España.ICONA-M.A.P.A., Madrid
CASTAÑO, J.P. 1995. Efecto de la actividad de siega y causas de fracaso reproductivo en un población de Aguilucho cenizo *Circus pygargus* en el SE de Ciudad Real. *Ardeola*, 42: 167-172
CLEMENS, C. 1993. International Conference on Montagu's Harrier. *WWGBP Bull* 18:12
CORBACHO, C., J.M. SÁNCHEZ & A. SÁNCHEZ 1997. Breeding biology of Montagu's Harrier *Circus pygargus* L. in agricultural environments of southwest Spain; comparison with other populations in the western Palearctic. *Bird Study* 44: 166-175.
CRAMP, S. & K.E.L. SIMMONS (Eds.) 1980. The Birds of the Western Paleartic, Vol. 2. Oxford University Press, Oxford.
DEL HOYO, J., A. ELLIOT & J. SARGATAL (Eds.) 1994. Handbook of the Birds of the World. Vol 2. Lynx Edicions, Barcelona.
ELLIOT, G. 1988. Montagu's Harrier conservation. *RSPB Conserv. Rev.* 2: 20-21
FERRERO, J.J. 1995. La población ibérica de Aguilucho Cenizo *Circus pygargus*. *Alytes* 7: 539-560.
FLINT, V.E., R.L. BOEHME, Y.V. KOSTIN & A.A. KUZNETSOV 1984. A field guide to birds of the USSR. Princeton University Press, New Jersey.
IVANOVSKI, V. 1993. International Conference on Montagu's Harrier. *WWGBP Bull* 19:13
KROGULEC, J. 1993. International Conference on Montagu's Harrier. *WWGBP Bull* 18:13
LACY R.C., A.H. KIMBERLY & P.S. MILLER 1995. Vortex: A Stochastic Simulation of the Extinction Process. Version 7 User's Manual. IUCN/SSC Conservation Breeding Specialist Group, Apple Valley, MN, USA.
LEROUX, A.B.A. 1987. Recensement des busards nicheurs, *Circus aeruginosus* L. et *Circus pygargus* L. et zonage de l'espace dans les marais de l'ouest de la France. *Acta Oecol. Oecol. Applic.* 8: 387-402
MARTELLI, D. 1987. Datti sull'ecologia riproduttiva dell'albanella minore (*Circus pygargus*) in Emila-Romana. Nota preliminare. *Suppl. Ric. Biol. Selvaggina* 12: 125-137
PALMA, L. 1985. The present situation of birds of prey in Portugal. *In* I. Newton and R.D. Chancellor (Eds.), Conservation Studies of Raptors, Technical Pub. 5. International Council for Bird Preservation, Cambridge, U.K..
PANDOLFI, M. & P.R. PINO D'ASTORE 1990. Analysis of breeding behaviour in Montagu's Harrier *Circus pygargus* in a site of Central Italy. *Avocetta* 14: 97-102
PIREZ CHISCANO, J.L. & M. FERNÁNDEZ CRUZ 1971. Sobre *Grus grus* y *Circus pygargus* en Extremadura. *Ardeola* Vol esp: 509-574

POMAROL, M. 1994. Releasing Montagu's Harrier (*Circus pygargus*) by the method of hacking. *J. Raptor Res.* 28: 19-22

SALAMOLARD, M., A. LEROUX & V. BRETAGNOLLE (in press). Le Busard cendré. *In* Rocamora, G., Jarry, G. & Yeatman-Berthelot, D., (Eds.) *Les oiseaux à statut de conservation défavorable ou fragile en France. Listes rouges et priorités nationales*. S.E.O.F., Paris.

SEO/BIRDLIFE 1997. Atlas de las aves de España (1975-1995). Lynx Edicions, Barcelona, Spain.

TUCKER, G.M. & M.F. HEATH 1994. Birds in Europe: their conservation status. Birdlife International (Birdlife Conservation Series No. 3), Cambridge, UK.

YEATMAN-BERTHELOT, D. & G. JARRY 1994. Nouvel atlas des oiseaux nicheurs. S.O..F. Paris

Beatriz Arroyo and Vincent Bretagnolle
CNRS/CEBC
79360 Villiers en Bois
France

On the Demography of the Imperial Eagle *Aquila heliaca* in Kazakhstan

Evgeny A. Bragin

ABSTRACT

Although rare in most of its range, the Imperial Eagle is one of the most widespread eagles in Kazakhstan and there appear to be roughly 750-800 pairs. Its breeding distribution covers more than 60% of the country and excludes only the mountainous and northern forested regions. The population in and around the Naurzum Reserve has been studied since 1978. The location and occupancy of nesting sites have remained relatively constant. In Naurzum Reserve 86% of 336 nesting attempts were successful (1978-1997), but in surrounding areas it was approximately 40%. Within the reserve, wind is a major cause of nest failure, whereas outside it is human activity. Between 1994 and 1996 17 nestlings fitted with radio transmitters survived to dispersal. Five of the 10 eagles radio-tagged in 1994 were detected, three in 1995, two in 1996 and two in 1997.

Naurzum Reserve has four other endangered species and overall 17 species of raptors nest there. It needs International Biosphere Reserve status and support to establish a model for the sustainable population of eagles and other rare species, and to identify migration routes and plan for their protection. It is necessary to carry out in-depth research using new technology and methodology.

INTRODUCTION

The Imperial Eagle *Aquila heliaca* is one of the most widespread eagles in Kazakhstan. Its breeding distribution covers more than 60% of the country and excludes only the mountainous and northern forested regions. However, this species is very rare throughout most of its range. Breeding densities have only been determined in areas east of the Aral Sea, at 0.18 pairs/1,000 km^2 (Lobachev 1960) and in the Andasay Zakaznik (South Betpak-Dala) at 2 pairs/1,000 km^2 (Koshvar 1986).

One of the main factors limiting the breeding distribution of the Imperial Eagle is the scarcity of trees in the steppe and desert landscapes of Kazakhstan. The region south of Kostanai, where the steppe contains scattered small islands of pine forests, provides ideal conditions for the Imperial Eagle and many other predatory birds, including Saker Falcon *Falco cherrug*, Kestrel *F. tinnunculus*, Red-Footed Falcon *F. vespertinus*, Hobby *F. subbuteo*, Merlin *F. columbarius*, White-Tailed Eagle *Haliaeetus albicilla* and others.

STUDY AREA AND METHODS

The study was conducted in Naurzum Nature Reserve (877 km^2) and surrounding areas (Figure 1) from 1978-1997. In 1996-1997, additional areas were examined to establish the number of rare and endangered raptors in other forests in the Kostanai region, including an area covering more than 60,000 km², from the border of Russia to the Sary-Copa lake in the south.

The terrain of this region is flat, with the exception of slopes of the Turgai valley, and includes different steppe vegetation communities with isolated forests and salt and fresh lakes. In the north of this region, steppe landscapes contain approximately 4.3% birch woodland and mostly open country. About 60% of the region is used for cultivation of wheat . In the dry steppe landscape south of Kostanai woodland comprises only 0.3%. There are three main forested areas, which appear mainly to be pine: Kazanbasi, Amankaragai and Kuandagash. Naurzum (180 km²) and Tersek (41 km²) are pine and Sipsin (140 km²) is birch. There are also three isolated and highly fragmented forest areas in Naurzum Reserve (877 km²) which are the most southerly. About 50% of the steppe surrounding the reserve has not been ploughed and consequently Siberian Marmot *Marmota bobac* and three species of suslik (Table 1) occur. The other main landscape is wetland.

Figure 1. Geographic location of Kostanai Region, Naurzum Reserve and Imperial Eagle breeding ares in Kazakhstan.

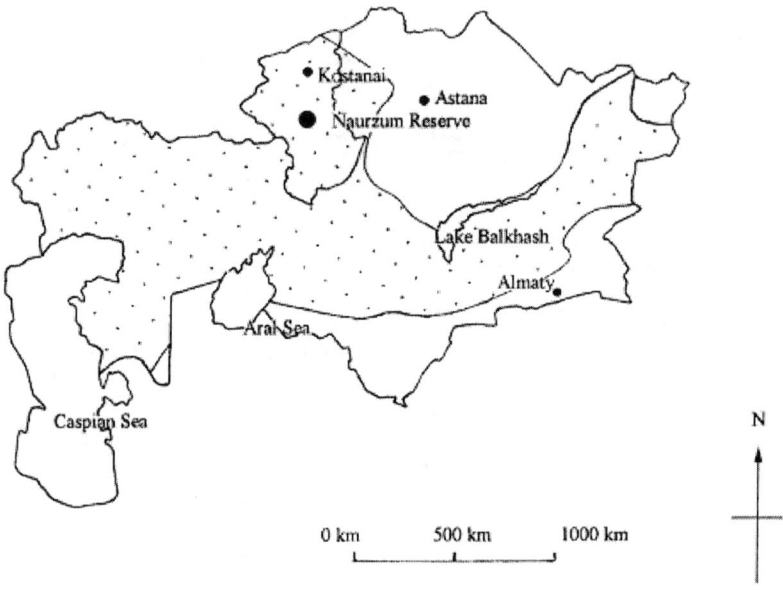

On the reserve and surrounding area, I identified nest locations and established productivity for each year 1978-1997. Prey data were collected from 1978-1985. In 1994 and 1996 17 young eagles from the reserve were marked with 5-year backpack radio-tags and were monitored to migration. In following years, attempts were made to find them returning from wintering areas. The distant nests found in 1996-97 were visited twice - after hatching and close to leaving the nest.

RESULTS AND DISCUSSION

In the Naurzum Reserve there were 40 eagle nest sites, of which 22-34 were occupied in any given year. Immature eagles were also present during the breeding season, sometimes concentrated in groups of 7-32 birds. The average ratio of immature to adult, breeding birds was 1:1.25.

The location and occupancy of nesting sites have remained relatively constant. In the 10-20 years of observation, occupancy averaged 85% (range 80-91%): 37% of nests were occupied each year; 33% were unoccupied for only 1-2 years; 15% were unoccupied 3- 4 years; and 4% were unoccupied for five or more years. The yearly average of pairs fledging young was 70% (range 67-92%) of the reserve population. Maximum duration of annual nesting in the same area was 11 years, plus an additional 6 years after a 1 year interval. However, more often the duration of continuous breeding has been 3-5 years, continued after one (sometimes two) or more years.

Some 290 (86.3%) of 336 Imperial Eagle nesting attempts were successful in the Naurzum Reserve (1978-1997), which is a very high rate. Here wind was a major cause of nest failure, whereas outside the reserve it was human activity (disturbance during incubation, including wilful destruction of eggs), reducing success to 40%. Average clutch size was 2.1 (range 1.7-2.4). The most successful nest produced an annual average of 1.8 fledged young (range 1.1-2. 2) and overall productivity was 1.5 young per active nest (range 1.1-1.8). Nesting success, measured as the proportion of fledged eaglets from eggs laid, was 77% in the reserve and 49% for the surrounding area. The mortality rate of nestlings was approximately 7%. After fledging, two young were known to have died on electric power lines.

All 17 nestlings fitted with backpack radio transmitters survived to dispersal. Between 1994 and 1997, five of the 10 eagles radio-tagged in 1994 were detected: three in 1995, two in 1996 and two in 1997. Three of the birds were detected twice: one in 1996 and 1997, and two in 1995 and 1997. Thus, the survival rate of young eagles to year 1 was at least 50% and to year 3 was at least 30%. However, none of the seven eagles radio-tagged in 1996 were detected a year later, possibly because they remained south of the Naurzum area.

The mortality of territorial eagles was estimated by indirect methods, assuming that an interval in the occupancy of a nesting site reflected the death of at least one bird from the pair. In some cases, the dead eagle was found. On this basis, a very rough estimate of adult mortality is 8-9% annually.

Monitoring the population of Imperial Eagles in the Naurzum Reserve has shown that the distribution and nesting density have not changed during the last 20-30 years. There are no complete data for the overall number of Imperial Eagles from earlier time periods. However, comparative analysis of Imperial Eagle's diet now, during 1935-1936, and during 1946-1949, 1955, 1966-1969 shows a stabilization between 1950 and 1960 (Table 1).

Table 1. Long-term changes of occurrence (%) of main prey species (or groups of species) in the diet of the Imperial Eagle in Naurzum pine forest.

PREY	1935-1936[1]		1946,1947,1955[2]		1966-69[3]		1978-1985[4]	
	RANGE	MEAN	RANGE	MEAN	RANGE	MEAN	RANGE	MEAN
Suslik[5]	13-19	15,9	7-24	18,6	22-23	27,1	34-49	45,7
Hamster *Cricetus cricetus*	2-3	2,4	7-26	13,4	1-4	2,1	0-1	0,5
Hedgehog *Erinaceus auritus*	0-15	7,4	1-3	1,5	0	0	1-2	1,3
Microtines *Microtus*	2-3	2,4	7-37	18,5	3-7	5,3	1-9	5,4
Corvidae[6]	9-15	11,8	1-10	5,9	10-25	16,1	14-30	23,5
Waterfowl[7]	7-16	11,6	2-5	3,7	17-38	29,7	17-34	22,9
Galliformes [8]	6-34	20,2	7-20	14	2-7	4,6	1-2	1.4
Little Bustard *Otus tetrax*	7-14	10,7	12-29	21,4	0	0	0-1	0,1
Owls [9]	0-2	0,9	3-15	4,7	0	0	0-1	0,1

[1]Osmolovskaja 1953; [2]Gibet 1960; [3]Solomatin 1970; [4]this study.
[5] Suslik: *Spermophillus fulvus*, *S. major*, *S. pygmeus* (before 1955 *S. pygmeus* only).
[6] Corvidae: Rook *Corvus frugilegus*, Jackdaw *C. monedula*, Carrion Crow *C. corone*, Magpie *Pica pica*.
[7] Waterfowl: ducks, coot, grebes, gulls, plovers, Heron *Ardea cinerea*
[8]Galliformes: Black Grouse *Tetrao tetrix*, Willow Grouse *Lagopus lagopus*, Grey Partridge *Perdix perdix*, Quail *Coturnix coturnix*.
[9]Owls: Long-eared Owl *Asio otus*, Marsh Owl *A. flammeus*

Before 1960, the main (>10%) kinds of prey in the diet of the Imperial Eagle changed almost every year (Table 1). After 1952 Large-toothed Suslik *Spermophilus fulvus* appeared and became widely distributed in the area until 1960, while numbers of Siberian Marmot also began to increase (Formozov 1959). Each year from 1966-1969 and 1978-1985, only three groups of prey were important (in different habitats): mammals (suslik or marmot) were the most important, followed by Corvidae (usually Rook *Corvus frugilegus*) and waterfowl. The most striking change was the increased proportion of suslik and marmot. It is possible that the distribution and population of Imperial Eagles also increased during 1950-1960. This eagle is now not so rare north of Naurzum reserve, although no data are available on nesting activities prior to this study. During April and May 1997 the following nests were found: 41 (33 active) in forests of the north of the reserve; five north of Kostanai town; and 36 in forests of the south dry steppe.

Present data do not allow us accurately to estimate the overall number of Imperial Eagles throughout Kazakhstan, because the breeding distribution of this species is very patchy. In at least 70% of the area, it is probable that the nesting density is close to 0.18 pairs/1000 km^2 as it is in the eastern Aral Sea region (Lobachev 1960). The main reason for this is that the eagles' breeding areas are located in relatively similar landscapes. In good habitats, which cover 400,000-500,000 km^2 (including the borders of desert with Haloxylon forest and some areas of isolated woodlands) the nesting density is about 1-1.1 pairs/1000 km^2, and a population size can be roughly estimated at 750-800 pairs. The Kostanai region holds more than 10% of the total number of Imperial Eagles in Kazakhstan, including approximately 5% in the Naurzum Reserve.

Nesting densities, productivity and survival of Imperial Eagles in the Kostanai region show that this population is now reaching stability. However, it is also vulnerable, because more than 50% of the nests outside the reserve fail as a direct result of human activities. The large nests of this eagle are usually located in the canopy of isolated trees or trees growing on the forest edge, where human activity is greatest, and such nests attract a lot of unwanted attention. Unfortunately, the attitude of the local people towards the eagles is not positive, due to the low level of cultural and ecological knowledge. It is conceivable that this situation could be dangerous to the eagle population as a whole.

The current social and economic crisis has had a large impact on some of the natural resources in rural areas, as the old system that provided local communities with these resources was destroyed. Extremely dangerous for the Imperial Eagle is the mass cutting of trees for fuel in cooking and heating homes. Furthermore it seems unlikely that a simple ban on the felling of trees that contain eagle nests will change the situation. Protection of the eagle needs the creation of a system that encourages local communities to protect trees that contain nests, both from disturbance and destruction.

It is clear that global conservation of birds of prey will require preservation of their habitats. Any definition of "key areas" of habitats for birds of prey would undoubtedly include the Naurzum Reserve. In addition to the Imperial Eagle, the area has four other endangered species, including 12 pairs of White-tailed Sea Eagles (11-13% of the total population in Kazakstan - which the Red Data Book [Anon1996] estimates at 95-110 pairs) and five pairs of Golden Eagles *Aquila chrysaetos*, as well as Steppe Eagles *A. rapax* and Saker Falcons. Overall, 17 species of birds of prey nest on the reserve. The forested areas of Naurzum support the highest densities of small-sized falcons, such as the Kestrel (mean = 850 pairs/100 km^2), Red-footed Falcon, Hobby and Merlin. Unfortunately, Naurzum reserve currently suffers from critical financial problems, which hinder protection and management activities. Therefore, Naurzum Reserve needs International Biosphere Reserve status and support. It is already contributing uniquely to the conservation of eagles and other rare raptors through the development of new population models, the identification of migration routes, and planning for the protection of these routes and the rare species that use them. It is essential to continue this in-depth research, and associated development of new conservation technologies.

ACKNOWLEDGEMENTS

The work to establish the number of rare and endangered predators in the Kostanai region was funded by the MacArthur Foundation. The International Association for Falconry and Conservation of Birds of Prey provided funds for radio-tracking. I thank Robert Kenward, for providing logistics and training with radio-tracking and for reviewing the manuscript.

REFERENCES

ANON. 1990. *The Red Data Book of Kazakhstan. In*: A.F. Koshvar (Ed.), *Vol. 3, Animals, Part I, Vertebrates.* Konjik Press, Almaty.

FORMOZOV, A.N. 1959. Movements and changing distribution of Mammals and Birds. *In* A. Formazov (Ed.) *Geography of Vertebrate Populations and Methods for their Study.* Academy of Science of the USSR Press, Moscow: 172-194.

GIBET, L.A. 1960. Connection of the number the Birds of Prey with Rodentia in the steppe zone of the North Kazakhstan. *Ornithology* 3: 278-291.

KOSHVAR, A.F. 1986. The Imperial Eagle in Andasai Zakaznik. *In* A.F. Koshvar, *Rare Animals of Kazakhstan.* Zoological Institute, Gilim Press, Almaty: 134.

LOBACHEV, V.S. 1960. On the biology of Imperial Eagle in the north-eastern Aral Sea Region. *Ornithology* 3: 306-315.

OSMOLOVSKAJA, V.I. 1953. Geographical distribution of the Birds of Prey of Plain Kazakhstan and their significance in exterminating harmful animals. *In* A.M. Formozov *Materials For Biogeography of the USSR.* Academy of Science of the USSR Press, Moscow: 219-307.

SOLOMATIN, A.O. 1970. The diet of the Imperial Eagles in the Naurzum Reserve. *Ecology* 3: 78-80.

Evgeny A. Bragin
The Naurzum National Nature Reserve
Altinsarina Street, 45
Kostanayskaja Oblast
Dokuchevka
459730 Kazakhstan

Chancellor, R. D. & B.-U. Meyburg eds. 2000
Raptors at Risk
WWGBP / Hancock House

Ecological Research and its Relationship to the Conservation Programme of the Golden Eagle and the Japanese Mountain Hawk-Eagle

T. Yamazaki

ABSTRACT

Two large raptors, the Golden Eagle *Aquila chrysaetos* and the Japanese Mountain Hawk-Eagle *Spizaetus nipalensis orientalis*, live in mountainous areas of Japan. Conservation plans have been established based on each raptor's ecology and population.

Golden Eagle: The population size is quite small. Two eggs are laid, but due to sibling aggression, only one eaglet survives. Since 1986 breeding success has dropped to crisis level. Conservation consists of two goals: 1) Increase fledgling numbers by fostering the second chick, and 2) protect from human disturbance the eagles' "high frequency use areas" which contain their nest site and main hunting areas during the breeding period.

Japanese Mountain Hawk-Eagle: Distribution is uniform throughout Japan even in mountainous areas covered with forest. Only one egg is laid. The fledglings' home range is located not only around the nest, but also within the parents' breeding territory, at least until the following spring. The principal conservation goal is to protect the breeding territory which contains the nest site and home range of the fledgling, thereby helping the fledgling reach independence. Because of the difficulty in determining the hunting areas outside of the breeding territory without radio-telemetry, a system of home range protection should be established to compensate for damage caused by human activities. Compiling accurate scientific data leads to appropriate conservation plans which are most likely to be accepted by the government agencies.

INTRODUCTION

Two large raptors, the Golden Eagle and the Japanese Mountain Hawk-Eagle, inhabit mountainous areas in Japan (Brown & Amadon 1968, Grossman & Hamlet 1964, Hidaka 1996). Although both eagles are listed as endangered species in the Japanese Red List (Environment Agency of Japan, EAJ 1991) and are under legal protection (EAJ 1993), in the past ten years both species have been jeopardized by environmental destruction caused by developers or forestry companies (Hirai 1994,

The Society for Research of the Golden Eagle, TSRGE 1983-1997, Yamazaki *et al.* 1996, Yamazaki 1997). Largely because of a lack of information about their ecology, no adequate and effective conservation plans have been put into practice (Yamazaki 1994a), and government officers and environmental impact assessment researchers have treated these two large raptors as the same species. Recently however, as a result of our research to understand their ecology and population status, effective plans for each raptor have been incorporated into conservation plans by the Government and construction companies.

STUDY AREA AND METHODS

Japan is located in the north-east part of South East Asia. The climate is temperate and most of the mountainous areas are covered with trees. The Society for Research of the Golden Eagle (TSRGE) was established in 1981 and consists of approximately 150 members throughout Japan. The Society has been monitoring every known pair of Golden Eagles and collecting data on their ecology. The Project Team for Research and Conservation of the Japanese Mountain Hawk-Eagle (PTRCJMHE) began research on the ecology of the Japanese Mountain Hawk-Eagle using wing markers and transmitters in 1987. We adopted radio-telemetry because Mountain Hawk-Eagles cannot be easily observed during their usual behaviour under the forest canopy.

RESULTS

1) Legal status

Both the Golden Eagle and the Japanese Mountain Hawk- Eagle are listed as endangered species in the Japanese Red Data Book, and are under legal protection (EAJ 1991, 1993). Recently, conservation of both species has become the social argument against construction of dams, wide roads and resort facilities in mountainous areas. In most development cases, an environmental impact assessment is required by prefectural regulation, but most assessments and proposed conservation mitigation plans ignored the ecology of these two large raptors. As a result, effective conservation management has not been practised.

Figure 1. Distribution of Golden Eagle and Japanese Mountain Hawk-Eagle

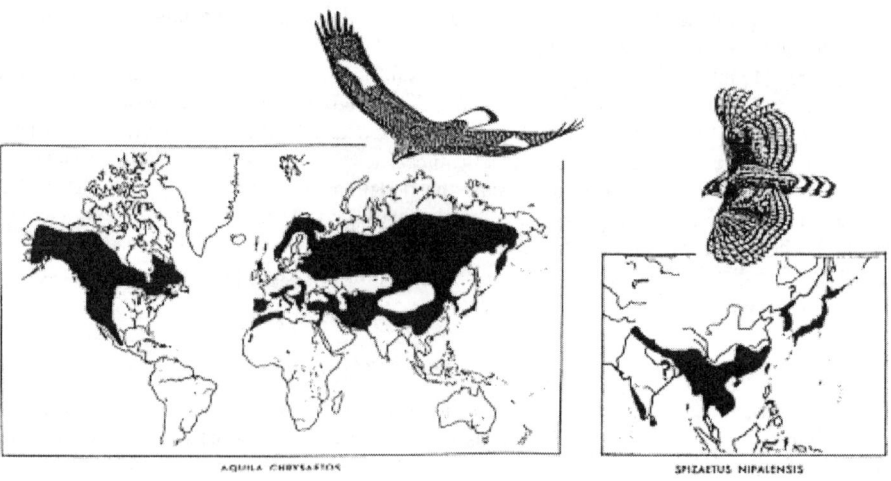

2) Distribution in the world

The Golden Eagle is widespread in the northern hemisphere and is distributed in all mountain landscapes with natural grassland to open woodland (Fig. 1). Six subspecies are normally recognized, the smallest of which, *A. c. japonica*, lives in Japan and Korea (Grossman & Hamlet 1964, del Hoyo *et al.* 1994). Mountainous areas of Japan appear to be covered more or less completely by dense forest so the Japanese subspecies of Golden Eagle has survived by somehow utilizing a scattered hunting area (Yamazaki 1997).

Three subspecies of the Mountain Hawk-Eagle are found from tropical S.W. India (*S. n. kelaarti*), the Himalayas of India and Nepal east through S. China and Hainan to E. China and Taiwan, and South to North Indochina and North Malay Peninsula (*S. n. nipalensis*), to temperate Japan (*S. n. orientalis*, Fig. 1, del Hoyo *et al.* 1994). Consequently, Japan supports two large raptor subspecies whose distribution is mostly limited to mountainous areas and whose specific ecological needs require unique conservation plans.

3) Population and home range in Japan

Due to the natural scarcity of open areas, the number of pairs of the Golden Eagle is estimated approximately at only 160 (TSRGE 1983-1997) and their distribution is not uniform (Table 1). Compared with the scarcity of the Golden Eagle, more than 1000 pairs of Mountain Hawk-Eagle are estimated to live uniformly throughout Japan (Table 1).

Table 1. Population and home range of Golden and Mountain Hawk- Eagles in Japan.

	Golden Eagle	Mountain Hawk-Eagle
Population Number of pairs	160	> 1000
Distribution	Scattered, 61% inhabit northern Japan	Uniform, same density throughout Japan
Home Range or density	21-237 km^2	1 breeding pair per 25-28 km^2
Distance between neighbouring nests	Irregular	Regular, mean = 4 km (1.5-5.6 km)

The home range of the Golden Eagle varies greatly between 21-237 km^2 (TSRGE 1983- 1997) depending on the distribution of hunting areas. The home range of the Mountain Hawk-Eagle is normally under about 20 km^2 and the mean density of breeding pairs is calculated at one per 25-28 km^2 uniformly throughout Japan (The Project Team for Research and Conservation of the Japanese Mountain Hawk-Eagle, TPTRCJHE 1995, Yamazaki *et al.* 1995). Nests were also spaced regularly at approximately 4 km apart.

4) Hunting pattern and hunting area

The Golden Eagle forages while flying above natural grassland, bush, forest edge and deciduous forest in winter (Table 2). The existence of the more open deciduous forest enables the Golden Eagle to live in forested mountain areas of Japan (Yamazaki 1997) by flying from one hunting area to another within their large home range. The proportion of " flight" time during the day was about 17%, and much greater than the 5% "flight" time of the Mountain Hawk-Eagle. Cooperative hunting among partners is a characteristic of Golden Eagles where prey hide inside bush or forest in winter (Hidaka 1996, Yamazaki 1997). Their main prey is the Japanese wild hare (*Lepus brachyurus*), Copper Pheasant (*Phasianus soemmerringii*), and large snakes during the breeding season and summer (TSRGE 1983-1997, Yamazaki 1997).

Mountain Hawk-Eagles mainly forage by "perch hunting" or "ambush hunting" inside or along forest edge (Table 2). They sometimes perch on a branch for an extensive amount of time waiting until prey appears. They never hunt cooperatively and the pair bond is maintained only during the breeding season (Yamazaki et al. 1995). They prey on various small and medium- sized mammals and birds (Yamazaki 1994b, Yamazaki 1997). This hunting strategy makes it very difficult to identify their location without the use of radio-telemetry.

Table 2. Hunting pattern and area of Golden Eagles and Mountain Hawk-Eagles in Japan.

	Golden Eagle	Mountain Hawk-Eagle
Hunting method	Soaring, single or cooperative	Perch and ambush, single
Hunting area	Grassland, bush, forest edge, deciduous forest in winter	Gap or forest edge, forest interior
Prey	Few species: hare, large snakes, copper pheasant	Varied: small to medium sized wildlife in forest
Distribution of prey	Distribution density varying within home range	Uniform distribution within home range

5) Breeding success

The breeding success of the Golden Eagle has been monitored since 1981 (TSRGE 1983-1997). Breeding success was 47.1% between 1981-1985, the same level as in other countries (Table 3). After 1986 breeding success dropped to a less than replacement level of 26.7% between 1991-1995. Fewer than 20 fledglings were observed.

Nationwide, monitoring of the Japanese Mountain Hawk-Eagle has not been completed so an accurate average value of breeding success is not available. A small sample of pairs that have been monitored for more than 10 years show that the trend is the same as the Golden Eagle: after 1991 the average breeding success dropped to around 10-35% (TPTRCJMHE 1996, Yamazaki et al. 1996, Table 3).

Table 3. Breeding success (%) of Golden Eagles and Mountain Hawk-Eagles in Japan.
*sample data from just one area.

	Golden Eagle	Mountain Hawk-Eagle*
1981-1985	47.1	85.7
1986-1990	41.0	62.5
1991-1995	26.7	36.8
Lowest	22.2 (1995)	16.7 (1996)

6) Breeding strategy

Golden Eagles usually lay two eggs, but due to sibling aggression, in 98.3% of breeding nests the second hatched eaglet dies (TSRGE 1983-1997). In contrast, only one egg is laid by Mountain Hawk-Eagle pairs (Table 4). After leaving the nest the fledgling Golden Eagle spends about one month near the nest, then it flies to the hunting area with its parents.

Table 4. Breeding stratey of Golden Eagles and Mountain Hawk-Eagles in Japan

	Golden Eagle	Mountain Hawk-Eagle
Clutch size	2-3	1
Home range of fledgling within one year	Home range of parent	Within 1000 m of nest
Food transfer from parent	Short period	Long period
Fledgling dispersal	6 months after fledging	2-3 years after fledging

The fledgling Mountain Hawk-Eagle resides within 1000 m (usually 500 m) of the nest site at least until the following spring (Yamazaki 1994b). The fledgling acquires its hunting skills around the nest site while receiving food from its male parent. The result of radio-tracking of fledglings revealed that although they gradually enlarge their home range after the next April, they do not disperse rapidly from their nest sites and appear there again even two to three years after fledging (TPTRCJMHE 1996).

7) Structure of home range

The analysis of the home range is important to establish an adequate conservation area. Because the Golden Eagle flies while foraging, it is not difficult to observe its behaviour and to analyse the inner structure of the home range. Through three years of intensive research of one pair, we were able to model the inner structure of the Golden Eagle home range (Table 5, TSRGE 1994). There is a core area we called the "high frequency use area", which is delineated by the higher frequency of the parents' appearance than in the rest of the home range. This area contains a nesting place and most of the main hunting areas during the breeding period. Connected to this "high frequency use area" is a "buffer zone" where alternative and potential hunting areas for the breeding season are located.

Table 5. Structure of home range of Golden Eagles and Mountain Hawk-Eagles in Japan

	Golden Eagle	*Mountain Hawk-Eagle*
Territory	Occupied all year	Breeding territory is occupied inside the core area only during the breeding period.
Home range	Nearly equals the territory	Centre is home range of the fledgling; breeding territory is occupied during the breeding period.
Home range	Almost the same between pairs	Not completely the same; breeding territory is almost the same.

Analysis of the Mountain Hawk-Eagle home range is almost impossible without the use of radio-telemetry because they spend most of the daytime perched on branches either resting or foraging. With more than 10 years of telemetry research we were able to discern the structure of its home range (Table 5). The home ranges of hawk-eagle neighbours overlap (Hidaka 1996), and the breeding territory is occupied by the pair only during the breeding period (Yamazaki et al. 1995). The core area accommodates nesting sites, the home range of the fledgling, the breeding territory, and most hunting areas throughout year and it is approximately 7-8 km surrounding the nest site. The range centre of the breeding territory is described as the home range of the fledgling.

8) Problems of environmental impact assessment without using radio-telemetry

From our intensive study of both species, their ecology and behaviour, the structure of their home range differs and depends on their habitat and ecological needs. Research of the Golden Eagle is not difficult, but because the home range structure fluctuates annually, one year of research is not adequate to correctly evaluate habitat use (Yamazaki 1994a). It is very difficult to observe hunting behaviour and to identify individuals of Mountain Hawk-Eagle and almost impossible to visually analyse the structure of the home range. The most serious problem of Mountain Hawk-Eagle research is overestimation of the high frequency use area from the course of flights because only flight behaviour is observable by visual methods (Table 6).

Table 6. Problems with environmental impact assessment studies without the use of radio-telemetry for Golden Eagles and Mountain Hawk-Eagles in Japan.

	Golden Eagle	*Mountain Hawk-Eagle*
Observation	Easy	Difficult
Appearance of other individuals	Not often	Often
Identify individuals	Easy	Difficult (fledgling is easy)
Finding the nest site	Comparatively easy	Usually difficult
Identify hunting area	Not difficult	Almost impossible
Analysis of home range structure	Possible	Impossible
Serious problems	Annual fluctuation of home range structure	Overestimation of the high frequency use area from flight observations

9) Minimum information necessary to establish conservation plans

Before completing the conservation model of each species we decided on the following minimum necessary information (Table 7). Although both eagles are listed as endangered species the critical levels of their respective populations are different. Currently, the annual number of Golden Eagle fledglings is too small to maintain the population in Japan (Yamazaki 1997). Because the habitat of the Golden Eagle is not distributed uniformly, the home range size of each pair varies greatly (TSRGE 1983-1997). We can easily imagine that the structure of the home range is different for each pair. Fortunately, it is possible to analyse the structure of the home range of the Golden Eagle because of its aerial hunting style. The most important area to protect is at least the minimum area necessary for reproduction, the "high frequency use area", but annual fluctuation of this area must be measured and included in the protected area (Yamazaki 1994a).

Table 7. Minimum information needed to establish conservation plans for Golden Eagle and Mountain Hawk-Eagles in Japan.

	Golden Eagle	*Mountain Hawk-Eagle*
Population size	Critical	Vulnerable
Breeding success	Drastic decrease	Drastic decrease
Home range variation among pairs	Varies greatly	Similar
Hunting area	Scattered in home range	Distributed uniformly
Specifying the hunting area	Not difficult	Almost impossible
Hunting area for breeding	High frequency use area	Core area (usually within 1.5km of the nest)
Minimum area needed for reproduction	High frequency use area; annual fluctuation occurs	Breeding territory (core area desirable); range centre (home range of fledgling is easy to identify and mostly the same between years)

By contrast, the home range of the Mountain Hawk-Eagle is similar throughout Japan, but it is difficult to locate its hunting areas and the range of each pair due to the densely forested habitat. However, we realized that most of the hunting areas for breeding are located within the core area. We also discovered that the most important range to protect for breeding success is that area where the fledgling resides until the following spring (TPTRCJMHE 1996, Yamazaki 1994b). Fortunately, it is comparatively easy to determine this area because the fledgling tends to perch on top of trees and has a conspicuous whitish breast.

10) Conservation models

The Golden Eagle: The emergency plan is to increase fledgling numbers by fostering the second chick, thereby maintaining the minimum population (Yamazaki 1997). Captive breeding is also necessary. In addition to these attempts, we have repaired nests which are not in good condition (Table 8, TSRGE 1983-1997). Habitat conservation is also needed. Due to the variation of each home range and the yearly fluctuation of its high frequency use area, at least three years of research is necessary to reveal the structure of the home range (Yamazaki 1994a). Once known, the "high frequency use area", which includes the nesting area and hunting areas during the breeding period, must be protected from human disturbance.

Table 8. Conservation models for Golden Eagles and Mountain Hawk-Eagles in Japan.

	Golden Eagle	*Mountain Hawk-Eagle*
Emergency plan to increase fledglings	Foster the second chick; captive breeding; nest repairing	Not necessary
Habitat conservation plan	Must be designed for each territory	Can establish a typical conservation model
Purpose and length of assessment research	Analyze structure of home range; at least three years of study	Specify home range of fledgling; at least one breeding period
Area to be strictly protected	High frequency use area	Breeding territory, especially home range of fledgling before independence
Theme for conservation of hunting area	Protection of hunting area used in breeding	Compensation for damaged areas
Special research	Causes of breeding failures	Causes of breeding failures

The Japanese Mountain Hawk-Eagle: An emergency plan for increasing fledgling rate is not necessary right now. The principal of conservation is to establish protection of the home range and to apply it to every pair throughout Japan. The most important point is to protect the home range of fledglings (Yamazaki 1994b) and the breeding territory to help maintain their number. Concerning the remaining area of the breeding territory, because of the difficulty in determining hunting areas by observation, we propose that construction companies compensate for damaged forest by providing adequate hunting area in alternative locations inside or close to the core area. In addition to these plans, it is a matter of course that research to analyse the causes of breeding failure is also necessary for both species.

CONCLUSION

Raptors are at the top of the food chain. Their conservation can therefore support the conservation of the entire ecosystem. If their conservation model is not defined and effective, we fail to protect not only the endangered raptors but also our natural environment.

First, sufficient scientific research about the ecology and habitat use of raptors is needed to establish an effective conservation model. Compiling accurate data leads to appropriate conservation decisions. Approximately 40% of raptors in the world are found in tropical forest (Thiollay 1985) and most of them are soon to be endangered. Up to today, the conservation models for raptors were decided upon in European and American countries (Newton 1990), but they are not always effective for raptors living in tropical forest. Even more information about the basic ecology of large tropical forest raptors in Asia is needed to adequately conserve and protect them and their habitat.

We completed our conservation models according to our special research for each species. These accurate conservation models persuaded the government and construction companies to accept and implement recommended plans.

REFERENCES

BROWN, L. & D. AMADON 1968. *Eagles, Hawks and Falcons of the World.* Country Life Books, Feltham.
del HOYO, J., A. ELLIOT & J. SARGATAL 1994. *Handbook of birds of the world, Vol. 2.* Lynx Edicions, Barcelona.
Environment Agency of Japan, EAJ 1991. *Endangered species of wildlife in Japan—the Red Data Book.* Japan Wildlife Research Centre, Tokyo (in Japanese).
Environment Agency of Japan, EAJ 1993. *The law of the conservation of endangered species of wildlife and plants* . Chuo-hoki Press, Tokyo (in Japanese).
GROSSMAN, M. L. & J. HAMLET 1964. *Birds of prey of the world.* Bonanza Books, New York.
HIDAKA, T. (Ed.) 1996. *The encyclopaedia of animals of Japan. Vol. 3: Birds I.* Heibonsha Limited Publishers, Tokyo (in Japanese).
HIRAI, K.(Ed.) 1994. *The research report of environmental contamination based on the ecology and diseases of wildlife in Chubu mountainous area.* Faculty of Agriculture, Gifu University (in Japanese).
NEWTON, I. 1990. *Birds of Prey.* Merehurst Press, London.
THE PROJECT TEAM FOR RESEARCH AND CONSERVATION OF THE JAPANESE MOUNTAIN HAWK-EAGLE, TPTRCJMHE 1995. Proceedings of the first Symposium on the Japanese Mountain protect Hawk-Eagle (in Japanese).
THE PROJECT TEAM FOR RESEARCH AND CONSERVATION OF THE JAPANESE MOUNTAIN HAWK-EAGLE, TPTRCJMHE 1996. Proceedings of the second Symposium on the Japanese Mountain Hawk-Eagle (in Japanese).
THE SOCIETY FOR RESEARCH OF THE GOLDEN EAGLE, TSRGE 1983-1997. *Aquila chrysaetos* No. 1- No. 13. Shiga, Japan (in Japanese).
THE SOCIETY FOR RESEARCH OF THE GOLDEN EAGLE, TSRGE 1994. *The research report of the Golden Eagle pair that live at the foot of the Tazawa Komagatake Mountain.* Nature Conservation Society of Japan, Tokyo (in Japanese).
THIOLLAY, J.-M. 1985. Falconiforms of tropical rainforests: A review: 155-165. *Conservation Studies on Raptors.* ICBP Technical Publication No. 5, England.
YAMAZAKI, T. 1994a. The Ecology of the Golden Eagle and its conservation against development activities. The Conservation Strategy of Regional Environment by Self-governing Body Vol. 3:249- 264. Gyosei Press, Tokyo (in Japanese).
YAMAZAKI, T. 1994b. The Conservation Programme for the Japanese Mountain Hawk-Eagle, the largest forest raptor in Japan. Research report of Pro Natura Fund: 173-180. Nature Conservation Society of Japan, Tokyo (in Japanese).
YAMAZAKI, T., T. INOUE, M. FUJITA, K. KAMIKODAI, Y. NITANI, K. KATO, H. ICHINOSE, N. NAKAGAWA & T. SUGIMOTO 1995. The Conservation Programme for the Japanese Mountain Hawk-Eagle, the largest forest raptor in Japan. Research report of Pro Natura Fund: 48-55. Nature Conservation Society of Japan, Tokyo (in Japanese).
YAMAZAKI, T., Y. KOJIMA & T. IIDA 1996. The Conservation of Raptors. Nature Conservation No. 408: 2-17. Nature Conservation Society of Japan, Tokyo. (in Japanese).
YAMAZAKI, T. 1997. The Ecology of the Golden Eagle and the Japanese Mountain Hawk-Eagle in relation to the Conservation of the Ecosystem. The Journal of Lake Biwa Research Institute: 66-73 (in Japanese).

Toru Yamazaki
482-57, Yukihata,
Yasu-cho, Yasu-gun,
Shiga Prefecture, 520-2341,
Japan

Part 5

Raptors in Urban Environments

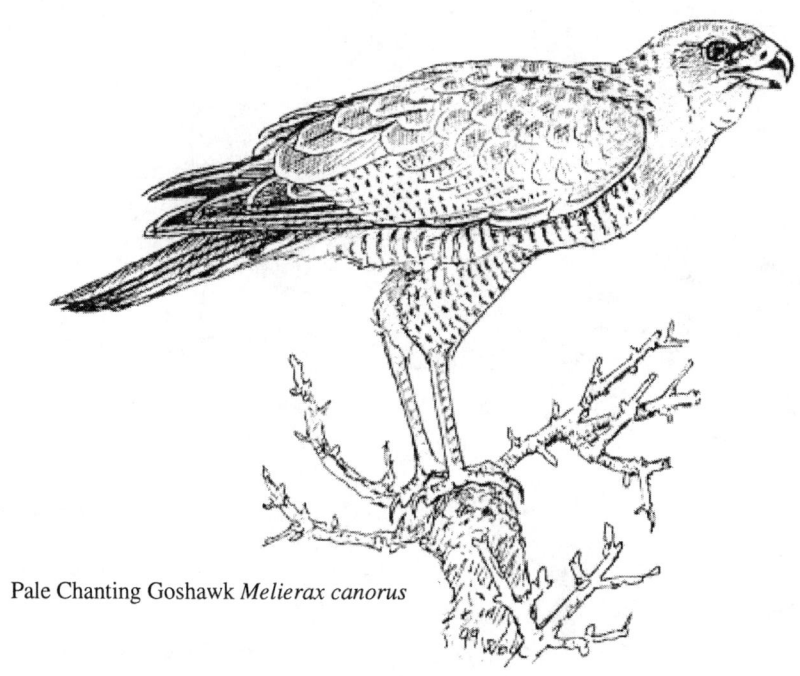

Pale Chanting Goshawk *Melierax canorus*

Conveners:
David M. Bird & Greg Septon

Chancellor, R. D. & B.-U. Meyburg eds. 2000
Raptors at Risk
WWGBP / Hancock House

Raptors in Urban Landscapes: A Review and Future Concerns

Oliver P. Love and David M. Bird

ABSTRACT

Over 25 of the world's raptor species can now be found living in or near modern urban settings. They are adapting by taking advantage of new food sources including refuse dumps and commercial slaughterhouses, accepting artificial and unusual nest structures and locations and by over-wintering in urban areas. However, competition for limited resources combined with a drastic reduction of suitable traditional habitat may be potential problems as raptors inhabit urban areas. In addition, it is not known with certainty whether species are thriving, or merely surviving, since the reproductive success of urban raptor populations has rarely been compared with those of former habitats. Furthermore, modern cities bring new sources of danger to raptors, as buildings, vehicles, refuse, chemicals, and people themselves pose a myriad of potential problems. Finally, urban areas may in fact foster the proliferation of single species rather than encourage raptor community diversity. This paper reports on current urban raptor research, emphasizing the vital need to encourage diversity in our cities as well as determine whether these new landscapes are important sources, or destructive sinks, for future raptor populations.

INTRODUCTION

Many reports as well as documented research describe raptors frequenting and nesting within urban centres the world over (Oliphant & McTaggart 1977, Stahlecker & Beach 1979, Shaw 1985, James & Smith 1987, Gennaro 1988, Cade & Bird 1990, Sodhi *et al.* 1991, James 1992, England *et al.* 1995, Bell *et al.* 1996, Bird *et al.* 1996, Bloom & McCrary 1996, Cade *et al.* 1996, Parker 1996, Rosenfield *et al.* 1996, Stout *et al.* 1996, Tella *et al.* 1996, Bosakowski & Smith 1997, Blanco 1997).

Some noted success stories include the Peregrine Falcon *Falco peregrinus* in North America, where almost one hundred pairs are nesting during 1997 (Tordoff & Redig 1997); increased reproductive success of the urban-nesting Red-shouldered Hawk *Buteo lineatus* compared well with that of rural areas in California (Bloom & McCrary 1996) and the Mississippi Kite *Ictinia mississippiensis* may be the most widespread urban raptor in North America (Parker 1996). Even accipiters, traditionally regarded as nervous, secretive birds, are adapting to urban habitats. Besides some of the highest breeding densities of Cooper's Hawks *Accipiter cooperii* in urban areas of the U.S state of Wisconsin (Rosenfield *et al.* 1996), Black Sparrowhawks *A. melanoleucos* are nesting within the city limits of Durban, South Africa (G. Malan, pers. comm.) and European Goshawks *A.*

gentilis have established urban populaetns in both Moscow, Russia (V. Galushin, pers. comm.) and in Cologne, Germany (E. Guthmann, pers. comm.).Table 1 summarizes the species known to be utilizing urban centres.

Table 1: Raptors Typically Associated with Urban Centres

Common Name	Scientific Name	Source
Peregrine Falcon	*Falco peregrinus*	Bell *et al.* 1996; Cade *et al.* 1988; Cade *et al.* 1996; Cade & Bird 1990; Wooton & Bell 1992; Sweeney 1997; Tordoff & Redig 1997
Bat Falcon	*Falco rufigularis*	Seijas 1996
Merlin	*Falco columbarius*	Oliphant & Mctaggart 1977; Oliphant & Haug 1985; Oliphant & Haug 1985; Sodhi *et al.* 1991; James *et al.* 1994
American Kestrel	*Falco sparverius*	Palmer 1988
Eurasian Kestrel	*Falco tinnunculus*	Village 1989
Lesser Kestrel	*Falco naumanni*	Tella *et al.* 1996
Mississippi Kite	*Ictinia mississippiensis*	Gennaro 1988; Parker 1996
Black Kite	*Milvus migrans migrans*	Blanco 1994, 97
Goshawk	*Accipiter gentilis*	Bosakowski & Smith 1997; Galushin, pers. comm.; Guthmann, pers. comm.
Cooper's Hawk	*Accipiter cooperii*	Stahlecker & Beach 1979; Rosenfield *et al.* 1996
Black Sparrowhawk	*Accipiter melanoleucus*	Malan, pers. comm.
Eurasian Sparrowhawk	*Accipiter nisus*	Frimer 1989*a*, 1989*b*
Broad-winged Hawk	*Buteo platypterus*	Bosakowski & Smith 1997
Red-tailed Hawk	*Buteo jamaicensis*	Stout *et al.* 1996, 98; Bosakowski & Smith 1997
Red-shouldered Hawk	*Buteo lineatus*	Bloom & McCrary 1996; Bosakowski & Smith 1997
Swainson's Hawk	*Buteo swainsonii*	James 1992; England *et al.* 1995
Harris Hawk	*Parabuteo unicinctus*	Dawson & Mannan 1995
Osprey	*Pandion haliaetus*	Poole 1989
Crested Caracara	*Polyborus plancus*	Rodríguez-Estrella & Rodríguez 1997
Black Vulture	*Coragyps atratus*	Iñigo 1987
Great-horned Owl	*Bubo virginianus*	Laidig & Dobkin 1995
Barred Owl	*Strix varia*	Laidig & Dobkin 1995; Bosakowski & Smith 1997
Burrowing Owl	*Athene cunicularia*	Botelho & Arrowood 1996
Screech Owl	*Otus asio*	Loos & Kerlinger 1993; Gehlbach 1996
Tawny Owl	*Strix aluco*	Zalewski 1994

URBAN SUCCESS STORIES

As noted by Bird *et al.* (1996), in these times of massive changes to natural environments leading to dwindling wildlife populations, it is a relief to hear that some organisms can adapt to and even benefit from human-altered areas. Survival of raptors from fledging to first year of age is one of the greatest factors involved in the success of any raptor population (Newton 1979), and cities may be fostering increased survivorship in some raptor species. Tordoff and Redig (1997), in their study of mid-west Peregrine Falcon demography between 1982 and 1995, found that a greater number of city-hacked birds (19%) survived than did wild fledged birds (12%). The authors stressed that actual first-year survival is higher than minimum first-year survival and probably exceeds 30%. With 80% of the Peregrines in their study area nesting on man-made structures, with human help, this population should continue to show steady growth to its current carrying capacity, with city pairs being largely responsible.

Reproductive output in some urban-nesting raptor species has been found to be greater than in traditional rural habitats due largely to the factors discussed earlier. In a study of western Red-shouldered Hawks, Bloom and McCrary (1996) found that reproductive success of pairs nesting in urban locations was greater than that previously reported in natural areas in the same region of California. Rosenfield *et al.* (1996) investigated various aspects of the nesting biology of Cooper's Hawks in central Wisconsin and found the highest nesting density known for the species, as well as clutch size and number of bandable young per nest being comparable to the highest known for these accipiters.

In addition to the fulfilment of basic needs such as adequate prey and nesting locations, city areas can offer some degree of relief from traditional habitat loss at a number of other levels. Urbanized green spaces can become sanctuaries for raptors, offering refuges for nesting, as well as for inexperienced juvenile birds. Cities not only offer vital stopovers during migration, but can even be so attractive as to allow for over-wintering to such raptors as Peregrines (Septon, this volume) and Merlins (Oliphant & Haug 1985). In addition, cities may act as potential genetic reservoirs allowing some species to survive genetically, as well as offering a potential source for reintroduction to new and reclaimed habitats. Sometimes even more important is the public relation and educational value of city raptors, as their high visibility and general allure make them ideal candidates for public education and general awareness of wildlife issues within our downtown cores. The Peregrine Information Centre in Montreal, Canada attracts thousands of visitors annually not only to the building where the birds nest and where information about saving endangered wildlife is located, but also to a world-wide-web site which links similar projects from all over the world.

WHAT ATTRACTS RAPTORS TO URBAN HABITATS?

Resources, including food, nesting sites and shelter from predators, are known to be important factors which limit or encourage raptor expansion and proliferation in any new environment, including the urban world. Raptors are attracted to cities because of abundant food sources such as urban passerines and pigeons, prey attracted to night lights, refuse dumps and commercial slaughterhouses. Modern refuse dumps and slaughterhouses, a by-product of the urban landscape, offer important sources of food for both breeding and migrating raptors in urbanized areas. In their study area in the Cape Region of Baja California, Mexico, Rodríguez-Estrella *et al.* (1997) found that most immature Crested Caracaras *Polyborus plancus* foraged near slaughterhouses and garbage sites rather than in natural areas. These predictable sources of food not only brought in adult and young birds, but also attracted invertebrates as yet another food source for the Caracaras. Blanco (1994) noted that Black Kites *Milvus migrans* in Spain also utilize urban refuse dumps as an abundant and predictable food supply during both pre- and post-breeding migratory passages.

Predatory birds that increasingly colonize urban areas must either find a habitat containing natural food resources close by or change their feeding ecology. The Tawny Owl *Strix aluco* is an example of the latter, a polyphagous species (Mikkola 1983) that can inhabit many environments and adapt to preying upon the most abundant species (Zalewski 1994). In his study comparing the diet of urban and suburban Tawny Owls in Poland, Zalewski found that urban owls preyed upon significantly more diurnal passerines, especially the abundant House Sparrow *Passer domesticus*, than suburban owls which preyed mainly upon nocturnal mammals.

Urban environments can also provide prey for other adaptable raptor species such as the Bat Falcon *Falco rufigularis* in Venezuela. This species augmented its diet of bats from approximately 16% in rural areas to almost 64% of its diet in an urban area of Venezuela (Seijas 1996). As the author suggested, these findings emphasize the ecological plasticity of the Bat Falcon and may make it an excellent candidate for an urban lifestyle.

Urban raptors also make successful use of the many city structures for nesting, as traditional haunts such as cliffs and trees are replaced by ever-advancing urban centres. Peregrine Falcons and Merlins *Falco columbarius* utilize high-rise buildings, smokestacks, and bridges (Oliphant & Haug 1985, Cade *et al.* 1996); Ospreys *Pandion haliaetus* use transmission towers (Poole 1989) and Red-tailed Hawks *Buteo jamaicensis* accept power poles and billboards as suitable nesting sites (Stout *et al.* 1996). Another raptor which appears to show nesting plasticity is the Saker Falcon *Falco cherrug* in Mongolia. Ellis *et al.* (1997) noted the Saker's remarkable adaptability in using a wide range of breeding situations, including a number of man-made structures, making it a possible breeding contender for urban environments.

Lowered predation in cities as compared to rural habitats may be another important factor which attracts raptors to urban centres. In a comparison of Lesser Kestrels *Falco naumanni* in Spain, Tella *et al.* (1996) found that rural nesting kestrels were faced with nine possible predators, whereas urban-nesting birds were faced with only three.

DRAWBACKS TO URBAN LIVING

Alterations of Foraging Behaviour

Although the number of raptor species inhabiting and breeding in urban locations is increasing, there are many drawbacks and shortcomings of city life, the first being alterations in foraging and nesting behaviour. From their study of reproductive performance of urban-nesting Swainson's Hawks *Buteo swainsonii* in California's Central Valley, England *et al.* (1995) found that fewer young fledged from nests in urban than in rural settings. Also, the numbers of young fledged per nesting attempt and per successful nest for urban nests were among the lowest reported for this species. The cost for these urban-nesting buteos appears to be the long-distance transport of prey throughout the entire nesting cycle due to the lack of suitable foraging areas located near nesting locations. The authors suggested that rapid urbanization could cause the long-term decline of Swainson's Hawks in existing urban neighbourhoods. Lower reproductive success in urban areas as compared to rural ones means that urban populations may be acting like sinks, pulling breeding adults from potentially productive habitats.

Similarly, Seijas (1996) noted that although aquatic birds made up over 35% of the diet of Bat Falcons in Venezuela, the urban falcons were capturing prey from a river some 6km outside the city. With this long-distance travel, prey may be available, but not in quantities sufficient to produce successful reproductive outputs.

Ecological shifts, such as changes in prey as raptors move into cities from non-urban areas, can also lead to problems. In his study comparing the diets of urban and suburban Tawny Owls in Poland, Zalewski (1994) found that diurnal passerines, the most numerous prey in cities, are probably more difficult to catch than the majority of nocturnal, terrestrial and vocally 'noisy' small mammals. However, because this owl relies upon hearing to locate prey, higher noise levels in cities may be interfering with prey location and capture. This may be a drastic problem for those nocturnal owls which cannot switch to day hunting of passerines, and furthermore cannot capture mammals at night due to increased noise levels.

Inherent Dangers of Cities

As noted by Cade and Bird (1990), Bird *et al.* (1996) and Cade *et al.* (1996), urban sites present unique hazards to raptors that can lead to juvenile and adult mortality. Hazards such as collisions with airplanes, vehicles and windows, secondary poisoning from pigeon control efforts, illegal shooting, as well as disturbance associated with building and city maintenance, are all factors with which city raptors must deal with.

A large potential problem for raptors in urban locations is collisions with the vast numbers of motor vehicles present throughout the day and night in our cities. Certain species, age-classes and even sexes may be affected to greater degrees than others. In their examination of morbidity, survival and breeding success of free-ranging Peregrine Falcons submitted to The Raptor Centre of the University of Minnesota for veterinary care during 1984-94, Sweeney *et al.* (1997) found that 81% of these raptors suffered traumatic injuries resulting from collisions with buildings, motor vehicles and utility lines. Almost 75% of these were first-year birds, indicating an increased risk for young, inexperienced raptors in cities. These findings support previous work showing that collisions with man-made objects are the leading cause of injury and death among midwestern Peregrines.

In a 1993 study of road mortality of raptors in New Jersey, Loos and Kerlinger found that Northern Saw-whet Owls *Aegolius acadicus* and eastern Screech Owls *Otus asio* accounted for 45% and 36% of all raptor road kills, respectively. A large percentage of the Saw-whet (79%) and Screech Owls (88%) found were less than one year old. In addition, more than 87% of the Saw-whets and 71% of the Screech Owls were found between November and January, thought to be the key times of wintering and migration. Thus, certain species may be more vulnerable than others to road mortality due to factors such as age, geographic distribution, specific hunting or nesting requirements (including sexually biased hunting), as well as the seasonal tendency of various species to be in or near cities.

Electrocution is also responsible for many raptor deaths, and as urban areas are cores of power usage, they may be significant sources of mortality, especially for younger birds and larger species. In a report on electrocution as a mortality factor in an urban population of Harris' Hawks *Parabuteo unicinctus*, Dawson and Mannan (1995) found that although nesting success by urban breeding groups was high, survival of fledglings was low due to electrocution. In fact, electrocution was the most common mortality factor encountered during the study, accounting for 112 of 177 deaths. Furthermore, they found that nests located near or on power poles were particularly susceptible to electrocution during the first two weeks after fledging, the time period when young are practicing and preparing for flight. Urban raptors are attracted to utility poles as nesting sites, and further measures must be taken to reduce mortality, especially for vulnerable fledglings.

A number of factors which may play a role in attracting and sustaining raptors in urban areas can also have dangerous tradeoffs, such as the ingestion of synthetic products from refuse dumps (Inigo 1987, Donázar 1992). As mentioned earlier, although Blanco (1994) found that Black Kites in Spain utilize urban refuse dumps as an abundant and predictable food supply, he also noted that kites may face some dangers from entanglement in plastic materials and other rubbish. In his study, five kites were observed with pieces of rope, plastic bags, and pieces of plastic (up to 40cm long) entangled in their legs, and one immature was seen with an empty can caught on a leg. The effects of these and other potential dangers of modern refuse dumps remain unknown.

RAPTOR DIVERSITY IN CITY LANDSCAPES

Although a number of noteworthy species such as the Peregrine Falcon, Merlin and Mississippi Kite are definite success stories in urban environments, other genera such as *Elanus, Circus, Aquila* and many of the nocturnal owls and raptors with specific habitat requirements, may never nest in urban areas (Bloom & McCrary 1996). The importance and dynamics of raptor community diversity within urban centres remains to be studied and fully understood. However, factors that have been found to promote raptor diversity, such as high habitat heterogeneity (White 1974), are often limited in urban situations. Conversely, forest fragmentation and reduced forest interior are also known to reduce raptor community diversity (Thiollay & Meyburg 1988).

Habitat Fragmentation in Urban Landscapes

Raptors are sensitive to habitat fragmentation due to their large foraging ranges, low population densities, sensitivity to disturbance, and their reluctance to cross large open areas (Thiollay 1998, Watson 1998). Highly subdivided cities containing isolated patches of inadequately sized green space may reduce diversity and viability of raptors in urban spaces. In a study comparing nesting habitat and reproductive success of urban and rural Red-tailed Hawks, Stout *et al.* (1998) found that the density of the rural population was greater than in suburban areas and lowest in urban locations. The authors noted that cover was an important component of the nesting habitat for the species.

The biological consequences of habitat fragmentation for raptors are numerous and far-reaching. One of the first and obvious effects of fragmentation on raptor populations is the elimination of a species that occurred in portions of natural habitat not preserved when a city begins or expands. In effect, the species will be excluded from urban areas because suitable habitat has been replaced, and if habitat outside the urban area is also eliminated, those species will be lost by exclusion from the city area (Meefe *et al.* 1997).

Isolation of habitats by barriers to movement such as buildings, roads and even city commotion, is a consequence of fragmentation as important as reduction in habitat size (Meefe *et al.* 1997). Many animals including the majority of raptor species require a mixture of different habitats with distinct resources for nesting, hunting and roosting in order to meet their life history requirements. If barriers separate critical areas such as large parks and greenspaces in cities, raptor populations may decline, as human-created structures can greatly inhibit the movements of even highly mobile birds. Moreover, forest raptors may be especially sensitive due to their reluctance to cross large, open areas (Thiollay 1998). In a multi-species context, the overall landscape of a city in which habitat "islands" may be embedded is better seen as a filter, rather than a barrier, as it allows individuals of some species, but not others, to pass through (Meefe *et al.* 1997). As discussed earlier, this may cause problems for raptor communities, as competition and even monopolization of limited resources can occur. As the landscape departs more and more from a raptor's natural habitat, isolation will increase as individuals may be less willing to travel from one patch of habitat to another.

Core Habitat and Edge Effects

Even planned urban green spaces may not contain sufficient core habitat area, increasing edge effects and limiting community diversity. Temple (1986) looked at two wildlife areas each with a total area of 40 hectares. Habitat A had zero hectares of core area and contained no breeding bird species, whereas habitat B, of which half was core area, contained six breeding bird species.

Within a New Jersey watershed, Bosakowski and Smith (1997) found a strong correlation between species richness of forest raptors and the increasing size of wilderness core area. No area less than 1000 ha had more than four species present, while 4 to 8 species were found in areas from 1000 to 8000 ha in size. Furthermore, several species preferring extensive, remote areas of deep woods, the Red-shouldered Hawk, Northern Goshawk and the Barred Owl, had a greater vulnerability to urbanization, whereas Eastern Screech Owls and Broad-winged Hawks were less sensitive to urbanization. Furthermore, Great-horned Owls and Red-tailed Hawks clearly benefited from forest fragmentation and urbanization.

The structural contrast between a habitat island such as a forested park and surrounding urban landscape is not only an indicator of isolation, but also demonstrates the strength of edge effects. The outer boundary of any habitat, especially an urban one, is not a line, but rather a zone of influence that varies in width depending on what is measured (Murcia 1995). According to Wilcove (1985) nest predation rates in birds are higher in woodlots surrounded by suburbs than in those surrounded by agriculture, probably because refuse and other food subsidies in suburban areas encourage opportunistic predators.

Similarly, the diversity and abundance of birds in forest blocks surrounded by suburbs was much lower than in forests with few, or no nearby houses (Friesen *et al.* 1995). Habitat patches below a certain size will lack the true interior or "core" habitat that many raptorial species, especially forest-dwelling owls and hawks, require. In areas with limited core forest area, edge effects are increased, which eliminates forest species and encourages opportunistic competitors and predators. The best urban areas for community diversity are those with large core areas of green space such as Tucson, Arizona (Mannan *et al.*, this volume) and those with limited distance from traditional habitats. Effective planning and management can allow for adequately sized and shaped habitats that can support raptor community diversity.

Competition limits Urban Diversity

As more and more raptors are forced to inhabit smaller and more isolated habitats, competition may play a destructive role in maintaining raptor diversity. Laidig and Dobkin (1995) found that fragmentation of forests in southern New Jersey caused an extraordinary degree of habitat overlap between Barred Owls, closely associated with undisturbed mature forests, and Great-horned Owls, found in highly fragmented landscapes. This overlap resulted in substantial competition and predation on the former by the latter species and emphasizes that competition for limited space in urban areas can lead to permanent diversity loss.

URBAN LANDSCAPES: SINKS OR SOURCES?

The fate of an entire raptor population may depend on whether the reproductive success of individuals in the productive habitats outweighs the lack of success by individuals in the poorer habitats, that is, source and sink dynamics (Meefe *et al.* 1997). Good habitats are sources, areas where local reproductive success is greater than local mortality. Poor habitats are termed sinks, that is areas where local productivity is less than local mortality. Without immigration from source areas, populations in sink areas inevitably spiral "down the drain" into extinction.

Wooton and Bell (1992) modelled the Californian Peregrine Falcon population as two sub-populations (northern and southern) linked by dispersal. Their analysis suggested that the northern population acts as a source for the southern population. The regional management strategy for this species includes the release of captive-reared young aimed primarily at the southern population, which the authors showed to be a sink. As Meefe *et al.* (1997) stated, management efforts would be more productive if efforts were directed at stabilizing the northern source population rather than the southern sink population.

Traditional landscapes, being suited for their resident organisms, may be important sources for raptor populations, whereas cities, which may lack many key elements, may be destructive sinks, pulling birds from the population without adding to them. If, in the worst possible case scenario, non-urban habitat for a given species becomes entirely replaced by an urban one, city populations will not be able to support themselves and will eventually become extinct.

Determining whether a habitat is a source or a sink requires a great deal of knowledge about the natural history of organisms. Researchers must know the birth and death rates of individuals in each habitat type, details of dispersal behaviour, and many other aspects of a species' life history. The gathering and interpretation of this basic information is absolutely fundamental in the planning of management and conservation strategies for our newest and one of the least understood environments, the city. Without this knowledge, it will be impossible to design a conservation plan that considers realistic population dynamics, and the idea of raptor diversity in cities will be a mute concern next to that of maintaining a single species, or even a single bird of prey, in an urban landscape.

FUTURE RESEARCH AND DISCUSSION

Analyses of the requirements of each potential urban species, as well as comparisons between urban and non-urban populations, are necessary in order to determine the viability of cities as raptor refuges. Population Viability Analyses (PVA's) can determine how habitat loss/alteration, environmental uncertainty, population structure and gene flow are affecting the survival and viability of urban raptor populations (James *et al.* 1994). However, little research has thus far centred upon comparisons between urban and traditional habitats in an attempt to assess the costs and benefits of urban-related resources, or reasons for raptors to leave or move from traditional habitats into urban ones (Blanco 1994, Tella et al. 1996). Raptor community diversity in urban areas has yet to be studied, and must be encouraged, as it is the best indicator that the green spaces are truly integrated, working ecosystems, rather than merely a visually pleasing yet empty framework. As stated earlier, the question of source and sink dynamics must be addressed for each raptor species inhabiting urban areas.

The key to the survival and productivity of urban raptors is to change the perception that cities are "areas of last resort". Instead, they must be looked at as potential refuges for raptors seeking shelter and success from an ever-shrinking natural world. They are areas that must be planned, maintained, studied and even altered as more information is gathered. It is simply not enough to build up an urban area with a few green spaces, and expect raptors to move in without worry or consequences. The ultimate value of raptors in urban areas may be their umbrella effect, as their high visibility and allure make them ideal species for conserving critically endangered habitats.

ACKNOWLEDGEMENTS

We would like to sincerely thank Ian Ritchie and Peter Thomas for their helpful comments on various portions of the manuscript and McGill University for its support of avian research. O.P.L would like to truly thank Christina Semeniuk for her constant and useful ideas, help and encouragement which made this manuscript possible.

REFERENCES

BELL, D.A, D.P. GREGOIRE & B.J. WALTON 1996. Bridge use by Peregrine Falcons in the San Francisco Bay area. *In* D.M. Bird, D. Varland & J. Negro (Eds.) *Raptors in human landscapes*. Academic Press and The Raptor Research Foundation, London, U.K.

BIRD, D.M., D.E. VARLAND & J.J. NEGRO (eds.) 1996. *Raptors in human landscapes: Adaptations to built and cultivated environments*. Academic Press and The Raptor Research Foundation, London, U.K. 396pp

BLANCO, G. 1994. Seasonal abundance of Black Kites associated with the rubbish dump of Madrid, Spain. *J.Raptor Res.* 28(4):242-245.

BLANCO, G. 1997. Role of refuse as food for migrant, floater and breeding Black Kites. *J.Raptor Res.* 31(1):71-76.

BLOOM, P.H. & M.D. MCCRARY 1996. The urban buteo: Red-shouldered Hawks in southern California. *In* D.M. Bird, D. Varland & J. Negro (Eds.) *Raptors in human landscapes*. Academic Press and The Raptor Research Foundation, London, U.K.

BOSAKOWSKI, T. & D.G. SMITH 1997. Distribution and species richness of a forest raptor community in relation to urbanization. *J.Raptor Res.* 31(1):26-33.

BOTELHO, S & P.C ARROWOOD 1996. Nesting success of western Burrowing Owls in natural and human-alterred environments. *In* D.M. Bird, D. Varland & J. Negro (Eds.) *Raptors in human landscapes*. Academic Press and The Raptor Research Foundation, London, U.K.

CADE, T.J., J.H. ENDERSON, C.G.THELANDER & C.M. WHITE (eds.) 1988. *Peregrine Falcon populations: their management and recovery*. The Peregrine Fund, Inc., Boise, Idaho.

CADE, T.J., M. MARTELL, P. REDIG, G.A. SEPTON & H.B. TORDOFF 1996. Peregine Falcons in urban North America. *In* D.M. Bird, D. Varland & J. Negro (Eds.) *Raptors in human landscapes*. Academic Press and The Raptor Research Foundation, London, U.K.

CADE, T.J. & D.M. BIRD 1990. Peregrine Falcons nesting in an urban environment: a review. *Can. Field-Nat.* 104:209-218.

DONÁZAR, J.A. 1992. Muladares y basureros en la biología y conservación de las aves en Espanã. *Ardeola* 39:29-40.

DAWSON, J.W. & R.W. MANNAN 1995. Electrocution as a mortality factor in an urban population of Harris Hawks. *J.Raptor Res.* March 1995 No. 1

ELLIS, D.H., M.H. ELLIS & P. TSENGEG 1997. Remarkable Saker Falcon breeding records from Mongolia. *J.Raptor Res.* 31930:234-240.

ENGLAND, A.S., J.A. ESTEP & W.R. HOLT 1995. Nest-site selection and reproductive performance of urban-nesting Swainson's Hawks in the central valley of California. *J.Raptor Res.* 29 (3):179-186.

FRIESEN, L.E, P.F.J. EAGLES & R.J. MACKAY 1995. Effects of residential development on forest-dwelling neotropical migrant songbirds. *Conserv. Biol.* 9:1408-1414.
FRIMER, O. 1989*a*. Food and predation in suburban Sparrowhawks *Accipiter nisus* during the breeding season. *Dansk ornitologisk Forenings Tidsskrift* 83: 35-44.
FRIMER, O. 1989*b*. Breeding performance in a Danish suburban population of Sparrowhawks *Accipiter nisus*. *Dansk ornitologisk Forenings Tidsskrift* 83: 151-156.
GEHLBACH, F.R. 1996. Eastern Screech Owls in suburbia: A model of raptor urbanization. *In* D.M. Bird, D. Varland And J. Negro (Eds.) *Raptors in human landscapes*. Academic Press and The Raptor Research Foundation, London, U.K.
GENNARO, A.L. 1988. Breeding biology of an urban population of Mississippi Kites in New Mexico. *In* R.L. Glinski, B. Pendleton, M.B. Moss, M.N. LeFranc, Jr., B.A. Millsap S.W. Hoffman (Eds.) *Proc. SW Raptor Manage. Symp. and Workshop*. Natl. Wildl. Fed. Wash; D.C
IÑIGO, E.M. 1987. Feeding habits and ingestion of synthetic products in a Black Vulture population from Chiapas, Mexico. *Acta Zool. Mex Nueva Ser.* 22:1-15.
JAMES, P.C. 1992. Urban-nesting of Swainson's Hawks in Saskatchewan. *Condor* 94:773-774, 101:592-594.
JAMES, P.C., I.G. WARKENTIN & L.W. OLIPHANT 1994. Populations viability analysis of urban Merlins. *J.Raptor Res.* 28(1):47.
LAIDIG, K.J. & D.S. DOBKIN 1995. Spatial overlap and habitat associations of Barred Owls and Great-horned Owls in southern New Jersey. *J.Raptor Res.* 29(3):151-157.
LOOS, G. & P. KERLINGER 1993. Road mortality of Saw-Whet and Screech Owls on the Cape May peninsula. *J.Raptor Res.* 27(4):210-213.
MEEFE, G.K. & R.C. CARROLL 1997. *Principles of Conservation Biology*. 2nd ed. Sinauer Assoc., Inc. Massachusetts.
MIKKOLA, H. 1983. *Owls of Europe*. T. & A.D. Poyser, London, UK.
MURCIA, C. 1995. Edge effects in fragmented forests: Implications for conservation. *Trends Ecol.Evol.* 10:58-62.
NEWTON, I. 1979. *Population ecology of raptors*. T. & A.D. Poyser, Calton, UK.
OLIPHANT, L.W. & E. HAUG 1985. Productivity, population density and rate of increase of an expanding Merlin population. *J. Raptor Res.* 19:56-59.
OLIPHANT, L.W. & S. MCTAGGART 1977. Prey utilized by urban Merlins. *Can Field-Nat* 91:190-192.
PARKER, J.W. 1996. Urban ecology of the Mississippi Kite. *In* D.M. Bird, D. Varland And J. Negro (Eds.) *Raptors in human landscapes*. Academic Press and The Raptor Research Foundation, London, U.K.
POOLE, A. F. 1989. *Ospreys: A natural and unatural history*. Cambridge Univ. Press, Cambridge, England.
RODRÍGUEZ-ESTRELLA, R. & L.B.RIVERA RODRÍGUEZ 1997. Crested Caracara food habits in the Cape Region of Baja California, Mexico. *J.Raptor Res.* 31(3):228-233.
ROSENFIELD, R.N., J. BIELEFELDT, J.L. AFFELDT, & D.J. BECKMANN 1996. Urban nesting biology of Cooper's hawks in Wisconsin. *In* D.M. Bird, D. Varland & J. Negro (Eds.) *Raptors in human landscapes*. Academic Press and The Raptor Research Foundation, London, U.K.
SEIJAS, A.E. 1996. Feeding of the Bat falcon in an urban environment. *J.Raptor Res.* 30(1):33-35.
SHAW, D. M. 1985. The breeding biology of urban-nesting Mississippi Kites (*Ictinia mississippiensis*) in west central Texas. MS thesis, Angelo State Univ; San Angelo, Texas.
SODHI, N.S., I.G. WARKENTIN & L.W. OLIPHANT 1991. Hunting techniques and hunting rates of urban Merlins. *J.Raptor Res.* 25:127-131.
STAHLECKER, D. W. & A. BEACH 1979. Successful nesting by Cooper's Hawks in an urban environment. *Inland Bird Banding News* 51: 56-57.
STOUT, W.E., R.K. ANDSERSON & J.M. PAPP 1996. Red-tailed Hawks nesting on human-made and natural structures in southeast Wisconsin. *In* D.M. Bird, D. Varland & J. Negro (Eds.) *Raptors in human landscapes*. Academic Press and The Raptor Research Foundation, London, U.K.
STOUT, W.E., R.K. ANDSERSON & J.M. PAPP 1998. Urban, suburban and rural Red-tailed Hawk nesting habitat and populations in southeast Wisconsin. *J.Raptor Res.* 32(3):221-228.
SWEENEY S.J., P.T. REDIG & H.B. TORDOFF 1997. Morbidity, survival and productivity of rehabilitated Peregrine Falcons in the upper midwestern U.S. *J.Raptor Res.* 31(4):347-352.
TELLA, J.L., HIRALDO, F., DONÁZAR-SANCHO, J.A. & J.J. NEGRO 1996. Costs and benefits of urban nesting in the Lesser Kestrel. *In* D.M.Bird, D. Varland & J. Negro (Eds.) *Raptors in human landscapes*. Academic Press and The Raptor Research Foundation, London, U.K.
TEMPLE, S.A. 1986. Predicting impacts of habitat fragementaion on birds: A comparison of two models. *In* J. Verver, M.L. Morrison & C.J. Ralph (Eds.) *Wildlife 2000: Modelling Habitat Relationships of Terrestrial Vertebrates*. University of Wisconsin Press, Madison.

THIOLLAY, J.M. 1998. Current status and conservation of Falconiformes in tropical Asia. *J.Raptor Res.* 32(1):40-55

THIOLLAY, J.M. & B.U. MEYBURG 1988. Forest fragmentation and the conservation of raptors: a survey of the island of Java. *Biol. Conserv.* 44:229-250.

TORDOFF, H.B. & P.T. REDIG 1997. Midwest Peregrine Falcon demography, 1982-1995. *J.Raptor Res.* 31(4):339-346.

VILLAGE, A. 1989. Factors limiting European Kestrel *Falco tinnunculus* numbers in different habitats. *In* B.U. Meyburg & R.D. Chancellor (Eds.) *Raptors in the Modern World.* WWGBP, London.

WATSON, R.T. 1998. Conservation and ecology of raptors in the tropics. *J.Raptor Res.* 32(1):1-2.

WHITE, C.W. 1974. Current problems and techniques in raptor management and conservation. *Transac. Thirty-ninth North American Wildlife Conference.*

WILCOVE, D.S., C.H. MCLELLAN & A.P. DOBSON 1986. Habitat fragmentation in the temperate zone. *In* M.E. Soulé (ed.) *Conservation Biology: The Science of Scarcity and Diversity.* Sinauer Assoc., Inc. Sunderland, MA.

WOOTON, T.J. & D.A. BELL 1992. A meta-population model of the Peregrine Falcon in California: Viability and management strategies. *Ecol. Applic.* 2:307-321.

ZALEWSKI, A. 1994. Diet of urban and suburban Tawny Owls in the breeding season. *J.Raptor Res.* 28(4):246-252.

Oliver P. Love & David M. Bird
Avian Science and Conservation Centre
Macdonald Campus of McGill University
21,111 Lakeshore Road
Ste. Anne de Bellevue, Quebec
H9X 3V9
Canada

Chancellor, R. D. & B.-U. Meyburg eds. 2000
Raptors at Risk
WWGBP / Hancock House

Urban Landscapes and Raptors: a Review of Factors affecting Population Ecology

David E. Andersen and David L. Plumpton

ABSTRACT

Many species of raptors occur in urban environments and recently some raptors have reinhabited many urban landscapes both as a result of purposeful reintroduction (e.g., Peregrine Falcon *Falco peregrinus*) and through recolonization (e.g., Cooper's Hawk *Accipiter cooperii*). Factors affecting use of urban environments are varied and raptors may use urban landscapes because of urbanization, in spite of urbanization, or because urban landscapes are indistinguishable from non-urban landscapes. To distinguish among these possibilities, we reviewed and summarized existing published information on use of urban landscapes by raptors, and found examples of all three conditions. In addition, we summarized published information dealing with survival, reproduction, and density of raptors in urban landscapes, and indicated where concurrent studies allowed direct comparison of these parameters in non-urban landscapes. Factors that affect population ecology of the same taxa in urban and non-urban landscapes can be different, and these differences need to be considered in conservation of raptors in urban landscapes.

INTRODUCTION

Many species of raptors (members of the order Falconiformes) occur in urban landscapes both during breeding (e.g., Bloom & McCrary 1996, Cade *et al.* 1996) and non-breeding (e.g., Sodhi *et al.* 1991) seasons. Considerable recent attention (e.g., Bird *et al.* 1996) has been afforded the occurrence of raptors in urban landscapes, yet reasons why raptors use urban landscapes, and whether raptors in urban landscapes are capable of maintaining their populations without augmentation through immigration, have not been thoroughly evaluated. By itself, occurrence of raptors in urban landscapes, often reported as anecdotal accounts of nesting (e.g., James 1992), does not equate to urban raptor populations that are self-sustaining.

Raptors may use urban habitats because of urbanization, in spite of urbanization, or because urban habitats are indistinguishable from non-urban habitats. In addition, whether contemporary urban populations result from persistence of raptor populations that pre-date urbanization, natural colonization of landscapes following urbanization, or purposeful introduction of raptors, may influence characteristics of raptor populations in urban landscapes. Similarly, whether raptors use urban landscapes for breeding, during migration, as winter habitat, or as non-breeding habitat may affect the relative importance of characteristics of urban landscapes that makes them suitable for raptors. Finally, the extent of direct persecution by humans of raptors in urban landscapes is likely to affect whether raptors use and persist in those habitats.

Our purpose herein is to summarize information on population ecology of raptors using urban landscapes. For the purposes of this paper, we define urban landscapes as those dominated by structures constructed to house the activities of humans, and supporting infrastructure such as roads, and urbanization as the conversion from some other landscape to one that is urban. For a more thorough discussion of what constitutes urban landscapes as related to raptors, we refer the reader to Cringan and Horak (1989). Further, we restrict the scope of this review to reports where the expected daily or seasonal activity range of the birds under consideration coincides geographically with the scale of landscapes (i.e., at the scale of 10s and 100s of km^2). We present limited summaries of our own studies of Ferruginous Hawks *Buteo regalis* in eastcentral Colorado (Plumpton 1996; Plumpton & Andersen 1997, 1998), but primarily review published research pertaining to density, reproduction, survival, and habitat use of diurnal raptors in urbanized settings. We may unintentionally have emphasized North American species due to greater availability of these literature sources to us. However, we have attempted to include all published accounts without regard to geographic location.

In our review of literature pertaining to the impacts of human activity on raptor populations, we reviewed numerous accounts that addressed various human influences not related to urbanization (e.g., agriculture, forestry, and mining). Similarly, we encountered many published accounts that made reference to raptors and the effects of human disturbance. However informative, if these accounts failed to address the response of raptors specifically to urbanization, provided no basis for comparison with raptors inhabiting non-urban landscapes, or made no mention of quantifiable differences in ecology attributable to urbanization, we did not include them in this review. We note however, that it is important to realize that often urbanization is not the first anthropogenic influence affecting local raptor populations. Agriculture, silviculture, human infrastructure establishment (e.g., roads, electric transmission rights-of-way, mineral extraction, water impoundments) and other human changes to the landscape often precede urbanization, and may therefore exert an influence upon the fauna inhabiting an area before changes due strictly to urbanization are detected. For this reason, one must recognize the potential for gross changes in raptor populations that may have occurred because of various human pressures prior to urbanization.

The specific objectives of our review then, were to: (1) provide a summary of published information on density, reproduction, survival, and habitat use by raptors in urban landscapes; (2) categorize existing descriptions of urban raptor populations based on factors such as when during the year raptors occur in those habitats and the likely source of the urban population, and; (3) suggest conditions under which raptors occur in urban landscapes in spite of, because of, or without regard to urbanization.

METHODS

We reviewed published literature by searching electronic databases and recent overviews of the potential impacts of human activity on raptors (e.g., Bird *et al.* 1996), and through our own familiarity with the literature. Based on manuscript titles and keywords, we selected those manuscripts that may have included information about population ecology of raptors in urban landscapes. One or both of us then evaluated the original manuscript to determine whether it was pertinent for this review.

We then categorized those manuscripts that included information about population ecology of raptors in urban landscapes based on (1) the nature of the study (anecdotal observation or descriptive or comparative study), (2) season (breeding or non-breeding), and (3) the likely source of the population (persistence from pre-urbanized landscape, colonization, or introduction). Based on this review and any other pertinent information included in the published account, we then assessed whether raptors described in the study were likely using a specific landscape in spite of, because of, or without regard to urbanization. For studies that included estimates of density, survival, or reproduction, we summarized comparisons of these parameters from populations in non-urban landscapes, based either on concurrent study of non-urban populations or comparison with previous studies, as reported in published manuscripts.

RESULTS AND DISCUSSION

1. Summary of Published Literature

We reviewed > 150 published manuscripts that reported on raptors or owls (owls are often included within the definition of raptors, and were sometimes included in the results of electronic literature searches) in human-modified landscapes, or the impacts of human activity on birds of prey, based on key words and titles. The majority of these were removed from further consideration, as they did not address raptor ecology in urban landscapes (we also excluded manuscripts that dealt solely with owls), leaving approximately 50 manuscripts for further consideration. Upon careful review of these, only 36 reported information on density, reproduction, survival, or habitat use of raptors in urban landscapes. Of these 36 manuscripts, we classified 6 (17%) as anecdotal descriptions of nesting by raptors in urban habitats (Stahlecker & Beach 1979, Hull 1980, Newton 1986, Murphy *et al.* 1988, James 1992, Bell *et al.* 1996; for an overview of nesting of raptors in urban habitats, we refer the reader to Love and Bird [this volume]), leaving 30 published studies of raptor ecology in urban landscapes (Tables 1-3). Several manuscripts included in these 30 resulted from a single research programme (e.g., Plumpton 1996; Plumpton & Andersen 1997, 1998). In those instances, we considered manuscripts together that resulted from the same study and reported related results, reducing the number of studies considered further from 30 to 21.

Fifteen (71%) of these 21 published studies reported on nesting success and productivity of raptors nesting in urban landscapes (Table 1), and emphasized breeding-season population ecology. Thirteen (62%) of these were primarily descriptive, in that they presented results from studies of raptors in urban landscapes without providing comparative information from non-urban raptor populations. The remaining 8 (38%) compared characteristics of ≥ 2 populations, at least one of which was located in an urban landscape. Only five studies included habitat use and behaviour as a primary component (Table 2) and in only three were raptor populations studied primarily outside of the breeding season (Table 2). Five (including several incorporated into previous categories) reported on nest site selection as the sole or a significant component (Table 3).

Relatively few species were represented in published studies of raptors in urban landscapes; 2 accipitrine hawks (Cooper's Hawk *Accipiter cooperii*, Sparrowhawk *A. nisus*), 4 buteonine hawks (Red-tailed Hawk *Buteo jamaicensis*, Red-shouldered Hawk *B. lineatus*, Swainson's Hawk *B. swainsoni*, and Ferruginous Hawk), 3 falconids (Merlin *Falco columbarius*, Peregrine Falcon *F. peregrinus*, Lesser Kestrel *F. naumanni*), 1 New World kite (Mississippi Kite *Ictinia mississippiensis*), and 1 sea eagle (Bald Eagle *Haliaeetus leucocephalus*) (Tables 1-3). In addition, the majority of published studies that we reviewed were of North American raptors. We located only three descriptions of raptors in urban landscapes from Europe (Newton 1986, Tella *et al.* 1996; Frimer 1989a, 1989b), and none from South America, Asia, Africa, or Australia. The reason(s) for our inability to locate published accounts of raptor ecology in urban habitats from outside of North America is unclear. If such literature exists, it does not appear to be readily accessible in electronic literature databases, nor cited in English-language scientific journals.

In most instances, it was not possible to discern whether raptor populations described in the published accounts we reviewed had colonized urban landscapes, or whether they had persisted in landscapes that had undergone urbanization. The nature of urbanization differs geographically (e.g., North American and European landscapes; Cringan & Horak, 1989), and thus the likely source of urban raptor populations may also vary geographically. In at least some accounts, however, authors speculated that raptors had colonized urban landscapes as nesting habitat. Colonization seemed most likely for Cooper's Hawks (Rosenfield *et al.* 1995, 1996; Boal 1997, Boal & Mannan 1998), Sparrowhawks (Frimer 1989a, 1989b), Merlins (Oliphant & Haug 1985, Warkentin & James 1988), Swainson's Hawks (England *et al.* 1995), and Mississippi Kites (Gennaro 1988, Parker 1996) (Table 1). Introduction into urban landscapes was an important consideration for Peregrine Falcons (Cade & Bird 1990, Cade *et al.* 1996, Tordorff & Redig 1997). For Red-tailed Hawks (Speiser & Bosakowski 1988, Stout *et al.* 1996), Red-shouldered Hawks (Bloom & McCrary 1996), and Lesser Kestrels (Tella *et al.* 1996), some combination of persistence and colonization probably resulted in populations

Table 1. Published studies of breeding raptors in urban landscapes that report estimates of nesting success, productivity, or both nesting success and productivity.

Study	Years	Location	Species	Study Type	Population Source	Parameters Reported	Sample Size and Type
Parker 1996	1977 1979-1980 1982-1987	Kansas	Ictinia mississippiensis	Comparative	Colonization Persistence	Nesting density Hatching success Nesting success Productivity	$n = 34$-41 nests
Gennaro 1988	1982-1984	Clovis, New Mexico	Ictinia mississippiensis	Descriptive	Colonization Persistence	Nesting success Productivity	$n = 124$ nests
Boal 1997 Boal and Mannan 1998	1994-1997	Tucson, Arizona	Accipiter cooperii	Descriptive Comparative	Colonization Persistence	Nest site selection Clutch size Productivity Nestling survival Adult survival	$n = 51$ territories $n = 275$ banded birds
Rosenfield et al. 1995, 1996	1993	Central Wisconsin	Accipiter cooperii	Descriptive	Colonization Persistence	Nesting density Clutch size Productivity	$n = 13$ nests
Frimer 1989a, 1989b	1979-1987	Denmark	Accipiter nisus	Comparative	Colonization	Nesting density Productivity	$n = 48$ breeding attempts
Stout et al. 1996	1987-1993	Milwaukee, Wisconsin	Buteo jamaicensis	Comparative	Colonization Persistence	Nesting success Nest site selection Nesting density Productivity	$n = 99$ nests
Minor et al. 1993	1980-1989	Central New York	Buteo jamaicensis	Descriptive	Persistence	Nesting density Productivity	$n = 134$ nests
Rottenborn In preparation	1994-1995	Central California	Buteo lineatus	Descriptive	Persistence Colonization	Nesting density Nesting success Productivity	$n = 85$ nests
England et al. 1995	1990-1994	Central Valley, California	Buteo swainsoni	Descriptive Comparative	Colonization Persistence	Nesting success Nest site characteristics	$n = 65$ nesting attempts
Bloom and McCrary 1996	"25 years"	Southern California	Buteo lineatus	Descriptive	Colonization Persistence	Nesting success Productivity	$n = 86$ nests
Oliphant and Haug 1985	1971-1982	Saskatoon, Saskatchewan	Falco columbarius	Descriptive	Colonization	Nesting success Nesting density Productivity	$n = 82$ nests

Table 1. continued

Study	Years	Location	Species	Study Type	Population Source	Parameters Reported	Sample Size and Type
Tella et al. 1996	1993	Southern Spain	Falco naumanni	Comparative	Colonization Persistence	Adult survival Nestling survival Clutch size Productivity	$n = 465$ nests $n = 16$ colonies
Cade and Bird 1990	1988	North America	Falco peregrinus	Comparative	Introduction Colonization	Nesting success Nestling success Productivity Survival (introduction)	$n = 24$ nests
Cade et al. 1996	1993	North America	Falco peregrinus	Descriptive	Introduction Colonization	Occurrence Nesting	$n = 88$ nests
Tordoff and Redig 1997	1982-1995	Central North America	Falco peregrinus	Descriptive	Introduction	Survival Dispersal Reproduction Fidelity	$n = 747$ released birds $n = 493$ wild birds

Table 2. Published literature reporting behaviour and habitat use of raptors using urban landscapes.

Study	Years	Location	Species	Study Type	Season	Population Source	Parameters Reported	Sample Size and Type
Bloom et al. 1993	1979-1981 1986-1988	Southern California	Buteo lineatus	Descriptive	Breeding	Persistence	Habitat use	$n = 2$ radio-marked birds
Plumpton 1996 Plumpton and Andersen 1997, 1998	1992-1995	Eastcentral Colorado	Buteo regalis	Comparative	Non-breeding (winter)	Persistence	Behaviour Home range size	$n = 38$ radio-marked birds
Warkenton et al. 1991, 1992 Warkenton and James 1988, 1990	1985-1990	Saskatoon Saskatchewan	Falco columbarius	Descriptive	Breeding	Colonization	Assortative mating Site fidelity Nest site characteristics Mate switching	$n = 149$ pairs $n = 120$ nesting attempts $n = 58$ nest sites $n = 41$ roosts
Sodhi et al. 1991	1987-1990	Saskatoon Saskatchewan	Falco columbarius	Descriptive	Breeding Non-breeding (winter)	Colonization	Hunting behaviour	$n = 27$ radio-marked birds
Buehler et al. 1991	1985-1989	Virginia and Maryland	Haliaeetus leucocephalus	Descriptive	Non-breeding	Persistence	Habitat use	$n = 75$ radio-marked birds

Table 3. Published studies reporting nest site characteristics of raptors nesting in urban landscapes.

Study	Years	Location	Species	Study Type	Population Source	Parameters Reported	Sample Size and Type
Boal 1997	1994-1997	Tucson, Arizona	*Accipiter cooperii*	Descriptive	Colonization	Nest site selection	$n = 51$ territories
Boal and Mannan 1998				Comparative	Persistence	Clutch size Productivity Nestling survival Adult survival Nesting density	$n = 275$ banded birds
England et al. 1995	1990-1994	Central Valley, California	*Buteo swainsoni*	Descriptive Comparative	Colonization Persistence	Nesting success Nest site characteristics	$n = 65$ nesting attempts
Speiser and Bosakowski 1988	1977-1987	New York and New Jersey	*Buteo jamaicensis*	Descriptive	Colonization Persistence	Nest site selection	$n = 61$ nests
Stout et al. 1996	1987-1993	Milwaukee, Wisconsin	*Buteo jamaicensis*	Comparative	Colonization Persistence	Nest site selection Nesting density Productivity	$n = 99$ nests
Rottenborn *In preparation*	1994-1995	Central California	*Buteo lineatus*	Descriptive	Persistence Colonization	Nesting success Productivity	$n = 85$ nests
Warkenton et al. 1991, 1992	1985-1990	Saskatoon, Saskatchewan	*Falco columbarius*	Descriptive	Colonization	Assortative mating Site fidelity Nest site characteristics Mate switching	$n = 149$ pairs $n = 120$ nesting attempts $n = 58$ nest sites $n = 41$ roosts
Warkenton and James 1988, 1990							

in urban landscapes (Tables 1 and 3). In contrast, published accounts of urban Ferruginous Hawks (Plumpton 1996; Plumpton & Andersen 1997, 1998), Bald Eagles (Buehler et al. 1991), and at least some Red-shouldered Hawks (Bloom et al. 1993) were likely based on raptors that persisted in landscapes that had become urbanized.

Few studies addressed aspects of population dynamics (reproduction, survival, and density) of urban raptors, and most addressed only nesting success and/or productivity (Table 1). We located only four studies of breeding urban raptors that included discussion of survival rates (Cade & Bird 1990, Tella et al. 1996, Boal 1997, Tordoff & Redig 1997), and only two of these (Boal 1997, Tordoff & Redig 1997) estimated population growth rates based on schedules of fecundity and survival. Several authors compared reproductive success in urban and non-urban raptor populations (e.g., Boal 1997), and examples of both higher and lower nesting success and productivity in urban landscapes (compared with non-urban) were reported. Similarly, estimates of nesting density in urban landscapes have been reported as higher compared with that in non-urban landscapes (e.g., Cooper's Hawks; Rosenfield et al. 1995, 1996), and lower than in adjacent non-urban areas (e.g., Red-tailed Hawk, Stout et al. 1996). We note, however, that nesting density has only infrequently been estimated for breeding raptors concurrently in both urban and non-urban populations.

We found few published accounts of habitat use and behaviour. Characteristics of nest sites have been measured concurrently in breeding urban and non-urban raptor populations in only a few instances (e.g., Red-tailed Hawk, Stout et al. 1996), but more commonly as part of study of urban-nesting raptors (e.g., Swainson's Hawk, England et al. 1995). We found relatively little information regarding habitat use and behaviour of urban raptors based on marked birds during the breeding season -- home range (e.g., Bloom et al. 1993; Boal & Mannan 1998) mating strategies (e.g., Warkentin & James 1988, 1990; Warkentin et al. 1991, 1992), and hunting behaviour (e.g., Sodhi et al. 1991) have been described for only a few urban raptors. Outside the breeding season, even less information is available regarding habitat use and behaviour. Plumpton (1996) and Plumpton and Andersen (1998) compared behaviour and habitat use of Ferruginous Hawks in urban and non-urban habitats in east-central Colorado, Buehler et al. (1991) documented avoidance of urban landscapes by wintering Bald Eagles in the Chesapeake Bay, and Sodhi et al. (1991) described hunting behaviour of wintering Merlins in Saskatoon, Saskatchewan.

2. Comparison with non-urban raptor populations

We found very few examples of published studies that compared urban and non-urban raptor populations, where data from both populations were collected coincident in time. Most studies that compared characteristics of urban and non-urban raptor populations reported reproductive parameters, usually nesting success and productivity. Boal (1997) reported larger clutches and more nestlings for Cooper's Hawks in urban than non-urban landscapes, but higher nestling mortality resulted in lower net productivity in urban landscapes. He also reported on potential differences in nesting phenology and breeding-season diet between Cooper's Hawks in urban and non-urban habitats. In contrast, Tella et al. (1996) reported lower nesting success and productivity for urban-nesting Lesser Kestrels, compared with kestrels nesting in non-urban landscapes. Predation of adult kestrels at the nest was lower, as were prey delivery rates to nests in urban landscapes, suggesting higher adult survival but poorer prey availability. England et al. (1995) reported lower nesting success and productivity of urban-nesting Swainson's Hawks compared with rural-nesting hawks in central California. Stout et al. (1996) presented nearest-neighbour distances for nesting Red-tailed Hawks in urban, suburban, and rural landscapes, indicating higher breeding densities in more rural landscapes. Conversely, in a correlative study of Red-shouldered Hawks in California, Rottenborn (in preparation) found no evidence for an effect of extent of urbanization on nesting success and productivity. Similarly, Cade and Bird (1990) reported comparable productivity of urban versus rural-nesting Peregrine Falcons in North America.

Because reproductive parameters can vary temporally in raptors (e.g., Newton 1979), comparisons of these characteristics for populations that are not coincident in time is difficult. Similarly, comparisons of populations separated geographically must account for underlying differences in landscape characteristics that might influence reproduction and behaviour. Bearing these constraints in mind, it may still be informative to compare reproductive parameters and habitat use in urban raptor populations to the range of values observed in non-urban populations of the same species. Boal (1997) and Rosenfield *et al.* (1995, 1996) both reported high nesting densities of Cooper's Hawks in urban landscapes, compared with published nesting densities in non-urban landscapes. Similarly, estimated clutch sizes were high for both studies, and in central Wisconsin (Rosenfield *et al.* 1995, 1996), indices to productivity were also relatively high. In Arizona, however, Boal (1997) reported a high incidence of disease in nestling Cooper's Hawks, resulting in low productivity. He further suggested that exposure to disease in urban habitats resulted in survival rates so low that the population was unable to sustain itself in the absence of immigration.

In California, Bloom and McCrary (1996) reported higher nesting success and productivity for urban-nesting Red-shouldered Hawks, compared with non-urban hawks (Wiley 1975). Oliphant and Haug (1985) reported higher nesting densities for urban-nesting Merlins in Saskatchewan, compared with rural Saskatchewan (Schmutz 1982). Conversely, England *et al.* (1995) reported low nesting success and productivity of Swainson's Hawks breeding in central California cities, compared with estimates from other studies conducted in non-urban landscapes (e.g., Olendorff 1978, Schmutz *et al.* 1980). Parker (1996) reported higher nest densities, nesting success, and productivity for urban Mississippi Kite colonies compared with rural colonies.

Fewer data exist comparing habitat use and behaviour of urban versus non-urban raptors. In east-central Colorado (Plumpton 1996; Plumpton & Andersen 1997, 1998), Ferruginous Hawks wintering in urban landscapes foraged in isolated, remnant Black-tailed Prairie Dog (*Cynomys ludovicianus*) towns, and modified perch use, time budgets, and roosting habits compared with hawks occurring in non-urban habitats. In a study of winter behaviour and habitat use, Buehler *et al.* (1991) reported that Bald Eagles avoided urban habitats, using them less than expected based on their availability.

3. Use of urban landscapes by raptors

Based on our review of published literature regarding raptor population ecology in urban landscapes, we propose three categories of landscapes, based on their ability to support raptor populations. First, raptors may use urban landscapes because these exceed the ability of non-urban landscapes to support raptor populations. This may be the case for urban-nesting Peregrine Falcons in eastern North America (e.g., Cade & Bird 1990, Cade *et al.* 1996) and Cooper's Hawks in central Wisconsin (Rosenfield *et al.* 1995, 1996) and Arizona (Boal & Mannan 1998), where parameters related to breeding indicated that food was abundant, and where nest sites were not limiting. Second, raptors may use urban landscapes in spite of urbanization. Ferruginous Hawks in east-central Colorado (Plumpton 1996; Plumpton & Andersen 1997, 1998) continued to forage in remnant Prairie Dog colonies, even as those colonies become more and more isolated due to urbanization. These hawks appear to modify their behaviour to persist in urban landscapes. Similarly, wintering Bald Eagles in Chesapeake Bay (Buehler *et al.* 1991) appeared to avoid urban landscapes, although they continued to use urban sites to some extent. Finally, whether a landscape is urban or non-urban may be a neutral factor in terms of the ability of that landscape to support a raptor population. Several authors (e.g., Bloom & McCrary 1996, Boal 1997) have indicated that at the level of an individual territory or home range, habitat features (both structural and compositional) are similar to characteristics of non-urban, high quality habitat. In some instances, where mortality is not increased through direct or indirect impacts of human activity, urban landscapes may be capable of supporting self-sustaining, high-density raptor populations.

CONCLUSIONS

Relatively few quantitative data exist regarding population ecology of raptors in urban landscapes, far too few to make generalizations about characteristics of urban landscapes that enhance the potential for raptors to occur there in self-sustaining populations (other than what is known generally about raptor populations [e.g., Newton 1979]). Several difficulties confound any attempt to quantify the effects of urbanization on raptors. One difficulty we encountered was in delimiting the topic of urbanization; it is neither as narrow and specific a causal agent as is direct human persecution or environmental contamination, nor is it as broad and all-encompassing as are human disturbance and habitat loss. The relative paucity of published information on population ecology of raptors in urban landscapes reflects this difficulty. Another problem we encountered was in separating the potential effects of multiple factors. For example, road construction, often a harbinger of urbanization, improved access into certain areas of Italy. This improved access led to widespread shooting of Red Kites *Milvus milvus* (Cortone et al. 1994), and caused significant population decline. Finally, there are a number of accounts of population declines or local extinctions of raptors following human population growth in previously undeveloped areas (e.g., Abuladze 1994), yet these accounts are not often supported by population counts or other data collected during the period of urbanization.

With a few notable exceptions, most studies of urban raptors have not estimated population attributes that allow thorough evaluation of population dynamics, nor have comparable data been collected on non-urban raptor populations coincident in time and in close geographic proximity. What is clear, is that a number of raptor species breed in urban landscapes, sometimes at relatively high densities and with high reproductive success and productivity. However, there is not a consistent pattern of breeding density and reproduction across species, or within the same species, and in most instances survival has not been measured, limiting the ability to project population trajectory. Although behaviour has been studied in only a few urban raptor populations, some species appear able to adapt their behaviour to forage and breed successfully in urban landscapes.

Although we believe that it is not currently possible to make broad generalizations about the effects of urbanization on raptor population ecology, we suggest that future studies could improve understanding about specific populations, and about urban raptor populations in general. Before-and-after studies (e.g., Bloom & McCrary 1996) and simultaneous comparison of areas with different levels of urbanization (e.g., Plumpton 1996; Plumpton & Andersen 1998; Boal & Mannan 1998) provide deeper insight than simple descriptions of urban-nesting raptors. Higher priority assigned to understanding their population ecology, combined with well-designed studies, would provide important information necessary to conserve raptors in urban landscapes.

REFERENCES

ABULADZE, A. 1994. Birds of Prey in Georgia in the 20th century. *In* B.U. Meyburg & R. D. Chancellor (eds.) *Raptor Conservation Today*. Proceedings of the IV World Conference on Birds of Prey and Owls. 799pp.

BELL, D.A., D.P. GREGOIRE & B.J. WALTON 1996. Bridge use by peregrine falcons in the San Francisco Bay area. *In* D. M. Bird, D. E. Varland, & J. J. Negro (eds.) *Raptors in human landscapes: adaptations to built and cultivated environments*. Academic Press, San Diego. 396pp.

BIRD, D.M., D.E. VARLAND & J.J. NEGRO (eds.) 1996. *Raptors in human landscapes: Adaptations to built and cultivated environments*. Academic Press, Harcourt Brace & Company, London, United Kingdom. 396pp.

BLOOM, P.H. & M.D. MCCRARY 1996. The urban buteo: Red-shouldered Hawks in southern California. *In* D. M. Bird, D. E. Varland & J. J. Negro (eds.) *Raptors in human Landscapes: adaptations to built and cultivated environments*. Academic Press, Harcourt Brace & Company, London, United Kingdom.

BLOOM, P.H., M.D. MCCRARY & M.J. GIBSON 1993. Red-shouldered Hawk home range and habitat use in southern California. *J. Wildl. Manage.* 57:258-265.

BOAL, C.W. 1997. An urban environment as an ecological trap for Cooper's Hawks. Ph.D. Diss., Univ. Arizona, Tucson. 85pp.

BOAL, C.W. & R.W. MANNAN 1998. Nest-site selection by Cooper's Hawks in an urban environment. *J. Wildl. Manage.* 62:864-871.

BUEHLER, D.A., T.J. MERSMANN, J.D. FRASER & J.K.D. SEEGAR 1991. Effects of human activity on Bald Eagle distribution on the northern Chesapeake Bay. *J. Wildl. Manage.* 55:282-290.

CADE, T.J., & D.M. BIRD 1990. Peregrine Falcons, *Falco peregrinus* nesting in an urban environment: A review. *Can Field-Nat.* 104:209-218.

CADE, T.J., M. MARTELL, P. REDIG, G. SEPTON & H. TORDOFF 1996. Peregrine falcons in urban North America. *In* D.M. Bird, D.E. Varland & J.J. Negro (eds.) *Raptors in human landscapes: adaptations to built and cultivated environments*. Academic Press, Harcourt Brace & Company, London, United Kingdom.

CORTONE, P., A. MINGANTI, M. PELLEGRINI, F. RIGA, A. SIGISMONDI & A. ZOCCHI 1994. Population trends of the Red Kite *Milvus milvus* in Italy. *In* B.U. Meyburg & R. D. Chancellor (eds.) *Raptor Conservation Today*. Proceedings of the IV World Conference on Birds of Prey and Owls. 799pp.
CRINGAN, A.T. & G.C. HORAK 1989. Effects of urbanization on raptors in the western United States. *In* Proceedings of the Western Raptor Management Symposium and Workshop, National Wildlife Federation, Washington, D. C.
ENGLAND, A.S., J.A. ESTEP & W.R. HOLT 1995. Nest-site selection and reproductive performance of urban-nesting Swainson's Hawks in the Central Valley of California. *J. Raptor Res.* 29:179-186.
FRIMER, O. 1989*a*. Food and predation in suburban sparrowhawks *Accipiter nisus* during the breeding season. *Dansk ornitologisk Forenings Tidsskrift* 83: 35-44.
FRIMER, O. 1989*b*. Breeding performance in a Danish suburban population of sparrowhawks *Accipiter nisus*. *Dansk ornitologisk Forenings Tidsskrift* 83: 151-156.
GENNARO, A.L 1988. Breeding biology of an urban population of Mississippi Kites in New Mexico. *In* Proceedings of the Southwest Raptor Management Symposium and Workshop, National Wildlife Federation, Washington, D. C.
HULL, C.N. 1980. Additional successful nesting of a Red-tailed Hawk in an urban subdivision. *Jack Pine Warbler* 58:30.
JAMES, P.C. 1992. Urban-nesting Swainson's Hawks in Saskatchewan. *Condor* 94:773-774.
MINOR, W.F., M. MINOR & M.F. INGRALDI 1993. Nesting of Red-tailed Hawks and Great-horned Owls in a central New York urban/suburban area. *J. Field Orni.* 64:433-439.
MURPHY, R.K., M.W. GRATSON & R.N. ROSENFIELD 1988. Activity and habitat use by a breeding male Cooper's Hawk in a suburban area. *J. Raptor Res.* 22:97-100.
NEWTON, I. 1979. *Population ecology of raptors*. Buteo Books, Vermillion, South Dakota, USA. 399pp.
NEWTON, I. 1986. *The Sparrowhawk*. T & A D Poyser, Ltd., Staffordshire, United Kingdom.
OLIPHANT, L.W. & E. HAUG 1985. Productivity, population density and rate of increase of an expanding Merlin population. *J. Raptor Res.* 19:56-59.
OLENDORFF, R.R. 1978. Population status of large raptors in northeastern Colorado 1970-1972. *Raptor Res. Rep.* 3:185-205.
PARKER, J.W. 1996. Urban ecology of the Mississippi Kite. *In* D.M. Bird, D.E. Varland & J.J. Negro (eds.) *Raptors in human landscapes: adaptations to built and cultivated environments*. Academic Press, San Diego. 396pp.
PLUMPTON, D.L. 1996. Anthropogenic effects on winter habitat use by Ferruginous Hawks in Colorado. Ph.D. Dissertation, University of Minn., St. Paul. 85pp.
PLUMPTON, D.L. & D.E. ANDERSEN 1997. Habitat use and time budgeting by wintering Ferruginous Hawks. *Condor* 99:888-893.
PLUMPTON, D.L. & D.E. ANDERSEN. 1998. Anthropogenic effects on winter habitat use and behavior of Ferruginous Hawks. *J. Wildl. Manage.* 62:340-346.
ROSENFIELD, R.N., J. BIELEFELDT, J.L. AFFELDT, & D.J. BECHMANN 1995. Nesting density, nest area reoccupancy, and monitoring implications for Cooper's Hawks in Wisconsin. *J. Raptor Res.* 29:1-4.
ROSENFIELD, R.N., J. BIELEFELDT, J.L. AFFELDT & D.J. BECKMANN 1996. Urban nesting biology of Cooper's Hawks in Wisconsin. *In* D.M. Bird, D.E. Varland & J.J. Negro (eds.) *Raptors in human landscapes: adaptations to built and cultivated environments*. Academic Press, San Diego. 396pp.
ROTTENBORN, S.C. In preparation. Nest-site selection and reproductive success of urban Red-shouldered Hawks in central California.
SCHMUTZ, J.K. 1982. An estimate of Ferruginous Hawks in Alberta and the relationship between their density and land use. Unpublished report for the Fish and Wildlife Division of Alberta Energy and Natural Resources.
SCHMUTZ, J.K., S.M. SCHMUTZ & D.A. BOAG 1980. Coexistence of three species of hawks in the prairie-parkland ecotone. *Can. J. Zoo.* 58:1075-1089.
SODHI, N.S., I.G. WARKENTIN & L.W. OLIPHANT 1991. Hunting techniques and success rates of urban Merlins. *J. Raptor Res.* 25:127-131.
SPEISER, R. & T. BOSAKOWSKI 1988. Nest site preferences of Red-tailed Hawks in the highlands of southeastern New York and northern New Jersey. *J. Field Orn.* 59:361-368.
STAHLECKER, D.W. & A. BEACH 1979. Successful nesting by Cooper's Hawks in an urban environment. *Inland Bird Banding News* 51:56-57.
STOUT, W.E., R.K. ANDERSON & J.M. PAPP 1996. Red-tailed Hawks nesting on human-made and natural structures in southeastern Wisconsin. *In* D.M. Bird, D.E. Varland & J.J. Negro (eds.) *Raptors in human landscapes: adaptations to built and cultivated environments*. Academic Press, San Diego. 396pp.

TELLA, J.L., F. HIRALDO, J.A. DON ZAR-SANCHO & J.J. NEGRO 1996. Costs and benefits of urban nesting in the Lesser Kestrel. *In* D.M. Bird, D.E. Varland & J.J. Negro (eds.) *Raptors in human landscapes: adaptations to built and cultivated environments.* Academic Press, San Diego. 396pp.
TORDOFF, H.B. & P.T. REDIG 1997. Midwest Peregrine Falcon demography, 1982-1995. *J. Raptor Res.* 31:339-346.
WARKENTIN, I.G. & P.C. JAMES 1990. Winter roost-site selection by urban Merlins. *J. Raptor Res.* 24:5-11.
WARKENTIN, I.G., P.C. JAMES & L.W. OLIPHANT 1991. Influence of site fidelity on mate switching in urban-breeding Merlins. *Auk* 108:294-302.
WARKENTIN, I.G., P.C. JAMES & L.W. OLIPHANT 1992. Assortative mating in urban-breeding Merlins. *Condor* 94:418-426.
WARKENTIN, I. G. & P. C. JAMES 1988. Nest-site selection by urban merlins. *Condor* 90:734-738.
WILEY, J.W. 1975. The nesting and reproductive success of Red-tailed Hawks and Red-shouldered Hawks in Orange County, California. *Condor* 77:133-139.

David. E. Andersen
Minnesota Cooperative Fish and Wildlife Research Unit
200 Hodson Hall, 1980 Folwell Avenue
St. Paul, MN 55108
USA

David. L. Plumpton
H.T. Harvey & Associates Ecological Consultants
906 Elizabeth Street
P.O. Box 1180, Alviso, CA 95002
USA

Nest Sites of Five Raptor Species Along an Urban Gradient

R. W. Mannan, C. W. Boal, W. J. Burroughs, J. W. Dawson, T. S. Estabrook and W. S. Richardson

ABSTRACT

We surveyed the metropolitan area of Tucson, Arizona, USA, from 1993-1997 for breeding Cooper's Hawks *Accipiter cooperii*, Harris' Hawks *Parabuteo unicinctus*, Red-tailed Hawks *Buteo jamaicensis*, Great-horned Owls *Bubo virginianus*, and Burrowing Owls *Athene cunicularia*, and found 227 nests. We were interested in determining whether these five species nested in identifiable and different environments along the gradient of developed to undeveloped land. Therefore, we randomly selected 20 nests of each species and plotted their locations on aerial photographs (scale: 2.5 cm = 360 m) taken in 1995. Within 200 m of each nest, we counted the number of houses and non-commercial buildings, and estimated the percent cover of major roads and commercial buildings, native vegetation, land developed for public activity (e.g., parks and golf courses), and undeveloped land from which native vegetation had been removed. We also measured the distance from each nest to the centre of the nearest square block of undeveloped land ≥ 16 ha in size. We compared the means of each variable among species with one-way analysis of variance. Mean values of all variables, except percent cover of commercial buildings and roads, differed among species ($P<0.001$). In general, Cooper's Hawks nested in high density residential areas or parks and golf courses, Harris' Hawks nested in moderate density residential areas interspersed with native vegetation, Red-tailed Hawks and Burrowing Owls nested in areas dominated by undeveloped land, and Great-horned Owls nested in a variety of environments. The distribution of nesting hawks and owls in Tucson appeared to be influenced by the distribution of nest structures or sites (e.g., large trees, burrows), favoured prey species, and environments in which the raptors are adapted to hunt.

INTRODUCTION

Urbanization generally creates a gradient of environments with highly developed land on one end of the continuum and moderately developed or undeveloped land on the other (Blair 1996). For example, towns and cities frequently have on their outskirts a mixture of native vegetation, agricultural fields, and a few private residences or other buildings. In contrast, centres of urban environments often are almost wholly covered by buildings and pavement, and vegetation, if present, is dominated by exotic species. The gradient of environments created by urbanization provides an array of resources (e.g., food, cover, nest sites, water) required by birds for nesting. Not surprisingly, species composition of breeding birds changes markedly along this gradient (e.g., Batten 1972, Emlen 1974, Beissinger & Osborne 1982, Rosenberg et al. 1987, Mills et al. 1989, Blair 1996).

Hawks, owls, and falcons also should respond to the gradient of resources created by urbanization, but information about the distribution of raptor species in urban settings is lacking for two reasons. First, standard survey methods for birds do not effectively estimate raptor abundance; raptors are, therefore, often excluded from bird counts in urban environments. And second, most reports of raptors nesting in urban environments focus on a single species and many describe only a few nests (see Adams 1994 for review). We report, herein, on urban-nesting by five species of hawks and owls in an urban centre in the southwestern United States, and identify and compare the environments in which they nest.

STUDY AREA

We studied the distribution of nesting raptors in the greater Tucson metropolitan area (32^0 12'N, 110^0 57'W) in southeastern Arizona, USA, from 1993 to 1997. The area encompasses about 70,000 ha, with an approximate human population of 800,000. Tucson includes developments ranging from commercial districts and high density housing to suburban areas with low density housing. Tucson is located in the Sonoran Desert. Vegetation communities common in the area prior to development were lower and upper Sonoran vegetation types and riparian corridors (Brown et al. 1979). Remnants of these vegetative communities are still found within Tucson, particularly in the suburban developments, but much of the native vegetation has been removed and replaced with exotic species.

METHODS

1. Surveys

Nests examined in this study were located over a period of five years (1993-1997) in a series of different surveys. In 1993, Dawson and Mannan (1994) attempted to find all Harris' Hawk nests in Tucson. From 1994 to 1997, Boal and Mannan (1998) attempted to locate all Cooper's Hawks nests in Tucson, and in 1997, Estabrook and Mannan (1998) searched for Burrowing Owls nests there. The effort to find nests in each of the above studies was maximized in a specific area where the subject species was most abundant. The areas did not overlap and totalled about 65,000 ha. Nests of all raptor species were noted in each of the study areas.

Beginning in 1993, W. Burroughs began to locate and map nest sites of all raptor species in Tucson, independent of the surveys conducted by Dawson and Mannan (1994), Boal and Mannan (1998), and Estabrook and Mannan (1998). Burroughs located nests partly from reports of injured or sick birds made to wildlife rehabilitators. A sample of nests ($n=50$) from this survey was revisited each year (1994-1997) by personnel from the Urban Raptor Conservation Project or the Arizona Game and Fish Department. In all of the surveys described above, except Estabrook and Mannan (1998), the general public was encouraged through newspaper articles and television news programmes to report the locations of nesting raptors.

Nests from all survey efforts described above were combined to form our overall sample. We believe the sample of nests for each species is representative of the kinds of environments which they occupy because most of the city was thoroughly searched at some time during the study, the general public aided in the location of nests, many nests were located independently in different surveys, and occupancy of a sample of nests was tracked over time.

2. Selection and Measurement of Nest Sites

We randomly selected 20 nests of five common species of raptors found in Tucson: the Cooper's Hawk, Harris' Hawk, Red-tailed Hawk, Great-horned Owl, and Burrowing Owl. We restricted our sample within a species to nests that were separated by at least 400 m to avoid sampling the same area more than once (see below). We plotted the locations of all nests on aerial photographs (scale: 2.5 cm = 360 m) taken in 1995. Within 200 m of each nest, we counted the number of houses and non-commercial buildings, and estimated the percent cover (by counting grid points) of major roads and commercial buildings, native vegetation, land developed for public activity (e.g., parks and golf courses), and undeveloped land from which native vegetation had been removed. We also measured the distance from each nest to the centre of the nearest square block of undeveloped land ≥ 16 ha in size and outside the 200 m radius. These measurements characterized the level of development surrounding nests and were selected to help identify where nests were positioned along the urban gradient.

Variance among variables was unequal (i.e., standard deviations often were positively correlated with means), and the distributions of our samples were skewed. We therefore transformed our count and distance measures with "log y" and our proportion measures with "log[y/(1 - y)]" (Sokal & Rohlf 1995). We then compared the means of each variable among species with one-way analysis of variance (Sokal & Rohlf 1995); P<0.001 was used to determine significance because of the number of tests conducted ($n=6$). For ease of interpretation, means and standard deviations are presented in their untransformed states.

Table 1. Means and standard deviations (SD) (untransformed) of variables describing conditions within 200 m of nests of five species of raptors ($n=20$ nests/species) in Tucson, Arizona, USA, 1993-1997. Species are ranked (high to low values) under each variable to facilitate assessment of their position along the urban gradient. Variables were estimated or counted from aerial photographs taken in 1995. P values are from one-way analyses of variance.

	Number of Houses/Bldgs[1]			Percent Commercial Bldgs/Roads[2]			Percent Land For Public[3]	
Sp[4]	Mean	SD	Sp	Mean	SD	Sp	Mean	SD
CH	32.7 (2.6)	44.7	GO	14.9	27.6	CH	31.7	36.7
HH	14.1 (1.1)	16.9	BO	11.5	13.4	GO	25.6	40.5
GO	10.7 (0.9)	12.8	RH	9.9	14.2	RH	7.9	23.5
BO	6.7 (0.5)	13.6	CH	7.9	10.5	BO	3.9	10.3
RH	4.5 (0.4)	5.6	HH	2.4	7.0	HH	1.3	5.6
	$P<0.0001$			$P>0.05$			$P<0.0004$	

[1]Number of houses and non-commercial buildings within 200 m of nests; number/ha in parentheses.
[2]Percent cover of commercial buildings and major roads.
[3]Percent cover of land developed for public activity (e.g., parks, golf courses).
[4]Species: CH=Cooper's Hawk; HH= Harris' Hawk; RH=red-tailed Hawk; GO=Great-horned Owl; BO=Burrowing Owl.

	Percent Undeveloped Land/Disturbed[1]			Percent Undeveloped Land/Native[2]			Distance to Undeveloped Land (m)[3]	
Sp	Mean	SD	Sp	Mean	SD	Sp	Mean	SD
BO	75.3	18.3	RH	55.6	36.9	CH	1541	1153
RH	12.7	21.9	HH	50.6	32.6	GO	1534	1201
HH	9.8	22.2	GO	23.8	29.8	HH	1001	816
GO	6.2	14.0	CH	11.7	22.6	RH	799	484
CH	6.1	14.1	BO	3.0	7.9	BO	526	526
	$P<0.0001$			$P<0.0001$			$P<0.0001$	

[1]Percent of undeveloped land from which native vegetation had been removed.
[2]Percent of undeveloped land supporting native vegetation.
[3]Distance from nest to the centre of the nearest square block of undeveloped land ≥ 16 ha in size. The block had to be outside the 200 m radius.
[4]Species: CH=Cooper's Hawk; HH= Harris' Hawk; RH=Red-tailed Hawk; GO=Great-horned Owl; BO=Burrowing Owl.

RESULTS

We selected our sample of 100 nests from a total of 227 nests (Cooper's Hawks [n=46], Harris' Hawks [n=53], Red-tailed Hawks [n=23], Great-horned Owls [n=32], and Burrowing Owls [n=73]). Cooper's Hawks generally nested in neighbourhoods where housing density was relatively high (n=11 nests; $\bar{x}$=4.5 houses/ha), or in lands developed for public activity (e.g., parks and golf courses; n=9 nests; Table 1). The sites where they nested had little undeveloped land around them and were relatively far from large blocks of undeveloped land (Table 1). Harris' Hawks nested in neighbourhoods where housing density was moderate to low ($\bar{x}$=1.1 houses/ha), and the areas between houses often supported native vegetation (Table 1). Both Red-tailed Hawks and Burrowing Owls nested in areas with undeveloped land where housing density was low (<0.5 houses/ha; Table 1). Red-tailed Hawks however, generally nested in areas dominated by native vegetation, whereas Burrowing Owls nested in areas where the native vegetation had been removed (Table 1). Great-horned Owls nested in a variety of environments, although they selected areas near the most urbanized end of the gradient most frequently. Coverage of major roads and commercial buildings around nests was variable and did not differ among species (Table 1).

DISCUSSION

All species of hawks and owls we examined, except Great-horned Owls, generally nested in identifiable places along the urban gradient. The gradient in this study was characterized at its most developed end by high-density residential neighbourhoods and parks and golf courses, and at its opposite end by low-density housing and undeveloped land. Cooper's Hawks nested in areas near the most urbanized end of the gradient, Harris' Hawks in moderately developed areas, and Burrowing Owls and Red-tailed Hawks in places with the least development. We speculate that selection of nest sites along the urban gradient by hawks and owls is influenced by the availability of nest structures, the abundance of favoured prey species, and the structure of vegetation as it relates to hunting behaviour.

Cooper's Hawks and Harris' Hawks in Tucson build their nests most frequently in aleppo pines (*Pinus halepensis*) and eucalyptus trees (*Eucalyptus* spp.) (Boal & Mannan 1998, unpubl. data). These trees are exotic to the southwestern United States and those used as nest sites are taller than the native trees or cacti in Tucson (e.g., Boal & Mannan 1998). Nest trees in urban settings also are taller than the trees or cacti used as nest sites in undeveloped desert outside the urban environment (e.g., Boal & Mannan 1998). Tall trees may provide the necessary level of security needed by nesting hawks to tolerate human activities in urban settings (Boal & Mannan 1998). However, tall, exotic trees occur in Tucson in a variety of environments, and thus only partly explain the distribution of urban-nesting raptors.

A relatively constant supply of water and green vegetation in Tucson, compared to undeveloped desert, probably increases the abundance of prey species for raptors and reduces fluctuations in prey populations during periods of drought. Availability of water and abundant prey explain, at least in part, why hawks and owls nest in urban environments at all, and why some species (e.g., Cooper's Hawks) nest in higher densities in the city than in exurban areas (Boal & Mannan 1998). Distribution of hawks and owls along the urban gradient likely is determined largely by species-specific prey preferences and hunting strategies. For example, Red-tailed Hawks, although generalists in their selection of prey, hunt in open areas (Monson 1998). We speculate that they nest most frequently along the outskirts of Tucson because undeveloped land with open vegetation is most common there. Minor *et al.* (1993) also attributed the success of Red-tailed Hawks nesting in urban areas in New York to their diet and their ability to move between isolated greenspaces.

Harris' Hawks in the United States hunt in areas with dense ground cover and rely primarily on ground-dwelling prey (Mader 1975), such as Cottontail Rabbits (*Sylvilagus auduboni*) and Gambel's Quail (*Callipepla gambelii*). Emlen (1974) studied birds in a Tucson suburb dominated by exotic vegetation and concluded that urbanization leads to the reduction of ground-dwelling birds, due partly to predation by domestic cats. However, in areas where native species, such as *Opuntia* cacti, are used as ornamental ground cover, some ground-dwelling birds and mammals persist and even flourish after development. Both rabbits and quail are common in Tucson in areas with desert landscaping or native desert vegetation. Harris' Hawks probably nested most frequently in suburbs with relatively low housing density because their favoured prey were present in these areas and their hunting strategies (Dawson 1988) were effective in the desert vegetation that existed around and between houses.

Cooper's Hawks in Tucson prey primarily on birds, especially Inca Doves (*Columbina inca*) and Mourning Doves (*Zenaida macroura*) (Boal 1998). We speculate that Cooper's Hawks nest in highly urbanized areas for two reasons. First, they are physically adapted to hunt in forests and shrublands (Rosenfield & Bielefeldt 1993) and thus are capable of capturing birds in structurally complex, urban environments. And second, developed areas generally support higher bird abundance than undeveloped areas (e.g., Beissinger & Osborne 1982, Mills *et al.* 1989). In Tucson, Emlen (1974) reported that the density of birds was 26 times higher in urban areas than in undeveloped desert. Furthermore, numbers of Mourning Doves and Inca Doves, the second and fourth most abundant birds in Tucson, are positively correlated with increasing housing density and exotic vegetation (Germaine 1995).

Great-horned Owls in Tucson appeared to be partly dependent upon diurnal raptors for nest sites and they occupied nests built by all three species of hawks we examined. Minor *et al.* (1993) also found that most pairs of Great-horned Owls in urban/suburban areas in New York nest in vacated hawk nests. We suspect that the tendency of Great-horned Owls in Tucson to nest near the urbanized end of the gradient was a result of the availability of nest structures and not selection for conditions around the nest. Cooper's Hawks and Harris' Hawks were more abundant in Tucson than Red-tailed Hawks; thus, stick nests were most abundant in areas with moderate to high development. We note, however, that Great-horned Owls in Tucson also nested in naturally formed cups at the base of fronds in palm trees (*Phoenix dactylifera*), and on buildings and other man-made structures (unpublished data). The flexibility of Great-horned Owls in selecting nest sites and their catholic diet (Dawson 1998) probably allows them to nest almost anywhere along the urban gradient.

Burrowing Owls in the western United States depend on burrows dug by mammals (e.g., ground squirrels [*Spermophilus* spp.]), or holes created in other ways (e.g., by erosion) as nest sites (Bent 1938, Thomsen 1971, Martin 1973). They usually nest in burrows in areas where vegetation is low or nonexistent (Rich 1986, Green & Anthony 1989, Haug *et al.* 1993, Plumpton and Lutz 1993), ostensibly so that they can see and avoid predators. In Tucson, it appears that even expanses of structurally simple, native, vegetation, such as Creosotebush (*Larrea tridentata*), do not provide the visibility they require. Burrowing Owls in Tucson, therefore, nest most frequently in areas where natural vegetation has been removed and grass or bare ground is maintained (Estabrook & Mannan 1998). These areas in Tucson are most common around airports, along river corridors where flood plains are periodically scraped, in vacant lots, and in new subdivisions where vegetation is removed before development (Estabrook & Mannan 1998). Wesemann and Rowe (1987) also found that Burrowing Owls in urban areas in Florida nest most commonly in places where development is limited.

The conditions which trigger different species of hawks and owls to nest in urban environments potentially could be duplicated and expanded in existing developments, or created in future developments, if hawks and owls are a desired component of urban avifaunas. However, nesting by raptors in towns and cities does not mean that urban environments provide high quality habitats for them. Developed areas present environmental challenges to raptors, such as electrocution, disease, poison, collisions with vehicles and windows, and human disturbance that may preclude self-sustaining populations (e.g., Dawson & Mannan 1994, Boal & Mannan 1999, Love & Bird, this volume). It is incumbent on biologists and city planners to understand the dynamics of populations of urban raptors and their species-specific habitat requirements before extensive habitat management efforts are undertaken.

ACKNOWLEDGEMENTS

We thank the many field technicians and volunteers who assisted in locating nests. We also thank W. Shaw and M. Tuegel for their helpful comments on a draft of the manuscript. The study was funded primarily by the Arizona Game and Fish Department Heritage Fund (Grants U94010, U95009, U96006).

REFERENCES

ADAMS, L. W. 1994. *Urban wildlife habitats. A landscape perspective*. Univ. Minnesota Press.
BATTEN, L. A. 1972. Breeding bird species diversity in relation to increasing urbanisation. *Bird Study*, 19:157-166.
BEISSINGER, S. R. & D. R. OSBORNE 1982. Effects of urbanization on avian community organization. *Condor*, 84:75-83.
BENT, A. C. 1938. Life histories of North American birds of prey. *United States National Museum Bull.*, 170.
BLAIR, R. B. 1996. Land use and avian species diversity along an urban gradient. *Ecol. Appl.*, 6:506-519
BOAL, C. W. 1997. An urban environment as an ecological trap for Cooper's Hawks. Ph.D. Dissertation. Univ. Arizona, Tucson.
BOAL, C. W. & R. W. MANNAN 1998. Nest-site selection by Cooper's Hawks in an urban environment. *J. Wildl. Manage.*, 62:864-871.
BOAL, C. W. & R. W. MANNAN 1999. Comparative breeding ecology of Cooper's hawks in urban and exurban areas of southeastern Arizona. *J. Wildl. Manage.* 63: 77-84.
BROWN, D. E., C. H. LOWE & C. P. PASE 1979. A digitized classification system for the biotic communities of North America, with community (series) and association examples for the Southwest. *J. Ariz.-Nev. Acad. Sci.*, 14 (1, Supplement).
DAWSON, J. W. 1988. The cooperative breeding system of the Harris' hawk in Arizona. M. S. Thesis, Tucson, Univ. Arizona.
DAWSON, J. W. 1998. Great-horned Owl. *In* R. L. Glinski (ed.) *The raptors of Arizona*. Univ. Arizona Press and Arizona Game and Fish Department.
DAWSON, J. W. & R. W. MANNAN 1994. Population dynamics of Harris' hawks in urban environments. Report to Arizona Game and Fish Department, Phoenix, Ariz. Heritage Grant Program.
EMLEN, J. T. 1974. An urban bird community in Tucson, Arizona: derivation, structure, and regulation. *Condor* 76:184-197.
ESTABROOK, T. S. & R. W. MANNAN 1998. Burrow selection by burrowing owls in urban environments. Report to Arizona Game and Fish Dep., Phoenix, Ariz., Heritage Grant U96006.
GERMAINE, S. S. 1995. Relationships of birds, lizards, and nocturnal rodents to their habitat in the Greater Tucson Area, Arizona. *Arizona Game and Fish Department Technical Report 20*.
GREEN, G. A. & R. G. ANTHONY 1989. Nesting success and habitat relationships of burrowing owls in the Columbia Basin, Oregon. *Condor* 91:347-354.
HAUG, E. A., B. A. MILLSAP & M. S. MARTELL 1993. Burrowing owl (*Speotyto cunicularia*). *The birds of North America*, number 61, A. Poole, and F. Gill (eds.) The American ornithologists' Union, Washington, D.C., USA, and the Academy of Natural Sciences, Philadelphia, Pennsylvania, USA.
MADER, W. J. 1975. Biology of the Harris' hawk in southern Arizona. *Living Bird* 14: 59-85.
MARTIN, D. J. 1973. Selected aspects of burrowing owl ecology and behavior. *Condor*, 75:446-456.
MILLS, G. S., J. B. DUNNING, JR. & J. M. BATES 1989. Effects of urbanization on breeding bird community structure in southwestern desert habitats. *Condor*, 91:416-428.
MINOR, W. F., M. MINOR & M. F. INGRALDI 1993. Nesting of Red-tailed hawks and Great-horned Owls in a central New York urban/suburban area. *J. Field Ornithol.*, 64:433-439.
MONSON, G. (ed.) 1998. Red-tailed hawk. *In* R. L. Glinski. *The raptors of Arizona*. Univ. Arizona Press and Arizona Game and Fish Department.
PLUMPTON, D. L. & R. S. LUTZ 1993. Nesting habitat use by burrowing owls in Colorado. *J. Raptor Res.*, 27:175-179.
RICH, T. 1986. Habitat and nest site selection by burrowing owls in the sagebrush steppe of Idaho. *J. Wildl. Manage.*, 50:548-555.
ROSENFIELD, R. N. & J. BIELEFELDT 1993. Cooper's hawk (*Accipiter cooperii*). *The birds of North America*, number 75, A. Poole, and F. Gill (eds.) The American ornithologists' Union, Washington, D.C., USA, and the Academy of Natural Sciences, Philadelphia, Pennsylvania, USA.

ROSENBERG, K. V., S. B. TERRILL & G. H. ROSENBERG 1987. Value of suburban habitats to desert riparian birds. *Wilson Bull.*, 99:642-654.
SOKAL, R. R. & F. J. ROHLF 1995. *Biometry*. Third edition. W.H. Freeman, New York, New York.
THOMSEN, L. 1971. Behavior and ecology of burrowing owls on the Oakland municipal airport. *Condor*, 73:177-192.
WESEMANN, T. & M. ROWE 1987. Factors influencing the distribution and abundance of burrowing owls in Cape Coral, Florida. *In* L. W. Adams and D. L. Leedy (eds.) *Integrating man and nature in the metropolitan environment*. National Institute of Urban Wildlife, Columbia, MD.

R. W. Mannan, J. W. Dawson and T. S. Estabrook
School of Renewable Natural Resources
University of Arizona
Tucson, Arizona
85721, USA

C. W. Boal
Minnesota Cooperative Fish and Wildlife Research Unit
200 Hodson Hall
1980 Folwell Avenue
University of Minnesota
St. Paul, Minnesota
55126, USA

W. J. Burroughs
Urban Raptor Conservation Project
4140 S. Aldon Road
Tucson, Arizona
85735, USA

W. S. Richardson
Arizona Game and Fish Department
555 N. Greasewood Road
Tucson, Arizona
85745, USA

Chancellor, R. D. & B.-U. Meyburg eds. 2000
Raptors at Risk
WWGBP / Hancock House

Overwintering by Urban-nesting Peregrine Falcons *Falco peregrinus* in Midwestern North America

Greg Septon

ABSTRACT

In January of 1997 a survey was conducted to determine the degree of overwintering by urban-nesting Peregrine Falcons in Midwestern North America. A survey was sent to 58 Peregrine observers and managers in 10 Midwestern states and the province of Ontario, Canada. Twenty-one observers (36%) responded representing all 10 states surveyed. No responses were received from Canada. The responses covered overwintering activity at 58 known urban Peregrine nest sites/territories. This paper will report on the results of the survey and describe the different types of man-made structures where Peregrines overwintered. Also discussed will be the attractiveness of cities versus near-urban sites. The results of this survey may provide useful management insights pertaining to the overwintering requirements and preferences of urban-nesting Peregrines in Midwestern North America and elsewhere.

INTRODUCTION

In an effort to restore the extirpated population of Peregrine Falcons *Falco peregrinus* in midwestern North America, a reintroduction programme was initiated in 1982. Since that time Peregrines have been making a comeback and the reintroduced population has continued to increase. In 1996 there was a total of 48 known successful nests (eggs and or young produced) within the region. Of these, 41 pairs (85%) nested in urban areas on human-built structures. Although the population of urban-nesting Peregrines in the midwest has been closely observed and documented during the nesting season, little has been collectively known about the degree to which this population overwinters in the region.

METHODS

In an attempt to determine the degree of overwintering by urban-nesting Peregrines in midwestern North America, a survey was conducted in mid-winter (January) of 1997. The survey aimed to answer related overwintering questions including site preferences, sex ratios, numbers of adults versus immatures and which urban areas had the highest numbers of overwintering falcons. The survey was sent to 58 prospective Peregrine managers and observers in 10 midwestern states and the province of Ontario, Canada. There were no survey responses from Canada, hence the resulting midwestern survey region can be defined as the ten state area map in Figure 1.

Figure 1. Midwestern overwintering survey area.

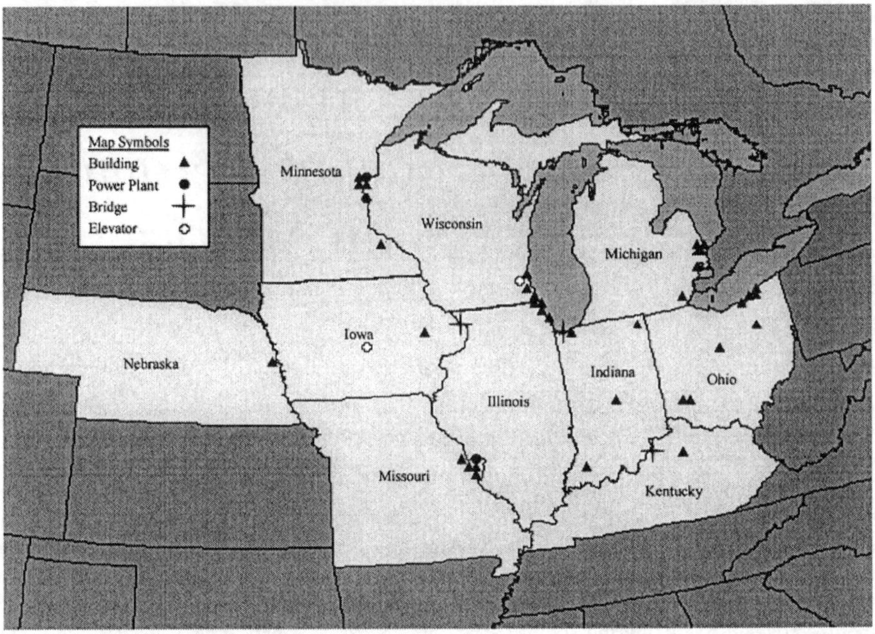

HISTORY OF OVERWINTERING IN NORTH AMERICA

Because overwintering accounts on the historic cliff-nesting population of Peregrines in the midwest are scarce, it is not known whether these Peregrines overwintered locally. It is generally believed however that the pre-DDT population from this region normally migrated and wintered in more southerly latitudes. One report from Berger and Mueller (1969) which indicates Peregrines may have at least spent some winters in the region includes a quote by W.E. Green who saw two Peregrines on 2 December 1949 on the Upper Mississippi River National Wildlife Refuge. This observation in Green's opinion indicated that some midwestern (nesting) birds might be year-round residents. However, the report was inconclusive as to whether these falcons actually overwintered on the refuge, wintered in a nearby city, or were merely passing through from somewhere further north.

More detailed overwintering records do exist for Peregrines in cities in eastern North America. Some of the more extensive observations from this region were documented by Herbert and Herbert (1965). Their detailed observations of Peregrines in the New York City region which ended in 1961 covered a span of 30 years. Herbert and Herbert (1965) reported that as many as 16 Peregrines regularly overwintered on some 20 different New York skyscrapers in mid-town and downtown Manhattan and on three bridges, a gas tank and a high school in the Bronx. They also indicate that females dominated the New York skyscrapers and seemed to have territorial attachments for certain buildings. In addition to unattached wintering females, a pair would occasionally overwinter and one year-round resident pair overwintered from 1943 - 1953. In reference to the Peregrines that nested at the Sun Life building in Montreal from 1936 - 1952 Hall (1955), stated that "after rearing young, they (the adults) did not migrate from the city, and during winter were seen from time to time in the vicinity; frequently towards evening they came in to roost on the building."

In the first 75 years of this century, city nesting Peregrines were a rare occurrence and an exception to the rule in North America. Consequently, aside from early accounts of nesting pairs in Hartford, Connecticut, New York City and Montreal, Canada, documented historical records of Peregrines nesting in cities in North America are few. Even though the vast majority of overwintering Peregrines referred to in the New York City region were not urban-nesters, their attraction to large cities as overwintering sites was well documented.

Since efforts to restore Peregrine populations in North America began in the 1970's, a steadily increasing number have nested in cities. In 1993, Cade *et al.* (1996) were able to document 88 pairs of Peregrines located in 61 urban areas in the US. Many of these falcons have been found to overwinter at these sites as well. According to D. Bird (pers. comm.) Peregrines that breed in Montreal, Canada overwinter there too. Frank (1994) noted that New York City Peregrines had shown a distinct predilection for remaining on their territorial grounds all year round. In contrast to where Herbert and Herbert (1965) observed mostly unattached, non-urban-nesting females overwintering in the New York City region, Frank's findings indicate that both males as well as females in the reintroduced population (often territorial pairs) overwintered in the region. Where the Peregrines in the New York City region before reintroduction were mainly non-resident winter visitors, the overwintering falcons noted by Frank were often resident urban-nesting pairs.

RESULTS AND DISCUSSION

Overwintering survey responses were received from 21 observers (Appendix I) who reported on a total of 58 urban Peregrine sites (i.e., known nest sites or territories) in ten midwestern states. Of the 58 sites surveyed, 43 (74%) had overwintering Peregrines (n = 77). Table 1 lists these sites by state, city and site name. The map in Figure 1 shows the midwestern survey area, overwintering sites (n = 43) and site types. An overview of the demographics of the overwintering population is provided in Table 2. Of special note is the fact that the majority of overwintering Peregrines (83%) were associated with buildings within cities and that most (88%) of these were identified as adults. Conversely, it is also important to note that only 3% of overwintering falcons at all site types combined were identified as immatures. Maturity of nine (12%) of the falcons observed in the survey was questionable and undetermined.

An interesting point regarding site preference is that 13 of the 15 sites (87%) covered in the survey where Peregrines were not found overwintering were "near-urban" sites. Near-urban sites can be described as those solitary yet prominent human-built structures such as power plants and grain elevators which are located away from large cities. These sites are generally visible from great distances and are quite attractive to Peregrines. Interestingly, the two remaining surveyed sites where Peregrines were not found overwintering were prominent state capitol buildings (Madison, Wisconsin and Lincoln, Nebraska) located in cities without numerous tall buildings. These state capitol sites, much like near-urban sites, are also prominent landmarks that attract Peregrines during the nesting season. However, they seemingly may not provide adequate prey nor the shelter provided by surrounding tall buildings in cities during the winter months. It appears then that cities, especially larger cities with numerous tall buildings and the associated prey available during the winter, i.e., Rock Doves (*Columba livia*) Mourning Doves (*Zenaida macroura*) and Starlings (*Sturnus vulgaris*), probably provide a fairly comfortable and secure existence for overwintering Peregrines. Even though some adult Peregrines from within this urban-nesting population have been known to migrate (as noted by band recoveries), it would still appear that most adult midwestern Peregrines stay fairly close to home throughout the year.

Table 1. Overwintering sites (n = 43) of peregrine falcons in Midwestern North America, 1996-97.

State	City	Site
Minnesota	Rochester	Mayo Clinic
	Bayport	NSP King Plant
	Minneapolis	Multifoods Tower
	Minneapolis	Colonnade Building
	Minneapolis	Riverside Plaza
	Saint Paul	North Central Life Tower
Ohio	Columbus	Rhodes State Office Tower
	Toledo	Commodore Perry Motor Inn
	Dayton	Lazarus Building
	Akron	Key Bank
	Cleveland	Terminal Tower
	Cleveland	Metro Health Hospital
	Lakewood	Gold Coast
	Cincinnati	PNC Building
Indiana	East Chicago	Cline Avenue
	Gary	U.S. Steel
	Burns Harbor	Bailly Power Plant
	Fort Wayne	One Summit Square
	Indianapolis	Market Tower
	Evansville	Downtown area
Wisconsin	Milwaukee	Firstar Center
	Milwaukee	Landmark on the Lake
	Milwaukee	Froedtert Malt Complex
Missouri	St. Louis	Chase Park Plaza
	St. Louis	Downtown area
	South St. Louis	J.B. Bridge
	Clayton	Interco Building
	Portage De Sioux	Ameren UE Power Plant
Illinois	Chicago	125 S. Wacker
	Chicago	5821 Broadway
	Chicago	Lakeview
	Chicago	Wacker & Michigan
	Chicago	Unitarian Church
Michigan	Detroit	Whittier Apartments
	Detroit	New Center/Fisher Building
	Detroit	Ameritech/Book Building
	Detroit	Monroe Edison Power Plant
Iowa	Des Moines	American Republic Insurance
	Davenport	Centennial Bridge
	Cedar Rapids	Firstar Bank
Kentucky	Louisville	Big Four Bridge
	Lexington	KY Central
Nebraska	Omaha	Woodman Tower

Table 2. Demographics of overwintering peregrines in midwestern North America. Numbers represent total survey counts by site type and include available sex and age data.

State	Buildings	Power plants	Elevators	Bridges	Total
Minnesota	3 ad. males 1 ad. female	1 ad. male 3 ad. females			4 ad. males 4 ad. females
Ohio	8 ad. males 7 ad. females 1 ad. ? 2 imm. ?				8 ad. males 7 ad. females 1 ad. ? 2 imm. ?
Indiana	4 ad. males 4 ad. females			1 ad. male 1 ad. female	5 ad. males 5 ad. females
Wisconsin	2 ad. males 2 ad. females		1 ad. male 1 ad. female		3 ad. males 3 ad. females
Missouri	2 ad. males 2 ad. females 2 ad. ? 2 unknown	1 ad. male			3 ad. males 2 ad. females 2 ad. ? 2 unknown
Illinois	5 ad. males 5 ad. females				5 ad. males 5 ad. females
Michigan	4 ad. males 4 ad. females				4 ad. males 4 ad. females
Iowa	1 ad. male		1 unknown	1 ad. male	2 ad. males 1 unknown
Kentucky	1 unknown			1 ad. male 1 ad. female	1 ad. male 1 ad. female 1 unknown
Nebraska	1 ad. male 1 ad. female				1 ad. male 1 ad. female
Sex and age breakdown by site type	30 ad. males 26 ad. females 3 ad. ? 2 imm. ? 3 unknown	2 ad. males 3 ad. females	1 ad. male 1 ad. female 1 unknown	3 ad. males 2 ad. females	36 ad. males 32 ad. females 3 ad. ? 2 imm. ? 4 unknown
Totals	64	5	3	5	77

In attempting to determine the makeup of the overwintering urban population in the midwest, one might also ask whether any of the overwintering falcons could be visitors from the north or from outside the region? This is certainly a possibility as some unbanded overwintering falcons have been observed and their origins are unknown.

However, these could also be urban-nesters from within the region as several urban-nesting midwestern Peregrines are unbanded. So although there may be some winter visitors in the region, the fact that several Peregrine observers participating in this survey identified known urban-nesting falcons from band numbers at their respective nest sites/territories, it is probably safe to say that the majority of overwintering Peregrines in the midwest are urban-nesters and comprise a non-migratory resident population.

From the findings of this survey, it appears that urban-nesting Peregrines are now regularly overwintering in cities across the midwest much like the New York City falcons described by Frank (1994). As cities have continued to grow in size across North America and the number of tall buildings has likewise increased within these cities, the urban-nesting component of the Peregrine population has increased as well. With urban nest sites/territories in the midwest occupied mainly by resident adult pairs during the winter, the question arises, where do the immatures produced at these sites spend their winters? And, if these immatures migrate, do they only migrate for their first winter or until such time they are able to establish nesting territories? Finally, do Peregrines from more northern cities overwinter in warmer cities to the south and do nesting Peregrines from near-urban sites move into nearby cities during the winter to take advantage of the more available prey and shelter? It is hoped that these questions and more will be answered in the coming years as satellite telemetry techniques are applied to urban-nesting falcons.

ACKNOWLEDGEMENTS

I would like to sincerely thank all of the survey respondents for identifying overwintering sites and for providing detailed information on the demographics of the overwintering Peregrine population. I would also like to recognize Clayton White who first coined the term "near-urban" to define prominent human-built structures located away from cities.

REFERENCES

BERGER, D. & H.C. MUELLER. 1969. Nesting peregrine falcons in Wisconsin and adjacent areas. P. 119 in J.J. Hickey, ed. *Peregrine falcon populations: their biology and decline.* Univ. of Wisconsin Press, Madison, Wisconsin USA.

CADE, T.J., M. MARTELL, P. REDIG, G. SEPTON & H. TORDOFF. 1996. Peregrine Falcons in urban North America. *In* D.M. Bird D. Varland & J. Negro (Eds.) *Raptors in human landscapes.* Academic Press and The Raptor Research Foundation, London, U.K.

FRANK, S. 1994. *City Peregrines: A ten-year saga of New York City peregrines.* Pp. 158-159. Hancock House Publishers, Blaine, WA USA

HALL, G.H. 1955. *Great Moments in Action: The Story of the Sun Life Falcons.* P. 11. Mercury Press, Montreal, Quebec, Canada

HERBERT, R.A. & K.G.S. HERBERT. 1965. Behavior of peregrine falcons in the New York City region. *Auk*, 82: 62-94

Greg Septon
c/o Milwaukee Public Museum
800 West Wells Street
Milwaukee
WI 53233, U.S.A.

APPENDIX I

Survey Respondents	State	Affilliation
Bob Anderson	Minnesota	Raptor Resource Project
Harrison Tordoff	Minnesota	Bell Museum of Natural History
Tom Hennessey	Minnesota	Mayo Clinic
Ted Bartel	Minnesota	Mayo Clinic
Sara Jean Peters	Ohio	Ohio Division of Wildlife
David P. Scott	Ohio	Ohio Division of Wildlife
John Castrale	Indiana	Indiana Division of Fish & Wildlife
Greg Septon	Wisconsin	Milwaukee Public Museum
Jim Marks	Wisconsin	Wisconsin Peregrine Society
Tim & Mary Ellestad	Wisconsin	Wisconsin Peregrine Society
Bill Holton	Wisconsin	Wisconsin Electric Power Company
Bob Miedl	Wisconsin	Wisconsin Electric Power Company
JoAnn Thiel	Wisconsin	Wisconsin Power & Light
Alan Trick	Wisconsin	Wisconsin Public Service
Mike Cook	Missouri	World Bird Sanctuary
Mary Hennen	Illinois	Chicago Academy of Sciences
Vernon Kleen	Illinois	Illinois Department of Conservation
Judith Yerkey	Michigan	Michigan Department of Natural Resources
Jaime Edwards	Iowa	Iowa Department of Natural Resources
Laura Burford	Kentucky	Kentucky Department of Fish & Wildlife
John Dinan	Nebraska	Nebraska Game & Fish Department

Adaptation of two Falcon species *Falco femoralis* & *Falco subbuteo* to an Urban Environment

Klaus Dietrich Fiuczynski and Paul Soemmer

ABSTRACT

Falco subbuteo in Europe and the New World *Falco femoralis* have been shown to be birds of open country with prey such as larks (Alaudidae) and swallows (Hirundinidae) in *Falco subbuteo* and a variety of passerine birds and small pigeons (Columbidae) in *Falco femoralis*. In contrast, pairs of both species can be found near or even in the cities of Berlin in Germany, and Rio de Janeiro in Brazil. *Falco subbuteo* exploit urban birds like sparrows (*Passer*), greenfinches (*Carduelis*), swifts (*Apus*) and escaped budgerigars (*Melopsittacus*), while *Falco femoralis* predate on passerine birds especially ground doves (*Columbina*). This phenomenon could be widespread, and the authors suggest further studies, especially in the Aplomado Falcon *Falco femoralis*.

INTRODUCTION

Like other vertebrates, birds of prey may exploit abundant food resources, shelter and protection that human settlements can offer (Klausnitzer 1988; Wandeler & Lüps 1993; Sukopp 1990). We studied two falcon species in Brazil and Germany and demonstrate here that even more stenotic species can adapt themselves to breed and hunt in big cities such as Rio de Janeiro and Berlin.

MATERIALS AND METHODS

Falco femoralis was studied in the city of Rio de Janeiro, Brazil, 22° 55' S / 43° 10' W, on excursions along the coast of the Atlantic ocean in the state ("estado") of Rio de Janeiro and Espírito Santo, 20° S / 40° W by KDF when he was living in Rio since 1991 and was joined by the co-author (PS) in Nov 1995, 1996 and Oct 1997, who trapped a resident male Aplomado and also the small birds in the home range of that Falcon. In Dec-Jan 1994-95 special attention was given to a pair of falcons with their offspring during the post-fledging period in a rural habitat in the Lake Region east of Rio de Janeiro; a pair of Aplomado Falcons were observed from July to September 1996 breeding (unsuccesfully) in an urban enviroment.

Falco subbuteo has been studied intensively in Berlin, Germany, 52° 30' N / 13° 20' E, since 1956 (Fiuczynski 1987), when falcons were abundant in city forests and even bred in gardens in city districts like Steglitz, Frohnau and the cemetery of Pankow. Additional observations in the area (Wendland 1953) north of Berlin and a extension of the study area by P. Soemmer led to studies on all aspects of population ecology including colour banding of young and trapping of adults. Today an area of approx. 1,000 km² is covered every year by regular observations between April and Aug/Sep; 1009 nestlings and 9 adults have been banded from 1956-1997 (Fiuczynski & Sömmer 1995).

Rural habitat of *F. femoralis*

We found this hunter of birds, bats and insects in its typical habitat of "open country, rural areas" (Sick 1988) at 60 - 1 m a.s.l. with clumps of trees or small woods between pastures, cattle or horse raising areas and scattered farm houses between the fringe of the Atlantic rain forest (Mata Atlântica) and dune vegetation (Restinga) or the coast of the Atlantic ocean in the south-eastern region of Brazil, state of Rio de Janeiro up to Espírito Santo. The composition of the avicoenosis of one well studied pair in the Restingas de Maricá is given in Table 1. Trees were mainly *Eucalyptus, Mangifera indica,* Coconut palm trees, Casuarina (all planted), various Bignoniaceae like the yellow flowering Ipê amarelo, *Tabebuia chrysotricha,* and others, *Chorisia speciosa, Gochnatia polymorpha.*Of the 20 km² home range (including hunting territory), about 30 % were covered with trees (between 0 5 and 75 % at the mountain slope). Typical shrubs were *Tibouchina, Eugenia, Clusia,* among ground vegetation (cover 90 - 100 %), we found Bromeliads like *Aechmea nudicaulis, Neoregelia cruenta, Vriesa* and *Dyckia* in the Restinga dune zone (Rizzini *et al.* 1991).

Urban habitat of *F. femoralis*

After sporadic observations in the city a breeding pair was found in 1996 in an old *Milvago chimachima* nest in a coconut palm tree, 80 m a.s.l. on the SE slope of Corcovado mountain about 100 m from the densely populated district of Botafogo, 1302.9 ha with a human population of 251 668 (1991), i.e. 193.2 inhabitans / ha (Anuário Estatistico Da Cidade Do Rio De Janeiro) with apartment blocks, tall office and administration buildings, schools, hospitals. Also 50 m off the favela Dona Marta, there are approximately 1,000 inhabitants. The vegetation was the very fringe of Tijuca forest, a National Park of 33 km², formerly Atlantic rain forest, now secondary forest with characteristic trees like *Cecropia pachystachya, C. hololeuca, Artocarpus integrifolia* and *A. incisa, Caesalpinia echinata, Cariniana legalis, Chorisia speciosa, Ficus, Cassia* and members of the Bignoniaceae (Cezar *et al.* 1992). Parks and streets in Rio de Janeiro contain numerous trees such as *Cassia, Ficus, Triplaris, Mangifera, Pinus elliotti, Schizolobium parahyba, Pachira aquatica, Caesalpinia leucostachya* and others (Soares *et al.* 1994).

Forest-type and rural habitat of *F. subbuteo*

In the Berlin area, the falcons nest in old open Scots pinewoods of the *Pino - Quercetum* type, *Pinus sylvestris* with *Pteridium aquilinum* and *Avellana flexuosa,* near forest clearings and new growth not far from the city where they hunt small birds. North of Berlin and outside the Scots pine forest, smaller woods and clumps of pine trees are also inhabited by *F. subbuteo.* As in the Berlin region, the falcons breed in nests of *Corvus corone cornix, Corvus corax* and artifical baskets hung up by the authors (about 60 in Berlin and 30 outside) (Sömmer 1991).

Urban habitat of *F. subbuteo*

Some of the falcons of the Berlin Scots pine forests already nested near the city, and in some cases individual pairs moved into the city and bred for some years in the urban districts of Berlin-Steglitz, Berlin-Frohnau and Berlin-Pankow (cemetery), breeding amidst houses and gardens in tall Scots pines.

Hunting in and around the city and abroad: *F. subbuteo*

The majority of the "Berlin forest falcons" and the urban pairs of *Falco subbuteo* used to hunt exclusively in the city with males delivering sparrows, *Passer domesticus & P. montanus* (53 %), Swallows/Martins *Delichon urbica & Hirundu rustica* (10 %), escaped Budgerigars *Melopsittacus undulatus* (9 %), Swifts *Apus apus* (9 %), Greenfinches *Carduelis chloris* (6 %), Larks *Alauda*

Table. 1. Avicoenosis in a rural habitat (Maricá, rj, Brazil)

Crypturellus tataupa	*Ardea cocoi*	*Casmerodius albus*
Nycticorax nycticorax	*Cochlearius cochlearius*	*Egretta caerulea*
Egretta thula	*Bubulcus ibis*	*Butorides striatus*
Ixobrichus involucris	*Anas bahamensis*	*Dendrocygna vituata*
Amazonetta brasiliensis	*Cathartes burrovianus*	*Cathartes aura*
Coragyps atratus	*Pandion haliaetus*	*Eleanus leucurus*
Heterospizias meridionalis	*Parabueto unicinctus*	*Chondrohierax unicinatus*
Buteo magnirostris	*Buteo albicaudatus*	*Polyborus plancus*
Milvago chimachima	*Herpetotheres cachinnans*	*Falco sparverius*
Falco femoralis	*Gallinula chloropus*	*Porphyrula martinica*
Rallus sanguinolentus	*Porzana albicollis*	*Jacana jacana*
Vanellus chilensis	*Charadrius collaris*	*Himantopus palliatus*
Nycticryphes semicollaris	*Columba picazuro*	*Claravis pretiosa*
Columbina talpacoti & minuta	*Brotogeris tirica*	*Amazona amazonica*
Crotophaga ani	*Guira guira*	*Tapera naevia*
Coccyzus americanus	*Coccyzus melacoryphus*	*Speotyto cunicularia*
Hydropsalis brasiliana	*Macropsalis creagra*	*Nyctidromus albicollis*
Podager nacunda	*Eleothreptus anomalus*	*Streptoprogne zonaris*
Chaetura anrei	*Thalurania claucopsis*	*Anthracothorax nigricollis*
Amazilia fimbriata	*Eupetomena macroura*	*Ceryle torquata*
Chlorocleryle americana	*Nystalus chacuro*	*Colaptes campestris*
Leuconerpes candidus	*Veniliornis passerinus*	*Picumnus cirrhatus*
Progne chalybea	*Phaeoprogne tapera*	*Riparia riparia*
Notiochelidon cyanoleuca	*Stelgiopteryx ruficollis*	*Tachycineta leucorrhoa*
Furnarius figulus	*Furnarius rufus*	*Thamnophilus punctatus*
Myrmotherula axillaris	*Pachyramphus polychopteri*	*Manacus manacus*
Machetornis rixosus	*Tyrannus melancholicus*	*Pitangus sulphuratus*
Myiozetetes cayanensis	*Myiozetetes similis*	*Myiodynastes maculatus*
Muscivora tyrannus	*Elaenia flavogaster*	*Gubernetes yetapa*
Tolomias flaviventris	*Fluvicola nengeta*	*Myiophobus fasciatus*
Serpophaga subcristata	*Culicivora caudacuta*	*Arundinicola leucocephala*
Turdus rufiventris	*Turdus leucomelas*	*Mimus saturninus*
Donacobius atricapillus	*Troglodytes aedon*	*Thryothorus genibarbis*
Hylophilus thoracicus	*Conirostrum speciosum*	*Dacnis cayana*
Coreba flaveola	*Cacicus cela*	*Agelaius ruficapillus*
Leistes militaris	*Parula pitiayumi*	*Ramphocelus bresilius*
Ramphocelus carbo	*Thraupis sayaca*	*Thraupis palmarum*
Nemosia pileata	*Saltator maximus*	*Emberizoides herbicola*
Zonotrichia capensis	*Sicalis flaveola*	*Passer domesticus*
Estrilda astrild	*Sporophila frontalis*	*Sporophila caerulescens*
Sporophila bouvreuil	*Volatinia jacarina*	

arvensis & *Lullula arborea* (0.3 %) (Fiuczynski 1987; Gawlik & Otto 1982) of 758 avian prey items. In contrast to this ranking, falcons in rural areas usually feed on Swallows (40%), Larks (21 %), Sparrows (6 %) and Swifts (2 %) out of 916 prey items all over Germany (Uttendörfer 1952). In Holland Bijlsma (1980) found 18 % Swallows, 11 % Larks, 28 % Sparrows and 6 % Swifts of 5728 prey items. Similar results were obtained in the falcons north of Berlin hunting in agricultural areas: 37% Swallows/Martins, 21% Sparrows, 18 % Sky Larks and 5 % Swifts 254 prey items 1987-1997, (Soemmer unpubl.).

Falco femoralis
In open *rural habitat,* we found an adult pair hunting using the known pair-hunting strategy which was synchronized from the beginning, i.e. leaving the lookout in an eucalyptus tree to attack a bird. The male flew above waiting for a chance to stoop while the female flushed out a hiding passerine from a shrub for the waiting male. Other methods included a communal "stoop and chase" pursuit of higher flying small pigeons like *Columbina minuta*. After having left the nest, young falcons preyed heavily and successfully on large tree-sitting cicadas (*Quesada gigas*), which they located acoustically and optically, this attracted other fledged young of the region to join until 7 young perched in trees on the hill, competing for those singing cicadas. The male of the *urban pair* in Rio de Janeiro brought avian prey to the female during the courtship and brooding period. Concluding from time and direction of the male's arrival around sunrise and sunset - minimum 6 minutes before sunrise in the short tropical dawn - the male hunted 1.5, maximum 10, km from the nest in the city districts of Botafogo and Lagoa, where "rolinhas" *Columbina talpacoti* bred and also gathered in flocks being fed by humans, thus constituting a numerous and easily available prey among other members of the urban avicoenosis such as Tyrannidae *(Pitangus sulphuratus, Tyrannus melancholicus)*, Turdidae *Turdus rufiventris* and - less numerous - House Sparrow *Passer domesticus*. The columbid food resource is also exploited by Peregrine Falcons *Falco peregrinus* coming from the northern hemisphere and spending the southern summer from November to March regularly in Rio de Janeiro (Sick 1988; pers. obs.). Their hunting methods are similar to the Aplomado Falcons hunting the numerous bats (*Chiroptera*) at dusk above the favela Dona Marta and at the fringe of Tijua National Park forest.

CONCLUSION

Apparently the abundance of food and also lack of human persecution towards *F. femoralis* and *F. subbuteo* offer them an opportunity to breed and hunt inside cities if at least a few trees are available. We presume that this phenomenon is more widespread for *F. femoralis* and suggest further study in its distribution area in Latin America.

ACKNOWLEDGEMENTS

In Germany we had support from many field observers, forest administrations and private house owners in whose gardens *Falco subbuteo* bred. Financial aid was granted to KDF by Volksbund & Stiftung Naturschutz, Berlin and Naturschutzbund Deutschland, Lv. Berlin. In Brazil, we were grateful to landowners and their employees for permitting operations on their farms and to friends offering housing facilities.

REFERENCES

ANUÁRIO ESTATISTICO DA CIDADE DO RIO DE JANEIRO Aspectos Sociodemográficos. IPLAN Rio de Janeiro 1995.
BIJLSMA, R. 1980 *De Boomvalk*, Amsterdam & Antwerp.
CEZAR, P.B. & R. R. DE OLIVEIRO 1992 *A floresta da Tijuca*. Rio de Janeiro: Editora Nova Tronteira
CLARK, W.S. 1987 *A field guide to hawks of North America*. Boston: Houghton Mifflin.
CRAMP. S. & K.E.L. SIMMONS 1980 *Handbook of the Birds of Europe, the Middle East and North Africa*. The Birds of the Western Palearctic vol. 2 Oxford etc.: Oxford Univ. Press.

DUNNING, J.S. 1988 *South American Birds*. Newton Square, Pa.
FIUCZYNSKI, D. 1987 *Der Baumfalke (Falco subbuteo)* Wittenberg: Ziemsen (Die Neue Brehm-Bücherei 575).
FIUCZYNSKI, K.D. & P. SÖMMER 1995 Baumfalke *(Falco subbuteo)*. In: A. Kostrzewa & G. Speer (Eds.) *Greifvögel in Deutschland*. Wiesbaden: Aula p. 73-76.
GAWLIK, H. & W. OTTO 1982 Zur Ernährung Berliner Baumfalken *(Falco subbuteo) Pica (Berl.)* 6: 54-59.
KLAUSNITZER, B. 1988 *Verstädterung von Tieren*. Wittenberg. 315 pp. (Die Neue Brehm-Bücherei vol. 579).
RIZZINI, C.T., A.F. COIMBRA, & A. HOUAISS 1991 *Ecossistemas brasileiros - Brazilian ecosystems*. o.O. (Rio de Janeiro): Editora Lyra/Editora.
SICK, H. 1988 *Ornitologia Brasileira*, Uma Introduçao. 3a ed. Brasilia: Editora Universidade da Brasîlia.
SOARES, & C. B. DA VEIGA 1994 *As mais belas árvores da mui formosa cidade da Sao Sebastiao do Rio de Janeiro*. Rio de Janeiro: Editora Nova Fronteira. Texto português e inglês.
SÖMMER, P. 1991 Zur Horstplatzwahl des Baumfalken *(Falco subbuteo)* in Verbindung mit künstlichen Nistunterlagen. *Pop. Greifv. Eulen* 2: 375-386.
UDVARDY, F. 1992 *The Audubon Society Field Guide to North American Birds*. Western Region. New York:Knopf
UTTENDÖRFER, O. 1952 *Neue Ergebnisse über die Ernährung der Greifvögel und Eulen*. Stuttgart: Ulmer.
WANDELER, A.I. & P. LÜPS 1993: p. 161-162 in *Handbuch Der Säugetiere Europas*, (Eds.) J. Niethammer & F. Krapp. vol. 5 Raubsäuger - Carnivora (Fissipedia). Teil 1 (Eds.) v. M. Stubbe & F. Krapp. Wiesbaden: Aula.
SUKOPP, H. (Ed.) 1990 *Stadtökologie. Das Beispiel Berlin*; Berlin: Dietrich Reimer. 455 pp.
WENDLAND, V. 1953 Populationsstudien an Raubvögeln. II. Bruterfolg 1940-1951 untersucht an 7 Arten. *J. Orn.* 94: 103-113.

Dr. Klaus-Dietrich Fiuczynski
Mettestr. 8
D 10825 Berlin
Germany

Paul Soemmer
Naturschutzstation Woblitz
D 16798 Himmelpfort
Germany

Chancellor, R. D. & B.-U. Meyburg eds. 2000
Raptors at Risk
WWGBP / Hancock House

Red-Shouldered Hawks *Buteo lineatus* Nesting on Human-Made Structures in Southwest Ohio

Jeffrey L. Hays

ABSTRACT

During 1996-1998, two different pairs of Red-shouldered Hawks *Buteo lineatus* nested on human-made structures in southwest Ohio. The first pair nested successfully in the same location on a roof of an occupied building in 1996, 1997 and 1998. A total of 12 chicks fledged from the roof in three years. The daily human activity around the building appeared to have no effect on the productivity of the hawks. The second pair nested unsuccessfully on the deck of a suburban home in 1997 and 1998. In 1997 three eggs were laid but did not hatch; in 1998 a new nest was constructed but no eggs were laid. To my knowledge, there is no previous documentation of Red-shouldered Hawks nesting on such structures.

INTRODUCTION

Many species of raptors have been reported nesting successfully on a wide range of human-made structures including power poles, high-voltage transmission towers, power plants, billboards, coal chutes, railway signal gantry, bridges, irrigation systems, abandoned and occupied buildings (Palmer 1988, Temple 1988, James 1992, Niemuth 1992, Varland & Loughin 1993, Blue 1996, Stout *et al*. 1996). To my knowledge, there is no documentation of Red-shouldered Hawks nesting on human-made structures. I here describe the nesting of two different pairs of Red-shouldered Hawks on occupied dwellings in southwest Ohio.

Red-shouldered Hawk habitat requirements and nest site selections are well-documented. Red-shouldered Hawks nest in mature, large trees in riparian zones or wet woodlands, (Bednarz & Dinsmore 1982, Morris & Lemon 1983, Woodrey 1986, Howell 1997), near water, (Titus & Mosher 1981, Preston *et al* . 1989), and often far from human disturbances (Bednarz & Dinsmore 1982, Johnson 1989, Bosakowski & Smith 1997). The nests described herein are two of 48 nests that were observed in a study of Red-shouldered Hawk nest-site selection in southwest Ohio. Many of the nests in this suburban area were located close to occupied dwellings (mean distance 75.2 +/- 19.6 m, n=48 1997-1998; Dykstra & Hays, unpubl. data).

NEST OBSERVATION

Pair 1

The first pair, both in adult plumage, nested successfully on the roof of a three-story multi-family dwelling, one of many such buildings in a large complex in Hamilton County, Ohio, in the suburban area surrounding the city of Cincinnati (39°11'N, 84°40'W). The building was located 25.3 m from a small wooded area and 16.8 m from a seasonal stream that runs through the woodlot. Within 90 m of the building were a minimum of 10 apparently suitable nest trees having a dbh > 33 cm (33 cm dbh = the smallest nest tree observed in the previously mentioned study). The building had two different roof heights and the nest was located 8.16 m from the ground at the bottom of the lower roof just above the gutters, resting against the siding of the higher-roofed section of the building. The first nest built by the hawks was removed from the roof on 28 February 1996 because of a possible conflict between the tenants and the hawks. By mid-March the hawks had rebuilt the nest and had begun incubation; therefore the landowners decided to allow the nest to remain. The nest was successful and all four nestlings fledged by 31 May 1996. To avoid moisture damage to the asphalt-shingled roof, the landowners removed the nest on 1 July 1996.

A pair of Red-shouldered Hawks, presumably the same pair, began construction of a third nest at precisely the same location on the 31 of January 1997. Incubation began on the 16 of March 1997, and the four chicks were banded on the 29 of April 1997. All four nestlings successfully fledged by 2 June. The third nest, measuring 76 cm in diameter x 30 cm deep, was removed on the 12 of June and was found to weigh 7.2 kg.

In 1998, a new nest was constructed in the same location by February 14th 1998, and incubation began approximately the 15th of March. Four nestlings were banded on May 13, and all had fledged by May 28.

Pair 2

The second nest site was located 6.0 km from the roof site (39°13'N, 84°36'W). The nest was built on a gas grill on the deck of an occupied house. The nest was 17.5 m from a woodlot and 60 m from a permanent stream. As with the roof site, there was a minimum of 10 apparently suitable nest trees having a dbh > 33 cm within 90 m. Construction of the nest began on February 20th, 1997. Incubation started the 8th of April; however, by the 4th of May, both adults had stopped incubating and the nest failed. Although the reason for the failure cannot be known for certain, the fact that the nesting female was in immature plumage and showed little interest during nest building and incubation may indicate the cause. The daily activities of the landowners did not change from February 20th to May 4th. The hawks were still seen and heard in the area after the nest failed. The nest was removed on 15 June 1997.

In late January of 1998, two adult Red-shouldered Hawks began construction of a new nest at the same location on the grill as in 1997. The nest was completed by early March, but no eggs were laid in the nest. The adults were seen in the area through April 1998.

DISCUSSION

Little has been published on suburban/urban nesting Red-shouldered Hawks. Red-shouldered Hawks have nested successfully in suburban areas of California (Bloom & McCrary 1997) and occasionally near homes and roads in Quebec (Morris & Lemon 1983). The close proximity to humans apparently did not impair reproductive rates for Red-shouldered Hawks nesting in suburban California (Bloom & McCrary 1997) and in surburban Hamilton County, Ohio (1.7 young per active nest, nestlings > 3 weeks old, n=48, 1997-1998, Dykstra & Hays, unpubl. data).

ACKNOWLEDGEMENTS

I thank the landowners of both of the sites, Bud and Donna Black, and David and Shirley Wiesman, for their cooperation during the observation of these nests. Earlier drafts of this short communication were improved through careful review and thoughtful comments by Cheryl Dykstra and Lisa Hays.

REFERENCES

BEDNARZ, J.C. & J.J. DINSMORE 1982. Nest-sites and habitat of Red-shouldered and Red-tailed Hawks in Iowa. *Wilson Bull.* 94:31-45.

BLUE, R. 1996. Documentation of raptor nests on electric utility facilities through a mail survey. *In* D.M. Bird, D.E. Varland & J.J. Negro (eds.) *Raptors in human landscapes.* Academic Press, San Diego, California USA.

BLOOM, P.H. & M.D. MCCRARY 1996. The urban buteo: Red-shouldered Hawks in southern California. *In* D.M. Bird, D.E. Varland & J.J. Negro (eds.) *Raptors in human landscapes.* Academic Press, San Diego, California USA.

BOSAKOWSKI, T. & D.G. SMITH 1997. Distribution and species richness of a forest raptor community in relation to urbanization. *J. Raptor Res.* 31:26-33.

HOWELL, D.L. & B.R.CHAPMAN 1997. Home range and habitat use of Red-shouldered Hawks in Georgia. *Wilson Bull.* 109:131-144.

JAMES, P.C. 1992. Urban nesting of Swainson's Hawks in Saskatchwan. *Condor.* 94:773-774.

JOHNSON, G. 1989. Status and breeding ecology of the Red-shouldered Hawk in north central New York. M.S. Thesis. State University of New York, Syracuse, NY.

MORRIS, M.J.M. & R.E. LEMON 1983. Characteristics of vegetation and topography near Red-shouldered Hawk nests in southwestern Quebec. *J. Wildl. Manage.* 47:138-145.

NEIMUTH, N. 1992. Use of man-made structures by nesting Ferruginous Hawks in Wyoming. *The Prairie Naturalist.* 24:43.

PALMER, R.S. (ed.) 1988. *Handbook of North American birds.* Vol. 4. Yale Univ. Press, New Haven, Connecticut USA.

STOUT, W.E., R.K. ANDERSON & J.M. PAPP 1996. Red-tailed Hawks nesting on human-made and natural structures in southeast Wisconsin. *In* D. M. Bird, D. E. Varland, & J. J. Negro (eds.) *Raptors in human landscapes.* Academic Press, San Diego. 396pp.

TEMPLE, S.A. 1988. Future goals and needs for the management and conservation of the Peregrine Falcon. *In* T.J. Cade, J.H. Enderson, C.G. Thelander & C.M. White (eds.) *Peregrine falcon populations: their management and recovery.* The Peregrine Fund, Inc., Boise, Idaho USA.

TITUS, K. & J.A. MOSHER 1981. Nest-site habitat selected by woodland hawks in the central Appalachians. *Auk* 98: 270-281.

VARLAND, D.E. & T.H. LOUGHIN 1993. Reproductive success of American Kestrels nesting along an interstate highway in central Iowa. *Wilson Bull.* 105:465-474.

WOODREY, M.S. 1986. Characteristics of Red-shouldered Hawk nests in southeast Ohio. *Wilson Bull.* 98:466-469.

Jeffrey L. Hays
7867 Bankwood Lane
Cincinnati
OH 45224
USA

Part 6

Understanding Distribution - the Whys and Wherefores of Geographical Ranges of Raptors

Jackal Buzzard *Buteo rufofuscus* - light morph

Conveners:
Nick Mooney & David Pepler

Chancellor, R. D. & B.-U. Meyburg eds. 2000
Raptors at Risk
WWGBP / Hancock House

Understanding the Distribution of Australia's Diurnal Raptors

William K. Steele and David J. Baker-Gabb

INTRODUCTION

Australia has a depauperate diurnal raptor community considering the size of the continent and the diversity of habitats it supports, with only 24 species of Falconiformes occurring regularly (Marchant & Higgins 1993). Of these, the Red Goshawk *Erythrotriorchis radiatus* is categorised as vulnerable, the Square-tailed Kite *Lophoictinia isura* and Grey Falcon *Falco hypoleucos* as rare (Endangered Species Protection Act 1992; Garnett 1993), and the Letter-winged Kite *Elanus scriptus* is uncommon. By way of contrast, southern Africa, which has a similar total number of bird species to Australia, supports 66 species of Falconiformes (Maclean 1993).

Nevertheless, the Australian Falconiformes form an important guild of native predators. Furthermore, as top-order predators with a high degree of mobility and because of their comparative conspicuousness, the more common diurnal raptors are ideal 'indicator species' for monitoring environmental change. But a knowledge of the present breeding and non-breeding distributions, relative abundances and movements of these birds is necessary before such monitoring studies can be initiated, or effective management policies implemented. Therefore, between 1986 and 1990 Birds Australia co-ordinated the first nation-wide survey of Australia's Falconiformes, using roadside counts to collect basic distribution and relative abundance data for all 24 species. A second national survey of diurnal raptors which repeated the methods of the first was initiated during 1996, ten years after the initial survey.

This paper presents and compares results of the two surveys and specifically addresses the questions:

1. Which areas of Australia support unusually high, or low, diversity and relative abundances of diurnal raptors, which might indicate a need for further study and appropriate management?
2. What changes to the large-scale distribution and abundance patterns of Australia's Falconiformes, if any, are evident from a comparison of results of two national surveys conducted ten years apart?

METHODS

Data Collection

The first national survey of Australian Falconiformes was conducted between 1986 and 1990. The second national survey commenced in July 1996, and is planned to continue until mid-2000.

During these surveys, roadside counts were conducted throughout Australia by knowledgeable volunteers from the birdwatching community while driving along rural roads at normal speeds. All birds of prey seen during counts were identified whenever possible and scored on a standard datasheet together with the date, time and duration of the journey, and the distance travelled. All road-killed raptors were identified and recorded.

After a review of relevant literature and consultation with a number of ecologists and biogeographers, Australia was divided into 61 biogeographic zones for the purposes of data collection (Fig. 1). Previously defined floral (Barlow 1984, 1985) and avian biogeographic regions (Blakers *et al.* 1984) were instrumental in devising these 61 zones, together with factors such as climate and altitude. In order to simplify data collection and to allow comparisons with other databases, boundaries between biogeographic zones follow 1° lines of latitude and longitude.

Figure 1. The 61 biogeographical zones used during the study.

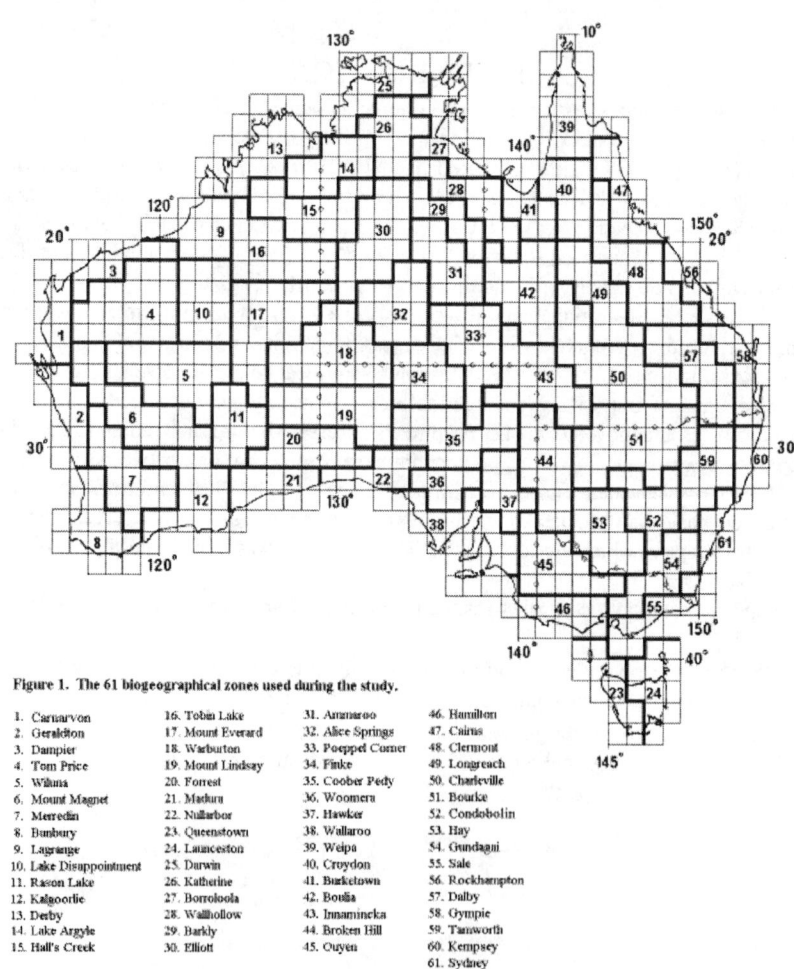

Figure 1. The 61 biogeographical zones used during the study.

1. Carnarvon
2. Geraldton
3. Dampier
4. Tom Price
5. Wiluna
6. Mount Magnet
7. Merredin
8. Bunbury
9. Lagrange
10. Lake Disappointment
11. Rason Lake
12. Kalgoorlie
13. Derby
14. Lake Argyle
15. Hall's Creek
16. Tobin Lake
17. Mount Everard
18. Warburton
19. Mount Lindsay
20. Forrest
21. Maduru
22. Nullarbor
23. Queenstown
24. Launceston
25. Darwin
26. Katherine
27. Borroloola
28. Wallhollow
29. Barkly
30. Elliott
31. Ammaroo
32. Alice Springs
33. Poeppel Corner
34. Finke
35. Coober Pedy
36. Woomera
37. Hawker
38. Wallaroo
39. Weipa
40. Croydon
41. Burketown
42. Boulia
43. Innamincka
44. Broken Hill
45. Ouyen
46. Hamilton
47. Cairns
48. Clermont
49. Longreach
50. Charleville
51. Bourke
52. Condobolin
53. Hay
54. Gundagai
55. Sale
56. Rockhampton
57. Dalby
58. Gympie
59. Tamworth
60. Kempsey
61. Sydney

Counts were conducted during daylight, or within half an hour of sunrise or sunset. All counts covered a minimum of 20 km, and few did not exceed 50 km. Counts with an average speed greater than 120 km/h were considered unreliable and excluded from the study. However, because of the continental scale of the study and the consequent need to involve a large number of volunteer observers it was not possible to establish too stringent rules governing the methods used to collect data. Therefore, unlike similar studies conducted elsewhere on a smaller scale (e.g. Tarboton & Allan 1984, Bunn *et al.* 1995), the speed at which vehicles travelled during counts, the timing of counts and the number of observers per vehicle were not standardised and the distance of each bird from the road was not measured or recorded.

Data collected during counts were used to calculate the relative abundance of Falconiformes within each zone, by season, in terms of the number of individuals recorded per 100 km. Following the *Atlas of Australian Birds* (Blakers *et al.* 1984), seasons were defined as: 'Summer' (December–February), 'Autumn' (March–May), 'Winter' (June–August) and 'Spring' (September–November).

The data also allow variation in Falconiformes species diversity across Australia to be determined. In general, the number of species recorded in any region will increase with the number of surveys conducted, and in an attempt to correct for this a simple index of species diversity was derived by dividing the number of species recorded in each zone by the logarithm of the number of counts conducted within that zone.

In order to assess how well lone drivers were able to detect raptors, when compared with counts conducted by more than one observer, 105 trial counts were carried out in southern New South Wales during the latter part of 1985. During these counts the number of raptors seen by the driver and by three additional observers in the same vehicle were recorded and compared. The same driver and observers were used in all counts.

Overall, the vehicle driver saw 2,963 (85%) of the 3,501 raptors recorded by the additional observers. The driver saw similar proportions of both large raptors, such as Wedge-tailed Eagles *Aquila audax*, and smaller ones, such as Nankeen Kestrels *Falco cenchroides*. In light of this result, a 'lone driver correction factor' was applied to the results of all counts carried out by a single person, whereby the total number of all birds of prey recorded during these counts was divided by 0.85.

The visibility of birds, and hence their detectability during roadside counts, is determined largely by three factors: the structure and density of local vegetation; local weather conditions; and the size, colouration and behaviour of the species. Although the biogeographic zones are differentiated largely on the basis of vegetation, it is difficult to determine a realistic correction factor for this variation which might be applied across the entire dataset. A simple test of the effectiveness of the methods used during the study produced equivocal results but indicated that roadside surveys recorded less than 60% of the raptors actually present, varying between species, habitat and land use types (Baker-Gabb 1986). Therefore, no attempt was made to estimate a correction factor for vegetation but rather the large-scale variations in vegetation between zones should be emphasised when interpreting results of the study.

The majority of Falconiformes are relatively conspicuous birds, which is why the roadside count methodology is generally considered appropriate for this group (e.g. Fuller & Mosher 1981, 1987; Diesel 1984; Tarboton & Allan 1984; Andersen *et al.* 1985; Taylor *et al.* 1985). Differences in conspicuousness or 'detectability' between species are not relevant in this study since no interspecific comparisons were considered. Only a few of the Australian species, such as the Red Goshawk, Collared Sparrowhawk *Accipiter cirrhocephalus* and Grey Falcon are difficult to observe from a motor vehicle (DJB-G pers. obs.; Mooney & Holdsworth 1988). In this study, both the observed distribution and the calculated relative abundance of these more secretive species are certain to be under-estimated.

RESULTS

Data Collection

Between 1986 and 1990, a total of 271 volunteer observers conducted 25,103 counts across Australia covering a distance of 3,818,471 km. Since 1996, 415 observers have submitted 23,611 completed datasheets. Of these, the results of 15,136 counts covering 1,971,787 km are used in this analysis. A further 94 roadside counts were conducted on an *ad hoc* basis during the 1990-1995 interim period between the two national surveys. Approximately 2% of datasheets submitted were considered unreliable, excluded from results and are not included in the totals given above.

As expected, there was great variation in the degree of coverage of the different zones, with those containing large cities having the greatest number of counts. In contrast, the arid central areas of Australia were not well covered, with fewer than 50 counts per season for some zones.

Species Diversity

Figures 2 and 3 show the Falconiformes species diversity recorded within each biogeographical zone during the course of the study, both as the number of species recorded and as a simple species diversity index which, to some extent, corrects for the varying number of counts conducted within zones.

As expected, species diversity generally increases from the temperate south of the country to the tropical north, with very low species diversity recorded in some particularly arid areas of central Australia (Fig. 3). The greatest number of species to be recorded within a zone was 20 in Zones 13 and 25, whereas the fewest species recorded was a mere four in Zone 19 in the Great Victoria Desert. The average number of species to be recorded in all zones was 14 ± 3.7.

Figure 2. Falconiformes species richness across Australia.

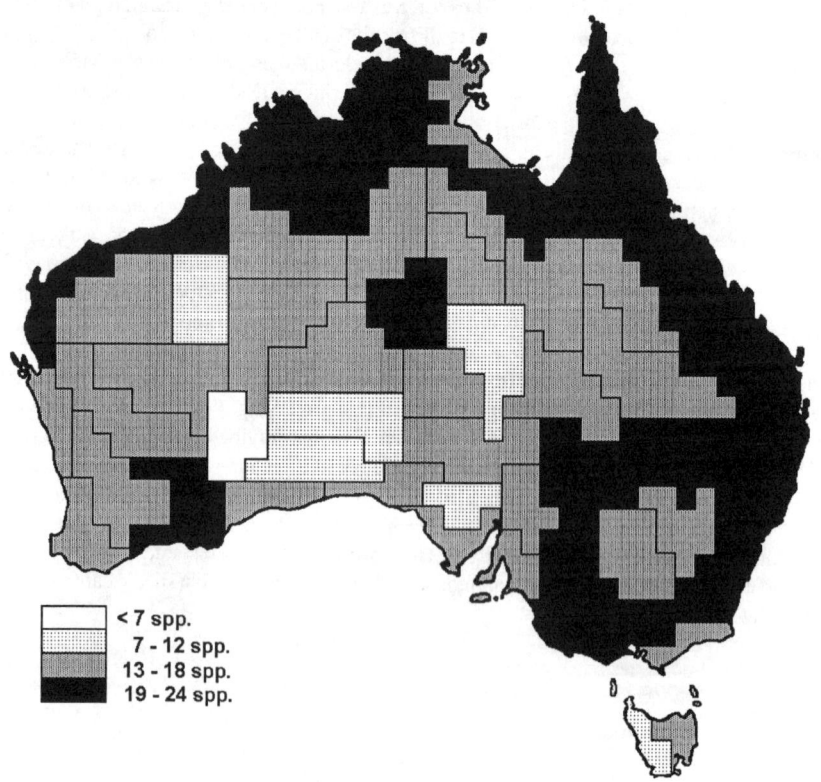

Figure 3. Index of Falconiformes species richness across Australia.

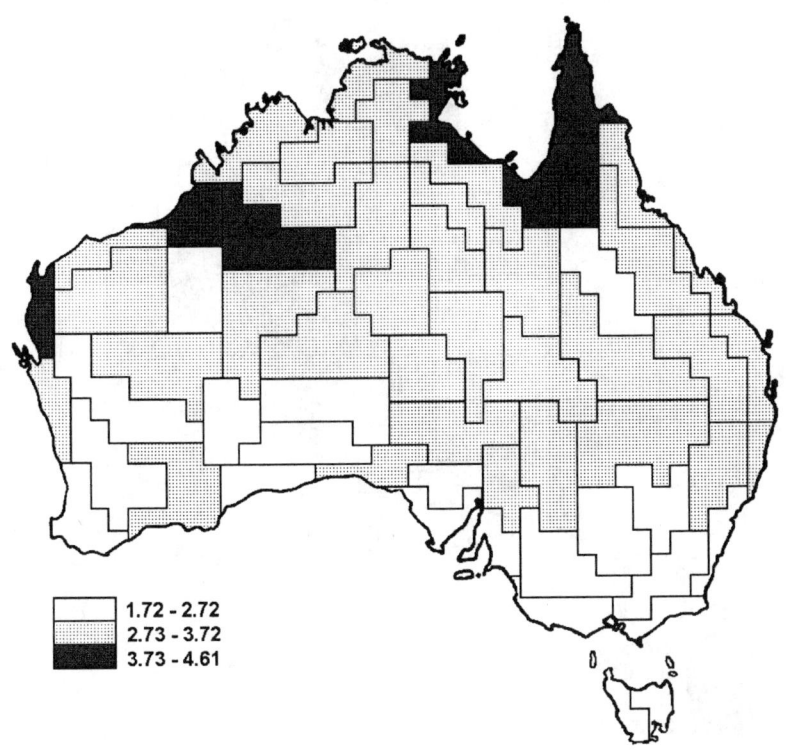

Distribution

Figure 4 presents survey results showing the relative abundance (birds/100 km) for all 24 resident species of Falconiformes together. Figure 5 presents the relative abundance of Falconiformes by season.

These results indicate that the area of the Mitchell Grass Downs south to the Cooper's Creek drainage basin (covering much of inland Queensland), and the Northwest coast of the Northern Territory are of major importance to Falconiformes. In contrast, Tasmania, the southeastern coastal region and much of Western Australia support comparatively low densities of raptors (Fig. 4).

Figure 5 illustrates a number of seasonal changes in the distribution of Falconiformes. The relative abundance of raptors in the Wet Tropics of northeastern Queensland (i.e. Zone 47) decreases markedly during the wet summer months from a winter peak. There is a similar decline during summer in the relative abundance of raptors in the Wet-Dry Tropics of northern Australia (e.g. Zones 13 and 25), which is least pronounced in the drier Gulf of Carpentaria (Zone 41). The summer decline in these areas is likely to be a result of wet weather leading to poor atmospheric conditions for soaring raptors. Simultaneously with the summer decrease in the relative abundance of raptors in northern and northwestern Australia there is an increase in numbers recorded to the south in the Riverina (Zone 53) and Nullarbor (Zone 22).

A large area from northern Western Australia extending through the Pilbara and Kimberley to the Arnhem Land coast assumes great importance during the dry autumn and winter but supports few raptors during the wet summer months. Also, there is an apparent overall decrease in the relative abundance of raptors throughout Australia during spring, which may be attributable to breeding birds at nests being less easy to detect from road-bound motor vehicles (Fig. 5).

Figure 4. Relative abundance (birds/100 km) of Falconiformes across Australia.

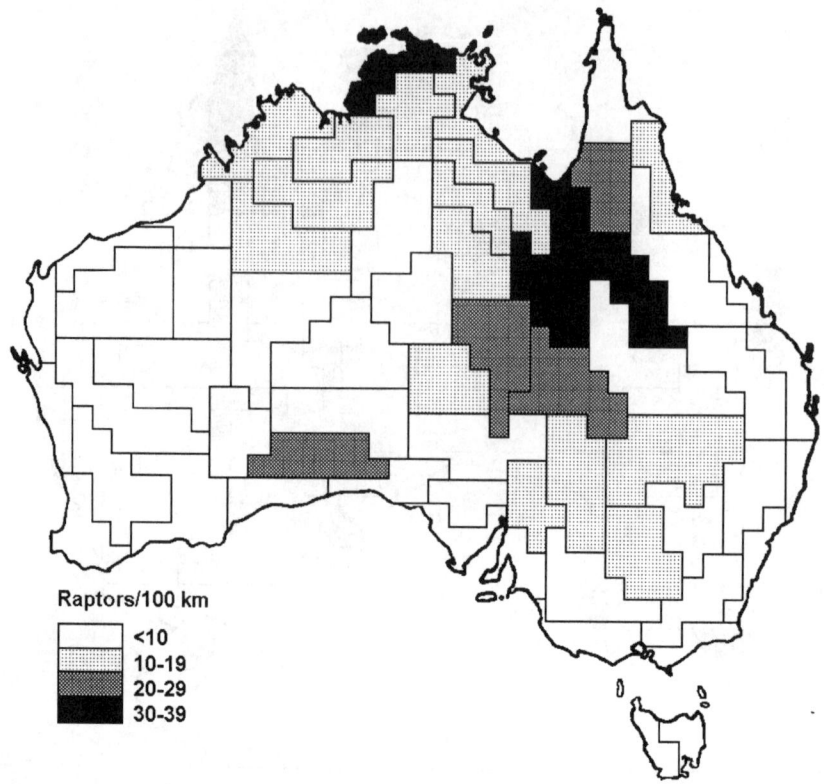

Inter-annual Variation

The number of diurnal raptors recorded per kilometre of survey varied significantly between years ($\chi^2 = 1,827.6$; d.f. = 4; $P < 0.01$), with 1987 having the lowest calculated relative abundance (Table 1).

Variation between Surveys

When the relative abundances of Falconiformes determined in each of the two national surveys, conducted 10 years apart, are compared, great differences become apparent. Those biogeographic zones where changes in the relative abundance of Falconiformes between the two surveys is 50% or greater (either an increase or decrease) are shown in Figure 6.

DISCUSSION

Data Collection

A potential criticism of this study is the simple methodology used to collect the data. In order to collect these data on a continent-wide scale a large number of competent volunteer observers was required, and this necessitated a simple data collection and recording procedure. Nevertheless, the unprecedented, continental database this study has produced provides useful information regarding the large-scale spatial distribution, movements and relative abundance of raptors throughout Australia. Such information could not have been collected in any other way without prohibitive cost to government research organisations.

Species Diversity

It is generally true that species diversity increases as one moves from the higher to the lower latitudes, which is explained by the Stability-Time Hypothesis (Colinvaux 1973). To a certain extent this rule is evident in the species diversity index for Falconiformes across Australia (Fig. 3). However, it is apparent that, in Australia, this general pattern of variation in species diversity is overlaid by a second pattern. When measured simply in terms of the actual number of species recorded across Australia, it was found that arid areas of the interior support the fewest species (Fig. 2). This is also explained by the Stability-Time Hypothesis, as the interior is subject to an unpredictable and extreme climate. Furthermore, the arid interior lacks many of the habitats which are attractive to some Falconiformes, such as the woodlands preferred by some accipiters, and the coastlines and wetlands frequented by the Osprey *Pandion haliaetus*, White-bellied Sea-Eagle *Haliaeetus leucogaster*, Brahminy Kite *Haliastur indus*, Pacific Baza *Aviceda subcristata* and Swamp Harrier *Circus approximans*.

Distribution

Roadside counts of raptors have previously been conducted in Australia, although on a very much smaller scale (e.g. Genelly 1978; Brickhill 1992). This large-scale study has brought to light a number of previously unknown facts. Important concentration areas for Australia's Falconiformes occur in the northeast of the country, from the Gulf of Carpentaria through the Mitchell Grass Downs to the Cooper's Creek drainage area, and along the coast of Arnhem Land. The 10 most important concentration areas for Australian raptors throughout the year are Zones 41, 42, 25, 49, 33, 43, 40, 20, 47 and 53.

Figure 5. Relative abundance (birds/100 km) of Falconiformes across Australia by season.

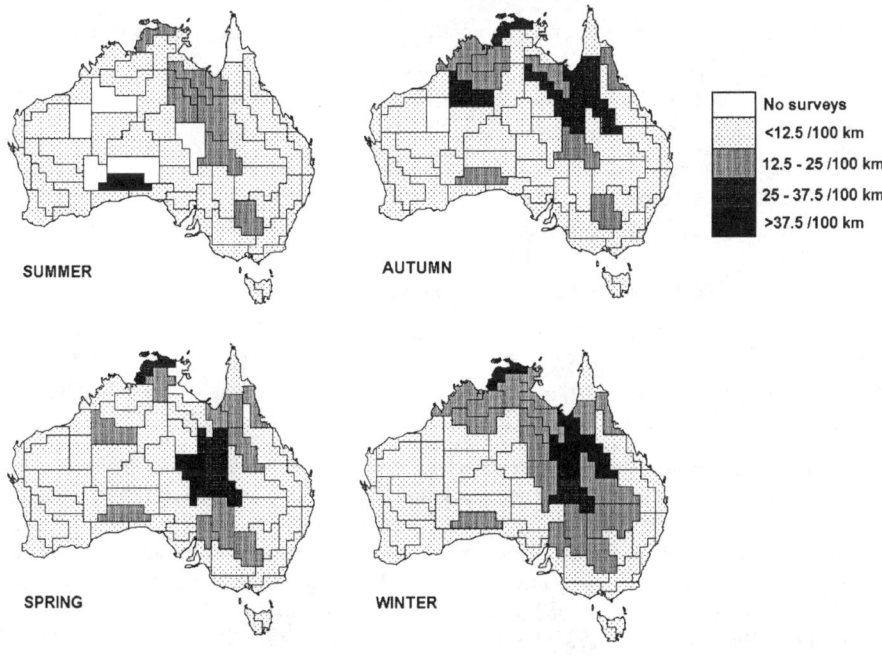

It is notable that most of these zones lie in the north of Australia, and that these zones support the greatest density of raptors during autumn and winter. In contrast, only Zones 20 and 53 lie in southern Australia: Zone 20 having the greatest density of raptors over summer, and Zone 53 supporting large numbers of raptors throughout the year (Fig. 5). Many of these zones are characterised by flat grasslands with few trees, which means raptors are easily seen and recorded. This result may be biased by the methods used and it is likely that some wooded zones are also of great importance to raptors, particularly accipiters.

The high relative abundance of raptors recorded in Zone 53 compared with surrounding zones (Figs 4 and 5) may be due to differences in land use as the Hay area is generally uncultivated grazing land whereas surrounding zones are important for crop production (Division of National Mapping 1979).

The importance of the Kimberley as a wintering ground for several species of Falconiformes (Fig. 5) has been noted previously (Aumann 1993; Olsen 1995). The MacDonnell Ranges in central Australia appear to be used as a migration corridor from the Murray-Darling and Cooper's Creek drainages to these northern wintering grounds and avoiding the arid Western Deserts (Fig. 5).

The 10 zones which display the lowest relative abundances of diurnal raptors are 23, 7, 55, 8, 11, 24, 10, 17, 6 and 12.

Thus the lowest relative abundance of Falconiformes occurs in Tasmania, southwestern Australia and the arid central areas of the Gibson and Great Victoria Deserts. However, the low numbers of raptors recorded in some of these zones may simply be related to their forested habitats (e.g. Zones 8, 23, 24 and 55). In contrast, the arid central zones are largely treeless, so vegetation cover is unlikely to have prevented birds from being seen and to have resulted in the low relative abundances observed.

Inter-annual Variation

Some variation in the number of Falconiformes recorded each year is normal, but there appears to be a trend towards decreased numbers in recent years (Table 1).

Table 1. Relative abundance of diurnal raptors throughout Australia between 1986 and 1998.

Year	No. of Surveys	Distance Covered (km)	No. of Survey Hours	No. of Falconiformes Recorded	Falconiformes / 100 km	Falconiformes/ 100 h
1986	4,221	697,291	9,631.2	58,899.2	8.45	611.54
1987	5,222	836,067	11,131.8	57,030.8	6.82	512.33
1988	5,505	816,721	10,705.6	71,167.5	8.71	664.77
1989	5,509	813,815	10,581.4	70,391.1	8.65	665.24
1990	4,400	619,901	8,075.2	53,902.4	8.70	667.51
1996	3,241	446,589	6,071.2	33,242.5	7.44	547.55
1997	10,628	1,367,550	19,059.0	96,737.8	7.07	507.57
1998	1,267	157,648	2,080.1	10,151.5	6.44	488.04

The introduced European Rabbit *Oryctolagus cuniculus* is a major environmental pest in Australia, causing widespread habitat degradation and restricting new growth of vegetation. During 1995/96, Rabbit Calicivirus Disease (RCD), which can kill up to 95% of infected rabbits, was introduced to Australia as a pest-control mechanism. However, the rabbit is now also a significant component in the diets, at least over a part of their ranges, of several Australian raptors (Leopold & Wolfe 1970; Brooker & Ridpath 1980; Mooney 1983; Baker-Gabb 1984a, 1984b, 1985; Debus 1984; Hull 1986; Aumann 1988, 1989; Robertson 1987; Olsen et al. 1990; Marchant & Higgins 1993).

The effect of a wide-scale reduction in rabbit numbers following the introduction of RCD has apparently been detrimental to some populations of Australia's larger Falconiformes, although effects vary between species and geographical areas. The overall relative abundance of Falconiformes is known to have declined in rabbit-infested areas after the introduction of RCD. A notable exception was southwestern Australia (Steele 1998) but the effectiveness of RCD was patchy rather than widespread in this area (M. G. Brooker pers. comm.).

It is difficult to assess to what degree this reduction in abundance of Falconiformes over large areas of southeastern Australia is attributable to the impact of RCD on rabbit numbers as 1997 was unusually hot and dry in southeastern Australia and it is likely that this will have had some influence on the number of birds recorded. However, there apparently is not a linear relationship between seasonal rainfall and the numbers of raptors recorded during counts in southeastern Australia (Baker-Gabb & Steele 1998). Thus one cannot use lower than average seasonal rainfall to predict lower than average relative abundances of diurnal raptors in this region.

Variation between Surveys

A broad comparison between the results of the 1986–90 and 1996–98 national surveys indicates that there have been major changes in the distribution patterns of Falconiformes during the last 10 years (Fig. 6). Some of these apparent changes are explicable but many can only be the subject of conjecture at this stage.

Figure 6. Biogeographic zones showing 50% or greater change in the recorded relative abundance (birds/100 km) of Falconiformes between 1986–90 and 1996–98.

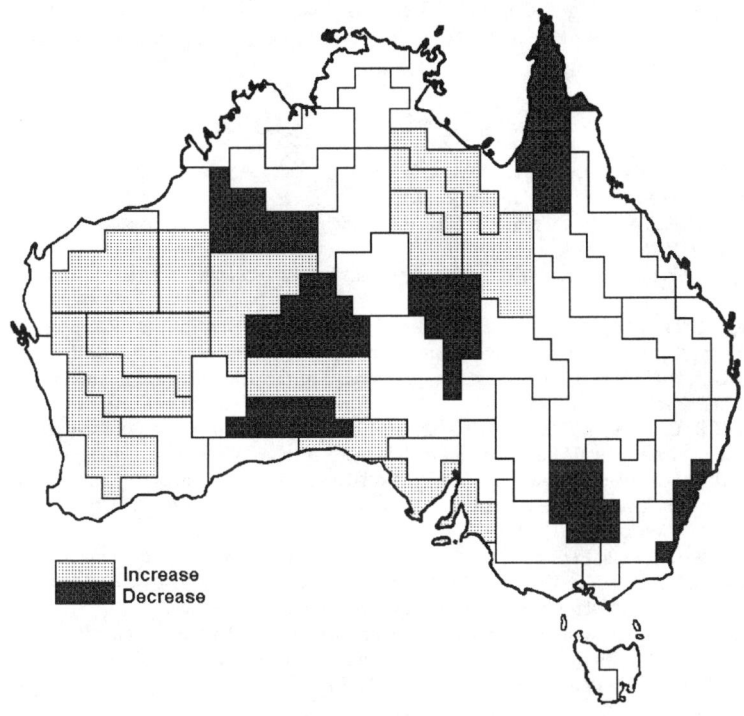

Major declines in the relative abundance of Falconiformes recorded in Zone 53 and Zone 61 reflect the increased intensity and extent of land use by Man over the past decade.

The decline recorded in Zone 33 is suspected to be due to two factors: the impact of reduced rabbit numbers following the introduction of RCD to this area (Steele 1998), and the very low number of counts conducted in this Zone during the 1986–90 survey, which lead to artificially high values for relative abundance (Baker-Gabb & Steele 1998).

Similarly, the decline observed in Zone 20 may be attributable to a combination of factors. During 1986–90 this zone was surveyed most often by a train driver. The Nullarbor is characterised by a lack of trees and it is likely that some Falconiformes, particularly habitual pole-perchers such as the Nankeen Kestrel, were attracted to structures, such as telephone poles, alongside the railway line which meant that unnaturally high numbers were recorded from trains. With new technology, most telephone poles have been removed from this area and so it might be expected that fewer birds are now recorded during roadside counts.

Apparent increases in the relative abundance of Falconiformes over inland areas of Western Australia from 1986–90 to 1996–98 (Fig. 6) are difficult to explain. Although these areas have become more accessible, following the construction of new roads, the number of counts conducted there has not increased significantly.

ACKNOWLEDGEMENTS

A great debt of gratitude is owed to the many volunteer observers who contributed both time and money through their participation in the national surveys and who made this study possible. Data entry was undertaken by Gudrun Arnold, Shelly Benson, Louise Currie, Rebecca Hayward, Margie Heinreich, Bronwyn Laycock, David Pool and Lyle Smith.

Although the 1986–90 national survey was run by DJB-G in a volunteer capacity, Birds Australia bore all the costs of printing and postage. Generous financial donations by the M. A. Ingam Trust and Dr Joost Brouwer provided much needed financial support for the project. Financial assistance from Environment Australia is gratefully acknowledged.

REFERENCES

ANDERSEN, D.E., O.J. RONGSTAD & W.R. MYTTON 1985. Line transect analysis of raptor abundance along roads. *Wildlife Society Bulletin* 13: 533–539.

AUMANN, T. 1988. The diet of the Brown Goshawk *Accipiter fasciatus* in southeastern Australia. *Australian Wildlife Research* 15: 587–594.

AUMANN, T. 1989. Prey at a Brown Goshawk nest near the You Yangs Range, Victoria. *Australian Bird Watcher* 13: 134.

AUMANN, T. 1993. Seasonal movements of the Brown Goshawk *Accipiter fasciatus* in Australia. In: Olsen, P. (Ed.). *Australian Raptor Studies*. Melbourne, Australian Raptor Association, pp. 228–242.

BAKER-GABB, D.J. 1984a. The breeding ecology of twelve species of diurnal raptor in northwestern Victoria. *Australian Wildlife Research* 11: 145–160.

BAKER-GABB, D.J. 1984b. The feeding ecology and behaviour of seven species of raptor overwintering in coastal Victoria. *Australian Wildlife Research* 11: 517–532.

BAKER-GABB, D.J. 1985. The feeding ecology and behaviour of seven species of raptor overwintering in coastal Victoria. Supplement to Baker-Gabb, D.J. 1984. Australian Wildlife Research 11, 517-532. *Australasian Raptor Association News* 6: 4–9.

BAKER-GABB, D.J. 1986. BOP Watch Update. *Royal Australasian Ornithologists Union Newsletter* 69: 4–5.

BAKER-GABB, D.J. & W.K. STEELE 1998. The relative abundance, distribution and seasonal movements of Australian Falconiformes, 1986-90. *Birds Australia Report Series No. 6*. 102 pp.

BARLOW, B.A. 1984. Proposal for delineation of botanical regions in Australia. *Brunonia* 7: 195–201.

BARLOW, B.A. 1985. A revised natural regions map for Australia. *Brunonia* 8: 387–392.

BLAKERS, M., S.J.J.F. DAVIES & P.N. REILLY 1984. *The Atlas of Australian Birds*. Melbourne, Melbourne University Press.

BRICKHILL, J. 1992. Abundance of raptors in the Riverina, 1978-1987. In: Olsen, P. (Ed.). *Australian Raptor Studies*. Melbourne, Australian Raptor Association, pp. 262–272.

BROOKER, M.G. & M.G. RIDPATH 1980. The diet of the Wedge-tailed Eagle, *Aquila audax*, in Western Australia. *Australian Wildlife Research* 7: 433–452.

BUNN, A.G., W. KLEIN & K.L. BILDSTEIN 1995. Time-of-day effects on the numbers and behaviour of non-breeding raptors seen on roadside surveys in eastern Pennsylvania. *Journal of Field Ornithology* 66: 544–552.

COLINVAUX, P.A. 1973. *Introduction to Ecology*. New York, John Wiley and Sons.

DEBUS, S.J.S. 1984. Biology of the Little Eagle on the Northern Tablelands of New South Wales. *Emu* 84: 87–92.

DIESEL, D.A. 1984. Evaluation of the road survey technique in determining flight activity of Red-tailed Hawks. *Wilson Bulletin* 96: 315–318.

DIVISION OF NATIONAL MAPPING. 1979. *Australia: Land Use. 1:5 000 000 map sheet.* Atlas of Australian Resources. Canberra, Division of National Mapping.

FULLER, M.R. & J.A. MOSHER 1981. Methods of detecting and counting raptors: a review. *Studies in Avian Biology* 6: 235–246.

FULLER, M.R. & J.A. MOSHER 1987. Raptor survey techniques. In: Giron Pendleton, B.A., Millsap, B.A, Cline, K.W. & Bird, D.M. (eds). *Raptor management techniques manual.* Washington, D.C., National Wildlife Federation, pp. 37–66.

GARNETT, S. 1993. Threatened and extinct birds of Australia. *Royal Australasian Ornithologists Union Report* 82 (second, corrected edition).

GENELLY, R.E. 1978. Observations of the Australian Kestrel on northern tablelands of New South Wales, 1975. *Emu* 78: 137–144.

HULL, C. 1986. The diet of the Wedge-tailed Eagle (*Aquila audax*) breeding near Melbourne. *Corella* 10: 21–24.

LEOPOLD, A.S. & T.O. WOLFE 1970. Food habits of nesting Wedge-tailed Eagles, *Aquila audax*, in southeastern Australia. *CSIRO Wildlife Research* 15: 1–17.

MACLEAN, G.L. 1993. *Roberts' Birds of Southern Africa.* Cape Town, John Voelcker Bird Book Fund.

MARCHANT, S. & P.J. HIGGINS (Eds) 1993. *Handbook of Australian, New Zealand and Antarctic Birds. Volume II: Raptors to Lapwings.* Melbourne, Oxford University Press.

MOONEY, N.J. 1983. Food of Swamp Harriers in Tasmania. *Australasian Raptor Association News* 4 (3): 12–13.

MOONEY, N.J. & M. HOLDSWORTH 1988. Observations of the use of habitat by the Grey Goshawk in Tasmania. *Tasmanian Bird Report* 17: 1–12.

OLSEN, P.D. 1995. *Australian Birds of Prey.* Sydney, University of NSW Press.

OLSEN, P.D., S.J.S. DEBUS, G.V. CZECHURA & N.J. MOONEY 1990. Comparative feeding ecology of the Grey Goshawk *Accipiter novaehollandiae* and Brown Goshawk *Accipiter fasciatus. Australian Bird Watcher* 13: 178–192.

ROBERTSON, G.G. 1987. Effect of drought on a breeding population of Wedge-tailed Eagles, *Aquila audax. Emu* 87: 220–223.

STEELE, W.K. 1998. Initial assessment of the impact of Rabbit Calicivirus Disease on Australian Birds of Prey, 1996–98. *Report for Phase II: Monitoring the Impact of Rabbit Calicivirus Disease on the Abundance, Movements and Concentrations of Australian Birds of Prey. Environment Australia Project No. ISP 09.* 27 pp.

TARBOTON, W. & D. ALLAN 1984. The status and conservation of Birds of Prey in the Transvaal. *Transvaal Museum Monograph* 3: 1–115.

TAYLOR, K., R.J. FULLER & P.C. LACK 1985. *Bird census and atlas studies: Proceedings of the VIII International Ornithological Conference on Bird Census and Atlas Work.* Hertfordshire, British Trust for Ornithology.

William K. Steele and David J. Baker-Gabb
Birds Australia
415 Riversdale Road
Hawthorn East
Victoria 3123
AUSTRALIA

Radio Telemetry studies of Dispersal and Survival in juvenile White-tailed Sea Eagles *Haliaeetus albicilla* in Norway

Torgeir Nygård, Robert E. Kenward and Kjell Einvik

INTRODUCTION

Norway holds approximately half of the current European population of the White-tailed Sea Eagle *Haliaeetus albicilla* (Folkestad, 1997). After having been persecuted for decades, this large long-lived raptor was eventually protected in 1968. Since then it has increased and expanded its range. Little is known, however, about the details of juvenile dispersal and mortality of this species, as ringing recoveries only give crude information on movements. The advent of long-life radio tags has provided more continuous data on movements and a rapid method of estimating survival for rare species, which generally provide too few ring recoveries for reliable survival estimates (Kenward, 1993).

METHODS

Study area

We studied dispersal of juvenile White-tailed Sea Eagles on the coast of Central Norway during 1989-97. The study area was located in the province of North Trøndelag, central Norway 64°-65°N (Fig. 1). Area 1 is located in the inner part of Trondheimsfjorden, a sheltered fjord where the landscape is dominated by forestry (mainly spruce forest) and agriculture (dairy and cereal farms). Area 2 is a coastal area indented with shorter fjords, richly interspersed with small islands. There is some coastal fishing and salmon farming, with small scale forestry and agriculture (dairy farms). The hills are covered with Scots pine and some birch up to an elevation of *ca*. 300 m. Area 3 is an island set off from the mainland, with small-scale agriculture and a growing fish-farming industry. The island is quite barren, especially toward the west, with some birch and mixed deciduous forest in more sheltered sites. The areas 1-3 form a gradient from sheltered inland to exposed outer coast.

Figure 1. The study area in central Norway, 63°-66°N, showing where the fledgling White-tailed Sea Eagles were tagged (Areas 1-3) and the general flight paths regularly travelled by fixed-wing aircraft to track their movements.

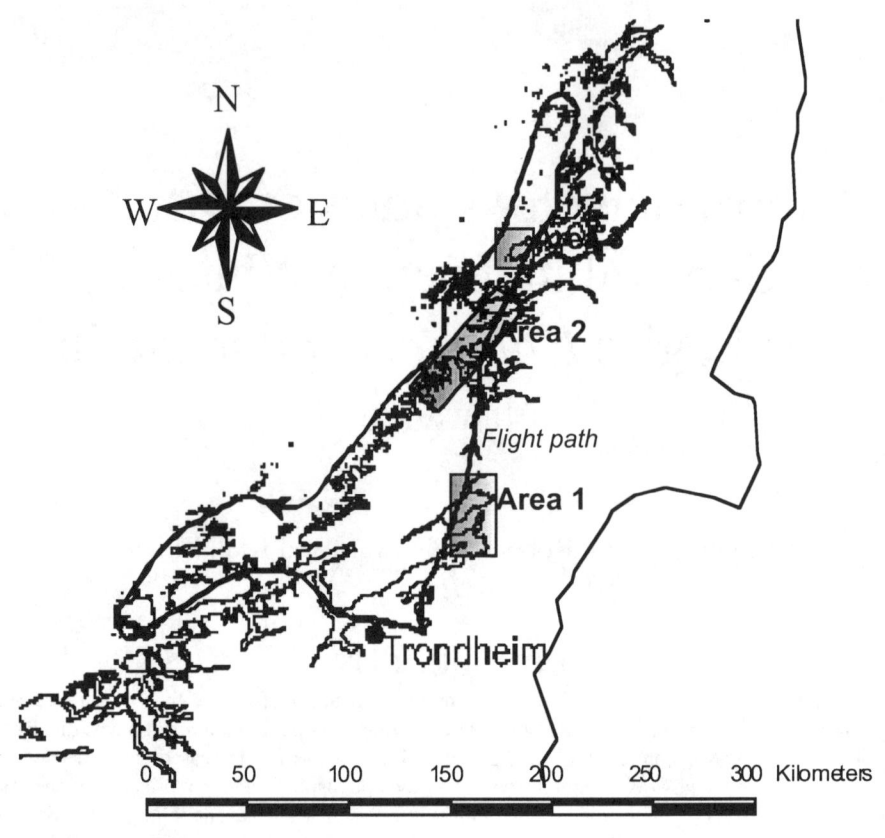

Sexing of nestlings

Nests were generally visited only once, but ten eaglets were measured 2-3 times at different intervals during the nest period to estimate growth rates. At our visits at nests, measurements (mm) of culmen length, bill height, tarsus width (at the thinnest point), tarsus breadth (at the same point perpendicularly to the first) were taken with a slide calliper to the nearest 0.1 mm (Bortolotti, 1984c). The wing length (straight flattened chord) was measured with an inch rule to the nearest mm. The tail length was measured by inserting a ruler between the central rectrices. The mass of the birds were taken with a 10 kg Pesola spring balance to the nearest 100 g. The filling of the crop of the nestlings was recorded, and the weight of the content was subtracted as follows: full crop = 300 g, more than half full crop = 200 g, less than half full crop = 100 g, empty crop = 0 g (Helander, 1981). The sex of the eaglets was assigned subjectively based on appearance, behaviour and biometrics. In the cases of twins, the relative size of birds facilitated the sexing. When the mass of an eaglet was more than 6.0 kg, it was assumed to be female. Two males and two females later had their sex verified by post mortem gonad inspection.

Radio tracking

Forty-one eaglets were radio-tagged with 75 g VHF transmitters from Biotrack Ltd, Wareham, UK using back-packs attached with a 1.25 cm wide teflon ribbon in a Y-type attachment and a loose fit (a least three fingers between the transmitter and the back of the nestling). This method has proven non-harmful to Bald Eagles *Haliaeetus leucocephalus* (Buehler *et al.*, 1995). The batteries of the tags from 1989-90 lasted approximately two years, while the tags used in 1991-1993 lasted five years and more. The backpack design has been extensively tested on Common Buzzards *Buteo buteo* without evidence of adverse impacts on behaviour or survival (Kenward & Walls, 1994). Only one of our birds (a presumed male) that was later recovered alive, showed slight signs of wear and also had some pressure sores on its back. Examination of the tagging-data showed that this was the smallest and probably the youngest bird we tagged. Three others that were examined post mortem showed no such adverse external effects. Radio-tracking was done from land, boat and air. After the birds had left their natal area in autumn, they were tracked from a fixed-wing single-engined aircraft, if possible once a month. The flights were normally of five to six hours, covering a total linear distance of up to 800 km. The signals were detected at a distance of 100 km and more, but usually less, depending on the terrain. Flying altitude was typically 1000-1500 m, at a cruising speed of 100 mph. A total of 943 fixes were collected during the course of study.

The statistical testing was performed using SPSSPC ver 8.0 software.

Table 1. Tracking of 41 fledgling White-tailed Sea Eagles radio-tagged to study movements and dispersal from the nest in central Norway 1989-93.

Year	No. of birds tagged	Signal lost 1st year, no further contact	Signal lost 2nd year, no further contact	Signal lost 3rd year, no further contact	Signal lost 4th year, no further contact	Found dead <4 years	Signal lost >4th year, no further contact	Alive >4 years, active signal	Controlled alive >4y, signal lost	Found dead >4y, signal lost
						Status of signal and bird				
1989	5		3						1	1
1990	7		2	4		1				
1991	10	1		1	3	1	1	1	1	1
1992	12	1		2	1		5	3		
1993	7		1		1	1		4		
Total	41	2	6	7	5	3	6	8	2	2

RESULTS

Measurements and sexing

Linear growth of flight feathers between the 24th and the 72th day after hatching has been demonstrated for Bald Eagle (Bortolotti, 1984b), who also found that the rectrices emerged at the age of 25-30 days (estimated from Figure 4 in Bortolotti, 1984a). We found the growth rate of the central tail-feathers to be on the average 5.6 mm/day, with only a slight difference between sexes: 5.5 mm/day for presumed males, and 5.7 for females. The birth date was estimated for each bird using the length of the central rectrices and a growth rate of 5.6 mm/day, and 30 days for their first emergence. A discriminant analysis was performed as a check on our sex-classification, using presumed sex as grouping variable and the different body measurements as independents. On the basis of our biometric data, the analysis divided the birds into two groups that conformed exactly with our subjective classification into males and females. The canonical correlation functions indicated that 49% of total variability between groups could be explained by tarsus width, 17% by bill depth, while 1.6% was explained by tarsus depth. No other measurement explained more than 1% of the total variability. Figure 2 shows the relation between presumed sex, tarsus width + bill depth and tail length. One would, of course, need a larger sample of fledglings of known sex to establish a reliable sexing formula. Bill depth *vs.* foot pad length have been used to discriminate between the sexes

(Bortolotti, 1984a). We found it difficult to use foot-pad, as the eaglets usually had considerable tension in their talons, making it difficult to obtain a good straight measurement. Helander (1981) suggested using tarsus width to separate the sexes, as he found little overlap between the (presumed) sexes in his material.

Figure 2. The relation between bill depth+tarsus width *vs.* tail length in 41 nestlings of White-tailed Sea Eagles in Norway. The birds were sexed on physical appearance, measurements and behaviour in the nest.

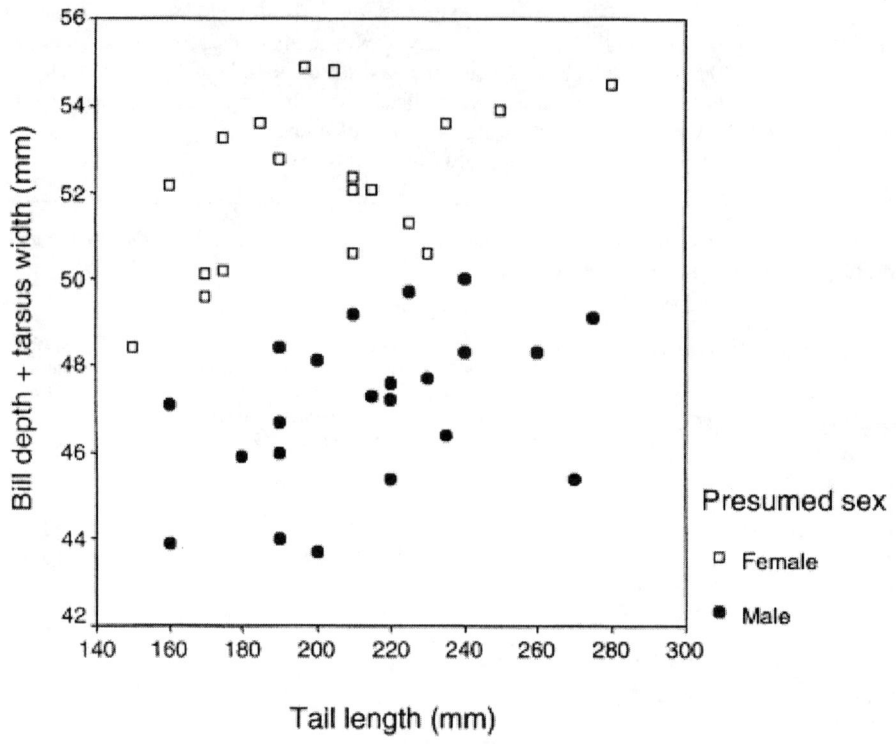

Dispersal age

For reasons connected with lack of personnel and logistics, the exact departure date was difficult to detect with certainty. A bird was considered dispersed when it was observed more than 4 km away from the nest, with no subsequent return that season. The date of dispersal was calculated as the mean of the last date present and the first date away. Two (5%) of the birds (one male, one female) did not leave during their first year of life. The estimated median age at time of permanent departure from the natal area was 161 (n = 23, SD = 61) days for males (median date 1 Oct), and 181 (n = 18, SD = 67) for females (median date 22 Oct); the difference was not significant (Mann-Whitney U test, $Z = -1.03$, $p = 0.31$, two-tailed). Excluding the birds that did not disperse during the first year, the median values were 160 (n = 22, SD = 45) days for males, and 180 (n = 17, SD = 30) for females; the difference was not significant (Mann-Whitney U test, $Z = -1.02$, $p = 0.31$, two-tailed). There was a tendency for birds tagged in the inner areas to disperse earlier than birds from the outer areas. Juveniles from Area 1 had a median age of departure of 141 days, while the ages for Areas 2 and 3 were 164 and 185 days, respectively. However, the differences were barely statistically significant (Spearman corr., $r_s = 0.29$, $p = 0.06$, two-tailed).

Patterns and directions of dispersal

Figures 3 a-d show the distances from nest with age of four juveniles, showing different patterns of dispersal. Male 153 (Fig. 3a) moved 100 km south in its first winter, then returned to its natal area during the next spring. The following autumn and winter he moved up to 200 km SW, with a subsequent return to his natal area in the spring the year after at the age of two years. The same pattern repeated in his third year of life. Male 351 (Fig. 3b) stayed close to the natal site the first whole winter: the longest excursions recorded were less that 10 km. He did not leave the natal area before his second autumn, and never went beyond 60 km. In contrast to most other birds, he moved north and east of his natal site. In his third year, he returned close to his birth-place in the spring, followed by a northerly movement next autumn. Female 271 (Fig. 3b) dispersed more than 180 km SW in her first winter, with a slight return movement next spring. This pattern repeated the following year, but she was never recorded closer that 80 km from her natal site. She was later found weak but alive in a snow-drift at the age of 5 years, and she was rehabilitated and later released. Female 473 (Fig 3d) exhibited a very regular alternating pattern between being 200 km away during winter and *ca.* 40 km from the nest in summer, but the second winter she stayed NE of her natal site, all other winters SW. Most recordings of all the birds were made in a SW direction relative to the nest during winter. 57.5% of all the initial movements (first fix after departure date) were in the south-west direction of the nest, and 27.5% were to the north-east. Only 2.5% were to the south-east, which was a movement inland.

Figure 3 a-d. The dispersal and distance from nest in relation to age of two male and two female radio-tagged juveniles of White-tailed Sea Eagle, showing different movement patterns. The broken line indicates 4 km from the nest.

Figure 3a.

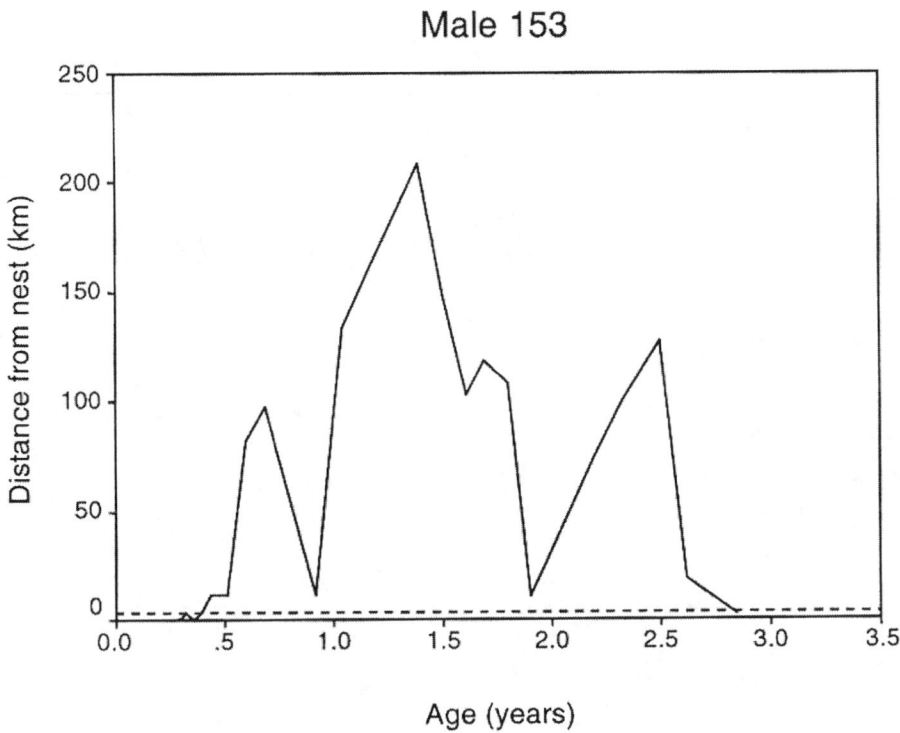

Figure 3b.

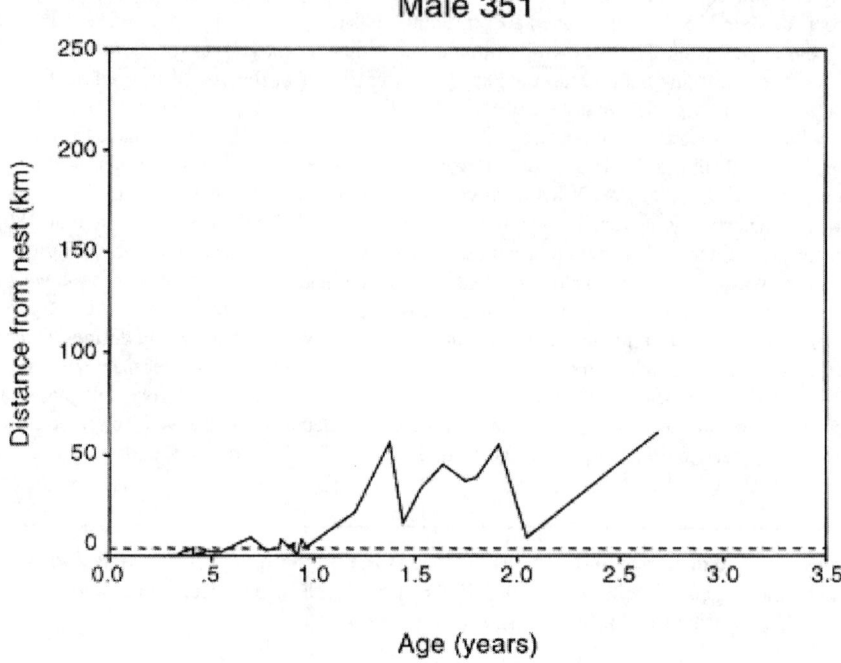

Figure 3c.

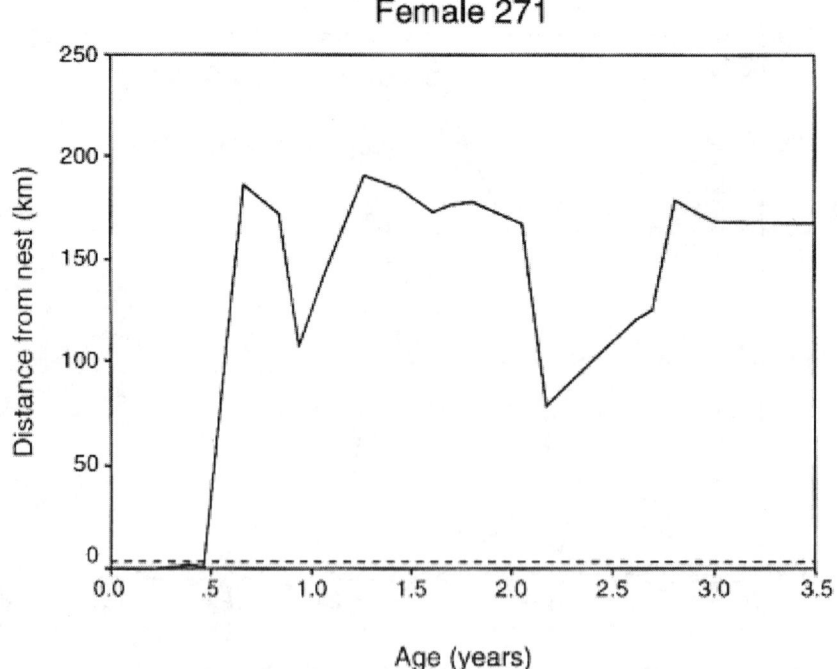

Figure 3d.

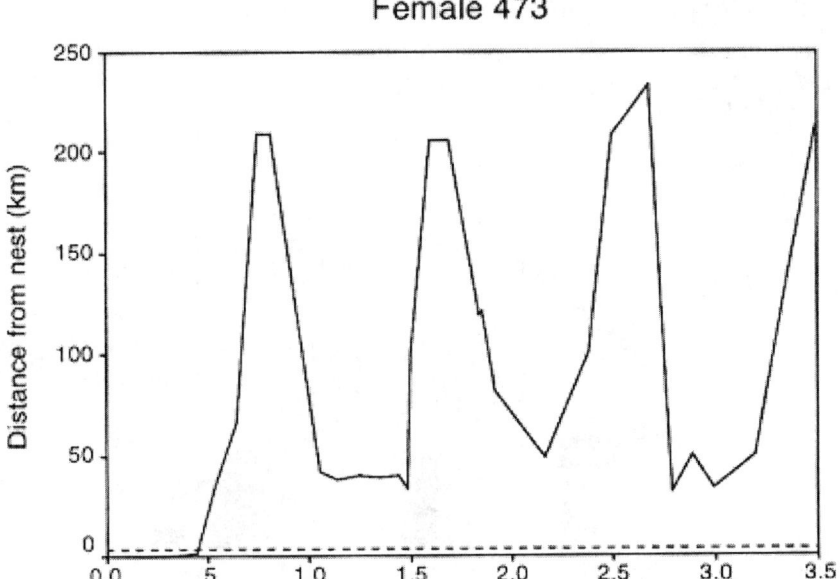

Effects of sex and natal area

Birds from Area 1 stayed further away from the nest in their second and third year than birds from Area 2 and 3, while birds from Area 2 stayed further away from the nest during November-February than birds from Area 3 in their second and third year (Figure 4). Females were observed further away from their natal site than males in winter. This tendency was strong during the second and the third winter, when the median distance from the nest was 44 km for males during November-February (50 fixes), while it was 121 km for females (49 fixes). An ANOVA on $\log_{10}$-transformed distances from the natal site (the dependent variable) was performed, using presumed sex, natal area, and brood size as independents. (Table 2). Among these variables, only sex and natal area had significant effect on the distance from natal site, and only in July-February. In the spring/early summer, there were no significant differences.

Table 2. The effect of presumed sex, natal area, brood size, year of study and birth year on distance from nest at different seasons in the second and third year of life. The significance of the differences was tested using general factorial ANOVA on $\log_{10}$-transformed distances.

Season	Jul-Oct	Nov-Feb	Mar-Jun
Presumed sex	**	**	N.S.
Natal area	*	**	N.S.
Brood size	N.S.	N.S.	N.S.
Year	N.S.	N.S.	N.S.
Birth year	N.S.	N.S.	N.S.
Year*Natal area	N.S.	N.S.	N.S.

* $p < 0.05$, **, $p < 0.01$, N.S. = not significant.

Figure 4. Distance from nest in relation to natal area in the second and third year of life of radio-tagged juvenile White-tailed Sea Eagles in Central Norway.

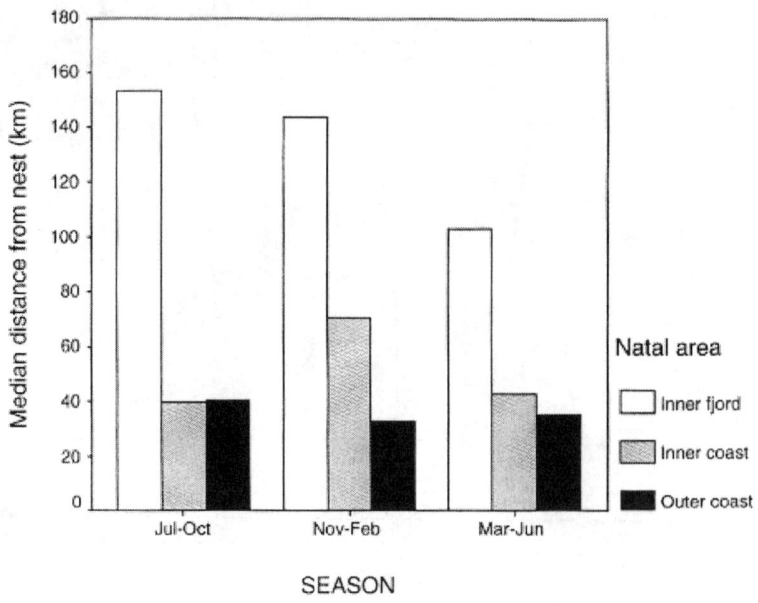

Survival

As seen from Table 1, the tracking records of the different cohorts were different. The performance of the tags mounted in 1989 and 1990 was poorer than in subsequent years, when an improved transmitter design was available. It was therefore necessary to treat the 1989-90 and 1991-93 cohorts separately, having estimated battery lives of approximately 2 vs. 5 years. All the birds from 1989-90 survived the first twelve months, but after that signal loss makes the survival estimates unreliable. Two of the birds whose signals were lost during their second year, were later proven to have obtained adult plumage. Loss of signal before 24 months without further recovery happened to only three of the 29 birds from the 1991-93 cohorts. A Kaplan Meier survival analysis estimated the maximum survival of these cohorts to be 94% (based on only recorded deaths), and the minimum survival 86% (assuming loss of signals is death). The true figure will lie somewhere between these extremes. The effect of the transmitters must be small, in view of the overall high survival rate found.

DISCUSSION

The age of independence found in our birds was slightly higher than found in the Spanish Imperial Eagle *Aquila heliaca adalberti* (123-145 days after hatch) (Alonso *et al.*, 1987). They also found that the time of independence was determined by parental "meanness", i.e. the young wanted more parental investment than the adults were inclined to give (Trivers, 1974). As the White-tailed Sea Eagle is able to and may attempt to breed each year, it may be adaptive to switch the investment effort from its offspring to its own body resources at a certain point of time in the autumn. However, Kenward *et al.*, (1993) showed with experimental feeding and parent removal in Northern Goshawks *Accipiter gentilis* that although dispersal was brought forward slightly by inadequate feeding, it was ultimately a maturation process. Dispersal may normally be a maturation process in Sea Eagles too. Other eagle species may have different strategies, i.e. the Crowned Eagle *Stephanoaetus coronatus* in East Africa, in which the parents continue to feed young for up to a year after hatching, the normal breeding frequency of this species being every second year (Brown, 1966).

The general SW direction found in the present data is against the prevailing winds in the autumn, contrary to what was found in dispersing juvenile Spanish Imperial Eagles (Ferrer, 1993). One reason for this may be that many species of birds suitable as prey for the White-tailed Sea Eagles (e.g. cormorants, geese, gulls) migrate SW along the coastline at this time of the year. This may be a triggering factor for the initial dispersal flights. The coastline runs in a general SW-NE direction, and it may also be advantageous to move south for slightly better climatic conditions in winter. However, within the distances we covered, (*ca.* 300 km linearly) there will be only small differences in general climate. Perhaps there are elements of chance involved in the decision whether to travel up or down the coast, but inland travels seem to be avoided.

Juveniles that moved more than 250 km in any direction from the nest would remain undetected, due to limitations of the flying routes. Two individuals were later found dead at distances in north- and easterly directions beyond those normally covered by the tracking-flights. Ringing-data have revealed that juvenile Sea Eagles may travel long distances, in some cases several hundred kilometres (Love, 1983). However, on most tracking flights the majority of the birds were present, indicating that most birds kept within the surveyed area most of the time.

The tendency for female juveniles to disperse further than males is also demonstrated in many other species of birds of prey, e.g. the European Sparrowhawk *Accipiter nisus* (Newton, 1986). If this is accompanied by a tendency for the males to settle closer to the natal site one may speculate on the possible adaptive significance. The male may have an advantage in an area where he is well known. It may therefore be adaptive for the female to behave differently, in order to avoid inbreeding. Under these circumstances there are, of course, chances that young males may pair up with their mothers if the father dies. Why females disperse further than males, and not *vice versa* is not easy to answer. Female biased dispersal seems to be a general pattern among birds (Clarke *et al.*, 1997). Greenwood (1980) explained male-biased philopatry in birds (which are, by and large, monogamous and territorial) by the greater need for males to establish territory (defend resources) and settle in familiar surroundings. Dobson (1982) argued similarly but also pointed out that in monogamous species the competition for mates should be more nearly equal between the sexes and, hence, that both sexes should disperse in equal proportions. Female White-tailed Sea Eagles may defend their territories vigorously, and can engage in violent female-female territorial fights (Einvik, 1989). Also male-male territorial fights are reported (Love, 1983). Birds in juvenile plumage (dark bill, dark-edges rectrices) seem to be tolerated in territories of breeding adults (Willgohs 1961, own obs.), as also has been recorded in Common Buzzards (Walls & Kenward, 1998). Among Swedish Northern Goshawks, it is the males that travel furthest, possibly because of differences in food supply, probably connected to the large size dimorphism between the sexes in this species (Kenward *et al.*, 1993).

Nest site fidelity of marked individuals is demonstrated in Bald Eagles (Gerrard *et al.*, 1992) as in this study. The very slow rate of geographical expansion of the White-tailed Sea Eagle since it was protected in 1968 in Norway may have to do with the tendency of immature birds of this species to return to their natal territories, presumably in search of vacant breeding territories.

The difference observed in moving distance between birds from the inner fjord area and the coastal areas may be explained by the need of the birds from the fjord to move to the outer coastal areas in winter to improve their foraging situation. We believe that the coastal archipelagos, with their extensive shallow areas created by the numerous islands and skerries, provide better fishing opportunities than the rather steeply shelving fjords. The coast has more local fishery, resulting in more available offal, and it also has more wintering birds suitable as prey, such as cormorants and large gulls. These factors may also be responsible for the earlier dispersal of the birds from the fjord.

Our results, indicating annual survival rates in the first two years of life at 90-95%, are remarkably high. They contrast strongly to with reports from Amchitka Island, Alaska in 1972 for Bald Eagles, where the estimated mortality in the juvenile stages up to adulthood was 90%, based on the numerical relationships between brown and mottled (juvenile) and adult-coloured birds (Sherrod *et al.*, 1977). Their calculations were made under the assumption of no immigration or emigration, which may not hold. In a study of released juveniles translocated from Norway to Scotland, Green *et al.* (1996) estimated an annual survival rate at 73% prior to settlement (normally at 4-7 years), and 94% thereafter.

The precision of their estimates was probably reduced as the birds were not radio-tagged, making individual identification in the field more difficult. Survival of large eagles in their first year of life has shown to be high in other studies using radio-tags. Buehler *et al.* (1991) found 100% survival in the first year of Bald Eagles in Maryland, USA. Our findings support the view that radio tagging is able to give better (and usually higher) survival estimates for medium-sized and large philopatric raptors (Kenward, 1993). The annual survival estimates of first-year Common Buzzards in Britain were 43-49% using ringing records, while in a study using radio-tags with back-pack mounts it was 73% (Kenward & Walls, 1994).

The study has provided details of the juvenile-life stage of White-tailed Sea Eagles that would have been very difficult to obtain using traditional methods. Ecological and life-history parameters of the type shown in this study are essential when it comes to constructing population models, predicting population growth, and assessing conservation and management.

REFERENCES

ALONSO, J. C., L. M. GONZALES, B. HEREDIA & J. L. GONZALES 1987. Parental care and transition to independence of Spanish Imperial Eagle *Aquila heliaca* in Doñana National Park, southwest Spain. *Ibis* 129:212-224.

BORTOLOTTI, G. R. 1984a. Criteria for determining age and sex of nestling Bald Eagles. *J. Field Ornithol.* 55:467-481.

BORTOLOTTI, G. R. 1984b. Physical development of nestling Bald Eagles with emphasis on the timing of growth events. *Wilson Bull.* 96:524-542.

BORTOLOTTI, G. R. 1984c. Sexual size dimorphism and age-related size variation in Bald Eagles. *J. Wildl. Manage.* 48:72-81.

BROWN, L. H. 1966. Observations on some Kenya Eagles. *Ibis* 108:531-572.

BUEHLER, D. A., J. D. FRASER, J. K. D. SEEGAR, G. D. THERRES & M. A. BYRD 1991. Survival rates and population dynamics of Bald Eagles on Chesapeake Bay. *J. Wildl. Manage.* 55:608-613.

BUEHLER, D. A., J. FRASER, D., M. R. FULLER, L. S. MCALLISTER & J. K. D. SEEGAR 1995. Captive and field-tested radio transmitter attachment for Bald Eagles. *J. Field Ornithol.* 66:173-180.

CLARKE, A. L., B.-E. SAETHER & E. RØSKAFT 1997. Sex biases in avian dispersal: A reappraisal. *Oikos* 79:429-438.

DOBSON, F. S. 1982. Competition for mates and predominant juvenile male dispersal in mammals. *Anim. Behav.* 30:1183-1192.

EINVIK, K. 1989. Havørndrama på Namdalskysten (White-tailed Sea Eagle drama on the Namdal Coast). *Vår Fuglefauna* 12:118-119. In Norwegian.

FERRER, M. 1993. Wind-influenced juvenile dispersal of Spanish Imperial Eagles. *Ornis Scand.* 24:330-333.

FOLKESTAD, A. O. 1997. Havsörnens status i Norge. (The status of the White-tailed Sea Eagle in Norway) *Kungsörnen* 1997:2-8. In Norwegian.

GERRARD, J. M., P. N. GERRARD, P. N. GERRARD, G. R. BORTOLOTTI & E. H. DZUS 1992. A 24-year study of Bald Eagles on Besnard Lake, Saskatchewan. *J. Raptor Res.* 26:159-166.

GREEN, R. E., M. W. PIENKOWSKI & J. A. LOVE 1996. Long-term viability of the re-introduced population of the White-tailed Eagle *Haliaeetus albicilla* in Scotland. *J. App. Ecol.* 33:357-368.

GREENWOOD, P. J. 1980. Mating systems, philopatry and dispersal in birds and mammals. *Anim. Behav.* 28:1140-1162.

HELANDER, B. 1981. Nestling measurements and weights from two White-tailed Eagle populations in Sweden. *Bird Study* 28:235-241.

KENWARD, R. 1993. Modelling raptor populations: to ring or to radio-tag? Pages 157-167 *in* J.-D. Lebreton & P.M. North (eds). *Marked individuals in study of bird population*. Birkhauser, Basel.

KENWARD, R. E., V. MARCSTRÖM & M. KARLBOM 1993. Post-nestling behaviour in Goshawks, *Accipiter gentilis*: I. The causes of dispersal. *Anim. Behav.* 46:365-370.

KENWARD, R. E. & S. WALLS 1994. The systematic study of radio-tagged raptors: I: Survival, home-range and habitat use. Pages 303-315 *in* Meyburg, B.-U. & Chancellor, R. D. (eds.). *Raptor conservation today*. WWGBP/ The Pica Press.

LOVE, J. A. 1983. *The return of the Sea Eagle*. Cambridge University Press, Cambridge.

NEWTON, I. 1986. *The Sparrowhawk*. T & A D Poyser, Calton.

SHERROD, T., C. M. WHITE & F. S. WILLIAMSON 1977. Biology of the Bald Eagle on Amchitka Island, Alaska. *Living Bird* 15:143-182.

TRIVERS, B. L. 1974. Parent-offspring conflict. *Am. Zool.* 14:249-264.
WALLS, S. S. & R. E. KENWARD 1995. Movements of radio-tagged Common Buzzards *Buteo buteo* in their first year. *Ibis* 137:177-182.
WALLS, S. S. & R. E. KENWARD 1998. Movements of radio-tagged Buzzards *Buteo buteo* in early life. *Ibis* 140:561-568.
WILLGOHS, J. F. 1961. The White-tailed Eagle *Haliaeetus albicilla* (Linné) in Norway. *Årbok Univ. Bergen, Mat.-Nat. Ser.* 12:1-211.

Torgeir Nygård
Norwegian Institute for Nature Research
Tungasletta 2
N-7485 Trondheim
Norway

Robert E. Kenward
Institute of Terrestrial Ecology
Furzebrook Research Station
Wareham, Dorset BH20 5AS
UK

Kjell Einvik
Office of the County Governor
Department of Environmental Affairs
Statens hus, N-7700 Steinkjer
Norway

The ups and downs of a Northern Goshawk *Accipiter gentilis* population over a 30 year period - Natural dynamics or an artefact?

Volkher Looft

INTRODUCTION

The population of the Northern Goshawk *Accipiter gentilis* increased in Central Europe since 1970 and has stabilised at a high level (Kostrzewa & Speer 1995, Olech 1998). This observation raises the question as to which are the factors responsible for the development.

Longterm investigations are well suited to find out the most important factors as well as to project the future population development. The ability of the Northern Goshawk to respond to changing environmental conditions mainly influenced by human beings is analysed in the study. Focus of further investigations should be put on human persecution and to what extent the population development depends on the availability of food.

STUDY AREA AND METHODS

A Northern Goshawk *Accipiter gentilis* population was studied from 1968 to 1997 using the same methods. The study area was located in Schleswig-Holstein (54.5°N / 9.4°E), in the very north of the Federal Republic of Germany close to the Danish border. It is nearly square in shape with sides approximately 41x48 km long and covering 2,000 km^2. The landscape consists of geological formations of younger and older moraine of glacial origin in similar proportions. The forested area amounts to about 8%, consisting of mainly deciduous trees (with a predominance of beech and oak) on the moraine and coniferous trees (mainly pine) in the sandy areas (Fig.1).

During the investigation period the study area was searched every year, using the same procedures and similar effort. Only in the first years, effort was larger due to some open questions which have been answered in the meantime (for the results see Looft and Busche 1981). The search for Northern Goshawk nests was initially based on previous known sites and then, later on, searches for other nests were made in relevant patches of forests 40 or more years old. In the first 15 years additional nest visits were carried out in order to determine the average clutch size.

During the 30 years all known nesting trees in the study area were climbed at the beginning of June in order to ring the nestlings and to record their age and sex. On this occasion further data were collected, such as the number of unhatched eggs which were buried below the fresh twigs and foliage placed on the nest as the chicks grow. Also, moult feathers around the breeding places were collected, marked and afterwards associated with nest sites and individuals.

Figure 1. North-east part of the study area. This open landscape is characterised by small woods and hedges on walls. Two to four pairs of Goshawk were breeding in this part.

RESULTS

Development of the breeding population

Over the 30 years, the development of the breeding population was markedly irregular, divided roughly into three phases of almost equal length (Fig.2).

Figure 2. Population trends of Northern Goshawk in northern Germany (Study area: 2000 km²)

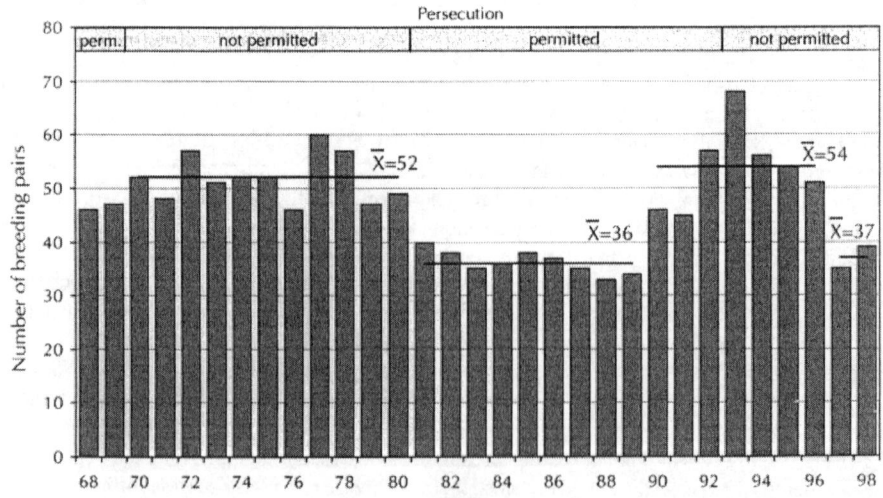

In the first eleven years after the termination of all persecution began in 1970, the number of breeding pairs was on a relatively constant high level of about 52 pairs. However, the annual fluctuations were occasionally large, up to 15 breeding pairs between 1976 and 1977.

From 1981 to 1989 the population decreased to a considerably lower constant level of 36 breeding pairs on average. In the following 8 years the absolute peak of this long-term study was already reached after 4 years (1993) with a total of 68 breeding pairs. Afterwards the population decreased again to a minimum of 35 breeding pairs in 1997 and 1998.

Breeding biology

Beginning of laying

The time of laying has usually been counted back by using the estimated age of nestlings at time of ringing and an incubation period of 38 days (Brüll 1964). Only in the first ten years was the beginning of laying recorded exactly in some individual cases.

During the 30 years the average varied by only 11 days (Fig. 3)- between 6th April (1968, 1989) and 16th April (1979, 1980, 1987).

Figure 3. Mean laying date

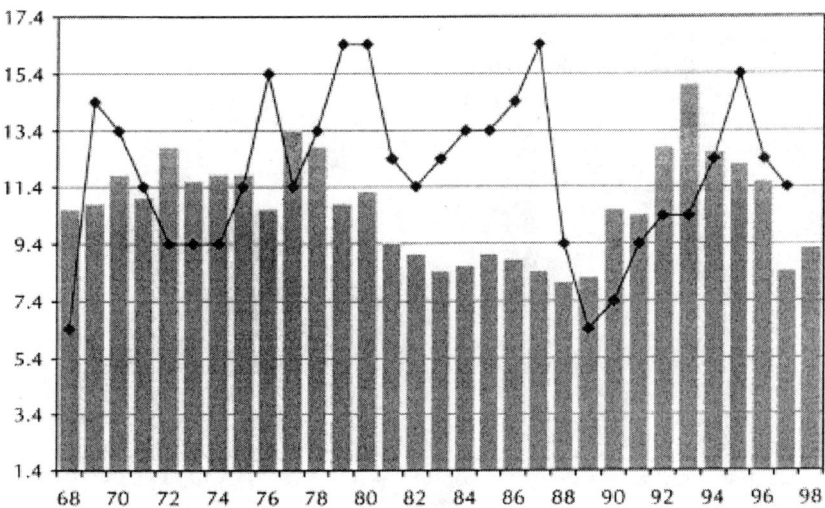

Clutch size

This parameter does not appear to correlate with the population trends. However, a clear statement cannot be made as random samples in the second half of the investigation period were too small, so that the average had to be calculated for six year blocks (Fig.4). Thus, it became evident that clutch size decreased by nearly one egg on average during the 30 years, possibly from 1975 onwards. As the development of the reproductive rate is also declining this finding would have been partly able to explain the decrease in the population development during the following years. It is, however, in contradiction to the large increase in the 1990s.

Number of young (Partial breeding success / Reproductive rate)

The number of young also does not correlate with the population development (Fig.5). It is, however, remarkable that the figures for young per successful breeding pair (Fig.6) are higher in the second half of the investigation period and that the reproductive rate increased by about two young until 1993, which could have resulted in the population peak.

Figure 4. Average clutch size (average values, weighted with annual number of clutches)

Average clutch size (weighted average values¹)

¹ weighted with annual number of clutches

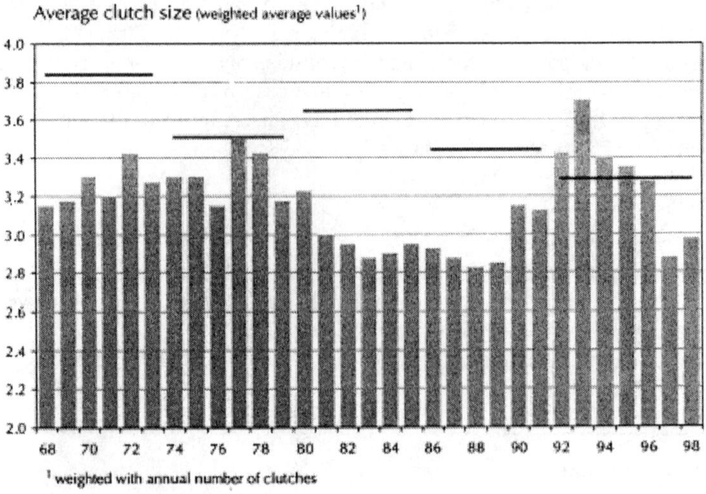

Figure 5. Average number of young per pair (all pairs)

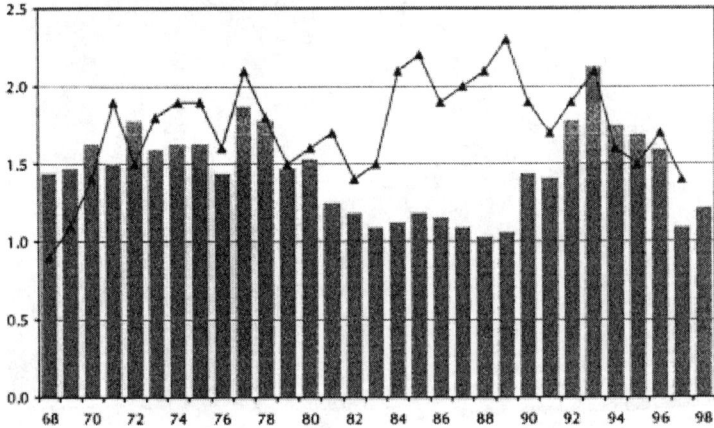

Figure 6. Average number of young per successful pair (at least one young fledged)

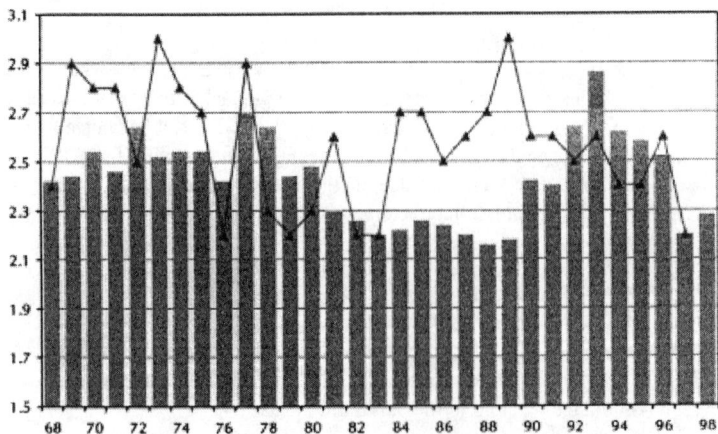

After the closure of hunting in 1970 the breeding success remained relatively constant at 75% (60-80%), while the decade from 1984 to 1993 produced the highest figures (Fig.7). It could thus have been expected also that the Northern Goshawk population would have profited thereby in the longterm and would not have suffered from a new population decline.

Figure 7. Percent pairs fledging young

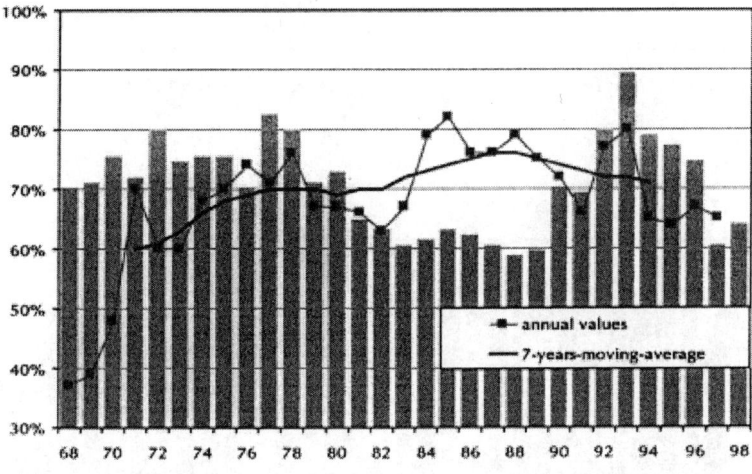

First breeders

"First breeders" were female Northern Goshawks which, irrespective of their age, occurred for the first time as breeders in the study area. Apart from the expected high figures during the first years up to 1970 (start of documentation, hunting season closed) there is no clear trend (Fig. 8). The proportion of first breeders usually ranged from 30 to 45%; except from 1983 to 1984 with over 50%.

Figure 8. Proportion of females breeding for the first time in the study area

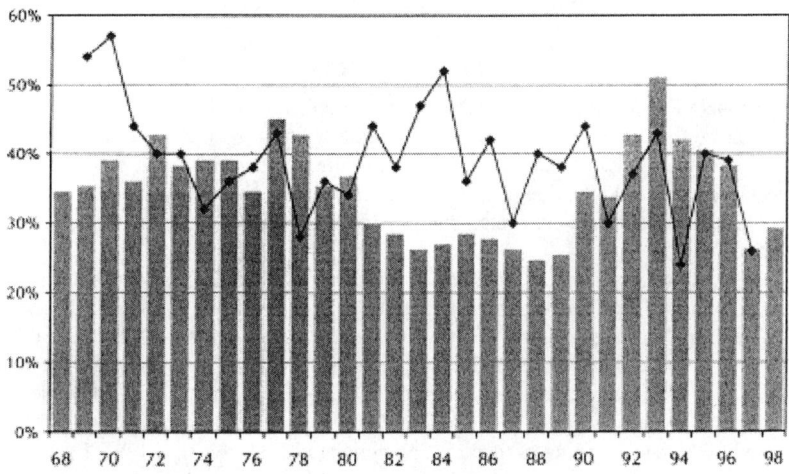

A comparison of the graphics does not show any correlation between the Northern Goshawk population and the number of first time female breeders.

Age structure of breeding females

Moulted feathers allow the exact definition of age in the first two years as well as the lifetime identification of an individual. These feathers were used to define the yearly age classes of females. Too few feathers from males were collected to apply this method to them. Thus, the one- and two-year-old females were compared with the older Northern Goshawks (Fig.9).

Figure 9. Proportion of females in the breeding stock aged less than three years

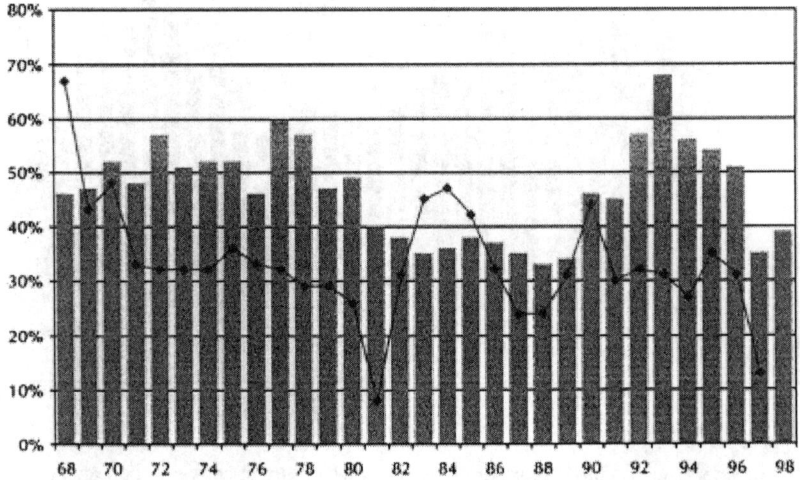

Over the 30 year period, the younger breeding females represent a very constant proportion of about one third of the breeding population. However, years when human persecution was legal show an exception: A limited, legal hunting period existed until 1970, and then between 1980 and 1993 with so-called "Goshawk Traps". The use of the latter probably showed an effect as late as 1983 to 1985. In this case, the Northern Goshawk population seems to have reacted to high, short-term losses by recruiting younger birds into the breeding population (Looft 1984).

DISCUSSION

As the population development over the 30 year period showed three distinct phases, there was reason to believe that these phases were, at least partially, influenced by reproductive parameters. However, individual breeding factors do not explain the fluctuations in the breeding population, neither over the whole study period nor for shorter periods. The size of the breeding population was related neither to reproductive nor demographic parameters (rank correlation analysis after Spearman; Table 1).

Since separate comparisons of breeding parameters versus breeding population size did not show any correlation, it might be expected that the bringing together of individual factors would show a correlation. However, none of the comparisons offered conclusive results. Since the survival rate of the adult females (Ziesemer 1983 and the author´s unpublished data) and the number of young produced remained on a relatively constant level, the fluctuations in the population could be due to changes in the survival rate of young birds before they reach sexual maturity. This can partly be explained by human cropping of the breeding population (Bezzel, *et al* 1997, Bilsma 1993). In the initial investigation period, from 1968 to 1970, shooting and trapping of Goshawks was allowed outside the breeding season (November to February), which might also have caused a reduction of the breeding population. After 1980 (with certain reservations until 1993), a further decline can be detected. During this period, the bordering Danish population was also affected by a similar decline (Jorgensen 1989), probably resulting from a large-scale homogenous development. After the hard winter of 1978/79, which resulted in a shortage of prey, Goshawks could be easily caught by means of traps (August to February). According to official figures 846 Goshawks were caught in Schleswig-Holstein (mainly in the southern part of the study area) between 1980 and 1993, i.e. an average of 60 per year (Ministry of Enviromental Affairs, unpublished documents). The rapid increase of the breeding population in the last four years of trapping could partly be explained by a decrease in this persecution.

Table 1: Rank correlation between the number of Northern Goshawk breeding pairs and some biological parameters during a 30-year-study in Northern Germany.

	Spearman's rho	P	N	
Mean number of eggs	0,164	p=0.55	14	only for years with 10 values
Mean date of the beginning of incubation	0,002	p=0.99	30	
Mean total breeding success	-0,076	p=0.68	30	
Mean partial breeding success	0,106	p=0.57	30	
Proportion of first-time-breeding females	-0,046	p=0.81	29	excl. the first year
Proportion of breeding females 3 years old	0,148	p=0.43	29	excl. the first year

I can only speculate as to the reasons for the surprising decline of the population in the end of the investigation period. It is possible that the rapid increase of the Eagle Owl *Bubo bubo* population during the last years together with this species' settlement in the few forested areas of Schleswig-Holstein has put enormous pressure on the Northern Goshawk population, i.e. they might not be able to settle close to Eagle Owls and alternative sites are lacking. Newton (1979) and Kenward (1982) pointed out that the development of the population depends on the availability of food, the most important avenue for further study.

ACKNOWLEDGEMENTS

Many friends have supported me during this long period of Goshawk study with their help and advice. Thanks to all of them for their commitment. Especially I thank Thomas Grünkorn, Jörg Reimers and Gerd Biesterfeld, who helped me with the fieldwork and Kai Abt and Joachim Kaiser for supporting me logistically.

REFERENCES

BEZZEL, E., R.RUST & W. KECHELE 1997. Revierbesetzung, Reproduktion und menschliche Verfolgung in einer Population des Habichts *Accipiter gentilis*. *J. Orn.* 138. pp. 413-441.
BIJLSMA, R. G. 1993. *Ecologische Atlas van de Nederlandse Roofvogels*. Harlem.
BRÜLL, H. 1964. *Das Leben deutscher Greifvögel*. Fischer, Stuttgart.
JØRGENSEN, H. E. 1989. *Danmarks rovfugle - en statusoversigt*. Frederikshus, Øster Ulslev.

KENWARD, R.E. 1982. *Goshawk* hunting behaviour, and range size as a function of food and habitat availabilty. *J. Animal Ecology* 51. pp 69-80.
KOSTREWA, A. & G. SPEER 1995. *Greifvögel in Deutschland.* Aula, Wiesbaden.
LOOFT, V. & G. BUSCHE 1981. *Vogelwelt Schleswig - Holstein.* Bd. 2: Greifvögel, Wachholtz, Neumünster.
LOOFT, V. 1984. Die Entwicklung des Habichtbestandes (*Accipiter gentilis*) in Schlewig - Holstein. *Corax* 10. pp. 395-400.
OLECH, B. 1998. Population Dynamics and Breeding Performance of the Goshawk *Accipiter gentilis* in Central Poland in 1982 - 1994. In Chancellor, R.D., B.-U. Meyburg & J.J.Ferrero (eds.) : *Holarctic Birds of Prey. ADENEX-WWGBP.* pp. 101-110.
NEWTON, I. 1979. *Population Ecology of Raptors*, Poyser Ltd, London.
ZIESEMER, F. 1983. Untersuchungen zum Einfluß des Habichts (*Accipiter gentilis*) auf Populationen der Beutetiere. *Beitr. z. Wildbiol.* 2. pp.1-127.

Volkher Looft
Verwalterhaus
24250 Gut Bothkamp
Germany

Part 7

Predation and Feeding Ecology

Black Eagle *Aquila verreauxii*

Conveners:
Ian Newton & Rob A. G. Davies

Chancellor, R. D. & B.-U. Meyburg eds. 2000
Raptors at Risk
WWGBP / Hancock House

Effects of Predators on their Prey: some generalisations

I. Newton

ABSTRACT

1. To reduce the breeding numbers of a prey species, mortality from predation must be additive to other mortality, and not merely 'compensatory', replacing other forms of death, such as starvation.

2. In any study of predation it is helpful to distinguish effects on prey breeding numbers from effects on prey post-breeding numbers. It is on breeding numbers that the immediate future of the prey population depends, but post-breeding numbers may be important to game hunters.

3. Predation might eliminate some prey species from particular areas, or it might lower prey breeding density below the level that would occur in the absence of predation, cause marked fluctuations in prey breeding density, or have no obvious effects on prey breeding density.

4. From studies in Britain, the Sparrowhawk has been found to have no obvious effects on the breeding densities of some common woodland prey species.

INTRODUCTION

Because many raptors eat other birds and mammals, their predation often causes conflicts between people interested in the raptors and those interested in the prey species. Yet there have been relatively few studies of the impacts of raptor predation on prey populations (for examples, see Kenward 1977, Kenward et al. 1981, 1991, Perrins & Geer 1980, Newton et al. 1997). In this paper, I make some general points about predation and summarise some empirical evidence for the effects of predators on bird populations. Not all examples concern raptors and emphasis is placed on those aspects not covered by other papers in this session, notably those of Thirgood & Redpath (this volume) and Davies (this volume).

SOME GENERAL POINTS

1. Additive and compensatory mortality.
Practically all animals are subject to predation at some stage of their lives, whether juvenile or adult. Many bird species, for example, suffer heavy predation at the egg and chick stages, and some

also at the fledgling and adult stages. In some bird species, predation is the major cause of loss at all stages of the life cycle, accounting for almost every nest that fails and almost every adult that dies. Yet, despite the prevalence of predation, it is not easy to assess its effects on prey population sizes. The numbers of many bird and mammal species can more than double each year through breeding so that, if they are to remain stable from year to year, more than half the individuals present at the end of one breeding season must die before the next, if not from predation then from something else. For predators to reduce a breeding population below the level that the habitat would otherwise support, at least part of the mortality they inflict must be 'additive' to other mortality, and not simply 'compensatory', replacing other forms of death. Whether losses from predation are subsequently offset by improved reproduction or by improved survival (or both) among remaining individuals, depends on whether these aspects vary in a density-dependent manner, increasing with reduction in density.

2. Predation and the annual cycle.

The numbers of individuals in any population that is exposed to predation must be reduced, at least temporarily, because some individuals die earlier than they would in the absence of predation. Inevitably, then, predators influence the dynamics of prey populations, and could reduce their average level over the year as a whole. But the important question is whether the predation to which many species are subject throughout the year reduces their overall breeding numbers. In any seasonally-breeding species, like almost all birds and mammals, the start of breeding is when numbers are at their lowest in the year, after most mortality on adults has occurred but before reproduction begins. If predation does not reduce breeding numbers, it has no effect on numbers entering the next generation and is not limiting in the long-term. It is thus irrelevant to the long-term persistence of the population at that level.

Game managers have a different perspective because they are interested in producing birds and mammals for human hunters to kill. They are thus concerned, not only with maintaining breeding stocks from year to year, but also with producing as large a post-breeding population as possible. Any predation or other mortality which lowers the production of young might reduce the numbers of game birds and mammals available for hunters, even though it may have no effect on breeding numbers. It is not contradictory, therefore, that predation might reduce the size of the post-breeding population peak each year, but have no impact on the pre-breeding low.

In assessing impacts of predation, much hinges on the fact that the annual cycle of most birds and mammals falls into two distinct phases, a breeding season when numbers increase because reproduction exceeds mortality, and a non-breeding season when numbers decline because only mortality operates.

In general, we can envisage three scenarios involving predation effects in the annual cycle of any bird or mammal species (Figure 1).

(1) Predation reduces the post-breeding numbers below what would otherwise occur, but not the breeding numbers. This scenario requires total compensation in over-winter survival.

(2) Predation reduces the breeding but not the post-breeding numbers below what would otherwise occur. This scenario requires total compensation in reproductive output.

(3) Predation reduces both breeding and post-breeding numbers below what would otherwise occur. In this scenario, compensation is insufficient to offset the full effects of predation.

Figure 1. Models showing possible effects of predation on the annual cycle of numbers in seasonal-breeding prey species. Solid line - no predation effects, dashed line - with predation effects. For further details, see text. From Newton 1998.

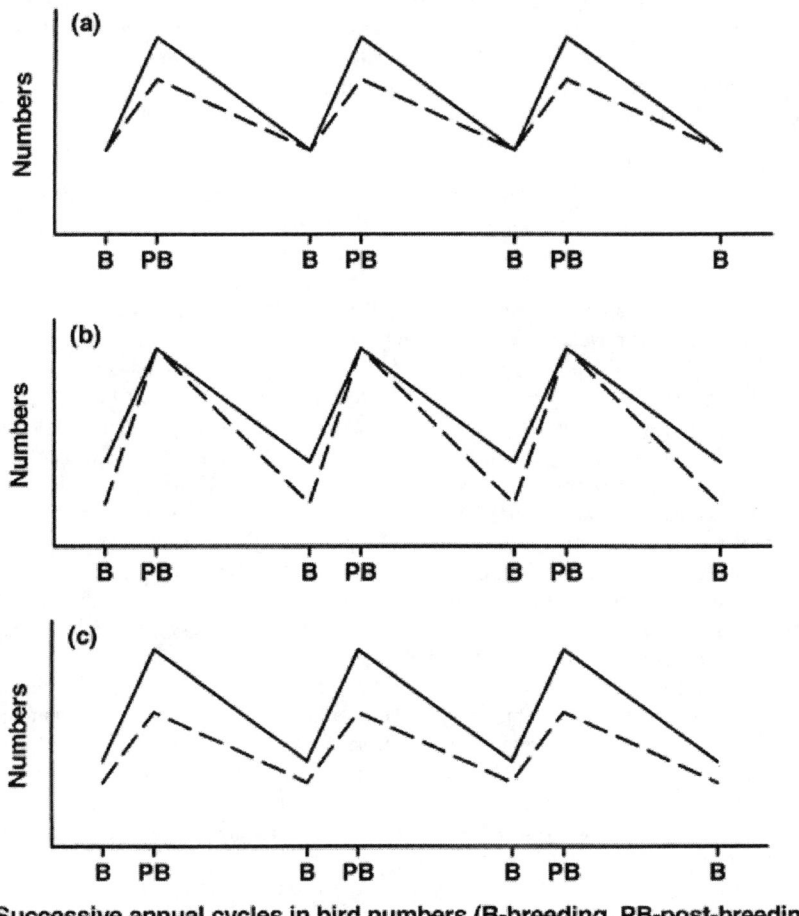

Successive annual cycles in bird numbers (B-breeding, PB-post-breeding)

MAIN IMPACTS OF PREDATORS ON PREY

The following are the major types of impact that predators have been found to have on their prey (see also Kenward 1986, Newton 1993, 1998):

1. Annihilation of prey.

The only documented examples known to me concern generalist predators, such as rats and cats, introduced by human action to offshore islands (Newton 1993, 1998). Because of their isolation, the avifaunas of oceanic islands have mostly evolved in the absence of mammalion predation. Many island bird species are tame, show no escape response to predators, and may nest in unprotected sites; some species are also flightless. For these reasons, some endemic island bird-species have proved highly vulnerable to introduced predators because they had no natural defences. Such predators are held responsible for at least 40% of the extinctions of endemic island birds known to have occurred in the past 400 years (King 1985). Clearly, this special situation is of limited relevance in the context of continental areas where most predator and prey species have persisted together for thousands or millions of years.

2. Lowering of prey breeding numbers.

The ability of predators to hold prey breeding density well below the level that could occur in the absence of predation is exemplified by research on the Grey Partridge *Perdix perdix* and Red Grouse *Lagopus l. scoticus* in Britain (Potts *et al.* 1980, Potts 1986, Thirgood & Redpath, this volume), and also by predator removal studies on a range of other gallinaceous birds and waterfowl (discussed in Newton 1993, 1994, 1998). Such limitation usually involves density-dependent predation on either eggs, chicks or adults, that regulates breeding numbers at a level lower than the habitat and food-supply would otherwise permit.

3. Oscillations in prey numbers.

Many grouse species, especially in northern latitudes, undergo cycles of abundance in which successive peaks and troughs in numbers occur at fairly regular intervals (Elton 1942, Lack 1954, Keith 1963, Keith *et al.* 1977). In boreal North America, for example, Ruffed Grouse *Bonasa umbellus* and others fluctuate in approximate ten-year cycles, in parallel with similar cycles in Snowshoe Hare *Lepus americanus* numbers. In much of boreal Europe, Hazel Grouse *Bonasa bonasia* and others fluctuate in 3-5-year cycles, in parallel with the numbers of voles. Moreover, some species, such as Willow Ptarmigan *Lagopus lagopus*, may follow a 3-5 year cycle in parts of Europe and a ten-year cycle in parts of North America (Watson & Moss 1979, Bergerud *et al.* 1985).

Predation is one of several hypotheses proposed to explain cycles in grouse numbers (Watson & Moss 1979), with predators causing regular crashes in the prey, which are followed by recoveries. In seeking causes of the cycles, however, it is important to separate the primary prey species (voles or hares) from the secondary (scarcer) ones (grouse). The evidence for predators causing the cycle is much stronger for the secondary species than for the primary (mammalian) ones. The supposed mechanism is as follows: as the numbers of herbivorous mammals rise over a period of years, so do the numbers of the predators that depend on them. Then, when mammal numbers crash, the abundant predators switch their emphasis to grouse and other birds (eggs, chicks or adults), reducing their numbers, and eventually themselves declining through starvation, emigration and non-breeding (Hagen 1952, Lack 1954, Keith 1974). This then enables both mammal and grouse numbers to rise again to start another cycle, and the remaining predators to shift their emphasis back to mammals. In these circumstances, grouse breeding numbers can be said to be limited by predation, at least in the decline phase of the cycle. Another likely effect of avian predators is in helping to synchronise the fluctuations in their prey over wide areas, as their movements lead them to concentrate at any one time in localities with the highest prey densities. What causes the cycles in mammal numbers is a more controversial question, but it is probably not predation.

On this basis, ten-year cycles in the numbers of Ruffed Grouse *Bonasa umbellus* in North America have been attributed to predators, such as Goshawks *Accipiter gentilis*, switching their attention to grouse in years when the primary prey (Snowshoe Hares) decline (Keith & Rusch 1988). Similarly, 3-5 year cycles in the nesting success (and hence numbers) of certain bird-species in northern Eurasia have been attributed to predators switching to birds in years when their rodent prey decline. This switch gives regular years of heavy nest predation in a wide range of bird-species, from passerines (Dunn 1977, Järvinen 1985, 1990, Orell 1989, Högstad 1993, Viestola *et al.* 1996) to waterfowl and waders (Pehrson 1976, Roselaar 1979, Summers & Underhill 1987). The pattern is exemplified in Brent Geese *Branta b. bernicla* and two shorebird species which nest on the Taimyr peninsula of Siberia and winter in western Europe (geese) or southern Africa (shorebirds), where the proportion of young in winter flocks has tended to fluctuate in synchrony and on a 3-year cycle, in inverse relation to lemming numbers (Figure 2). In these studies, therefore, predation by specialist predators was seen as an important cause of cycles in the numbers of avian prey. In contrast, in a study by Thirgood & Redpath (this volume) predation by generalist predators proved capable in preventing a cyclic increase in Red Grouse and holding their numbers at a low level.

Figure 2. Proportion of first-year birds in wintering populations of various bird species that breed in arctic Siberia, in relation to the numbers of lemmings on the breeding grounds in different years. High production of young in Sanderling *Calidris alba*, Curlew Sandpiper *C. ferruginea* and Brent Goose *Branta bernicla* occurred about every three years when lemming numbers were also high, providing alternative food for predators. From Summers & Underhill 1987.

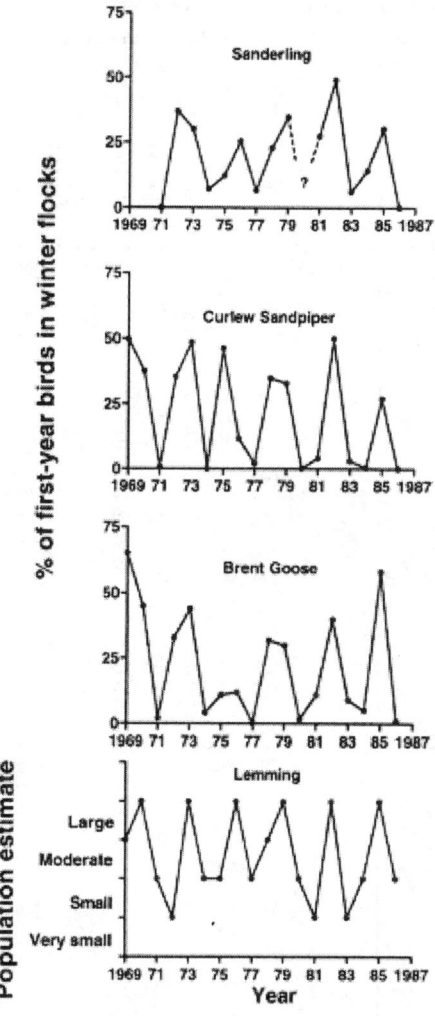

4. No effects on prey breeding numbers.

In some bird and mammal species, predation might remove so few individuals that it has no discernible effects on breeding numbers. In other species, which are subject to substantial year-round predation, the losses involved could be fully compensated by reductions in other losses. This might happen, for example, when total mortality is density-dependent and 'pre-determined' by the extent to which numbers exceed the available territories or other resources, giving rise to the idea of a 'doomed surplus' (Errington 1946, Jenkins *et al.* 1964). An example of a system in which a raptor has been found to have no apparent effects on the breeding numbers of its prey is discussed below.

A CASE STUDY: SPARROWHAWKS AND THEIR SONGBIRD PREY

The Sparrowhawk *Accipiter nisus* is one of the commonest raptors in Europe, nesting in woodland and hunting small birds, in both woods and open country. It can remove a large proportion of prey individuals each year, yet seems to cause no obvious depression of breeding densities (Tinbergen 1946, Perrins & Geer 1980, Newton 1986, McCleery & Perrins 1991, Newton *et al.* 1997). This was shown incidentally over much of Europe around 1960, when Sparrowhawks were eliminated from large areas through the use of organochlorine pesticides, recovering and recolonising years later when organochlorine use was reduced (Newton 1986). During the period of Sparrowhawk absence, woodland songbirds were not noticeably more numerous than before or after.

Table 1. Means of annual numbers of various songbird species in a 16 hectare oakwood plot during three successive periods when Sparrowhawks were present, absent or present respectively. From data in Bevan (1976) and Kettle (1982), based on counts of singing males.

SD - standard deviation, SE - standard error. The terms increasing, decreasing and no significant trend refer to long term trends over the whole 34 year period (see Table 2).

Species	1946-59 Sparrowhawks present			1960-72 Sparrowhawks absent			1973-79 Sparrowhawks present		
	Mean	SD	SE	Mean	SD	SE	Mean	SD	SE
Increasing									
Great Tit (*Parus major*)	9.0	±2.4	(0.77)	13.8	±2.5	(0.71)	16.0	±2.2	(0.82)
Blue Tit (*Parus caeruleus*)	11.8	±2.9	(0.96)	18.0	±2.1	(0.57)	18.6	±3.9	(1.46)
Coal Tit (*Parus ater*)	2.3	±0.9	(0.30)	4.4	±2.0	(0.55)	7.1	±2.2	(0.83)
Nuthatch (*Sitta europaea*)	2.1	±1.4	(0.43)	4.3	±1.3	(0.36)	4.6	±1.0	(0.37)
Wren (*Troglodytes troglodytes*)	14.8	±4.3	(1.37)	17.0	±8.1	(2.26)	25.7	±5.1	(1.92)
Song Thrush (*Turdus philomelos*)	3.7	±1.9	(0.62)	6.6	±1.9	(0.53)	5.3	±1.5	(0.57)
Blackbird (*Turdus merula*)	8.7	±2.6	(0.79)	10.5	±2.1	(0.60)	10.7	±2.3	(0.87)
Robin (*Erithacus rubecula*)	26.8	±4.3	(1.18)	30.1	±7.6	(2.09)	36.3	±3.4	(1.27)
Starling (*Sturnus vulgaris*)	0.1	±0.3	(0.10)	6.3	±3.0	(0.82)	8.3	±1.2	(0.67)
Decreasing									
Chaffinch (*Fringilla coelebs*)	8.0	±3.1	(0.98)	5.6	±1.8	(0.51)	2.6	±0.8	(0.30)
Willow Warbler (*Phylloscopus trochilus*)	13.8	±4.7	(1.48)	2.3	±1.6	(0.45)	1.0	±0.8	(0.31)
No significant trend									
Blackcap (*Sylvia atricapilla*)	3.0	±0.7	(0.21)	3.9	±1.7	(0.47)	3.4	±1.1	(0.43)
Chiffchaff (*Phylloscopus collybita*)	3.1	±1.6	(0.49)	3.3	±2.1	(0.58)	3.6	±1.3	(0.48)

This was apparent, for example, in a single 16 ha oakwood, on Bookham Common, Surrey, where all breeding birds were counted every year during 1949-1979 (except for 1957). These counts covered both the decline and the recovery periods of the Sparrowhawk, which bred in the wood up to 1959 (inclusive) and again from 1973 (Beven 1976). This gave three periods for comparison: 1947-59 (hawks present), 1960-72 (hawks absent) and 1973-79 (hawks present). The 1960s corresponded with the period when Sparrowhawks were scarcest in the general area, reaching their lowest numbers around 1964.

Figure 3. Counts (log values) of various songbird species in an English oakwood each year during three successive periods when Sparrowhawks were present, absent and present respectively. Mean values show average numbers of singing males (untransformed values) present each year over the whole period. None of the species shown was significantly most numerous in the middle period when Sparrowhawks were absent. From Newton *et al.* 1997.

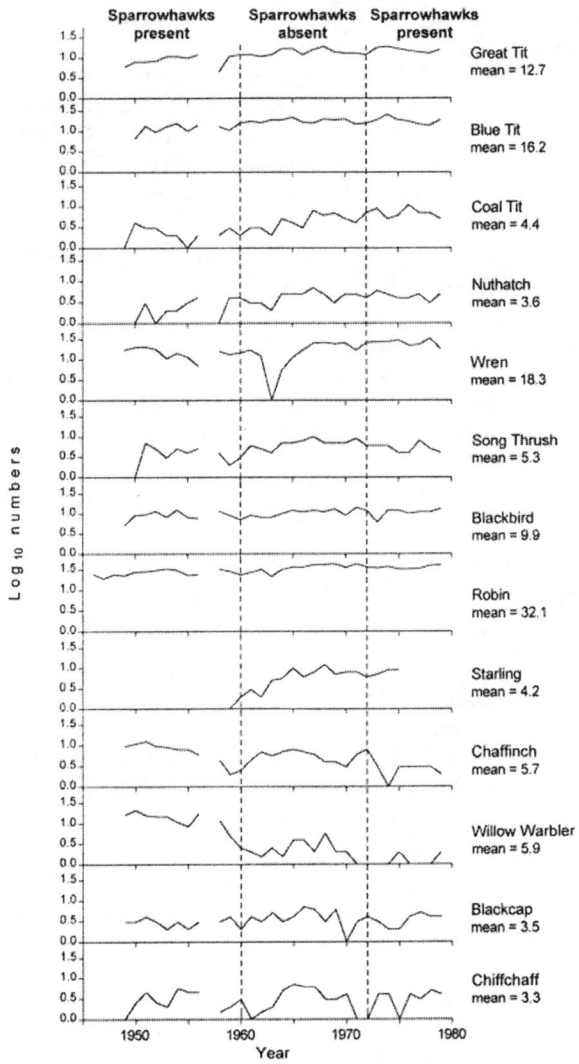

Thirteen songbird species were judged sufficiently numerous for analysis (Newton et al. 1997). In nine such species, significant variation occurred between the mean counts for the three successive periods (Table 1). In seven species, this was attributable to a sustained increase over the whole period, and in two species to a sustained decrease. These trends occurred regardless of Sparrowhawk numbers, and coincided with changes in the internal structure of the wood (less understorey and more canopy) (Beven 1976). Not a single species was present in significantly greater numbers in the middle period when Sparrowhawks were absent from the wood and at their lowest numbers in the surrounding area (Table 1, Figure 3). One species, the Starling *Sturnus vulgaris,* colonised the wood after Sparrowhawks ceased to nest there, but remained in good numbers after they returned. In the Wren *Troglodytes troglodytes,* the main noticeable effect was the hard winter of 1962-63. Hence, these data gave no evidence that Sparrowhawks had any negative impact on the breeding densities of woodland songbirds.

How is it that Sparrowhawks had no obvious impact on counts of singing males in the study area? Four explanations seem possible: (a) the proportions taken from the wood were too small to be detectable in the overall counts; (b) killed birds were quickly replaced from a non-territorial surplus so that the numbers of territorial (singing) birds in the wood were maintained in the face of continuing predation; (c) the census plot represented optimal habitat for most species in which their densities were maintained by continual immigration from suboptimal habitats where the effects of predation might have been more apparent; or (d) when Sparrowhawks were absent, songbird mortality from other causes (including other predators) increased in compensation. In retrospect, it is not possible to separate these possibilities, but evidence for the existence of surplus birds, able to take the places left by removed territorial ones, has been obtained for a wide range of bird species, including several of those discussed here (Newton 1992).

Some additional findings emerged from a detailed study of hawk predation on box-nesting tits in a 320 ha wood near Oxford (Geer 1978, Perrins & Geer 1980):

(1) Within 60m of each successful hawk nest, both the occupancy and the success of nest boxes were depressed, compared with boxes further away. This was attributed to the hawks eating more of the tits near their own nests than elsewhere in the wood. Findings were consistent between years, even though the locations of hawk nests changed from year to year. However, the effects of this localised high predation on the overall tit population of the wood was immeasurably small.

(2) The hawks ate many fledgling tits, removing an estimated 34%, 18% and 33% of young Great Tits in three different years, and 27%, 18% and 27% of young Blue Tits. More than six young tits per pair (including failed pairs) were raised in these years, but only about one chick per pair was needed to replace the annual losses of adults in order to maintain the population at constant level. Hence, many young tits must have died from predation or other mortality causes at other times of year.

(3) Great Tit and Blue Tit breeding numbers fluctuated greatly from year to year, but in general the numbers of nest boxes occupied each year were no higher in the period when hawks were absent than when they were present. These results thus gave no evidence that Sparrowhawks, despite their predation, depressed the breeding populations of these tit species.

These various findings for tits could probably be generalised to many other prey species, in that the main effects of Sparrowhawk predation were to: (1) change the seasonal pattern of mortality; (2) reduce the size of the post-breeding peak in the population; and (3) change the main agents of death; all without causing any noticeable decline in breeding numbers. In practice, this meant that, instead of dying mainly in winter from food shortage, for example, potential prey individuals died at all seasons, and largely from predation.

Despite the long-term findings from woodland birds, some people writing in the popular press in Britain have claimed that increasing numbers of Sparrowhawks (in recovery from organochlorine impacts) have caused declines in farmland birds. There is no doubt that most farmland bird-species have declined in the past 30 years (some species by more than 50%, Fuller et al. 1995), but these declines have coincided with a period of agricultural intensification which has enormously reduced the habitat and food-supplies available for most farmland bird-species. In fact, all studies of declining species on farmland have excluded predation as a significant causal factor (Newton 1998).

CONCLUDING REMARKS

Among animals in general, predator-prey relationships vary from closely-coupled interactions at one extreme, in which the numbers of prey and predators are inter-dependent, to neutral feeding links at the other extreme which are of no consequence for the population dynamics of either consumer or consumed. In between are prey-controlled dynamics in which the numbers of prey influence the numbers of predators but not vice versa, and predator-controlled dynamics in which the numbers of predators influence the numbers of prey but not vice versa. Studies of predation by raptors are relatively few in number, and while some raptors had no obvious effects on prey breeding numbers, others helped to hold prey breeding numbers below the level they would otherwise achieve, or contributed to cyclic fluctuations in prey numbers.

REFERENCES

BERGERUD, A.T., D.H. MOSSOP, & S. MYRBERGET 1985. A critique of the mechanics of annual changes in Ptarmigan numbers. *Can. J. Zool.* 63: 2240-2248.
BEVEN, G. 1976. Changes in breeding bird populations of an oak-wood on Bookham Common, Surrey, over twenty-seven years. *London Naturalist* 55: 23-42.
DAVIES, R.A.G. 1999. The influence of predation by Black Eagles *Aquila verreauxii* on Rock Hyrax numbers in the arid Karoo. This volume.
DUNN, E.K. 1977. Predation by Weasels (*Mustela nivalis*) on breeding tits (*Parus* spp.) in relation to the density of tits and rodents. *J. Anim. Ecol.* 46: 633-652.
ELTON, C.S. 1942. *Voles, mice and lemmings*. Oxford, University Press.
ERRINGTON, P.L. 1946. Predation and vertebrate populations. *Quart. Rev. Biol.* 21: 145-177, 221-245.
FULLER, R.J., R.D. GREGORY, D.W. GIBBONS, J.H. MARCHANT, J.D. WILSON, S.R. BAILLIE & N. CARTER 1995. Population declines and range contractions among lowland farmland birds in Britain. *Conserv. Biol.* 9: 1425-1441.
GEER, T.A. 1978. Effects of nesting Sparrowhawks on nesting tits. *Condor.* 80: 419-422.
HAGEN, Y. 1952. *Rovfuglene og viltpleien*. Oslo, Gyldendal Norsk Forlag.
HOGSTAD, O. 1993. Structure and dynamics of a passerine bird community in a spruce-dominated boreal forest - a 12-year study. *Ann. Zool. Fenn.* 30: 43-54.
JÄRVINEN, O. 1985. Predation causing extended low densities in microtine cycle: implications from predation on hole-nesting passerines. *Oikos* 45: 157-158.
JÄRVINEN, O. 1990. Changes in the abundance of birds in relation to small rodent density and predation rate in Finnish Lapland. *Bird Study* 37: 36-39.
JENKINS, D., A. WATSON & G.R. MILLER 1964. Predation and Red Grouse populations. *J. Appl. Ecol.* 1: 183-195.
KEITH, L.B. 1963. *Wildlife's ten-year cycle*. Madison, University Wisconsin Press.
KEITH, L.B. 1974. Some features of population dynamics in mammals. *Proc. Int. Congr. Game Biol.* 11: 17-58.
KEITH, L.B., A.W. TODD, C.J. BRAND, R.S. ADAMCIK & D.H. RUSCH 1977. An analysis of predation during a cyclic fluctuation of Snowshoe Hares. *Int. Congr. Game Biol.* 13: 151-175.
KEITH, L.B. & D.H. RUSCH 1988. Predation's role in the cyclic fluctuations of Ruffed Grouse. *Proc. Int. Orn. Congr.* 19: 699-732.
KENWARD, R.E. 1977. Predation on released Pheasants (*Phasianus colchicus*) by Goshawks (*Accipiter gentilis*) in central Sweden. *Viltrevy* 10: 79-112.
KENWARD, R.E. 1986. Problems of Goshawk predation on pigeons and some other game. *Proc. Int. Orn. Congr.* 18: 666-678.
KENWARD, R.E., V. MARCSTRÖM & M. KARLBOM 1981. Goshawk winter ecology in Swedish Pheasant habitats. *J. Wildl. Manage.* 45: 397-408.
KENWARD, R.E., V. MARCSTRÖM & M. KARLBOM 1991. The Goshawk (*Accipiter gentilis*) as predator and renewable resource. *Gibier Faune Sauvage* 8: 367-378.

KETTLE, R.H. 1982. Common Bird Census results on a woodland plot on Wimbledon Common 1973 to 1980. *London Bird Report* 47: 91-96.
KING, W.B. 1985. Island birds: will the future repeat the past? *ICBP Tech. Pub.* 3: 3-15.
LACK, D. 1954. *The natural regulation of animal numbers*. Oxford, University Press.
MCCLEERY, R.H. & C.M. PERRINS 1991. Effects of predation on the numbers of Great Tits *Parus major*. Pp. 129-147 in '*Bird Population Studies.*', ed. C.M. Perrins, J.-D. Lebreton & G.J.M. Hirons. Oxford, University Press.
NEWTON, I. 1986. *The Sparrowhawk*. Calton, T. & A.D. Poyser.
NEWTON, I. 1992. Experiments on the limitation of bird numbers by territorial behaviour. *Biol. Rev.* 67: 129-173.
NEWTON, I. 1993. Predation and limitation of bird numbers. *Curr. Ornithol.* 11: 143-198.
NEWTON, I. 1994. Experiments on the limitation of bird breeding densities: a review. *Ibis* 136: 397-411.
NEWTON, I. 1998. *Population limitation in birds*. London, Academic Press.
NEWTON, I., L. DALE & P. ROTHERY 1997. Apparent lack of impact of Sparrowhawks on the breeding densities of some woodland songbirds. *Bird Study* 44: 129-135.
ORELL, M. 1989. Population fluctuations and survival of Great Tits *Parus major* dependent on food supplied by man in winter. *Ibis* 131: 113-127.
PEHRSON, O. 1976. Duckling production of Long-tailed Duck in relation to spring weather and small rodent fluctuations. Unpubl. Ph.D. thesis, University of Gothenburg, Sweden.
PERRINS, C.M. & T.A. GEER 1980. The effect of Sparrowhawks on tit populations. *Ardea* 68: 133-142.
POTTS, G.R. 1986. *The Partridge: pesticides, predation and conservation*. London, Collins.
POTTS, G.R., J.C. COULSON & I.R. DEANS 1980. Population dynamics and breeding success of the Shag, *Phalacrocorax aristotelis*, on the Farne Islands, Northumberland. *J. Anim. Ecol.* 49: 465-484.
ROSELAAR, C.S. 1979. Fluctuaties in aantallen Krombek strandlopers *Calidris ferruginea*. *Watervogels* 4: 202-210.
SUMMERS, R.W. & L. UNDERHILL 1987. Factors related to breeding production of Brent Geese *Branta b. bernicla* and waders (*Charadrii*). *Bird Study* 34: 161-171.
THIRGOOD, S.J. & S.M. REDPATH 1999. Can raptor predation limit Red Grouse populations? This volume.
TINBERGEN, L. 1946. Sperver als Roofvijand van Zangvogels. *Ardea* 34: 1-123.
VIESTOLA, S., E. LEHIKOINEN, T. EEVA & L. ISO-IIVARI 1996. The breeding biology of the Redstart *Phoenicurus phoenicurus* in a marginal area of Finland. *Bird Study* 43: 351-355.
WATSON, A. & R. MOSS 1979. Population cycles in the Tetraonidae. *Ornis. Fenn.* 56: 87-109.

I. Newton
Institute of Terrestrial Ecology
Monks Wood, Abbots Ripton
Huntingdon
Cambridgeshire
PE17 2LS
United Kingdom

The Influence of Predation by Black Eagles *Aquila verreauxii* on Rock Hyrax Numbers in the Arid Karoo

R A G Davies and J W H Ferguson

INTRODUCTION

Black Eagles *Aquila verreauxii* occupy a controversial position on karoo farmland: whether they harm the sheep farmer by preying on livestock; and/or whether they benefit the farmer by limiting their principal prey, rock hyrax *Procavia capensis* which can compete with domestic sheep for available forage. Under normal conditions there may be 1.2 million hyrax living in the rocky habitats of the karoo biome with an appetite equivalent to 7% that of the entire sheep flock for the region. Hyrax numbers vary noticeably in the Karoo and there have been several reported irruptions of the species during the twentieth century when farmers have experienced significant harm to the veld resource at times when they need it most for their sheep. It was a visit to a farm where hyrax had irrupted in 1984 that prompted a five year doctoral field study on this predator-prey system (Davies 1994: referred to herein as the field study). The extent and cost of livestock predation by Black Eagles as revealed by the study were reported elsewhere (Davies in press.) The present paper presents the influence of Black Eagles on rock hyrax numbers and thus the benefits that these birds may offer to farmers. Many of the inferences presented herein are drawn from a novel and high-resolution hyrax population model.

KEY ELEMENTS IN THE SYSTEM

Rock hyrax are excellent subjects for population modelling. They are easily classified by sex and into annual age classes from the dentition of maxillary remains. They have a high propensity for population increase and reproduce in a synchronised annual birth-pulse, the size of which is usually predictable from rainfall events during the gestation period. There is much reference work available from research studies on hyrax reproduction (including some modelling, e.g. Fourie 1983, Swart *et al.* 1986). Rock hyrax occur in discrete and countable groups. They are well adapted to life in rocky habitats (Sale 1970). At night they allow their body temperature to drop to conserve energy. This obliges them to sunbathe every morning, providing an opportunity for counting.

The adaptations that equip hyrax for life in rocky habitats enable them to evade nearly all predators when they are within this refuge but the same adaptations render them highly vulnerable to an efficient guild of predators when they are away from their rocks. Refuge in this predator-prey system is unusual in that it is highly effective and it is permanent. This can be expected to confer stability on the system. Hyrax feed close to their rocks and were not observed further than 15m from shelter in the field study. These feeding patterns result in a distinct vegetation zone around rock outcrops which are highly visible from the air. Previous hyrax models have not included measurement of refuge.

While the safe feeding zone determined by rock outcrops is fixed, the number of hyrax that it supports varies with rainfall. In the semi-arid Karoo rainfall is highly stochastic. Alternating periods of enrichment and drought can be expected to destabilise the system in the manner observed for environmentally-modulated predation systems in Australia. Enrichment through the lower trophic level has an obvious and profound effect on hyrax population processes (not accommodated in previous hyrax models).

Livestock rarely venture into rocky habitats in the Karoo (Lensing 1982) so we assess the cost of hyrax to the sheep farmer as the surplus of hyrax whose food requirement is not met within their safe feeding zone. The food requirements of ten hyrax are equivalent to that of one sheep and this grazing is valued at $8.70 per annum.

Paradoxically the breeding performance of Black Eagles shows an inverse relationship with rainfall (Allan 1988). Hyrax become more available to eagles when they are forced to move further from their refuges to find food during drought. This mismatch of prey availability and prey abundance appears to be a unique attribute of the system. All diet studies using prey remains collected beneath eyries have indicated that Black Eagles are obligate predators of rock hyrax. However time-lapse cameras positioned at eagle nests during the field study revealed that Black Eagles captured significant numbers of red rock rabbits *Pronolagus rupestris*, not indicated by the prey remains. A population study of the rabbits indicated that this predation related merely to changes in the availability of alternate prey, not changes in hunting emphasis by the eagles. Black Eagles behaved as specialist predators in the present study by pursuing their preferred hyrax prey despite low abundance and low availability. Predation of hyrax by Black Eagle pairs varied between 70 and 180 per annum (per pair) and has been estimated to exceed 350 elsewhere (Gargett 1972, 1990). The assumption of a constant annual kill by Black Eagles in previous hyrax models is unrealistic.

Caracals are the other major predator of rock hyrax in the Karoo, but they are generalist predators and scat analyses conducted in the field study revealed that they were subsisting on alternative prey. Diet studies show that the hyrax component can vary between 2-50% of caracal prey. This instantaneous 'functional response' is known to greatly empower the influence of generalist predators in regulating their prey. Caracals are also able to show a numerical response. Farm trapping records indicate that numbers can change by up to 30% per annum, usually following a six month time-lag after rainfall events. Caracals probably occur at a density of 4.9 adult units per eagle territory in the study area (it is estimated that they consume six times as much food as the resident eagles). Studies elsewhere in the Karoo indicate that this density might vary between 2.4 and 7.4 adult units per eagle territory (Stuart 1982; Moolman 1986a & b).

STUDY AREA AND APPROACH

All key elements were comprehensively evaluated in a five year field study. The results were combined with other research findings and with long-term rainfall data in a population model designed to escape the limitations of the field study and forecast hyrax population change in the long-term. The field study was conducted in the Karoo National Park where predators had not been persecuted for seven years. Counts at hyrax colonies indicated a fourfold decline in hyrax numbers in the park immediately prior to the present study (Fairall 1991). Synchronous declines in hyrax populations were reported throughout southern Africa and an explanation of this was sought. Twenty-two pairs of eagles were located in the vicinity of the park. Overlap between neighbouring territories was minimal (<10%). All hyrax refuge habitats spanning four complete territories and parts of two others (149km^2) were classified and mapped out. Density of hyrax was not found to be predictable in these refuge habitats so a population estimate was obtained by plotting all groups (n=303) and determining mean group size (16.2). The average eagle territory was found to accommodate 63 groups and 1062 hyrax. Variation in hyrax numbers and the extent of refuge habitats across eagle territories was very low.

We assumed that territories were stable and used the territory (24km^2) as the unit area for all measures in the model. Direct observations of hyrax groups indicated that the safe feeding area (358ha) in an average territory should be able to accommodate 112 groups. This indicated a carrying capacity of 1816 hyrax per territory in a standard year and that the refuge habitat was currently 60% saturated.

IMMEDIATE ACTION OF PREDATION

All field data were collated in a spreadsheet model (Microsoft Excel) to represent what was happening to the hyrax population over the study period (Figure 1). Black Eagles removed 11% of the hyrax standing crop from their territories in an average year. This amount was equivalent to 29% of the numbers added to the hyrax population annually. Clearly Black Eagles were not important mortality factors for juvenile hyrax but they took a greater toll of immature hyrax and they could account for most of the mortality of adult age classes. Many of the hyrax captured by eagles were from age classes with good survival expectancy rates. For some adult hyrax age classes Black Eagles were responsible for three quarters of all deaths. By removing an amount of rock hyrax equivalent to almost a third of the annual recruitment to the population, Black Eagles qualify as one of the limiting factors affecting hyrax population change. By removing breeding adults Black Eagles have a greater inhibitory influence on hyrax population growth than a predator which removes surplus elements such as young or old individuals. The emphasis of this predation on adult hyrax age classes (which are otherwise unlikely to die) also suggests that these losses would not readily be compensated by other, non-violent, mortality factors in the absence of eagles. For this predation to be regulatory, current theory demands that it should be density-dependent. There was no evidence of this during the field study, but losses to the population did explain more of the variation in population change than additions which proved to be highly correlated with rainfall. The spreadsheet model represents an annual snapshot of the population but it gives a hypothetical structure that represents a hyrax population in a constant environment. In reality, hyrax population structure responds in a highly dynamic fashion to variation in mortality and especially the birth pulse. The model provides a convenient point of departure for how the hyrax population behaves under average conditions.

Figure 1. A diagrammatic summary of age- and sex-specific predation by Black Eagles in relation to the availability and the annual mortality of the hyrax population classes. This summary was derived by computer simulation of a stable hyrax population which best represents the population under study.

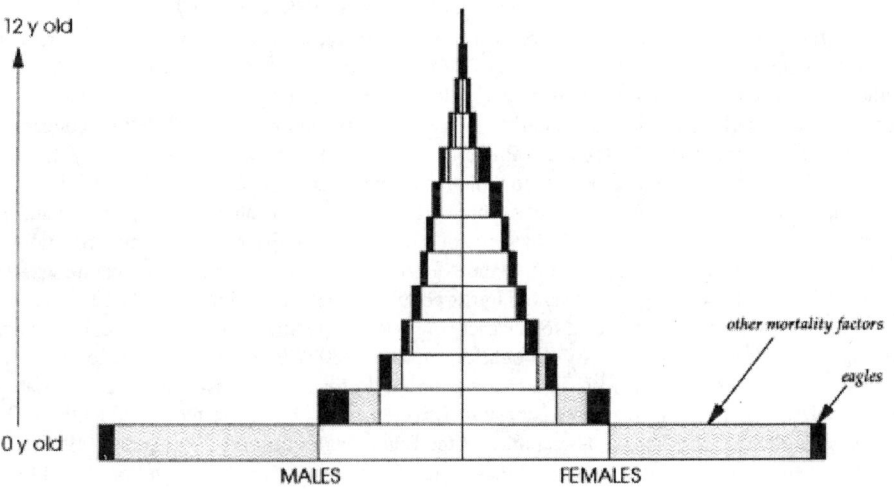

LOWER TROPHIC INTERACTION

Various field observations confirm that hyrax suffer heavier predation during drought and lighter predation after rain. We assume that hyrax populations experience lowest mortality and show greatest recruitment when small populations (relative to the carrying capacity of the safe feeding zone) benefit from good rains, and we assume the reverse when large populations are stressed by drought (i.e. processes modelled on P:K). The refuge habitat accommodates 1816 hyrax under average conditions but the same vegetation would support more hyrax in good years and fewer during drought. Variation in plant production on arid range-lands is generally one and a half times greater than the variation in rainfall (Le Houérou et al 1988). We therefore assume that the refuge habitat will support 15% more hyrax than average when there is 10% more rainfall than usual. Estimates of 'K' derived in this way did not reflect cumulative effects of several years of drought or several years of good rain. To accommodate these effects, we separated the vegetation resource into winter phytomass which can be thought of in a simple financial analogy as the capital, and fresh summer growth which can be thought of as the interest on that capital. We allowed capital to appreciate by up to 30% per annum in years of good rains and depreciate or decay by up to 6% per annum during drought. In a second step we allowed herbivory by hyrax to accelerate the depreciation when hyrax appetite outweighed the available fresh growth. We constrained the capital between likely limits derived from veld studies.

UPPER TROPHIC INTERACTION

Mortality and conception rates were set in accordance with P:K ratio. Prenatal mortality was allowed to claim 2-20% of foetuses in accordance with rainfall during gestation. Eagle kill was modelled both on hyrax abundance (P) and availability (P:K). Caracal functional response was modelled on hyrax surplus (P-K) and the numerical response on fresh growth (an indicator of enrichment which included a time-lag of six months). Compensatory mortality of hyrax for simulations of eagle removal was handled in two ways: first it was assumed that 10% of the eagle kill would have died anyway (old animals made up 16% of eagle prey); second we invoked a starvation mortality of 0.75 affecting all age classes whenever hyrax appetite exceeded the food supplies by a factor of 4.5 or more. This was based on observations of population declines. This starvation mortality factor was latent in the model whether eagles were removed or not. For most runs of the model the caracal kill was estimated but treated as part of non-eagle mortality.

STANDARD RUN OF THE MODEL UNDER NATURAL CONDITIONS (PREDATORS PRESENT)

In a standard run of the model (Figure 2), it was evident that veld condition could totally recover or totally deteriorate over four or five years. We felt that this was realistic for karoo biota and it tallied with the contentions of range managers. The model predicted phases of increase and decline for the hyrax population reflecting underlying changes in its food supplies. Modelling conception on previous summer rainfall rather than P:K ratio did not alter this pattern significantly. Historic reports of hyrax irruptions corresponded to drought and predicted decline phases. The 1946 irruption coincided with numerous springbok treks which are generally associated with pasture exhaustion (Skinner 1993). It seems likely that these were not 'population explosions' but rather perceptions of increase created by dispersal of hyrax out of the safe feeding zone. A most important feature was that the model correctly predicted the observed hyrax population decline during the early 1980's ($r=0.9$; $p<0.001$). This decline was predicted for a variety of regions in southern Africa wherever enrichment during the 1970's was followed by drought during the 1980's. Predator interference was not a requirement and this complies with field observations of declines in conserved areas. Using Matobo Hills rainfall data, the model predicted change in hyrax density which correlated significantly ($r=0.5$; $p<0.01$) with the limited numerical response of the Black Eagles observed by Gargett (1993). The breeding performance of these eagles correlated significantly ($r=0.5$; $p<0.01$) with predicted hyrax surplus.

Figure 2. Changes in 'relevant' winter phytomass (heavy shading) and fresh growth (light shading) occurring within the 'safe feeding area', and in hyrax population density (per eagle territory), predicted by a standard run of the model with the full complement of predation, using Beaufort West rainfall data. Asterixes denote timing of hyrax irruptions reported in the literature. Phytomass values are expressed as kg dry matter in the 'safe feeding area'.

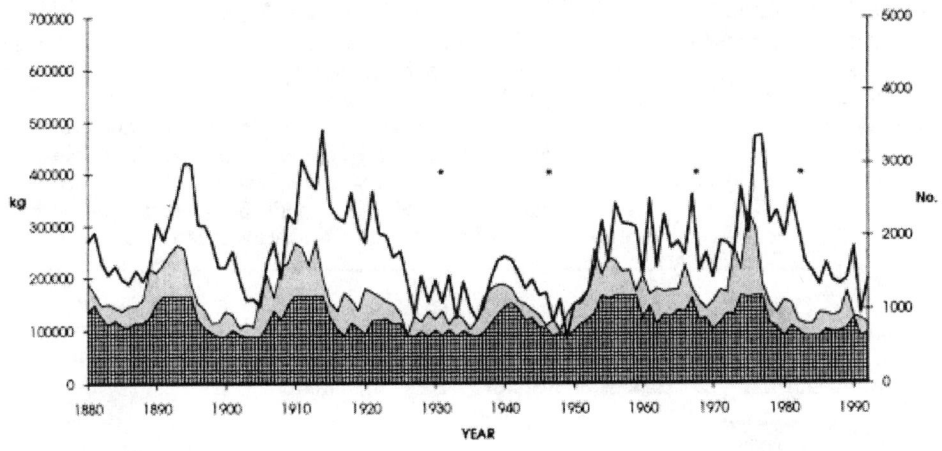

SIMULATED REMOVAL OF BLACK EAGLES

In the absence of Black Eagles the model predicts rapid increase in hyrax numbers and impaired decline (Figure 3). There is a 17% depression in the phytomass and so carrying capacity is set lower. Despite this, hyrax density is 32% greater in this simulation, and regularly attains levels where gross imbalance occurs between hyrax and their food supplies, resulting in heavy starvation mortality. It is important to remember that the recruitment rate of the hyrax population and non-eagle mortality rate

Figure 3. Changes in 'relevant' winter phytomass (heavy shading) and fresh growth (light shading) occurring within the 'safe feeding area', and in hyrax population density (per eagle territory), predicted by a run of the model (Beaufort West rainfall) with predation by Black Eagles removed. Assumptions on compensatory mortality in the absence of predation by eagles are explained in the text.

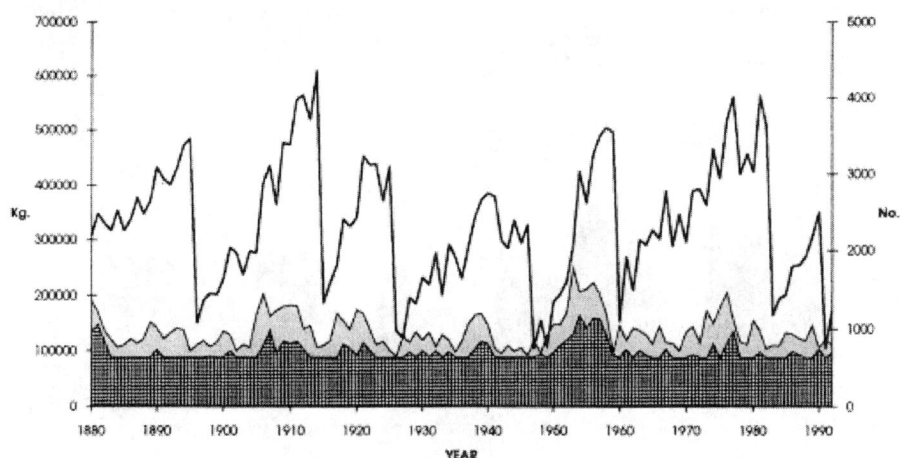

are still accorded opportunity for density-dependent feedback in this simulation. Juvenile mortality is relatively unaffected by the removal of eagles, so the rapid increase in the population can be ascribed primarily to enhanced survivorship of adult hyrax (and their subsequent contribution to reproduction) in the absence of eagles.

HYRAX SURPLUSES WITH AND WITHOUT EAGLE PREDATION

Under natural conditions hyrax numbers appear to be able to comfortably track the dramatic changes in the carrying capacity of their refuge environment (Figure 4a). By removing predation we impair this ability of hyrax numbers to track changes in carrying capacity. Average departure of density from carrying capacity was 50% greater in simulations after eagle removal. This results in a far greater surplus of hyrax not supported within the safe feeding zone (Figure 4b). The amount of grazing consumed by the additional hyrax surplus in the absence of Black Eagle predation on the average karoo farm (two territories) is valued at US$ 1080. This benefit of having eagles on the farm outweighs the cost of occasional lamb predation by the eagles by a factor of 155 times.

Figure 4a. Changes in the carrying capacity of food supplies in the 'safe feeding area' of a standard eagle territory for hyrax, K, and concordant changes in hyrax population density, P, (visible black area represents surplus) predicted by a standard run of the model with the full complement of predation, using Beaufort West rainfall data.

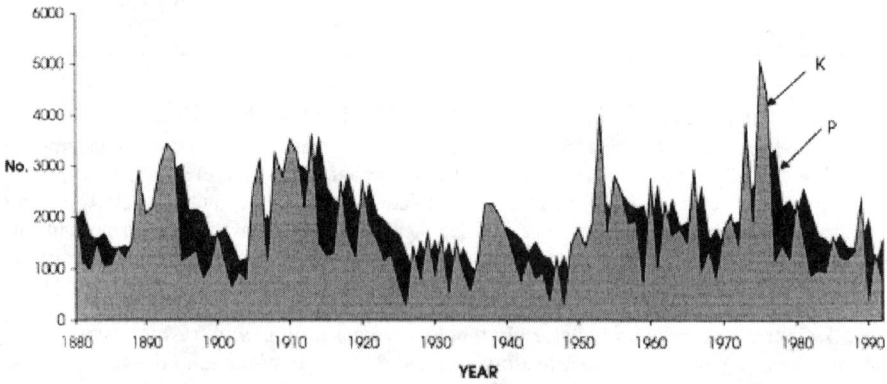

Figure 4b. Changes in the carrying capacity of food supplies in the 'safe feeding area' of a standard eagle territory for hyrax, K, and changes in hyrax population density, P, (visible black area represents surplus) predicted by a run of the model where predation by Black Eagles has been removed (Beaufort West rainfall data).

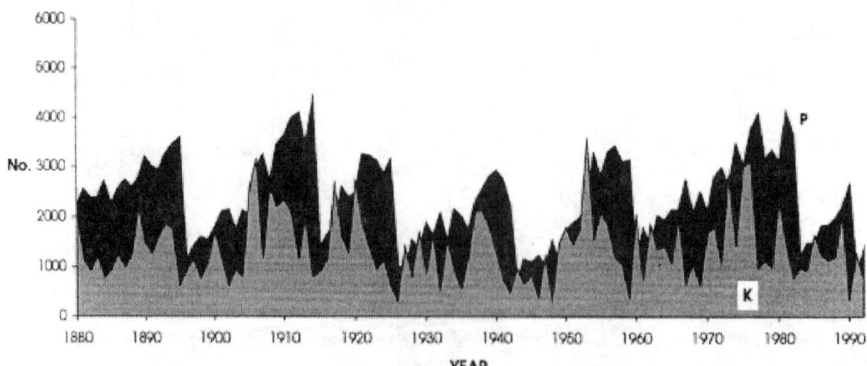

RESPECTIVE ROLES OF THE PREDATORS

During increase phases of the hyrax population (when K exceeded P) specialist predation by Black Eagles (as modelled here) greatly exceeded predation by caracals and so acted as more of a brake on the hyrax population. Predation by caracals was minimal at these times and the concordant demand for alternate prey (by both predators) was maximal. But caracals removed many more hyrax during the decline phases and exhibited a far greater capacity than Black Eagles for removing surpluses in excess of the carrying capacity. The range in hyrax numbers removed by caracals was three times greater than that taken by Black Eagles. Compensation by caracals (not incorporated into the model) is likely to lessen the effect of removing eagles, but most karoo farmers persecute caracals before eagles and just a 10% impedance (=removal) of both predators (i.e. 10% of both predicted kills survive) resulted in a significant predicted increase in hyrax density. Hyrax surplus increased as a linear function of predator impedance such that a 40% impedance of both predators resulted in a similar cost to the farmer as did total removal of the eagles.

SENSITIVITY ANALYSIS AND CONCLUSION

The model predicts that removing or impeding predators has a profound effect upon hyrax population change, but how robust is this prediction? We tested this robustness by running the model with and without eagles while varying the most important parameters dramatically. For each perturbation the model returned the same prediction, that hyrax density and its variability increase significantly when predators are interfered with. So why is predation such an essential ingredient for close tracking of changing food supplies by the hyrax population? For a standard run of the model we measured losses through the upper trophic level (predation) and losses through the lower trophic (loss of full breeding potential plus non-violent mortality). Losses in the lower trophic level explained only 2% of the predicted change in hyrax numbers whereas losses to predators could explain as much as 64%. Losses through the lower trophic level, although much larger than losses to predators, were less variable and appeared instrumental to population change only during periods of enrichment such as the 1970's when they explained 41% of the change. Predators prove to be essential facilitators of the decline phase. An important bearing of this is that the results of field studies will be highly dependent on whether the study is conducted during an increase or decline phase. Losses through the lower trophic level exert a profound influence on hyrax population structure but they primarily affect only the first age class. Perhaps the build-up in hyrax numbers during the 1970's (and subsequent crash) was amplified by the lack of effective density-dependent feedback in this component. It is easy to see that hyrax numbers in the arid Karoo could be as unstable as rabbit numbers in Australia were it not for the effective and permanent refuge resource, and the stability induced by this refuge facilitates the highly effective co-existence of the specialist Black Eagles and generalist caracals. The model demonstrates that these predators have the capacity to remove surplus hyrax not supported by the refuge habitat even after extraordinary birth-pulses. Stochastic climate-induced variation in the number of protected prey obscures any direct relationship between this predation and hyrax density. We offer this as an example of how predation can still regulate prey numbers between limits without showing density-dependence (where density is measured as animals per unit area).

ACKNOWLEDGEMENTS

We would like to thank SA Eagle Insurance Co Ltd for financial assistance; Elsabe Aucamp for providing information on red rock rabbits; Sascha Klemm and Gus van Dyk for providing information on caracals; GIMS and GIS lab for assistance with a geographical information system of the study area; Professor Ian Newton for comments on the manuscript.

REFERENCES

ALLAN, D.G. 1988. Breeding success, nest spacing and territory size of Black Eagles in the Magaliesberg, South Africa. *Gabar* 3: 76-81.

DAVIES, R.A.G. 1994. Black eagle *Aquila verreauxii* predation on rock hyrax *Procavia capensis* and other prey in the Karoo. Ph.D. thesis, University of Pretoria.

DAVIES, R.A.G. (extended abstract in press). The extent, cost and control of livestock predation by eagles with a case study on Black Eagles *Aquila verreauxii* in the Karoo. 'Solving Raptor-Human Conflicts' symposium, Canterbury, Sept. 1993. *J. Raptor Res.* 33.
FAIRALL, N. 1991. Factors affecting the dynamics of hyrax populations. *Proc. XXth Congr. Int. Union Game Biol.*, (Gödöllö, Hungary), part 1: 372-377.
FOURIE, L.J. 1983. The population dynamics of the rock hyrax *Procavia capensis* (Pallas, 1766) in the Mountain Zebra National Park. Ph.D. thesis, Rhodes University, Grahamstown.
GARGETT, V. 1972. Observations at a Black Eagle's nest in the Matopos, Rhodesia. *Ostrich* 43: 77-108.
GARGETT, V. 1990. *The Black Eagle, a Study*. Acorn Books, Johannesburg. 279pp.
GARGETT, V. 1993. Territory boundaries and occupancy and related behaviours of Black Eagles (*Aquila verrreauxii*) in the Matobo Hills. Report to Department of National Parks and Wildlife Management, Zimbabwe, January 1993, (unpubl. mimeograph),142pp.
LE HOUÉROU, H.N., R.L. BINGHAM, & W. SKERBEK 1988. Relationship between the variability of primary production and the variability of annual precipitation in world arid lands. *J. Arid Environ.* 15: 1-18.
LENSING, J.E. 1982. Feeding strategy of the rock hyrax and its relation to the rock hyrax problem in southern South West Africa. *Madoqua* 13: 177-196.
MOOLMAN, L.C. 1986a. Aspekte van die ekologie en gedrag van die rooikat *Felis caracal*, Schreber, 1776 in die Bergkwagga Nasionale Park en op die omliggende plase. M.Sc. thesis, University of Pretoria.
MOOLMAN, L.C. 1986b. Aspekte van die ekologie en gedrag van die rooikat *Felis caracal* (Schreber 1776) in die Bergkwagga Nasionale Park en op die omliggende plase. *Pelea* 5: 8-21.
SALE, J.B. 1970. Unusual external adaptations in the rock hyrax. *Zool. Afr.* 5: 101-113.
SKINNER, J.D. 1993. Springbok (*Antidorcas marsupialis*) treks. *Trans. Roy. Soc. S.* Afr. 48: 291-305.
STUART, C.T. 1982. Aspects of the biology of the caracal (*Felis caracal* Schreber, 1766) in the Cape Province, South Africa. M.Sc. thesis, University of Natal, Pietermaritzburg.
SWART, J., M.R PERRIN, J.W. HEARNE & L.J. FOURIE 1986. Mathematical model of the interaction between rock hyrax and caracal lynx, based on demographic data from populations in the Mountain Zebra National Park, South Africa. *S. Afr. J. Sci.* 82: 289-294.

R A G Davies
Mammal Research Institute
University of Pretoria
Pretoria 0001
South Africa
(current address: P O Box 1390, Halfway House 1685, South Africa)

J W H Ferguson
Department of Biology,
University of Pretoria
Pretoria 0001
South Africa

ved's eds. 2000
Chancellor, R. D. & B.-U. Meyburg eds. 2000
Raptors at Risk
WWGBP / Hancock House

Can Raptor Predation limit Red Grouse Populations?

S.J. Thirgood and S.M. Redpath

ABSTRACT

Whether vertebrate predators can limit their prey has long been a controversial question in ecology. This paper summarises a study of predation by Hen Harriers *Circus cyaneus* and Peregrines *Falco peregrinus* on Red Grouse *Lagopus lagopus scoticus* populations in Scotland. Harrier breeding densities were highest in areas and years where passerines and microtines were most abundant. Peregrine breeding densities were highest on southern moors, probably as a result of high pigeon densities. Harriers showed a Type III functional response to grouse chicks. Peregrines showed a Type II response to adult grouse. The implication of these findings is that the greatest proportion of grouse will be removed by raptors from low density grouse populations on southern, grassy grouse moors were alternative prey are abundant. On a moor where breeding densities of harriers and peregrines were high, predation by these raptors during April to September reduced autumn grouse densities by 50% within a single breeding season. On this moor, an increase in raptor densities coincided with a large decline in the numbers of grouse shot. Our data were strongly suggestive that predation by generalist raptors limited Red Grouse populations at low density.

INTRODUCTION

The question of whether predators can limit their prey has long been controversial. An earlier view was that vertebrate populations were limited by habitat constraints and that predators took only the so-called 'doomed surplus' (Errington 1946). However, there is an emerging consensus that predation can in some circumstances limit populations of microtine rodents and lagomorphs (Boutin 1995; Nordahl 1995). Current evidence for predator limitation of bird populations is equivocal - with studies on songbirds suggesting that predation has little effect but studies on waterfowl and gamebirds suggesting that predation can reduce both breeding success and breeding density (Newton 1998).

Red Grouse *Lagopus lagopus scoticus* fall prey to a range of avian and mammalian predators and there has been much debate regarding the impact of predation on grouse populations. Early studies on Red Grouse populations at high density concluded that predators concentrated on non-territorial grouse as opposed to territory owners and that predation was unimportant in limiting populations (Jenkins *et al* 1964; Watson 1985). Later research on Red Grouse populations at low density demonstrated that overwinter survival of territorial and non-territorial grouse was similar, and suggested that winter predation could be partially additive (Hudson 1992). The importance of the relative densities of grouse and their predators was also highlighted in two studies of predation by Hen Harriers *Circus cyaneus* on grouse chicks. Picozzi (1978) estimated that harriers removed only 7.4% of grouse chicks from a moor where grouse were at high density, whilst Redpath (1991) suggested that on moors with lower grouse densities, harriers could remove up to 17% of grouse chicks.

These studies suggested that the relative abundance of raptors and grouse was important in determining whether raptor predation could limit grouse populations. Little information was available, however, on the mechanisms involved, or on the factors influencing raptor numbers and diet on moorland. Here we summarise a recent study (Redpath & Thirgood 1997), which addressed the following questions:

1. What influences the numbers (numerical response) and diet (functional response) of Hen Harriers and Peregrines *Falco peregrinus* on grouse moors?
2. What impact does predation by Hen Harriers and Peregrines have on grouse populations and grouse shooting bags?

STUDY AREAS AND METHODS

The study was conducted during 1992-96 at Langholm in southern Scotland on a grouse moor where harriers and peregrines had been protected since 1990. We extended the work in part to six other moors where raptors were also protected. On all of these moors mammalian predators and corvids were controlled by gamekeepers. Langholm was historically one of Scotland's finest moors, but in common with many moors, grouse bags had been in decline since early this century at approximately 1.7% per anum. It is very unlikely that raptors were involved in this decline as they were uncommon prior to 1990. Comparison of aerial photographs taken at Langholm during 1948 and 1988 indicates that heather cover declined by 48% in this period and this loss of grouse habitat was considered to be the most likely cause of the long-term decline in grouse bags.

On each moor we estimated the density of Red Grouse and obtained a measure of abundance of moorland passerines and small mammals. Grouse densities were estimated in April, July and October using standard counts with pointing dogs. We also used dogs to obtain estimates of grouse brood size and grouse chick abundance in early June. Passerines were counted in June using line transects on random grid squares. Small mammal abundance was estimated by snap trapping in April. The numbers of harriers and peregrines attempting to breed on each moor were determined in spring by systematically watching the moor from vantage points for displaying harriers and by visiting peregrine nesting sites for signs of occupancy. Harrier diet was assessed during 2678 hours of observations from hides placed at harrier nests. Peregrine diet was assessed from prey remains and pellets collected during regular searches at eyries throughout the breeding season. Intensive studies on the effects of raptor predation on grouse populations and shooting bags were conducted at Langholm. In addition to the estimates of grouse densities described above, we systematically searched for grouse corpses on counting sites throughout each winter 1992-96. We also captured and radiotagged 308 grouse during 1994-96 and monitored their weekly survival. Finally, we had access to detailed bag records of the numbers of grouse shot in each year at Langholm and on neighbouring moors since the late 19th century. Full details of methods used and tests of potential biases are given in Redpath & Thirgood (1997) and references cited therein.

RESULTS AND DISCUSSION

Numerical response of harriers and peregrines

Before considering the numerical response of harriers, we assessed how densities varied after illegal control had stopped. Breeding densities of harriers on our study moors increased year-on-year for four years, on average, following protection. At Langholm, harrier numbers increased from two females in 1992 to 20 females in 1997. Having removed the effects of illegal control, breeding

Figure 1. Mean (± se) Hen Harrier density km² for (a) males and (b) females in relation to mean (±) meadow pipit abundance on six study moors.

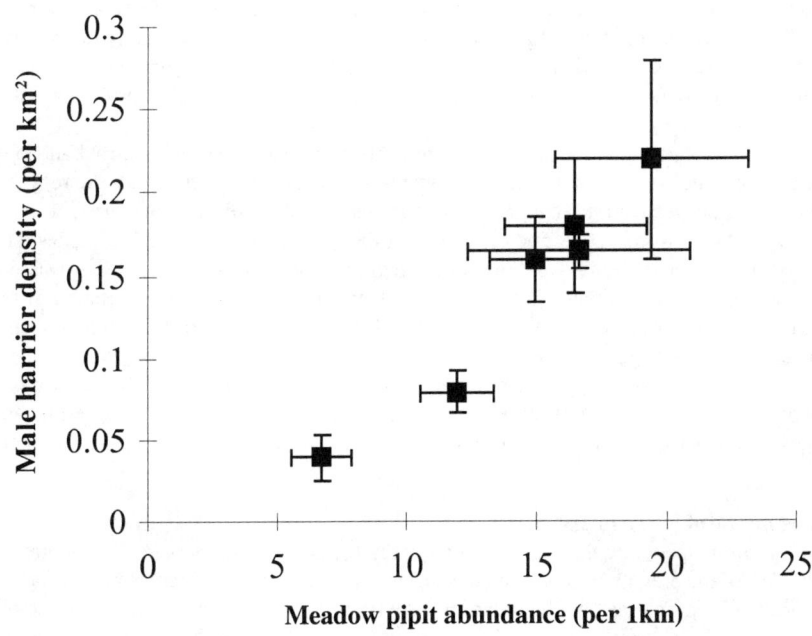

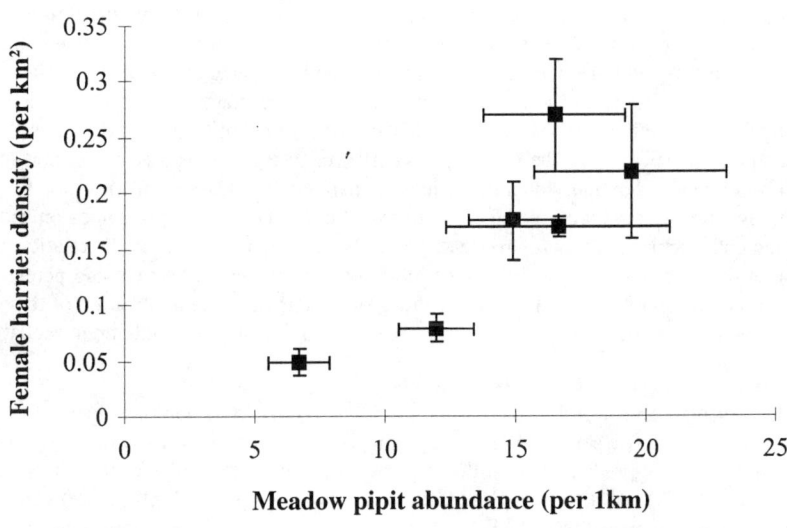

densities of harriers varied considerably between moors and were not primarily related to grouse density in April. Comparison of harrier densities between moors indicated that densities of males and females were positively associated with Meadow Pipit *Anthus pratensis* abundance and to a lesser extent females were positively associated with small mammal abundance (Figure 1). Within moors, variation in male and female densities from year to year were related to small mammal abundance. This is an important finding, because it has implications for how many harriers we would expect on grouse moors in the absence of illegal control. Meadow pipits and field voles occur at higher densities on moors with a mosaic of heather and grass, so we can expect more harriers on these moors in the absence of control.

Breeding densities of peregrines tended to be more stable from year to year, although at Langholm they increased from three to six pairs over the course of the study. Comparing areas, there was a positive relationship between latitude and the average nearest neighbour distance between peregrine nests (Figure 2). In other words, peregrine nests were further apart at more northerly latitudes. The relationship between grouse density in April and peregrine nearest neighbour distance was not significant, nor was it significant after removing the effects of latitude. Our interpretation of the relationship between peregrine nesting density and latitude is that it is an indirect measure of racing pigeon abundance. Racing pigeons are a major prey of peregrines.

In summary - neither harrier nor peregrine breeding densities were related to grouse densities. In the absence of illegal control, we would expect more harriers on grassy moors where passerines and voles are more abundant and more peregrines on southern moors where racing pigeons are more abundant.

Functional response of harriers and peregrines

Passerines were numerically the most important prey for breeding harriers (63%) and grouse formed only 15% of the prey items identified to species. Of the 263 grouse seen brought to harrier nests, 96% were chicks. The rate at which harriers provisioned grouse chicks varied considerably between different years and different moors. The main factor influencing this variation was the density of grouse chicks, with more grouse chicks resulting in higher provisioning rates. The relationship between grouse chick density and male provisioning was sigmoidal (Type III), with a sharp increase in provisioning of grouse chicks at densities between 50 and 70 chicks per km^2 (Figure 3). The shape of this relationship indicated that the greatest proportion of grouse chicks were removed by individual harriers at relatively low grouse chick densities.

A total of 868 prey remains was collected during the breeding season from 20 peregrine eyries on six moors. Racing and feral pigeons formed the bulk of the items (49%), whilst Red Grouse formed only 15%. The majority of Red Grouse collected were adults (92%), although the remains of 10 chicks were found. As with the harriers, there was considerable spatial and temporal variation in the occurrence of Red Grouse in the diet of peregrines. The percentage of biomass provided to peregrines by Red Grouse increased with grouse density but levelled off at grouse densities above 20 birds per square km (Figure 4). The shape of this curve suggested that the greatest proportion of adult grouse were removed by individual peregrines at relatively low grouse densities.

In summary - Red Grouse were not the main prey of either harriers or peregrines on grouse moors, though both species took more grouse as grouse became more abundant. The relationships between raptor diet and Red Grouse abundance indicated that individual harriers and peregrines took a greater proportion of grouse at relatively low grouse densities. The implication of this was that grouse populations at low density were more susceptible to limitation through raptor predation.

Impact of raptor predation on grouse populations

The data presented here were derived from counts of grouse with pointing dogs and from systematic searches for grouse corpses. We also radiotagged 308 grouse to look at mortality patterns in more detail. Overall, these data showed that raptors killed on average 30% of the grouse over winter (October - March) and a further 30% during the following spring (April - June) when the grouse were attempting to breed (Table 1). We were unable to distinguish between the kills of harriers

Figure 2. Mean nearest neighbour distance between Peregrine eyries in relation to latitude for seven study moors.

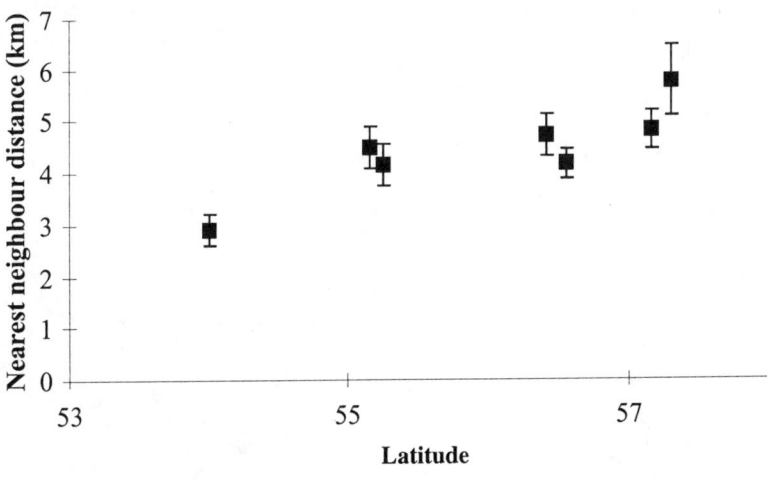

Figure 3. Rate at which Red Grouse chicks brought to harrier nests by male and female harriers combined in relation to the density of grouse chicks. Points represent means ($\pm$ se) for one moor in one year. Line is fitted Type III relationship. Curve fitted to model $Y = 0.21 x^{5.1} / (515.1 + x^{5.1})$.

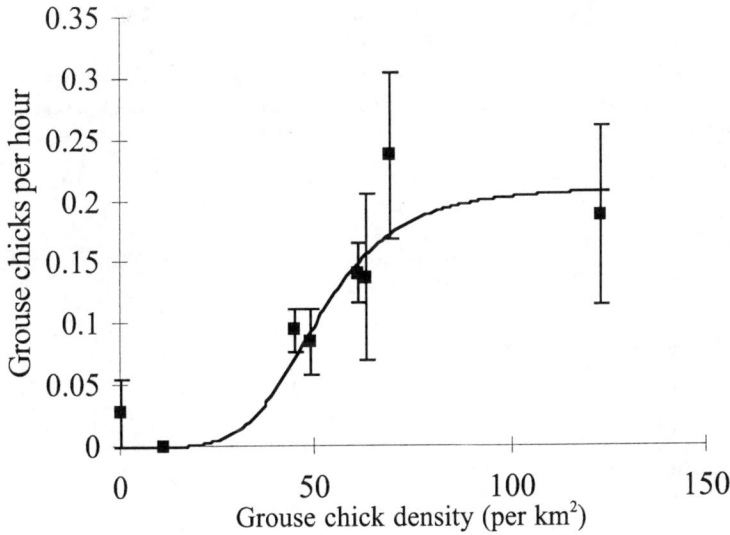

Figure 4. Percentage of Red Grouse in Peregrine prey items (by biomass) in relation to estimates of grouse abundance within a two kilometre radius of each eyrie. Line is fitted Type II relationship. Curve fitted to model $Y = 53.4x / (8.4 + x)$.

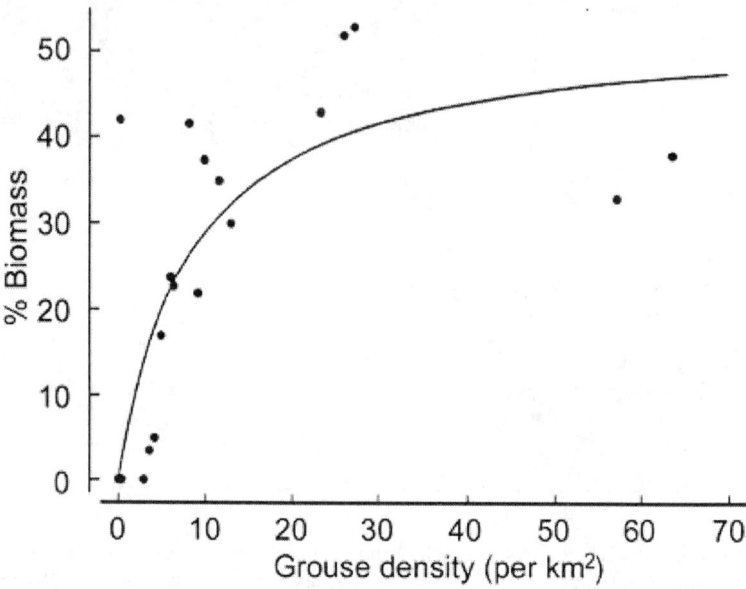

Figure 5. Numbers of Red Grouse shot on Langholm moor during 1975-97 in comparison to numbers shot on nearby moors F and G during the same period. Grouse bags on all three moors fluctuated in synchrony during 1975-93. After 1993, grouse bags on moors F and G increased, while bags on Langholm moor continued to decline. Harrier and peregrine numbers on Langholm moor increased between 1990 and 1997, whereas numbers of these raptors on moors F and G remained low.

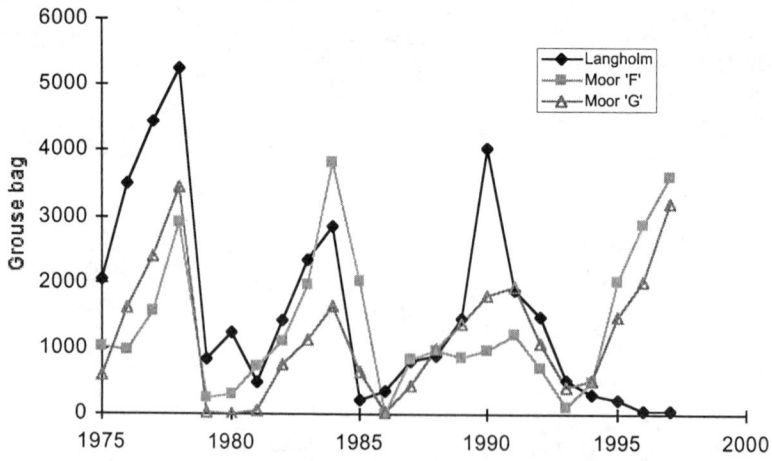

and peregrines during these periods. Predation on adult grouse during the summer was low but when harriers were abundant in the latter years of the study they removed up to 40% of the chicks produced by the surviving hens (Table 1). We were unable to determine whether or not the losses to raptors during the winter were compensated by reductions in other losses. However, losses to raptors of adult grouse in spring and grouse chicks in summer appeared to be additive to other mortality and we estimated that they reduced autumn densities of grouse by 50% within a single breeding season. A simple model of the grouse population, combining the estimated reduction in breeding productivity with the observed density dependence in winter loss, predicted that over two years, in the absence of breeding raptors, grouse breeding numbers would have increased by 30% and post breeding numbers by 150%.

Table 1. Grouse mortality to raptors at Langholm during 1995 and 1996. Data on adult mortality derived from radio-tagging studies. Data on chick mortality derived from observations at harrier nests and counts of grouse chicks with pointing dogs. Further details in Redpath & Thirgood (1997).

Year	1995	1996
Live grouse in October (km^2)	49	41
Killed by raptors October - March (%)	28	47
Killed by raptors April - September (%)	30	39
Live grouse chicks at hatch (km^2)	78	71
Killed by raptors June - July (%)	35	39

Impact of raptor predation on shooting bags

Analysis of long-term bag records demonstrated that, in common with many moors, grouse bags at Langholm fluctuated with an approximately six year cyclic pattern. The last peak year at Langholm was in 1990, when more than 4000 grouse were shot, and the next peak was thus expected in 1996. Grouse bags declined year on year from 1990 until only 51 grouse were shot in 1997. A model based on the Langholm bags from 1950-90 suggested that the observed bags in 1995-97 were significantly lower than expected. We compared the grouse bags at Langholm to those from two nearby moors where harriers and peregrines bred at low density because of illegal control (Figure 5). Between 1975 and 1993 the bags from all three moors cycled in relative synchrony. Since 1993, when raptor numbers at Langholm started to increase, grouse bags at Langholm declined. In contrast, grouse bags on the nearby moors increased to high levels. The simplest explanation was that raptors prevented the grouse population at Langholm from increasing to a cyclic peak as expected.

CONCLUSIONS

Whilst raptors were unlikely to be responsible for long-term declines in British Red Grouse populations, they appeared to be capable of holding grouse at low density. Our data were strongly suggestive that predation by the large numbers of harriers and peregrines prevented the grouse population at Langholm from increasing to a cyclic peak and can thus be considered a limiting factor. This suggestion now needs testing through predator reduction experiments.

The numbers of harriers and peregrines were high at Langholm because of the abundance of alternative prey such as meadow pipits, field voles and pigeons. Meadow pipits and voles were abundant because of the mosaic of heather and grass and pigeons were more abundant on southern moors than northern moors. Information on the diet of harriers and peregrines suggests that the greatest proportion of adult grouse and grouse chicks were removed by individual raptors when grouse populations were at low density. The numerical and functional responses suggested that the potential for harriers and peregrines to limit grouse populations varied between moors. The impact of raptor predation was expected to be greatest on low density grouse populations on grassy southern moors where alternative prey and raptors were at high density. A key area for further research is to determine how many other grouse moors would resemble Langholm, with high harrier densities and low grouse bags, if illegal control of harriers were to cease.

ACKNOWLEDGEMENTS

Many people helped in this research but we particularly thank Ian Newton for his support and guidance throughout. The study was funded by the Buccleuch Estate, Game Conservancy Trust, Game Conservancy Scottish Research Trust, Institute of Terrestrial Ecology, Joint Nature Conservation Committee, Natural Environment Research Council, Royal Society for the Protection of Birds, Scottish Natural Heritage and Westerhall Estate. SJT is grateful to the Royal Society for supporting his attendance at this conference.

REFERENCES

BOUTIN, S. 1995. Testing predator-prey theory by studying fluctuating populations of small mammals. *Wildlife Research*, 22, 89-100.
ERRINGTON, P.L. 1946. Predation and vertebrate populations. *Quarterly Review of Biology*, 21, 144-177.
HUDSON, P.J. 1992. *Grouse in Space and Time*. Fordingbridge: Game Conservancy Trust.
JENKINS, D., A. WATSON & G.R. MILLAR 1964. Predation and Red Grouse. *Journal of Applied Ecology*, 1, 183-195.
NEWTON, I. 1998. *Population Limitation in Birds*. London: Academic Press.
NORDAHL, K. 1995. Population cycles in northern small mammals. *Biological Reviews*, 70, 621-637.
PICOZZI, N. 1978. Dispersion, breeding and prey of the hen harrier in Glen Dye, Kincardineshire. *Ibis*, 120, 489-509.
REDPATH, S.M. 1991. The impact of Hen Harriers on Red Grouse breeding success. *Journal of Applied Ecology*, 28, 659-671.
REDPATH, S.M. & S.J. THIRGOOD 1997. *Birds of Prey and Red Grouse*. London: Stationary Office.
WATSON, A. 1985. Social class, socially induced loss, recruitment and breeding in Red Grouse. *Oecologia*, 67, 493-498.

S. J. Thirgood
Game Conservancy Trust
Institute of Cell, Animal and Population Biology
University of Edinburgh, Kings Buildings
Edinburgh, EH9 3JT
UK.

S. M. Redpath
Institute of Terrestrial Ecology
Banchory, Kincardineshire
AB31 4BY
UK.

Chancellor, R. D. & B.-U. Meyburg eds. 2000
Raptors at Risk
WWGBP / Hancock House

The Impact of Rabbit Calicivirus Disease on Raptor Reproductive Success in the Strzelecki Desert, South Australia: A Preliminary Analysis.

I.D. Falkenberg, V. G. Hurley and E. Stevenson

INTRODUCTION

The Strzelecki Drainage System is recognised as one of Australia's most important raptor breeding areas. In September 1981 along a 20 km stretch of the Strzelecki Creek floodplain extending to a maximum width of 3 km, 73 pairs of ten species were recorded nesting (Mace 1981). The area provides one of the highest known concentrations of breeding raptors in the world and highlights the importance of tree-lined drainage systems in arid areas (Olsen 1995). A number of species that regularly breed there are listed as rare or threatened (eg. Grey Falcon *Falco hypoleucos* & Black-breasted Buzzard *Hamirostra melanosternon*, Olsen 1995).

The introduced European rabbit *Oryctolagus cuniculus* is one of Australia's major environmental pests, particularly in arid and semi arid areas and is a significant component of the diet of seven species of raptors found breeding in the Strzelecki. This study was initiated in November 1995 as a response to the unplanned release of the Rabbit Calicivirus from Wardang Island, South Australia, where field tests were being performed to assess its possible use as a biological control agent in Australia. A highly infectious virus, Rabbit Calicivirus Disease (RCD) kills rabbits quickly, without infecting other animals, including predators of rabbits.

RCD was first confirmed in the Strzelecki Creek area in mid November 1995, having arrived through natural spread. This project aims to study the reproductive responses of raptors to the expected RCD-induced decline in rabbit numbers. Combined with historical productivity data (post-1981), this study will provide a bench mark against which to measure any future changes in raptor productivity as a result of the removal of a major prey source. This project is ongoing and the results presented are preliminary.

Few previous opportunities have arisen to study the indirect effects of a biological control agent on native wildlife species in Australia, particularly in environmentally important and ecologically sensitive areas.

Figure 1. Far north east of South Australia showing study location and area surveyed for raptor breeding.

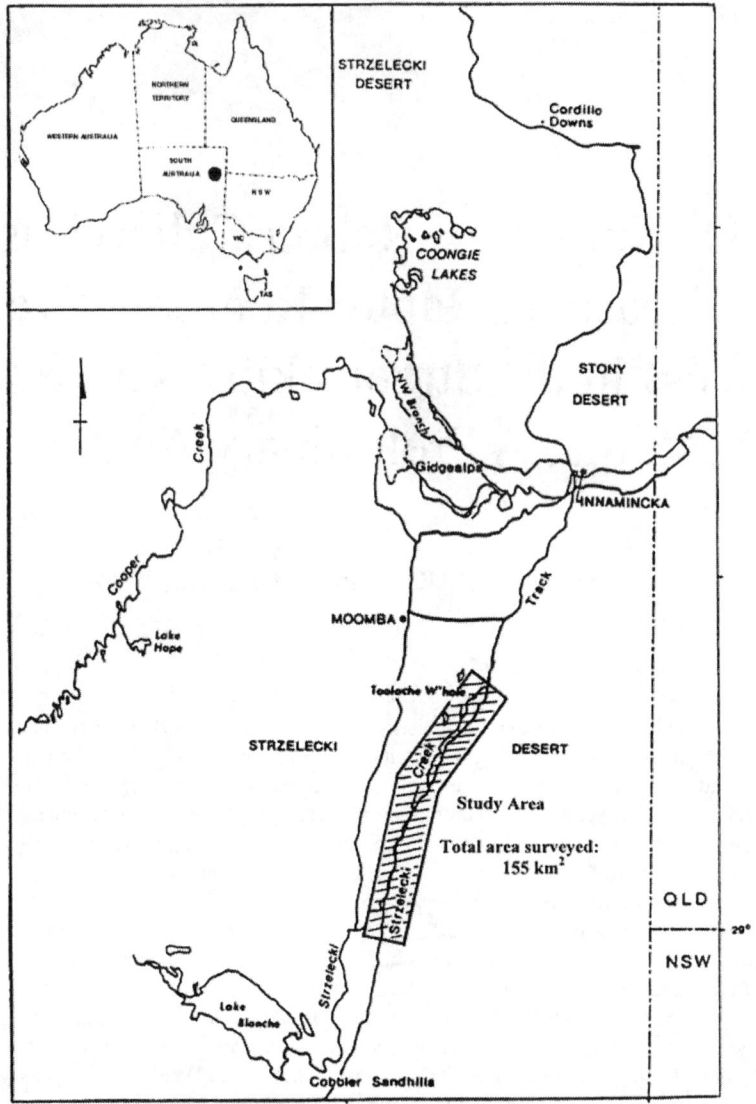

STUDY AREA AND METHODS

The Strzelecki Creek is lined by relatively narrow riparian woodland surrounded by a complex system of longitudinal red sand dunes in the Strzelecki Desert located in the far northeast corner of South Australia (Figure 1). The Strzelecki Creek is unusual in that it receives flows from the Cooper Creek only under extreme flood conditions. In consequence the inundation of this system is much less frequent than that of the Cooper.

The study area comprises mostly a dry creek and associated floodplain extending 40km south from Merty Merty Station to Tinga Tingana Crossing (110km^2) and 15km from Toolache Waterhole to Tilparee Waterhole (45km^2) (Figure 1). Distance from the creek bed to the edge of the floodplain varies from about 500 metres to 3 km.

RAPTOR PRODUCTIVITY

A systematic search was undertaken in the study area to locate all active raptor nests. In 1995 one survey was undertaken, in 1996 and 1997, two surveys were undertaken during each breeding season to determine raptor productivity and nesting success based on the terminology of Postupalsky (1974).

The survey was conducted by three teams who searched prescribed transects using a combination of 4WD vehicles, four-wheel quad motorcycles and walking in order to sample all habitat types including the dry creek bed. Transects crossed the creek bed and associated flood plain at intervals ranging from 100 to 150 metres, depending upon vegetation density and terrain.

A series of dry tree-lined clay pans beyond the defined drainage channel were also checked for nesting activity. Two four-wheel motorcycles were used to investigate nests that were located in particularly remote saltbush *Atriplex vesicaria*, lignum *Muehlenbeckia florulenta* and cane grass *Eragrostis australasica* flats. Each nest site was inspected for breeding activity. Active nests were determined by the presence of fresh nesting material and prey remains, castings and excreta below the nest and, if birds were seen at the nest, were checked whether eggs, young or fledglings were present using telescopic poles with mirror attached at 450 angle. Locations of nests were recorded using Garmin GPS instruments which provided sufficient accuracy to locate nest sites during the next survey.

All prey remains were collected from each nest and identified to species where possible. Prey items were quantified by determining percentage by number of the total number collected from each nest.

Historical Productivity

Historical reproductive data for the area were sourced from the Australian Bird and Bat Banding Schemes (Environment Australia), the Nest Record Scheme (Birds Australia) and from surveys undertaken by bird banders. Other data collected by the authors during 1984-87 were also included.

Rabbit Distribution and Density

For each year from 1995 to 1997, rabbit numbers were assessed by spotlight surveys, conducted at night between 2000 hrs and 2300 hrs. Twenty one (21) transects, each two (2) kilometers long and one hundred (100) meters wide were established in the study area. Each survey was undertaken by a team of 3 persons, comprising a driver, recorder and observer. Each team repeated the counts two days later, at approximately the same time. A speed of 10 km/hr was maintained during the surveys. All transects were established along existing tracks and exploration survey lines.

RESULTS

Reproductive Success of Raptors (1981-97)

Generally raptors were observed in very low numbers throughout the study area. A total of 18 active nests of rabbit-dependent raptor species were recorded with young in 1995, 6 in 1996, and 4 in 1997 (Table 1). In five of the seven species no nests with young were recorded in 1997.

Productivity for Black Kites *Milvus migrans*, Whistling Kites *Milvus sphenurus*, Black-breasted Buzzards *Hamirostra melanosternon* and Black Falcons *Falco subniger* decreased during the period 1995-97 (Table 1).

Brown Falcons *Falco berigora*, Black Kites and Black-breasted Buzzards were the only species to successfully produce young during 1996 and Brown Falcons and Little Eagles *Hieraaetus morphnoides* were the only species to successfully produce young in 1997. All monitored nesting of other species failed to successfully produce young.

The number of successful pairs for each species in the study area, post RCD was considerably lower than pre RCD historical data, however a clear trend appears to be emerging from these preliminary results indicating lower productivity for Black Kites, Whistling Kites, Black-breasted Buzzards and Black Falcons. Wedge-tailed Eagles *Aquila audax* have failed to successfully breed since 1995.

Non rabbit-dependent raptor species were found with young during the study, including Australian Kestrels *Falco cenchroides*, Grey Falcon *Falco hypoleucos* and Australian Hobby *Falco longipennis*, but have not been included in these results.

Historically the combined total number of productive nests for Wedge-tailed Eagles, Black Kites, Whistling Kites, Little Eagles, Black-breasted Buzzards, Brown Falcon and Black Falcon found in the area peaked in 1985 with 212 nests (Figure 2). The number of active nests then declined to 38 in 1986 and to 19 in 1987. No data were obtained in 1989 to 1994.

Table 1. Numbers of pairs and productivity of various raptor species, Strzelecki Creek.

Species	Pre-RCD				Post-RCD		
	1984	1985	1986	1987	1995	1996	1997
Wedge-tailed Eagle							
Number of Pairs	4	12			1		
Number of Young	6	17			1		
Mean Young / pair	1.50	1.40	na	na	1.00	F	F
Black Kite							
Number of Pairs	42	144	29	17	4	2	
Number of Young	65	181	42	22	4	2	
Mean Young / pair	1.54	1.25	1.44	1.29	1.00	1.00	F
Whistling Kite							
Number of Pairs	4	14	3		3		
Number of Young	9	25	6		4		
Mean Young / pair	2.25	1.78	2.00	na	1.30	F	F
Little Eagle							
Number of Pairs	14	3			3		1
Number of Young	16	3			3		1
Mean Young / pair	1.14	1.00	na	na	1.00	F	1.00
Black-breasted Buzzard							
Number of Pairs	3	10	4	2	2	2	
Number of Young	4	15	6	2	1	1	
Mean Young / pair	1.33	1.50	1.50	1.00	0.50	0.50	F
Brown Falcon							
Number of Pairs	12	24	1		3	2	3
Number of Young	23	45	1		4	3	6
Mean Young / pair	1.90	1.87	1.00	na	1.33	1.5	2.00
Black Falcon							
Number of Pairs	2	5	1		2		
Number of Young	4	10	2		2		
Mean Young / pair	2.00	2.00	2.00	na	1.00	F	F

Note: na = not available; F = failed:
1984-87 - data collected by Waterman.

Productive nests for 1995 to 1997 declined from 18 to 4 (Figure 2 and Table 1). The high peak in active nests for the area during 1985 followed a year of relatively high rainfall. The 270 mm of rain recorded during 1997 compares with 1984 when 276 mm of rain were recorded (Figure 2). Yet the difference in numbers of raptor nests recorded in these two years is striking.

Prey Analysis

During the 1995 survey, the most common prey item in the diet of raptors was rabbit, followed by reptiles (Table 2). Rabbits made up the bulk of the breeding season diet (86% to 100%) of Wedge-tailed Eagles, Whistling Kites, Black Kites and Brown Falcons. For Black-breasted Buzzards, Black Falcon and Little Eagles, rabbit comprised 75% and 63% of the diet respectively. The sample size of prey items was low and no great weight should be put on these results.

Figure 2. Annual rainfall (mm) for Merty Merty Station and number of active raptor nests recorded in the study area.

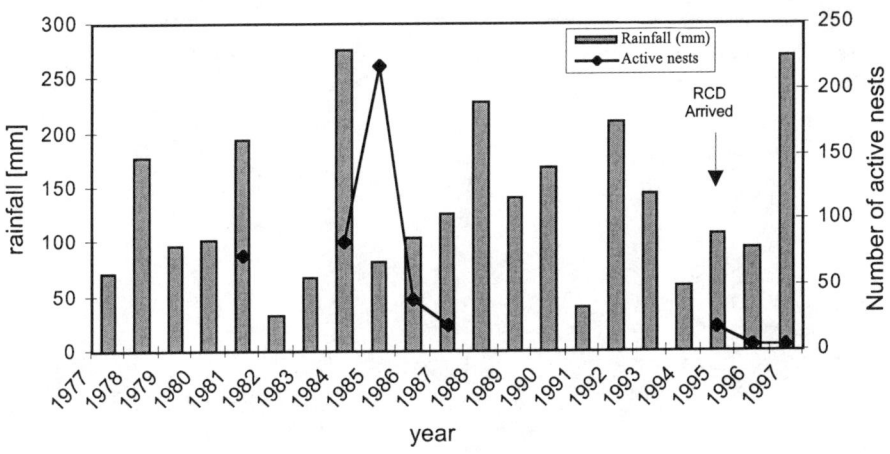

Other prey remains included one Fat-tailed Dunnart *Sminthopsis crassicaudata* found in a Whistling Kite's nest, and Netted Dragons *Ctenophorus nuchalis*, Bearded Dragons *Pagona vitticeps* and Sand Goanna *Varanus gouldii*, found in Little Eagle and Black-breasted Buzzard nests (38% and 25% of all prey items respectively).

Table 2. Prey remains represented as a percentage of total collected from each raptor nest - November 1995.

Species	Rabbit	Birds	Reptile	Small Mammal	Other	Total no of items
Wedge-tailed Eagle	88 [7]		12[1]			8
Whistling Kite	89[8]			11[1]*		9
Black-breasted Buzzard	75[9]		25[3]			12
Little Eagle	62[5]		38[3]			8
Black Kite	100[14]					14
Brown Falcon	86[6]				14[1]ψ	7
Black Falcon	75[3]	25[1]*f*				4

Note: * Fat-tailed Dunnart, *f* Galah, ψ unable to identify remains
Figures in parenthesis represent number of prey items

Few prey remains were found in or beneath active nests during the 1996 and 1997 surveys. However, prey remains recorded include; Little Corella *Cacatua pastinator* from a Little Eagle nest

539

and Bearded Dragon and Netted Dragon from a Brown Falcon nest. Two pellets collected from beneath a Black-breasted Buzzard nest in 1997 comprised bird feathers (species unknown) and rabbit. Most of the items from rabbit-feeding species in these years were not rabbits, reflecting the shortage of the primary prey.

Rabbit Density and Presence of RCV

Two rabbit carcasses excavated from burrows near Toolache Waterhole (Site 2) during the 1995 survey tested positive to RCD. Spotlight counts indicated a 94% decrease in numbers from November 1995 through November 1996 to November 1997 (5.7, 0.4 and 0.3 rabbits/km respectively, figure 3 and 4).

Figure 3 Number of rabbits seen per kilometre at Tinga Tingana and Merty Merty (mean over two nights). Total length of spotlight transects = 24 km.

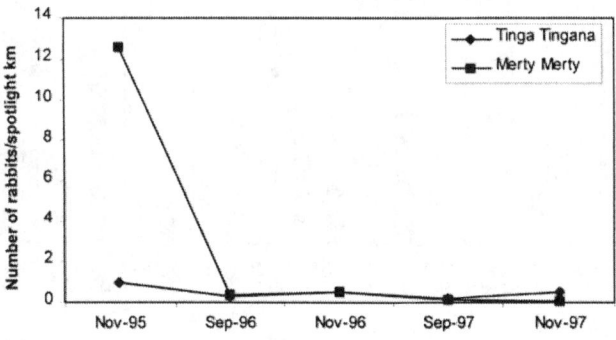

Figure 4 Number of rabbits seen per kilometre at Toolache and Daralingie (mean over two nights). Total length of spotlight transects = 18 km.

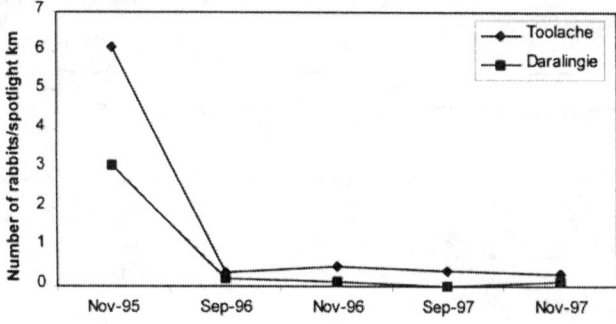

Serological testing was not undertaken on rabbits in 1996, but we presume that the virus was the major influence in the observed decline in rabbit numbers. During September 1997, four rabbits were collected, ranging in age from 150 to 220 days. Three were seropositive for RCD antibodies, reflecting possible RCD outbreaks in August-September 1996 and again in February-March 1997.

By contrast at Bollards Lagoon Station in September 1997 about 70 km east of Merty Merty Station and outside our raptor study area, rabbit numbers were relatively high. The spotlight survey of the Bollards Lagoon area found 7.5 rabbits/km and 40 rabbits/km. It seems, therefore, that rabbit density was highly variable over the region as a whole.

DISCUSSION

The 1995 results indicate a high degree of dependence of seven species of raptors on rabbits for food. During the 1995 breeding season, the population of Wedge-tailed Eagles (3 pairs) produced one young. Two pairs were present at nests but did not produce young and were not included in the results. During the 1997 season a total of 17 Wedge-tailed Eagle nests were checked for activity. No adults were observed near any of the nests, but two had been lined with fresh leaves, perhaps a month prior to our visit. These nests are not included in the above figures for total active nests, as adults were not present. Many of these nests were in a bad state of repair, showing considerable deterioration from previous years.

A study in Western Australia found that Wedge-tailed Eagles did not breed unless the late summer or early winter index of rabbit abundance had reached at least 1.6 per kilometre (determined by spotlight counts, Ridpath and Brooker (1985). Consistent with this, the mean number of rabbits per spotlight km for the Strzelecki Creek in 1997, when no Wedge-tailed Eagles successfully produced young in the study area, was less than 0.5 per km.

In their arid-zone study of Wedge-tailed Eagles, Ridpath and Brooker (1985) found that, where the mean annual rainfall was distributed more erratically between years and was combined with less diverse flora, there were periods of up to 4 years between the successful breeding of particular pairs.

Given the good rainfall figures in our area for 1997, it would appear that factors other than rainfall contributed to the decline in nesting activity of raptors there. Whilst lower rainfall during 1994 to 1996 may have accounted for lower raptor breeding during this period there appears to have been no increase coinciding with good rains in 1997. We can suggest no explanation other than the disease-induced scarcity of rabbits.

During the 1997 survey very few raptors were observed compared to previous years. Even Black Kites, which are normally very common and conspicuous as they soar above the floodplain, were noticeably scarce.

The observed decrease in rabbit numbers, resulting from the combined effects of drought and RCD and apparent low populations of potential alternative prey may have had an effect on the number of raptors breeding in the area.

Severe storms occurred in the area prior to the November 1997 survey and may have contributed to some nesting failure. Although no carcases were found beneath nests, other predators and scavengers might have removed any that occurred.

Bird-eating species of raptors may well benefit in time from the increased vegetation cover and resulting increased seed and herbage production for prey species (ie improved habitat conditions for prey species).

In Britain, where rabbit numbers were greatly reduced by the disease Myxomatosis, the numbers and productivity of Common Buzzards *Buteo buteo* were much reduced. In some areas, most pairs failed to breed, as alternative prey were insufficient. As rabbit numbers recovered buzzard breeding improved (Newton 1979. Sumption and Flowerdew 1985).

Studies undertaken by Olsen & Marples (1992) demonstrated that the clutch sizes in raptors such as Whistling Kites, Brown Goshawks *Accipiter fasciatus* and Wedge-tailed Eagles decreased significantly following rabbit control with myxomatosis. In raptors which occurred in the same areas, but which rarely took rabbits, clutch size remained unchanged (Olsen & Marples 1992). North of 26° S where rabbits are rare, clutch sizes remained unchanged as well.

Myxomatosis has had little impact on rabbits in arid regions of Australia, which may explain why many raptor populations remain in a relatively healthy state. A major decline in numbers of rabbits is likely to result in a decline in the breeding success of many raptor species; since the 1995 breeding season, Wedge-tailed Eagles have failed to reproduce.

In conclusion, the decline in raptor breeding activity in the Strzelecki Creek would appear to be linked to the RCD induced decline in the rabbit population. We consider that further investigation into this little known aspect of predator/prey relationships is important for the future preservation of our raptor populations.

ACKNOWLEDGMENTS

This project has been financed by the Bureau of Resource Science, Department Primary Industries and Energy, Canberra and National Parks and Wildlife, South Australia (NPWSA). A special thanks to Nick Mooney for presenting this paper at the conference and for support and advice with the field work since 1995. Also a special thanks to Jim Robinson for his dedication and commitment to this project each season and thanks to Mark Holdsworth, Tim Collins, Mark Boulet, Nick Birks, Katrina Gray, Dawn Hay, Pat Kennedy, Wally Klau, Bill Brown and Niel Jarvis for their commitment to the field work often under harsh and hot conditions. Also thanks to Ron Sinclair and Peter Bird of the Animal Plant Control Commission SA for their assistance and support during the September 1997 survey.

Thanks to Steve Coulthard (Aboriginal Ranger) for his expertise and skill with identifying animal tracks and to Pam and Martin Rieck, Managers of Merty Merty Station for supplying rainfall information and allowing the survey teams to camp on the station. Ron Sinclair and Peter Bird also provided helpful advice and comments on this report. Thanks to Peter Alexander (Wildlife Management NPWSA) and Phil Strachan (Balcanoona NPWSA) for assistance with vehicles and equipment, Cheryl Vale (NPWSA) for preparation of illustrations and diagrams, to the Australian Bird and Bat Banding Schemes (Environment Australia) and Nest Record Scheme (Birds Australia) for access to data and records. Also special thanks to Mr Max Waterman for allowing access to his comprehensive banding records from the Strzelecki Creek.

REFERENCES

MACE, B. 1981. ARA Field Trip to the Strzelecki Creek, North-east of South Australia. *Australasian Raptor Association News*, 2 (4):3.
NEWTON, I. 1979. *Population Ecology of Raptors*. Berkhamsted, Poyser.
OLSEN, P.D. 1995. *Australian Birds of Prey, The Biology and Ecology of Raptors*. University of New South Wales Press.
OLSEN, P.D. & MARPLES, T.G. 1992. Alteration of clutch size of Raptors in response to a change in prey availability: evidence from a control of a broad scale rabbit infestation. *Wildlife Research* 19: 129-135.
POSTUPALSKY, S. 1974. Raptor Reproductive Success: some problems with methods, criteria, and terminolgy. *Raptor Research Report* 2, 21-31.
REDPATH, M. & BROOKER, M.G. 1985. The breeding of the Wedge-tailed Eagle *Aquila Audax* in relation to its food supply in arid Western Australia. *Ibis* 128: 177-194
SUMPTION, K.J. & FLOWERDEW, J.R. 1985. The Ecological Effects of the Deline in Rabbits (*Oryctolagus cuniculus* L) due to myxomatosis. *Mammal Review* Volume15, No 4 151-186.

Ian D. Falkenberg
Department Environment, Heritage and Aboriginal Affairs
National Parks and Wildlife South Australia
Murraylands Region
Vaughan Terrace, Berri
South Australia 5343

Victor G. Hurley
Department Natural Resources and Environment
253 Eleventh Street, Mildura
Victoria 3500
Australia

Elizabeth Stevenson
City of Melbourne
GPO Box 1603M
Melbourne
Victoria 3001
Australia

Chancellor, R. D. & B.-U. Meyburg eds. 2000
Raptors at Risk
WWGBP / Hancock House

Can the Common Kestrel *Falco tinnunculus* provision Increased Broods in a mid-latitude environment?

Anthony J. van Zyl

ABSTRACT

Brood manipulations have traditionally been used to test Lack's hypothesis (1954) that birds lay a clutch size that maximizes the number of offspring they fledge. Results of manipulations vary from those that show parents are unable to raise experimentally enlarged broods to those where parents successfully raise extra nestlings without obvious detrimental effects. I reviewed the literature on brood manipulations to evaluate whether latitudinal differences between study areas partly explain the variation in experimental results. Three previous brood manipulations at mid-latitudes (24° - 45°) demonstrated that parents were unable to provide sufficient food to their offspring. To test whether other species are unable to raise enlarged broods in mid-latitudes, I manipulated Common Kestrel broods in the Western Cape Province, South Africa (34°S) and monitored provisioning rate, nest attendance and nestling growth and survival. Parents of enlarged broods (+2) were able to increase their provisioning rates to such an extent that their nestlings obtained as much food as control broods. While females of enlarged broods did not make any increased effort to hunt around the nest site while attending the brood, there was a decrease in the amount of food caching in the enlarged broods, suggesting that they were probably being provisioned at close to their maximum rate. The results of this study do not support the hypothesis that birds are constrained by food during reproduction at mid-latitudes.

INTRODUCTION

Clutch size is regarded as a major trait in life-history evolution (Stearns 1992) and is one of the easiest parameters to measure. Lack (1954; 1966) hypothesized that birds should lay a clutch size which maximizes their number of offspring. In a proximate sense, this means that they create a brood size which they can adequately nourish. Several other clutch size hypotheses have been proposed relating to seasonality of resources and resultant population levels (Ashmole 1963; Ricklefs 1980), habitat use (O'Connor 1982), adaptive lifetime response (Williams 1966; Klomp 1970) and energy allocation (Cody 1966; 1971). Brood manipulations are an easy experimental method of testing Lack's ideas and in the last four decades, broods of many species have been manipulated (51 studies reviewed by Dijkstra *et al*. 1990; Dann 1988; Navarro 1991; Beissinger 1990; Gard & Bird 1992;

Robinson & Rotenberry 1991; Kallander & Smith 1990; Husby 1986; Sanz 1997). Some studies have supported Lack's hypothesis, but many found that birds were able to raise more chicks than the average clutch size (Gustafsson & Sutherland 1988; Pettifor *et al.* 1988; Hegner & Wingfield 1987). The cost of reproduction to parents was used as a possible explanation for these discrepancies (Reznick 1985; Nur 1988a) and studies subsequently addressed the issues of future reproduction of parents following experimental manipulation as well as the survival of offspring after fledging (Dijkstra *et al.* 1990).

Obtaining data on lifetime reproductive success is difficult and few brood manipulation studies have been published during the 1990s. The results of studies that address the issues of reproductive costs are divided amongst those showing definite reproductive costs when raising more chicks than determined by clutch size (Roskaft 1985; Hegner & Wingfield 1987; Dijkstra *et al.* 1990) and those showing no effect on the parents (Korpimaki 1988). Monaghan and Nager (1997) point out that most brood manipulations do not take into account the costs of laying and incubation and are restricted to one part of the breeding phase, namely chick-rearing. They suggest that by including all components of the breeding phase in the manipulation, increased broods may show an effect on the cost of reproduction. Reznick (1992) goes further and argues that experimental manipulations are not good indicators of reproductive costs and that costs can better be determined by quantitative genetics.

Most brood manipulations have been conducted in high latitude regions (48° - 76°latitude) where clutch sizes are generally larger than in mid- (29°- 42°latitude) and tropical (0°- 18°latitude) regions (Klomp 1970; Hussel 1985). The breeding season is short in high latitude regions and some raptor prey populations such as voles are known to show large year-to-year variations in numbers (Hansson & Henttonen 1985; Korpimaki & Rita 1996). Food supply has been postulated as a reason for the differences in clutch size between low and high latitude regions in raptors (Simmons 1989a; Beissinger 1990). I hypothesize that birds at high latitudes are, on average, able to cater for the increased number of chicks in manipulations because of the high food availability during peaks in these large prey population fluctuations. Assuming that these birds allow for a greater food resource margin than those at mid- and low latitudes because of a higher variation in food availablity, these birds would have more food available to raise increased broods. In brood manipulations at mid- and low latitudes, parents in three species were unable to increase provisioning rates to provide sufficient food for the enlarged broods (Simmons 1986; 1989a; 1997).

I manipulated the broods of Common Kestrel in a mid-latitude environment where prey populations appear to have smaller year-to-year fluctuations than those in high latitudes (Hansson & Henttonen 1985). The aim of the manipulation was to test whether kestrels were able to provide sufficient food to chicks in a mid-latitude environment when having to feed broods larger than the maximum number determined by clutch size.

STUDY AREA

The study was conducted in the Western Cape Province, South Africa (34°S, 18°E) at sites between the Cape Peninsula and Langebaan, 130 km to the north. The area includes the city of Cape Town roughly in the central western section of the study area. The topography varies from quartzitic sandstone mountains on the Cape Peninsula (including Table Mountain) to siliceous and calcareous sandy flats north to Langebaan. The area experiences a Mediterranean-type climate characterized by cool, wet winters and warm, dry summers. Rainfall is highly variable depending on the exact location. On the Cape Peninsula it varies from 400 mm per annum in the southern Peninsula to 2270 mm per annum on Table Mountain. The flat, low-lying areas north of Cape Town have an annual rainfall of 500-600 mm per annum (Cowling *et al.* 1996). Temperatures are relatively constant and mild, with mean annual values ranging between 16°C and 22°C and with a range of mean minimum and maximum temperatures of 6°C and 10°C. The study area experiences strong winds from the northwest during the winter ranging from 20-30 km per hour. During summer, southeast winds blow at speeds of 20-40 km per hour.

Kestrel pairs were scattered over the whole area including urban habitats, mountain slopes and open scrub. Nests were found on the cliffs of the mountains on the Peninsula, on buildings in urban or suburban areas and in quarries when no natural nesting sites were available.

METHODS

Brood manipulations were conducted between October and December 1994: brood size was increased in 4 nests and reduced in 5 nests. Five additional nests were used as controls. Manipulations were randomly allocated to nests of different laying dates, clutch sizes and habitats (Table 1). Hatching dates were determined by checking the nests regularly and inspecting the eggs for pipping. Some nests were not checked on the day the eggs hatched and the hatching date for these broods were determined by backdating after estimating the age of the nestlings. Estimations were done within the first two weeks after hatching and the age of nestlings was estimated by comparing size and down-plumage changes with photographs taken of chicks of known ages (Van Zyl 1993). Because nestlings hatched on different days with a maximum of 5 days between the first and last hatching (Van Zyl in press), the estimated date of hatching of the oldest nestling was used in the calculations of nestling age for the brood. Broods were manipulated by adding two more chicks than the original clutch size to increase the brood size or by subtracting two chicks from the original clutch size (Dijkstra et al. 1990). Controls were not manipulated unless all the eggs did not hatch, in which case nestlings were added so that the brood size equalled the clutch size. An extra chick had to be provided to two control broods because of nestling fatality soon after hatching. Ages of introduced chicks did not differ by more than three days from the study brood ($x = 0.7$ days, range 0 - 3 days, $n = 7$) and introductions were made when chicks were between 3 and 16 days old ($x = 9.3$ days, $n = 7$).

Food delivered to the nestlings was monitored by full day watches at the nest. During these watches, nest attendance by parents was scored to the minute. The nest site was observed from a concealed position 40 - 100 m from the nest and all food brought to the nest was identified where possible. When prey items were clearly seen, they were rated according to size by estimating the length of the item in centimeters relative to tarsus length for small items and to tail length for large items. The prey items were placed into three size categories for analysis based on their estimated body length (Table 2). It was impossible to determine if nestlings ate all food provided to them but it was assumed that all items delivered to the nest were consumed by the nestlings. However, especially when chicks were young, food was sometimes left on the nest and later eaten by the adults. It was also impossible to determine the exact mass of the food provisioned. Thus, data were initially analysed using two prey mass estimates. Prey mass was estimated for all the size categories (Table 2) in the first analysis and the total mass of prey delivered to the observed nests totalled 3386.8 grams. In the second analysis, published estimates based on consumption times of average invertebrate (0.6 grams) and average vertebrate (12.8 grams) prey items were used (Van Zyl 1994) and the total mass of prey delivered to the nests totalled 3685.4 grams. This calculation is less than 9% more than the analysis based on estimated prey sizes.. Findings from the two analyses were found not to be statistically different (Mann Whitney U-test, $p=0.81$). For comparison in this study, all calculations of prey mass were performed using the two published estimates for kestrel vertebrate and invertebrate prey (Van Zyl 1994). Using these generalized masses can be justified because of errors inherent in estimating prey size and hence prey mass. Prey brought to the nest is often plucked and partly eaten so prey mass is overestimated, while on the other hand, nestlings do not necessarily eat all prey provided. This procedure also provides comparable results to a study of Common Kestrels in the Eastern Cape Province, South Africa where similarly-sized prey were provisioned (Van Zyl in press).

Provisioning rates have been correlated to the hunger calls of the brood (Bengtsson & Ryden 1983; Masman et al. 1989). Screaming intensities of nestlings were not explicitly recorded in this study but no excessive screaming was heard.

Nestling mass and wing length were measured at various ages and were used as indices of nestling growth. However, measurements were taken only once or twice during the development of the nestlings which allowed a very limited comparison of growth. Nestling survival was equated to the number of nestlings surviving beyond 25 days: most nestlings surviving to this age fledge successfully (Van Zyl 1993).

Two or three days of observations were conducted during the nestling cycle at each nest to avoid biases by days of unusually high or low provisioning rates (Simmons 1989b). These observations were then averaged to avoid pseudoreplication (*sensu* Hurlbert 1984). However, while all statistical tests and differences between groups use these averaged data, figures also include the raw data points for each observation day to indicate the range of the data. To allow comparison of provisioning rates and nest attendance scores for nestlings of different ages, provisioning rates and nest attendance were adjusted for nestling mass. Nestling mass was estimated from sigmoid growth curves plotted from nestling measurements ($r2 = 0.979$, $n = 19$) using the formula:

$$\text{estimated chick mass} = 228.428/(1+\exp(-(\text{age}-8.482)/3.753))$$

Kruskal-Wallis one-way analysis of variance and Mann Whitney U-tests were used in data analyses from the statistical software packages StatGraphics version 4.0 (STSC 1984) and Statistix for Windows version 1.0 (Analytical Software 1996).

Table 1. Information on breeding sites of Rock Kestrels used in the brood manipulation experiment

Nest Site	Exp	Eggs	Hatched	Add/Remove	Est. Hatch Date	Manip. Date	Nest Site	Habitat
Rondeberg Quarry Upper east	Red.	4	3	-2+1	9 October	13 October	Quarry	Scrub
Tafelsig/Seesig	Enlarg.	4	4	+2	10 October	13 October	Building	Suburbia
Rondeberg Quarry Lower west	Contr.	4	3	+1	19 October	27 October	Quarry	Scrub
Tygerberg Quarry	Red.	4	4	-2	22 October	3 November	Quarry	Scrub/suburbia
Dorstberg Upper section	Enlarg.	5	5	+2	22 October	3 November	Quarry	Scrub
Escom Nestbox	Contr.	4	4	0	26 October	-	Building	Suburbia
Durbanville Quarry	Contr.	4	4	0	28 October	-	Quarry	Scrub/suburbia
Tygerberg Hospital	Contr.	4	4	0	4 November	-	Building	Suburbia
Rondeberg Quarry Lower Middle	Red.	4	4	-2	6 November	18 November	Quarry	Scrub
Kommetjie	Enlarg.	4	4	+2	6 November	18 November	Cliff	Scrub
Devil's Peak	Red.	3	2	-1	9 November	28 November	Cliff	Scrub
Lion's Head - South	Contr.	4	3	+1	12 November	28 November	Cliff	Scrub
*Scarborough	Red.	4	4	-2	6 November	16 November	Cliff	Scrub
**Dorstberg Quarry North	Enlarg.	3	3	+2	6 November	18 Novermber	Quarry	Scrub

* Nestlings disappeared within 10 days of manipulation. Possibly predated by baboons.
** Nestlings killed by a snake 14 days after manipulation.

Table 2. Provisioning and estimated sizes and masses of prey fed to enlarged, control and reduced broods. Number of prey items per prey type and size are in the order of enlarged/control/reduced broods.

Vertebrates:

Mammalia	Small (<4cm; 6g)	Medium (4-6cm; 15g)	Large (>6cm; 22g)
Rhabdomys pumilio	0/0/0	1/1/2	0/0/3
Unidentified moles	0/0/0	0/0/1	0/0/0
Unidentified rodents or shrews	4/1/1	3/5/4	1/1/1
Total prey items	4/1/1	4/6/7	1/1/4

Reptilia	Small (<4cm; 4g)	Medium (4-12cm; 8g)	Large (>12cm; 15g)
Agama spp	0/0/0	1/0/0	0/0/0
Bradypodion occidentale	0/0/0	11/1/1	0/0/0
Cordylus spp	0/0/0	0/0/3	0/0/0
Unidentified geckos	0/0/0	0/0/1	0/0/0
Unidentified lizards	1/0/0	41/11/14	4/1/8
Meroles spp	0/0/0	0/4/1	0/4/4
Nucras spp	0/0/0	0/0/0	0/0/1
Mabuya spp	1/0/0	6/2/2	4/3/8
Unidentified snakes	0/0/0	0/2/0	0/1/1
Total prey items	2/0/0	59/20/22	8/9/22

Aves	Small (<4cm; 8g)	Medium (4-5cm; 15g)	Large (>5cm; 25g)
Unidentified birds	13/5/3	25/18/6	1/0/0
Passer melanurus	0/0/0	1/1/1	0/0/0
Cisticola spp	1/0/0	0/0/0	0/0/0
Numida meleagris day-olds	0/0/0	1/0/0	1/0/0
Streptopelia spp	0/0/0	0/0/0	0/1/0
Streptopelia senegalensis	0/0/0	0/0/0	1/0/0
Passer spp	0/2/0	4/4/2	1/0/0
Sturnus vularis	0/0/0	0/0/0	1/2/0
Parus afer	0/0/0	1/0/0	0/0/0
Motacilla capensis	0/0/0	0/2/0	0/0/0
Total prey items	14/7/3	32/25/9	5/3/0

Unidentified vertebrates	Small (<4cm; 6g)	Medium (4-6cm; 8g)	Large (>6cm; 15g)
	4/7/1	0/0/0	1/0/0

Invertebrates	Small (<3cm; 0.6g)	Medium (3-4cm; 1g)	Large (>4cm; 3g)
Solifugidae spp	3/1/0	1/1/0	0/0/0
Orthoptera spp	4/0/0	3/1/3	0/0/2
Arachnidae spp	1/0/0	0/0/0	0/0/0
Unidentified invertebrates	19/8/12	7/1/10	0/0/1
Total prey items	27/9/12	11/3/13	0/0/3

Unknown	(size unknown; 1g)
Total prey items	17/4/8

RESULTS

Nest attendance

Nest attendance declined with age of the nestlings in both treatments and controls (y = -1.49x + 109.7, r2 = 0.32, n = 25, excluding two outlier points at 15 and 20 days old, Fig. 1). Except for the low nest attendance by one pair over two observation days, there appeared to be a minimum nest attendance time depending on the age of the nestlings which could be represented by the following equation:

$$\% \text{ time at the nest site} = 113.27 - (2.64 * \text{nestling age}) \quad (r2 = 0.99, n = 7)$$

Figure 1: The relation of nest attendance of parent kestrels and age of nestlings for enlarged (□), control (∆) and reduced (O) broods. The solid line (_____) is the average regression of nest attendance per nestling age (y = -1.49x + 109.7, r^2 = 0.32, n = 25, excludes two outlier points at 15 and 20 days old). The dashed line (———) is the regression of the threshold for nest attendance and nestling age (y = -2.64x + 113.27, r^2 = 0.99, n = 7).

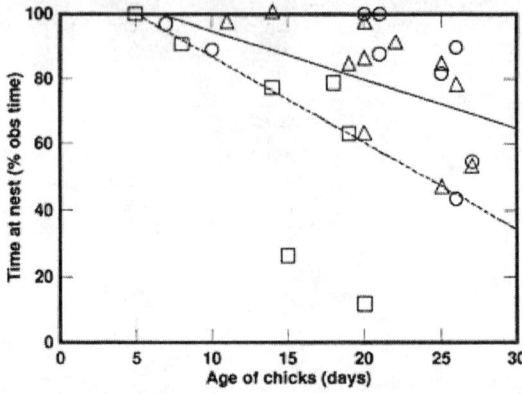

Figure 2: Nest attendance corrected for nestling age for enlarged (□), control (∆) and reduced (O) broods. The individual points are age corrected nest attendance figures for each observation day, while the average and standard deviation for means for 2 or 3 observation days are shown as vertical bars.

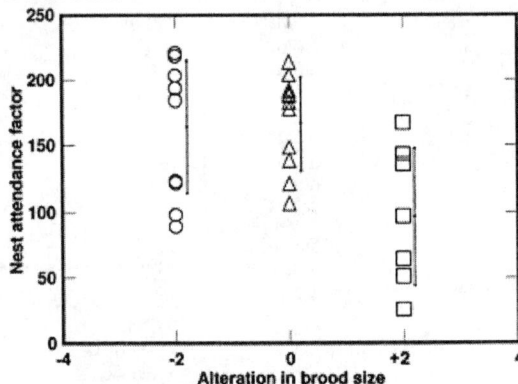

Figure 3: Nest attendance of males and females at various ages of the chicks for enlarged (□), control (∆) and reduced (O) broods. Points connected are for males (solid) and females (open) of the same pair representing one day of observation.

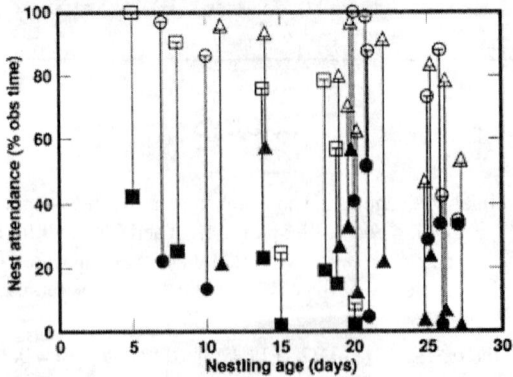

Figure 4: Parental contributions to the nestlings for enlarged (□), control (Δ) and reduced (O) broods as number of items brought to the nest. Dotted lines (............) indicate values for which the male contributes 75% of the items, where both male and female make equal contributions and for which the female contributes 75% of the items.

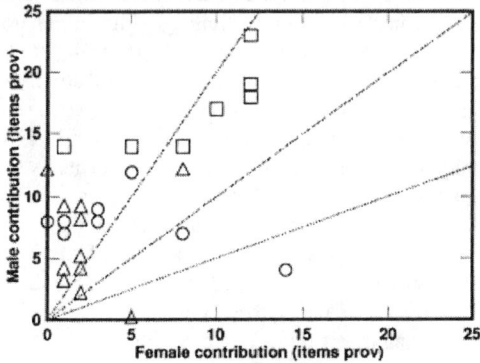

Figure 5: Provisioning rate to nestlings of different ages for enlarged (□), control (Δ) and reduced (O) broods in units of (a) items per 14 hour day, (b) grams provisioned to the brood per 14 hour day and (c) grams provisioned per nestling per 14 hour day.

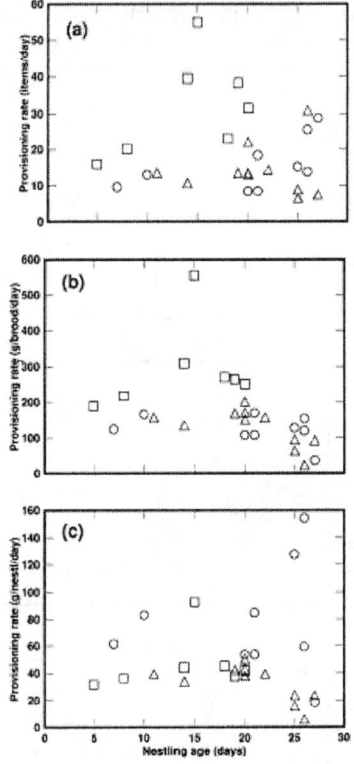

Nest attendance was lower in enlarged compared to control and reduced broods although this difference was not statistically significant (Kruskal-Wallis, p=0.15; Fig. 2). Females spent much more time at the nest than males (Paired t-test, $t = 10.23$, $n = 27$, $p<0.001$). The low nest attendance at the nest where attendance on two days was below the threshold attendance time was mostly due to the female who was away for similar periods to the male (Fig. 3).

Provisioning rate

Provisioning rate was measured as the number of food items delivered to the brood per day, estimated mass of food provided to the brood per day and estimated mass of food provided per nestling per day. Both male and female provided food to the nestlings, although the male provided most (Fig. 4). Provisioning rate increased with nestling age (Fig. 5a). There was a decrease in mass of prey delivered to control broods of 25 days old and older (Fig. 5b) and hence a decrease in mass of prey delivered per nestling (Fig. 5c). However, the mass of food provisioned to broods of 25 days old and older was not significantly lower than that provisioned to younger broods (Mann-Whitney U-test, $Z=1.01$, $p>0.05$). When provisioning rates were corrected for the age of the nestlings, parents of enlarged broods provided significantly more food in terms of items (Fig. 6a) and mass to the brood (Kruskal-Wallis, $p<0.05$; Fig. 6b) than did parents of controls and reduced broods. There was, however, no significant difference between treatments in the amount of food provisioned per nestling (Fig. 6c). Parents of reduced broods did not decrease the amount of food brought to the nest (Fig. 6b) resulting in more food per nestling in some reduced broods (Fig. 6c) than in control and enlarged broods. Parents of enlarged broods appeared to over-compensate for the extra nestlings and provided on average more food per nestling than parents of control broods (Fig. 6c).

Figure 6: Provisioning rates corrected for nestling age by standardizing rates for 218 gram nestling mass (20 days old) for enlarged (□), control (Δ) and reduced (O) broods in units of (a) items per 14 hour day, (b) grams provisioned to the brood per 14 hour day and (c) grams provisioned per nestling per 14 hour day. The individual points are age corrected provisioning rates for each observation day while the average and standard deviations are shown as vertical bars. Asterisks indicate significant differences of $p<0.05$.

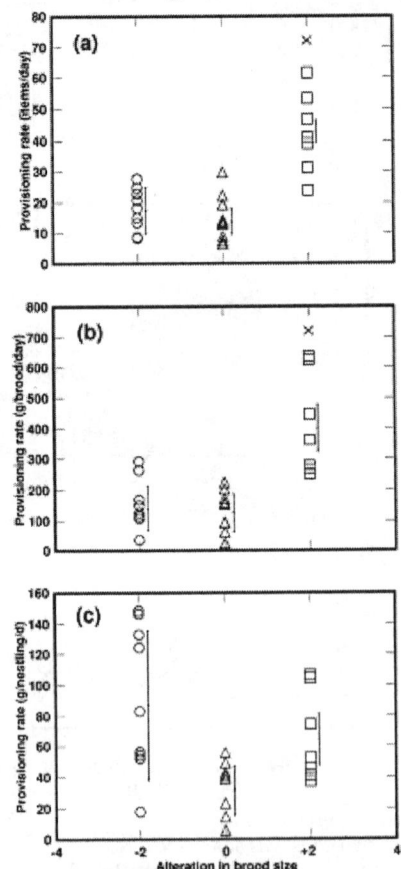

Prey species provisioned to the nest - proportion of vertebrates vs invertebrates

A variety of mammals, birds, reptiles and invertebrates ranging in size from Laughing Doves (*Streptopelia senegalensis*) to small grasshoppers was brought to the nest (Table 2). There was no difference in the number of prey items for each size category brought to the nest for the various animal taxa (Kruskal-Wallis, p>0.05). The majority of prey provisioned was vertebrate (Mann-Whitney U-test, p<0.001; Table 3). A slightly higher proportion of vertebrates was provisioned to the control and enlarged broods than to reduced broods, but this was not statistically significant (Kruskal-Wallis, p>0.05).

Table 3. Proportions of vertebrate and invertebrate prey delivered to the nests of enlarged (n=3), control (n=5) and reduced broods (n=4). Proportions are not significantly different from one another (Kruskall-Wallis, p>0.05).

NEST SITE	*Vertebrates*	*Invertebrates*	*Unknown*
Enlarged:			
Tafelsig/Seesig	51	4	2
Dorstberg Upper section	39	26	2
Kommetjie	46	6	13
TOTAL	136 (72%)	36 (19%)	17 (9%)
Control:			
Rondeberg Quarry Lower west	30	4	3
Escom Nestbox	21	0	0
Durbanville Quarry	15	2	0
Tygerberg Hospital	9	0	1
Lion's Head - South	3	6	0
TOTAL	78 (83%)	12 (13%)	4 (4%)
Reduced:			
Rondeberg Quarry Upper east	33	5	0
Tygerberg Quarry	16	0	0
Rondeberg Quarry Lower Middle	6	21	6
Devil's Peak	14	3	2
TOTAL	69 (65%)	29 (27%)	8 (8%)

Strike rates within 100 metres of the nest site

Females made significantly more strikes around the nest (<100m away) than males (2.28 vs. 0.71 strikes per 14 hour day respectively; Mann Whitney U-test, p<0.005). There was no difference in strike rates or strike success close to the nest for either sex between treatments and controls.

Caching

Prey was cached when chicks refused the food, when food had been recently provided to the brood or when the female refused food from the male. There was no significant variation in the delivery rate through the day for reduced, control and enlarged broods (ANOVA, F=0.07, p=0.97; F=0.69, p=0.57; F=2.31, p=0.15 respectively) suggesting that food was not cached becuase of irregular food supply through the day. There was no significant difference in the number of days that caching was observed or in the rate of caching by pairs with different brood sizes (Kruskal-Wallis, p>0.05). However, caching of prey brought to the nest site was performed more frequently for reduced (89%; 8 of 9 observation days) than control (36%; 4 of 11 observation days) and enlarged (43%; 3 of 7 observation days) broods. All pairs of the four reduced broods cached prey, while three of the five control pairs and only one of three pairs with enlarged broods cached prey. On average, reduced broods also had a higher caching rate (3.2 caches per day) than control and enlarged broods (1.3 and 1.0 caches per day respectively).

Provisioning rate and nest attendance

There was a negative correlation between provisioning rate and nest attendance for daily values for all the pairs combined (items provided per hour = 98.2 - (15.98 * nest attendance); p=0.002; r^2=31.75; n=27). This suggests that parents sacrificed time spent attending the nest in order to hunt.

Nestling survival and growth

Sample sizes were too small to statistically analyse the effect of increased brood size on nestling survival and growth. However, there were no differences in either mass or wing lengths of similarly-aged nestlings in enlarged, control and reduced broods (Fig. 7). All nestlings of observed broods survived past 25 days old, although one fledgling was recovered dead below the nest of an enlarged brood soon after leaving the nest. All the nestlings of one enlarged brood were killed by a snake and one reduced brood disappeared between the manipulation and first observation day (Table 1).

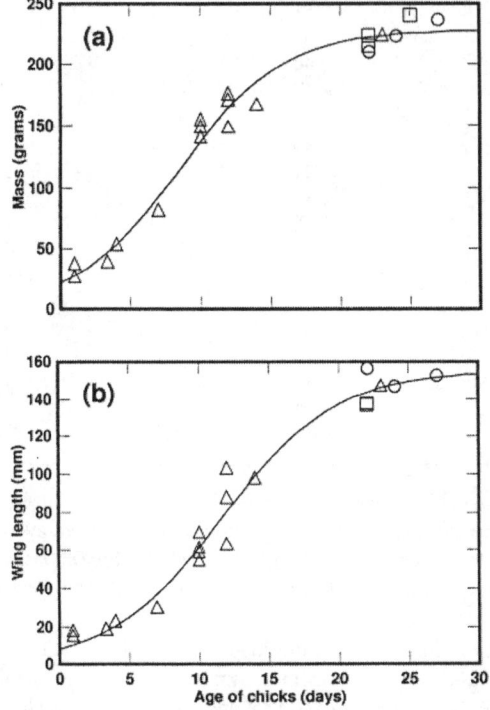

Figure 7: Growth rates of nestlings of enlarged (□), control (Δ) and reduced (O) broods using (a) nestling mass and (b) nestling wing length as indicators of growth.

Other brood manipulations

The majority of brood enlargements have shown that birds are able to raise more nestlings than determined by clutch size (reviewed in Dijkstra *et al.* 1990; Stearns 1992; Table 4). However, this has been demonstrated less conclusively at low and mid-latidudes, (10 of 17 studies, 59%) than at high latitudes (24 of 29 studies, 83%; c^2=3.74, d.f.=1, p=0.052; Table 4). Studies at low and mid-latitudes have more frequently demonstrated decreases in fledgling body mass (11 of 15 studies, 73%) and survival to fledging (11 of 16 studies, 69%) than have studies at high latitudes (10 of 20 studies, 50%, c^2=6.07, d.f.=1, p=0.013 and 13 of 25 studies, 52%, c^2=7.32, d.f.=1, p=0.007; Table 4). The influence of brood enlargements was lower at low and mid-latitudes than at high latitudes on the body mass (0% vs 83%), survival (0% vs 43%) and future reproductive performance of parents (25% vs 57%; Table 4).

Table 4. Results of brood manipulation experiments at low, mid- and high latitudes. Life-history details of offspring and parents are indicated as an increase (+), decrease (-) or no difference from controls (0). Fledge = number of offspring that left the nest; Survival -fledge = survival of nestlings until fledging; Survival-season = survival of fledglings until autumn or the next breeding season; Future breeding = future breeding performance of the parents

Species	Offspring Fledge	Body mass	Survival -fledge	Survival -season	Parents Body mass	Survival	Future breeding	Latitude	Hemisphere	Reference
Low latitudes (0° - 23° latitude)										
Puffinus puffinus	-	-	-		0			0	S	Harris (1969)
Oceanodroma castro	-		-					0	S	Harris (1969)
Creagrus furcatus	+	0	0		0	0		0		Harris (1970)
Sula sula	-		-					8	S	Nelson (1966)
Rostrhamus sociabilis			-					10	N	Beissinger (1990)
Quelea quelea	0	0	-					10	N	Ward (1965)
Aerodramus spodiopygius	0	-	-					18	S	Tarburton (1987)
Mid-latitudes (24° - 45° latitude)										
Accipiter rufiventris		-	-					29	S	Simmons (1986)
Diomedea immutabilis	-	-						30	N	Rice & Kenyon (1962)
Sula capensis	+				0			32	S	Jarvis (1974)
Sula capensis	+	-						33	S	Navarro (1991)
Falco tinnunculus	+	0	0					34	S	this study
Ficedula hypoleuca	+	-	-		0		0	40	N	Sanz (1997)
Passer domesticus	+	-	0		0	0	-	40	N	Hegner & Wingfield (1987)
Troglodytes aedon	+	0	0		0		0	40	N	Finke, Milinkovich & Thompson (1987)
Troglodytes aedon	+	-					0	40	N	Robinson & Rotenberry (1991)
Eudyptula minor	+	-	0					40	S	Dann (1988)
Puffinus tenuirostris	0	-	-					41	S	Norman & Gottish (1969)
Agelaius phoeniceus	+	-	-					42	N	Cronmiller & Thompson (1980)
High latitudes (46° - 90° latitude)										
Larus glaucescens	+		0					50	N	Vermeer (1963)
Fratercula arctica	-		-					50	N	Nettleship (1972)
Larus argentatus	+	0	0					50	N	Haymes & Morris (1977)
Falco sparverius	+	-						50	N	Gard & Bird (1992)
Ficedula hypoleuca	+	-	0	0				51	N	Von Haartman (1954)
Parus caeruleus	+		0	0	-		0	51	N	Nur (1984a, 1984b, 1988b)
Alca torda	+	-						51	N	Lloyd (1977)
Delichon urbica	+	0	0					51	N	Bryant (1975)
Fratercula arctica	+							52	N	Corkhill (1973)
Columba palumbus	+	-		0				52	N	Murton, Westwood & Isaacson (1974)
Passer domesticus	+	-						52	N	Schifferli (1978)
Apus apus	-		-					52	N	Perrins (1964)
Parus major	+				0			52	N	Boyce & Perrins (1987); Pettifor, Perrins & McCleery (1988)
Larus fuscus	+	0	0					52	N	Harris & Plumb (1965)
Branta canadensis	0	0	0	0	-		-	53	N	Lessels (1986)
Falco tinnunculus	+	-	-	0	-	-	0	53	N	Dijkstra, et al. (1990)
Ficedula hypoleuca	0	-	-	-	-		-	55	N	Askenmo (1977, 1979)
Parus major	+	-	-	-			-	55	N	Smith, Kallander & Nilsson (1987, 1989)
Corvus corone	+	0	-					55	N	Loman (1980)
Sula bassna	+	-	-					56	N	Nelson (1964)
Pica pica	-	0	-					56	N	Hogstedt (1980)
Ficedula hypoleuca	+	-	-		-			56	N	Kallander & Smith (1990)
Delichon urbica	+	-	-					56	N	Bryant & Westerterp (1983)
Cepphus grylle	+	0	0					57	N	Asbirk (1979)
Ficedula albicollis	+			-		0	-	57	N	Gustafsson & Sutherland (1988)
Stercorarius longicaudus	+		0					60	N	Andersson (1976)
Corvus frugilegus	+				0		-	62	N	Roskaft (1985)
Aegolius funereus	+	0	0		0	0	0	63	N	Korpimaki (1988)
Pica pica		0	0	-				63	N	Husby (1986)
Turdus pilarus	+	0	0					63	N	Slagsvold (1982)

553

DISCUSSION

Among Common Kestrels studied by Dijkstra et al. (1990) in the Netherlands, a high latitude environment, nestlings in enlarged broods had slower growth rates and higher mortality rates than control broods. Nonetheless, parents were still able to fledge more young than determined by natural clutch size. As in this study, these birds were able to increase their provisioning rate by both parents allocating more time to hunting for the brood, resulting in enlarged broods receiving as much food per nestling as control broods. Unnaturally large broods did, however, have a negative impact on fledgling survival and reproductive success of the adults in the following year. Prey population dynamics are different at different latitudes (Hansson & Henttonen 1985) and it is possible that prey availability is lower at mid- or low latitudes (Beissinger 1990). This study showed, however, that kestrels are able to raise artificially increased broods, suggesting that clutch size is not limited by the ability of adults to provision offspring. However, this study could not determine whether such provisioning compromised future reproductive output of the adults.

Kestrels can increase the amount of food delivered to a nest by increasing their time spent hunting, increase the proportion of hover hunting to perch hunting, increasing their strike rate or by catching larger prey. Most hunting was away from the nest, so hunting duration was not recorded in this study and nor were strike rate and prey capture success. Parents of enlarged broods spent on average more time away from the nest than parents of control and reduced broods (Fig. 2). As there was a significant correlation between provisioning rate and time away from the nest, these results suggest that strike rate and prey capture success were similar between control and manipulated broods and that the differences in food deliveries were due to differences in the time spent hunting. A comparison of the number of prey items provisioned per day (Fig. 6a) and the number of grams provided to the brood per day (Fig. 6b) could be used to determine whether the increased time hunting was used only to increase the number of prey provisioned or if there was also an increase in the size of prey brought to the nest. The extent of increase in the number of prey items delivered per day and the number of grams of prey provisioned per day did not differ, indicating that parents increased the amount of food for the nestlings by increasing the hunting time and thus the number of prey items caught. There was no difference in the frequency of prey delivered for the various size categories (Table 2), nor for the proportions of vertebrate and invertebrate prey (Table 3) between the manipulations.

Parents of enlarged broods were able to provide as much food per nestling to their brood as control pairs (Fig. 6c). Evidence from this study suggests that kestrels at mid-latitudes are easily able to provision enough food to their chicks. If the females were under pressure to provision more food to enlarged broods, it would have been expected that they would have spent a proportion of their time hunting around the nest site while attending the brood. Females hunted more than males at the nest site but those tending enlarged broods did not make more strikes there than females with control and reduced broods.

When surplus food is available, kestrels cache food during the breeding season to spread the food delivery to the nest throughout the day and to exploit hunting opportunities during the best time of day (Village 1990). In this study, food was delivered regularly throughout the day by males in control and manipulated broods. This suggests that food was not cached because of food resources only being available during certain hours of the day. In situations where food was short, parent kestrels fed prey items directly to the brood rather than cache food. Although kestrels provisioning enlarged broods did cache some prey, most prey caching was recorded for the control and, especially, the reduced broods. This suggests that broods of six or seven are close to the maximum size that the kestrels were able to successfully raise. The advantages of food surpluses, as seen in reduced broods, may be reflected later by allowing the parents to be in better condition the following breeding season or to have a second brood in the same season (Van Heerden et al. 1994).

Dijkstra et al. (1990) showed that male kestrels tending reduced broods reduced their hunting time and females virtually stopped hunting. The response of parents to reduced broods in this study varied. Some pairs were no different to control birds in terms of nest attendance and provisioning rates. Individual nestlings in reduced broods received on average more food than control and increased broods due to the fewer nestlings in the nest (Fig. 6c) although this was not reflected in chick growth or fledging success.

Clutch and brood sizes increase with latitude within and among several bird species (Payne 1976; Ricklefs 1980; Hussel 1985) and it has been suggested that food availability constrains clutch sizes at low latitudes (Simmons 1986; Beissinger 1990). The purpose of this study was to test whether birds at mid-latitudes are able to raise enlarged broods. Most brood manipulation studies have been conducted at high latitudes (Table 4) making latitudinal comparisons difficult. Results of the brood manipulations suggest that clutch sizes of birds at low and mid-latitudes are constrained, possibly by food supply, but also that parents fare better raising smaller broods. Other factors may also be involved. For instance, reduced offspring survival in enlarged broods of Barn Swallows *Hirundo rustica* has been attributed to a lowered immunocompetence (Saino *et al.* 1997).

This study does not support the hypothesis that brood size at mid-latitudes is regulated by food availability. However, there are several studies which do provide evidence in support of this hypothesis (Simmons 1986; 1989a; 1997). American Kestrels at a high latitude (50°N) were able to successfully raise enlarged broods during a year with high rodent numbers but not in a poor year (Gard & Bird 1992). However, Common Kestrels in Finland (63°N) were unable to successfully raise enlarged broods in both good and bad vole years (Korpimaki & Rita 1996). My own study on Common Kestrels was conducted during one season to minimize seasonal effects on the experimental manipulation and it is possible that it was conducted in a particularly "good" year, resulting in better success than normal. However, there are no data to support this and rodent counts conducted by Jarvis in the Cape Peninsula nature reserve were not unusually high during the year of this study (*pers. comm.*). Common Kestrels lay on average smaller clutches in South Africa than in Europe (Van Zyl 1994) but are able to raise larger broods (this study). The restraint to produce larger broods could possibly be due to having more than one brood per season as has been recorded in the study area (Van Heerden, *et al.* 1994) or because they live longer than their high latitude counterparts.

ACKNOWLEDGEMENTS

I would like to thank my supervisors, Alan Kemp and Phil Hockey for their support during this study. Sally Newton, Rob Simmons and Andrew Jenkins provided critical comments on previous drafts of this paper and MornÇ du Plessis is thanked for his encouragement. Bill Branch, Martin Whiting, Bill Bateman and Rob Toms helped to identify prey items from descriptions in my field notes. This study was funded by the Transvaal Museum and Dr Rautenbach is thanked for allowing time away from the museum to conduct the field work. The Percy FitzPatrick Institute of African Ornithology provided logistic support and office space during the fieldwork.

REFERENCES

ANDERSSON, M. 1976. Clutch size in the Long-tailed Skua *Stercorarius longicaudus*: some field experiments. *Ibis* 118:586-588.
ANALYTICAL SOFTWARE 1996. Statistix for Windows version 1.0.
ASBIRK, S. 1979. The adaptive significance of reproductive pattern in the black guillemot *Cepphus grylle*. *Videnskaplige Meddelelser Dansk naturhistorisk Forening* 141:29-80.
ASKENMO, C. 1977. Effects of addition and removal of nestlings on nestling weight, nestling survival and female weight loss in the Pied Flycatcher *Fidelcula hypoleuca* (Pallas). *Ornis Scand.* 8:1-8.
ASKENMO, C. 1979. Reproductive effort and return rate of male Pied Flycatchers. *Am. Nat.* 114:748-753.
BEISSINGER, S. R. 1990. Experimental brood manipulations and the monoparental threshold in snail kites. *Am. Nat.* 136:20-38.
BENGTSSON, H., & O. RYDEN 1983. Parental feeding rate in relation to begging behaviour in asynchronously hatched broods of the Great Tit *Parus major*. *Behav. Ecol. Sociobiol.* 12:243-251.
BOYCE, M. S., & C. M. PERRINS 1987. Optimizing Great Tit clutch size in a fluctuating environment. *Ecology* 68:142-153.
BRYANT, D. M. 1975. Breeding biology of House Martins *Delichon urbica* in relation to aerial insect abundance. *Ibis* 117:180-215.

BRYANT, D. M., & K. R. WESTERTERP 1983. Time and energy limits to brood size in House Martins (*Delichon urbica*). *J. Anim. Ecol.* 52:905-925.

CODY, M. L. 1966. A general theory of clutch size. *Evolution* 20:174-184.

CORKHILL, P. 1973. Food and feeding ecology of Puffins. *Bird Study* 20:207-220.

CRONMILLER, J. R., & C. F. THOMPSON 1980. Experimental manipulation of brood size in Red-winged Blackbirds. *Auk* 97:559-565.

COWLING, R. M., I. A. W. MACDONALD & M. T. SIMMONS 1996. The Cape Peninsula, South Africa: physiographical, biological and historical background to an extraordinary hot-spot of biodiversity. *Biodiv. Conserv.* 5:527-550.

DANN, P. 1988. An experimental manipulation of clutch size in the Little Penguin *Eudyptula minor*. *Emu* 88:101-103.

DE STEVEN, D. 1980. Clutch size, breeding success, and parental survival in the Tree Swallow (*Iridoprocne bicolor*). *Evolution* 34:278-291.

DIJKSTRA, C., A. BULT, S. BIJLSMA, S. DAAN, T. MEIJER & M. ZIJLSTRA 1990. Brood size manipulations in the kestrel (*Falco tinnunculus*): Effects on offspring and parent survival. *J. Anim. Ecol.* 59:269-285.

FINKE, M. A., D. J. MILINKOVICH & C. F. THOMPSON 1987. Evolution of clutch size: An experimental test in the House Wren (*Troglodytes aedon*). *J. Anim. Ecol.* 56:99-114.

GARD, N.W. & D.M. BIRD 1992. Nestling growth and fledging success in manipulated American Kestrel broods. *Can. J. Zool.* 70:2421-2425.

GUSTAFSSON, L. & W. J. SUTHERLAND 1988. The costs of reproduction in the collared flycatcher *Ficedula albicollis*. *Nature* 335:813-815.

HANSSON, L. & H. HENTTONEN 1985. Gradients in density variations of small rodents: the importance of latitude and snow cover. *Oecologia* 67:394-402.

HARRIS, M. P. 1969. The biology of stormpetrels in the Galapagos Islands. *Proceedings of the California Academy of Science* 37:95-166.

HARRIS, M. P. 1970. Breeding ecology of the Swallow-tailed Gull, *Creagrus furcatus*. *Auk* 87:215-243.

HARRIS, M. P. & W. J. PLUMB 1965. Experiments on the ability of Herring Gulls *Larus argentatus* and Lesser Black-backed Gulls *L. fuscus* to raise larger than normal broods. *Ibis* 107:256-257.

HAYMES, G. T, & R. D. MORRIS 1977. Brood size manipulations in Herring Gulls. *Can. J. Zool.* 55:1762-1766.

HEGNER, R. E. & J. C. WINGFIELD 1987. Effects of brood-size manipulations on parental investment, breeding success and reproductive endocrinology of House Sparrows. *Auk* 104:470-480.

HOGSTEDT, G. 1980. Evolution of clutch size in birds: adaptive variation in relation to territory quality. *Science* 210:1148-1150.

HURLBERT, S.H. 1984. Pseudoreplication and the design of ecological field experiments. *Ecological Monographs* 54: 187-211.

HUSBY, M. 1986. On the adaptive value of brood reduction in birds: experiments with the Magpie *Pica pica*. *J. Anim. Ecol.* 55:75-83.

HUSSEL, D. J. T. 1985. Clutch size, day length, and seasonality of resources: comments on Ashmole's hypothesis. *Auk* 102:632-634.

JARVIS, M. J. F. 1974. The ecological significance of clutch size in the South African Gannet (*Sula capensis*), (Lichtenstein). *J. Anim. Ecol.* 43:1-17.

KALLANDER, H. & H. G. SMITH 1990. Manipulation of the brood size of Pied Flycatchers. In: J. Blondel, A. Gosler, J. D. Lebreton & R. McCleery (Eds.); Population biology of passerine birds, *NATO ASI Series* G24: 257-268. Springer-Verlag, Berlin.

KLOMP, H. 1970. The determination of clutch size in birds. *Ardea* 58:1-124.

KORPIMAKI, E. 1988. Costs of reproduction and success of manipulated broods under varying food conditions in Tengmalm's Owl. *J. Anim. Ecol.* 57:1027-1039.

KORPIMAKI, E. & H. RITA 1996. Effects of brood size manipulations on offspring and parental survival in the European Kestrel under fluctuating food conditions. *Ecoscience* 3: 264-273.

LACK, D. 1954. *The natural regulation of animal numbers*. Clarendon Press Oxford.

LACK, D. 1966. *Population studies of birds*. Clarendon Press Oxford.

LESSELS, C.M. 1986. Brood size in Canada Geese: a manipulation experiment. *J. Anim. Ecol.* 55:669-689.

LLOYD, C. S. 1977. The ability of the Razorbill *Alca torda* to raise an additional chick to fledging. *Ornis Scand.* 8:155-159.

LOMAN, J. 1980. Brood size optimization and adaption among Hooded Crows *Corvus corone*. *Ibis* 122:494-500.

MASMAN, D., C. DIJKSTRA, S. DAAN & A. BULT 1989. Energetic limitation of avian parental effort: Field experiments in the kestrel (*Falco tinnunculus*). *J. Evol. Biol.* 2:435-455.
MEIJER, T., S. DAAN & M. HALL 1990. Family planning in the kestrel (*Falco tinnunculus*): The proximate control of covariation of laying date and clutch size. *Behaviour* 114:117-136.
MONAGHAN, P. & R.G. NAGER 1997. Why don't birds lay more eggs? *TREE* 12: 270-274.
MURTON, R. K., N. J. WESTWOOD & A. J. ISAACSON 1974. Factors affecting egg-weight, body-weight and moult of the woodpigeon *Columba palumbus*. *Ibis* 116:52-73.
NAVARRO, R. A. 1991. Food addition and twinning experiments in the Cape Gannet: effects on breeding success and chick growth and behaviour. *Colonial Waterbirds* 14:92-102.
NELSON, J. B. 1964. Factors influencing clutch-size and chick growth in the North Atlantic Gannet *Sula bassana*. *Ibis* 106:63-77.
NELSON, J. B. 1966. Clutch size in the Sulidae. *Nature* 210:435-436.
NETTLESHIP, D. N. 1972. Breeding success of the common puffin (*Fratercula artica L.*) on different habitats at Great Island, Newfoundland. *Ecological Monographs* 42:239-268.
NORMAN, F. I. & M. D. GOTTISH 1969. Artificial twinning in the short-tailed shearwater *Puffinus tenuirostris*. *Ibis* 111:391-393.
NUR, N. 1984a. The consequences of brood size for breeding blue tits. I. Adult survival, weight change and the cost of reproduction. *J. Anim. Ecol.* 53:479-496.
NUR, N. 1984b. The consequences of brood size for breeding blue tits. II. Nestling weight, offspring survival and optimal brood size. *J. Anim. Ecol.* 53:497-517.
NUR, N. 1988a. The cost of reproduction in birds: An examination of the evidence. *Ardea* 76:155-168.
NUR, N. 1988b. The consequences of brood size for breeding blue tits. III. Measuring the cost of reproduction: survival, future fecundity, and differential dispersal. *Evolution* 42:351-362.
PAYNE, R.B. 1976. Clutch size and number of eggs of Brownheaded Cowbirds: Effects of latitude and breeding season. *Condor* 78:337-342.
PERRINS, C. 1964. Survival of young Swifts in relation to brood size. *Nature* 201:1147-1148.
PETTIFOR, R. A., C. M. PERRINS & R. H. MCCLEERY 1988. Individual optimization of clutch size in great tits. *Nature* 336:160-162.
REID, W. V. 1987. The cost of reproduction in the glaucous-winged gull. *Oecologia* 74:458-467.
REZNICK, D. 1985. Costs of reproduction: an evaluation of the empirical evidence. *Oikos* 44:257-267.
REZNICK, D. 1992. Measuring the costs of reproduction. *TREE* 7:42-45.
RICE, D. W. & K. W. KENYON 1962. Breeding cycles and behavior of Laysan and black-footed albatrosses. *Auk* 79:517-567.
RICKLEFS, R. E. 1980. Geographical variation in clutch size among passerine birds: Ashmole's hypothesis. *Auk* 97:38-49.
ROBINSON, K. D. & J. T. ROTENBERRY 1991. Clutch size and reproductive success of House Wrens rearing natural and manipulated broods. *Auk* 108:277-284.
ROSKAFT, E. 1985. The effect of enlarged brood size on the future reproductive potential of the Rook. *J. Anim. Ecol.* 54:255-260.
SAINO, N., S. CALZA & A. P. MOLLER 1997. Immunocompetence of nestling barn swallows in relation to brood size and parental effort. *J. Anim. Ecol.* 66:827-836.
SANZ, J.J. 1997. Clutch size manipulation in the Pied Flycatcher: effects on nestling growth, parental care and moult. *J. Avian Biol.* 28:157-162.
SCHIFFERLI, L. 1978. Experimental modification of brood size among House Sparrows *Passer domesticus*. *Ibis* 120:365-369.
SIMMONS, R. 1986. Food provisioning, nestling growth and experimental manipulation of brood size in the African Redbreasted Sparrowhawk *Accipiter rufiventris*. *Ornis Scandinavica* 17:31-40.
SIMMONS, R. 1989a. Adaptation and constraint in the breeding of subtropical harriers and eagles. Ph.D. Dissertation, University of the Witwatersrand, Johannesburg.
SIMMONS, R. 1989b. The importance and assessment of food provisioning rates for African birds. *Tauraco* 1:211-216.
SIMMONS, R. 1997. Why don't all siblicidal eagles lay insurance eggs? The egg quality hypothesis. *Behav. Ecol.* 8: 544-550.
SLAGSVOLD, T. 1982. Clutch size, nest size, and hatching asynchrony in birds: Experiments with the Fieldfare (*Turdus pilaris*). *Ecology* 63:1389-1399.
SMITH, H. G., H. KALLANDER & J. A. NILSSON 1989. The trade-off between offspring number and quality in the great tit *Parus major*. *J. Anim. Ecol.* 58:383-402.
STEARNS, S. C. 1992. *The evolution of life histories*. Oxford University Press, New York.
STCS, INC. 1984. Statgraphics version 4.00.

TARBURTON, M. K. 1987. An experimental manipulation of clutch and brood size of White-rumped Swiftlets *Aerodramus spodiopygius* of Fiji. *Ibis* 129:107-114.
TINBERGEN, J. M. 1987. Cost of reproduction in the Great Tit: Intraseasonal cost associated with brood size. *Ardea* 75:111-122.
VAN HEERDEN, P., A. ELLMANN & B. VAN ZYL 1994. Multiple breeding by Rock Kestrels in the Tygerberg residential area. *Birding in SA* 46:119-122.
VAN ZYL, A. J. 1993. Aspects of the foraging and breeding ecology of the Southern African Kestrel, *Falco tinnunculus rupicolus*. M.Sc. Thesis, University of Cape Town, Cape Town.
VAN ZYL, A. J. 1994. A comparison of the diet of the Common Kestrel *Falco tinnunculus* in South Africa and Europe. *Bird Study* 41:124-130.
VAN ZYL, A. J. in press. Breeding biology of the Common Kestrel in southern Africa (32°S) compared to studies in Europe (53°N). *Ostrich*.
VERMEER, K. 1963. The breeding ecology of the glaucous-winged gull *Larus glaucescens* on Mandarte Island. *Occasional Papers British Columbia Provincial Museum* 13:1-104.
VILLAGE, A. 1990. *The Kestrel*. T & AD Poyser, London.
VON HAARTMAN, L. 1954. Der Trauerfliegenschnapper. III. Die Nahrungsbiologie. *Acta Zoologica Fennica* 83:1-196.
WARD, P. 1965. The breeding biology of the black-faced dioch *Quelea quelea* in Nigeria. *Ibis* 107:326-349.

Anthony J. van Zyl
Bird Department, Transvaal Museum
P.O Box 413
Pretoria 0001, South Africa

Chancellor, R. D. & B.-U. Meyburg eds. 2000
Raptors at Risk
WWGBP / Hancock House

Feeding ecology of Javan Hawk-eagle *Spizaetus bartelsi* during the nestling period

Dewi M. Prawiradilaga, Nils Rov, Jan Ove Gjershaug, Hapsoro and Adam Supriatna

ABSTRACT

The Javan Hawk-eagle is one of the least known raptors in the world, an endangered and endemic bird of prey of Indonesia. Its distribution is limited to forest on the island of Java. The decline in its population has prompted concerns about the availability of prey species. The Javan Hawk-eagle is a medium-sized eagle with a total length of 60-70 cm, with females slightly larger than males. Its feeding behaviour and diet have been studied by observations and analyses of regurgitated pellets and prey remains. In West Java, this species preys upon a wide range of animals including small and medium-sized mammals, birds and reptiles. In our study, the most common prey species were squirrels (Sciuridae), treeshrews (Tupaiidae), rodents (Muridae) and bats (Chiroptera). During the nestling period, both parents brought prey to the nest, the male more often in the morning and the female more often in the afternoon. The estimated total number of prey brought to the nest during the nestling period ranged between 109 and 116 animals.

INTRODUCTION

The Javan Hawk-eagle (*Spizaetus bartelsi* Stresemann, 1924) is one of the least known raptors in the world and endemic to Java island, Indonesia. Its distribution is confined to rain forest. In the last few decades, its population has been considered to decline and now it is classified as an endangered species according to current IUCN threat categories (Collar *et al.* 1994).

Many factors may be implicated in the decline of the Javan Hawk-eagle population, including loss of prey and habitat and illegal trapping by people. The role of prey-supply in the declining population is still obscure, because the diet of the Javan Hawk-eagle is poorly documented. Casual observations indicate that domestic chickens (*Gallus* sp.), a large fruit bat (*Cynopterus* sp.), stink badger (*Mydaus javensis*) (Bartels 1924; Becking 1989), squirrels (Linsley in Sozer and Nijman 1995), lizards (van Balen 1991), snakes and medium-sized mammals (Sozer and Nijman 1995) are eaten. In this paper, we present recent information gained on the diet and feeding behaviour, and estimate the total number of prey items taken during the nestling period.

STUDY AREA AND METHODS

Information was gathered by analysing regurgitated pellets and prey remains, by interviewing local people and by field observations.

Study area

General observations on feeding behaviour to identify prey species were conducted during nest surveys at G. Halimun (6°50' S and 106° 32' E), G. Salak (6043í S and 106042í E) and Cibulao, Puncak (6°42' S and 106°59' E).

Pellet collections and analysis

Twelve samples of regurgitated pellets and prey remains were collected from under roosting tree at Cibulao, Puncak and from inside the nest at G. Salak. In the laboratory, samples were sometimes washed with water to remove dirt and then dried for analysis. Prey items were identified by comparison with museum collections, in consultation with the staff.

Feeding observations and analysis

Feeding activities were recorded during intensive nest observations on a pair of breeding Javan Hawk-eagles with their single young at G. Salak between August and October 1997. The pair members were sexed by individual recognition based on plumage differences and size, the female being larger than the male. Data were analysed in one hour intervals. A chi square test was used to examine whether the number of prey brought to the nest in the morning was the same as in the afternoon and a univariate ANOVA test was applied to see if the parents brought prey at mainly different times.

In order to estimate prey consumption, we recorded the rate at which various prey species were delivered to the eaglet. The nest was watched for 37 days, for a total of 276 hours.

RESULTS

Prey species

Small to medium-sized mammals, birds, snakes and lizards were identified either from prey remains, observations or interviews (Table1). Small mammals, in particular squirrels (Sciuridae), tree shrews (Tupaidae), rodents (Muridae) and bats (Chiroptera), were most commonly taken. Because during observations squirrels and treeshrews were often difficult to tell apart, they were lumped in the analysis.Predation pattern

Both male and female parents often came to the nest with prey. If the prey could not be eaten in one meal, they left the remains in the nest. When feeding the eaglet, both parents seemed to feed the oldest prey first.

Prey were often brought to the nest between 06.00 and 12.00 hours and between 14.00 and 16.00 hours (Figure 1), but at a greater frequency in the morning than in the afternoon ($\chi^2 = 13.12$; df = 1; $p < 0.001$)). The male brought prey more often in the morning and female more often in the afternoon (F = 6.3; df = 1; p = 0.02) (Table2).

Table 1. Prey of Javan Hawk Eagle *Spizaetus bartelsi*
Method codes: 1 = field observation
2 = identified prey remains from nest or perching site
3 = information from local people

Species	No. of observations	Method
Mammals		
Common Treeshrew (*Tupaia glis*)	3	1
Ebony Monkey (*Trachypithecus auratus*), young	1	3
Flying lemur (*Cynocephalus variegatus*)	1	3
Diadem Roundleaf Bat (*Hipposideros diadema*)	2	1
Fruitbat (*Cynopterus* sp.)	1	1
Bat (*Chiroptera*)	6	1
Black Giant Squirrel (*Ratufa bicolor*)	1	1
Black-banded Squirrel (*Callosciurus nigrovittatus*)	1	2
Plantain Squirrel (*Callosciurus notatus*)	1	1
Squirrel (*Callosciurus* sp.)	5	1 & 2
Squirrel or Treeshrew	24	1
Rat (*Rattus* sp.)	2	2
Small rodent (*Muridae*)	6	1
Total mammals	**54**	
Birds		
Domestic Chicken (*Gallus gallus*)	2	3
Barred Button-quail (*Turnix suscitator*)	1	2
Emerald Dove (*Chalcophaps indica*)	2	2
Dove (*Streptopelia* sp.)	1	2
Javan Frogmouth (*Batrachostomus javensis*)	1	2
Unidentified bird (Aves)	1	1
Total birds	**8**	
Snakes (Reptilia)	1	3
Lizards (Reptilia)	1	3
Total reptiles	**2**	

Figure 1. Estimated number of prey brought to the nest per hour during nestling period. Numbers above bars depict total observation hours.

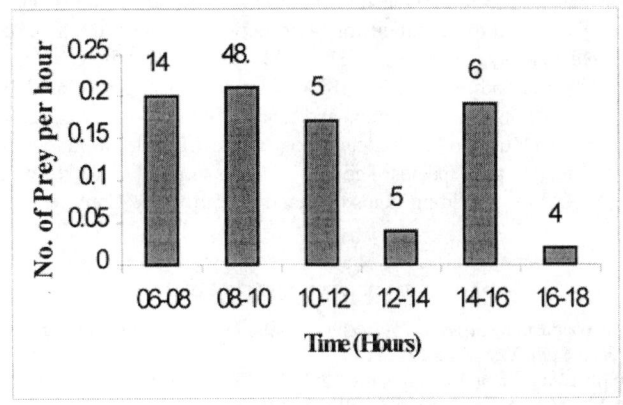

Estimate of total number of prey items during the nestling period

Prey were delivered to the nest during 13.4% of the nest watches. Most prey taken were small mammals (Table 1). Assuming (1) that each watch when prey was brought to the nest represented a predation event, (2) that predation largely involved small mammals,(3) that there were 12 hours of feeding during a day, and (4) that the nestling period ranged from 68 to 72 days, then each pair of Javan Hawk-eagles would kill about 109 to 116 individual small mammals to raise their single chick. The total prey killed is likely to have been much greater, because this figure took insufficient account of prey consumed by the parents.

Table 2.   Number of prey brought to the nest during observations (n=276 hours)

Sex	Time	
	Morning (Before 12 noon)	Afternoon (After 12 noon)
Male	16	5
Female	6	10
Total	22	15

DISCUSSION

The diet of the Javan Hawk-eagle we studied consisted of a wide variety of animals, including mammals, birds and reptiles (Table 1). Evidently, the species was an opportunist predator. However, small to medium-sized mammals, especially squirrels and treeshrews, were often taken. Such species are arboreal and live on low to high branches in primary, as well as in secondary, forests (PPA 1978). At the nest watched, the male brought prey more often in the mornings and the female in the afternoons (Table 2), but further study on sexed individuals is necessary to see whether this behaviour is general.

It seems that the Javan Hawk-eagle took birds less often than the Changeable Hawk-eagle *Spizaetus cirrhatus*, but otherwise their diets are fairly similar (Hoogerwerf 1949).

ACKNOWLEDGEMENTS

We proudly acknowledge that this study was carried out as a part of an environmental cooperation between Indonesia and Norway. We are grateful to the Indonesian Institute of Sciences (LIPI) for giving research permits to the Norwegian researchers, the State Ministry for Environment (LH) for fruitful cooperation and the Directorate General of Forest Protection and Nature Conservation (PHPA)-Ministry of Forestry and Perum Perhutani for permission to work in the study areas. We thank BirdLife International-Indonesia Programme, Harry, Mulyadi, Bob, Arbi, Dwi (Telapak members), Usep Suparman, Eddy, Mulyadi, Bapa Dili (CIBA members), local people at G. Salak, especially Pak Ocen, Pak Otang, Pak Onyon, G. Halimun and especially Pak Kokon for their help during field work, and M.H. Sinaga (Museum Zoologicum Bogoriense-LIPI) for valuable assistance during identification of mammalian prey species. The first author is grateful to the Norwegian Institute for Nature Research (NINA) for providing funds to attend the 5th World Conference on Birds of Prey and Owls.

REFERENCES

BARTELS, M. 1924. Waarnemingen omtrent *Spizaetus cirrhatus limnaetus* Hors. en *Spizaetus nipalensis kelaarti* Legge op Java. *Jaarber. Club. Ned. Vogelk.*14: 11-21.
BECKING, J.H. 1989. *Henry Jacob Victor Sody (1892-1959). His Life & Work.* Leiden: E.J. Brill. Netherlands.
COLLAR, N.J., M.J. CROSBY & A.J. STTAERSFIELD 1994. Birds to watch 2: The world list of threatened birds. *BirdLife Conservation Series* No. 4. BirdLife International, Cambridge.
DIREKTORAT PERLINDUNGAN DAN PENGAWETAN ALAM (PPA), DIT.JEN. KEHUTANAN 1978. *Mamalia di Indonesia.* Pedoman Inventarisasi Satwa. Bogor.
HOOGERWERF, A. 1949. *De avifauna van Tjibodas en omgeving (Java).* Koninklijke Plantetuin van Indonesie, Buitenzorg.

SOZER, R. & V. NIJMAN. 1995. Behavioural ecology, distribution and conservation of the Javan Hawk-eagle *Spizaetus bartelsi* Stresemann, 1924. Verslagen en Technische Gegeven No. 62. University of Amsterdam. The Netherlands.

VAN BALEN, S. 1991. The Java Hawk eagle *Spizaetus bartelsi*: WWGBP project report No. 1, March 1990. WWGBP Birds of Prey Bulletin 4: 33-40.

Dewi M. Prawiradilaga
R & D Centre for Biology-LIPI
Flora and Fauna International
Indonesia Programme
P.O. Box 230, Bogor 16002
Indonesia

Nils Rov and Jan Ove Gjershaug
NINA.NIKU
Tungasletta 2
7005 Trondheim
Norway

Hapsoro
Telapak Indonesia
Jalan Sempur Kaler No. 16
Bogor 16154
Indonesia

Adam Supriatna
KPB CIBA, Kotak Pos 66
Sindanglaya
Cianjur 43253
Indonesia

Chancellor, R. D. & B.-U. Meyburg eds. 2000
Raptors at Risk
WWGBP / Hancock House

Socio-Economic Problems and Solutions in Raptor Predation

R.E. Kenward

ABSTRACT

Raptors can cause problems (a) for farmers through killing domestic animals, (b) for hunters by competing for a sustainable yield of game, and (c) for conservationists through direct and indirect impacts on other species in managed landscapes. Predation on domestic animals, and on game at release or feeding sites, can sometimes be prevented by (i) exclusion or (ii) landscaping techniques. Occasional use has also been made of (iii) deterrent, (iv) distraction and (v) pre-emption measures, all of which offer scope for further study. Economic loss from predation may also usefully be offset by eco-tourism, by predation on other problem species or by statutory compensation, provided that such payments do not drain conservation resources with no net gain for biodiversity. With few human resources available for maintaining biodiversity in increasingly managed landscapes, it is important that groups interested in different aspects of wildlife conservation should cooperate and not divert resources into disputes about total protection. New data show that early analyses overestimated juvenile mortality of some raptor species, and thus underestimated the density of non-breeders in healthy habitats and the ability of populations to sustain removal of first-year individuals without reduction in numbers breeding. Live-trapping on kills can selectively remove problem individuals, which are often dispersing juveniles. Selective removal of live raptors, based on agreements between interested parties to seek non-lethal approaches, to prevent general persecution or gratuitous killing of raptors and to monitor health of the managed populations, may be preferable to the illegal poisoning and shooting that can result when raptor predation is thought to threaten human livelihoods.

INTRODUCTION

The study of predation raises questions that are fundamental to the conservation of wildlife and wild places. A first question could be "is there a genuine problem for humans from this predation?" A follow-up might well be "can the problem be solved economically without putting any species at risk of local extinction?" However, it is important also to ask "is the solution cost-effective for conservation?"

As a hypothetical example, imagine a wild prey species that is abundant enough for humans to harvest, provided that numbers of natural predators are reduced; humans are competing with other predators for the prey. Let's say that areas of ground are at first reserved for harvesting that prey, to the benefit of associated species, but that public opinion then moves towards protecting the predators. One solution to the resulting conflict between prey-harvesters and predator-protectors could be to breed the prey in enclosures. This might be a very cost-effective solution, enabling a higher stocking density than in the wild, with efficient growth and harvest of the prey's food as an intensive crop. However, the result would also be an increasingly managed landscape, that might well support fewer wild prey and fewer predators overall. What if public desire to protect predators then evolved into antipathy towards hunting or even eating animals at all? In Britain, such attitudes are leading to greatly changed land-use, habitat fragmentation and increasing isolation of wildlife in reserves.

The following is a brief review of ways to alleviate problems caused by predation. It does not repeat the more detailed considerations given in previous publications (Kenward & Marcström 1981, Kenward 1986, Kenward 1999), but draws attention to the wider economic and conservation implications of different solutions to problems from raptor predation. Some ways to reduce predation are convenient because they are inexpensive and relatively effective. Others deserve further study, because even if they prove impractical, the research into them may tell us more about predation mechanisms and give us new ideas for solving problems. However, it is important also to note new findings that raptors in prey-rich habitats can be as robust a renewable resource as many of their prey. When failure of measures to alleviate predation economically puts other aspects of conservation at risk, it may be appropriate to relax demands for absolute protection of raptors in favour of population management, provided that a return to wholesale persecution can be avoided.

SUFFERING FROM PREDATION

Raptors can cause problems (a) for livestock owners through killing domestic animals, (b) for hunters by competing for a sustainable yield of game, and (c) for conservationists through direct and indirect impacts on biodiversity in managed landscapes. Often, these problems are not distributed equally across all situations, but are severe in some cases and unimportant elsewhere (Lloyd 1976, Davies in press). This may be because prey are in some circumstances unusually vulnerable to any predator, or because an individual predator becomes a specialist on the prey, or both. For example, surveys of Buzzard *Buteo buteo* predation at pens of released Pheasants *Phasianus colchicus* showed an average take of 4%, but a distribution of kills ranging from none at many pens to more than 20% of the pheasants at a minority (Kenward *et al.* in review a). The pens with heavy predation had little shrub cover, much deciduous canopy and few Pheasants relative to the size of pen. Independent tracking of radio-tagged Buzzards showed that only 8% associated strongly with Pheasant pens, and especially where there was much deciduous canopy to provide perches and few Pheasants.

Where circumstances render prey especially vulnerable, prevention may be practical in ways outlined below. However, this may not stop individual predators from specialising, for example when Peregrine Falcons *Falco peregrinus* become wedded to a loft of racing Pigeons *Columba livia* near their nest (Musgrove 1996) or a Kestrel *Falco tinnunculus* to a local colony of rare Little Terns *Sterna albifrons* (James 1996). Nor may problems be solved easily when a prey species is strongly preferred by predators, such that they do not switch from it to alternative prey at low density of the favoured prey (functional response Type II rather than Type III of Holling 1959), and may thus have a severe impact if drawn to an area by abundant alternative prey. This was the situation for Goshawks *Accipiter gentilis* taking wild Pheasants in an area where Rabbits *Oryctolaus cunniculus* were abundant (Kenward 1986), and of Hen Harriers *Circus cyaneus* taking Red Grouse *Lagopus lagopus scotticus* in an area with high passerine density (Redpath & Thirgood 1997).

In the past, predation on game and livestock motivated general persecution of raptors, often supported by bounty payments (Newton 1979). This persecution was sometimes intense enough for local extirpation of raptor species, especially in Britain where early industrialisation produced an increased density of humans, an increase in leisure to hunt game and a reduction of woodland habitat below 4% of the land area. More recently, growth of leisure interest in raptors motivated legal protection for them, with added urgency when organochlorines were found to threaten extinction of some populations. Present emphasis is on restoring diversity of raptors to areas from which they were eliminated (Evans *et al.* 1994), but this and the recovery of populations that were previously depressed has increased the call for solutions to predation problems.

BEHAVIOURAL SOLUTIONS

At least five possible behavioural solutions are available to those suffering from raptor predation on domestic animals, or on game at release or feeding sites. The most common are the prevention of predation by (i) exclusion or (ii) landscaping techniques. Excluding raptors from livestock in pens is as old as chicken netting, and justifies its cost by effects on predatory mammals too. Penning livestock for birthing has reduced losses to sheep from Golden Eagles *Aquila chrysaetos* (Murphy 1977), and wires that hinder access can reduce predation at fish farms (Draulens 1987). Landscaping can involve adding cover, as in Pheasant release pens (Lloyd 1975, Kenward *et al.* in review a) or removing trees that offer hunting perches above game release pens or feeding stations (Mikkelsen 1984). The improvement of general landscapes to minimise raptor predation on game is a seductive idea. However, although there are general indications, for example that Grey Partridges *Perdix perdix* suffer reduced raptor predation in areas with few trees (Potts 1984), experimental examples of its value are surprisingly lacking. One possible problem is that the agricultural intensification which removed cover may also have removed food for prey. There is also a risk that improved cover might conceal predators better than prey. Landscaping solutions are easy to suggest, but require experimental studies to show they are effective, economic and free from possible adverse impacts on other species.

Other possible behavioural solutions to raptor predation involve (iii) deterrence, (iv) distraction and (v) pre-emption. Deterrence by visual or auditory stimuli has been proposed, but not shown by robust laboratory or field experiments to be effective. However, following laboratory experiments with taste-repellent chemicals on food for raptors (Brett *et al.* 1976, Musgrove 1996, Nicholls & Bird this volume), the application of repellent or aversive chemicals seems worth trying in the field to deter predators during a short period of high prey vulnerability, such as when game is released. Where raptors are fed artificially at nests, they do not kill so many wild prey or travel so far to hunt, raising the possibility that similar artificial feeding might be used to distract raptors from unwanted predation during the breeding season. Initial trials with Hen Harriers have given promising results (S.M. Redpath and S.G. Thirgood, *pers. comm.*). However, this is an expensive approach, and it is important that increased settlement density in areas where food is provided does not offset reduced predation during breeding with an increase at other times of year. In Sweden, where Goshawk predation on wild Pheasants was low until the arrival of snowcover, it was recommended that shooting should be moved forward to late autumn from its traditional time at Christmas, not only to pre-empt the Goshawk predation but to leave fewer Pheasants to attract hawks into the area (Kenward & Marcström 1981).

FINANCIAL SOLUTIONS

Where none of the five behavioural solutions is practical, conservation bodies may consider paying compensation, for example to farmers that have livestock killed by eagles (Davies in press). However, it is important that statutory compensation payments, and the checks necessary to validate claims, should not drain conservation resources without a net gain for biodiversity.

Compensation for raptor predation can also be indirect. For example, income from eco-tourism might be sought at sites where predation is conspicuous in small areas, such as fish farms. Another consideration is that raptors may themselves compensate for occasional killing of game or livestock by suppressing numbers of other competitors or predators. A fine example is the predation by Black Eagles *Aquila verauxii* on Rock Hyrax *Procavia capensis*. Although the eagles occasionally kill lambs (Davies 1999), they can also suppress hyrax populations, which compete with livestock for food (Davies this volume).

DEMOGRAPHIC SOLUTIONS

When other solutions are impractical or uneconomic, a last resort may be the removal of individual raptors that cause problems. In this case, the principle should be that conservation gains outweigh costs. A potential conservation gain from minimising predation is the maintenance of diverse land-use. If landowners are obliged to tolerate high predation on stock or game, or to pay a high price to reduce it, a marginal land-use may no longer be economic. If this will motivate changes that reduce biodiversity, it seems best to seek cooperation and compromise rather than to create single-species conflicts. A current example from Britain is the problem of Hen Harrier predation on Red Grouse, where joint research in Scotland by the Game Conservancy, Institute of Terrestrial Ecology and Royal Society for the Protection of Birds has shown that Harrier numbers on moorland can increase to a level where few Grouse remain to be shot (Redpath & Thirgood 1997, Thirgood & Redpath this volume), at which point the moorland is likely to be replaced by the more profitable land-uses of intensive forestry or sheep rearing.

Under such circumstances, there may be concern that relaxation of total protection will produce persecution to extinction. However, this fear is not supported by recent experience in countries where limited removal of problem raptors has been allowed. The probable reason is that healthy raptor populations are larger and more resilient than indicated by early population models based on ringing data.

In 26 early analyses of ring recoveries from raptors, the lowest estimate of first-year mortality was 50%, and 17 were more than 60% (Newton 1979). In contrast, extensive radio tagging during the 1980s showed that Goshawks on the Swedish island of Gotland had a first-year mortality of only 42%, and mortality of first-year Buzzards in southern Britain was a maximum 34% in the early 1990s (Kenward et al. in press, in review b). In each case, the proportion of deaths due to humans or impact with human artefacts was overestimated by contemporary ringing data, simply because birds (mainly juveniles) that die in association with people are most likely to be found and reported. On Gotland, 48% of ring recoveries were from Goshawks killed by humans (which was legal to protect poultry) compared with 35% of deaths among radio-tagged hawks, and the ringing data estimated more than 60% first-year mortality. A recovery bias may also have been augmented by persecution and pesticides to give the high first-year mortality estimates from early ringing data.

Juvenile mortalities of 42% for radio-tagged Goshawks and 34% for Buzzards predicted that populations in spring contained 2-4 times as many hawks as were breeding, and this was confirmed by independent tests. The data also predicted that the Goshawk population could have sustained 64% first-year losses without decline in breeding numbers, and the Buzzard population 76% (Kenward et al. in press, in review b). Even lower first-year mortalities, of 10-29%, have been recorded in studies of radio-tagged *Haliaeetus* eagles (Buehler et al. 1991, Bowman et al. 1995, Nygård et al. this volume). Although it has long been recognised that raptor populations contain non-breeders that can replace adults shot at breeding sites (Newton 1979), the underestimation of juvenile survival has resulted in underestimation of non-breeder density, and hence of the ability of some raptor populations to sustain removal.

Nevertheless, where removal of raptors might be the most cost-effective approach for conservation, it is important that techniques should be selective, humane and unlikely to damage overall biodiversity. For example, tests with spring nets set on Pheasant kills showed that all captured birds could be released unharmed and that, unlike box traps baited with live Pigeons, the spring nets caught only Goshawks that were killing Pheasants (Kenward et al. 1983). Moreover, the traps rarely caught hawks of breeding age, so hawks removed were primarily juveniles, which tended to accumulate in areas of high prey density after dispersal, and not the breeding adults (Marcström & Kenward 1981, Kenward et al. 1993). In Sweden, with relatively few areas of released Pheasants, it was practical to release Goshawks alive, because few returned after being translocated more than 30 km away from the site of capture (Marcström & Kenward 1981).

Permitting the setting of spring nets on kills was effectively fail-safe, because it could only be applied where there was a predation problem, and selectively removed only the minority of juvenile hawks that caused problems. Moreover, the live raptors were available for fostering cooperation between different interest groups, through reintroduction projects, research, education and falconry. Conditions of any discussions to consider removal of problem raptors should be the seeking of all possible alternatives to killing, and the promulgation by all parties of the view that general persecution or gratuitous killing of raptors is unacceptable. Another desirable condition would be contribution of effort and resources to monitor impact on the affected populations, for example through mark-recapture estimates based on the live-trapping. All sorts of innovative contributions to conservation may be possible through management of raptor predation problems if minds are opened to all possible solutions.

CONCLUSIONS

Protection of raptors from deliberate destruction has been important for signalling that persecution to extinction is unacceptable, and for drawing attention to the needs of raptors and to the wishes of the wider community. However, where raptors can become abundant enough for their predation to put human livelihoods at risk (Redpath & Thirgood 1997), total protection does not prevent deliberate killing (Etheridge *et al.* 1997). Moreover, rigid protection can hinder management-based conservation projects, waste resources and detract attention from issues of more long-term importance (Kenward 1987). It also motivates illegal use of the least selective techniques, because these often leave the least evidence: poisoning is quieter than shooting which in turn provides less evidence than the safest of all management techniques, live-trapping.

While we are inspired by raptors and may wish their numbers never to be reduced deliberately by humans, we must also appreciate the relative importance of different constraints on persistence of their populations. The pressures on raptor habitats for human agriculture, forestry and living space are huge. Against them, all the human and material resources to conserve wildlife are tiny. However, the interests of farmers and game hunters, against other developers, often overlap with those of other conservationists. Grassland habitats for farming and ranching suit many raptors, as do the even more varied habitats needed for game abundance. It therefore behoves us wherever possible to work with different interest groups, and not to waste resources by fighting to protect each species; persecution to extinction is not the only alternative to total protection. In prey-rich habitats, most raptor populations can probably sustain selective loss of some individuals to protect livestock or to increase the human share of game crops. As an alternative to conflict between groups that could cooperate, an emphasis on tolerance, engagement, analysis and management would give a TEAM approach to conservation. Convergent use of all available human resources, by maintaining diverse use of wildlife resources, may prove the best way to preserve a diversity of wildlife and wild places.

ACKNOWLEDGEMENTS

My very grateful thanks to those who have helped me to understand the realities of raptor conservation, especially Vidar Marcström, Ian Newton and Chris Perrins. I also acknowledge the many others who have helped me see the dangers of over-protection, and am humbled by all the World Working Group members who expressed agreement, by unanimous endorsement of conference resolution 11, with the view that flexible cooperation rather than conflict is the way to solve raptor predation problems to mutual satisfaction.

REFERENCES

BOWMAN, T.D., P.F. SCHEMPF & J.A. BERNATOWICZ 1995. Bald eagle survival and population dynamics in Alaska after the Exxon Valdez oil spill. *Journal of Wildlife Management* 59:317-324.
BRETT, L.P., W.G. HANKINS & J. GARCIA 1976. Prey-lithium aversions: III *Buteo* hawks. *Behavioural Biology* 17:87-98
BUEHLER, D.A., J.D. FRASER, J.K.D. SEEGAR, G.D. THERRES & M.A. BYRD 1991. Survival rates and population dynamics of bald eagles in Chesapeake Bay. *Journal of Wildlife Management* 55:608-613.

DAVIES R.A.G. 1999. The extent, cost and control of livestock predation by eagles with a case study on black eagles *Aquila verreauxii* in the Karoo. *Journal of Raptor Research*.33:67-72

DRAULANS, D. 1987. The effectiveness of attempts to reduce predation by fish-eating birds: a review. *Biological Conservation* 41:219-232.

ETHERIDGE, B., R.W. SUMMERS & R.E. GREEN 1997. The effects of illegal killing and destruction of nests by humans on the population dynamics of the hen harrier *Circus cyaneus* in Scotland. *Journal of Applied Ecology* 34:1081-1105.

EVANS, I.M., J.A. LOVE, C.A. GALBRAITH & M.W. PIENKOWSKI 1994. Population and range restoration of threatened raptors in the United Kingdom. pp.447-457 in B.-U. Meyburg & R.D. Chancellor (eds) *Raptor Conservation Today*. World Working Group on Birds of Prey.

HOLLING, C.S. 1959. *Canadian Entomologist* 91:293:320.

JAMES, P. 1996. *The Birds of Sussex*. Sussex Ornithological Society, Haywards Heath.

KENWARD, R.E. 1986. Problems of goshawk predation on pigeons and some other game. *Proc. of XVIII International Ornithological Congress*, 666-678.

KENWARD, R.E. 1987. Protection versus management in raptor conservation: the role of falconry and hunting interests. pp 1-13 in D.J. Hill (ed.) *Breeding and Management in Birds of Prey*. Bristol University Press.

KENWARD, R.E. 1999. Raptor predation problems and solutions. *Journal of Raptor Research*. 38:73-75

KENWARD, R.E., D.G. HALL, S.S. WALLS & K.H. HODDER. (in review b). Predation impact and risk factors when buzzards (*Buteo buteo*) attack released pheasants (*Phasianus colchicus*).

KENWARD, R.E., M. KARLBOM & V. MARCSTRÖM 1983. The price of success in goshawk trapping. *Journal of Raptor Research* 17:84-91.

KENWARD, R.E., V. MARCSTRÖM & M. KARLBOM 1993. Post-nestling behaviour in goshawks, *Accipiter gentilis*: I. The causes of dispersal. *Animal Behaviour* 46:365-70.

KENWARD, R.E., V. MARCSTRÖM & M. KARLBOM (in press). Demographic estimates from radio-tagging: models of age-specific survival and breeding in the goshawk (*Accipiter gentilis*). *Journal of Animal Ecology*.

KENWARD, R.E., S.S. WALLS,, K.H. HODDER, M. PAHKALA, S.N. FREEMAN & V.R. SIMPSON (in review a). The prevalence of non-breeders in raptor populations: evidence from ringing, radio-tagging and survey data.

LLOYD, D.E.B. 1975. Avian predation on reared pheasants. *Game Conservancy Annual Review* 7:65-66.

MARCSTRÖM, V. & R.E. KENWARD 1981. Movements of wintering goshawk in Sweden. *Swedish Game Research* 12:1-35.

MIKKELSEN, J.D. 1984. *Effekt af duehøge, og andre rovfugle, ved fasanudsaetningsteder*. Kalø Viltbiologisk Station, Kalø [in Danish].

MURPHY, J.R. 1977. Eagles and livestock - some management considerations. pp. 307-314 in R.D. Chancellor, (ed.) *Proceedings of World Conference on Birds of Prey*. ICBP, Cambridge.

MUSGROVE, A. 1996. *Peregrines and pigeons: investigations into a raptor-human conflict*. PhD thesis, University of Bristol.

NEWTON, I. 1979. *Population Ecology of Raptors*. Berkhamsted, Poyser.

POTTS, G.R. 1986. *The partridge*. Collins, London.

REDPATH, S.M. & S.J. THIRGOOD 1997. *Birds of prey and red grouse*. Stationery Office, London.

Robert E. Kenward
Institute of Terrestrial Ecology,
Furzebrook Research Station,
Wareham BH20 5AS,
United Kingdom

Part 8

Conservation Biology of the World's Migratory Raptors

Red Kite *Milvus milvus*

Conveners:
Keith Bildstein & Reuven Yosef

Conservation Biology of the World's Migratory Raptors: status and strategies

Keith L. Bildstein, Jorje Zalles, Jennifer Ottinger and Kyle McCarty

ABSTRACT

At least 162 (55%) and possibly as many as 193 (67%) of the world's 294 species of raptors migrate. Among known migratory raptors, 19 species (6% of all raptors) are complete migrants, 100 (34%) are partial migrants, and 43 (15%) are local, irruptive, or altitudinal migrants. Africa and Asia have 76 and 68 species of migratory raptors, respectively. Australia has 22 species, Europe 38, Central and South America 39, North America 41, and the Pacific Islands 34. The geography of raptor migration is better studied in the Northern than in the Southern Hemisphere, particularly in North America, Europe, and the Middle East. Relatively little is known about raptor migration in Asia and Africa.

Twenty-eight (37%) of the world's 75 Near Threatened, Vulnerable, Endangered, and Critically Endangered raptors are known or suspected migrants. Principal threats to known or suspected migratory raptors include habitat loss (97 species), environmental contaminants (40 species), and direct persecution (59 species).

Migratory raptors are secretive, wide-ranging birds that operate over enormous ecological neighborhoods. Their protection is neither simple nor easy. Global raptor conservation depends upon a practical mix of intercontinental networks, longterm databases, and local community support. The development and widespread use of prismatic binoculars and modern field guides earlier this century provided raptor enthusiasts with the tools needed to begin documenting the geography of raptor migration, as well as to monitor populations along important migration corridors. Programs at well-established migration watchsites, including Hawk Mountain Sanctuary's *Hawks Aloft Worldwide* (*HAWW*), offer useful models for recently activated and incipient watchsites, particularly in areas where raptor migration is little studied.

INTRODUCTION

Diurnal birds of prey (Falconiformes) represent a diverse group of highly mobile, wide-ranging, area-sensitive predators, whose populations occur across a broad range of habitats on six continents (Brown & Amadon 1968). Each year, millions of these birds travel long distances— in many instances across and among entire continents—en route to their breeding and wintering grounds. Although raptors often migrate across broad fronts (Bednarz & Kerlinger 1988), individuals of many species congregate along established corridors on migration, particularly along specific geographic features including mountain chains, coastal plains, isthmuses, and peninsulas (Bildstein 1998). Considerable potential exists for using these concentrated movements to monitor local, regional, and continental populations, as well as to introduce local inhabitants to these normally secretive and dispersed birds (Broun 1949, Bildstein 1998, Bildstein et al. 1995).

Long-distance raptor migration represents one of the most spectacular movements of land-based predators on earth (Bildstein & Zalles 1995). The charismatic and evocative nature of the birds, together with their trophic status as area-sensitive predators, make them useful flagship species for broader conservation issues. Hawk Mountain Sanctuary, the world's first refuge for birds of prey (Broun 1949), maintains the longest and most complete record of raptor migration in the world (Bildstein 1998). The Sanctuary has used the spectacle of raptor migration to introduce more than a million Americans to these birds and their habitat needs since 1934. In 1987, Hawk Mountain launched *Hawks Aloft Worldwide* (*HAWW*), a cooperative global conservation initiative designed to export aspects of the Sanctuary's practical and effective conservation efforts elsewhere, and to amass, analyze, and distribute information on the movements of the world's migratory raptors (Senner & Brett 1989, Bildstein et al. 1995, Bildstein & Zalles 1995).

As of mid-1998, *Hawks Aloft Worldwide* had identified 384 raptor-migration watchsites in 87 countries on six continents.

Here, we summarize the results of these efforts, documenting the distribution of migratory raptors, together with that of active and incipient raptor-migration watchsites. We then use these data to highlight opportunities for increased conservation efforts in Africa, where the geography of raptor migration has yet to be studied in detail.

THE GEOGRAPHY OF RAPTOR MIGRATION

Raptor migration is complex and confusing. Most migratory raptors are partial rather than complete migrants (*sensu* Kerlinger 1989), and it is not always possible to determine the extent to which raptors migrate into and out of an area, particularly in regions where migration occurs across a broad front. Nevertheless, it appears that populations of at least 48 of 99 species of New World, and 120 of 201 species of Old World raptors migrate on a regular or irregular basis (Table 1). In the New World, all 36 species of Nearctic breeders are known or suspected migrants, as are 39 of 86 Neotropical breeders, and 30 of 62 Austral breeders (Table 2). In the Old World, 22 Australian, 60 African, 66 Asian, 19 Pacific Islands, and 38 European breeders are suspected or confirmed migrants (Table 3). The continental distribution of known complete and partial migrants is depicted in Figure 1.

Figure 1. Continental distribution of known complete and partial migratory raptors. The Pacific Islands, including New Guinea, are considered separately from Asia and Australia.

Table 1. Continental distribution of the world's complete, partial, irruptive, and local migrant raptors[a].

Species[b]	Continental distribution[c]						
	AUS	AFR	NAM	SAM	ASI	PIS	EUR
Complete migrants							
Osprey *Pandion haliaetus*	+	+	+	+	+	+	+
Western Honey Buzzard *Pernis apivorus*		+			+		+
Eastern Honey Buzzard *P. ptilorhynchus*					+	+	
Mississippi Kite *Ictinia mississippiensis*			+	+			
Short-toed Eagle *Circaetus gallicus*		+			+		
Gray-faced Buzzard *Butastur indicus*					+	+	
Montagu's Harrier *Circus pygargus*		+			+		+
Gray Frog Hawk *Accipiter soloensis*					+	+	
Broad-winged Hawk *Buteo platypterus*			+	+			
Swainson's Hawk *B. swainsoni*			+	+			
Rough-legged Hawk *B. lagopus*			+		+		+
Lesser Spotted Eagle *Aquila pomarina*		+			+		+
Greater Spotted Eagle *A. clanga*[d]		+			+		+
Lesser Kestrel *Falco naumanni*[d]		+			+		+
Western Red-footed Falcon *F. vespertinus*		+			+		+
Eastern Red-footed Falcon *F. amurensis*		+			+		
Northern Hobby *F. subbuteo*		+			+		+
Eleonora's Falcon *F. eleonorae*		+			+		
Sooty Falcon *F. concolor*		+			+		
Partial migrants							
Black Vulture *Coragyps atratus*			+	+			
Turkey Vulture *Cathartes aura*			+	+			
African Cuckoo Hawk *Aviceda cuculoides*		+					
Asian Baza *A. jerdoni*					+	+	
Crested Baza *A. subcristata*					+	+	
Black Baza *A. leuphotes*					+	+	
Swallow-tailed Kite *Elanoides forficatus*			+	+			
White-tailed Kite *E. leucurus*			+	+			
Black-shouldered Kite *Elanus caeruleus*		+			+	+	+
African Swallow-tailed Kite *Chelictinia ricourii*		+					
Snail Kite *Rostrhamus sociabilis*			+	+			
Plumbeous Kite *Ictinia plumbea*			+	+			
Red Kite *Milvus milvus*		+			+		+
Black Kite *M. migrans*	+	+			+	+	+
Whistling Kite *Haliastur sphenurus*	+					+	
Brahminy Kite *H. indus*	+				+	+	
Pallas' Fish Eagle *Haliaeetus leucoryphus*[d]					+		
White-tailed Eagle *H. albicilla*			+		+		
Bald Eagle *H. leucocephalus*			+				
Steller's Sea-Eagle *H. pelagicus*[d]					+		
Lesser Fishing Eagle *Icthyophaga humilis*					+	+	
Cinereous Vulture *Aegypius monachus*		+			+		+
Lappet-faced Vulture *A. tracheliotus*		+			+		
Eurasian Griffon *Gyps fulvus*		+			+		+
Ruppell's Griffon *G. rueppellii*		+					
Asian White-backed Vulture *G. bengalensis*					+		
African White-backed Vulture *G. africanus*		+					
Egyptian Vulture *Neophron percnopterus*		+			+		+
Bearded Vulture *Gypaetus barbatus*		+			+		+
Palmnut Vulture *Gypohierax angolensis*		+					
African Harrier Hawk *Polyboroides typus*		+					
Madagascar Harrier Hawk *P. radiatus*		+					
Eastern Chanting Goshawk *Melierax poliopterus*		+					
Dark Chanting Goshawk *Melierax metabates*		+			+		
Gabar Goshawk *M. gabar*		+			+		
Grasshopper Buzzard *Butastur rufipennis*		+					
White-eyed Buzzard *B. teesa*					+		
Spotted Harrier *Circus assimilis*	+					+	

Species[b]	AUS	AFR	NAM	SAM	ASI	PIS	EUR
Northern Harrier *C. cyaneus*		+	+	+	+	+	+
Cinereous Harrier *C. cinereus*				+			
Pallid Harrier *C. macrourus*		+			+		+
Pied Harrier *C. melanoleucus*					+	+	
Western Marsh Harrier *C. aeruginosus*		+			+		+
Eastern Marsh Harrier *C. spilonotus*					+	+	
Swamp Harrier *C. approximans*	+				+		
African Marsh Harrier *C. ranivorus*		+					
Long-winged Harrier *C. buffoni*				+			
Gray-bellied Hawk *Accipiter poliogaster*				+			
Levant Sparrowhawk *A. brevipes*		+			+		+
Shikra *A. badius*		+			+		
Japanese Sparrowhawk *A. gularis*					+	+	
Besra *A. virgatus*					+	+	
Ovambo Sparrowhawk *A. ovampensis*		+					
Eurasian Sparrowhawk *A. nisus*		+			+		+
Sharp-shinned Hawk *A. striatus*			+	+			
Cooper's Hawk *A. cooperii*			+				
Bicolored Hawk *A. bicolor*			+	+			
Northern Goshawk *A. gentilis*			+	+		+	+
Gray Hawk *Asturina nitida*			+	+			
Common Black Hawk *Buteogallus anthracinus*			+	+			
Savanna Hawk *B. meridionalis*				+			
Harris' Hawk *Parabuteo unicinctus*			+	+			
Red-shouldered Hawk *Buteo lineatus*			+				
White-tailed Hawk *B. albicaudatus*			+	+			
Red-backed Hawk *B. polyosoma*				+			
Zone-tailed Hawk *B. albonotatus*			+	+			
Red-tailed Hawk *B. jamaicensis*			+				
Eurasian Buzzard *B. buteo*		+			+		+
Mountain Buzzard *B. oreophilus*		+					
Long-legged Buzzard *B. rufinus*		+			+		+
Upland Buzzard *B. hemilasius*					+		
Ferruginous Hawk *B. regalis*			+				
Red-necked Buzzard *B. auguralis*		+					
Steppe Eagle *Aquila nipalensis*		+			+		+
Imperial Eagle *A. heliaca*[d]		+			+		+
Golden Eagle *A. chrysaetos*		+	+		+		+
Black Eagle *A. verreauxi*		+					
Wahlberg's Eagle *Hieraaetus wahlbergi*		+					
Bonelli's Eagle *Hieraaetus fasciatus*		+			+	+	+
Booted Eagle *H. pennatus*		+			+		+
Martial Eagle *H. bellicosus*		+					
Chimango Caracara *Milvago chimango*				+			
American Kestrel *Falco sparverius*			+	+			
Old World Kestrel *F. tinnunculus*		+			+		+
Australian Kestrel *F. cenchroides*	+				+		
Fox Kestrel *F. alopex*		+					
Gray Kestrel *F. ardosiaceus*		+					
Red-headed Falcon *F. chicquera*		+			+		
Aplomado Falcon *F. femoralis*			+	+			
Merlin *F. columbarius*			+	+	+	+	+
Oriental Hobby *F. severus*					+	+	
Australian Hobby *F. longipennis*	+				+		
New Zealand Hobby *F. novaeseelandiae*	+						
Brown Falcon *F. berigora*	+				+		
Prairie Falcon *F. mexicanus*			+				
Lanner Falcon *F. biarmicus*		+			+		+
Saker Falcon *F. cherrug*		+			+		+
Gyrfalcon *F. rusticolus*			+		+		+
Peregrine Falcon *F. peregrinus*	+	+	+	+	+	+	+
Barbary Falcon *F. pelegrinoides*		+			+		

Species[b]	AUS	AFR	NAM	SAM	ASI	PIS	EUR
Local and irruptive migrants							
Savanna Vulture *Cathartes burrovianus*			+	+			
California Condor *Gymnogyps californianus*[d]			+				
Andean Condor *Vultur gryphus*				+			
Black-winged Kite *Elanus notatus*	+						
Letter-winged Kite *E. scriptus*	+						
Hook-billed Kite *Chondrohierax uncinatus*			+	+			
Rufous-thighed Kite *Harpagus diodon*				+			
Square-tailed Kite *Lophoictinia isura*	+						
Black-breasted Buzzard *Hamirostra melanosternon*	+						
White-bellied Sea-Eagle *Haliaeetus leucogaster*	+					+	+
African Fish Eagle *H. vocifer*		+					
Hooded Vulture *Necrosyrtes monachus*		+					
Himalayan Griffon *Gyps himalayensis*					+		
Cape Griffon *G. coprotheres*		+					
Brown Snake Eagle *Circaetus cinereus*		+					
Banded Snake Eagle *C. cinerascens*		+					
Bateleur *Terathopius ecaudatus*		+					
Crested Serpent Eagle *Spilornis cheela*					+	+	
Brown Goshawk *Accipiter fasciatus*	+					+	
Australasian Collared Sparrowhawk *A. cirrhocephalus*	+					+	
Rufous-breasted Sparrowhawk *A. rufiventris*		+					
Black and White Goshawk *A. melanoleucus*		+					
Great Black Hawk *Buteogallus urubitinga*			+	+			
Black-collared Hawk *Busarellus nigricollis*			+	+			
Short-tailed Hawk *Buteo brachyurus*			+	+			
Puna Hawk *B. poecilochrous*				+			
Hawaiian Hawk *B. solitarius*						+	
Rufous-tailed Hawk *B. ventralis*				+			
Madagascar Buzzard *B. brachypterus*		+					
Jackal Buzzard *B. rufofuscus*		+					
Harpy Eagle *Harpia harpyja*			+	+			
Tawny Eagle *Aquila rapax*		+					
Wedge-tailed Eagle *Aquila audax*	+					+	
Little Eagle *Hieraaetus morphnoides*	+					+	
Ayres' Hawk Eagle *H. ayresii*		+					
Mountain Hawk Eagle *Spizaetus nipalensis*					+	+	
Secretarybird *Sagittarius serpentarius*		+					
Crested Caracara *Polyborus plancus*			+	+			
African Pygmy Falcon *Polihierax semitorquatus*		+					
White-eyed Kestrel *Falco rupiculoides*		+					
African Hobby *F. cuvierii*		+					
Gray Falcon *F. hypoleucos*	+						
Black Falcon *F. subniger*	+						
Continental totals	**22**	**76**	**41**	**39**	**68**	**35**	**38**
Continental totals (without locals and irruptives)	**11**	**60**	**33**	**28**	**64**	**27**	**38**

[a]Complete migrants are species in which more than 90% of all individuals leave the breeding range during the nonbreeding season. Partial migrants are those in which 90% or fewer of all individuals leave the breeding range. Irruptive and local migrants are species whose movements are correlated with less predictable environmental fluctuations, and whose migratory habits are less regular than those of complete or partial migrants. (Based primarily on Kerlinger 1989 as updated in del Hoyo et al. 1994.)

[b]Taxonomic status and distribution are based primarily on Amadon and Bull 1988.

[c]AUS = Australia and New Zealand, AFR = Africa, NAM = North America, SAM = South America, ASI = Asia, PIS = Pacific Islands, EUR = Europe.

[d]Species listed in *Birds to watch 2: the world list of threatened birds* (Collar et al. 1994). See Table 4 for details.

Table 2. Migratory populations of Western Hemisphere raptors.

Type migrant	Breeding population		
	Nearctic	Tropical	Austral
Complete migrants			
Osprey *Pandion haliaetus*	+[a]		
Mississippi Kite *Ictinia mississippiensis*	+		
Broad-winged Hawk *Buteo platypterus*	+		
Swainson's Hawk *B. swainsoni*	+		
Rough-legged Hawk *B. lagopus*	+		
Partial migrants			
Black Vulture *Coragyps atratus*	+	+	—
Turkey Vulture *Cathartes aura*	+	+	+
Swallow-tailed Kite *Elanoides forficatus*	+	+	+
White-tailed Kite *Elanus leucurus*	?	?	+
Snail Kite *Rostrhamus sociabilis*	+	+	+
Plumbeous Kite *Ictinia plumbea*	+	+	+
Bald Eagle *Haliaeetus leucocephalus*	+		
Northern Harrier *Circus cyaneus*	+		
Cinereous Harrier *C. cinereus*		+	+
Long-winged Harrier *C. buffoni*		+	+
Gray-bellied Hawk *Accipiter poliogaster*		+	+
Sharp-shinned Hawk *A. striatus*	+	—	+
Cooper's Hawk *A. cooperii*	+		
Bicolored Hawk *A. bicolor*			+
Northern Goshawk *A. gentilis*	+		
Gray Hawk *Asturina nitida*	+	?	
Common Black Hawk *Buteogallus anthracinus*	+	?	
Savanna Hawk *B. meridionalis*		+	+
Harris' Hawk *Parabuteo unicinctus*	+	—	—
Red-shouldered Hawk *Buteo lineatus*	+		
White-tailed Hawk *B. albicaudatus*	?	—	+
Red-backed Hawk *B. polyosoma*			+
Zone-tailed Hawk *B. albonotatus*	+	?	?
Red-tailed Hawk *B. jamaicensis*	+		
Ferruginous Hawk *Buteo regalis*	+		
Golden Eagle *Aquila chrysaetos*	+		
Chimango Caracara *Milvago chimango*		+	+
American Kestrel *Falco sparverius*	+	—	+
Aplomado Falcon *F. femoralis*	+	+	+
Merlin *F. columbarius*	+		
Prairie Falcon *F. mexicanus*	+		
Gyrfalcon *F. rusticolus*	+		
Peregrine Falcon *F. peregrinus*	+	+	+
Local and irruptive migrants			
Savanna Vulture *Cathartes burrovianus*		+	+
Forest Vulture *C. melambrotus*		+	
California Condor *Gymnogyps californianus*	+		
Andean Condor *Vultur gryphus*		+	+
King Vulture *Sarcoramphus papa*		+	?
Hook-billed Kite *Chondrohierax uncinatus*	+	—	—
Rufous-thighed Kite *Harpagus diodon*		?	+
Great Black Hawk *Buteogallus urubitinga*	+	?	?
Black-collared Hawk *Busarellus nigricollis*		?	+
Black-chested Eagle *Geranoaetus melanoleucus*		?	?
White-rumped Hawk *Buteo leucorrhous*		+	?
Short-tailed Hawk *B. brachyurus*	+	—	—
Puna Hawk *B. poecilochrous*		+	?
Rufous-tailed Hawk *B. ventralis*			?
Harpy Eagle *Harpia harpyja*		+	
Striated Caracara *Phalcoboenus australis*			?
Crested Caracara *Polyborus plancus*	+	+	+
Bat Falcon *Falco rufigularis*		+	
Orange-breasted Falcon *F. deiroleucus*		+	
Total number of known (suspected) migrants	34 (2)	22 (8)	22 (8)

[a] + = known migratory population; ? = suspected migratory population; — = no known migratory population.

Table 3. Migratory populations of Old World raptors.

Species	AUS	AFR	ASI	PIS	EUR
Complete migrants					
Osprey *Pandion haliaetus*	+	+	+	+	+
Western Honey Buzzard *Pernis apivorus*			+		+
Eastern Honey Buzzard *P. ptilorhynchus*			+	?	
Short-toed Eagle *Circaetus gallicus*		+	+		+
Gray-faced Buzzard *Butastur indicus*			+		
Montagu's Harrier *Circus pygargus*		+	+		+
Gray Frog Hawk *Accipiter soloensis*			+		
Rough-legged Hawk *Buteo lagopus*			+		+
Lesser Spotted Eagle *Aquila pomarina*			+		+
Greater Spotted Eagle *A. clanga*			+		+
Lesser Kestrel *Falco naumanni*		?	+		+
Western Red-footed Falcon *F. vespertinus*		+	+		+
Eastern Red-footed Falcon *F. amurensis*			+		
Eleonora's Falcon *F. eleonorae*		+	+		+
Sooty Falcon *F. concolor*		+	+		
Northern Hobby *F. subbuteo*		+	+		+
Partial migrants					
African Cuckoo Hawk *Aviceda cuculoides*		+			
Asian Baza *A. jerdoni*			+	+	
Crested Baza *A. subcristata*			+		
Black Baza *A. leuphotes*			+		
Black-shouldered Kite *Elanus caeruleus*		+	+	+	+
African Swallow-tailed Kite *Chelictinia ricourii*		+			
Red Kite *Milvus milvus*		+	+		+
Black Kite *M. migrans*	+	+	+	?	+
Whistling Kite *Haliastur sphenurus*	+				
Brahminy Kite *H. indus*	+		+	?	
Pallas' Fish Eagle *Haliaeetus leucoryphus*			+		
White-tailed Sea Eagle *H. albicilla*			+		+
Steller's Sea Eagle *H. pelagicus*			+		
Lesser Fishing Eagle *Ichthyophaga humilis*			+	?	
Cinereous Vulture *Aegypius monachus*			+		+
Lappet-faced Vulture *A. tracheliotus*		+	+		
Eurasian Griffon *Gyps fulvus*		?	+		+
Ruppell's Griffon *G. rueppellii*		+			
Asian White-backed Vulture *G. bengalensis*			+		
African White-backed Vulture *G. africanus*		+			
Egyptian Vulture *Neophron percnopterus*		+	+		+
Bearded Vulture *Gypaetus barbatus*		?	?		+
Palmnut Vulture *Gypohierax angolensis*		+			
African Harrier Hawk *Polyboroides typus*		+			
Madagascar Harrier Hawk *P. radiatus*		+			
Eastern Chanting Goshawk *Melierax poliopterus*		+			
Dark Chanting Goshawk *M. metabates*		+			
Gabar Goshawk *M. gabar*		+			
Grasshopper Buzzard *Butastur rufipennis*		+			
White-eyed Buzzard *B. teesa*			+		
Spotted Harrier *Circus assimilis*	+			+	
Black Harrier *C. maurus*		+			
Northern Harrier *C. cyaneus*			+		+
Pallid Harrier *C. macrourus*			+		+
Pied Harrier *C. melanoleucus*			+	+	
Western Marsh Harrier *C. aeruginosus*			+		+
Eastern Marsh Harrier *C. spilonotus*			+		
Swamp Harrier *C. approximans*	+				
African Marsh Harrier *C. ranivorus*		+			
Levant Sparrowhawk *Accipiter brevipes*			+		+
Shikra *A. badius*		+	+		
Japanese Sparrowhawk *A. gularis*			+		
Besra *A. virgatus*			+		
Ovambo Sparrowhawk *A. ovampensis*		+			

Species	AUS	AFR	ASI	PIS	EUR
			Breeding population		
Eurasian Sparrowhawk A. nisus			+		+
Northern Goshawk A. gentilis			+		+
Eurasian Buzzard Buteo buteo			+		+
Mountain Buzzard B. oreophilus		+			
Long-legged Buzzard B. rufinus		?	+		+
Upland Buzzard B. hemilasius			+		
Red-necked Buzzard B. auguralis		+			
Asian Black Eagle Ictinaetus malayensis			+		
Steppe Eagle Aquila nipalensis			+		+
Imperial Eagle A. heliaca			+		+
Golden Eagle A. chrysaetos			+		+
Black Eagle A. verreauxii		+			
Wahlberg's Eagle Hieraaetus wahlbergi		+			
Bonelli's Eagle H. fasciatus		?	?		+
Booted Eagle H. pennatus		+	+		+
Rufous-bellied Eagle H. kienerii			+	+	
Martial Eagle H. bellicosus		+			
Old World Kestrel Falco tinnunculus		?	+		+
Australian Kestrel F. cenchroides	+			+	
Fox Kestrel F. alopex		+			
Gray Kestrel F. ardosiaceus		+			
Red-headed Falcon F. chicquera		+	+		
Merlin F. columbarius			+		+
Oriental Hobby F. severus			+	+	
Australian Hobby F. longipennis	+				
New Zealand Hobby F. novaeseelandiae	+				
Brown Falcon F. berigora	+				
Lanner Falcon F. biarmicus		+	+		+
Saker Falcon F. cherrug			+		+
Gyrfalcon F. rusticolus			+		+
Peregrine Falcon F. peregrinus	?	+	+	?	+
Barbary Falcon F. pelegrinoides		+	+		

Local or irruptive migrants

Species	AUS	AFR	ASI	PIS	EUR
Black-winged Kite Elanus notatus	+				
Letter-winged Kite E. scriptus	+				
Square-tailed Kite Lophoictinia isura	+				
Black-breasted Buzzard Hamirostra melanosternon	+				
White-bellied Sea Eagle Haliaeetus leucogaster	+		?	?	
African Fish Eagle H. vocifer		+			
Red-headed Vulture Aegypius (Sarcogyps) calvus			+		
Hooded Vulture Necrosyrtes monachus		+			
Long-billed Griffon Gyps indicus			+		
Himalayan Griffon G. himalayensis			+		
Cape Griffon G. coprotheres		+			
Brown Snake Eagle Circaetus cinereus		+			
East African Snake Eagle C. fasciolatus		+			
Banded Snake Eagle C. cinerascens		+			
Bateleur Terathopius ecaudatus		+			
Crested Serpent Eagle Spilornis cheela			+	?	
Pale Chanting Goshawk Melierax canorus		+			
Lizard Buzzard Kaupifalco monogrammicus		+			
Malagasy Marsh Harrier Circus maillardi		+			
Asian Crested Goshawk Accipiter trivirgatus			+	+	
Little Sparrowhawk A. minullus		+			
Brown Goshawk A. fasciatus	+			?	
Australasian Collared Sparrowhawk A. cirrhocephalus	+			?	
Rufous-breasted Sparrowhawk A. rufiventris		+			
Black and White Goshawk A. melanoleucus		+			
Hawaiian Hawk Buteo solitarius				+	
Madagascar Buzzard B. brachypterus		+			
Augur Buzzard Buteo augur		+			
Jackal Buzzard B. rufofuscus		+			
Tawny Eagle Aquila rapax		+			

Species	AUS	Breeding population AFR	ASI	PIS	EUR
Wedge-tailed Eagle *A. audax*	+			?	
Little Eagle *Hieraaetus morphnoides*	+			?	
Ayres' Hawk Eagle *H. ayresii*		+			
Long-crested Eagle *Spizaetus occipitalis*		+			
Crested Hawk Eagle *S. cirrhatus*			+	?	
Mountain Hawk Eagle *S. nipalensis*			+		
Secretarybird *Sagittarius serpentarius*		+			
African Pygmy Falcon *Polihierax semitorquatus*		+			
White-eyed Kestrel *Falco rupiculoides*		+			
African Hobby *F. cuvierii*		+			
Gray Falcon *F. hypoleucos*	+				
Black Falcon *F. subniger*	+				
Laggar Falcon *F. jugger*			+		
Total number of known (suspected) migrants	21(1)	62(6)	70(3)	10(12)	38(0)

Key

Species

Complete migrants	species in which >90% of all individuals leave the breeding range during the nonbreeding season
Partial migrants	species in which £90% of all individuals leave the breeding range
Irruptive or local migrants	species whose movements are associated with less predictable environmental fluctuations, and whose migratory habits are less regular than those of complete or partial migrants (based primarily on Kerlinger 1989, as updated in del Hoyo *et al.* 1994 and this volume)

Continental distribution
- AUS Australia and New Zealand
- AFR Africa
- ASI Asia
- PIS Pacific Islands
- EUR Europe

Breeding population
- + known migratory population
- ? suspected migratory population

In the Western Hemisphere, raptor migration is best understood in Canada and the United States. Although considerable effort is underway in Middle America (i.e., Mexico south to Panama), migration in South America is yet to be studied in detail (but see Davis 1989, Zuquim Antas 1994, Woodbridge *et al.* 1995).

In the Old World, raptor migration is well studied in Europe, particularly in southern Sweden (Rudebeck 1950, 1951), the Pyrenees, southernmost Iberia (Finlayson 1992), and Bulgaria (Ruskov *et al.* unpubl. ms.); and in the Middle East, particularly Israel (Shirihai 1996). Except for Japan (Brazil 1991, Brazil & Hanawa 1991) and Taiwan (Severinghaus 1991), the geography of raptor migration is little studied in Asia (McClure 1998). Much remains to be learned regarding the passage of European and Asian raptors into and out of, as well as within Africa, particularly West Africa (Brown *et al.* 1982).

HAWW AND RAPTOR CONSERVATION

Fifty percent of all migratory raptors are threatened by habitat loss, 21% by environmental contaminants, and 31% by direct persecution. Twenty-two percent are threatened by two of these factors, 7% by all three. Seventy percent of all Asian, 79% of all Pacific Island, 67% of all African, 82% of all European, 53% of all Central and South American, and 59% of all North American raptors are threatened by one or more of these factors. Overall, world populations of 10 migratory species—5% of all suspected or known migratory raptors—are listed as Critically Endangered or Vulnerable by the international conservation community (Collar *et al.* 1994). Another 9% (18 species) are listed as Near-threatened (Table 4).

Table 4. Critically Endangered, Endangered, Threatened, Vulnerable, and Near-threatened species of suspected and known migratory raptors from *Birds to watch 2: the world list of threatened birds* (Collar et al. 1994).

Species	Type migrant	Continental distribution
Critically Endangered		
Gymnogyps californianus	Irregular, irruptive migrant	North America
Vulnerable		
Lophoictinia isura	Irregular, irruptive migrant	Australia
Haliaeetus leucoryphus	Partial migrant	Asia
Haliaeetus pelagicus	Partial migrant	Asia
Gyps coprotheres	Irregular, irruptive migrant	Africa
Harpyhaliaetus coronatus[a]	Irregular, irruptive migrant	Central and South America
Aquila clanga	Complete migrant	Africa, Asia, Europe
Aquila heliaca	Partial migrant	Africa, Asia, Europe
Falco naumanni	Complete migrant	Africa, Asia, Europe
Falco hypoleucos	Irregular, irruptive migrant	Australia
Near-threatened		
Aviceda jerdoni	Partial migrant	Asia
Haliaeetus albicilla	Partial migrant	Asia, Europe, North America
Icthyophaga humilis	Partial migrant	Asia
Gyps bengalensis	Partial migrant	Asia
Gyps indicus[a]	Irregular, irruptive migrant	Asia
Gyps calvus[a]	Irregular, irruptive migrant	Asia
Aegypius monachus	Partial migrant	Africa, Asia, Europe
Circaetus fasciolatus[a]	Irregular, irruptive migrant	Africa
Circus maurus[a]	Irregular, irruptive migrant	Africa
Circus macrourus	Partial migrant	Africa, Asia, Europe
Accipiter poliogaster	Partial migrant	South America
Harpyhaliaetus solitarius[a]	Irregular, irruptive migrant	Central and South America
Buteo solitarius	Irregular, irruptive migrant	Asia
Buteo ventralis	Irregular, irruptive migrant	South America
Harpia harpyja	Irregular, irruptive migrant	Central and South America
Phalcoboenus australis[a]	Irregular, irruptive migrant	South America
Falco chicquera	Partial migrant	Africa, Asia
Falco novaeseelandiae	Partial migrant	Australia

[a]Suspected, not confirmed migrant.

Hawks Aloft Worldwide has identified 384 raptor migration watchsites in 87 countries on six continents. The distribution of raptor migration watchsites is closely tied both to the distribution of migratory raptors and to the distribution of the conservationists who study them. In part because of differences in land mass, and in part because of differences in conservation effort, the Northern Hemisphere is home to 90% of all *HAWW* watchsites. Europe and North America, continents with long traditions in migration-watchsite activity (Broun 1949, Rudebeck 1950, 1951) have 97 and 126 watchsites, respectively. Africa and Central and South America have considerably fewer watchsites (Figure 2). Africa, an important wintering area for many Asian and European raptors (Newton 1995), is particularly underrepresented in this regard.

Figure 2. Continental distribution of *Hawks Aloft Worldwide* raptor-migration watchsites.

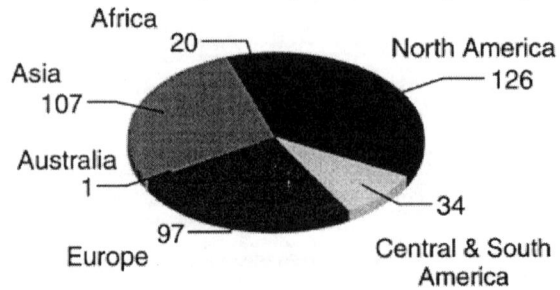

Although two-thirds of all *HAWW* watchsites are on protected lands, percentages vary considerably among continents, from a low of 45% in Africa, to a high of 74% in North America. More watchsites are active in autumn than in spring. Overall, 8 African, 33 Asian, 19 European, 12 Central and South American, and 37 North American watchsites report more than 10,000 raptors, annually (Figure 3); 16 watchsites report more than 100,00 raptors, annually. With an autumn average of more than two million raptors, and a spring average of 600,000 individuals, the Veracruz Coastal Plain watchsite in Gulf Coast Veracruz, Mexico, ranks as the world's greatest active watchsite. Elat, Israel, with 830,000 migrants in spring and >40,000 migrants in autumn ranks as the most numerically significant Old World site.

Active raptor-migration watchsites can function as centres of environmental education, as well as important sources of information regarding the status of local, regional, and sometimes, continental populations of raptors (Bildstein 1998, Bildstein *et al.* 1995).

HAWK AND RAPTOR CONSERVATION IN AFRICA

Africa may be the most important wintering area for migratory raptors anywhere. The continent hosts 34 species of endemic, *intra*continental migrants, together with significant populations of 34 European and 42 Asian breeders, several of which travel from as far as Scandinavia, Siberia, and Amurland to over-winter in Africa's grasslands, savannas, and wet and dry forests. Four African countries—Kenya, Ethiopia, Sudan, and Tanzania—rank among the world's top 10 in numbers of species of raptors overall; while 9—Kenya, Ethiopia, Sudan, Uganda, South Africa, Tanzania, Zaire, Eritrea, and Mozambique—rank among the top 10 in terms of numbers of species of *migratory* raptors. In spite of such diversity, the geography of raptor migration is little studied in the Africa, especially in comparison with what is known about raptor migration in Europe and North America.

Leslie Brown's treatment (Brown 1971) remains the best overview of the geography of raptor migration in Africa, while Brown *et al.* 1982 and Mundy *et al.* 1992, provide the best species treatments, overall. Taken as a whole, these three references serve as an essential primer to raptor migration on the continent. Below we use these sources, together with seminal regional references and information provided by *Hawks Aloft Worldwide* cooperators to sketch a synoptic overview of the geography of raptor migration in the region and to suggest ways in which activities at raptor-migration watchsites can increase our understanding of the phenomenon.

Although some migrants, including many harriers (*Circus* spp.) and small falcons (*Falco* spp.),

Figure 3. Locations of 109 *Hawks Aloft Worldwide* **raptor-migration watchsites reporting at least 10,000 migrants, annually.**

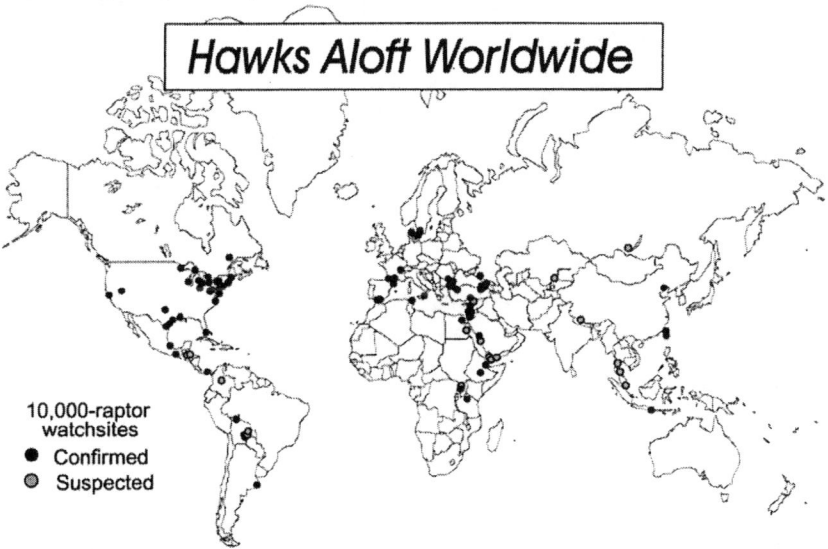

enter North Africa across a broad front via the Mediterranean Sea; and while Eastern Red-footed Falcons *Falco amurensis* enter equatorial East Africa via the Indian Ocean; populations of most migrants enter the continent at well-established bottlenecks that minimize the extent of water crossings. East to west, principal points of arrival and departure include: (1) The northeastern coast of Djibouti along the **Bab-el-Mandeb Straits**, <30 km from Yemen in southern Arabia, and the shortest crossing point between Asia and Africa south of Sinai. More than 240,000 raptors, including 98,000 Common Buzzards *Buteo buteo* and >76,000 Steppe Eagles *Aquila nipalensis* have been recorded in a single autumn at the site (Welch & Welch 1988). (2) **Suez,** in northeastern Egypt at the southern end of the isthmus linking the Sinai Peninsula to mainland Africa. Autumn and spring counts of migrants in the area reveal totals of 134,000 and 125,000 raptors, respectively (Bijlsma 1983). (3) Coastal Tunisia, in and around **Cap Bon**. Spring reports from the site indicate movements of at least 10,000 raptors, presumably en route to Sicily (Steinbacher 1958, Thiollay 1975a). (4) Cape Spartel on **the Strait of Gibraltar**, 12-km south of southernmost Iberia. Autumn and spring reports along the Spanish coast suggest movements of more than 100,000 migrants (Finlayson 1992) (Table 5; Figure 4).

Within Africa, movements of most raptors are decidedly less well understood. In West Africa, particularly in the Sahara and Sahel, most Palaearctic migrants appear to move north-south across a broad front (Moreau 1961, 1972; Brown 1971; Thiollay 1989). There also appear to be significant coastal movements of Peregrine Falcons *Falco peregrinus* in the region (Gatter 1987). Except for Western Honey Buzzards *Pernis apivorus*, which appear to overwinter in the region's humid tropical forests, most Palaearctic migrants in the region concentrate in the more arid Sahel, directly south of the Sahara; whereas the region's Afrotropical migrants tend to spend the wet season (July-September) in the Sahel, and the dry season (December-February) farther south in the more humid savannas of the Guinea Belt (Thiollay 1989). Seasonally flooded wetlands associated with Lake Chad in extreme northern Cameroon may be an important wintering area for Palaearctic migrants (Thiollay 1978). West African wetlands appear to be important wintering areas for *Pandion haliaetus* from northwestern Europe (Österlöf 1977). African Fishing Eagles *Haliaeetus vocifer* undertake sporadic movements in the Niger Inundation Zone and other seasonal wetlands in the region (Thiollay 1977). *HAWW* watchsites in this part of Africa include Hassi Marroket, Algeria, and Bougouni and Niger Inundation Zone, Mali (Table 5, Figure 4).

In East Africa, most Palaearctic migrants travel north-south along the Western and Eastern Rift Valleys. In Egypt, where many raptors enter Africa via the Sinai Peninsula, movements are especially pronounced along the Eastern Desert on the Red Sea. Southeast of Egypt, raptors entering northern Djibouti via the Bab-el-Mandeb Straits continue inland en route to the Ethiopian highlands and the Eastern Rift Valley. Farther south, Western Honey Buzzards, Black Kites *Milvus migrans*, Common Buzzards *Buteo buteo*, and Wahlberg's Eagle *Hieraaetus wahlbergi* migrate along the Western Rift Valley in Rwanda (Vande Weghe 1978) and, presumably, Burundi; while reports from Kenya suggest that large numbers of Steppe Eagles and Lesser Kestrels *Falco naumanni* (the latter, at least in spring) use the Eastern Rift Valley corridor (Curry-Lindahl 1981, Brown *et al.* 1982, and Lewis & Pomeroy 1989). By the time Palaearctic migrants reach South Africa, most movements, except for concentrations along the Drakensbergs and, possibly, the Waterburgs and the Lebombo Range on the border with Mozambique, appear to occur across a broad front (Newman 1977, Broekhuysen 1971, Schmitt *et al.* 1980). *Hawks Aloft Worldwide* watchsites in the region include Bur Safaga, Egypt; Lake Langano, Ethiopia; Lewa Downs and Tsavo, Kenya; Akagera, Rwanda; Mti Mwili and Lake Manyara, Tanzania; Murchison Falls-Budongo Forest and Kibale Forest, Uganda; Lundazi and Chizongwe Hill, Zambia; and Lake Chivero and Mvurwi, Zimbabwe (Table 5, Figure 4).

Table 5. *Hawks Aloft Worldwide* raptor-migration watchsites in Africa.

Name and country[a]	Season(s)[b]	Numbers of: Species	Endangered species[c]	Individuals
Hassi Marroket, northcentral Algeria	Autumn (Aug.-Oct.)	10	0	?
Bab-el-Mandeb Straits, northern Djibouti	Spring (Mar.)	7	1	1,000s
	Autumn (Oct.-Nov.)	27	3	240,000
Suez, northeastern Egypt	Spring (Feb.-May)	30	4	>125,000
	Autumn (Sep.-Nov.)	33	5	134,000
Bur Safaga, eastern Egypt	Spring (Mar.)	12	2	>>6000
Lake Lagano, central Ethiopia	Spring (Mar.-Apr.)	14	3	?
	Autumn (Sep.-Oct.)	10	3	10,000
Lewa Downs, central Kenya	Autumn (Nov.)	3	0	>>4,000
Tsavo, southeastern Kenya	Austral Summer (Dec.-Mar.)	24	3	?
Bougouni, southwestern Mali	Spring (Apr.-Jun)	12	0	?
	Autumn (Oct.-Nov.)	12	0	?
Niger Inundation Zone, central Mali	Autumn-Spring (Oct.-May)	14	2	?
Akagera, eastern Rwanda	Austral spring (Aug.-Nov.)	13	2	?
	Austral autumn (Feb.-Apr.)	13	2	1000s
Mti Mwili, northcentral Tanzania	Austral autumn (Mar.)	3	2	145,000
Lake Manyara, northcentral Tanzania	Austral autumn (Feb.-Mar.)	5	2	?
Cap Bon, northeastern Tunisia	Spring (Feb.-Jun.)	22	2	>10,000
Murchison Falls-Budongo Forest, northwestern Uganda	Spring (Mar.)	4(+2?)	1?	10,000s
	Autumn (Jul.)	4	0	?
Kibale Forest, western Uganda	Spring (Mar.)	1	0	100s
	Autumn (Jul.-Aug.)	1	0	100s
Lundazi, eastern Zambia	Austral spring (Sep.-Nov.)	11	2	?
	Austral autumn (Jan.-Mar.)	11	2	100s
Chizongwe Hill, eastern Zambia	Austral summer (Aug.-Apr.)	8	?	1000s
Lake Chivero, northcentral Zimbabwe	Austral summer (Aug.-Apr.)	15	2	1000s
Mvurwi, northcentral Zimbabwe	Austral summer (Aug.-Apr.)	4	0	10,000

[a]Sites are listed alphabetical by country.
[b]Seasons are based on a site's position north or south of the Equator. Boreal spring and summer are listed as spring and autumn.
[c]Includes all Critically Endangered, Endangered, Threatened, Vulnerable, and Near-threatened species listed in Collar *et al.* 1994.

Thoughts and suggestions regarding the conservation of migratory raptors in Africa

Four of 10 globally Vulnerable species of migratory raptors, and 5 of 18 Near-threatened species, occur in Africa (Table 4). Six of the nine species are intercontinental visitors whose migratory geography and conservation status is better studied outside of the continent than within (*HAWW* unpubl. data). Two or more of these species have been counted at 15 of 20 incipient or currently-active *HAWW* migration watchsites in Africa (Table 5). Monitoring the movements and numbers of these birds at these watchsites—particularly if it were done in conjunction with counts at important watchsites in the Middle East—would provide conservationists with important new information regarding the distribution, status, and potential threats to these birds in Africa.

Even without the 9-million-km^2 Sahara Desert, 30-million-km^2 Africa forms the driest and most open of the world's three mainly tropical continents (Brown 1965, Sayer *et al.* 1992). The wet and dry savannas and grasslands of Africa support some of the highest land-based herbivore biomasses anywhere (Frank *et al.* 1998). Although vertebrates comprise some of this biomass, much of the total consists of invertebrates, including termite alates and migratory locusts (*Schistocerca gregaria*) (cf. Brown 1965). Many Palaearctic and Afrotropical migrants, including many harriers, eagles, and falcons, depend upon these ephemeral insects for much of their "winter" food (Brown 1971, Brown *et al.* 1982). This relatively concentrated, albeit geographically episodic resource, together with the nomadic behaviour of many insect-dependent migratory raptors in Africa, probably explains how these intercontinental migrants manage to overwinter in areas in Africa that are several times smaller than their European and Asian breeding ranges (cf. Newton 1995).

Figure 4. Locations of 20 African *Hawks Aloft Worldwide* raptor-migration watchsites. The sites include: Hassi Marroket, Algeria; Bab-el-Mandeb Straits, Djibouti; Suez and Bur Safaga, Egypt; Lake Langano, Ethiopia; Lewa Downs and Tsavo, Kenya; Sarir, Libya; Bougouni and Niger Inundation Zone, Mali; Akagera, Rwanda; Mti Mwili and Lake Manyara, Tanzania; Cap Bon, Tunisia; Murchison Falls-Budongo Forest and Kibale Forest, Uganda; Lundazi and Chizongwe Hill, Zambia; and Lake Chivero (McIlwaine) and Mvurwi, Zimbabwe.

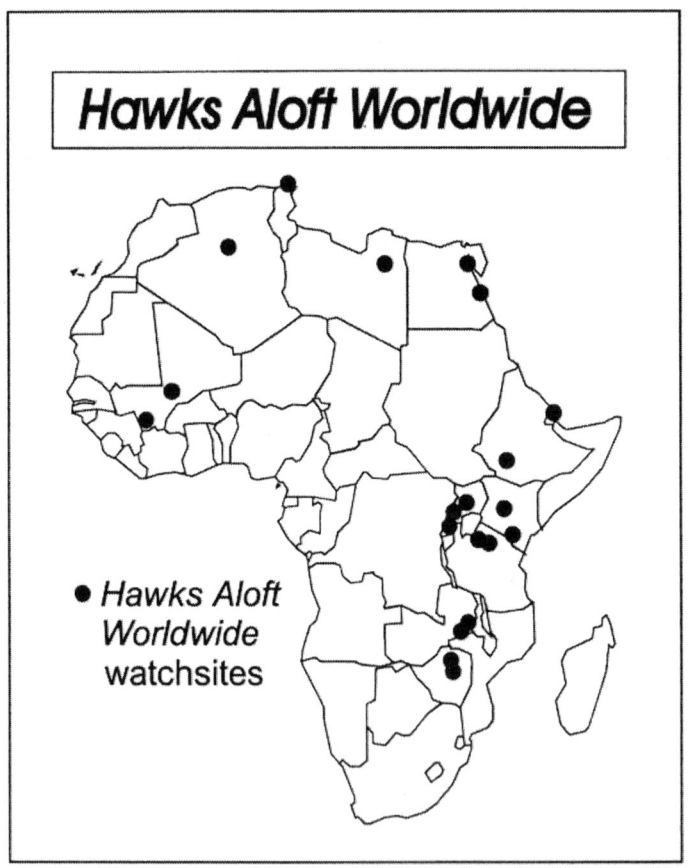

Table 6. Points of inquiry for students of African raptor migration.

1. Where do Western Honey Buzzards *Pernis apivorus* go once they reach Africa? Most appear to enter Africa via Cape Spartel, Morocco, and, to a lesser degree, northeastern Egypt (Brown 1971). Nowhere, however, are they known to be common Africa, except, perhaps in Zimbabwe, and the presumed centre of their wintering range in the Miombo (*Brachystegia*) woodland belt south of the Equator, and the continent's equatorial moist forests (Brown 1971). The species is a rare migrant in most of West Africa (Thiollay 1975b), which largely disappears once it enters the continent (Brown *et al.* 1982). The degree to which its migratory movements on the continent changes among years remains unclear.

2. What are the migratory movements of the three subspecies of Black Kites M*ilvus migrans migrans*, *M. m. parasitus*, and *M. m. aegyptius* in Africa? How do the three subspecies interact there? Detailed radio-telemetry studies of this, one of the most conspicuous raptors of tropical Africa, are long overdue.

3. Where do European populations of Egyptian Vultures *Neophron percnopterus* go once they reach Africa; and how long do first-year birds stay on the continent? The extent to which European and Asian birds in juvenal plumage over-summer in Africa remains an understudied topic (Mundy *et al.* 1992).

4. Where do populations of Levant Sparrowhawks *Accipiter brevipes* and European Sparrowhawks *A. nisus* go once they reach Africa? Presumably both species overwinter in grassy woodlands South of the Sahara Desert and north and east of the continent's equatorial forests, but the distributions of both species, not to mention their wintering ecology, remain understudied (Brown *et al.* 1982).

5. Where do Lesser *Aquila pomarina* and Greater Spotted Eagles *A. clanga* go once they reach Africa? The former, which has been reported southbound in Kenya in November, appears to winter in the region's Miombo (*Brachystegia*) woodlands; while the latter, which may be largely nomadic in winter, appears to remain mainly in northeastern Africa. Unfortunately, the movements of both appear to be masked somewhat by those of the far more numerous Steppe Eagle *A. nipalensis* (Brown 1971, Brown *et al.* 1982).

6. How do Eastern Red-footed Falcons *Falco amurensis* reach Africa in autumn? Whether the species does so across the Arabian Peninsula, or via the Indian Ocean from southwestern India, is not yet known (Ash & Miskell 1989, Brown *et al.* 1982). Equally importantly, how do the birds return to their breeding areas in spring (Steyn 1982).

Unfortunately, many of the natural grasslands and savannas that host these arthropods include some of the most endangered terrestrial ecosystems on the planet (Hannah *et al.* 1994, Frank *et al.* 1998). Africa's human population is increasing at an estimated 2.9% annually, with a doubling rate of 24 years (Sayer *et al.* 1992). As the primary productivity of African grasslands and savannas shifts from natural grazers to row-crop agriculture and cattle and wild-game ranching (Frank *et al.* 1998) to feed growing human populations, populations of migratory raptors, particularly insect-dependent species such as Lesser Kestrels, Lesser Spotted Eagles and Steppe Eagles; and semiendemics (*sensu* Gomez de Silva Garza 1996) such as Levant Sparrowhawks, are likely to decline (cf. Brown 1971), particularly if chemical pesticides toxic to raptors are used to control insects and birds in the region (cf. Woodbridge *et al.* 1995, Keith & Bruggers 1998). Counts at African migration watchsites offer the potential of acting as an early warning system for such declines.

Many African migration watchsites occur in areas of high avian diversity and endemism (Thirgood & Heath 1994, Newton 1995). Because such areas often overlap areas of high diversity and endemism for other vertebrate groups (Thirgood & Heath 1994), and because raptors are excellent bioindicators (Bildstein & Zalles 1995), migration counts at these sites also offer the promise of monitoring the ecological health of globally significant centres of biological diversity, as well as populations of migrating raptors.

Although field work in as vast a continent as Africa is both difficult and expensive, Africa offers raptor biologists and conservationists exciting opportunities for meaningful study (Table 6). We strongly recommend the expansion of field studies of migratory raptors in continental Africa. The region's highly diverse but largely understudied fauna, all but ensure considerable and immediate progress for those working in this area. International, continental, and regional initiatives that use the spectacle of long-distance raptor migration to strengthen local conservation activities along major migration corridors, together with meetings that focus on African raptors such as this one, should be continued and expanded.

The fate of African migratory raptors, including many Asian and European breeders, almost certainly rests in the hands of the human inhabitants of Africa's rural landscapes. In 1971, Leslie Brown lamented that "Rural Africans, who have the best opportunities for observing [raptor] migration note these movements, but neither comprehend them nor record them." Unfortunately, this statement remains largely true today. Community supported and locally operated raptor-migration watchsites along major migration corridors offer the promise of practical and effective raptor conservation, as well as considerable ecotourism revenue (Kerlinger & Brett 1994, Bildstein & Zalles 1995). Training opportunities for conservationists and ecotourism operators working the region, including internships at established watchsites elsewhere, designed to strengthen monitoring activity at these sites, should be encouraged and supported (Bildstein & Zalles 1995, Caldecott *et al.* 1996). Given what remains to be discovered and protected, the benefits of such efforts most certainly outweigh their costs.

ACKNOWLEDGMENTS

Our work at Hawk Mountain Sanctuary and with *Hawks Aloft Worldwide* would not be possible without the enthusiastic cooperation of hundreds of local, regional, and global volunteers and cooperators. We thank them all for their efforts and encouragement over the years. A number of individuals, organizations, and foundations have supported our efforts financially. They include the National Fish and Wildlife Foundation, the Prospect Hill Foundation, the McLean Contributionship, Nancy Frederick, and the many members of the Hawk Mountain Sanctuary Association. We thank them all. We thank Bernd Meyburg, Robin Chancellor, Gerhard Verdoorn, and John Ledger for inviting us to South Africa to present the results of our work. Nancy Keeler and Reuven Yosef helped improve earlier drafts of this manuscript. This is Hawk Mountain Sanctuary contribution number 70.

REFERENCES

AMADON, D. & J. BULL 1988. Hawks and owls of the world: A distributional and taxonomic list. *Proceedings of the Western Foundation of Vertebrate Zoology* 3: 294-357.

ASH, J. S. & J. E. MISKELL 1989. Eastern Red-footed Falcons *Falco amurensis* and Red-footed Falcons *F. vespertinus* in Somalia and Ethiopia. *Scopus* 12:61-64.

BEDNARZ, J. C. & P. KERLINGER 1988. Monitoring hawk populations by counting migrants. Pages 328-342 *in Proc. Northeast Raptor Management Symposium and Workshop*. National Wildlife Federation scientific and technical series no. 3, Washington D. C., USA.

BILDSTEIN, K. L. 1998. Long-term counts of migrating raptors: a role for volunteers in wildlife research. *Journal of Wildlife Management* 62:435-445.

BILDSTEIN, K. L. & J. I. ZALLES (eds.) 1995. Raptor migration watch-site manual. Hawk Mountain Sanctuary Association, Kempton, Pennsylvania, USA.

BILDSTEIN, K. L., J. J. BRETT, L. J. GOODRICH & C. VIVERETTE 1995. Hawks Aloft Worldwide: a network to protect the world's migrating birds of prey and the habitats essential to their migrations. Pages 504-516 *in* D. A. Saunders, J. L. Craig, & E. M. Mattishe (eds.) *Nature Conservation IV: networks*. Surrey Beaty & Sons, Chipping Norton, New South Wales, Australia.

BIJLSMA, R. G. 1983. The migration of raptors near Suez, Egypt, Autumn 1981. *Sandgrouse* 5:19-44.

BRAZIL, M. A. 1991. *The birds of Japan*. Smithsonian Institution Press, Washington, D.C., USA.

BRAZIL, M. A. & S. HANAWA 1991. The status and distribution of diurnal raptors in Japan. *WWGBP Birds of Prey Bulletin* 4:175-238.
BROEKHUYSEN, G. J. 1971. Third report on bird migration in southern Africa. *Ostrich* 42:41-64.
BROUN, M. 1949. *Hawks aloft: the story of Hawk Mountain.* Dodd, Mead Co., New York, New York, USA.
BROWN, L. 1965. *Africa: a natural history.* Random House, New York, New York, USA.
BROWN, L. 1971. *African birds of prey.* Houghton Mifflin, Boston, Massachusetts, USA.
BROWN, L. & D. AMADON. 1968. *Eagles, hawks and falcons of the world.* McGraw-Hill, New York, USA.
BROWN, L. H., E. K. URBAN & K. NEWMAN 1982. *The birds of Africa.* Vol. 1. Academic Press, London, England.
CALDECOTT, J. O., M. D. JENKINS, T. H. JOHNSON & B. GROOMBRIDGE 1996. Priorities for conserving global species richness and endemism. *Biodiversity and Conservation* 5:699-727.
COLLAR, N. J., M. J. CROSBY & A. J. STATTERSFIELD 1994. Birds to watch 2: the world list of threatened birds. *Birdlife Conservation Series No. 4.* Birdlife International, Cambridge, England.
CURRY-LINDAHL, K. 1981. *Bird migration in Africa.* Academic Press, London, England.
DEL HOYO, J. A., A. ELLIOT, & J. SARGATAL 1994. *Handbook of the birds of the world.* Vol. 2. Lynx Edicions, Barcelona, Spain.
DAVIS, S. E. 1989. Migration of Mississippi Kite *Ictinia mississippiensis* in Bolivia, with comments on *I. plumbea*. *Bulletin British Ornithologists' Club* 109:149-152.
FINLAYSON, C. 1992. *Birds of the Strait of Gibraltar.* T&AD Poyser, London, England.
FRANK, D. A., S. J. MCNAUGHTON & B. F. TRACY. 1998. The ecology of the Earth's grazing systems. *BioScience* 48:514-521.
GATTER, W. 1987. Vogelzug in Westafrika: Beobachtungen und hypothesen zu zugstrategien und wanderrouten vogelzug in Liberia, Teil II. *Die Vogelwarte* 34:80-92.
GOMEZ DE SILVA GARZA, H. 1996. The conservation importance of semiendemic species. *Conservation Biology* 10:674-675.
HANNAH, L., D. LOHSE, C. HUTCHINSON, J. L. CARR & A. LANKERANI 1994. A preliminary I inventory of human disturbance of world ecosystems. *Ambio* 23:246-250.
KEITH, J. O. & R. L. BRUGGERS. 1998. Review of hazards to raptors from pest control in Sahelian Africa. *Journal of Raptor Research* 32:151-158.
KERLINGER, P. 1989. *Flight strategies of migrating hawks.* University of Chicago Press, Chicago, USA.
KERLINGER, P. & J. BRETT 1994. Hawk Mountain Sanctuary: a case study of birder visitation and birding economics at a private refuge. Pp. 271-280 *in Wildlife and recreationists: coexistence through management and research* (ed. by R. Knight and K. J. Gutzwiller). Island Press, Washington, D. C., USA.
LEWIS, A. & D. POMEROY 1989. *A bird atlas of Kenya.* A. A. Balkema, Rotterdam, Netherlands.
MCCLURE, H. E. 1998. *Migration and survival of the birds of Asia.* White Lotus press, Bangkok, Thailand.
MOREAU, R. E. 1961. Problems of Mediterranean-Saharan migration. *Ibis* 103a:373-427, 580-623.
MOREAU, R. 1972. *The Palaearctic—African bird migration systems.* Academic Press: London, England.
MUNDY, P., D. BUTCHART, J. LEDGER & S. PIPER 1992. *The vultures of Africa.* Academic Press, London, England.
NEWMAN, K. B. 1977. Observations on raptor migration. *Bokmakierie* 29:75-79.
NEWTON, I. 1995. Relationships between breeding and wintering raptors in Palaearctic-African migrants. *Ibis* 137:241-249
ÖSTERLÖF, S. 1977. Migration, wintering areas, and site tenacity of the European Osprey *Pandion h. haliaetus* (L.). *Ornis Scandinavica* 8:61-78.
RUDEBECK, G. 1950, 1951. The choice of prey and modes of hunting of predatory birds with special reference to their selective effect. *Oikos* 2:67-88, 3:200-231.
SAYER, J. A., C. S. HARCOURT & N. M. COLLINS 1992. *The conservation atlas of tropical forests: Africa.* Macmillan, Hants, England.
SCHMITT, M. B., S. BAUER & F. VON MALTITZ 1980. Observations on the Steppe Buzzard in the Transvaal. *Ostrich* 51:151-159.
SENNER, S. E. & J. J. BRETT 1989. A proposal to create a registry of sites of international importance to raptors, especially on migration. Pages 33-37 *in Raptors in the modern world* (B.-U. Meyburg and R. D. Chancellor, eds.). WWGBP, Berlin, Germany.
SEVERINGHAUS, L. L. 1991. The status and conservation of Grey-faced Buzzard-eagles and Brown Shrikes migrating through Taiwan. Pages 203-223 *in* T. Salathé (ed.) *Conserving migratory birds.* ICBP Technical Publication No.12. Cambridge, England.
SHIRIHAI, H. 1996. *The birds of Israel.* Academic Press, London, England.
STEINBACHER, J. 1958. Migration de printemps en Tunisie. *Alauda* 26:199-227.

STEYN. P. 1982. *Birds of prey of southern Africa*. David Philip, Cape Town & Johannesburg, South Africa.
THIOLLAY, J. -M. 1975a. Migration de printemps au Cap Bon (Tunisie). *Nos Oiseaux* 33:109-121.
THIOLLAY, J. -M. 1975b. Migrations de rapaces africains en Ouganda at au Rwanda. *L'Oiseau et RFO* 45:192-194.
THIOLLAY, J. -M. 1977. Distribution saisonnière des rapaces diurnes en Afrique Occidentale. *L'Oiseau et R.F.O.* 47:253-294.
THIOLLAY, J. -M. 1978. Les plaines du nord Cameroun, centre d'hivernage de rapaces Paléarctiques. *Alauda* 46:319-326.
THIOLLAY, J. -M. 1989. Distribution and ecology of Palearctic birds of prey wintering in West and Central Africa. Pages 95-107 *in* B. -U. Meyburg and R. D. Chancellor (eds.) *Raptors in the modern world*. WWGBP, Berlin, Germany.
THIRGOOD, S. J. & M. F. HEATH 1994. Global patterns of endemism and the conservation of biodiversity. Pages 207-227 *in* P. I. Forey, C. J. Humphries, and R. I. Vanc-Wright (eds.) *Systematics and conservation evaluation*, Clarendon Press, Oxford, England.
VANDE WEGHE, J. -P. 1978. Les rapaces Paléarctiques au Rwanda. *Le Gerfaut* 68:493-519
WELCH, G. & H. WELCH 1988. The autumn migration of raptors and other soaring birds across the Bab-el-Mandeb Straits. *Sandgrouse* 10:26-50.
WOODBRIDGE, B., K. K. FINLEY & S. T. SEAGER 1995. An investigation of the Swainson's Hawk in Argentina. *J. Raptor Res.* 29:202-204.
ZUQUIM ANTAS, P. DE T. 1994. Migration and other movements among the lower Paraná River valley wetlands, Argentina, and the s Brazil/Pantanal wetlands. *Bird Conservation International* 4:181-190.

Keith L. Bildstein, Jorje Zalles, Jennifer Ottinger and Kyle McCarty
Hawk Mountain Sanctuary
1700 Hawk Mountain Road
Kempton, Pensylvania 19529
USA

Chancellor, R. D. & B.-U. Meyburg eds. 2000
Raptors at Risk
WWGBP / Hancock House

Conservation Strategies for the World's Largest Known Raptor Migration Flyway: Veracruz the River of Raptors

Ernesto Ruelas Inzunza, Stephen W. Hoffman, Laurie J. Goodrich, and Ruth Tingay

INTRODUCTION

Each autumn and spring across the North American continent, hawk watchers take to the hills and coastlines to enjoy raptor migration. Daily counts per site range from 10 to thousands of hawks and a few count sites in the United States and Canada exceed 40,000 hawks in a season (Bildstein 1998). Hawk Mountain Sanctuary, Pennsylvania, the longest running migration count site in the world, averages 20,000 hawks each autumn (Goodrich 1997). Overall, hawk migration watching has grown by leaps and bounds in the past 20 years with count sites established in nearly every U.S. state and Canadian province with thousands of sites monitored (Bildstein 1998).

Until recent years, little was known about the raptor migration patterns and numbers passing through Mexico. Periodic observations of migrating raptors in central Veracruz, Mexico, had suggested that it might harbour a significant raptor migration flyway (Andrle 1968, Thiollay 1980, Tilly *et al.* 1990). However, no season-long migration counts had been conducted and the volume of migration was unknown.

In spring 1991, Hawk Mountain Sanctuary, HawkWatch International and Pronatura Veracruz, in Xalapa, Mexico, established a partnership to begin the first standardized count of migrant raptors ever to be conducted in Mexico. During that first spring, more than 400,000 hawks were counted at four sites over a 45-day count, verifying prior observations (e.g., Thiollay 1980). Thousands of waterbirds and songbird migrants were also observed, suggesting that this corridor was used by more than just raptors. These early observations confirmed that most of the migrants were passing east of the central Sierra Madre mountain range and west of the Gulf of Mexico (Figure 1). In central Veracruz, these two geographic features converge to form a narrow 70 kilometre bottleneck constricting the migration flow across the Gulf coastal plain. Most of the migrants concentrate in the area with strongest thermal activity stretching approximately 30 kilometres from the coast to the lowest foothills.

Exciting though this discovery was, it raised conservation concerns due to extensive threats facing resident and migrating birds in this region (Ruelas 1997). Regional deforestation, pesticide use (including DDT), illegal pet and falconry trade, and shooting of hawks, all were increasing.

Veracruz population growth was estimated at 2.4% per year, and only 30 percent of the natural habitat remained. Several of the most abundant migrants using this corridor were suspected to be declining (e.g., Swainson's and Broad-winged Hawks).

Figure1. Location of the Veracruz Raptor Migration Flyway.

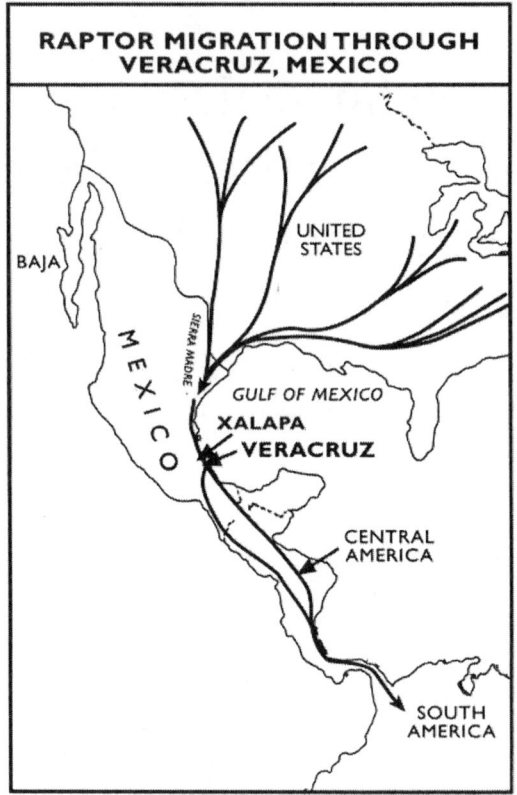

During autumn 1992, the three partner organizations launched a long-term conservation initiative to monitor and conserve this critical migration corridor. The initiative was spearheaded by Pronatura and christened the Veracruz Rio de Rapaces or Veracruz River of Raptors project (VRR). It included several short and long-term objectives, one of which was to determine the seasonal and geographic patterns of raptor migration and which site(s) might be appropriate for long-term hawk migration monitoring. Another important objective was to launch environmental education programmes focused on the migration. In this paper, we present an overview of the first five years of work and the initial strategies developed for long-term conservation of the flyway.

METHODS

Monitoring

Autumn migration counts were conducted between 20 August and 20 November from 1992 through 1996 at one to three sites per year within the flyway. Counts were conducted from 0900 to 1800 daily. Only one site was monitored in 1994 due to funding difficulties. Counts were conducted by one to three observers at each site and counts recorded hourly along with weather variables. In recent years, the counts have been conducted at two towns near the central part of the flyway, Cardel and Chichicaxtle. The Cardel watch site is on top of the largest building in this medium sized town, 6.5 kilometres from the coast. The Chichicaxtle count was conducted from on top of a scaffold in a ball field at the edge of the village, approximately 18 kilometres from the coastline.

In the later years of the study monitoring techniques were modified to cope with the large volume flights. Count teams of three observers were necessary to record both the volume of the large flocking migrants, such as the Broad-winged Hawk *Buteo platypterus*, as well as recording the single dispersed migrants such as American Kestrel *Falco sparverius* and Peregrine Falcon *Falco peregrinus*. Counters are trained in flock size estimation and hawk identification before the season begins. Count teams rotate through with two days counting and one day off to protect against fatigue.

Education

Education outreach consisted of handing out brochures and conservation posters through the flyway region, holding bird festivals in local towns, and presenting formal education programmes at schools during the autumn season. Educators have also held teacher training workshops and shared activities focused on general ecological principles and migration ecology. School programmes have developed into an eight-week formal programme for fourth grade students with pre and post testing of students. Informal education occurs at the count sites with students that may stop by to assist the counters.

RESULTS AND DISCUSSION

The first autumn migration count was conducted in autumn 1992 and tallied more than 2.5 million hawks at three count sites spaced across the coastal plain from the Gulf of Mexico west to the foothills of the Sierra Madre mountains. The four most abundant migrants were the Broad-winged Hawk, Turkey Vulture *Cathartes aura*, Swainson's Hawk *Buteo swainsoni* and the Mississippi Kite *Ictinia mississippiensis*. Other than the Turkey Vulture, these species are not well-monitored within other North American monitoring programmes or hawk migration counts. Count estimates suggested that over 90 percent of the world's population of these three species, (excluding Turkey Vulture) were concentrated in this narrow corridor each spring and autumn. These phenomenal numbers placed Veracruz as the world's most concentrated flyway for raptors, surpassing counts from sites such as Eilat, Israel, and Panama. These data also suggest that Veracruz could serve as a long-term monitoring station for continental populations of some raptor species.

In the years since 1992, improved count methodology has revealed an annual autumn migration of three to five million raptors in central Veracruz (Table 1). Twenty species of raptors have been recorded together with over 220 other species of neotropical migrant birds (Ruelas *et al.* 1997). Regular rarer migrants have included species such as the Hook-billed and Plumbeous Kites, Zone-tailed Hawk, and Golden Eagle (Table 1).

The timing of the migration varies among species. Mississippi Kites peak in late August with daily counts of over 10,000 birds in a record day, and a peak flight number exceeding 30,000 in some years. Broad-wings peak in late September and early October with daily peak flights of up to 600,000 birds. Swainson's Hawks peak in early to mid-October when the combined total of Swainson's, Turkey Vultures, and Broad-wings may surpass one million birds in a record day. Peak flights of falcons and accipiters are recorded during October as well. The Turkey Vulture is the last abundant migrant in autumn. Their migration is prolonged with peak numbers occurring in mid to late October, although substantial flights are recorded into mid-November. By late November, most of the hawks have passed through, well on their way to non-breeding ranges in Central and South America (Ruelas *et al.*, 1997), to help estimate and monitor the flight volume through the region.

Environmental education has been a critical component of the VRR project since its inception. Without the awareness and subsequent support of the local people, there will be no hope of protecting migrating raptors or the habitat critical to their survival. The first formal education efforts took place in 1992 and focused on elementary school students and their teachers, as well as the general public.

Posters and brochures were developed to help inform the adult public about the migration and the importance of these birds to the ecosystem. The first teacher's guide and teacher training workshops were held in autumn 1992 (Silva & Gaughan 1992). Further development of the educational approach and materials resulted in a soft-bound teacher's manual with lesson plans and topics designed to suit the fourth grade curriculum in Veracruz (Mesa et al. 1995). Many of the topics have focused on simple ecological concepts as well as bird migration patterns and identification. Student testing has suggested that many of the students are retaining the ecological concepts contained in the Veracruz River of Raptors programme (Mesa et al. 1997). Some of the local students in Chichicaxtle area that have spent the most time with the hawk counters are now in training to become hawk counters in the future. Several of them are taking English classes so that they may attend internships in the United States in the future. In 1998 one of them served as an assistant bird counter.

Table 1. Five-year averages for each raptor species monitored during the autumn migration in Veracruz.

Species	Five-Year Average, 1992-96*
Turkey Vulture (*Cathartes aura*)	1,202,000
Osprey (*Pandion haliaetus*)	1,500
Swallow-tailed Kite (*Elanoides forficatus*)	50
Mississippi Kite (*Ictinia mississippiensis*)	34,900
Plumbeous Kite (*Ictinia plumbea*)	5
Hook-billed Kite (*Chondrohierax uncinatus*)	60
Northern Harrier (*Circus cyaneus*)	200
Sharp-shinned Hawk (*Accipiter striatus*)	2,800
Cooper's Hawk (*Accipiter cooperii*)	1,100
Harris Hawk (*Parabuteo unicinctus*)	2
Zone-tailed Hawk (*Buteo albonatus*)	23
Red-shouldered Hawk (*Buteo lineatus*)	20
Broad-winged Hawk (*Buteo platypterus*)	1,452,000
Swainson's Hawk (*Buteo swainsoni*)	513,000
Red-tailed Hawk (*Buteo jamaicensis*)	140
Ferruginous Hawk (*Buteo regalis*)	<1
Golden Eagle (*Aquila chrysaetos*)	<1
American Kestrel (*Falco sparverius*)	4,400
Merlin (*Falco columbarius*)	50
Peregrine Falcon (*Falco peregrinus*)	290
Unidentified Raptor	80,000
TOTAL	3,295,000

*The numbers shown are LESS than the numbers known to pass through this area, because in some years we had incomplete coverage. In 1996, a complete count yielded 4.6 million hawks with over two million Broad-winged Hawks, and this number is believed to be closer to the true number of migrants passing each autumn.

Conservation outreach to the adult population has proven more difficult. Poster distribution and occasional talks at agricultural meetings have been only moderately successful. During 1996 and 1997 funds were raised to build a small education centre and bird monitoring station at the heart of the flyway. One of the purposes of this centre is to operate a nature centre and museum focusing on bird migration and the importance of raptors in the ecosystem. Modelled after the successful Hawk Mountain Sanctuary, in Pennsylvania, the centre should serve as a nucleus of public outreach year-round. The centre, the Veracruz Bird Observatory, will be built during 1999, and will house a full-time naturalist/educator. It will serve as one of the main count sites for the monitoring programme and provide comfortable hawk watching for visiting tourists. Nature trails and habitat restoration areas will serve to introduce local residents to local birds and bird-watching.

The extreme concentration of migrants in this narrow corridor has also highlighted the need for habitat protection within this area. Many of the migrants, particularly Broad-winged Hawks, seek out wooded areas for evening roosts. Long-term project goals include identification and conservation of roosting habitat for raptor migrants. Much of the grassland habitat has been converted into sugar cane plantations in recent years, further restricting the habitat for feeding and resting migrants, as well as native raptors. Other goals include establishing outreach programmes to local farmers to reduce pesticide use, and promote native habitat protection.

One of the important critical challenges of the VRR project has been to maintain funding to continue the monitoring and education initiatives. To support long-term conservation and monitoring programmes in the flyway, the VRR project launched a membership programme in 1996. To date nearly 200 people have become founding members, supporting the annual hawk count and education programmes. Pronatura-Veracruz is also developing ecotourism as another avenue to support their monitoring and education programmes. From 1994 to 1998 the numbers of visiting tours has grown from one to seven in 1998. Local businesses that benefit from the tourism are also beginning to contribute to the conservation programme.

In summary, hawk migration counts in central Veracruz have established this site as the most concentrated raptor migration site in the world, hosting three to five million raptors each autumn. Most the world's Broad-winged and Swainsons' Hawks, and Mississippi Kites pass through this narrow corridor each spring and autumn. Habitat loss and alteration continues throughout this region, highlighting the need for focused conservation efforts. Long-term conservation strategies include enhanced environmental education and public outreach, continued long-term monitoring, research on raptor and waterbird migration including use of radar to estimate flight volumes, and habitat conservation initiatives focused on protection of forests and other native habitats.

ACKNOWLEDGEMENTS

The authors thank Keith L. Bildstein for his comments on an earlier version of this manuscript. We also thank volunteers and staff who have assisted the project over the years, particularly Sandra Mesa and Sharon Gaughan. Support for the VRR project has been provided by: National Fish and Wildlife Foundation; United States Fish and Wildlife Service; Secretaría de Desarollo Social, Mexico; The John D. And Catherine T. MacArthur Foundation; U.S. Agency for International Development; Center for the Study of Tropical Birds, Inc.; Hawk Migration Association of North America; Hawk Mountain Zeiss Research Award; Bobbie Dent Memorial Fund; Scott Neotropic Fund, Lincoln Park Zoo; Lighthawk, Inc.; Lannan Foundation; and by Hawk Mountain Sanctuary Association, HawkWatch International, and their respective members. This is Hawk Mountain contribution number 77.

REFERENCES

ANDRLE, R. 1968. Raptors and other North American migrants in Mexico. *The Condor* 70:393-395.

BILDSTEIN, K. 1998. Long-term counts of migration raptors: a role for volunteers in wildlife research. *J. of Wildlife Management* 62:435-445.

GOODRICH, L. 1997. The Migration Report, Hawk Mountain News No. 86:8-14.

MESA, S.L., L. CORONADO, & S.M. GAUGHAN 1995. Veracruz: Río de Rapaces, Manual de Educación Ambiental para la Conservación de las Aves Rapaces y sus Hábitats en Veracruz, Dirigido a Maestros de Enseñanza Primaria. Pronatura Veracruz and National Fish and Wildlife Foundation. In-house Publication.

MESA, S.L., E. RUELAS INZUNZA & X. OSORIO M. 1997. Programa de educación ambiental Veracruz Río de Rapaces: su inserción en el curriculum de 4o. grado de enseñanza primaria. Pp. 101-114. *In*: de Alba y E. González Gaudiano. *Evaluación de programas de educación ambiental, experiencias de America Latina y El Caribe*. CESU-UNAM/Cecadesu. México, D.F.

RUELAS INZUNZA, E. 1997. The River of Raptors: What's going on in Veracruz? *Amigos del Río de Rapaces newsletter* 1, 1:1-3.

RUELAS INZUNZA, E., S.W. HOFFMAN, L.J. GOODRICH, & S.L. MESA 1997. Veracruz River of Raptors II, Project 96-124 Progress Report. Submitted to National Fish and Wildlife Foundation, Washington, D.C.
RUELAS INZUNZA, E., S.L. MESA., & J. MONTEJO 1997. Veracruz River of Raptors I, Project 94-236 Final Report. Submitted to National Fish and Wildlife Foundation, Washington, D.C.
SILVA R., E. & S.M. GAUGHAN, 1992. México: un Puente para la Migración, una guía de referencia para maestros sobre educación para la conservación de las aves rapaces. Hawk Mountain Sanctuary Association/ Pronatura, Veracruz In-house Publication. Kempton, PA.
THIOLLAY, J. 1980. Spring hawk migration in eastern Mexico. *Raptor Research* 14:12-14.
TILLY, F., S. HOFFMAN, & C. TILLY. 1990. Spring hawk migration in southern Mexico, 1989. *J. of Hawk Migration Studies* 15:21-29.

Ernesto Ruelas Inzunza
Pronatura Veracruz
Apartado Postal 399
Xalapa, Veracruz
Mexico, 91000

Stephen W. Hoffman
HawkWatch International
P.O. Box 660
Salt Lake City
Utah 84110
USA

Laurie J. Goodrich
Hawk Mountain Sanctuary
1700 Hawk Mountain Road.
Kempton, PA 19529
USA

Ruth Tingay
Dept. Geography
Nottingham University
United Kingdom

The Value of Extensive Raptor Migration Monitoring in Western North America.

Jeff P. Smith and Stephen W. Hoffman

ABSTRACT

Monitoring raptor migration at migratory concentration points is an efficient and cost-effective method for tracking raptor populations over long periods and large geographic scales. HawkWatch International (HWI) and its organizational precursors have been monitoring fall and spring raptor migrations in western North America since the late 1970s. HWI has gathered more than a decade of annual count data for primarily 16 diurnal raptor species in Nevada (fall), Utah (fall), and New Mexico (fall and spring), and coordinates counts at another 13 sites (3 spring, 10 fall) from Texas to Montana and Washington state to Veracruz, Mexico. The HWI effort is unique in applying standard methods across a geographically extensive network of sites, which is critical for accurately tracking regional population trends. However, several other annual counts in the region also add important nodes to the monitoring network and contribute valuable information about regional population trends and flyway dynamics. HWI also conducts banding programs at five sites (2 spring, 3 fall). Together with data from other projects, band encounters from these sites document three distinct regional flyways west of the Great Plains, which we call the Pacific Coast, Intermountain, and Rocky Mountain flyways. Count data from four of HWI's long-term sites and elsewhere document widespread population increases for Ospreys *Pandion haliaetus*, Merlins *Falco columbarius*, Peregrine Falcons *F. peregrinus*, and Turkey Vultures *Cathartes aura*, but indicate concern for Northern Goshawks *Accipiter gentilis* in the northern Rocky Mountains and Golden Eagles *Aquila chrysaetos* in the Great Basin since the late 1970s. The effort to monitor raptor migrations in western North America, although young, is yielding substantial understanding about the dynamics of raptor migrations through the region, valuable information to guide conservation actions, and much additional information concerning the biology and migratory ecology of diurnal raptors. Three primary needs remain: (1) expand the monitoring network to include more of western Canada, the central Rocky Mountains in Colorado and Wyoming, the Sierra Nevada and southern mountains of California, and northern and central Mexico; (2) establish intensive nest productivity studies on selected species to help validate migration monitoring as an effective indicator of population trends; and (3) further improve analytical methods for overcoming biases and summarizing trend data.

INTRODUCTION

Raptors typically occupy top positions in biological food pyramids, occur in most habitats, use resources over broad areas, and are sensitive to chemical contamination and other forms of habitat disturbance. For this reason, raptors represent important biological indicators of environmental change and ecosystem health (Bednarz et al. 1990a, b; Bildstein & Zalles 1995). However, many raptors occur at relatively low densities, are secretive in nature, occupy habitats that are difficult to access, and use large home ranges. Accordingly, developing monitoring programs to track the status of populations over long periods and appropriate geographic scales is difficult (Fuller & Mosher 1981, 1987; Titus et al. 1989; Bildstein 1998; Kirk & Hyslop 1998). Although not free from inherent biases and methodological problems, monitoring raptors at migratory concentration points is an efficient and cost-effective alternative for gathering substantial information on the population dynamics of multiple species (Kerlinger 1989, Bednarz & Kerlinger 1989, Bildstein et al. 1995, Bildstein & Zalles 1995, Dunn & Hussell 1995). Moreover, using standardized methods at multiple sites is essential for yielding accurate information about regional changes in status and population trends (Titus et al. 1989, Dixon et al. 1998), which today is often the scale of interest for assessing the impact of human activities.

Specific benefits of long-term, geographically extensive monitoring of raptor migrations include: (1) standardized counts are an efficient, cost-effective method for tracking long-term population trends of multiple raptor species, and help develop understanding of migratory ecology by documenting variation in the timing of migratory activity for different species, sexes, and age classes in relation to various environmental parameters (e.g., weather); (2) banding enables large-sample studies of raptor morphology, moult, physiology, genetics, and health (e.g., parasites, fat levels), and foreign encounters with banded birds help identify migratory routes, connections between breeding and wintering grounds, causes of injury and mortality, and longevity in the wild; (3) migration studies provide opportunities to engage the public in monitoring activities and to promote grass roots conservation on behalf of raptors and the ecosystems that support them; and (4) a standardized network of monitoring sites enables detailed delineation of flyways and subpopulations, increases statistical power for detecting regional population trends, enables fine-scale tracking of threats to raptor populations, increases the diversity of samples for biological studies, and greatly expands opportunities for public outreach.

In this paper, we review the status of raptor-migration monitoring in western North America, emphasizing the value and results of pioneering efforts by HawkWatch International (HWI) to establish a broad network of counting and banding sites in the region. Although raptor migration has been intensively studied in the eastern United States for more than 50 years (e.g., Allen & Peterson 1936, Broun 1949, Mueller & Berger 1967, Heintzelman 1975), intensive efforts to document migration patterns in western North America did not commence until the late 1970s (Binford 1979, Hoffman 1985). Now, with information spanning more than a decade at several western sites, migration counts and banding are beginning to reveal the intricacies of western flyways and provide valuable information about regional population trends.

WESTERN NORTH AMERICA RAPTOR MONITORING NETWORK

HWI and its organizational precursors have been monitoring fall and spring raptor migrations in western North America since 1977. HWI has gathered more than a decade of full-season, daily count data at four sites in Utah (fall), Nevada (fall), and New Mexico (spring and fall), and coordinates counts that have proceeded for more recently initiated counts at another 13 sites (3 spring, 10 fall) ranging from Montana to Texas and Washington to Veracruz, Mexico (Table 1, Fig. 1). Supervision by a single organization ensures a high degree of methodological standardization across this extensive network of sites, which greatly facilitates integrating multi-site data and tracking regional population trends (Titus et al. 1989, Bildstein & Zalles 1995, Dunn & Hussell 1997, Link & Sauer 1998). HWI monitoring sites encompass three of the largest known concentrations of migratory raptors in North America: Veracruz, Mexico; Corpus Christi, Texas; and the Goshute Mountains, Nevada (Table 1).

Figure 1. Locations of established full or near full-season diurnal raptor migration counts and multi-species raptor banding projects in western North America (numbers refer to sites as listed in Tables 1 and 2).

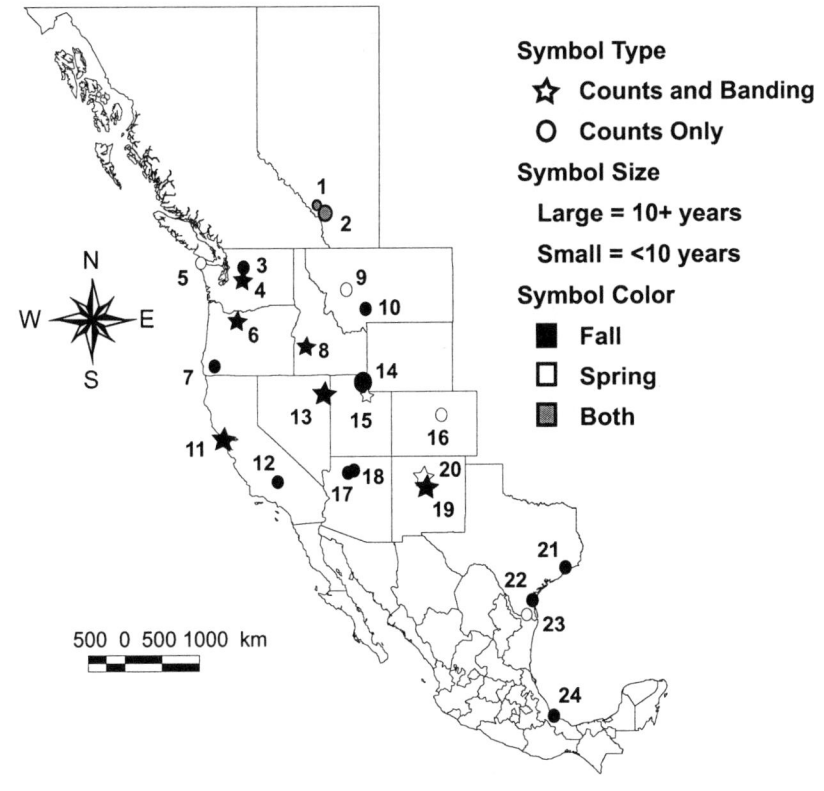

Several other noteworthy raptor migration monitoring programs exist in the region besides the HWI efforts (Table 1, Fig. 1). Establishment of fall counts at Boise Ridge, Idaho in 1994 (run by the Idaho Bird Observatory [IBO]) and Dinosaur Ridge, Colorado in 1990 (run by the Denver Museum of Natural History) benefited from HWI technical support. Since 1986, the Golden Gate Raptor Observatory (GGRO) has monitored movements at Pt. Diablo, California that rival the concentration in the Goshute Mountains (Binford 1979, GGRO 1997). A sharp rise in raptor migration monitoring activity has recently occurred in western Canada. Windy Point and Mt. Lorette are two prominent sites in Alberta where both spring and fall counts have been conducted since 1986-88 and 1992, respectively, and several other sites in British Columbia, Alberta, and the Yukon Territory offer additional promise for the future in western Canada (Sherrington 1997, 1998). Since 1994, the Kern River Research Center has been monitoring the fall migration through the Kern River Valley of California, which may attract as many as 40,000 Turkey Vultures *Cathartes aura* each year (Rowe & Gallion 1996, McDermot 1997). Variation in methods ultimately may preclude direct comparison of data from these and HWI's network of sites. Nevertheless, all nodes in the raptor monitoring network of western North America can provide valuable comparative information on population trends and flyway dynamics (Kirk & Hyslop 1998). This will be particularly true if all operations follow standardized data recording procedures of the Hawk Migration Association of North America (HMANA) and other guidelines outlined in the Raptor Migration Watch-site Manual prepared by Hawks Aloft Worldwide (Bildstein & Zalles 1995).

Table 1. Ongoing, annual, full or near full-season, multi-species diurnal raptor migration counts in western North America.

Map #	Site	Organization	Season	Year Initiated	Species	Annual Counts	References
1	Mt. Lorette, Alberta	Peter Sherrington et al.	spring/fall	1992	18	4000–5000[2]	Sherrington 1997, 1998
2	Windy Point, Alberta	Wayne Smith	spring/fall	1986/88[3]	15	3000–5000	Sherrington 1997, 1998
3	Chelan Ridge, Washington	HWI	fall	1997	15	1500–2000	Rossman 1998
4	Diamond Head, Washington	HWI	fall	1993	16	1300–1700	Prosser and DeSorbo 1998
5	Cape Flattery, Washington	HWI	spring	1990	16	3000–9000	Clark et al. 1998
6	Bonney Butte, Oregon	HWI	fall	1993	18	2300–2700	Grindrod and Smith 1998a
7	Dutchmans Peak, Oregon	HWI	fall	1997	16	≈5400[4]	HWI unpubl. data
8	Boise Ridge, Idaho	Idaho Bird Observatory	fall	1994	18	3500–5900	Tilly 1997
9	Rogers Pass, Montana	HWI	spring	1988	13	1200–2200	Tilly and Tilly 1998
10	Bridger Mts., Montana	HWI	fall	1991	17	2500–3500	Beason and Scifres 1998
11	Pt. Diablo, California	Golden Gate Raptor Observatory	fall	1986	19	14000–30000[5]	GGRO 1997
12	Kern River Valley, California	Kern River Research Center	fall	1994	14	20000–40000[4]	McDermot 1997
13	Goshute Mts., Nevada	HWI	fall	1983	18	17000–23000	Hoffman et al. in review
14	Wellsville Mts., Utah	HWI	fall	1977[5]	18	3000–6000	Hoffman et al. in review
15	Jordanelle, Utah	HWI	spring	1997	17	1300–1500	Miller and Smith 1998
16	Dinosaur Ridge, Colorado	Denver Museum of Natural History	fall	1990	19	2200–5400	Grindrod 1998
17	Yaki Pt., Arizona	HWI	fall	1997	18	4000–5000	Thomas and Smith 1998
18	Lipan Pt., Arizona	HWI	fall	1991	18	6000–10000	Thomas and Smith 1998
19	Manzano Mts., New Mexico	HWI	fall	1985	18	4000–7000	Hoffman et al. in review
20	Sandia Mts., New Mexico	HWI	spring	1985	20	3000–6000	Hoffman et al. in review
21	Smith Point, Texas	HWI; Gulf Coast Bird Observatory	fall	1997	19	≈43000[5,7]	Grindrod and Smith 1998b
22	Corpus Christi, Texas	HWI	fall	1997	24	≈84000[7]	Simon and Grindrod 1998
23	Santa Ana NWR, Texas	Santa Ana NWR	spring	1992	15	6000–60000	Economidy 1998
24	Veracruz, Mexico	Pronatura Veracruz; HWI; Hawk Mountain Sanctuary Association	fall	1992	22	2–5 million	Pronatura/HWI/HMSA unpubl. data

[1] Number-coded locations shown in Figure 1.
[2] 80–90% Golden Eagles.
[3] Partial, intermittent counts since 1967.
[4] 85–99% Turkey Vultures.
[5] Values are indicative of passage activity but not necessarily numbers of individuals because of multi-directional flight paths.
[6] Sampled 1977–1979 and 1987–present.
[7] 70% (Smith Pt.) and 99% (Corpus Christi) Broad-winged Hawks.

Table 2. Annual, multi-species migratory raptor banding operations in western North America.

Map #[1]	Site	Organization	Season	Year Initiated	Species	Total Captures Through Spring 1998	Reference
4	Diamond Head, Washington	Falcon Research Group	fall	1993	10	≈1000	J. Bettesworth pers. comm.
6	Bonney Butte, Oregon	HWI	fall	1995	9	371	Grindrod and Hallett 1998
8	Boise Ridge, Idaho	Idaho Bird Observatory	fall	1993	12	3322	G. Kaltenecker pers. comm.
11	Pt. Diablo, California	Golden Gate Raptor Observatory	fall	1983	15	12274	GGRO 1997
13	Goshute Mts., Nevada	HWI	fall	1980	13	36961	Meehan and Carver 1998
15	Jordanelle, Utah	HWI	spring	1998	6	50	Covert 1998
19	Manzano Mts., New Mexico	HWI	fall	1990	11	7179	Stravers and Smith 1998
20	Sandia Mts., New Mexico	HWI	spring	1990	12	2193	Smith and Smith 1999

[1] Number-coded locations shown in Figure 1.

HWI also conducts raptor banding programmes at five sites (Table 2, Fig. 1). Banding programmes provide essential information on breeding and wintering ranges, migratory routes, and the health and morphology of migrants. Knowledge of migratory routes and associated breeding and wintering ranges is critical for establishing the spatial context for specific migration counts and for tracking the causes of observed population trends (Senner & Fuller 1989). Other large-scale, multi-species, migratory raptor banding projects in the region that we are aware of include GGRO Pt. Diablo, IBO Boise Ridge, and the Falcon Research Group (FRG) project at Diamond Head, Washington (also the location of a HWI count station since 1993; Table 2, Fig. 1). Long-term banding by Peter Bloom and colleagues in California at nests and elsewhere also has yielded valuable information about migratory pathways along the Pacific Coast (e.g., Bloom 1985).

Regional Flyways

A primary value of long-term banding programmes is that foreign encounters with previously banded birds help delineate migratory routes and flyway boundaries (Kerlinger 1989). Band-encounter information from HWI Goshute and New Mexico sites (HWI unpubl. data), FRG Diamond Head (J. Bettesworth pers. comm.), GGRO Pt. Diablo (Scheuermann 1996), IBO Boise Ridge (G. Kaltenecker pers. comm.), and Bloom (1985) indicate at least three distinct regional flyways, which we call Pacific Coast, Intermountain, and Rocky Mountain (Fig. 2). These flyways ultimately converge in southern Mexico for species known to winter in Latin America (e.g., Turkey Vulture and Swainson's Hawk *Buteo swainsoni*. However, for the four species that constitute the bulk of birds banded at migration monitoring sites in the West—Sharp-shinned Hawk *Accipiter striatus*, Cooper's Hawk *A. cooperii*, Red-tailed Hawk *Buteo jamaicensis*, and American Kestrel *Falco columbarius*—all three flyways terminate within North America.

Figure 2. Major raptor migration flyways in western North America.

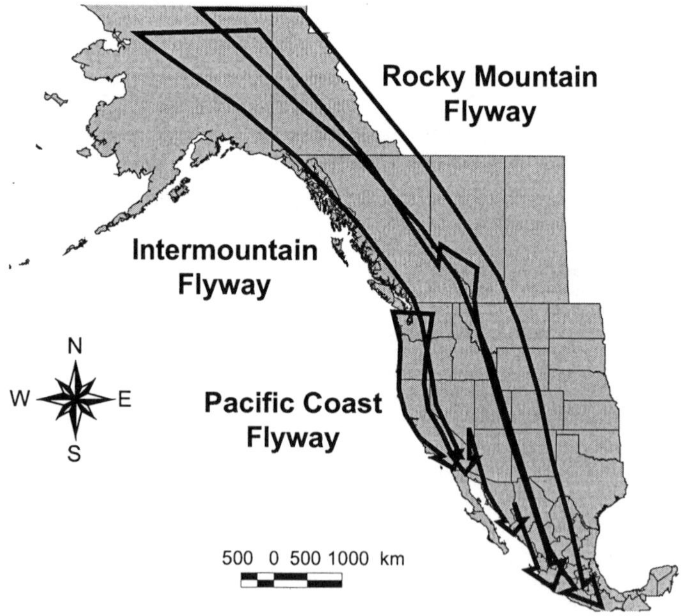

Based on data for these species from GGRO Pt. Diablo, Bloom (1985), and FRG Diamond Head, the Pacific Coast flyway extends from the Cascade Mountains in northwestern Washington to primarily southern California, but also occasionally into Baja California and along the west coast of Mexico, running primarily west of the Cascade Mountains and Sierra Nevada. Based on data from

HWI Goshute Mountains and IBO Boise Ridge, the Intermountain flyway extends from interior Alaska, along the western flanks of the Rocky Mountains through Canada, between the Rocky Mountains and Cascade/Sierra Nevada ranges in the United States, to Baja California and the coastal states of Mexico primarily along or west of the Sierra Madré Occidental. Based on data from HWI's two New Mexico sites, the Rocky Mountain flyway extends from northern Alaska to southern Mexico, running primarily along the eastern and central Rocky Mountains and within the belt extending from the eastern flanks of the Sierra Madré Occidental to the western flanks of the Sierra Madré Oriental. In addition to these truly western flyways, the HWI sites along the gulf coast of Texas and in Veracruz monitor a continuation of eastern and midwestern flyways that funnel large numbers of raptors, especially Broad-winged Hawks *Buteo platypterus*, into Latin America for the winter (e.g., see Goodrich *et al.* 1996).

As additional information accumulates, other aspects of major flyways will be revealed. Encounter information from the HWI Bonney Butte and FRG Diamond Head sites will be of particular interest for delineating boundaries between the Pacific Coast and Intermountain flyways, whereas information from the HWI Jordanelle site will help delineate boundaries between the Intermountain and Rocky Mountain flyways (Fig. 1). For example, several exchanges between the HWI Goshute and IBO Boise Ridge sites indicate a strong connection within the Intermountain flyway; however, winter encounters of Boise Ridge birds thus far have been concentrated slightly northwest (northwestern Mexico, Baja California, and southern California) of most Goshute encounters (mostly central and southern coastal states of Mexico).

Figure 3. Probable raptor migration flyways near the Great Salt Lake and Great Salt Lake Desert of Utah.

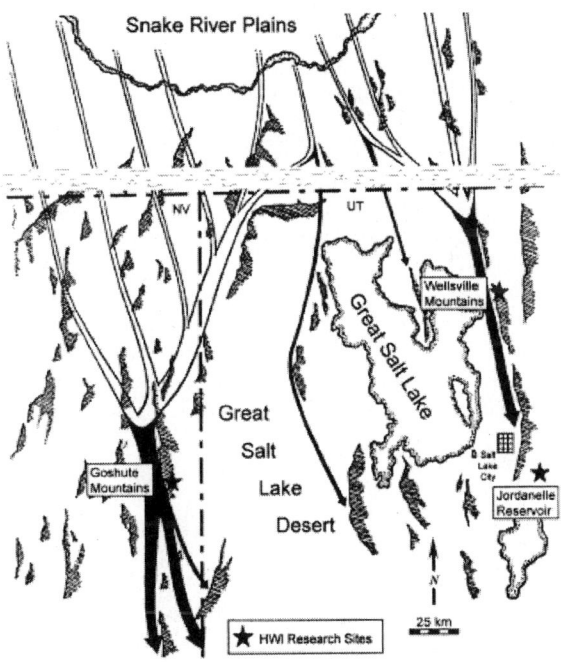

Comparing band-encounter information from the HWI Utah and Nevada sites also will be important for determining how migrants respond to the Great Salt Lake and Great Salt Lake Desert. Large bodies of water and otherwise inhospitable habitat often act as major barriers for migrating raptors (Kerlinger 1989). We believe that the Goshute Mountains are a major concentration point for migrating raptors largely because the range lies at the western edge of the Great Salt Lake Desert at the point where many birds accumulate after skirting around the desert from the northeast (Fig. 3). Encounter data from the newly established HWI Jordanelle banding site in Utah near the eastern edge of the Great Salt Lake will help determine if the Wasatch and Goshute flyways attract distinct subpopulations. Inconsistencies in count data from the HWI Goshute and Wellsville, Utah sites suggest that this may be the case for some species (Hoffman *et al.* in review); however, additional verification of flyway affinities is needed to enable definitive interpretation of the count trends.

Population Trends

The primary value of long-term migration counts is that they facilitate tracking of population trends, especially when combined with knowledge of flyway dimensions and information about regional variation provided by a multi-site monitoring network. Hoffman *et al.* (in review) recently analyzed long-term trends in annual passage rates (total raptors counted / total hours observed) through spring 1998 for 16 species counted in the Wellsville, Goshute, Manzano (fall), and Sandia (spring) mountains (Fig. 1). They adjusted daily counts for variation in observer numbers based on Smith and Hoffman (in review), and conducted site-specific trend analyses using primarily linear regression on the log scale (Bednarz & Kerlinger 1989, Titus & Fuller 1990, Hatfield *et al.* 1996). Although a variety of methods are available for combining multi-site data in integrated analyses (e.g., Hussell 1981, Titus *et al.* 1990, Link & Sauer 1998), Hoffman *et al.* elected to follow the recommendation of Dunn and Hussell (1995) for independent, site-specific analyses because of uncertainties about the monitored populations each count represents. Table 3 summarizes the results of these analyses.

These analyses (hereafter called "HWI analyses") consistently reveal significant increases in annual passage rates for Turkey Vulture, Osprey *Pandion haliaetus*, Broad-winged Hawk, Merlin *Falco columbarius*, and Peregrine Falcon *F. peregrinus* at the four sites (Table 3, Fig. 4). Data on the regional status of western Turkey Vultures and Merlins are limited (Pattee & Wilbur 1989, Sodhi *et al.* 1993); thus, the insight provided by migration count data is particularly valuable. North American Breeding Bird Survey (BBS) data for the western region (Sauer *et al.* 1997) and Canada (Kirk & Hyslop 1998), and migration count data from GGRO Pt. Diablo (A. M. Fish, GGRO, pers. comm.) and Hawk Ridge, Minnesota (Hussell & Brown 1992) also indicate increasing trends for Turkey Vultures. This population growth may reflect expansion of open habitat from logging and rural development, and increases in carrion availability associated with an expanding human population (Wilbur 1983, Hoffman *et al.* in review).

Evidence from several migration count sites and BBS routes suggests a possible widespread decline among Broad-winged Hawks in eastern North America (Titus & Fuller 1990, Hussell & Brown 1992, Goodrich *et al.* 1996, Kirk & Hyslop 1998). However, recent increases in general sightings in the western United States and signs of breeding activity in western Canada suggest that the species is expanding its breeding range in the West (Goodrich *et al.* 1996, Hoffman *et al.* in review).

Ospreys, Merlins, and Peregrine Falcons continue to rebound after suffering during the DDT era (Speitzer *et al.* 1978, Henny & Anthony 1989, Cade *et al.* 1988, Sodhi *et al.* 1993). Widespread availability of artificial nesting platforms and reservoirs also has helped Ospreys (Swenson 1981, Henny & Kaiser 1995). Similarly, aggressive conservation action and widespread artificial propagation and release bolstered recovery of Peregrine Falcons, and artificially reared stocks contributed to expansion of Merlins in southern Alberta and Saskatchewan (Platt & Enderson 1989). BBS data confirm the increasing trend for Ospreys in the western region and the increasing trend for Merlins in Canada (Sauer *et al.* 1997, Kirk & Hyslop 1998). Migration counts from GGRO Pt. Diablo confirm increasing detection rates for Merlins and Peregrine Falcons (A. M. Fish, GGRO, pers. comm.), migration counts from Hawk Ridge Minnesota confirm increasing trends for all three species (Hussell & Brown 1992), and nesting surveys in Canada also indicate stable or increasing Peregrine populations (Holroyd & Banasch 1996).

Table 3. Summary of trend results for four raptor migration count sites in western North America (adapted from Hoffman et al. in review).[1]

Raptor species	Scientific name	Wellsville Mts., UT (fall) 1977–79 vs 87–97 t-test	Wellsville Mts., UT (fall) 1987–1997 Regression	Goshute Mts., NV (fall) 1983–1997 Regression	Manzano Mts., NM (fall) 1985–1997 Regression	Sandia Mts., NM (spring) 1985–1998 Regression
Turkey Vulture	Cathartes aura	(I)	(I)[2]	I*	I*	I*
Osprey	Pandion haliaetus	I*	(I)[2]	I*	I*	I*
Northern Harrier	Circus cyaneus	–	–	I[3]	–	–
Broad-winged Hawk	Buteo platypterus	I*	–	I	–	I*
Swainson's Hawk	Buteo swainsoni	I*	(I)[2]	–	I[3]	–
Red-tailed Hawk	Buteo jamaicensis	I*	–	–	–	–
Ferruginous Hawk	Buteo regalis	I*	–	I[3]	D	–
Golden Eagle	Aquila chrysaetos	D	–	–	–	–
Bald Eagle	Haliaeetus leucocephalus	–	D	–	–	–
Sharp-shinned Hawk	Accipiter striatus	–	–	I	–	–
Cooper's Hawk	Accipiter cooperii	–	–	–	–	–
Northern Goshawk	Accipiter gentilis	D*	D[3]	–	–	I[3]
American Kestrel	Falco sparverius	–	–	I*	I*	I*
Merlin	Falco columbarius	I	–	I*	I*	–
Prairie Falcon	Falco mexicanus	–	–	I	I*	–
Peregrine Falcon	Falco peregrinus	I*[4]	–	I*	I*	I*

[1] I* = highly significant increase, $p \leq 0.01$; I = significant increase, $0.01 < p \leq 0.05$; (I) = marginally significant increase, $0.05 < p \leq 0.10$; D* = highly significant decrease; D = significant decrease; – = not significant, $p > 0.10$. Note that all linear regressions were also tested using nonparametric rank trend analysis (Titus et al. 1990), and cases where the two approaches yielded substantially different conclusions are indicated by footnotes 2 and 3.
[2] Nonparametric rank trend analysis indicates significant increasing trend ($0.01 < p \leq 0.05$).
[3] Nonparametric rank trend analysis indicates no trend ($p > 0.10$).
[4] Based on nonparametric Mann-Whitney U-test because of zero counts during 1970s.

The HWI analyses indicate significant declines for five species, but in each case only at one site (Table 3). Moreover, only Sharp-shinned Hawk, Northern Goshawk *Accipiter gentilis*, and Golden Eagle *Aquila chrysaetos* showed a decline at one site and no increasing trends. The apparent, recent decline in Sharp-shinned Hawk passage rates at the Wellsville site may be an artifact of inclement weather leading to a poor count in 1997 (Hoffman *et al*. in review). Although no significant long-term trends were evident, data from the other three HWI sites showed recent increases (Hoffman *et al*. in review). Moreover, BBS data for the western region indicate no trend for 1980–1996 (Sauer *et al*. 1997), most evidence summarized by Kirk and Hyslop (1998) for Canada indicated stable or increasing trends, and migration counts from Hawk Ridge, Minnesota indicate stable trends for Sharp-shinned Hawks (Hussell & Brown 1992).

Figure 4. Examples of increasing population trends as discerned from raptor migration counts in Utah, Nevada, and New Mexico (adapted from Hoffman *et al.* in review).

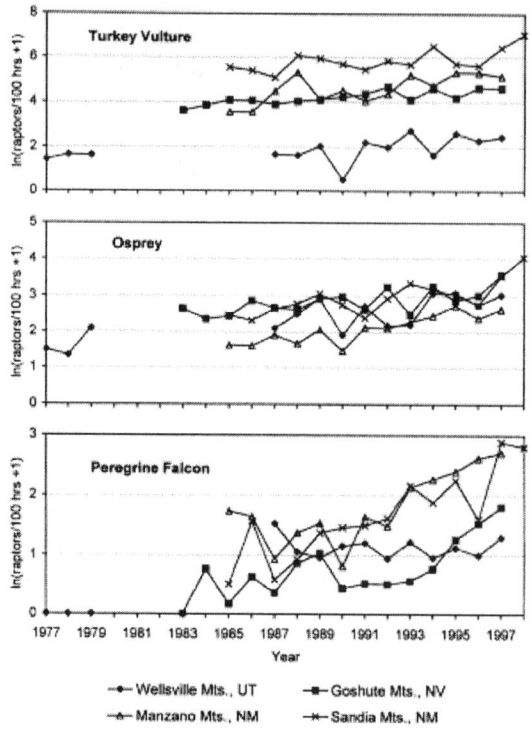

For Northern Goshawks and Golden Eagles, the HWI analyses indicated no significant long-term trends except in the Wellsvilles (Table 3). Passage rates of immature Northern Goshawks and Golden Eagles declined significantly in the Wellsvilles between the late 1970s and late 1980s (Fig. 5), suggesting that productivity declined in the north-central Rocky Mountains during this period and has not recovered. In comparison, Goshute Northern Goshawks showed two previously unequalled spikes in immature detection rates during the past six years, suggesting that productivity in the Great Basin may be improving for this species (Hoffman *et al*. in review). Passage rates of adult Golden Eagles also have generally increased in recent years at the three HWI fall sites. However, because adults of both species are largely non-migratory in many areas (Palmer 1988), indications of increased migratory movements among adults may reflect poor winter conditions on breeding grounds rather than increasing populations (Hoffman et al. in review). Recent decreases in immature : adult ratios at the three HWI fall count sites also probably reflect poor breeding conditions for Golden Eagles in the Intermountain region (Hoffman et al. in review).

Figure 5. Declines in migration passage rates of immature Northern Goshawks and immature/subadult Golden Eagles in the Wellsville Mountains of Utah between the late 1970s and late 1980s (adapted from Hoffman et al. in review).

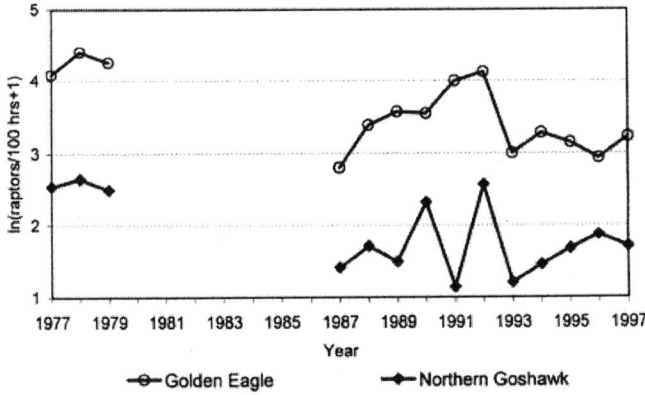

The United States Fish and Wildlife Service (USFWS) recently concluded that Northern Goshawks are a forest generalist and that listing under the U.S. Endangered Species Act was not warranted for populations west of the 100th meridian (USFWS 1998). Nonetheless, many indications suggest that Northern Goshawks do best in relatively undisturbed tracts of mature or old-growth forest, are sensitive to excessive forest fragmentation, and have declined in several local areas as a result of habitat disturbance (e.g., Crocker-Bedford 1990, Reynolds et al. 1992, Woodbridge & Detrich 1994, Iverson et al. 1996, Squires & Reynolds 1997). Thus, we suggest that Northern Goshawks at least warrant additional careful monitoring, particularly in the northern and central Rocky Mountains and Pacific Northwest.00

Indications of trouble for Golden Eagles are consistent with evidence of declining territory occupancy and productivity in the Snake River area of Idaho (Steenhof et al. 1997) and among breeding populations in Utah (K. Keller, Salt Lake City, Utah, pers. comm.). Throughout much of the interior West, the reproductive success of Golden Eagles is tightly coupled with the abundance of Black-tailed Jackrabbits *Lepus californicus*; (Beecham & Kochert 1975, Steenhof & Kochert 1988, Steenhof et al. 1997, K. Keller, Salt Lake City, Utah, pers. comm.). Jackrabbits naturally undergo cyclic population fluctuations; however, the current low-abundance period has been more severe and prolonged than normal, and peak abundances in the early 1990s were substantially lower than during previous high years (Steenhof et al. 1997). In the Great Basin, jackrabbits occupy shrub habitats and avoid thick grassland habitats (Knick & Dyer 1997). Consequently, widespread degradation and conversion of native sagebrush habitats caused by poor management of livestock grazing and fire, expanding agriculture, and especially invasions of exotic grasses (primarily cheatgrass, *Bromus tectorum*) has negatively affected jackrabbit populations in many areas (Harlow & Bloom 1989, United States Department of Interior 1996, Steenhof et al. 1997, Marzluff et al. 1997). Thus, aggressive efforts to restore shrub-steppe ecosystems in the Great Basin and monitor the future status of Golden Eagle populations in the region is warranted (Hoffman et al. in review).

Causes of Mortality

Another important benefit of raptor banding is information about longevity and causes of injury and mortality derived from foreign encounters with previously banded birds. Encounter information may be biased towards human factors because the probability of recovery is highest near centres of human activity. Therefore, analysts must pursue assessing the relative importance of natural and human-related causes of mortality with caution. Regardless, the knowledge gained about human-related causes of mortality or removal from wild populations is important for establishing conservation and education agendas. For example, as of 1997, 35% of the 190 foreign encounters with birds banded in the Goshute Mountains (44% of mortalities) resulted from shooting incidents, primarily in Mexico (HWI unpubl. data). At the same time, encounter rates in Mexico have declined during the past decade, which suggests that educational efforts may be reducing shooting pressure. In the United States and Canada, the disposition of most foreign encounters with injured or dead HWI-banded birds is "found dead-unknown cause" (67%; HWI unpubl. data). Otherwise, collision with human structures (e.g., fences, cars, windows, and power lines) accounts for at least 44% of HWI encounters with a known cause of injury or death (Hoffman et al. in prep).

Long-term band encounter data from HWI sites also indicate noteworthy differences in the probability of recovering males and females (HWI unpubl. data). Male : female banding ratios for Sharp-shinned Hawks, Cooper's Hawks, Northern Goshawks, American Kestrels at the Goshute, Manzano, and Sandia sites average between 0.7–1.5 : 1, whereas foreign encounter ratios average from 0–0.5 : 1 and HWI recapture ratios average 0–0.3 : 1. These results suggest three possibilities: (1) accident and mortality rates are higher for females; (2) females are more likely to be discovered after death because they occupy more open habitats where they are more easily discovered by humans, and (3) females are less wary or selective in pursuing prey—in this case lure birds at trapping stations—than males and therefore are more likely to be retrapped. Clark (1985) also documented higher recovery rates for female Sharp-shinned Hawks, and suggested that greater exposure to humans through use of relatively open habitats explained this result. He suggested that greater exposure to humans probably results in both a higher probability of discovery and higher injury and mortality rates from shooting, trapping, and collisions with structures, automobiles, and power lines. A potential, alternative explanation is that males are less prone to accidents and repeating unproductive pursuit of lure birds because their hunting skills are more refined. Lower absolute metabolic energy requirements may allow males to be more selective in pursuing prey because they generally experience less energetic stress than larger females (Mosher & Matray 1974). In addition, for most raptor species, the principal role of males during nesting is to provide prey to females and nestlings (Brown & Amadon 1968). Therefore, males probably develop better hunting skills and more finely tuned pursuit strategies, which may make them more wary and less apt to engage in careless and unproductive hunting pursuits.

Migration Ecology

For raptor species with readily distinguishable age classes or sexes, long-term monitoring of migratory flights offers an opportunity to study differences in timing across sex–age groups. For some species, addition of a migrant banding program is essential for providing useful sex–age-specific information. In addition, location information gleaned from winter and summer encounters with previously banded birds enable determinations of how distances travelled vary across sex–age classes. Evidence from raptor migration and nesting studies generally indicate the following concerning differential migration (see Kerlinger 1989 for review): (1) immature birds generally depart from breeding grounds before adults in the fall, with adult males the last to depart; (2) adults winter farther north than immatures; (3) adults depart from wintering grounds and arrive on breeding grounds before immatures; and (4) among short-distance or partial migrants, adult males often winter farther north and return to breeding grounds before adult females; however, among long-distance or complete migrants, adults of both sexes usually winter at similar latitudes and return to breeding grounds at similar times, often already paired. Kerlinger (1989) reviews six hypotheses evoked to explain various aspects of differential migration, but concurs with Ketterson and Nolan (1983) that only three merit strong consideration. These three hypotheses concern social dominance structures, age and sex-specific variation in body size, and the importance of spring arrival times.

Migration count data from HWI sites generally confirm these sex and age-specific trends (Jewell 1998, Jewell & Smith 1998). Goshute band encounter data, although still limited by small sex and age-specific sample sizes, also appear to confirm that adults tend to winter farther north than immatures and males tend to winter farther north than females among American Kestrels and Sharp-shinned, Cooper's, and Red-tailed hawks (HWI unpubl. data). DeLong and Hoffman (in press) recently used data on migratory timing from HWI Goshute and New Mexico sites to test hypotheses about relationships between foraging efficiency and differential migration.

Weather may be the most important source of extraneous variation in migration counts, potentially affecting the timing and pace of migratory movements, flight paths, and the visibility of migrants at monitoring sites (Mueller & Berger 1961, Kerlinger 1989, Hall *et al.* 1992, Allen *et al.* 1996, Maransky *et al.* 1997). Documenting how weather affects counts over time at different sites and developing analytical methods to account for weather-related variation is therefore of great importance for increasing statistical power to detect underlying population trends (Hussell 1981, 1985). Fall migration research in eastern North America has revealed that migratory activity often is greatest 1–3 days after passage of a cold front when northwest winds are strong (Allen *et al.* 1996). In contrast, although no comprehensive statistical analyses have been conducted yet, HWI's inland migration data suggest that raptor migration activity in the West is heaviest just ahead of advancing cold fronts when west winds create strong ridge updrafts but montane temperatures remain moderate, or during periods of warm, fair weather when either light southwest or calm winds prevail and thermal activity is high (Millsap & Zook 1983, Hoffman 1985).

Thus, as long-term data accumulate and in-depth analyses become possible, western migration studies likely will add important new dimensions to our understanding of how weather and climate affect raptor migration. In addition, as the network of western banding operations expands and matures, we will be able to generate greater understanding of the migratory ecology of different subpopulations. In turn, this information will facilitate tailoring local and regional conservation activities and management plans to accommodate subtle differences in the ecology of associated raptor populations.

Morphology, Physiology, and Health Assessments

Banding operations also offer a rich opportunity to study a variety of morphological and physiological parameters. Banding at migration sites, in particular, often yields very large sample sizes for such studies, which greatly increases statistical power for analyzing patterns and trends. Knowledge of size characteristics derived from migratory banding enabled accurate classification of accipiters (Mueller *et al.* 1976, 1981a, b; Hoffman *et al.* 1990; Smith *et al.* 1990) and contributed to understanding of ecological relationships between morphological variation and adaptation to different environments (e.g., Smith 1988, Smith *et al.* 1990). Migratory banding enables advances in understanding of the moult process and associated energetics (e.g., Gorney & Yom-Tov 1994), raptor hematology and hemoparasites (Gessaman *et al.* 1986, Powers *et al.* 1994), and metabolic physiology (e.g., Gessaman & Hoffman 1990, Kennedy & Gessaman 1991). Blood samples also can yield information about chemical contamination (e.g., Wood *et al.* 1996) and enable genetic studies that may help track migrant source populations (Haig & Avise 1995). In addition, HWI migration banding has led to accumulation of considerable data on external parasites and body fat levels of migrants, which will facilitate health assessments in relation to environmental conditions (HWI unpubl. data). Another potential project that we envision in conjunction with HWI banding efforts is collecting feather samples to enable stable isotope analyses. Stable isotope analysis is a cutting-edge tool that offers promise for supplementing band encounter information to identify the geographic origins of migrants (Chamberlain *et al.* 1997, Hobson & Wassenaar 1997).

Public Outreach

Raptors constitute an invaluable tool for promoting public interest in the natural world and conservation activities, because they are incredibly dynamic and impressive creatures. At HawkWatch International, as at other institutions such as Hawk Mountain Sanctuary and Golden Gate Raptor Observatory, our mission is to promote raptor conservation through scientific research and an extensive education programme. Having live, captive raptors on hand during educational programmes at schools and in the community often is the key to captivating audiences and ultimately motivating greater interest in HWI activities. However, we have observed that witnessing the migration spectacle first hand and experiencing live, wild birds up close through trapping and banding at migration monitoring sites is by far the most powerful tool for producing life-long raptor enthusiasts and conservationists. Accordingly, the more extensive the monitoring network, the more opportunities we will have to effectively engage the public and expand awareness of raptor ecology and conservation needs (Bildstein et al. 1995, Bildstein 1998).

Needs For the Future

Substantial progress has been made in developing an extensive, standardized network of raptor migration monitoring sites in western North America. Nevertheless, aside from needing more time to accumulate long-term data, there remain several needs for improvement. The first need is further expansion of the monitoring network. Canadian researchers recently have made considerable progress in identifying new potential sites and setting up annual, standardized counts at known concentration points, especially in Alberta (Sherrington 1997, 1998). Areas of primary interest for additional count coverage include the Coast Mountain and Rocky Mountain regions of British Columbia, the Yukon Territory, and far west Northwest Territories (Fig. 1). Establishment of one or more migratory banding operations in western Canada also would be a valuable addition to the network. In the United States, primary needs for expansion include better coverage of the central and southern Rocky Mountains in Wyoming and Colorado, along the Sierra Nevada in California and western Nevada, and in montane areas of southern California, southern Nevada, and southern Arizona (Fig. 1). Further south in Mexico and Baja California, little is known about migratory flyways and activity other than what has been learned from the Veracruz count in southern Mexico; this region is therefore wide open for exploratory work.

The second primary need for improvement of the raptor monitoring network in western North America is to establish intensive breeding productivity studies of selected species in carefully selected areas to provide more specific and stronger validation of migration monitoring as an effective indicator of regional and perhaps local population trends. This will require prior knowledge gained from band encounters or telemetry studies to ensure that breeding and migration studies represent the same monitored populations (*sensu* Dunn & Hussell 1995). Many authors have sought and found reasonable agreement between trends indicated by raptor migration counts and breeding-season surveys like the BBS (e.g., Hussell & Brown 1992, Kirk & Hyslop 1998, and see Dunn & Hussell 1995 for a general review). Moreover, qualitative agreement between the history of DDT use in the United States and trends in long-term migration counts from Hawk Mountain, Pennsylvania (Bednarz et al. 1990b) and Cedar Grove, Wisconsin (Mueller et al. 1988) clearly demonstrated that migration counts are a useful indicator of regional population trends. Nevertheless, we are not aware of any past or present efforts to conduct well-matched breeding and migration studies that would provide strong, quantitative corroboration of the premise that migration counts accurately track actual trends in population size and productivity.

Finally, during the past two decades a variety of approaches have been developed to account for various confounding factors and enable robust statistical analysis and interpretation of trends in migration counts (e.g., Hussell 1981, 1985; Titus & Fuller 1990; Titus et al. 1989, 1990; Bednarz & Kerlinger 1989; Bednarz et al. 1990b; Dunn & Hussell 1995; Allen et al. 1996; Hatfield et al. 1996; Smith & Hoffman in review). Standardization of data collection methods likely will solve many problems with methodological biases (Bednarz & Kerlinger 1989, Dunn & Hussell 1995). Much more effort is needed, however, to document the effects of weather on flight dynamics and visibility, and to develop efficient statistical methods for removing weather-related variation in counts to improve statistical power for detecting underlying population trends (Dunn and Hussell 1995). We also believe that age-specific trend analyses offer promise for tracking the reproductive success of monitored populations, particularly for species such as the Northern Goshawk where most adults are non-migratory or irruptive migrants but most immatures undergo regular migration (Hoffman et al. in review; also see Bednarz et al. 1990b). However, one important potential bias that has been little studied concerns the effects of variation in proportions of unaged individuals on the accuracy of age-specific analyses.

ACKNOWLEDGEMENTS

The HawkWatch International research discussed herein is made possible by funding and logistical support provided by a long list of government agencies, corporations, foundations, HWI members, and other private individuals. Moreover, HWI research relies on extensive teams of largely volunteer field technicians that dedicate incredible energy in the interest of promoting raptor conservation. The list of supporters and volunteers is too long for detailed recording here; suffice it to say that the HWI staff are eternally grateful for the enthusiasm and support of the many organizations and individuals that have made our work possible. We also thank Keith Bildstein and Reuven Yosef for convening and inviting us to participate in the migration symposium, and Dr. Bildstein for his comments on the manuscript.

REFERENCES

ALLEN, P. E., L. J. GOODRICH & K. L. BILDSTEIN 1996. Within- and among-year effects of cold fronts on migrating raptors at Hawk Mountain, PA, 1934–1991. *Auk* 113:329–338.

ALLEN, R. P. & R. T. PETERSON 1936. The hawk migrations at Cape May Point, New Jersey. *Auk* 53:393–404.

BEASON, J. & P. SCIFRES 1998. Fall 1997 raptor migration study in the Bridger Mountains, Montana. HawkWatch International, Inc., Salt Lake City, Utah. 44 pp.

BEDNARZ, J. C. & P. KERLINGER 1989. Monitoring hawk populations by counting migrants. Pages 328–342 *in* B. Pendleton (Ed.). *Proc. Northeast raptor management symposium and workshop*. National Wildlife Federation, Washington, D.C.

BEDNARZ, J. C., T. J. HAYDEN & T. FISCHER 1990a. The raptor and raven community of the Los Medanos area in southeastern New Mexico: a unique and significant resource. Pages 92–101 *in* R. S. Mitchell, C. J. Sheviak, and D. J. Leopold (Eds.). *Ecosystem management: rare species and significant habitats*. New York State Museum Bulletin No. 471, Albany, New York.

BEDNARZ, J. C, D. KLEM, JR., L. J. GOODRICH & S. E. SENNER 1990b. Migration counts of raptors at Hawk Mountain, Pennsylvania, as indicators of population trends, 1934–1986. *Auk* 107:96–109.

BEECHAM, J. J. & M. N. KOCHERT 1975. Breeding biology of the Golden Eagle in southwestern Idaho. *Wilson Bull.* 87:506–513.

BILDSTEIN, K. L. 1998. Long-term counts of migrating raptors: a role for volunteers in wildlife research. *J. Wildl. Manage.* 62:435–445.

BILDSTEIN, K. L., J. J. BRETT, L. J. GOODRICH & C. VIVERETTE 1995. Hawks Aloft Worldwide: a network to protect the world's migrating birds of prey and the habitats essential to their migrations. Pages 504–516 *in* D. A. Saunders, J. L. Craig, and E. M. Mattiske (Eds.). *Nature conservation 4: the role of networks*. Surrey Beatty & Sons, Chipping Norton, New South Wales, Australia.

BILDSTEIN, K. L. & J. I. ZALLES (editors) 1995. Raptor migration watch-site manual. Hawk Mountain Sanctuary Association, Kempton, Pennsylvania.

BINFORD, L. C. 1979. Fall migration of diurnal raptors at Pt. Diablo, California. *Western Birds* 10:1–16.

BROUN, M. 1935. The hawk migration during the fall of 1934, along the Kittatinny Ridge in Pennsylvania. *Auk* 52:233–248.

BROWN, L. & D. AMADON 1968. *Eagles, hawks and falcons of the world*. McGraw Hill, New York, New York.

CADE, T. J., J. E. ENDERSON, C. G. THELANDER & C. M. WHITE 1988. *Peregrine falcon populations, their management and recovery*. The Peregrine Fund, Inc., Boise, Idaho. 949 pp.

CHAMBERLAIN, C. P., J. D. BLUM & R. T. HOLMES 1997. The use of isotope tracers for identifying populations of migratory birds. *Oecologia* 109:132–141.

CLARK, W. S. 1985. The migrating Sharp-shinned Hawk at Cape May Point: banding and recovery results. Pages 137–148 *in* M. Harwood (Ed.). *Proc. Hawk Migration Conference IV*. Hawk Migration Association of North America.

CLARK, W., V. CLARK, K. E. WIERSMA & L. LIU 1997. Spring raptor migration studies at Cape Flattery, Washington in 1990–1997. HawkWatch International, Salt Lake City, Utah. 35 pp.

COVERT, K. 1998. Spring 1998 raptor banding study at Jordanelle Reservoir in northern Utah. HawkWatch International, Salt Lake City, Utah. 18 pp.
CROCKER-BEDFORD, D. C. 1990. Goshawk reproduction and forest management. *Wildl. Soc. Bull.* 18:262–269.
DELONG, J.P. & S. W. HOFFMAN. In press. Differential migration of fall-migrant accipiters: investigating the foraging efficiency hypothesis. *Condor.*
DIXON, P. M., A. R. OLSEN & B. M. KAHN 1998. Measuring trends in ecological resources. *Ecological Applications* 8:225–227
DUNN, E. H. & D. J. T. HUSSELL 1995. Using migration counts to monitor landbird populations: review and evaluation of status. Pages 43–88 *in* D. M. Power (Ed.). *Current Ornithology*, Vol. 12. Plenum Press, New York, New York.
ECONOMIDY, J. 1998. Texas. *Hawk Migration Studies* 23(2):20.
FULLER, M. R. & J. A. MOSHER 1981. Methods of detecting and counting raptors: a review. Pages 235–246 *in* C. J. Ralph and J. M. Scott (Eds.). Estimating numbers of terrestrial birds. *Studies in Avian Biology* 6.
FULLER, M. R. & J. A. MOSHER 1987. Raptor survey techniques. Pages 37–65 *in* B. G. Pendleton, B. A. Millsap, K. W. Cline, and D. M. Bird (Eds.). *Raptor management techniques manual*. National Wildlife Federation, Scientific and Technical Series No. 10.
GESSAMAN, J. A. & S. W. HOFFMAN 1990. Body temperatures of migrant accipiter hawks just after flight. *Wilson Bulletin* 102:133–137.
GESSAMAN, J. A., J. A. JOHNSON & S. W. HOFFMAN 1986. Hematocrits and erythrocyte numbers for Cooper's and Sharp-shinned Hawks. *Condor* 88:95–96.
GOLDEN GATE RAPTOR OBSERVATORY [GGRO] 1997. Season summary 1997. Golden Gate Raptor Observatory, San Francisco, California.
GOODRICH, L. J., S. C. CROCOLL & S. E. SENNER 1996. Broad-winged Hawk (*Buteo platypterus*). No. 218 *in* A. Poole and F. Gill (Eds.). *The birds of North America.* Academy of Natural Sciences, Philadelphia, Penn., and American Ornithologists' Union, Washington, D.C.
GORNEY, E. & Y. YOM-TOV 1994. Fat, hydration condition, and moult of steppe buzzards *Buteo buteo vulpinus* on spring migration. *Ibis* 136:185–192.
GRINDROD, P. & C. E. HALLETT 1998. Fall 1997 raptor banding project at Bonney Butte, Oregon. HawkWatch International, Salt Lake City, Utah. 13 pp.
GRINDROD, P. & J. P. SMITH 1998a. Fall 1997 raptor migration study at Bonney Butte, Oregon. HawkWatch International, Salt Lake City, Utah. 25 pp.
GRINDROD, P. & J. P. SMITH 1998b. Fall 1997 raptor migration study at Smith Point, Texas. HawkWatch International, Salt Lake City, Utah. 21 pp.
HAIG, S. M. AND J. C. AVISE 1995. Avian conservation genetics. Pages 160–189 *in* J. C. Avise and J. L. Hamrick (Eds.). *Conservation genetics: case histories from nature.* Chapman & Hall, New York, New York.
HALL, L. S., A. L. FISH & M. L. MORRISON 1992. The influence of weather on hawk movements in coastal northern California. *Wilson Bull.* 104:447–461.
HARLOW, D. L. & P. BLOOM 1989. Buteos and the Golden Eagle. Pages 102-110 *in* B. G. Pendleton, editor. *Proc. western raptor management symposium and workshop*. National Wildlife Federation, Washington, D.C.
HATFIELD, J. S., W. R. GOULD IV, B. A. HOOVER, M. R. FULLER & E. L. LINDQUIST 1996. Detecting trends in raptor counts: power and Type I error rates of various statistical tests. *Wildl. Soc. Bull.* 24:505–515.
HEATH, J. & D. COOPER 1998. Fall 1997 raptor migration study in the Wellsville Mountains of northern Utah. HawkWatch International, Salt Lake City, Utah. 47 pp.
HEINTZELMAN, D. S. 1975. *Autumn hawk flights: the migrations in eastern North America.* Rutgers University Press, New Brunswick, New Jersey.
HENNY, C. J. & R. G. ANTHONY 1989. Bald eagle and osprey. Pages 66-82 *in* B. G. Pendleton (Ed.). *Proc. Western Raptor Management Symposium and Workshop.* National Wildlife Federation, Washington D.C.
HENNY, C. J. & J. L. KAISER 1995. Osprey population increase along the Willamette River, Oregon, and the role of utility structures, 1976–1993. Pages 97–108 *in* D. M. Bird, D. E. Varland, and J. J. Negro (Eds.) *Raptors in human landscapes: adaptations to built and cultivated environments.* Academic Press, London, England.
HOBSON, K. A. & L. I. WASSENAAR 1997. Linking breeding and wintering grounds of neotropical migrant songbirds using stable isotopic analyses of feathers. *Oecologia* 109:142–148.
HOFFMAN, S. W. 1985. Raptor movements in inland western North America: a synthesis. Pages 325–338 *in* M. Harwood (Ed.). *Proc. Hawk Migration Conference IV.* Hawk Migration Association of North America.
HOFFMAN, S. W., J. P. SMITH, W. R. DERAGON & J. C. BEDNARZ. In review. Recent population trends of migratory raptors in western North America. *Ecolog. Applications.*
HOFFMAN, S. W., J. P. SMITH & J. A. GESSAMAN 1990. Size of fall-migrant accipiters from the Goshute Mountains of Nevada. *J. Field Ornithol.* 61:201–211.

HOLROYD, G. L. & U. BANASCH 1996. The 1990 Canadian Peregrine Falcon (*Falco peregrinus*) survey. *J. Raptor Res.* 30:145–156.
HUSSELL, D. J. T. 1981. The use of migration counts for detecting population trends. *Studies in Avian Biology* 6:92–102.
HUSSELL, D. J. T. 1985. Analysis of hawk migration counts for monitoring population levels. Pages 243–254 in M. Harwood (Ed.). *Proc. Hawk Migration Conference IV*. Hawk Migration Association of North America.
HUSSELL, D. J. T. & L. BROWN 1992. Population changes in diurnally-migrating raptors at Duluth, Minnesota (1974–1989) and Grimsby, Ontario (1975–1990). Ontario Ministry of Natural Resources, Maple, Ontario, Canada.
IVERSON, G. C., G. D. HAYWARD, K. TITUS, E. DEGAYNER, R. E. LOWELL, D. COLEMAN CROCKER-BEDFORD, P. F. SCHEMPF & J. LINDELL 1996. Conservation assessment for the Northern Goshawk in southeastern Alaska. General Technical Report PNW-GTR-387. USDA Forest Service, Pacific Northwest Research Station, Portland, Oregon. 101 pp.
JEWELL, J. V. 1998. Spring raptor migration study in the Sandia Mountains of central New Mexico. HawkWatch International, Salt Lake City, Utah. 39 pp.
JEWELL, J. & J. P. SMITH 1998. Fall 1997 raptor migration study in the Goshute Mountains of northeastern Nevada. HawkWatch International, Salt Lake City, Utah. 43 pp.
KENNEDY, P. L. & J. A. GESSAMAN 1991. Diurnal resting metabolic rates of accipiters. *Wilson Bull.* 103:101–105.
KETTERSON, E. D. & V. NOLAN, JR. 1983. The evolution of differential bird migration. Pages 357–402 in R. F. Johnston (Ed.). *Current ornithology*, Vol. 1. Plenum Press, New York, New York.
KIRK, D. A. & C. HYSLOP 1998. Population status and recent trends in Canadian raptors: a review. *Biol. Conserv.* 91–118.
KNICK, S. T. & D. L. DYER 1997. Distribution of black-tailed jackrabbit habitat determined by GIS in southwestern Idaho. *Journal of Wildlife Management* 61:75–86.
LINK, W. A. & J. R. SAUER 1998. Estimating change from count data: application the North American Breeding Bird Survey. *Ecological Applications* 8:258–268.
MARANSKY, B., L. GOODRICH & K. BILDSTEIN 1997. Seasonal shifts in the effects of weather on the visible migration of Red-tailed Hawks at Hawk Mountain, Pennsylvania, 1992–1994. *Wilson Bull.* 109:246–252.
MARZLUFF, J. M., S. T. KNICK, M. S VEKASKY, L. S. SCHUECK & T. J. ZARRIELLO 1997. Spatial use and habitat selection of Golden Eagles in southwestern Idaho. *Auk* 114:673–687.
MCDERMOT, F. 1997. California region. *Hawk Migration Studies* 23(1):66–68.
MEEHAN, T & L. CARVER 1998. Fall 1997 raptor banding project in the Goshute Mountains of northeastern Nevada. HawkWatch International, Salt Lake City, Utah. 45 pp.
MILLER, T. & J. P. SMITH 1998. Spring 1998 raptor migration study at Jordanelle Reservoir in northern Utah. HawkWatch International, Salt Lake City, Utah. 30 pp.
MILLSAP, B. A. & J. R. ZOOK 1983. Effects of weather on accipiter migration in southern Nevada. *Raptor Res.* 17:43–56.
MOORE, K. R. & C. J. HENNY 1983. Nest site characteristics of three coexisting accipiter hawks in north-eastern Oregon. *Raptor Res.* 17:65-76.
MOSHER, J. A. & P. F. MATRAY 1974. Size dimorphism: a factor in energy. *Auk* 91:325–341.
MUELLER, H. C. & D. D. BERGER 1961. Weather and the fall migration of hawks at Cedar Grove, Wisconsin. *Wilson Bull.* 73:171–192.
MUELLER, H. C. & D. D. BERGER 1967. Fall migration of Sharp-shinned Hawks.. *Wilson Bull.* 79:397–415.
MUELLER, H. C., D. D. BERGER & G. ALLEZ 1976. Age and sex variation in the size of goshawks. *Bird-Banding* 47:310–318.
MUELLER, H. C., D. D. BERGER & G. ALLEZ 1979. Age and sex differences in the size of Sharp-shinned Hawks. *Bird-Banding* 50:34–44.
MUELLER, H. C., D. D. BERGER & G. ALLEZ 1981. Age, sex, and seasonal differences in the size of goshawks. *J. Field Ornithol.* 52:112–126.
MUELLER, H. C., D. D. BERGER & G. ALLEZ 1988. Population trends in migrating peregrines at Cedar Grove, Wisconsin, 1936-1985. Pages 497–506 in T. J. Cade, J. H. Enderson, C. G. Thelander, and C. M. White (Eds.) *Peregrine falcon populations, their management and recovery*. The Peregrine Fund, Boise, Idaho.
O'CONNOR, S. & J. OGBURN 1998. Fall 1997 raptor migration study in the Manzano Mountains of central New Mexico. HawkWatch International, Salt Lake City, Utah. 40 pp.
PALMER, R. S. 1988. *Handbook of North American birds*. Vols. 4 and 5: Diurnal raptors (Parts 1 and 2). Yale University Press, New Haven, Connecticut.

PATTEE, O. H. & S. R. WILBUR 1989. Turkey vulture and California Condor. Pages 61–65 in B. G. Pendleton (Ed.). *Proc. Western Raptor Management Symposium and Workshop.* National Wildlife Federation, Washington, D.C.

PLATT, S. W. & J. H. ENDERSON 1989. Falcons. Pages 111–117 in B. G. Pendleton (Ed.). *Proc. Western Raptor Management Symposium and Workshop.* National Wildlife Federation, Washington, D.C.

POWERS, L. V., M. POKRAS, K. RIO, C. VIVERETTE & L. GOODRICH 1994. Hematology and occurrence of hemoparasites in migrating Sharp-shinned Hawks (*Accipiter striatus*) during fall migration. *J. Raptor Res.* 28:178–185.

PROSSER, S. & C. DE SORBO 1998. Fall 1997 raptor migration study at Diamond Head, Washington. HawkWatch International, Salt Lake City, Utah. 34 pp.

REYNOLDS, R. T., R. T. GRAHAM, M. H. REISER, R. L. BASSETT, P. L. KENNEDY, D. A. BOYCE, JR., G. GOODWIN, R. SMITH & E. L. FISHER 1992. Management recommendations for the Northern Goshawk in the southwestern United States. General Technical Report RM-217. USDA Forest Service, Rocky Mountain Forest and Range Experiment Station, Fort Collins, Colo. 90 pp.

ROSSMAN, D. J. 1998. Fall 1997 exploratory raptor migration study for Chelan Ridge, Washington. HawkWatch International, Salt Lake City, Utah. 42 pp.

ROWE, S. P. & T. GALLION. Fall migration of Turkey Vultures and raptors through the southern Sierra Nevada, California. *Western Birds* 27:48–53.

SAUER, J. R., J. E. HINES, G. GOUGH, I. THOMAS & B. G. PETERJOHN 1997. The North American Breeding Bird Survey results and analysis. Version 96.4. Patuxent Wildlife Research Center, Laurel, Maryland.

SCHEUERMANN 1996. GGRO band recoveries 1992 to 1996. *Pacific Raptor Report* 17:11–16.

SENNER, S. E. & M. R. FULLER 1989. Status and conservation of North American raptors migrating to the Neotropics. Pages 53–58 in B. –U. Meyburg and R. D. Chancellor (Eds.). *Raptors in the modern world*. Proc. III World Conference on Birds of Prey and Owls. WWGBP, Berlin, Germany.

SHERRINGTON, P. 1997. Canadian Rockies and plains region. *Hawk Migration Studies* 23(1):62–65.

SHERRINGTON, P. 1998. Canadian Rockies and plains. *Hawk Migration Studies* 23(2):16–19.

SIMON, J. & P. GRINDROD 1998. Fall 1997 raptor migration study at Hazel Bazemore Park, Corpus Christi, Texas. HawkWatch International, Salt Lake City, Utah. 22 pp.

SMITH, J. P. 1988. Morphometric variation in accipiter hawks with emphasis on western North America. M.Sc. Thesis, Utah State University, Logan.

SMITH, J. P. & S. W. HOFFMAN. In review. Observer and visitor effects on counts of migrating raptors. *J. Wildl. Manage.*

SMITH, J. P., S. W. HOFFMAN & J. A. GESSAMAN 1990. Regional size differences among fall-migrant accipiters in North America. *J. Field Ornithol.* 61:192–200.

SMITH, R. J. & J. P. SMITH 1999. Spring 1998 raptor banding project in the Sandia Mountains of central New Mexico. HawkWatch International, Salt Lake City, Utah.

SODHI, N. S., L. W. OLIPHANT, P. C. JAMES & I. G. WARKENTIN 1993. Merlin (*Falco columbarius*). No. 44 in A. Poole and F. Gill (Eds.). *The birds of North America*. Academy of Natural Sciences, Philadelphia, Pennsylvania, and American Ornithologists' Union, Washington, D.C.

SPEITZER, P. R., R. W. RISEBROUGH, W. WALKER, II, R. HERNANDEZ, A. POOLE, D. PULESTON & I. C. T. NISBET 1978. Productivity of Ospreys in Connecticut-Long Island increases as DDE residues decline. *Science* 202:333–335.

SQUIRES, J. R. & R. T. REYNOLDS 1997. Northern Goshawk (*Accipiter gentilis*). No. 298 in A. Poole and F. Gill (Eds.). *The birds of North America*. Academy of Natural Sciences, Philadelphia, Pennsylvania, and American Ornithologists' Union, Washington, D.C.

STEENHOF, K. & M. N. KOCHERT 1988. Dietary responses of three raptor species to changing prey densities in a natural environment. *Journal of Animal Ecology* 57:37–48.

STEENHOF, K., M. N. KOCHERT & T. L. MCDONALD 1997. Interactive effects of prey and weather on Golden Eagle reproduction. *Journal of Animal Ecology* 66:350–362.

STRAVERS, J., JR. & J. P. SMITH 1998. Fall 1997 raptor banding project in the Manzano Mountains of central New Mexico. HawkWatch International, Salt Lake City, Utah. 31 pp.

SWENSON, J. E. 1981. Status of the Osprey in southeastern Montana before and after construction of reservoirs. *Western Birds* 12:47–51.

THOMAS, S. M. & J. P. SMITH 1998. Fall 1997 raptor migration study in the Grand Canyon of Arizona. HawkWatch International, Salt Lake City, Utah. 67 pp.

TILLY, F. C. 1997. Northern U.S. mountains and plains. *Hawk Migration Studies* 23(1):59–61.

TILLY, F. C. & C. R. TILLY 1998. Spring 1998 raptor migration study in west-central Montana near Roger's Pass. HawkWatch International, Salt Lake City, Utah. 30 pp.

TITUS, K. & M. R. FULLER 1990. Recent trends in counts of migrant hawks from northeastern North America. *J. Wildl. Manage.* 54:463–70.
TITUS, K., M. R. FULLER & D. JACOBS 1990. Detecting trends in hawk migration count data. Pages 105-113 *in* J. R. Sauer and S. Droege (Eds.). *Survey designs and statistical methods for the estimation of population trends*. U.S. Fish and Wildlife Service, Biological Report 90.
TITUS, K., M. R. FULLER & J. L. RUOS 1989. Considerations for monitoring raptor population trends based on counts of migrants. Pages 19-32 *in* B. U. Meyburg and R. D. Chancellor (Eds.). *Raptors in the modern world*. Proc. III World Conference of Birds of Prey and Owls. WWGBP, Berlin, Germany.
UNITED STATES DEPARTMENT OF INTERIOR 1996. Effects of military training and fire in the Snake River Birds of Prey National Conservation Area. BLM/IDARNG Research Project Final Report. U.S. Geological Survey, Biological Resources Division, Snake River Field Station, Boise, Idaho. 130 pp.
UNITED STATES FISH AND WILDLIFE SERVICE 1998. Endangered and threatened wildlife and plants; notice of 12-month finding on a petition to list the Northern Goshawk in the contiguous United States west of the 100th Meridian. Federal Register 63(124):35183–35184.
WILBUR, S. R. 1983. The status of vultures in the Western Hemisphere. Pages 113–123 *in* S. R. Wilbur and J. A. Jackson (Eds.). *Vulture biology and management*. University of California Press, Berkeley.
WOOD, P. B., C. VIVERETTE, L. GOODRICH, M. POKRAS & C. TIBBOTT 1996. Environmental contaminant levels in Sharp-shinned Hawks from the eastern United States. *J. Raptor Res.* 30:136–144.
WOODBRIDGE, B. & P. J. DETRICH 1994. Territory occupancy and habitat patch size of Northern Goshawks in the southern Cascades of California. *Studies in Avian Biology* 16:83–87.

Jeff P. Smith and Stephen W. Hoffman
HawkWatch International, Inc.
1800 South West Temple, Suite 226
Salt Lake City, UT 84115
U.S.A.

Chancellor, R. D. & B.-U. Meyburg eds. 2000
Raptors at Risk
WWGBP / Hancock House

Conservation of Migrating Raptors through Banding; results of over 30 years of the Cape May Raptor Banding Project

William S. Clark, Christopher Schultz, and Olin Allen

ABSTRACT

Almost 100,000 migrating diurnal raptors have been captured and banded at Cape May, New Jersey since 1967; fewer than 200 of them had been banded previously. Almost 1550 of the banded raptors have been encountered later elsewhere during every month of the year. Maps of selected species will show winter and summer ranges and migratory pathways. Over 90% captured were juveniles. Sex ratios were different from 50:50; more males in some species, more females in others. Most captured raptors were in excellent condition, only a few showed injuries or abnormalities. Banding results followed trends of the annual raptor count at Cape May. Banding and count results were able to predict seasonal trends for Northern Harrier. Declines in captures during the late 1980's of Sharp-shinned Hawks and in recent years of American Kestrels suggest some reproductive failure in eastern Canada and northeastern USA. On the other hand, increases in captures of Cooper's Hawk from the same area indicate a gradual population increase over the past 30 years. Swainson's Hawks are a regular visitor. A vagrant Common Kestrel captured most likely rode a ship from Europe. Banded raptors were shown to tens of thousands of people and released after an educational message to the spectators.

INTRODUCTION

Placing numbered or lettered bands on birds legs, called 'banding' in North America and Australia and 'ringing' elsewhere, is one method used to study raptor migration, as the banded birds can be encountered elsewhere at any time during the year: either on migration or on breeding or wintering grounds. These areas can be determined if enough recoveries of bands are made. In addition, the bird in hand can also provide much useful information, such as age, sex, measurement data, blood sample, plumage details, parasites, moult, etc.

There are over 20 banding stations in North America that specialize in raptors. The Cape May Raptor Banding Project has been in operation for 32 years and has banded more raptors than any of the others, almost 100,000 (Table 1). From these has come information on almost 1550 recoveries (Table 2), many of which were recovered alive and released and some of which have been encountered more than once. However, few have returned to be captured again at Cape May and few have already been banded, as over 90% of the raptors captured are juveniles, less than 6 months of age. For over the past 25 years, a few raptors were taken on weekends to the local State Park and shown to the public while presenting a raptor conservation message and then released. More than 30,000 people have seen this.

Table 1. Total raptors captured at Cape May by species.

Species	No. caught
Osprey *Pandion haliaetus*	17
Bald Eagle *Haliaeetus lecocephalus*	4
No. Harrier *Circus cyaneus*	2440
Sharp-shinned Hawk *Accipiter striatus*	57089
Cooper's Hawk *A. cooperi*	9253
No. Goshawk *A. gentilis*	262
Red-tailed Hawk *Buteo jamaicensis*	4923
Red-shouldered Hawk *B. lineatus*	259
Broad-winged Hawk *B. platypterus*	283
Rough-legged Hawk *B. lagopus*	7
Swainson's Hawk *B. swainsonii*	15
Golden Eagle *Aquila chrysaetos*	15
Peregrine *Falco peregrinus*	1026
Merlin *F. columbarius*	6236
Am. Kestrel *F. sparvertus*	15990
Com. Kestrel *F. tinnunculus*	1
TOTAL	**97820**

Table 2. Recoveries from Cape May banded raptors.

Species	No.
Sharp-shinned Hawk *Accipiter striatus*	705
Cooper's Hawk *A. cooperi*	216
American Kestrel *F. sparvertus*	207
Red-tailed Hawk *Buteo jamaicensis*	174
Merlin *F. columbarius*	109
Peregrine *Falco peregrinus*	91
Six other species	40
TOTAL	**1542**

METHODS AND MATERIALS

A raptor banding project has been operated at Cape May Point, New Jersey in the United States every autumn from 1967 until the present. Clark (1970, 1976, 1981) described the capture devices and procedures used to capture the migrant raptors. Raptors were aged and sexed and most had measurements of wing chord and weight recorded. Blood samples and colour tags were placed on some raptors in some years.

Banding and recovery information were input to two DBASE IV files. The geographic information system (GIS) program ARCVIEW was used to generate maps of recovery locations for Sharp-shinned and Cooper's Hawks by season, sex, and species.

Researchers not directly associated with the banding projects were invited to sample the migrant raptors as part of their research.

Twice every weekend in the autumn for six or seven weeks, one of the project's banders or helpers gathered from one to seven raptors from the banding stations and took them to the Cape May Point State Park. Here he or she exhibited each of the raptors for a short period while talking to the observers about raptor conservation. The raptors were released in front of the spectators. From four to eight private presentations were made every year as well.

RESULTS

Almost 100,000 raptors of 15 species have been captured (Table 1). Only 211 of these were previously banded. A total of 1452 recoveries, both live and dead, of the banded raptors were reported to the Bird Banding Lab (Table 2). Fewer than 20 raptors were recaptured at Cape May in subsequent years.

Maps of recoveries for Sharp-shinned Hawk and Cooper's Hawk show that the wintering area is mainly in the southeastern United States on the coastal plain (Figs. 1-7). Migration is primarily on the Atlantic coastal plain but is farther west in the spring compared to the autumn. Female Cooper's Hawks tended to winter farther south compared to males. The summer range and presumed breeding area for these species is north and east of Cape May.

Sex ratios were different from the expected 50-50 in most species (Table 3).

Table 3. Percent female of Cape May captured raptors by species.

Species	Banding	Recovery
No. Harrier *Circus cyaneus*	37	61
Cooper's *A. cooperi*	38	51
Kestrel *F. sparverius*	54	45
Merlin *F. columbarius*	55	64
Peregrine *Falco peregrinus*	60	69
Sharp-shin *A. striatus*	60	76

Results for individual species have been published for Peregrines (Henny & Clark 1982), Northern Harriers (Bildstein et al. 1984), Merlins (Clark 1985), and Sharp-shinned Hawks (Clark (1986).

Schultz (1996) showed that counts and numbers captured of Northern Harriers show a significant positive correlation with breeding bird surveys in New York State and that counts and capture numbers are strongly correlated.

Both count and banding results showed a steep decline in numbers of Sharp-shinned Hawks from the mid-1980's into the early 1990's; since that time their numbers have been somewhat steady. Kerlinger (1993) suggested that this drop was due to a population decline in the New England and far eastern Canada, as banding stations and counts farther west did not record this decline. However, Viverette et al. (1996) suggested that the decline was due to many more Sharp-shinned Hawks stopping their migration north of Cape May, as supported by the annual Christmas Count data. Presumably they did so because of the increase in the use of backyard bird feeders, providing a winter food source.

Kirkpatrick and Lauer (1985) found that almost 60% of 259 raptors of 12 species examined were infected with protozoan parasites. Kirkpatrick and Trexler-Myren (1986) found Salmonella in cloacal samples from two juvenile Red-tailed Hawks but not in 103 individuals of 6 other species examined.

A juvenile female Common Kestrel was captured in 1972 (Clark 1974a), for the second North

Figure 1. Recoveries of Cape May banded female Sharp-shinned Hawks during autumn and spring migration.

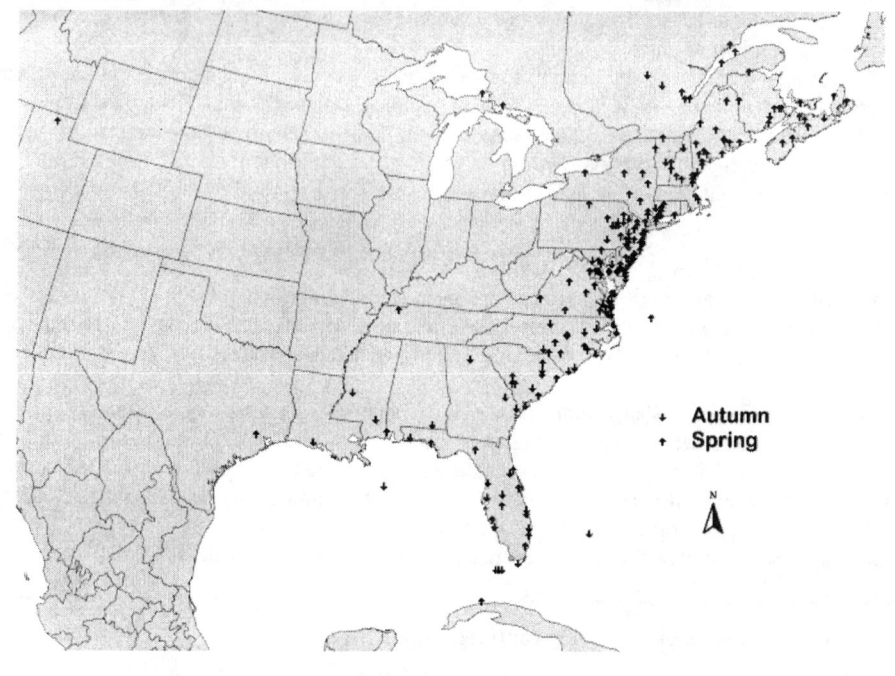

Figure 2. Recoveries of Cape May banded male Sharp-shinned Hawks during autumn and spring migration.

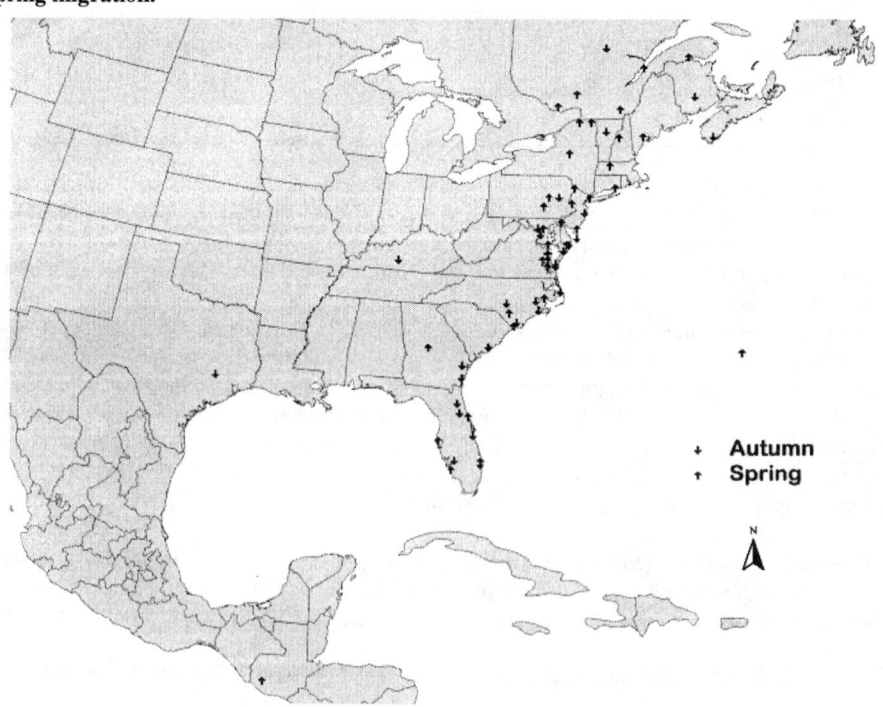

Figure 3. Recoveries of Cape May banded female Sharp-shinned Hawks during winter.

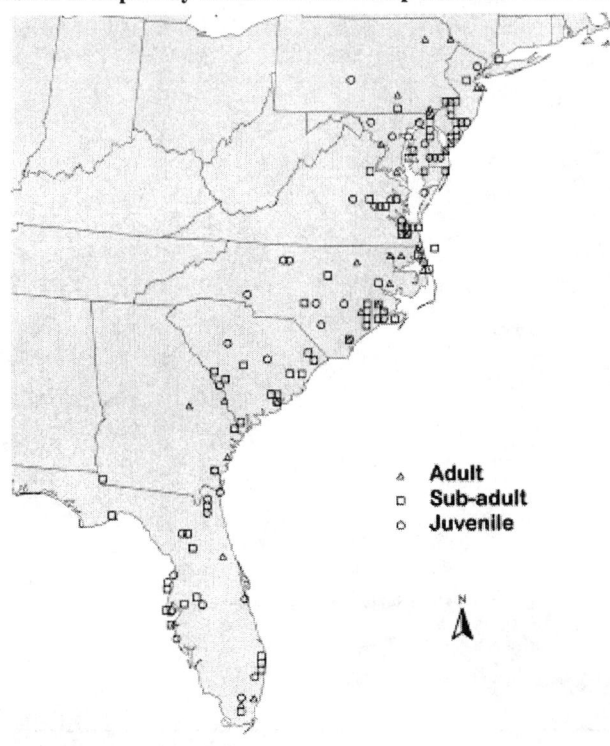

Figure 4. Recoveries of Cape May banded male Sharp-shinned Hawks during winter.

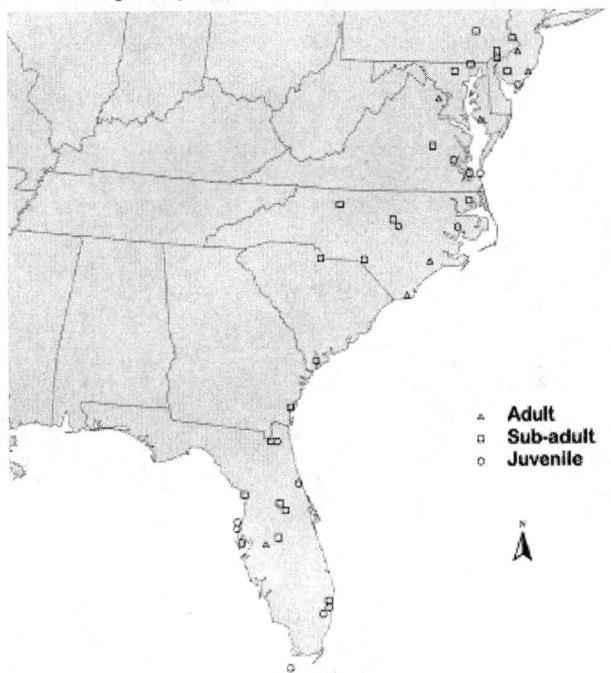

Figure 5. Recoveries of Cape May banded Sharp-shinned Hawks during summer.

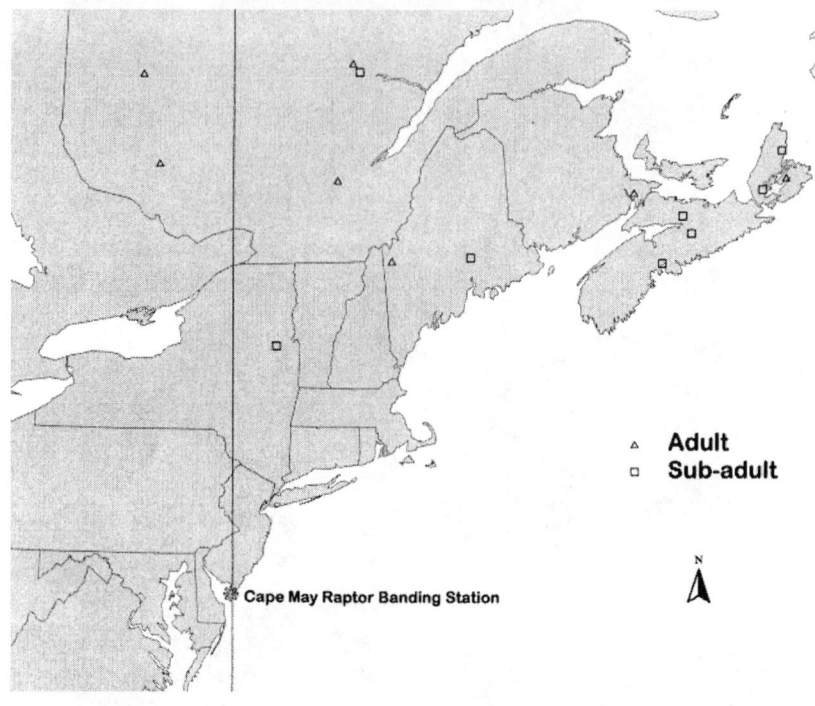

Figure 6. Recoveries of Cape May banded female Cooper's Hawks.

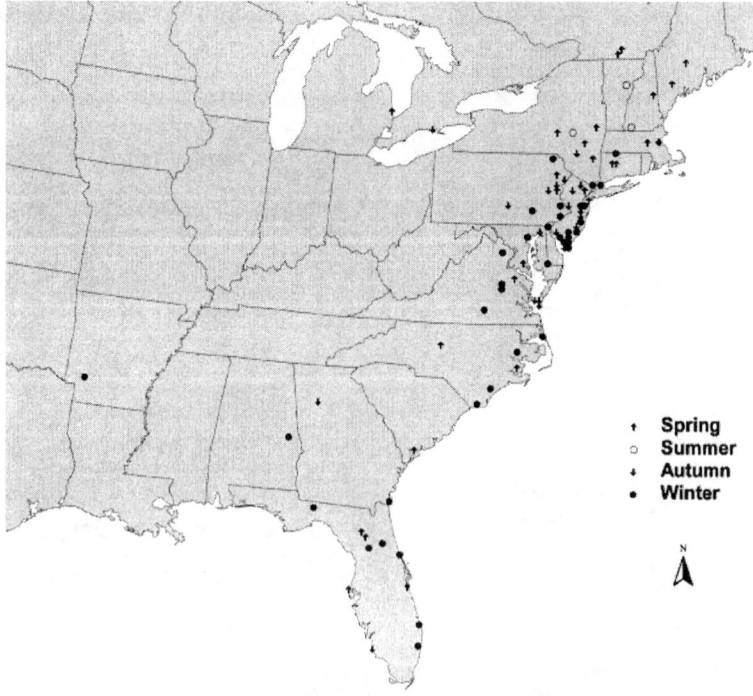

Figure 7. Recoveries of Cape May banded male Cooper's Hawks.

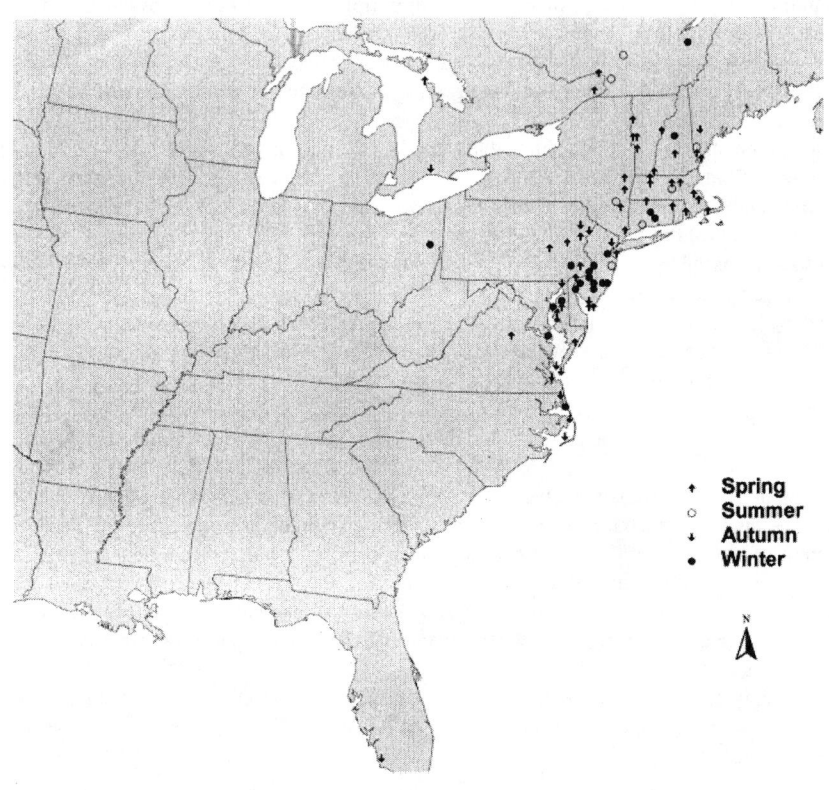

Swainson' Hawks, which breed in western North America, have been captured regularly since the first was caught in 1973 (Clark 1974b), for a total of 15. One banded in October of 1988 was found dead in New Brunswick in May of 1989, northeast of the banding location.

Over 30,000 people have witnessed the showing of banded raptors and received a raptor conservation message over the past 25 years, or about 1300 every year. We estimate an average attendance of 100 people at every public showing and around 15 for each private showing.

Table 4. Recovery rates of Cape May banded raptors by species.

Species	Recovery rate
No. Harrier *Circus cyaneus*	0.7 %
Sharp-shinned Hawk *A. striatus*	1.3
Cooper's Hawk *A. cooperi*	2.6
Red-tailed Hawk *Buteo jamaicensis*	2.5
Broad-winged Hawk *B. platypterus*	5.7
Peregrine *F. peregrinus*	9.0
Merlin *F. columbarius*	1.8
Am. Kestrel *F. sparverius*	0.6
OVERALL	**1.6%**

DISCUSSION

Banding (ringing) numbers of raptors at migration concentration areas can provide much information useful for their conservation, such as their condition, age and sex ratios, and, in particular, their migration pathways, wintering areas, and summer breeding areas. However, to get sufficient recoveries for the seasonal areas to be determined, large numbers of raptors must be banded, as recovery rates are rather low.

If a raptor count is also conducted in that area, then the data are even better, as it has been shown that counts and banding data are correlated. Counts and banding data can yield long-term trend data if they are conducted in the same manner annually.

Making captured raptors available to other researchers facilitates their studies as they can concentrate on taking their samples or measurements and do not have to be concerned with capturing a large enough sample size.

Age ratios from banding can be important in evaluating the banding results. For example, because over 90% of the raptors captured at Cape May Point are juveniles, annual variations in numbers are reflective of breeding success rather than population changes.

Sex ratios are interesting, particularly when they differ noticeably from 50:50, as is the case with many species in our data. Possible causes are differential migratory pathways, differential survivability, and capture bias. Further discussion of this is outside the scope of this article but will be addressed in later publications. However, we feel that capture bias alone does not explain our results.

Our showing of banded raptors to the public, although a secondary objective for the project, has allowed us to reach tens of thousands of people with a strong raptor conservation message.

Our future plans include concentration on capturing more of the species that occur in lower numbers to get more recoveries, to continue to make raptors available to other researchers, and to put a few satellite transmitters on species that occur in low numbers, e.g. Swainson's Hawk, to learn their wintering and breeding areas.

In summary, raptor banding stations can provide important conservation information, especially the migration pathways and wintering and breeding areas, but also to gather information from the individual migrants.

ACKNOWLEDGEMENTS

We thank the Cape May Bird Observatory, especially P. Dunne and P. Kerlinger, for providing support for the project over the long term. The National Wildlife Federation also provided support. Banders and helpers far too numerous to list are thanked for their important contribution to this project.

REFERENCES

BILDSTEIN, K. L., W. S. CLARK, D. L. EVANS, M. FIELD, L. SOUCY & E. HENCKEL 1984. Sex and age differences in fall migration of Northern Harriers. *J. Field Ornith.* 55:145-150.

CLARK, W. S. 1970. Migration trapping of hawks (and owls) at Cape May N.J.-3rd year. *EBBA News* 33:181-89.

CLARK, W. S. 1974a. Second record of the Kestrel (*Falco tinnunculus*) for North America. *Auk* 91:172.

CLARK, W. S. 1974b. Occurrence of Swainson's Hawk substantiated in New Jersey. *Wilson Bull.* 86:284-285.

CLARK, W. S. 1976. Cape May Point raptor banding station - 1974 results. *No. Am. Bird Bander.* 1:5-13.

CLARK, W. S. 1985. Migration of the Merlin along the coast of New Jersey. *Raptor Res.* 19:85-94.

CLARK, W. S. 1986. The migrating Sharp-shinned Hawks of Cape May Point, N. J. (*In*) Harwood, M. (ed.) *Proc. Hawk Conf. IV*, Rochester, March 1983. Hawk Migr. Assn. of N. Am.

HENNY, C. J. & W. S. CLARK 1982. Measurements of fall migrant Peregrine Falcons from Texas and New Jersey. *J. Field Ornith.* 53:326-332.

KERLINGER, P. 1993 Sharp-shinned Hawk populations in free fall. *Winging it* 5:10-11.

KIRKPATRICK, C. E. & D. M. LAUER 1985. Hematozoa of raptors from southern New Jersey and adjacent areas. *J. Wildl. Dis.* 21:1-6.

KIRKPATRICK, C. E. & V. P. TREXLER-MYREN. 1986. A survey of free-living falconiform birds for *Salmonella. J. Am Vet. Med. Assoc.* 189: 997-998.

SCHULTZ. C.W. 1996. Migration trend and morphometric characteristics of Northern Harriers during autumn migration at Cape May Point, New Jersey. M.S. Thesis, Utah State University, Logan, 90pp.
VIVERETTE, C. B., S. STRUVE & L.J. GOODRICH. 1996. Decreases in migrating Sharp-shinned Hawks (*Accipiter striatus*) at traditional raptor-migration watchsites in eastern North America. *Auk* 113:32-40.

William S. Clark
7800 Dassett Court, Apt. 101
Annandale, VA 22003
USA

Christopher W. Schultz
305 Pine Valley Road
Bayfield, CO 81122
USA

Olin S. Allen
Rt. 1, Box 188-C
Shepherdstown, WV 25443
USA

Where have 30,000 Lesser Spotted Eagles *Aquila pomarina* gone?

Dan Alon

INTRODUCTION

Israel is well known as a bottleneck for migrating Palearctic birds, particularly soaring birds, migrating from their breeding grounds in Eastern Europe and Western Asia to their wintering grounds in Africa and back (Leshem & Yom-Tov 1996, Alon et. al. 1992). Medium to large soaring birds avoid crossing large bodies of water such as the Mediterranean during migration and hence use land bridges, such as Israel, to reach their destinations.

Autumn migration of Palearctic soaring birds over Israel has been surveyed by ground observers systematically since 1977 (Dovrat 1991, Tsoval & Alon 1991, Leshem & Yom-Tov 1996). From 1977 - 1987, surveys were conducted over the central part of Israel (Kefar Kassem) (Dovrat 1991). As of 1988, the autumn soaring bird migration survey is conducted across the Northern Valleys. Both surveys were and are conducted by the Israeli Ornithological Center. In autumn, the majority of soaring birds pass Israel along two major flyways, the western flyway along the central mountain range and the eastern flyway along the Jordan Rift Valley (Leshem & Yom-Tov 1998). Thirty-five species of birds of prey (Accipitriformes) were observed, along with two species of storks *Ciconia ciconia, C. nigra* and White Pelicans *Pelecanus onocrotalus*.

Unlike in the spring, the southern route through Eilat is almost inactive in autumn. The only species with significant numbers migrating along the southern route at that time of year is the Steppe Eagle *Aquila nipalensis* (Shirihai & Christie 1992).

The Lesser Spotted Eagle *Aquila pomarina* is one of the predominant migrating birds of prey during autumn migration in Israel along the western flyway (Dovrat 1991, Tsoval & Alon 1991, Leshem & Yom-Tov 1996. There are five bottlenecks along their migration route (Burgus, Bosphorus, Belen Pass, Iscadron Gulf, Israel and the Suez Gulf) (Meyburg et. al 1997, 1995). Lesser Spotted Eagles pass through Israel from the third week of September to the second week in October. According to most studies the entire population of Lesser Spotted Eagles passes through the above-mentioned migration route, except for a few individuals that were recorded crossing the Mediterranean Sea through Cyprus (Meyburg et. al 1995).

Although autumn counts have been conducted in other regions, in contrast to this survey, they are only conducted at a few stations, over only a few years, or both.

METHODS

This study is based on annual autumn counts conducted between 1982-1997 in Israel. From 1982-1987 counts were conducted in the Kfar Kassem region. Since 1988 counts have been conducted across the Northern Valleys.

The Autumn Migration Soaring Bird Survey across the Northern Valleys begins each year on 1 August with the beginning of the White Stork migration and in the past on 20 August in Kfar Kassem. Until 25 August, 3-4 stations are opened from the Jordanian border (61 km from the coast) to 54 km from the coast. During the migration season, as the species composition changes, the survey moves west. During the period of Lesser Spotted Eagle migration (25.9-15.10), the stations are run between 11-46 km from the coast in the Northern Valleys and 5-30 km from the coast in Kfar Kassem.

Station locations

Stations occur more or less in a straight line across the migration front and at a distance which will allow maximal identification of all the raptors crossing the front. For minimal coverage of a 35 km wide migration front, at least 12 stations, placed 3 km apart, are used.

All stations are opened approximately 1 hour after sunrise, as raptors start taking off, and close an hour before sunset, as diurnal migration stops. The bird watcher at each station is equipped with binoculars, a telescope and radio communications. The bird watchers record the following information: hour, species, number, distance from station, estimated altitude, direction of migration. This helps in learning about hourly changes in the migratory axis and facilitates the elimination of duplications (those birds that were recorded in two or more different stations).

RESULTS

Figure 1. Annual counts of Lesser Spotted Eagles, 1982 - 1997

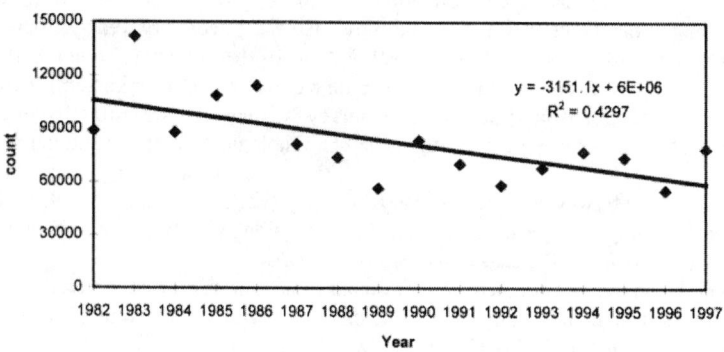

Figure 2. Annual counts of Lesser Spotted Eagles, 1982 - 1986

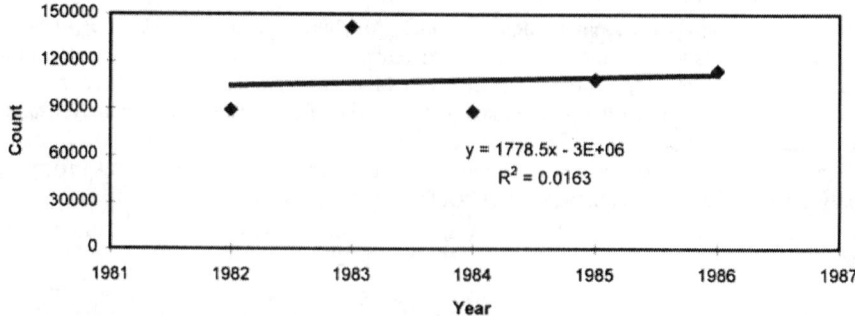

Figure 3. Annual counts of Lesser Spotted Eagles, 1987 - 1997

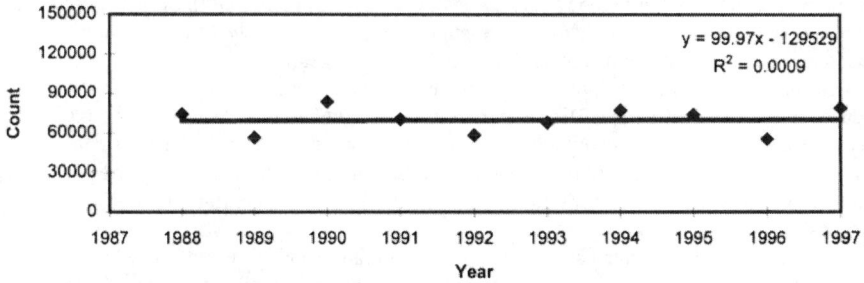

Figure 4. Annual counts of Lesser Spotted Eagles, 1985 - 1990

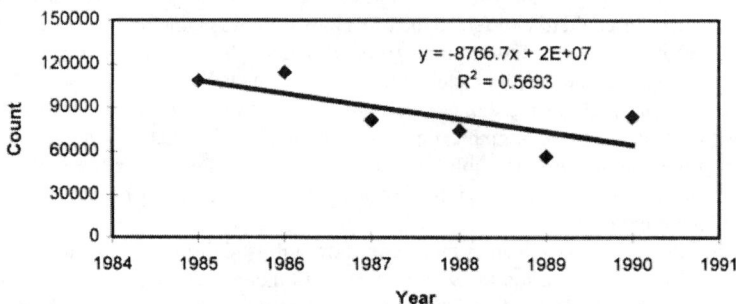

Figure 5. Annual counts of Lesser Spotted Eagles, 1992 - 1997

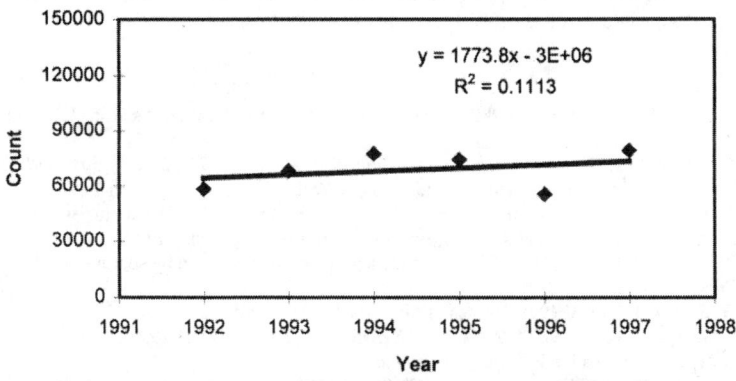

DISCUSSION

Figure 1 shows a clear decline in numbers of Lesser Spotted Eagles from 1982-1997. However, no decline is noted between the years 1982-1986, in fact a slight increase may even be seen (Figure 2). The same is true for Figure 3, regarding the years 1987-1997, with almost no change between the years. The average count for 1982-1986 is significantly higher then the average for 1987-1997. Figure 4, summarizing 1985-1990, shows a sharp decrease in numbers from 1987 onwards. From 1992-1997, a slight positive trend is seen (Figure 5).

Titus *et. al.* (1989) suggested that the main factors affecting the difference in counts between migration survey years are the quality of observers and changes in the weather. These factors do affect seasonal counts; however, long term studies decrease the significance of the between year variance. Leshem and Yom-Tov (1998) doubt the applicability of annual counts in estimating population size because of this variance. For short term surveys, lasting only a few years, this may be true (their paper dealt with nine years compared to fifteen in this study). Survey counts may not be an efficient tool to monitor changes in population size immediately, as long-term monitoring is needed to draw firm conclusions regarding population changes.

The change in the Lesser Spotted Eagle population size, according to the survey counts in this study, occurred suddenly and was first apparent in the count of autumn 1987. Only an extreme event can cause such a drastic drop in numbers, unlike many cases where a gradual decrease in numbers is a result of the gradual destruction of habitat. The breeding distribution of Lesser Spotted Eagles includes West Germany eastwards to Russia and the largest concentration of birds is found in Belorussia.

One event that could have caused such a dramatic and sudden decrease in May 1986 indeed occurred during the Chernobyl nuclear disaster in the Ukraine, bordering Belorussia. The area is the core nesting region of the Lesser Spotted Eagles (Meyburg *et. al.* 1997) (Cramp & Simmons 1980). The Lesser Spotted Eagle is the only raptor whose central breeding region is so close to the disaster. Radioactive emissions could have affected the birds in several ways, including direct damage to the eagle's productivity, damage to food sources (rodents and amphibians), and damage to the habitat which can directly affect the breeding sites of the eagles or the habitat of the prey.

It is unclear if the slight increase in population size shown in the results indicates a recovery of the population. From personal communications, some regions, such as Latvia and Estonia, are noting an increase in populations. It is possible that this increase is being recorded in the survey and if indeed the cause of the drastic decrease is habitat destruction, the birds may be moving to other areas within their breeding range.

In conclusion, the results shown in this study show a drastic drop in the population size of the Lesser Spotted Eagle that occurred in 1987, or near that time, and not a gradual decrease that may result from gradual habitat destruction. This raises the theory that the cause of the drastic change is the disaster at the nuclear plant that occurred in the centre of the eagle's breeding region in spring 1986. These results demand in depth research, though this would be much more difficult today because of the long time that has passed since the disaster.

REFERENCES

ALON, D., Y. LESHEM, E. DOVRAT & A. TSOVEL 1992. Autumn migration of soaring birds across Samaria and northern valleys. *Torgos* 20.
CRAMP, S. & K. SIMMONS 1980. *Handbook of the Bird of Europe, The Middle East and North Africa*, volume 2. Oxford University Press, Oxford, London, New York.
DOVRAT, E. 1991. The Kefar Kassem raptor migration survey autumn 1977-1987: a brief summary. Raptors in Israel, Israel Raptor Information Center and International Birdwatching Center, Eilat.
LESHEM, Y. & Y. YOM TOV 1996. The magnitude and timing of migration by soaring raptors, Pelicans and Storks over Israel. *Ibis* 138 :188-203.
LESHEM, Y. & Y. YOM TOV 1998. Routes of migrating soaring birds. *Ibis* 140:41-52.
MEYBURG, B.-U., L. HARASZTHY, M. STRAZDS & N. SCHAFFER 1997. European Union species action plan for Lesser Spotted Eagle (*Aquila pomarina*). RSPB.
MEYBURG, B.-U., W. SCHELLER & C. MEYBURG 1995. Migration of Lesser Spotted Eagle *Aquila pomarina*: A study by means of satellite telemetry. *Journal für ornithologie* 136:401-422.
SHIRIHAI, H. & D. CHRISTIE 1992. Raptor migration at Elat. *British Birds* 85:141-185
TITUS, K., M. FULLER & J. L. RUOS 1989. Considerations for monitoring raptor population trends based on counts of migrants. *Raptors in the Modern World.* WWGP Berlin, London, and Paris.
TSOVEL, A. & D. ALON 1991. Soaring bird migration survey in the Northern Valleys of Israel, Raptors in Israel, Israel Raptor Information Center and International Birdwatching Center, Elat.

Dan Alon
Israeli Ornithological Center
SPNI, 155 Herzel St.
Tel Aviv 68101
Israel

Part 9

Islands and Raptors

Black-shouldered Kite *Elanus caeruleus*

Conveners:
Clayton M. White & Luis Felipe Oliveira

Biodiversity, Island Raptors and Species Concepts

Clayton M. White and Lloyd F. Kiff

ABSTRACT

The biological species concept (BSC), which emphasizes reproductive isolation, and the phylogenetic species concept (PSC), based on unique combinations of characters, yield different numbers of raptor species. Based on the former approach, only taxa that are morphologically diagnosable are designated as species or subspecies, but new molecular techniques may reveal the existence of taxa ("putative" and "cryptic" species) unrecognizable by traditional morphological characters. Additionally, there are population groups, termed "evolutionarily significant units" (ESU's), which are on their own evolutionary trajectory, are usually identifiable by molecular characteristics, and often considered the same as phylogenetic species. In the extreme, many subspecies of the BSC are simply elevated to the species level of the PSC (Cracraft 1992). The taxonomic level at which conservation efforts are concentrated may have profound financial and logistical ramifications. A preliminary analysis reveals that 22% of 477 biological species (Sibley & Monroe 1990), at least 30% of a conservative estimate of about 592 phylogenetic species, occur on islands with about 28% and 44%, respectively, being insular endemics.

Regardless of the taxonomic approach, populations of island raptors usually have unique gene pools. In a biogeographic sense, islands may be any disjunct block of habitat, ranging from mountaintops and other isolated mainland habitats to bodies of land surrounded by water, but only the latter are considered here. According to the treatment of Sibley and Monroe (1990), a BSC-based list, there are 238 species of Accipitridae, 64 Falconidae, 17 Tytonidae and 159 Strigidae. A large proportion occur on islands (excluding Australia), as follows: Accipitridae; 45% (18% endemic), Falconidae; 41% (17%), Tytonidae; 83% (53%), and Strigidae; 48% (26%). A high percentage occur only on single islands or clusters of small islands. Of raptor species designated as threatened by the IUCN (Baillie & Groombridge 1996), 58% of Accipitridae are on islands, as are 50% of Falconidae, 80% of Tytonidae, and 67% of Strigidae. Of near-threatened, islands have 38% of listed Accipitridae, 14% of Falconidae, 100% of Tytonidae, and 21% of Strigidae. Examples of the importance of islands to overall raptor species diversity and problems of determining species status (BSC vs.PSC) of insular taxa on islands are provided by *Tyto* owls, owls of the genus *Otus* from SE Asia, Indonesia and Philippines, the serpent-eagle genus *Spilornis* in SE Asia and Indonesia, and the goshawks *Accipiter novaehollandiae* that range from Australia through Indonesia.

INTRODUCTION

Currently, one of the major concerns in conservation biology is the preservation of unique genetic combinations in the effort to maintain biodiversity (Vogler & DeSalle 1994, Barrowclough & Flesness 1996). From the standpoint of preserving biodiversity, the maintenance of unique island taxa is a critical conservation concern, since they tend to be evolutionarily isolated groups possessing the vulnerabilities peculiar to restricted-range species (King 1985, Long et al. 1996). Indeed, beginning with Darwin himself, it has long been understood that, as a result of isolation, islands tend to be unique places occupied by endemic and novel taxa; such a radiation or modification has often been called the "insular syndrome" (Masseti & Mazza 1996). Regrettably, the majority of documented avian extinctions have occurred on islands (Diamond 1984, Olson & James 1982), owing mostly to their often small populations, coupled with the effects of introduced biota and new forms of predation.

In the process of defining biodiversity and taxonomic boundaries, there is no present consensus on which of several major concepts should be followed (National Research Council 1995, Sites & Crandall 1997, Woodruff 1989). Some suggest that the diversity is best expressed at the species level (see discussion in Whittemore 1993), others argue that the polytypic subspecies concept better expresses that diversity, and still others contend that conservation efforts should be focused at taxonomic levels below the subspecies (National Research Council 1995). From a conservation standpoint relative to raptors, the choice of taxonomic concepts becomes important in trying to define the number of "species," especially when dealing with island-dependent or endemic taxa, because higher conservation priorities are accorded to species than to subspecies or populations (Collar et al. 1994, Haig 1998).

Traditionally, the most widely used species definition, and still the basis for most contemporary species lists and conservation laws, is the **biological species concept (BSC)**, the limits of which are set by isolation that requires geographic sympatry to test reproduction compatibility (Mayr 1969). However, many workers now advance the **phylogenetic species concept (PSC)**, which defines species as unique combinations of characters, whether morphometric or molecular (Zink & McKitrick 1995, Haffer 1997). The PSC accommodates the existence of "cryptic" and "putative" species, taxa that may have virtually imperceptible morphological differences, but which may be readily separated by molecular techniques (Davis & Nixon 1992). Further, the PSC is said to give a better description of the spatial patterns of biodiversity and produces units required by conservation biology (Zink 1997). Most island raptor subspecies as defined by the BSC possess unique combinations of characters; thus, they are generally elevated to the species level using the PSC.

However, it is an increasingly widely held notion that it is the population and not the species that is the ultimate currency of biodiversity (Crozier 1997). Various authors (e.g., Whitney et al. 1995) have made a persuasive case for the conservation of unique, isolated taxa, whether the "taxon" is currently judged to be a valid subspecies or not. How, then, does one define the unit of greatest evolutionary or conservation significance (Ryder 1986)? In recently assessing the effectiveness of the United States Endangered Species Act a committee of biologists proposed that an "evolutionary unit" (we prefer the earlier, but similar term "evolutionarily significant unit," or ESU) "is a group of organisms that represents a segment of biological diversity that shares evolutionary lineage and contains the potential for a unique evolutionary future," and they noted that each of these units is distinct from all other equivalent units in morphological, behavioural, biochemical, and/or physiological attributes (National Research Council 1995). This essentially follows the **evolutionary species concept (ESC)**, as described by Wiley (1981).

Definition of what is significant and how one makes such determinations remains complex, somewhat arbitrary, and accompanied by its own suite of characteristics and problems (Fleischer 1998). It is beyond the scope and intent of this paper to attempt to reconcile competing species definitions. However, we tend to agree with ESU adherents (e.g., O'Hara 1993) who argue that the evolutionary process is simply too dynamic to describe within the fixed boundaries of the BSC or PSC, or, as the National Research Council committee noted, "Speciation is a dynamic process with many factors involved, and science cannot delineate what nature itself does not." It is the maintenance of biodiversity and not so much the "species" that is of conservation importance.

Our goal is to review some of the issues of raptors on islands, discuss something of their biodiversity, and call attention to their distribution. "Islands," in a biogeographic sense, include a wide variety of geographical features ranging from lakes and isolated mountains, surrounded by dissimilar or inhospitable habitat (see Vuilleumier 1970), to land islands surrounded by water, all of which produce genetic isolation. Among the numerous examples of raptor taxa on habitat "islands" are the Red-chested Owlet *Glaucidium tephronotum elgonense*, which is confined to Mt. Elgon in Kenya, and Long-whiskered Owlet *Xenoglaux loweryi* known only from cloud forests around 1900 m elevation in central Peru (O'Neill & Graves 1977).

For the purpose of this paper, however, only land islands surrounded by water will be considered. Such islands may earlier have been connected to a continental land mass and contain continental rock or fragments of continents (a variety of islands such as Fiji and the Seychelles), or, in various fashions, may have arisen from ocean floors and are called oceanic islands. (Williamson 1981). Many of the former islands, especially in the seas between peninsular India and the greater Australian regions, approximate oceanic islands in the processes that produced their biological patterns and contents (Gorman 1979, Williamson 1981). Good accounts of tropical island raptors and their current status are found in Bildstein *et al*. (1998), Virani and Watson (1998), Thiollay (1998) and van Balen (1998).

MATERIAL AND METHODS

We have attempted to assess the differences in island raptor biodiversity as measured by the numbers of "species/taxa" according to the BSC, and PSC concepts (Table 1). Lacking detailed analyses of character data sets of the 580 raptor taxa considered here, our judgement is based on (1) morphological and (where available) molecular criteria and their relation to known distribution and the degree of isolation from other bird taxa, (2) our combined knowledge and experience in raptor taxonomy and raptor ecology, and (3) implications by others that can be used to estimate numbers of PSC species.

Table 1. Comparison of projected number of "species" within the families of raptors based on the biological species concept (BSC) and phylogenetic species concept (PSC). First number is for total species, second number for island endemics, and third number is percentage of total that are insular endemics. Numbers of BSC species were taken from Sibley and Monroe (1990). See text for the basis and rationale underlying PSC totals. These are given as a range of estimated numbers with the lower one representing the most conservative PSC approach and the higher figure representing the number of "stocks" or ESU's embedded within the PSC and often considered to equate with it. Percents rounded to the nearest whole number. Note increasing importance of islands as the number of taxa increases from BSC to PSC treatments.

Families	BSC			PSC		
Accipitridae	239	45	**19 %**	288 - 405	80 - 179	**28 - 44 %**
Falconidae	63	9	**14 %**	84 - 115	19 - 43	**23 - 37 %**
Tytonidae	17	9	**53 %**	21 - 55	13 - 41	**62 - 75 %**
Strigidae	158	42	**27 %**	198 - 276	63 - 130	**32 - 47 %**
TOTALS (MEANS)	477	105	**(28%)**	(721	284	**44%**)

In general, we have followed the treatment of Sibley and Monroe (1990) for our estimates of the numbers of biological species and their generic designations. Because of its contemporary widespread adoption, their list was also followed for the most part by del Hoyo (1994). Our few departures from strict adherence to the Sibley and Monroe list were based mostly on supplementary information in Amadon and Bull (1988). The approximate number of raptor species recognized under the BSC is rather straightforward and relatively little changed during the last half of this century, although there remain perennial subjective judgements about reproductive compatibility among many allopatric taxa.

Peters (1940), Mayr and Cottrell (1979), and Howard and Moore (1991) contain valuable information on raptor subspecies names and ranges. The latter reference was especially useful for determining the ranges of insular subspecies. Our determinations of what constitutes a phylogenetic species are largely subjective, but are based on degree of morphological differences, degree of geographic isolation, or a combination of both when one or the other is somewhat weak or questionable. In actual practice, we have mostly elevated well-marked subspecies under the BSC concept to phylogenetic species rank where specific taxonomic or molecular studies were lacking. This is not entirely satisfactory, since some avian subspecies may have been described on the basis of genetically insignificant plumage or other variations (Barrowclough & Flesness 1996). Ideally, species designated under the PSC should require cladistic or molecular analyses (Zink 1997, Haffer 1997), but such data are not yet available for most raptor taxa.

ESU's are best defined by the disjunctness of populations as usually identified by molecular data, regardless of where presumed taxonomic boundaries may be set by the other two systems. We recognize the diagnosis of them as important to issues in conservation especially if one considers them more equivalent to the "stocks" in wildlife biology, as have others (see Fleischer 1998). To be conservative, however, we will for the purpose of this paper, be content to view ESU's as synonymous with taxonomic units of the PSC in accordance with the argument of Barrowclough and Flesness (1996) and will not consider them further. In the following discussion, we use the term "taxon" (*pl.* taxa) to refer to a taxonomic entity, including genera, species or subspecies, as traditionally described, but not for unnamed ESU's.

For our analysis, Australia is not considered an island, as is often customary. For perspective, it is only about 16% smaller than the continental United States, or 35% larger than the size of continental Europe, and its conservation problems and types of endemic taxa more resemble those of larger continental land masses than islands. The largest islands incorporated into our analyses are those of New Guinea (over 85% smaller than the U.S.), Borneo, and Madagascar.

Traditional geographical regions (Neill 1969, Müller 1981) are used with a few modifications, i.e., some of our categories are a mixture of parts or all of two or more traditional regions. The regions include: **Nearctic** (North America north of the Mexican Plateau), **Neotropical** (South and Middle America south of the Mexican Plateau, except for most associated islands), **Caribbean** (islands in the Caribbean between North and South America), **Eurasia** or **Palearctic** (Europe and Asia, except Japan, Sakhalin, and associated islands), **Holarctic** (Palearctic and Nearctic combined), **Afrotropical** (Africa south of the Sahara and Madagascar, but not including other associated islands), **South Asia** (Pakistan east through India to Burma [Myanmar], but not Sri Lanka), **Indian Ocean** (islands from Madagascar east to Andaman and Nicobar Islands including Sri Lanka), **Indomalayan** (Thailand east to Philippine Islands and Indonesia), **Wallacea** (eastern Indomalayan area from Wallace's Line lying west of Sulawesi and between Bali and Lombok east to Lydekker's Line, i.e., to the east of the Moluccas and Lesser Sundas; see Coates and Bishop (1997)), **Australasia** (from the Moluccas in the centre of Wallacea eastward to Fiji and New Caledonia and Australia), **Australopapuan** (Australia, New Guinea, New Zealand and islands between New Zealand and New Guinea; generally used term for a region that is essentially a subset of Australasia but takes in New Zealand), **Pacific Ocean** (remaining islands in that ocean), and **Atlantic Ocean** (remaining islands in that ocean).

For the purposes of our analysis we have either retained some genera separate or combined them as described below. In this choice we used what we deemed to be the most persuasive evidence, a procedure that is unavoidably subjective. Thus, we include *Asturina* (2-5 species) with *Buteo* (del Hoyo 1994), place *Ketupa* (4-5 species) with *Bubo* (Amadon & Bull 1988), unite *Ciccaba* (4 species) with *Strix,* and maintain *Speotyto* separated from *Athene* (Sibley & Monroe 1990). It is likely that the curious monotypic island endemic genus *Mimizuku* (Giant Scops-owl) should be included with *Otus* (Miranda *et al.* 1997), although we have maintained it as a separate genus as did Miranda *et al.* (1997).

Putative species are taxa that may be allocated to one species but, based on other criteria, could be a valid species in their own right. An example is shown by the disagreement over whether the so-called Harlan's Hawk *Buteo harlani,* represented by dark-coloured populations in interior Alaska and the Yukon, should be treated as a distinct species, or as a geographic race of the Red-tailed Hawk *Buteo jamaicensis harlani*. A similar question exists over whether the pale falcons of central Asia and North Africa are a separate species, the so-called "Barbary" Falcon *Falco pelegrinoides*, or merely geographic races of the Peregrine Falcon *Falco peregrinus*, i.e., *F. p. pelegrinoides* and *F. p. babylonicus,* or divided in some other manner (see Wink *et al.* this vol.).

One of many examples of unresolved taxonomic questions among raptors is provided by the goshawk on Christmas Island in the Indian Ocean. That taxon, given the trinomial *natalis*, is currently allocated as a subspecies of the Australasian Goshawk *Accipiter fasciatus,* but some authorities regard it as a subspecies (?) in the Variable Goshawk *Accipiter novaehollandiae* complex, and others as a full species in its own right. Regardless of the taxonomic treatment, *natalis* possesses distinct morphological traits; thus, at the least, it appears to be an ESU with a unique gene pool, evolutionary history, and evolutionary future. Many similar examples exist throughout the Falconiformes and Strigiformes.

Cryptic species are similar and defined as those taxa that appear, or are suspected, to be a species in their own right, but for which sufficient data or analyses have not been acquired to confirm their status. This is the situation with the *Tyto* owl on the Galapagos Islands, which is currently regarded as a subspecies, *Tyto alba punctatissima,* of the cosmopolitan Barn Owl complex. The term "species group" has been used similarly to indicate taxa lumped by some as one species, but separated as valid species by others, as shown in insular Indian Ocean "superspecies" of the Madagascar Scops-Owl *Otus rutilus*, with the Malagasy representative nominate *rutilus*, and two "groups," Pemba Scops-Owl *O.[r.] pembaensis* and Adjouan Scops-Owl *O. [r.] capnodes* (Sibley & Monroe 1993). As we proceed through the discussion it will be evident that some of the taxa considered probably properly fall into the category termed "megasubspecies", that is, defined as a subspecies (or cluster of subspecies) known or judged to be approaching species status; many were originally described as full species (Stresemann & Amadon 1979, Amadon & Short 1976, 1992) and some may be restored to full species, even under the BSC, in the future.

RESULTS

The concepts:

It is of perhaps coincidental interest that the numbers of island-dependent Falconiformes and Strigiformes are about equal based on the BSC. About 220 taxa of Falconiformes and 225 taxa of Strigiformes are island-dependent; of these we regard 51-53 and 52-53, respectively, as full species. The island endemic "species" are also about equal between hawks and owls with 54 and 51 respectively (Table 1). It is also clear in Table 1 that the numbers of island endemics increase, in some cases slightly more than double, if one uses the PSC rather than the BSC. In most of the cursory analyses done on a variety of groups of birds, the number of species overall with the PSC increases by a factor of about 2.5 over the number of species with the BSC (R. Zink pers. comm.). The important information in Table 1 is that the percentage of island endemics increases as the focus becomes finer and the resulting populations viewed in some taxonomic fashion are smaller. It should be remembered that: 1). There is not full agreement among workers as to which of the island taxa or populations are full species in their own right so the number is tentative, and 2). Our assessment of the numbers of species with the PSC are not based on rigorous analyses and there is a range of values depending on the inclusion of the ESU's within the larger units.

In nearly each case for the larger genera included in our analysis, the numbers given by Amadon and Bull (1988) were fewer, usually only by one or two but as many as five in the case of *Otus,* since their list is BSC-based. The number of named taxa may change as knowledge increases, but also in part based on the penchant by investigators to lump or split.

As shown in Table 2 the number of taxa listed by the IUCN (based on the BSC) as threatened is nearly equal between Falconiformes and Strigiformes, although more of the Strigiformes occur on islands, but not significantly so ($\chi^2 = 0.52$). There are, however, nearly three times more Falconiforms than Strigiforms listed as near-threatened (significant difference, $\chi^2 = 29$, $p < 0.001$) with about the same differential on islands ($p < 0.01$). The differences may simply reflect our poorer knowledge of Strigiformes; thus, fewer species have been assigned to that category.

Table 2. Distribution of taxa considered by the IUCN to be in the threatened and near-threatened category for Falconiformes and Strigiformes. The threatened category includes: CE = critically endangered, E = endangered, V = vulnerable.

Locations	Number Threatened Taxa (percent of IUCN listed total [1])						Near-threatened	
	Falconiformes			Strigiformes			Falconi- formes	Strigi- formes
	CE	E	V	CE	E	V		
Mainlands	2 (6)	2 (6)	10 (32)	1 (4)	2 (8)	6 (23)	31 (70)	9 (60)
Australia	-----	1 (3)	2 (6)	-----	-----	1 (4)	-----	1 (7)
Islands								
Atlantic Ocean	-----	-----	-----	-----	-----	-----	-----	1 (7)
Indian Ocean	2 (6)	1 (3)	1 (3)	3 (12)	1 (4)	----	4 (9)	3 (30)
Indo- malayan	1 (3)	1 (3)	4 (13)	1 (4)	1 (4)	7 (27)	2 (5)	1 (7)
Australo- papuan	-----	-----	2 (6)	-----	1 (4)	3 (12)	5 (11)	-----
Pacific Ocean	-----	1 (3)	1 (3)	-----	-----	-----	2 (5)	-----
Carib- bean	-----	1 (3)	-----	-----	-----	-----	-----	-----

[1] Percent rounded to next nearest 0.5% so totals may not equal 100%.

Several genera, owing partly to their primarily tropical distribution (see Bildstein et al. 1998), contain more island endemics and more putative or cryptic species than genera with a more temperate distribution (Table 3). To recognize each of these forms taxonomically, especially using the BSC, may simply be an exercise in oversplitting. Most are insular taxa.

Because of the trends in the interpretation of molecular data we would predict that some unique island taxa will be raised to the species level We especially expect this to occur in populations on certain islands where other species of birds have differentiated enough to be allocated species rank. Some of these taxa and the islands where they might be expected to differentiate are shown in Table 4. With the use of molecular techniques differences in the level of magnitude of change found in other well recognized species are being uncovered. For example, Wink et al. (1998), using cytochrome b evidence, argued that the Merlins of North America are a separate species from those of Eurasia and that the Red-necked Falcons of Africa are separate from two groups in India. Based on DNA findings, Norman et al. (1998) concluded that the species complex of *Ninox squamipila* is comprised of three separate species; treatments based on traditional morphological characters had considered it to be a single species (Peters 1940, Schodde & Mason 1997).

Table 3. Ten genera and their taxa (BSC) with particularly rich island endemic representation (Part A) compared with 5 genera and their taxa (Part B) with rather poor island representation. Putative or cryptic species are taxa (frequently termed subspecies) that may be differentiated at the species level but still taxonomically hidden within another described taxon (see text). The majority of putative or cryptic forms not described or formally named species are island-dependent endemic taxa. Only one of the putative species in Part B is an island endemic. Number of named species taken from Sibley and Monroe (1990) but may be oversplit.

PART A

			Island Endemics as % of Species and % of Total Taxa [3]	
	No. Traditionally Named Species		No. Additional Putative or Cryptic	
Genera	Total Taxa [1]	Species [2]	Species	Total Taxa
Aviceda (Cuckoo Hawks)	5/31	0	20 %	61 %
Pernis (Honey Buzzards)	3/9	8	33 %	55 %
Spilornis (Serpent Eagles)	5/26	7	80 %	81 %
Accipiter (Goshawks/Sparrowhawks)	48/142	9	46 %	63 %
Spizaetus (Hawk Eagles)	13/23	0	8 %	43 %
Falco (Falcons)	37/108	5	19%	26%
Tyto (Barn/Grass Owls)	12/64	2	50 %	55 %
Otus (Scops Owls)	56/224	7? [4]	43%	74 % [5]
Ninox (Southern Hawk Owls)	19/73	3?	74 %	74 %
Asio (Long/Short Eared Owls)	7/29	0	14 %	41 %

1. Includes monotypic species in addition to polytypic ones in the total number of taxa.
2. Category indicates that some named subspecies are allocated by some taxonomists to independent species; taxonomy and systematics not clear with new molecular data changing the number on a regular basis..
3. Rounded to the nearest 0.5 %.
4. *Otus* is difficult. In addition to the putative species at least 10 insular taxa and 5 continental taxa treated by Sibley and Monroe (1990) as full species have been considered subspecies of other taxa.
5. Of the taxa, 46 % are in the New World of which only 5 % are island endemics

PART B

Buteo (True Buzzards) [6]	26/73	3 ? [6]	15 %	25 %
Aquila (True [booted] Eagles) [7]	12/19	?	8 %	11 %
Bubo (Eagle Owls) [8]	18/27 [8]	1 + ?	6 %	14 %
Strix (Wood Owls) [9]	18/65	2 ± ?	0 %	26 %
Glaucidium (Pygmy Owls)	20/66	3 ± ?	5 %	15 %

6. Between 2-5 species are sometimes placed in the genus *Asturina* rather than *Buteo* as here (see Amadon & Bull 1988 and Sibley &Monroe 1990). As recently as 1998, the species *poecilochrous* and *polyosoma* were said to be conspecific (Farquhar 1998).
7. Opinions differ on the species limits in the *A. rapax/nipalensis* and *A. heliaca/adelberti* complexes.
8. Herein the genus *Ketupa* (Fish Owls) are included in *Bubo* (see Sibley and Monroe 1990).
9. The Neotropical genus *Ciccaba* (Neotropical Wood Owls) is included in *Strix* (see Sibley and Monroe 1990)

While there is not general agreement even among molecular workers themselves, as to what level of molecular divergence might suggest the species level, we can use an example from among passerines where the average sequence divergence (D) values between subspecies is 0.0058 and between species 0.174 (Barrowclough 1980). Boyce (1989) found that the divergence (D) value between a sample of North American and Argentine American Kestrels *Falco sparverius* was 0.144, suggesting differentiation at the species level, and at least six other populations of kestrels seemingly have equivalent levels of genetic divergence. Whether to regard these various taxa as species or subspecies under the BSC remains problematical, but they presumably qualify as phylogenetic species. The different populations of Merlins, Red-necked Falcons and American Kestrels mentioned here are certainly on their own evolutionary trajectories.

Table 4. Traditional taxa (BSC), often geographically widespread, that occur on certain islands but not differentiated enough on those islands to be given separate binomial or trinomial names. The islands on which they occur are islands where other raptor taxa (as well as many birds) have differentiated sufficiently to be given *nomen*. As shown below in the second column, many of the taxa listed are not prone to differentiation while others are, and probably have done so on the islands listed (see text for discussion). Where a trinomial name is in parenthesis the islands involved refer only to that subspecies.

Taxon No.	Taxa / No.	Total Named Geographic Area	Island Endemics Islands Occupied But Taxa Not Differentiated
Pandion haliaetus subspp.	6 / 0	Indomalayan, Pacific Ocean	some in Indomalayan but also w Caledonia and Tasmania
Machaerhamphus alcinus	3 / 1	Australopapuan Indomalayan	Sumatra, Borneo
Milvus migrans	9 / 3	Indomalayan, Australopapuan	several, but mainly New Guinea
Milvus milvus	2 / 1	Eurasia	Canary Islands
Haliastur indus	4 / 1	Indomalayan, Indian Ocean	mainly Sri Lanka, New Guinea
Ichthyophaga humilis	2 / 0	Indomalayan	Sulawesi
Spilornis cheela (malayensis)	20 / 15	Indomalayan	North Borneo
Butastur liventer	1 / 0	Indomalayan	Java, Sula Islands
Butastur indicus	1 / 0	Indomalayan	Japan, Philippine Islands
Circus spilonotus	2 / 1	Indomalayan	Philippine Islands, Borneo
Circus approximans	1 / 0	Australopapuan, Pacific Ocean	various, including New Zealand
Circus buffoni	1 / 0	Neotropical	Trinidad
Accipiter badius	6 / 0	Africa, Asia	Sri Lanka, Taiwan
Accipiter novaehollandiae	23 / 22	Indomalayan, Australopapuan	Tasmania
Accipiter fasciatus	12 / 10	Indomalayan, Australopapuan	Tasmania
Accipiter virgata (besra)	8 / 6	Asia, Indian Ocean	Sri Lanka, Andaman Islands
Accipiter cirrhocephalus	4 / 2	Australopapuan	Tasmania
Leucopternis albicollis	4 / 0	Neotropical	Trinidad
Buteogallus urubitinga	2 / 0	Neotropical	Trinidad
Buteo polyosoma	2 / 0	Neotropical	Falkland (Malvinas) Islands

Table 4. continued

Buteo jamaicensis	14 / 4	Nearctic, Neotropical	Bahamas
Ictinaetus malayensis	2 / 0	S. Asia, Indomalayan	Sri Lanka,
Hieraaetus kienerii	2 / 0	S. Asia, Indomalayan	several, mainly Sri Lanka, Sulawesi
Spizaetus cirrhatus	6 / 4	S. Asia, Indomalayan	Several, mainly Borneo, Java
Spizaetus nanus	2 / 1	Indomalayan	Several, mainly Sumatra
Spizaetus alboniger	1 / 0	Indomalayan	Borneo
Polyborus plancus	4 / 2	Nearctic, Neotropical	Cuba, Falkland (Malvinas) Islands
Microhierax fringillarius	1 / 0	S. Asia, Indomalayan	Sumatra
Falco tinnunculus subspp.	11 / 4	Pacific Ocean, Indian Ocean	Socotra, Philippines
Falco cenchroides	2 / 1	Australopapuan	Tasmania
Falco severus	1 / 0	S. Asia east to Australopapuan	New Guinea
Falco longipennis	3 / 0	Australopapuan	Tasmania
Tyto alba subspp	35 / 20	Indian Ocean to Australopapuan	several, Sri Lanka, Solomon Islands
Tyto capensis	10 / 4	Africa, Asia to Australropapuan	Lesser Sundas
Phodilus badius	5 / 3	S. Asia, Indomalayan	Java, Borneo
Otus scops	9 / 4	Eurasia, Indomalayan	Taiwan
Otus bakkamoena	7 / 0	Eurasia, S. Asia	Sri Lanka
Otus lempiji subspp	13 / 8	Asia, Indomalayan	Sakhalin, Sumatra
Bubo virginianus (heterocnemis)	20 / 0	Nearctic, Neotropical	Newfoundland
Bubo bubo (tenuipes)	20 / 1	Eurasia	Kurile Islands, Hokkaido
Bubo sumatrana	2 / 1	Indomalayan	Sumatra
Bubo ketupu	4 / 2	S. Asia, Indomalayan	Java-Borneo
Strix seloputo	3 / 2	S. Asia, Indomalayan	Java
Strix uralensis	11 / 4	Eurasia	Hokkaido
Speotyto cunicularia	19 / 2	Nearctic, Neotropical	Bahamas
Ninox scutulata	11 / 4	Asia to Indomalayan	Sri Lanka, Sumatra

Table 5. Islands or areas and their endemic formerly named taxa from greatest number (top) to lowest. In some cases (especially Madagascar, Sulawesi and New Guinea), the island named also includes smaller satellite or adjacent islands that also have the species. Sulawesian species must also be included in the Wallacea group and thus Wallacea has the greatest number with 20 species although the two entities are listed separately.

Island/Area	Species count	Species
Madagascar	15 species	*Aviceda madagascariensis* *Haliaeetus vociferoides* *Eutriorchis astur* *Circus maillardi* *Polyboroides radiatus* *Accipiter francesii* *Accipiter madagascariensis* *Accipiter henstii* *Buteo brachypterus* *Falco newtoni* *Falco zoniventris* *Tyto soumagnei* *Otus rutilus* *Ninox superciliaris* *Asio madagascariensis*
Philippines	including Palawan, 12 species	*Spilornis holospilus* *Pithecophaga jefferyi* *Spizaetus philippensis* *Microhierax erythrogenys* *Otus mirus* *Otus longicornis* *Otus megalotis* *Otus mindorensis* *Otus fuliginosus* *Mimizuku gurneyi* *Bubo philippensis* *Ninox philippensis*
Sulawesi	11 species–see below for remainder of Wallacea	*Spilornis rufipectus* *Accipiter griseiceps* *Accipiter trinotatus* *Accipiter nanus* *Accipiter rhodogaster* *Spizaetus lanceolatus* *Tyto inexspectata* *Tyto rosenbergii* *Otus manadensis* *Ninox ochracea* *Ninox punctulata.*
Bismarck Archipelago	9 species * = endemic to New Britain	*Henicopernis infuscatus** *Accipiter luteoschistaceus** *Accipiter princeps** *Accipiter brachyurus** *Tyto manusi* *Tyto aurantia** *Ninox meeki* *Ninox variegata* *Ninox odiosa**
Wallacea	9 species on islands other than Sulawesi where there are 11, thus 20 total for Wallacea	*Accipiter henicogrammus* *Accipiter erythrauchen* *Tyto nigrobrunnea* *Tyto sororcula* *Otus alfredi* *Otus silvicola* *Otus* sp.

Region	Species count	Species
New Guinea	8 species	Ninox rudolphi
		Ninox squamipila
		Henicopernis longicauda
		Accipiter melanochlamys
		Accipiter poliocephalus
		Accipiter meyerianus
		Erythrotriorchis buergersi
		Harpyopsis novaeguineae
		Ninox theomacha
		Uroglaux dimorpha
Caribbean	8 species on various islands * = Cuba, ** = Hispaniola	Chondrohierax spp.*
		Accipiter gundlachi*
		Buteo ridgwayi**
		Tyto glaucops**
		Otus nudipes
		Otus lawrencii*
		Glaucidium siju*
		Pseudoscops grammicus
Pacific Ocean	6 species to include New Caledonia and New Zealand	Accipiter haplochrous
		Accipiter rufitorques
		Buteo galapagoensis
		Buteo solitarius
		Falco novaezeelandiae
		Otus podarginus.
Solomons	5 species	Haliaeetus sanfordi
		Accipiter imitator
		Accipiter albogularis
		Ninox jacquinoti
		Nesasio solomonensis
Andaman and Nicobar	4 species	Spilornis minimus
		Spilornis elgini
		Spilornis klossi
		Otus balli
		Ninox affinis
Indian Ocean other than Andaman and Nicobar	3 species, * = Sri Lanka, see below	Falco punctatus
		Falco areae
		Glaucidium castanonotus*
Java	3 species	Spizaetus bartelsi
		Otus angelinae
		Glaucidium castanopterum
Sumatra	3 species [1]	Otus umbra
		Otus enganensis
		Otus mentawi
		Otus brookii [2]
Borneo	3 species [3]	Spilornis kinabaluensis
		Microhierax latifrons
		Otus mantanensis [3]
		Otus brookii [2]
Atlantic Ocean	1 species	Otus hartlaub.
Tasmania	1 species	Tyto castanops
Sri Lanka	1 species- also listed separately because somewhat distant from the other islands in the Indian Ocean	Glaucidius castanonotus
Mediterranean	1 species	Falco eleonorae

1. Van Marle and Voous (1988) recognize the Stresemann's Mountain Scops-Owl *Otus stresemanni* as an endemic species thus giving Sumatra four endemics but suggest that it may be a subspecies of the Mountain Scops-Owl *O. spilocephalus*, where it is also placed by Sibley and Monroe (1990).
2. In both Sumatra and Borneo
3. Off coast of N.W. Borneo but counted.

Table 6. Comparison of raptor taxa (species and subspecies, BSC) endemic to islands in the Caribbean and Mediterranean seas. Some small islands and islets, e.g., along eastern coast of Mexico and western coast of Italy, where no endemics occur, are not listed. Islands in the Caribbean are in Part A and those in the Mediterranean in Part B. Abbreviations in Part A are: CU = Cuba and Isle of Pines, HI = Hispaniola, PR = Puerto Rico, JA = Jamaica, BH = Bahamas, LA = Lesser Antilles except Trinidad and Tobago, TT = Trinidad and Tobago, NA = Netherlands Antilles. X = present, – = absent. Percents are rounded to nearest whole number.

PART A Taxa endemic in Caribbean Islands

	% taxa island endemics / % taxa							
		CU	HI	PR	JA	BH	LA	TT	NA
Chondroheirax uncinatus [1]	50 / 100	X	–	–	–	–	X	–	–
Rostrhamus sociabilis [2]	25 / 100	X	–	–	–	–	–	–	–
Accipiter striatus [3]	30 / 100	X	X	X	–	–	–	–	–
Accipiter gundlachii	100 / 100	X	–	–	–	–	–	–	–
Buteogallus anthracinus [4]	67 / 50	X	–	–	–	–	–	–	–
Buteo ridgwayi	100 / 100	–	X	–	–	–	–	–	–
Buteo platypterus [5]	83 / 100	X	–	X	–	–	X	X	–
Buteo jamaicensis [6]	29 / 50	X	X	X	X	–	–	–	–
Falco sparverius [7]	31 / 80	X	X	X	–	X	X	–	X
Tyto alba [8]	57 / 25	X	–	–	X	X	X	–	X
Otus nudipes	100 / 100	–	–	X	–	–	–	–	–
Otus lawrencii	100 /1100	X	–	–	–	–	–	–	–
Speotyto cunicularia [9]	16 / 66	X	X	–	–	–	–	–	X
Glaucidium siju	100 / 100	X	–	–	–	–	–	–	–
Pulsatrix perspicillata [10]	17 / 100	–	–	–	–	–	–	X	–
Asio stygius [11]	33 / 100	X	X	–	–	–	–	–	–
Asio clamator [12]	33 / 100	–	–	–	–	–	–	X	–
Asio flammeus [13]	60 / 33	–	X	X	–	–	–	–	–
Pseudoscops grammicus	100 / 100	–	–	–	X	–	–	–	–

1. Population on CU sometimes treated as separate species, the Cuban Kite *Chondrohierax wilsonii*; population on Granada (LA) = *C.h. mirus*
2. CU = *R.s. levis*
3. Populations named *ventralis, chionogaster* and *erythronemius*, here considered full species; CU = *A.s. fringilloides*, HI = *striatus*, PR = *venator*.
4. CU = *B.a. gundlachii*
5. CU = *B.p. cubanensis*, PR = *brunnescens*, LA and TT = *insulicola, rivierei*, and *antillarum*.
6. CU = *B.j. solitudinis*, HI, PR, and JA = *jamaicensis*.
7. CU and BH = *F.s. sparveroides*, HI = *dominicensis*, PR and LA = *caribearum*, NA = *brevipennis*.
8. CU and JA = *T.a. furcata*, BH= *lucayana*, LA = *nigrescens* and *insularis*, NA = *bargei*.
9. Has been placed in the genus *Athene*, CU = *S.c. siguapa*, HI = *noctipetens*, NA = *arubensis*.
10. TT = *P.p. trinitatis*.
11. CU = *A.s. sipuapa*, HI = *noctipetens*.
12. Often in genus *Rhinoptynx*, TT = *A.c. oberi*.
13. HI = *A.f. domingensis*, PR = *portoricensis*.

Table 6, continued PART B. Islands on the Mediterranean Sea. See part A for description of Table content. SY = Sicily, SR = Sardinia, CR = Corsica, CY = Cyprus, GI = Greek Islands (Cyclades, Crete), BA = Balearics, NA = offshore of North Africa.

	Taxa Percent (see Part A)	SY	SR	CR	CY	GI	BR	NA
Accipiter nisus [1]	23 / 50	–	X	X	–	–	–	–
Accipiter gentilis [2]	33 / 33	–	X	X	–	–	–	–
Falco eleonorae	100 / 98 ±	X	X	X	X	X	X	X
Tyto alba [3]	57 / 10	–	X	X	–	–	–	–
Otus scops [4]	44 / 50	–	–	–	X	X	–	–
Athene noctua [5]	7 / 100	–	X	–	–	–	–	–

1. SR, CR = *A.n. wolterstorffi*
2. SR, CR = *A.g. arrigonii*
3. SR, CR = *T.a. ernesti*
4. CR = *O.s. cyprinus*; GI = *O.s. cyclodum*
5. SR = *A.n. sarda*

The data we present for the family Strigidae are admittedly tentative since owls are not as well known taxonomically as Falconiformes. The dynamic nature of strigid taxonomy is illustrated by the recent splitting of the Least Pygmy-owl *Glaucidium minutissimum* into six species (with the naming of a new one and the elevating of subspecies to species level), based on differences in vocalizations thought to isolate the taxa reproductively in zones of present or potential contact (Howell & Robbins 1995). At least three of the taxa, *G. palmarum, G. minutissimum,* and *G. sanchezi,* differ only slightly morphologically, but are allopatric and have been regarded as subspecies under the BSC. Aside from the vocalization characters, they may not differ sufficiently to qualify as species under the PSC.

Based on the *Glaucidium* example and the distribution of other isolated strigid taxa, it is possible to predict that among the genus *Otus* the Spotted Scops Owl *O. spilocephalus* may be composed of five species, Eurasian Scops Owl *O. scops* of nine species, Madagascar Scops Owl *O. rutilus* of two species, and Collared Scops Owl *O. lempiji* of six species. If this sort pattern holds true for the entire family, we may have underestimated the number of species of Strigidae based on the PSC concepts by 10-15% and perhaps even as much as 30-40%.

Conversely, we have not shown the numbers of species (BSC) that might be considered conspecific with other species. However, among the Falconiformes a minimum of 30, of which five are island endemics, have been suggested to be conspecific with other taxa. Among the Strigiformes a minimum of 36 have been suggested to be conspecific (Sibley & Monroe 1990) and 12 of these are island endemics. For example, the island-dependent, highly endemic Moluccan Scops-Owl *Otus magicus* complex includes several forms that may properly belong to either the Madagascar Scops-Owl *Otus rutilus* or the Sulawesi Scops-Owl *Otus manadensis* (see Sibley & Monroe 1990, Howard & Moore 1991, Coates & Bishop 1997).

The Islands: Contemporary taxonomy.

As a geographic unit, Wallacea has the most (20) endemic island-dependent species of Falconiformes and Strigiformes combined. This is not significantly different from Madagascar with the next greatest number of endemics ($c^2 = 1.05$). Although Wallacea has 60% more island endemics than the Philippines, both have nearly the same percentage of polytypic species - 35% and 33%, respectively (Dickinson *et al.* 1991, Coates & Bishop 1997) with no significant difference between those that show subspeciation and those that do not ($c^2 = 0.009$). However the Philippines seemingly have higher rates of differentiation among its 7,000+ islands than Wallacea does among 13,500+ islands. The apparent high rate of speciation producing endemic *Otus* owls in the Philippines may reflect taxonomic oversplitting, or simply more thorough study than in Wallacea (Marshall & King *in* Amadon & Bull 1988). There may be as high a rate of endemics in equivalent insular situations in other regions, but existing as overlooked cryptic species.

Within the Madagascaran fauna we have included the Malagasy Scops-Owl *Otus rutilus*, which occurs not only in the Comoros, but also as an isolated subspecies some 1,300 km away on Pemba Island off the coast of Tanzania; perhaps the latter population is actually a different species (Sibley & Monroe 1993, Langrand 1990). The Madagascar Marsh-Harrier *Circus maillardi* is frequently treated as a subspecies of the very widespread Western Marsh-Harrier *Circus aeruginosus*, as is the Eastern Marsh-Harrier *Circus spilonotus*, which has insular forms on New Guinea, the Philippines, and Borneo (Nieboer 1973).

For New Guinea we include the East and West Papuan Islands, Aru, and islands in the Bay of Geelvink (Beehler *et al.* 1986). Although we have listed here only the three endemic *Accipiter* species (Table 5), there are seven resident species, with three of these more or less centred in Australia. This is rivalled by the Bismarck Archipelago with at least five resident *Accipiter* species, although both regions contain fewer species than Wallacea. The greatest radiation of insular species of *Accipiter* occurs in a region called "Australasia", running from the centre of Wallacea to Fiji and New Caledonia and including Australia, where 17 *Accipiter* species are island residents (see Wattel 1973). It is not surprising that Sulawesi has numerous endemic raptors since it has a generally rich endemic flora and fauna (Whitten *et al.* 1987a). The number of endemics there contrasts remarkably with adjacent Borneo, Java and Sumatra (Table 5), which also have a much poorer endemic fauna overall (Smythies 1960, Whitten *et al.* 1987b, MacKinnon & Phillipps 1993)

It is interesting that at least one additional type of endemic with specific ecological and behavioural traits does not now occur in the Caribbean region (Tables 5 and 6). Walter (1979) commented on the curious lack of a colonial falcon species in the islands of the Caribbean as there is in the Mediterranean islands with the Eleonora's Falcon *Falco eleonorae*. Ecological conditions in the Caribbean, including the biannual stream of migrating passerine species, appear at least superficially similar to those of the Mediterranean. It is possible that early extinctions may have eliminated one or more raptors that filled that role, since ecological changes from European colonization in the last 500 years in the Caribbean have been extensive (Wiley 1986). However, no Caribbean raptor species is known to have become extinct historically, although the Short-eared Owl *Asio flammeus*) on Puerto Rico has come close to extinction (Wiley 1986), the Hook-billed Kite *Chondrohierax uncinatus* on Cuba (traditionally considered a subspecies, *C. u. wilsonii*, but recently elevated to full species rank by Raffaele *et al.* 1998) is on the verge of extinction, and the Hook-billed Kite form *C. u. mirus* endemic to Grenada is even more critically endangered.

A comparison of the endemic island taxa in the Caribbean (Voous 1983, ffrench 1991, Raffaele *et al.* 1998) with those in the Mediterranean (Cramp & Simmons 1980, Cramp 1985) clearly shows a significantly greater ($\chi^2 = 6.76$, p. < 0.01) contemporary number of taxa in the Caribbean than the Mediterranean (Table 6). At the species level, however, the significance level drops ($\chi^2 = 5$, p < 0.05 > 0.02). It is curious that only one Mediterranean endemic, the Eleonora's Falcon, occurs on Sicily or its satellite islands; it is also the most widespread.

DISCUSSION

Island Influences on Differentiation

It is well known that some taxa (e.g., *Tyto* and *Otus*) have a marked penchant for colonizing islands and undergoing differentiation at the species or subspecies levels. A major influence on this issue is the exposure to, or opportunity for, isolation on islands. Taxa occurring in areas of abundant islands have the greater exposure to the possibility of isolation. Also, taxa in tropical environments, where there is a greater chance of permanent residency, have more opportunity for the fixation of unique character traits. For all bird species, including the Falconiformes and Strigiformes, it has been shown that there is a significant positive association between the number of island-endemic species and the number of continental species in the family and the number of islands in the vicinity, but this factor only accounts for 50% of the variance (G=1571, P<0.0001, df=66) (McCall *et al.*

1996). This clearly does not explain all the differences seen, since the frequency of gene flow or genetic liability in the taxa is not unusually known. Gene flow, however, cannot be great, or at least is less than the influences and pressure for differentiation.

The degree of island influence on differentiation depends on whether the perspective is at the species or subspecies level. This is illustrated by the comparisons of the Caribbean and Mediterranean sea avifaunas. Since our present knowledge of events in either sea is limited to the relatively short-term historical records and the incomplete fossil record, we cannot know the actual extent of differentiation that has occurred. As a general rule, however, differentiation at the species level (BSC) follows the "island area curve" (MacArthur 1972) as seen in Figure 1. The larger the island the more taxa there are. There are a great many exceptions, however, that may have to do with climate (tropical or arctic as in the case of Greenland), or the age of the island, as examples. Islands long inhabited by humans have usually lost species regardless of their size or degree of isolation. We suspect this may be the case with Madagascar and its fewer than expected species based on island size.

Figure 1. Relationship of raptor species (BSC) to size of some selected islands or group of islands. Generally the relationship follows the "island area curve"(see text) with three important departures. Madagascar is highly depauperate which may be related to vegetational changes since colonization (1,500 years BP). Wallacea represents a group of islands some of which have their own suite of endemics. Greenland is mainly composed of uninhabitable ice, thus for all its size it is an arctic island which typically have fewer species than tropical or temperate islands. The regression is not significant with P = 0.094. Without the two outliers of Wallacea and Greenland (see text) the relationship becomes significant at P = 0.004.

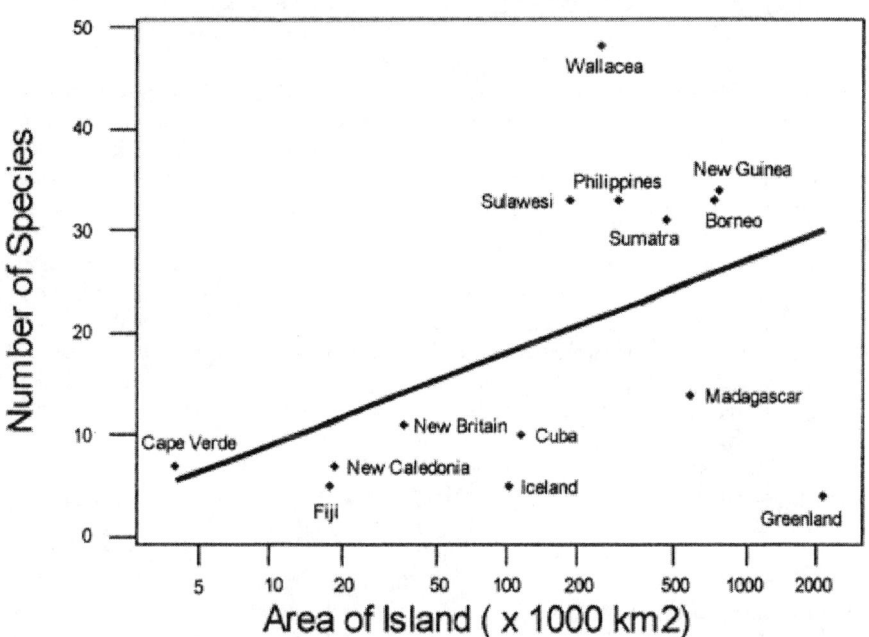

Striking differences in levels of raptor endemism between adjacent islands is shown between Borneo and Sulawesi, the Philippines and Sulawesi, and New Britain and New Ireland. Borneo has only two endemic raptor species, and none of *Accipiter,* the Philippines has at least 12, but no endemic *Accipiter* species, while Sulawesi has four endemic *Accipiter* species. While the Philippines has five endemic *Otus* species, Sulawesi has but one (see Table 5). Perhaps most unexpected is the low number of endemic raptors on Borneo. New Britain contains 67% of the endemic species, including three of *Accipiter,* in the Bismarck Archipelago, while adjacent New Ireland, although more than 70% smaller, has no completely endemic species, and the only breeding *Accipiter* species there is the widespread Variable Goshawk *Accipiter novaehollandiae.*

Loss of Diversity on Islands

The IUCN lists six taxa of raptors known to have become extinct since about 1600, and all were island endemics (Baillie & Groombridge 1996). They include a *Falco* sp. (Réunion, Indian Ocean), the Guadalupe Caracara *Polyborus lutosus* (Guadalupe Island, Mexico), an owl *Sauzieri* sp. and the Mauritian Owl *Scops commersoni* (Mauritius, Indian Ocean), Rodrigues Little Owl *Athene murivora* (Rodrigues Island, Indian Ocean) and the Laughing Owl *Sceloglaux albifacies* (New Zealand).

While the IUCN category of "threatened" includes the categories "critical," "endangered," and "vulnerable," we think it worthwhile to separate the first two categories from the latter. In the Falconiformes there are 31 taxa listed as threatened, and 11, including nine (82%) island endemics, are in the first two categories. Among the Strigiformes, 26 are listed as threatened and of the nine in the first categories, six (67%) are island endemics. At a lower level of concern are what IUCN terms "near threatened" species, a less precise term, but a category that nevertheless may include taxa requiring conservation action. This category includes 44 species of Falconiformes, of which 13 (30%) are island endemics, while in the Strigiformes, three (12%) of the 25 species are island endemics. Large-sized owls, in fact, the largest known (*Ornimogalonyx*) and a radiation of large-sized insular *Tyto* owls (*T. alba, T. noeli, T. riveroi, T. osstologa* and *T. pollens*) occur in the Quaternary fossil record of the Caribbean (Olson 1985); there was likewise a radiation of raptors, now extinct, in the Mediterranean (Bochenski 1992, Alcover *et al.* 1992). It is not yet clear what impact the long history of human occupancy in the Mediterranean has had on the extinction rates of former endemics there, but Olson and James (1982) have documented the profound effects of man on avian extinctions in Polynesia in recent, but prehistoric times.

The Island Conundrum: Biodiversity and Conservation.

The issue of raptor conservation on islands poses some interesting problems, as with many other groups of insular birds. As previously noted, the tendency, whether administrative, political, or biological, is to devote conservation efforts to birds and other vertebrates at the species level (Collar 1997). However, if we concentrate only on full species, unique genetic combinations and distinctive evolutionary variations stand a chance of being lost. We think this is especially true as consensus on a universally accepted species concept become increasingly unlikely as new technology and different interpretations emerge. This partly reflects generational tensions between adherents of the imperfect traditional species concepts, and molecular researchers, whose search for perfect understanding of raptors' genomes is still subject to the limitations of current analytical techniques. Because of this, certain species of raptors, as identified by future, more sophisticated analyses, will doubtless be lost unknowingly, because of actions taken "too little too late," or because the political climate and geography work against conservation efforts. Increasingly, choices must be made about conservation, as described by Mann and Plummer in their book "Noah's Choice: The future of endangered species" (1995). The complexity of the species definition issue and thus of conservation efforts is demonstrated with several island taxa that are comprised totally, or in part, by island endemics, as is the case among the owls *Tyto, Otus,* and *Ninox* and among the diurnal raptors *Accipiter* and *Spilornis*.

At the species level *Tyto alba* is one of the most widespread land birds, having, in the broadest taxonomic sense, an almost cosmopolitan range. With such a widespread species one could argue that the loss of the populations from, say, the Galapagos Islands (currently *T. a. punctatissima*) is not that much of a loss of biodiversity because there are still Barn Owls remaining over large portions of the earth. However, as previously noted, both this taxon and *T. a. delicatula* of Australia and the Solomon Islands almost certainly constitute phylogenetically independent species (Sibley & Monroe 1990). By any approach other than the BSC, the loss of either of these taxa would, therefore, be a significant conservation event, equivalent to the long-lamented loss of the Guadalupe Caracara *Polyborus butosus*.

Among falconiform genera, *Accipiter* contains the greatest number of species listed by the IUCN in one of the threatened categories. Of the 11 listed, nine are island endemics, namely, the New Britain Sparrowhawk *A. brachyurus* of New Britain Island, Gundlach's Hawk *A. gundlachi* from Cuba, Imitator Sparrowhawk *A. imitator* from the Solomon Islands, Nicobar Sparrowhawk *A. butleri* from the Nicobar Islands, Henst's Goshawk *A. henstii* of Madagascar, Slaty-mantled Sparrowhawk *A. luteoschistaceus* of New Britain Island, Madagascar Sparrowhawk *A. madagascariensis* of Madagascar, Small Sparrowhawk *A. nanus* of Sulawesi, and the New Britain Goshawk *A. princeps* of New Britain Island. Part of the problem with this genus is our present lack of taxonomic knowledge. For example, one of the more complex issues with *Accipiter* involves the current makeup of the Variable Goshawk *A. novaehollandiae* complex. As the name suggests, the species is incredibly variable in size and colour, ranging from pure white forms to those with gray barred breasts to those with rufous breast and nuchal collars. Size is variable with mean wing length ranging in males from about 184 mm (an island endemic) to 262 mm in Australia (a 30% difference). The insular Moluccan *griseogularis* complex (213 mm average wing length in males) of three recognized forms with rufous breast and faint barring and rufous nuchal collars may represent a separate species. The yet several smaller insular forms in the Moluccas (represented by *A. hiogaster*) have solid rufous to chestnut breast and lack a collar may be other species. There is no way to use the BSC to test species (reproductive) limits among them, and their status has been mired in controversy among traditional taxonomists. From an empirical standpoint, the PSC supports full species separation.

The serpent eagles, *Spilornis*, are particularly characteristic of islands, and as many as 24 taxa in five species have been recently accorded formal status, with 19 of them being island endemics. The number of species, however, usually varies from two, with eight megasubspsecies, to five. Sumatra and her satellite islands are particularly rich in taxa. Within short inter-island distances they have pronounced morphological differences. The form *malayensis* on northern Sumatra is rather dark in colour and large with an average wing length of 364 mm while 125 km westward on Nias Island the form *asturinus* is very pale and small with an average wing of 299 mm. There is clearly no gene flow nor is there a character cline between them. Are these good species? How does one treat them relative to the conservation of species? There are at least two distinct forms on the Nicobar Islands, *kolssi* and *minimus*, both of which are small and similar in colour. Even here, however, the issue is not that simple, and views on their systematic relationship (species or subspecific status) vary from author to author. Pending molecular investigations, the evolution and species limits of this genus is complex, unresolved, and the number of published opinions probably exceeds the number of actual species.

Bock (1995) stated that one concept or one manner of recognizing species is no better than the other when it comes to the issue of conservation, although he recognized the need to conserve unique gene pools. Because of legal, political, financial, and biological considerations, we do not agree that all taxonomic approaches will yield the same conservation result. We would contend that, depending on the level of taxonomic concentration, whether at the traditional BSC level, the PSC, or the fine-grained ESU level, the economic and logistical implications are profound. It is estimated that the cost of the captive breeding and reintroduction programme that brought the Mauritius Kestrel *Falco punctatus* back from near extinction was at least US$500,000 (W. Burnham, pers. comm.). The expense of rescuing similar endangered raptors will naturally vary widely, depending on such factors as the size of the population, the nature of the conservation problem, and the complexity of the solution. In the future, however, the most important variable of all may be whether we decide to concentrate our conservation resources at the BSC or PSC levels, or whether we will spread them thinner by concentrating on smaller units. In practice, the latter approach may include every disjunct raptor population on every island of any significant size.

In the foregoing discussion, we have selected a small sample from a very much larger array of possible taxa that could be offered as examples of taxonomic uncertainty. They all indicate the folly in being too definitive -- or too premature -- in judgements on species limits. Without adequate knowledge of taxonomic relationships, there is additional folly in conservation efforts, especially if the goal of the conservation is to preserve genetic diversity. How, then, does one proceed with conservation efforts in politically unstable countries with differing priorities of whether one saves "species" or "evolutionarily significant units," compounded by the problem of taxa with unresolved systematics? Resolution of this conundrum is a challenging task for the future and the preservation of biodiversity. Islands may well present the ultimate test of our commitment and abilities.

REFERENCES

ALCOVER, J.A., F. FLORIT, C. MOURER-CHAUVIER & P.D.M. WEESIE. The avifauna on the isolated Mediterranean islands during the Middle and Late Pleistocene. *J. Nat. Hist. Mus. Los Angeles County, Sci. Ser.* 36:273-283.

AMADON, D. & J. BULL 1988. Hawk and owls of the world: a distributional and taxonomic list. *Proc. Western Foundation Vert. Zool.* 3(4):294-357.

AMADON, D. & L.L. SHORT 1976. Treatment of subspecies approaching species status. *Syst. Zool.* 25:161-167.

AMADON, D. & L.L. SHORT 1990. Taxonomy of lower categories -- suggested guidelines. *Bull. Brit. Ornithol. Club* 112A:11-38.

BAILLIE, J. & B. GROOMBRIDGE (eds.) 1996. 1996 IUCN red list of threatened animals.IUCN., Gland Switzerland.

BARROWCLOUGH, G.F. 1980. Genetic and phenotypic differentiation in the wood warbler (Genus *Dendroica*) hybrid zone. *Auk* 97:655-668.

BARROWCLOUGH, G.F. & N.R. FLESNESS 1996. Species, subspecies, and races: the problem of units of management in conservation. Pp. 247-254 in D.G. Kleiman, M.E. Allen, K.V. Thompson, S. Lumkin & H. Harris (eds), *Wild mammals in Captivity: Principles and Techniques*. Univ. Chicago Press, Chicago, IL.

BEEHLER, B.M., T.K. PRATT & D.A. ZIMMERMAN 1986. *Birds of New Guinea*. Princeton Univ. Press, Princeton, NJ.

BILDSTEIN, K.L., W. SCHELSKY & J. ZALLES 1998. Conservation status of tropical raptors. *J. Raptor Res.* 32:3-18.

BOCHENSKI, Z. 1992. History of European owls. *Przeglad Zoologiczny* 36:77-90.

BOCK, W.J. 1995. The species concept versus the species taxon: their roles in biodiversity analyses and conservation, Pp. 47-72 in A.R. Kato, M. Doi & Y. Doi (eds), *Biodiversity and Evolution*. The National Science Museum Foundation, Tokyo.

BOYCE, D.A., Jr. 1989. A systematic study of the family Falconidae: protein electrophoretic analysis of genera, gene expression in the American Kestrel, and morphological analysis of the subgenus *Tinnunculus* (kestrels). Ph.D. dissertation, Brigham Young University, Provo, UT.

COATES, B.J. & K.D. BISHOP 1997. *A guide to the birds of Wallacea: Sulawesi, The Moluccas and Lesser Sunda Islands, Indonesia*. Dove Publications, Alderley, Queensland, Australia.

COLLAR, N.J. 1997. Taxonomy and conservation: chicken and egg. *Bull. Brit. Ornithol. Club* 117:122-136.

COLLAR, N.J., M.J. CROSBY & A.J. STATTERSFIELD 1994. *Birds to watch 2: the world list of threatened birds*. Birdlife Conservation Series no. 5, BirdLife International, Cambridge, UK.

CRACRAFT, J. 1992. The species of the birds-of-paradise (Paradisaeidae): applying the phylogenetic species concept to a complex pattern of diversification. *Cladistics* 8:1-43.

CRAMP, S. (ed). 1985. *The birds of the western Palearctic*, Vol. IV. Oxford Univ. Press., Oxford, UK.

CRAMP, S. & K.E.L. SIMMONS (eds) 1980. *The birds of the western Palearctic*, Vol II. Oxford Univ. Press, Oxford, UK.

CROZIER, R.L. 1997. Preserving the information content of species: genetic diversity, phylogeny, and conservation. *Ann. Rev. Ecol. Syst.* 28:243-68.

DAVIS, J.I. & K.C. NIXON 1992. Populations, genetic variation, and the delimitations of phylogenetic species. *Systematic Biol.* 41:421-435.

DEL HOYO, J., A. ELLIOTT & J. SARGATAL (eds) 1994. *Handbook of the birds of the world*. Vol. 2, New World vultures to guineafowl. Lynx Edicions, Barcelona.

DIAMOND, J.M. 1984. Historic extinctions: a rosetta stone for understanding prehistoric extinctions. Pp. 824-862 in P.S. Martin & R.G. Klein (eds.). *Quaternary extinctions: a prehistoric revolution.* Univ. Arizona Press, Tucson, AZ.
DICKINSON, E.C., R.S. KENNEDY & K.C. PARKES 1991. The birds of the Philippines; an annotated checklist. *BOU Check-list No. 12*, British Ornithologists' Union, Tring, UK
FARQUHAR, C.C. 1998. *Buteo polyosoma* and *B. poecilochrous*, the "Red-backed Buzzards" of South America, are conspecific. *Condor* 100:27-43.
FLEISCHER, R.C. 1998. Genetics and avian conservation. Pp. 29-47 in J.M. Marzluff & R. Sallabanks (eds.), *Avian Conservation: Research and Management.* Island Press, Washington, D.C.
FFRENCH, R. 1991. *Birds of Trinidad & Tobago.* Cornell Univ. Press, Ithaca, NY.
GORMAN, M. 1979. *Island Ecology. Outline Studies in Ecology.* Chapman and Hall, London.
HAFFER, J. 1997. Species concepts and species limits in ornithology. Pp. 11-24 in: J. del Hoyo, J. Elliott & J. Sargatal (eds.), *Handbook of the Birds of the World.* Vol. 4. Sandgrouse to Cuckoos, Lynx Edicions, Barcelona.
HAIG, S.M. 1998. Molecular contributions to conservation. *Ecology* 79:413-425.
HOWARD, R. & A. MOORE 1991. *A complete checklist of the birds of the world.* 2nd ed., Academic Press, London.
HOWELL, S.N.G. & M.B. ROBBINS 1995. Species limits of the Least Pygmy-Owl *(Glaucidium minutissimum)* complex. *Wilson Bull.* 107:7-25.
KING, W.B. 1985. Island birds: will the future repeat the past? Pp. 3-15 in P.J. Moors (ed.), *Conservation of island birds.* ICBP Tech. Publ. 3, Cambridge, UK.
LANGRAND, O. 1990. *Guide to the birds of Madagascar.* Yale Univ. Press, New Haven, CT.
LONG. A.J., M.J. CROSBY, A.J. STATTERSFIELD & D.C. WEGE 1996. Towards a global map of biodiversity: patterns in the distribution of restricted-range birds. *Global Ecol. Biogeogr. Letters* 5:281-304.
MACARTHUR, R.H. 1972. *Geographical Ecology: patterns in the distribution of species.* Harper & Row, Publ., NY.
MACKINNON, J. & K. PHILLIPPS 1993. *A field guide to the birds of Borneo, Java, Sumatra and Bali.* Oxford Univ. Press, Oxford, UK.
MANN, C.C. & M.L. PLUMMER 1995. *Noah's choice: the future of endangered species.* Alfred A. Knopf, NY.
MASSETI, M. & P. MAZZA 1996. Is there any paleontological "treatment" for the "insular syndrome"? *Vie et Milieu* 46:355-363.
MAYR, E. 1969. *Principles of systematic zoology.* 2nd ed. McGraw-Hill, NY.
MAYR, E. & G.W. COTTRELL (eds.) 1979. *Check-list of birds of the world.* Vol. 1. 2nd ed. Museum of Comparative Zoology, Harvard University, Cambridge, MA.
MCCALL, R.A., S. NEE & P.H. HARVEY 1996. Determining the influence of continental species -richness, island availability and vicariance in the formation of island-endemic bird species. *Biodiversity Letters* 3:137-150.
MIRANDA, H.C. Jr., R.S. KENNEDY & D.P. MINDELL 1997. Phylogenetic placement of *Mimizuku gurneyi* (Aves: Strigidae) inferred from mitochondrial DNA. *Auk* 114:315-324.
MÜLLER, P. 1981. *Arealsysteme und biogeographie.* Verlag Eugen Ulmer, Stuttgart, Germany.
NEILL, W.T. 1969. *The geography of life.* Columbia Univ. Press, NY.
NIEBOER, E. 1973. Geographical and ecological differentiation in the genus *Circus.* Ph.D. dissertation, Free Univ., Amsterdam, The Netherlands.
NATIONAL RESEARCH COUNCIL 1995. *Science and the endangered species act.* National Academy Press, Washington, D.C.
NORMAN, J.A., L. CHRISTIDIS, M. WESTERMAN & F.A.R. HILL 1998. Molecular data confirms the species status of the Christmas Island Hawk-owl *Ninox natalis. Emu* 98:197-208.
O'HARA, R.J. 1993. Systematic generalization, historical fate, and the species problem. *Syst. Biol.* 42:231-246.
OLSON, S.L. 1985. The fossil record of birds. Pp. 80-256 in D.S. Farner, J.R. King & K.C. Parkes (eds), *Avian Biology*, Vol. III. Academic Press, NY.
OLSON, S.L. & H.F. JAMES 1982. Fossil birds from the Hawaiian Islands: evidence for wholesale extinction by man before Western contact. *Science* 217(4560):633-635.
O'NEILL, J.P. & G.R. GRAVES 1977. A new genus and species of owl (Aves: Strigidae) from Peru. *Auk* 94:409-416.
PETERS, J.L. 1940. *Check-list of birds of the world.* Vol. IV. Museum of Comparative Zoology, Harvard University, Cambridge, MA.
RAFFAELE, H., J. WILEY, O, GARRIDO, A. KEITH & J. RAFFAELE 1998. *A guide to the birds of the West Indies.* Princeton Univ. Press, Princeton, NJ.

RYDER, O.A. 1986. Species conservation and systematics: the dilemma of subspecies. *Trends in Ecology and Evolution* 1:9-10.
SCHODDE, R. & I.J. MASON 1997. Aves (Columbidae to Cracticidae). in W.W.K. Houston & A. Wells (eds.). *Zoological Catalogue of Australia*. Vol 37.2, 440 pp, Melbourne, Australia.
SIBLEY, C.G. & B.L. MONROE, Jr. 1990. *Distribution and taxonomy of birds of the world*. Yale Univ. Press, New Haven, CT.
SIBLEY, C.G. & B.L. MONROE, Jr. 1993. *A supplement to distribution and taxonomy of birds of the world*. Yale Univ. Press, New Haven, CT.
SITES, J.W., Jr. & K.A. CRANDALL 1997. Testing species boundaries in biodiversity studies. *Cons. Biol.* 11:12-89-1297.
SMYTHIES, B.E. 1960. *The birds of Borneo*. Oliver and Boyd, Edinburgh.
STRESMANN, E. & D. AMADON 1979. Order Falconiformes. Pp. 271-425 in E.Mayr & G.W. Cottrell (eds). *Check-list of Birds of the World*, 2nd ed. Museum of Comparative Zool., Cambridge, MA.
THIOLLAY, J-M. 1998. Current status and conservation of Falconiformes in tropical Asia. *J. Raptor Res.* 32:40-55.
VAN BALEN, S. 1998. Tropical forest raptors in Indonesia: recent information on distribution, status, and conservation. *J. Raptor Res.* 32:56-63.
VAN MARLE, J.G. & K.H. VOOUS 1988. *The birds of Sumatra*. British Ornithol. Union Check-list No. 10.
VIRANI, M. & R.T. WATSON 1998. Raptors in the East African tropics and western Indian Ocean islands: state of ecological knowledge and conservation status. *J. Raptor Res.* 32:28-39.
VOGLER, A.P. & R. DESALLE 1994. Diagnosing units of conservation management. *Conser. Biol.* 8:345-363.
VOOUS, K.H. 1983. *Birds of the Netherlands Antilles*. De Walburg Pers, Utrecht, The Netherlands.
VUILLEUMIER, F. 1970. Insular biogeography in continental regions. I. The northern Andes of South America. *Amer. Nat.* 104: 373-388.
WALTER, H. 1979. *Eleonora's Falcon. Adaptation to prey and habitat in a social raptor*. Univ. Chicago Press, Chicago, IL.
WATTEL, J. 1973. Geographical differentiation in the genus *Accipiter*. *Publ. Nuttall Ornithol. Club* No. 13.
WHITNEY, B.M., J.F. PACHECO & R. PARRINI 1995. Two species of *Neopelma* in southeastern Brazil and diversification within the *Neopelma/Tyranneutes* complex: implications of the subspecies concept for conservation (Passeriformes: Tyrannidae). *Ararajuba* 3:43-53.
WHITTEMORE, A.T. 1993. Species concepts: a reply to Ernst Mayr. *Taxon* 42: 573-583.
WHITTEN, A.J., M. MUSTAFE & G.S. HENDERSON 1987A. *The ecology of Sulawesi*. Gadjah Mada Univ. Press, Yogyakarta, Indonesia.
WHITTEN, A.J., S.J. DAMANIK, J. ANWAR & N. HASYAM 1987B. *The ecology of Sumatra*. Gadjah Mada Univ. Press, Yagyakarta, Indonesia.
WILEY, E. 1981. *Phylogenetics: the theory and practice of phylogenetic systematics*. John Wiley and Sons, NY.
WILEY, J.W. 1986. Status and conservation of raptors in the West Indies. *Birds of Prey Bull.* 3:57-70.
WILLIAMSON, M. 1981. *Island populations*. Oxford Univ. Press, Oxford, UK.
WINK, M., H. DÖTTLINGER & M.N. NICHOLLS this volume. Phylogenetic relationships between the Shaheen group *Falco peregrinus babylonicus* and *Falco peregrinus peregrinator* and the Peregrine Falcon *Falco peregrinus*.
WINK, M., I. SEIBOLD, F. LOTFIKHAH & W. BEDNAREK 1998. Molecular systematics of Holarctic raptors (Order Falconiformes). Pp. 29-48 in R.D. Chancellor, B.-U. Meyburg & J.J. Ferrero (eds), *Holarctic Birds of Prey*: Proceedings of an International Conference. WWGBP/ADENEX, Badajoz, Extremadura, Spain.
WOODRUFF, D.S. 1989. The problems of conserving genes and species. Pp. 76-88 in D. Western & M. Pearl (eds.), *Conservation for the twenty-first century*. Oxford University Press, Oxford, UK.
ZINK. R.M. 1997. Species concepts. *Bull. British Ornithol. Club* 117:97-109.
ZINK, R.M. & M.C. MCKITRICK 1995. The debate about species concepts and its implications for ornithology. *Auk* 112:701-710.

Clayton M. White
Department of Zoology
Brigham Young University
Provo, Utah 84602
U.S.A.

Lloyd F. Kiff
The Peregrine Fund
566 West Flying Hawk Lane
Boise, Idaho 83709
U.S.A.

Chancellor, R. D. & B.-U. Meyburg eds. 2000
Raptors at Risk
WWGBP / Hancock House

Biology and molecular genetics of Eleonora's Falcon *Falco eleonorae*, a colonial raptor of Mediterranean islands*

Michael Wink and Dietrich Ristow

ABSTRACT

Eleonora's Falcon breeds colonially on Mediterranean islands, especially of the Aegean Sea. Colonial breeding provides the advantage that intruding raptors (17 species of raptors, owls, and raven have been observed in 23 years) can be successfully warded off in a social mobbing reaction. Eleonora's Falcon is a socially monogamous species. Breeding colonially on islands in close vicinity could facilitate extra-pair paternity. But a DNA fingerprinting study revealed that extra-pair young (EPY) could not be detected; thus social and genetic monogamy is the breeding system in this species. As copulations were observed almost every 30 min during the days prior to egg-laying, sperm competition could be the means to avoid EPY; mate guarding is less efficient, as mates are often separated when away for hunting.

DNA sequences of the cytochrome b gene show that Eleonora's Falcon, Sooty Falcon *Falco concolor*, and Hobby *F. subbuteo* are a closely related monophyletic group. Red-footed Falcon *F. vespertinus* and Amur Falcon *F. amurensis* are sibling species which cluster as a sister group to *eleonorae/concolor/subbuteo*. These species also share a number of ecological and behavioural characters, which they apparently obtained from a common ancestor. These 5 species prey on insects and small birds to a large extent; they winter in Africa south of the Sahara, but breed in Europe or Asia. Some of these falcons live socially or even colonially (*F. eleonorae, F. concolor, F. vespertinus, F. amurensis*). In this falcon complex dark and light plumage morphs are apparent; it is likely that the distant ancestor was polymorphic.

INTRODUCTION

Eleonora's Falcon *Falco eleonorae* is one of the rarer falcon species with about 3800-4500 breeding pairs on Mediterranean and the Canary islands; the majority (2500-3000 pairs) breed on Aegean islands (Cramp 1990; Wink, 1994a). *F. eleonorae* migrates via East Africa to Madagascar where this falcon winters in mixed flocks with Sooty Falcons *Falco concolor*; a detailed summary

---

*This contribution represents part 24 of a series on Eleonora's Falcon

of all known records outside the breeding season is given in Ristow and Wink (1995). The biology of Eleonora's Falcon has been summarized and reviewed in Cramp (1980) and Walter (1979a).

We have been studying the biology of Eleonora's Falcon in a large South Aegean colony since 1965, and since 1975 we have been working in the colony almost yearly for prolonged periods. In this paper we summarize data obtained over the last 23 years and will discuss the advantages/ disadvantages of colonial breeding and the phylogenetic relationships of Eleonora's Falcons with other falcons.

STUDY SITE

The falcon colony we studied is situated on a small, uninhabited rocky island in the South Aegean Sea (the exact site is not given for reasons of conservation). The number of breeding falcons varied between 200 and 350 pairs. Nests were under bushes, on cliffs or in small crevices and about 70% of them were monitored by us (Wink *et al.*, 1982a). Field research was carried out by 1 to 4 scientists every year for periods between 2 and 8 weeks each year. We were thus able to monitor the whole breeding season from May until October. For about 40 nests, breeding, egg laying, hatching, development of the young and fledging have been recorded in detail. In addition to a normal ring, all young falcons were colour-ringed between 1980 and 1990 (each year had a different colour), to enable us to determine their age in subsequent years.

PLUMAGE & MORPHOLOGY

Eleonora's Falcons are polymorphic, showing a light and a dark morph, but intermediate plumage variations have also been described (Wink *et al.*., 1978; Ristow *et al.*, 1998). Plumage morphs are inherited in a Mendelian fashion with dark being the dominant allele. Our description with DD (the dominant and homozygote dark morph), ll (recessive homozygote light morph) and Dl (heterozygote dark morph) represents a simplified model for the observed colour polymorphism (Ristow *et al.*, 1998). Abundance of the homozygote dark morph DD is 3.4%, the heterozygote dark morph Dl 30.1% and that of the recessive light morph ll 66.5% (Wink *et al.*, 1978). A detailed description of plumage variation in immature and adult falcons has been documented (Wink *et al.*, 1978; Ristow *et al.*, 1998). The abundance of the dark morph varies through its range and between years. The dark morph has an abundance of about 20-30% in Aegean colonies (Wink *et al.*, 1978; Ristow *et al.*, 1989; 1998) and appears to decrease to 6-20% in west Mediterranean colonies (Ristow *et al.*, 1998).

Sexual dimorphism

As in all falcons, Eleonora's Falcon also shows a strong size dimorphism (males 327±22 g; females 399±27 g) which is also reflected in other morphological characters (Wink *et al.*, 1982b). Also colouration of the ceres is indicative during the breeding season; ceres are orange-yellow in adult males and bluish-green in females (Walter, 1979; Ristow *et al*, 1998). The orange-yellow colour derives from carotinoids; carotene based colouration is frequent in animals and it has been speculated that the intensity could be a cue for females to select healthy males (Ferny & Bird, 1998).

BREEDING BIOLOGY

Adult falcons always return to their breeding colony once they have started breeding there. In several instances adults maintained their breeding territory through consecutive years, indicating a high degree of site tenacity (Ristow *et al.*, 1979). Also mate tenacity could be confirmed by trapping and retrapping for several pairs (Ristow *et al.*, 1979).

Egg-laying and Clutch size

Eleonora's Falcons return to their breeding colony in May and occupy territories (20-50 m in diameter) which later hold their nests. From May to the middle of July most of the falcons are absent during the day, because there is hardly any food near the colony and only a minor portion returns to the territories for roosting each night.

Egg-laying in a colony is synchronized and starts in the second half of July (24.5 July ± 3.3 days for the first egg) with laying intervals of 2.6-2.9 days between first and second, and second and third egg, respectively (Wink *et al.*, 1985, 1993). Generally, by the beginning of August almost 95% of all eggs are laid. There is no replacement clutch upon egg loss. Also hatching is a synchronized process and falls in the same time period each year: Hatching starts at August 14 and reaches a maximum betwen August 23 and August 28 (Wink *et al.*, 1993). Mean clutch size was 2.28. 3-egg clutches were started earlier than 2- or 1-egg clutches, a circumstance which results in a negative correlation between laying date and clutch size. Within a clutch, 3rd eggs are significantly smaller and darker than 1st and 2nd eggs (Wink *et al.*, 1985). Egg size was positively correlated with female weight (Wink *et al.*, 1985).

Basically, insects represent the major food in winter, spring, and early summer. A shift in diet begins prior to egg laying, when the first migrants, although scarce, can be caught. Males with a higher weight have a better hunting success (Wink *et al.*, 1980b) and deliver more food during courtship feeding than smaller males. Clutch size is correlated with the number and total weight of prey items delivered by the male before and during the time of egg laying (Wink *et al.*, 1980b). Interestingly, male weight increases during the first years of life and gains a maximum between 6 and 8 years (Wink *et al.*, 1993), indicating that the experienced and older males sire more young than inexperienced males which breed for the first time at an age of 3 or 4 (Wink *et al.*, 1987b). On the other hand, female weight decreases with age; females reach their maximum weight during the first 2 to 5 years (Wink *et al.*, 1993) and 30% start breeding when 2 years old (Ristow *et al.*, 1983b).

After 28-30 days of incubation the first two young hatch within 36 h, whereas the third chick, deriving from the smallest 3rd egg, hatches 2-3 days later. Whereas growth of the two first-born chicks is very similar, the 3rd young usually lags behind. Young falcons are able to fly between 30 and 40 days and are fully fledged after 35 days. In the second half of October Eleonora's Falcons leave the breeding colony and depart for East Africa and Madagascar, their wintering quarters (Ristow and Wink, 1995).

In a total of 1016 nests studied between 1985 and 1990 a mean clutch size of 1.92 was found, 1.58 young hatched (egg loss due to predation by rats, sun irradiation, or other factors amounted to 17.5%) and 1.51 young fledged per nest. Later losses are due to siblicide, disease or predators (Wink *et al.*, 1993). These figures result when assessments were made in September, when earlier egg losses could not be recognized with certainty. If the whole season was evaluated, a clutch size of 2.3 and 1.2 fledged young per nest was found (Ristow & Wink, 1985).

Food and feeding

Eleonora's Falcons raise their young at a time (September-October) when food abundance is high because of the autumn migration of palaearctic migrants (Walter 1979). Migrants usually start on the mainland in the evening and reach the breeding islands of Eleonora's Falcon in the early morning hours. The island operates like a funnel and attracts the migrating birds close to the island where a phalange of falcons usually surf in the wind waiting for the prey to come. Prey items include: *Phylloscopus trochilus* (29%), *Lanius collurio* (10.5%), *Saxicola rubetra* (9.6%), *Muscicapa striata* (9.6%), *Anthus trivialis* (4.3%), *Sylvia communis* (4.2%),*Calandrella brachydactyla* (3.5%), *Oenanthe oenanthe* (3.4%), *Phylloscopus sibilatrix* (3.2%), *Hippolais icterina* (2.9%), *Motacilla flava* (2.2%), *Ficedula hypoleuca* (1.6%), *Luscinia megarhynchos* (1.2%), *Passer domesticus* (1.5%), *Oriolus oriolus* (0.85%), *Lanius minor* (0.8%), *Jynx torquilla* (0.65%), *Streptopelia turtur* (0.65%) and *Upupa epops* (0.45%) (Ristow *et al.*, 1983a; 1986; Wink *et al.*, 1993). On favourable mornings, falcons hunt more than they use and food caching in the territory is a regular event. More than 4% of prey items are cached, in the shade beside bushes, stones or rocks (Wink *et al.*, 1993). They are retrieved later in the day, usually by the female.

Migration is not a continuous process but depends on wind velocity and wind directions and food supply for the young is sufficient on days with winds from north or northwest between 10-30 km/h. During periods without wind, which can last as long as 10% of the nestling period, prey abundance is very low. During these intervals, nestlings lose weight and then, in case of clutches with 3 young (the third young usually being the smallest), siblicide is a regular event (from 140 nests with 3 chicks, the 3rd young was killed in 17 instances = 12%) and the 3rd young is eaten by the survivors (Ristow et al., 1983a; Wink et al., 1993).

Food items (insects, birds) taken by Eleonora's Falcon appear to have low pesticide levels; a pesticide analysis of failed eggs in 1977 and 1990 revealed low levels of HCB, PCBs, DDE and dieldrin, indicating that this falcon is not yet directly endangered by organochlorine contamination (Clark & Peakall, 1977; Ristow et al., 1980; Wink et al., 1993)

Physiology

The body temperature T_b is 41.6±0.48°C in males and 41.4±0.19°C in females. Incubation temperatures (measured inside the egg) accounted for 38.6±1.24°C (Wink et al., 1980a). Ambient and especially soil temperatures during the day exceed 45-55°C, indicating that incubation rather serves to cool than to heat the eggs under these conditions. If nest sites are disturbed and eggs exposed to the open sun, lethal temperatures are obtained and can lead to egg losses. Even without disturbance, breeding success was significantly lower in open eyries (0.8-1.3 chick/nest) than in sheltered nests under rocks or in crevices (1.75 chick/nest) (Wink et al., 1982a). Continuous brooding is essential during the first 5 days of hatching, since young falcons gain the capability for independent thermoregulation at an age of 6 days (Wink et al. 1980a). This finding would explain why female falcons brood their newly hatched young so firmly.

Eleonora's Falcons take regular dust and sun baths and, during rare occasions of rain, also rain baths (Ristow et al., 1979b). In cases when open water is available, Eleonora's Falcons were seen bathing in open water (Walter 1979; A. Martin pers. comm.; P. Marriott in Ristow et al., 1995).

Dispersal of young falcons

Non-breeding juvenile falcons in their 1st year form a small proportion of a colony (4.5%); most birds disperse during their first year and ringing recoveries of birds ringed near Crete were obtained from Spain to Turkey during the breeding season. After the second year nearly all recoveries or retraps during the breeding season were from the natal colony, indicating a high degree of natal philopatry (Ristow et al., 1979a; Wink et al., 1987a). Mean distance to the natal territory was 192±153 m in males and 738±1104 m in females, indicating that females tend to settle further away from their site of birth or even migrate to different colonies (Swatschek et al., 1993). Because of the high philopatry genetic relatedness of birds from a single colony was higher between each other than between unrelated birds from other colonies (Swatschek et al., 1993).

Survival

Adult survival estimates, based on analysis of colour-ringed birds, indicate an adult yearly survival of 87-89% and an immature survival until first breeding of 22% (Wink et al., 1987a; Ristow et al., 1991). The oldest Eleonora's Falcon retrapped was 16 years old; others 14 (2x), 13 (1x), 11 (5x), 10 (7x), 9 (6x), and 8 years (7x). We have calculated an age model of breeding Eleonora's Falcons and found that 50% of the breeding birds were older than 8.7 years (Ristow et al., 1989; 1991).

Parasites

Eleonora's Falcons were found to be parasitized by a malaria parasite, *Leucocytozoon toddi*, and several ectoparasites, including hippoboscid flies (*Ornithophila gestroi*), Mallophaga (*Laemobotrion tinnunculi*, *Degeeriella rufa*) and ticks (*Haemaphysalis hoody*). Ectoparasite infection increases during growths of the nestlings and reaches about 70-85% in adult falcons (Wink et al., 1979).

COLONIAL BREEDING AND ITS CONSEQUENCES

Breeding colonially on isolated islands provides a number of advantages: nest sites are usually protected from predators, such as mammals, raptors & owls and snakes. This is also true for Eleonora's Falcon. Predators rarely occur on the breeding islands, exceptions are rats (which were introduced during historic times) and occasionally Peregrines *Falco peregrinus*, Lanner Falcons *Falco biarmicus*, and Bonelli's Eagle *Hieraaetus fasciatus* and probably Sparrowhawk *Accipiter nisus*, Eagle Owl *Bubo bubo*, and Raven *Corvus corax*. Because Eleonora's Falcons have a delayed breeding period which coincides with the onset of migration of palaearctic birds to Africa, also a number of migrating raptors (eagles, harriers, owls) pass the island and may prey on falcon nestlings.

In common with other falcon species, Eleonora's Falcon shows a defence reaction at its nest. Due to its colonial breeding a social defence reaction has evolved towards aerial intruders. If an aerial predator approaches the island closer than 0.5 km, an alarm call is given (which resembles the call of solitary falcon species in such situations) and a combined effort of the nearest falcons drives the intruder away through direct mobbing. In case of a terrestrial intruder or when a raptor lands within the territory of an individual pair, the neighbours respond to the alarm call, but stay outside the territory and circle above it. Individual nest defence is left to the pair concerned, which attack the intruder by a series of stoops. As the alarm call is usually not given when a pair has eggs, but readily when young are present, the colonial/social function of the alarm call has to be interpreted cautiously (Ristow *et al.*, 1982). In Table 1, we have listed the instances of social defence reactions towards raptors and ravens (other interactions with herons, gulls, shearwaters and other larger birds, which are sometimes mobbed by Eleonora's Falcons, were omitted from this tabulation, but see Ristow *et al.*, 1982) observed during 11 spring/summer and 20 autumn seasons of our field studies. As can be seen, only occasional defence responses occur from May to July, because most falcons are absent. From mid July onwards the sensitivity towards intruders increases (see data for *F. tinnunculus*) and from August onward all intruders are mobbed, except sometimes Peregrine and Kestrel that are resident on the island. Social mobbing appears effective because we found only 14 nestlings killed by predators as compared to 4350 successfully fledged young.

Sooty Falcons apparently show the same colonial defence behaviour, as Walter (1979b) describes two instances when 20 or several Sooty Falcons mobbed an Egyptian Vulture and a Pallid Harrier, respectively. An apparent difficulty of breeding colonially is the maintainance of a monogamous breeding system. In the period before and during egg-laying, sufficient food is not available in the direct neighbourhood of the breeding colony. As far as we know, both partners hunt individually 20-60 km away and meet in the territory for casual courtship. The synchrony of their prolonged presence in the breeding territory increases during July as well as the male's share in supporting its mate by courtship feeding. In the time of absence, any male which stays in the colony could try to intrude a foreign territory and try to copulate with the respective female. A high rate of extra-pair young (EPY) would be a logical expectation (Birkhead & Møller,1992). We have analyzed 60 young falcons from 17 families by multilocus DNA fingerprinting and found for all families that the social mothers and fathers were also the genetical parents, i.e. EPY could not be detected (Swatschek *et al.*, 1993). This finding corresponds with other falcons in which EPY are rare (Oliphant *et al.*, 1993). So the question is, how do Eleonora's Falcons avoid EPYs? A week prior to the onset of laying a male will sometimes sit alone in the territory for several hours waiting to feed its mate, being away for hunting, thus mate guarding would be difficult. If the female is present, copulations take place quite often and we observed copulations every 30 min. Half a week before egg laying, the copulation frequency remains the same, but the pair spends more time together. On the day of egg laying, only a single copulation was seen in 5 hours. Because of the high copulation frequency we can expect sperm competition; i.e. even if there was an extra-pair copulation, the sperm of the extra-pair male would be diluted in such a way that its chance to fertilize an egg becomes very small. More field work needs to be done, to elucidate the actual rate of extra-pair and intra-pair copulations.

MOLECULAR PHYLOGENY OF ELEONORA'S FALCONS AND ALLIES

Using nucleotide sequences of the mitochondrial cytochrome b gene it is possible to reconstruct the evolutionary past of birds, including Accipitridae and Falconidae (Mindell, 1997; Seibold *et al.*, 1993; Wink 1995; Wink & Seibold, 1996; Wink *et al.*, 1996; Wink *et al.*, 1998). For the present analysis we have sequenced approx. 1100 nucleotides of the cytochrome b gene of several individuals of *F. eleonorae, F. concolor, F. subbuteo, F. vespertinus, F. amurensis, F. peregrinus, F. cherrug, F. biarmicus, F. rusticolus, F. chicquera, F. tinnunculus* and *F. punctatus* using an automatic sequencer (ALFexpress, Pharmacia). Aligned sequences were analysed with the phylogeny programme PAUP* (Swofford, 1998) and Maximum Parsimony (MP), Maximum Likelihood (ML), and Neighbour Joining (NJ) methods were used to reconstruct the underlying molecular phylogeny. For details of methodology see Avise (1994), Wink (1998), Wink *et al.*, (1996, 1998) and Leisler *et al.*, (1997).

Table 1. Occurrence of social defence reactions against raptors, owls, or ravens in a colony of more than 200 pairs of Eleonora's Falcon

Species	date	frequency	number of mobbing falcons
Aquila nipalensis	7.9.1977	1x	80
Aquila pomarina	20.9.- 2.10.	2x	10
Aquila spec.	22.9.83	1x	10
Hieraaetus fasciatus	12.-15.6.	2x	0
	2.8.-13.10.	26x	2-100
Hieraaetus pennatus	21.8.-28.9.	3x	3-10
Milvus migrans	20.8.-11.9.	6x	15-50
Circaetus gallicus	4.10.95	1x	20
Circus aeruginosus	26.5.-9.6.	4x	0
		1x	3
	2.9.-5.10.	26x	3-100
Circus macrourus (?)	12.9.80	1x	10
Falco tinnunculus	26.5.-7.7.	14x	0
		2x	1-2
	17.7.-2.10.	10x	0
		11x	2-20
Falco biarmicus	2.9.-8.10.	8x	8-70
Falco peregrinus	5.6.-7.7.	9x	0
		5x	1-5
	4.8.-7.10.	10x	0
		11x	2-50
Accipiter nisus	1.6.93	1x	0
	19.9.-2.10.	4x	10-100
Buteo buteo	10.-27.9.	3x	4-20
Buteo rufinus	5.-11.9.	2x	3-100
Pernis apivorus	26.5.-7.6.	7x	0
		1x	1
	7.9.-2.10.	9x	3-40
Otus flammeus	1.10.77	1x	150
Corvus corax	20.6.92	1x	0
	4.9.-11.10.	15x	4-70

Tyto alba: 4 carcasses were found on the island, one of them might have been killed by the falcons

All three methods used for tree building (MP, ML and NJ) produce identical trees, as shown in Figures 1 and 2, indicating that the reconstructed phylogeny can be regarded as a solid base for further discussions and interpretations.

Figure 1. Molecular phylogeny of Eleonora's Falcons and allies.

A. The NJ bootstrap cladogram represents the results of 1000 replications (distance algorithm logdet); origins of birds is indicated after each taxon name

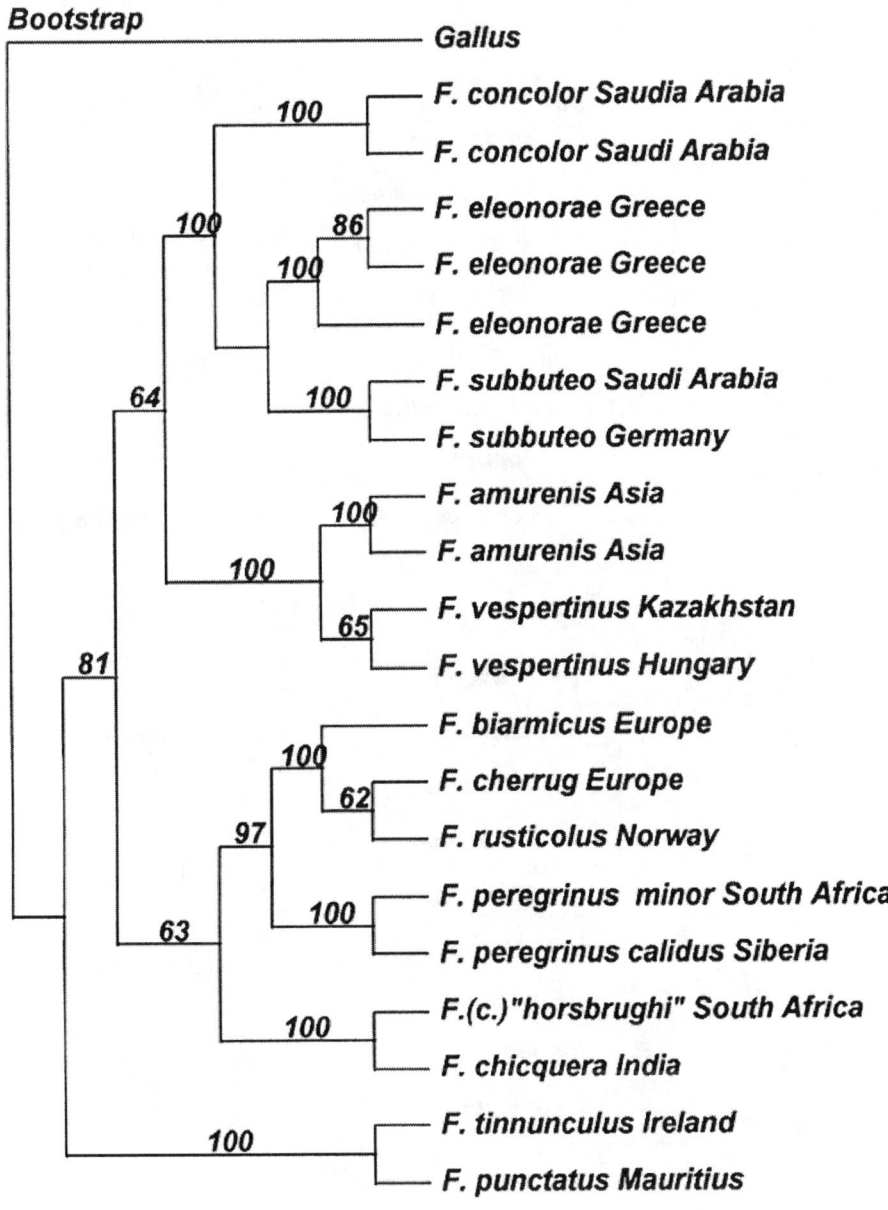

B. Branch lengths in the Maximum Likelihood tree are proportional to evolutionary distances; MLE settings: Assumed nucleotide frequencies: A=0.298, C=0.341, G=0.121, T=0.238; all sites were assumed to evolve at same rate; transition/transversion ratio was set to 2; score of the best tree found= 4609

Maximum Likelihood

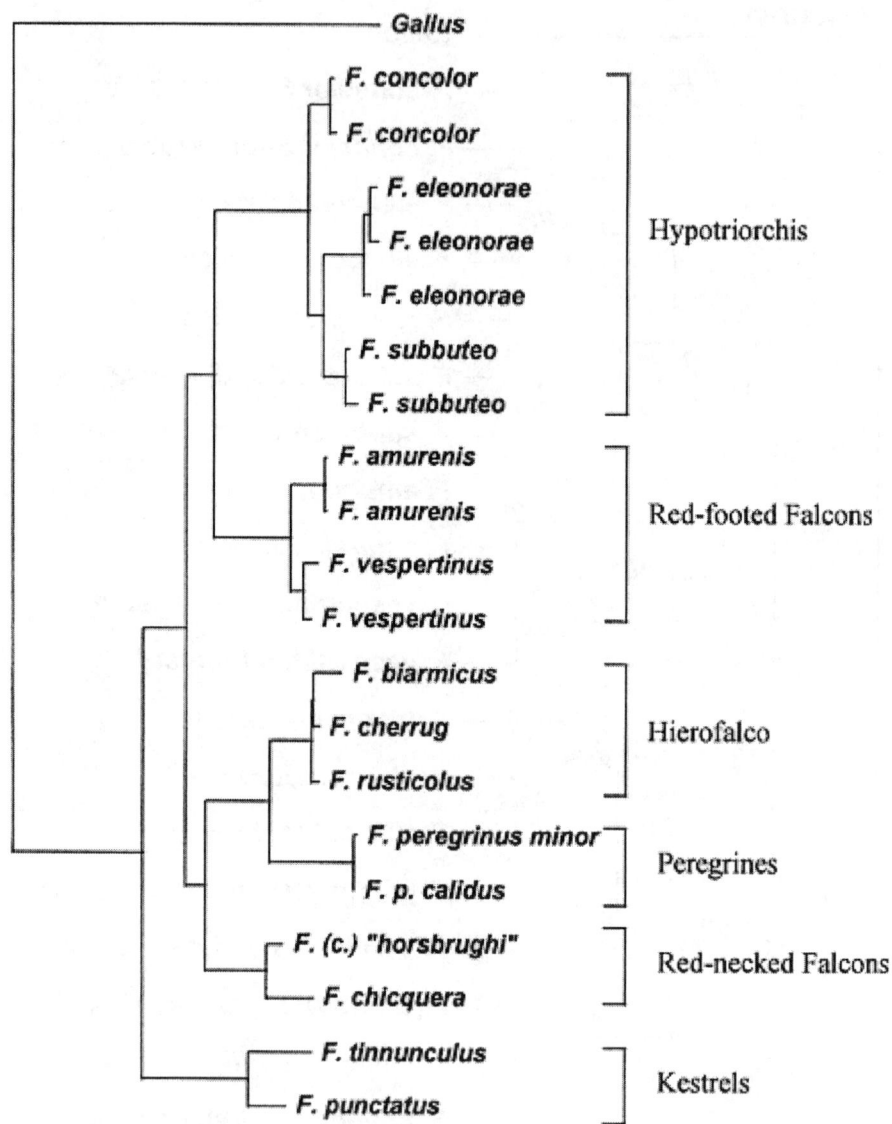

Figure 2. Correlation between phylogeny and ecological/behavioural traits of Eleonora's Falcons and allies

Base is a Maximum parsimony tree (length 570 steps; CI=0.767; RI=0.834; HI=0.233) (heuristic search, unweighted characters)

A. Distribution

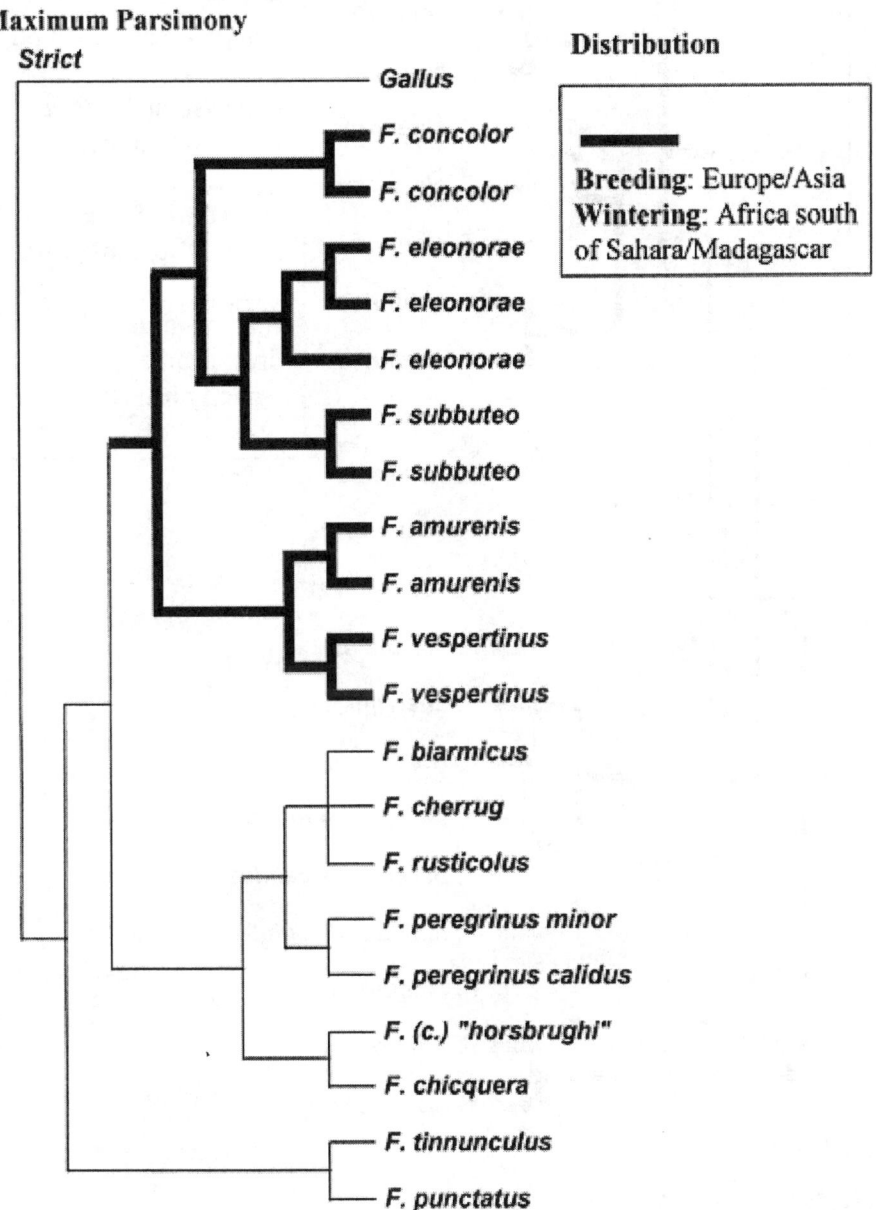

B. Food and feeding

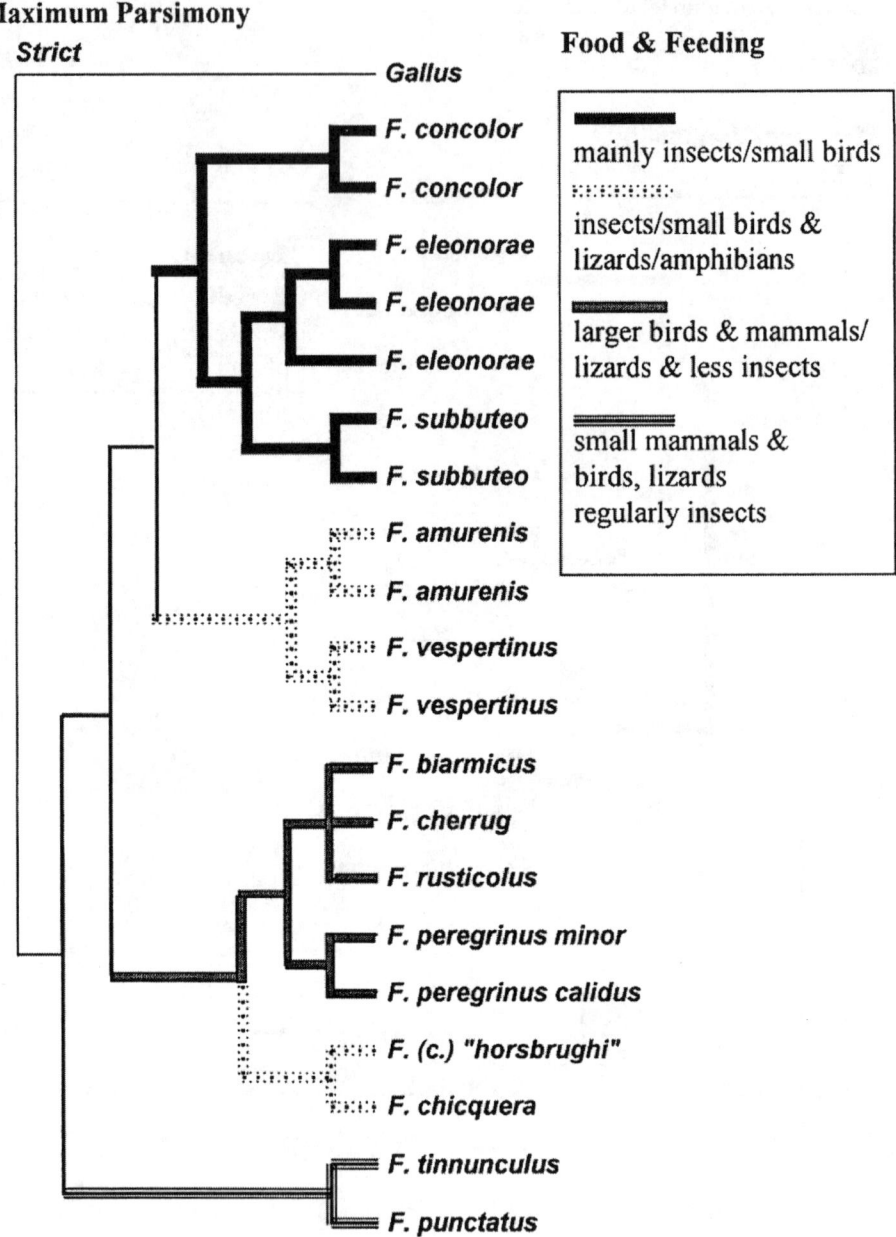

C. Occurrence of colonial breeding

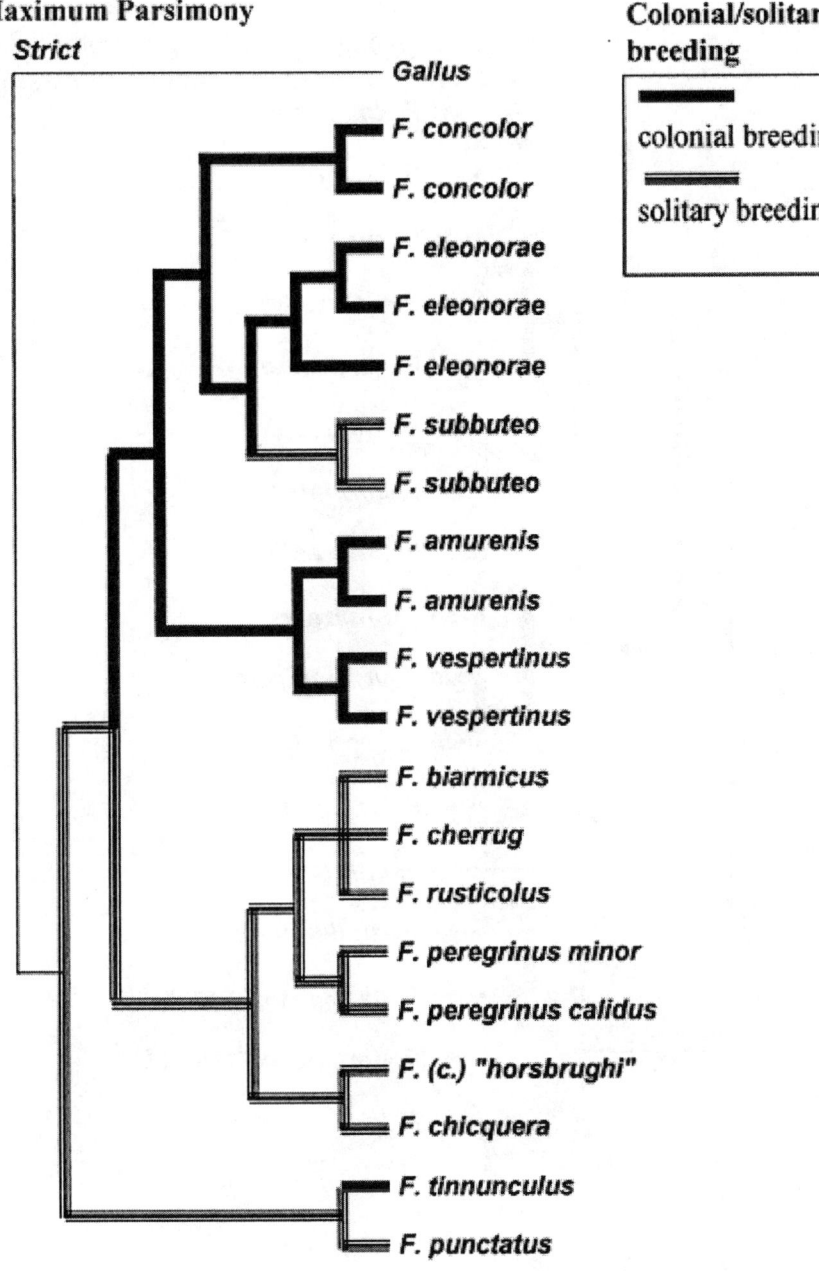

D. Occurrence of dark plumage or dark morph

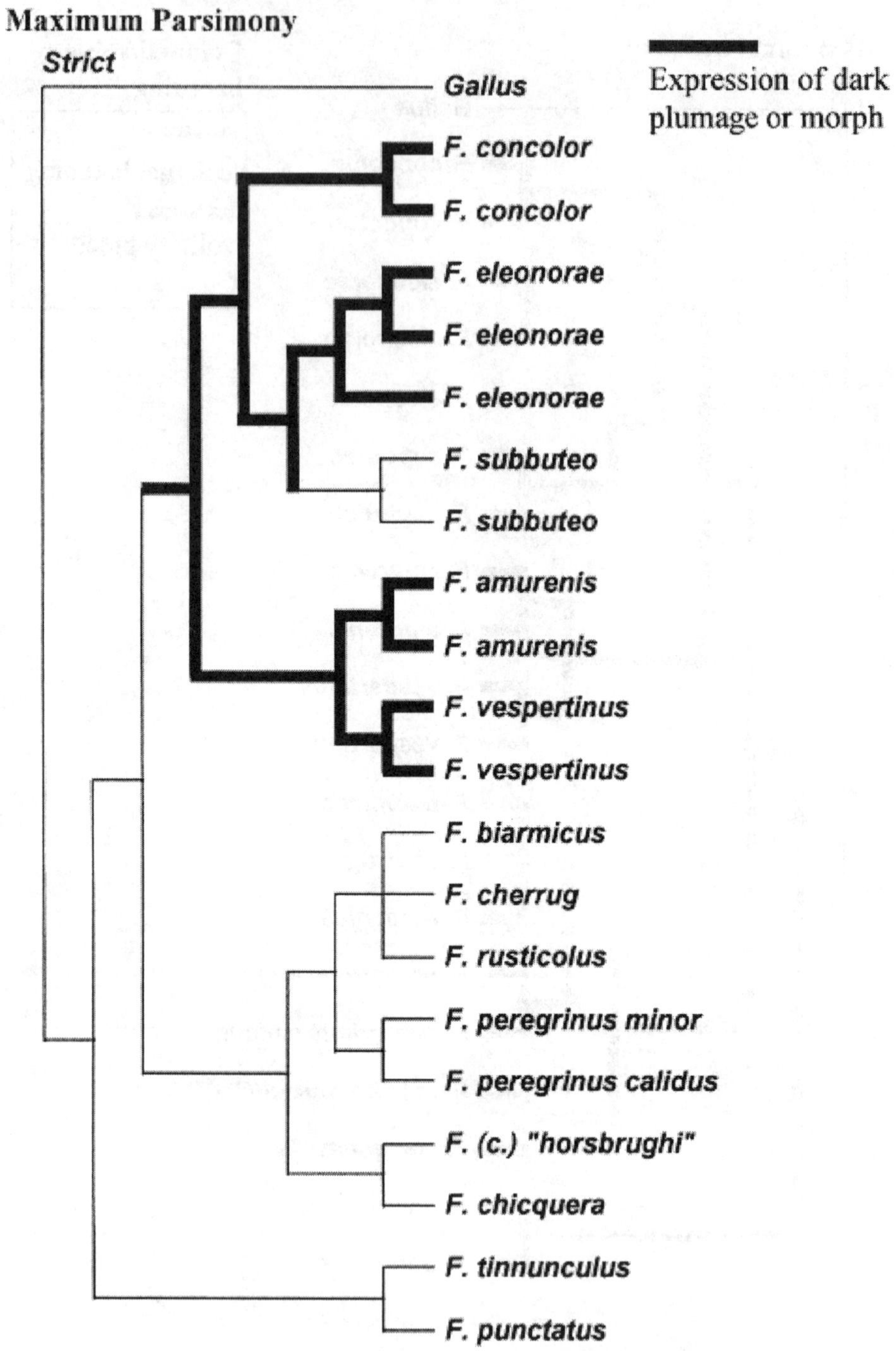

Maximum Parsimony
Strict

 Expression of dark plumage or morph

- Gallus
- F. concolor
- F. concolor
- F. eleonorae
- F. eleonorae
- F. eleonorae
- F. subbuteo
- F. subbuteo
- F. amurenis
- F. amurenis
- F. vespertinus
- F. vespertinus
- F. biarmicus
- F. cherrug
- F. rusticolus
- F. peregrinus minor
- F. peregrinus calidus
- F. (c.) "horsbrughi"
- F. chicquera
- F. tinnunculus
- F. punctatus

According to these analyses, *F. eleonorae, F. concolor*, and *F. subbuteo* form a closely related monophyletic group which has been recognized as the "Hobby" group or Hypotriorchis, confirming earlier results (Seibold *et al*., 1993; Wink & Seibold, 1996; Wink *et al*., 1998). Distances between these taxa range between 2.2 and 3.2% nucleotide substitutions. Assuming a crude calibration of a molecular clock for mitochondrial genes (Shields & Wilson, 1979, Tarr & Fleischer, 1993) which equates 2% nucleotide substitutions with 1 million years of divergence, the three falcon species must have evolved about 1 to 1.5 million years ago.

Also *F. vespertinus* and *F. amurensis* form a closely related pair of sibling species (sequence divergence 2% = 1 million years) which cluster as a sister clade to the Hobby-group (distance 7.2-8.1%; = 3.6-4 million years). According to these data, both clades share common ancestry and appear to be monophyletic (Fig. 1, 2).

Kestrels diverge at the base of the falcon tree, leading to the Hypotriorchis-complex on one hand and the Peregrine/Hierofalco complex on the other hand; these relationships are discussed by Wink & Sauer-Gürth (1999) in this volume.

Because *F. concolor, F. subbuteo, F. eleonorae, F. vespertinus* and *F. amurensis* share common ancestry we have a chance to analyse whether common traits can also be discovered in their biology and ecology. Data on *F. concolor, F. subbuteo, F. vespertinus,* and *F. amurensis* were taken from Glutz *et al*., (1989), Cramp (1980), and Frumkin (1988, 1993, 1994), Frumkin & Clark (1988), Gaucher *et al*., (1988, 1994, 1995), and Walter (1990).

In Figures 2 A-D the molecular phylogeny is used as a frame-work to analyse behavioural, ecological and morphological traits seen in these falcons and to ask which of these traits reflect common ancestry and sequential or parallel evolution.

In Figure. 2 A, branches leading to taxa which have their breeding grounds in the Mediterranean, Europe or Asia, but migrate to South Africa or Madagascar, are printed in bold. *F. concolor, F. subbuteo, F. eleonorae, F. vespertinus,* and *F. amurensis* share these properties as opposed to the other falcons which are either resident or make local movements only. This result indicates that the ancestor to the *F. concolor/ F. subbuteo/ F. eleonorae/ F. vespertinus/ F. amurensis* -assemblage, which could have evolved 4-5 million years ago, must have been a falcon which wintered or lived in Africa south of the Sahara and started to migrate north for exploiting food sources or directly for breeding.

If the feeding ecology is classified in four categories 1. mainly insects and small birds, 2. some insects, small birds, lizards, and amphibians, 3. larger birds & mammals, lizards but less insects, and 4. small mammals & birds, lizards and also insects, Figure 2B is obtained. The Hypotriorchis clade share properties of category 1; i.e. prey which is only hunted while in the air, whereas *F. amurensis* and *F. vespertinus* are in category 2, which adds lizards and amphibians to the diet; i.e. prey is also taken from the ground. The larger falcons of the Peregrine/Hierofalco group are in category 3, whereas kestrels are in group 4. Food and feeding habits are obviously similar in closely related monophyletic groups, but show adaptive traits, as can be seen in Red-necked Falcons *F. chicquera*, which share category 2 with *F. amurensis*, but are not directly related to them.

In Figure 2 C we have analyzed whether falcons breed solitarily or colonially. Again we find that colonial breeding appears as a shared character in *F. concolor, F. eleonorae, F. vespertinus,* and *F. amurensis*, with the exception of *F. subbuteo* which usually breeds solitarily. Also the degree of coloniality differs between these taxa, with *F. eleonorae* as the most colonial species and colony sizes of up to 300 breeding pairs. Colonial breeding is also known for some *F. tinnunculus* populations (and for *F. naumanni*, which has not been incorporated in this analysis but clusters as a true kestrel) but not for any of the other falcons (in this analysis). We can draw the evolutionary scenario that already the ancestor of *F. concolor, F. subbuteo, F. eleonorae, F. vespertinus,* and *F. amurensis* had evolved the colonial breeding habit, but that *F. subbuteo* has lost this trait.

In Figure 2 D we have marked those falcons which either have dark plumage (*F. concolor*) or in which dark plumage or morphs occur. Again we see a common heritage in *F. concolor, F. eleonorae, F. vespertinus* and *F. amurensis* with the exception of *F. subbuteo*, in which only light coloured falcons are known. If various plumage morphs are interpreted as a signal to conspecifics, it is hardly a coincidence that *F. subbuteo* as the least colonial species in the group has lost the polymorphic trait. In *F. vespertinus* and *F. amurensis*, we see both a dark and a light colour morph, which depends on gender, males are dark (with reddish "trousers") whereas females show the typical light colour type. In *F. eleonorae* we have a light and dark morph (see above), which is independent of gender. If we accept the phylogenetic relationships shown in Figures 1-2, we can draw the following evolutionary scenario. The ancestor of the *F. concolor, F. subbuteo, F. eleonorae, F. vespertinus*, and *F. amurensis* complex must have been a polymorphic falcon, possibly the result of a hybridisation between a dark and a light falcon. In its descendants the light and dark plumage reappears, either depending on sex (*vespertinus/amurensis*) or independently of gender (*eleonorae*) or in only a single light (*subbuteo*) or dark (*concolor*) form. It is worthwhile mentioning that fledglings of *F. concolor, F. vespertinus*, and *F. amurensis*, and normal *F. eleonorae* resemble light plumage falcons and develop their dark plumage when one year old.

ACKNOWLEDGEMENTS

We thank our Greek and German friends for their support in the field, Mrs H. Sauer-Gürth for skillful assistance in the laboratory, and the Greek Ministry of Agriculture for a permit to study Eleonora's Falcons in Greece.

REFERENCES

BIRKHEAD, T.R. & A.P. MOLLER 1992. *Sperm competetion in birds: Evolutionary causes and consequences.* Poyser, London.
CLARK, A.L. 1982. Ecology of the Eleonora's Falcon in Morocco. Dissertation Cornell University, USA.
CLARK, A.L. & D.B. PEAKALL 1977. Organochlorine residues in Eleonora's Falcon *Falco eleonorae*, its eggs and its prey. *Ibis* 119, 353-358.
CRAMP, S. 1980. *Handbook of the birds of Europe, the Middle East and North Africa.* Vol. II: Hawks to Bustards. Oxford University Press, Oxford.
FERNIE, K.J. & D.M. BIRD 1998. Carotenoids: Do they indicate individual-mate quality? In: Adams, N.J. & Slotow, R.H. (eds) *Ostrich* 69, 319-320.
FRUMKIN, R. 1988. Biologie und Bestimmung des Schieferfalken *Falco concolor. Limicola* 2, 83-109.
FRUMKIN, R. 1993. Breeding ecology of the sooty falcon (*Falco concolor*) in Israel. In: Nicholls, M.K. & Clarke, R. [Eds]. *Biology and conservation of small falcons:* Hawk and Owl Trust, London, pp. 51-58.
FRUMKIN, R. 1994. The sooty falcon *Falco concolor*: the breeding biology and ecology of a desert raptor.*Torgos* 23. 15-23, 66.
FRUMKIN, R. & W.S. CLARK 1988. Is there a dark morph of the sooty falcon *Falco concolor*?*Ibis* 130 569-571.
GAUCHER; P., T. PETIT & P. SYMENS 1988. Notes on the study of the sooty falcon (*Falco concolor*) during its breeding season in Saudi Arabia. *Alauda* 56, 277-283.
GAUCHER, P., W.D. DAUNICHT & X. EICHACHER 1994. The Sooty Falcon in Saudi Arabia. In Meyburg, B.-U. & Chancellor, R.D.eds. *Raptor Conservation Today.* WWGBP & Pica Press. 109-116.
GAUCHER, P., J-M. THIOLLAY & X. EICHACHER 1995. The sooty falcon *Falco concolor* on the Red Sea coast of Saudi Arabia: distribution, numbers and conservation. *Ibis* 137, 29-34.
GUTZ VON BLOTZHEIM, U., K.M. BAUER & E. BEZZEL 1989. *Handbuch der Vögel Mitteleuropas.* Vol 4, Falconiformes. Aula-Wiesbaden.
LEISLER, B., P. HEIDRICH, K. SCHULZE-HAGEN & M. WINK 1997. Taxonomy and phylogeny of reed warblers (genus *Acrocephalus*) based on mtDNA sequences and morphology. *Jounal für Ornithologie* 138, 469-496.
MINDELL, D.P. 1997. *Avian molecular evolution and systematics.* Academic Press, San Diego.
OLIPHANT, L.W., I.G. WARKENTIN, N.S. SODHI & P.C. JAMES 1993. Ecology of urban merlins in Saskatoon. Pp 42-44, in: *Biology and Conservation of small falcons* (M.K.Nicholls & R. Clarke, eds), The Hawk & Owl trust, London.
RISTOW, D., B. CONRAD, C. WINK & M. WINK 1980. Pesticide residues of failed eggs of Eleonora's Falcon, *Falco eleonorae*, from an Aegean colony. *Ibis* 122, 74-76.

RISTOW, D., F. FELDMANN, W. SCHARLAU, C. WINK & M. WINK 1991. Population dynamics of Cory's Shearwater (*Calonectris diomedea*) and Eleonora's Falcon (*Falco eleonorae*) in the Eastern Mediterranean. In: *Species conservation: A population-biological approach* (Eds. A. Seitz & V. Loeschcke), Birkhäuser Verlag, Basel,1991) pp 199-212.

RISTOW, D., W. SCHARLAU & M. WINK 1989. Population structure and mortality of Eleonora's Falcon *Falco eleonorae* In: Meyburg, B.-U. & Chancellor, R.D. eds., 321-326 (1989) *Raptors in the Modern World*, WWGBP: Berlin, London & Paris.

RISTOW, D., C. WINK & M. WINK 1979a. Site tenacity and pair bond of the Eleonora's Falcon. *Il-Merill* 20, 16-18.

RISTOW, D., C. WINK & M. WINK 1979b. On the bathing behaviour of Eleonora's Falcon, *Falco eleonorae*. *Bird Study* 27, 54-56.

RISTOW, D., C. WINK & M. WINK 1982. Biology of Eleonora's Falcon.1. Individual and social defense behavior. *Raptor Research* 16, 65-70.

RISTOW, D., C. WINK & M. WINK 1983a. Biologie des Eleonorenfalken. 12. Die Anpassung des Jagdverhaltens an die vom Wind abhängigen Zugvogelhäufigkeiten. *Vogelwarte* 32, 7-13.

RISTOW, D., M. WINK, C. WINK & H. FRIEMANN 1983b. Biologie des Eleonorenfalken. 14. Das Brutreifealter der Weibchen. *Journal für Ornithologie* 124, 291-293.

RISTOW, D., C. WINK & M. WINK 1986. Assessment of Mediterranean autumn migration by prey analysis of Eleonora's Falcon. *Supplemento alle richerche di biologia della selvaggina* 10,. 285-295.

RISTOW, D., C. WINK, M. WINK & W. SCHARLAU 1998. Colour polymorphism in Eleonora's Falcon, *Falco eleonorae*. *Sandgrouse* 20, 56-64.

RISTOW, D. & M. WINK 1985. Breeding success of the Eleonora's Falcon and conservation management. In: *Conservation studies on raptors* (Eds. I, Newton & R.D. Chancellor). ICBP Technical publication No.5., pp 147-152.

RISTOW, D. & M. WINK 1995. Distribution of non-breeding Eleonora's Falcons. *Il-Meril* 28, 1-10.

SEIBOLD, I., A. HELBIG & M. WINK 1993. Molecular systematics of falcons (family Falconidae). *Naturwissenschaften* 80, 87-90.

SHIELDS, G.F. & A.C. WILSON 1987. Calibration of mitochindrial DNA evolution in geese. *J. Mol. Evol.* 24, 212-217.

SWATSCHEK, I., D. RISTOW, W. SCHARLAU, C. WINK & M. WINK 1993. Populationsgenetik und Vaterschaftsanalyse beim Eleonorenfalken (*Falco eleonorae*). *Journal für Ornithologie* 134, 137-143.

TARR, C.L. & R.C. FLEISCHER 1993. Mitochondrial DNA variation and evolutionary realtionships in the amakihi complex. *Auk* 110, 825-831.

WALTER, H. 1979a. *Eleonoras's falcon. Adaptations to prey and habitat in a social raptor*. The University of Chicago Press, Chicago & London. 1-410.

WALTER, H. 1979b. The Sooty Falcon *Falco concolor* in Oman. Results of a breeding survey. *J. Oman Studies* 5, 9-59.

WALTER, H. 1990. Colonial nesting in Eleonora's and sooty falcons. In: Newton, I. & Olsen, P. [Eds]. *Birds of prey*. Merehurst, London. 1990: 1-240.

WINK, M. 1994. *Falco eleonorae*. In: *Birds in Europe- Their conservation status* (G.M.Tucker & M.F.Heath, eds), pp 194-195, Birdlife International, Cambridge.

WINK, M. 1994. Molekulare Methoden in der Greifvogelforschung. *Greifvögel & Falknerei* 17-28.

WINK, M. 1995. Phylogeny of Old and New World vultures (Aves: Accipitridae and Cathartidae) inferred from nucleotide sequences of the mitochondrial cytochrome b gene. *Z. Naturforsch.*50c, 868-882.

WINK, M. 1998. Application of DNA-markers to study the ecology and evolution of raptors. In: *Holarctic Birds of Prey*. (R.D. Chancellor, B.-U.Meyburg, J.J. Ferrero, eds), Adenex & WWGBP, pp 49-71.

WINK, M., H. BIEBACH, F.FELDMANN, W. SCHARLAU, I. SWATSCHEK, C.WINK & D. RISTOW 1993. Contribution to the breeding biology of Eleonora's Falcon (*Falco eleonorae*). In: *Biology and Conservation of small falcons*. (M.K.Nicholls & R. Clarke, eds), The Hawk & Owl trust, London, 59-72.

WINK, M. & I. SEIBOLD 1996. Molecular phylogeny of Mediterranean raptors (Families Accipitridae and Falconidae). In: *Biology and Conservation of Mediterranean raptors*, (Muntaner, J. & J. Mayol, eds), SEO/BirdLife, Madrid 1996, Monografia 4: 335-344.

WINK, M., C. WINK & D. RISTOW 1978. Biologie des Eleonorenfalken (*Falco eleonorae*). 2. Zur Vererbung der Gefiederphasen (hell- dunkel). *Journal für Ornithologie* 119, 421-428.

WINK, M., D. RISTOW & C. WINK 1979. Biologie des Eleonorenfalken. 3. Parasitenentwicklung während der Brutzeit und Jugendentwicklung. *Journal für Ornithologie* 120, 64-68.

WINK, M., C. WINK & D. RISTOW 1980a. Biologie des Eleonorenfalken. 9. Eitemperaturen und Körpertemperaturen juveniler und adulter Falken. *Vogelwarte* 30, 320-325.

WINK, M., C. WINK & D. RISTOW 1980b. Biologie des Eleonorenfalken: 8. Die Gelegegröße in Relation zum Nahrungsangebot, Jagderfolg und Gewicht der Altfalken. *Journal für Ornithologie* 121, 387-390.
WINK, M., C. WINK & D. RISTOW 1982a. Biologie des Eleonorenfalken (*Falco eleonorae*): 10. Der Einfluß der Horstlage auf den Bruterfolg. *J. Ornithol.* 123, 401-408.
WINK, M., C. WINK & D. RISTOW 1982b. Biologie des Eleonorenfalken. 11. Biometrie des Sexualdimorphismus adulter und flügger Falken. *Vogelwelt* 103, 225-229.
WINK, M., D. RISTOW & C. WINK 1985. Biology of Eleonora's Falcon. 7. Variability of clutch size, egg dimensions and egg colouring. *Raptor Research* 19, 8-14.
WINK,M., C.WINK, W.SCHARLAU & D. RISTOW 1987. Ortstreue und Genfluß bei Inselvogelarten: Eleonorenfalke (*Falco eleonorae*) und Gelbschnabelsturmtaucher (*Calonectris diomedea*). *Journal für Ornithologie* 128, 485-488.
WINK, M., W. SCHARLAU & D. RISTOW 1987. Population structure in a colony of Eleonora's Falcon (*Falco eleonorae*). *Supplemento alle Richerche di Biologia della Selvaggina* 12, 301-305.
WINK, M., P. HEIDRICH & C. FENTZLOFF 1996. A mtDNA phylogeny of sea eagles (genus *Haliaeetus*) based on nucleotide sequences of the cytochrome b gene. *Biochemical Systematics and Ecology* 24, 783-791.
WINK, M., I.SEIBOLD, F. LOTFIKHAH & W. BEDNAREK 1998. Molecular systematics of holarctic raptors (Order Falconiformes). In *Holarctic Birds of Prey*. (R.D. Chancellor, B.-U.Meyburg, J.J. Ferrero, eds), Adenex & WWGBP; pp. 29-48.

Prof. Dr. M. Wink
Universität Heidelberg
Institut für Pharmazeutische Biologie
INF 364, D-69120 Heidelberg
Germany

Dr. Dietrich Ristow
Pappelstr. 35
D-85579 Neubiberg
Germany

Status of Réunion Marsh Harrier *Circus maillardi* on Réunion island

V. Bretagnolle, J.M. Thiollay and C. Attié

ABSTRACT

On Réunion Island, Indian Ocean, the only surviving resident raptor is the endemic Réunion Marsh Harrier, *Circus m. maillardi*. This taxon is traditionally considered conspecific with the Madagascar Marsh Harrier, *C. m. macrosceles* (but see Sibley & Monroe 1990). We present evidence that the population on Réunion is indeed different from the Madagascar birds, both in body size, shape, sexual dimorphism, juvenile and male patterns, and habitat use. Thus a full species status for Réunion birds may be warranted. They are also compared to *C. spilonotus,* the closest species in the *aeruginosus* group. An intensive survey was carried out on the island in 1997-1998 and the breeding population was found to be probably lower than 100 pairs, mostly concentrated in forested areas at mid elevation. Therefore this taxon as a whole must be considered as vulnerable, though it may not be currently declining.

INTRODUCTION

The Mascarene Islands (Mauritius, Réunion and Rodrigues) are located in the Western Indian Ocean. Two species of diurnal raptors are known today from the Mascarenes: the Mauritius Kestrel, *Falco punctatus*, on Mauritius and the Madagascar Marsh Harrier, *Circus maillardi*, on Réunion. Another falcon, *F. duboisi*, is extinct on Réunion and a harrier is extinct on Mauritius, so probably a falcon and a harrier were actually sympatric on each island. None seems to have ever existed on Rodrigues Island, according to the fossil or subfossil records (review in Cowles 1987). These two raptors are considered endemics and threatened (see Virani & Watson 1998), but the taxonomic status of *Circus maillardi* is still debated. The latter is currently divided into two well-marked subspecies (e.g. Howard & Moore 1978), *C. m. maillardi* (Réunion) and *C. m. macrosceles* (Madagascar and Comoros), but other treatments have been proposed. Some authors have considered these two populations as separate taxa (e.g. Sibley & Monroe 1990), others have regarded *maillardi* as a subspecies of the Marsh Harrier (*C. aeruginosus*). The population which breeds on Réunion Island might be a key link between African and Asiatic taxa.

Moreover, most taxa within the large *aeruginosus* group are poorly known. Detailed information is only available for *æruginosus* in Europe (see review in Clarke 1995) and *approximans* in Australasia (review in Marchant & Higgins 1993). This prompted an investigation i) to assess differences between Réunion birds and other populations and ii) to determine the current status, population size and trends of the Réunion Marsh Harrier, in order to identify its conservation needs.

Previously, two little documented assessments had tentatively estimated the population size at 200 pairs (Clouet 1978) and 300 pairs (Barré *et al.* 1996). In earlier times, the species was considered to be abundant (Dubois 1672, in Barré *et al.* 1996), but the only detailed study has been that of Clouet (1978). Therefore we undertook a comprehensive survey aimed at locating most breeding pairs of harrier. Because of a high landscape heterogeneity and a perceived uneven distribution of the species, we preferred to avoid population estimates, relying on extrapolations from a limited number of sample areas. Instead, we surveyed most areas of natural and semi-natural vegetation in order to monitor as many potentially suitable breeding habitats for harriers as possible. Habitat suitability was established on the basis of previous extensive experience of the species on Réunion, and the survey was facilitated by the fairly dense network of roads, forest tracks, mountain trails and view points that allowed an adequate coverage of otherwise seemingly inaccessible areas.

METHODS

Study area

Réunion Island (21°15 S-55°30 E) is a 2515 km² (maximum 50x70km) oceanic island of volcanic origin, 2-3 million years old, 165 km from Mauritius, the nearest island, and 700 km east of Madagascar. Most of the island is mountainous and steep. Three cirques (caldeiras), namely Mafate, Cilaos and Salazie, surround the highest peak (Piton des Neiges, 3069 m). An often active volcano (Piton de la Fournaise, 2631 m) in the southeast, is the second highest summit. Urban settlements are essentially in the now totally cultivated lowlands along the coast. Below about 1300 m, native forest tends to be restricted to steep sides of valleys. The island, discovered in the 16th century, was heavily deforested (Fig. 1) when the human population grew from 250 in 1676 to 110,000 in 1848 and six times higher today. Massive extinctions, including at least 22 bird species, occurred from the early stages of colonization through hunting pressure, introduced mammals (rats, cats, goats and pigs) and habitat destruction (Maurer Chauviré pers. com.). Intensive agriculture, spreading urbanization and construction of many roads are still severely affecting natural habitats.

Habitats on Réunion Island

The native flora comprises 750 species, but 1100 additional species have been introduced, of which at least 62, including weeds (*Hedychium*), shrubs (*Rubus, Psidium, Lantana, Solanum*) and trees (*Eugenia*) are severely invading natural forest remnants, altering their structure and preventing their regeneration (MacDonald *et al.* 1991). All forest types together, at most 55,000 ha of forest remain (Cadet 1980, Doumenge & Renard 1989, Dupont 1990), i.e. 22% of the island area. Five major natural habitats are usually recognized (see Fig. 1; Rival 1952, Cadet 1980, Barré *et al.* 1996):

(1) A dry savanna woodland and semi-sclerophylous forest on the coastal lowlands. Almost nothing of the former western dry woodlands remains, and it is now completely replaced by cultivation, urbanization and introduced vegetation.

(2) A humid lowland mixed evergreen forest ("*Bois de Couleur des Bas*") originally covered the eastern lowlands up to 800-900 m and the western side, from 750 to 1100 m. Degraded remnants have a dense understorey, dominated by an open canopy 6-15 m high, but the only primary stand (Marelongue Reserve) has a continuous canopy up to 25 m high. Approximately < 1% of original lowland mixed forest remains today.

(3) An upland wet mixed evergreen forest ("*Bois de Couleur des Hauts*"), from 800 to 1900 m in the east and 1100 to 2000 m in the west, is richer in epiphytes and treeferns.

(4) Between 1600-2000 m, a montane forest is dominated by large *Acacia heterophylla* ("*Tamarins des Hauts*"), higher (15-20 m) and bigger (up to 1.5-m d.b.h.) than trees in mixed evergreen stands. The understorey is locally rich in native bamboos, *Nastus borbonicus*, giant heath, *Philippia montana* or stands of *Pandanus montanus*. It still represents *ca.* 60% of the original montane forest.

Figure 1: Distribution and extent of natural vegetation types, before human settlements (above) and today (below). From coastal to central areas: dry woodlands, lowland wet forest, upland wet forest; *Acacia heterophylla* forest and high altitude heather. White areas below are cultivated and urbanized areas.

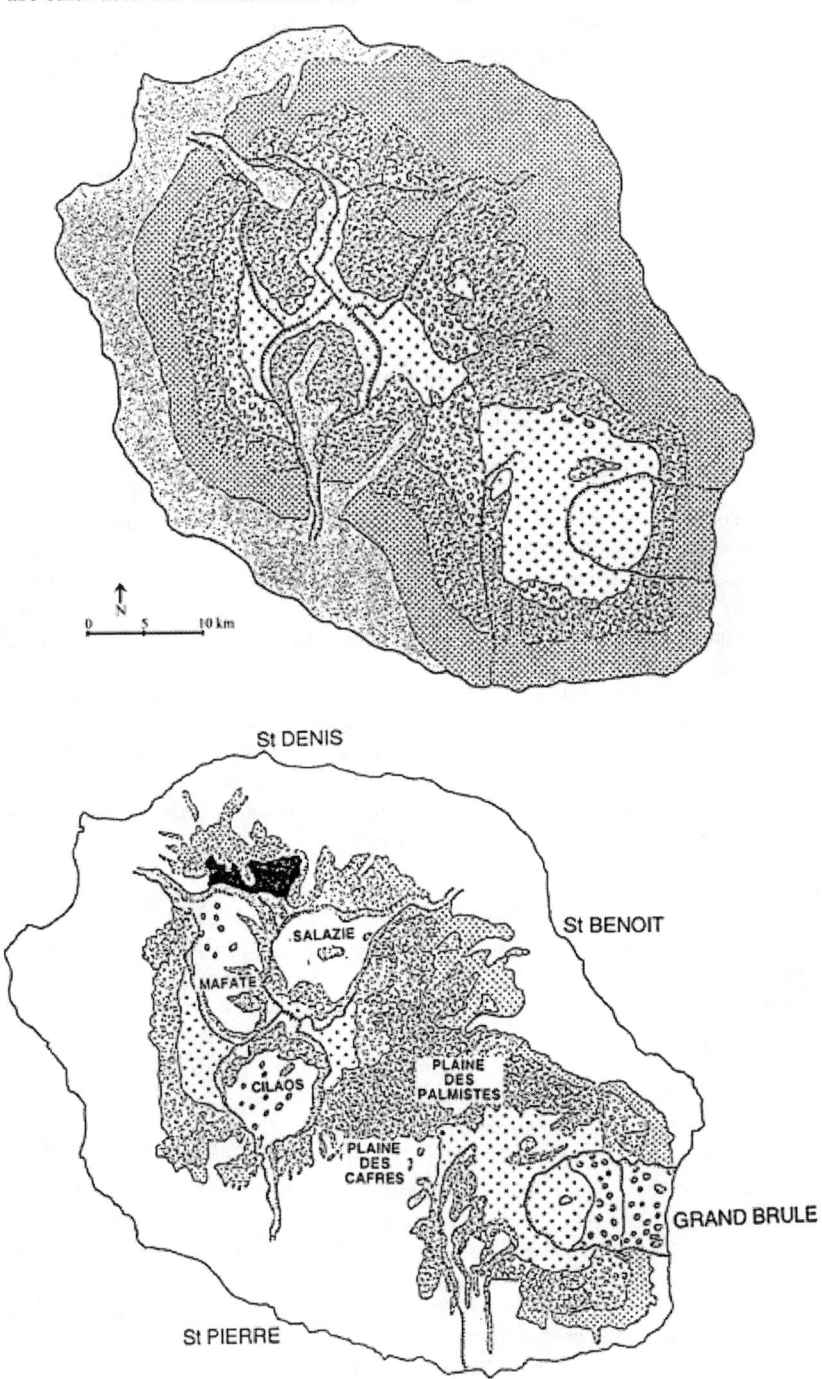

(5) Above the tree line are large extents of dense 1-2-m high heath and shrubs. >80% of original high altitude vegetation is still present.

Apart from natural habitats, five other broad habitat categories were distinguished:

(6) Monospecific exotic tree plantations, most often dense coniferous patches (*Cryptomeria*) or *Eucalyptus* and *Pinus*.
(7) More prominently in the western lowlands, dry derived savannas and abandoned shrubby areas.
(8) Cultivated areas, often large fields of sugar cane, sometimes more diversified crops with tree rows, woodlots and orchards.
(9) Urban and suburban areas including associated gardens and tourist resorts.
(10) Wetlands, i.e. either coastal ponds and marshes or lakes in mountains. Both are highly restricted and modified, by exotic vegetation and deforested surroundings.

Population census

The most suitable areas were surveyed from dominant lookouts during 2-hour periods in fine weather, between 07h00 and 18h00, during the breeding season (November-June). All individuals seen and their behaviour, sex and age were recorded and their movements monitored on 1/25,000 topographical maps. From December 1996 to March 1998, 168 sample periods were carried out in as many different localities, most often with two people at a time. However, most surveys were done during the 1997-1998 breeding season, which was the only year of reference for the population estimate.

Because of the wide-ranging habits of this harrier, we focused on the identification and localization of actually breeding pairs, excluding the numerous observations of individual birds only foraging or that did not fit any of the breeding criteria. We distinguished between *possible* breeding pairs (e.g. pair of adults flying together), *probable* breeding pairs (i.e. showing territorial or sexual behaviours), and *confirmed* breeding pairs (that exhibited typical breeding behaviour or for which we found nests or fledglings).

Using a Geographic Information System (ArcView 3.b.), a grid was superimposed on the island map, dividing the area into 577 2x2-km squares. When a nest site was not precisely located and the record overlapped the limits of a square, it was assigned to a single and most appropriate square. Two pairs on the same or adjacent squares were considered different if they had been seen simultaneously. The total population size as given here was the minimum cumulative number of pairs in each category, and was thus a conservative estimate.

Biometrical data

All available skins from known breeding localities of the Indian Ocean were measured at the Museum of Saint-Denis (Réunion), Museum National d'Histoire Naturelle (Paris), British Museum (Tring) and American Museum of Natural History (New-York). We measured culmen, tarsus, wing and tail and also recorded colour patterns, especially of back, head, rump and presence of tail bar in males, and white on rump, body colour and streaks on underside in females and immatures.

RESULTS

Distribution patterns over the island

Overall, harriers were found throughout the island, with no marked preference for any of the major geographic areas, despite important differences in rainfall and associated environmental conditions (Fig. 2). Pairs were irregularly spaced, with large areas where the species was quite rare, and 6-8 patches where several pairs were aggregated, e.g. up to 7-8 pairs within a 8-km valley segment, or 5-7 pairs over *c.* 16 km^2 (Fig. 2; see also Clouet 1978). Such a patchy distribution was not apparently correlated with the occurrence of a markedly more suitable habitat. Breeding pairs of harriers were distributed from sea-level to 1200 m, and possibly to 1600-1800 m if unconfirmed breeding cues were included. Most pairs, however, were concentrated between 300-700 m. The mean elevation of confirmed and probable breeding pairs was 530 ± 290 (n = 32). Surprisingly, harriers were quite rare within the three large cirques (1-2 pairs in each). All the flat bottoms of these cirques are heavily populated, but their surrounding steep slopes would provide suitable breeding sites below the elevation threshold. Conversely, most breeding pairs were concentrated downstream at the entrance of cirques and more generally along lower narrow valleys and canyons (here called "*ravines*"), a shift also apparent in many breeding seabirds. Breeding sites may be safer in little populated areas and more inaccessible slopes.

Figure 2: Distribution of breeding pairs of Réunion Harrier in 1997-1998.

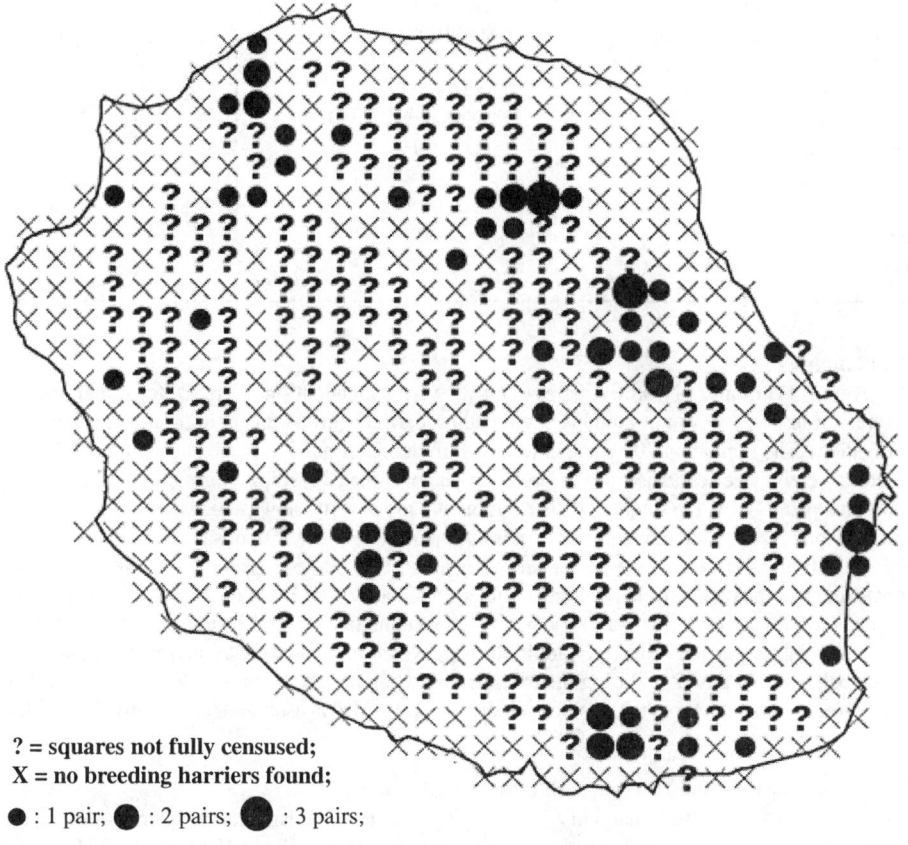

? = squares not fully censused;
X = no breeding harriers found;
● : 1 pair; ● : 2 pairs; ● : 3 pairs;

Habitat selection

Because most habitat types, as defined above, have a limited altitudinal distribution, there was a strong correlation betwen habitat choice and elevation range. All known harrier breeding zones were in forested areas, except one in the dense vegetation of a coastal swamp (Etang Saint-Paul). The forest cover involved was relatively low, dense and degraded native woodlands, but nest sites actually checked were never under a tree canopy. Rather, they were in open patches within forest (n = 6), in savanna with shrubs (n = 12) and in vegetation on cliffs or steep grassy slopes (n = 10). None has been found or suspected in the widespread sugarcane fields. Foraging habitats, however, were much less restricted and included almost any habitat type except usually urban and suburban areas, probably for safety reasons rather than food availability, since they were used in older times (Dubois, in Barré et al. 1996). This raptor in fact seems to be very ubiquitous and adaptable. Prey abundance and accessibility are probably major determinants of foraging habitat choice. Although it usually shuns high closed canopy forest, it is much more of a forest bird than any other of the 12 species of harriers (*Circus* sp.) in the world (pers. obs.).

Table 1. Distribution of breeding pairs of Réunion Harrier among habitat types.

Habitat	Habitat reference	Elevation range	Number of breeding pairs			Total
			confirmed	probable	possible	
Dry savanna woodland	1	<500	0	2	1	3
Lowland evergreen forest	2	200-800	8	10	17	35
Upland wet evergreen forest	3	800-1600	3	5	11	19
Montane forest of *Acacia*	4	1600-2000	0	0	0	0
High altitude heathland	5	2000-3000	0	0	0	0
Exotic tree plantations	6	200-1400	0	0	0	0
Derived shrubland	7	100-600	4	2	3	9
Cultivated areas	8	0-1500	1	0	2	3
Urban and suburban areas	9	0-1300	0	0	0	0
Wetlands	10	0-600	2	0	1	3
Total			**18**	**19**	**35**	

Population size

Overall, 331 of all 577 4-km^2 squares (57.4 %) were searched for harriers. Of the remaining 246 squares, at least 44 were not suitable for breeding harriers (urban areas, high altitude, intensive cultivation). The remaining 202 squares were insufficiently or not surveyed. During the 1997-1998 breeding season, we identified 36-39 probable or confirmed breeding pairs and *ca.* 35 possible additional pairs. Using the frequency distribution of pairs in well known squares, we can add *ca.* 20 breeding pairs, and a similar number of possible pairs (from the 202 unsampled squares). Total estimated figures are therefore 55-60 breeding pairs, and 50-55 possible pairs. We suggest in conclusion that the total current breeding population of harriers on Réunion Island must be between 50 pairs (conservative estimate) and 100 pairs (upper estimate). Most of the uncertainty comes from the substantial proportion of birds in adult plumage which did not exhibit convincing territorial or sexual behaviour at any time during the extended breeding period. It is possible that some of them do not breed every year. From the number of individuals recorded in each square, the harrier population must be over 400 birds.

Comparison of Réunion Harrier with other populations

Plumage pattern differs markedly between Réunion and Madagascar or Comoros birds The major differences with Madagascar birds are (see illustration of males in Hoyo et al. 1994):

1/ adult males : terminal bar more often present on tail (75% of specimens from Réunion as against 25% in those from Madagascar), head darker and mostly black, back darker, grey on upperwings lighter.

2/ adult females : more rufous, more heavily streaked on body (although this may possibly vary with age), nape always lighter, and most often white (never white on Madagascar birds).

3/ juvenile : completely dark rufous brown, without white rump (which is cream coloured), large white nape (apparently larger in females than in males) ; juvenile in Madagascar birds is similar to females.

4/ immature plumage intermediate between juvenile and adult, and maturation apparently requires several years (possibly less in Madagascar birds).

Réunion birds are much smaller than those from Madagascar or Comoros (Table 1) while there is no difference between Madagascar and Comoros birds. Results hold for both males and females. Réunion birds differed significantly from those of Madagascar and Comoros for tarsus, wing and tail lengths (ANOVA and Scheffe's a posteriori tests, all $p < 0.05$), but not culmen, while females showed significant differences for all parameters. Madagascar and Comoros birds did not differ statistically for any of these parameters.

Table 2. Specimen measurements of Réunion and Madagascar harriers

Taxon	Locality	Sex	Sample size	Culmen	Tarsus	Wing	Tail
maillardi	Réunion	male	15	32.1(2.1)	81.6(4.0)	354.8(8.1)	214.0(13.6)
		female	10	33.9(2.0)	81.1(4.3)	368.3(20.1)	221.8(16.5)
macrosceles	Madagascar + Comoros	male	27	32.7(1.8)	89.4(3.4)	410.1(12.7)	230.9(11.1)
		female	13	36.6(1.5)	93.6(2.4)	436.5(6.4)	247.6(10.3)

DISCUSSION

Biometry and plumage patterns convincingly argue for a full species status of the Réunion Harrier. Behavioural and genetical differences (to be developed later) provide additional evidence for a taxonomic segregation between Madagascar and Réunion birds. Many tropical raptors (56%) have restricted distributions and most of them (91%) occur on islands (Bildstein et al. 1998).

Current population size of the Réunion Harrier is below 100 pairs. There is no evidence for a recent decline, though harriers are still shot (at least 2 or 3 records each year since 1990). It is not known whether this harrier was more abundant in the past, though it is likely, as it was said to be common (Barré et al. 1996). During the last decades however, there was no conclusive evidence that the harrier population had declined significantly, despite higher population estimates that were not based on systematic surveys throughout the island. Urbanization and roads are increasing dramatically, though they affect mostly lowlands and areas that had long been deforested. Such a population size is precariously low by genetic, demographic and conservation standards, especially on an island where habitat loss, human disturbance, direct persecution, frequent cyclones, heavy rains and wild fires may increase the risk of local stochastic extinctions. The harrier breeding population is now the smallest of all the native non-marine bird species on Réunion. It is now even lower than that of the current recovering population of the Mauritius Kestrel, *Falco punctatus*, once the most endangered raptor species in the world. The populations on Madagascar (Langrand 1990) and in the Comoros (Louette 1988) are also very low. Therefore we suggest that the Réunion Harrier is vulnerable according to BirdLife criteria.

REFERENCES

BARRE, N., A. BARAU & C. JOUANIN 1996. *Oiseaux de la Réunion*. Editions du Pacifique, Paris.
BILDSTEIN, K.L., W. SCHELSKY & J. ZALLES 1998. Conservation status of tropical raptors. *J. Raptor Research* 32: 3-18.
CADET, T. 1980. *La végétation de l'île de la Réunion*. Imprimerie Cazal, St. Denis, Réunion.
CLARKE, R. 1995. *The Marsh Harrier*. Hamlyn, London.
CLOUET, M. 1978. Le Busard de Maillard, *Circus aeruginosus maillardi*, de l'île de la Réunion. *O.R.F.O.* 48: 95-106.
COWLES, G. S. 1987. The fossil record. Pages 90-100. *In* A. W. Diamond (Ed.) *Mascarene Island Studies*. British Ornithologists' Union.
DEL HOYO, J., A. ELLIOTT & J. SARGATAL 1994. *Handbook of the birds of the world*. Vol.2. Lynx Edicions, Barcelona.

DOUMENGE, C. & Y. RENARD 1989. *La conservation des systèmes forestiers de l'Ile de la Réunion.* IUCN, Cambridge, UK. 95 p.
DUPONT, J. 1990.*Cartes de végétation de la Réunion.* SREPEN, Saint-Denis, Réunion.
HOWARD, R. & A. MOORE 1980. *A complete checklist of the birds of the world.* Academic Press, London.
LANGRAND, O. 1990. *Guide to the birds of Madagascar.* Yale University Press, New-Haven.
LOUETTE, M. 1988. *Les Oiseaux des Comores.* Ann. Musée Royal Afrique Centrale, Tervuren. Sciences Zoologiques, n° 255.
MACDONALD, I.A.W., C. THEBAUD, W.A. STRAHM & D. STRASBERG 1991. Effects of alien plant invasions on native vegetation remnants on La Réunion (Mascarene Islands, Indian Ocean). *Environmental Conservation* 18: 51-61.
MARCHANT, S.& P.J. HIGGINS 1993. *Handbook of Australian, New Zealand and Antarctic birds.* Vol 2. Oxford Univ. Press., Melbourne.
RIVALS, P. 1952. *Etudes sur la végétation naturelle de l'Ile de La Réunion.* Travaux du Laboratoire Forestier de Toulouse, V, 3rd section, Vol. I (2). Faculté des Sciences de Toulouse. 216 p.
SIBLEY, C.G. & B. MONROE 1990. *Distribution and taxonomy of birds of the world.* Yale University Press, New Haven, Connecticut.
VIRANI, M. & R.T. WATSON 1998. Raptors in the east African tropics and western Indian Ocean Islands: state of ecological knowledge and conservation status. *Raptor Research* 32: 28-39.

V. Bretagnolle
CEBC-CNRS
79360 Beauvoir-sur-Niort
France

J.M.Thiollay
Laboratoire d'Ecologie, ENS
46, rue d'Ulm
75230 Paris
Cedex 05
France

C. Attié
79360 Vauballier
France

Population Density, Territory Size and Habitat Use of Gurney's Eagle *Aquila gurneyi* in the North Moluccas, Indonesia

Nils Røv and Jan Ove Gjershaug

ABSTRACT

The study was carried out in 1996 as part of an environmental co-operation between Indonesia and Norway. Almost nothing is known about the biology and status of this rain-forest eagle. It is assumed that it is possibly threatened by deforestation. We studied the abundance and distribution of eagle territories within three study areas covering 439 km². An average density of one pair of eagles per 33 km² of land area was found. Mean territory size varied between 19 and 29 km², dependent on the forest productivity. Hunting most often took place in primary rain-forest (55 and 76 % of observed hunting time in two different areas), although that forest type covered a minor part of the eagles' habitats (12 and 34 % respectively). Our results indicate that about 800-900 pairs of Gurney's Eagles might be found in the North Moluccas, and it is concluded that at present the population is highly viable in that area. However, the species' dependence on primary forests makes it particularly vulnerable to reduction or degradation of the remaining rain-forest areas.

INTRODUCTION

In 1990 a bilateral agreement on environmental co-operation between Indonesia and Norway was established. As part of this co-operation, a project on Conservation biology of Rain Forest Eagles in Indonesia started in 1995. The ultimate aim of the study was to obtain basic knowledge about large raptor species in the rain forest ecosystems in Indonesia so that their habitats can be managed in such a way that viable populations could be maintained in the future.

In 1996 a field study of Gurney's Eagle in the North Moluccas was carried out. This area forms a sub-biogeographic region characterised by a very special fauna of terrestrial mammals dominated by rodents, bats and marsupials. It includes the islands within Halmahera Tenga and Maluku Utara in the Maluku province (Fig. 1). Since terrestrial carnivores are absent, big raptors are the top-predators in the forest ecosystems. In order to maintain the diversity and the particular characteristics of the natural environment in this area, the preservation of those raptors might be considered as particularly important.

Gurney's Eagle is the largest top-predator in the lowland rain forest. Almost nothing has been known of its status and biology (Thiollay 1985, Burton 1989, del Hoyo et al. 1994). In BirdLife's last list of the threatened bird species of the world (Collar *et al*. 1994), Gurney's Eagle is classified as near threatened, but was assumed by Burton (1989) to be threatened with extinction because of the destruction of its habitat. Meyburg (1986) has also included it in his list of threatened species. However, the fact is that very little information has been available about its population status.

Figure 1. Map of Indonesia showing the location of the North Moluccas.

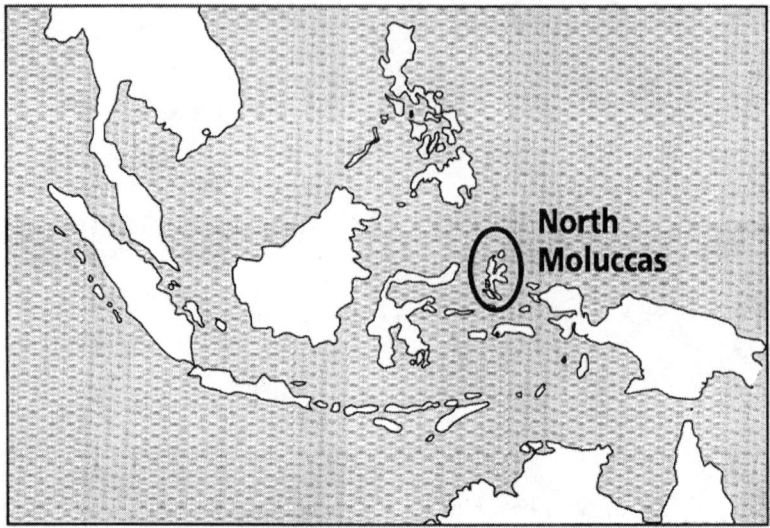

The forest management authority and BirdLife International have recently proposed that a large forest area in Halmahera should be protected. It is assumed that the proposed reserve will effectively conserve a rich genetic reservoir and a unique and valuable component of the national biodiversity resource. However, the importance of the proposed protected area to large raptor species has not been considered, although those species are likely to be of particular importance. They usually need large areas for their territories and might be dependent on primary forest. It is reasonable to believe that if one can safeguard viable populations of the most area-demanding species within a protected area, the total biodiversity of the area will be conserved for future generations.

The objectives of the present study have been to obtain knowledge on population status and habitat selection of Gurney's Eagle in the North Moluccas, and to evaluate the importance of the proposed conservation of forest areas in Halmahera for the future survival of the species in the area. Fieldwork was carried out in September - October in 1996.

STUDY SITES

Three study areas covering 439 km^2 have been investigated, two on Halmahera mainland and one including Ternate and Tidore islands (Fig. 2). It is assumed that these areas represent common rain-forest habitats in the North Moluccas. Apandi & Sudana (1980) give the geology of the study areas on geological maps.

Ternate and Tidore islands

These volcanic islands have very fertile soil of volcanic origin. On most of the islands highly productive forests have been transformed into cultivated habitats, mostly clove, nutmeg and coconut plantations and gardens. There are considerable amounts of urban areas along the coast, including an airport on Ternate. The height above sea level of the mountains of both islands is about 1700 m and the total area of the islands is approximately 214 km^2, about 14 % of which is covered by primary montane forest. Above the tree lines, there are narrow bands with alpine grassland, which makes the border against the bare volcanic rocks around the crater at the top of the mountains, particularly on Ternate.

Figure 2. Map of the North Moluccas showing the study areas (enlarged). The areas of primary forest are indicated (shaded).

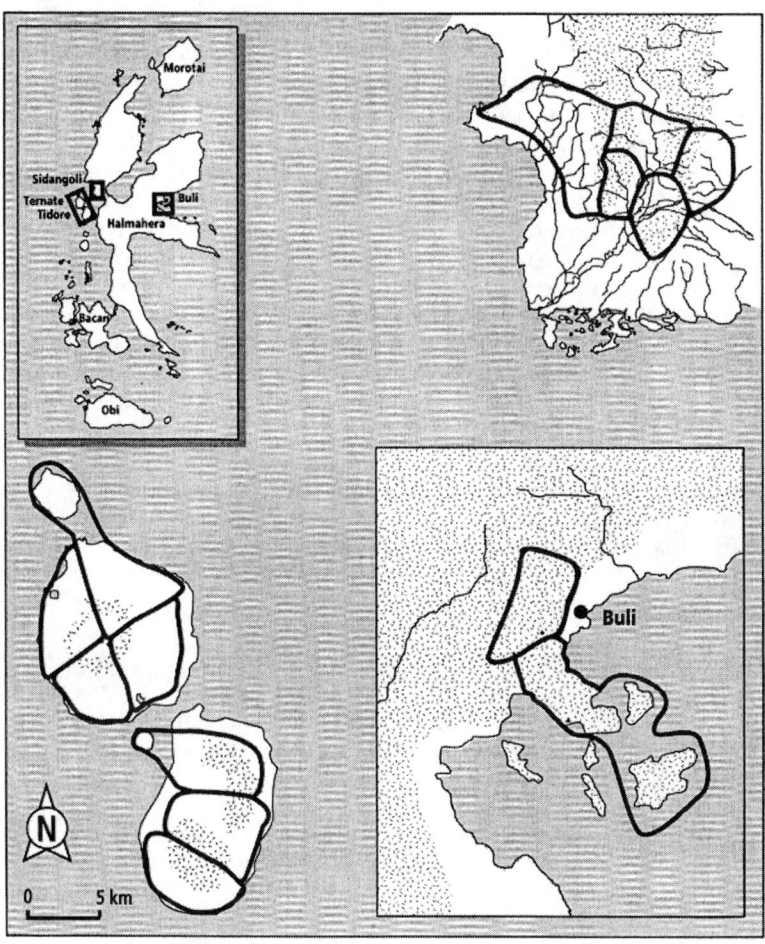

Sidangoli area

Most of the 156-km²-study area consists of forested hills on volcanic rocks belonging to the Bacan formation. Part of the lowland forest is situated on rich sedimentary rocks from late Tertiary belonging to the Weda formation. Near Sidangoli town, there is flat lowland on quaternary sediments (volcanic tuff and alluvial/coastal deposits). Today, most of this area is degraded grassland. The coastline limits the southern and western parts of the study area. Outside Sidangoli there is an area of mangrove forest. Most of the forest areas have been selectively logged or transformed into plantations and gardens. An estimated area of 33 km² of primary lowland and lower montane rain forest is found on the upper hills.

Buli

An area of 69 km² around Buli was studied during one week in September 1996. More than 84 % of the area consists of natural rain forest of lowland and lower montane types. This forest is situated on igneous ultrabasic rocks on hilly terrain. One large peninsula and two islands are found within the study area. The flat lowland around the village Buli is situated on alluvium or coastal sediments. Most of these areas are cultivated. The forests on the peninsula and the islands are partly degraded. We were informed that part of the forest has been burned some years ago.

RESEARCH APPROACH AND METHODS

Choice of investigation areas and methods was based on our own experience during visits to the study area in 1994 and 1995. The methodological approach to estimate eagle density is based on the eagles' territorial behaviour. Gurney's Eagles (usually the pair together) often soar high above the forest or perform territorial display to indicate the range of their territories. Observations were usually carried out from places with good views of the surrounding terrain. We identified the different territories by simultaneous observations of neighbouring pairs, or individual recognition on the basis of variation in plumage. Occasionally the home ranges of neighbouring pairs overlap. To calculate the average density of eagle territories, we divided the total size of the study areas by the number of recorded pairs. In the calculations, areas not used by the eagles were included, mostly plantations, gardens and grassland. Large areas of such land are found in the North Moluccas. However, on the basis of the available statistics and maps, we have not been able to estimate the areas of the different habitat types in the North Moluccas. Our population estimates are therefore based on the assumption that the study areas represent the general situation in the North Moluccas.

The seashores limit the land areas on Ternate and Tidore. In Sidangoli, the coastline limits the southern and western parts of the study area. The inland limit to the north has been defined on the basis of observations of neighbouring pairs, while to the east, the limit indicates the area which was covered by observations. In Buli, the eastern limit of the northernmost home range indicates where the eagles have been observed. Because of the high mountains we were not able to observe any neighbouring pairs in that territory. Accordingly, the size of that territory should be considered as a minimum estimate.

For each territory we calculated the total size and estimated the area of primary forest. The habitat-preference was studied by recording the forest types where hunting eagles were observed. The total time used and the frequency of observations have been compared with the estimated area of available primary forest within each territory. The area calculations were made on the basis of the available maps and a satellite spot image.

RESULTS

Population density

No significant differences in population density between the study areas were found (Table 1). On the average, one pair of Gurney's Eagle was found in each 31 km² of land area. However, one should keep in mind that in Buli, only two pairs have been studied and the home-range size of one of the pairs is a minimum estimate. Accordingly, the area requirement of eagles on igneous rocks might be more than the present results indicate.

Table 1. Abundance of Gurney's Eagle territories within the study areas.

Study area	Total area (km²)	No. of pairs	Mean area (km²) per pair
Ternate and Tidore	214	7	31
Sidangoli	156	5	31
Buli	69	2	34
Total	439	14	31

Territory size

On Ternate and Tidore seven pairs divided the islands in almost equal parts. Some overlap between the different home ranges was recorded. Overall, territory size varied between 9.5 and 40.5 km^2 (average 25.8 km^2) (Table 2). In the highly fertile islands of Ternate and Tidore on the average only 4.3 km^2 of primary forest were available for each territorial pair, while in nearby Sidangoli a mean area of 6.5 km^2 of primary forest was found. In Buli, the two recorded home ranges were found in forested areas on igneous ultrabasic rocks. Although natural forests covered the entire areas of those two home ranges, they were of the same size as in the other study areas. However, part of the forest was degraded, probably because of earlier forest fires.

Table 2. Territory size and area of primary forest within the territories of Gurney's Eagles within the study areas. Means, minimum and maximum values are given in km^2.

Study area	No. of pairs	Territory size		Area of primary forest within territories	
		Mean	Min.-Max.	Mean	Min.-Max.
Ternate & Tidore	7	29.4	18.5-40.5	4.3	3.2-6.8
Sidangoli	5	19.4	9.5-38.3	6.5	5.0-9.3
Buli	2	28.9	25.0-32.8	28.9	25.0-32.8

Habitat use

Each time a single or a pair of eagles were observed, we recorded its behaviour and the number of minutes that particular behaviour was observed. Flying low over forest canopy or sitting on a branch of a tree obviously looking for prey were recorded as hunting. However, because of long distances, most observations of sitting eagles were recorded as unknown. Therefore, most observations of hunting behaviour were of flying birds.

Within the study areas in Ternate and Sidangoli, hunting behaviour was recorded on 93 occasions. The total duration of the hunting observations was more than four hours. Hunting birds were mostly observed in primary forest although that habitat covered a minor part of the eagles' territories (Figs. 3 and 4). This indicates that the area of primary forest is of particular importance for Gurney's Eagles.

Figure 3. Hunting time in primary forest compared to habitat availability of Gurney's Eagles on Ternate island.

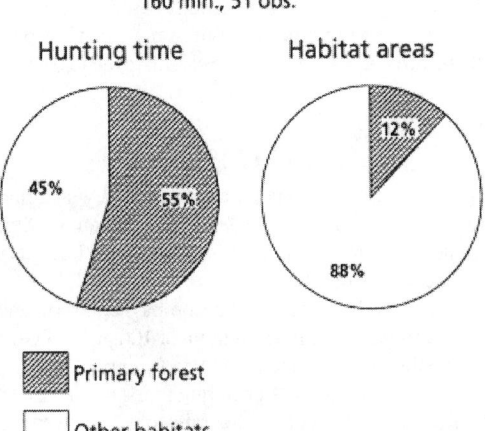

Figure 4. Hunting time in primary forest compared to habitat availability of Gurney's Eagles in Sidangoli study area.

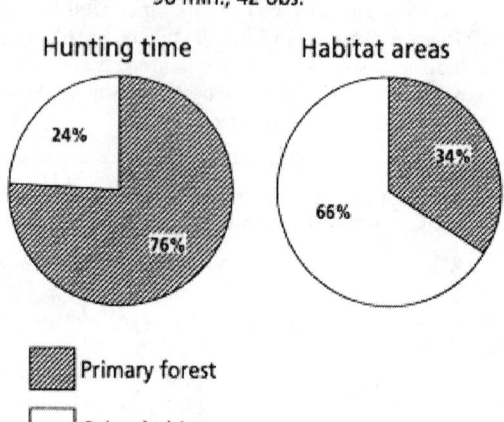

DISCUSSION

Both population density and territory size are within the ranges of what has been found in other studies of large *Aquila* eagles, e.g. Wedge-tailed Eagles *Aquila audax* (cf. Marchant & Higgins 1993) Golden Eagles *Aquila chrysaetos* (cf. Cramp & Simmons 1980) and Verreaux's Eagle *Aquila verreauxii* (cf. Gargett 1990).

Population status in the North Moluccas

Our results indicate an average density of approximately one pair of Gurney's Eagle per 30 km^2 of forested areas on Halmahera (satellite islands included). It is known that within the North Moluccas, Gurney's Eagles are also found on the islands of Morotai, Bacan and Obi, but not in the Sula islands (Coates & Bishop 1997, White & Bruce 1986). According to the available statistics, there are approximately 27,500 km^2 of forested areas available for the eagles in the North Moluccas (areas of Sula islands subtracted). On the assumption that the average density of Gurney's Eagles within these large areas is about the same as has been found in our study areas, there would be an approximate number of 900 pairs of Gurney's Eagles in the North Moluccas. We have not been able to evaluate the reliability of the assumption on which this estimate is based. The maps of forested areas, which form the basis of the statistics, seem to represent future management plans rather that reflect the present situation. It has therefore not been possible to calculate the exact area of primary forest in the North Moluccas.

CONCLUSIONS

Our results indicate that there is a viable population of Gurney's Eagles in the North Moluccas. Moreover, the species is found in the large forests that still remain on Seram and New Guinea. A reasonable conclusion would therefore be that at present Gurney's Eagle is not a threatened species, in contrast to what has been earlier suggested.

The proposed protected area in Halmahera will encompass approximately 350,000 ha. Based on our results, an area of that size might support a minimum of 100 pairs of Gurney's Eagle. In addition, large areas of forest will probably be protected as "Hutan Lindung" (special protected forests). One might therefore conclude that if a continuous area of rain forest of the size indicated above would be protected for the future, the total biodiversity of the rain-forest ecosystems in the North Moluccas will probably be safeguarded for future generations.

ACKNOWLEDGEMENTS

We are grateful to our Indonesian sponsor, the Ministry of State for Environment (LH) for fruitful co-operation and to the Indonesian Institute for Sciences (LIPI) for permission to carry out research in the Moluccas. We are furthermore grateful to BirdLife International Indonesia Programme for their support and valuable advice during our stay in Indonesia.

REFERENCES

APANDI & SUDANA 1980. Systematic Geological Map, Indonesia, Lembar: Ternate 2516/2517, scale 1:250 000.
BURTON, P. 1989. *Birds of Prey*.. Gallery Books, New York.
COATES, B.J. & K.D. BISHOP 1997. *A Guide to the Birds of Wallacea*. Dove Publications.
COLLAR, N.J., M.J. CROSBY & A.J. STATTERSFIELD 1994. *Birds to watch 2*. The World List of threatened Birds. BirLife Conservation Series No. 4.
CRAMP, S. & K.E.L. SIMMONS 1980. *Handbook of the birds of Europe, the Middle East and North Africa*. Vol. 2: Hawks to Bustards. Oxford Univ. Press, Oxford.
GARGETT, V. 1990. *The Black Eagle*. Acorn Books and Russel Friedman Books, South Africa.
DEL HOYO, J., A. ELLIOTT & J. SARGATAL (eds.) 1994. *Handbook of the Birds of the World*. Vol. 2. New World Vultures to Guineafowl. Lynx Edicions, Barcelona.
MARCHANT, S. & P.J. HIGGINS (eds.) 1993. *Handbook of Australian, New Zealand and Antarctic Birds*. Vol. 2: Raptors to Lapwings. Oxford Univ. Press, Melbourne.
MEYBURG, B.-U. 1986. Threatened and near-threatened diurnal birds of prey of the World. *Birds of Prey Bull.* 3: 1-12.
THIOLLAY, J. M. 1985. Falconiformes of tropical rain forest: a review. In: Newton, I. & Chancellor, R.D. (eds.). *Conservation studies of raptors*. Vol. 5. ICBP Tech. Publ., Cambridge, pp. 155-165.
WHITE, C.M.N. & M.D. BRUCE 1986. *The Birds of Wallacea*. B.O.C. Check-list No. 7. British Ornithologists' Union.

Nils Røv and Jan Ove Gjershaug
Norwegian Institute for Nature Research
Tungasletta 2
N-7005 Trondheim
Norway

Chancellor, R. D. & B.-U. Meyburg eds. 2000
Raptors at Risk
WWGBP / Hancock House

Recent Observations on Peregrine Falcons *Falco peregrinus* of the Cape Verde Islands, Atlantic Ocean

Clifford M. Anderson and Clayton M. White

ABSTRACT

Surveys were made in March and April of 1997 and 1998. In all, eight islands in the Cape Verde group were visited including Cima, the location of the first published breeding record in 1963. Anderson saw a total of ten individuals on three of the islands but none on Cima. The most recent summary by Hazevoet (1995) indicates definite sightings or specimen records for only six islands and suggests that the species is rare. Observations from 1997 and 1998 support the notion of its rarity.

INTRODUCTION

The Peregrine Falcon *Falco peregrinus* is one of the most widely distributed bird species and some 19 subspecies have been recognized (White & Boyce 1988). The majority of them (16) occur either continentally or within large island groups such as Madagascar (*F. p. radama*) or Indonesia (*F. p. ernesti*). Only 3 subspecies (*F p nesiotes, furuitii* and *madens*) are completely limited to small archipelagos (the Fijian, Volcano, and Cape Verde Islands respectively). The latter two are considered the rarest and most threatened races of Peregrines in the world (White 1994). From 16 March to 14 April 1997 and 18 March to 14 April 1998 Anderson (CMA) visited the Cape Verde Islands off western Africa to look for resident Peregrines to determine if Peregrines still existed on the islands, check the status of the only historically known nest site, and better document their breeding phenology

AN HISTORICAL PERSPECTIVE

The first literature record of Peregrines in the Cape Verde Islands was reported by Bocage (1902) He refers to a female taken at an unknown date and locality, but apparently not at a breeding site, on São Nicolau island in 1901 at 300 m elevation. This specimen was destroyed in 1978 during a fire in the Museu Bocage, Lisbon, Portugal, but had been previously examined and described by de Naurois (1970).

The next records were provided by the Yale University American *Blossom* expedition in 1923-1924 (Bannerman 1968). This expedition collected three more specimens; an adult female at Povação (now Vila Nova Sintra) on the island of Brava, an immature female also from Brava taken in February or March 1924, and an adult male on the island of Santiago near Pedra Badejo, 22 April 1924. Based on these three specimens Ripley and Watson (1963) described a new race of Peregrine *F. p. madens*. The trinomium *madens* means saturated, apparently in reference to the rufous suffusion to the plumage.

On 6 August 1951 Bourne (1955) observed what he concluded were Peregrines around cliffs at the highest point between Praia and Pedra Badejo. Then, in 1963, the first known Peregrine nest site was recorded (de Naurois 1969) when on 6 March a breeding pair was found on Cima in the Rombos islands. The eyrie, on cliffs at the south end of the island, contained a week old nestling and two infertile eggs.

de Naurois returned to Cima again, on 26 January 1965, and found falcons nesting on the same cliff, although on a different ledge. He found a single egg judged to have been laid between 14-26 January but later found three eggs indicating that onset of egg laying was 24-26 January. He also collected the adult female. de Naurois wrote that local fishermen had reported a second nesting pair on the north coast of Brava, near Furna, and presumed it to be the location where the *Blossom* falcons were collected.

By far the best and most complete summary of modern Peregrine sightings in the Cape Verde Islands is provided by Hazevoet (1995) who lists definite sightings (including collected specimens) from five islands: Santiago (7 sightings), Brava (2), Cima (4), Branco (1), and São Nicolau (1). He also includes tentative sightings from 4 other islands: Fogo (1), São Vicente (1), Santo Antão (?) and Boavista (1). The total number of definite sightings up to 1995, excluding specimens, was 11, and 15 including specimens. Addition of all tentative records raised the total to 19. Hazevoet (pers. comm.) had an additional record from near Praia since his publication, bringing to 20 the total sightings of Peregrines in the Cape Verde Islands.

RESULTS

Sightings

The five islands visited in the Cape Verde's in 1997 were: Sal (16-18 March, 14 April), Santiago (18-24 March, 9-14 April), Brava (25 March-5 April), Fogo (5-8 April), and Cima (31 March). In 1998 CMA visited three more islands: São Vicente (21-22 March), Santo Antão (23 March- 6 April), and São Nicolau (7-12 April). In 1997 CMA observed a minimum of ten individual Peregrines (Table 1) on three of the islands (Sal, Santiago, and Fogo). CMA saw no Peregrines on Cima or Brava, despite a 12 d visit. In 1998 no Peregrines were seen on the three islands surveyed.

Most (70%) of the Peregrines seen were adults and on the island of Santiago. One group of four involved a family of both adults and two young. CMA observed two other probable pairs of adults again on Santiago. On Fogo, an adult female occupied the crater south of Chã das Caldeiras and on Sal, a single immature approximately two miles north of Espargos represent range extensions for the species in the Cape Verdes, although Hazevoet states accurately that Peregrines probably occur in very small numbers on all islands and islets.

Breeding data

Historical Nesting Site.

CMA visited Cima 31 March 1997 (1100-1400 hrs). The island is long, low, and narrow with a basalt headland, *ca.* 400 m long and 30 m high, at the south end. The highest point of the island is some 77 m. Although some of the cliffs drop directly into the Atlantic, most are accessible from below. CMA was able to examine the entire, but fairly limited, cliff habitat either from above or below. Although CMA spent only 3 hrs on Cima he was confident that Peregrines were not nesting during the time of his visit. However, it is possible that Peregrines may now inhabit the more inaccessible islets of the Rombos group, primarily Ilhéu Luiz Carneiro to the west, although he was not able to survey either it or Ilhéu Grande or Sapado. These islands should be a high priority in future surveys.

Table 1. Peregrine Falcon sightings on the Cape Verde Islands, 1997.

DATE	ISLAND	COMMENT
17 March	Sal	Immature, male?
21 March	Santiago	Adult male
		Adult female
23 March	Santiago	New eyrie with
		Adult male
		Adult female
		Immature female
6 April	Fogo	Adult female
11 April	Santiago	On mountain peaks
		Adult male
		Adult female
13 April	Santiago	Same family group seen on 23 March (above)
		Adult male
		Adult female
		Immature male
		Immature (sex?)

Since de Naurois' visits in the 1960's, human visitation to Cima has increased substantially, primarily because of the availability of outboard motor boats. Residents told CMA that the best local fishing occurred in the shallow waters surrounding Cima and fishermen often camped there. He found evidence of campsites below most of the cliffs. In addition, a large concrete light station has been constructed at the top of the cliffs. Harvesting of seabirds for human consumption is still practiced and CMA observed it on Cima. There were thousands of petrel nesting burrows distributed throughout the sandy parts of the island. CMA thought that the absence of falcons was due to human interference although 12 old petrel kills (eaten in typical falcon fashion) suggested that one or more falcons still hunt on Cima.

New Nesting Site

On 23 March 1997 CMA found a new Peregrine nest on Santiago. That eyrie was located in a mountainous region near the centre of the island and at this writing it is the only known active site on Cape Verde. The eyrie is located on a high, precipitous, fin-shaped ridge, about 93 m high and completely inaccessible to humans as relatively loose basalt rock prevents safe climbing. The eyrie was situated at the end of a lava tube which formed a small cave opening to the SSW. The abundant faecal stains (whitewash) suggested that they had used at least two other ledges on this rock.

It seems significant that the site is high in elevation, commands an extraordinary view with good winds, is inaccessible, remote from humans and in one of the wettest areas on Cape Verde.

Breeding Phenology and Reproduction

It has not been established whether there is a distinct breeding season for Peregrines in the Cape Verde Islands. However, de Naurois (1969) confirmed that egg laying on Cima in 1965 ranged from 14-26 January. He determined a hatch date of approximately 28 February in 1963. These two dates are in synchrony for both years and suggest fledging dates (assuming a 34 d incubation, 42 d development period) of about 11 April.

Anderson used this chronology to time his visits. However, at the nest discovered on 23 March 1997, one young female had fledged and was flying strongly. Its fledging date was estimated to be about 15-17 March, suggesting egg laying and hatching dates of 29 December and 1 February respectively, approximately one month earlier than occurred on Cima in the 1960's.

Behavioural observations

Adults were present at the nesting site for at least 18-21 d. after the young fledged. On 4 April, sunset occurred at 1825 hrs. By 1905 hrs, darkness had set in. At 1918 hrs. the adult male flew to the cliff wailing; and "chup" vocalizations took place for 3 min. At 1925 hrs., well after dark, the male uttered "chupping" calls approximately 20 more times with the female answering. Vocalization continued until 1930 hrs.

On l0 April, dawn calls began at 0542 hrs. with the male "wailing" and female uttering "chups" over an 8 min period. Because it started at astronomical dawn the indication was that the pair had roosted at the eyrie cliff. Nothing was heard during the 3 hr period thereafter.

Description of immatures

On 13 April 1997 CMA observed the two fledglings repeatedly within 100 m as they perched on the radio tower near Pico da Antónia. Plumages of sexes were identical. The breasts were tan-cream with narrow, darker brown streaking extending from the upper breast into the undertail coverts. The tail had a broad creamy terminal band, typical of many other young Peregrines. A narrow tan forehead band was above the cere and their throats were clear cream-tan. Feet and tarsus were pale yellow. Dorsally, colouration was "typically" brown, similar to some North American *F.p. anatum*. There appeared to be reddish highlights in the nape. Auriculars were well defined, clear and creamy in colour. Malar stripes were distinct. Slight amounts of down remained on both the heads and tail tips. CMA was surprised at their similarity to the North American *anatum*. In his experience, had he trapped them on migration at South Padre Island, Texas, they would not be recognized as a separate race of Peregrine.

Notes on adult moult

On 12 April, the adult female at the eyrie had new central rectrices about 3 cm long. This indicated that her tail moult began near fledging of the young, not during egg laying as in many north temperate Peregrines.

Notes on prey

de Naurois (1969) reported "petrels and sparrows" as prey on Cima. Presumably these included the White-faced Storm Petrel *Pelagodroma marina* and the Cape Verde Little Shearwater *Puffinus boydi*. He identified the sparrow as Iago Sparrow *Passer iagoensis*. CMA observed the adult female on Fogo unsuccessfully attacking a group of Spanish Sparrows *Passer hispaniolensis*. At the Santiago eyrie CMA found prey remains of several Rock Dove *Columba livia* and a Grey-headed Kingfisher *Halcyon leucocephala*.

CONCLUSIONS AND DISCUSSION

New information on a little known population

Overall there had been a lack of published information on the Peregrines of the Cape Verde Islands, even following their diagnosis and naming as a distinct subspecies. While several of the observations or collection dates suggested that the individuals might have been near or at breeding sites, only one nesting location with two different sites was known. CMA confirmed breeding at an additional location on a separate island. Projected dates of the egg laying fell within the general timing of earlier known breeding dates suggesting there was a distinct "breeding season" and that egg laying may start as early as late December and as late as late January.

Moult (based on the single female) may differ slightly from other Northen Hemisphere populations. It seemed not to start in the female during incubation but rather after young had fledged. If this is the case, implications as to what drives the moult would be interesting to investigate.

Estimates of population size of Cape Verde Peregrines

Population size or density on islands is of particular importance in understanding conservation. Usually small island populations have limited genetic heterozygosity and consequently may be prone to extinction. Further, in the case of the Cape Verde Islands it is not known if all islands have suitable conditions for Peregrines or how far the falcon might wander to find such conditions, e.g., from island to island. Few authors have attempted to address the difficult issue of determining the size of the Cape Verde Peregrine Falcon population. Estimates vary widely, because of the limited knowledge of this species on the islands. Most of the projected numbers are relatively low although most values given for falcons, in general, tend to underestimate their populations.

The least reliable numbers for the Cape Verde's are those on the low end of estimates. They are based on second hand information. King (1981) relied heavily on the fact that falcons had been reported from few islands and from discussions with R. de Naurois (pers. comm.). King suggested no more than 6 pairs. White (1994) used similar sources to arrive at the value of 6-8 pairs and when White discussed the matter with de Naurois in 1990 (pers. comm.) a higher value seemed warranted. Interestingly de Naurois earlier (1969) was more optimistic and suggested a total population of 30-50 individuals but fewer than 10 pairs for the archipelago. Lastly, Hazevoet (1995) used recent information and literature sources to arrive at a population of perhaps less than 20 birds.

Finally, current studies on the Common Kestrel *Falco tinnunculus* by S.M. Hille (this volume) and on the Osprey *Pandion haliaetus* by J. Ferreira and L Palma (this volume) on the Cape Verde Islands shed some light on Peregrine densities. Researchers on both studies have spent considerable time in the field in Peregrine habitat, especially so for the coastal studies on Ospreys, and they have failed to see Peregrines. Our studies, taken together with all the other information, support the notion that the Peregrine Falcon in the Cape Verde Islands is a rare bird.

ACKNOWLEDGMENTS

I thank the following individuals for their help and assistance with this study; Cornelius Hazevoet, Sabine Hille, Bill Clark, Dana Baer and his family (Andre, Emily, and Andrew), Peter Swavely of the U S Embassy in Praia, Tom Gardiner of the ACDI, Jose Levy, Maria Teresa Veracruz and João Mendes of Inida, the U.S. Peace Corps in Praia, including Susan Prising and Rebecca Figgins in Brava. I thank Dick and Bonnie Robbins, Pat Hitchens and Dan Brimm for providing financial support for this study.

REFERENCES

BANNERMAN, D.A. & W. M. BANNERMAN 1968. History of the Birds of the Verde Islands, *in*: *Birds of the Atlantic Islands*, Vol 4. Oliver and Boyd, Edinburgh. 458pp.
BOCAGE, J.V. BARBOSA DU. 1902. Aves e Reptis de Cabo Verde. *Journ. Sci. Math. Phys. Nat. (Lisbon)* 6:206-210.
BOURNE, W.R.P. 1955. The birds of the Cape Verde Islands. *Ibis* 97:508-556
HAZEVOET, C.J. 1995. *The birds of the Cape Verde Islands, an annotated checklist*. British Ornithologists' Union Checklist No. 13. Nat. Hist. Museum, Tring. 192 pp
HICKEY, J.J. 1969. *Peregrine Falcon populations; their biology and decline*. Univ. Wisconsin Press, Madison. 596 pp
KING, W. B. 1981. *Endangered birds of the world*. The ICBP bird red data book. Smithsonian Press, Wash. D.C.
NAUROIS, R. DE. 1969. La population de Faucons Pèlerins *(Falco peregrinus madens* Ripley et Watson) de L'archipel du Cap-Vert: Effectifs, écologie et signifcation zoogéographique. *Alauda* 37:301-14.
NAUROIS, R.DE. 1970. Le plus ancien specimen de Faucon Pèlerin *(Falco peregrinus* L.) obtenu dans L'archpiel du Cap Vert. *Arq. Mus. Bocage* (2) 11:33-37.
RIPLEY, S.D. & G. E. WATSON 1963. A new Peregrine Falcon from the Cape Verde Islands, eastern Atlantic Ocean. *Postilla* 77:1-4.
WHITE, C. M. 1994. Falconidae, 00. 249-279 *in*: *Handbook of the birds of the world*. J. del Hoyo, A. Elliott & J. Sargatal (eds.). Vol 2. New World Vultures to Guineafowl. Lynx Edicions, Barcelona.
WHITE, C. M. & D.A. BOYCE, Jr. 1988. An overview of Peregrine Falcon subspecies, pp. 789-810 *in*: T.J. Cade, J.H. Enderson, C.G. Thelander & C.M. White (eds.), *Peregrine Falcon populations: their management and recovery*, The Peregrine Fund, Boise, Idaho.

Clifford M. Anderson
Falcon Research Group
Box 248, Bow
WA 98232
U.S.A.

Clayton M. White
Department of Zoology
Brigham Young University
Provo, UT 84602
U.S.A.

The Status of the Christmas Island Hawk-Owl *Ninox natalis*

F.A. Richard Hill

ABSTRACT

Island birds are particularly vulnerable to extinction. The Christmas Island Hawk-Owl *Ninox natalis* is a small, forest-dwelling owl restricted to Christmas Island in the Indian Ocean. The island is small (13,500 ha) of which 75% remains naturally forested. Approximately 1,000 adult owls occupy territories in primary forest across the island with a small number of adults living in second growth vegetation. The owl is considered Vulnerable due to its small population size and particularly because it occurs as a single population on a remote oceanic island. Settlement of the island and anthropogenic factors appear to be the main threats to the owl population. Forest clearance has reduced the total population size by *ca.* 25%. Numerous exotic plants and animals have arrived and the risk of introduction of new diseases has markedly increased since settlement. Global climate change may alter the frequency of cyclones on the island, and increase environmental variability. Although most of the original forest is now protected in national park, significant areas remain without legislative protection. Greater economic independence is one of the most important goals for the island community and is inextricably linked to the future of conservation efforts on the island.

INTRODUCTION

Island birds are particularly vulnerable to extinction (King 1985). Sixteen species of birds have become extinct in historical times and of these ten were island birds (Collar *et al.* 1994). Island birds often have a small total population size and small populations are, in general, more vulnerable to extinction than large populations (Shaffer 1981; Soulé 1987). A small, declining population is one of the key criteria for recognising a taxon as being threatened (Collar *et al.* 1994). Island birds have often evolved in the absence of predators and disease, making them particularly vulnerable to the introduction of exotic biota (Caughley & Gunn 1996). Island birds also tend to show high rates of endemism, so a loss of a single population can mean the extinction of an entire taxon (King 1985). A single population is particularly vulnerable to extinction because there is no chance of recolonisation by neighbouring populations if it becomes extinct (King 1985). Island birds all over the world have suffered as a result of direct human activity such as hunting and habitat destruction. For example, in the Pacific, including New Zealand, at least 151 species and subspecies of birds are known to have become extinct since the late Holocene (Milberg & Tyrberg 1993) and the number could be much larger. Humans probably hunted some species to extinction, as did their pigs, domestic dogs, and Polynesian Rats *Rattus exulans*, and others may have been affected by introduced diseases (Warner 1968; Diamond 1985; Caughley & Gunn 1996).

Christmas Island is in the Indian Ocean (10°25'S, 105°40'E) approximately 1,400 km northwest of Australia, and is 360 km south of Java in the Republic of Indonesia. It is an external territory of Australia. The island is 135km^2 in area, of which 75% is covered with original vegetation. Most of the natural vegetation, and 63% of the island, is protected within the Christmas Island National Park (ANCA 1994). Christmas Island is oceanic and all its flora and fauna have arrived from neighbouring areas by sea or air (Gray & Clark 1995).

Christmas Island's avifauna is highly endemic, with at least nine endemic taxa out of a total of 18 resident taxa (excluding introduced species). No bird species on Christmas Island has become extinct since settlement. Although four of the taxa are considered to be threatened due to small population size and forest clearance, only one, Abbott's Booby, is considered endangered (Garnett 1993).

Unusually for a remote oceanic island, Christmas Island had three endemic mammals. MacLear's Rat *R. macleari* was very large (total length *ca.* 50cm), very common at the time of settlement, nocturnal and a proficient climber, and the similar-sized Burrowing Rat *R. nativitatis* both appeared to be extinct within 10 years of human settlement (Andrews 1909). A shrew *Crocidura fuliginosa trichura* was also very common at the time of settlement (Andrews 1909) and is now very rare (ANCA 1994). A number of vertebrates have been introduced to Christmas Island, including the Black Rat *R. rattus,* a species which occurs throughout the island and is semi-arboreal, the Domestic Cat *Felis catus*, Tree Sparrows *Passer montanus,* and Java Sparrows *Lonchura oryzivora* (ANCA 1994).

HISTORY

The Christmas Island Hawk-Owl *Ninox natalis* (Norman *et al.* 1998) is a small (*ca.* 180 g), nocturnal raptor restricted to Christmas Island. The population size of the owl is assumed to have declined with forest clearance (Stokes 1988; Olsen & Stokes 1989). Van Tets (1975) suggested that the total population size was in the order of 10-100 pairs and Stokes (1988) thought the upper limit of this estimate might be more accurate. The Christmas Island Hawk-Owl is currently listed as Vulnerable (Schedule 1; Endangered Species Protection Act 1992). During 1994-96 Christmas Island Hawk-Owls were widespread across the island in all largely undisturbed habitats but also used secondary vegetation and the vegetation in the suburbs of the single township and Hill & Lill (1998) estimated the total population size to be 562 ± 105 territories comprising at least one adult owl. Owls occurred in largely undisturbed or primary forests at densities similar to those of the few other published studies of similar-sized rainforest owls (eg. Gerhardt *et al.* 1994), but were much less common in secondary vegetation and suburban areas (Hill & Lill 1998).

The total population size of Christmas Island Hawk-Owls has undoubtedly declined since settlement of the island occurred and clearance of primary forests commenced. By 1987, when clearing of primary forest ceased, 25% of the island had been cleared (ANCA 1994). Hill & Lill (1998) showed that density was relatively uniform at all census sites in primary forest, and the total owl population at the time of settlement was estimated from the original area of primary forest. If densities found in primary forest in 1995/96 are not significantly different from those at the time of settlement, then the population at that time was between 640 and 840 occupied territories (95% confidence limits). The impact of forest clearance has probably been slightly offset by the areas of secondary vegetation growing along roadsides and on old mine stockpiles which are occupied by owls, but at much lower densities (Hill & Lill 1998). Thus the total population size may have decreased by slightly less than 25% since settlement and this decrease is probably primarily due to loss of habitat. Such a decline has probably increased the risk of extinction.

Christmas Island Hawk-Owls appear, so far, to have been unaffected by the introduction of Black Rats and domestic cats. Both species arrived on the island in the early 1900's (Andrews 1909) and are now widespread and common (ANCA 1994; Tidemann *et al.* 1994). Christmas Island's avifauna must have coexisted with its endemic rats for many generations, to some extent pre-adapting it to introduced predators. Only birds which could coexist with these species, at least one of which was was a proficient climber (Maclear's Rat, Andrews 1900), would have been able to persist. Owls sometimes roost close to the ground and may occasionally be at risk of being caught by cats. Cat densities in primary forest are currently low (Tidemann et al. 1994; G. Van Der Lees 1995. pers.comm.). However, if cat densities increase significantly there may be cause for concern. The Galapagos Islands also had a number of endemic rodents and the introduction of the Black Rat there appears not to have had a significant impact on its avifauna (Atkinson 1985). The presence of partly-arboreal crabs on Christmas Island may also have selected for anti-predator behaviours in the endemic avifauna.

Island birds have often evolved in the absence of diseases that are common in continental bird faunas and the introduction of such diseases to island bird populations can be disastrous. For example, the introduction of avian malaria to Hawaii in 1826 is implicated in the extinction of almost the entire endemic bird fauna below 600m in altitude, and was probably the main cause of such extinctions (Warner 1968). The range of many surviving species was also severely reduced and fragmented, which in turn markedly increased their probabilities of extinction. Once established, a 'new' disease may persist on an island in introduced populations of continental bird species which have resistance to the disease. For example, the Black Francolin *Francolinus francolinus*, introduced to Guam, may have provided a reservoir of disease-carrying hosts accentuating the impact of disease on the island's endemic birds (Savidge 1984). Thus it is not only important to maintain strict quarantine controls to minimise the risk of introduction of new bird diseases, but it is probably also undesirable to have wild populations of feral birds on Christmas Island such as Eurasian Tree Sparrows and Java Sparrows. A quarantine barrier between the island, Indonesia and Australia has only been in place since 1994 and the benefits of this barrier for wildlife conservation on the island are recognised (ANCA 1994; Hill 1988).

PRESENT STATUS AND THREATS

The Christmas Island Hawk-Owl is endemic to Christmas Island; no other population of this species exists, so there is no potential for recolonisation if this species becomes extinct. The island is small, of which 75% is primary forest, and it seems unlikely that any population of the owl is isolated from any other. Thus in assessing the species' population viability, it would seem reasonable to consider it a single, small, completely isolated population. Of the 75% of primary forest, 84% is protected within national park (ANCA 1994). The 12% of primary forest outside the national park is to some extent protected from clearing by legislation; however, some of it may eventually be cleared. Modelling the effect of clearance of this unprotected forest on the population using Population Viability Analysis suggested that the rate of increase of the smaller population would be reduced, and that the likelihood of survival of the population over 100 years would be reduced (Hill 1998).

A number of other threats to the Christmas Island Hawk-Owl have been suggested. All four nests recorded for this species have been in hollows in Gowok *Syzygium nervosum* and all nest sites are likely to be in tree hollows (Hill & Young 1995). Gowok is a common emergent tree, particularly in plateau forests, where it forms approximately 18% of the forest canopy and constitutes 30% of the emergent species (ABRS 1993). It is commonly greater than 35m high and has abundant hollows, unlike most other tree species in plateau forest (author, pers obs). Gowok may, therefore, be a very important tree species for Christmas Island Hawk-Owls. Most Gowok on the island are large, old trees and there are few seedlings due to their predation by Red Crabs *Gercacoidia natalis*, an endemic land crab (P. Green, CSIRO, Atherton, pers. comm.). Thus the recruitment of large Gowok is currently limited. If Gowok is a major source of nest sites for Christmas Island Hawk-Owls, nest sites may eventually be in short supply. Terrace forest appears to have more species of trees with hollows than plateau forest (author, pers. obs) and may have more potential nest sites for the owls. Further nest tree data may show that owls can nest in a number of tree species.

Garnett (1992) suggested that road-kill by vehicles might be a threat to Christmas Island Hawk-Owls; however, from data collected between 1994 and 1996, this appears unlikely. In 2.5 years on

Christmas Island eight Hawk-Owls were found dead on the road, presumably killed by cars (author, unpubl.data), and the number killed on the road is probably not much greater than this. Although these road-killed birds could not be aged conclusively, it seems unlikely, even if all of them were adults, that this level of mortality would have a significant impact on population viability. It is conceivable that road kills may limit population density in the settled areas of the island where traffic volumes are high and owl densities low (Hill & Lill 1998). There are suggestions that the human population, and therefore the number of cars on the island, will increase markedly in the future. If this eventuates, collisions with cars might become an issue in the conservation of owl populations in settled areas.

A secure economic future for the island is essential to ensure continued support for the high standard of environmental management the island requires. Christmas Island is very remote and has a small human population. These factors conspire to make economic activity on the island uncertain. Maintaining services to the human community equivalent to Australian mainland standards is very expensive and governments are anxious for the community to be as self-supporting as possible. This environment can encourage uncritical enthusiasm for proposed development which might bring investment to the island. It was very encouraging to see the Australian government recently resist pressure to fast-track a proposed space launch facility on Christmas Island and instead to require a full environmental effects study. Such a development *may* help safeguard both the economic and environmental well-being of the island if the proposal is carefully assessed.

CONCLUSION

In summary the Christmas Island Hawk-Owl is vulnerable to extinction for a number of reasons: it has a small population size which has been reduced by habitat clearance and is restricted to one oceanic island with no opportunity for recolonisation. It has probably been isolated for a long time and is likely to be immunologically 'naïve' to avian diseases common in nearby continental avifaunas. Unusually for oceanic island fauna, it appears to some extent to be pre-adapted to cope with terrestrial predators, probably because it has coexisted with endemic arboreal rats and land crabs*. Currently it is only known to nest in one species of tree, which itself may be declining in abundance. Finally the island's economic vulnerability also increases the risk of extinction for the Hawk-Owl along with all its endemic biota.

The following recommendations were made to the wildlife management agency on Christmas Island for the long term conservation of wild populations of Christmas Island Hawk-Owls:

- To monitor the Christmas Island Hawk-Owl population every five years to detect any significant change in the distribution or abundance of the species. The recommended monitoring programme can detect changes in total population size of more that 20%.
- To maintain ongoing negotiations with all landowners to ensure protection of primary forests outside the national park
- To maintain [and regularly review] a quarantine barrier between Christmas Island and all other land masses minimising the risk of 'new' avian diseases becoming established on Christmas Island.
- To establish a community education programme to raise awareness and interest in the conservation of Christmas Island Hawk-Owls.
- To investigate options for control/removal of feral populations of Eurasian Tree Sparrows and Java Sparrows.

---

* Footnote: In December 1998 'supercolonies' of an exotic invasive ant *Anoplolepis gracilipes* were reported for the first time on Christmas Island (P. Green, CSIRO, Atherton, Australia), although the ant had been recorded on the island for many years. This 'Crazy Ant' forages in all strata of the forest and supercolonies of it may prevent successful breeding by most or all of the avifauna of Christmas Island (C. Beare, WildWings Bird Management, Surrey, UK, pers.comm.). An Action Plan for the control of Crazy Ants is currently being implemented by the Australian Government.

REFERENCES

ABRS. 1993. Flora of Australia, Volume 50. Oceanic Islands 2. Australian Biological Resource Study, Canberra.
ANCA 1994. Christmas Island National Park Plan of Management. Australian Nature Conservation Agency, Commonwealth of Australia.
ANDREWS, C.W. 1900. *A Monograph of Christmas Island.* London, British Museum of Natural History.
ANDREWS, C.W. 1909. On the Fauna of Christmas Island. *Proceedings Zoological Society of London*: 101-103.
ATKINSON, I.A.E. 1985. The spread of commensal species of *Rattus* to oceanic islands and their effects on island avifaunas. *In Conservation of Island Birds* (ed.) P.J. Moors, ICBP/Technical Publication No 3:79-96.
CAUGHLEY, G. & A. GUNN 1996. *Conservation Biology in theory and practice.* Blackwell Science, Inc. USA.
COLLAR, N.J., M.J. CROSBY & A.J. STATTERSFIELD 1994. *Birds to Watch 2.* The World List of Threatened Birds. Birdlife Conservation Series No. 4. Birdlife International, United Kingdom.
DIAMOND, J.M. 1985. Population processes in island birds: immigration, extinction and fluctuations. *In* P.J. Moors (ed.) *Conservation of Island Birds.* ICBP/Technical Publication No 3: 214-231
GARNETT, S. 1992. *The Action Plan for Australian Birds.* Australian National Parks and Wildlife Service, Canberra.
GRAY, H.S. & R. CLARK 1995. *Christmas Island Naturally.* 2nd Edition. Christmas Island Natural History Association.
HILL, F.A.R. & A. LILL, 1998. Density and Total Population Estimates for the Threatened Christmas Island Hawk-Owl *Ninox natalis*. *Emu* 98: 209-220.
HILL, F.A.R. 1998. The Conservation Biology of the Christmas Island Hawk-Owl *Ninox natalis*. Unpublished MSc thesis, Monash University, Melbourne, Australia.
KING, W.B. 1985. Island birds: will the future repeat the past? *In Conservation of Island Birds*. ICBP, Technical Publication No 3: 276-295.
MILBERG, P. & T. TYRBERG, 1993. Naïve birds and noble savages-a review of man- caused prehistoric extinctions of island birds. *Ecography* 16: 229-250.
NORMAN, J. A., L. CHRISTIDIS, M. WESTERMAN & F.A.R. HILL, 1998. Molecular data confirm the species status of the Christmas Island Hawk-Owl *Ninox natalis*. *Emu* 98: 197-206.
OLSEN, P.D. & T. STOKES, 1989. State of knowledge of the Christmas Island Hawk- Owl *Ninox squamipila natalis*. *In* B.U. Meyburg & R.D. Chancellor (eds) *Raptors in the Modern World.*, WWGBP, Berlin:411-414.
SAVIDGE, J.A. 1984. Guam: paradise lost for wildlife. *Biological Conservation* 30: 305-317.
SHAFFER, M.L. 1981. Minimum population sizes for species in conservation. *Bioscience* 31: 131-143.
SOULÉ, M.E. 1987(Ed). *Viable Populations for Conservation.* Cambridge University Press, Cambridge.
STOKES, T. 1988. *A review of the birds of Christmas Island, Indian Ocean.* Australian National Parks and Wildlife Service, Occasional Paper No. 16.
TIDEMANN, C., H.D. YORKSTON, & A.J. RASSACK, 1994. The diet of cats, *Felis catus*, on Christmas Island, Indian Ocean. *Wildlife Research* 21: 279-286.
VAN TETS, G.F. 1975. *A report on the conservation of resident birds on Christmas Island.* ICBP Bulletin XII.
WARNER, R.E. 1968. The role of introduced diseases in the extinction of endemic Hawaiian avifauna. *Condor* 70: 101-120.

F.A. Richard Hill
Birds Australia
415 Riversdale Rd
East Hawthorn
Australia. 3123

Chancellor, R. D. & B.-U. Meyburg eds. 2000
Raptors at Risk
WWGBP / Hancock House

Dispersion in the Seychelles Kestrel *Falco araea*

Jeff Watson

ABSTRACT

A study of Seychelles Kestrel dispersion behaviour was carried out in a 1270 ha area on Mahé in 1975/76, with a re-survey of part of the area in 1998. Nest sites were over-dispersed with nearest-neighbour-distances typically around 450m. Some 34 pairs nested within the study area which was mainly dense secondary forest. The kestrels occupied year-round territories that were actively defended along boundaries between pairs, and territorial defence was most frequent in March-June, immediately after the breeding season. Disputes typically involved prolonged bouts of vocalisation with birds perched in trees or on small rock faces. Territory size varied from 33.5-46.5 ha (mean 40.3 ha) and smaller territories contained proportionately more 'structured' forest and less 'open' habitat. Occupancy of the territory was advertised by characteristic display flights that occurred most frequently in May-July, prior to the breeding season. The same study area was re-surveyed in February 1998 and occupancy was checked in 22 of the original territories. Mated pairs or adult birds with recently fledged young were detected in 20 of these territories confirming the expected long-term stability in the pattern of dispersion in this tropical island raptor living in a forest environment.

INTRODUCTION

The Seychelles Kestrel is endemic to the remote Indian Ocean archipelago of Seychelles (Fig. 1) where it is the only breeding diurnal raptor (Penny 1974). Early accounts of the Seychelles avifauna described the native landbirds and recorded their distribution throughout the islands (Newton 1867, Oustalet 1878). Gaymer *et al.* (1969) stated that the kestrel was 'territorial, with only one pair in most plateau areas'. Subsequently, Feare *et al.* (1974) used colour-ringed birds to estimate home range size for five pairs of kestrels and used these data to estimate population size on the 145 km^2 island of Mahé. My work on the species involved intensive research on population ecology, food and conservation during 1975-77 (Watson 1981) with additional data gathered during subsequent visits, including a fairly comprehensive re-survey of dispersion in part of the 1975 study area during February 1998.

With a body weight of 70-80g the Seychelles Kestrel is the smallest member of the genus *Falco*. Adult males and females are indistinguishable by plumage, with both sexes having grey heads, rich chestnut backs and wing-coverts, and black and grey banded tails, all of which are among typically male characteristics of kestrel species in which sexual plumage dimorphism occurs (Village 1990).

Seychelles Kestrels have a distinct breeding season with egg-laying in September/October and the young leave the nest in November/December (Watson 1992). Food is predominantly lizards with arboreal green geckos (*Phelsuma*) captured from branches and trunks of trees, and ground-living skinks (*Mabuya*) that are typically taken on, or close to the ground (Watson 1981).

Past and current distribution of the kestrel is reviewed in Collar & Stuart (1985). Nowadays the main population (c. 370 pairs) is on Mahé with another 35-40 pairs on Silhouette (Fig. 1). Small numbers occur on most of the satellite islands off Mahé (including Conception where presence was confirmed in 1998), and on the island of Praslin to which birds were reintroduced in 1977 (Watson 1989). Kestrel habitat on Mahé comprises variously dense and more open secondary woodland in the mountains, and a range of lowland habitats including coconut plantation, gardens and mixed-woodland as well as agricultural crops and urban areas.

Figure 1 Map of the granitic Seychelles showing the location of the kestrel study area on Mahé.

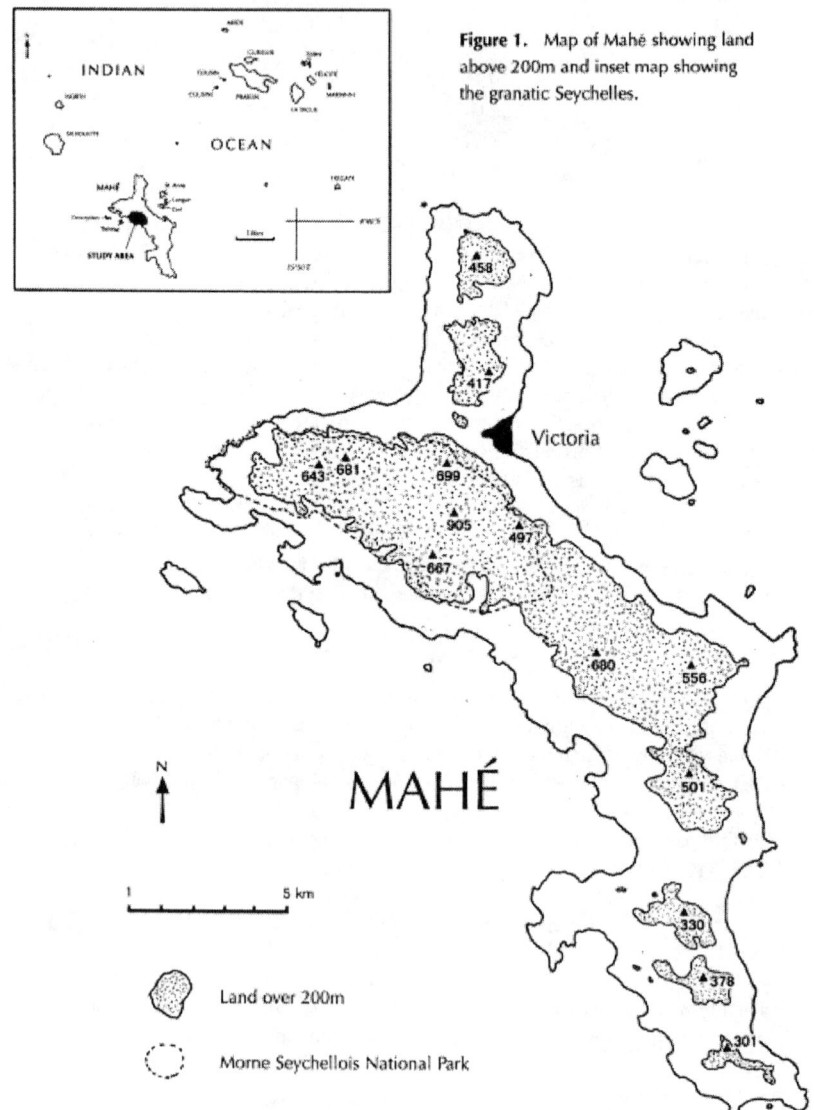

Figure 1. Map of Mahé showing land above 200m and inset map showing the granatic Seychelles.

This paper describes dispersion behaviour and documents the pattern of dispersion in the Seychelles Kestrel. It also reports on kestrel distribution in an area of Mahé in 1998, some 23 years after the same area was first surveyed in 1975.

STUDY AREA AND METHODS

Study Area

An area of 1270 ha in north-west Mahé (Fig. 1) was used for work on dispersion. This included a range of altitudes from the summit ridge around 500 m to sea level. Around 50% of Mahé lies above and below the 200 m contour and proportions within the study area were broadly similar to this. The main vegetation communities of Seychelles are described in Vesey-Fitzgerald (1940), Sauer (1967) and Procter (1984).

Within the study area, four broad habitat types were recognised. In upland areas, above the 200 m contour, *mixed upland forest* was predominant. This is a structurally diverse habitat with a canopy height of 12-15 m. In the highest altitude areas the dominant tree species are the endemic *Northia seychellarum* and *Dillenia ferruginia* but more typically this habitat type comprises secondary woodland dominated by exotic species such as the acacia-like *Albizia falcata* and the shrub *Cinnamon zeylanicum*. The second and more restricted upland habitat of *open scrub woodland* is structurally more simple with a typical maximum height of 5m or less. It is often associated with bare-rock areas, known locally as *glacis* where the dominant species are *Memecylon elaegni* and *Randia* spp., but also includes the structurally comparable tea plantations that were quite widespread in the study area.

Below the 200 m contour much of the land is covered by *mixed coconut plantation and lowland forest* habitat which is structurally varied and typically reaches a height of 15 m or more. Here coconut palms *Cocos nucifer* are associated with trees such as *Calophyllum inophyllum*, *Terminalia catappa* and *Artocarpus* spp. and a wide range of exotic shrubs. Finally, *open lowland habitat* occurs below 200 m and is characterised by structural simplicity. This includes monoculture coconut plantations with a canopy height of 5-20 m depending on age, as well as areas holding a range of other agricultural crops.

Individually Marked Birds

To provide information on home range use, kestrels were individually colour-ringed. Adult birds were trapped at a range of sites using a bal-chatri (Berger & Mueller 1975) containing a Madagascar Fody (*Foudia madagascariensis*) during the period January - June. During the subsequent breeding season (September - November) a selection of nestlings or dependent young were also marked with colour rings. Sightings of marked adults were recorded over a 12 month period from March on a systematic basis. At least twice each month, all localities where marked adults occurred were searched, with the aid of tape recordings in especially dense forest. Once located, colour-ringed birds were observed for around one hour. The bird's position and subsequent movements were recorded and sightings were transferred to a map with an overlying 1 ha grid. Movements of dependent young were recorded in a similar way from the time they fledged in November/December until they began to disperse in February.

Territorial Boundary Disputes

Boundary disputes between Seychelles Kestrels are characterised by intense and prolonged vocal activity. Individuals in dispute perch conspicuously in the upper layers of the vegetation and all birds present give vent to a loud *keez* call (Willoughby & Cade 1964), repeated at a rate of two notes per second for 20 seconds or so. In prolonged conflicts the interaction sometimes intensifies with birds displacing one another from their prominent perches, and in its most extreme form this displacing behaviour can involve actual contact. During work on home ranges and other fieldwork activity, all territorial disputes were noted and their locations plotted on maps.

Display Flights

Aerial display in the Seychelles Kestrel is distinctive and can be exhibited by either member of a mated pair. Typically a bird takes to the air and, with a series of flaps and glides, circles up to a height of 50-100 m when calling begins. The call comprises an erratic series of truncated notes, each followed by a distinct but variable pause. A bird may continue circling for as long as 20 minutes, calling intermittently. Based on evidence from territorial disputes, this circling behaviour generally occurred close to territorial boundaries. After circling a bird may descend directly to a prominent perch or may enter a straight, level or slightly descending flight with erratic, forced wing-beats and during the course of the flight it typically gives the truncated call note. These straight flights can cover up to 800 m before the bird perches, or alternatively enters a second bout of ascending, circling flight before finally dropping to a perch. As with boundary disputes, records were kept of the frequency of occurrence of display flights and the location of these was recorded on maps.

Nest Sites and Spacing Analysis

Nest sites were located as described in Watson (1992). Within the study area, most nest sites were in cliffs with smaller numbers in holes in trees and in the crowns of coconut palms. The distribution of sites was plotted on maps and spacing of nest sites was assessed using an analysis of nearest-neighbour-distance. To test for regular nest spacing, the G-statistic (GMASD) was used as recommended by Brown (1975). Values of GMASD range from 0 to 1. Larger values indicate greater regularity of spacing and values less than 0.65 indicate that nest sites are randomly spaced (Nilsson et al. 1982).

Re-survey in 1998

During a 10-day period in February 1998 I re-surveyed a substantial part of the kestrel study area in north-west Mahé. In the time available I was able to visit 22 of the original 34 territories, spending a minimum of 3 hours close to the location of the 1975 nest site, sometimes spread over 2 or 3 visits.

RESULTS

Home Range

Individually marked adults and/or dependent young were present among 25 of the 34 pairs of kestrels that nested in the study area in 1975. All 1 ha squares from which marked birds were recorded are shown in Fig. 2. Data for the 12-month period from March 1975 have been pooled. Evidence from sites N and U, where the largest number of records were obtained, indicated no significant difference in the pattern of range use between the non-breeding period (March-August) and the breeding period (September-February. Results for adult males and females (separated on size difference, Watson 1981) have been pooled since no significant difference occurred in the number of 1 ha squares visited by males ($x = 17.43 \pm sd\ 4.65$, n=7) compared with females ($x = 18.20 \pm sd\ 5.77$, n = 15). For ranges where both marked adults and young were present, all records of adults are shown in Fig. 2 and records of young are shown only for squares where no sightings of marked adults occurred.

Territorial Boundary Disputes

Most data on boundary disputes refer to the 14-month period from January 1975, with some further records from the second half of 1976. A dispute frequency index was calculated based on the amount of time spent by me on fieldwork during each month (Fig. 4). Although some disputes occurred in all months of the year, there was a clear peak in frequency between March and June and dispute frequency was low from September - February (the main breeding period). No data were available for April/May 1976 but otherwise the pattern was similar to 1975. Altogether 107 boundary conflicts were recorded at 64 localities in the study area during the 12-months from March 1975 (the period when home range use was recorded). Disputes are shown on Fig. 3 and each point may refer to more than one conflict as these have been plotted separately only where they occurred more than 100 m from another recorded conflict. Comparison between Figs. 2 and 3 reveals that, where the edges of ranges were known from movements of marked birds, the location of dispute points closely coincided with range boundaries.

Figure 2 Recorded ranges of colour-ringed Seychelles kestrels within the study area on Mahé. Upper-case letters refer to sightings of colour-ringed adult birds and lower-case to dependent young. All records denote occurrence within 1-ha squares.

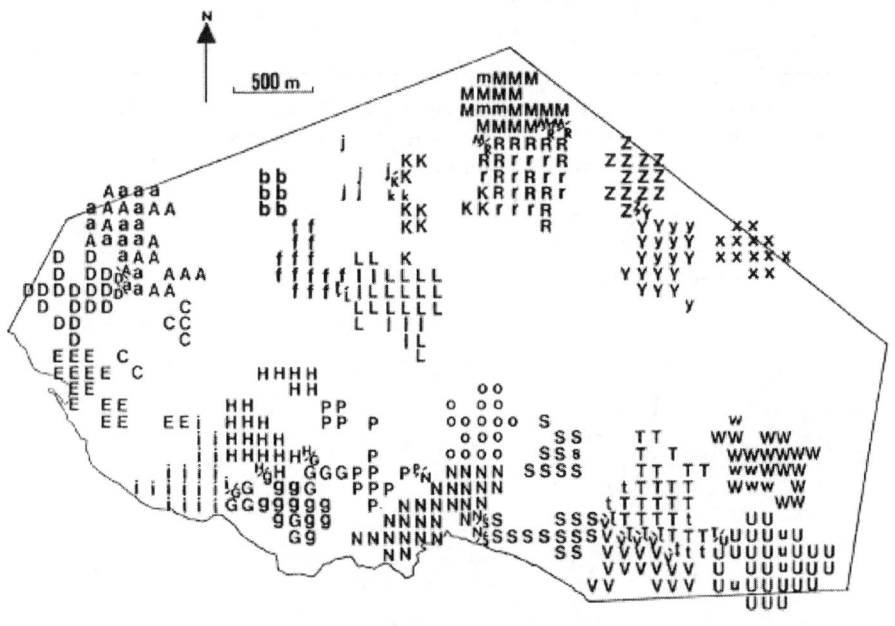

Figure 3. Territorial boundaries of Seychelles kestrels in the Mahé study area. Locations of nest sites (•), dispute points (▲), and display flights (---) are shown. Boundaries were drawn using this information and the range data in Fig. 2. See text for explanation of solid and hatched lines.

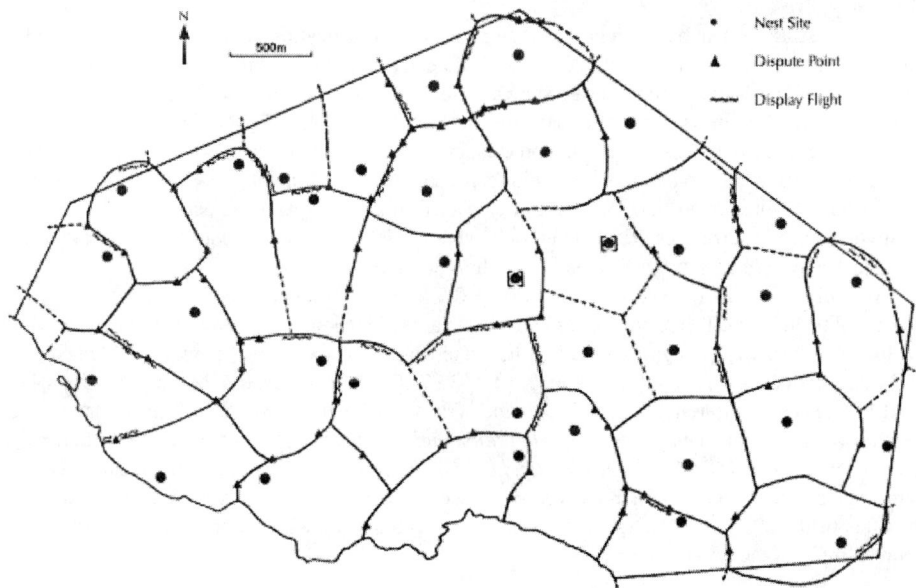

Display Flights

The frequency of display flights was highest in July/August 1975 and this pattern was repeated at the same time in 1976 (Fig. 4); in both years this was immediately prior to the onset of breeding. The locations of display flights that were recorded during the 12-month period from March 1975 are shown in Fig. 3.

Figure 4. Frequency of boundary disputes and of display flights by Seychelles kestrels during each month in 1975 and 1976. Frequency data are standardised to number of disputes/display flights per 50 hours fieldwork.

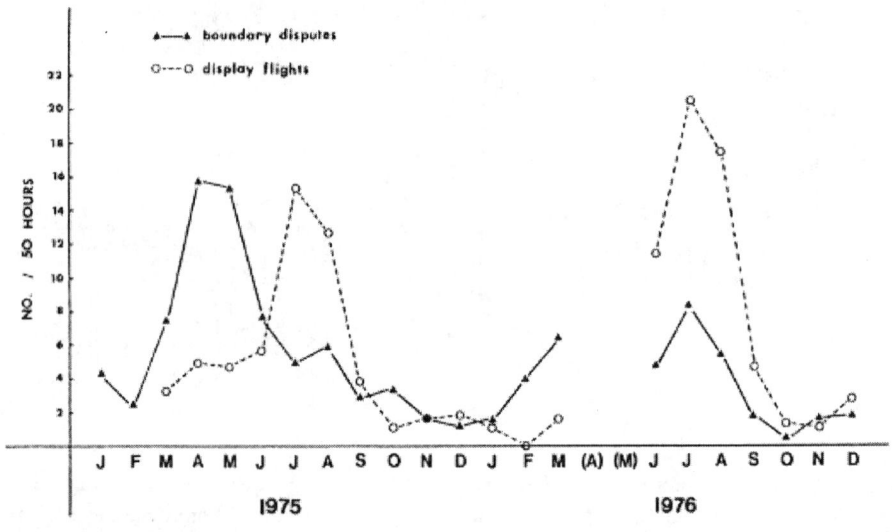

Territory Size

The close agreement between home range boundaries, the location of boundary disputes, and of display flights confirms that Seychelles Kestrels defend an exclusive home range (Type A territory, Hinde 1956). Territorial boundaries are shown as solid lines in Fig. 3 where evidence was available from either marked birds, from boundary disputes or from display flights. Dotted lines are used where boundaries were less certain. In some cases these were determined from the movements of unmarked birds known to be associated with particular nest sites, and in a few cases where no data were available, the dotted lines are arbitrarily placed midway between adjacent nest sites. In the following analysis territories are included only where 75% or more of the boundary was known for certain. There were 22 such territories within the study area.

Territory size was measured to the nearest 0.5 ha using squared paper and a traced map of territorial boundaries. The 22 territories had a mean area of 40.3 ha ± sd 3.99 with a range from 33.5 to 46.5 ha. There was no significant difference in territory size above and below the 200 m contour (12 territories centred above 200 m; x = 39.5 ± sd 3.77: 10 territories centred below 200 m; x = 41.2 ± sd 4.24). Habitat differences did explain some of the variation in territory size. The habitat types of *mixed upland forest* and *mixed coconut plantation and lowland forest* are structurally more diverse than *open scrub woodland* and *open lowland habitat*. There was a significant relationship between territory size and the proportion of the territory that contained the structurally more complex habitats ($r = -0.686$, df = 20, $p < 0.001$). Specifically, smaller territories held a higher proportion of structurally more complex vegetation.

Analysis of Spacing

Nest sites were located for 32 of the 34 pairs within the study area in the 1975 breeding season (Fig. 3). Nearest-neighbour-distances ranged from just over 200 m to more than 600 m with a mean of around 450 m. Testing for randomness/regularity of nest spacing gave a G-statistic of 0.94 indicating that nest sites were significantly over-dispersed. A small number of sites in the north-west of the study area showed a more clumped distribution and this was caused by several pairs nesting on a very extensive area of cliff at Morne Blanc. Here it appeared that some of the separation between adjacent pairs was being effected by vertical distances on a particularly large cliff face.

Re-survey in 1998

During survey work in February 1998 kestrels were detected within 100 m of the 1975 nest site at 20 out of 22 territories visited. None of the original marked birds were seen and it is almost certain that all the 1998 birds were different individuals form those of 1975. In eight territories, at least one adult kestrel was seen in association with one or more dependent young, and in the remaining 12 territories the adult pair only was recorded. In the two territories where no kestrels were seen within 100 m of the 1975 nest site this may have been a product of the relatively short time available for the survey, or it may have reflected loss or movement of birds from these sites. Comprehensive survey was not possible throughout the area and it is possible that some pairs of kestrels that had moved their nesting sites were missed. Nor was it possible from this quick survey to be sure that no new pairs had become established in places that had not been occupied in 1975.

DISCUSSION

Pairs of Seychelles Kestrels occupied individual home ranges and these were used throughout the year. Ranges were contiguous and boundaries between pairs were actively defended. Home range in the Seychelles Kestrel is therefore synonymous with territory. Boundary disputes occurred throughout the year but were most frequent between March and June, immediately following the period when fledged young became independent. An aerial display behaviour served to reaffirm territorial boundaries and was most frequent during July/August, just prior to breeding. A re-survey of the study area 23 years after the initial research revealed a highly stable pattern of dispersion over time. More than 90% of localities containing nesting kestrels in 1975 revealed evidence of occupancy by pairs or families of kestrels in 1998.

The majority of non-colonial raptors have nest sites that are spaced out, with a small surrounding area (the nesting territory, Newton 1976) defended against conspecifics. Food is typically obtained from hunting ranges that overlap widely (e.g. European Kestrel *Falco tinnunculus*, Village 1990; Peregrine Falcon *Falco peregrinus*, Cade 1960; Goshawk *Accipiter gentilis*, Kenward 1977; European Sparrowhawk *Accipiter nisus*, Newton 1979). Rather fewer species have exclusive home ranges (e.g. Buzzard *Buteo buteo*, Mebs 1964; Greater Kestrel *Falco rupicoloides*, Kemp 1968 in Newton 1979; Black Eagle *Aquila verreauxii*, Gargett 1975; Galapagos Hawk *Buteo galapagoensis*, de Vries 1975). The dispersion continuum from colonialism, through overlapping home ranges to exclusive defended areas probably reflects progressive adjustment to an increasingly even and predictable food supply (Newton 1979). Factors leading to a more even and predictable food supply include dependence on vertebrate (rather than invertebrate) prey, stability (as opposed to unpredictability) of climate, and structural complexity of habitat (complex woodland as opposed to structurally simply grassland/ tundra). The conditions for the Seychelles Kestrel meet each of the above requirements and it is unsurprising to find that this species has a relatively extreme dispersion pattern (exclusive home ranges).

The mean territory size of Seychelles Kestrels was 40.3 ha with a range of 33.5-46.5 ha among 22 pairs. Range size in raptors is generally positively correlated with the size of the bird (Newton 1979). As the smallest member of the genus *Falco*, it is not surprising that the Seychelles Kestrel has one of the smallest home ranges recorded for any diurnal raptor, only beaten by the Frog Hawk *Accipiter soloensis* (Kwon & Won in Newton 1979). Grant (1966) showed that the numbers and biomass of passerine birds was greater per unit area on islands compared with equivalent mainland areas. If this is also true for lower vertebrates such as the lizards that are the Seychelles Kestrel's staple diet, then this could be another factor contributing to the exceptionally small home range in the Seychelles Kestrel.

Several raptors have been shown to have smaller ranges in areas where food availability was measurably greater (e.g. Buzzard, Picozzi & Weir 1974; Black Eagle, Gargett 1975; European Sparrowhawk, Newton et al. 1986). The relationship between territory size and habitat in the Seychelles Kestrel is probably linked to differences in food availability, since an important prey species, the arboreal gecko *Phelsuma* is likely to be more plentiful in the structurally more complex woodland habitat where Seychelles Kestrels occupied appreciably smaller ranges (Watson 1981).

Significant over-dispersion of nest sites occurred in the Seychelles Kestrel and has been reported for many species of raptor (e.g. European Sparrowhawk, Newton et al. 1977; Buzzard, Tubbs 1974; Peregrine Falcon, Ratcliffe 1962; Golden Eagle *Aquila chrysaetos*, Watson 1997). The phenomenon of over-dispersion is consistent with the view that populations are, at least proximately, limited by the territorial behaviour of individual pairs (Newton 1979). Further support for this view comes from the removal experiments of Seychelles Kestrels that were carried out in 1977 (Watson 1981, 1989) and these confirmed the existence of a non-breeding surplus. Finally, the exceptionally stable dispersion pattern that was evident between surveys 23 years apart, in 1975 and 1998, further supports the hypothesis that territorial behaviour is an important factor regulating population size in the Seychelles Kestrel.

REFERENCES

BERGER, D.D. & H.C. MUELLER 1959. The bal-chatri: a trap for birds of prey. *Bird Banding* 30: 18-26.
BROWN, D. 1975. A test of randomness of nest spacing. *Wildfowl* 26: 102-103.
CADE, T.J. 1960. Ecology of the peregrine and gyrfalcon populations in Alaska. *Univ. California pubis. Zool.* 63: 151-290.
COLLAR, N.J. & S.N. STUART 1985. *Threatened birds of Africa and related islands*. Cmbridge: ICBP & IUCN.
DE VRIES, T.J. 1975. The breeding biology of the Galapagos hawk *Buteo galapagoensis*. *Le Gerfaut* 65: 29-57.
FEARE, C.J., S.A. TEMPLE & J. PROCTER 1974. The status, distribution and diet of the Seychelles kestrel *Falco araea*. *Ibis* 116: 548-551.
GARGETT, V. 1975. The spacing of black eagles in the Matopos, Rhodesia. *Ostrich* 46: 1-44.
GAYMER, R., R.A.A. BLACKMAN, P.G DAWSON,. M. PENNY & C.M. PENNY 1969. The endemic birds of Seychelles. *Ibis* 111: 157-176.
GRANT, P.R. 1966. The density of land birds on the Tres Marias Islands in Mexico. 1. Numbers and biomass. *Can. J. Zool.* 44: 391-401.
HINDE, R.A. 1956. The biological significance of the territories of birds. *Ibis* 98: 350-369.
KENWARD, R.E. 1977 Predation on released pheasants by goshawks in central Sweden. *Vitrevy* 10: 79-12.
MEBS. TH. 1964 Zur Biologie und Populationsdynamik des Mausebussards *Buteo buteo*. *J. Orn.* 105: 247-306.
NEWTON, E. 1867. On the land-birds of the Seychelles archipelago. *Ibis* (2)3:335-360.
NEWTON, I. 1976. Population limitation in diurnal raptors. *Can. Field Natur.* 90: 274-300.
NEWTON, I. 1979. *Population Ecology of Raptors*. Berkhamsted: T. & A.D. Poyser.
NEWTON, I., M. MARQUISS, D.N. WEIR, & D. MOSS 1977. Spacing of sparrowhawk nesting territories. *J. Anim. Ecol.* 46: 425-451.
NEWTON, I., J. WYLLIE, & R. MEARNS 1986. Spacing of sparrowhawks in relation to food supply. *J. Anim. Ecol.* 55: 361-370.
NILSSON, I.N., S.G. NILSSON & M. SYLVEN 1982. Diet choice, resource depression and the regular nest spacing of bird of prey. *Biol. J. Linn. Soc.* 18: 1-9.
OUSTALET, M.E. 1878. Etude sur la faune ornithologique des Iles Seychelles. *Bull. Soc. Philomath. Paris* (7)2: 161-206.
PENNY, M. 1974. *The birds of the Seychelles and the outlying islands*. London: Collins.
PICOZZI, N. & D.N. WEIR 1974. Breeding biology of the buzzard in Speyside. *British Birds* 67: 199-210.
PROCTER, 1984. Vegetation of the granitic islands of the Seychelles. In: *Biogeography and Ecology of the Seychelles Islands*. D.R. Stoddart (ed.). The Hague: W.Junk.
RATCLIFFE, D.A. 1962. Breeding density in the peregrine *Falco peregrinus* and raven *Corvus corax*. *Ibis* 104: 13-39.

SAUER, J.D. 1967. *Plants and man on the Seychelles coast.* Madison: Univ. Wisconsin Press.
TUBBS, C.R. 1974. *The Buzzard.* Newton Abbot: David & Charles.
VESEY-FITZGERALD, D. 1940. On the vegetation of Seychelles. *J. Ecology* 28: 465-483.
VILLAGE, A. 1990. *The Kestrel.* London: T. & A.D. Poyser.
WATSON, J. 1981. *Population ecology, food and conservation of the Seychelles kestrel* Falco araea *on Mahé.* Ph.D. thesis, University of Aberdeen.
WATSON, J. 1989. Successful translocation of the endemic Seychelles kestrel *Falco araea* to Praslin. In: *Raptors in the Modern World.* B.-U. Meyburg and R.D. Chancellor (eds.). Berlin, London, Paris: WWGBP.
WATSON, J. 1992. Nesting ecology of the Seychelles kestrel *Falco araea* on Mahé, Seychelles. *Ibis* 134: 259-267.
WATSON, J. 1997. *The Golden Eagle.* London: T. & A.D. Poyser.
WILLOUGHBY, E.J. & T.J. CADE 1964. Breeding behaviour of the American kestrel. *The Living Bird* 3:75-96.

Jeff Watson
Scottish Natural Heritage
9 Culduthel Road
Inverness
IV2 4AG
Scotland

Chancellor, R. D. & B.-U. Meyburg eds. 2000
Raptors at Risk
WWGBP / Hancock House

The Peregrine Falcon *Falco peregrinus* in Fiji and Vanuatu

Clayton M. White, Daniel J. Brimm and Jon H. Wetton

ABSTRACT

We studied the Peregrine Falcon *Falco peregrinus* in Fiji 1985-1997 and in Vanuatu 1993-1995. Based on preliminary findings in 1985-86 and data from Fergus Clunie, Fiji Museum, we projected a population of about 100 pairs for Fiji. By 1987 we had adjusted our population projection downward to about 70 pairs and based on the history of inactivity and our continual checking of various regions we concluded that perhaps only 20 effective breeding pairs were a reasonable estimate for Fiji, although in any one year possibly 30 pairs breed. In 1994 of 6 nesting sites checked only 1 was active, and 2 had lone females; of 6 checked in 1997, 2 were active. Through time we have seen a reduction in occupancy of nesting sites. If our sample is indicative of the entire population in Fiji, especially for places we have not checked such as much of Vanua Levu, Kadavu, and the Lau Group, then the species is extremely rare and may be down to a few pairs within Fiji. We discuss other interpretations that might explain our findings of an apparent downward trend in occupancy rate, speculate on this aspect of their biology, and compare it with better known northern hemisphere populations. Breeding chronology in Fiji has been regular with young leaving the nest about early to mid-September while in Vanuatu the phenology is *ca.* 6 weeks later despite being on the same latitude. Effects of such factors as food and weather in regulating breeding, as opposed to photoperiodic control, are discussed. Peregrines in Fiji, Vanuatu and New Caledonia are allocated to the same subspecies (*F. p. nesiotes*). Those in Fiji show signs of inbreeding and we discuss the DNA differences and similarities between those of Fiji, Vanuatu, and Australia. Such differences are important from the point of view of conservation if in fact the Peregrine in Fiji has declined and this will be discussed.

INTRODUCTION

While allusions to the breeding of the Peregrine Falcon *Falco peregrinus* in Fiji were made as early as 1877 (Gordon 1897-1912) there was no clear consensus in the literature (Mayr 1941), even as late as 1968 (Brown & Amadon 1968), that they even occurred in Fiji. It was not until the studies of Clunie (1972) that some of their breeding status and biology was chronicled. His study was first restricted to a single breeding pair on Joske's Thumb. Clunie suggested breeding for Viti Levu, Vanua Levu, Wakaya, Ovalau, and Kadavu but little else was known about their breeding distribution. While the Peregrine may be among the most studied and best known species of birds in many parts of the northern hemisphere, and while in the southern hemisphere they are well studied in temperate

South America, Africa and Australia, little has been done on the species in tropical climes. The species is cosmopolitan in distribution and in Fiji represents the easternmost outlier in Oceania and thus a peripheral population. Since the species had also been affected by synthetic chemicals (mainly chlorinated hydrocarbons) in the northern hemisphere, and in some places declined into extinction, its status within Fiji was of interest.

With this in mind we started to study the birds in some detail in 1985. The questions we had in mind were: 1) what is their breeding density and geographical distribution? 2) what is their breeding chronology for a tropical population of the species? 3) what do they eat? 4) have they been affected by synthetic chemicals in a similar fashion to populations of the northern hemisphere? 5) to which population are they most closely related evolutionarily (phylogenetically)? and 6) what effect do the above parameters have on their long term conservation in Fiji? Some of these questions have been briefly explored in White *et al.* (1988, 1993).

MATERIALS AND METHODS

Field Work

Peregrines normally nest on cliffs and in the northern hemisphere, at least, cliff size is important with large (high) cliffs having priority selection. In 1985 we spent 10 hours with a helicopter examining major cliff areas, over the range of types of cliffs Peregrines occupy, on Viti Levu, Vanua Levu (part), Moturiki, Ovalau, Wakaya, Makogai, Koro and Kioa islands. Three observers (including the pilot) examined each cliff closely for nesting ledges with excreta (faecal stain) on them and for falcons. We flew the helicopter about 10 kph past cliffs and perhaps 20-50 m from them. When a falcon flushed from a cliff we searched the cliff slowly for an eyrie. Locations and observations were plotted on maps and elevation and orientation of each cliff was recorded. We later visited several accessible areas on foot and by car. Cliffs visited were recorded as small (<50 m tall), or large (>50 m tall). Values for the numbers of cliffs examined were somewhat arbitrary as it was often hard to determine exactly where one cliff ended and another began. Islands without cliffs were not examined. Extrapolations on distribution in the Lau group came mainly from Clunie (northern Lau), from Fijians, and from P. Geraghty, none of which we were able to confirm. In 1986, 6.5 hours were spent in a helicopter examining most eyries on Viti Levu, Wayaka and Kioa and some eyries on Vanua Levu. Food remains and eggshell fragments were gathered from 6 eyries and the shell fragments were examined for their thickness at the Western Foundation of Vertebrate Zoology. In 1989 only eyries that could be visited from automobile and by foot were examined. In 1991 helicopter was again used and in addition to visiting all known eyries we examined other parts of Viti Levu not previously seen, Taveuni, and the Mamanuca-I-Cake, Mamanuca-I-Ra, and Yasawa Groups. In 1993 only 4, 1994 only 7, and in 1997 only 6 easy of access eyries were examined.

We worked in Vanuatu between 18-30 August 1993, and surveyed by helicopter some 30% of the linear area (24% of the land area) covered by islands in Vanuatu. Within that area, however, some islands without cliffs such as Emae, of 33 km^2 area, were not examined. Large inland regions devoid of cliffs were also not examined so in some cases only shorelines were surveyed. We used Efate (*ca.* 17° 45' S. Lat.) as a starting point because of helicopter service, and from there examined cliffs on 21 islands from Tanna (*ca.* 19° 30' S. Lat.) in the south to Epi (ca. 16° 30' S. Lat.) in the north. This covered a linear distance of about 310 km. Cliffs were categorized into 3 groups based on estimated heights; 1) 20 m or less, 2) 20-70 m, and 3) over 70 m. Numbers of cliff, by size, were recorded for each island. Only those cliffs that were devoid of heavy vegetation were examined. We timed our survey to occur during what we deemed to be the peak of fledgling development (1-4 wk old young). This was based on the breeding chronology at the same latitude in Fiji (White *et al.* 1988) and locations 10° latitude farther south in adjacent Queensland, Australia (Czechura 1984). In 1994 we examined 6 eyrie locations (Efate and Erromango) from helicopter and climbed into 1 eyrie to look for eggshells and get blood samples. In 1995 our helicopter pilot examined 3 locations from helicopter and we obtained a blood sample from 1 bird.

Molecular Data

DNA was extracted from a variety of tissues; primarily aliquots of whole blood or pectoral muscle stored at ambient temperature (some later frozen) in an equal volume or larger volume of Blood Lysis Buffer (0.1 M Tris-HCl-pH 8.0; 0.1 M EDTA; 0.1M NaCl; 0.5% SDS). Samples from Vanuatu included a pectoral muscle sample in formalin, feather tips, and egg contents ranging from embryonic material to egg membrane. Aliquots of clotted whole blood or finely chopped pieces of tissue ($ca.20\mu g$) were resuspended in 650µl SET (150mM NaCl, 50mM Tris/HCl pH 8.0, 1mM EDTA Na2) with 15µl of 10mg ml-1 Proteinase K solution, 7.5µl of 25% SDS (w/v), and 7.5µl 10% Triton 100 followed by two phenol, two phenol/chloroform and one chloroform extractions with subsequent ethanol precipitation. The DNA was dried at 37°C for 30 minutes and resuspended by overnight incubation in 150µl TE (1mM EDTA Na2, 10mM Tris/HCl pH 8.0).

PCR amplification of the two microsatellite loci *Fpe*µ1 & *Fpe*µ2 was achieved using 30ng of DNA per 25µl PCR reaction comprising 20 pmoles of each primer, 0.2 mM each of dATP, dGTP, dTTP and 0.05 mM dCTP, 0.25mCi[alpha-^{32}P]-dCTP, 3mM MgCl2, 20mM $(NH_4)_2SO_4$, 0.01% (w/v) Tween, 75mMTris-HCl pH 9.0 and 1 unit "Red Hot" DNA polymerase (Advanced Biotechnologies). After an initial denaturing step of 180 seconds at 94°C, the reaction proceeded for 30 cycles as follows; 45 seconds at 94°C, 60 seconds at 58°C then 90 seconds at 72°C (DNA Thermal Cycler PTC-100, MJ Research). The PCR products were electrophoresed through 6 or 7% denaturing polyacrylamide gels and visualized by autoradiography after an overnight exposure. Allele sizes were determined by reference to standards.

RESULTS

Cliffs Examined-Fiji

Of the various surveys, the primary areas not checked were major cliffy areas in east and west Vanua Levu, Kadavu, and the Lau Group. Overall more than 263 total cliffs were examined. On Viti Levu those cliffs checked varied in elevation from 122-920 m; mean elevation for a sample of 49 large cliffs was 598 m and mean for 49 small cliffs was 483 m in elevation. More than half of the inland cliffs were checked but very small (< 8 m) coastal cliffs were not. As an indication of the distribution of cliff sizes examined, other than on Viti Levu, a sample is: 35 large and 55 small cliffs on Vanua Levu, 6 large and 15 small on Ovalau, 1 large and 2 small on Wakaya (all the cliffs), 3 small on Kioa (all the cliffs), 2 small on Matage. Of the 33 cliffs checked in the Mananuca and Yasawa Groups about half were considered large.

Cliffs Examined-Vanuatu

While numbers of cliffs in each category were recorded by island we do not present the data for each island. Cliffs in many cases were extensive and nearly continuous, with only short breaks, and it was at those places we divided them for convenience. Therefore, the numbers of cliffs are only approximate since the determination of the end of one cliff and the start of the next was often arbitrary. We suspect the number of cliffs 20 m or less is overestimated because from the helicopter angle and distance from the cliff, the actual size is misleading and thought to be smaller. The 70 m category may be correspondingly underestimated. It may well be that the 20 m or smaller category is 20-30% fewer and those in the 70 m over may be 15-20% more. A large number of cliffs in the 70 m or more category were higher than 100-125 m. Numbers of cliffs by island varied greatly. For example, Ewose in the Shepherd Island group and Veto Manung near Erromango, are small islands of less than 1 km^2 in area and completely ringed with cliffs 20-40 m in height. Most cliffs are on the perimeter of islands. Tanna and Erromango contained the most cliffs, probably partly because of their size. Although Efate and Erromango have about the same land area, the former had 28 and the latter 123 coastal cliffs. In all, 421 cliffs were examined; 85 (20 m or less), 181 (20-70 m), and 155 (70m or more).

Numbers of Falcons

For Fiji during the breeding season usually only those falcons associated with cliffs are seen (Clunie 1976, pers. obser.). The 12 locations where we found young or other positive signs of nesting or where we knew that eyries occur are shown on Table 1. For the total 263 cliffs examined falcons were at only about 7%. In addition, however, there are several areas with typical falcon faecal staining on cliffs on eastern Vanua Levu and behind Lautoka on Viti Levu where falcons doubtless nest but we never found eyries. Overall, falcons were found by us or collaborators or reported by Fijians (not all were documented eyries but most presumed to be) at 42 locations (see White *et al.* 1988 for earlier discussion of this); we only have some "history" of occupancy for 12 (Table 1). The eyrie at Sawa-i-Lau has long been talked about but we never found young there as clear proof of nesting. Based on the total numbers we originally estimated about 100 pairs for Fiji but as we continued to search and look at cliffs over and over again our data suggest that perhaps only 30 pairs nest in any one year and the average effective population size may only be 20 pairs or less. We lack data from Kadavu and the Lau group, however. The decreasing eyrie occupancy rate of our sample will be discussed below.

Table 1. Occupancy[1] rate of Peregrine eyries[2] visited in Fiji (F) and Vanatu (V), 1985-1997.

Eyrie name		\-\-\-\-\-\-\-\-\-\-\-\-\-\-\-\- Year Visited (1985-1997) \-\-\-\-\-\-\-\-\-\-\-\-\-\-\-\-							
		85	86	89	90	91	93	94	95[3]	97
Joske's Thumb	(F)	2	2	---		---	---[6]	---		
Namosi	(F)	2	2	2			---[6]			
Nausori Road	(F)	2	1	2		2	1	1		2
Wakaya	(F)		2			---				
Kioa	(F)	2	2			---				
Sigatoka	(F)		2	2		2	---	1		---
Nalato Range	(F)		2?[4]			2				---
"The Saddle"	(F)		2?[4]			---		2		---
Raki Raki	(F)		2[4]		2[5]	2		---		2
Matagi	(F)					2		2		---
Swa-i-Lau	(F)		2[4]	---		---				
Lautoka	(F)		2[4]					---		
Nguna	(V)						2	---	2	
Goat Island	(V)						2	---		
Erromango I	(V)						2	2	2	
Efate	(V)						2	---	2	
Tongoa	(V)						2			
Erromango II	(V)						2	---		
Tanna Volcano	(V)						---	2	2	

[1]Occupancy by pair, usually breeding=2; only single adult found although pairs may have been present but not breeding=1. Eyries visited but no breeding falcons seen=---. Blank areas indicate eyrie was not checked. Presumed eyries on Vanua Levu had no falcons, were never checked again, and are not on table.

[2]Eyries are defined as areas with evidence of use and breeding (faecal stains, "whitewash" in eyrie) and falcon seen nearby.

[3]Checked by G. Cloete

[4]Found by C. Anderson

[5]Young found by Fijians

[6]Checked by helicopter pilots

Peregrines have been recorded on 13 of the more than 83 named islands of Vanuatu (Diamond & Marshall 1976, Pickering 1982, Bregulla 1992, W. Eakle pers. comm.). In all, we found 11 peregrines, 4 pairs, 2 single adults (1 male, 1 female) and 1 sub-adult female occupying cliffs; about a 2% cliff occupancy rate. All pairs or adults, the latter we believe to have been at breeding stations because of their behaviour, were only on islands where they were previously known even though we searched 15 islands where they had not been recorded. We include as part of Erromango, where we found 2 pairs and a single bird, a small volcanic upthrust (less than 1 km area and 1.5 km offshore) called locally Goat Rock or Veto Manung, where we also found falcons. The rock is not specifically mentioned in any of the above literature as having falcons but it also may have been included with Erromango in that literature. We found a sub-adult female on Mataso, for which falcons were also not listed, but she showed no signs of being a breeder. Although the literature lists Peregrines for 12 islands we do not doubt that they may breed on many other islands with cliffs, especially in areas difficult of access where ornithologists have not visited.

After our departure, a pair was found by Garrett Cloete on Emae, an island that we considered to be poor because of the lack of good cliffs. Falcons had not before been recorded and perhaps the pair seen were post-breeding wanderers or were from nearby neighbouring Nguna, where they do breed. Cloete also saw a lone falcon on Ambryum, another island where they had not been recorded and found a pair on Tanna near the volcano.

Breeding Chronology and Success

All the nests with young we examined on Fiji between 1985-1997 have been well synchronized relative to the month of fledging. Most young are of fledging age by early September; eggs were then laid during the first part of July. Clunie (1972), however, found that eggs in the Joske's Thumb eyrie were laid in the first week of August 1971. If that was the first clutch then young would have fledged the second week of October. All young we have seen are within 2 to 2-1/2 weeks age of one another and it is difficult to believe that in any one year some pairs lay in June and others in August. There may, however, be variation from year to year, the timing of which is dictated by some of the factors we discuss below. If there were considerable variation from pair to pair within any one year the absence of pairs and young in eyries that are visited in late August might be explained. This will also be discussed below. The 5 active eyries examined in 1986 all had young for an average of 2.6/eyrie. In 1994, when only 1 eyrie of 6 checked had young, they too were near fledging on 15 September.

Based on our Fiji work we were surprised to find falcons either incubating eggs or not yet having laid on Vanuatu in mid-August. On 20 August the pair at Nguna had c/3, and on 28 August a pair at Erromango had c/3. On 20 August we found a pair inland on Efate that flew together as a territorial pair, but clearly had not laid eggs. Upon returning on 30 August the female flushed from a ledge after the helicopter was but 7 m from it and had been so for several seconds. She flew back past the ledge and looked at it in the common practice of falcons "checking" eggs or young. Her intensity at trying to return to the ledge indicated that she was on eggs. We could not, however, see the ledge adequately from the helicopter because of a screen of vegetation on it but subsequently found young on that ledge. A second pair at Erromango and a pair on Veto Manung were territorial and "aggressive" at our presence but clearly had not laid (or had lost clutches?). A male on Tongoa was very territorial but we could not flush a mate from the cliff. Lastly, at a third location on Erromango, a female flushed from a cliff was territorial but nonetheless acted as though she had not laid eggs. The female at Nguna was still incubating with great intensity on 30 August. She was so intent on returning to the clutch after she was first flushed that she flew under the helicopter and landed on the ledge while the helicopter was about 15 m from the ledge. She then commenced to incubate while the helicopter hovered there and even moved to within about 6 m of her, without flushing. After our departure, G. Cloete checked the eyrie on Nguna and inland on Efate but could not determine the latter's contents. At one eyrie young were 3-4 d old on 16 August and on Efate there were 2 young about one week from fledging on 23 September. The eyrie on Nguna produced 3 young but only 1 survived.

Overall, the breeding cycle on Vanuatu was in the pre- to mid-incubation stage in late August. This breeding schedule averaged about 6 weeks behind Fiji even though on the same latitude and with essentially the same temporal climatic patterns. In 1986, in 5 eyries on Fiji, the largest young (a female) was about 1 ½ weeks from fledging on 22 August [tail *ca.* 60 mm, wt. 680 g.,(adult female wt. *ca.*850 g.)], and the youngest nestlings in 5 eyries were about 1 week old (wt. 200 g.) on 23 August. On 31 August 1991 on Fiji we found young ranging from those with tail feathers out 55 mm (3 weeks old) to those within a week of fledging (4 eyries). Unfortunately, we could not verify the breeding stage in Fiji on 2 September 1993, the year we first examined Vanuatu, because no eyrie checked was occupied. The breeding schedule on Fiji, however, has been within this same time period on 5 surveys between 1985 and 1997 and there was no reason to expect they would not have been on that timing in 1993.

Figure 1. Comparison of genetic (DNA) diversity at two microsatellite loci, $Fpe\mu1$ and $Fpe\mu2$ in *Falco peregrinus macropus* (Australia and Tasmania) and *Falco peregrinus nesoites* (Fiji and Vanuatu). Five to six individuals were used at each locus for each population. At locus $Fpe\mu1$, Vanuatu data were too faint to interpret. The falcons indicated by the term Australia were from the state of Victoria.

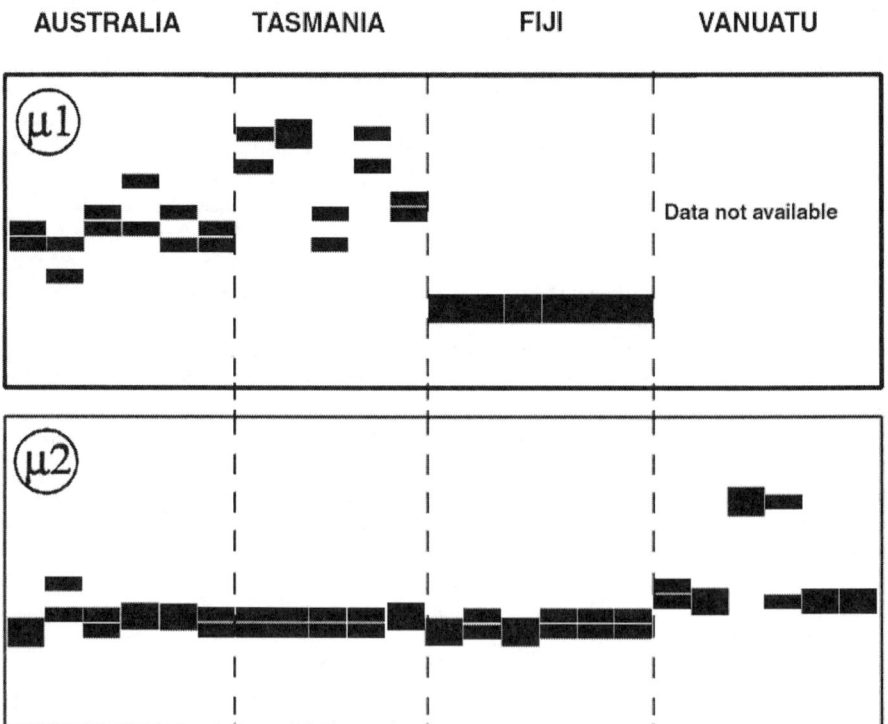

Molecular Findings

As was described earlier for DNA fingerprinting analysis (White *et al.* 1993) Peregrines from Fiji show essentially no genetic variation and high inbreeding (though perhaps not deleterious) based on that technique. The microsatellite technique presented here (Fig. 1) confirms the earlier data. This is especially graphic when compared to the Australian (state of Victoria) and adjacent Tasmanian samples; typical of large outbred populations. The differences in frequency of the observed genetic variants between Victoria and Tasmania suggests restricted gene flow although the 2 locations are only separated by the narrow (200 km) Bass Strait. Recoveries of ringed birds also indicate no movement between the two locations (W.B. Emison, C.M. White ms). The little genetic data available indicate that Fiji falcons may be more inbred than those of Vanuatu. This makes sense if one looks only at isolation as the principal factor. Unfortunately we obtained no data from the $Fpe\mu 1$ locus to see if falcons from Vanuatu posses similar genetic variants to those of Fiji. In order to gain better insight to their relationship this would be important to know. Further analyses of other loci may help resolve that point. Based on this analysis we were also not able to resolve the question of relationships among the Australian/Vanuatu/Fiji groups and thus the question of origin of the Fiji population remains open.

DISCUSSION

Genetic Information

We had hoped that the genetic information might have provided at least two sorts of information. 1) What is the extent of genetic variability within the subspecies *nesoites* (Fiji and Vanuatu) and 2) What might have been the source of the populations on Fiji/Vanuatu/New Caledonia that differentiated into the subspecies *nesoites*; Australia (*F.p. macropus*) or Solomon Islands/New Guinea (*F.p. ernesti*) of which *nesoites* is nearly morphologically intermediate? To date we have not been able to resolve those questions.

Breeding Density

Earlier we suggested that Peregrines might be as frequent on Vanuatu as on Fiji provided that food and nesting resources were as abundant (White *et al.* 1988). However, based on our results, Peregrines appear to be less frequent on Vanuatu, by more than half, given the abundant habitat, than they were on Fiji. We also suggested earlier, based on our Fiji experience, that if habitat and food resources were similar on Fiji, Vanuatu and New Caledonia then the subspecies *nesoites*, whose range encompasses those islands, may contain 200-250 pairs. We now believe that to be a significant overestimate. Y. Letocart (pers. comm.) indicated that the Peregrine was encountered very infrequently on New Caledonia and that the Loyalty Islands contained most of the likely Peregrine habitat. Our experience now, having examined some of both Vanuatu and Fiji, suggests that the subspecies *nesoites* may not consist of more than 100 pairs being scattered over 51,610 km^2 of land area that itself occurs over many times that amount of ocean surface. *F. p. nesoites* is thus a rare subspecies of the Peregrine.

Our misestimate of nesting chronology for Vanuatu came as a complete surprise. We may have missed some pairs because during our survey some females may have been sitting tightly on clutches. Males, however, should have been "on guard" near eyries and we think we missed few areas where they are known. For example, Aniwa is a small island (8 km^2 area) where Peregrines have been recorded and has a limited series of easily examined cliffs. We found none, however, suggesting they did not nest the year of our survey. We have good confidence in our findings although a larger sample may have altered our views of temporal sequence..

On Fiji in 1986 of 263 cliffs examined we located 7 cliffs with pairs or territorial birds and several other obvious eyries, in distinct territories, without pairs. For Vanuatu, twice the number of cliffs were examined and 7 locations (probably representing 6 pairs) were found. In Fiji, many of the cliffs used were black volcanic rock making white faecal stains easy to see which resulted, in part, in our being able to find used cliffs even though falcons were not present (see discussion in White et al. 1988 on cliff use by birds in general on Fiji). In Vanuatu, however, many of the coastal cliffs (e.g., Erromango) were of uplifted marine limestone, white in colour, thus making it difficult to see faecal stains even when pairs were present. Not being able to find even unused eyries adds to the impression of rareness. Nonetheless, if our results are a rough indicator of density then not more than 20-30 pairs occur in Vanuatu; considerably fewer than we expected. We are thus as perplexed, as we were by Fiji data, at the low numbers of falcons. Peregrines may, however, be inexplicably spotty in what is seemingly excellent habitat. Kodiak Island, in the Gulf of Alaska for example, appears "identical" in habitat quality and food base abundance to the adjacent Aleutian Islands. Yet Kodiak has only about one-fourth the number of breeding pairs of falcons for amount of habitat available and examined (C.M. White, R.J. Ritchie, pers. observ.)

Table 2. Comparative densities per pair of Peregrines expressed as linear distances and areas (see text for discussion of area comparisons). Linear distances are shorelines, rivers or simply average straight line distances between a sample of eyries. Areas are for entire land masses, not just regions where falcons occur.

Name	Islands (Location) Density		Name	Mainlands (Location) Density	
	Linear (km)	Area (km^2)		Linear (km)	Area (km^2)
Zembra (Mediterranean Sea)	0.9	0.04	Spain	8.7[2]	300
Amchitka (Aleutian Islands)	10.1	136	Arctic Canada	3.3[3]	17
Buldir (Aleutian Islands)	2.6	0.40	Victoria (Australia)	16[4]	700
Tasmania (Australia)	13.8[1]	939	New South Wales (Australia)	6.1[5]	154
Vanuatu	130	507	Transvaal (South Africa)	6.4[6]	7150

[1]Sample of 10 eyries (Mooney & Brothers 1988)
[2]Sample of 41 eyries in southern Spain (Heredia et al. 1988)
[3]Sample of 18-26 eyries over several years (Court et al. 1988)
[4]Sample of 14 eyries (Emison et al. 1988)
[5]Sample of 21 eyries (Olsen & Olsen 1988)
[6]Sample of 4 eyries in a river canyon (Tarboton & Allen 1984)

Peregrines' territories can become rather dense with averages of about 4-6 km apart over large portions of their worldwide range. It is difficult to calculate a density for Fiji because of the scattered nature of cliffs and because some likely areas with cliffs were not examined. Within Vanuatu the most realistic way to calculate Peregrine density is by linear shoreline distance since most cliffs are on island perimeters. Calculation by area, as in much of the literature, can be misleading because large regions may not have cliffs; pairs per km^2 has little meaning and in part accounts for the large variance of values in Table 2. Since Peregrines frequently have a clumped distribution, distances between pairs in areas where falcons occur, often have quite similar average nesting densities. For comparative purpose, however, we have presented data in linear distances (where available) and also by area (Table 2). Some of the highest densities known are on the island of Zembra in the Mediterranean Sea off the coast of Tunisia where 10-12 pairs of Peregrines occur along 9.5 km of coastline (Thiollay 1988). In some regions such as Africa, Peregrine densities are unexpectedly thin and tend to be spotty or regional (Hustler 1988, Mendelsohn 1988, Tarboton & Allen 1984, Thomson 1984). For the Transvaal of South Africa the average might be 1 pair / 9533 km^2 (Tarboton & Allen 1984) whereas south of the Transvaal Peregrines have still lower densities until again near the Cape (Jenkins 1991). North of the Transvaal in Zimbabwe some local populations are extremely dense. The low overall densities for Africa are surprising, especially in relation to densities in other parts of the southern hemisphere such as much of Australia and southern Chile and Argentina. The low densities for Vanuatu are likewise surprising because of the abundance of habitat. For Africa, such factors as competition with congeners (Lanner Falcons, *Falco biarmicus*), nest sites in short supply, and limited amounts of appropriate foods have been hypothesized to explain the rareness of Peregrines there; all logical factors. In Vanuatu there are no congeners or other cliff nesting raptors. Appropriate cliffs for nest sites are in superabundance and not limiting. In addition to cliffs, however, suitable nesting ledges on the cliffs are necessary. While many cliffs, especially on Fiji, are more or less smooth basalt without horizontal ledges, this was not the case on Vanuatu; the majority of cliffs we examined had suitable ledges. As with Fiji, we are left with the possibility of some form of food dictated breeding limitation. There are at least 45 widespread bird species in Vanuatu, however, that are in the size class and taxonomic composition that Peregrines feed on elsewhere. Seven are doves and pigeons and 2 are parrots; high preference foods for Peregrines. While we did not see many birds flying above the canopy, from the helicopter we saw forest pigeons and kingfishers "commonly" on Erromango and parts of Tanna in 1993 and fruit bats (at least three species) were abundant in large camps at least on southwestern Efate and Tangoa. In fact they were so abundant in Tangoa that on several occasions we were afraid they would collide with the helicopter. After our departure large numbers of bats were seen on Erromango in inland areas where we did not visit. On a similar flight in 1994 we saw few if any birds. Aside from bats, we have no good impressions about the vulnerability of likely prey species; but in fact we saw no bat remains in eyries.

Breeding Chronology

We are also at a loss to explain the difference in timing of breeding between 2 locations on essentially the same latitude (and thus the same photoperiod) with similar climatic and ecological conditions. In addition to photoperiodic control of breeding, we are aware that environmental cues, such as weather (rain, temperature) and food, may also drive reproductive cycles (Cody 1971, Murton & Westwood 1977). Although rainfall varies considerably, depending on the side of the island, both island groups are within the same precipitation range (1800-4000 mm). The lee and windward sides of islands in Fiji were on the same breeding schedules. Wet and dry and hot and cold seasons occur essentially over the same period on both island groups. Cyclones hit both island groups during a similar temporal period. Thus, the difference in timing is especially difficult to understand, because breeding on Fiji has been so constant in timing over a 10 year spread. On the other hand, Peregrines in equatorial regions have reduced photoperiodic cues and so breeding cycles must be driven largely by environmental factors. At 1 eyrie in Ecuador, at nearly 2400 m, egg laying varied between late June and mid-December (Hilgart 1988) and in Kenya egg laying occurred between June and December (Thomsett 1988). Both authors concluded that food availability was the factor determining onset of laying.

It was suggested to us that cyclones early in 1993 in Vanuatu were so disturbing to fruit bats that they became largely unavailable as food to Peregrines. However, by the time falcons were ready to breed (June, July) bats were once again in large camps as we found them. Both Peregrines and bats have had a long evolutionary history together on the islands in the presence of temporally regular cyclones. Falcon breeding seasons in general are quite regular on Fiji and there are no data to suggest they would not be on Vanuatu. We saw no evidence that cyclones caused Peregrine food shortages in 1993 that might have affected onset of breeding and, further, the breeding schedule was the same in 1994.

One factor that might alter onset of breeding of an entire population in one direction or the other is rainfall. For example, in temperate Australia, a dry, warm winter may shift egg laying earlier, but by less than a week (Olsen & Olsen 1989b). Wet years were those in which the mean increase in rainfall came within two months of the normal onset of laying. However, in Queensland, Australia, onset of laying has been as early as July and as late as early November (the latter date was one case, anomalous and perhaps a replacement clutch, Czechura 1984). Australian birds in general, however, are noted for being very dependent on weather related breeding responses and in Australia weather is varied. We encountered the "normal" variation in weather in Fiji (some "wet," some "dry" seasons) over the 10 years of looking at breeding, but because of the few nests could not "measure" any real difference or relationship in onset of laying. Certainly mean differences were not more than 2 weeks apart. Generally speaking, our experience is that food abundance or quality drives either onset of laying or clutch size while environmental conditions affect success of the nesting attempt or fledging rate (see also Olsen & Olsen 1989a).

Lack of Breeding

We are disturbed by our findings in Fiji between 1985 and 1997 of the gradual decrease (perhaps actually only extreme variation) in occupancy of nest sites. In mid-October 1985, we found flying young and adults at 4 locations and observed 6 other nest sites that appeared active. Adjusting survey time in 1986, based on age of young the previous year, we covered most of the same area except for parts of Vanua Levu and located young in nests in late August at 7 locations, 4 at the same places from 1985. In 1986 pairs were seen at 3 other locations by colleagues but eyries were not found. In 1989, we covered the same area as previously on Viti Levu and found 2 eyries containing young and 1 had flying adults but no young. In 1991, we made a thorough examination of the cumulative total of 10 eyries with some history of activity and the results are shown on Table 1. Following 1989 there was a rather sharp drop in activity, representing about a 50% overall inactivity rate. In 1993 we checked 2 reliable eyries that had been active on all previous years and two were checked by our helicopter pilots; there was no breeding although a solitary female was at one. If the rest of Fiji (e.g., Kadavu, Lau group, parts of Vanua Levu) has a similar inactivity rate to our sample then the falcon has become extremely rare as a breeding species in Fiji.

We are at a loss to explain the gradual loss in activity of these eyries over such a short period of time. But F. Clunie (pers. comm.) found that the eyrie on Joske's Thumb was used intermittently and D. Watling (pers.comm,) mentioned the inactivity (see White et al. 1988) of the eyrie we called "Signatoka" in Table 1. The latter may have been because of human disturbance since the eyrie is relatively accessible and can be walked to. Generally, there is no evidence that direct human interference at eyries is involved since most of the eyries are relatively inaccessible. However, we heard of several cases of adults being shot. In 1995 we know of 1 adult shot by a farmer during the breeding season, prior to our visit, near a known eyrie. That eyrie was unoccupied that season. The same farmer told us he had shot 3 others over the previous 4 years as they sat in trees at his farm.

There are several events that might have happened to explain our findings. First, adults were lost at a higher rate (perhaps a result of human shootings) than they could be replaced because of an extremely low floating, non-breeding population. Second, pairs might have had early egg loss and thus not been attached to breeding stations on a permanent basis so they were not seen. Third, the single birds we saw at eyries in 1994 could be a result of either one of these. Lastly, they may be tied to variable weather and food resources as they are in Australia; this could result in non-breeding or at least adjustments in the breeding cycle as in Queensland. In Australia, for example, breeding dynamics of some raptors have evolved to compensate for periodic weather phenomena, such as El Niño events of which there have been a series over the past 4-5 years (Trenberth & Hoar 1996), that in turn affect food availability and thus their breeding condition. Weather, however, seems to have been "average" through this time period except for the especially wet typhoon Kina that occurred in January 1993. In a species with naturally low adult mortality one evolutionary strategy used when food is undependable or periodically affected, is to have intermittent breeding (many northern hemisphere raptors do just that). As with the Australian populations (Sherrod 1983), falcons in Fiji and Vanuatu may also have long juvenile dependency periods that help increase survivorship of young as a response to that very situation. On Vanuatu, we were at a nest containing a newly hatched young when a juvenile of the previous year came food begging from the flying adults. It was not driven away by the pair as would be the case in other populations we have studied.

Population Dynamics-A Scenario

Based on the fact that Peregrines seem to be, 1) poorly suited or adapted to tropical climates and generally occur in low densities there, 2) that few year-old birds are seen away from eyries (Clunie in White et al. 1988) suggesting a low floating population and that, 3) there seemed to be variable amounts of breeding year to year. A plausible scenario for those island populations might be as follows: Adults have evolved to be relatively long lived once reaching breeding age because mortality is high in the years prior to breeding. A relatively substantial pre-breeding age mortality may be related to food availability. Food availability (or perhaps choice or vulnerability) require that young have an extended period of dependence on adults (our observations in Vanuatu; Sherrod 1983). Food or weather vagaries, rather than interaction for nest sites or with adults, thus account for the major mortality of young. All of this then results in a low density non-breeding (floating) population to act as replacements at eyries once adults are lost. Under normal compensatory mortality rates (mortality adjusted so that there is a balance with carrying capacity) population density is maintained at a given level. However, once additive mortality (mortality over and above the natural compensatory levels) increases, from shooting of adults for example, replacement populations are not sufficient to maintain eyrie activity. Some adults may occur at eyries (our observations of lone adults) without finding mates for a time period. Slowly the population builds up and eyries are reoccupied again.

IMPLICATIONS FOR BIODIVERSITY AND CONSERVATION

There are at least 3 important items that emerge from the data on Peregrines from Fiji and Vanuatu. First, the race *F.p. nesiotes* occurs in low densities and breeding pairs are widely scattered. However, Peregrines may occur in very low densities over long time periods if adult survivorship is not drastically altered or if mortality is not additive. Effective breeding populations of only a few pairs persisted in some regions of North America for apparently a couple of decades during the pesticide era in the 1960's-70's. The subspecies *madens*, confined to the Cape Verde Islands, may contain 10-12 pairs and *furuitii* is apparently confined to one island in the Volcano Islands, North Pacific Ocean, so far as is known (King 1978,79). Second, even if such small populations may persist over some time periods it gives us little comfort with regards to Fiji if our impressions of a highly fluctuating breeding population are accurate (Brimm 1994), especially because of the lack of any feasible scenario causing such changes. This is especially alarming in the face of a rapidly developing island nation. Because of the falcon's presence, its historical roots and folklore within Fiji (the *ganivatu* of legend), the loss of the species from Fiji would certainly diminish the biodiversity by more than simply the loss of one species. Perhaps annual census data over at least one falcon breeding generation is necessary to understand breeding phenology and to help answer the questions of any relationship between the loss of eyrie occupation we have witnessed and disturbance, weather, food, and the regularity of breeding. An Australian population near Melbourne with 21 eyries steadily declined 25% between 1976-1984 and the regression line predicted nearly a 50% decline by 1992. However, a survey in 1992 showed nearly a 90% reoccupancy again (Emison & Hurley 1995). Also, during the exceptionally dry year of 1994 over 50% of a well studied sample of 22 eyries near Canberra, Australia, did not occupy breeding sites but were back to the previously high occupancy rate (around 90%) the following year (P.D. Olsen, pers. commun,). Overall, this population generally had a 82-100% occupancy per year by at least one bird. Annual eyrie occupancy rates in continuously monitored populations may be extremely different from region to region and from one another as shown in a sample of studies in Table 3. No particular relationship between occupancy rates and food or weather was established for these studies although the Utah sample is in a region of inordinately abundant food resources. Thus, better knowledge is needed on the control of breeding dynamics in tropical or southern latitudes and assumptions based on northern hemisphere breeding biology may not be accurate. Third, the impact of inbreeding on population viability is not understood especially for populations that may have successfully passed through several "bottlenecks" and where the breeding strategy may be one of inbreeding. Regardless, genetic variability (and the so-called hybrid vigour) may help the populations we have studied. The notion of infusion of genes from Vanuatu

Table 3. Examples of variation in eyrie occupancy rates between regions as compared with Fiji. Occupancy is defined as the presence of at least one falcon at the eyrie whether breeding took place or not. The South African sample[1] was specifically used because all sites were checked in a given year and the regions had more or less distinct populations. Percent occupancy is for a constant sample except in Fiji where it represents occupancy of those that were checked and the sample size varied from year to year.

Region	Percent by Year						
	Yr. 1	Yr. 2	Yr. 3	Yr. 4	Yr. 5	Yr. 6	Yr. 7
So. Africa 1 (n=10)	70%	80%	90%	90%	90%	90%	100%
So. Africa 2 (n=6)	100%	100%	100%	100%	100%	100%	83%
So. Africa 3 (n=7)	86	71%	71%	57%	71%		
Utah[2] (n=7)	100%	100%	100%	100%	100%	100%	100%
Fiji	100% (n=4)	100% (n=11)	60% (n=5)	50% (n=10)	25% (n=4)	57% (n=7)	40% (n=6)

[1]Unpublished data provided, at our request, by Andrew Jenkins from his study areas.
[2]Data were taken from "hack" towers around the shores of the Great Salt Lake from which falcons had been originally released for a reintroduction programme. Data furnished by Don Paul.

---

into Fiji by translocating birds, and *vice versa*, may be a worthwhile consideration for populations declining or in low densities. Based on a phylogenetic analysis of morphological traits (White & Boyce 1988) it was not clear if Peregrines from Australia or those from the New Guinea/Solomon Islands complex are the source gene pool although *nesoites* did cluster with that clade. So far, genetic analysis has also not been adequate to resolve this question. The likely answer may lie in a broader DNA analysis of birds from New Caledonia, northern Australia, and the Solomon Islands.

ACKNOWLEDGEMENTS

Numerous people helped in this study over the years. We cannot mention them all for the list would be too long but helicopter pilots Lisa Patterson, Ian Simpson, Nick Ragg, and Robbie MacKenzie in Fiji, and Garrett Cloete on Vanuatu, were invaluable and made our study possible. Fergus Clunie, Clifford "Bud" Anderson, and Dick Watling provided or helped with data from Fiji. Penny Olsen, Dean Amadon, Tom Cade and Andrew Jenkins provided important comments. Vickie and Marcus Tompson, Tuku Tuku Ranch, Vanuatu, allowed us to stay at their ranch in 1995. The governments of Fiji and Vanuatu have provided unrestricted help; particularly being aided by Niumaia Tebunakawai and Peter Manuele of Fiji and Ernest Bani of Vanuatu.

REFERENCES

BREGULLA, H.L. 1992. *Birds of Vanuatu*. Anthony Nelson, UK
BRIMM, D.J. 1994. Falcons of Fiji. *Wild Birds* 8(8):281-290.
BROWN, L.H. & D. AMADON 1968. *Eagles, hawks and falcons of the world*. McGraw Hill Book Co., New York.
CLUNIE, F. 1972. A contribution to the natural history of the Fiji peregrine. *Notornis* 19:302-322.
CLUNIE, F. 1976. A Fiji peregrine in an urban-marine environment. *Notornis* 23:8-28.

CODY, M. 1971. Ecological aspects of reproduction. In: *Avian Biology*, Vol. 1, (eds D.S. Farner & J.R. King) pp 461-512, Academic Press, New York.

COURT, G.S., BRADLEY, D.M., GATES, C.C., & BOAG, D.A. 1988. The population biology of Peregrine Falcons in the Keewatin District of the Northwest Territories, Canada. In: *Peregrine Falcon Populations: Their Management and Recovery* (eds T.J. Cade, J.H. Enderson, C.G. Thelander & C.M. White) pp. 729-739. The Peregrine Fund Inc., Boise, Idaho.

CZECHURA, G. V. 1984. The Peregrine Falcon (*Falco peregrinus macropus* Swainson) in southeastern Queensland. *Raptor Res.* 18:81-91.

DIAMOND, J. M. & MARSHALL, A. G. 1976. Origins of the New Hebridean avifauna. *Emu* 76:187-200.

EMISON, W.B, BREN W.M., & ARCHER, H.F. 1988. Victoria - Agricultural areas. In: *Peregrine Falcon Populations: their Management and Recovery*. (eds T.J. Cade, J.H. Enderson, C.G. Thelander & C.M. White) pp 267-268. The Peregrine Fund Inc., Boise, Idaho.

EMISON, W.B. & V.G. HURLEY 1995. Occupancy of peregrine falcon eyries near Melbourne during 1976-84 and 1992. *The Victorian Nat.* 112:100-101.

GORDON, A.C.H. (LORD STANMORE) (Ed.). 1897-1912. Fiji: records of private and of public life, 1875-1880, vol I-IV. Edinburgh, private printing.

HEREDIA, B., HIRALDO, F., GONZALEZ, L.M. & GONZALEZ, J.L. 1988. Status, ecology, and conservation of the Peregrine Falcon in Spain. In: *Peregrine Falcon Populations: their Management and Recovery* (eds T.J. Cade, J.H. Enderson, C.G. Thelander & C.M. White). pp. 219-226. The Peregrine Fund Inc., Boise, Idaho.

HILGERT, N. 1988. Aspects of breeding and feeding behavior of peregrine falcons in Guayllabamba, Ecuador. In: *Peregrine Falcon Populations: their Management and Recovery* (eds T.J. Cade, J.H. Enderson, C.G. Thelander, & C.M. White) pp 749-755. The Peregrine Fund, Inc., Boise, Idaho.

HUSTLER, K. 1988. Why are peregrines so rare in South Africa? *Ostrich* 58:86-88.

JENKINS, A. 1991. Latitudinal prey productivity and potential density in the peregrine falcon. *Gabar* 6:20-24

KING, W.B. 1978-79. *Endangered Birds of the World*-The ICBP Bird Red Data Book. Vol. 2, Aves. 2nd ed. IUCN, Morges, Switzerland.

MAYR, E. 1941. Birds collected during the Whitney South Sea expedition. XLV. The geographical variation of *Falco peregrinus* in the Papuan and Australian regions. *Amer. Mus. Novitates* No 1133.

MENDELSOHN, J.M. 1988. The status and biology of the peregrine in the Afrotropical region. In: *Peregrine Falcon Populations: Their Management and Recovery*. (eds T.J. Cade, J.H. Enderson, C.G. Thelander & C.M. White) pp. 297-306. The Peregrine Fund, Boise, Idaho.

MOONEY, N. & BROTHERS, N. 1988. Tasmania. In: *Peregrine Falcon Populations: their Management and Recovery*. (eds T.J. Cade, J.H. Enderson, C.G. Thelander & C.M. White) pp. 271-272. The Peregrine Fund Inc., Boise, Idaho.

MURTON, R.K. & WESTWOOD, N.J. 1977. *Avian Breeding Cycles*. Oxford Univ. Press, Oxford, UK.

OLSEN, P.D. & OLSEN, J. 1988. Southern Tablelands, New South Wales. In: *Peregrine Falcon Populations:their Management and Recovery*. (eds T.J. Cade, J.H. Enderson, C.G. Thelander & C.M. White) pp. 266-267. The Peregrine Fund Inc., Boise, Idaho.

OLSEN, P.D. & OLSEN, J. 1989a. Breeding of the Peregrine Falcon (*Falco peregrinus*). III. Weather, nest quality and breeding success. *Emu* 89:6-14.

OLSEN, P.D. & OLSEN, J. 1989b. Breeding of the Peregrine Falcon (*Falco peregrinus*). II. Weather, nest quality and the timing of egg-laying. *Emu* 89:1-5.

PICKERING R. 1982. Birds of Vanuatu 5: birds of prey. *Naika* 7:11-12.

TARBOTON, W. & ALLEN, D. 1984. The Status and Conservation of Birds of Prey in the Transvaal. Monog. No. 3., Transvaal Museum, Pretoria, South Africa.

THIOLLAY, J.-M. 1988. Prey availability limiting on island population of Peregrine Falcons in Tunisia. In: *Peregrine Falcon Populations: their Management and Recovery*. (eds T.J. Cade, J.H. Enderson, C.G. Thelander & C.M. White). pp 701-710. The Peregrine Fund, Inc. Boise, Idaho.

THOMSON, W.R. 1984. Comparative notes on the ecology of Peregrine, Lanner and Taita Falcons in Zimbabwe. In: Proceedings of the 2nd Symposium on African Predatory Birds. (eds J.M. Mendelsohn & C.W. Sapsford) pp. 15-18. Natal Bird Club, Durban, South Africa.

THOMSETT, S. 1988. Distribution and status of the Peregrine in Kenya. In: *Peregrine Falcon Populations: their Management and Recovery*. (eds T.J. Cade, J.H. Enderson, C.G. Thelander & C.M. White). pp 289-295. The Peregrine Fund, Inc., Boise, Idaho.

TRENBERTH, K.E. & T.J. HOAR 1996. The 1990-1995 El Niño-Southern Oscillation event: Longest on record. *Geophysical Res. Lett.* 23:57-60.

SHERROD, S.K. 1983. *Behavior of fledging peregrines*. The Peregrine Fund, Boise, Idaho

WHITE, C.M. & D.A. BOYCE, Jr. 1988. An overview of peregrine falcon subspecies. In: *Peregrine Falcon Populations: their Management and Recovery.* (eds. T.J. Cade, J.H.Enderson, C.G. Thelander & C.M.White). pp.789-810. The Peregrine Fund, Boise, Idaho.

WHITE, C. M., BRIMM, D.J., & CLUNIE, F. 1988. A study of Peregrines in the Fiji Islands, South Pacific Ocean. In: *Peregrine Falcon Populations: their Management and Recovery.* (eds T.J. Cade, J.H. Enderson, C.G. Thelander & C.M. White) pp. 275-287. The Peregrine Fund, Boise, Idaho.

WHITE, C.M., J.R. PARRISH, D.J. BRIMM & J.L. LOMNGMIRE 1993. Aspects of variation between peregrine falcon *Falco peregrinus*: a review with emphasis on southern hemisphere populations. In: *Australian Raptor Studies.* (ed. P.D. Olsen) pp. 13-24. Australasian Raptor Association, R.A.O.U., Melbourne.

Clayton M. White
Department of Zoology
Brigham Young University,
Provo, Utah 84602
USA

Daniel J. Brimm
Endangered Species Recovery Council
2461 Vallecitos, La Jolla,
California 92037
USA

Jon H. Wetton
Forensic Science Service
Priory House, Gooch Street North
Birmingham
B5 6QQ
UK

The Osprey *Pandion haliaetus* in the Cape Verde Islands: Distribution, Population Trends and Conservation problems

João Ferreira and Luis Palma

SUMMARY

The Osprey population of the Cape Verde Islands has been estimated since the 1960's at about 50 pairs, hence the most important in Macronesia. However, this was only based on incidental observation. In 1998, we started a systematic survey of Ospreys in the archipelago in order to investigate the present situation, recent demographic trends and conservation status. A comprehensive survey of breeding pairs and nests as well as of abandoned historic nesting sites is currently ongoing. Population trends have been checked on the basis of observed abandoned nest sites and information on former breeding sites obtained from published data, personal communications and enquiries among local residents. Incidental data on breeding biology, success and failure are being collected, along with basic ecological information on breeding habitats, diet and preferred foraging areas. Human impacts were identified and evaluated in terms of their potential direct or indirect effect upon breeding. An important loss of eggs and nestlings linked with widespread human depredation is supposed to take place in the more accessible breeding sites. Increasing touristic activities may also be a disturbing factor in some areas. The number of abandoned territories and nests in the southern margins of the distribution range and in the more accessible locations of the northeastern islands seems to be an indication of a general decline of the population.

INTRODUCTION

The historical presence of resident populations of Ospreys *Pandion haliaetus* is known from all the island groups of Macronesia with the exception of the Azores (Naurois, 1987; González *et al*, 1992; Palma, in press). As in the Mediterranean and along the Portuguese coast, in Macaronesia breeding Ospreys are exclusively marine dwelling birds. The species is long absent from the Madeira archipelago, where toponymics recalling traditional breeding sites in the coasts of Madeira and Porto Santo are now the only trace of its former existence. Ospreys also heavily declined in the Canaries and only a small remnant of their former numbers survive.

In the Cape Verde islands Ospreys were reputedly common and even abundant at least during the last century and that was probably still the case during the first half of the present century, although references are scarce and diffuse (cf. Naurois, 1987). The latter provided a detailed report on the species' occurrence in the islands but, as he admitted himself, his observations were incomplete and mainly resulted from general ornithological work in the archipelago rather than from a specific study. In particular, his assessment of the species situation in the islands with a more rugged topography is only approximate due to the obvious logistic difficulties encountered. Therefore, the estimate of 45-60 pairs for the 1960's has to be cautiously accepted. Nevertheless, his work is of value in terms of the general information about the Osprey population in the Cape Verdes and an important reference to evaluate population trends since the 1960's.

Naurois' estimate of c. 50 pairs is maintained by Hazevoet (1995) for the 1988-1993 period and a slightly larger figure of 55-65 pairs has recently been advanced by Dennis and Hille (in press) for the years 1996-97. However, in both cases, no systematic survey was undertaken and hence these numbers are also to be taken with precaution. Poole (1989) and Dennis & Hille (in press) stressed the importance of further investigations on the population.

The aims of the current research were: 1) to characterise the present situation and the conservation status of the species in the Cape Verde islands and 2) to provide basic management measures for the conservation of the population. To achieve these aims we intended:
   a) to make a complete census of the population and map nests or breeding locations, and to characterise the breeding habitat;
   b) to check breeding success, nestling mortality and productivity;
   c) to evaluate population trends during the last three decades, interactions between Osprey and man and associated conservation problems;
   d) to study the genetic distance between this and other populations of the Western Palearctic;
   e) to provide conservation and land management indications.

Information supplied here is preliminary and reports only on the results of the partial survey carried out in 1998 and on the discussion of population trends and general conservation issues. References and stretches of coast that remained unchecked during 1998 will be visited the following breeding season. Known breeding sites will be monitored to check for breeding success.

METHODS

For the assessment of the size, distribution and trends of the breeding population, an extensive survey of territorial pairs and nest sites was carried out. As a starting point we used all previous information available (Naurois, 1964, 1969 and 1987; Hazevoet & Haafkens, 1989; Hazevoet, 1995) as well as unpublished data provided by several observers (C. J. Hazevoet, S. Hille, N. Onofre, pers. comm.). Additionally, we checked all 1:25 000 maps of the archipelago for toponymic references. The Osprey has a distinctive popular name in Portuguese - guincho - which remains widespread in toponymics, not only along the coasts of Portugal but also along the coastal areas of Madeira, the Canaries and the Cape Verdes, probably spread by the Portuguese along their navigation routes during the 15th century. Fishermen and peasants were questioned about the current and the past occurrence of breeding "guinchos" and the existence of occupied or deserted nests.

All previous information on breeding sites, both along the coast as well as inland, were investigated for their occupancy status. The search was, however, not restricted to these locations, being carried out wherever possible all along the coastline and neighbouring areas up to several kilometres inland on the basis of suitable geographic and topographic features and/or tranquillity, according to a search image based on literature and direct observation. The mountainous centres of some islands were searched only if the presence of the species was suspected.

From December 1997 to August 1998 fieldwork was carried out by motorcycle and on foot, with the aid of 10x50 binoculars and a 32x80 telescope. Parts of the coast unsuited for observation from inland will be surveyed by boat in 1999.

The survey coverage level (SCL) of each island was assessed by first dividing its coastline into 5 categories: 0 - not searched; 1 - searched but unsuited for observation from inland; 2 – not fully searched (i.e. pairs and nests possibly overlooked); 3 - satisfactorily searched (possibly undetected nests but not undetected pairs) and 4 - fully searched (every pair or nest detected). Each category was then weighed by multiplying it by the corresponding number of UTM 1x1 km units of the coastline. Finally SCL was calculated by dividing the weighed total by the total number of UTM units. Values range between 0 and 4.

Actual or potential anthropic threats were evaluated on the basis of observed or implied human presence and activity near occupied and unoccupied nests, and residents were asked about interactions between man and Osprey. The degree of public awareness about the presence of each pair or nest was subjectively assessed. Whenever possible, escape distance to the observer was recorded as a measure of response to human presence.

To evaluate the degree of exposure to human impact, nests were categorised by their relative vulnerability in terms of ease of access without climbing equipment. Categories of relative accessibility are: high – very easily accessed by motorcycle or normal walk (e.g. ground nests); moderate – accessible on foot or by boat and easily climbed without equipment; low – accessible on foot or by boat involving difficult/dangerous approach and access; and inaccessible - with no access without sophisticated climbing equipment.

RESULTS AND DISCUSSION

Area surveyed

In 1998, during 98 days of fieldwork, 9 of the 10 islands of the archipelago were surveyed. Among these, 5 belong to the northern Barlavento (windward) group – Santo Antão, São Nicolau, São Vicente, Sal and Boavista – and the remaining 4 to the southern Sotavento (leeward) group – Maio, Santiago, Fogo e Brava. Furthermore, the islet of Raso was visited by other ornithologists (N. Ratcliffe, C. J. Hazevoet and L. Monteiro) in February 1998 (C. J. Hazevoet, pers. comm.).

The island of Santa Luzia and the islet of Branco (Barlavento), and the islets of Rombos (Sotavento) have not been surveyed so far. Santo Antão and São Nicolau were also only partially surveyed.

Table 1 shows the survey effort and coverage (SCL) undertaken in 1998, and the ratio between checked and unchecked references during that phase. About *c.* 70% of the area was surveyed corresponding to an average SCL of the islands of 57.5%.

Table 1. Osprey population survey effort in 1998 (* visited by Hazevoet and others).

ISLANDS ISLETS	No. of field days	SCL (%)	Toponymics checked	Toponymics unchecked	Other ref's checked	Other ref's unchecked
Sto. Antão	8	40	1	1	2	2
S. Vicente	16	77.5	3	0	8	0
Sta. Luzia	0	0	0	0	0	2
Branco	0	0	0	0	0	2
Raso	*	100	0	0	0	4
S. Nicolau	6	25	1	2	2	2
Sal	9	100	2	0	7	0
Boavista	11	95	3	0	11	4
Maio	4	97.5	0	0	4	0
Santiago	24	77.5	0	2	6	2
Fogo	11	72.5	6	0	4	0
Brava	9	70	0	0	1	0
Rombos	0	0	0	0	0	2
Total/Mean	98	57.5	16	5	45	20

Reference checking

In the next table we present the results of checking for the Osprey's current presence in locations with references to its former occurrence (last 3 decades), either nests or pairs observed, obtained from publications, toponymics and personal communications.

Table 2. Results of checking Osprey reference sites in surveyed islands (+ = positive results, - = negative results).

ISLANDS	Nests +	Nests -	Observ. +	Observ. -	Total +	Total -
Sto. Antão		1	2		2	1
S. Vicente	4		3		7	0
S. Nicolau		1	1		1	1
Sal	2	5		1	2	6
Boavista	1	6	1		2	6
Maio	1			2	1	2
Santiago		1	2	3	2	4
Fogo		4		1		5
Brava				1		1
Total	**8**	**18**	**9**	**8**	**17**	**26**

The number of reference sites where the present occurrence of Ospreys was confirmed (17) are clearly less than those with negative result (26). This can be viewed as a first indication that important changes in the location or the number of pairs have occurred recently.

Nest census and occupancy

During the 1998 field work, 38 nests were found of which 19 were occupied, 12 unoccupied (unattended) and 8 abandoned (decaying), plus one occupied nest found in Raso by Ratcliffe, Hazevoet and Monteiro. Unoccupied nests were probably alternative nests in most cases.

Taking into consideration only the islands and islets thoroughly surveyed, the percentage of abandoned nests is quite high (20.5%). These are located in the eastern and Sotavento islands and indicate at least serious disturbance or, as in the cases of Fogo and Sal, a clear decline. In the case of unoccupied nests, however, they may be alternative nests of extant pairs in many cases. It must be stressed that the rates of unoccupancy are particularly high in the eastern islands – Sal and Boavista – where nests are often quite accessible, hence vulnerable, to disturbance and human depredation. Moreover, these islands also yielded several deserted territories with abandoned nests.

Table 3. Nest census and occupancy (* At least 1 nest must exist but could not be located)

ISLANDS ISLETS	No. nests observed	Occupied	Unoccupied	Abandoned	Territories w/ aband. nests
São Vicente	7	7	0	0	0
Raso	1	1	0	0	0
Sal	7	2	3	2	2
Boavista	17	7	7	3	0-2
Maio	0	0*	0	0	?
Santiago	4	2	2	0	?
Fogo	3	0	0	3	3
Brava	0	0	0	0	?
Total	**39**	**19**	**12**	**8**	

Based on the number of pairs observed (with or without nest), we estimate 32-39 pairs of Osprey in the part of the country already surveyed (c. 70%). We compared this estimate with the one made by Naurois (1987) in the 1960's to assess the population trend of the species during the last 3 decades in those islands and islets sufficiently studied (Table 4).

We believe that numbers in São Vicente and Boavista must have remained stable though present estimates are higher than Naurois'. In Boavista the difference is slight whereas in São Vicente the lower numbers for the 1960's may be due to underestimating by Naurois because of the rugged nature of the island. Conversely, it is not impossible that some increase may have occurred. This is the only island where local people do not refer to the traditional human consumption of eggs and nestlings. An increase may also have occurred in Raso.

In all other already well surveyed islands there was a clear decrease in the number of pairs, both in Sal and all islands of the Sotavento, especially in Fogo and Brava where the species vanished.

Table 4. Population sizes and trends of the Osprey in the Cape Verde islands (*Rough estimates according to Naurois because of logistic difficulties due to the rugged topography of the islands)

ISLANDS ISLETS	Naurois' estimate	Current estimate	Trend	Approximate % change
Santo Antão	8-11 *	> 6		
São Vicente	3-6	7-9	⇑ (?)	+ 44
Santa Luzia	3-4			
Branco	3-4			
Raso	1-2	3	⇑	+ 62
São Nicolau	5-8 *	> 3		
Sal	6-8	2-3	⇓	- 64
Boavista	5-8	7-9	⇔ (?)	
Maio	2-3	1	⇓	- 60
Santiago	4-6 *	2-4?	⇓	- 40
Fogo	2-5 *	0?	⇓	- 100?
Brava	3-5	0?	⇓	- 100?
Rombos	1?			
Total	**45-60**	**31-38**		

As we can see in the table above, with the exception of Sal, population decrease becomes stronger as one approaches the southwest end of the archipelago. For reasons not yet established though probably linked with ecological factors such as food or suitable nest-site availability, the abundance of Ospreys has always been much lower in the Sotavento than in the Barlavento islands (Naurois, 1987). Therefore, we can speculate that the Sotavento constitutes a demographic periphery of the population. If that is the case, the species can hold itself in the less favourable areas of the Sotavento only by dispersal from the Barlavento.

Thus, if a significant decrease of productivity occurs in the Barlavento population, an insufficient number of emigrants reach the Sotavento to compensate for mortality and low productivity. This can eventually cause the decline and extinction of the species in the sub-region. Hence, the negative trend verified in the southern islands may be rather a reflection of a general decline of the species in the archipelago than a local or regional phenomenon. This may be due to the overharvesting of eggs and nestlings by humans (cf. Naurois, 1964).

The Osprey decline in Sal may also reflect the general trend of the population, but this island is located among others with stable Osprey nuclei so local human impacts are more likely to be an explanation. In fact, this is the island where the intensification of human activities seems to have had a stronger detrimental effect upon the species. This can both be due to human depredation and disturbance by tourist activities. The small size and sloping topography of the island can explain its vulnerability.

We anticipate that the spreading of tourism in the other eastern "flat" islands – Boavista and Maio – will with time cause a similar situation, of which the recent retreat of several nesting sites to the hinterland of Boavista seems to be a first indication. Considering its numeric importance and geographic position, the decline and possible loss of the Boavista population would be especially serious to the whole population of the archipelago and to the southern islands' sub-populations in particular.

The response of Ospreys to the probable increase of stress from human impacts is clearly shown in the relationship between the vulnerability of nests and their present occupancy. All but one of the highly accessible nests (namely ground nests) were inactive; this happens in Boavista and the only exception is on the island of São Vicente, so far a stronghold of the species. Most ground nests in flat areas referred to in the literature have also disappeared. Of the moderately accessible nests (Sal and Boavista, n=16), 63% were inactive or abandoned. Thus, retreat has begun first in the most vulnerable sites and is gradually affecting safer locations. In the end, even inaccessible locations are deserted as has happened in Fogo, where all the (decaying) nests found are of this type.

CONCLUSIONS

Considering the present estimate of 31-38 pairs of Ospreys in the 70% of the islands already surveyed it seems reasonable to accept that at least a total of 44 pairs may exist. From another perspective, if the part of Santo Antão already studied (40%) is representative for the rest, then the island can hold up to $c.$ 15 pairs. The same exercise for São Nicolau (25% surveyed) would give $c.$ 12 pairs in the island. For comparison, the figures given by Naurois (1987) for these islands are 8-11 and 5-8 respectively but this author stressed the uncertainty of his estimate. The anticipation of 18 pairs more than the number censused so far in both islands (9 pairs) seems reasonable for there are no reasons to suspect a decline in these islands. Thus, the total population in the archipelago may roughly rise up to $c.$ 60 pairs.

Because Naurois' observations were made before the strong decrease that occurred in the islands of the Sotavento and Sal, the actual Osprey population in the 1960's must have been significantly larger than his upper estimate (60 pairs). The decrease verified probably reflects the long-term effect of the traditional use of eggs and nestlings for food by man. Also the increase of disturbance caused by a growing number of urban people and four-wheel-drive cars near the nests is liable to cause desertion, especially in vulnerable sites near the coastline in the eastern islands where tourism is gradually encroaching. Both factors lower productivity and force the birds to retreat from the most vulnerable yet probably favoured breeding locations, this in turn further lowering productivity, and hence being susceptible of implicating a wider retraction of the range and loss of pairs. The situation in the islands of Santiago, Maio and Sal, and also Boavista to some extent, seems precarious. In particular, Boavista still is a stronghold of the species and losses due to unplanned tourism would be disastrous to the whole population.

Notwithstanding, the Osprey population of the Cape Verdes is still by far the most important in Macaronesia and its fate may determine the future of the species in the whole region. The Osprey is quite tolerant of moderate human presence and indeed very tolerant in the Cape Verdes due to the fact that the adults are not persecuted. Technically its recovery and survival in the islands should not be a difficult task provided education of rural populations and coastal tourist management is carried out within time. For tourism, the Osprey is of undoubtful value because of its attractiveness and liveliness and for the environmental quality of the islands it is one of the most faithful wardens.

ACKNOWLEDGEMENTS

We are especially indebted to the Instituto Nacional de Desenvolvimento das Pescas (INDP) of Cape Verde in Mindelo for the continuous support provided. We are particularly grateful to its President

Dr. Aníbal Medina and the fisheries biologist Edério Almada. We also thank the Instituto Nacional de Investigação e Desenvolvimento Agrário (INIDA) of Cape Verde in Praia, its President Dr. João Levy and Isildo Gomes.

This work has been made much easier and greatly improved by the valuable unpublished data kindly provided by Sabine Hille, Nuno Onofre and especially Dr. Cornelis Hazevoet, to whom we are deeply indebted. The latter also helped with the revision of the manuscript.

Special thanks are due to Dr. Francisca Inocêncio in Mindelo and to Eng. Osvaldo Cruz in Praia for their kind hospitality and support. We are also deeply grateful to the many new friends all over the country for their warm and friendly companionship. A final word goes to the prompt and genuine "morabeza" of the people of the Cape Verde islands.

The Parque Natural do Sudoeste Alentejano e Costa Vicentina of Portugal and a grant from FAO-Pescas of Cape Verde have financially supported this work.

REFERENCES

DENNIS, R & S. HILLE IN PRESS. Ospreys in the Cape Verdes. *Vogelwarte.*
HAZEVOET, C.J. 1995. The birds of the Cape Verde islands. *BOU Check-list 13*. British Ornithologists' Union, Tring.
HAZEVOET, C.J. & L.B. HAAFKENS 1989. Nature Reserve development and ornithological research in the República de Cabo Verde. Report on Phase 1, ICBP, Amsterdam.
GONZÁLEZ, G., J.M. SANTIAGO & L. FERNÁNDEZ 1992. *El águila pescadora (Pandion haliaetus) en España. Censo, reproducción y conservación.* Colección Técnica. ICONA, Madrid.
NAUROIS, R. DE 1964. Les oiseaux des îles du Cap Vert. *Garcia da Orta* 12 (4): 609-620.
NAUROIS, R. DE 1969. Notes brèves sur l'avifaune de l'archipel du Cap-Vert. Faunistique, endémisme, écologie. *Bulletin de l'Institut Fondamental d'Afrique Noire.* Tome XXXI, série A, n° 1: 143-218.
NAUROIS, R. DE 1987. Le Balbuzard (*Pandion haliaetus* L.) aux îles du Cap Vert. *Annali del Museo Civico di Storia Naturale (Genova)* 86: 657-682.
PALMA, L. In press. Ospreys *Pandion haliaetus* in the Portuguese coast. Past, present and recovery potential. *Vogelwelt.*

João Ferreira and Luis Palma
Universidade do Algarve
UCTRA, Campus de Gambelas
P-8000 Faro
Portugal

Ecomorphology of island populations of the Kestrel *Falco tinnunculus* on Cape Verde

S. Hille and H. Winkler

ABSTRACT

Data comprising 23 morphological characters from 55 Kestrels *Falco tinnunculus* from three island populations of the Cape Verde archipelago show significant variation in shape of bill, tarsus, and talon. Since the variation refers to trophic structures, we suggest that ecological factors are largely responsible for the morphological differences in these island populations. Kestrels of the population on Brava (*Falco tinnunculus alexandri*) are intermediate between those of Boavista (*Falco tinnunculus alexandri*) and Santo Antao (*Falco tinnunculus neglectus*).

The data also revealed a distinct sexual dimorphism in morphological shape. The differences pertain mainly to trophic structures. This suggests that the dimorphism, previously only discussed with respect to body size, is due, at least in part, to ecological factors relating to prey type and availability. This assumption is strengthened by the fact that the degree of sexual dimorphism varies among these ecologically very different islands.

INTRODUCTION

Islands offer divergent environments with geographically separated animal populations that are subject to several evolutionary forces like genetic bottle-necks, drift, gene flow and selection driven by local conditions. Therefore, islands are an ideal field laboratory to study differentiation within a species and the corresponding covariation among behavioural and morphological characteristics and ecological conditions. Studies of the morphological variation of island vertebrate populations range from comparisons between continental and island forms to meticulous analyses of micro evolutionary change (Gorman 1979, Losos *et al.* 1997). Ecomorphological arguments were also used to describe and explain extant biogeographic patterns (Wunderle 1983).

Populations of the same species often differ among islands of an archipelago. These differences may be caused by genetic drift or selection for individuals best equipped for the prevailing local conditions. Drift is strongly dependent on population size and constitutes the major force counteracting selection in isolated populations. Gene flow from other islands or from continental populations can effectively swamp local adaptations. Population bottle-necks have ambiguous effects. On the one hand they exacerbate drift, but they may also increase additive genetic variance and hence allow for bursts of effective selection (Carson & Templeton 1984). Selection of individuals well adapted to local ecology can be strong and island populations may differentiate within astonishingly few generations (Losos *et al.* 1997).

One precondition for answering functional questions using comparative studies of island populations is that these populations are sufficiently different in the characters of interest. These differences should mainly be due to adaptations to local conditions rather than drift. Gene flow from large continental populations and phylogenetic inertia leading to adaptive differences should be low or absent.

In many bird species sexual dimorphism contributes greatly to within population differentiation. The so-called reversed sexual dimorphism, with females being larger than males, occurs in most birds of prey (hawks, owls, skuas) and in some charadriiform waders. It is greatest in species that feed on large prey (Amadon 1975). Explanations for sexual dimorphism abound (Mueller 1986, Owens & Hartley 1998). They can be grouped as those that invoke sexual selection, reproductive biology, or competition.

Small-sized males may be favoured if small and agile prey is abundant and important for small nestlings (Storer 1966). Small males also spend less energy while hunting (Reynolds 1972, Balgooven 1976). Big females are best suited to contribute to offspring care when food demand of the young is high. The female's size will offer her a variety of advantages concerning reproduction, including better nest defence (Storer 1966, Selander 1972). Selection for female dominance seems to be a major reason for the reversed sexual dimorphism, too (Amadon 1975, Mueller 1986).

Morphological differences between the sexes may also be due to niche differentiation to avoid competition for food (Storer 1954, van Valen 1965, Selander 1966, Wilson 1969, Snyder & Wiley 1976, Newton 1979). They should be more common if fewer competing species are present (Willson 1969, Ebenmann 1986) as is generally the case on islands. However, it has also been argued that a large number of competitors would select for greater efficiency and hence higher dimorphism (van Valen 1965, Willson 1969). In woodpeckers, at least, sexual dimorphism is more pronounced on islands (Wallace 1974).

The Kestrel *Falco tinnunculus* is an ideal study object for this kind of question because it is widespread on the mainland and occurs with two allopatric taxa *Falco tinnunculus neglectus* (Schlegel, 1873) and *Falco tinnunculus alexandri* (Bourne, 1955) on the entire Cape Verde archipelago (for distribution see Figure 1). They are ubiquitous and generalists in hunting modes and prey choice.

We have chosen the Cape Verde archipelago as a study area because it exhibits a variety of different environments. It consists of nine inhabited islands and some remote islets, and is situated 460 km off the West African coast. The islands in the east differ greatly from those in the west. The former are flat and sandy and aeolian activity including wandering dunes determine geomorphological traits. The western islands are less eroded and exhibit a mountainous relief with peaks up to 3000 m and little flat land. The monsoon rains are unpredictable and not annual. The islands belong to the hyper-arid areas (Barrow 1991) and there is continuing desertification of the land. Humidity and precipitation outside the monsoon are only possible at higher elevations (over 600 m).

Because of the differences in the environments on the islands adaptation may lead to divergence in morphological structures in the Kestrel among island populations. Many ecomorphological studies have shown the close relationship between habitat, behaviour and morphology (Leisler *et al.* 1989, Stiles 1995, Gamauf *et al.* 1998). The larger islands may have greater environmental heterogeneity, and so a greater width of environmental selective pressures (Williamson 1981). Further, morphological features correlate with hunting behaviour (Leisler *et al. 1989,* Carrascal *et al.* 1994).

Gene flow that potentially retards differentiation among island populations may occur between the island populations and between the archipelago and resident or migratory mainland populations (*Falco t. tinnunculus* (Linnaeus, 1758) and *Falco tinnunculus rufescens* (Swainson, 1837)).

Data sets for the analysis of morphological parameters in bird populations are mostly restricted to a basic set of a few parameters. But larger sets of morphological characters are crucial for detecting variation within one species. Leisler *et al.* (1997) stress that the number of relevant characters is still low in most studies. By taking 23 characters into account, including some which play a crucial role in subduing (tarsus, toe, talon) and manipulating prey (bill), we made sure that we could detect even low levels of morphological variation.

The study focuses on three islands which represent main Cape Verdian landscape units: Santo Antao, Brava and Boavista (see Fig. 1). Santo Antao and Brava offer a mountainous relief, the latter showing most intensive agriculture and land degradation due to drought and human impact. Boavista is one of the eastern flat and sandy islands, where agriculture is only possible in oasis-like riverbeds.

In this paper we will assess variation of external morphological characters among island populations and between sexes of the Kestrel on the archipelago to test the basic assumption that divergence among islands does occur and that it is driven by ecological factors rather than random processes.

Figure 1: Map of the Cape Verde Islands. The line separates the island populations of *F. t. neglectus* and *F t. alexandri*.

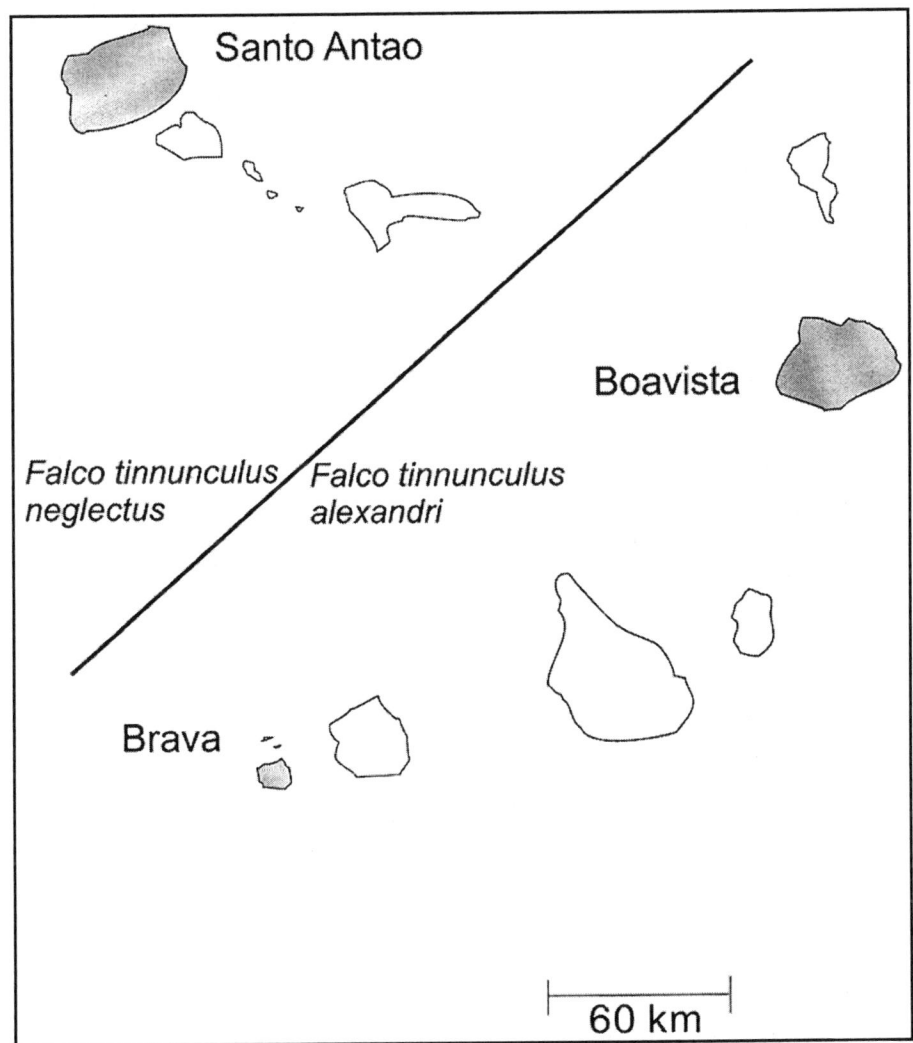

MATERIAL AND METHODS.

To examine morphometric variation in three populations of both subspecies, we measured 55 living birds from 3 islands (Boavista 21, Santo Antao: 17, Brava: 17). On the head, feet, wing and tail we measured 23 variables. These comprised bill width (gape), maxilla height from nostril until lower edge, nostril distance, cere length, cranium maximum length, tarsometatarsus length, diameter of intertarsal joint, length of toes (middle, hind, inner), length of claws (outer, middle, hind), height of claws (outer, middle, hind, inner), wing-length, Kipp's distance (wing tip to secondary 1), wing tip to primary 6, wing tip to primary 7, wing tip to primary 8 and ulna length. For details see Leisler &Winkler (1985,1991).

Data were adjusted by dividing all characters by the cube root of the weight and transformed to natural logarithms. We analyzed data with canonical variate analysis (CVA, ter Braak 1995).

RESULTS

First we grouped the individuals according to their geographical origin (island). With CVA we obtained one highly significant factor (Chi-Square= 95.925, F.G.= 24., p < .0001). It correlates mainly with seven variables: height of hind claw, gape, maxilla height, height of inner claw, distance between wing tip and 6p, height of outer claw and nostril distance (Table 1).

Table 1. Univariate F-tests and correlations of the first factor with the original characters in a CVA of 23 external characters with the birds grouped according to their origin (three islands).

Character	univariate F	p	factor
Gape	17.7827	.00000	-0.661
Maxilla height	11.6228	.00007	-0.584
Nostril distance	9.3425	.00034	-0.542
Cere			
Cranium			
Tarsometatarsus			
Knuckle			
L. toe middle			
L. toe hind			
L. toe inner			
L. claw outer			
L. claw middle	8.9692	.00045	-0.533
L. claw hind			
H. claw outer	9.5791	00029	0.543
H. claw middle			
H. claw hind	20.7185	.00000	0.702
H. claw inner	10.8255	.00012	0.571
Wing length			
kipp			
Ulna			
Tip to p6	9.4112	00032	-0.544
Tip to p7			
Tip to p8			
Percentage of total variance			91.7

Then the individuals were grouped according to sex. The highly significant factor (Chi-Square=77.721; F.G= 23; p < .0001) (Table 2). relates mainly to maximum cranium length, tarsometatarsus, nostril distance, cere length, and length of the hind claw.

Table 2: Univariate F-tests and correlations of the factor with the original characters in a CVA of 23 external characters, with the birds grouped according to sex.

Character	univariate F	p	factor
Gape			
Maxilla height			
Nostril distance	20.0439	.00004	-0.572
Cere	16.7181	.00015	-0.534
Cranium	55.1159	.00000	-0.779
Tarsometatarsus	23.3671	.00001	-0.604
Knuckle			
L. toe middle			
L. toe hind			
L. toe inner			
L. claw outer			
L. claw middle			
L. claw hind	15.6326	.00023	-0.521
H. claw outer			
H. claw middle			
H. claw hind			
H. claw inner			
Wing length			
kipp			
Ulna			
Tip to p6			
Tip to p7			
tip to p8			
Percentage of total variance			100.03

A plot of the scores on one plane obtained from these analyses (Figure 2) shows how the six groups separate according to sex and island. On the first, the "island" axis, *Falco tinnunculus neglectus* of Santo Antao is found at the far positive end, the Brava Kestrels hold an intermediate position, and the Kestrels of Boavista are on the far left (negative) end of the axis. This corresponds to the high and short claws of the Santo Antao Kestrels, their small bill (gape, maxilla height, nostril distance), and their short and somewhat rounded wings. Towards the left (negative) of the axis, bills get bigger, claws longer and flatter, and the wings are more elongated, as is typical for the Kestrels on Boavista (Figure 2). The second axis separates the sexes with the females being found on the upper (positive) end. Since the data were corrected for size, this analysis reveals that females are not only the bigger sex, but also different in shape with respect to trophic structures. They differ from the males by their shorter cranium, shorter tarsometatarsus, smaller cere, shorter distance between nostrils, and shorter claws.

The females do not overlap morphologically between islands, but the males do as differences between the males are less strong. Sexual dimorphism according to those variables appears to be larger on Santo Antao than on Brava and Boavista. Also the females on Santo Antao vary more in these variables than do the males.

Figure 2: Plot of the results (first axes) of CVAS with respect to island and sex. Unit of scale is the standard deviation of the scores relative to the mean. For details of the analyses see Tables 1 and 2, and text.

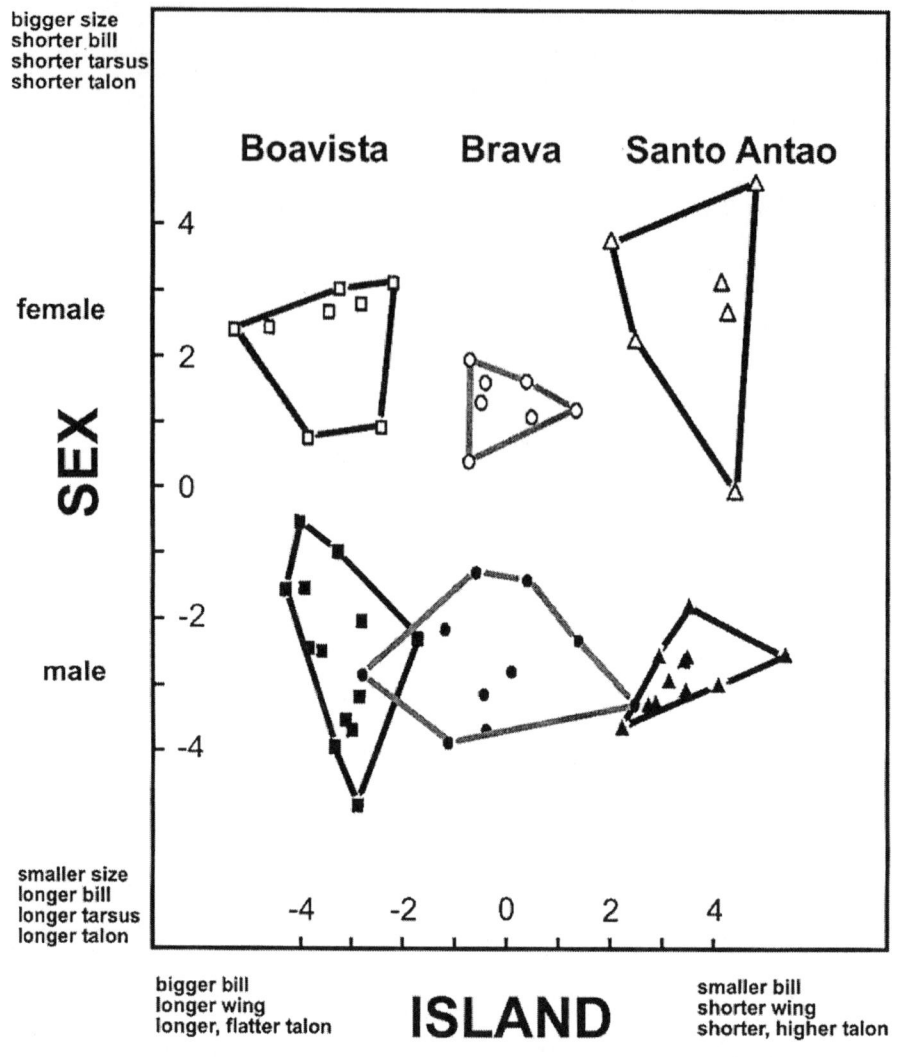

DISCUSSION

There is variation in morphological structures between the island populations of the Kestrel. This variation occurs not just in size, but also in shape, related to traits of the prey-catching apparatus, namely the bill, talons, as well as tarsus and wing. These differences in trophic structures lead us to the assumption that adaptation to local environments with their respective habitat characteristics and prey abundance played a crucial role in forming morphologically distinct island populations (Figure 2). We suggest that small bill, short distal wing, and shorter and higher talons are well adapted to capture small, terrestrial prey. The longer wing, bigger bill, and longer and flatter talons of Boavista Kestrels may indicate frequent aerial hunting of bigger prey types.

The data also open new aspects for the discussion of the sexual dimorphism in birds of prey. Sexual dimorphism in birds of prey has been exclusively discussed in terms of differences in size. Our study shows that sexual dimorphism does not only refer to the difference in size but also to shape. The heavier females possess relatively short tarsi and a short bill (Figure 2). As far as we know, variation in shape has not been described and analyzed in previous studies on sexual dimorphism in raptors. As the data reveal sexual dimorphism in trophic structures, it indicates that ecological factors like availability of different prey types are important for the evolution of sexual dimorphism in raptors. Since environments differ among islands it is not surprising in this context that the extent of sexual dimorphism in the Kestrels varies among islands.

ACKNOWLEDGEMENTS

This work was not possible without the help of the field assistants Armin Nemitz, Uli Nienaber, Sandra Kraetschmer, Ute Nau, Gernot Segelbacher and the advisory help of Roy Dennis. Great support came also from the local Institute of Agriculture, Institutio Nacional de Desenvolvimento e Agrigcultura, and the German Society for Technical Cooperation (GTZ). The project was funded by the European Commission through a Marie Curie Fellowship grant.

REFERENCES

ANDERSSON, M. & R.A. NORBERG 1981. Evolution of reversed sexual size dimorphism and role partitioning among predatory birds, with a size scaling of flight performance. *Biol. J Linn. Soc.*15:105-130.

BALGOOYEN, T.G. 1976. Behaviour and ecology of the American Kestrel (*Falco sparverius* L.) in the Sierra Nevada of California. University of California *Publications in Zoology* 103:1-88.

BARROW, C.J. 1991. *Land degradation: development and breakdown of terrestrial environments*. Cambridge, University of Cambridge.

CARRASCAL, L.M., E. MORENO & A. VALIDO 1994. Morphological evolution and changes in foraging behaviour of island and mainland populations of Blue Tit (*Parus caeruleus*) - a test of convergence and ecomorphological hypotheses. *Evolutionary Ecology* 8: 25-35.

CARSON, H.L. & A.R. TEMPLETON 1984. Genetic revolutions in relation to speciation phenomena: the founding of new populations. *Annu. Rev. EcolSyst* 15: 97-131.

EBENMANN, B. 1986. Sexual size dimorphism in the great tit *Parus major* in relation to the number of coexisting congeners. *Oikos* 43: 355-359.

GAMAUF, A., M. PRELEUTHNER & H. WINKLER 1998. Philippine birds of prey: interrelations among habitat, morphology, and behaviour. *The Auk* 115:713-726.

GORMAN, M.L. 1979. *Island ecology*. University Press, Cambridge.

GRANT, B.R. & P.R. GRANT 1989. *Evolutionary Dynamics of a Natural Population: The Large Cactus Finch of the Galapagos*. The University of Chicago Press.

HUNT, G.R. & I.G. MCLEAN 1993. The Ecomorphology of Sexual Dimorphism in the New Zealand Rifleman *Acanthisitta chioris*. *Emu* 93: 71-78.

LEISLER, B., H.-W. LEY, & H. WINKLER 1989. Habitat, behaviour and morphology of *Acrocephalus* warblers: an integrated analysis. *Ornis Scandinavia* 20:181-186.

LEISLER, B. & H. WINKLER 1985. Ecomorphology. *Current Ornithology* 2: 155-186.

LEISLER, B. & H. WINKLER 1991. Ergebnisse und Konzepte ökomorphologischer Untersuchungen an Vogeln. *Journal für Ornithologie* 132: 373-425.

LEISLER, B., H. WINKLER & K.-H. SIEBENROCK 1997. Ökomorphologische Untersuchungen am Beispiel der Webervögel (Ploceidae) und Eisvögel (Alcedinidae). *Annalen für Ornithologie* 21:17-43.

LOSOS, J.B., K.I. WARHEIT, & T.W. SCHOENER 1997. Adaptive differentiation following experimental island colonisation in *Anolis* lizards. *Nature* 387: 70-73.

MUELLER, H.C. 1986. The evolution of reversed sexual dimorphism in owls: an empirical analysis of possible selective factors. *Wilson Bulletin* 98:387-407.

NEWTON, 1.1979. *Population ecology of raptors*. T & A Poyser, London.

OWENS, I.P.F. & I.R. HARTLEY 1998. Sexual dimorphism in birds: why are there so many different forms of dimorphism?. *Proceedings of the Royal Society London, Biology* 265: 397-407.

REYNOLDS, R.T. 1972. Sexual dimorphism in *Accipiter* Hawks: A new hypothesis. *The Condor* 74:191-197

SELANDER, R.K. 1966. Sexual dimorphism and differential niche utilisation in birds. *The Condor* 68:113-151.

SELANDER, R.K. 1972. Sexual selection and dimorphism in birds. In: *Sexual Selection and the descent of man 1871-1971* (ed. B. Campbell), pp.180-230. Aldine, Chicago.
SNYDER, N. F. R. & J. W. WILEY 1976. Sexual size dimorphism in hawks and owls of North America. *Ornithological Monographs* 20,1-96.
STILES, F.G. 1995. Behavioral, ecological and morphological correlates of foraging for arthropods by the hummingbirds of a tropical wet forest. *The Condor* 97: 853-878.
STORER, R.W. 1954. Weight, wing areas, and skeletal proportions in three accipiters. *Acta XI Congressus Internationalis Ornithologici*: 287-290.
STORER, R.W. 1966. Sexual dimorphism and food habits in three North American accipiters. *The Auk* 83, 423-436.
Ter BRAAK, C.J.F. 1995. Ordination. In: *Data analysis in community and landscape ecology* (eds R.H.G. Jongman, C.J.F. ter Braak & O.F.R. van Tongeren), pp.91-173. Cambridge University Press, Cambridge & New York.
VAN VALEN, L. 1965. Morphological variation and width of ecological niche. *The American Naturalist* 99: 377-390.
WALTER, H. 1979. *Eleonora's falcon, adaptations to prey and habitat in a social raptor.* Chicago University Press, Chicago.
WILLIAMSON, M.H. 1981. *Island populations.* Oxford University Press, Oxford.
WILLSON, M.F. 1969. Avian niche size and morphological variation. *American Naturalist* 103: 531-542.
WUNDERLE, J.M. 1983. A shift in the morph ratio cline in the bananaquit on Grenada, West Indies. *The Condor* 85: 365- 367.
WALLACE, R.A. 1974. Ecological and social implications of sexual dimorphism in five melanerpine woodpeckers. *The Condor* 76: 238-248.

S. Hille & H. Winkler
Konrad-Lorenz Institut für Vergleichende Verhaltensforschung
Savoyenstrasse 1a
1160 Vienna
Austria

Part 10

Impact of Electricity Utility Structures on Raptors

Crowned Eagle *Stephanoaetus coronatus*

Conveners:
Chris van Rooyen & Peter Nelson

Chancellor, R. D. & B.-U. Meyburg eds. 2000
Raptors at Risk
WWGBP / Hancock House

Raptor Mortality on Powerlines in South Africa

Chris S. van Rooyen

INTRODUCTION

Eskom is the largest electrical utility in Africa. To accomplish its mission "to supply the world's lowest cost electricity to encourage growth and prosperity", without negative environmental effects presents a significant challenge to the company. In 1996, Eskom's network of powerlines amounted to 255,745 km (158,847 miles) (Eskom 1996). After numerous vultures were electrocuted on an 88 kV powerline, a subsequent study revealed that bird mortalities on the electricity network were much higher than originally envisaged.

The southern African experience with regard to wildlife interactions and electricity structures is (with some notable exceptions) generally characterised by an *ad hoc* approach, fragmented documentation, inconsistency of data and few "before and after" studies. The vast distances, poor coordination and integration of mitigation efforts as well as discontinuity and duplication further exacerbated the problem.

Eskom has had an informal alliance with the Endangered Wildlife Trust (EWT), an environmental non-government organisation focusing on promoting the region's biodiversity, since 1978. In view of the complexity, scope and persistence of the problem of interactions between wildlife and utility networks, Eskom and EWT formalised their long-standing relationship by entering into a partnership at the end of 1995 to address the problem in a systematic manner on a national basis.

HISTORICAL OVERVIEW

There are no records of interactions between raptors and electricity structures in southern Africa documented in biological literature prior to 1972 (Ledger 1996). In that year a note on mortality of Cape Griffons on 88 kV distribution lines in the former Transvaal province of South Africa was published in the journal *Nature* (Markus 1972). Later Ledger and Annegarn (1981) revealed a serious problem for vultures on 88 kV lines where the so-called kite structure was used. In response to this problem, the South African national supplier of electricity, Eskom (then known as the South African Electricity Supply Commission), established the Bird Research Committee in 1978, which later developed into the voluntary Eskom Wildlife Impacts Advisory Committee (EWIAC). Dr. John Ledger, the current director of the Endangered Wildlife Trust (EWT), acted as consultant on wildlife matters to EWIAC from 1978 to 1996.

Considerable progress was made in terms of finding solutions for the problem of raptor electrocutions. The knowledge and experience gained were summarised in 1988 in the Eskom Bird

Identification Guide, which offered practical advice on how to deal with bird related problems (Ledger 1988).

Despite efforts by members of EWIAC to communicate recommendations throughout the organisation, implementation of solutions did not always take place in a satisfactory manner. In 1995 a serious incident involving the electrocution of vultures on 88 kV structures in the North-West Province of South Africa prompted Eskom to look afresh at the problem of wildlife interactions with its electricity structures (Verdoorn 1996).[1] A subsequent investigation into the matter revealed that the following factors had, (and to some extent still have) a major impact on the effective management of this issue (Van Rooyen 1996):

- Discontinuity due to staff turnover.
- *Ad hoc* approach to problems.
- Lack of ornithological expertise among Eskom technical staff.
- Little integration and coordination of efforts to reduce wildlife mortalities on electricity structures.
- Ineffective communication resulting in duplication of efforts and/or application of ineffective solutions to problems.
- Very little monitoring of the effectiveness of implemented mitigation measures.
- Lack of systematic data collection

The problem of negative interactions between wildlife and electricity structures is an international one, and has given rise to a vast amount of literature. Studies in southern Africa deal largely with biological and engineering perspectives i.e. the impact on species that may be biologically significantly affected, and engineering solutions to the problem (Ledger & Annegarn 1981; Ledger 1983; Ledger 1984; Hobbs & Ledger 1986a; Hobbs & Ledger 1986b; Hobbs *et al.* 1990; Mundy *et al.* 1992; Ledger 1992; Ledger *et al.* 1992;). This has also been the case elsewhere (Hess 1996; Galushin 1996; Harness 1996; Janss & Ferrer 1996;) Studies often take the form of a pre- or post-construction study with regard to specific structures (McCann & Wilkens 1995).

Co-operative management has only lately been recognised as a vitally important aspect in the field of electricity/wildlife interactions (Olendorff *et al.* 1996). Without a proper, integrated management system, incorporating biological, engineering and economic perspectives, any large-scale effort to reduce or eliminate negative interactions between wildlife and electricity structures is bound to run into difficulties sooner or later (Van Rooyen 1996; Van Rooyen *et al.* 1998).

Persistent problems previously thought to have been solved, led to the formation of an Eskom-Endangered Wildlife Trust Strategic Partnership (the Partnership) in 1996. The goal of the Partnership is the establishment of an integrated management system to reduce negative interactions between wildlife and electricity infrastructures to within acceptable levels, by systematically managing it in an integrated manner[2].

METHODS

Systematic data capturing on raptor electrocutions started on 1 August 1996, and is still continuing. Raptor electrocutions are reported to the Partnership co-ordinator by Eskom staff and members of the public through a toll-free line at the headquarters of the Endangered Wildlife Trust. Whenever possible, volunteer field investigators follow up with field investigations at the site of the incident to

---

[1] The remains of many electrocuted Cape Griffons and African Whitebacked Vultures were found under an 88 kV line after farm labourers alerted the landowner, who then contacted Eskom.

[2] It goes without saying that any attempt to completely eliminate negative interactions between birds and electricity structures would inevitably fail due to the sheer number of interactions, as well as the enormous size of the electricity grid. For the same reasons detailed bird impact assessment studies *for each incident* fall outside the scope of the Partnership. The focus is on the provision of hands-on, practical advice to Eskom staff to deal with problems encountered in the course of their everyday duties. However, the identification of opportunities for dedicated research and the facilitation of such research fall well within the scope of the Partnership.

capture as much data as possible, *inter alia*:
- Species impacted upon
- Type of structure involved

The following wildlife mortalities have been reported to the Partnership:

Table 1. Birds killed through collisions with electricity structures during the period 1 August 1996 to 1 August 1998

All species	Raptors
480	25

Table 2. Raptors killed through collisions with electricity structures during the period 1 August 1996 to 1 August 1998

Species	Number	Conservation status
Cape Griffon *Gyps coprotheres*	7	Vulnerable*
Secretarybird *Sagittarius serpentarius*	7	
African Whitebacked Vulture *Pseudogyps Africanus*	4	
Tawny Eagle *Aquila rapax*	2	Endangered**
African Hawk Eagle *Hieraaetus spilogaster*	1	
Barn Owl *Tyto alba*	1	
Blackbreasted Snake Eagle *Circaetus pectoralis*	1	
Martial Eagle *Polemaetus bellicosus*	1	Vulnerable*
TOTAL	**25**	

*   South African Red Data book - Birds (Brooke, 1984)
**   The Atlas of Southern African Birds (Harrison *et al.* (eds), 1997)

Table 3. Wildlife killed through electrocution on electricity structures during the period 1 August 1996 to 1 August 1998

All species	Raptors
232	158

DISCUSSION

1. Collision

Raptors comprised only 5% (n=25) of all reported collision mortalities (n=480). The relatively low collision rate corresponds with other studies (Ferrer *et.al.* 1991), and indicates that generally speaking collisions with powerlines are not a major cause of unnatural raptor mortality. The only southern African raptor that seems to be relatively susceptible to collisions with powerlines, is the solitary, semi-terrestrial Secretarybird. No detailed study has been made to date to clarify this phenomenon, but from anecdotal accounts from farmers and Eskom field staff, it would seem that human disturbance that causes birds to flush and fly blindly into overhead lines may play a major role.

2. Electrocution

Raptors (n=158) make up 68% of all reported wildlife electrocutions (n=232). This may be a function not only of raptor behaviour i.e. using electricity structures for perching roosting and nesting purposes, but also of the high profile that raptors currently enjoy among the general public and Eskom staff in particular (pers.obv.).

Table 4. Raptors killed through electrocution on electricity structures during the period 1 August 1996 to 1 August 1998

Species	Number	Conservation status
African Fish Eagle *Haliaeetus vocifer*	1	
African Hawk Eagle *Hieraaetus spilogaster*	1	
African Whitebacked Vulture *Pseudogyps africanus*	31	
Barn Owl *Tyto alba*	12	
Black Eagle *Aquila verreauxii*	7	
Blackbreasted Snake Eagle *Circaetus spilogaster*	2	
Blackshouldered Kite *Elanus caeruleus*	2	
Brown Snake Eagle *Circaetus cinereus*	1	
Cape Griffon *Gyps coprotheres*	40	Vulnerable*
Eastern Redfooted Kestrel *Falco amurensis*	1	
Giant Eagle Owl *Bubo lacteus*	3	
Greater Kestrel *Falco rupicoloides*	2	
Gymnogene *Polyboroides typus*	1	
Jackal Buzzard *Buteo rufofuscus*	5	
Lanner Falcon *Falco biarmicus*	1	
Longcrested Eagle *Lophaetus occipitalis*	3	
Marsh Owl *Asio capensis*	1	
Martial Eagle *Polemaetus bellicosis*	10	Vulnerable*
Pale Chanting Goshawk *Melierax canorus*	2	
Peregrine Falcon *Falco peregrinus*	1	Rare*
Spotted Eagle Owl *Bubo africanus*	8	
Steppe Buzzard *Buteo buteo*	3	
Tawny Eagle *Aquila rapax*	1	Endangered**
"Eagle"	2	
"Owl"	7	
"Raptor"	1	
"Vulture"	10	
TOTAL	**158**	

*   South African Red Data book - Birds (Brooke, 1984)
** The Atlas of Southern African Birds (Harrison *et al.* (eds), 1997)

Table 5. Type and number of structures implicated in the electrocution of raptors for the period 1 August 1996 to 1 August 1998

Type of structure	Number	Percentage of total
Predominantly steel *	59	42.1%
Non-earthed T-structure	8	5.7%
Earthed T-structure	22	15.7%
Terminal structure**	31	22.1%
Other	20	14.2%

*   Includes both an all-steel structure and a wooden structure with energised components attached to a steel cross-arm.
** A typical terminal structure incorporates surge arrestors, a transformer, jumper cables and a bonded and earthed cross-arm.

African Whitebacked Vultures (n=31) and the closely related Cape Griffons (n=40) together make up 44% of all reported raptor electrocutions. If it is assumed that the unidentified electrocuted vultures (n=10) are Cape Griffons and African Whitebacked Vultures, the percentage is 51%[3]. It is submitted that the comparatively high number of electrocutions reported for these species can be attributed to a combination of the following factors:
- Both species are large with wingspans of more than 2 metres, that makes them vulnerable to electrocution, as they easily bridge the air gap between two energised components or an energised and an earthed component.
- Both species congregate in large numbers when feeding. This leads to multiple electrocutions on electricity structures in close proximity to carcasses utilised for feeding.
- Feeding vultures of these species are often the first indication to a farmer of possible stock losses, who finds and reports electrocuted birds on closer inspection.

It is difficult to assess the impact of electrocution on Martial Eagles. Electrocution of this species on Eskom structures is not a new phenomenon (Smith 1992).[4] The relatively low number of Martial Eagles (n=10) reported to the Partnership may be due to a combination of low numbers and low reporting rate, but does not necessarily mean that the impact is not biologically significant:
- Although widespread, Martial Eagles are thinly distributed on the ground, with extensive territories, anything from a 100 to a 150 km^2 (Tarboton *et.al.* 1989). The electrocution of a single eagle or a pair of eagles in such a vast area could easily escape attention, unless it causes a permanent electrical fault (which rarely happens).
- Apart from electrocution, Martial Eagles face a host of other man-induced threats i.e. direct persecution by small-stock farmers, indirect persecution through poisoning, drowning in sheer-walled reservoirs and reduction of natural prey through habitat alteration and degradation (Boshoff 1997). It is therefore not surprising that a decrease in numbers has been reported from many parts of southern Africa (Boshoff 1997).[5]

Tawny Eagle numbers have crashed dramatically over the past two decades and the species is now considered to be one of the most threatened eagles in southern Africa, with centres of distribution now confined to major protected areas and sparsely inhabited regions (Simmons 1997). Electrocution no doubt poses a real threat to existing populations, and despite the fact that only a single electrocution was reported, it remains a cause for concern. This figure no doubt does not reflect the true electrocution induced mortality, and/or could be a function of the already low numbers of this species. Further investigation of this issue is urgently required.

3. Structure types

Steel structures comprised 42.1% of all structures that were implicated in raptor electrocutions. This emphasises the lethal nature of steel structures to raptors, as the number of steel structures used in the reticulation network is far outnumbered by wood poles (pers. obv.), yet they seem to cause the majority of electrocutions. The steel structures most commonly implicated are the so-called 88 kV Kite-structure and the 88/132 kV Delta suspension structure.

The problem of electrocutions on Kite-structures was thought to have been solved after they were fitted with perches and PVC spirals wrapped around the centre conductor clamp to form a "basket" to prevent birds from touching them.

However, investigations into continued electrocutions on Kite-structures thought to have been rendered safe in the manner described above, revealed that the problem had not been solved (Van Rooyen 1998).

---

[3] The area from where these electrocutions were reported has a history of electrocutions of Cape Griffons and African Whitebacked Vultures, and these two species are the only vultures known to occur there in large numbers.
[4] During an Eskom survey in 1992 among farmers in what was then the north-eastern Cape Province of South Africa in an area of ? square kilometres, farmers reported 22 Martial Eagles and 16 unidentified eagles presumably killed through electrocution on electricity structures, over an unknown period of time.
[5] At least two farmers from the Burgersdorp region in the north Eastern Cape have categorically stated to the author that they each lost Martial Eagle pairs breeding on their farms through electrocution about a decade ago, which have not been replaced since.

Figure 1. Delta suspension structure

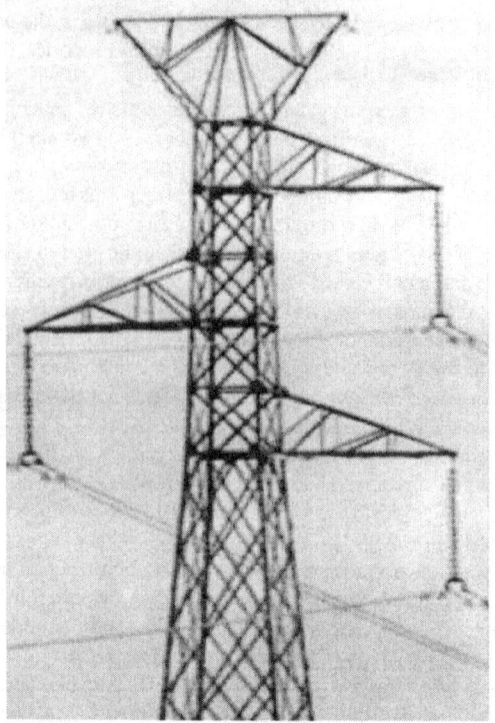

Figure 2. Kite structure

Figure 3: Kite structure modified with perch and PVC "basket" wrapped around the centre conductor clamp.

A new approach was tried i.e. to stretch two inter-linked PVC spirals directly above the bottom cross-arm to form an obstacle, thereby effectively preventing the vultures from landing on the bottom cross-arm. This seems to have reduced the rate of electrocutions, but the problem has not been entirely solved[6].

On the Delta suspension structure, birds are electrocuted presumably when they take off from or land on the lowest cross-arm. The vultures prefer to perch on the extreme end of the cross-arm, right above the string insulator (pers.obs.). Another possibility (believed widely by Eskom field staff) is that the birds often excrete before taking off, thus bridging the critical gap between conductor and cross-arm, and causing a phase to earth fault.

Various bird guards have been proposed to prevent the birds from perching above the insulator, but by preventing the bird from perching on the structure, the problem is simply transferred to the next structure. An attempt was made to accommodate the birds by fixing PVC spirals to the conductor around the insulator clamp to create a barrier to the wing-tips touching the conductor at the moment of landing (as was done with the 88 kV Kite constructions). Although this method initially rendered positive results, electrocutions were again reported from poles modified in this manner. A possible explanation might be that the spirals themselves become energised after a couple of years, and/or the fact the Cape Sparrows *Passer melanurus* have taken to nesting inside the spirals (pers.obs.), thereby seriously reducing their insulating effect. Steps are currently being taken to physically modify the design of these poles in order to eliminate the electrocution problem.

A design that is becoming increasingly popular with Eskom for 88 kV and 132 kV feeders due to its relatively cheap construction, little impact on the physical environment, ease of construction and limited visual impact, is the new 259 series. These are single, earthed steel poles with three staggered insulators, each 1.5 metres in length. The areas through which many of these powerlines will run harbour populations of large scavenging birds such as Cape Griffons and African Whitebacked Vultures, and large eagles such as Martial and Black Eagles. These birds will almost certainly attempt to perch on the new poles, and specifically the insulators. In the process, the bird will most probably not be able to secure a firm foothold on the slippery insulator. Given the length of the insulator relative to the wingspan of these species, the chances of a phase to earth fault in the process are considerable, not only resulting in the electrocution of the bird, but also causing problems in the power supply.

The EWT through the Partnership expressed concern over the electrocution potential of this design. Eskom design engineers have undertaken that poles of this design will be fitted with a wooden perch fastened to the top of the pole as a standard feature in specific areas, to create perching space for birds, if so advised by the EWT.

The next most common structures implicated in electrocutions (22.1%), are terminal structures. The lethal nature of terminal structures has been recognised elsewhere (Harness 1997), as well as in southern Africa (Smith 1992, Ledger *et al.* 1992).

---

[6] On a 10km stretch of line modified in this manner, electrocutions have dropped to two to three a year.

Figure 4. Steel suspension structure Type 259

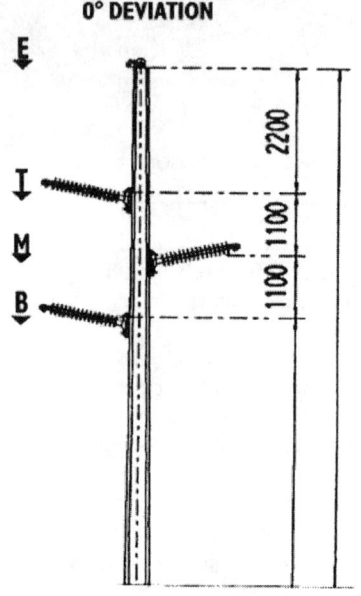

Figure 5. Terminal structure with pole mounted transformer

These structures are particularly lethal because of the following reasons:
- Minimal phase to phase and phase to ground spacing between the energised components, particularly the bare jumper cables connecting transformers, protective switches and surge arrestors.
- Terminal structures often serve water pumps in remote, arid areas to provide surface water for livestock. Raptors are drawn to the water for drinking and bathing purposes, and get electrocuted on the terminal structure. This problem is likely to be aggravated by wet feathers.
- Virtually every farmyard in South Africa has one or two terminal structures. Barn Owls and Spotted Eagle Owls often frequent farm yards, presumably for the nesting opportunities in barns, and the large rodent populations often associated with farm yards. They use the terminal structures as convenient hunting perches with fatal consequences. Neither the Barn Owl nor the Spotted Eagle Owl is presently regarded as threatened in southern Africa, but the situation needs careful monitoring.

A factor that may also explain the high incidence of reports of birds electrocutions on terminal structures, is that birds killed on these structures are more likely to be noticed and reported than those on other structures, since terminal structures are frequently visited by landowners, or Eskom staff (for maintenance purposes).

To render the terminal structures safe for raptors and other birds, suitable insulation is fitted to all the jumper leads above the cross-arm, and to the jumpers running to the transformer. Lightning arrestors are now fitted on the transformer rather than the cross-arm, eliminating the need for jumper leads on the top cross-arm. In several areas, the systematic modification of terminal structures to render them harmless for birds, have started. The process is however far from being completed and many thousands of these lethal structures still dot the landscape of South Africa.

T-structures accounted for 21.4% of reported raptor electrocutions. The T-structure is a very common design, and probably comprises the majority of 11 and 22kV rural structures in southern Africa. In many cases, an earthwire for lightning protection runs up the pole and terminates in a spike between the middle and an outer insulator on the 2.5 metre cross-arm. The potential for phase to phase, or phase to earth electrocutions on such structures is clearly high.

Figure 6. T-structure with earthwire

T-structures can be rendered safe by cutting a 500 mm gap in the earth wire (or removing the earth spike completely and terminating the earthwire just below the cross-arm braces), in conjunction with insulation of the middle phase conductor. This is done by fitting the locally developed RP 3 Raptor Protector (Ledger 1992).

An important milestone for the Partnership was Eskom agreeing to fit approximately 683 km (6830 poles) of reticulation lines in the raptor rich Molopo area in the North-West Province of South Africa with RP3 Raptor Protectors. The programme started in March 1998 and will run over the next six years, at a cost of approximately R 600,000 (US$ 120,000) to Eskom[7]. This action was decided upon after a risk assessment was conducted by the Partnership to establish the risk that the reticulation network posed to raptors in the area. The possibility to fit RP3 Raptor Protectors with a link-stick under live-line conditions to save costs and speed up the programme is currently being investigated, and field tests with an experimental link-stick will soon commence.

---

[7] To date, approximately 1800 out of a total of 6830 structures have been retrofitted.

Figure 7: T-structure fitted with RP3 Raptor Protector

4. Implementation of mitigation measures to minimise raptor electrocutions

The following table illustrates the progress made with the retrofitting of lines in South Africa at locations where raptor electrocutions occurred as identified by the Partnership in the period 1 August 1996 to 1 August 1998 (Eskom structures only)[8].

Number of locations identified	Number of locations recommended to be retrofitted	Number of locations retrofitted by Eskom	Percentage retrofitted
78	48	15	31%

These statistics should be interpreted in the light of the following:
- The 48 locations for which retrofitting was recommended accounted for 77.8% of reported raptor mortalities.
- Supplies of mitigation measures seem to be generally low. The long waiting period (6 weeks) from date of order to delivery are causing bottlenecks.
- The complexity of the problem prevents the immediate application of mitigation measures in some instances. No suitably tested device exists at this stage that can be fitted to alleviate the problem of electrocution of vultures on 132 kV structures.
- Mitigation measures thought to have solved problems in the past are not entirely effective. This seems to be the case with vulture electrocutions on 88 kV and 132 kV structures.
- Field services staff, as reasons for delays, often cite budget, time and manpower constraints. The various Eskom procedures to be followed to obtain authorisation for capital expenditure can seriously hamper mitigation efforts, since obtaining the necessary funding for mitigation measures is often a protracted process.
- Confusion among field services staff as to what mitigation measures to apply and the procedures involved in acquiring them. This is in the process of being addressed by Eskom's line design departments after it was brought to their attention by the Partnership in order to standardise procedures and standards where possible.
- Difficult terrain and adverse weather conditions (wet conditions) prevent the speedy fitting of mitigation measures in some instances.

---

[8] This does not take into account the Molopo retrofitting scheme.

- The remoteness of certain areas where negative interactions occur. This leads to delays in the investigation of incidents, as field investigators sometime have to travel hundreds of miles to conduct investigations.
- Work pressure and other priorities often prevent action from being taken. Unfortunately, not all Eskom employees regard attempts to address wildlife interactions as an important part of their work, as awareness and attitude vary greatly within Eskom from region to region.
- Organisational restructuring within Eskom leads to huge delays in the completion of projects, or even *de facto* termination of projects in certain cases.

In conclusion it must be mentioned that the fitting of mitigation devices to powerlines has also produced other positive spin-offs for Eskom, particularly in terms of their image with their customers. Many landowners have contacted the EWT to express their appreciation at Eskom's response to their concerns about birds being killed on their property.

CONCLUSION

The EWT/Eskom Strategic Partnership has been in existence for two years. In that time it has made some progress towards achieving its goal of an integrated management system to reduce negative interactions between wildlife and electricity infrastructures. It is equally clear, however, that a lot remains to be done. The problem of raptor electrocutions in South Africa (and the rest of the world) is far from solved and remains a difficult and unavoidable challenge to engineers, conservationists and managers.

REFERENCES

BOSHOFF, A.F., 1997. Martial Eagle *Polemaetus bellicosus*. *In* Harrison, J.A., Allan, D.G., Underhill, L.G., Herremans, M., Tree, A,J., Parker, V. & Brown, C.J. (Eds.) *The atlas of southern African birds. Vol. 1: Non-passerines*. BirdLife South Africa: Johannesburg, p.192-193.

BROOKE, R.K. 1984. *South African Red Data book-Birds*. South African National Scientific Programmes Report No. 97. FRD, CSIR, Pretoria.

ESKOM. 1996. *Continual Improvement*. Environmental Report 1996. Johannesburg.

FERRER, M., DE LA RIVA, M. & CASTROVIEJO, J. 1991. Electrocution of Raptors on Power Lines in Southwestern Spain. *Journal of Field Biology* 62(2):181-190.

GALUSHIN, V.M. 1996. Contradictory Significance of Powerlines for Raptors in Russia and her Neighbouring Countries. *Abstracts of the 2nd International Conference on Raptors*. Raptor Research Foundation/University of Urbino. p.5.

HARNESS, R. 1996. Raptor Electrocutions on Electric Utility Distribution Overhead Structures. *Abstracts of the 2nd International Conference on Raptors*. Raptor Research Foundation/University of Urbino. p.6.

HARNESS, R.E. 1997. Raptor Electrocutions Caused by Rural Electric Distribution Powelines. Thesis. Colorado State University, Fort Collins.

HESS, J. 1996. Reducing Bird Electrocution and Collision Mortality due to Power Assets: the Wedge-tailed Eagle (*Aquila audax fleayi*) and the Grey Goshawk (*Accipiter novaehollendiae*) in Tasmania, Australia.. *Abstracts of the 2nd International Conference on Raptors*. Raptor Research Foundation/University of Urbino p.4.

HOBBS, J.C.A. & LEDGER, J.A. 1986A. The Environmental Impact of Linear Developments; Powerlines and Avifauna. Third International Conference on Environmental Quality and Ecosystem Stability. Israel, June 1986.

HOBBS, J.C.A. & LEDGER, J.A. 1986B. Powerlines, Birdlife and the Golden Mean. *Fauna and Flora*. 44:23-27.

HOBBS, J.C.A., LEDGER, J.A. & AUDITORE, T. 1990. The Impacts of Powerlines on Wildlife. *Electricity SA*.. March/April 1990: 43-47.

JANSS, G. & FERRER, M. 1996. Procedure to select Power Poles which cause Bird Electrocution. *Abstracts of the 2nd International Conference on Raptors*. Raptor Research Foundation/University of Urbino p.7.

LEDGER, J. 1983. Guidelines for Dealing with Bird Problems of Transmission Lines and Towers. Escom Test and Research Division Technical Note TRR/N83/005.

LEDGER, J. 1988. *Eskom Bird Identification Guide*. Eskom, Johannesburg.

LEDGER, J. 1992. Protecting Eagles and Other Large Birds from Electrocution on Rural Powerlines. South African Eagle Insurance Company Limited.

LEDGER, J.A. & ANNEGARN, H.J. 1981. Electrocution Hazards to the Cape Vulture *(Gyps coprotheres)* in South Africa. *Biological Conservation* 20:15-24.

LEDGER, J.A. 1984. Engineering Solutions to the Problem of Vulture Electrocutions on Electricity Towers. *The Certificated Engineer* 57:92-95.

LEDGER, J.A., HOBBS J.C.A. & SMITH T.V. 1992. Avian Interactions with Utility Structures: Southern African Experiences. *Proceedings of the International Workshop on Avian Interactions with Utility Structure.* 1992. Electric Power Research Institute. Miami, Florida

MARKUS, M.B. 1972. Mortality of Vultures Caused by Electrocution. *Nature:* 238:228.

MCCANN, K.I. & WILKINS H.J.. 1995. Ariadne-Venus 400kV Transmission Powerline: A Study of the Annual Biology and Movement Patterns of the three Crane Species in the KwaZulu/Natal Midlands for Purposes of Aiding in the Selection of the Route for the Ariadne-Venus 400kV Powerline. Eskom and Endangered Wildlife Trust. Unpublished report.

MUNDY, P., BUTCHART, D., LEDGER, J. A. & PIPER, S.E. 1992. *The Vultures of Africa.* Acorn Books/Russel Friedman Books, Johannesburg.

OLENDORFF, R. R., ANSELL, A.R., GARRETT, M.G., LEHMAN, R.N. & MILLER, A.D. 1996. *Suggested Practices for Raptor Protection on Powerlines: The State of the Art in 1996.* Avian Power Line Interactions Committee (APPLIC). Edison Electric Institute/Raptor Research Foundation. Washington. D.C.

OLENDORFF, R.R., MILLER, A.D. & LEHMAN, R.N. 1981. *Suggested Practices for Raptor Protection on Powerlines: The State of the Art in 1981.* Prepared by the Raptor Research Foundation, St. Paul, Minnesota. Prepared for the Edison Electric Institute, Washington, D.C.

SIMMONS, R.E., 1997. Tawny Eagle *Aquila rapax. In* Harrison, J.A., Allan, D.G., Underhill, L.G., Herremans, M., Tree, A,J., Parker, V. & Brown, C.J. (Eds.) *The atlas of southern African birds. Vol. 1: Non-passerines.* BirdLife South Africa, Johannesburg, p.178-179.

SMITH, T.V., 1992. Questionaire: Bird Fatalities. Internal Eskom Report. Eskom, East London.

TARBOTON, W., PICKFORD, P. & B. PICKFORD. 1989. *Southern African Birds of Prey.* Cape Town: Struik Publishers.

VAN ROOYEN, C. S. 1996. Towards an Integrated Management System for the Management of Wildlife Interactions with Electricity Structures. *Abstracts of the 2nd International Conference on Raptors.* Raptor Research Foundation/University of Urbino. p.9

VAN ROOYEN, C.S., 1998. Proposed Mitigation Measures to Address the Issue of Ongoing Bird Electrocutions on 88 kV Distribution Lines in the North-West Province. Unpublished report to Eskom. Endangered Wildlife Trust, Johannesburg.

VAN ROOYEN, C.S., KRUGER, R., NELSON, P.A & FEDORSKY, C.A. 1998. The Eskom/EWT Strategic Partnership: The South African Approach towards the Management of Wildlife/Utility Interactions. *EEI Natural Resources/Biologist National Workshop.1998.* Edison Electrical Institute, Washington, D.C.

VERDOORN, G.H.1996. Mortality of Cape Griffons *Gyps coprotheres* and African Whitebacked Vultures *Pseudogyps africanus* on 88 kV and 132 kV Powerlines in Western Transvaal, South Africa, and Mitigation Measures to Prevent Future Problems. *Abstracts of the 2nd International Conference on Raptors* Raptor Research Foundation/University of Urbino. pp. 7-8.

C. S. van Rooyen
Endangered Wildlife Trust
Private Bag X11
Parkview 2122
South Africa

Chancellor, R. D. & B.-U. Meyburg eds. 2000
Raptors at Risk
WWGBP / Hancock House

Steel Distribution Poles – Environmental Implications

Richard E. Harness

ABSTRACT

Steel poles are becoming popular in distribution powerline construction. Steel poles have a high strength to weight ratio and are resistant to insect, animal and bird damage. They are also recyclable and do not require treatment with chemical preservatives. Although steel distribution class poles offer some environmental advantages over wood poles, they can be extremely lethal to raptors and other large perching birds. Constructing distribution lines with metal poles in a traditional manner typically results in reduced phase to ground clearances. These reduced clearances can result in electrocuted raptors, which are protected by United States federal and state laws. Distribution steel pole construction requires alternative construction materials and framing to mitigate these potential electrocutions. Alternative construction methods including the use of fibreglass crossarms, pole-top pin extensions, perch guards and pole top insulating material are discussed.

INTRODUCTION

Traditional overhead construction is expanding to include the use of distribution steel poles. Utilities are increasingly employing steel poles in their new low voltage construction, partially because steel offers certain environmental advantages over wood. First, steel poles are not susceptible to woodpecker damage. In some regions of the United States, woodpecker damage to wood poles is the most significant cause of pole deterioration (Abbey *et al.* 1997). Second, steel poles are harder for animals such as Eastern Fox Squirrels *Sciurus niger*, Raccoons *Procyon lotor* and Opossums *Didelphis marsupialis* to climb and keeping animals off utility structures can help reduce outages. Although steel can rust, it is also not susceptible to fungal, bacterial, and insect damage. Lastly, steel is recyclable.

Despite these environmental benefits, steel poles can be extremely lethal to birds of prey. Distribution powerlines constructed with steel poles utilizing standard utility configurations can significantly reduce phase to ground clearances. These reduced clearances can result in electrocuted birds of prey.

Raptors are especially vulnerable to electrocution when the birds are wet. Although dry feathers can withstand voltages up to 70 kV, wet feathers arc and burn at 5 kV (Nelson 1979). Most rural systems in the United States distribute power at 7.2 kV. Since a Golden Eagle's *Aquila chrysaetos* tail can extend 25 cms below its perch, large birds of prey can be electrocuted while perching on centre phase pins under wet conditions if tail feathers contact grounded surfaces, such as a steel pole.

MITIGATION MEASURES

The American industry standard for 15 kV Class construction at equipment locations is 95 kV Basic Impulse Insulation Level (BIL). The Rural Utilities Service (RUS) provides power in many rural areas and also adheres to this standard. Traditionally wood has been used as insulation between primary current and ground, using a wood impulse flashover value of approximately 80 kV per foot (Raytheon Engineers & Constructors 1994). Wood also has an arc quenching ability. The use of wood typically results in a BIL rating in excess of 350 kV BIL between primary conductors mounted on wood pole tops and crossarms, excluding equipment. The use of wood has proven to be a good design because values over 300 kV BIL reduce lightning flashovers. RUS advocates a minimum of 300 kV BIL on steel tangent poles to minimize these flashovers. RUS requires the 300 BIL at deadend steel structures (Rural Utilities Service 1996). The additional required insulation and air gap on steel poles is typically accomplished by adding longer deadend insulators and installing insulated pole top brackets. Fortunately this additional insulation and separation also increases clearances for birds.

One solution currently employed to increase the centre phase separation from the top of the steel pole is the use of a poletop pin employing an insulated pultruded solid fibreglass rod (Fig. 1). Although the increased distance eliminates the possibility of electrocutions to birds perching on the pin insulator, the modification makes it possible for a raptor to perch directly below the phase wire on the grounded metal pole top. This new condition can be lethal to birds sufficiently large to bridge the gap between the steel pole top and centre phase wire (Detail 1, Fig. 1). Therefore, steel structures using extended pole top pins need additional modification to keep large birds off the pole top or away from the centre phase.

Figure 1. Increased centre pin seperation using a pultruded solid fibreglass rod.

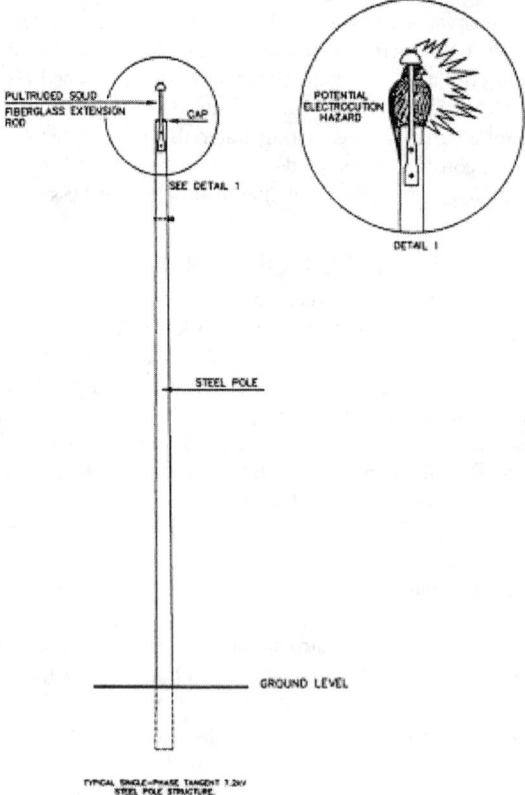

One solution to keep birds off the pole top is the use of plastic end caps. Steel poles are typically fitted with end caps to prevent small birds from nesting inside the structures. The caps also minimize noise from air blowing across the pole top. In preliminary tests utilizing captive raptors at the Rocky Mountain Raptor Center, these caps discouraged birds from perching on pole tops because of the caps' slick surface. It is uncertain however how these caps will perform long term in the field.

The Raptor Research Foundation recommends a minimum of 152 cm spacing between phases and phase to ground to minimize eagle electrocutions (APLIC 1996). A large female Golden Eagle can have a 229-cm wingspan, 137 cms between wrists. The 152-cm spacing was selected to minimize electrocutions of eagles when they begin or terminate a flight.

Figure 2. Three-phase clearances and mitigating measures

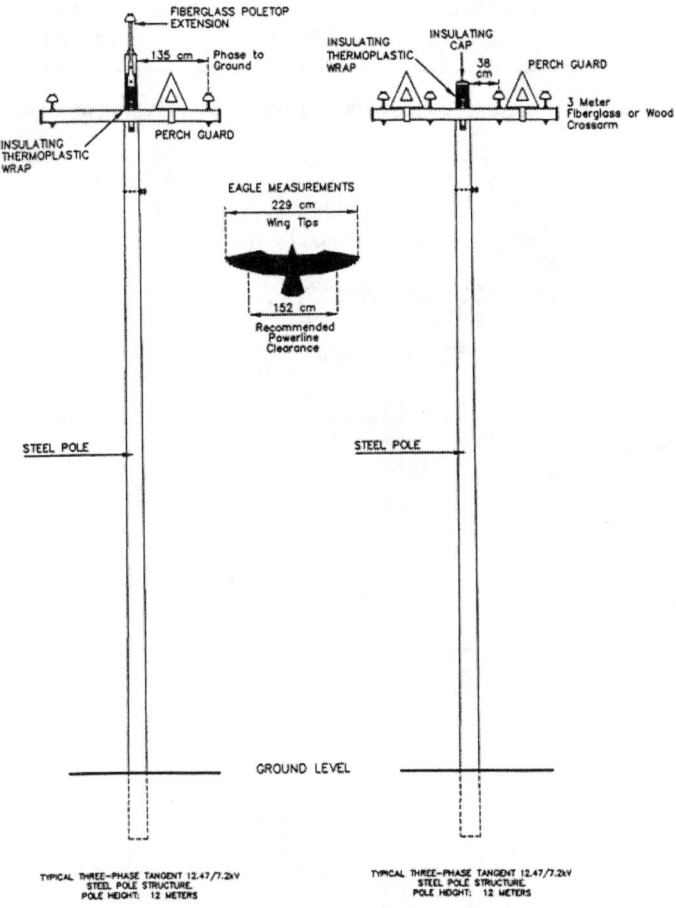

A typical RUS three-phase pole constructed with 3 metre wood crossarms provides the required 152 cms of clearance. However, when a steel pole is substituted the wire to ground (steel pole) separation becomes the critical distance, not the wire to wire separation. The steel pole to energized wire separation is often reduced to 135 cms or less (Fig. 2). If all the conductors are supported on a single crossarm, the horizontal clearances can be further reduced to 38 cms (Fig. 2), clearly placing both small and large birds at electrocution risk. The reduced phase to ground clearances on steel poles can be mitigated by wrapping the pole with a band of thermoplastic wrap above the crossarm

(Figure 2). The wrap consists of a 40-mil thermoplastic polymer membrane backed with a pressure sensitive adhesive. The thermoplastic wrap is produced by Valmont as a below grade corrosive protective system. Carbon Power and Light Company, Inc., performed a dielectric test of the pole wrap, determining that a 46-cm x 167-cm piece allows no appreciable current leakage at 35 kV for a three-minute duration. The thermoplastic wrap can also effectively reduce phase to ground clearances in narrow profile construction.

Perch guards can also be mounted on crossarms (Fig. 2) to keep raptors away from unsafe areas (APLIC 1996). The required clearances can also be obtained by snapping insulating Kaddas Bird Guards* over problem phase wires and insulators. Additionally, nonconducting wood or fibreglass crossarms should always be used. Steel crossarms mounted on steel poles are extremely hazardous due to minimal phase to ground clearances and should always be avoided. Raptors landing on steel arms are grounded and need only touch one energized conductor to become electrocuted.

An alternative to constructing lines in a traditional manner is to frame them in a form that allows safe perching. This can be accomplished by suspending two of the energized conductors under the

Figure 3. Three-phase suspension structure designed to allow perching on cross-arms

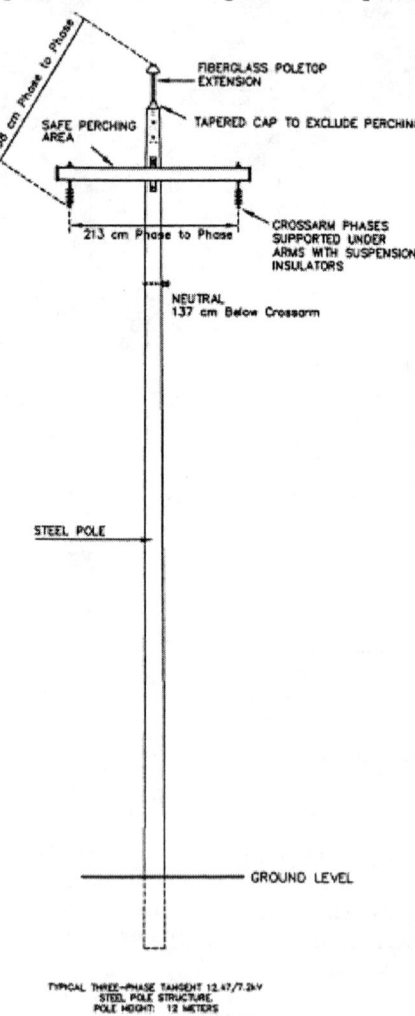

crossarm, instead of supporting them on the arm (Fig. 3). Suspending the conductors allows birds to perch on the crossarm without coming in close proximity to energized conductors. A poletop cap must still be employed to discourage perching on the top of the pole. Suspending the insulators and conductors will also allow utilities to achieve the Raptor Research Foundation's recommended 152 cms with shorter crossarms. Constructing new lines in a manner that allows raptors to safely utilize utility structures is preferable to retrofitting structures after a problem is detected.

CONCLUSION

A reduced Basic Impulse Insulation Level can result in electrocuted raptors, which are protected by State and Federal laws. All migratory birds are protected by the Migratory Bird Treaty Act (MBTA) and electrocutions can result in $10,000 (U.S.) fines per incident per organization. Both Bald *Haliaeetus leucocephalus* and Golden Eagles are additionally protected under the Eagle Protection Act. Eagle electrocutions can result in felony charges resulting in a $500,000 fine and up to 2 years in prison. The Endangered Species Act (ESA) also protects rare birds such as the Peregrine Falcon *Falco peregrinus*, Northern Spotted Owl *Strix occidentalis*, and Bald Eagles. Utilities killing birds will also usually be required by the U. S. Fish and Wildlife Service to reconstruct lethal poles in a manner that eliminates the electrocution hazard.

Utilities using non-traditional materials should review design tolerances to ensure that there are adequate clearances for birds and animals that traditionally use utility structures. Incorporating new designs before construction is preferable to costly fines and retrofits. This process will also avoid a negative impact on consumer relations.

ACKNOWLEDGMENTS

Electrical Systems Consultants, Inc funded this study. John Ulven of Viking Utility Products provided utility products employed in the raptor trials and provided his expertise gained as a utility lineman. Bob Hartman of Kaddas Enterprises, Inc. was extremely responsive and provided new product samples to test. I also thank Judy Scherpelz and Colorado State University for providing the birds used to study clearances on the mock utility powerline structures. I also thank the dedicated volunteers of the Rocky Mountain Raptor Center for handling the birds. Jerry Hager, Russell Waldner, Dennis Rankin, Jody Skyberg, and Jim Bohlk also helped gather data and review this paper.

REFERENCES

ABBEY, M., A. STEWART & J. MORRELL 1997. Existing strategies for control/remediation of woodpecker damage. *Proceedings of a workshop on the mitigation of woodpecker damage to utility lines*. Electric Power Research Institute.
APL1C. 1996. Cf Olendorff *et al.* below.
NELSON, M.W. 1979. Power lines progress report on eagle protection research. Unpublished report. Boise, Idaho. 13pp.
OLENDORFF, R. R., ANSELL, A.R., GARRETT, M.G., LEHMAN, R.N. & MILLER, A.D. 1996. *Suggested Practices for Raptor Protection on Powerlines: The State of the Art in 1996*. Avian Power Line Interactions Committee (APPLIC). Edison Electric Institute/Raptor Research Foundation. Washington. D.C. 125pp.
RAYTHEON ENGINEERS & CONSTRUCTORS 1994. Electric distribution systems engineering handbook. McGraw-Hill Energy Information Services Group, New York. 424pp.
RURAL UTILITIES SERVICE. 1996. Summary of items of engineering interest – August 1996. United States Department of Agriculture. Washington, D.C. 29 pp.

Richard E. Harness
Environmental Specialist
EDM International
4001 Automation Way
Colorado, 80525
USA

Evaluating the Risk existing Powerlines pose to large Raptors by utilising Risk Assessment Methodology: the Molopo Case Study

Rudi Kruger & Chris. S. van Rooyen

ABSTRACT

Eskom is the largest electrical utility in the Republic of South Africa. Prior to 1991, Eskom powerlines were designed and built without awareness of electrocution risk to birds, especially large raptors. In the late 1980's, Eskom launched an electrification project (the Molopo Project) along the border between South Africa and Botswana. Because of the absence of a policy dictating the use of a bird friendly design, a bird unfriendly line was constructed. This prompted various conservationists and non-Governmental organisations to approach Eskom with a request that the line be modified to make it bird friendly. In response to these requests a risk assessment was undertaken and recommendations made to Eskom's management on how to deal with the issue. The following factors were taken into account as part of a comprehensive risk assessment:
- topography and vegetation;
- land use;
- raptor populations;
- powerline design;
- environmental performance of the powerline;
- interested and affected parties; and
- cost of mitigating measures.

Management accepted the recommendations and 6830 structures will be pro-actively fitted with raptor protectors, an insulating device used to prevent birds from being electrocuted. This paper provides an overview of the risk assessment methodology, results and recommendations.

INTRODUCTION

During the late 1980's the previous South African Government launched various programmes to encourage farmers along the border between South Africa and Botswana to inhabit their farms on a permanent basis. Part of this programme was the supply of electricity to farms along the corridor to the border. Eskom launched an electrification project referred to as the Molopo Project which was subsidised by the Government and completed during 1990.

At the time of the design of the powerline, Eskom had a policy of constructing powerlines in the most cost effective method within electrical parameters. Some of these designs were not always compatible with wildlife, and large raptors were particularly at risk of being electrocuted (Hobbs & Ledger 1986a; Hobbs & Ledger 1986b; Hobbs *et al.* 1990; Ledger & Annegarn 1981; Ledger 1984; Ledger 1992; Ledger *et al.,* 1992; Van Rooyen *et al.,* 1998). Subsequent to the completion of the project, Eskom adopted a policy during 1991 that all future powerline designs would be compatible with birds - or so-called "bird friendly designs".

Concern was expressed at various forums by conservationists and non-Governmental organisations, regarding the potential hazard the powerlines (approximately 680 km of the Molopo Project[1]) pose to large raptors. To address the various concerns, as well as some allegations, it was proposed to Eskom management that as part of the Eskom/EWT[2] partnership, a risk assessment be undertaken to provide them with information enabling them to make informed decisions on how to deal with the issue. The risk assessment was based on risk management[3] methodology, focusing on identifying the biological risk of electrocutions, negative perception of interested and affected parties, cost implications to Eskom's business, and pro-active actions to either terminate, treat, tolerate or transfer these risks. Eskom management accepted the recommendations of the risk assessment and a programme has commenced by fitting raptor protectors[4] to an estimated 6830 structures, over the next five years.

METHODS

An investigation team consisting of the authors conducted the risk assessment. The fundamental principles of risk management were used to assess the risk the powerlines pose to large raptors, and the risk of raptor electrocutions to Eskom's business. According to Valsamakis *et al.,* (1992) risk management can be defined as *"a managerial function aimed at protecting the organisation, its people, assets, and profits, against the consequences (adverse) of pure risk, more particularly aimed at reducing the severity and variability of losses".*

Risk implies the presence of uncertainty (uncertainty prevails because outcomes of situations are not known in advance) which is the foundation of any discussion of risk in a risk management context. The degree of uncertainty surrounding an event determines the extent of risk[5]. Risk can be defined as *"the presence of uncertainty, where there may be uncertainty as to the occurrence of the event producing a loss[6], and uncertainty as regards the outcome of the event"* (Valsamakis *et al.,* 1992). Outcome in itself can assume various forms, however, for this study the concern was primarily about the environmental outcomes of risk, as well as the risk to Eskom's business.

---

[1] The powerlines assessed during the study were erected in the North West Province's districts of Tosca, Bray, Terra Firma, Pomfret and Vorstershoop as part of the Molopo Project.

[2] Eskom and the Endangered Wildlife Trust (EWT), an environmental non-government organisation focusing on promoting the region's biodiversity, entered into a partnership at the end of 1995 to address the problem of wildlife interactions and electricity structures, in a systematic manner on a national basis.

[3] The concept of risk management is extensively marketed by insurance brokers, who, by nature of their business, have a strong leaning towards insurance. However, risk management is becoming more pro-active, holistic and systematic. In this way, risk management becomes an integral part of general management (Valsamakis *et al.,* 1992).

[4] The RP3 Raptor Protector is an insulating device intended to permanently cover up energised conductors at support structures for the purpose of preventing accidental contact with the conductor by birds, as they perch in close proximity to the conductors. The device consists of one moulded alkaline product approximately 2 metres in length, and is fitted over the insulator.

[5] In the context of the risk assessment the term "event" is considered to be the electrocution of a raptor. The extent of risk (biological) is determined by the conservation status of the species.

[6] Loss is considered to be financial loss due to supply interruptions (loss of income), damage to equipment as a result of an electrocution, third party claims due to veld fires as a result of a flashover during electrocution, and loss of biodiversity due to raptor mortalities.

The present understanding of risk management as a process (Valsamakis et al., 1992), adopted for the study, comprised four distinct stages:
- risk identification,
- risk evaluation,
- risk control directed at loss elimination, or more usually loss (or risk) reduction,
- risk financing *via* transfer.

Any risk management programme must be put in motion by the process of risk identification, for obviously a risk cannot be managed if it is not identified. Risk identification is considered to be the single most important step in the risk management programme, and should not be entertained in a spurious fashion, but in as systematic a manner as possible (Valsamakis et al., 1992). The obvious and most commonly used method to identify the risks is to conduct a physical inspection. The main advantage of this method is that the terrain and network are seen firsthand and, importantly, such a visit brings one into contact with those people on whom reliance is placed for much of the information concerning risks and hazards[7]. Some of the drawbacks, however, are that it is time consuming, and the effectiveness of any inspection is directly related to the competence and expertise of the individual(s) carrying out the survey (Valsamakis et al., 1992).

In the current case study, the following factors were considered and evaluated to determine the risks:
- Topography and vegetation: riverbed or otherwise; trees, shrubs or grassland; nesting substrates.
- Land-use: type of farming and intensity; human population density.
- Raptor populations: species diversity; active breeding in the area; and conservation status of species.
- Powerline design: distance between conductors; distance between grounded hardware (i.e. earthwires) and energised conductors.
- Environmental performance of the powerlines: perusing line performance reports determining whether reason for outage was birds.
- Interested and affected parties: meetings with local Eskom staff, landowners, and a local conservationist to obtain their perspectives on the perceived problem.
- Cost of mitigation measures: financial and resource implications in connection with the implementation of mitigation measures.

It should be noted that it is unlikely that any particular method or technique of identification will be sufficient to identify all the risk exposures, and address all the problems associated with such risks. It is more appropriate to consider a combination of methods (viz. fault-tree analysis, hazard indices, audits, research etc.) in order to ensure risk identification is as complete and encompassing as possible. The process of identification is greatly assisted and enhanced by consultation with as many interested and affected parties as possible. Finally, risk identification entails a certain degree of imagination. Whilst past routines used in risk identification do provide some system and rigour to the activity, there should be no limit imposed on any lateral approach to identification (Valsamakis et al., 1992).

RESULTS AND DISCUSSION

Topography and Vegetation

The route of the powerline along the Molopo Riverbed is characterised by large camelthorn trees *Acacia erioloba* which are used by raptors for nesting substrates (Steven Dell, Conservation Officer - Molopo Nature Reserve, pers. comm.). The presence of the exposed powerline within this breeding territory, especially to juvenile raptors, was considered to be a real and potential risk and threat to raptor populations.

---

[7] Hazard relates to the environment surrounding the cause of loss (Valsamakis et al., 1992).

The sections of the route away from the riverbed are characterised by grassland, scattered trees, shrubs and fallow agricultural lands. Raptors use power poles as perches from which to establish territorial boundaries, hunt, rest, feed and sun themselves (APLIC, 1996). The presence of fallow lands attracts large numbers of foraging Helmeted Guineafowl *Numida meleagris*. Electricity poles are often used as hunting perches which attract raptors. Despite the presence of trees, electricity poles are evidently used a lot by the raptors[8], probably because the pylons offer an unrestricted view and are often on average significantly higher than the surrounding trees. In view of this, the electricity poles were regarded as both a real and potential risk to raptors.

Land Use

Land use consists mostly of extensive cattle and game farming, with very large farms, or even blocks of farms managed as a single unit. Such units are anything from 5,000 to as big as 50,000 hectares. Given the low intensity of the farming operations, the impact on the vegetation is minimal. This area is one of the very few places in South Africa where a large predator like the cheetah is still regularly encountered on commercial farmland (Steven Dell, Conservation Officer - Molopo Nature Reserve, pers. comm.). A local landowner in the area consulted during the investigation was very aware and positive about the large raptors in the area.

The good rains that the region experienced prior to the inspection resulted in dense ground cover which makes it very difficult to locate carcasses of electrocuted raptors below structures. The vastness of the area as well as the limited human activities make it unlikely that carcasses will be found in the event of an incident. Furthermore, the possibility that scavengers such as jackal will scavenge and remove carcasses in the event of an incident may be one of the reasons why no incidents have been reported to date. These factors contributed to one of the conclusions of the assessment, namely that the lack of past reports of raptor electrocutions may not be a true reflection of actual raptor mortality rates.

Raptor Populations

The Molopo area was found to be rich in raptor populations, both in species numbers and species diversity. It is one of the few areas in South Africa where raptors and vultures, such as the Martial Eagle *Polemaetus bellicosus*, Bateleur *Terathopius ecaudatus*, Tawny Eagle *Aquila rapax*, African Whitebacked Vulture *Gyps africanus* and Lappetfaced Vulture *Torgos tracheliotus*, are found and even breed in large numbers outside proclaimed game reserves and national parks. In the course of 1997, the vulture restaurant at the Molopo Nature Reserve attracted up to 196 African Whitebacked Vultures and 15 Lappetfaced Vultures at a time.

In the past three years, the following active raptor nests were recorded in the study area (Table 1).

Table 1. Active raptor nests in the period 1995-1997 (Steven Dell, Conservation Officer - Molopo Nature Reserve, pers. comm.).

Nests	*Species*	*Conservation status: South African Red Data book-Birds (Brooke, 1984)*
2	Martial Eagle	Vulnerable
6	Bateleur	Vulnerable
1	Tawny Eagle	Not endangered
2	Brown Snake Eagle	Not endangered
8	Wahlberg's Eagle	Not endangered
7	Giant Eagle Owl	Not endangered
200	Whitebacked Vulture	Not endangered

---

[8] In the course of three days, the investigation team personally recorded four Martial Eagles *Polemaetus bellicosus*, all of which perched on electricity poles. An adult Bateleur *Terathopius ecaudatus*, a large unidentified raptor and two immature Martial Eagles, on electricity poles, were observed in the course of one morning's drive from Bray to Vostershoop (approximately 150 km) along the banks of the Molopo river. The investigation team also encountered scores of Pale Chanting Goshawks *Melierax canorus*.

Martial Eagles, Bateleurs and Lappetfaced Vultures are regarded as vulnerable in the South Africa Red Data book - Birds (Brooke, 1984). Even though the Tawny Eagle is not included in the Red Data book, its numbers outside protected areas have declined disastrously in the past 15 years, and do not show any signs of recovery. It should also be added that the South African Red Data book - Birds is almost 13 years old and in dire need of updating. The recent Atlas of Southern African Birds (Harrison *et al.* 1997) confirms the decline of the Tawny Eagle and Bateleur to a fraction of their previous distribution in South Africa, and clearly shows that humans are responsible for these distribution patterns. The Atlas also confirms that healthy populations of all the birds mentioned in Table 1 still occur in adjacent Botswana. It may well be that there is a natural influx of large raptors from Botswana into the region, re-populating areas where farmers exterminated large raptors in the recent past (before education and awareness programmes were launched, aimed at changing farmers' attitudes to raptors). Conservationists were of the opinion that the persecution by farmers have to a great extend been eliminated as the major cause of decline, and that the exposed poles were considered to be a risk to the high and growing raptor population of the area.

Powerline Design

Electrocutions of raptors are directly related to powerline design and spacing between elements that can comprise a phase-to-phase or phase-to-ground contact (APLIC, 1996). According to APLIC (1996) two design factors make a line hazardous to raptors: (1) phase conductors separated by less than the wingspread of the bird that is landing, perching or taking off; (2) a distance between grounded hardware and an energised conductor that is less than the wingspread or the distance from the tip of the bill to tip of the tail.

The majority of the reticulation poles in the study area are three phase T-structures with raised pin insulators (Figure 1a). The cross-arms are 2.5m in length, with the earthwire terminated below the attachment point of the bracing strap to the pole. The design of these poles constitutes a threat to the large raptors and vultures with a wingspan of more than 1.7m. Martial Eagles, Tawny Eagles and Brown Snake Eagles and all of the vulture species are particularly vulnerable in this respect, due to their large size and wingspan and habit of using electricity poles as hunting or roosting perches.

The main 22kV line from Tosca to Vesel substation is built for some distance on a wooden SCF type structure (Figure 1b). This three-phase structure has an earthwire running all the way to the top of the supporting pole(s) extending to approximately 100mm above the pole top. This leaves a gap of only about 450mm between the earthwire and the outer conductor which creates a very dangerous situation as even small raptors risk electrocution when perching within this space. During the course of the inspection, an adult Martial Eagle perched on one of the structures. These structures are also significantly higher than the surrounding vegetation, and are therefore ideal perches for large raptors.

Figure 1. Wooden SCF Structure

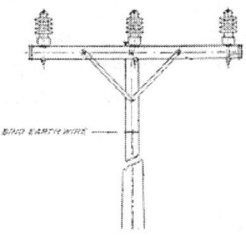
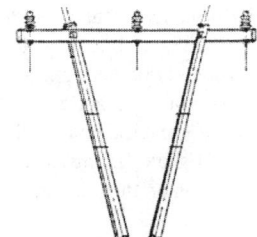

A. Three phase T-Structure   B. SCF Structure

Based on the above parameters, the assessment found that the design of the powerlines poses a real and potential risk of electrocution to raptors.

Environmental Performance of the Powerlines

To assess the environmental performance of the powerlines, the Network Availability and Performance Indicator (NAPI) system reports[9] for the powerlines in the study area from the period January 1995 - August 1997, were analysed to determine possible trends. The only other system to indicate whether incidents occurred, was the internal reporting of electrocution incidents. However, no incidents were reported through this system.

The NAPI reports of the study area for the period January 1995 - August 1997 recorded no incidents where birds were the reason for the outage. There were however 25 incidents without positive identification of what caused the interruption (reason unknown). However, if incidents did occur between two phases, the bird would not have caused a permanent fault and hence not required a line patrol. The number of outages without positive identification of what caused the interruption (reason unknown), could possibly be linked to birds; however, this could not be verified. The NAPI report system did therefore not contribute materially to the knowledge about the situation.

Interested and Affected Parties

Meetings were held with the local Eskom staff, as well as the conservation officer at the Molopo Nature Reserve, to obtain their views. One landowner was also consulted. From these meetings the following information was obtained:
- Eskom at that stage had already pro-actively fitted approximately 1800 structures with raptor protectors, but the process was time consuming;
- Local Eskom staff were of the opinion that due to their limited manpower and budget capacity the request for an acceleration of the process from conservationists was unrealistic;
- Conservationists from the Raptor Conservation Group[10] and provincial Nature Conservation bodies launched various programmes[11] amongst the farmers to actively promote the conservation of raptors on their properties. They were of the opinion that the powerlines posed a significant threat to large raptors, but they would be satisfied if a systematic programme was instituted to fit raptor protectors to the powerlines.

Cost of Mitigation Measures

The total cost to fit raptor protectors to the powerlines in the study area was calculated at R683, 191,24 (US$ 110, 192), and the implementation period approximately 6 years and 10 months.

CONCLUSION

The investigation team found no conclusive evidence of any bird mortalities as a result of electrocution or collisions with the powerlines. Although no formal reports of wildlife incidents were reported to Eskom since the time the powerlines were built, various factors such as high raptor populations, low human population density, vegetation cover, scavenger activities and infrequent Eskom patrols, suggest that the number of incidents reported may not present a true reflection of the environmental performance of the powerline.

The investigation team concluded that the parameters discussed during the risk assessment indicated that the reticulation network in the Molopo area constituted a real and potential threat to the growing population of large raptors in the area. It furthermore concluded that the general awareness of the local landowners and the potentially negative consequences for Eskom's image which might result in the event of Eskom failing to take any action, should be evaluated by Eskom management when making a decision on this matter.

---

[9] NAPI is an electronic fault recording system used by some of the divisions within Eskom's Distribution Group.
[10] The Raptor Conservation Group is a working group of the Endangered Wildlife Trust, a non-Governmental Organisation focusing on the conservation of biodiversity in southern Africa.
[11] Programmes were launched to educate farmers about the dangers that poisoning, drowning in farm reservoirs, as well as direct prosecution pose to the local raptor populations. Since these programmes were launched, the number of sightings of large raptors as well as nests recorded have risen sharply.

Having identified the risks and evaluated their possible impacts, the stage was reached where it had to be treated through design and implementation of a physical risk management programme. According to Valsamakis *et al.,* (1992) risk control entails *"any activity which is aimed at preventing losses that may arise from all pure risks facing an organisation; even those which are relatively unpredictable and which pose a threat to the organisation's existence"*. It can also be defined as *"a method of countering risk and includes all activities conducted for the purpose of"*:
- eliminating or reducing the factors that may cause loss to a person or organisation, and
- minimising the actual loss that occurs when preventative methods have not been fully effective.

The approach adopted to risk control was through an engineering approach and perspective to control the physical aspects of the risk situation. Attention was thus directed at physical factors such as design and protective devices and the following recommendations as part of the risk assessment were forwarded to Eskom management:
- That a formal communication programme be launched to inform all interested and affected parties on Eskom's decision and, if recommendations were accepted, the progress of the project, and that the project be marketed as a success story.
- That the earthwire on the mainline SCF structure from Tosca to Vesel substation be terminated to a distance below the cross-arm as specified by the Eskom Design Section.
- That all the powerlines of the Molopo Project be fitted with RP3 Raptor Protectors according to a fixed schedule.
- That a systematic programme be compiled with set targets and management information (Key Performance Indicators) to track project progress.
- That a formal audit programme be compiled to ensure compliance with set targets.
- That intensive market research be conducted and incentives developed for suppliers to design a Raptor Protector, which can be fitted with a link-stick without having to interrupt the electricity supply.

Eskom management accepted all the recommendations and at the time of this paper the project was in progress.

Effective management of risks is often sacrificed in the quest for progress and usually only leaps to the forefront when a major incident occurs. A systematic approach to the management of risks is necessary. Emphasis should not be placed on short-term cost to benefit relationships, but on maximising or achieving risk-return trade-off efficiency in the long term.

By using risk management methodology and systematically evaluating the biological and business risks, the risk existing or prospective powerlines pose to raptors can be determined and pro-active measures taken to either terminate, treat, tolerate or transfer these risks. It should also be noted that risk management must be viewed as an ongoing process, and not as a single event.

REFERENCES

APPLIC 1996. Cf. Olendorff *et al.* below.
BROOKE, R.K. 1984. *South African Red Data book-Birds.* South African National Scientific Programmes Report No. 97. FRD, CSIR, Pretoria.
HARRISON, J.A., ALLAN, D.G., UNDERHILL, L.G., HERREMANS, M., TREE, A,J., PARKER, V. & BROWN, C.J. (EDS.)1997. *The atlas of southern African birds. Vol. 1: Non-passerines.* BirdLife South Africa, Johannesburg.
HOBBS, J.C.A. & LEDGER, J.A. 1986a. The Environmental Impact of Linear Developments; Powerlines and Avifauna. Third International Conference on Environmental Quality and Ecosystem Stability. Israel, June 1986.
HOBBS, J.C.A. & LEDGER, J.A. 1986b. Powerlines, Birdlife and the Golden Mean. *Fauna and Flora.* 44:23-27.
HOBBS, J.C.A., LEDGER, J.A. & AUDITORE, T. 1990. The Impacts of Powerlines on Wildlife. *Electricity SA..* March/April 1990: 43-47.
LEDGER, J. 1992. Protecting Eagles and other Large Birds from Electrocution on Rural Powerlines. South African Eagle Insurance Company Limited.

LEDGER, J.A. & ANNEGARN, H.J. 1981. Electrocution Hazards to the Cape Vulture *(Gyps coprotheres)* in South Africa. *Biological Conservation* 20:15-24.
LEDGER, J.A. 1984. Engineering Solutions to the Problem of Vulture Electrocutions on Electricity Towers. *The Certificated Engineer* 57:92-95.
LEDGER, J.A., HOBBS J.C.A. & SMITH T.V. 1992. Avian Interactions with Utility Structures: Southern African Experiences. *Proceedings of the International Workshop on Avian Interactions with Utility Structure.* 1992. Electric Power Research Institute. Miami, Florida
OLENDORFF, R. R., ANSELL, A.R., GARRETT, M.G., LEHMAN, R.N. & MILLER, A.D. 1996. *Suggested Practices for Raptor Protection on Powerlines: The State of the Art in 1996.* Avian Power Line Interactions Committee (APPLIC). Edison Electric Institute/Raptor Research Foundation. Washington. D.C.
VALSIMAKIS, A.C., VIVIAN, R..W. & DU TOIT, G.S. 1992. *The Theory and Principles of Risk Management.* Butterworths. Durban.
VAN ROOYEN, C.S., KRUGER, R., NELSON, P.A & FEDORSKY, C.A. 1998. The Eskom/EWT Strategic Partnership: The South African Approach towards the Management of Wildlife/Utility Interactions. *EEI Natural Resources/Biologist National Workshop.1998.* Edison Electrical Institute, Washington, D.C.

Rudi Kruger
Senior Environmental Advisor
Eskom
P.O.Box 606
Kimberley
8301
South Africa

Chris S. van Rooyen
Endangered Wildlife Trust
Private Bag X11
Parkview
2122
South Africa

Chancellor, R. D. & B.-U. Meyburg eds. 2000
Raptors at Risk
WWGBP / Hancock House

Raptor Electrocutions and Outages – A Review of Rural Utility Records spanning 1986-1996

Richard E. Harness and Kenneth R. Wilson

ABSTRACT

Raptor mortality records spanning the years 1986 through 1996 were gathered from 58 electric utilities located in the western United States. These 1,450 records were reviewed to determine the types of utility structures causing outages and placing raptors at risk. The most commonly reported species electrocuted were eagles, with Golden Eagles *Aquila chrysaetos* reported 2.3 times more frequently than Bald Eagles *Haliaeetus leucocephalus*. Juvenile eagles were reported more frequently than adult birds. Eagle mortality was detected at an elevated rate during the late winter. Red-tailed Hawks *Buteo jamaicensis* and Great Horned Owls *Bubo virginianus* were the most commonly reported hawk and owl species. Hawk and owl electrocutions resulting in electric outages were elevated in the late summer. Six hundred and forty-six raptor deaths were tied to specific utility construction units. These data suggest that although transformers are relatively rare on rural overhead distribution systems, they are associated with most rural electric raptor electrocutions. Three- phase transformer banks were associated with a disproportionate number of detected electrocutions. These units are particularly lethal to raptors because of minimal phase-to-phase and phase-to-ground separation between bare energized jumper wires connecting transformers, protective cutouts and surge arresters. Three-phase transformer banks may also be dangerous because they often serve irrigation pumps located in remote areas likely to support numerous raptors.

INTRODUCTION

Distribution powerline raptor electrocutions have been studied extensively since 1971. Numerous methods to modify powerline structures to eliminate the potential for electrocutions and outages have been developed, published, and utilized by the electric industry. Two recent publications, *Suggested Practices for Raptor Protection on Power Lines: The State of the Art in 1996* and *Animal-Caused Outages* have provided utilities with numerous construction alternatives to minimize animal electrocutions and outages. Some of the modified overhead distribution line construction units have been adopted as standards by utilities, dramatically reducing raptor electrocutions. However, despite the utility construction improvements some electrocutions persist. These electrocutions often cause outages resulting in damaged equipment, safety problems and loss of service to consumers.

A 1993 Institute of Electrical and Electronics Engineers, Inc. (IEEE) survey stated the majority of their respondents still experience outages caused by squirrels, birds, raccoons and snakes (IEEE Power Engineering Society 1993). Southern Engineering Company (SC&E) recently surveyed 560 electric utilities nationwide to determine where and how outages occur. According to their survey results, animals are the third leading identifiable cause of all power outages, and birds cause more outages than any other animal (Southern Engineering Company 1996). According to the surveyed utilities, raptors and other birds were the number one cause of transmission outages in the Western United States. The respondents also indicated that birds were the most frequently reported cause of substation outages. Detroit Edison (1997) reported 255 animal caused substation outages and 39 bird caused outages between 1987 to 1994. Historically, 186 (27%) of Detroit Edison's 688 substations experienced one or more animal or bird caused outages in the past ten years. Historically, animals are the second greatest cause of all Edison's substation outages and animal outages have been increasing from 1987 to 1994. Although most of these outages were momentary, approximately 25% were sustained, resulting in lost revenue and consumer confidence. Georgia Power Company (1998) reported that animal caused substation outages on their system last an average 50.62 minutes and cost $15,000 (U.S.) each.

JUSTIFICATION

Reducing electrocutions will result in reduced outages, representing an opportunity to gain a competitive edge by reducing operating and maintenance costs. When utilities have a better understanding of which construction units cause most animal electrocutions, they will also be able to optimize their resources to mitigate the electrocutions. Since United States Federal law protects all birds-of-prey, successful research and development directed at mitigating animal- caused outages would have environmental benefits. The main laws employed by the United States Fish and Wildlife Service (USFWS) to protect raptors from electrocutions and wire strikes are the Migratory Bird Treaty Act (MBTA), Bald and Golden Eagle Protection Act and the Endangered Species Act (ESA). A proactive approach would also address pressures that may inevitably be aimed at electric utilities by environmental groups.

METHODS

Raptor mortality records spanning the years 1986 through 1996 were gathered from 58 electric utilities located in the western United States. The records provided data on 1,450 raptor deaths. These records were reviewed to determine the number of outages and types of utility structures potentially placing raptors at risk. Fifty- eight electric utilities located in the western United States provided 1,366 records. Wildlife rehabilitators and the USFWS provided 38 accounts. Additional records (n = 131) were obtained from Canada, and falconers provided 22 records.

RESULTS

Species Electrocuted

Twenty-six different electrocuted species of North American raptors are reported in the scientific literature (APLIC 1996). Sixteen species were recorded in this study, spanning in size from small American Kestrels *Falco sparverius* to Bald Eagles *Haliaeetus leucocephalus*. Non- raptor electrocuted species included a Sandhill Crane *Grus canadensis*, Great Blue Heron *Ardea herodias* and Common Ravens *Corvus corax*. Wildlife rehabilitators located in Texas and New Mexico reported one Brown Pelican *Pelecanus occidentalis*, and four Franklin's Gull *Larus pipixcan* electrocutions. Powerline collisions were also recorded for a Sandhill Crane and swan (species unknown). Table 1 tabulates the raptor electrocutions using six taxonomic groups; eagle, hawk, falcon, owl, osprey and vulture.

Table 1. Summary of all detected raptor electrocutions from 1986-1996.

Taxonomic Groups	Electrocutions
Eagle Total	748
Hawk Total	278
Falcon Total	14
Owl Total	344
Osprey Total	11
Vulture Total	18
Unidentified Raptors	15
Total	**1,428**

The most frequently reported raptors were eagles (n = 748). Golden Eagles *Aquila chrysaetos* are historically electrocuted more frequently than any other North American bird of prey (APLIC 1996). This study documented 272 Golden Eagle and 118 Bald Eagle electrocutions. Golden Eagle juveniles (n = 44) were electrocuted 2 times more frequently than adults (n = 22). Bald Eagle juveniles (n = 15) were electrocuted 1.6 times more frequently than adults (n = 9).

This study also tabulated 278 confirmed hawk electrocutions, mainly represented by buteos. The most frequently electrocuted species were Red-tailed Hawks *Buteo jamaicensis* (n = 35). Similarly, the most common hawk species to interact with power facilities in the Salt River Project's Avian Protection Program near Phoenix, Arizona were buteos; Harris' Hawks *Parabuteo unicinctus* and Red-tailed Hawks (Nobel 1995).

Although buteos comprise the largest non-eagle group of electrocutions (APLIC 1996), this study collected 344 owl electrocutions, surpassing the 278 hawk records. Historically, Great Horned Owls *Bubo virginianus* have been the most commonly electrocuted North American nocturnal raptor (Olendorff et al. 1981). Great Horned Owls were the most commonly electrocuted raptor on Salt River Project's power facilities located in Phoenix, Arizona (Nobel 1995). Likewise, Great Horned Owls (n = 86) were the most commonly reported nocturnal raptor in this study. Great Horned Owls may be more vulnerable, because of their large size and ability to thrive in urban areas with greater concentrations of overhead powerlines.

Seasonal Mortality

One-thousand one-hundred and forty-six of the 1,428 confirmed electrocution records included either a carcass discovery (n = 735) or precise electrocution (n = 411) date. Eighty-two percent of the precise raptor electrocution dates were tied to power outages.

There were 612 eagle electrocution outage (n = 96) and carcass discovery (n = 516) dates (Figure 1). Most detected eagle mortality and outages noted in this report occurred January, February, March and April. March carcass detections (n = 136) were disparately greater than any other month. Most eagle electrocutions (n = 516) were not tied to outages and therefore did not define precise electrocution dates. Therefore, it is possible that many eagles detected in March were actually killed in previous months. The carcasses may have avoided detection until spring thaws when utility crews became more active, especially in remote areas. Winter carcass detections may also be greater because cold temperatures delay the decaying process. Scavenging pressure may also be less in winter.

A late summer increase in the number of electrocuted hawks and owls was noted in this study. There were 210 hawk electrocution outage and carcass discovery dates (Figure 2) and 273 owl electrocution outage and carcass discovery dates (Figure 3). July, August and September had twice as many hawk deaths as any other month. Non-outage hawk mortality, not coinciding with the actual time-of-death, was similarly highest in September. Forty-seven percent of the 182 owl outage electrocutions also occurred in late summer months, peaking in August (n = 26). The elevated mortality in this study may similarly have been due to increased numbers of inexperienced fledgling birds since temperate breeding raptors often fledge during the late summer (Newton 1979). In a study of urban Harris' Hawks in Tucson, Arizona, Dawson and Mannan (1995) reported that birds at some nests are particularly susceptible to electrocution during the initial 2 weeks after fledging.

Figure 1. Eagle electrocution monthly mortality 1986-1996

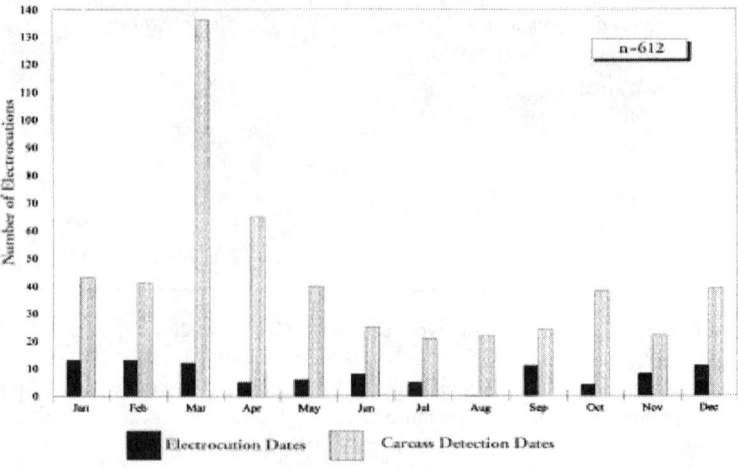

Figure 2. Hawk electrocution monthly mortality

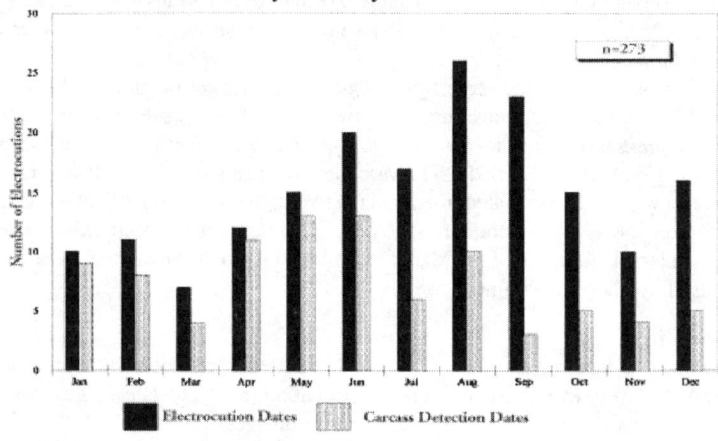

Figure 3. Owl electrocution monthly mortality

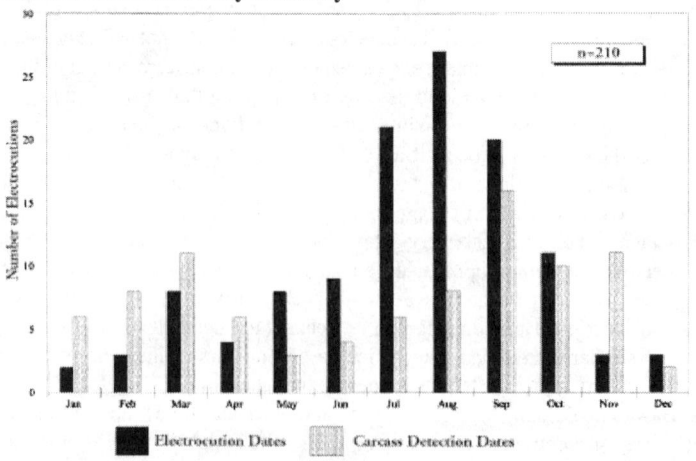

Structure Comparisons

Six hundred and forty-six raptor deaths were tied to specific utility construction units. These data suggest that although transformers are relatively rare on rural overhead distribution systems they are associated with most rural electric raptor electrocutions (Harness 1997). An urban study of Harris' Hawks in Tucson, Arizona also recorded more electrocutions by transformers than any other unit (Dawson & Mannan 1995). Dedon and Colson (1987) reported that Pacific Gas and Electric (PG&E) troublemen indicate that most PG&E electrocutions are also associated with incidental wiring and hardware on pole equipment (e.g. transformers, capacitors, etc.).

Most raptor electrocutions in this study were recorded at three-phase transformer banks (Figure 4). This is significant because three-phase transformer banks (n = 125) show comparable mortality rates to single phase transformers (n = 109) even though the number of three phase banks in rural areas is much lower. Rural multi- phase transformer banks often serve remote irrigation or oil pumps and may be particularly harmful, because they are often situated near open agricultural fields likely to support numerous raptors. These units are particularly lethal to raptors because of minimal phase-to-phase and phase-to-ground separation between bare energized jumper wires connecting transformers, protective cutouts and surge arresters.

Figure 4. Typical three-phase rural distribution structure with three-phase transformer.

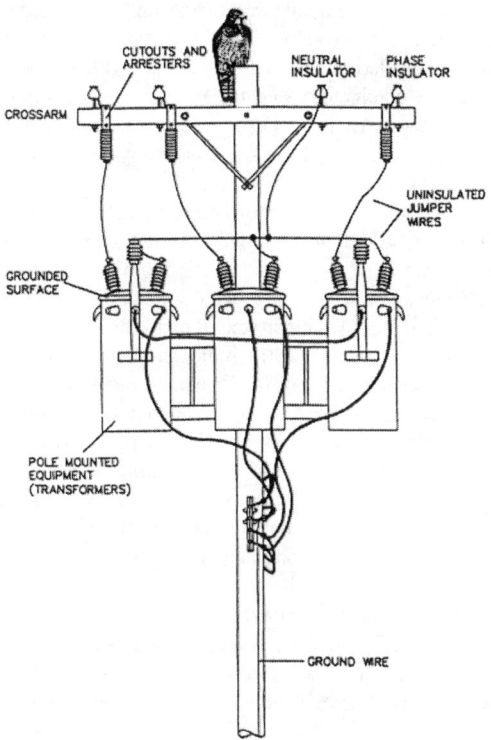

DISCUSSION AND RECOMMENDATIONS

Each year animals cause a significant number of outages on overhead distribution lines. PacifiCorp recently reported an average of 346 annual system outages from 1986 through 1995 caused by large perching birds (PacifiCorp, unpubl. data). Pacific Gas and Electric Company (PG&E) reported that 8 % of all their overhead outages from 1979 through 1983 were also due to birds (Dedon & Colson

1987). Some PG&E districts reported as many as 23 % of their outages were due to birds. Starlings *Sturnus vulgaris* and Blackbirds flocking in late fall and early winter primarily caused these outages.

Unfortunately the total number of outages caused by raptors and other animals is predicted to be large but cannot be estimated with current information. Although some utilities record and report all documented electrocutions, many do not because they are not required to do so. In addition, the few utilities that voluntarily keep records of the cause of all outages often have incomplete reporting. There is also no standardized raptor electrocution reporting form. The forms vary to meet the participating utilities' needs.

The use of automatic reclosers on rural electric powerlines further reduces the potential for detecting electrocutions. Reclosers automatically clear most short duration faults on primary conductors without tripping a fuse. Because the lines reenergize within seconds, outages are avoided and line crews are not required to investigate the service interruption causes. Electronic equipment and computers are sensitive to transient "blinks" due to recloser operations. Therefore, power quality suffers from even these momentary outages.

The data in this report indicate that an emphasis on providing insulated jumpers on all electrical equipment and at tap and deadend locations should reduce outages and provide the greatest amount of protection for all raptor species, including eagles. Fortunately, transformer units can be raptor-proofed without making major structural changes. The amount of exposed energized hardware can be dramatically reduced on new transformer installations by using 600 volt insulated jumper wire and installing insulated bushing covers. Existing transformer units can be retrofitted by either replacing bare wire with 600 volt insulated jumpers or by sliding insulating material over bare jumpers. Several utility manufacturers produce insulating material constructed with an open seam, allowing it to be easily slipped over existing bare conductors. Because the insulating material and bushing covers are relatively inexpensive and easy to install, this option is also economically attractive compared to increasing separation between conductors. Increased phase separation should continue to be used in remote areas with eagle populations.

All utilities should be encouraged to report raptor electrocutions/outages annually on a standardized form. The form should include detailed information on the types of construction units contacted and address the presence or absence of existing raptor-proofing on structures contacted. This knowledge would provide an indication as to what sorts of mitigating measures are working or failing. Recording measurements from the electrocuted raptor would also help determine clearances required to mitigate raptor electrocutions. Wildlife biologists should aid utility personnel with raptor species identification, and necropsies should be performed whenever possible to rule out other causes of mortality. These data should be compiled and shared annually. An observational study designed to monitor distribution line raptor electrocutions would also help determine if information contained in the outage reporting forms is representative of electrocutions detected.

Utilities should also actively look for electrocutions on their systems. Utilities annually inspect a percentage of the wood poles in their service territory to determine if they are deteriorating. Searching for raptor carcasses should be combined with ongoing pole inspection programmes to identify problem areas.

Promising protective methods and devices have recently been developed to mitigate electrocutions and outages. Unfortunately, insufficient data are available to assess their effectiveness. Documentation on existing protective methods and devices is also quite limited and there are minimal data on their relative cost-effectiveness. Research should be conducted to determine the effectiveness of these devices.

ACKNOWLEDEGMENTS

Electrical Systems Consultants, Inc funded this study. Jerry Hager was especially helpful with the technical details of this study. Dennis Rankin of the Rural Utilities Service, Monte Garrett of PacifiCorp, and Sam Milodragovich of Montana Power Company were invaluable in their assistance with gathering raptor electrocution data.

I am especially indebted to my committee members, Dr. Ken Wilson, Dr. Pat Kennedy and Dr. Denis Dean for enthusiastically supporting my work while taking the time to learn the difference between "telephone" and "power" poles. Ken Wilson and Dave Smith were indispensable with their statistical advice. I also thank my wife Sue and my two sons, Chris and Dan, for tolerating many side trips on family outings to scout electrocuted raptor carcasses.

REFERENCES

OLENDORFF, R. R., A.R ANSELL, M.G GARRETT, R.N. LEHMAN & A.D. MILLER 1996. *Suggested Practices for Raptor Protection on Powerlines: The State of the Art in 1996.* Avian Power Line Interactions Committee (APPLIC). Edison Electric Institute/Raptor Research Foundation. Washington D.C.

DAWSON, J.W. & R.W. MANNAN 1995. Electrocution as a mortality factor in an urban population of Harris' hawks. *The Journal of Raptor Research* 29-1.55.

DEDON, M.F. & E.W. COLSON 1987. *Bird-caused outages in the PG&E electrical distribution system.* Pacific Gas and Electric Company.

DETROIT EDISON 1997. Substation maintenance in 2000 – substation animal intrusion. T&D Management Conference – April 1997, Lansing, Michigan.

GEORGIA POWER 1998. Wildlife proofing to prevent animal- caused outages in substations. EPRI Transmission & Substation with Distribution Systems Targets Conference on Wildlife and Pest Control in Transmission Systems – April 1998. Scottsdale, Arizona.

HARNESS, R.E. 1997. Raptor Electrocutions caused by rural electric distribution powerlines. M.S. Thesis, Colorado State University, Fort Collins, Colorado.

IEEE POWER ENGINEERING SOCIETY 1993. *IEEE guide for animal deterrents for electric power supply substations.* Institute of Electrical and Electronics Engineers, Inc., New York.

NEWTON, I. 1979. *Population ecology of raptors.* Buteo Books, Vermillion, South Dakota.

NOBEL, T.A. 1995. Salt River Project's Avian Protection Program. *The Journal of Raptor Research* 29: 64.

OLENDORFF, R.R., A.D. MILLER & R.N. LEHMAN 1981. Suggested practices for raptor protection on powerlines: the state of the art in 1981. Raptor research report no. 4. Raptor Research Foundation, University of Minnesota, St. Paul, Minnesota.

SOUTHERN ENGINEERING COMPANY. 1996. Animal-caused outages. Electric Power Research Institute, National Rural Electric Cooperative Association. Arlington, Virginia.

Richard Harness
Environmental Specialist
EDM International
4001 Automation Way
Fort Collins, Colorado 80525
USA

Dr. Kenneth Wilson
Colorado State University
Department of Fishery and Wildlife Biology
135 Wagar
Fort Collins, CO 80523
USA

Chancellor, R. D. & B.-U. Meyburg eds. 2000
Raptors at Risk
WWGBP / Hancock House

Powerlines and Raptors, using Regulatory Influence to prevent Electrocutions

Leo R. Suazo II

ABSTRACT

The United States Fish and Wildlife Service hereafter (Service) has documented migratory bird electrocutions and collisions for almost four decades. Although great strides have been made to modify powerlines and utility structures, problems still exist. With the continuing expansion of human populations into rural areas, avian interactions with structures and lines are expected to increase. United States law protects migratory birds with treaties, statutes, and regulations. Congressional legislation used to protect birds include the Migratory Bird Treaty Act, the Bald and Golden Eagle Protection Act, and the Endangered Species Act. Aldo Leopold listed regulatory influence as one of five wildlife management tools. Accordingly, the Service uses its regulatory influence to generate voluntary compliance to protect the Nation's avian resources. The Service encourages electric utilities to retrofit old lines and to construct all new lines in a bird-friendly manner. Because many utilities are too small to have staff biologists, the Service helps these utilities identify migratory corridors and other sensitive areas, by forming partnerships and sharing biological data. Sharing biological data helps utilities identify existing or potential problem areas. If utilities do not comply voluntarily, the Service has the option of forcing compliance through civil and criminal action. Penalties can range from $10,000 to $500,000 and imprisonment for up to two years.

INTRODUCTION

Many papers and books have been published identifying the specific problems raptors encounter with utility structures and related powerlines. These structures and lines cause raptor mortality, mostly through electrocution (Harness 1997). Since electrocution has been identified as a significant mortality factor, government agencies and the utility industry have developed many design solutions to protect raptors (Suggested Practices for Raptor Protection on Powerlines—State of the Art 1996). Often, however, electric utilities are reluctant to implement design changes on existing equipment structures and lines, due to cost constraints. When such reluctance is encountered, regulatory influence becomes the driving force to bring about modification.

The United States Fish and Wildlife Service's mission is "to conserve, protect and enhance the Nation's fish and wildlife and their habitat for the continuing benefit of people." Every Service employee has a stewardship obligation to ensure the fulfilment of the mission statement. Special

Agents are charged with enforcing the laws passed by Congress and regulations promulgated by the Service. Special Agents have been fulfilling the protection portion of the mission statement for over one hundred years.

The Service's Office of Law Enforcement has been involved with the electrocution of migratory birds for many decades. In the early 1970s, Service Special Agents conducted an investigation into the poisoning and shooting of over 1200 eagles by residents of Wyoming and Colorado. During the investigation Special Agents and other conservationists found more than 300 eagles and other raptors near powerlines. The raptors died primarily from electrocution (Olendoff 1972). This paper discusses the involvement of the Service's Law Enforcement Office in activities associated with migratory bird electrocutions and collisions.

HISTORY

To best understand the role of the Special Agent, we must look at the history of law enforcement within the Service. At the end of the 19th century, concern arose over the slaughter and decline of game animals and migratory birds throughout the United States. These concerns attracted the attention of the American Sportsmen. The Federal government offered no protection to migratory birds. Market hunters took literally tons of game each year in violation of state laws, and shipped large quantities of illegal wildlife tocity markets.

States were unable to cope with market hunting because of a disinterested public, political interference, lack of authority, insufficient law enforcement officers and finally due to the of lack of jurisdiction of states when game was transported across state lines.

In 1900, John F. Lacey, United States Congressman from Iowa, introduced a bill in Congress which passed on May 25, called the Lacey Act. The purpose of the Lacey Act was to make it a violation of Federal law to transport wildlife in interstate commerce which had been taken in violation of state law. Unfortunately, due to a lack of Special Agents, the Lacey Act failed to provide adequate protection to migratory birds.

The Weeks-McLean Bill, generally known as the "Migratory Bird Law" was passed in Congress on March 4, 1913, but was vigorously attacked as unconstitutional by states righters, resort owners, spring shooters and market hunters. The Migratory Bird Law was abandoned following the passage and ratification of the Migratory Bird Treaty Act in 1918. The Migratory Bird Treaty Act was vigorously contested in a famous test case: Missouri vs. Holland. Ray P. Holland, one of the original "Special Agents-Migratory Bird Law" arrested Frank McAllister, the Attorney General of Missouri, for "Spring Hunting" with friends during a closed season. The case was appealed to the United States Supreme Court where the Honorable JusticeOliver Holmes, on April 19, 1920, ruled the Migratory Bird Treaty Act was constitutionally valid (Bean 1983).

REGULATORY INFLUENCE

Three pieces of Congressional legislation mandate the Service's role in preventing avian electrocutions and collisions. The first and earliest piece of legislation is the Migratory Bird Treaty Act. Treaties were negotiated with Great Britain on behalf of Canada in 1916, Mexico in 1936, Japan in 1974 and Russia in 1978. The purpose of the Act was to afford protection to migratory birds, their parts, nests and eggs. All raptors are considered migratory and fall under the protection of the Migratory Bird Treaty Act, Title 16 United States Code, Sections 703-712. The Migratory Bird Treaty Act states that, unless permitted by regulation, it is unlawful to pursue, hunt, take, capture, kill, possess, sell, barter purchase, ship, export, or import any migratory birds, or any part, nests, eggs, or product thereof. Culpability is strict liability, that is no degree of knowledge need be proven. There are no civil provisions in the Act.

Maximum criminal penalties for the violations under the felony provisions include fines up to $250,000 per individual, and $500,000 per organization and up to two years imprisonment. [Note: The felony provisions apply to the sale of Migratory Bird Treaty Act species or their parts, eggs or nests.] For misdemeanours the penalties include fines up to $5,000 per individual, and $10,000 per organization and up to 6 months imprisonment. Migratory bird electrocutions violate the misdemeanour provisions of the Migratory Bird Treaty Act. The Service has determined that electrical utilities fall under the provisions of the Act, as their utility structures and lines are causing a "take" when electrocutions occur.

The second piece of legislation which protects eagles is the Bald and Golden Eagle Protection Act, Title 16 United States Code, Section 668a. This bill was first signed into law June 8, 1940, affording protection to Bald Eagles *Haliaeetus leucocephalus*. On October 24, 1962, the Bald and Golden Eagle Protection Act was amended to afford protection to the Golden Eagle *Aquila chrysaetos*. The law states that no person shall take, posses, sell, purchase, barter, offer for sale, purchase or barter, transport, export, or import any bald or golden eagle alive or dead, or any part, nests or eggs, thereof without a valid permit to do so. Provisions of this Act also define molest or disturb as a take. Thus, when eagles are electrocuted or collide with powerlines and utility structures the individual or organizations involved can be held in violation of the Act. Culpability for Bald and Golden Eagle Protection Act violations are knowingly or with wanton disregard for the consequences of their act. Under this Act there are civil provisions and the degree of culpability is strict liability.

Maximum criminal penalties for misdemeanour violations of the Bald and Golden Eagle Protection Act, include fines up to $100,000 per individual and $200,000 per organization and up to one year of imprisonment. For felony violations the penalties include fines up to $250,000 per individual, and $500,000 per organization and up two years imprisonment. Civil penalties are $12,500.

The last legislation which protects some raptors is the Endangered Species Act, Title 16 United States Code, Sections 1531 - 1543 which was signed into law on December 28, 1973. The law affords protection to fish, wildlife, and plants listed as endangered or threatened. The Endangered Species Act makes it is unlawful to import, export, take, transport, sell, purchase, or receive in interstate or foreign commerce any species listed as endangered or threatened. "Take" under the Endangered Species Act means an act which kills, injures, or harms a listed species. Violations may include significant habitat modification or degradation where it actually kills or injures wildlife by significantly impairing essential behavioural patterns, including breeding, feeding or sheltering. When utility companies locate a powerline or other structures in an area where it is likely to result in an electrocution or collision, thus causing death or injury to an endangered or threatened species, the utility would be in violation of Endangered Species Act. Culpability for Endangered Species Act violations is knowingly and culpability for civil actions are knowingly or strict liability.

Maximum penalties (misdemeanour) for violations include fines up to $100,000 per individual, and $200,000 per organization, as well as up to one year of imprisonment. Civil penalties can be assessed up to $25,000.

LAW ENFORCEMENT ACTIONS

In 1978, the first organized electrocution project was initiated by Special Agent Lucinda Schroeder in Utah. Schroeder discovered large numbers of electrocuted eagles and other raptors in an area known as Skull Valley,Utah.

Along one mile of powerline, nine Golden Eagle carcasses were found and the birds' deaths attributed to electrocution. (Schroeder 1998, pers. comm.) Schroeder pioneered the first educational programmes and formed the first enforcement-industry partnership. Schroeder formed a partnership with Utah Power and Light to retrofit equipment structures and lines which were responsible for killing migratory birds.

The first documented prosecution occurred in 1993. Special Agents Roger Gephart and Frank Kuncir conducted an investigation into the electrocution of ten Swainson's Hawks *Buteo swainsoni* and Great Horned Owls *Bubo virginianus* under one equipment power pole. As a result of the investigation, Gephart issued a violation notice to Pacific Gas and Electric (PG&E) located in California for Migratory Bird Treaty Act violations. PG& E representatives met with Gephart and Kuncir and agreements were made to retrofit problem lines in a timely manner. Kuncir discovered

32 Red- tailed Hawks *Buteo jamaicensis*, Barn Owls *Tyto alba*, Ravens *Corvvus corax*, and four Golden Eagles. During the course of the investigation, Kuncir also discovered several Red-tailed Hawks and Swainson's Hawks, on San Luis National Wildlife Refuge and Merced National Wildlife Refuge. After repeated and continued electrocutions of protected species by PG&E's power poles and powerlines, Kuncir filed additional criminal charges against PG&E for Endangered Species Act violations. Kuncir, working through the Regional Solicitor, also filed civil proceedings against PG&E. In all PG&E paid $1500 in fines. Agreements were set into place for the continued retrofitting of PG&E equipment structures and lines. Policies and procedures also were developed to further protect raptors. (Gephart & Kuncir 1998, pers. comm.)

Since 1993 the role of the enforcement office has been one of mostly a silent partner. Service Special Agents and their regulatory influence have been used by other Service divisions, non-government organizations, other natural resource agencies, and industry biologists in a joint effort to bring the utility industry into compliance. The enforcement office in many cases is the driving force behind many utility companies forming bird protection programs and polices in their respective companies. Since the 1970s, Service Special Agents have used their regulatory influence with industry and along with other conservationists have been responsible for millions of dollars in retrofits as well the construction of new powerlines in a bird friendly manner. In most cases legal action is not necessary.

Figure 1. Reported raptor deaths in Region 6 from 1978-1998.

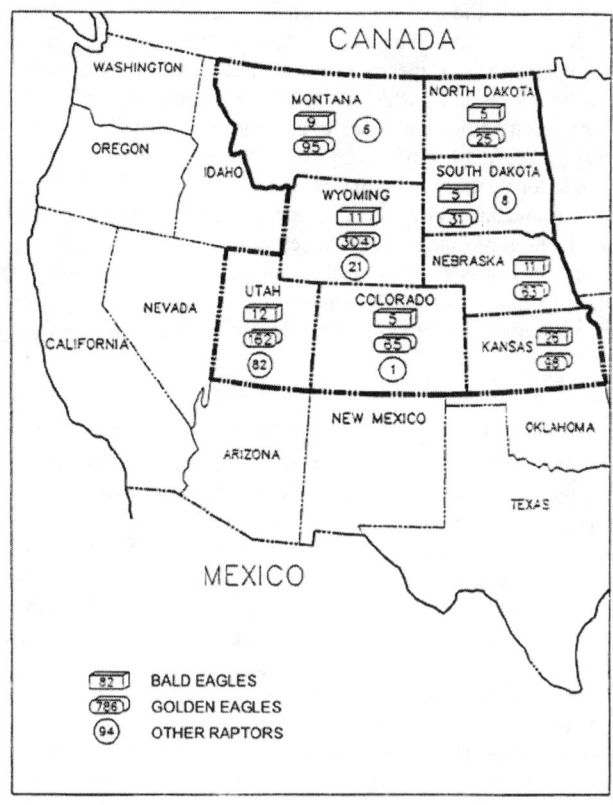

REACTIVE/PROACTIVE

In the past, Special Agents have investigated electrocutions and collisions of migratory birds primarily in a reactive manner. Reports of electrocuted birds are received from various sources including the utility company responsible. Once utility companies are notified of problem equipment structures or lines they usually move rapidly to repair the structures or lines causing the electrocutions or collisions. Currently, the Service is taking a proactive approach. Using the partnership approach the Service advises utility companies of impending problems with utility structures and lines before birds are killed. In many cases electrical utilities working with Service biologists and Special Agents implement proactive solutions, however some utility companies for a variety of reasons tend to only fix the specific problem as it is reported. It is in the best interest of all partners involved to act in a proactive manner. The Service will be conducting inspections on retrofits as well as new line construction, to insure that repairs meet compliance requirements.

The Service is involved with raising industry awareness by providing training on legal ramifications and providing biological support to the industry. The Service has taken a major proactive step by appointing a Special Agent to act as the first electrocution program coordinator. The role of the coordinator provides guidance to Service agents when conducting investigations and to act as a liaison with industry officials, and other conservationists. The coordinator is to provide training to all concerned participants, including the general public. This is a significant step for the enforcement office, since it is one of the smallest divisions within the Service.

ENFORCEMENT MORTALITY DATA

The Service is divided into seven geographic regions nationwide. Region 6 includes Colorado, Wyoming, Montana, Utah, Kansas, Nebraska, North Dakota, and South Dakota. Working in partnership with Industry, other Federal agencies and Conservation Organizations, the Service established a National Mortality Reporting System in 1973. During 1972 through 1975 the system documented about 300 Golden Eagles. After 1975 the system was discontinued for reasons that remain unclear (Bob Lehman 1998). However, from 1978 to date the effort has continued in Region 6; the Office of Law Enforcement has recorded all migratory bird mortality (primarily raptors). Data were obtained from 1978 to 1998 (Figure 1). The fatality reports indicated electrocution of 1045 migratory birds including 786 Golden Eagles (75%), and 82 Bald Eagles (8%). The Electrocution fatalities listed by state are in Table 1.

Table 1. Region 6: Migratory Bird Mortalities related to Power Distribution Lines

	Utah 1985-1995	Wyoming 1978-1994	Montana 1979-1997	Kansas 1989-1997	Nebraska 1980-1992	Colorado 1979-1998	N. Dakota 1985-1996	S. Dakota 1980-1993	Total
B. EAGLE	12	11	9	26	11	5	5	5	82
G. EAGLE	162	304	95	98	63	65	25	31	786
GHO	0	14	4	0	0	0	0	3	21
RTH	28	6	2	0	0	1	0	5	18
OWLS	24								
WTRBRD	1								
CROWS	28								
UNKN.	1								
P.FALCN	0	1	0	0	0	0	0	0	1
	256	336	110	124	74	71	30	44	1045

D. WIRCENSKE/L.SUAZO 4/98 REVISED 6/04/98

Note: One (1) Sandhill Crane and one (1) unidentified owl in Wyoming flew into powerlines.

Region 6 data indicate a strong need for the renewal of a national reporting plan within the Federal government as well as the electrical industry. The need to compile all the available data is essential to help determine the scope of the problem and to determine if ongoing mitigated measures are having the desired effect.

ACKNOWLEDGEMENTS

I wish to thank the Service for looking into the future and allowing me the opportunity to work on this project. I also thank Kevin Ellis, Roger Gephart, Lucinda Schroeder, Jim Klett, Dominic Domenici, Andrew Archuleta, Clay Ronish, Debra Wircenske and Rick Harness for helping in data collection and reviewing the manuscript.

REFERENCES

BEAN, M. J. 1983. The evolution of national wildlife law. 449 pp.
HARNESS, R.E. 1997. Raptor electrocutions caused by rural electric distribution powerlines. Master's Thesis, Colorado State University, Fort Collins. 110 pp.
LEHMAN, R.N. 1998. Raptor electrocutions on powerlines: A discussion of issues and needs For the next century. Unpublished.
OLENDORFF, R.R. 1972. Eagles, sheep and powerlines. *Colorado Outdoors* 2:3-11.
SUGGESTED PRACTICES FOR RAPTOR PROTECTION ON POWERLINES: THE STATE OF THE ART IN 1996. 1996. Edison Electric Institute/Raptor Research Foundation. 125pp.

Leo R. Suazo II
755 Parfet Suite 230
Lakewood
Colorado 800215
USA

Part 11

Biology of Owls with with Emphasis on Vocalisations

Sokoke Scops Owl *Otus ireneae*

Convener:
Claus König

ch
Owl-Vocalizations as Interspecific Differentiation-Patterns and their Taxonomical value as Ethological Isolating Mechanisms between various Taxa

Claus König

ABSTRACT

Owls are mainly active by night or at dusk Therefore plumage-patterns and colourations are less important for mutual recognition than vocalizations. This may explain the sometimes enormous individual variability of plumage patterns, as well as the existing different colour-morphs in various species. On the contrary the whole vocabulary of each species is totally inherited and therefore taxonomically specific. Keeping this in mind, vocalizations seem to be the most important differentiating patterns between species, playing apparently also a role as ethological isolating mechanisms between separate species. In comparison with passerine birds, owls show rather little geographical variation of vocal patterns and the specifically typical parameters are always kept. Therefore we have no very distinctive geographical "dialects" within the range of the same species! Geographical differences in voice are often even less obvious than individual variation within the same population.

The author has studied owls in the wild and in aviaries for more than 35 years. Most of his field-work was done in Europe, South America and Africa. His studies proved the hypothesis mentioned above, which has been supported by molecularbiological studies (PCR, DNA-sequences). According to these investigations we can speak of about 213 species of Strigiformes in the world.

* * *

Owls are chiefly active at dusk or at night. Therefore plumage-patterns and colourations are obviously less important for interspecific recognition than are vocalizations - in spite of the birds' increased visual perception under faintest light-conditions. Keeping this in mind, the sometimes enormous variability of plumage-patterns, as well as the different colour-morphs in several species of owls may be understood quite well. Indeed many species can "afford" a large individual polymorphy (e.g. *Strix aluco* or some *Glaucidium* and *Otus*), while on the contrary in all species of owls the complete vocabularies are totally inherited and taxonomically specific. The variability of vocalizations is generally rather low as well individually as on a geographical level. In no case the specific vocal parameters are altered in different races of the same species. Distinct regional "dialects", very obvious in many passerine birds, do not exist in owls! If, in two owl-specimens very similar in plumage, striking differences in voice may be noted, they doubtless are good candidates for specific separation. Therefore bioacoustics is highly important as a taxonomical criterion in "difficult" species-groups of owls (e.g. *Glaucidium* and *Otus*), showing no obviously distinctive patterns in plumage or size. This knowledge has led to the discovery of "new" species. Meanwhile the specific status of the latter could be proved by molecularbiological studies (PCR, DNA-sequences) and ecological investigations in the field.

Supported by the German Scientific Community (Deutsche Forschungsgemeinschaft) my wife Ingrid König and myself have studied taxonomical problems in Neotropical owls, comparing the results with studies on Old World Strigidae. The hypothesis of the importance of vocalizations for taxonomy, based on investigations of Marshall (1978) and Scherzinger (1978), could be proved by the studies mentioned above: Vocal patterns are doubtless the most important interspecific isolating mechanisms in owls! Studies on DNA-evidence stress the bioacoustical results in a convincing manner.

We actually know that concerning the taxonomy of owls, the nucleotide substitutions by DNA-sequencing are varying at subspecific level between 0 to about 1 %. Greater distances (e.g. more than 1,5 %) of the nucleotide substitution suggest species status of the compared taxa. But, this is not valid for every order of birds! In species of Passeriformes the nucleotide substitutions may be much greater than in Strigiformes, and the vocal differences due to geographical dialects may be very striking.

Based on bioacoustic studies on a large scale on Old and New World Owls it may be quoted that:

1.) Clearly distinguishable vocal patterns (e.g. songs) speak for different species. This counts especially for sympatrically living taxa.

2.) In allopatrically distributed species many vocal patterns may be similar or even rather identical. But, this must not be taken as evidence for closer relationship! The areas of distribution of allospecies normally are separated by large distances. Therefore it is very unlikely that they might ever meet or get into contact with each other in any way, unless they are migratory species. Isolating mechanisms between allopatric, superficially similar species are therefore not necessary. This holds true for morphological as well as for vocal patterns. Here the phenomenon of convergence quite often plays an important part too, having fooled many taxonomists in the past.

3.) In parapatric species specific vocal parameters may be distinguished in all cases. But, the latter may be sometimes difficult to be told apart by the human ear; they are obviously sufficient for the owl-species in question, to recognize specific differences. Nevertheless interspecific hybridizations may occasionally occur, but hybrids will rather soon be exterminated by natural selection. Populations of hybrids (as it is usually the case between subspecies) of longer duration never will be established in such cases.

Now some examples for the mentioned topics:

1.) The Eurasian Pygmy Owl (*Glaucidium passerinum*) and the Sub-Saharan Pearl-Spotted Owlet (*Glaucidium perlatum*) are allospecies, although some authors have considered them to be geographical races of the same species(Eck & Busse 1973). Indeed they look very similar, as do most species of the genus *Glaucidium*. But there are totally different vocalizations, different habitat and different behaviour. Beyond DNA-evidence shows clearly the specific status of both taxa (Heidrich & Wink, pers. comm.) and proved the hypothesis of being doubtless two separate species.

Of the relatively large vocabularies of both species, which are very different, I wish to give here only few examples: The territorial song of male *Glaucidium passerinum* consists of long series of single notes uttered at intervals of about 1-2 s between each note (Fig. 1). If the bird is very excited, it utters a short "staccato"-trill after each note (Fig. 2). The female has a similar, but higher-pitched and less clear song. When begging for food, it delivers a high-pitched "seeht", mostly to be heard near the nesting-site (Figs. 1- 3).

Figure 1. "Normal" territorial song of a male *Glaucidium passerinum* from SW Germany. *

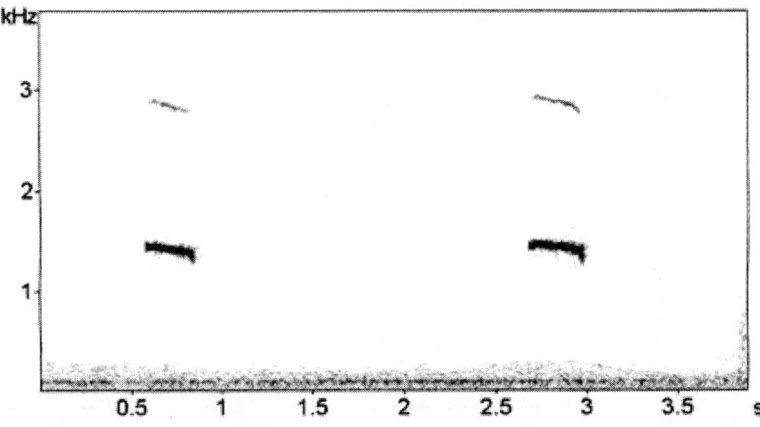

Figure 2. Phrase of the "excited" song of *Glaucidium passerinum*: the single note is followed by a short staccato trill. This song may be uttered in long sequences like the "normal" song.

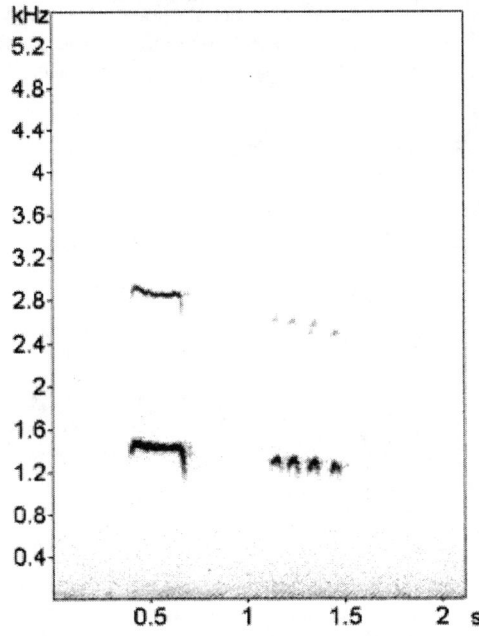

*If no recordist is mentioned, the records are made by C. König, who also made the sonograms with "Avisoft" programme. Some sonograms have been prepared by Richard Ranft with the same programme at the British Library National Sound Archive.

Figure 3. Contact-calls of *Glaucidium passerinum:* **female (left) and male (right).**

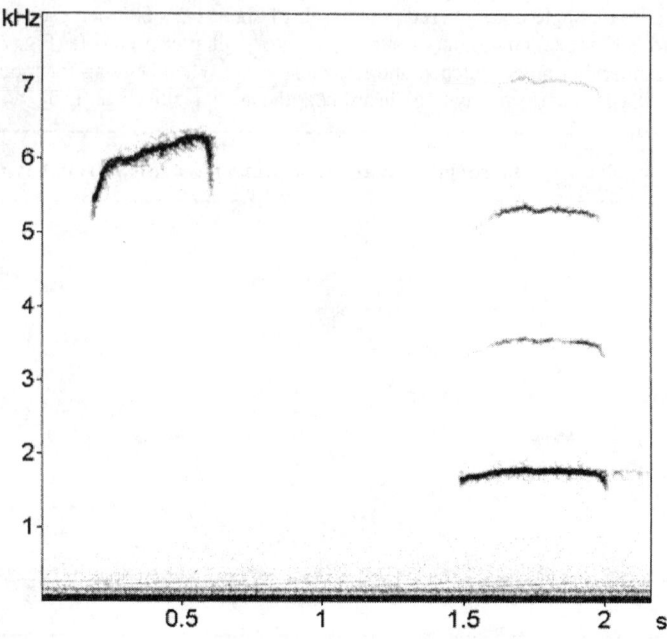

The territorial song of *Glaucidium perlatum* is a relatively rapid sequence of notes with intervals of about 0.2 s between each. Further, the notes increase in volume and also slightly in pitch and finally end in several very loud "glissando"-notes "peeoh" with emphasis on the "ee" (Fig. 4 and 5). The contact-call (also begging-call) is a short "peowit" (Fig. 6).

Figure 4. Section of territorial song of *Glaucidium perlatum* from South Africa.

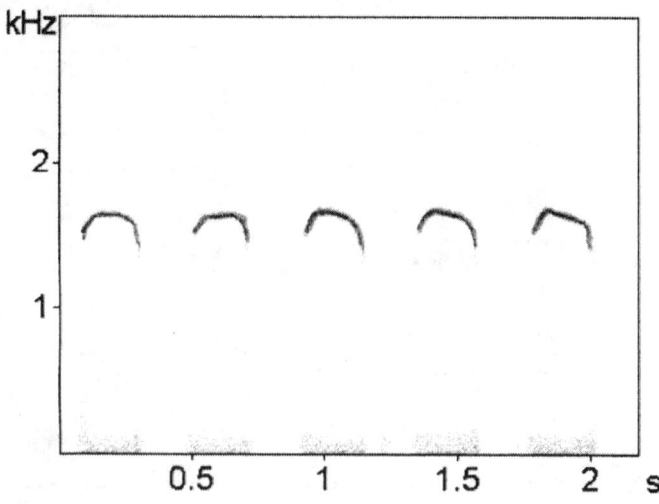

Figure 5. The "glissando" notes, which mostly follow the territorial song of *Glaucidium perlatum*.

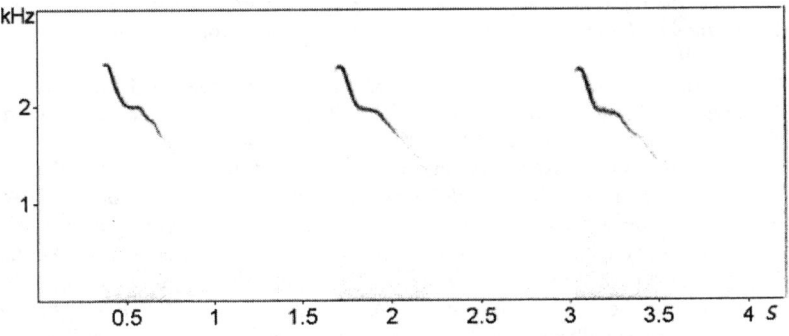

Figure 6. Contact-call of a female *Glaucidium perlatum*.

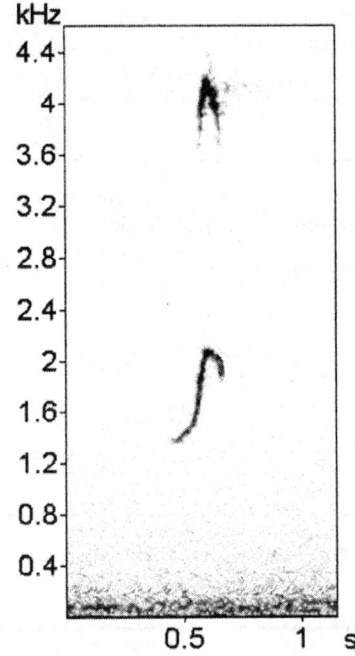

2.) On behalf of the American Pygmy Owls studies on vocalizations have shown, that there are much more species present, as most authors had supposed before (König 1991, 1994, 1998, Heidrich, König & Wink 1995, Howell & Robbins 1995, Vielliard 1989). According to bioacoustical, ecological and zoogeographical studies the taxonomical status of these taxa could be cleared up, as e.g. *Glaucidium californicum, G. gnoma, G. palmarum, G. sanchezi* and *G. griseiceps* being different species. In some of them DNA-evidence could in addition prove the results. This is for example the case on behalf of *Glaucidium nanum, Glaucidium peruanum* and *Glaucidium tucumanum,* being specifically distinct from *Glaucidium brasilianum*. Because of vocalizations, ecology and DNA-evidence the Andean Pygmy Owl (*Glaucidium jardinii*) is only distributed in north-western South America from mountains in Venezuela to about the Marañón-depression in the northern Andes, while from Peru to N

Argentina the cloud forests of the eastern Andes are inhabited by the Yungas Pygmy Owl (*Glaucidium bolivianum*). The Central American taxon *costaricanum* is either a subspecies of *Glaucidium gnoma,* resp. *cobanense* or even a separate species, but never a race of *Glaucidium jardinii* ! (König 1991, and in prep., Heidrich, König & Wink 1995; Robbins & Stiles 1999).

3.) The American Great Horned Owl (*Bubo virginianus*) and Magellan Great Horned Owl (*B. magellanicus*) have proved separate species (König, Heidrich & Wink 1986, König 1998). They are parapatric taxa with totally different vocalizations.

A similar situation we have to recognize in the African Spotted Eagle-Owl (*Bubo africanus*) and the Vermiculated Eagle-Owl (*Bubo cinerascens*) (König, Weick & Becking 1999). The latter has been regarded as northern race of the Spotted Eagle-Owl (Fry *et al.* 1988, Voous 1988). But both are specifically distinct and have different songs. Beyond the Vermiculated Eagle-Owl has dark brown (not yellow!) irides with a fleshy-red edge of the eyelids, which are blackish in the more southern counterpart *Bubo africanus*. Male *Bubo africanus* start singing in general with an incomplete song, consisting of a rather loud hoot, often followed by a deeper, somewhat drawn-out one, while the "full" song, often in duet with the female, consists of the "incomplete song", followed by 2 rather loud hoots (Fig. 7), leading finally to a sequence of 3 slurred notes followed by a drawn-out, somewhat downward inflected hoot: "wuohu - whooh". These phrases are repeated at intervals of several seconds. *Bubo cinerascens* never utters more than two notes in a phrase, nor does he give the described "wuohu - whooh". He utters instead a song of bisyllabic notes uttered at intervals. The first note is always rather loud and explosive and followed after a short break by a softer hoot (Fig. 8).

Figure 7a. "Full song" (notes 1,3,4) of a female *Bubo africanus* from South Africa. The second note is a call of a nearby male. Rec. O. Prozesky.

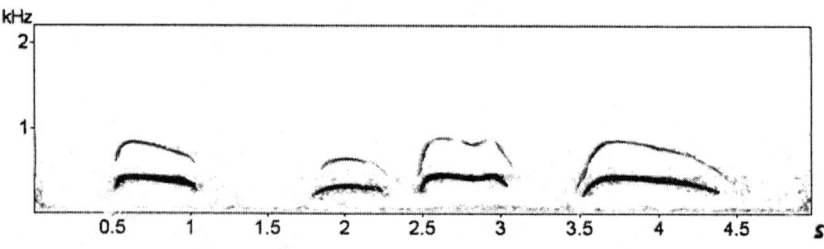

Figure 7b. One phrase of the "full song" of a male *Bubo africanus* from Tanzania. Rec. R. Stjernstedt. Spectogram by R. Ranft (NSA).

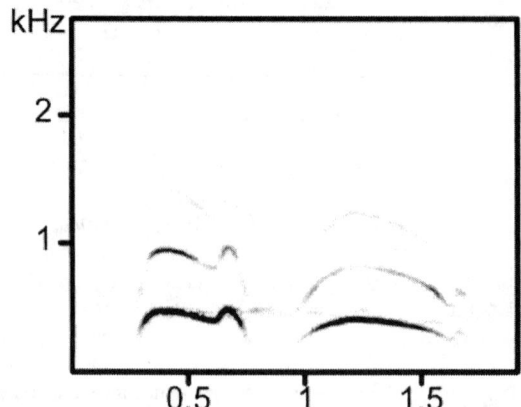

Figure 8. "Full song" of *Bubo cinerascens* from Mali. Rec. C. Chappuis. Spectogram by R. Ranft (NSA)

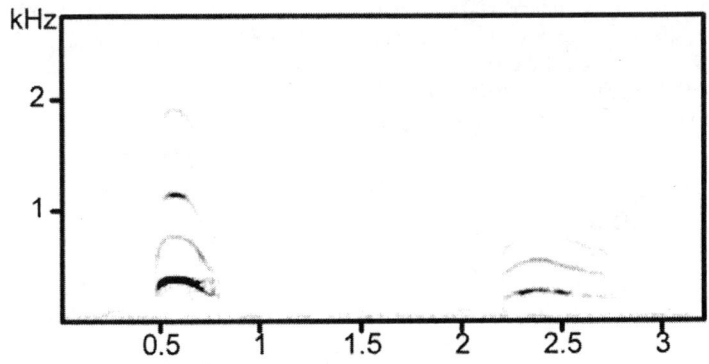

4.) The Scops Owls are a taxonomically very difficult, large group of owls (Eck & Busse 1973). We actually recognize about 68 species. As in other Strigiformes the vocalizations are a good help for specific separation (Marshall 1978). The Common Scops Owl (*Otus scops*) is distributed from southern Central Europe to North Africa (north of the Sahara) and east to about Pakistan. There are no remarkable differences in song to be noticed (Figs. 9 and 10).

Figure 9. Territorial song of a male *Otus scops* from Mallorca (Balearic Islands).

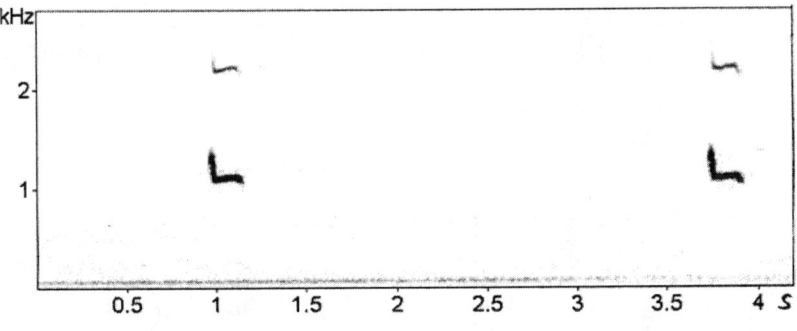

Figure 10. Territorial song of *Otus scops* from Pakistan. Rec. T. Roberts.

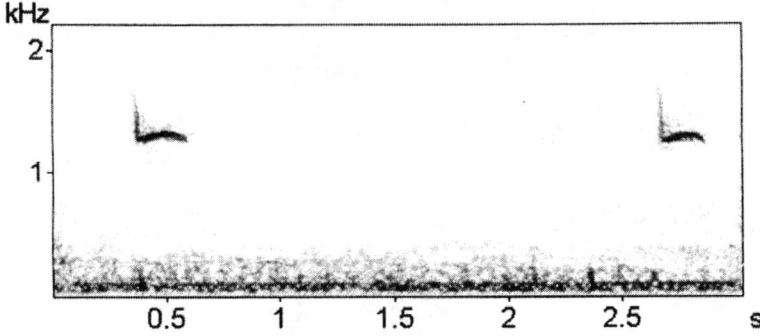

The Sub-Saharan African Scops Owl (*Otus senegalensis*) utters a purring song, while the Asian Scops Owl (*Otus sunia*) gives a tri-syllabic song. It is a typical Scops Owl in China and Japan. The southern races (*malayanus, rufipennis, leggei*) differ vocally and might perhaps be specifically distinct (Figs.11 and 12). In that case these 3 taxa would best be treated as geographical races of the taxon *malayanus*: *Otus malayanus* (Hay 1847) the Malay Scops Owl. The Seychelles Scops Owl (*Otus insularis*) utters a hoarse rasping song, similar to the sound of sawing a dry branch with a hand-saw. It is doubtless a separate species (Fig. 13).

Figure 11. Territorial song of *Otus sunia* from Japan. Rec. T. Kabaya.

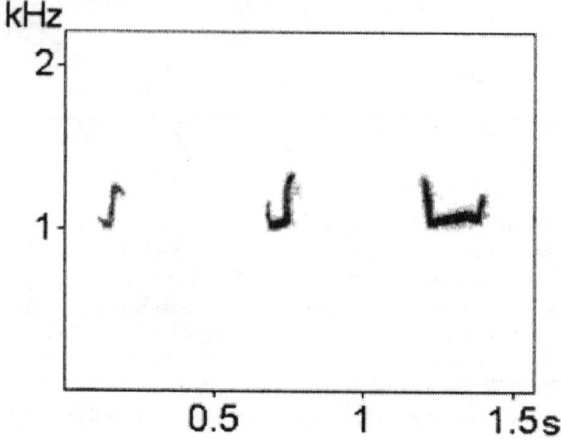

Figure 12. Territorial song of *Otus (sunia ?) malayanus* from Thailand. Rec. J.T. Marshall.

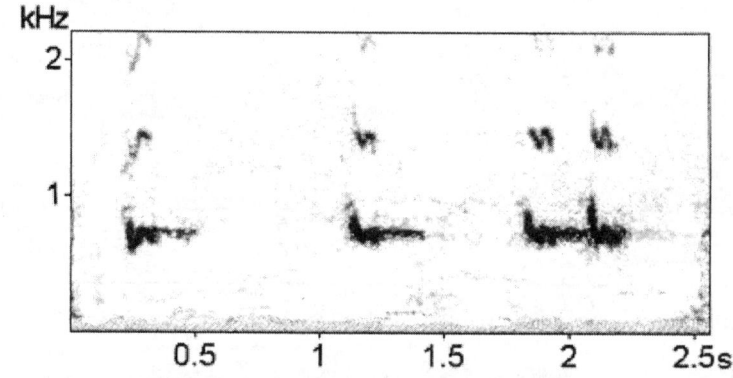

Figure 13. Territorial song (after playback) of *Otus insularis* from Mahé (Seychelles). Rec. R. Ertel.

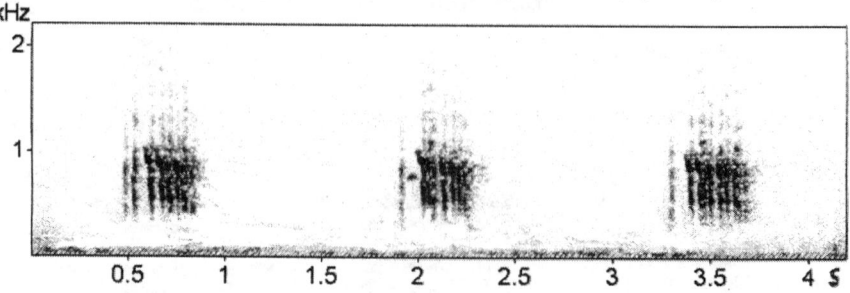

Otus bakkamoena represents a species-group of the following taxa with specific rank, all differing vocally: *Otus bakkamoena* the Indian Scops Owl (eastern Middle-East to India), *Otus lempiji* the Sunda Scops Owl (Malaysia, Greater Sunda Islands), *Otus lettia* the Collared Scops Owl (from the Himalayas to China and Taiwan) and *Otus semitorques* the Japanese Scops Owl (Japan and coastal S Siberia). Probably one more species might be attributed to this group: the Singapore Scops Owl (*Otus cnephaeus*) which has been thought a race of *bakkamoena* or *lempiji*, but differing very much vocally (König, Weick & Becking 1999). It is found around Singapore.

All members of the *bakkamoena*-superspecies-group are very similar in appearance. *Otus lettia,* the Collared Scops Owl, has the most pronounced collar on its hindneck, together with an indistinct second collar (Fig. 14 and 15). It has brown irides. The male's song is a downwards inflected note, uttered at rather long distances (Fig. 16). The very similar in size and outside appearance *Otus semitorques,* the Japanese Scops Owl, has only an indistinct collar on its hindneck and dark red or orange-yellow eyes. The song consists of rather deep, uniform hoots without any inflections (Fig. 17).

Figure 14. Adult *Otus lettia glabripes* from Taiwan. Photo. R. Harling, Mus. Stuttgart.

Figure 15. *Otus lettia glabripes* from Taiwan showing the double collar. Fot. R. Harling, Mus. Stuttgart.

Figure 16. A note of the song of *Otus lettia* from Taiwan. Rec. J.-H. Becking.

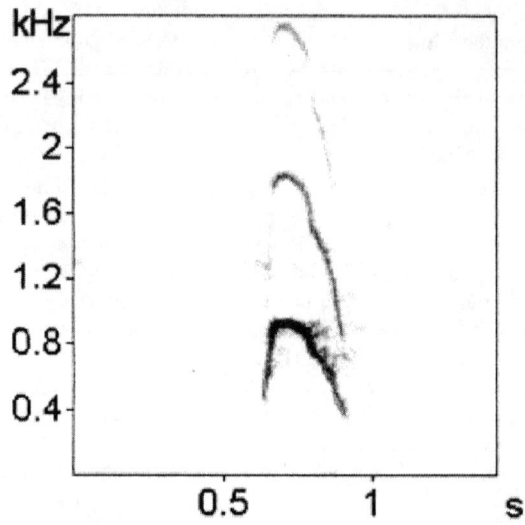

Figure 17. A note of the song of *Otus semitorques* from Japan. Rec. T. Kabaya.

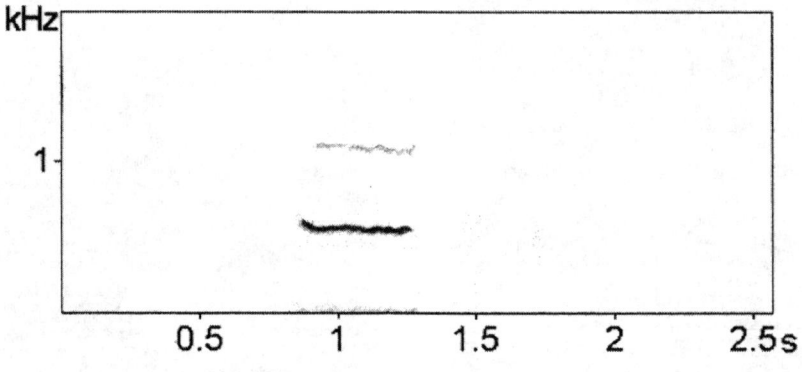

5.) The American Screech Owls are the ecological counterparts to Old World Scops Owls. They are generally treated as species of the same genus, but should be given another generic name: *Megascops*. But there is one exception: the Flammulated Owl (*Otus flammeolus*) is related to Old World Scops Owls and not to New World Screech Owls! The latter have two different songs: the A-song uttered in a territorial function and the B-song given during courtship or in an aggressive sense; sometimes as an introduction to the A-song. The Montane Forest Screech Owl (*Otus hoyi*) of the "Yungas" of northern Argentina and southern Bolivia is a new species described in 1989 (König & Straneck 1989, König 1994) with typical vocalizations, while similar in plumage patterns to many other Screech Owls.

In the Peruvian Screech Owl (*Otus roboratus*) two "subspecies" differing very much in size have to be recognized. Their vocalizations are said to be similar (Johnson & Jones 1990), but there are differences, which might suggest specific separation. Like other Screech Owls, the Peruvian Screech Owl has two different songs: the territorial advertising (A-song) and a courtship, resp. aggressive song (B-song). In the dwarfish lowland form *pacificus* the A-song shows a distinctly slower sequence of notes in a trill than in *roboratus*, while in the latter the harmonics (overtones) are much more pronounced. In the B-song of *pacificus* the notes are accelerated towards the end of the short trill, first rising and finally falling in pitch (Hardy et al. 1989). In *roboratus* the B-song is longer and consists of equally-spaced "staccato"-notes uttered with a somewhat "undulating" quality in pitch (Figs. 18 and 19). Larger differences may be noted in the calls (see Johnson & Jones 1990!). I therefore cannot support the idea of Johnson & Jones (1990), who treat the taxon *pacificus* as subspecies of *Otus roboratus*, which is a relatively large *Otus*, living in mountainous regions. I suggest to give the dwarfish Pacific taxon from northwestern coastal Perú and western coastal Ecuador specific rank, calling it *Otus pacificus*, the Tumbes Screech Owl.

Figure 18. 2 phrases of the B-song of *Otus pacificus* from Tumbes, NW Perú. Rec. J.P. O'Neill (ARA-Records 16).

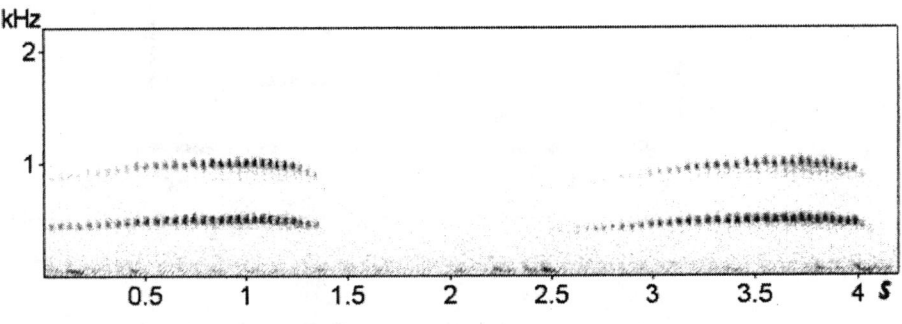

Figure 19. Phrase of the B-song of *Otus roboratus* from near Bagua, N Perú. Rec. J.P. O'Neill (ARA Records 16)

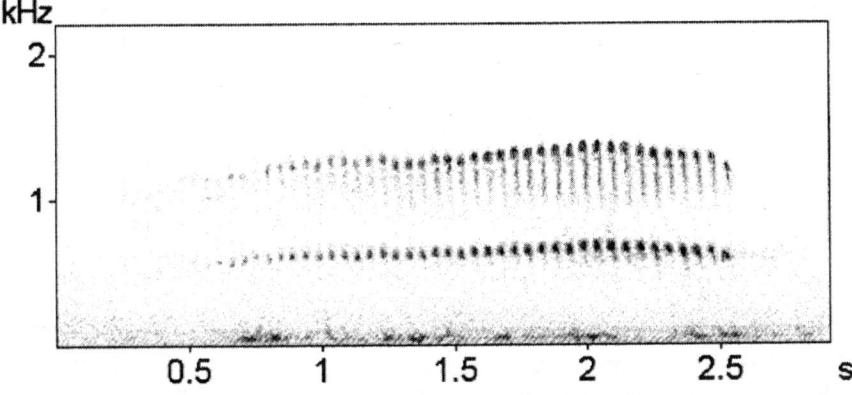

6.) The African White-Faced Owls should be split into two different species according to voice: The Northern White-Faced Owl (*Ptilopsis leucotis*) and the Southern White-Faced Owl (*Ptilopsis granti*) (Figs. 20 and 21). It was W. van der Weyden (1975) who first showed the differences in spectrograms. The distribution of the first taxon reaches from Senegambia accross the Sahel-zone to N. Kenya and Ethiopia, while the second is distributed from southern Kenya south to South Africa and Namibia, avoiding the dense rain forest of Central Africa and the deserts.

Figure 20. Phrase of the territorial song of *Ptilopsis leucotis*. Rec. C. Chappuis. Spectogram by R. Ranft (NSA).

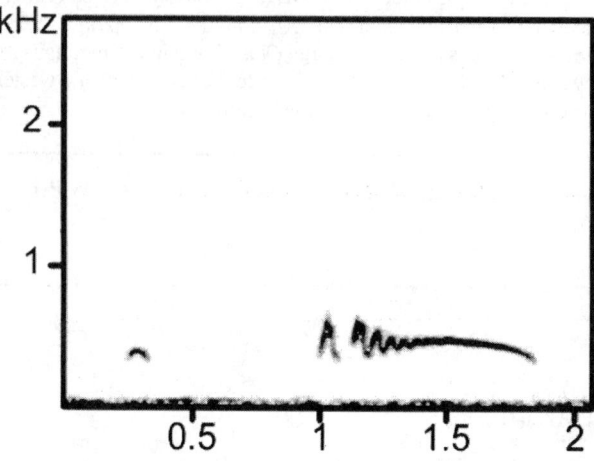

Figure 21. Phrase of the territorial song of *Ptilopsis granti* from Zambia. Rec. R. Stjernstedt. Spectogram by R. Ranft (NSA).

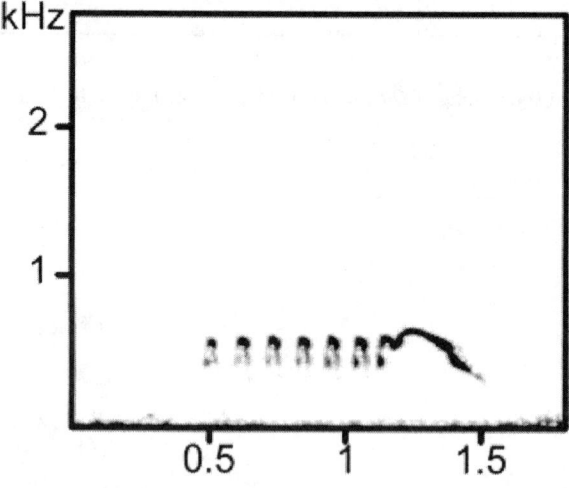

Further investigations on vocalizations, ecology and zoogeography will doubtless enlarge the number of owl species in the world, especially in South America and South East Asia, as several taxa regarded as races of one species might prove specific distinction (Lambert & Rasmussen 1998; König, Weick & Becking 1999; Robbins & Stiles 1999).

According to our most recent knowledge the number of living owl-species in the world is about 213. Many of them have been described during the last years, or have been separated from existing species by bioacoustical, ecological and molecularbiological investigations. The specific status of most of them could be proved by such studies and may therefore be regarded as secured. Doubtless some more species will be found in the near future, not only in South America, but also in SE-Asia, as some taxa described as races might prove separate species. Bioacoustical studies doubtless will be very essential for taxonomy of "difficult" groups of owl-species, as they will help to complete the "taxonomical mosaic" in a sensible and effective way. Finally molecularbiological and ecological studies are needed to prove the results. Up to now we always found our hypothesis confirmed, that vocal patterns are the most important interspecific ethological isolating mechanisms (Osche 1966) in owls and being therefore very important for the taxonomy of the Strigidae (Marshall 1978, Scherzinger 1978, König 1994, 1998).

ACKNOWLEDGEMENTS

I wish to thank my dear colleagues from Heidelberg University Michael Wink and Petra Heidrich, who put the results of their molecularbiological studies on the DNA-evidence of several species at my disposal for a final decision of some taxonomical problems. Beyond I owe many thanks to Jan-Hendrik Becking, Wageningen, The Netherlands, Cornell Laboratory of Ornithology, Ithaca, Rainer Ertel, Remseck (Germany), John William Hardy, Gainesville, (USA), Tsuruhiko Kabaya, Tokyo (Japan), Joe T. Marshall, Washington, (U.S.A.), Otlef Prozesky, Pretoria (South Africa), Richard Ranft (British Library, Wildlife Sounds), London, and Tom Roberts, (U.K.), for providing me with bioacoustical material.

REFERENCES

ECK, S. & H. BUSSE 1973. Eulen. Die rezenten und fossilen Arten. - NBB Wittenberg-Lutherstadt.
FRY, C. H., S. KEITH & E.K. URBAN 1988. The Birds of Africa. Vol. III. - Acad. Press. London, San Diego, etc.
HEIDRICH, P., C. KÖNIG & M. WINK 1995. Bioakustik, Taxonomie und molekulare Systematik amerikanischer Sperlingskäuze (Strigidae: *Glaucidium* spp.). - *Stuttgarter Beitr. Naturk.*, Ser. A, no. 534: 1-47.
HOWELL, S.N.B. & M. B. ROBBINS 1995. Species limits of the Least Pygmy Owl (*Glaucidium minutissimum*) complex. - *Wilson Bull.* 107 (1): 7-25.
JOHNSON, N.K. & R. E. JONES (1990. Geographic differentiation and distribution of the Peruvian Screech Owl. - *Wilson Bull.* 102 (2): 199-212.
KÖNIG, C. & R. STRANECK 1989. Eine neue Eule (Aves: Strigidae) aus Nordargentinien. - *Stuttgarter Beitr. Naturk*, Ser. A., no. 428: 1-20.
KÖNIG, C. 1991. Zur Taxonomie und Ökologie der Sperlingskäuze (*Glaucidium* spp.) des Andenraumes. - *Ökol. Vögel (Ecol. Birds)* 13 (1): 15-76.
KÖNIG, C. 1994. Biological patterns in owl taxonomy, with emphasis on bioacoustical studies on Neotropical Pygmy (*Glaucidium*) and Screech Owls (*Otus*). - In: Meyburg & Chancellor (eds.): *Raptor Conservation Today*. - WWGBP/ Pica Press: 1-19.
KÖNIG, C. 1994. Lautäußerungen als interspezifische Isolationsmechanismen bei Eulen der Gattung *Otus* (Aves: Strigidae) aus dem südlichen Südamerika. - *Stuttgarter Beitr. Naturk.*, Ser. A., no.511: 1-35.
KÖNIG, C. 1998. Lautäußerungen als interspezifische Differenzierungsmerkmale bei Eulen und ihre Bedeutung für die Taxonomie (Aves: Strigiformes). - *Zool. Abh. Staatl. Mus. Naturk.* Dresden, 50 (suppl.): 51-62.
KÖNIG, C., P. HEIDRICH & M. WINK 1996. Zur Taxonomie der Uhus (Strigidae: *Bubo* spp.) im südlichen Südamerika. - *Stuttgarter Beitr. Naturk.*, Ser. A., no. 540: 1-9.
KÖNIG, C., F. WEICK & H.-J. BECKING 1999. Owls. An Identification Guide to the Owls of the World. - Pica Press, Mountfield (UK).
LAMBERT, F.R. & P.C. RASMUSSEN 1998. A new Scops Owl from Sangihe Island, Indonesia. - *Bull. B.O.C.* 118 (4):204-217.
MARSHALL, J. 1978. Systematics of smaller Asian Nightbirds based on Voice. - *Orn. Monogr.* 25: 1-58.
OSCHE, G. 1966. Grundzüge der allgemeinen Phylogenetik. In: Gessner, F. (ed.): *Handbuch der Biologie* (Allg. Biol.), 3 (2): 817-906. Frankfurt a.M.

ROBBINS, M.B. & F.G. STILES 1999. A new species of Pygmy Owl (Strigidae: *Glaucidium*) from the Pacific slope of the Northern Andes. - *Auk* 116 (2):305-315.
SCHERZINGER, W. 1978. Vergleich der Stimmeninventare von fünf Arten der Gattung *Glaucidium*. - *J. Ornith.* 119 (4): 475.
VIELLIARD, J. 1989. Uma nova espécie de *Glaucidium* (Aves, Strigidae) da Amazônia. - *Revta. bras.Zool.* 6 (4): 685-693.
VOOUS, K.H. 1988. Owls of the Northern Hemisphere. - London (Collins).
WEYDEN, W.J. VAN DER 1975. Scops and Screech Owls: Vocal evidence for a basic subdivision in the genus *Otus*. - *Ardea* 63: 65-77.

Prof. Dr. Claus König
Staatliches Museum für Naturkunde
Rosenstein 1
D - 70191 Stuttgart
Germany

Chancellor, R. D. & B.-U. Meyburg eds. 2000
Raptors at Risk
WWGBP / Hancock House

Distribution and population size of the Sokoke Scops Owl *Otus ireneae* in the Arabuko-Sokoke forest, Kenya.

Munir Virani

ABSTRACT

The Sokoke Scops Owl *Otus ireneae* is known only from the Arabuko-Sokoke forest, Kenya and the foothill forests of the east Usambara mountains in Tanzania. The Arabuko-Sokoke forest is ranked as the second most important forest in mainland Africa for bird conservation. The forest faces many threats, among them the clearing of its valuable trees and proposed forest excisions to settle the growing local human population. These threats pose a potential risk to the Sokoke Scops Owl as its numbers were believed to be on the decline. An ecological study was conducted on the species in 1993. Call-playback surveys were used to study the owls' distribution and population size. The owls were mainly found in dense *Cynometra* woodland where they occurred at densities of about 7 pairs/km^2. They occurred at lower densities in adjacent habitats with a lower canopy height. The total owl population in the forest was estimated at 1000 pairs. Based on this study, the owls' status was downlisted from endangered to its present status, vulnerable. Follow-up census studies to monitor the owls are urgently required as illegal logging in the forest continues unabated. This study recommends a two-yearly census of the owls in the forest as part of a long-term monitoring programme.

INTRODUCTION

The Sokoke Scops Owl *Otus ireneae* was discovered in 1965 when a specimen was collected during an American Museum expedition to the Arabuko-Sokoke forest (Ripley 1966). In Kenya, the owl is found only in the Arabuko-Sokoke forest, a vestige of the coastal forest that once stretched along the entire coastline of East Africa (Fig 1). Arabuko-Sokoke forest is a vital refuge for a large number of rare and threatened animals and is ranked as the second most important forest in mainland Africa for bird conservation (Collar & Stuart 1985). The Sokoke Scops Owl occurs mainly in the *Cynometra-Manilkara-Brachylaena* (now referred to as *Cynometra*) woodland habitat type found along the western half of the forest (Britton & Zimmerman 1979). The species also occurs in the foothill forests of the east Usambara mountains in Tanzania, and this has led to speculation that the owls may have once ranged throughout suitable habitat along the East African coast (Fanshawe 1993; Hipkiss *et al.*, 1993).

The Arabuko-Sokoke forest faced a major threat from clearance of its valuable timber trees, which seemed to negatively affect the owl population (Kelsey & Langton 1984). A reliable assessment of the owls' conservation status was difficult since virtually nothing was known of the biology of this rare species. Information gathered about a species' distribution and density has been critical in the implementation of successful management and conservation policies aimed at ensuring the survival of viable populations (Wood 1991).

Figure 1. Map of Kenya showing position of Arabuko-Sokoke forest

An ecological study of the Sokoke Scops Owl was conducted in the Arabuko-Sokoke forest between February and December 1993 (Virani 1995). The aims were to understand the owls' ecological requirements specifically with respect to distribution and abundance, behaviour and habitat use. Information gathered would be used to maintain or improve the status of the Sokoke Scops Owl throughout its range (Virani 1995; Virani this volume). This paper presents results on the distribution, density and population size of the owls in the forest.

STUDY AREA AND METHODS

The study was conducted in all the different forest types of the Arabuko-Sokoke forest (Virani 1995) (Fig 2). These are mixed forest, mixed *Hymenaea* forest, *Brachystegia* woodland and *Cynometra* woodland (Fig 1). Mixed forest and mixed *Hymenaea* forest are semi-deciduous type forests occurring on white sandy soils with a canopy height of about 10-12 m (Britton & Zimmerman 1979; Kelsey & Langton 1984). *Brachystegia* woodland is more open woodland dominated by *Brachystegia spiciformis* trees up to 18 m high. This woodland, which also occurs on white sandy soils, forms a narrow belt running from the southern to the northern part of the forest (Fig 2). The *Cynometra* woodland lies on red Margarini sands and is further divided into woodland, intermediate woodland and thicket. This sub-division was necessitated due to the different canopy heights of the dominant *Cynometra webberi* trees. The *Cynometra* woodland which occurs in two separate regions of the forest (Fig 2) has an average canopy height of about 15 m, whilst the intermediate *Cynometra* and the *Cynometra* thicket have canopy heights of 7 m and 4 m respectively (Virani 1995; Kelsey & Langton 1984; Britton & Zimmerman 1979). In *Cynometra* woodland, the illegal removal of *Brachylaena huillensis*, a strong hardwood tree, much sought after by wood carvers, is believed to have a negative impact on the owl population as the tree is considered a potential nesting site for the owls due to the numerous holes and cavities in it (Kelsey & Langton 1984).

Figure 2. Map of Arabuko-Sokoke forest showing various forest habitat types.

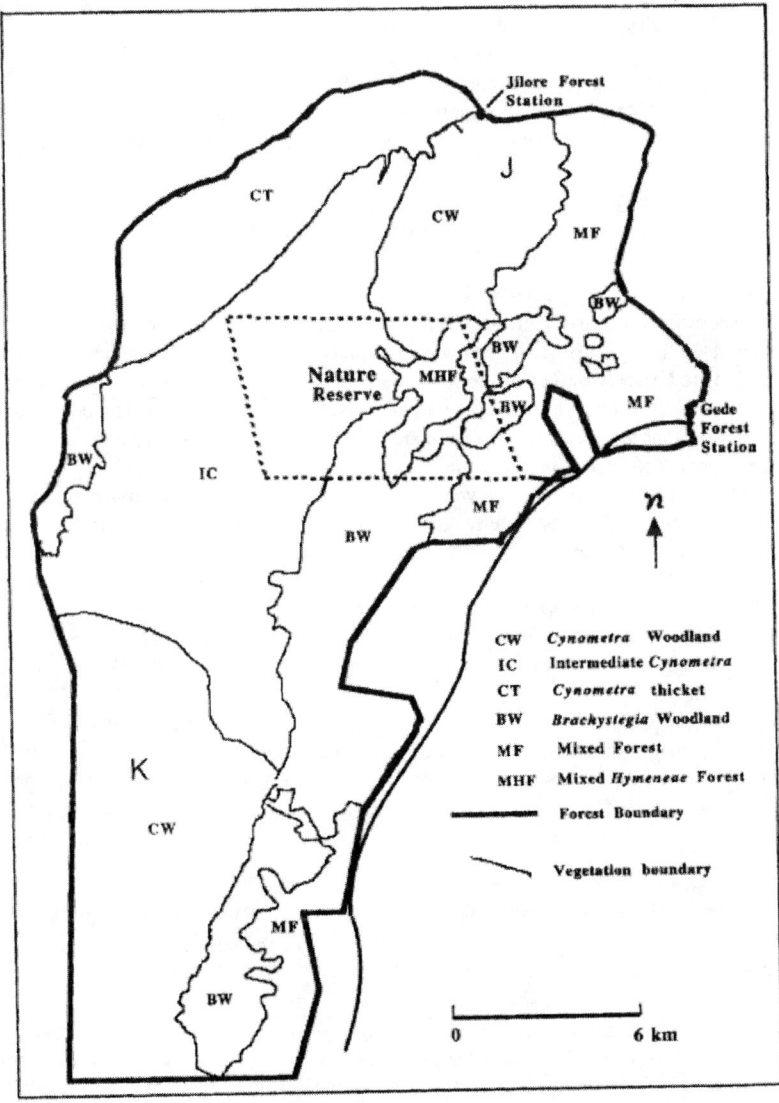

Nocturnal call surveys were conducted between April 1 and June 7 1993. Two blocks of *Cynometra* woodland (J and K), in the north and south of the forest were selected as prime locations for conducting call surveys, while supplementary study sites were selected in the intermediate *Cynometra* and mixed *Hymenaea* forests (Fig 2). Owl surveys based on call-playback (Southern 1954) were conducted in representative areas of all the habitat types of the Arabuko-Sokoke forest which were accessible by vehicle. Call surveys involved walking transects and playing-back owl calls. Six 1-km long transects were chosen at locations J and K respectively (A-F) while supplementary 1-km long transects were chosen in intermediate *Cynometra* (a-f) and mixed *Hymenaea* forest (mhfD) (Fig 3). One-minute-long owl calls were played at each transect at intervals of 200 m and owls responding in the ensuing 5 minutes were recorded. This exercise was repeated at each transect point. Based on the work of Kelsey & Langton (1984), each responding owl was considered to be a territorial male and hence representing a pair. Prior to commencement of owl surveys, we spent two weeks familiarizing ourselves with owl responses and estimated that the maximum distance an owl could be heard from was 250 m. Thus all responses heard in an area of 1 km by 0.5 km gave a reasonable indication of owl density. Owl distribution patterns in the forest were determined by presence or absence of responding owls (all species of owls heard were recorded) while owl population density (based on four replicates of 6 transects per location) was calculated using the method described by Kendeigh (1944) and Emlen (1974). All transect counts were conducted on calm, clear nights. It was assumed that the owls responded to play-back calls irrespective of the time of the night or the stages of the moon.

RESULTS AND DISCUSSION

General distribution of owl species

Sokoke Scops Owls occurred throughout the *Cynometra* woodland habitats to the north-east and south-west parts of the forest (Fig 3). They were also patchily present in mixed *Hymenaea* forest and in the intermediate *Cynometra* habitat. Sokoke Scops Owls were not recorded in *Cynometra* thicket to the north-west of the forest nor in any plantation areas adjacent to *Cynometra* woodland or thicket. They were not present in *Brachystegia* woodland and hence the collection of the type specimen in *Brachystegia* woodland is considered as anomalous (Kelsey & Langton 1984).

Barred Owlets *Glaucidium capense* were dominant in the *Brachystegia* woodland while a few responses were recorded in the peripheries of *Cynometra* thicket and intermediate *Cynometra* (Fig 3). The Sokoke Scops Owl and the Barred Owlet were heard calling together in the intermediate *Cynometra*.

African Wood Owls *Strix woodfordii* were present in all habitat types of the forest and in surrounding plantations, while Verreaux's Eagle Owls *Bubo lacteus* were present only in the *Brachystegia* woodland and in the mixed forest. One Barn Owl *Tyto alba* was recorded in the *Cynometra* woodland.

The presence of Sokoke Scops Owls in intermediate *Cynometra* and mixed *Hymenaea* forest confirmed earlier suggestions that these areas might hold owls (Kelsey & Langton 1984). The distribution of Sokoke Scops Owls and Barred Owlets was remarkably disjunct although overlap was observed in degraded areas around the edges of *Cynometra* woodland and in intermediate *Cynometra*.

Population density and size

In the northern and southern parts of the *Cynometra* woodland, the Sokoke Scops Owls occurred at densities of 7.3 pairs/km^2 (s.d = 0.80) and 6.9 pairs/km^2 (s.d = 1.01) respectively. These densities did not differ significantly (Mann-Whitney U = 569.0, p > 0.05) and hence the overall mean density of the owls in *Cynometra* woodland was calculated at 7.1 pairs/km^2 (n = 44, 95% limits: 6.1 – 8.0). In intermediate *Cynometra* and mixed *Hymenaea* forest, the owls occurred at densities of 1.2 pairs/km^2 (n = 7, 95% limits: 0.00 – 3.31) and 3.0 pairs/km^2 (n = 7, 95% limits: 2.37 – 3.58) respectively. There was no significant difference between the mean population density of owls in these two habitats although the p value obtained was small (Mann-Whitney U = 29.0, p = 0.06).

Figure 3. Locations of vocal responses (and non- responses) of Sokoke Scops Owls and Barred Owlets in visted areas of the Arabuko-Sokoke forest, 1993.

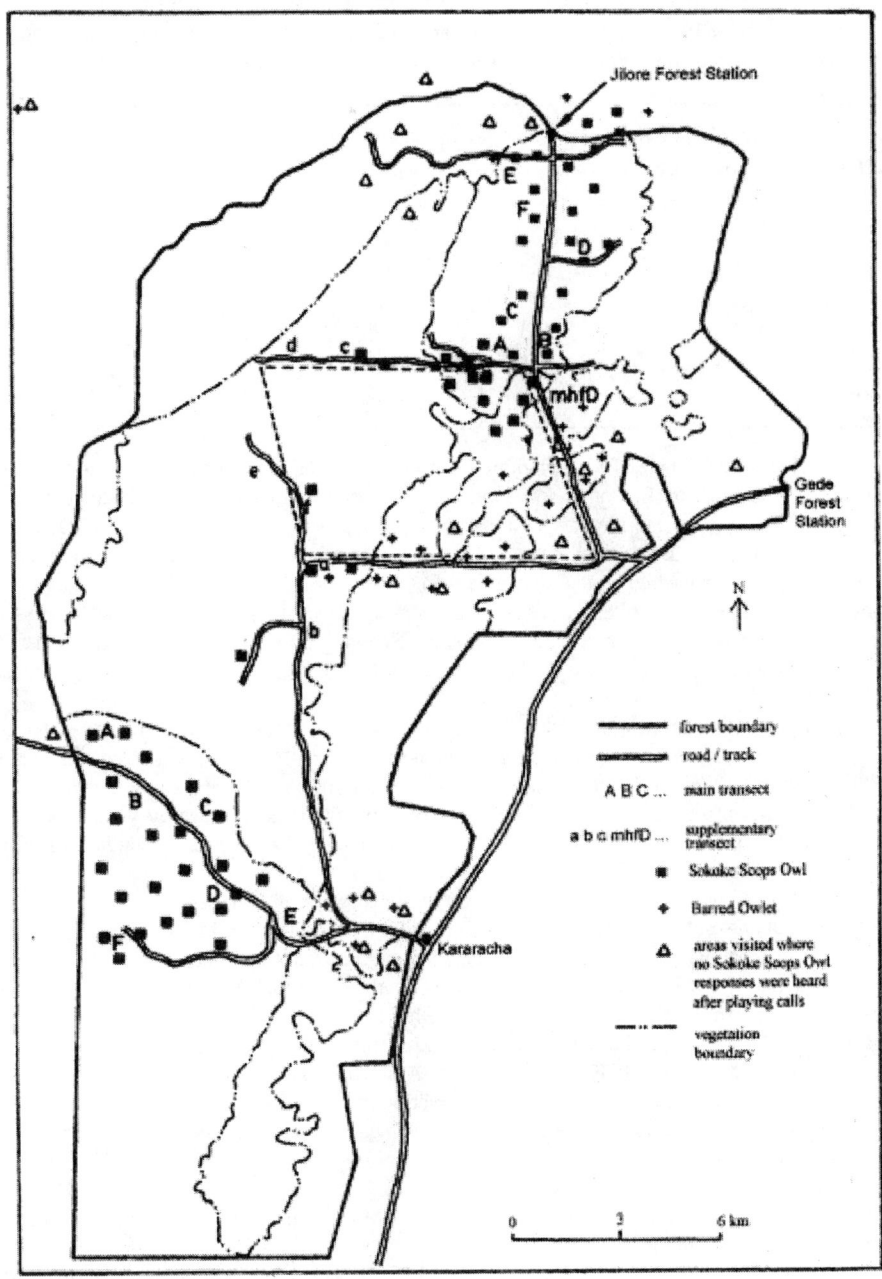

The Sokoke Scops Owl population size was estimated by extrapolating the population density estimates obtained from transect surveys. Since all forest types were homogenous, this extrapolation assumed that owl pairs were uniformly distributed in their habitats. Based on density estimates and areas of available habitat, the population size of Sokoke Scops Owls was estimated at 750 pairs in *Cynometra* woodland, 250 pairs in intermediate *Cynometra* and about 25 pairs in mixed *Hymenaea* forest giving a total of 1025 pairs in the entire forest (Table 1). The small p value (0.06) obtained for the differences in owl density between intermediate *Cynometra* and mixed *Hymenaea* forest suggest that fewer owls may be present in intermediate *Cynometra* than the estimated number.

Table 1. Areas of various habitat types showing mean and maximum (based on upper 95% limits) densities and population size of Sokoke Scops Owls in the Arabuko-Sokoke forest, Kenya, 1993.

Habitat Type	Area (km2)	Density (pairs/km2)	Total (pairs)	Maximum (pairs)
Cynometra woodland	99	7.1	703	796
Intermediate *Cynometra*	113	1.2	136	374
Mixed *Hymeneae* forest	7	3.0	21	26
Total	**219**		**860**	**1196**

The owl density estimate of 7.1 pairs/km^2 in *Cynometra* woodland compares to previous density estimates of 7-8 pairs/km^2 (Britton & Zimmerman 1979; Kelsey & Langton 1984). The lower density estimates of the owls in intermediate *Cynometra* and mixed *Hymenaea* forest may be due to the "lower" quality of these habitats compared to *Cynometra* woodland. *Cynometra* woodland appeared to provide the owls with a higher quality habitat than did intermediate *Cynometra* which had a lower canopy height, fewer mature trees and evidence of more scattered stumps which gave the impression of an altered woodland. Lower densities of Sokoke Scops Owls have also been associated with heavily-degraded areas, such as the lowland forests of the East Usambara mountains in Tanzania (Evans 1997).

Sokoke Scops Owl densities in the *Cynometra* woodland appear to have remained stable for many years. However, reduction in area of this suitable owl habitat from 111 km^2 (Kelsey & Langton 1984) to 99 km^2 (Virani 1995) may indicate that the population (in suitable habitat) may have only slightly declined as forest clearance continued. Based on the findings of this study, the conservation status of the Sokoke Scops Owl was downlisted from endangered to its present status, vulnerable (Collar et al., 1994).

At the time of writing, no follow-up census studies have been conducted on the owls in the forest. The Arabuko-Sokoke forest continues to be under tremendous pressure from adjacent (densely populated) villages, mainly for settlement. Illegal logging practices continue to be on the increase, while the recent discovery of large Titanium deposits along the east African coastal forests may exert further pressure on Arabuko-Sokoke (D. Obura, pers comm.,). Local and international conservationists have fought hard against the de-gazettement of 3000 ha proposed for excision in the southern part of the forest. The survival of the Arabuko-Sokoke forest will depend on a firm commitment by local conservation groups, conservation-minded villagers and strong political will by authorities in charge. The success of community based conservation projects such as the involvement of local villagers to farm butterflies for export (Kipepeo Project) and the formation of a local bird-guide association has provided some financial incentives for local villagers to conserve the forest. This study recommends a two-yearly census of the owls in the forest as part of a long-term monitoring programme.

ACKNOWLEDGEMENTS

I would like to thank the Peregrine Fund Inc. World Center for Birds of Prey for funding the Sokoke Scops Owl study. I am grateful to Rick Watson, David Harper, Simon Thomsett and Leon Bennun for their advice. I am indebted to David Ngala and Wellington Kombe for their field assistance.

The National Museum of Kenya provided logistical support. Funding to attend the V World Conference on Birds of Prey was provided by the South African Raptor Conservation Group through the Endangered Wildlife Trust. This paper is dedicated to Barbara Simpson for her conservation efforts in Kenya.

REFERENCES

BRITTON, P.A. & D.L. ZIMMERMAN. 1979. The avifauna of Sokoke Forest, Kenya. *J. Ea. Afr. Nat. Hist. Soc. and Nat. Mus.* 169:1-15.
COLLAR, N.J. & S.N. STUART. 1985. Threatened Birds of Africa and related islands: the ICBP/IUCN Red Data Book. *ICBP/IUCN*, Cambridge, U.K.
COLLAR, N.J., M.J. CROSBY & A.J. STATTERSFIELD. 1994. Birds to Watch 2. The world list of threatened birds. Birdlife Conserv. Ser. No. 4. Birdlife International, Cambridge U.K.
EMLEN, J.T. 1974. An urban bird community in Tucson, Arizona: deviation, structure, regulation. *Condor* 76:184-197.
EVANS, T. 1997. Preliminary estimates of the population density of the Sokoke Scops Owl *Otus ireneae* Ripley in the East Usambara lowlands, Tanzania. *Afr. J. Ecol.* 35:303-311.
FANSHAWE, J. 1993. Sokoke Scops Owl. *World Birdwatch* 15:18-19.
HIPKISS, A.J., L.G. WATSON & T. D. EVANS. 1994. The Cambridge-Tanzania Rainforest Project 1992. Brief account of ornithological results and conservation proposals. *Ibis* 136:107-108.
KELSEY, M.G. & T.E.S. LANGTON. 1984. The conservation of Arabuko-Sokoke forest, Kenya. *ICBP Study Report No. 4*. Cambridge, U.K.:ICBP.
KENDEIGH, S.C. 1944. Measurement of bird populations. *Ecological Monographs* 14:67-106.
SOUTHERN, H.N. 1954. Tawny Owls and their prey. *Ibis* 96:384-408.
RIPLEY, S.D. 1966. A notable owlet from Kenya. *Ibis* 108:136-137.
VIRANI, M.Z. 1995. Ecology of the endangered Sokoke Scops Owl *Otus ireneae*. M.Sc. thesis, Dept. of Biology, University of Leicester U.K.
WOOD, G.W. 1991. Owl conservation strategy flawed. *J. of Forest.* 89:39-41.

Munir Virani
Dept. of Ornithology
National Museums of Kenya
P.O Box 40658
Nairobi Kenya

Relationships between Foraging Range, Prey Density and Habitat Structure in the Tawny Owl *Strix aluco*

C.F. Coles, S.J. Petty and C.J. Thomas

ABSTRACT

1. We examined the ranging behaviour of Tawny Owls *Strix aluco* in relation to the structure of their foraging habitat, and spatio-temporal variations in the abundance and dispersion of field voles *Microtus agrestis*, their main prey. We plotted 15 home ranges of radio-tagged owls on a GIS coverage of Kielder Forest, northern England.
2. Males (n = 7) generally had larger ranges than females (n = 4). There was no significant difference between the range sizes of male owls in two valley systems.
3. Owl home ranges comprised a similar proportion of vole habitat. There was no relationship between home range size and vole density, although birds studied in consecutive years showed some range contraction as vole densities increased.
4. Home range size was not correlated with habitat structure. Larger home ranges contained more patches of clear-cut than smaller ones.
5. We discuss potential influences on home range size. Resource-sharing and heterogeneity of the habitat mosaic may explain why home range size was not strongly affected by prey density and habitat structure, respectively.

INTRODUCTION

Unlike nomadic raptors that specialise on microtine prey, such as European Kestrels *Falco tinnunculus* (Village 1982) and Short-eared Owls *Asio flammeus* (Village 1987), Tawny Owls *Strix aluco* are highly sedentary predators (e.g. Cramp 1985). In Kielder Forest, northern England, Tawny Owls feed largely on field voles *Microtus agrestis*, which exist in discrete populations, in isolated islands of grassy habitat created by clear-cutting (the felling of mature trees) (Petty 1987, 1992). Most authors assume that resident Tawny Owls carry out most of their activities within their territorial boundaries (e.g. Southern & Lowe 1968, Southern 1970, Galeotti 1994) and range exclusivity has been demonstrated by radio tracking for a population in fragmented farmland (Hardy 1992). However, in Kielder several territories may adjoin a clear-cut, so that these patches could represent shared resources, with implications for the pattern of range dispersion. Recent work showed that ranges of territorial Tawny Owls, determined by radio-telemetry, in a broadleaved woodland overlapped, and differed from the area defended (Appleby 1995). Redpath (1995) also suggested this possibility.

Home range and territory sizes have been shown to vary with landscape characteristics (Southern 1970, Hardy 1992, Galeotti 1994; Carey & Peeler 1995, Redpath 1995) social characteristics (Galeotti, 1994) and food density and dispersion (Lockie 1955, Village 1982, 1987, Carey & Peeler 1995, Zabel et al. 1995), leading to the construction of optimal feeding-territory size models (e.g. Dill 1978, Schoener 1983).

Here we ask whether habitat characteristics of Tawny Owl home ranges, and population fluctuations of field voles in time and space, are related to home range size in the landscape mosaic of our study area.

STUDY AREA

The study area was in Kielder Forest, Northumberland, northern England (55°N, 2°W) an extensive man-made upland conifer forest (Figures 1 and 2). Kielder Forest measures 480 km^2 and was planted mainly with Sitka spruce (*Picea sitchensis*) and Norway spruce (*Picea abies*) grown on 40-60 year rotations. Broadleaved trees grew along many of the watercourses and there were some larger areas of deciduous trees, including alder (*Alnus glutinosa*) and birch (*Betula pubescens*).

In 1996 and 1997 the forest was comprised of a mosaic of tree stands of different species and ages. Extensive clear-cut patches which, once colonised by grasses (*Deschampsia* spp., *Molinia caerulea*) and rushes (*Juncus* spp.), provided ephemeral islands of habitat suitable for voles. Some other grassy areas, such as powerline wayleaves, deer glades and unplanted areas along watercourses, also provided suitable habitat for voles.

Figure 1. Location of the Kielder study area in Great Britain.

METHODS

In 1996 and 1997, we radio-tagged eight (four pairs), and seven (two pairs, two breeding males, one non-breeding male) adult Tawny Owls, respectively. All Tawny Owls in the study area bred in nest boxes. We caught males using nest-box traps (Petty 1992), except the non-breeding bird, which was caught in a small modified Chardonneret trap (Newton 1986). Brooding females were caught with a net.

Tawny Owl pairs, of which two were studied in both years, had territories in the Deadwater Burn valley system (Figure 2). Three male birds studied in 1997 had territories in the Kielder Burn valley system (Figure 2). Birds were radio-tracked from July (1996) and June (1997) until November (both years). Locations of females during the incubation and nestling periods were not included, but were during the fledging period.

A soft nylon harness was used to fix the transmitter to the back of the owls (Petty & Thirgood 1989). Radio tags (Biotrack Ltd) transmitted on 173.233-173.973 MHz and had a lifespan of approximately one year. The combined mass of the radio and harness was 7.3g. This represents 1.3%-1.9% of the mean mass of males and females, respectively. A TRX 1000S receiver (Wildlife Materials Inc.) with a hand-held three element Yagi antenna were used to find the position of radio-tagged birds.

Figure 2. The study area, represented by the rectangular box, included two valleys, the Deadwater and Kielder Burns.

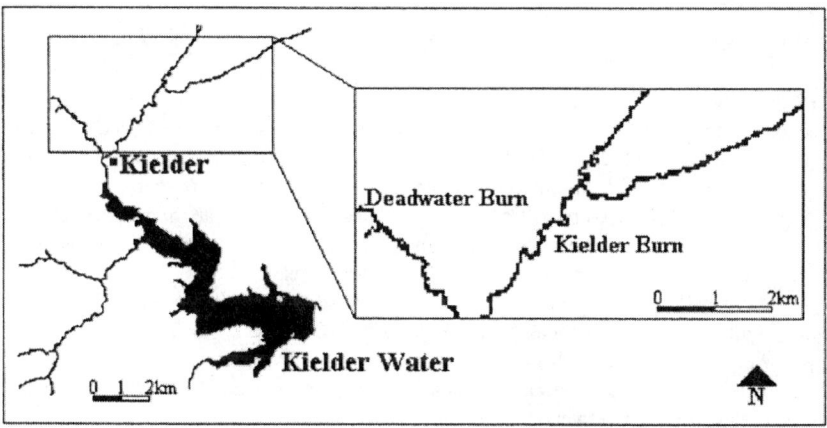

Triangulation of signal bearings taken from at least two fixed points within a ten-minute period gave owl "fixes".

Analyses used harmonic mean home ranges, so that ranges were biased toward the centres of activity (Dixon & Chapman, 1980), calculated with Ranges V software (Kenward 1995). Home ranges were calculated from 18 to 35 (mean 24.4) fixes per bird. Utilisation plots on 15 individuals revealed that home range areas became asymptotic at about 20 fixes, on average. An isoline incorporating 95% of fixes was used to exclude occasional excursions outside the normal foraging range from area calculations. No more than one fix per night per bird was included, thus ensuring statistical independence. Minimum convex polygon (MCP) home range sizes were also calculated for comparison with other studies. MCP and harmonic mean home range sizes were compared using a paired samples T test.

Harmonic mean contours were overlaid on a Geographical Information System (GIS), based on a Forestry Commission database. We grouped the resulting habitat outputs into three categories: areas suitable for field voles, agricultural land and other land largely unsuitable for field voles, and tree crops over 11 years old that were also unsuitable for field voles. "Patches" were defined as grassy clear-cuts up to 11 years after planting. These were often connected by corridors of the other types of habitat suitable for field voles.

Linear regression was used to examine the relationships between home range size and eleven variables (Table 1). Home ranges were averaged for each bird studied in both years. Data were normalised by log or arcsine (for percentages) transformation.

Variables that related to habitat structure were measured from GIS coverages. We assessed field vole abundance near Tawny Owl radiolocations using a vole sign index (VSI). This was based upon the presence or absence of fresh grass clippings in 25 quadrats thrown within a 0.25 ha area of suitable habitat (Petty 1992). Vole abundance indices were converted to densities using a formula derived from the regression of VSI scores on abundance data collected by live trapping (J.L. MacKinnon, unpublished data). There were 0-9 (mean 3.1) clear-cut patches per owl home range. In addition to these clear-cuts, VSI scores were also obtained for other habitats suitable for voles, such as streamsides and powerline wayleaves.

Distances between occupied nestboxes in territories were used as an indication of breeding dispersal.

Differences between male and female owls, valley systems, and birds tagged in both years were analysed using the Mann-Whitney U test. A Spearman's Rank correlation matrix was constructed to examine relationships between variables. Spearman's Rank correlation coefficient was used to examine the relationship between the magnitude of temporal changes in range size and average vole densities. Data were analysed using Systat, Inc., Illinois (1993).

RESULTS

Radio telemetry

Recaptured individuals had no apparent injuries caused by tags and bred successfully in both years. One female was killed by a Goshawk *Accipiter gentilis*, the main natural predator of Tawny Owls in Kielder Forest, and one male, found dead next to a road, had probably been killed by a vehicle. In both cases, there were sufficient numbers of fixes to calculate their home ranges.

Increment plots on 15 individuals showed that, on average, ranges reached size asymptotes at about 20 fixes. Home ranges were constructed from 18-32 (mean 24) fixes. Harmonic mean ranges were generally smaller than MCP ranges (mean = 122.22 and 165.59, respectively; Tables 2 and 3), but this difference was not statistically significant (d.f. = 10, t = 1.62, P = 0.136).

Owls were rarely recorded crossing large open spaces, such as clear-cuts, and moved up and down stands of mature trees or along streamsides. On several occasions, owls were seen flying across roads when moving between tree stands.

Table 1. Variables measured in home ranges. Vole habitat includes grassy clear-cuts as well as features such as deer glades, unplanted streamsides and wayleaves. Hard edge refers to the boundary between vole habitat and tree crops, suitable for perching on by foraging owls.

Variable	Description
SEX	Sex of bird
PCVH	Percentage composed of field vole habitat
VPH	Number of field voles per hectare, calculated from sign indices using formulae derived from live trapping.
HEPH	Length of hard edges (suitable for perch-foraging) per hectare
APTPD	Average inter-patch (clear-cut) distance
ABTPD	Average box to patch (clear-cut) distance
NP	Number of patches (clear-cuts and adjoining grassy habitat)
APA	Average patch area (ha)
ANND	Average distance (m) to nearest occupied territories

Table 2. Harmonic mean home range sizes, in hectares, for males, females, two pairs studied in consecutive years, and two valley systems in 1997. All Kielder Burn birds were males. Home range sizes of birds studied in both years were averaged, except for year to year comparisons.

Group	n	Minimum	Maximum	Mean	Median	S.E.
Male	7	17.75	396.56	166.72	113.76	52.98
Female	4	14.86	89.99	44.38	36.35	18.18
2 pairs, DW 1996	4	16.36	189.21	93.51	84.24	39.76
2 pairs, DW 1997	4	13.33	73.58	46.56	49.66	13.23
Deadwater (males)	4	17.75	134.59	90.02	103.87	25.48
Kielder Burn (males)	3	8	81.10	14.86	396.56	134.59
Deadwater (all birds)	269.06	67.20	329.53	73.68	95.93	16.86

Table 3. Minimum convex polygon home range sizes, in hectares, for 11 owls. Again, range sizes of birds tagged in consecutive years were averaged.

Group	n	Minimum	Maximum	Mean	Median	S.E.
Male	7	42.02	545.05	192.53	113.19	67.95
Female	4	16.34	272.53	128.45	112.46	57.00
All	11	16.34	545.05	169.23	113.19	47.04

Table 4. Changes in home range area and field vole density from 1996 to 1997 for two pairs of owls studied in consecutive years. Vole densities were extrapolated from indices based upon signs of vole feeding activity.

Bird	Pair	Change in area, ha	Change in voles/ha
Female 919/817	1	+32.3	+6.2
Male 279/562	1	-150.7	+3.3
Male 296/573	2	-66.4	+27.7
Female 909/829	2	-3.0	+21.6

Table 5. Densities of field voles per hectare in 11 Tawny Owl home ranges.

	n	Maximum	Minimum	Mean	S.E.	Variance
2 years	15	178.08	49.58	98.25	12.74	2434.93
1996	8	60.36	49.58	56.03	1.45	16.82
1997	7	178.08	118.07	146.57	9.01	567.71

Table 6. Correlations between variables of 11 home ranges. Few of the variables were interrelated.

	PCVH	VPH	HEPH	ABTPD	APTPD	NP	APA
VPH	—						
HEPH	—	—					
ABTPD	—	0.067*	—				
APTPD	—	0.005**	—	0.016*			
NP	—	—	—	0.026*	—		
APA	—	—	—	—	—	—	
ANND	—	—	—	—	—	—	—

(Spearman's rank test, significance of coefficients: * = $P < 0.05$, ** = $P < 0.01$, — = not significant.)

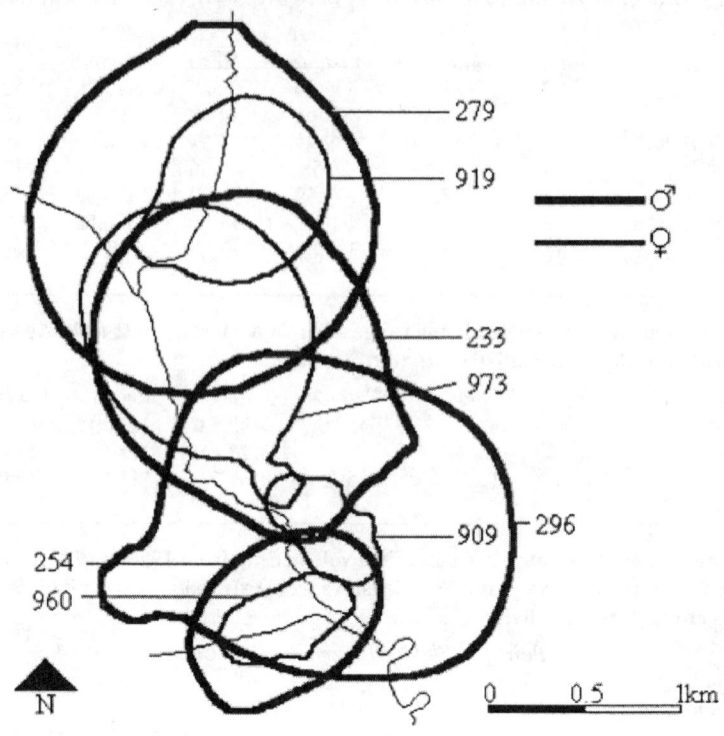

Figure 3. Harmonic mean 95% isoline home ranges for 8 owls in the Deadwater valley system in 1996. Numbers indicate radio frequencies.

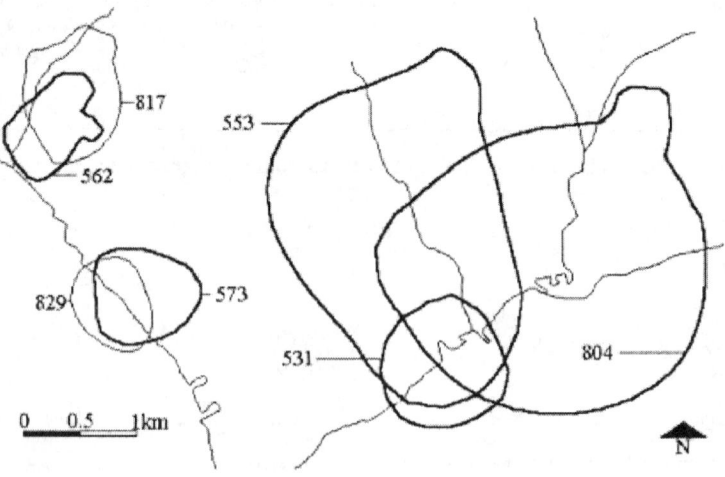

Figure 4. Harmonic mean 95% isoline home ranges for 7 owls in the Deadwater and Kielder Burn valleys in 1997. Again, males are represented by thicker lines. The two pairs in Deadwater (left) were also tagged in the previous year (table 4).

Figure 5 There was no relationship between home range area and the proportion of vole habitat within them (n = 11, r = 0.021, P = 0.95)

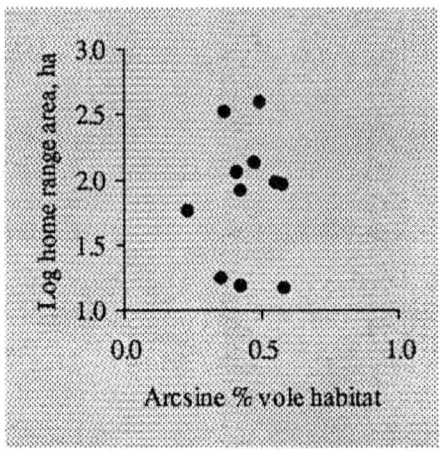

Figure 6. There was no statistically significant relationship between home range area and field vole density (n=11, r = 0.468, P = 0.147).

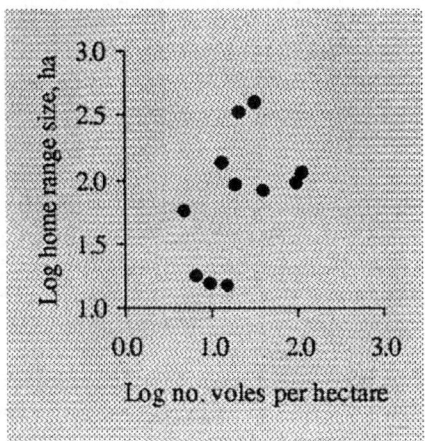

Sex and temporal differences

Generally, male owls had larger home ranges than females (d.f. =7,4, Mann-Whitney U = 3, P = 0.05, Table 2, Figures 3 and 4). Female home ranges overlapped less than those of males and male ranges included those of several females (Figure 3).

Comparing the home ranges of two pairs tagged in both years, all but one bird reduced its range size in 1997 (Table 4, Figures 3 and 4). However, this difference was not statistically significant (d.f. =4,4, Mann-Whitney U = 5, P = 0.486). There was no correlation between the change in range size and change in average vole densities (Spearman's rank coefficient S = 0.200, P = 0.800, n.= 4), which increased in every home range studied in consecutive years (Tables 4 and 5).

In 1996, in all cases but one, female ranges were totally enclosed by those of their mates (Figure 3). The two largest and two smallest female ranges were grouped together at the northern and southern ends of the Deadwater Burn, respectively. This was not the case in 1997, when male/female differences in range size and shape became less marked and inter-pair overlap decreased (Figures 3 and 4).

Spatial differences

The home ranges of male Tawny Owls were compared between the Deadwater Burn and the Kielder Burn. On average, male range sizes were larger in the Kielder Burn than in the Deadwater Burn but this relationship was not statistically significant (d.f. = 4,3, Mann-Whitney U = 3, P = 0.400, Figure 4).

Adding the generally smaller ranges of Deadwater Burn females to the comparison still failed to produce a statistically significant difference between range sizes in the two valley systems (d.f. =8,3, Mann-Whitney U = 4, P = 0.043). There was no difference between the areas of clear-cut patches in the two valleys (d.f. = 11,18, Mann-Whitney U = 37, P = 0.930). Home ranges in the Deadwater and Kielder Burns showed a high degree of overlap (Figures 3 and 4). On one occasion all three males from the Kielder Burn were located foraging at the edge of the same clear-cut.

Relationship between variables and home range size

Of the nine variables, only NP (n = 11, r = 0.659, P < 0.05) and ABTPD (n = 11, r = 0.826, P < 0.01) were significantly correlated with home range size. Both correlations were positive. The number of voles per hectare and proportion of ranges comprised of habitat suitable for field voles did not vary significantly with home range size (Figs. 5 and 6).

Vole densities varied relatively little between home ranges in the same year and in 1997 were higher in each home range than in any of the ranges studied in 1996 (Table 5).

Correlation between numerical variables

Few of the variables were highly inter-related (Table 6), but those which were, precluded the use of multivariate models in the analysis.

DISCUSSION

Sex differences in home range size

The most striking result was the large size difference in home range size between sexes in 1996. Males appeared to respond more to increased prey densities than females, based upon their greater degree of range contraction in the increasing phase of the vole cycle. They also generally ranged over much larger areas than their mates. This difference was not so marked in 1997 when voles were more abundant. This suggested that males foraged more widely than females and are more sensitive to variation in prey densities. Females may have been more tied to the area in which breeding had just occurred, when there were dependent chicks within the territory during some of the tracking period. Female Tawny Owls are more predisposed to protect nestlings than males (Wallin 1987) and this defensive role may extend until after fledging, while they still have dependent juveniles.

Spatio-temporal differences

The inverse relationship between range size and prey abundance, consistent with previous studies (e.g. Village 1982, 1987, Zabel et al. 1995), over time but not in space suggests that this interaction was affected here by other factors. That all home ranges contained a similar proportion of habitat suitable for field voles may reflect uniform distribution of such patches throughout the area we studied. A comparison between areas (elsewhere in the forest) with and without Tawny Owl territories may show if owls are selecting areas similar to those in the study area. It is possible that owls require prey availability to equal or exceed a threshold for breeding and survival, and that in larger home ranges the extra area was associated with other factors. Not all habitat suitable for voles within a home range boundary would necessarily have been used for foraging.

Tawny Owls need older forest for roosting and breeding, and clear-cuts for feeding. Therefore, fine-grained (rather than coarse-grained) habitat mosaics are likely to hold a higher density of breeding owls (Petty 1989). This may go a long way in explaining the lack of relationships between home range size and habitat variables.

Topography may explain differences in range size between the two valleys where, at any one time, vole densities were similar. Territories in Kielder Burn were generally at higher altitude than those in Deadwater, and had their centres at a greater distance from the main patches of habitat suitable for field voles, which were located in the valley bottoms. Immediately after the fledging period, the male 553 foraged along streamsides of a Kielder Burn tributary near to the nesting area. It was then seen to switch its efforts to a more distant clear-cut, possibly after depleting the vole population on the smaller patch. Unfortunately, our prey index did not operate on a small enough temporal scale to detect such short-term changes.

Given that clear-cuts in the Kielder Burn were generally no larger than those in the Deadwater Burn, and that there was not a general relationship between home range and patch sizes, differences in range sizes between the valleys did not relate to the graininess of the habitat mosaics.

Up to three tagged males were found around the same clear-cut simultaneously, and it is likely that untagged individuals were also using the same area (pers. obs.). This pattern of resource sharing could invalidate the assumptions of feeding territory size models based upon animals foraging within exclusively defended areas (Dill 1978, Schoener 1983). In habitats with great spatial variation, it may be advantageous to share resources. Thus, defence costs were not a limiting factor in foraging range size as they only applied to territories. Territorial owls could sub-divide clear-cuts, so although the high degree of range overlap that we observed suggested that this was not the case, more information is needed before this possibility can be fully rejected.

Topographical constriction at the southern end of the Deadwater valley may have caused owls to encounter others more regularly. This situation leads to increased vocal behaviour, in contrast to birds which only rarely encounter conspecifics (Redpath 1995). Here, birds may allocate more time to territorial defence and range less widely than birds in more open country, thus causing the observed range constriction, which was not explained by nearest neighbour distance *per se*.

Accurate territorial mapping may have given further insight into the social factors in operation, particularly given that territories are not necessarily centred on the nestbox (Appleby 1995).

ACKNOWLEDGEMENTS

We thank Claire McSorley and Sam Smart for help with the fieldwork. Graham Gill of Forest Enterprise allowed us to work in Kielder Forest and provided student accommodation. The British Trust for Ornithology provided licences to fit owls with radio tags. Dr. Steve Redpath kindly commented on an earlier manuscript. The research was conducted with funding from a studentship as part of a NERC Large Scale Processes in Ecology and Hydrology Special Topic, grant GST/02/1218.

REFERENCES

APPLEBY, B.M. 1995. The behaviour and ecology of the tawny owl *Strix aluco*. PhD thesis, University of Oxford.
CAREY, A.B. & K.C. PEELER 1995. Spotted owls: resource and space use in mosaic landscapes. *Journal of Raptor Research* 29(4): 223-239.
CRAMP, S. (Ed.) 1985. The birds of the Western Palearctic, Volume IV. Oxford University Press, Oxford.
DILL, L. 1978. An energy-based model of optimal feeding territory size. *Theoretical Population Biology* 14: 396-429.
DIXON, K.R. & J.A. CHAPMAN 1980. Harmonic mean measures of animal activity areas. *Ecology* 61(5): 1040-1044.
GALEOTTI, P. 1994. Patterns of territory sizes and defence level in rural and urban Tawny Owl (*Strix aluco*) populations. *Journal of Zoology (London)* 234: 641-658.
KENWARD, R.E. 1995. Ranges V. Software for analysing animal location data. ITE, NERC. Cambridge.
LOCKIE, J.D. 1955. The Breeding Habits and Food of Short-Eared Owls After a Vole Plague. *Bird Study* 2: 53-69.

NEWTON, I. 1986. *The Sparrowhawk.* Poyser, Calton.
NILSSON, I.H. 1978. Hunting in flight by Tawny Owls *Strix aluco*. *Ibis* 120: 528-531.
PETTY, S.J. 1987. Breeding of Tawny Owls (*Strix aluco*) in relation to their food supply in an upland forest. In: Jenkins, D. (ed.), Trees and wildlife in the Scottish Uplands: 121-128. Institute of Terrestrial Ecology, Huntingdon.
PETTY, S.J. 1989. Productivity and density of Tawny Owls *Strix aluco* in relation to the structure of a spruce forest in Britain. *Annales Zoologici Fennici* 26: 227-233.
PETTY, S.J. 1992. The Ecology of the Tawny Owl *Strix aluco* in the Spruce Forests of Northumberland and Argyll. PhD Thesis, The Open University.
PETTY, S.J. & S. J. THIRGOOD 1989. A radio tracking study of post-fledging of Tawny Owls in Argyll. *Ringing and Migration* 10: 75-82.
REDPATH, S.M. 1995. Habitat fragmentation and the individual: Tawny Owls *Strix aluco* in woodland patches. *Journal of Animal Ecology* 64: 652-661.
SCHOENER, T.W. 1983. Simple models of optimal feeding territory size: a reconciliation. *American Naturalist* 121: 608-629.
SOUTHERN, H.N. 1970. The natural control of a population of Tawny Owls (*Strix aluco*). *Journal of Zoology (London)* 162: 197-285.
SOUTHERN, H.N. & V.P.W. LOWE 1968. The pattern of distribution of prey and predation in Tawny Owl territories. *Journal of Animal Ecology* 37: 285-304.
VILLAGE, A. 1982. The home range and density of kestrels in relation to vole abundance. *Journal of Animal Ecology* 51: 413-428.
VILLAGE, A. 1987. Numbers, territory size and turnover of Short-Eared Owls *Asio flammeus* in relation to vole abundance. *Ornis Scandinavica* 18: 198-204.
WALLIN, K. 1987. Defence as parental care in Tawny Owls (*Strix aluco*). *Behaviour* 102:213-230.
ZABEL, C.J., K., MCKELVEY & J.P. WARD JR. 1995. Influence of primary prey on home-range size and habitat-use patterns of northern spotted owls (*Strix occidentalis caurina*). *Canadian Journal of Zoology* 73: 433-439.

C.F. Coles and C.J. Thomas
Department of Biological Sciences
University of Durham
South Road
Durham DH1 3LE
UK

S.J. Petty
Woodland Ecology Branch
Forest Research
Northern Research Station
Roslin
Midlothian EH25 9SY
UK

How Many Seychelles Scops Owls *Otus insularis* are there?

Jeff Watson

ABSTRACT

The endemic Seychelles Scops Owl *Otus insularis* was reported extinct in the 1950s, and rarely seen by ornithologists for over a decade following its 'rediscovery' around 1960. It has been definitely recorded only from the island of Mahé although suitable habitat exists on several other Seychelles islands. A tape recording of the Scops Owl call was obtained in 1975 and was used to locate pairs of owls by eliciting response to playback of recordings. Over a two year period, mated pairs were consistently located by this method in 12 places along a series of tracks and roads in the mountains of Mahé. Typical Scops Owl habitat was dense secondary forest growing in deep ravines and river valleys where there were accumulations of large boulders. Based on the average distance between these pairs, and extrapolating from the known extent of potentially suitable habitat, the population on Mahé was estimated to be a minimum of 80-90 pairs. During a follow-up study in October 1993, eight of the original study sites were checked and in each locality a pair of owls was detected close to sites that were occupied in 1975/76.

INTRODUCTION

Almost nothing was written about the endemic Seychelles Scops Owl between its discovery and initial description (Tristram 1880) and its rediscovery by Philippe Lalanne in 1960 (Loustau-Lalanne 1961). At least one author believed the bird extinct (Greenway 1958). The key to understanding this retiring, nocturnal species is its vocalisation and, since good quality tape recordings were obtained in 1975, substantially more is now known about the bird's distribution and habits. This paper summarises observations made during a range of visits to Seychelles over a 20-year period from 1974. The Scops Owl has only ever been recorded from the island of Mahé, the largest of the granitic Seychelles (Fig. 1).

VOCALISATION

The typical call of the Seychelles Scops Owl is a deep, monotonous and rhythmic grunting given at the rate of around one note per second. Birds tend to call in bursts ranging from 15-20 seconds to several minutes or more. Scops Owls very rarely call during daylight hours and the most reliable time to hear calling is during the first hour or two after sunset. Simultaneous calling by both members of a mated pair is quite common, and since the rate of calling by different individuals is generally slightly different, there is typically an asynchronous quality to this dueting. In prolonged bouts of dueting the call of one or both birds can change quite markedly, from the usual grunting note to a sharper, quacking note. Sometimes this is accompanied by a short snapping noise that sounds like bill-snapping. A duet can reach a crescendo when the pair copulate, and the note changes completely to a very distinctive short series of whiffling, high-pitched whistles. A quite different call is given by birds that were presumed to be dependent young. This is a short and strongly directional call, best represented as '*whsst*', and given as single notes at intervals of 5-10 seconds. This presumably serves a locational function for the parents when feeding fledged young.

Figure 1. Map of Mahé showing land above 200 m and inset map showing the granitic Seychelles.

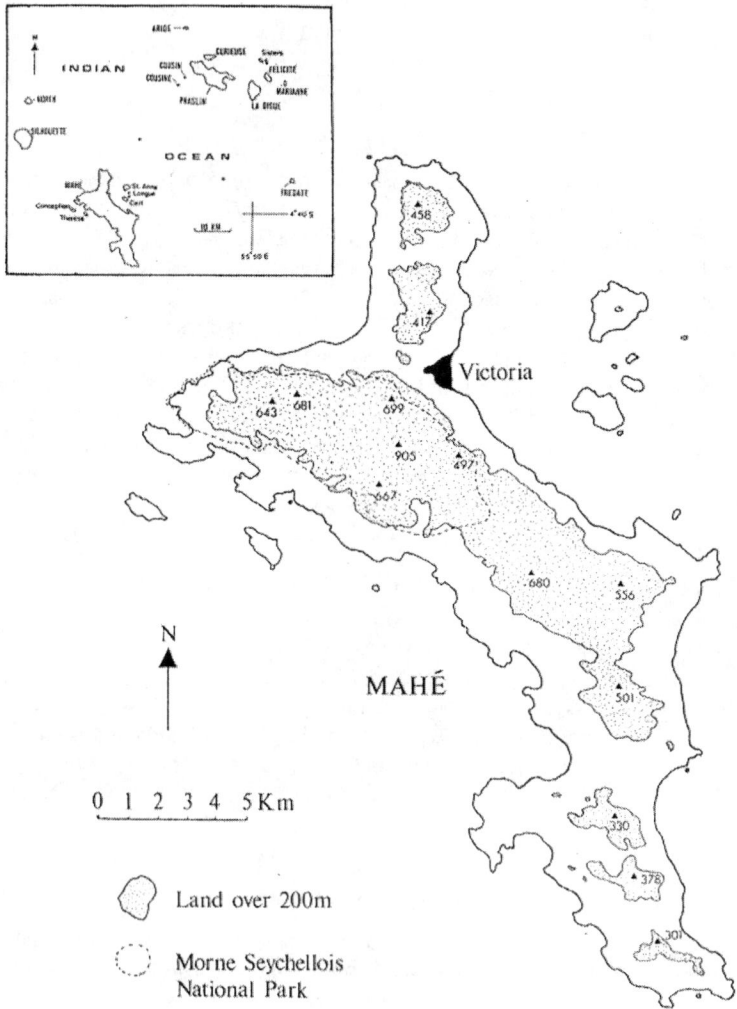

BREEDING BIOLOGY

The Scops Owl remains the one Seychelles endemic for which the nest has yet to be found (Collar & Stuart 1985). Some information is, however, available on timing of breeding. Over the years I have recorded recently fledged young on five occasions. One bird was killed by a dog and given to me freshly dead in the month of June. I have also heard a young bird on site (evidenced by the *'whsst'* call referred to above) on four separate occasions, once in June, once in October and twice in November. These minimal data suggest that either breeding occurs through the year or, perhaps more likely, that there is a twice-yearly breeding season, either side of the heavy rains which occur from December to March. In each case only a single young bird was detected and this would suggest the clutch size is small, and possibly only a single egg (Watson 1979).

HABITAT PREFERENCE

Scops Owls are nowadays confined to upland areas on Mahé, typically from around 250 m up to 600 m. It is not known whether the bird was more widespread at lower altitudes before people arrived in Seychelles some 200 years ago, and before much of the original forest was cleared. Today the preferred habitat in the mountains is mature forest in river valleys. Mostly this is now secondary forest with dense stands of the exotic acacia-like *Albizia falcata* and the introduced shrub *Cinnamon zeylanicum*. The river valleys and ravines in these steep mountain areas typically hold large accumulations of massive granite boulders and such boulder fields are a common feature of Scops Owl locations on Mahé. Whether there is a functional connection between Scops Owls and boulders is not clear, but one possibility is that the owls nest deep within these rock piles, and this could be one reason why no nest has yet been found. Scops Owls seem to avoid the drier ridges between the valleys where the vegetation tends to be sparser and shorter and where there are often extensive areas of bare rock known locally as *'glacis'*.

DISTRIBUTION

Because of the accessibility provided by the Sans Souci road between Victoria and Port Glaud, the great majority of Scops Owl records have come from the area between Mission and the Tea Factory. Over the period 1974-93, however, there have been a range of sightings from Jasmin and Mare aux Cochons in the north, to Trois Frères and Cascade in the east and Castor in the south. The concentration of records from around Mission, as well as the range of outliers, is shown in Figure 2. Overall, around 50 km^2 of Mahé lies above the 250 m contour between Jasmin in the north-west and Castor in the south. Most of this provides potentially suitable habitat for Scops Owls.

OTHER ISLANDS

Judging by the known preferred habitat on Mahé, the other island that could potentially hold Scops Owls is Silhouette, although some of the higher areas on Praslin could also be suitable. Collar & Stuart (1985) review the history of possible records from Praslin, but as yet there has been no definite sighting from that island. Neither has it proved possible to locate birds there using playback recordings. In 1975 and again in 1993 I spent several evenings in the mountains of Silhouette searching for Scops Owls with aid of tape recordings. No birds were found on these occasions and there have been no confirmed records from Silhouette despite the abundance of apparently suitable habitat there. Perhaps the bird never chanced to colonise Silhouette, or perhaps it became extinct there in the early period of intensive forest clearance in Seychelles. In terms of conservation management, there is a strong argument to consider the translocation of Scops Owls to Silhouette as an insurance against threats to the single small population on Mahé.

POPULATION ESTIMATE

During 1975-76 Scops Owls were found at 12 localities near tracks and roads in the mountains immediately south of Morne Seychellois. Eight of these localities were systematically checked with the aid of tape recordings during a brief visit in October 1993. The average nearest-neighbour-distance between these eight sites was 850 m. Sites were regularly spaced and, on that basis, an estimate of the spacial needs of a pair can be made by assuming a circular 'territory' with a radius of $\frac{1}{2}$ the average nearest-neighbour-distance. This gives an estimate of 'territory' size for each pair of Scops Owls of 57 ha. On the assumption that around 50 km^2 of suitable habitat exists within the mountains of Mahé (see above), this gives an estimate of 80-90 pairs of Scops Owls. I believe this is probably a minimum figure as there have been occasional records of Scops Owls below 250 m, and there is some suitable habitat south of Castor and some pairs may occur there.

Figure 2. Map of Mahé based on 1 km grid squares. Filled squares indicate localities where Seychelles scops owls were recorded during the period 1974-93.

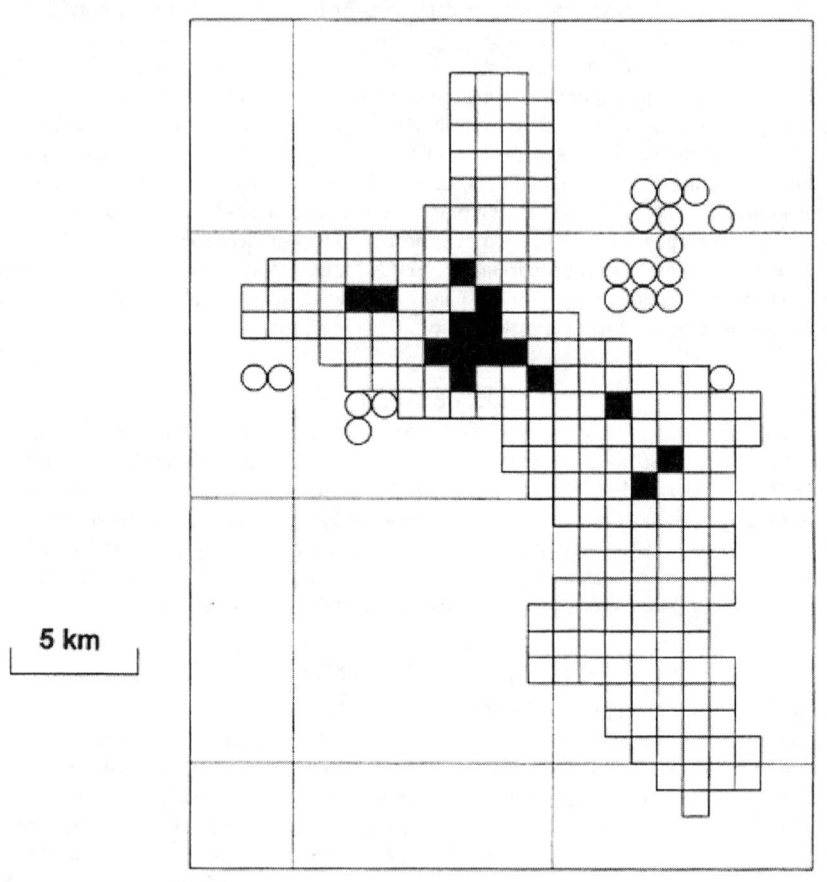

ACKNOWLEDGEMENTS

I am grateful to my many friends and colleagues in Seychelles who have helped search for, and contributed information on Scops Owls, and especially to Lindsay Chong Seng.

REFERENCES

COLLAR, N.J. & S.N. STUART 1985. *Threatened Birds of Africa and related islands.* Cambridge: ICBP & IUCN.
GREENWAY, J.C. 1958. *Extinct and vanishing birds of the world.* New York: American Committee for International Wildlife Protection.
LOUSTAU-LALANNE, P. 1961. Land-birds endemic to the granitic group of the Seychelles Islands. *Journal of the Seychelles Society* 1: 22-31.
TRISTRAM, H.B. 1880. Description of a new genus and species of owl from the Seychelles Islands. *Ibis* (4) 4: 456-459.
WATSON, J. 1979. Clutch sizes of Seychelles endemic birds. *Bull. Brit. Orn. Club* 99: 102-105.

Jeff Watson
Scottish Natural Heritage
9 Culduthel Road
Inverness
IV2 4AG
Scotland

Chancellor, R. D. & B.-U. Meyburg eds. 2000
Raptors at Risk
WWGBP / Hancock House

Molecular Systematics of Owls (*Strigiformes*) based on DNA-sequences of the mitochondrial cytochrome b gene

Michael Wink and Petra Heidrich

ABSTRACT

Sequence data of the mitochondrial cytochrome b gene provide a powerful tool (besides morphology, anatomy, behaviour and bioacoustics) to elucidate and reconstruct the evolutionary past and speciation of owls. We have already analyzed 35% of species and 68% of genera of owls. The phylogenetic relationships inferred from sequences of the cytochrome b gene are generally in a good agreement with the classical taxonomy of owls and the attribution of species to a given genus. However, paraphyly and polyphyly are evident in the genus *Otus* and in the *Bubo* complex and we have proposed to split *Otus* into three genera *Otus*, *Ptilopsis*, and *Megascops*, but to merge *Nyctea*, *Ketupa*, and *Scotopelia* in *Bubo*.

INTRODUCTION

In order to occupy the ecological niche of a nocturnal raptor, owls had to evolve several adaptations (Burton 1992, Hume 1991, Mikkola 1983, König *et al.*, 1999). Besides specialized hunting strategies, owls developed a sophisticated acoustical communication system. On the other hand their morphology is often invariant but the distinctive calls which are inherited and not learned are of considerable taxonomic value (König, 1991a,b, 1994a,b; Hekstra, 1982). If phylogenetic relationships are reconstructed on the basis of the morphological characteristics alone, wrong conclusions might be drawn since some of these characters may be convergent traits that are unrelated to the true phylogeny.

The amplification of marker genes by polymerase chain reaction (PCR) followed by DNA sequencing (overviews in Avise 1994; Hillis & Moritz, 1990; Mindell 1997) provide a powerful tool to elucidate phylogenetic and phylogeographic relationships. The molecular approach does not make the traditional analysis obsolete; just the opposite, it is rather complementary and the right questions can only be asked if we have a solid frame-work based on morphology, geography, behaviour, or acoustics. The analysis of mitochondrial genes is central today in most molecular studies on birds (Mindell 1997), since mtDNA evolves much faster than nuclear DNA. Among mitochondrial genes, many studies use the cytochrome b gene, as this gene usually is a good marker at the species and genus level, but it loses resolution on divergence events which are more than 30-50 million years away. This is mainly due to multiple nucleotide substitutions at the same position, which can lead to homoplasy.

We have chosen the mitochondrial cytochrome b gene to study speciation and phylogeny of owls (Heidrich & Wink 1994, 1998, Heidrich et al., 1995a,b, 1996, 1997, 1998; Wink & Heidrich 1999). In this communication we present results of our molecular investigation on phylogenetic relationships in the genera *Tyto, Phodilus, Otus, Bubo, Ketupa, Nyctea, Scotopelia, Strix, Pulsatrix, Glaucidium, Athene, Speotyto, Aegolius, Ninox, Asio,* and *Surnia*. So far we have covered 35% of species and 68% of genera of owls. The missing genera mostly belong to monotypic genera, so that a general picture on the phylogeny of owls becomes possible with the present data set. (We would be happy to receive blood, tissue or feather samples from species that are not included in our trees, since we hope to arrive at a complete tree of Strigiformes some day).

MATERIAL AND METHODS

Details on materials and methods used for DNA isolation, PCR, PCR primers, DNA sequencing, and tree reconstruction have been published (Heidrich 1998; Heidrich & Wink, 1994, 1998; Heidrich et al., 1995, 1996, 1997, 1998; Wink 1995; Wink et al., 1996). Sequences have been deposited with Gene Bank.

For most species we have determined cytochrome b sequences (1040 bp) from two and more individuals, so that the sequences used in this analysis are unequivocal and reliable (Heidrich, 1998). For the molecular analysis (Fig. 1) we have assembled a data set consisting of a single cytochrome b sequence per taxon in those cases, that significant haplotype differentiation was absent.

Distances (p-distance) are calculated as the proportion of nucleotide substitutions (in %) between pairs of taxa (Wink & Heidrich, 1999). Distances correlate with divergence time and a crude estimate equals 2% nucleotide substitution with 1 million years of separation (Shields & Wilson, 1987). This molecular clock provides a rough estimate for a temporal frame-work (Moore & DeFilippis, 1997), but needs to be interpreted with caution, since the clock was not calibrated for owls. Distances can be used to decide whether a taxon can be regarded as a distinct species; in owls a divergence of >1.5% is usually indicative for species level and in a case where morphological, acoustical, and geographic characters support a separation, we have advocated to treat such a taxon as a distinct species.

Phylogenetic trees were reconstructed using Maximum Parsimony, Maximum Likelihood (PAUP*; Swofford 1993) or Neighbour Joining methods (MEGA; Kumar et al., 1993). Bootstrap values provide an estimate how good a furcation is supported by the sequence data. Although bootstrap values are discussed controversially by many authors, they can be helpful. Hillis & Bull (1993) concluded that nodes with calculated bootstrap values of 70% and higher actually occurred in 95% and more of the simulated phylogenies. This means that a bootstrap value of 70% can be regarded as evidence for a well-supported node (Moore & DeFilippis, 1997).

Phylogenetic relationships within the Strigiformes

The sequence dataset with one sequence per taxon was analyzed by Neighbour joining (NJ), Maximum Likelihood (ML), and Maximum parsimony (MP). A few non-related families of birds (such as Passeres, Falconidae, Accipitridae, Lariidae, Procellariidae, Phasianidae) were selected as ingroups and *Tinamus major* as a distant outgroup. The owl tree was stable and rather independent of different ingroups and outgroups. The resulting trees are congruent in most groupings (compare Fig. 1 A, B, and C). Differences were found in the placement of individual taxa within a few genera, e.g., in New World *Otus* and in the positioning of the genera *Strix, Asio,* and *Ptilopsis*.

As can be seen from Fig. 1 the owl families Tytonidae and Strigidae form a monophyletic group, i.e. they share common ancestry. Passeriformes cluster at the base of the bird tree, a finding recently suggested when complete mitochondrial genomes were analyzed (Mindell & Sorenson, 1998). Falcons do not form a sister group to owls, as had been concluded from a cladistic analysis (Cracraft 1981).

Figure 1. Genetic relationships within the *Tytonidae* and *Strigidae* (based on 1040 nt of the cytochrome b gene)

A. Maximum parsimony strict consensus tree of 60 equally parsimonious trees. Conditions: Heuristic search (TBR branch swapping; tree length 5175 steps; consistency index CI= 0.217; retention index RI= 0.511).

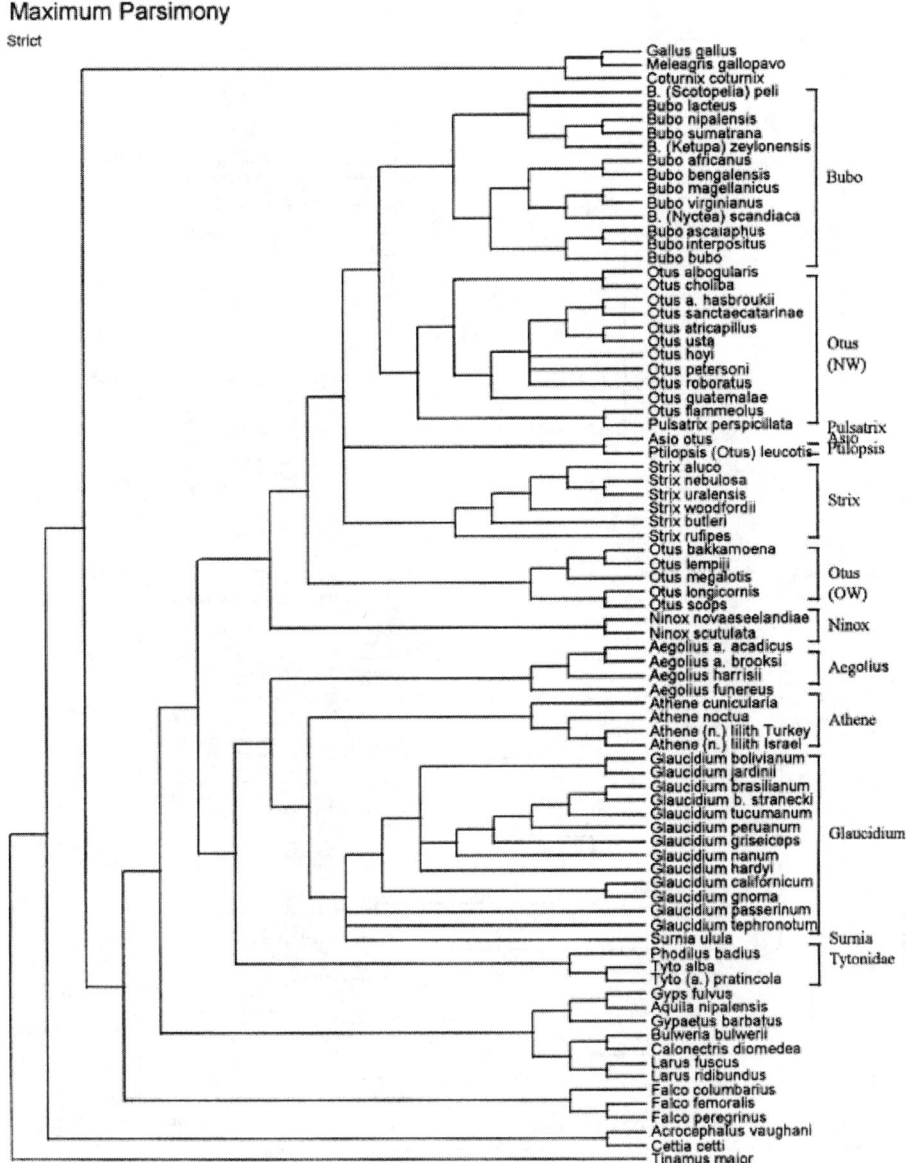

B. Neighbour Joining phylogram employing Jukes-Cantor as a distance algorithm (other algorithms, such as Kimura 2, Tamura-Nei) do not change tree topology). Bootstrap values from 500 replications (above 50%) above 70% are indicated. Arrows point to the branches leading to the Strigiformes and Strigidae.

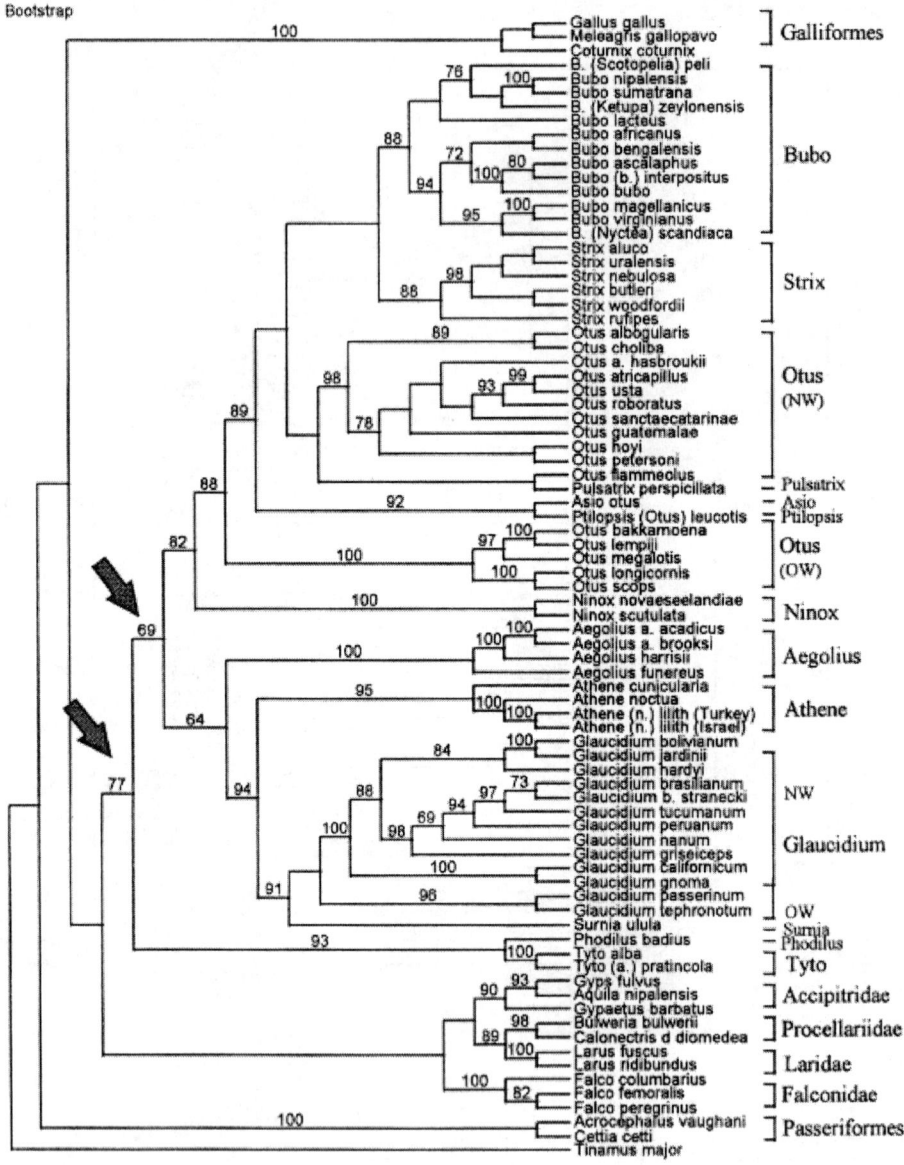

C. Maximum Likelihood tree constructed by heuristic search with TBR branch swapping. Number of substitution types 2; all sites had same evolution rates; transition/transversion ratio 2; score of best tree was 26657; nucleotide frequencies: A= 0.269, C= 0.353, G= 0.136, T= 0.242. Branch lengths are proportional to genetic distances.

Maximum Likelihood

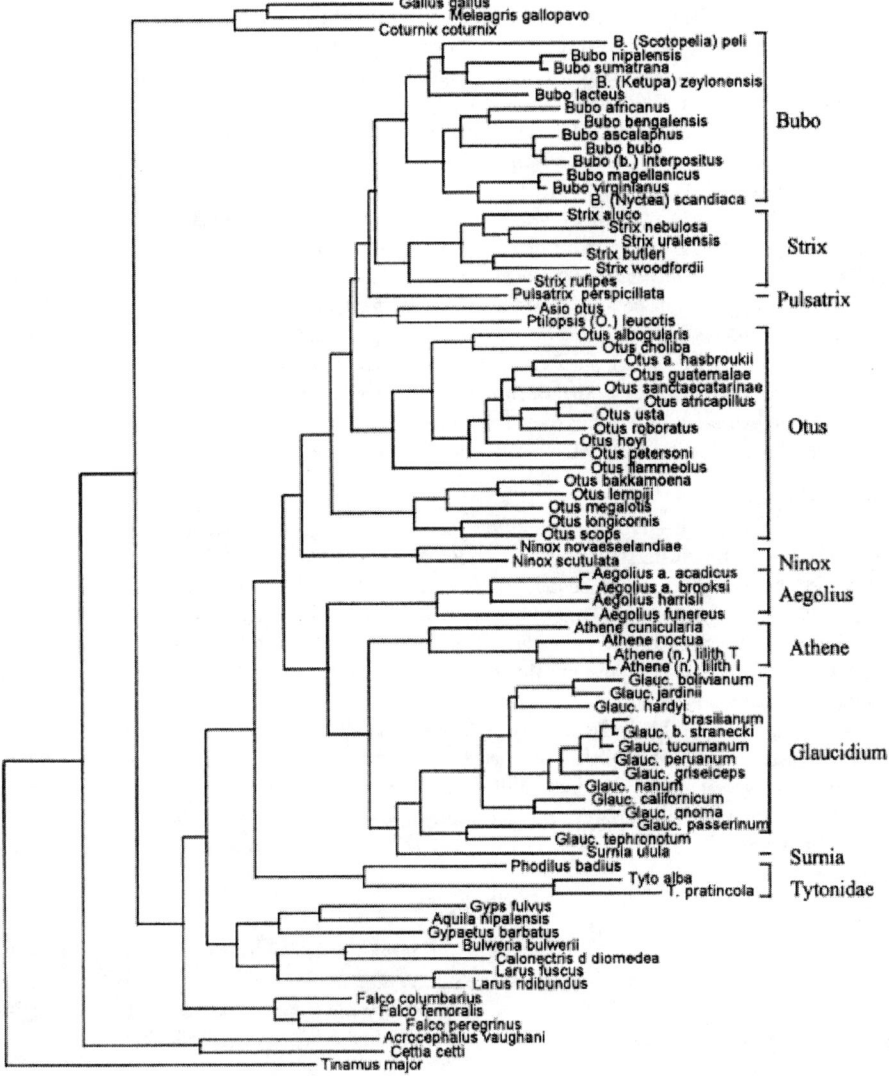

Sequence data were from our own laboratory, except *Meleagris, Coturnix, Gallus,* and *Tinamus* which were obtained from GeneBank.

OW= Old World; NW= New World

Relationships within the families *Tytonidae* and *Strigidae*

Tyto and *Phodilus*

Traditionally, two genera are distinguished within the Tytonidae: Tyto and Phodilus. This view is clearly supported by the sequence data (Fig. 1 B,C). the distances between both genera are large; i.e. they must have diverged from a common ancestor more than 9 million years ago.

Glaucidium

Pygmy owls of the genus *Glaucidium* which occur in the Old and New World show very similar plumage patterns, but can be distinguished by a unique repertoire of vocalizations (König, 1994b). Taxonomical classifications based on differing acoustic signals (König, 1994b) could be corroborated by DNA sequence data (Heidrich *et al.*, 1995). Fig. 1 clearly shows that Old and New World species cluster in separate monophyletic clades which share common ancestry but have diverged more than 7 to 8 million years ago. *G. gnoma/californicum* and *G. passerinum* are definitely not conspecific as sometimes assumed because of similar plumage patterns (Sibley & Monroe, 1990).

Within the South American *G. brasilianum* complex, several distinct haplotypes have been recognized (Fig. 1) that occur in different regions of Argentina, and Brazil. Because vocalisation and size also differ, *G. tucumanum* has been considered a distinct species (Heidrich *et al.*, 1995) and *G. b. stranecki* a new subspecies (König & Wink, 1995). *G. brasilianum* shares common ancestry with *G. peruanum, G. griseiceps* and *G. nanum* (Fig. 1); they form a monophyletic group. *G. bolivianum, G. jardinii*, and *G. hardyi* also cluster in a common, apparently monophyletic group in NJ and ML trees (Fig. 1 B, C). Both the *brasilianum* and the *bolivianum* complex are clearly separated from the small *Glaucidium* species, *G. californium* and *G. gnoma* which have distinctive calls and live in North America, especially the Rocky mountains, south to Central America.

Athene/Speotyto

Two species have been recognized in the genus *Athene*, i.e. *A. noctua* and *A. brama*. Within *A. noctua*, two genetic clusters are apparent which are supported by high bootstrap values; genetic differences between both groups account for 6.4% nucleotide substitutions suggesting species level. Birds from cluster I derive from Israel and Turkey [they could be treated as *Athene lilith* as suggested by Wink & Heidrich (1999)] whereas those from cluster II represent *A. noctua* from Europe.

Speotyto cunicularia represents the genus *Athene* in the New World, and this species has sometimes been considered as a member of the genus *Athene*. Since DNA-DNA hybridization suggested significant differences (Sibley & Monroe, 1990), a separation into a monotypic genus appeared justified. According to the sequence data, it is clear that *Speotyto* and *Athene* share common ancestry (divergence approximately 6 million years ago) and that they form a monophyletic group. Due to similarities in morphology, general outlook, vocal patterns, and behaviour, we suggest to merge *Speotyto* back in *Athene*. *Athene* always clusters as a sister group to the *Glaucidium/Surnia* complex (Fig. 1 A-C).

Surnia

The Northern Hawk Owl (*Surnia ulula*) of northern Eurasia and North America shares common ancestry and forms a monophyletic group with the *Glaucidium* complex of Old World origin but clusters at its base (Fig. 1 B,C). A separation as a monotypic genus could be debated, but might be justified because of morphological, behavioural and, last but not least, genetic differences.

Aegolius

Tengmalm's owls (genus *Aegolius*) can be found as a third major monophyletic group (Fig. 1) at the base of the branches leading to *Athene/Surnia/Glaucidium* (Fig. 1 A-C). The North American *A. acadius* diverges with 12.9% nucleotide substitutions from *A. funereus*, implicating a divergence time of more than 6 million years. Two geographically separated subspecies, *A.a. acadius* and *A.a. brooksii* can be recognized (distance 0.7%). As expected, the South American *A. harrisii* is closer related to the North American *A. acadius* than to *A. funereus* (Fig. 1), suggesting a common ancestor for the New World species.

Ninox

The genus *Ninox* comprises 19 species with Australasian distribution. *Ninox* clusters at the base to the branches leading to the genera *Otus/Strix/Bubo* in NJ,MP, and ML trees (Fig. 1 A-C). These groups apparently share common ancestry.

Strix

Tawny and wood owls (genus *Strix* with ca 21 species including the former genus *Ciccaba*) are always in a monophyletic clade (Fig. 1) and share ancestry with the *Bubo* complex (according to NL and MP reconstructions; Fig. 1 B,C). This sister group relationship is not supported by high bootstrap values (Fig. 1 B).

DNA data show that *S. butleri* is a distinct species (and not a subspecies of *S. aluco*) and rather related to the African *S. woodfordii* than to *S. aluco* (Heidrich & Wink, 1994). *S. uralensis* appears as a sister taxon of *S. aluco*, as suggested from behaviour and general appearance; genetic distances imply that both taxa diverged from a common ancestor more than 4 million years ago. The South American *S. rufipes* always clusters at the base of the *Strix* complex and could constitute a sister group of the Old World *Strix*, that was separated from a common ancestor 5-6 million years ago.

Pulsatrix

Four species are recognized in the Central and South American genus *Pulsatrix*, of which we could study *P. perspicillata* and *P. koeniswaldiana*. The phylogenetic position of *Pulsatrix* cannot be resolved with certainty: In NJ and MP trees (Fig. 1) it clusters with the *Otus flammeolus*, and in ML trees in the neighbourhood of *Strix* and *Asio* (Fig. 1C); but these relationships are not supported by high bootstrap values.

Otus, Mimizuka, Asio, and *Ptilopsis*

According to our genetic analysis (Fig. 1), members of the genus *Otus* appear in at least 3 different monophyletic clades, indicating that the presently recognized genus is polyphyletic. The Screech Owls of the New World represent a distinct group which is separated from Old World members of *Otus* by genetic distances between 12 and 16% (equivalent 6-8 million years). Within the Screech Owl complex, which has its radiation centre in South and Central America, several species have been recognized on account of different acoustic repertoires (König, 1994a). Sequence data could corroborate these findings (Heidrich et al., 1995), stressing the importance of vocalization for speciation and taxonomy. *O. atricapillus* and *O. usta*, are distinct sibling species. *O. sanctaecatarinae*, *O. roboratus* and probably *O. guatemalae* and *O. asio* (from North America) also belong to this monophyletic cluster. *Otus hoyi* and *O. petersoni* appear as sibling species (in NL trees), as do *O. albogularis* and *O. choliba* (Fig. 1).

Of the large group of Old World Scops owls (overview in Sibley & Monroe, 1990) *O. scops, O. lempiji, O. megalotis, O. longicornis, O. brucei,* and *O. bakkamoena* have been included here as representatives for this group. As can be seen from Fig. 1 these Scops owls fall into a common clade which is very distinct from the New World Otus complex. Using 12S mt rDNA sequences, Mindell et al. (1997) showed that *O. mirus, O. mindorensis,* and *Mimizuku gurneyi* cluster together with *O. megalotis* and *O. longicornis*. As we also studied the latter two species we can conclude that *O. mirus, O. mindorensis,* and *Mimizuku gurneyi* are members of the Old World *Otus* group. Since *Mimizuku* clusters within this group we suggested merging *Mimizuku* in *Otus* (Wink & Heidrich, 1999).

The African *O. leucotis* (West Africa) and *O. granti* (South Africa) differ both morphologically and genetically from the other Old World *Otus* species and have been placed in the genus *Ptilopsis*. In all reconstructions (Fig. 1) *P. leucotis* figures as a sister group to the genus *Asio* in NJ, MP, and ML reconstructions (Fig. 1 A-C).

Genera should comprise monophyletic groups in phylogenetically orientated systematics. As polyphyletic groups are artificial, the present genus *Otus* needs a revision. Therefore, *Ptilopsis* and *Megascops* have been proposed as additional genera.

Bubo, Ketupa, Scotopelia, and *Nyctea*

Eagle Owls of the genus *Bubo* represent another prominent group of "eared owls". According to phylogenetic relationships and distances (Fig. 1), most taxa are distinct species, although some of them have been treated as subspecies of *B. bubo* (Sibley & Monroe, 1990). The southernmost taxon of South American Eagle Owls differs in size, vocalisations and DNA (Fig. 1) from *B. virginianus* and has been treated as a distinct species, *B. magellanicus* (König et al., 1996).

B. (b.) ascalaphus, which occurs in North and West Africa, has been classified as a distinct species (Sibley & Monroe, 1990). In our analysis distances differ by 3.5% between *B. bubo* and *B. ascalaphus*. Also *B. b. interpositus*, which is morphologically distinct from *B. bubo* and lives in the Israelian desert, is also genetically distinct (distance 2.8%) (Fig. 1). As a sequence divergence of more than 1.5% is indicative of species level, it could be justified to treat both taxa as distinct species.

The Snowy Owl (*Nyctea scandiaca*) shares common ancestry with *Bubo* (Fig.1), especially with the New World species *B. virginianus* which would be in agreement with the arctic distribution of *N. scandiaca*. The separation from a common ancestor took place more than 4 million years ago. Since *Nyctea* represents a monotypic genus but unambiguously clusters within the *Bubo*-complex, the taxonomic consequences would be to merge *Nyctea* in *Bubo* and call the species *Bubo scandiaca*.

A similar situation can be found for *Ketupa*, of which 4 species have been described from Southeast Asia. *Ketupa zeylonensis* and *K. ketupa* cluster as close relatives of the Asian *Bubo* species, such as *B. nipalensis* and *B. sumatrana* (Fig. 1). Also the general appearance of *Ketupa* is similar to that of *Bubo*; because of genetic relationships (distance 9-10%) we agree with Amadon & Bull (1988) to merge *Ketupa* in *Bubo*. Three Fishing Owls (genus *Scotopelia*) are known which feed on fish as *Ketupa*. Both taxa are in a monophyletic clade with *Bubo lacteus, B. sumatrana* and *B. nipalensis*. We suggest to consider *Scotopelia* as a member of the monophyletic *Bubo* complex (Fig. 1 A-C).

CONCLUSION

Trees which are based on sequence data are not necessarily unequivocal and correct. If a dataset is incomplete (as in our study) and does not contain all related taxa for a comparison, errors are possible due to "long branch attraction". Nuclear copies of mitochondrial genes ("paralogous genes") can bias a phylogeny (Quinn 1997), although we found no evidence for this phenomenon in the owl data set. For mitochondrial genes it should be remembered that we can only trace maternal lineages ("gene trees") and that trees can be distorted by inbreeding and introgression. Some of these limitations have to be kept in mind when interpreting the phylogenetic trees presented in this communication which represents a form of progress report from an ongoing study.

As can be seen from Fig. 1 A-C the phylogenetic relationships inferred from sequences of the cytochrome b gene, are generally in a good agreement with the classical taxonomy of owls (Sibley & Monroe, 1990; Burton, 1992; Hume, 1991; König et al, 1999) and the attribution of species to a given genus. Paraphyly and polyphyly are evident in the *Otus* and in the *Bubo* complex and we have proposed to split *Otus* into three genera *Otus, Ptilopsis,* and *Megascops,* but to merge *Nyctea, Ketupa,* and according to this study also *Scotopelia* with *Bubo*.

Summarizing, sequence data of the mitochondrial cytochrome b gene provide a powerful tool (besides morphology, anatomy, behaviour and bioacoustics) to elucidate and reconstruct the evolutionary past and speciation of owls. As the analysis of a single gene only provides a window for a particular evolutionary period, we need to include more progressive or more conservative genes (i.e., both mtDNA and ncDNA) to solve other problems of microevolution or of higher level classifications.

ACKNOWLEDGEMENTS

We thank W. Bednarek, G. Ehlers, O. Hatzofe, R. Krahe, D. Reynolds, A. Kemp, C. Fentzloff, W. Grummt, C. König, J. Yom-Tov, D. Ristow, E. Thaler, B. Etheridge, D. Engelbrecht, and U.

Schneppat for providing blood, feathers or tissues of owls. The study of owl phylogenetics has been performed in close collaboration with C. König (Stuttgart) whom we would like to thank for his help and encouragement.

REFERENCES

AMADON, D., & J. BULL 1988. Hawks and owls of the world. *Proc. W. Found. Vertebr. Zool.* 3, 297-357.
AVISE, J.C. 1994. *Molecular Markers, Natural History & Evolution.* Chapman & Hall, New York, London.
BURTON, J.A. 1992. *Owls of the World, their Evolution, Structure and Ecology.* Peter Lowe, London.
CRACRAFT, J. 1981. Towards a phylogenetic classification of recent birds of the world (class Aves). *The Auk*, 98, 681-714
HEIDRICH, P. 1998. Untersuchungen zur molekularen Phylogenie ausgewählter Vogelgruppen anhand von DNA-Sequenzen des mitochondriellen Cytochrom b-Gens. PhD thesis, Universität Heidelberg
HEIDRICH, P. & M. WINK 1994. Tawny Owl (*Strix aluco*) and Hume's tawny Owl (*Strix aluco*) are distinct species, Evidence from nucleotide sequences of the cytochrome b gene. *Z. Naturforsch.*, 49c,230-234.
HEIDRICH, P, C. KÖNIG & M. WINK 1995. Molecular phylogeny of the South American Screech Owls of the *Otus atricapillus* complex (*Aves, Strigidae*) inferred from nucleotide sequences of the mitochondrial cytochrome b gene. *Z. Naturforsch.* 50c: 294-302.
HEIDRICH,P., C. KÖNIG & M. WINK 1995. Bioakustik, Taxonomie und molekulare Systematik amerikanischer Sperlingskäuze (Strigidae: *Glaucidium* spp.). *Stuttgarter Beiträge zur Naturkunde* A, 534, 1-47,
HEIDRICH, P., J. AMENGUAL, & M. WINK 1998. Phylogenetic relationships in Mediterranean and North Atlantic *Puffinus* Shearwaters (*Aves: Procellariidae*) based on nucleotide sequences of mtDNA. *Biochemical Systematics and Ecology* 26, 145-170
HEIDRICH, P., & M. WINK 1998. Phylogenetic relationships in holarctic owls (Order Strigiformes): Evidence from nucleotide sequences of the mitochondrial cytochrome b gene. In *Holarctic Birds of Prey*. (R.D. Chancellor, B.-U.Meyburg, & J.J. Ferrero eds), Adenex & WWGBP.
HEIDRICH, P., D. RISTOW & M. WINK. 1996. Molekulare Differenzierung von Gelb- und Schwarzschnabelsturmtauchern (*Calonectris diomedea, Puffinus puffinus, P. yelkouan*) und Großmöwen des Silbermöwenkomplexes (*Larus argentatus, L. fuscus, L. cachinnans*). *Journal für Ornithologie* 137, 281-294, 1996
HEKSTRA, G.P. 1982. Description of twenty-four new subspecies of American *Otus* (*Aves*, Strigidae). *Bull. zool. Mus. Amsterdam* 9:49-63.
HILLIS, D.M. & J.J. BULL 1993. An empirical test of bootstrapping as a method for assessing confidence in phylogenetic analysis. *Syst. Biol.* 42, 182-192
HILLIS, D.M. & C. MORITZ 1990. *Molecular systematics.* Sinauer Publishers, Sunderland.
HUME, R. 1991. *Owls of the World.* Dragons World, Limpfield.
KÖNIG, C. 1991a. Taxonomische und ökologische Untersuchungen an Kreischeulen (*Otus* spp.) des südlichen Südamerika. *J. Orn.* 132: 209-214.
KÖNIG, C. 1991b. Zur Taxonomie und Ökologie der Sperlingskäuze (*Glaucidium* spp.) des Andenraumes. *Ökol. Vögel* 13: 15-76.
KÖNIG, C. 1994a. Lautäußerungen als interspezifische Isolationsmechanismen bei Eulen der Gattung *Otus* (*Aves:* Strigidae) aus dem südlichen Südamerika. *Beitr. Naturkde.* Ser. A.
KÖNIG, C. 1994b. Biological patterns in owl taxonomy, with emphasis on bioacoustical studies on neotropical pygmy (*Glaucidium*) and screech owls (*Otus*). In *Raptor Conservation Today* (B.-U.Meyburg & R.D. Chancellor, eds), pp 1-19, Pica press.
KÖNIG, C., F. WEICK, & J.H. BECKING 1999. *Owls. An Identification Guide to the Owls of the World.* Pica Press.
KÖNIG, C., P. HEIDRICH, & M.WINK 1996. Zur Taxonomie der Uhus (Strigidae: *Bubo* spp.) im südlichen Südamerika. *Stuttg. Beitr. Naturk.* Ser.A., 540, 1-9,
KÖNIG, C. & M. WINK 1995. Eine neue Unterart des Brasilsperlingskauzes aus Zentralargentinien: *Glaucidium brasilianum stranecki* n. ssp. *J. Orn.*136, 461-465
KUMAR, S., K. TAMURA, & M. NEI 1993. *MEGA - Molecular Evolutionary Genetics Analysis.* Version 1.0. Pennsylvania State University.
MAYR, E., & D. AMADON 1951. A classification of recent birds. *Americ. Mus. Novit.* 1496
MIKKOLA, H. 1983. *Owls of Europe.* Poyser, Calton
MINDELL, D.P. 1997. *Avian molecular evolution and systematics.* Academic Press San Diego.
MINDELL, D.P. & M. D. SORENSON 1998. Testing the root of the avian tree and the phylogenetic position of Passeriformes. *Ostrich* 69, 43.

MINDELL, D.P., M.D. SORENSON, C.J. HUDDLESTON, J. MIRANDA, A. KNIGHT, S.J. SAWCHUK, & T. YURI 1997. Phylogenetic relationships among and within select avian orders based on mitochondrial DNA. In: Mindell, D.P. (Ed.) *Avian molecular evolution ans systematics*. Academic Press San Diego, pp. 213-247

MOORE, W.S. & V.R. DEFILIPPIS 1997. The window of taxonomic resolution for phylogenies based on mitochondrial cytochrome b. In: Mindell, D.P. (ed.) *Avian molecular evolution and systematics*. Academic Press San Diego, pp. 83-119.

QUINN, T.W. 1997. Molecular evolution of the mitochondrial genome. In: Mindell, D.P. (ed.) *Avian molecular evolution ans systematics*. Academic Press San Diego, pp. 3-28.

SHIELDS, G.F. & A.C. WILSON 1987. Calibration of mitochondrial DNA evolution in geese. *J. Mol. Evol.* 24, 212-217.

SIBLEY, C.G. & B.L. MONROE 1990. *Distribution and Taxonomy of Birds of the World*. Yale University Press, New Haven, London.

SWOFFORD, D.L. 1993. *PAUP, Phylogenetic analysis using parsimony. Version 3.1.1*, Illinois.

WINK, M. 1995. Phylogeny of Old and New World vultures (Aves: Accipitridae and Cathardidae) inferred from nucleotide sequences of the mitochondrial cytochrome b gene. *Z. Naturforsch.* (in press).

WINK, M., & P HEIDRICH. 1999. Molecular evolution and systematics of owls (Strigiformes). In *Owls of the World* (König, C. & Becking, J.H., eds), Pica Press (in press)

WINK, M., P. HEIDRICH, & C. FENTZLOFF 1996. A mtDNA phylogeny of sea eagles (genus *Haliaeetus*) based on nucleotide sequences of the cytochrome b gene. *Biochemical Systematics and Ecology* 24, 783-791

Prof. Dr. M. Wink & Dr. P. Heidrich
Universität Heidelberg
Institut für Pharmazeutische Biologie
Im Neuenheimer Feld 364
D-69120 Heidelberg
Germany

Part 12

Taxonomy, Phylogeny, Developments in Raptor DNA Studies and other Theoretical Aspects

Bat Hawk *Machaeramphus alcinus*

Conveners:
Michael Wink & Anthony van Zyl

Chancellor, R. D. & B.-U. Meyburg eds. 2000
Raptors at Risk
WWGBP / Hancock House

Advances in DNA studies of diurnal and nocturnal raptors

Michael Wink

ABSTRACT

Sequence variations in the nuclear and mitochondrial genome of raptors offer a unique chance to elucidate their evolutionary past, phylogeography and population structure as DNA contains a blueprint of most evolutionary events. In this overview the ongoing efforts to study the evolution and phylogeny of diurnal and nocturnal birds of prey has been summarized. DNA sequencing of marker genes is undoubtedly the method of choice for this question. Considering the large number of species concerned, the present data base is still fragmentary and much more work (e.g., more taxa, additional genes) is needed to obtain a complete evolutionary scenario. Two other recent examples of DNA studies (e.g., molecular sexing and turnover assessment) represent new molecular tools to analyse the behaviour and ecology of raptors.

INTRODUCTION

Sequence variation in the nuclear and mitochondrial genome of animals (including birds) offers a unique chance to obtain a deeper knowledge of their evolutionary past, both in terms of space and time as DNA contains a blueprint of most evolutionary events. DNA studies have become a powerful tool in most areas of biology, in order to understand the phylogeny, systematics, and phylogeography of species, their ecology, population structure, breeding biology, paternity, and many other aspects (overviews in Avise 1994; Hoelzel 1992; Karp *et al.*, 1998; Hillis *et al.* 1996; Mindell, 1997; Nei 1996; Wink 1998).

The nuclear genome of vertebrates consists of approximately 3×10^9 nucleotides (in humans). Theoretically, this large size could be a base for over 3 million distinct genes. In reality however, the number of protein encoding genes ranges between 60000 and 100000 in humans and should be even lower in less developed animals. Thus, only 3% of the genome represent low or single copy genes (Fig. 1). The other 97% are rDNA repeats or non-coding introns, regulatory sequences, retroelements, transposons, degenerate copies and pseudogenes (remnants of past evolutionary events), tandemly repeated DNA sequences, such as telomeres, satellite DNA, minisatellites and microsatellites (Fig. 1). The mitochondrial DNA in animals and chloroplast DNA in plants have originated from bacterial endosymbionts which fused with early eukaryotic cells. Organelle DNA consists mainly of protein encoding and rRNA genes; introns and uncoding regions are rare (except for the D-loop in mitochondria) (Fig. 2).

Depending on the evolutionary, ecological or biological question, we can analyse particular parts of the nuclear and mitochondrial genome. For studies in molecular evolution and systematics, marker genes are selected either from mtDNA, cpDNA or ncDNA. In animals, mitochondrial DNA evolves faster than nuclear genes and rDNA slower than protein encoding DNA. Interestingly, we find the opposite behaviour in plant DNA, where mtDNA evolves much slower than ncDNA or

Figure 1. Schematic illustration of DNA sequences in the nuclear genome

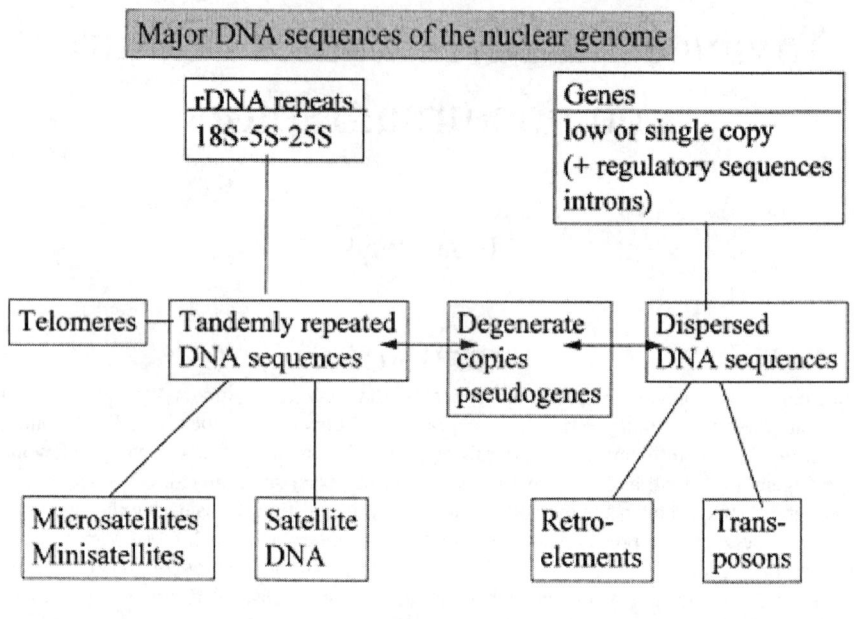

Figure 2. Mitochondrial genome of birds (after Quinn 1997) and chloroplast genome of higher plants

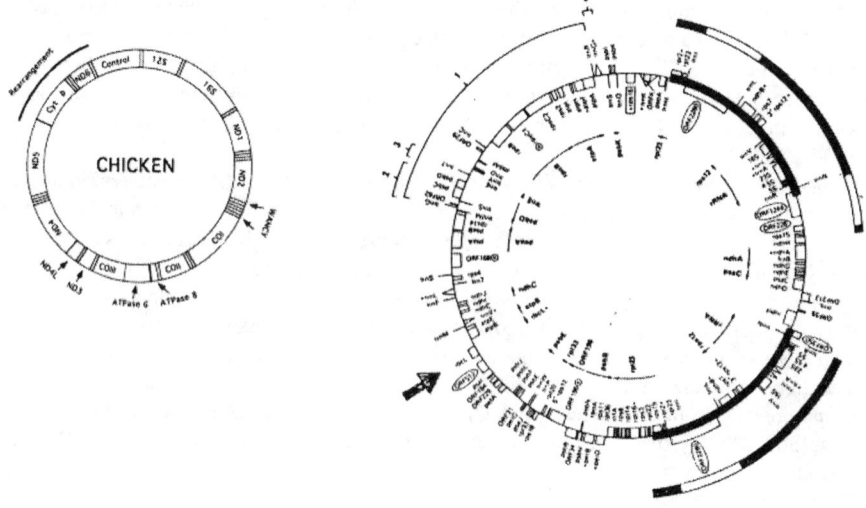

cpDNA (Fig. 3). For a finer analysis of phylogeographic patterns, population structures, breeding systems and individual profiling in animal, more variable DNA sequences are needed. These can be found in the mitochondrial D-loop, in introns of protein encoding genes, and especially in mini- and microsatellites (Fig. 1). Whereas DNA sequencing is the major tool for phylogenetic studies, RFLP analysis, DNA-fingerprinting with single and multilocus probes, and microsatellite PCR are the methods of choice if a higher resolution is needed (overviews in Avise 1994; Hoelzel 1992; Karp *et al.*, 1998; Hillis *et al.* 1996; Wink & Wehrle, 1994; Wink 1998).

Figure 3 Schematic view of the use and evolutionary tempo of marker genes

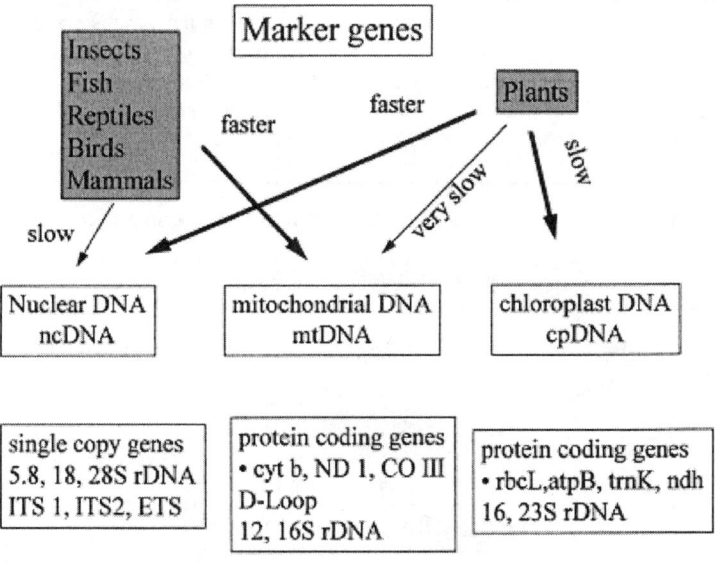

This review summarizes several papers given at the 5th World Conference of birds of prey and owls with special focus on advances in molecular systematics and molecular ecology of raptors.

1. Molecular phylogeny and evolution of birds of prey and owls

Charles Darwin wrote to T.H. Huxley in 1857: "The time will come I believe, though I shall not live to see it, when we shall have fairly true genealogical trees of each kingdom of nature...". Sequencing of marker genes from mitochondrial and ncDNA has made fast progress in the last 10 years, after the development of polymerase chain reaction (PCR) which has revolutionized most areas of biology and medicine. Using sequences of marker genes, data on the molecular phylogeny and systematics of all groups of organisms can be generated and are published at a fast speed, so that Darwin's dream will probably become true within the next decades. DNA results will not replace studies in morphology, anatomy, behaviour or vocalizations, but will complement them. Sequence analysis of marker genes are helpful

- to elucidate the evolutionary past of most organisms
- to distinguish between convergent and phylogenetic traits
- to identify monophyletic groups which share common ancestry
- to understand speciation
- to elucidate phylogeographic patterns, migration and colonisation
- together with morphology, anatomy, behaviour, acoustics etc. to reconstruct the "true" phylogeny of a group of organisms
- to understand and maintain biodiversity

Of major importance is the selection of the appropriate marker gene for the relevant evolutionary time window. In order to study genetic relationships within families down to the species level, sequences of mitochondrial DNA (Quinn 1997; Moore & DeFilippis 1977) are very helpful, such as cytochrome b, 12S rRNA, ND2 and others (Fig. 2).

Nucleotide sequences of the mitochondrial cytochrome b gene have already been employed to study the systematics and evolution of diurnal raptors and owls (Avise *et al.*, 1994; Griffiths 1997; Mindell 1997; from our laboratory: Seibold *et al.*, 1993, 1996; Heidrich & Wink, 1994, 1998; Heidrich *et al.*, 1995a,b, 1996; Helbig *et al.*, 1994; Wink 1995, 1998; Wink & Seibold, 1996; Wink *et al.*, 1996, 1998a,b; Wink & Heidrich, 1999; Seibold & Helbig, 1995, 1996).

In our studies, the mitochondrial cytochrome b gene was amplified and sequenced from approximately 35% of species and 50% of genera of diurnal raptors and 35% of species and 68% of genera of owls. Figures 4 and 5 provide a schematic overview on the various procedures between the starting point, a feather, tissue or blood sample and the final result as a phylogenetic tree. More details can be found in the following books and reviews: Avise (1994); Hoelzel (1992); Karp *et al.*, (1998); Hillis *et al.* (1996); Wink & Wehrle, (1994); Sambrook *et al.* (1989), Swofford (1993), Kumar *et al.*, (1993) and Felsenstein (1993).

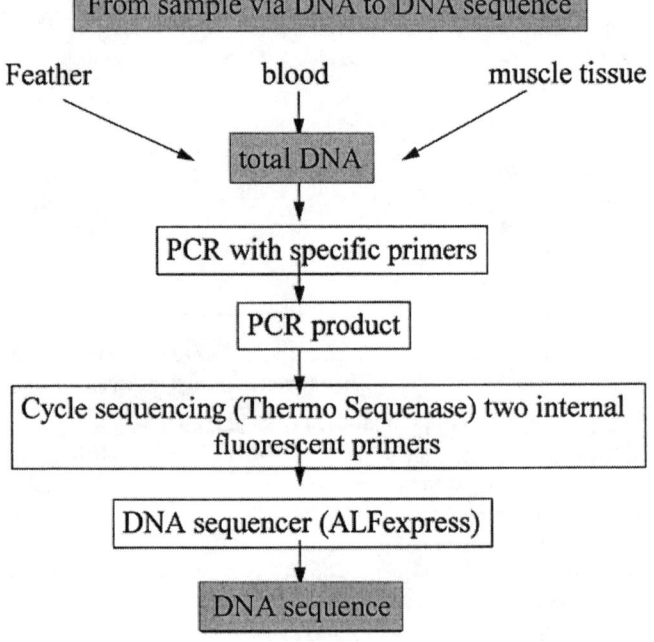

Figure 4. Schematic illustration of the steps from sample to DNA-sequence.

Fig. 6 represents a phylogenetic tree, reconstructed with Maximum Parsimony, for which we have analysed 1 to 3 taxa from each genus of diurnal and nocturnal raptors and members from a few other families. This tree should be regarded as a sort of "progress report" and not as a final result. A better resolution and higher reliability of the relationships between genera and families will be obtained when a complete data set is available, as long-branch attractions can be a major element of error (often found in incomplete data-sets) which could also distort some relationships between families in the tree shown in Fig. 6. Another reason, why we cannot resolve many of the deeper branches unambiguously is because of homoplasy due to multiple substitutions.

Figure 5: From DNA-sequence to phylogeny

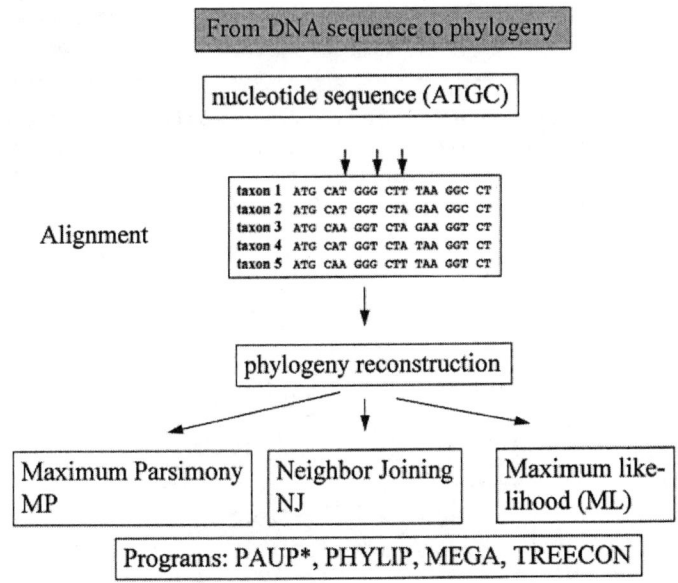

A few phylogenetic relationships appear unequivocal already- at present. In most instances, the taxa which have been grouped in a common genus represent a monophyletic assemblage. In some instances we obtained good evidence for para- or polyphyletic groups, indicating that the systematics need a revision. Such examples are:
- *Aquila* and *Hieraeetus* form a paraphyletic clade; it would be plausible that *Hieraeetus* should be merged in *Aquila* (Wink and Sauer-Gürth, this volume).
- *Bubo, Ketupa, Nyctea,* and *Scotopelia* form a monophyletic assemblage; a common genus *Bubo* would be more appropriate for this complex (Wink & Heidrich, in press).
- Members of the genus *Otus* are polyphyletic and 3 clades can be distinguished. Here a split into the genera *Otus, Megascops* and *Ptilopsis* has been proposed (Wink & Heidrich, in press)

Members within defined terminal monophyletic groups should carry a common genus name. We have several instances, that monotypic genera have been created, although they derive from the same ancestor and form a closely related clade of birds. Examples are:
- Within Old world vultures, 3 lineages are evident, a) *Gypaetus, Neophron* and *Gypohierax*, b) *Gyps* and c) the *Aegypius*-complex with *Aegypius/Torgos/Trigonoceps*, and *Sarcogyps* as monotypic genera. Because vulture group c constitutes a monophyletic clade of species which share many morphological and behavioural characters, it would be plausible to place them in a single genus: The name *Aegypius* has already been proposed for this assemblage (del Hoyo *et al.*, 1994; Mundy *et al.*, 1992).

The Black-shouldered kite, *Elanus caeruleus*, does not cluster within the Accipitridae, to which this taxon has been attributed (Fig. 6); *Elanus* falls between falcons and owls and seems to represent a unique group (family Elanidae?) of raptors. It would be interesting to find out whether *Elanoides, Gampsonyx,* and *Chelictinia* which share some characteristics with *Elanus* are true Accipitridae or more related to *Elanus*. The African Harrier-hawk *Polyboroides typus* shows many particular habits and morphological traits, which makes it difficult to classify this taxon correctly. *Polyboroides typus*, clusters at the base of the Accipitridae in the group of ancestral vultures of the *Gypaetus/Neophron/Gypohierax* group and honeybuzzards (Fig. 6).

Diurnal raptors have been grouped into 5 families, Accipitridae, Pandionidae, Sagittariidae, Falconidae, and Catharthidae and placed in a common order Falconiformes (del Hoyo *et al.*, 1994) or the infraorders Falconides and Ciconiides, respectively (Sibley & Monroe, 1990). Morphological and molecular data (Fig. 6) provide evidence that at least Cathartidae, Falconidae and Sagittariidae

Figure 6. Molecular phylogeny of diurnal and nocturnal birds of prey based on nucleotide sequences of the cytochrome b gene (sequences are either unpublished from my laboratory [Seibold, (1994); Heidrich (1998)], Griffiths (1997) or GenBank). Tree length 9268 steps, CI=0.145, HI=0.855, RI=0.412. Illustration of a strict consensus tree from 6 equally parsimonius trees.

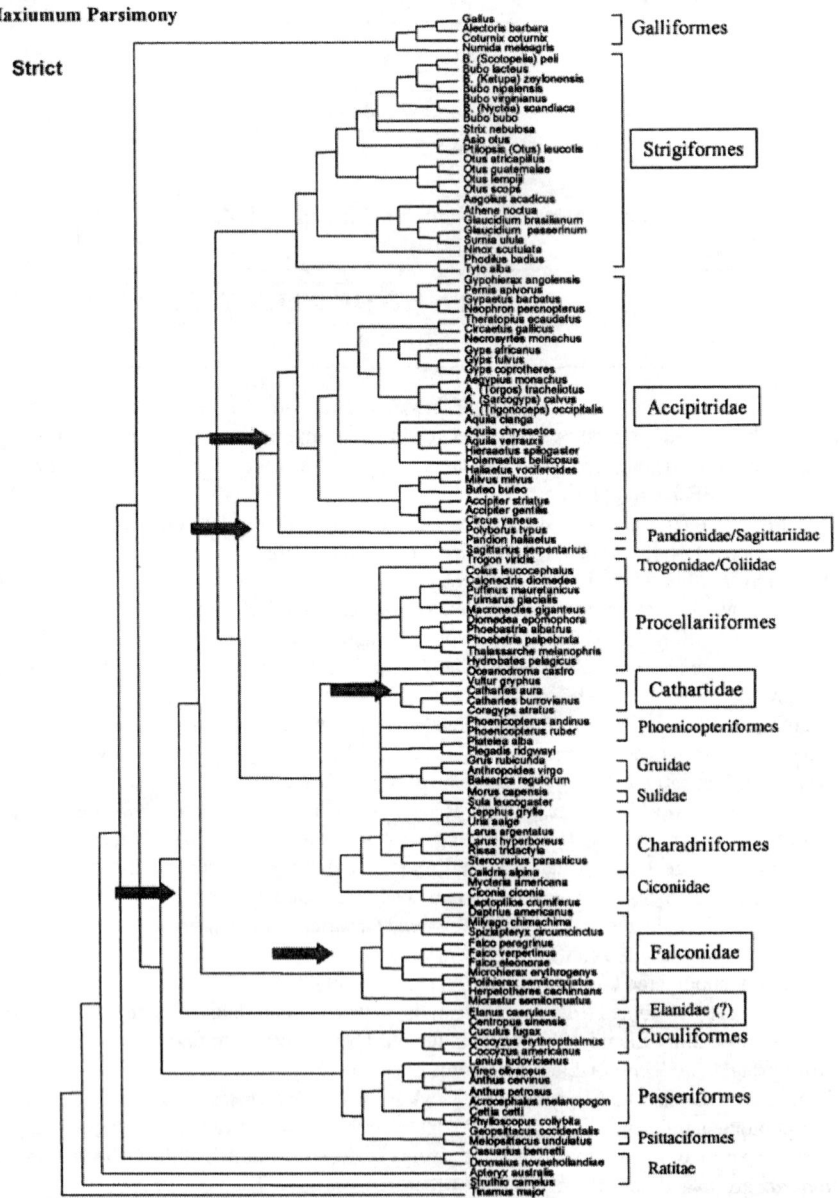

do not share direct ancestry with Accipitridae and Pandionidae, indicating that the order Falconiformes or infraorder Falconides are apparently artificial units (Wink 1995; Wink et al., 1998) which combine birds that share a common life style, especially behaviour and ecology.

For a more detailed discussion of phylogenetic relationships in diurnal and nocturnal raptors, see Wink & Ristow, Wink & Sauer-Gürth and Wink & Heidrich in this volume.

2. Molecular sexing of raptors

Falcons, hawks, and eagles show a high degree of sexual dimorphism, so that adult sexes are usually apparent. In vultures, however, a size or plumage dimorphism is not visible. But gender is important if ringing recoveries, recruitment rates or other ecological and behavioural data are to be analyzed. For reintroduction programs of Black vultures *Aegypius monachus*, Griffon vultures *Gyps fulvus* or Lappet-faced vultures *Torgos tracheliotus* knowledge of the sex of the birds is vital to create successful breeding pairs.

The gender of vultures can be determined macroscopically via endoscopy. But this procedure is stressful for the birds. Alternatively, sex chromosomes (female birds have ZW and males ZZ chromosomes) can be identified cytologically (Hatzofe & Getreide, 1990). If the size of the sex chromosomes differs, the DNA content of erythrocytes can be determined by flow cytometry (Nakamura et al. 1990).

A rapid and more flexible approach is molecular sexing (Ellegren and Sheldon 1997) by

- Hybridisation with oligonucleotide or W-specific DNA probes (Griffiths 1992, Griffiths & Holland 1990, Millar 1992, Millar et al. 1994, 1996, Rabenold et al. 1991)
- PCR-methods (Ellegren 1996, Ellegren & Sheldon 1997, Griffiths & Tiwari 1993, 1995; Griffiths et al., 1992, 1996, Ogawa et al. 1997, Sabo et al. 1994). Whereas most methods are specific for a single species, the methods of Ellegren (1996), Griffiths et al., (1996), and Ogawa et al. (1997) have a much wider application range.
- Instead of specific PCR primers RAPD have been applied that amplify part of the female W chromosome (Griffiths & Tiwari 1993).

Table 1. Molecular sexing of raptors by ISSR-PCR

Species	$(GACA)_4$	$(GACA)_4$ +RAPD	Kahn
Vultures			
Gyps fulvus	X	nd	X
Aegypius monachus	X	nd	X
Torgos tracheliotus	X	nd	X
Neophron percnopterus	no	no	X
Eagles			
Aquila adalberti	no	X	X
Aquila nipalensis	nd	nd	X
Hieraaetus fasciatus	X	nd	X
Haliaeetus albicilla	no	X	X
Falcons			
Falco eleonorae	no	no	X

X= method works successfully; no= method fails; n.d.= not determined; Kahn = Kahn et al., (1998)

We have applied a new strategy using the single primer MW4 $(GACA)_4$ (Wink et al., 1998). This method has been termed Inter Simple Sequence Repeat-PCR (ISSR-PCR). With $(GACA)_4$ several PCR products were obtained in DNA samples from *A. monachus, G. fulvus,* and *T. tracheliotus* of which one or more display a sex-specific pattern; i.e. they were only present in females but absent in males (Fig. 7,8). Specific PCR products of 450 or 550 nt length (marked with an arrow, Fig. 9), can be attributed to females only, but are absent in males. Since 65-75% of DNA in the W chromosome consists of repetitive sequences (Ellegren 1996, Ogawa et al. 1997, Rabenold et al. 1991), we assume that the distinctive PCR products derive from DNA regions between microsatellite DNA. The advantage of this protocol is that PCR can be performed at higher, more stringent annealing temperatures as compared to RAPD primers of 10 nt length which reduces artifacts.

Figure 7. Schematic illustration of a PCR for molecular sexing with a single primer (ISSR-PCR).

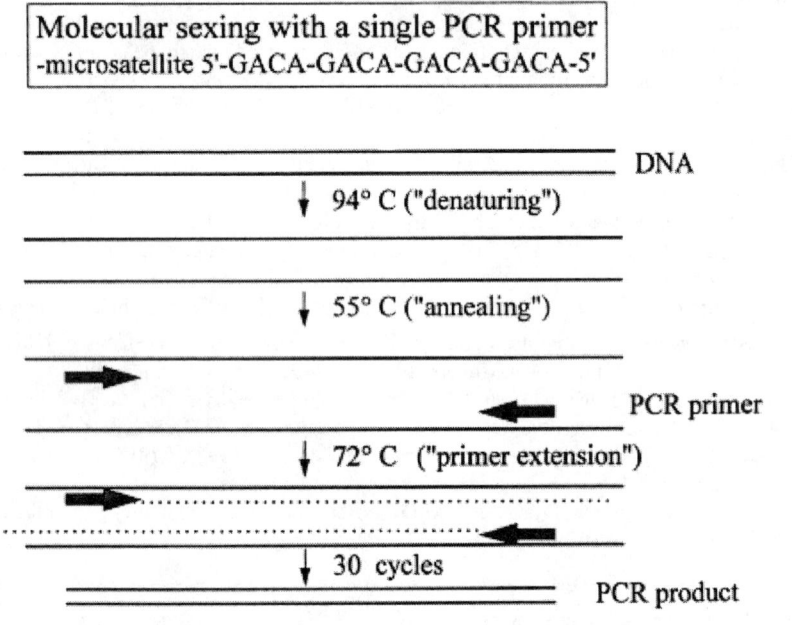

Figure 8: From DNA to molecular sexing

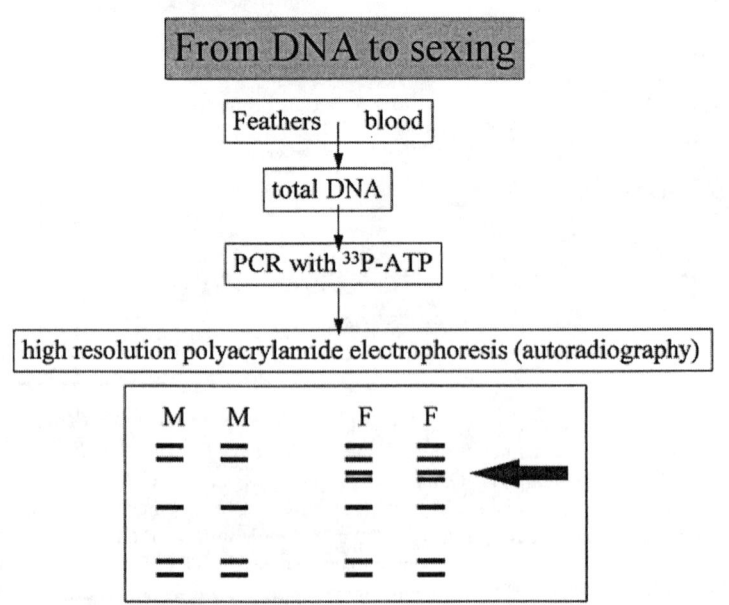

We have applied the $(GACA)_4$ PCR to a number of other species: It was successful with *Crex crex* (Wink, 1998), but failed with eagles (*Aquila adalberti*), sea eagles (*Haliaeetus albicilla*), terns, and bustards (*Chlamydotis undulata*). If the use of $(GACA)_4$ PCR fails then this primer can be used in combination with a RAPD primer according to the protocol outlined in (Matioli & de Brito 1995) (Table 1). Recently, Kahn *et al.* (1998) have published new PCR primers for molecular sex determination in birds. Preliminary analysis in our laboratory showed that these primers work in those species which could not be analyzed by our $(GACA)_4$-PCR (Table 1).

Figure 9. Examples of molecular sexing of raptors

A. Autoradiography of PCR products from $(GACA)_4$ PCR by high resolution gel electrophoresis. PCR products of *Gyps fulvus* with a size of 550 nucleotides are diagnostic for females (marked by arrow). Females of which the gender was established, are marked with a black dot.

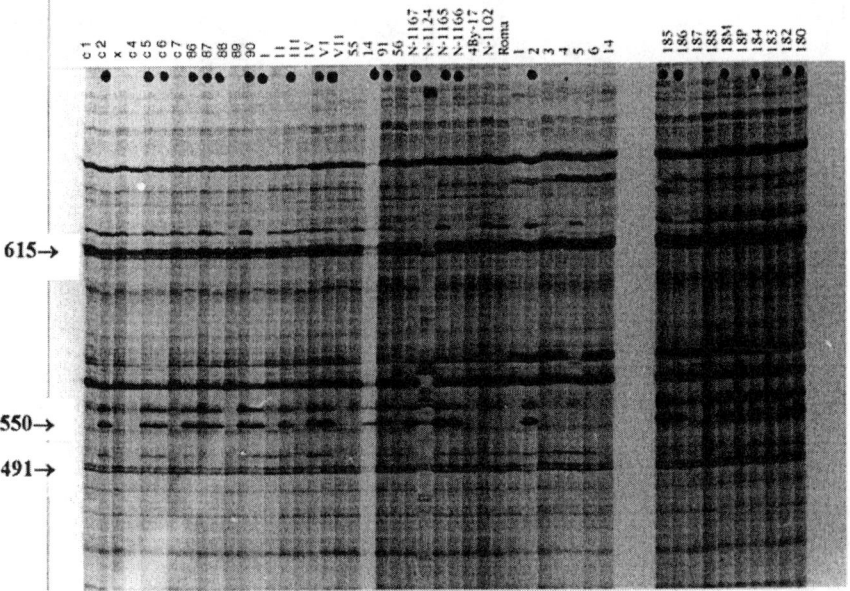

B. Autoradiography of PCR products from *Neophron percnopterus* using PCR primers for chromosome-specific intron size differences in the avian CHD gene (Kahn *et al.*, 1998). Females (marked with a dot) can be recognized by a second doublet of bands.

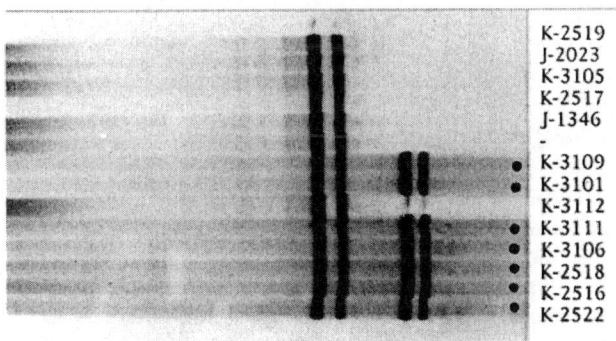

3. Determination of adult turnover and survival with DNA-Fingerprinting

Estimates for juvenile and adult survival are important population parameters in animals. Traditionally, survival data are obtained by marking juvenile and adult birds with tags, rings, or transmitters and to recover, trap, or monitor them during consecutive months and years. Reliable survival estimates are available for only a limited number of raptor species (Newton 1979) although knowledge of this parameter becomes increasingly important for conservation as many raptors are now rare or endangered. We have chosen multilocus DNA (Wetton et al., 1987; Burke et al., 1991, Hoelzel 1992) as a method for the determination of adult survival without the need to trap or mark the adult falcons (Wink et al., 1999). As a first example, we have used blood samples from the Saker Falcon *Falco cherrug* from Kazakhstan. As there is a high demand for this falcon in falconry, the future of the species is uncertain, and survival estimates are of prime importance in assessing likely trends in its populations.

Figure 10. Schematic illustration of the steps involved in DNA fingerprinting using multilocus probes

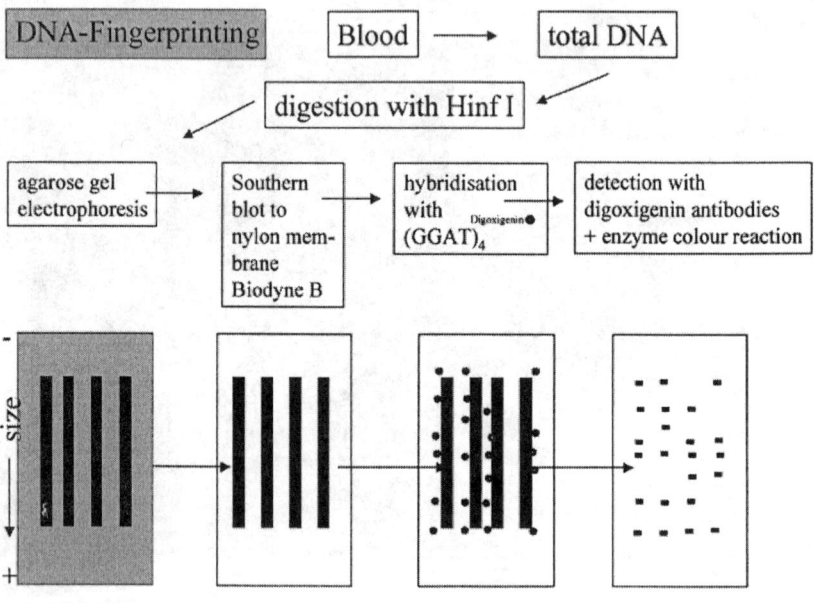

Our approach is based on the following assumptions: Many long-lived birds, especially raptors, show a high degree of site and mate tenacity and breed together in the same territory for consecutive years; this also applies to the Saker Falcon. Our strategy was to carry out multilocus fingerprinting (Fig. 10) of nestlings from the same territory in consecutive years as in indirect approach to estimate a minimal survival rate for adult Sakers.

- Nestlings of an individual brood are full sibs (band-sharing coefficients (BSC)= 0.5 to 0.8); accordingly, band-sharing coefficients (Fig. 11) between full sibs do not differ between years, but should differ significantly from those between unrelated birds (BSC=0.19)
- If the breeding adults are identical in a territory in consecutive years, the band-sharing coefficients of corresponding nestlings should not vary significantly between broods since all young are full sibs.
- If both partners have changed, then band-sharing coefficients between broods should be as low as between unrelated individuals (BSC=0.19) and differ significantly from the BSC value between broods (Fig. 11)

- In cases that one adult bird has been replaced, band-sharing coefficients between broods of the same territory should be significantly lower than those of full sibs but higher than those between unrelated birds.

We have analyzed Saker broods of 16 territories between 1993 and 1997 and obtained a minimal estimate of 82% for adult survival. A value of 82% is in the range found in other falcons: For *F. eleonora* annual survival and turnover is 87% (Ristow et al., 1991); for *F. columbarius* up to 70% (Oliphant et al., 1993), for *F. peregrinus* 78-90% (Mearns & Newton, 1984; Court et al., 1989), and for *F. mexicanus* 78-81% (Runde 1987).

Figure 11. Example of a DNA profiling of related (a,b) und unrelated birds (c) and the calculation of the corresponding band-sharing coefficients (BSC).

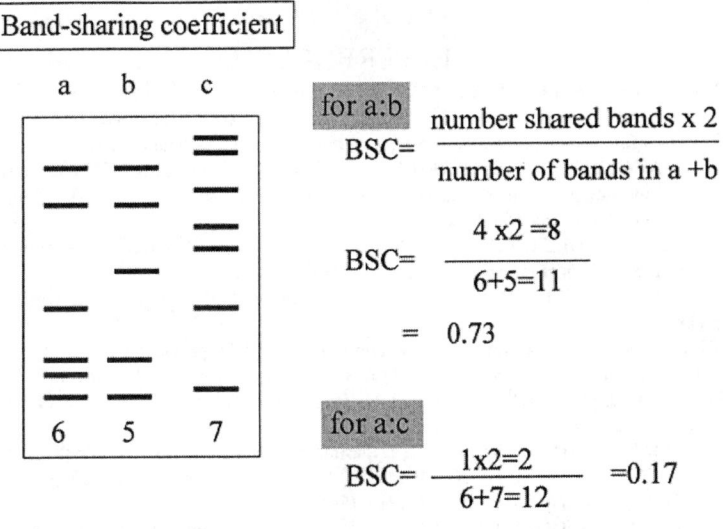

This new approach using DNA fingerprinting has a number of advantages and disadvantages:

Pros:
- no need to catch adult birds
- minimal survival rates can be obtained in a minimum of 2 years
- method probably works in other species with a high site tenacity and mate fidelity

Cons:
- data are reliable in case that no or a complete change took place
- exchange of one adult can lead to ambiguous results
- high "extra-pair paternity", high divorce, emigration, etc., increase the apparant mortality rate

However, the other methods used to determine turnover and survival, such as ringing, recapture and telemetry also provide only minimal estimates only and have their intrinsic shortcomings. We conclude that DNA fingerprinting provides a new and interesting alternative (Wink et al., 1999; Kenward et al., 1999).

CONCLUSIONS

In this overview I have shortly summarized our ongoing efforts to study the evolution and phylogeny of diurnal and nocturnal birds of prey. DNA sequencing of marker genes is undoubtedly the method of choice for this question. Considering the large number of species concerned, our data base, although quite large at present, is still fragmentary and much more work (e.g., more taxa, additional genes) is needed to obtain a complete picture. The other two examples (e.g., molecular sexing and turnover assessment) are new molecular tools to study the behaviour and ecology of raptors, which will not necessarily replace the traditional methods but rather complement them.

ACKNOWLEDGEMENTS

I would like to thank my present and former coworkers H. Sauer-Gürth, H. Staudter, I. Seibold, P. Heidrich, and my collaborators R. Kenward, O. Hatzofe, G. Blanco, C. König for their help and support and many colleagues world-wide for supplying blood, tissue and feather samples of dirunal and nocturnal raptors. The Deutsche Forschungsgemeinschaft and The Land Baden-Württemberg supported parts of the study.

REFERENCES

AVISE, J.C., W.S. NELSON & C.G. SIBLEY 1994. DNA sequences support for a close phylogenetic relationship between some storks and New World vultures. *Proc. Natl. Acad. Sci, USA*, 91, 5173-5177.

AVISE, J.C. 1994. *Molecular markers, natural history and evolution*. Chapman and Hall, London.

BURKE, T., O. HANOTTE, M.W. BRUFORD & E. CAIRNS 1991. Multilocus and single locus minisatellite analysis in population biological studies. In: Burke, T., Jeffreys, A.J., & Wolff, R. (eds): *DNA fingerprinting approaches and applications*: 154-168. Basel.

COURT, G.S., D.M. BRADLEY, C.C. GALES & D.A. BOAG 1989. Turnover and recruitment in a tundra population of Peregrine falcon (*Falco peregrinus*). *Ibis* 131: 487-496.

DEL HOYO, J., A. ELLIOTT & J. SARGATAL 1994. *Handbook of the birds of the world*. Vol. 2, Lynx edicion, Barcelona.

ELLEGREN, H. 1996. First gene on the avian W chromosome (CHD) provides a tag for universal sexing of non-ratite birds. *Proceedings of the Royal Society of London Series B Biological Sciences* 263, 1635-1641.

ELLEGREN H. & B.C. SHELDON 1997. New tools for sex identification and the study of sex allocation in birds. *Trends Ecology & Evolution* 12, 255-259.

FELSENSTEIN, J. 1993. PHYLIP, version 3.5c, Department of Genetics, Univ. Washington, Seattle.

GRIFFITHS, R., S. DAAN & C. DIJKSTRA 1996. Sex identification in birds using two CHD genes. *Proceedings of the Royal Society London B* 263, 1251-1256.

GRIFFITHS, R. & P.W.H. HOLLAND 1990. A novel avian W chromosome DNA repeat sequence in the lesser black-backed gull (*Larus fuscus*). *Chromosoma* 99, 243-250.

GRIFFITHS, R., B. TIWARI & S.A. BECHER 1992. The identification of sex in the starling *Sturnus vulgaris* using a molecular DNA technique. *Molecular Ecology* 1, 191-194.

GRIFFITHS, R. & B. TIWARI 1995. Sex of the last wild Spix's macaw. *Nature* 375, 454.

GRIFFITHS, R. 1992. Sex -biased mortality in the Lesser Black-Backed Gull. *Ibis* 134, 237-244.

GRIFFITHS, T. & B. TIWARI 1993. The isolation of molecular genetic markers for the identification of sex. *Proceedings National Academy of Sciences, USA* 90, 8324-8326.

GRIFFITHS, C.S. 1997. Correlation of functional domains and rates of nucleotide substitution in cytochrome b. *Mol. Phylog. Evol.* 7, 352-365.

HATZOFE, O. & S. GETREIDE 1990. Sex determination in vultures and other mono-morphic raptors. *Torgos* 8: 27-29.

HEIDRICH, P. 1998. Untersuchungen zur molekularen Phylogenie ausgewählter Vogelgruppen anhand von DNA-Sequenzen des mitochondriellen Cytochrom b-Gens. PhD thesis, Universität Heidelberg.

HEIDRICH, P. & M. WINK 1994. Tawny owl (*Strix aluco*) and Hume's tawny owl (*Strix butleri*) are distinct species, Evidence from nucleotide sequences of the cytochrome b gene. *Z. Naturforsch.*, 49c, 230-234.

HEIDRICH, P. & M. WINK 1998. Phylogenetic relationships in holarctic owls (Order Strigiformes): Evidence from nucleotide sequences of the mitochondrial cytochrome b gene. *In Holarctic Birds of Prey.* (R.D. Chancellor, B.-U.Meyburg, J.J. Ferrero, eds), ADENEX & WWGBP; pp. 73-87.

HEIDRICH, P., C. KÖNIG & M. WINK 1995a. Molecular phylogeny of the South American Screech Owls of the *Otus atricapillus* complex (Aves, Strigidae) inferred from nucleotide sequences of the mitochondrial cytochrome b gene. *Z.Naturforsch.* 50c: 294-302.

HEIDRICH,P., C. KÖNIG & M. WINK 1995b. Bioakustik, Taxonomie und molekulare Systematik amerikanischer Sperlingskäuze (Strigidae: Glaucidium spp.). *Stuttgarter Beiträge zur Naturkunde A*, 534, 1-47.

HELBIG, A.J., I. SEIBOLD, W. BEDNAREK, H. BRÜNING, P. GAUCHER, D. RISTOW, W. SCHARLAU, D. SCHMIDL & M. WINK 1994. Phylogenetic relationships among falcon species (genus *Falco*) according to DNA sequence variation of the cytochrome b gene. *in Raptor conservation today* (B.-U. Meyburg & R.D. Chancellor eds.), 593-599.
HILLIS, D.M., C MORITZ & B.K. MABLE 1996. *Molecular systematics*. 2nd ed., Sinauer Assoc. Sunderland.
HOELZEL, A.R. 1992. *Molecular genetic analysis of populations*. IRL-Press, Oxford.
KAHN, N.W., ST.JOHN & T.W. QUINN 1998. Chromosome-specific intron size differences in the avian CHD gene provide a simple and efficient method for sex determination in birds. *Auk* 115, 1074-1078.
KARP, A., P.G.ISAAC & D.S. INGRAM 1998. *Molecular tools for screening biodiversity*. Chapman & Hall, London.
KENWARD, R., M. WINK, V. MARCSTROM, S.S. WALLS, M. KARLBOM, R.H. PFEFFER, E.A. BRAGIN, K.H. HODDER & A. LEVIN. Rapid modelling of sustainable use for raptors with radio-tags and DNA fingerprints. (Ecology Letters submitted)
KUMAR, S., K. TAMURA & M. NEI. *MEGA-Molecular Evolutionary Genetics Analysis*. Version 1.0. Pennsylvania State University.
MATIOLI, S.R. & R.A. DE BRITO 1995. Obtaining genetic markers by using double-stringency PCR with microsatellites and arbitrary markers. *BioTechniques* 19, 752-755.
MEARNS, D. & I. NEWTON 1994. Turnover and dispersal in a Peregrine falcon (*Falco peregrinus*) population. *Ibis* 126: 347-355.
MILLAR, C.D., I. ANTHONY, D.L LAMBERT, P.M. STAPLETON, C.C. BERGMANN, R.A. BELLAMY & E.C. YOUNG 1994. Patterns of reproductive success determined by DNA fingerprinting in a communally breeding oceanic bird. *Biological Journal of the Linnean Society* 52, 31-48.
MILLAR, C.D., D.M. LAMBERT, S. ANDERSON & J.L. HALVERSON 1996. Molecular sexing of the communually breeding pukeko: an important ecological tool. *Molecular Ecology* 5, 289-293,.
MILLAR, C.D. 1992. Sex-specific restriction fragments and sex ratios revealed by DNA fingerprinting in the Brown Skua. *Journal of Heredity* 83, 350-355.
MINDELL, D.P. (ed.) 1997. *Avian molecular evolution and systematics*. Academic Press San Diego.
MOORE, W.S. & V.R. DEFILIPPIS 1997. The window of taxonomic resolution for phylogenies based on mitochondrial cytochrome b. *In*: Mindell, D.P. (ed.) *Avian molecular evolution ans systematics*. Academic Press San Diego, pp. 83-119.
MUNDY, P.J., D. BUTCHARD, J. LEDGER & S. PIPER 1992. *The vultures of Africa*. Academic Press, London.
NAKAMURA, D., T.R.TIERSCH, M. DOUGLASS & R.W. CHANDLER 1990. Rapid identification of sex in birds by flow cytometry. *Cytogenetics Cell Genetics* 53, 201-205.
NEI, M. 1996. Phylogenetic analysis in molecular evolutionary genetics. *Annu. Rev. Genet.* 30, 371-403.
NEWTON, I. 1979. *Population ecology of raptors*. Berkhamstead.
OGAWA, A., I. SOLOVEI, N. HUTCHISON, Y. SAITOH, J.E. IKEDA, H. MACGREGOR & S. MIZUNO 1997. Molecular characterization and cytological mapping of a non-repetitive DNA sequence region from the w chromosome of chicken and its use as a universal probe for sexing Carinatae birds. *Chromosome Research* 5, 93-101.
OLIPHANT, L.W., I.G. WARKENTIN, N.S. SODHI & P.C. JAMES 1993. Ecology of urban Merlins in Saskatoon. *In: Biology and conservation of small falcons* (M.K. Nicholls & R. Clarke, eds), pp 42-44, Hawk & Owl Trust, London.
QUINN, T.W. 1997. Molecular evolution of the mitochondrial genome. *In*: Mindell, D.P. (ed.) *Avian molecular evolution and systematics*. Academic Press San Diego, pp. 3-28.
RABENOLD, P.P., W.H. PIPER, M.D. DECKER & D.J. MINCHELLA 1993. Polymorphic minisatellite amplified on avian W chromosome. *Genome* 34, 489-493.
RISTOW, D, F. FELDMANN, W. SCHARLAU, C. WINK & M. WINK 1991. Population dynamics of Cory's shearwater (*Calonectris diomedea*) and Eleonora's falcon (*Falco eleonorae*) in the Eastern Mediterranean. *In*: A. Seitz & V. Loeschke (Eds.) *Species conservation: a population biological approach*: 199-212. Basel.
RUNDE, D.E. 1987. Population dynamics, habitat use and movement patterns of the Prairie falcon (*Falco mexicanus*). PhD thesis, University of Wyoming.
SABO, T.J., R. KESSELI, J.L. HALVERSON, I.C.T. NISBET & J.J. HATCH 1987. PCR-based method for sexing roseate terns (*Sterna dougallii*). *Auk* 111, 1023-1027.
SAMBROOK, J., E.F FRITSCH & T. MANIATIS 1989. *Molecular Cloning. A Laboratory Manual*. 2nd ed. CSHL, Cold Spring Harbour, New York.
SEIBOLD, I. 1994. Untersuchungen zur molekularen Phylogenie der Greifvögel anhand von DNA-Sequenzen des mitochondriellen Cytochrom b-Gens. Dissertation University Heidelberg, Hartung-Gorre Verlag, Konstanz.

SEIBOLD, I., A. HELBIG, B.-U. MEYBURG, J. NEGRO & M. WINK 1996. Genetic differentiation and molecular phylogeny of European *Aquila* eagles according to cytochrome b nucleotide sequences. pp. 1-15, *In*: *Eagle studies*. B.-U. Meyburg & R. Chancellor (eds). WWGBP, Berlin, London & Paris.
SEIBOLD, I., A. HELBIG, & M. WINK 1993. Molecular systematics of falcons (family Falconidae). *Naturwissenschaften* 80, 87-90.
SEIBOLD, I., A. HELBIG, B.-U. MEYBURG, J.J. NEGRO & M. WINK 1995. Genetic differentiation and molecular phylogeny of European *Aquila* eagles (Aves: Falconiformes) according to cytochrome b nucleotide sequences. *In: Eagle Studies* (B. Meyburg & R. Chancellor,eds.). WWGBP, Berlin, London & Paris.
SEIBOLD, I. & A.J. HELBIG 1995. Evolutionary history of New and Old World vultures inferred from nucleotide sequences of the mitochondrial cytochrome b gene. *Phil. Transact. Roy. Soc. London* Series B, 350, 163-178.
SEIBOLD, I. & A.J. HELBIG 1996. Phylogenetic relationships of the sea eagles (genus *Haliaeetus*): Reconstructions based on morphology, allozymes and mitochondrial DNA sequences. *J. Zool. Syst. Evol. Res.* 34, 103-112.
SIBLEY, C.G. & B.L. MONROE 1990. *Distribution and taxonomy of birds of the world*. Yale University Press, New Haven.
SWOFFORD, D.L. 1993. PAUP-Phylogenetic analysis using parsimony. Version PAUP.
WETTON, J.H., R.E. CARTER, D.T. PARKIN & D. WALTERS 1987. Demographic study of a wild house sparrow population by DNA fingerprinting. *Nature* 327: 147-149.
WINK, M. 1995. Phylogeny of Old and New World vultures (Aves: Accipitridae and Cathartidae) inferred from nucleotide sequences of the mitochondrial cytochrome b gene. *Z. Naturforsch.*50c, 868-882.
WINK, M. 1998. Application of DNA-markers to study the ecology and evolution of raptors. *In: Holarctic birds of prey*. (R.D. Chancellor, B.-U. Meyburg & J.J. Ferrero. eds), pp. 49-72, ADENEX-WWGBP.
WINK, M., P. HEIDRICH & C. FENTZLOFF 1996. A mtDNA phylogeny of sea eagles (genus *Haliaeetus*) based on nucleotide sequences of the cytochrome b gene. *Biochemical Systematics and Ecology* 24, 783-791.
WINK, M., & P. HEIDRICH 2000. Molecular evolution and systematics of owls (Strigiformes). *In*: C. König, F. Weick, & J.H. Becking (eds) *Owls of the world*. Pica Press.
WINK, M., H. SAUER-GÜRTH, F. MARTINEZ, G. DOVAL, G. BLANCO & O. HATZOFE 1998. Use of GACA-PCR for molecular sexing of Old World vultures (Aves: Accipitridae). *Molecular Ecology* 7, 779-782.
WINK, M. & H. SAUER-GÜRTH (this volume). Advances in the molecular systematics of African raptors.
WINK, M. & I. SEIBOLD 1994. Molecular phylogeny of Mediterranean raptors (Families Accipitridae and Falconidae). *In: Biology and Conservation of Mediterranean raptors*, 1994. (Muntaner, J. & J. Mayol, eds), SEO/BirdLife, Madrid 1996, Monografia 4: 335-344.
WINK, M., I. SEIBOLD, F. LOTFIKHAH & W. BEDNAREK 1998. Molecular systematics of holarctic raptors (Order Falconiformes). *In Holarctic Birds of Prey*. (R.D. Chancellor, B.-U.Meyburg, J.J. Ferrero, eds), ADENEX & WWGBP; pp. 29-48.
WINK, M., H. STAUDTER, Y. BRAGIN, R. PFEFFER & R. KENWARD (in press). The use of DNA fingerprinting to determine annual survival rates in Saker falcons (*Falco cherrug*). *Journal Ornithologie* (1999 in press).
WINK, M. & H. WEHRLE (eds.) 1994. *PCR im medizinischen und biologischen Labor*. GIT-Verlag, Darmstadt.

Prof. Dr. Michael Wink
Universität Heidelberg
Institut für Pharmazeutische Biologie
INF 364, D-69120 Heidelberg
Germany

Preliminary Genetic Analysis of some Western Palaearctic Populations of Bonelli's Eagle, *Hieraaetus fasciatus*.

Pedro Cardia, Bárbara Fráguas, Miguel Pais, Thomas Guillemaud, Luís Palma, M. Leonor Cancela, Nuno Ferrand and Michael Wink

ABSTRACT

Twelve allozyme loci were analysed from Bonelli's Eagles of Portugal; PEPD2, MPI, NP and PX proved to be polymorphic. All the remaining loci were found to be monomorphic. Two alleles were detected for PEPD2, MPI and NP loci and the PX locus exhibited three alleles. DNA sequences of the mitochondrial cytochrome b gene from birds originating from Saudi Arabia to Portugal, show a low degree of haplotypic differentiation. However, two clades comprising birds from the western and eastern Mediterranean are apparent. A single primer PCR analysis revealed 4 groups. DNA analysis shows some phylogeographic differentiation but also an obvious mixing of haplotypes in the Mediterranean region.

INTRODUCTION

Bonelli's Eagle, *Hieraaetus fasciatus*, is a medium-sized eagle whose numbers have strongly declined in west Palearctic, where it is restricted to the Mediterranean zone (Snow & Perrins, 1998). Of the 800 pairs estimated to exist in Western Europe, 10% (75-90 pairs) are found in Portugal (Palma *et. al.*, 1996) and considered to be endangered (Cabral *et al.*, 1990). It is distributed along two main areas of high density, northeast and southwest regions (Figure 1), separated by a diffuse distribution area of low density.

The genetic analysis of natural populations provides information on its genetic variability, their genetic relationships and the gene flow that may exist between them, allowing the development of sound conservation strategies. This work provides a preliminary genetic analysis of some Portuguese Bonelli's Eagle populations and their relationships with other Western Palaeartic populations. Allozyme studies were done in Portugal and DNA studies in Germany.

MATERIAL AND METHODS

Blood samples were collected from the brachial vein of Bonelli's Eagle nestlings, as well as from birds found "freshly" dead, and stored in EDTA buffer for preservation. Samples were divided in two fractions - serum and red cells - and both were stored at –20°C. Samples were obtained from individuals of southwest and northeast populations and from one individual caught in central Portugal.

Allozyme variation

The study of genetic variability at the protein level was based on a set of 12 loci (Table 1). It was performed by means of conventional electrophoretic techniques and isoelectric focusing in carrier ampholyte pH gradients.

Gene frequencies were obtained by direct count, and were used to calculate the average expected heterozygozity for each population. However, it was impossible to perform statistical test on the data because of the small sample size (23 individuals).

Figure 1. Portuguese Bonelli's Eagle populations studied in the present work by allozyme analysis

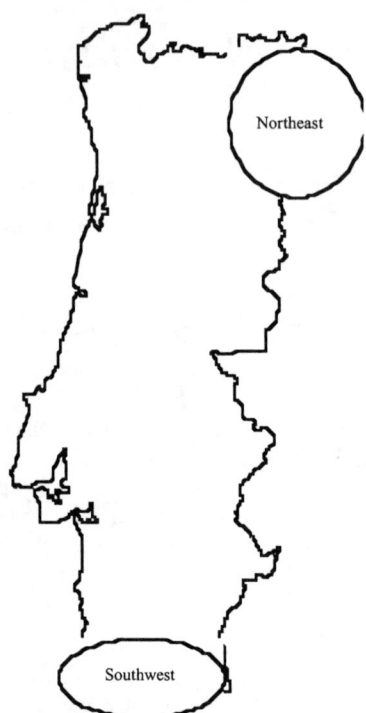

Table 1. Protein markers and separation methods used in this work.

Protein markers	Separation methods	Protein markers	Separation methods
Adenine deaminase (ADA)	CE	Peptidase B (PEPB)	CE
Albumin (ALB)	IEF	Peptidase C (PEPC)	CE
Glucosephosphate isomerase (GPI)	CE	Peptidase D1 (PEPD1)	CE
Isocitrate dehydrogenase (IDH)	CE	Peptidase D2 (PEPD2)	CE
Manosephosphate isomerase (MPI)	CE	Phosphogluconate dehydrogenase (PGD)	CE
Nucleoside phosphorylase (NP)	CE	unknown plasmatic protein (PX)	IEF

Abbreviations: IEF - isoelectric focusing; CE - conventional electrophoresis.

DNA variation

DNA was extracted from blood and feather samples of *H. fasciatus*, that derived from Europe: Spain, Portugal, Corsica and Greece; the Near East: Israel and Saudi Arabia; and North Africa: Tunisia and Morocco.

A PCR was performed with a single PCR primer $(GACA)_4$ which produced several DNA products (usually of nuclear DNA origin) in each individual (details in Wink *et al.*, 1998). In a second set of experiments we have amplified the mitochondrial cytochrome b gene by PCR and have sequenced it (1200 bp) with an ALFexpress DNA sequencer (for methods see Wink & Sauer-Gürth, this volume). The aligned sequences were analysed by the character state method Maximum parsimony (Swofford, 1993).

RESULTS AND DISCUSSION

Allozyme study

Of the 12 loci analysed, PEPD2, MPI, NP and PX proved to be polymorphic. All the remaining loci were found to be monomorphic. Two alleles were detected for PEPD2, MPI and NP loci and the PX locus exhibited three alleles. Allelic frequencies for PEPD2, MPI, NP and PX loci, and observed and expected average heterozygozities data are presented in Figures 2-6, respectively.

Figure 2. PEPD2 allele frequencies in Southwest (SW), Northeast (NE) and total populations

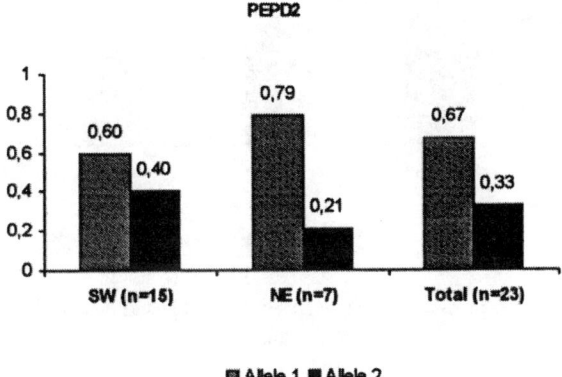

Figure 3. MPI allele frequencies in SW, NE and total populations.

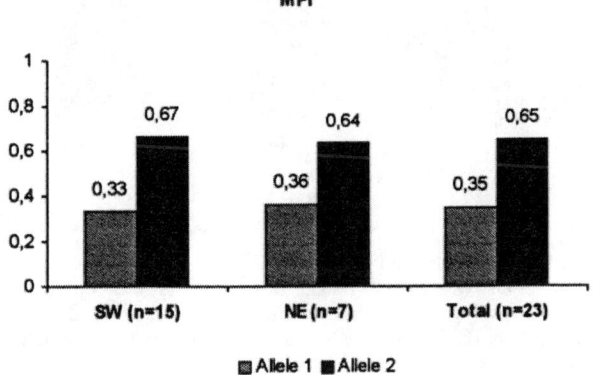

Figure 4. NP allele frequencies in SW, NE and total populations.

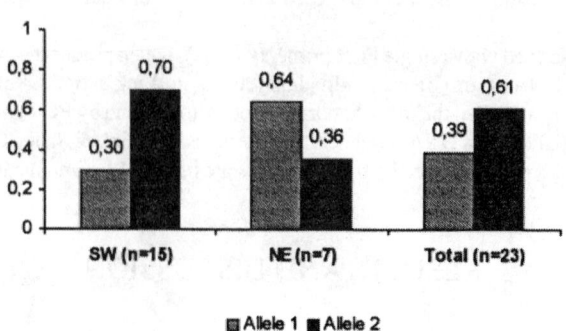

Figure 5. Px allele frequencies in SW, NE and total populations

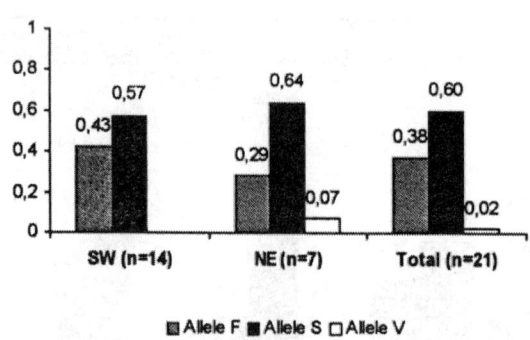

Figure 6. Observed and expected heterozygozities (H_o and H_e) in NE, SW and total populations.

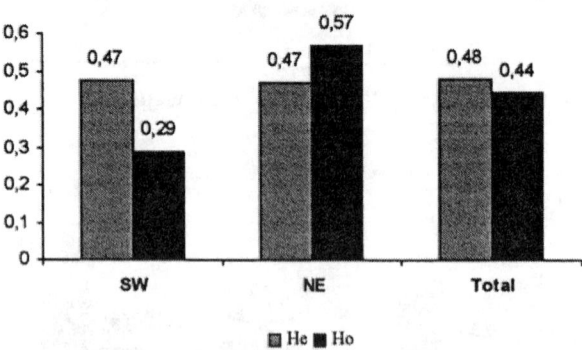

Fifty-three individuals were sampled and screened for the above stated *loci* (Table 1). However, as many of those individuals were closely related (*i. e.* brothers) only one individual per breeding pair was used for the calculation of gene frequencies. This resulted in an effective sample size of only 23 individuals (15 individuals from Southwest, 7 individuals from Northeast and 1 individual from central Portugal).

Gene frequencies at PEPD2, MPI and PX *loci* do not appear to differ significantly among the studied populations. However, the NP *locus* shows an asymmetric distribution of allele frequencies in Southwest and Northeast populations, NP*1 being the commonest in Northeast (64.3%) and NP*2 in Southwest (70%). This might be due to the existence of a North-South gradient in allele frequencies at this locus. Another difference between NE and SW is found when comparing the expected and observed average values of heterozygozity (H_e and H_o, respectively). NE population has a higher H_o than H_e while SW population has a higher H_e than H_o.

An interesting feature is the existence of the variant PX*V at the PX locus, identified in a single individual from the Northeast.

DNA study

DNA sequences of the mitochondrial cytochrome b gene show a low degree (< 1% sequence divergence) of haplotypic differentiation. As can be seen from the resulting MP consensus cladogram (Figure 7), two main clusters are apparent. Cluster 1 which corresponds to some degree to Cluster I in the GACA-analysis (Figure 8), contains birds from both Europe, North Africa and the Near East, whereas Cluster 2 has predominantly birds from the western Mediterranean region (group II-IV in Figure 8).

Figure 7. Phylogeography of *H. fasciatus* inferred from nucleotide sequences of the cytochrome b gene (>1000 nucleotides)
Analysis by Maximum Parsimony; illustration as a 50% consensus cladogram.

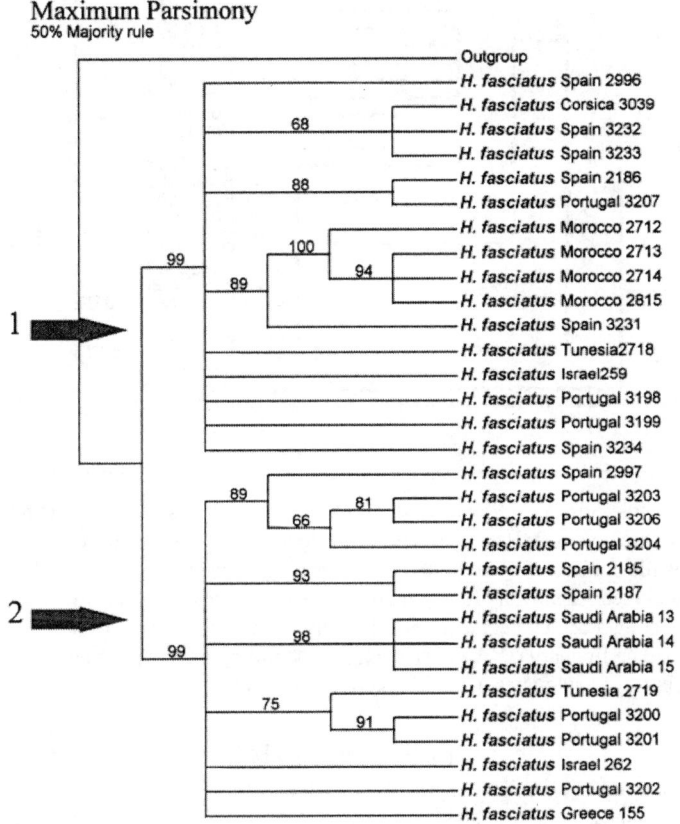

Figure 8. Phylogeographic relationships of *H. fasciatus*.
Dendrogram based on the presence or absence of 4 polymorphic alleles detected by GACA-PCR.

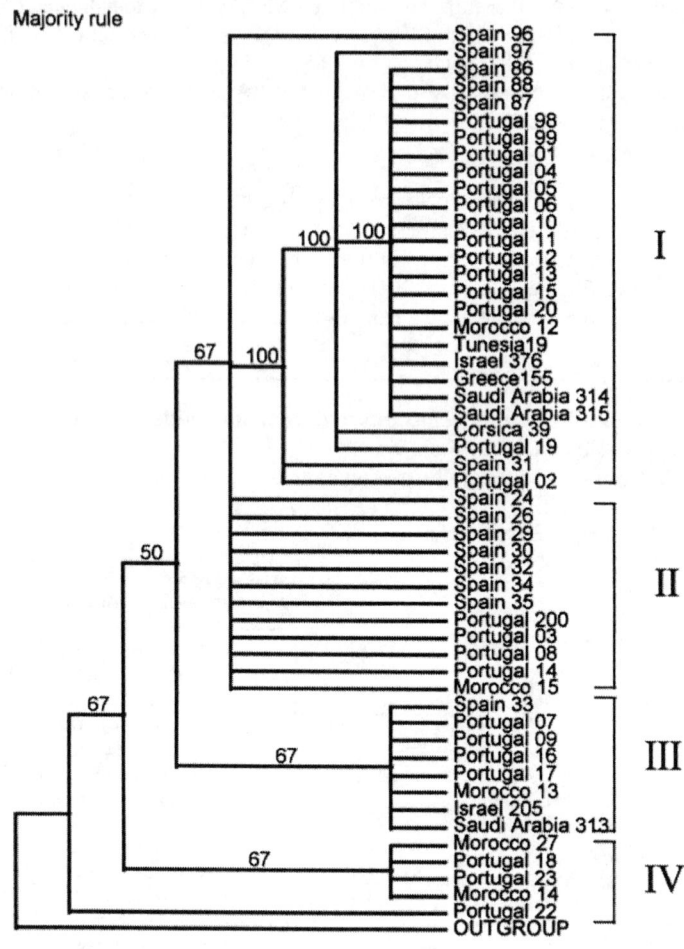

Using the single-primer PCR approach, complex DNA profiles can be generated. Most of the PCR products were invariant. However, 4 polymorphic "alleles" were discovered. A corresponding dendrogram is illustrated in Figure 8, in which 4 main groups can be recognised. Birds from the Eastern Mediterranean are mainly found in group I, but two birds from this origin also turned up in group III, indicating a certain degree of gene flow between east and western Mediterranean.

This first and preliminary DNA analysis suggests some phylogeographic differentiation but also an obvious mixing of haplotypes in the Mediterranean region.

PERSPECTIVES.

Work is currently underway to detect new enzyme polymorphisms, as well as to include new individuals from unsampled Portuguese populations. At the DNA level, microsatellites have already been cloned and will be used to further characterise Bonelli's Eagle populations.

ACKNOWLEDGEMENTS

This work was partially supported by Praxis Project BIA 132. M. W. would like to thank Mrs H. Sauer-Gürth for technical assistance and U. Höfle, C. Pacteau, S. Ostrowski, O. Hatzofe, D. Ristow for providing blood or feather samples

REFERENCES.

PALMA, L., M. C. PAIS & B. FRÁGUAS 1996. Status and distribution of Bonelli's Eagle, *Hieraaetus fasciatus* in Portugal. II Int. Conf. On Raptors. Urbino, Italy.
CABRAL, M. J. M., C. P. MAGALHÃES, M. E. OLIVEIRA & C. ROMÃO 1990. *Livro Vermelho dos Vertebrados de Portugal.* Vol. 1 - Mamíferos, Aves, Répteis e Anfíbios. Serviço Nacional de Parques Reservas e Conservação da Natureza, Lisboa.
SNOW, D. & C.M. PERRINS 1998. *Birds of the Western Paleartic - Concise Edition.* Oxford University Press, London.
SWOFFORD, D.L. 1993. PAUP-Phylogenetic analysis using parsimony. Version PAUP*, 4.0, 1998.
WINK, M. H. SAUER-GÜRTH, F. MARTINEZ, G. DOVAL; G. BLANCO & O. HATZOFE 1998. Use of GACA-PCR for molecular sexing of Old World vultures (Aves: Accipitridae). *Molecular Ecology* 7, 779-782.
WINK, M. & H. SAUER-GÜRTH (this volume). Advances in the molecular systematics of African raptors

Pedro Cardia[1,2], Nuno Ferrand[1,2] Bárbara Fráguas[2]
1-Centro de Estudos de Ciência Animal
Campus Agrário de Vairão
4480 Vila do Conde
Portugal
2-Departamento de Zoologia e Antropologia
Faculdade de Ciências da Universidade do Porto
4050 Porto, Portugal

Miguel Pais
Universidade de Évora
7000 Évora
Portugal

Thomas Guillemaud, Luís Palma and M. Leonor Cancela
Universidade do Algarve-UCTRA
Campus de Gambelas
8000 Faro, Portugal

Michael Wink
Institut für Pharmazeutische Biologie
Universität Heidelberg
Germany.

Phylogenetic relationships between Black Shaheen *Falco peregrinus peregrinator*, Red-naped Shaheen *F. pelegrinoides babylonicus* and Peregrines *F. peregrinus*

M. Wink, H. Döttlinger, M.K. Nicholls, and H. Sauer-Gürth

ABSTRACT

Nucleotide sequences of the mitochondrial cytochrome b gene from the Black Shaheen *F. p. peregrinator* from the Sri Lanka population, the Red-naped Shaheen *Falco pelegrinoides babylonicus* and from several subspecies of the Peregrine *peregrinus, calidus, anatum, minor, macropus* were used to reconstruct underlying phylogenetic relationships. Genetic variation is quite low (< 0.6% sequence divergence) in the *peregrinus/pelegrinoides* group, indicating that both taxa form a young species complex. Systematic consequences would be either to treat all subspecies of *F. peregrinus* and *F. pelegrinoides* as subspecies of *F. peregrinus* or to give species rank to all of them.

INTRODUCTION

The Peregrine Falcon *Falco peregrinus* shows cosmopolitan distribution and 19 geographic subspecies have been distinguished (Cade & Digby, 1987; del Hoyo *et al.*, 1994; Weick 1980). The Barbary Falcon with 2 subspecies *Falco pelegrinoides pelegrinoides* and *F. p. babylonicus* which occurs from North Africa to south and central Asia, has been either treated as a distinct species (Vaurie, 1965; Cramp 1980) or as a subspecies of *F. peregrinus* (del Hoyo *et al.*, 1994; Sibley & Monroe, 1990).

Some of the Peregrine subspecies show very characteristic plumage patterns and morphometric differences. Falconers from India, Pakistan or Arabia distinguished between Peregrine Falcons, Red-naped Shaheen and the Black Shaheen (Ratcliffe, 1871) and their different qualities in falconry. In a cladistic analysis performed on morphological data Kemp and Crowe (1993) showed that *Falco pelegrinoides, Falco peregrinus peregrinator* and *F.p. minor* are morphometrically very close and separated from *Falco peregrinus pealei*.

We have employed sequence data of the mitochondrial cytochrome b gene in order to analyse the phylogenetic relationships in the *peregrinus-pelegrinoides* complex and present first results in this communication.

MATERIAL AND METHODS

DNA was isolated from blood, muscle tissue or feathers and stored in EDTA buffer (Heidrich et al. 1998). The mitochondrial cytochrome b gene was amplified by PCR (ca 1250 base pairs). The PCR product was directly sequenced by "Cycle sequencing" using two internal overlapping fluorescent primers. A Thermo Sequenase labelled primer kit with 7-deaza-dGTP (Amersham LIFE SCIENCE) was employed, according to a protocol provided by the manufacturer. Sequencing was performed on an ALFexpress DNA sequencer, AMV 3.0 (Pharmacia).

Sequences (1250 nt) were aligned and analyzed with PAUP*, employing Maximum Parsimony (MP), Neighbour Joining (NJ), and Maximum Likelihood (MLE) to reconstruct phylogenetic trees. More details on the methodology can be found in Wink (1998, 1999), Heidrich et al., (1998), Leisler et al. (1997).

RESULTS AND DISCUSSION

Phylogenetic relationships were reconstructed using *Falco tinnunculus* as a distant outgroup and *F. rusticolus* as an ingroup; however, other ingroups or outgroups do not change tree topologies. Results are illustrated as NJ and MLE trees (Fig. 1).

Figure 1: Molecular phylogeny of Black and Red-naped Shaheens and allies.

A. NJ phylogram (p distance as distance algorithm)

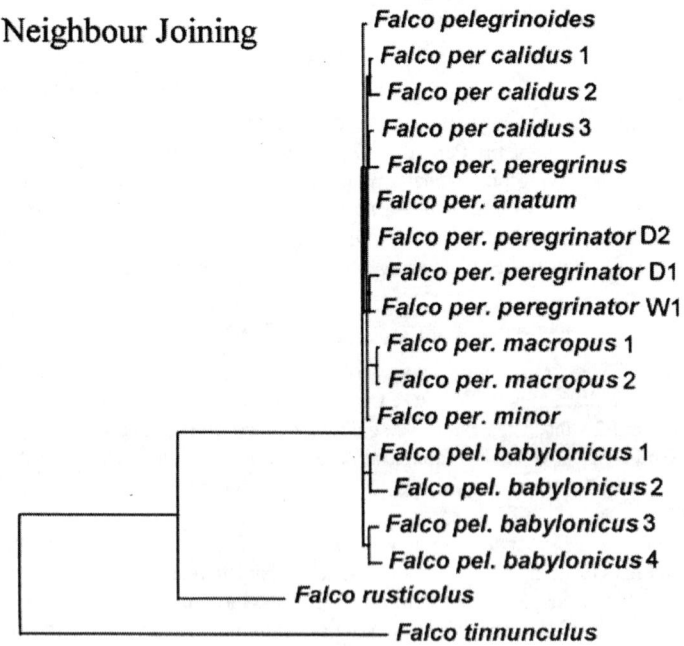

B. MLE settings: Assumed nucleotide frequencies: A=0.301, C=0.334, G=0.122, T=0.243; all sites were assumed to evolve at same rate; transition/transversion ratio was set to 2; score of the best tree found= 2456

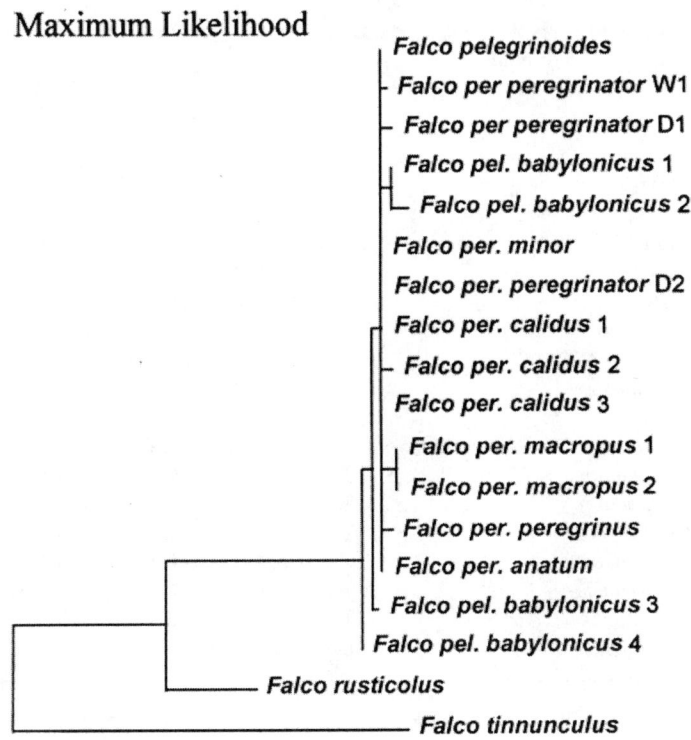

Maximum Likelihood

Branch lengths are proportional to evolutionary distances

In order to study the phylogenetic relationships of the *peregrinus/pelegrinoides* complex in more detail cytochrome b sequences were studied from 16 different specimens representing 6 subspecies of *F. peregrinus* and the 2 described subspecies of *F. pelegrinoides* (Table 1).

Falco peregrinus, and its subspecies *peregrinus*, *calidus*, *anatum*, *minor*, *macropus*, *peregrinator* and *F. pelegrinoides*, *F. pel. babylonicus* are closely related and share common ancestry. They represent

Table 1. Origins of the falcons studied

Taxon	Origin
F. p. pelegrinoides	captivity (D. Schmidl)
F. p. babylonicus	captivity (D. Schmidl)
F. p. peregrinus	Scotland
F. p. anatum	North America
F. p. calidus	Siberia
F. p. minor	South Africa
F. p. peregrinator	Sri Lanka

855

a sister group to the monophyletic Hierofalco complex (Wink & Sauer-Gürth, 1999). Genetic distances (expressed as % pairwise nucleotide substitutions) were below 0.6%, a level typical for intraspecific differentiation in falcons (Table 2).

Table 2. Illustration of variable nucleotide positions in the cytochrome b data set Diagnostic substitutions are printed in bold.

```
                                1 1 1 1 1 1 1
             1 1 3 5 5 5 6 7 8 9 9 1 1 1 1 1 1 2
             0 5 3 6 6 7 3 4 3 6 7 1 6 6 6 7 8 0
Taxon        0 2 3 3 5 2 0 6 0 5 4 0 0 5 8 0 4 5

Falco p.calidus 1        A T A ? ? ? A A A C C C C C T G A G
Falco p.calidus 2        A T A A A C A A A C C C G C T G A G
Falco p.calidus 3        A T A ? ? ? A A A C C C C C T G A G
Falco p.anatum           A T A A A A A A A C C C C C T G A G
Falco p.peregrinus       A T A G A A A G A C C C C C T G A G
Falco p.macropus 1       A T G A A A A A A C C C C C G A G
Falco p.macropus 2       A T G A A A A A A C C C C ? ? ? ? ?
Falco p.minor            A T A A A A A A A C C C C C T G A G
Falco p.peregrinator D1  A T A A A A A A A C C C C S T A A A
Falco p.peregrinator D2  A T A A A A A A A C C C C C T G A G
Falco p.peregrinator W1  A T A A A A A A A C C A C C T G A ?
Falco pelegrinoides      ? ? A A A A A A A C C C C C T G A G
Falco p.babylonicus 1    ? C A A A A G A G C C C C C T G A G
Falco p.babylonicus      A T A A A A G A G C C C C G T G C G
Falco p.babylonicus      C T A A A A A A A T C C C C T G A G
Falco p.babylonicus      C C A A A A A A A T T C C C T G C G
```

F. pelegrinoides hardly differs from *F. p. peregrinus*, *F.p. anatum*, and *F.p. peregrinator* (no character was parsimony informative), indicating the close ancestry between *peregrinus* and *pelegrinoides*. Within the *babylonicus* group, two haplotypes were detected (Fig. 1 A,B). Whether these haplotypes reflect different geographic origins or are the result of distant hybridisations needs to be analyzed in future studies.

Within the *peregrinus* group, unambiguous relationships could not be resolved. *F. p. macropus* from Australia and *F. per. calidus* from Siberia form distinct haplotypes and differ by 0.2 to 0.4% nucleotide substitutions from *F. p. peregrinus* indicating a low level of phylogeographic differentiation. The DNA sequence of Black Shaheen is almost identical with *F. p. peregrinus*, *F. p. calidus*, *F.p. minor* and *F. pelegrinoides* which would confirm findings of a morphometric analysis by Kemp and Crowe (1993).

Distances between *pelegrinoides* and *peregrinus* are below 0.6-0.7% nucleotide substitutions indicating a rather recent divergence of both groups. Distances found in "good" species within the Falconidae and Accipitridae are usually higher than 1.5% (Seibold et al., 1996). As a consequence, both falcon taxa could be either treated as a single species *F. peregrinus* with *pelegrinoides* and *babylonicus* as a subspecies or the other subspecies of *peregrinus* would deserve species rank.

ACKNOWLEDGEMENTS

We would like to thank W. Bednarek, N. Fox, C. Eastham, D. Schmidl, and N. Mooney for providing blood or feather samples, and the Elmar-Schlögl-Stiftung and the Department of Wildlife Conservation Sri Lanka for their support.

REFERENCES

CADE, T., & D.R. DIGBY 1987. *The falcons of the World*. Cornell University Press
CRAMP, S. 1980. *Handbook of the birds of Europe, the Middle East and North America*. Oxford University Press.
DEL HOYO, J., A. ELLIOTT & J. SARGATAL 1994. *Handbook of the birds of the world*. Lynx Edit., Barcelona
HEIDRICH, P., J. AMENGUAL & M. WINK 1998. Phylogenetic relationships in Mediterranean and North Atlantic *Puffinus* Shearwaters (Aves: Procellariidae) based on nucleotide sequences of mtDNA. *Biochemical Systematics and Ecology* 26, 145-170
KEMP, A.C. & T.M. CROWE 1993. A morphometric analysis of Falco species. In: *Biology and Conservation of Small Falcons* pp 223-243. The Hawk and Owl Trust, London.
LEISLER, B., P. HEIDRICH, K. SCHULZE-HAGEN & M. WINK 1997. Taxonomy and phylogeny of reed warblers (genus *Acrocephalus*) based mtDNA sequences and morphology. *Jounal für Ornithologie* 138, 469-496
RADCLIFFE, D.E. 1871. *Falconry- Notes on the Falconidae used in India in falconry*. Frampton, Reprint 1971
SEIBOLD, I., A.J. HELBIG, B. -U. MEYBURG, J. NEGRO & M. WINK 1996. Genetic differentiation and molecular phylogeny of European *Aquila* eagles according to cytochrome b nucleotide sequences. pp. 1-15, In: *Eagle studies* B.-U. Meyburg & R. Chancellor (eds.). WWGBP, Berlin, London & Paris
SIBLEY, C.G. & B.L.MONROE 1990. *Distribution and taxonomy of birds of the world*. Yale University Press, New Haven
VAURIE, C. 1965. *The birds of the palaearctic fauna. Nonpasseriformes*. Witherby, London
WEICK, F. 1980. *Die Greifvögel der Welt*. Parey, Hamburg
WINK, M. 1998. Application of DNA-Markers to Study the Ecology and Evolution of Raptors. In *Holarctic Birds of Prey*. R.D. Chancellor, J.J. Ferrero, B.-U.Meyburg, (eds), ADENEX & WWGBP. pp 49-71.
WINK, M. (this volume). Advances in DNA studies of diurnal and nocturnal raptors.
WINK, M., & H. SAUER-GÜRTH (this volume). Advances in the molecular systematics of African raptors.

Prof. Dr. Michael Wink, Hedi Sauer-Gürth
Universität Heidelberg
Institut für Pharmazeutische Biologie
INF 364, D-69120 Heidelberg
Germany

Dipl.Ing. Hermann Döttlinger, Dr Mike K. Nicholls
Ecology Research Group
Canterbury Christ Church College
North Holmes Road
Canterbury, Kent
U.K.

Chancellor, R. D. & B.-U. Meyburg eds. 2000
Raptors at Risk
WWGBP / Hancock House

The application of DNA technology to enforce Raptor Conservation Legislation within Great Britain

Nick P. Williams and Justin A. Evans

ABSTRACT

Raptor conservation within Great Britain is underpinned by the primary and secondary legislative controls introduced under the Wildlife and Countryside Act 1981. If kept in captivity, certain bird species are required to be ringed and registered with the Department of the Environment, Transport and the Regions. DNA-based research on certain birds of prey, sponsored by the Department between 1987-1994, led to the development of a range of genetic markers enabling individual raptors to be identified and familial relationships to be established.

In 1995, the Department's Wildlife Inspectorate introduced a programme of blood sampling inspections to obtain material for DNA profiling, which utilised these genetic markers to verify captive breeding claims made by registered keepers of Goshawks *Accipiter gentilis* and Peregrine Falcons *Falco peregrinus*. This paper describes the approach adopted for this innovative method of enforcing raptor conservation legislation, examines the constraints, results and benefits of the inspection programme and considers the implications for raptor keepers and enforcement officers alike.

BACKGROUND AND LEGISLATIVE FRAMEWORK

In 1979, Member States of the European Union (EU) negotiated the Council Directive on the Conservation of Wild Birds (1979/409/EEC) as a joint formal commitment to maintain European wild bird populations at favourable conservation status. In common with other EU Directives, each Member State is required to implement the 'Birds' Directive' by means of national legislation. Within Great Britain, the Government satisfied this obligation with the introduction of the Wildlife and Countryside Act (WCA) 1981. Part I of this statute deals solely with the protection and conservation of wild birds.

Under section 1 of the WCA 1981, all wild birds, their nests and their eggs are protected from capture, killing, destruction, etc. However, the level of this protection differs between species. For example, most species are protected at all times but game birds may be shot for sport during certain times of the year, and the so-called 'pest' species may be killed throughout the year, providing certain conditions are met.

In addition to this primary protection, section 7 of the WCA 1981 provides a 'secondary' level of regulation and states that: *'If any person keeps or has in his possession or under his control any bird included in Schedule 4 which has not been registered and ringed or marked in accordance with regulations made by the Secretary of State, he shall be guilty of a an offence'*. The species listed on Schedule 4 originally included all the diurnal birds of prey (worldwide), plus about 60 native non-raptor species considered to be rare breeding birds in Great Britain.

Additionally, section 7 empowers any person authorised in writing by the Secretary of State to enter and inspect any premises where birds included in Schedule 4 are kept. The Wildlife Inspectorate of the Department of the Environment, Transport and the Regions (DETR), formerly the Department of the Environment (DOE), discharges these inspection responsibilities.

This Inspectorate is managed by a Chief Wildlife Inspector (the first author), with support from one full-time Wildlife Inspector (the second author) and two administrative staff. It consists of a panel of *c.*70 part-time fee-paid home-based consultants who possess specialist expertise in the identification of species, predominantly birds. Annually, Wildlife Inspectors undertake a total of around 800 visits (both unannounced and by appointment) to the premises of keepers of registered birds and importers/exporters/traders of endangered species.

Section 19 of the WCA 1981 deals with enforcement. It identifies the Police as the statutory enforcement authority for offences created by Part I of the WCA 1981, including those relating to sections 1 and 7.

BIRD REGISTRATION SCHEME

Established in 1982, the Bird Registration Scheme for Great Britain is administered by the Global Wildlife Division of the DETR, from offices in the city of Bristol. It is a computer-based registration system, operated on similar lines to the scheme administered by the Driver and Vehicle Licencing Agency for motor vehicles. But whereas cars are identified by registration plates, individual birds are fitted with a uniquely-numbered leg-rings issued by the DETR.

In 1993, more than a decade after its introduction, the Bird Registration Scheme was examined as part of the DETR Review of Wildlife Sales and Related Controls. At that time, there were more than 16,000 registered birds (Hansard 1994a). This figure had increased dramatically from an initial estimate of 1,500 birds, for which the scheme had been originally designed. The review team concluded that the scheme had played a valuable role in assisting the maintenance and recovery of wild populations of certain native birds, particularly Britain's three commonest raptors (Common Buzzard *Buteo buteo*, Kestrel *Falco tinnunculus* and Sparrowhawk *Accipiter nisus*). Further, the costs involved in maintaining these secondary controls could not be justified for those species whose wild populations were no longer threatened. Accordingly, the team recommended that the scope of the existing scheme should be reduced by removing the requirement to register a significant number of species of birds, including the three commonest raptors and all non-native birds of prey, except 24 species considered to be threatened globally.

The team also recognised that there was evidence to support claims that an unknown number of birds and their eggs were being taken from the wild illegally, and were then being 'laundered' into the Bird Registration Scheme by unscrupulous keepers making false claims of captive breeding by birds in their care. To combat these activities, it recommended that the resources released by de-registration and other internal re-organisational changes be re-deployed to increase the enforcement of the controls. Moreover, that such efforts should be targeted particularly at those species considered to be most endangered or most at risk from illegal exploitation. One of the main ways proposed to achieve this increased level of enforcement was to expand the use of DNA testing techniques to verify captive breeding claims made by raptor keepers (Hansard 1994b).

Ultimately, the Police are the statutory authority tasked with the investigation and enforcement of offences created by Part I of the WCA 1981. Nevertheless, the DETR closely monitors the Bird Registration Scheme by combining a comprehensive range of administrative checks with programmes of inspections carried out by members of the Wildlife Inspectorate.

DNA PROFILING IN BIRDS OF PREY

Between 1986 and 1994, the DOE sponsored research at the University of Nottingham to investigate the genetic variation in birds of prey using DNA profiling techniques. Originally, the objective was to ascertain whether it would be possible to identify familial relationships for certain key species, namely Peregrine Falcon, *Falco peregrinus*, Merlin *Falco columbarius,* Goshawk *Accipiter gentilis* and Golden Eagle *Aquila chrysaetos*. These species were chosen because they were considered to be in particular demand by raptor keepers, and there was evidence to suggest that some of the young birds being claimed as captive-bred were in fact being illegally taken from wild nests.

Using the Jeffreys' 33.6 multilocus probe (Jeffreys 1985a & 1985b), the researchers confirmed that variability in the DNA of these, and other raptor species, existed. Moreover, they showed that DNA fingerprinting could be used for both individual recognition and parentage studies (Parkin 1987). Later research focussed on isolating single locus probes from minisatellite sequences, which occur naturally in the chromosomes of birds of prey, but which had been introduced into bacteria in order to mass produce them by means of artificial viral chromosomes known as charomids. Twelve probes were found to detect a single locus in at least one of the four target species. In addition, several of these probes were found to be equally informative when used on closely related species (e.g. other species within the genus *Falco*) (Wetton & Parkin 1994). Copies of these probes have since been transferred by the DETR to the Laboratory of the Government Chemist at Teddington in west London and are now freely available to any laboratory for use in law enforcement.

BLOOD SAMPLING INSPECTIONS FOR DNA TESTING

In early 1995, as a result of a Ministerial commitment (Hansard 1994b), the authors began work to plan and implement the introduction of DNA technology to check the captive breeding claims made by keepers of registered birds. A total budget of £8,000 was allocated for the task. This amount was calculated to meet all the costs associated with collecting the blood samples (including the fees and travelling expenses for the veterinary surgeons and Wildlife Inspectors) and the DNA analysis costs levied by the laboratory.

Constraints

A programme of blood sampling inspections was planned which would satisfy the following constraints:
- although DETR Wildlife Inspectors are granted certain powers of entry to premises where registrable birds are kept, the WCA 1981 contains no specific power to take blood samples. Therefore, no unannounced inspections could be undertaken because it would be necessary to obtain the advance co-operation of the registered keeper of each bird to be tested;
- in addition to the co-operation of the individual keepers, it was considered essential to win the support of the Hawk Board. (A national body elected to represent the views of falconers and keepers of diurnal birds of prey and owls);
- in Great Britain, blood sampling is classed as an invasive veterinary procedure by the Veterinary Surgeons Act 1966, and therefore it would be necessary to commission qualified vets to obtain each of the samples;
- although the inspection programme was being devised as a means of monitoring the Bird Registration Scheme, not as part of a forensic investigation, it was considered essential that the samples be collected, stored, transported and analysed using protocols which would meet the rigorous standards required for forensic use. Thus, if potential offences were discovered, the results could be passed to the Police for further investigation and, if necessary, be presented as evidence in court;
- because the success of the programme relied heavily on the co-operation of the registered keepers, in most cases it would be necessary to collect the samples between late September and early February to avoid disturbing birds unnecessarily by catching them up during periods when they would be breeding or moulting.

Benefits

It became clear that, provided the inspection programme was conducted properly, with due regard to the above constraints and in particular the welfare of the birds themselves, the following benefits could be achieved for those concerned:
- by co-operating with the DETR, legitimate raptor breeders with selected birds in their care could have them DNA profiled free of charge, and would be provided with a written report confirming the results. Broadcasting the fact that their birds had proven to be captive-bred was considered likely to publicly enhance their credibility within the raptor-keeping fraternity, and might also enable them to sell future captive-bred stock more quickly and at a higher market price;
- targeting the sampling effort in favour of family groups of Goshawks would increase the inadequate sample size for this species which had been previously available to the researchers at Nottingham University. This would provide an opportunity to further validate the single locus probes which had been isolated during previous research sponsored by the DETR (Wetton & Parkin 1994).
- the introduction of blood sampling inspections for DNA testing was considered likely to act as a major deterrent against unscrupulous individuals who might otherwise have attempted to launder illegally taken wild birds into the Bird Registration Scheme. Keepers would be unable to predict whether any of the birds in their care would be selected by the DETR for profiling. Moreover, failure to co-operate when selected would immediately arouse suspicion which could lead to details being passed to the Police for further investigation.

For the Phase I programme of blood sampling inspections, it was decided to concentrate on family groups of two species; Peregrine Falcons and Goshawks. These species are highly prized by falconers and austringers alike. Moreover, previous Police action which had utilised DNA technology in this field of wildlife law enforcement revealed that 22% of the combined number of Peregrine Falcons and Goshawks registered with the DOE as captive-bred in 1993 had been taken illegally from wild nests (Guy Shorrock, Royal Society for the Protection of Birds (RSPB), pers.comm.). To avoid the possibility of reducing the level of the deterrent effect exerted by the introduction of these inspections, the decision to restrict testing to these two species was not disclosed by the authors to anyone else.

Phase I inspections objectives

In the light of the above, the objectives of this first programme of blood sampling inspections were:
- to undertake a programme of approximately 20 inspections to collect blood samples from a total of $c.70$ birds ($c.40$ Goshawks and $c.30$ Peregrine Falcons), consisting of $c.20$ family groups;
- to actively negotiate to seek the full co-operation of each and every keeper of the birds selected for blood testing;
- to formulate and adopt procedures for the collection, storage, transportation and analysis of the blood samples which would, if required, meet the demanding standards necessary for forensic use;
- to keep total expenditure within a budget of £8,000 and to complete the whole exercise by the end of the 1995/96 financial year (i.e. 4 April 1996);
- on completion of the inspection programme, to provide written reports of the DNA profiling results to each keeper who had participated and to seek to widely publicise the results.

Preparatory work

On 10 April 1995, the first author wrote to each and every keeper of the $c.$ 4,000 birds registered in captivity in Great Britain at that time, advising them of the Department's intention to introduce a programme of blood sampling inspections for DNA testing to verify captive breeding claims. Making this announcement at the beginning of the breeding season was considered to possess the potential to deter some individuals who might otherwise have chosen to make false captive breeding claims. Consequently, this reduction in demand for illegally taken stock should decrease the number of nests of wild raptors plundered by robbers.

Following a period of intensive research and investigation, involving consultations with personnel at the Forensic Science Service (FSS), selected veterinary surgeons who specialised in avian medicine, and medical equipment suppliers, a unique blood sampling kit was devised and produced for the task. Each kit contained all the equipment that would be required by the veterinary surgeon to obtain a blood sample from a single bird, as follows:

> pre-injection swab; 2 x disposable needles (23G x 25mm long); 2 x disposable needles (25G x 16mm long); 2 x 2ml disposable syringes; 2 x 2.5ml EDTA plastic sealable blood sample tubes; 2 x cotton buds in 'minigrip' plastic bag; 1 pair of latex gloves; and 1 x 'tamper-proof' plastic evidence bag (140mm x 215mm).

Detailed letters were drafted to provide comprehensive advice and guidance for each registered keeper and their chosen veterinary surgeon. In addition, an instruction letter and report form was designed, for use by the Wildlife Inspector who was selected to witness each sampling procedure. Further, a three-sheet carbonised declaration form was specially produced to enable the veterinary surgeon to formally record details of each bird sampled and the identification details marked on each corresponding EDTA tube.

The DETR commissioned the FSS to undertake a two-day Quality Assurance audit of the selected DNA analysis laboratory, namely, the Department of Genetics at the University of Nottingham. Overall the report was favourable, and it acknowledged the high standard of expertise of the two main scientists involved. However, a number of recommendations emerged from the audit concerning the security arrangements in place at the laboratory, and some relatively minor criticisms of their documentation procedures. Accordingly, these recommendations were implemented by the University before any of the blood sampling inspections were carried out.

Prolonged negotiations with colleagues in the Home Office and within the DETR's Legal Directorate, proved necessary to secure approval that the planned inspection programme could be undertaken without the need to follow the lengthy licencing procedures required under the Animals (Scientific Procedures) Act 1986.

The full support of the Hawk Board was secured by consulting key members throughout the planning process, augmented by regular attendance at their quarterly meetings in order to present outline proposals for the inspection programme, in advance of any visits taking place.

Eventually, when the extensive preparatory work had been completed and finalised, a single pilot inspection was carried out by the second author to confirm that the proposed procedures were practical, and that they would operate efficiently.

Additionally, at the Department's annual training seminar for Wildlife Inspectors held in November 1995, this new type of inspection was introduced to the panel of consultant Inspectors by means of two workshop sessions. This strategy provided two major benefits: a) it allowed for the direct dissemination of detailed practical advice and guidance to the people who would be responsible for ensuring that the inspection procedures were correctly followed; and, b) it provided an opportunity for initial feedback to be obtained from the Inspectors themselves. As a result of these workshops, minor modifications were incorporated into the final inspection procedures.

APPROACH

Analysis of the DETR's comprehensive computer records dating back to 1987 allowed appropriate family groups of the two target species to be selected. It was considered important to inspect the breeders of the two key species because these were the individuals who, as part of the standard registration process, had been required to make written and signed declarations concerning the origins of their captive-bred stock. In order to optimise the number of inspections required to meet the stated objectives, the decision was taken to bias the selection of keepers towards those who were in possession of at least two or three related birds at the time the inspections were allocated.

In December 1995, letters were despatched to the keepers of the targeted birds seeking their co-operation and enclosing another letter containing instructions for their veterinary surgeon. To minimise inconvenience to keepers, the latter letter requested that the Department be invoiced directly for the fees incurred by the vet. Within 14 days, each keeper was contacted by telephone to arrange an appropriate appointment for a Wildlife Inspector to visit their premises to witness the blood sampling procedure. Keepers were expected to make contact with their chosen veterinary surgeon to check that they were content to undertake the necessary procedures, and to confirm their availability at the appropriate date and time. Once these arrangements had been agreed, a suitably qualified Wildlife Inspector was selected by the DETR. Telephone contact was made to confirm their availability to carry out the inspection. If unavailable, another Inspector was chosen. Next, a written inspection request, including detailed instructions and an appropriate number of sampling kits, was despatched to the Wildlife Inspector.

On the chosen day, the Inspector was required to attend the premises at the agreed time to deliver the sampling kits to the veterinary surgeon and to witness the blood being taken from each target bird. Keepers were asked to be wholly responsible for the catching and handling of the birds because Wildlife Inspectors have no statutory authority to undertake these procedures. To minimise the stress inflicted upon the birds, particularly those housed in aviaries (as opposed to falconry-trained birds kept tethered to blocks or bow perches), most keepers chose to catch them up immediately prior to the sampling procedure and then replace them in their aviaries straightaway afterwards. However, a small number of keepers preferred to catch the birds prior to the appointment and retain them in boxes, thus reducing the pressure on themselves of catching birds whilst the vet and Inspector were waiting (and watching too!).

In the guidance notes, the Department recommended that 1ml of blood be taken from the brachial vein at an appropriate location on the ventral surface of the bird's wing. The vet could then divide the sample into equal parts by carefully injecting the blood into two separate EDTA tubes. One tube was to be sent to the laboratory for the DNA analysis, and the other retained and stored by the registered keeper of the bird. Should the analysis results lead to a dispute between the keeper and the DETR, the stored sample could be made available for additional independent DNA analysis.

The Wildlife Inspector was required to label each specimen tube with the inspection reference number, a sample reference number and a consecutive exhibit number, the latter being unique to the veterinary surgeon involved. To ensure confidentiality for the keeper and the anonymity of the specimen tube received by the laboratory, no leg-ring numbers or personal identification information relating to the keeper were included on the label.

When the labelling had been completed, and the accuracy of the details confirmed with both the keeper and the vet, the Inspector was required to write his/her initials and the date on each EDTA tube. One tube of blood relating to each of the birds was then selected by the keeper for retention. The remaining tubes were wrapped in cotton wool and sealed inside in the special 'tamper-proof' plastic evidence bag by the Inspector. This bag was packed with additional padding, placed in a cardboard box and the whole package was then sealed inside a standard Royal Mail Registered Delivery envelope. This whole procedure was witnessed by the keeper who was then invited to sign across the final seal.

One sheet, of the special three-sheet carbonised sampling declaration form signed by the vet, was passed to the keeper, one copy was retained by the vet and the top copy was kept by the Inspector for return to the Department. On leaving the premises, the Inspector was required to go immediately to a Post Office and to send the package to the laboratory, not forgetting to obtain a 'Certificate of Posting' receipt for continuity of evidence purposes. Finally, an inspection report form was completed by the Inspector and submitted to the Department, attaching the vet's declaration form and the Certificate of Posting.

RESULTS

The extensive background research and preparatory work proved to have been a worthwhile use of time and resources because the procedures adopted worked remarkably well. No major or insurmountable problems were encountered. Minor difficulties included, for example, two of the keepers' local veterinary surgeons declining to participate because they did not feel confident or experienced enough to take blood samples from raptors. However, in both cases other vets were found who willingly carried out the task.

Despite concerns expressed by a few keepers at the outset of the inspection programme, no birds sustained injuries or died as a result of the blood sampling inspections. However, towards the end of the sampling period, two keepers who were originally selected declined to participate because they were concerned that, in the event of injury or death occurring to a bird as a direct result of the blood sampling procedure, the Department was not prepared to accept liability and to pay appropriate compensation. It was pointed out that, by agreeing to co-operate with the DETR, keepers were effectively forfeiting their ability to claim recompense should something go wrong. The Hawk Board supported this interpretation as sound and reasonable, a view which was subsequently shared by DETR's Legal Directorate.

Accordingly, the authors undertook further negotiations within the Department and eventually obtained Ministerial agreement to the effect that, *'providing certain reasonable conditions have been met by keepers, the DOE will accept financial liability in the unlikely event of injury or death occurring to a bird, where it can be shown to have been caused as a direct result of a blood sampling inspection commissioned by the Wildlife Inspectorate'*. This policy was not finalised until mid June 1996, after the completion of the 1995/96 Phase I inspection programme. However, once the liability issue had been addressed, both keepers agreed to participate in Phase II of the blood sampling inspection programme which was scheduled to begin in November 1996.

The inspection programme was completed within the agreed deadline and the final total expenditure was £8,032. The results are summarised below:

Table 1. Results of the DETR's 1995/96 programme of blood sampling inspections

BIRDS/INSPECTIONS	Goshawk	Peregrine Falcon	Total
Number of birds sampled	32	35	67
(ad=adults; o/s=offspring)	(ad=18; o/s=14)	(ad=18; o/s=17)	(ad=36; o/s=31)
Number of family groups	10	9	19
Number of keepers inspected	9	8	17
Number of inspections	9	8	17

The final report received from the scientists at Nottingham University showed that the Peregrine Falcon samples were subjected to DNA profiling analysis using a battery of eight single locus probes (four of these probes had originally been isolated from the DNA of Peregrine Falcons, two from Merlin DNA and one from Kestrel DNA). The Goshawk samples were profiled with a series of five single locus probes (four originally derived from Red Kite *Milvus milvus* DNA and one from Golden Eagle DNA). No mutations or incompatibilities were observed. Therefore, these results effectively verified the captive breeding claims made by each registered keeper and confirmed that all those offspring tested had been bred in captivity.

In addition to writing to each of the registered keepers who had participated to notify them of the results and to thank them for their co-operation, a DETR Press Release was issued in which Environment Minister James Clappison was quoted as saying: '...*These inspections provide two major benefits: first, they enable genuine bird keepers to substantiate their captive breeding claims unequivocally; and secondly, I believe they act as a major deterrent against the small number of unscrupulous keepers who may otherwise attempt to launder illegally taken wild birds into captivity. The success of this programme of inspections highlights the value of DNA testing techniques...*' (DOE 1996).

DISCUSSION

Due to the existing situation where the Department lacks the appropriate powers to undertake unannounced blood sampling inspections, it is perhaps not surprising that all the offspring proved to have been bred in captivity. The DETR is currently exploring the possibility of amending the legislation to rectify this perceived weakness in the WCA 1981.

Although it is impossible to quantify the actual impact that this programme of inspections exerted upon those keepers who might otherwise have been tempted to make false breeding claims, the Department received widespread public support from the Police; RSPB; Royal Society for the Prevention of Cruelty to Animals (RSPCA); the Hawk Board; and the vast majority of raptor keepers. Nonetheless, these inspections should be viewed as part of a two-pronged strategy, which also includes the application of DNA technology during intelligence-led investigations undertaken by the Police.

The numbers of Peregrine Falcons and Goshawks claimed to have been captive-bred and registered with the DETR annually since 1990 are detailed in Table 2.

Table 2: Numbers of captive-bred raptors registered with the DETR

SPECIES/YEAR	1990	1991	1992	1993	1994	1995	1996
Peregrine Falcon[1]	269	319	290	360	286	318	436
Goshawk	79	155	141	154	118	141	140
Total	**348**	**474**	**431**	**514**	**404**	**459**	**576**

Notes:[1] The totals for this species include Peregrine Falcon hybrids.

In Great Britain, DNA technology was first employed as a forensic tool as part of a wildlife law enforcement investigation to refute a raptor keeper's claims, relating to four Goshawks he alleged had been bred in captivity in 1991. Although the court case was not heard until October 1992, the Police investigation generated an immense amount of publicity which began soon after the search warrant was executed in June 1991. It can be argued that the deterrent effect generated by the high profile use of DNA technology in this case was responsible for a significant proportion of the $c.10\%$ drop in production of both Peregrine Falcon and Goshawks in 1992, compared with the 1991 breeding season. However, other factors may have contributed to this decline (e.g. weather conditions, changes in the number of breeding pairs, etc.)

In October 1992, captive-bred Goshawks were being freely advertised for sale in specialist national newspapers and magazines for between £650 and £850 each. So although that initial court case resulted in the falconer being successfully convicted, the £200 penalty imposed was clearly derisory. In effect, the message which circulated within the raptor-keeping fraternity following this conviction was that a potential offender would simply plan to take an extra bird from the wild to 'budget' for the possibility of being caught and prosecuted.

During 1993 and early 1994, with encouragement and practical assistance provided by the DETR and RSPB, the Police undertook a series of major investigations involving several raptor keepers who had claimed to have been captive breeding Peregrine Falcons and Goshawks. Blood samples were taken from more than 100 birds and DNA analysis was used to test each keeper's declarations. The results showed that 36 Peregrine Falcons (10% of the total 'captive-bred' young registered with the Department in 1993) and 18 Goshawks (almost 12% of those claimed as captive-bred in 1993) were not related to their alleged parents (Guy Shorrock, RSPB, pers.comm). It seems reasonable, therefore, to conclude that these high profile Police operations were largely responsible for the significant reduction in the number of 'captive-bred' birds of these two species registered with the DETR in 1994. Table 2 shows that, compared with the 1993 figures, the number of 'captive-bred' Goshawks registered in 1994 fell by more than 23%, and those of Peregrine Falcons fell by more than 20% (a combined total of more than 21%).

Seven men were subsequently prosecuted under the WCA in 1981, each case resulting in a conviction. The fines ranged from £522, imposed against a keeper who was shown to be in possession of a single illegal Goshawk, to £10,500 (reduced to £2,000 on appeal), exacted upon a breeder who was shown to be in illegal possession of 13 Goshawks and 2 Peregrine Falcons.

Two further cases, which followed on from these investigations and involved large-scale independent breeder/dealers of Peregrine Falcons, were heard at Crown Courts in Northumberland and Essex during May 1995 and September 1995, respectively. Rather than prosecute these two individuals for offences under the WCA 1981 (which does not currently provide for the imposition of custodial sentences), the Crown Prosecution Service chose to charge the men for being in possession of illegally-acquired Peregrine Falcons for the purpose of sale, under Regulations 3 and 8 of the Control of Trade in Endangered Species (Enforcement) Regulations 1985 (Statutory Instrument1985/ 1155). These Regulations implemented the original European CITES Regulation (EEC/3626/82). Both defendants were found guilty and imprisoned, one for 18 months and the other for 4 months. In addition, a total of 35 Peregrine Falcons were subject to forfeiture.

In summary, the utilisation of modern DNA technology via programmes of blood sampling inspections implemented by the DETR, combined with carefully targeted intelligence-led Police investigations, is considered to act as a powerful deterrent against potential offenders who might otherwise attempt to launder illegally-obtained birds into the captive raptor population in Great Britain. The application of such technology has also proved to be an effective means of enforcing the controls imposed by the Bird Registration Scheme, for the benefit of wild raptor populations. Clearly, there is real potential for similar techniques to be adopted within conservation strategies for the benefit of other threatened taxa (e.g. psittacines).

REFERENCES

DEPARTMENT OF THE ENVIRONMENT 1996. *DNA inspections help protect wild bird populations.* DOE News Release 340:30 July 1996.
HANSARD 1994a. *Wildlife Sales Controls.* Written answer to a question by John Carlisle MP to the Secretary of State for the Environment: 21 February 1994.
HANSARD 1994b. *Birds of Prey.* Written answer to a question by Tony Banks MP to the Secretary of State for the Environment: 25 April 1995.
JEFFREYS, A.J. 1985a. *Hypervariable 'minisatellite' regions in human DNA. Nature* 316: 76-79.
JEFFREYS, A.J. 1985b. *Individual-specific 'fingerprints' of human DNA. Nature* 316: 818-819.
PARKIN, D.T. 1987. *Genetic variation in birds of prey: Phase II.* Unpublished internal report to the Department of the Environment. by the University of Nottingham, Department of Genetics: Nottingham.
WETTON, J.H. & D.T. PARKIN 1987. *Genetic variation in birds of prey: Phase IV.* Research report to the Department of the Environment by the University of Nottingham, Department of Genetics: Nottingham.

Nick P. Williams
Department of the Environment
Transport and the Regions
Wildlife Inspectorate
Room 8/08, Tollgate House
Bristol, BS2 9DJ
United Kingdom

CITES refers to the Convention on International Trade in Endangered Species of Wild Fauna and Flora.

Part 13

General Studies

Little Owl *Athene noctua*

Convener:
R.D. Chancellor

Contaminants and Wintering Areas of Peregrine Falcons, *Falco peregrinus*, from the Kola Peninsula, Russia

Charles J. Henny, William S. Seegar, Michael A. Yates, Thomas L. Maechtle, Sergei A. Ganusevich, and Mark R. Fuller

ABSTRACT

Eggs collected from the small bog-associated nesting population of migratory Peregrine Falcons, *Falco peregrinus*, along the Ponoy River depression (67°N, 37°E) of the Kola Peninsula contained relatively low concentrations of p,p'-DDE (DDE) in 1991. Polychlorinated biphenyls (PCBs) were higher than DDE, comparable to the contaminant profile shown by peregrine populations from Fennoscandia, and were higher than those in Alaska eggs. Relatively high concentrations of polychlorinated dibenzo-p-dioxins and dibenzofurans also were found in several eggs. The source(s) of these industrial contaminants and the wintering grounds of the population were unknown. In fact, the peregrine subspecies nesting along the Ponoy River was not known for certain. In the summer of 1994, satellite telemetry equipment was attached to four adult nesting females, and standard morphometric measurements were recorded. Knowledge of the wintering grounds of the population could provide useful information for evaluating the source of the industrial contaminants and perhaps, together with measurements, for determining the appropriate subspecies. These peregrines wintered in western Europe (The Netherlands, France and Spain) with *F. p. peregrinus* from Fennoscandia and probably belong to the nominate subspecies. Industrialized western Europe is the probable source of most of the organic contaminants found in their eggs.

INTRODUCTION

Galushin (1977) noted a rapid and continuous decline in numbers of peregrines in the Soviet Union, although chemical residue levels were unavailable for pesticides or other contaminants in eggs or carcasses. Peakall and Kiff (1979) measured eggshells at the Zoological Museum, Moscow, and reported significant shell thinning (25%) in eggs of peregrines taken from Siberia in 1961-66. They also reported the presence of p,p'-DDE (DDE) in shell membranes of eggs measured. With this background and the general understanding that DDE residues in peregrine eggs decreased widely following DDT bans in the early 1970's (Cade *et al.* 1988), peregrine eggs were collected from the Kola Peninsula in 1991 (Henny *et al.* 1994). These eggs contained relatively low concentrations of DDE (geometric mean 3.5 µg/g) and the population had shown a recent increase in numbers. Eggshell thinning (11.4%) was similar to that found in Alaska; however, polychlorinated biphenyls (PCBs), an industrial contaminant that does not thin eggshells, were in higher concentrations than DDE. PCB concentrations were comparable to profiles shown by populations in Fennoscandia, and were higher than those found in the Alaskan eggs (see Henny *et al.* 1994). Two other industrial contaminants, polychlorinated dibenzo-p-dioxins (PCDDs) and polychlorinated dibenzofurans (PCDFs), were found at relatively high concentrations in a few of the eggs. Even though the peregrine population seemed to be released from decades of a DDT problem, exposure to several industrial contaminants continued, and this was cause for concern.

The source(s) of the industrial contaminants and the wintering grounds of the peregrine population from the Kola Peninsula were unknown. In fact, the peregrine subspecies nesting along the Ponoy River remains unknown (see White & Boyce 1988). Therefore, in the summer of 1994 we attached satellite telemetry equipment to four adult nesting females, and we recorded standard morphometric measurements. Knowledge of the wintering grounds of the Kola Peninsula nesting population could provide useful information for evaluating the source of the industrial contaminants and the peregrine subspecies.

STUDY AREA

Ganusevich (1988) reviewed the raptors nesting on the Kola Peninsula of extreme northwestern Russia (near the Finnish border), and began studying this peregrine population of the Ponoy River depression (above the Arctic Circle) in 1977. The 1000 km^2 study area was believed adequately surveyed from 1987 onward, and the peregrine population increased from 4 to 10 pairs between 1987 and 1991, with an average of 1.94 young produced per active nest (Henny *et al.* 1994). The peregrine population is locally distributed in the basin of the upper and middle course of the Ponoy River. The Ponoy depression is characterized by large bogs, many small and large lakes, rivers and hills with parcels of land elevated (above the bogs) with forests, rocks, and cliffs. An abundance of prey (primarily shorebirds associated with the bogs and lakes), suitable nesting sites, and the absence of human activities define optimum conditions for breeding of the peregrine, although easy access to many eyries by predatory animals sometimes causes nest failure.

METHODS

Blood was collected from the brachial vein of 9 nestlings as described by Henny *et al.* (1982). The whole blood (2 ml) was preserved with 0.10 ml formalin. The blood was analyzed for organochlorine pesticides and total polychlorinated biphenyls (PCBs) at the Patuxent Wildlife Research Center, Laurel, MD, following procedures described in Henny *et al.* (1996). DDE was the only pesticide reported and the detection limit was 0.01 µg/g wet weight; PCBs had a detection limit of 0.20 µg/g.

We captured adult peregrines at the nest site using a noose gin. This device is composed of two circular wire loops with nooses attached to ensnare incubating falcons at the scrape or egg location. Four adult female peregrines captured for the study were tracked by satellites via the Argos/Tiros satellite system (Taillade 1992, Fancy *et al.* 1988, Fuller *et al.* 1995). Each peregrine was equipped with a platform transmitter terminal (PTT, Microwave Telemetry Inc., Columbia, MD.) The PTT, model 100, weighed 28 g and was designed for 12 months of operation. The PTTs were attached in a backpack configuration using 6.35 mm teflon ribbon (Snyder *et al.* 1989). The PTT was centrally located on the peregrines back and held in place by a breast loop and a body loop (behind the wings, around the abdomen, Fuller *et al.* 1995). The PTTs were individually fitted to allow for all natural movement. In addition to the PTT each peregrine received a Russian leg band (ring) attached to the tarsus. The processing of each peregrine required about 1 hour and the birds were released in the exact location they were captured.

Measurements were taken following procedures of Baldwin *et al.* (1931) for exposed culmen without cere, tarsus, length of tail, middle toe and chord of the closed wing (not flattened wing).

RESULTS

Contaminants in Blood

In 1994 four young from the eyrie at Palnik Lake contained DDE concentrations of 0.01, <0.01, 0.02, and 0.01 µg/g; one young from the Kinemur River 0.01 µg/g; one young from Okunjevy Hill 0.02 µg/g; and two young from Devichy Hill 0.02 and 0.01 µg/g. The detection limit for estimated PCBs was 0.20 µg/g, which was unfortunately high, and all young were below the detection limit.

Figure 1. Autumn migration pathways and wintering localities of adult female Peregrine Falcons nesting on the Kola Peninsula, Russia.

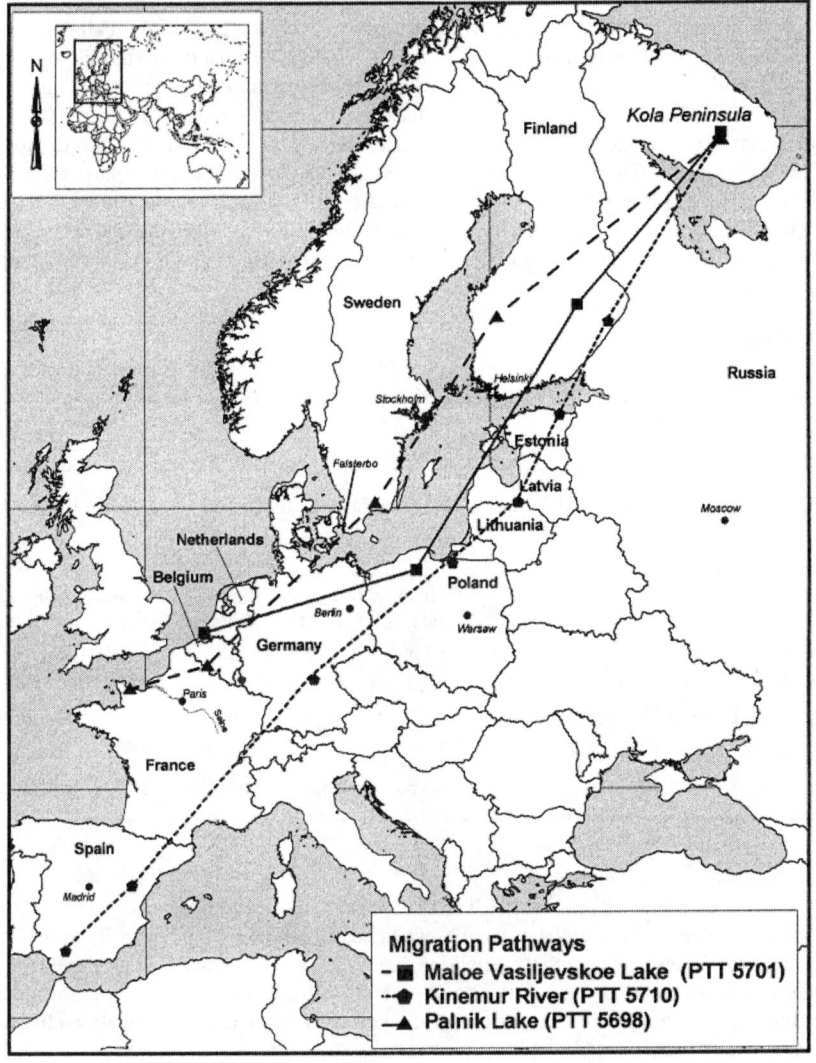

Migration Routes and Wintering Localities

Prior to this study, only one Peregrine Falcon banding record was available from the Kola Peninsula. A nestling banded by Ganusevich on July 31, 1980 (67°N, 39°E) was reported shot on

September 26, 1982 at Loire-Atlantique (near Les Moutiers), France (47°N, 2°W) which is coastal. Its autumn migration may not have been completed when it was shot.

Four adult female peregrines were trapped during incubation at their eyries from June 12-14, 1994, and PTT's attached. The Vuljavr Lake female (PTT 5700) either lost her PTT soon after attachment or died. The Maloe Vasiljevskoe Lake female (PTT 5701) departed the Ponoy River study area between September 2 and 7, was reported in southern Finland (Sept. 7), in Poland (W. Gdansk) (Sept. 12), and in The Netherlands (Sept. 23) where she stayed (Figure 1). Skeletal remains of this bird were found (and reported to Moscow Ringing Centre) in September 1995 on the island of Tholen, village of St. Martensdijk, The Netherlands. The Kinemur River female (PTT 5710) migrated from the study area between September 12 and 15, was reported in southern Finland (Sept. 15), in Estonia (Sept. 19), in Latvia (Sept.23), Poland (Sept. 26), Germany (Oct. 3), Spain (Oct. 7), and finally southern Spain (Oct. 10) where she wintered. The final female from Palnik Lake (PTT 5698) left the study area between September 17 and 21, and like the other two birds migrated through southern Finland (Sept. 21), southern Sweden (Sept. 24), northern France near the Belgium border (Oct. 1), and then to its wintering grounds in France near the mouth of the Seine River (Oct. 4). All three peregrines from the Kola Peninsula wintered in Western Europe, and appeared to take fairly direct migration routes. The adult females were first detected away from the Ponoy River nesting area on September 7, 15, and 21 (mean Sept. 14), but were still present in the study area on September 2, 12, and 17 (mean Sept. 10). The estimated time for migration (time from the first detection away from nesting area to first record on wintering area) was: to The Netherlands (17 days), France (14 days), and Spain (26 days).

Measurements

All four adult females were relatively large weighing 1198±26.3 g (mean±sd), with a wing chord of 364.5±3.7 mm (Table 1). At the time of capture, the females were incubating and did not have food in their crops.

Table 1. Measurements of adult female Peregrine Falcons trapped at eyrie sites on the Kola Peninsula.

Eyrie name	Date	Mass(g)	Culmen (mm)	Middle toe (mm)	Tarsus (mm)	Tail length (mm)	Wing chord (mm)
Kinemur River	12-Jun-94	1220	22.3	57.6	65	175	364
Palnik Lake	13-Jun-94	1180	23.4	56.2	65.5	170	360
Vasilijevskoe Lake	14-Jun-94	1170	24.5	55.6	66	178	365
Vulijavr Lake	14-Jun-94	1220	23.9	55	65	169	369
Mean	- -	**1198**	**23.5**	**56.1**	**65.4**	**173**	**364.5**

DISCUSSION AND CONCLUSIONS

The south-westerly flight of the peregrines we radio marked along the Ponoy River on the Kola Peninsula is closely associated with the peregrine migration through Fennoscandia. The Ponoy River peregrines were located in southern Finland and/or southern Sweden on September 7, 15, and 21-24. These dates were within the peak autumn migration of adult peregrines over Falsterbo in southern Sweden (Kjellén 1992).

Peregrines from Norway winter in western Europe (The Netherlands, Belgium, France, England, Scotland, and Wales) with some along the coast of Norway (Schei 1977, T. Nygård, pers. comm.). Lindberg (1977) showed Swedish peregrines also wintering primarily along the western portion of Europe (Denmark, Germany, The Netherlands, Belgium, France, England and Spain). Data from peregrines banded in Finland revealed those birds mostly moved to the southwest into the region occupied by peregrines from Sweden and Norway. A few peregrines from Finland were recovered in central Europe, and the most south easterly in Serbia (Saurola 1977). The general picture of the wintering area of Finnish peregrines has changed during the last two decades: the number of recoveries south of France has increased remarkably (Saurola 1998). Prior to 1970 almost all peregrines were ringed in southern Finland. In contrast, now there are no peregrines in southern Finland where eggshell thinning was more severe in earlier years, and all recent recoveries are from birds breeding in the northern part of the country (Saurola 1998). Thus, it appears that peregrines from Finnish Lapland have their wintering ground south of the area formally used by the peregrines that lived in the south of the country. These findings are in general agreement with Cramp (1980) who reports that *F. p. peregrinus* are non-migratory, except that birds from northern areas in Fennoscandia and Russia vacate their territories in the winter. He states that *F. p. calidus* breeds in the Arctic from east Finnmark to 130° E, and that the entire population migrates, including a transequatorial element. Peregrines from Norway and Sweden were considered *F. p. peregrinus* by White and Boyce (1988), and appeared to broadly winter within the same range as our three adult females from the Ponoy River (The Netherlands, France and Spain).

White and Boyce (1988) were uncertain about the taxonomy of the Ponoy River peregrines. Stepanyan (1995) notes that in the European region, distribution of subspecies is connected with zonal characteristics and *F. p. calidus* resides along the Arctic coast, southwards to forest-tundra zone (in agreeement with Vaurie 1965), down to about 66-67° N., and *F. p. peregrinus* occupies the major part of Europe, south of *calidus* range. The Ponoy River birds at 67° N. are therefore, near the boundary of the two subspecies, although Galushin (1995) referred to them as *calidus*. Vaurie (1961) noted that *calidus* differs only slightly morphologically from nominate *peregrinus* by being generally paler and by averaging slightly larger. Vaurie (1961) further noted that *calidus* is highly migratory, whereas nominate *peregrinus* is sedentary, or its migratory movements are very limited with some individuals spending the winter in the southern part of the breeding range or occasionally the Iberian Peninsula and Sardinia. Curry-Lindahl (1981: 19,52) describes *calidus* as migrating from the north to tropical Africa, "... south to Angola and Natal as well as on Fernando Poo and Mauritius..." Thus, our radio tracking data support the idea that Ponoy River peregrines are *peregrinus*.

Vaurie provides wing measurements (flattened, see Vaurie 1965) for 10 female *calidus* 350-370 mm (mean 361.8), and 21 female *peregrinus* (measured by Dementiev) from Russia and western and southern Siberia 343-375 mm (mean 356.6). Measurements of live adult female peregrines on the Ponoy River were 360-369 mm (mean 364.5) and within the limits for both subspecies. However, it is dangerous to compare live bird measurements with study skin measurements and flattened wing with wing chord. Clayton White (pers. comm) found wing chords of 10 adult females shorter than flattened wings (7.4±1.83 mm, range 5.2-10). It is also recognized that study skin shrinkage occurs and affects wing measurements (see Fjeldså 1980, Henny & Clark 1982). Fjeldså (1980) reported a 3% shrinkage in grebe wing measurements (i.e., about 10.9 and 10.7 mm for *calidus* and *peregrinus*, respectively). Thus, *calidus* adjusts to a mean live adult wing chord of about 361.8 + 10.9 (shrinkage) - 7.4 (flattened to chord) =365.3 mm, and *peregrinus* about 356.6 + 10.7 - 7.4 = 359.9 mm. This exercise with measurements has not clarified the situation much except that the Ponoy River mean wing is between *calidus* and *peregrinus* and with considerable overlap. However, because the Ponoy River peregrines breed near the tundra, but in a region with trees, and show a relatively short migration pattern that is similar to *peregrinus* from Fennoscandia, we believe that they more likely belong to *peregrinus*.

Peregrines from the Kola Peninsula are seemingly distributional extensions from Scandinavia rather than from eastward in Russia as suggested by the migration and winter ground pattern, a pattern shown by many other species (C. M. White, pers. comm). For example, the Arctic Warbler (*Phylloscopus borealis*) has extended out of Siberia into central Alaska, but returns to Asia to winter in southeast Asia rather than south into North America (AOU 1998). Likewise, the Snow Goose (*Chen caerulescens*) and Sandhill Crane (*Grus canadensis*) extend out of the North American arctic into Siberia and Wrangel Island to breed, but return to winter in North America and follow migration routes of North American birds rather than to follow a migration route south in Asia. Blood samples were collected from the four adults for genetic study and remain available for research; this may provide additional insight into the subspecies issue.

The source of the industrial contaminants found in the eggs is the other important issue for the small localized Ponoy River population. The tremendous variation in PCB concentrations among clutches (3.0 to 21.0 µg/g; Henny et al. 1994) implies a relatively large wintering area (with many point sources and PCB availability ranging from high to low) is the most likely source of PCBs and is responsible for the variability among clutches. The diet of peregrines on the wintering grounds remains unknown and is probably quite variable, which also can account for differences in exposure to industrial contaminants. No PCB point sources were known along the Ponoy River. While in the remote Ponoy River study area, we saw one village and its associated subsistence fishermen and reindeer herdsmen, one abandoned village, and nobody else and no other structures during the field work on the project.

While on the Ponoy River breeding grounds, peregrines preyed upon at least 30 species of birds (Henny et al. 1994). The dominant species included the Ruff (*Philomachus pygnax*), 52.0%; Common Snipe (*Gallinago gallinago*), 8.6%; Jack Snipe (*Lymnocryptes minima*), 4.8%; and Wood Sandpiper (*Tringa glareola*), 4.5%. No other species contributed to more than 3.4% of the diet. Ruffs were collected on the study area, but they did not make it successfully to the United States for chemical analyses; however, 3 of the 4 most important species (65.1% of the Ponoy River diet) had been collected at peregrine territories in northern Sweden in 1976-77 (Lindberg et al. 1985). All three species from northern Sweden (Ruff, Common Snipe, Wood Sandpiper) contained extremely low concentrations of PCBs, 0.02, 0.03, and 0.06 µg/g (wet weight), respectively. Likewise, DDT and its metabolites were low, 0.12, 0.02, and 0.12 µg/g, respectively. The young peregrines blood sampled along the Ponoy River during this study contained low DDE concentrations and no detectable PCBs, although the PCB detection limit was high. If (perhaps a big assumption) the principal prey species in the Ponoy River study area contained contaminant concentrations similar to those in northern Sweden two decades earlier (i.e., very low), this further supports the conclusion that wintering grounds of the peregrines were the primary source of the industrial contaminants in the eggs. Henny et al. (1982) reported a similar conclusion (based upon strategic blood sampling over time) for Arctic peregrines from North America, and Lindberg et al. (1985) reached the same conclusion (based upon breeding ground prey species residues) for peregrines in Sweden. We recognize that PCBs and other contaminants can be transported long distances and be atmospherically deposited thousands of kilometers from the original source (see Bidleman et al. 1990, Nakata et al. 1998), but the low chemical concentrations in the same prey species at a similar latitude in Sweden, and in the blood of nestlings in this study, argues against atmospheric deposition in the Arctic being critical in the Ponoy River peregrine-contaminant scenario.

In contrast to the relatively low DDE concentrations found in peregrine eggs from the Kola Peninsula in 1991 (Henny et al. 1994), one egg from a bog-associated nest site further south in Russia (Novgorod Region, 58°N, 32°E) in 1992 contained high DDE and PCB concentrations (27.3 and 14.3 µg/g wet weight, respectively) (Henny et al. 1998). The wintering locality for this more southern nesting peregrine is unknown. For birds from this latter locale, as well as those from the Ponoy River, information gathered by satellite telemetry equipment about wintering areas can be most useful for better understanding environmental contaminant exposure patterns.

ACKNOWLEDGMENTS

We are grateful to Vladimir Flint and Alexander Sorokin (Russian Ministry of Ecology and Natural Resources) and Steven Kohl (Office of International Affairs, U.S. Fish and Wildlife Service) for supporting this project. Sergei Kharitonov of the Moscow Ringing Centre kindly provided the ringing records from the Kola Peninsula. This study was carried out under Area V of the U.S.-Russia Environmental Agreement. This is the fourth paper in a series that deals with contaminants and raptors in Russia. Clayton White kindly provided unpublished information about peregrine measurements and other advice, and Torgeir Nygård provided unpublished information on winter band recoveries from Norway. Pertti Saurola reviewed the manuscript and had several suggestions to improve it. We thank Linda Schueck for management of the radio tracking data and for preparing the detailed map with the peregrine locations.

REFERENCES

AMERICAN ORNITHOLOGISTS' UNION 1998. *Check-list of North American Birds*, 7th Edition. American Ornithologists' Union, Washington DC 829 pp.

BALDWIN, S.P., H.C. OBERHOLSER & L.G. WORLEY 1931. Measurement of birds. *Sci. Publ. Cleveland Mus. Natural History.* 2:1-165.

BIDLEMAN, T.F., G.W. PATTON, D.A. HINCKLEY, M.D. WALLA, W.E. COTHAM & B.T. HARGRAVE 1990. Chlorinated pesticides and polychlorinated biphenyls in the atmosphere of the Canadian Arctic, pp.347-372. In: *Long range transport of pesticides.* D.A. Kurtz (ed.). Lewis Publishers, Chelsea, MI. 462pp.

CADE, T.J., J.H. ENDERSON, C.G. THELANDER & C.M. WHITE (eds) 1988. *Peregrine Falcon populations: Their management and recovery.* The Peregrine Fund, Inc., Boise, ID. 949pp.

CRAMP, S. (Chief Ed.) 1980. *Handbook of the birds of Europe, the Middle East and North Africa II.* Hawks to bustards. Oxford Univ. Press, Oxford 695 pp.

CURRY-LINDAHL, K. 1981. *Bird migration in Africa: movements between six continents.* Vol. 1. Academic Press. London. 444pp.

FANCY, S.G., L.F. PANK, D.C. DOUGLAS, C.H. CURBY, G.W. GARNER, S.C. AMSTRUP & W.F. REGELIN 1988. Satellite telemetry: A new tool for wildlife research and management. U.S. Fish and Wildl. Serv. Resour. Publ. 172, 54pp.

FJELDSÅ, J. 1980. Post-mortem changes in measurements of grebes. *Bull. Br. Ornithol. Club.* 100:151-154.

FULLER, M.R., W.S. SEEGAR & P.W. HOWEY 1995. The use of satellite systems for the study of bird migration. *Israeli J. Zool.* 41:243-252.

GALUSHIN, V.M. 1977. Recent changes in the actual and legislative status of birds of prey in the U.S.S.R., pp.152-159. In: R.D. Chancellor, (ed.) *World Conference on Birds of Prey.* Internat. Council Bird Preservation, London 442pp.

GALUSHIN, V.M. 1995. Recent population status of the Peregrine Falcon *Falco peregrinus* in European Russia. *Acta Ornithologica* 30:43-46.

GANUSEVICH, S.A. 1988. Raptors of the Kolsky Peninsula. *Ornitologiya.* 23:73-80, (in Russian).

HENNY, C.J. & W.S. CLARK 1982. Measurements of fall migrant Peregrine Falcons from Texas and New Jersey. *J. Field Ornithol.* 53:326-332.

HENNY, C.J., W.S. SEEGAR & T.L. MAECHTLE 1996. DDE decreases in plasma of spring migrant Peregrine Falcons, 1978-94. *J. Wildl. Manage.* 60:342-349.

HENNY, C.J., S.A. GANUSEVICH, F.P. WARD, & T.R. SCHWARTZ. 1994. Organochlorine pesticides, chlorinated dioxins and furans, and PCBs in Peregrine Falcon, *Falco peregrinus,* eggs from the Kola Peninsula, Russia, pp.739-749. In: B.U. Meyburg and R.D. Chancellor (eds). *Raptor Conservation Today,* WWGBP and Pica Press. 799pp.

HENNY, C.J., F.P. WARD, K.E. RIDDLE & R.M. PROUTY 1982. Migrating Peregrine Falcons, *Falco peregrinus,* accumulate pesticides in Latin America during winter. *Canadian Field-Naturalist.* 96:333-338.

HENNY, C.J., V.M. GALUSHIN, P. DUDIN, A.V. KHRUSTOV, A.L. MISCHENKO, V.N. MOSEIKIN, V. SARYCHEV & V. TURCHIN 1998. Organochlorine pesticides, PCBs, and mercury in hawk, falcon, eagle and owl eggs from the Lipetsk, Voronezh, Novgorod and Saratov Regions, Russia, 1992-1993. *J. Raptor Research.* 32:143-150.

KJELLÉN, N. 1992. Differential timing of autumn migration between sex and age groups in raptors at Falsterbo, Sweden. *Ornis Scandinavica.* 23:420-434.

LINDBERG, P. 1977. [Banding of peregrines (*Falco peregrinus*) in Sweden (preliminary report)], pp 39-42. In: *Pilgrimsfalken I Sverige.* Svenska Naturskyddsföreningen. Stockholm, 94pp.

LINDBERG, P., T. ODSJÖ & L. REUTERGÅRDH 1985. Residue levels of polychlorobiphenyls, ΣDDT, and mercury in bird species commonly preyed upon by the Peregrine Flacon (*Falco peregrinus* Tunst.) in Sweden. *Arch. Environ. Contam. Toxicol.* 14:203-212.

NAKATA, H., S. TANABE, R. TATSUKAWA, Y. KOYAMA, N. MIYAZAKI, S. BELIKOV & A. BOLTUNOV 1998. Persistent organochlorine contaminants in Ringed Seals (*Phoca hispida*) from the Kara Sea, Russian Arctic. *Environ. Toxicol. Chem.* 17:1745-1755.

PEAKALL, D.B. & L.F. KIFF 1979. Eggshell thinning and DDE residue levels among Peregrine Falcons, *(Falco peregrinus)*: A global perspective. *Ibis* 121:200-204.

SAUROLA, P. 1977. [Banded peregrines (*Falco peregrinus*) in Finland], pp. 33-38. *In*: *Pilgrimsfalken I Sverige*. Svenska Naturskyddsföreningen. Stockholm, 94pp.
SAUROLA, P. 1998. Rengastusvuosi (Summary: Bird ringing in Finland 1997). *Linnut- vuosikirja* 1997:61-70.
SCHEI, P.J. 1977. [The falcon project (*Falco peregrinus*) in Norway], pp16-23. *In*: *Pilgrimsfalken I Sverige*. Svenska Naturskyddsföreningen. Stockholm, 94pp.
SNYDER, N.F.R., S.R. BEISSINGER & M.R. FULLER 1989. Solar radio transmitters on snail kites in Florida. *J. Field Ornith.* 60:171-177.
STEPANYAN, L.S. 1995. A review of taxonomic concepts for the Peregrine Falcon *Falco peregrinus* subspecies in the Western Palearctic. *Acta Ornithologica* 30:27-29.
TAILLADE, M. 1992. Animal tracking by satellite, pp.149-160. *In*: I.G. Priede and S.S. Swift, (eds.) *Wildlife Telemetry, remote monitoring and tracking of animals*. Ellis Horwood, New York.
VAURIE, C. 1961. Systematic notes on palearctic birds. No. 44 Falconidae: The genus *Falco* (Part 1, *Falco peregrinus* and *Falco pelegrinoides*). American Museum Novitates No. 2035, 19pp.
VAURIE, C. 1965. The birds of the palearctic fauna - - *A systematic reference, Non - Passeriformes*. H.F. and G. Witherby Ltd., London 763pp.
WHITE, C.M. & D.A. BOYCE, JR. 1988. An overview of Peregrine Falcon subspecies, pp. 789-810. *In*: T.J. Cade, J.H. Enderson, C.G. Thelander, and C.M. White (eds). *Peregrine Falcon populations: Their management and recovery*. The Peregrine Fund, Inc., Boise, ID. 949pp.

Charles J. Henny
USGS Forest & Rangeland Ecosystem
Science Center
3200 SW Jefferson Way
Corvallis, OR 97331
USA

William S. Seegar
Edgewood Research Development and
Engineering Center
Aberdeen Proving Ground
MD 21010
USA

Michael A. Yates and Thomas L. Maechtle
Raptor Research Center
Boise State University
1910 University Avenue
Boise, ID 83725
USA

Sergei A. Ganusevich
Krasnostuden-Tcheskiy
PROEZD 21-45
Moscow, 125422
Russia

Mark R. Fuller
USGS Forest & Rangeland Ecosystem Science Center
Snake River Field Station
970 Lusk Street
Boise, ID 83706
USA

also for Seegar, Yates and Maechtle
Center for Conservation Research & Technology
University of Maryland

Chancellor, R. D. & B.-U. Meyburg eds. 2000
Raptors at Risk
WWGBP / Hancock House

A Multisensor Telemetry System for Studying Flight Biology and Energetics of Free-flying Griffon Vultures - *Gyps fulvus*. A Case Study

R. Bögel, R. Prinzinger, E. Karl and C. Walzer

INTRODUCTION

In the study of flight energetics, several approaches are common: 1) measuring oxygen consumption, 2) measuring turn-over-rates using double-labelled-water, 3) adapting models of flight mechanics to the dimension of birds, and 4) using heart rate as an estimate for metabolic rate. All of these approaches have specific disadvantages: method 1) is restricted to lab conditions, 2) delivers only average turn-over-rates within a defined period, 3) is a pure theoretical approach with little experimental evidence, and 4) delivers relatively rough estimates, which are influenced by other factors. However, several studies have proved that heart rate can be a reliable indicator for metabolic rate, especially if regression functions are individually correlated to different activities. To study flight energetics of free-flying Eurasian Griffon Vultures *Gyps fulvus* under natural conditions, a telemetry device was developed to measure flight-specific parameters and to correlate them with observed flight behaviour.

This study was supported by the GIF research grant No. I 0370-154.01/94.

METHODS

The multisensor telemetry transmitter which was developed, measures heart rate, body temperature, plumage/ambient temperature and air pressure/flight altitude. The transmitter is divided into 2 subunits: an intracorporal unit (64 x 35 x 12 mm, 42 g) detects heart rate from the ECG signal, measures body temperature and transfers this information to an external repeater via a short range telemetry link (100 kHz-band). A self-adaptable trigger circuit and adequate filter characteristics minimize interference with EMG-signals and ensure proper ECG-triggering over the long term. The external repeater which is fitted with a semi-flexible silicone/teflon-harness (78 x 37 x 27mm, 150g) decodes the parameters from the implant, measures plumage/ambient temperature and air pressure and transmits all information through a telemetry data link (150 MHz band). All parameters are transmitted in sequence with a PDM/PIM modulation scheme. During 24 hours, the following data rates are collected: heart rate 2880 data sets (which represent averaged values over a half minute period), air pressure 1440 data sets (which represent 4 averaged values each), body and plumage temperatures 720 data sets (which represent discrete values). Thus, depending on the fluctuations of the various parameters, update intervals range from 30 sec (heart rate) and 60 sec (air pressure) to 120 sec (body and plumage temperatures). On average, 85% of the theoretical data rates are recorded under field conditions. Lifespan of the transmitter is approx. 2 years, and the range under field conditions is approx. 5 kilometres. For datalogging a standard TELEVILT RX900 receiver is used.

For a detailed description of the transmitter and implantation techniques see Schober *et al.* (1998) and Walzer *et al.* (in press). For a calculation of altitudes from air pressure values under different weather conditions see Bögel (1996).

To calibrate energy turnover versus heart rate, detailed measurements on oxygen consumption under various conditions were made in a metabolic chamber at the Frankfurt University.

RESULTS AND DISCUSSION

Figure 1 shows the relation and regression function between heart rate, energy turnover and body temperature resulting from the measurements in the metabolic chamber. If data are pooled and averaged, and body temperature is implemented as an additional variable, residuals are below 0.2 J/g*h, indicating an excellent correlation coefficient of 0.974. However, under field conditions heart rates can easily exceed 200 bpm, and energy turnover rates have therefore to be extrapolated from laboratory measurements where heart rates did not exceed 100 bpm. Thus, energy turnover rates derived from heart rates >100 bpm cannot be confidently estimated at present.

Figure 1: Metabolic Rate (MR) versus heart rate (HR) and body temperature (BT), (a) pooled data and (b) surface regression for a Eurasian Griffon Vulture in a metabolic chamber.

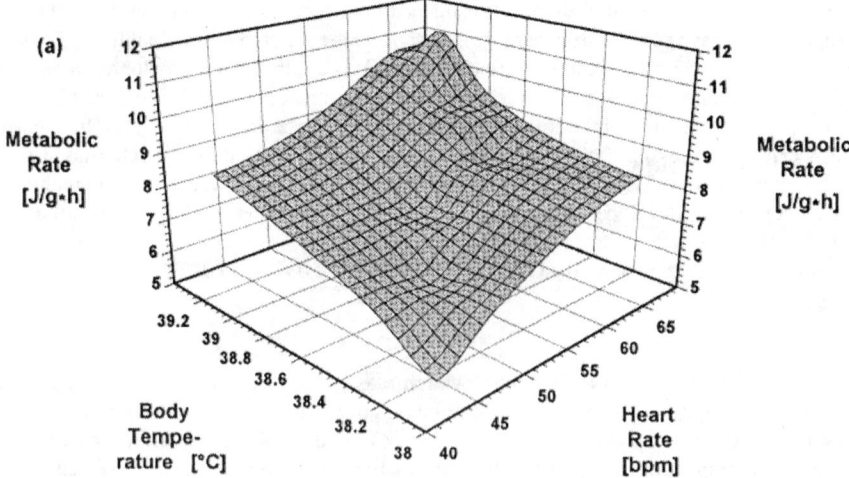

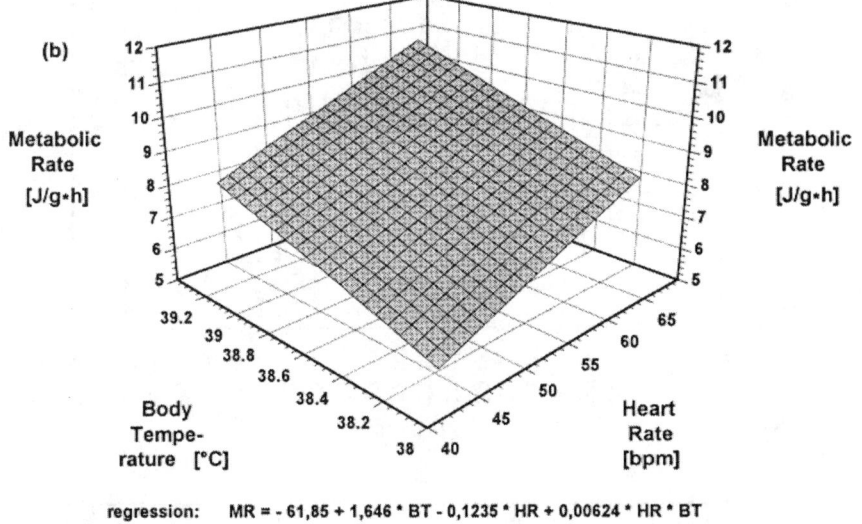

regression: MR = - 61,85 + 1,646 * BT - 0,1235 * HR + 0,00624 * HR * BT

Using the method described above, flight profiles of a Eurasian Griffon Vulture with corresponding heart rates and patterns of body and plumage temperatures were recorded in the northern European Alps (Karl 1998). Figure 2 shows these for 24th March 1998 over a 24-hour period. The bird left its nesting cliff at Mount Untersberg at 06.30 hrs and performed various flight activities and changes in roosting sites before it finally arrived at the zoo at 12.00 noon. After feeding, the vulture left around 15.45 hrs and perched at its nesting cliff at Mount Untersberg around 17.10 hrs. Heart rates ranged from <20 to almost 200 bpm and varied substantially over most of the diurnal cycle according to the

Figure 2 a-d: Patterns of (a) heart rate, (b) body temperature, (c) plumage temperature and (d) altitude for a free-fying Eurasian Griffon Vulture on 24th March 1998.

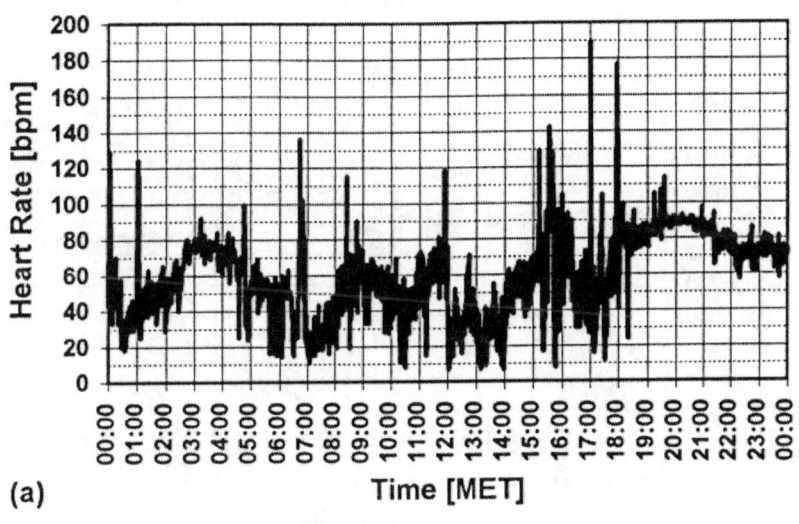

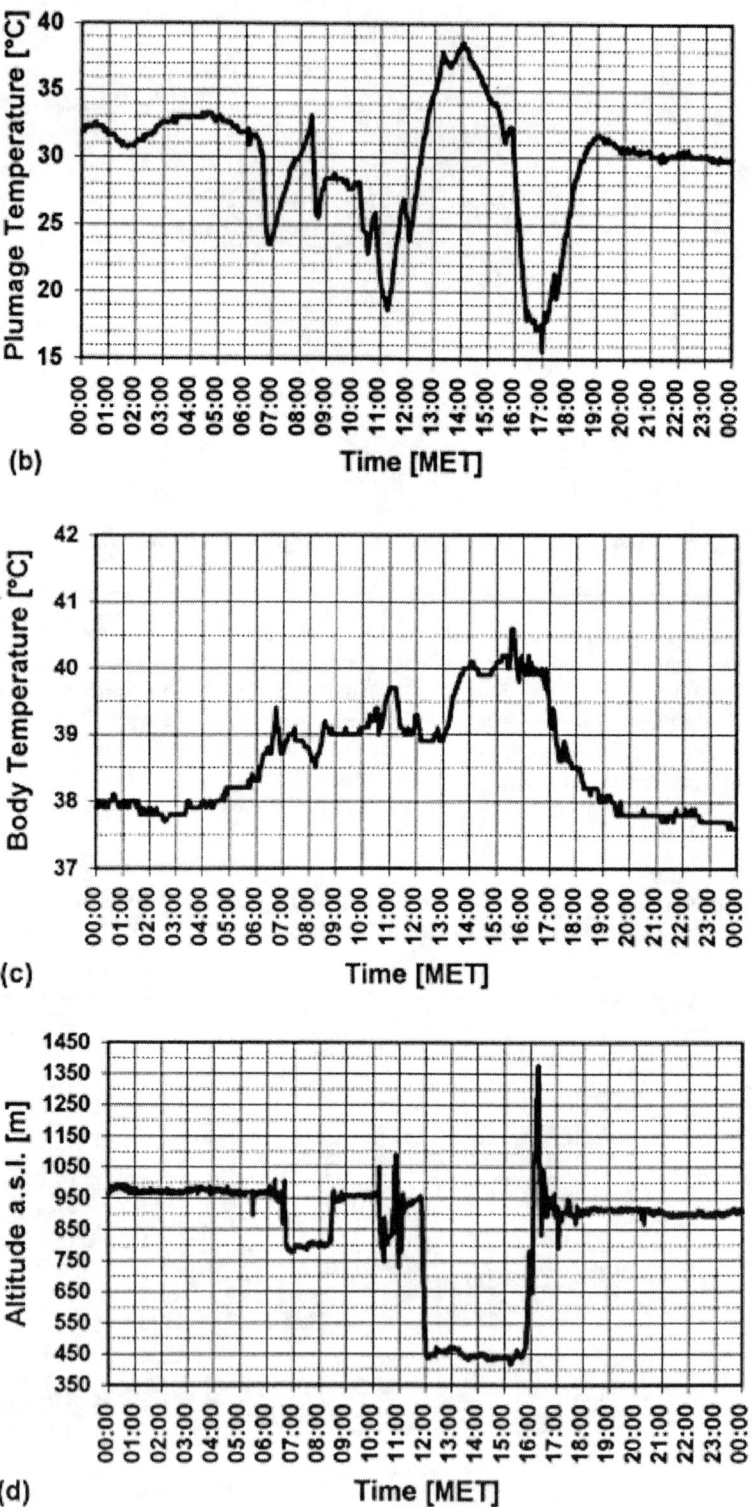

performed activities (Fig. 2a). Body temperature (Fig. 2b) showed a clear diurnal pattern with peaks which are caused by flight activities (around 06.45 hrs, 11.00 hrs, 15.45 hrs) but also by feeding activities that included a high level of intraspecific aggression (between 14.00 and 15.00 hrs). Plumage temperature (Fig. 2c) is an excellent indicator of flight activities (cooling effect) and clearly reflects changes in flight altitude (Fig. 2d). It can be seen that flight activities can be an energy-efficient mechanism for thermoregulation if flight conditions are favourable due to efficient updrafts (around 16.00 hrs). Peaks in body temperature and heart rate correlate, but due to different flight behaviour (gliding versus flapping flight) these peaks correlate closer around 06.45 hrs and 15.40 hrs than around 11.00 hrs. However, many bursts in heart rate which are not caused by physical stress, are not represented in the body temperature pattern. It is also interesting to note that heart rates during inactivity vary between approx. 40 and 80 bpm, and may even be decreased to lower levels, probably as a "compensatory mechanism" after stress (Fig. 2a). Correlating the selected flight tracks and profiles with the corresponding flight conditions as predicted by GIS-models on thermals and dynamic updrafts reveal that the vultures optimize their flight behaviour in order to minimize their energy consumption (Bögel 1996).

The described method is also very useful to detect and quantify perturbations in the vulture from disturbances which may be caused by various reasons. This has been documented, for example during fireworks on New Year's eve (Bögel et al. in press)!

REFERENCES

BÖGEL, R. 1996. Untersuchungen zur Flugbiologie und Habitatnutzung von Gänsegeiern (*Gyps fulvus*, HABLIZL 1783) unter Verwendung telemetrischer Meßverfahren. Dissertatition an der Universität Ulm. Published in: *Nationalpark Berchtesgaden 1996: Forschungsberichte* Nr. 33, pp.168.
BÖGEL, R., KARL, E., PRINZINGER, R. & C. WALZER. Die Reaktion der Herzfrequenz auf Silvesterfeuerwerk bei einem freifliegenden Gänsegeieer (*Gyps fulvus*). *Ecology of Birds*, in press.
KARL, E., 1998. Telemetrie von Herzfrequenz und Körpertemperatur an freilebenden Gänsegeiern (*Gyps fulvus*, HABLIZL 1783). Diplomarbeit an der Johann Wolfgang Goethe Universität Frankfurt, pp. 186 (unpublished).
SCHOBER, F., FLUCH, G. & R. BÖGEL 1998. Multichannel Microcontroller-Based Repeater Telemetry System with Digital Radio Data Link. In: Penzel, P., Salmons, S. & M.R. Neuman: *Biotelemetry XIV*, Proc. 14th Int. Symp. Biotel., Marburg, Germany, 1997: 77-82.
WALZER, C., BÖGEL, R., KARL, E., SCHOBER, F. & R. PRINZINGER. Intraabdominal Implantation of a Multisensor Telemetry System in a Free-Flying Griffon Vulture (*Gyps fulvus*). In: Lumeij, S. (ed.): *Raptor Biomedicine II. Proc. Raptor Biomed. Congress, Midrand, South Africa*: in press.

R. Bögel
Nationalpark Berchtesgaden
Doktorberg 6, D-83471
Berchtesgaden
Germany

C. Walzer
Salzburger Tiergarten Hellbrunn
A-5081 Anif
Austria

R. Prinzinger and E. Karl
AK Stoffwechselphysiologie
Universität Frankfurt
Siesmayerstraße 70
D-60323 Frankfurt/Main
Germany

Footedness Bias in Hunting Birds of Prey

Davide Csermely

ABSTRACT

Birds of prey use their feet to capture prey, particularly when occurring on the ground, and thus they are good candidates for studies on footedness, i.e. the preferential use of limbs. This preference is still poorly known among birds in general.

Several successful attempts at predation by rehabilitated Falconiformes and Strigiformes were analysed. Those birds' predatory ability is routinely tested to evaluate the success of their release to the wild. One laboratory mouse was usually offered, but other species, ranging from grasshopper to one-day-old chick or small rat, were used as well. Kestrels *Falco tinnunculus* and Common Buzzards *Buteo buteo* tended to grip with only one foot, but without side preference. The foot used in the first test was also used subsequently. In contrast, owl species such as the Barn Owl *Tyto alba* and Tawny Owl *Strix aluco* used mainly both feet. Young Barn Owls were more variable than adults in foot use. In contrast, the Little Owl *Athene noctua*, a rather diurnal owl, showed strong preference for using the right foot only.

Birds of prey then show various degrees of footedness, with limited difference between individuals, and such species differences are likely related to environmental constraints.

INTRODUCTION

Brain functions have for a long time been known to be asymmetrical. Such a difference in functions is connected to different morphology. The brain is defined as asymmetrical (or lateralized) when one side of it is structurally different from the other and/or performs different functions. Brain lateralization has been recorded in many species of birds as well as of mammals (Bradshaw & Rogers, 1993); it is questionable, however, whether this can be considered as a homologous or just as a polyphyletic character.

Brain lateralization, moreover, can be considered at *individual level* or at *population level*. In the first instance the population can consist of one half of individuals that are left-handed while the others are right-handed; as a result, the population itself, as a whole, cannot be defined as lateralized, although consisting of lateralized individuals. In the second case, the population is formed by coherently lateralized individuals, most of them left-handed or right-handed. In this situation it is possible that some sort of selective pressure worked for more than one-half of the population, although ontogenetic factors, other than the selection itself, can promote such a lateralization (Denenberg *et al.*, 1978). In contrast, selective pressure did not exist in the first situation.

Structural asymmetry seems to have a very distant origin. Some of the oldest chordate fossils, the Chalcichordates, appear to be rather asymmetrical in their cephalic extremity (Jeffries & Lewis, 1978); lateralization would then be a primitive character for the Vertebrates.

Birds, particularly birds of prey, are good candidates for the study of the preferential use of limbs for feeding (footedness), as they constantly rely on a firm grasp to hold prey when hunting. Our knowledge of this behaviour in birds is still limited. Footedness has been studied in several bird taxa. For instance, several species of African and Australian parrots, Cockatoos and Goldfinches *Carduelis carduelis* show footedness bias for feeding at population level; in contrast, Great Tits *Parus major* show such a preference only at individual level, while Pigeons *Columbia livia* show no lateral bias of foot use at all (Güntürkün et al., 1988; Harris, 1989; Rogers & Workman, 1993). Since birds of prey have not yet been investigated, this study aims to make a preliminary contribution towards filling this gap by studying the preferential use of either foot in individuals of several species when hunting a terrestrial prey.

MATERIAL AND METHODS

The birds used were all wild individuals of both Falconiformes and Strigiformes, temporarily kept in captivity at a Rehabilitation Centre near Parma (Italy), managed by the Italian Society for the Protection of Birds (LIPU). They were recovering from various kinds of injury and were chosen from among those ready for release. Thus, they were in perfect physical, plumage and flight condition. A variable number of individuals of five species was used: Common Buzzard *Buteo buteo* (n = 17), Eurasian Kestrel *Falco tinnunculus* (n = 73), Barn Owl *Tyto alba* (n = 32), Tawny Owl *Strix aluco* (n = 7) and Little Owl *Athene noctua* (n = 8).

In order to ascertain their ability to hunt prey, a fundamental requirement for their survival after the release, the birds are routinely tested at the Rehabilitation Centre to assess the probability of successful hunting. They have been individually tested in an aviary specifically equipped to record the predatory behaviour sequence. These tests were also useful in studying some details of the behaviour patterns involved, which are otherwise seen with difficulty in the wild.

I analysed the patterns of several successful predatory attempts by the rehabilitated individuals. The birds were usually each offered daily one adult live or dead laboratory Mouse *Mus musculus domesticus* (C3H strain, agouti pelage), but other species, ranging from young laboratory Rat *Rattus norvegicus* (Brown Norway strain, agouti pelage) to one-day-old chick *Gallus gallus*, adult Lizard *Podarcis muralis / P. sicula*, Grasshopper *Chorthippus* sp. and Earthworm *Lumbricus* sp., were used as well, depending on the food adaptations of the predator species.

For the purpose of this study, the parameters of the predatory behaviour considered were (1) which foot, if any, was used by the bird to grasp its prey, (2) the type of approach to the prey (i.e. *direct* = landing on the prey's body or *indirect* = landing a few centimetres away and gripping the prey after a few steps) and (3) the latency of predation, i.e. the time elapsed between the prey's appearance and its capture.

The sex and age of the birds, when ascertained without doubt, were considered. The first test the bird experienced was considered separately; in fact, some birds, but not all, were tested repeatedly, in which case subsequent tests were possibly influenced by the first one.

RESULTS

Prey type as well as sex and age of the birds and the latency of predation did not have any substantial influence on foot preference. Figure 1 shows that hawks preferred to use one foot only. However, there was no preference for a particular limb, although a greater proportion of Buzzards used the right one. The foot not involved in prey grasping was used for standing. These species appear then to be lateralized at individual level, as the sample is almost split equally concerning the foot preferred.

In contrast, the Barn Owl and Tawny Owl had tended to use both feet, the Barn Owl in particular. Tawny Owls also used the right foot as well, at a frequency slightly smaller than both feet together.

The Barn Owl, on the other hand, used the left- or right foot with similar frequency. It is then possible that these owl species are not lateralized at all.

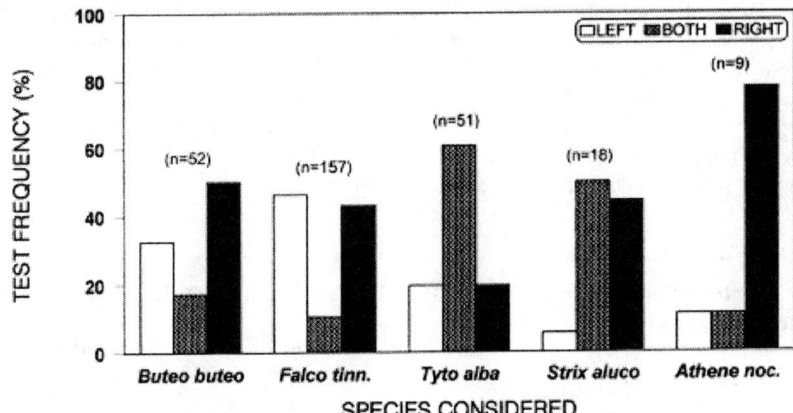

Figure 1. The preferential use of feet by the several species used when grasping the prey.

The Little Owl showed completely different results from the other owl species. In fact, it almost invariably used the right foot when gripping the prey, a tendency more similar to that displayed by buzzards and kestrels than by owls. This odd habit can be explained by the rather "diurnal" activity displayed by the Little Owl, that converged towards a "hawk" predatory habit.

Table 1. Number of tests in which either foot was used by age classes with different types of approach.

Species	Age	Approach	Left	Both	Right
Buteo buteo	Adults	Direct	5	4	2
		Indirect	1	0	6 **
	Juveniles	Direct	4	1	10 **
		Indirect	5	2	4
Falco tinnunculus	Adults	Direct	13	11	18 *
		Indirect	20 ***	1	10
	Juveniles	Direct	5	5	7
		Indirect	25 **	0	19 *
Tyto alba	Adults	Direct	5	15 **	3
		Indirect	1	5 **	0
	Juveniles	Direct	1	2	4 *
		Indirect	0	2	1
Strix aluco	Adults	Direct	0	2	2
		Indirect	0	0	0
	Juveniles	Direct	1	4	3
		Indirect	0	3	3
Athene noctua	Adults	Direct	0	1	6
		Indirect	1	0	1

* (More frequent than expected) = $P<0.05$; ** = $P<0.01$; *** = $P<0.001$.

Both adults and juveniles of any species approached the prey directly and indirectly with similar frequency (Table 1). Adult Buzzards used the right foot more often than expected (Chi-sq. Comp. 'z' value = 2.400, $P < 0.01$) in indirect attacks, while the opposite occurred in juveniles (Chi-sq. Comp.

'z' value = 2.236, P < 0.01). On the other hand, both adult and juvenile Kestrels tended to prefer using one foot only when performing indirect approach to the prey, but with just a little preference for the left foot (Chi-sq. Comp. 'z' value = 3.007, P < 0.001 for adults; Chi-sq. Comp. 'z' value = 2.698, P < 0.01 for juveniles), but used one foot or both feet with almost similar frequency when the prey was approached directly.

While Buzzards and Kestrels generally used both feet when approaching the prey directly, the Barn owl constantly used both feet more often than expected during both tests with direct and indirect approach (Chi-sq. Comp. 'z' value = 2.648, P < 0.01; Chi-sq. Comp. 'z' value = 2.121, P < 0.01, respectively). In contrast, both Tawny Owl and Little Owl used both feet together and the right foot only, respectively, without regard to the type of approach to the prey. Unfortunately, the small sample size prevents any statistical calculation concerning this pattern.

I also ascertained whether there was a constancy in the foot use in repeated tests compared with what was performed during the first test (Table 2). The results show that, once again, Buzzards and

Table 2. Number of birds using the same (≥ 66.7%) or different (< 66.7%) foot than the first test in repeated tests.

Species	1st Test	Same Foot	Different Foot
Buteo buteo	Left	3	1
	Both	3	0
	Right	10	0
	Total	**16 ****	**1**
Falco tinnunculus	Left	22 *	11
	Both	6	5
	Right	22 *	7
	Total	**50 ****	**23**
Tyto alba	Left	2	3
	Both	17 **	4
	Right	5	1
	Total	**24 ****	**8**
Strix aluco	Left	0	0
	Both	0	2
	Right	5	0
	Total	**5**	**2**
Athene noctua	Left	0	1
	Both	2	0
	Right	4	1
	Total	**6**	**2**

* (More frequent than expected) = P<0.05; ** = P<0.01.

Kestrels behaved similarly, continuing to use the same foot used in the first test (Chi-sq. Comp. 'z' value = 2.572, P < 0.01; Chi-sq. Comp. 'z' value = 2.235, P < 0.01, respectively), without regard to which one it was. The same occurred for the Barn Owl too (Chi-sq. Comp. 'z' value = 2.000, P < 0.01), but it used principally both feet, instead of only one. Unfortunately, the small sample prevents any statistical analysis in the Tawny Owl and Little Owl.

DISCUSSION

This study shows the existence of a striking bias in footedness between Falconiformes and Strigiformes. Although type of prey as well as sex and age of the bird had no influence on the use of feet, the Falconiformes preferred to use one foot only when grasping the prey. Individuals showed some preference for a particular limb, using the other one for standing. These species appear then strongly lateralized, but only at the individual level; in fact, the tests showed that one leg was used almost as frequently as the other.

Strigiformes preferred to use both legs to grip the prey. The Little Owl was an exception, as it held the prey mainly with the right foot only. Such an odd pattern can be explained by the rather diurnal activity of the species, leading it to adopt a "hawk-like" predatory habit.

These findings show degrees of footedness at *individual level in Falconiformes* and at *population level in the Strigiformes*. Such a bias recorded between species seems more related to environmental constraints, principally daylight, than to phylogenetic similarity. In fact, being active with dim light, owls have principally adopted an ambush predation technique and the grip with both feet gives them higher capture probability, enlarging the area useful for contacting the prey's body. In contrast, Falconiformes can also account on sight during the last phase of the approach to the prey and this gives them the possibility to use just one foot. Selective factors seem to have affected the species but not individual birds, which are indifferently left- or right-footed.

ACKNOWLEDGEMENTS

The whole staff of the Rehabilitation Centre of LIPU is thanked for the collaboration and the permission to use the Centre's facilities and the birds housed there. I am greatly indebted to Nicolantonio Agostini, Luca Bagni, Lisa Bertè, Roberta Camoni, Giorgia Gaibani, Roberto Girelli, Vittoria Maccagnoni, Marta Peretti, Stefano Sponza, and Alessia Visentini for their help in the collection of data. This study was financially supported by the Italian Ministero dell'Università e della Ricerca Scientifica e Tecnologica.

REFERENCES

BRADSHAW, J.L. & L.J. ROGERS 1993. The Evolution of Lateral Asymmetries, Language, Tool Use, and Intellect. *Academic Press.* New York.
DENENBERG, V.H., J. GARBANATI, G.F. SHERMAN, D.A. YUTZEY & R. KAPLAN 1978. Infantile stimulation induces brain lateralization in rats. *Science* 301: 1150-1152.
GÜNTÜRKÜN, O., S. KESCH & J.D. DELIUS 1988. Absence of footedness in domestic pigeons. *Anim. Behav.* 36: 602-604.
HARRIS, L.J. 1989. Footedness in parrots: three centuries of research, theory, and mere surmise. *Can. J. Physiol.* 43: 369-396.
JEFFRIES, R.P.S. & D.N. LEWIS 1978. The English Silurian fossil *Placocystites forbesianus* and the ancestry of the Vertebrates. *Phil. Trans. R. Soc. London B* 282: 283-286.
ROGERS, L.J. & L. WORKMAN 1993. Footedness in birds. *Anim. Behav.* 45: 409-411.

Davide Csermely
Dipartimento di Biologia Evolutiva e Funzionale
Università di Parma
Parco Area delle Scienze 11A
43100 Parma
Italy

Resolutions

RESOLUTION 1

RECOGNISING the co-operation existing between the World Working Group on Birds of Prey and Owls (WWGBP) and the Raptor Research Foundation (RRF)

REQUESTS the resolutions committee of RRF to submit these resolutions to participating members at the 1998 Fall Meeting in Ogden, Utah, for endorsement and joint submission with WWGBP.

RESOLUTION 2

RECOGNISING that the survival of the globally threatened Lesser Spotted Eagle *Aquila pomarina* is only possible in the last unfragmented and undisturbed areas of Central Europe, and that 80% of the remaining German population of this eagle is concentrated in small parts of Mecklenburg-Vorpommern

REQUESTS the government in Mecklenburg-Vorpommern to protect the areas with a high breeding concentration of Lesser Spotted Eagles from growing fragmentation and disturbance, and

URGES the authorities not to permit the proposed Oltschott wind-farm to be constructed in the most important breeding area for Lesser Spotted Eagles in Germany, and

RECOMMENDS the implementation of the EU Action Plan for this species.

RESOLUTION 3

RECOGNISING that the Lesser Spotted Eagle *Aquila pomarina* is the rarest and most threatened species of eagle that breeds regularly in Germany, and

RECOGNISING that despite intensive protection during the last 40 years the population of this species is not increasing

URGES the authorities of Mecklenburg-Vorpommern to take great care, during the privatisation of the state forests, that the forest ecology necessary for Lesser Spotted Eagles is not prejudiced by insensitive introduction of intensive forestry techniques, and thus that the environment necessary for this and other threatened German raptors is preserved.

RESOLUTION 4

RECOGNISING that recent studies clearly show that the European Griffon Vulture *Gyps fulvus* makes very long movements in their Mediterranean area and that there is a high exchange of individuals between different and distant colonies, and

RECOGNISING that the European Griffon Vulture is particularly threatened by poisoning, electrocution, direct killing and disturbance at the nesting colonies

URGES the Mediterranean countries involved to protect carefully the existing colonies and suitable buffer zones in order to prevent disturbance and habitat deterioration, to enforce legislation forbidding poisoning and to re-introduce Griffon Vultures where appropriate.

RESOLUTION 5

RECOGNISING that anti-poaching patrols by the National Forest Service guards in the Strait of Messina, Italy, and particularly on the Calabrian side, from the end of April to the beginning of June have reduced illegal killing of migrating raptors by about 90% in the last 10 years,

COMPLIMENTS the Italian government and the National Forest Service for the very efficient action taken against poaching and

STRONGLY RECOMMENDS that this action will continue in the same way in the future.

RESOLUTION 6

DEEPLY CONCERNED by the recent massive poisoning of Griffon Vultures *Gyps fulvus* in Israel,

SUPPORTS the very important decision of the Israeli Minister of the Environment to nominate a committee to investigate the incident and

STRONGLY URGES the Israeli Minister of the Environment to implement all recommendations of the committee at the earliest.

RESOLUTION 7

NOTES that the activities of the South African Poison Working Group of the Endangered Wildlife Trust have reduced the poisoning of raptors, and

NOTES the importance of focussing attention on education, and co-operation with agrochemicals manufacturers and government departments, and

URGES the European countries and other nations to follow this model by establishing similar Working Groups with assistance from the EWT.

RESOLUTION 8 (from The Workshop on Co-operative Management of Raptor Electrocutions)

RECOGNISING that negative interaction between birds and electricity structures remains a problem, URGES

1. Electricity utility companies to form co-operative management partnerships with recognised ornithological bodies,
2. That all new electricity structures be designed to be safe for raptors and other birds, and
3. That all existing structures be assessed by these partnerships to develop a timetable for the mitigation of those structures causing negative impacts on bird populations.

RESOLUTION 9

RECOGNISING that raptors can drown in farm dams

URGES the organised agricultural sector in countries where this is a problem to alert its members to this situation, and

URGES the members to effect the necessary measures to mitigate raptor mortality in their farm dams.

RESOLUTION 10 (from session on Raptor Predation and Feeding Ecology)

RECOGNISING that predation by raptors can create conflicts between owners of livestock, conservers of game and other interests, and

RECOGNISING that human resources, including skills and other contributions, are needed from all possible quarters to conserve wildlife, and

RECOGNISING that conflicts divert attention and resources from issues on which all interests can agree, especially the absolute priority of maintaining health of habitats and raptor prey populations

URGES governments, authorities, NGOs and other interest groups to seek all possible solutions to such conflicts, including if absolutely necessary the selective removal of identified problem raptors, if possible for other conservation programmes.

RESOLUTION 11 (from the 3rd International Raptor Biomedicine Conference)

RECOGNISING that scientific and veterinary studies on birds of prey play a vital part in the conservation of these birds and that such work often requires the international movement of samples (derivatives) taken from species subject to controls under the Convention on the International Trade in Endangered Species of Wild Flora and Fauna (CITES), and

NOTING that diagnostic and other samples usually need to be examined promptly if meaningful results are to be obtained, and

NOTING that CITES controls on the movement of such derivatives can cause delay in delivery of valuable material, prove excessively time-consuming and are at times impossible to follow, and

NOTING that some countries are not signatories to CITES or lack CITES issuing facilities,

THIS CONFERENCE urges the CITES Secretariat and Signatories to the Convention to devise a system which would permit the rapid movement between countries of samples (derivatives), for example, blood smears, biopsies and tissues for DNA studies, for scientific research or veterinary purposes.

RESOLUTION 12 (from the Trade and Legislation Workshop)

RECOGNISING that the CITES appendices require regular revision to encompass new understanding of animal demography and changes in patterns of trade, and

RECOGNISING that direct costs to CITES administration authorities and indirect costs, for example, to research workers, should be concomitant with conservation benefits that result from regulations

REQUESTS the CITES Secretariat to review its appendices with up-to-date recommendations from raptor biologists, taking note of IUCN criteria and with particular emphasis on:

1. Raptor species or sub-species with globally small and vulnerable populations in the wild.
2. Raptor species with population dynamics that cannot sustain a high yield.
3. Raptor species liable to be affected by Trade in the next decade.
4. Reviewing the status of raptor species in appendices on a 5-year basis.
5. Urging the European Union to adopt the same principles.
6. Down-listing species that no longer meet CITES criteria.

RESOLUTION 13 (from the Trade and Legislation Workshop)

RECOGNISING that captive breeding and reintroduction of endangered species can be important proven conservation methods and that speed and timing of movements are vital for the success of the methods.

RECOGNISING that the statistics from TRAFFIC in CITES movements show an increasing preponderance towards captive-bred birds, and consequently a decreasing proportion in the trade of wild birds, and

RECOGNISING that the current situation penalises the movement of captive-bred birds rather than encourages it.

REQUESTS CITES to urge all member countries to accelerate the process for issuing export/import permits to meet these conservation efforts.

RESOLUTION 14 (from the Middle East Falcon Research Group)

RECOGNISING that some bird of prey populations are under pressure from live harvesting

URGES all governments which issue permits to harvest birds of prey on an annual quota system to do so:

1. only where an adequate monitoring programme of the breeding population shows that such a harvest is sustainable long-term, and
2. only for juvenile birds, not for adults, in order to minimise impact on the donor population

RESOLUTION 15

RECOGNISING the important role that the Endangered Wildlife Trust (EWT) is playing in the conservation of African species, especially birds of prey and owls

CONGRATULATES the EWT on its 25th anniversary, and

THANKS the EWT for its generous hospitality in hosting the 5th World Conference and for the high level of patient, dedicated assistance by members during the Conference.